THE RESTORATION OF DIALOGUE

THE RESTORATION OF DIALOGUE

READINGS IN THE PHILOSOPHY OF CLINICAL PSYCHOLOGY

EDITED BY
RONALD B. MILLER

AMERICAN PSYCHOLOGICAL ASSOCIATION
WASHINGTON, DC

Published by the
American Psychological Association
750 First Street, NE
Washington, DC 20002

Copies may be ordered from
APA Order Department
P.O. Box 2710
Hyattsville, MD 20784
Item Number: 431-7260

This book was typeset in Goudy and Helvetica by Scott Photographics, Riverdale, MD

Printer: Braun-Brumfield, Inc., Ann Arbor, MI
Cover Designer: Grafik Communications Ltd., Alexandria, VA
Technical/Production Editor: Christine P. Landry

Library of Congress Cataloging-in-Publication Data

The restoration of dialogue : readings in the philosophy of clinical psychology /
Ronald B. Miller, editor.
p. cm.
Includes bibliographical references and index.
ISBN 1-55798-157-4 (cloth). — ISBN 1-55798-166-3 (paper)
1. Psychology and philosophy. 2. Psychology—Philosophy.
3. Clinical health psychology—Philosophy. I. Miller, Ronald B.,
1948- .
BF41.R47 1992
150′.1—dc20 91-46051
CIP

Printed in the United States of America
First Edition

For Naomi, Ari, and Maya

CONTENTS

CONTRIBUTORS

Gregory Bateson (1904–1980) is the acknowledged conceptual founder of the systems approach to family therapy. He began his career as a cultural anthropologist working with his first wife, Margaret Mead. After World War II, he began collaborating with psychiatrists and psychologists on developing new models of pathological behavior and is perhaps best known for his *double-bind theory of schizophrenia.*

Allen Bergin, PhD, is a professor of psychology at Brigham Young University, where he is also the director of the clinical psychology program.

Richard D. Chessick, MD, PhD, is a professor of psychiatry at Northwestern University and has a private practice in Evanston, Illinois.

Willard F. Day (1926–1989) was a professor of psychology at the University of Nevada, Reno.

Gerald D. Erickson, DPhil (1935–1989), was a professor in and the director of the School of Social Work, University of Windsor, Ontario, Canada.

Herbert Feigl, PhD, (1902–1989) was a professor of philosophy and the director of the Minnesota Center for the Philosophy of Science at the University of Minnesota, Minneapolis.

Kenneth J. Gergen, PhD, is a professor of psychology at Swarthmore College.

Adolf Grünbaum, PhD, is Andrew Mellon Professor of Philosophy at the University of Pittsburgh, where he is also a research professor of psychiatry and chairman of the Center for Philosophy of Science.

Barbara S. Held, PhD, is a professor of psychology at Bowdoin College and also has a private practice in Brunswick, Maine.

Arthur C. Houts, PhD, is a professor of psychology at Memphis State University.

George S. Howard, PhD, is a professor of psychology and fellow of the Reilly Center for Science, Technology, and Values at the University of Notre Dame.

Jerry L. Jennings, PhD, is the clinical director of the Bustleton Guidance Center in Philadelphia and lectures at the Osteopathic Medical College of Philadelphia.

Bradford P. Kenney, PhD, is professor and director of Scholarly Studies in the Department of Professional Psychology at the University of St. Thomas.

Seymour S. Kety, MD, is Professor Emeritus of Neuroscience at the Harvard Medical School and senior scientist in the Intramural Research Program, National Institute of Mental Health in Bethesda, Maryland.

Richard F. Kitchener, PhD, is a professor in and chairman of the Department of Philosophy at Colorado State University.

Leonard Krasner, PhD, is Professor Emeritus of Psychology at the State University of New York at Stony Brook and a clinical professor in the Department of Psychiatry at Stanford University School of Medicine.

James T. Lamiell, PhD, is a professor of psychology at Georgetown University.

Murray Levine, JD, PhD, is a professor of psychology, an adjunct professor of law, and director of the Research Center for Children and Youth at the State University of New York at Buffalo.

Alvin R. Mahrer, PhD, is a professor of psychology at the University of Ottawa, Ontario, Canada.

Michael J. Mahoney, PhD, is a professor of psychology at the University of North Texas.

Peter T. Manicas, PhD, is Professor Emeritus of Psychology at Queens College, City of New York, and the director of Liberal Studies at the University of Hawaii at Manoa.

Joseph Margolis, PhD, is a professor of philosophy at Temple University.

Rollo May, PhD, is a noted author, lecturer, and psychotherapist who resides in Tiburon, California.

Paul E. Meehl, PhD, is Hathaway-Meehl Professor of Clinical Psychology and Regents' Professor Emeritus of Psychology at the University of Minnesota.

Stanley B. Messer, PhD, is a professor of psychology in the Graduate School of Applied and Professional Psychology, Rutgers University, and an adjunct professor of psychiatry at the Robert Wood Johnson Medical School, University of Medicine and Dentistry of New Jersey.

Martin J. Packer, PhD, is an assistant professor in the Graduate School of Education at the University of Michigan.

Michael Polanyi (1892–1976) was a professor of physical chemistry and of social studies at the University of Manchester, England, and a fellow of Merton College, Oxford, England.

Edward Pols, PhD, is a research professor of philosophy at Bowdoin College, where he was formerly a professor of philosophy and Kenan Professor of Humanities.

Karl H. Pribram, MD, Professor Emeritus of Neuroscience at Stanford University, is currently James and Anna King University Professor and Eminent Scholar in the Commonwealth of Virginia and heads the Center for Brain Research and Informational Sciences at Radford University.

Frank C. Richardson, PhD, is an associate professor of educational psychology at the University of Texas at Austin.

Paul Ricoeur is John Nuveen Professor Emeritus in the Divinity School, a member of the Committee on Social Thought, and Professor Emeritus of Philosophy at the University of Chicago. He is dean of the Faculty of Letters and Human Sciences at the University of Paris X, Nanterre.

Carl R. Rogers (1902–1987) was a pioneer in the development of the humanistic approach to psychology and psychotherapy. At the time of his death, he was a resident fellow of the Center for Studies of the Person, having taught previously at Ohio State University, the University of Chicago, and the University of Wisconsin.

Joseph F. Rychlak, PhD, is the Maude C. Clarke Professor of Humanistic Psychology at Loyola University of Chicago.

Thomas E. Schacht, PsyD, is an associate professor in the Department of Psychiatry and Behavioral Sciences at the James H. Quillen College of Medicine, East Tennessee State University.

Paul F. Secord, PhD, is Research Professor of Psychology at the University of Houston.

B. F. Skinner (1904–1990) was considered the most influential proponent of the behavioral approach to psychology in the 20th century. At the time of his death, he was Professor Emeritus of Psychology at Harvard University. He taught at the University of Minnesota and Indiana University prior to accepting his appointment as professor of psychology at Harvard University in 1948.

Robert L. Spitzer, MD, is the chief of psychiatric research in the Biometrics Research Department of the New York State Psychiatric Institute and a professor of psychiatry at the College of Physicians and Surgeons of Columbia University.

Douglas Sprenkle, PhD, is a professor of marriage and family therapy and director of the Marriage and Family Therapy Program at Purdue University.

Hans H. Strupp, PhD, is Distinguished Professor in the Department of Psychology at Vanderbilt University.

Thomas Szasz, MD, is Professor Emeritus of Psychiatry at the State University of New York Health Science Center, Syracuse.

Charles Taylor, PhD, is a professor in philosophy and political science at McGill University, Monreal, Quebec, Canada.

Paul L. Wachtel, PhD, is Distinguished Professor of Psychology at City College, City University of New York Graduate Center, where he is also associate director of the doctoral program in clinical psychology.

Michael Wertheimer, PhD, is a professor of psychology at the University of Colorado at Boulder.

Meir Winokur, PsyD, is in private practice in psychology in Jerusalem, where he is also a candidate at the Israel Institute of Psychoanalysis, and Visiting Lecturer at the Hebrew University.

Robert L. Woolfolk, PhD, is a professor of psychology at Rutgers—the State University.

FOREWORD

Clinical psychology has always occupied a strained position in psychology, balancing precariously between the demands of a basic science and an applied profession. In 1946, the first year of the *American Psychologist*'s appearance, David Krech[1] published a warning of the growing fission then occurring between experimental and professional psychology. This prophetic piece outlined the problems of a basic science that did not meet the needs of an applied profession. It also showed how applied areas of interest can contribute to the fundamental or basic knowledge of a science such as psychology. A lot of water has passed over the dam since Krech's warnings were put forward. Unfortunately, "down river" the flow has bifurcated as Krech predicted. In fact, there seems to be a number of tributaries splashing off in different directions within the "applied flow" of this separation. I believe that clinical psychology is currently in a serious condition, in which the Boulder model has been challenged and, in many quarters, flatly rejected. What happened? How did we get here? Where are we going?

Questions of this sort, which should interest any clinical psychologist (not to mention his or her colleagues), must inevitably touch upon philosophical issues. No matter how much the practical considerations of economics or politics may have influenced psychology's seeming breakup, there are underlying philosophical positions that motor such developments. Pretending that one makes no philosophical assumptions in doing the work of a psychologist is naively foolish. Ronald Miller's excellent collection of philosophical readings is designed to help both the pre- and postdoctoral members of the clinical profession to understand the dynamics of change now taking place in psychology. As Dr. Miller points out, definitions of philosophy vary. A fairly literal translation of philosophy would be something like "the love of wisdom." But, I have always thought of philosophy as that endeavor that seeks to teach us what we already "know" by presumption.

I believe that there is a clear recognition in all of psychology today regarding what might be termed the role of an initiating organization on resulting knowledge, belief, learning, and so forth. Learning theorists have discovered that the framing organization of materials to be learned is more important to subsequent recall than sheer rehearsal without an effective initial patterning. Good heuristics make for good recall. Constructivists of all types (social, personal, etc.) tell us how important it is to understand the role played by the "viewpoint" of the behaving organism or cultural system of interest. We not only construct but deconstruct meanings based upon the perspective "reading" that we given to events. Family resemblances that are not clearly

[1]Krech, D. (1946). A note on fission. *American Psychologist, 1,* 402–404.

definable are nevertheless shown to influence how we frame and understand our experience. Prototypes, plans, scripts, metaphors, and schemata are said to shape ongoing cognition. The list of such precedent organizers is seemingly endless.

All such findings, it seems to me, are consistent with the view of human reason as fundamentally predicational, as relying upon assumptions, preferential biases, preferred paradigms, meaningful worldviews, and so forth. The terms we use to describe such precedent frames of reference are not important. It *is* important to appreciate that philosophy is the discipline that deals with such precedent organizers of thought. These framing predications are the very meat of philosophy. Through philosophy we flesh out the meanings that silently direct us this way and that. It is good to familiarize oneself with such silent conceptual–logical forces. By knowing more precisely where we are coming from we are more likely to direct our future with assurance, guided now by an enlightened course of action. The benefit here is not unlike the benefit attained by the client in psychotherapy. Knowledge, even the abstract knowledge of a philosophical analysis, is life's most practical tool.

The selections in this book are organized for the reader or classroom presentation into sections dealing with behaviorism, cognitivism, biological approaches, phenomenological–existentialism, psychoanalysis, family systems, and clinical research. The papers included within these sections focus on topics such as the philosophy of science, ethics, religion, the logic of psychology, mind versus brain, Lockean versus Kantian theoretical models, *DSM–III* problems, soft psychology, humanism, and epistemology. One finds classic papers by psychological luminaries such as Skinner, Meehl, Mahoney, Szasz, Rogers, Bergin, Strupp, and Gergen. Selections from the writings of important philosophers such as Feigl, Polanyi, Ricoer, and Manicas are included. I found all of the papers well chosen and obviously didactically pretested by Dr. Miller in his classroom teaching. It is clear that his book has been carefully molded and attended to with that love of wisdom that stamps the true philosophical quest.

Joseph F. Rychlak

PREFACE

This book is intended as a remedy, a bibliotherapy of sorts, for a serious malady that afflicts the mental health professions themselves but that remains largely undiagnosed. The disorder requiring urgent treatment is the splitting of clinical theory from its historical and logical foundation in Western philosophy, the resulting inability to speak effectively about theoretical differences, and the fragmentation into rival professions and theoretically isolated "schools" of treatment. What is required as an antidote to this tendency toward a dogmatic, schismatic, and often cultist approach to clinical theory is the recognition of the philosophical nature of these theoretical disputes and the restoration of philosophical methods of analysis and dialogue to a central role in the development of clinical theory. In this manner, the energies that currently are invested in the protection of professional turf and ideological diatribe may be devoted instead to collaborative discourse, research, and action. This is what will be required to make genuine headway in understanding that particular form of human misery and suffering that is variously called behavior disorders, emotional disturbance, problems in living, or mental illness.

This book is designed to make accessible to students, faculty, and practitioners in the various mental health disciplines an interdisciplinary literature on the philosophy of clinical practice. It may also be of interest to those in philosophy who are concerned with the philosophy of psychology or contemporary applications, as in the philosophy of medicine. I have attempted in the introductory chapter and in the introductory remarks to each section to provide the kind of background information that readers who are new to this interdisciplinary endeavor (from either psychology or philosophy) would require in order to work their way through this literature.

Despite the virtual neglect of philosophical issues by the mainstream training programs in the mental health professions over the past 40 years, a small but growing cadre of mental health professionals and philosophers have labored to bring these issues to the attention of their respective disciplines. Published in widely diverse sources, often by individuals working in relative isolation from one another, and with widely disparate technical languages, it has been as a body of thought rather inaccessible to both the student and the practitioner. In fact, its very existence as a *body* of thought or a literature within the mental health professions is not widely recognized. I hope that by bringing these selections together in this format and under one cover to raise the consciousness of psychologists and other mental health professionals concerning the centrality of philosophical issues in the development of clinical theory.

Papers were chosen for this book with five criteria in mind: (a) to recognize the lifelong commitment of a number of authors to this interdisciplinary endeavor; (b) to offer a balance of classic or formative papers and more recent contributions; (c) to demonstrate the contemporary relevance of metaphysics (ontology), epistemology, and moral philosophy to all the major theoretical approaches to clinical practice; (d) to extensively illustrate the process of philosophical dialogue and discourse; and (e) to expose readers to both the Anglo-American philosopohical tradition and European continental philosophy. I am sure that in my efforts to balance classic with recent papers, cover a broad range of psychological approaches, and sample both analytical and continental philosophy that important papers in each category have been regrettably excluded. In addition, in a few instances, articles were eliminated from the collection because of difficulty in obtaining copyright permissions. The lists of recommended readings after each section include important contributions to the literature that for one reason or another could not be reprinted here. In an attempt to respect the editorial conventions of the various disciplines represented, all articles (unless otherwise specifically noted) are reprinted here exactly as they originally appeared. The position of the article headings might have been changed so that the level of headings would be consistent throughout the book.

ACKNOWLEDGMENTS

I am indebted to the authors and original publishers of the articles in this book for both their contributions to the field and their gracious cooperation in this project. I am particularly grateful to those who not only agreed to having their work included, but expressed enthusiasm and support for the project *as a whole.*

The members of the Oberlin College philosophy department, particularly Norman Care, Robert Grimm, and Alfred MacKay, provided me as an undergraduate a model of philosophical discourse in which intellectual rigor, mutual respect, and human compassion were shown to be necessary and not incompatible elements of the pursuit of truth. It was a model that has served me well in the years since and that I strive to emulate in this book. Over the last 20 years of my involvement with clinical psychology, I have benefitted in thinking about the issues I address here from discussions with Joseph Hasazi, Peter Tumulty, and Jeffrey Adams. Few men understood or practiced the art of philosophical dialogue better than my good friend, the late Miles Davidson, whose cogent opinions and scholarly advice were sorely missed in the final prepration of this book. I have also been assisted by feedback from students enrolled in my graduate seminar on the philosophical foundations of clinical psychology and by a number of colleagues who have suggested articles for possible inclusion in the book. I am, of course, responsible for the final selections made and the positions articulated in this book.

One of the greatest benefits that work on this book has brought has been the opportunity to work with someone whose work I have greatly admired: Joseph F. Rychlak. He agreed to serve as a reviewer for the book, and he offered both his tremendous knowledge and perspective on the field, as well as his personal kindness and support. This is a much better book because of his efforts; the faults that remain are surely my own.

Without the loving, patient, good counsel of Naomi P. Shapiro, my partner in clinical practice as well as in life, this work could never have been begun, much less completed. She has read and faithfully critiqued the introductory chapter while at the same time shouldering more than her share of our other responsibilities. In fact, it was Naomi who pointed me in the direction of integrating my background in philosophy with my clinical work by introducing me to the work of Richard Chessick some 15 years ago.

I wish to thank the administration of Saint Michael's College for supporting the development of this book by providing the opportunity to teach the philosophical foundations of clinical psychology course and by providing a reduction in other teaching responsibilities so that I could complete it. The reference librarians of the Durick Library, Diane Boisnier, Christine Anderson, and Nancy Bianchi, were of great help in tracking down references and locating articles for consideration. The staff of the Graduate Office provided much technical support and secretarial assistance. Without the efforts of Marie Halsted, Monica Kellow, and Cora Frost, the preparation of the book would have been a far more difficult task.

I am greatly appreciative of the work of Julia Frank-McNeil, Director of Book Acquisitions and Development, and the staff of APA Books for their faith in this project, editorial guidance, technical expertise in bringing it to fruition, and their overall professionalism. I cannot imagine a more respectful publishing environment in which a writer could work.

RONALD B. MILLER

1

INTRODUCTION TO THE PHILOSOPHY OF CLINICAL PSYCHOLOGY

RONALD B. MILLER

For many clinical psychologists[1] and students entering the profession, few subjects could seem further removed from their intellectual interests than philosophy. Psychologists and other mental health professionals are looking for practical solutions to the pressing problems of human suffering that they are confronted by daily in clinical settings. Complex and abstract articles arguing the nature of being, knowledge, or virtue seem at best to be an academic luxury, or at worst, obsessive intellectualization that avoids the painful problems of daily living faced by the clinician. Nor has it been just the practitioners who have an aversion to philosophy. Clinical researchers reject philosophical discussion as a pernicious form of armchair psychology, an atavistic influence dragging clinical psychology back to its 19th-century prescientific status. As the 20th century comes to a close, practitioners, researchers, and scientist–practitioners find themselves increasingly divided as to the future course of American psychology. Yet, on one topic there has been virtual agreement: Twentieth-century philosophy has little to offer clinical psychology.

The disavowal of philosophical issues and discourse as a proper concern of clinical psychology comes in a variety of forms, some direct and others subtle. Few writers or theorists in

[1]Throughout this book my primary focus is on the discipline and profession of clinical psychology. However, the conflicting models of personality and psychotherapy that I discuss are found to some extent in all of the mental health professions (psychiatry, counseling psychology, school psychology, clinical social work, psychiatric nursing, mental health counseling, etc.). In fact, several of the articles reprinted in this book were written by individuals identified as leaders in these other mental health professions. I believe that the major thesis of this book—that contemporary philosophy has been neglected and needs to be reintegrated with theories of personality, psychopathology, and psychotherapy—holds true for work being done in all of the mental health professions. However, for purposes of economy of expression, and because I am more familiar with the nuances of the clinical psychology literature, I generally refer throughout the text to clinical psychology rather than to the mental health professions as a whole. This is in no shape or manner intended to imply a judgment on the relative importance of the various mental health professions or on their respective literature.

the discipline have been so bold as to ignore philosophy all together. Rather, the tendency has been to dismiss, disparage, or trivialize philosophical debate and thus to avoid the serious discussion of fundamental assumptions that is required.

The everyday language of the profession is instructive. Clinical psychologists can often be heard discussing their "philosophy" of something, but the discussion is rarely philosophical. Adopting the layperson's use of the term, clinical psychologists call their biases and prejudices "philosophies." When we do this, we mean to indicate that we do not think we have any real support for the belief in question, nor do we think that any is required. In other words, we use the term philosophy to indicate that what we are about to say is a bias we feel entitled to hold and about which discussion would be useless. This trivialization of the notion "every man (woman) a philosopher" is indicative of the hard times that befell philosophy during the heyday of logical positivism. The positivists (e.g., Ayer, 1952) argued that metaphysical or moral claims were actually expressions of personal feelings or attitudes and as such, could not be validated or invalidated as a system of beliefs about the world. Argument, even reasoned logical argument, about such matters was thus considered a waste of intellectual energy, if not downright foolish. The only acceptable form of philosophy, according to the logical positivists, was the philosophy of science, which was to be a sort of conceptual housekeeping for the natural sciences. (See the following discussion of logical positivism for a more thorough discussion of this view.)

One particularly virulent form of the trivialization of philosophy found in clinical psychology can be found in the response given to humanistic psychologists by their more "scientific" brethren. Even during the heyday of positivism, humanists were more open than most to acknowledging the importance of philosophy in formulating their positions (see Rogers, 1955 and chapter 17 of this book; Rychlak, 1969 and chapter 18 of this book). The response to this from mainstream psychology was either to dismiss their work as "not psychology" or to trivialize it by saying, in effect, "that's their philosophy; our philosophy is not to talk about philosophy, so we won't." In other words, if one wishes to talk about the philosophical issues in psychology, one can become a humanistic psychologist, which one is entitled to do, but the rest of psychology need not bother with it if that is its preference. Scientific psychologists are entitled to avoid that discussion, and to do so without their intellectual integrity or credibility being questioned.

What is absent from such a trivialized acceptance of philosophy, and in fact from all of the responses to be discussed, is the sense that philosophy is inherently a process of discourse, discussion, and debate. A philosophical position that is taken to restrict the opportunity for further philosophical dialogue is a philosophical position in name only. Of course, within philosophy itself, the logical positivists stimulated a tremendous debate as to the nature of philosophy and science. The discipline of philosophy could hardly respond otherwise to such bold claims. However, when these ideas were transported into psychology, they were used to end philosophical discussion itself.

I previously identified three other ways in which the discipline of clinical psychology has assiduously avoided philosophical discourse: *theoretical preciousness, terminal philosophical ambivalence,* and *philosophy by fiat* (Miller, 1983). *Theoretical preciousness* is modeled after the notion of "professional preciousness" introduced by Sarason, Levine, Goldenberg, Cherline, and Bennett (1966). Professional preciousness is essentially the attitude that only one's own profession is adequately trained to help people and that all the other professions in mental health work are not only unhelpful but actually doing harm.

Theoretical preciousness[2] is the explicit or implicit belief that only one's own theoretical approach to psychotherapy (e.g., psychoanalytic, cognitive-behavioral, person-centered, medical model, family systems, etc.) is rational, coherent, and true. Most, if not all, of the other

[2]Adapted in part from Miller (1983).

theoretical approaches are not only less adequate but fundamentally misguided, illegitimate, and false. Consequently, only one's own approach to psychotherapy is capable of helping those in need, whereas others are either ineffective or actually damaging people. Theoretical preciousness might be thought to be primarily associated with the kind of sectarian fervor that has developed around the various "schools" of psychotherapy with their favorite gurus and cultist trappings. However, as Toulmin (1979) argued, there is a "cult of empiricism" in academic psychology, or what Bakan (1969) called "methodolatry," that maintains that all important questions are empirical questions and that any method of arriving at the truth other than quantitatively controlled research is pernicious and unacceptable. Thus, theoretical preciousness is found even among those who have ostensibly eschewed grand theories in favor of empirical research.

In a climate of theoretical preciousness, people who disagree with one's own theory are treated more like heretics to be pitied or scorned than like colleagues whose views are to be respected and explored. To sit down and seriously examine theoretical differences is considered a waste of time and perhaps even a little dangerous due to risking contamination of one's own pure soul. Professional preciousness, although distasteful, is a relatively common feature of the professional world. Wherever professionals are competing for prestige and income, there is bound to be at least some chauvinism. It is predictable and tolerable, even if unfortunate.

However, when it comes to the marketplace of ideas and the pursuit of knowledge, theoretical preciousness is not nearly so benign. It undermines the entire intellectual enterprise and makes theoretical investigation and dialogue next to impossible. Rhetoric and ridicule replace reasoning, conceptual analysis, and logic. A field such as mental health, in which professional allegiances and identities are defined and symbolized by theoretical positions, runs the constant risk that its theoretical base will degenerate into propaganda serving the struggle for professional supremacy. When theoretical preciousness prevails over theoretical dialogue, a discipline becomes increasingly polarized and fragmented. It is marked by schisms, compartmentalized literature, and narrow universes of discourse. No framework or vehicle exists for rationally exploring and discussing theoretical differences. Those discussions that are attempted end quickly in impasse or stalemate. Nothing remains that can be done with theoretical positions except to reiterate them with greater force and assurance. Our scholarship and literature, which could serve as a bulwark against the fragmentation of the field into sects and cults, serves instead only to further "Balkanize" the discipline.

Witness the recent split in the American Psychological Association that resulted in the formation of the American Psychological Society. Ostensibly, this was a political schism over whether the professional practitioners or the scientific academics would control the American Psychological Association. In part, it surely was this. It was also, however, a split over a fundamental question in philosophy concerning the nature of science and its relationship to practical knowledge. The scientists did not see the practitioners paying sufficient attention to the development of the knowledge base of their work, and the practitioners did not find the academics' work on that knowledge base of much use. Because psychologists generally have little understanding of how to approach such philosophical differences on the meaning of knowledge, they converted the problem to a simple matter of power and influence. They "acted out" rather than understood the philosophical conflict.

The second obstacle toward progress in building a philosophical dialogue in clinical psychology is what I call *terminal philosophical ambivalence*. Here, psychologists acknowledge serious philosophical problems as being inherent to the discipline but then go on to focus on the technical problems of research or practice as if they can be discussed independently of the philosophical problems. This position certainly has more integrity than others mentioned earlier, for it neither trivializes nor dogmatizes philosophical issues. It seems to express in a straightforward manner the dilemma created by the separation of psychology from philosophy as an academic discipline during the late 19th century. To make the break, psychologists had to show how they were not philosophers any longer, that they did not "do philosophy." They "did psychology."

Psychology was like an adolescent trying to leave home. To establish an independent identity, it is sometimes necessary to deny any form of dependency on the parents. One can hardly be independent if one keeps bringing the dirty laundry home each weekend for mom to do. However, if one never learns how to clean up after oneself, then the dirty clothes just get thrown under the bed and in the closet, and ones hopes no one will notice. Sooner or later, though, one cannot go out in public any longer because there is nothing left to wear (or someone accidentally opens the closet door and is buried by the dirty laundry).

The third obstacle to philosophical discourse in clinical psychology is what I call *philosophy by fiat*. Here, a clinical theorist imports a whole line of philosophical arguments from philosophy to serve as a basis for a psychological theory but does so in a manner that suggests that it is the only legitimate philosophical position that can be taken on the subject. Thus, the behaviorists imported logical positivism, the Rogerians imported Husserl's phenomenology or Sartre's existentialism, Biswanger imported Heidegger's *Dasein,* and today a number of social systems, humanistic, and psychoanalytic theorists have adopted hermeneutics as their philosophy. Although this is yet another step in the right direction, in that a philosophical position is put forward as a philosophical position and is not hidden as a bias, trumpeted as an ideology, or withdrawn in ambivalence, it still falls far short of encouraging a philosophical dialogue. In fact, it implies that philosophy does not involve dialogue at all, and so in this sense may be said to be of little improvement over the other means of avoiding philosophy identified earlier.

Perhaps one of the most vivid illustrations of philosophy by fiat can be found in Wolman's (1965) classic textbook, *The Handbook of Clinical Psychology*. In his introductory chapter, "Clinical Psychology and the Philosophy of Science," Wolman offered a thorough review of the epistemological problems raised by clinical psychology. Writing from within the neopositivist tradition, he argued that a knowledge of practice is distinct from a knowledge of science and that practice must be governed by an ethical concern with the suffering of others, whereas science must be governed by experimental methodology. He also argued that theories always must go beyond the facts and that the facts of psychology must include introspective reports, individual behavior, and social fields. Theories must be checked against the facts as determined by experimental methods, but clinical practice can only be learned or captured well by case study methods. Wolman conceded that theories of personality and psychotherapy do represent different ethical values, but these differences cannot be resolved. Ethical positions are merely expressions of emotional reactions that cannot be justified through rational argument.

Wolman (1965) provided a scholarly and masterful philosophical apologia for the mainstream clinical psychology of mid-20th century America. Although this is certainly preferable to ignoring or avoiding the philosophical issues that are both pervasive and divisive in the field, it stops far short of inviting psychologists to enter into philosophical discourse. He wrote as though all of the important philosophical questions relevant to clinical psychology had been settled and the science and practice could proceed unhindered by further philosophical problems. Perhaps it is no coincidence that few if any contemporary textbooks or handbooks of clinical psychology devote much attention to the issues Wolman addressed. Clinical psychology had the green light it needed to be a respectable science. Philosophy had served its purpose and was no longer necessary as part of the discipline itself.

Feigl (see chapter 2) noted that philosophy, particularly logical positivist philosophy, was used in much the same manner by experimental psychologists during the early part of the 20th century. Ironically, about the time Wolman was pronouncing the solution to the philosophical problems of clinical psychology, experimental psychologists under the influence of the move to cognitive psychology found that 20th-century philosophy had much to offer in conceptualizing problems and interpreting results of empirical investigations. Conceptual analysis, philosophical argument, and empirical investigation are mutually reinforcing, rather than mutually exclusive, activities (Block, 1980; Gardner, 1985; Robinson, 1985; Valentine, 1982).

One might be tempted here to argue that because psychology has begun to reembrace philosophy, clinical psychology must do so as well. However, that would be repeating the mistakes of the past: assuming that the problems of clinical psychology are merely a subset of the problems of experimental psychology. This is an assumption that must be examined rather than made. Instead, what is needed is an examination of what the philosophical problems of clinical psychology might be and how they might be addressed.

THE PHILOSOPHICAL PROBLEMS OF CLINICAL PSYCHOLOGY

1. The fundamental philosophical problem of clinical psychology is metaphysical—conflicting models of the nature of psychological reality. (Philosophers sometimes refer to this as the problem of human nature.) Psychological textbooks abound with lists and comparisons of alternative models or paradigms of personality, psychopathology, psychological assessment, or psychotherapy. Although it is sometimes acknowledged that these different paradigms reflect different philosophical positions, rarely is the philosophical literature itself discussed. One is given the impression that there is little benefit to a psychologist in understanding the philosophical arguments for or against these positions.

What is the basic "stuff" with which clinicians work (subjective experience, behavior, social systems, unconscious forces, brain cells)? This is essentially a metaphysical question having to do with the nature of reality, being, and causality. There are a number of subsidiary problems that quickly follow: How do these different elements (i.e., experience, brain cells, behavior, etc.) relate to one another (the mind–body problem)? Do these "stuffs" obey the same laws of causality (the free will vs. determinism problem)? Can each of these "stuffs" be studied with the same methodology and truth criteria (the epistemological problem)? It is no wonder that clinicians have not been able to resolve their differences in theories of psychopathology or treatment "philosophies"; they have been acting out the most important philosophical conflicts in Western civilization without the benefit of awareness or the fruits of the labor of those who have openly faced and struggled with these questions.

2. The second fundamental philosophical problem of clinical psychology concerns the moral character of clinical psychology. Is mental health practice a moral undertaking from start to finish, as some have argued (Halleck, 1971; London, 1964; Margolis, 1966, also see chapter 5; Szasz, chapter 12), or is it possible to develop a morally neutral science of psychopathology and technology of behavior change, as theorists as diverse as Freud (1933/1965) and Skinner (1974) have argued (the meta-ethical problem [having to do with the nature of morality itself] and the fact–value dichotomy)? If models of personality, psychopathology, assessment, and psychotherapy do indeed implicitly or explicitly represent different value systems, what should the definition be of mental health or illness (the problem of normative ethics [defining the good life or virtue])? Furthermore, if these differences in assessment or treatment "philosophies" are the result of differing views on matters of moral philosophy, is consensus therefore impossible (the question of ethical relativism vs. absolutism and the nature of moral reasoning)? Moral philosophy naturally leads to social and political philosophy. Once clinicians acknowledge the moral character of clinical practice and their conceptions of mental illness, they must acknowledge their political character as well. How does a mentally healthy person regard personal liberty and social responsibility, and for whom is the therapist working, the client or the society (the problem

of individual rights vs. duties owed society or the state)? There are many challenging versions of this latter problem, including the morality of civil commitment, the right to suicide, and uses of clinical procedures to subdue political opposition.

3. The third fundamental philosophical problem of clinical psychology is implicit in what I said earlier, but it is so important that it needs to be stated explicitly here. It may be properly identified as the philosophy of science question addressed by Wolman (1965). What does it mean to call something an applied science, and how does that differ from a pure science? What kinds of knowledge, other than scientific knowledge, must a practitioner possess in order to function effectively? How is this other knowledge obtained, communicated, validated, if not by the scientific method? How is clinical knowledge to be integrated with scientific knowledge? These are the epistemological questions inherent in, and specific to, the development of a practice-oriented discipline of psychology. Of course, to the extent that clinical psychology is viewed as a scientific research discipline, it also shares in the general problems of the philosophy of science: the relationship of facts to theories, the role of values in both theoretical and factual claims, the logic of justification, and so forth.

For purposes of introduction, I have discussed each of these fundamental philosophical problems as though it were separate from the others. In fact, metaphysical, moral, and epistemological questions are highly interdependent, and it is a matter of considerable philosophical importance which questions are given priority. Philosophers have differed greatly in the urgency that they attach to metaphysical versus moral issues. So, for example, those who attach a greater significance to moral questions are more likely to view the basic "stuff" of psychology as being more nonmaterial (i.e., as being more than simply brain cells and behavior) and to view knowledge claims in psychology as partly resulting from an intuitive process of recognizing truth and goodness.

This interrelatedness of philosophical problems is part of what makes philosophy both so intellectually stimulating and so difficult for the uninitiated. In order to understand it better, and more fully appreciate the philosophical dimension of clinical psychology, it is necessary to digress temporarily from a discussion of the philosophical problems of clinical psychology and focus more directly on the nature of philosophy itself.

THE NATURE OF PHILOSOPHY

The definition of philosophy is itself a philosophical question that has been the subject of much discussion and critical analysis. This is in keeping with one of the most basic features of philosophy that it is to be an examination of the most fundamental assumptions and first principles of thought, bar none. No questions are off limits because they are too general, abstract, or far reaching. It is always fair game in philosophy to call into question philosophy itself, or the prevailing definition of philosophy.

The word philosophy was created from two Greek words that, taken together, mean "the love of wisdom." However, *wisdom* to the Greeks meant both knowledge and competence, both knowing and knowing how to do things (Passmore, 1967). It represents a commitment to the life of reason, to trying to understand how and why things happen, and then to doing something to better the human condition with that knowledge. Note, too, that this definition does not read "an interest in" but "a love of." Philosophy was not meant to be a sterile intellectual exercise, detached from the concerns or realities of daily life. It was to be a love, a passionate concern with the truth about human existence. (There is much here that attracts the attention of the clinical psychologist. It would appear that what makes clinical psychology suspect to many in academia—linking knowledge to action and the commitment to improving the human condition—are features of the oldest scholarly discipline in the world.)

Bertrand Russell, certainly the most widely read and perhaps the most outstanding philosopher of the 20th century, has defined philosophy in the following manner: "Philosophy is something intermediate between theology and science. Like theology it consists of speculation on matters as to which definite knowledge has so far been unascertainable, but like science it appeals to reason rather than authority" (1945, p. xiii).

Russell's (1945) definition is helpful because it indicates both a content and a method for philosophy. The content is derived from the ultimate concerns of religion: the meaning of human existence, one's place in the universe, and the dilemmas of life choices. The method is the application of rationality: thought, critical analysis, observation, logic, and reasoning. There are those like Hegel in the 19th century and Heidegger and the existentialists in the 20th century who have preferred to explore the content issues even when this strained the methodological restriction that philosophical propositions appeal to a common sense of reasonableness. Their philosophy tended to the mystical and poetic, and they offered no apologies when they found it necessary to communicate in such a manner in order to do justice to their subject matter (e.g., being vs. nonbeing). So, for example, Hegel defined philosophy in this way:

> This science is the unity of Art and Religion. Whereas the vision-method of Art, external in point of form, is but subjective production and shivers the substantial content into many separate shapes, and whereas Religion, with its separation into parts, opens it out in mental picture, and mediates what is thus opened out; Philosophy not merely keeps them together to make a totality, but even unifies them into the simple spiritual vision, and then in that raises them to self-conscious thought. Such consciousness is thus the intelligible unity (cognized by thought) of art and religion, in which the diverse elements in the content are cognized as necessary, and this necessary as free. (Weiss, 1974, p. 326)

This may be contrasted with a definition of philosophy as offered by one of the leading 20th-century British philosophers, G. E. Moore, who is credited with being one of the founders of the contemporary Anglo-American analytical approach to philosophy.

> I want, as a start, to try to give you a general idea of what philosophy *is*: or, in other words, what sort of questions it is that philosophers are constantly engaged in discussing and trying to answer.
>
> To begin with, then, it seems to me that the most important and interesting thing which philosophers have tried to do is no less than this; namely: To give a general description of the *whole* of the Universe, mentioning all the most important kinds of things which we *know* to be in it, considering how far it is likely that there are in it important kinds of things which we do not absolutely *know* to be in it, and also considering the most important ways in which these various kinds of things are related to one another. I will call all this, for short, "Giving a general description of the *whole* Universe," and hence will say that the first and most important problem of philosophy is: To give a general description of the *whole* Universe. (Moore, 1953/1962, p. 13–14)

Rorty (1979) argued that both of these traditional approaches to philosophy, as different as they are, share a common belief in foundationalism. Philosophy is viewed as establishing the foundation of knowledge for all disciplines in some sort of absolute, a priori sense. Following Charles Pierce, Williams James, and John Dewey, the late 19th- and early 20th-century American pragmatists, Rorty argued that philosophy is incapable of accomplishing this task because it is an impossible one. Each discipline must, by struggling with its own material or data, find its own foundation. Philosophy has no privileged position or method to allow it to intervene or supervene in this process. Developing Dewey's notion that philosophy is a catalyst for integration, consolidation, and change within the social, artistic, and intellectual tradition of a civilization or culture, Rorty (1974) wrote that "the only point on which I would insist is that the philosopher's moral concern should be with continuing the conversation of the West, rather than on insisting upon a place for the traditional problems of modern philosophy within that conversation" (p. 394).

It is the philosopher's job to be a guardian and overseer of the moral tradition of a civilization without recourse to criteria of absolute truth or certainty. This is a sort of sociological interpretation of philosophy and one attracting greater interest in contemporary philosophy. Note, also, that it is the only definition of the three to give precedence to moral philosophy over metaphysics.

Although much discussed, Rorty's (1979) view remains controversial in contemporary philosophical circles. There is one belief, however, that these diverse philosophers share: The philosopher works without need of technical augmentation of the everyday powers of observation and reasoning available to all human beings. An astronomer, microbiologist, or historian might argue that others lack the exposure to the facts that are needed to appreciate the position being offered or defended, but not so the philosopher. Pierce captured this feature of philosophy when he wrote of philosophy:

> Class II (of the theoretical sciences) is philosophy, which deals with positive truth, indeed, yet contents itself with observations such as come within the range of every man's normal experience, and for the most part in every waking hour of his life. Hence Bentham calls this class, *coenoscopic*. These observations escape the untrained eye precisely because they permeate our whole lives, just as the man who never takes off his blue spectacles soon ceases to see the blue tinge. Evidently, therefore, no microscope or sensitive film would be of the least use in this class. The observation is observation in a peculiar, yet perfectly legitimate sense. If philosophy glances now and again at the results of special sciences, it is only as a sort of condiment to excite its own proper observation. (cited in Buchler, 1940/1955, p. 66)

The philosopher wants to make sense of the puzzles of everyday human existence and to do so relies on the everyday powers of observation, inference, and deduction. As the tradition of Western philosophy has unfolded, it has, to be sure, become increasingly complex, differentiated, and to some extent technical or specialized (e.g., symbolic logic, Hegelian dialectic, or linguistic analysis). So, although not just anyone can open up a given work of philosophy and jump right in, it is a lack of familiarity with the history of the discussion or the tradition of the literature, rather than the inaccessibility of the relevant facts or problems, that stands in the way.

To "do" philosophy, one needs a commitment to looking for creative solutions to the most basic problems of human existence, a willingness to follow a line of argument wherever it leads, and submitting all proposed problems and solutions to the test of careful, detailed, critical analysis. This analysis involves checking the veracity of claims of fact for accuracy, and logic for consistency and coherence. Such an approach does not rule out a role for insight or intuition, but it would rule out positions supported solely by such means. Nor does it rule out the possibility that some philosophical problems will reemerge in conjunction with more technical or scientific investigations and that they will be more effectively discussed by those who are also conversant with that scientific literature. Nevertheless, it may be said fairly that philosophy is simply the attempt to bring the *full* powers of the human intellect to bear on the most basic, puzzling, and pervasive questions of human life.

However, as noted earlier, to enter into an ongoing philosophical discussion, one also needs an appreciation of the philosophical tradition that gives rise to that discussion. Consequently, before one can do the philosophy of clinical psychology, one must have some background in the historical tradition of Western metaphysics, epistemology, and moral philosophy.

PREDOMINANT THEMES IN WESTERN PHILOSOPHY

Western philosophy began with the writings and teachings of what have come to be called the pre-Socratic philosophers of Ionia in Asia Minor in the 6th century BC. Greek philosophy reached its zenith in Socrates (470–399 BC), Plato (428–347 BC), and Aristotle (384–322 BC). The questions posed and the answers offered during this period of little over 250 years have set the agenda and framework for philosophical speculation and debate for the last 2,000 years. Socrates and his student, Plato, are credited with articulating the fundamental moral and political dilemmas of Western civilization and demonstrating the virtue of rational discourse as the primary method of problem solving in human affairs through the use of the dialogue. Aristotle, who was a student of Plato, is credited with combining the moral concerns of his teacher with a passion for observation and analysis of natural phenomena. Aristotle was the founder of systematic Western science. This is a rich and broad tradition: Until the Renaissance, all learning and scholarship went by the name of "philosophy." Since that time, the various sciences—physics, mathematics, biology, history, and most recently psychology, anthropology, and sociology—have established independent identities. Their common roots in philosophy are vestigially recognized by the continued practice of awarding the degree of doctor of philosophy (PhD) in all academic research disciplines.

There is a certain strain of this tradition that remains the concern of philosophy proper, particularly as an academic discipline. These are the problems of metaphysics, epistemology, and moral philosophy. The modern era of philosophy is generally said to have begun with the work of Descartes (1596–1650). Unlike the scholastic philosophers of the Middle Ages before him, he did not consider all philosophy to be a commentary on Aristotle but saw himself capable of questioning the foundation of all knowledge. In his *Meditations*, Descartes (1641/1969) searched for a firm foundation for all knowledge by asking if there was anything that he knew that was so certain that he could not doubt it. In this Cartesian doubt and his famous cogito response—"I think, therefore I am"—Descartes set the agenda for philosophy in the modern era up to the present day. Some of the most interesting philosophical works of the past decade have challenged Descartes's agenda (e.g., Bernstein, 1983; Rorty, 1979), but still it is Descartes's epistemological agenda that is being discussed. Like Plato, Descartes found certainty in mathematics and pure thought, not in the data of the senses. Descartes found support in the work of the continental rationalists, particularly Leibnitz (1646–1716) and Spinoza, (1632–1677), whereas the British empiricists, Locke (1632–1704), Berkeley (1685–1753), and Hume (1711–1776), sought to redeem the senses as the foundation of knowledge, particularly in light of the growing success of the natural sciences. Despite the efforts of the best minds of the modern era to break away from the influence of The Philosopher (as the scholastics had referred to Aristotle), the argument had circled back to his position that knowledge begins with the senses.

At this point, toward the end of the 18th century, as the world was embroiled in revolution, Kant (1781/1929) published the *Critique of Pure Reason*. Many consider it the most profound philosophical treatise to have appeared since Aristotle's work, and it still exerts an enormous influence over philosophical thinking in modern times. Kant's intent was threefold: (a) to put an end to metaphysical speculation on matters that ultimately depend on empirical facts for their solution (a posteriori knowledge); (b) to recognize the rightful place of the natural sciences in deciding all a posteriori matters; and (c) to establish a legitimate area of nonempirical study, the a priori, which is the logical framework that makes it possible for there to be any empirical knowledge whatsoever. Kant distinguished between two kinds of a priori judgments: analytic and synthetic. Analytic statements are tautologies. The predicate is already contained in the subject. If one says, "All men are males," this does not require empirical confirmation because it is a true statement by definition. The concept of male is already included in the concept of men. If one were to deny its truth, one would simply be showing that one does not know the language. Logicians since at least the time of Aristotle have recognized this form of nonempirical truth.

Kant (1781/1929), however, in a stroke of analytical brilliance, maintained that there were some a priori claims that were more than just tautologies, in which the predicate was not contained in the subject (Körner, 1955). The predicate adds something to the subject, but it does so based not on experience but on pure thought. When people think about their own thinking, they enter the domain of transcendental logic or reason. As with Plato, the clearest examples of this kind of thought are mathematical. Although the mathematical proposition $5 = 5$ is an a priori analytic truth, the proposition $3 + 2 = 5$ is an a priori synthetic truth. "All men are males" is an a priori analytic truth, whereas "All men are free" is an a priori synthetic truth. The mental process of addition allows people to create true claims about numbers without resorting to either experience or mere tautologies. When confronting the empirical world people bring to it certain categories of understanding, just as they bring the capacity of addition to numbers. These categories of thought are the framework people place on the world and through which they can know anything whatsoever. The categories set the limits of experience. Rather than discuss Kant's (1781/1929) list of 12 categories of thought, of which many are controversial, it is important to note that Kant thought that the introduction of the categories permitted the solution of a number of crucial philosophical problems. Causation that Hume had dismissed as nothing more than a contingent association of events, and therefore a largely empty concept, Kant reclaimed as an inherent feature of experience. Similarly, Kant found that a number of troublesome philosophical concepts are prerequisites to empirical experience: universals, the infinite, necessity, existence, and nonexistence. Thought transcends the empirical world to discover the basic knowledge structures that make empirical experience possible.

Kant (1781/1929) also addressed the antinomies of human thought, the paradoxes in which both elements appear to be true but are mutually contradictory. He noted, for example, that both the freedom of human action and scientific determinism appear to be true, as do scientific materialism and Christianity. His solution relied on his theory of the categories. Human freedom and the belief in God are truths of transcendental reason: determinism and materialism are truths of empirical knowledge. No true contradiction results because each is in a different domain of knowledge. Kant's writings in the tradition of German academia are long and convoluted. When this is added to the profundity of his thought, the work is almost impenetrable. Yet, the outstanding proponents of a philosophical approach to clinical psychology (and psychiatry), Rychlak (1969) and Chessick (1977), relied heavily on the work of Kant.

It is customary in philosophy textbooks to try to capture the thematic development of Western philosophy in terms of various dichotomies (e.g., empiricism vs. rationalism, free will vs. determinism, idealism vs. materialism, objective vs. subjective, etc.). To the scholarly researcher studying the work of a great philosopher, these labels are an anathema, confusing rather than clarifying. Yet, to the novice, such terms are bench marks, even lifelines in a turbulent uncharted sea. They provide some guidance as well as comfort as one tackles a forbidding area. So, for purposes of discussion, these terms are a necessary but oversimplified point of departure.

For those interested in understanding the philosophical issues currently being discussed in clinical psychology, the key dichotomy is that of objective versus subjective: objective versus subjective reality, objective versus subjective knowledge, and objective versus subjective moral values. To some extent, this is a dichotomy with which psychologists are very familiar. William James (1907) noted that thinkers could be divided into those who preferred tough versus tender-minded approaches to their subject matter. Recently, Kimble (1984) has used C. P. Snow's notion of the "two worlds" of science and the humanities to survey the attitudes of psychologists on matters relating to objective versus subjective approaches to their discipline. What is missing generally, though, is a philosophical discussion of the merits or shortcomings of each viewpoint.

First, one needs to define these central terms, *objective* and *subjective*. This is a daunting task, doomed to failure, but I make at least a first effort. By *objective* I mean those philosophical positions that give priority to material or physical reality, to the kind of knowledge that can be gained of that physical substantial reality (i.e., clear-cut measurements that are publically confirmable), and to absolute standards of right and wrong, good and evil.

By *subjective* I mean those philosophical approaches that give priority to mental reality (ideas, images, feelings, dreams, etc.); to knowledge claims that are the result of introspection, intuition, or insight (and, consequently, very personal, private, and not usually confirmable by other people); and a relativistic concept of moral truth or goodness.

The distinction between objective and subjective approaches to philosophy is helpful and clarifying, but it will be confusing if one does not know that it is possible to maintain a position identified with one side of the dichotomy in one area of philosophy (e.g., metaphysics) while supporting the other side of the dichotomy in the other areas (e.g., epistemology and moral philosophy). For example, one finds Bishop Berkeley, who was a chief architect of British empiricism as a theory of objective knowledge, concluding that objects themselves are ideas—what I have been calling a subjective view of metaphysics (often referred to as idealism). Similarly, many logical positivists, who, following in the tradition of British empiricism, took a very objective approach to knowledge and truth, also maintained a phenomenalist (i.e., subjective or idealist) view of material objects and reality. In psychology, Skinner's radical behaviorism is strictly objective both about the nature of reality and knowledge, but on the matter of moral principles, it offers a confusing naturalized ethics that might be interpreted as subjective and lacking in any universal concrete principles of moral behavior.

It is generally assumed that the objective is less open to biased observation and that it is therefore more solid as a centerpiece of one's conception of the world or knowledge. On the other hand, the objective is seen as being more cold, less human, and somewhat forbidding. People would want the surgeon who is performing open-heart surgery on them to be objective, but they would resent it if they felt treated like objects, and not as people.

One of the leading philosophers of our day, Thomas Nagel, has selected this theme as central to his work. He begins his book, *The View From Nowhere,* with the following observation:

> This book is about a single problem: how to combine the perspective of a particular person inside the world with an objective view of the same world, the person and the viewpoint included. . . . It is the most fundamental issue about morality, knowledge, freedom, the self, and the relation of the mind to the physical world. (1986, p. 3)

Although the objective versus subjective dichotomy is clearly a central and critical one for philosophy, and ultimately for psychology, it is far from being a simple one. I return to this theme throughout the discussion to follow on the nature of metaphysics, epistemology, and moral philosophy. In doing so, one would do well to pay heed to this warning from Nagel (1986):

> There is a persistent temptation to turn philosophy into something less difficult and more shallow than it is. It is an extremely difficult subject, and no exception to the general rule that creative efforts are rarely successful. I do not feel equal to the problems treated in this

book. They seem to me to require an order of intelligence wholly different from mine. Others who have tried to address the central questions of philosophy will recognize the feeling. (p. 12)

Metaphysics

Metaphysics is defined by Aristotle in his *Metaphysics* as the "science of being as such" (cited in McKeon, 1941, Book 4). Metaphysical thought attempts to penetrate to the truth about the essence of reality, to find the first principles or causes of things being the way they are. How is an individual member of a class of objects related to that class (the problem of universals)? Is the world ultimately of one substance or many (the problem of reductionism)? How is the identity of one object distinguished from the identity of another (the problem of identity and difference)?

Beginning with Plato and Aristotle, and continuing through to the present, there have been two chief schools of thought in metaphysics: Platonic and Aristotelian. Plato's doctrine of the "forms" has been described as an idealist (or subjective) view of reality. The world is the most fundamentally real and stable at the level of thought, idea, or conceptualization (Copleston, 1946/1962a). Physical reality is but a shadow of mental reality. One can know universal categories of experience with certainty, but individual empirical events are always open to doubt and question. Aristotle, although greatly influenced by Plato, rejected the theory of the forms and saw the universal ideas of Plato as being too far removed from the natural world. For Aristotle, the natural order of things was fascinating and it is in the study of the particular (i.e., material objects) that the universal is revealed (Copleston, 1946/1962b, p. 35). Knowledge begins with sensory perception, and so there is a connection between the mental world of abstract truths and the physical world of sensible objects (Cornford, 1932). This view is usually identified by the term *realism,* meaning that reality is taken to be just what it appears to be in common sense. For the realist, ideas and things (mind and body) are separate and real aspects of life. The mind is elusive but clearly dependent on the body for its existence, and the realist sees the mental as an extension of the natural order of the universe. Since the time of Aristotle, many in the world of natural science have been willing to go one step farther and endorse materialism. Materialism is the view that reality consists of material objects in various combinations and configurations. Mental phenomena, the hallowed "Ideas of Plato," are dismissed as products of the physical realm, devoid of any power or importance in the final shape of things.

There is a strong pull toward monism in metaphysics. Statements of the sort, "Everything is really mental" or "Everything is really physical" are monistic and reductionistic because all aspects of life are reduced to one kind of substance. Realists are those in philosophy who reject both idealism and materialism in favor of granting reality status to both mental and physical events. Realism is antireductionistic or dualistic as a metaphysical position. The beauty of dualism is that it accepts people's commonsense notion of the reality of both the mental and physical dimensions of their lives. Its chief drawback is that once this dual reality is granted, it becomes very difficult to explain the interaction between these two radically different aspects of reality (i.e., the mind–body problem). Idealism flies in the face of people's experience that hands-on experiences in the world change what they think about that world in ways that fantasy and speculation do not, that the existence of physical objects persists regardless of whether people pay any attention to them, and that people cannot will them in and out of existence simply by changing their thoughts about the objects. Furthermore, idealism is hard-pressed to explain how people come to share common views of the world. What is it that allows the ideas in one person's mind to coincide with the ideas in another's (i.e., the development of commonly held beliefs), if not the press of an external, objective reality? If idealism is correct, there is the risk of solipsism (each person knowing a separate reality).

Materialism, too, has its problems: Although most people are willing to admit that minds need brains to exist, mental functioning or phenomenological experience seems to lack physicality in important ways. Thoughts just do not seem to occupy space, nor do they obey the laws of gravity or energy.

In clinical psychology, the fundamental debate triggered by Szasz's *The Myth of Mental Illness* (see chapter 12) is in part a question of metaphysics. How are clinicians to conceptualize the basic reality with which they work? It seems that the objections to other models put forth by biologically oriented psychologists come down to a rejection of subjective states as real, efficacious, or important. Similarly, the defense of psychodynamic and more humanistically oriented positions often amounts to a claim that nothing could be more real or central to a person than his or her own subjective states, values, and choices.

Faced with these sorts of dilemmas, philosophers have returned to the initial task that gave rise to them: the search for truth. Perhaps truth can be explored directly as a form of knowledge without having to decide its specific content (material or ideal)? In this way metaphysical questions give way to epistemology (the study of the nature of knowledge itself).

Epistemology: The Theory of Knowledge

What are knowledge and truth, and what criteria distinguish them from false beliefs? Again, one finds characteristically Platonic and Aristotelian positions. Plato's doctrine of the forms suggests that knowledge is discovered through insight and self-examination. Ultimately, it is a form of reminiscence. People must discover what they know, but they do not know or remember that they know. Taking mathematical knowledge as the paradigmatic case of knowing, Plato showed how the truth is arrived at through deductive reasoning. This view became known in the modern era as rationalism. Rationalists believe that truth is discovered via the powers of human insight and reason and never simply via observing the facts of the case. What people know to be true is a product of their own power of logical coherent thought. This is the coherence theory of truth. Ideas that are true fit together and form a unified body of knowledge.

By contrast, empiricists believe that truth is derived from careful and systematic observation or experience of events taking place in the world. Truth emerges because people, like good reporters, assiduously keep checking the facts of their stories. Truth is discovered when a person's picture of reality and reality itself match up. This is called the correspondence theory of truth. It is conducive to the development of the natural sciences and in psychology has many adherents.

The problem with the rationalist–empiricist dichotomy are twofold. First, neither can give a very good account of each other's paradigmatic case of knowing. Second, there is a built-in circularity to both criteria of truth. One can define truth in terms of coherence or correspondence, but then how does one define these terms? How does one "match" a picture to an event or decide that ideas "fit" together. These turn out to be metaphorical expressions for saying that something is true rather than simple descriptions of procedures to be followed to ascertain the truth.

These sorts of problems have led to various skeptical views that knowledge is impossible or to relativistic views that knowledge is very personal and nonobjective (i.e., not requiring mutually agreed on truth criteria). Epistemological positions may be characterized as subjective or objective in two very different senses of each term. *Subjective* may mean that knowledge originates from the realm of ideas or consciousness, or it may mean that the truth of the knowledge claim is relative to the person issuing it (i.e., relativistic). Something might be true for one person but not for another. *Objective* may be used to contrast with either of these two meanings of subjective. Objective may mean that a knowledge claim is thought to originate in the study of material objects rather than in human consciousness, or it may mean that a knowledge claim is intended to be universal or absolute and not relative to the speaker.

Rationalism emphasizes the subjective aspect of knowledge when it claims people find truth within their own powers of reason, but its findings are of an objective or absolute truth as in a mathematical formula that is true for all mathematicians. Empiricism is subjective in its emphasis on the experience of people's senses, but objective in seeing this experience as resulting from a material world that people can all sense and about which they can determine an objective truth. It is not an absolute truth because experience may lead people to revise their beliefs, nor is it relative truth because it assumes a common world as the basis of individual experience.

Frustration with the murkiness of concepts and issues such as these led in the 19th century to a number of radical attempts to break out of this cyclical empiricist–rationalist argument. Most familiar to psychologists is the group of experimental physiologists, physicists, and neurologists, who began to investigate just how the brain and senses operated and who hoped to show a direct, lawful link between physiological variables and psychological experience and therefore put an end to the philosophical debate. Experimental psychology developed as the result of the work of men such as Fechner and Wundt, whose concerns were deeply philosophical. They hoped to solve the mind–body problem and end the rationalism versus empiricism debate with their experimental research.

Observing this cycle of the alternating popularity of empirical and rationalistic theories of knowledge, Hegel (1770–1831) sought to embrace both sides of the controversy with his *dialectical method.* Both are true in part, but they miss the essential contradictory nature of all truth. Hegel embraced both horns of the dilemma and elevated this cycle to a theory of history and truth such that the truth always involves its own negation. This dialectical logic was in opposition to Aristotle's law of the excluded middle or contradiction: Something cannot be both "A" and "–A" at the same time.

Hegel's esoteric and convoluted style, even more difficult than Kant's, and as noted earlier so typical of German academic philosophy, led the existentialist writers such as Kierkegaard (1813–1855), Nietzsche (1844–1900), and Heidegger (1889–1976) to reject both sides of the dichotomy as being too cognitive and unemotional. Truth is more alive, intuitive, and passionate than either philosophical approach allows. One feels the truth as well as knows it.

Karl Marx (1818–1883) and Friedrich Engels (1820–1895), on the other hand, explained knowledge as depending on social and economic forces rather than on independent intellectual processes. The empiricist versus rationalist debate is therefore moot. It does not matter because the truth is an empty abstraction, an economic necessity masquerading as an intellectual necessity. The American pragmatists also took a functional view of truth—the truth is what works. Statements are true to the extent that they lead to effective action in one's environment.

In clinical psychology, the schism between research-based biobehavioral, or systems-oriented, clinicians and psychodynamic and humanistic practitioners also falls out along epistemological grounds. Research-based psychologists hold to an empiricist or pragmatic epistemology, whereas practitioners who rely on clinical experience, intuition, and empathy are more aligned with the existential–phenomenological (rationalist) position.

Three of the 19th-century attempts to escape the dichotomy of empiricism and rationalism (i.e., pragmatism, existentialism, and Marxism) emphasized the importance of human action or, in other words, the moral dimension. Truth is whatever leads people to human freedom or effective action. Life is lived by making choices. Some choices are better than others. How can people know in advance what they should do? How do they decide what to do when faced with tough choices and moral dilemmas? Are people really free to decide their own actions, or are they the unwitting product of forces beyond their control (determinism vs. free will)? Thus, by way this time of epistemology, one arrives back at the questions of moral philosophy that were so central to the thought of Socrates at the beginning of the Western philosophical tradition.

Moral Philosophy

Moral philosophy is that part of philosophy that attempts to determine the principles that should guide human conduct (normative ethics) and explores the nature of moral concepts and judgments (meta-ethics) pertaining to rights, duties, responsibility, good and bad, right and wrong, just and unjust. Again, one sees the connection of philosophy to religion, which prior to philosophy was the sole guardian of moral principles. However, the philosopher asks what the basis of such judgments might be rather than assuming that right and wrong are defined by a higher power. Again, one finds the influence of the two great traditions begun by Plato and Aristotle. The first, the Platonic (or deontological) ethics, attempts to preserve the conception of moral duty found in the theological ethics where there are universal and absolute principles of conduct. However, these principles are justified not through God but via a rational understanding of the "Good" (Kant) or moral intuition (as in G. E. Moore, the turn-of-the-century Cambridge philosopher) as the ultimate basis of these principles. Deontological theories argue that things may be good in themselves, intrinsically, regardless of what the consequences might be. Kant believed that certain duties derived from the *categorical imperative* provided such a basis. People should will only those acts in themselves that they would be comfortable with all people willing. Duty boundness is a common feature of these types of theories. Opposed to this view are the Aristotelian moral theories that claim that moral principles aim to maximize either individual or the social group's happiness or pleasure. Those that emphasize the individual are referred to as egoistic hedonism; those that emphasize the greatest happiness of the greatest number, a la J. Bentham and J. S. Mill, are referred to as utilitarian. Aristotelian approaches tend to be identified with teleological interpretations of moral principles, meaning that something is good only if it leads to good consequences.

Naturalistic Aristotelian moral theories are probably most familiar to psychologists because in these theories some descriptive state of the person is taken as an indicator of the moral good. For example, one may define "good" as some attribute or feeling (pleasure, happiness, peace of mind, etc.) and then attempt to measure this attribute in an individual or the population to determine whether a situation is producing a morally acceptable outcome. Skinner's behaviorism defined the good as that behavior that promotes survival of the species (i.e., adaptive). Not the first theorist to attempt to deduce a moral or political agenda from biological theory (the social Darwinists had done so in the mid-19th century), Skinner somewhat paradoxically argued both that values can be determined by observing what behaviors are reinforcing and that psychologists and social planners should move quickly to radically change the contingencies of reinforcement in Western society. Those who hope for an empirical science of values are generally described as supporting *ethical naturalism*. Philosophy reduces to psychology or social science and in so doing holds out hope of becoming objective knowledge, although it may depend on measuring and averaging in some manner the subjective states of moral agents. This kind of moral theory produces objective moral judgments, but not universal or absolute moral principles. (One can see how, as philosophical positions evolve, the earlier, useful distinctions between objective and subjective are increasingly problematic.)

This view, popular as it is in psychology, has been rejected by philosophers on a number of accounts. First, there are those such as G. E. Moore (1903), who coined the phrase "naturalistic fallacy" to describe the error of trying to derive an "ought" from an "is." Psychological facts about what is the case concerning some attribute of a person's behavior or psychological state does not determine whether the facts are desirable. Moore claimed that the fact–value dichotomy could not be bridged and consequently that people could not derive what they ought to do from some statement of what is the case. It is always an open question whether what is the case, should or ought to be the case. For example, if it is determined that beating children gives more pleasure (or some other desirable psychological state or attribute) to a group of parents than the amount of pain caused by the beatings to the children, could one not still ask, "But is it right to beat children?"

G. E. Moore shifted the ground of discussion from normative ethics to meta-ethics, from talking about what people should do to talking about how they talk about moral issues. He believed that the meaning of ethical terms had to be determined before ethical principles could be decided. Moore argued that "good" referred to an irreducible quality of experience that people intuitively grasped but shared with one another nonetheless.

Naturalists in ethics made a strong response to Moore in the work of Stevenson (1950), who claimed that ethical statements are not knowledge claims at all but merely reports of what a person feels, or feels like doing, at a given point in time. To say something is good, then, is simply to say that one likes it or feels good about it. This meta-ethical claim about the meaning of the concept of good and the nature of moral reasoning has led Hare (1963), Baier (1965), Toulmin (1958), and Rawls (1971) to defend the cognitive rationality in moral argument, although there is agreement that moral terms are not simply descriptive of reality. Rather than being emotive, moral claims are seen as prescriptive—prescribing actions that ought, or ought not, to be done. They pointed out how a central aspect of moral reasoning is having "good reasons" for a decision and that there are criteria that people use to evaluate reasons for actions that go beyond simple subjective preferences.

It can be seen, then, that both of these traditions (Platonic and Aristotelian) have their objective and subjective (or relativistic) versions. Utilitarianism might lead to a calculus of pleasure and pain that would pronounce certain actions as good or evil in a manner independent of the assessor. As noted earlier, this objective assessment depends on the physical or subjective states of all people affected by the moral decision and does not yield universal principles of moral conduct. *Egoistic hedonism,* on the other hand, would produce a different standard of good for each ego: "If I don't find pleasure in reading, then it is bad for me; if you do, then it is good for you." A Kantian rationalistic ethic is certainly objective in the sense of universal, but it depends on Kant's view that people find the universal categories of existence in their own thought (i.e., subjectivity). Contemporary philosophers of the cognitive "good reasons" school of thought are inclined to deny that all moral disagreements are decidable through rational discourse alone. Consequently, a certain degree of subjectivity enters into the attempt to find a rational, and thus universal, basis for moral reasoning.

Clinicians' clinical disagreements also represent differences in moral philosophy. Humanistic approaches tend to adopt an intuitive–subjective view of moral values such that the individual must decide what is right or good. Self-actualization, for example, although it involves a great deal of social concern or interest, is established within the individual's own subjective field by a process of introspection and self-knowledge. Subjective though this may be, self-actualization is asserted to be a universal value for all human beings and is therefore not relativistic in this sense. Behavioral, biological, and systems approaches hold generally to a utilitarian view of moral principles (i.e., appropriate or healthy behavior is that which maximizes social acceptance, adaptation, or harmony). Although the humanistic view of moral principles risks encouraging an egoistic morality that may undermine the fabric of social institutions, the others risk encouraging social conformity and the political repression of independent thought or unorthodox behavior under the guise of treatment.

TWENTIETH-CENTURY PHILOSOPHY

Twentieth-century Western philosophy has been deeply divided between Anglo-American analytical philosophy and Continental European existential–phenomenological philosophy. In the United States, there has been in addition to analytical philosophy, a somewhat parallel but smaller movement of pragmatism, that in recent years has reasserted itself in the work of Rorty (1979). On the European continent, Marxist philosophy has played a similar role and has seen a similar revival in the work of Habermas (1971, 1973). In both cases, the smaller movement was concerned primarily with social and political philosophy and the role of philosophy in the culture as a whole. Contemporary hermeneutical philosophy tends to draw out the epistemological implications of these lesser movements in forming a critique of both analytic and phenomenological schools of thought. I briefly review each of these contemporary movements that are the subject of much discussion in later chapters.

Anglo-American Analytical Philosophy

This approach had its beginnings in logical positivism, sometimes known as logical empiricism, and has had the greatest impact on American psychology of any 20th-century philosophy. The tenets of logical positivism have been incorporated into the discipline's very concept of adequate research methodology. Associated with the group of philosophers who gathered around Moritz Schlick and Rudolph Carnap, it came to be known in the 1920s as the "Vienna Circle." Logical positivism was put forth as a radical solution to the empiricism versus rationalism debate as to the nature of knowledge. Forging an integration of rationalism (the truths of logic) and empiricism (the fruits of the natural sciences), logical positivism claimed that metaphysical and moral philosophy had become outdated and unnecessary (Ayer, 1952). Epistemology, as philosophy of science, was a legitimate activity because it helped to clarify the questions posed and concepts used by the natural sciences. Its job was to examine the boundaries between the highly specialized branches of natural science that had emerged and to search for paths to integration and unification. Philosophy had become philosophy of science—all else was superfluous speculation—poetry perhaps, but not knowledge claims. Only statements that met their verification principle criteria of meaning could qualify as true knowledge claims. This principle claimed that all terms in a proposition had to be open to verification by the senses in order to be meaningful. The only exception to this rule was the logical operators from mathematical logic (e.g., all, a, and, or, not, if–then); thus, the phrase *logical positivism* came into being. No terms or concepts could be introduced into the principles of a discipline unless they were either empirical claims amenable to verification or logical operators (Urmson, 1956).

Although this program quickly stimulated much debate on the validity of its claims, social scientists and particularly American psychologists fell under its sway for at least 40 years (Koch, 1981). In fact, a recent American Psychological Association (APA) paper on graduate education cited logical positivism as one of its few specific content areas to be covered in a core graduate curriculum (APA, 1987, p. 1070). Many of the articles in this book address this hegemony held by positivist philosophies of science over the field of psychology (see chapters 3, 7, 35, 37, and 41) and others defend it (see chapters 2, 13, 23, 26, and 36).

Although few philosophers today accept the logical positivist program for the unification of all sciences in the image of physics, it has had an enormous influence on how philosophy is done in the United States and the United Kingdom. Philosophy is primarily seen as either an extension of science, as in philosophy of science, or to be done in a scientific or analytical manner. This is often called analytical philosophy and includes those carrying forth the logical positivist program of clarifying the nature of science, as well as those who believe philosophy must proceed by very detailed analyses of arguments and concepts. Ordinary language philosophers who, following G. E. Moore, J. L. Austin, G. Ryle, and most notably the later work of L. Wittgenstein, use ordinary language as the basic data from which to begin philosophical work are included in this grouping (Urmson, 1956). Wittgenstein (1958) believed that philosophical problems began when "language goes on holiday" (p. 19) and that the function of philosophy was therefore to analyze linguistic usage and show exactly how the philosophical problem vanishes when the linguistic confusions are clarified. For Wittgenstein, philosophy was a kind of conceptual therapy: Once the problem is understood, it goes away. In fact, it is said that Wittgenstein was inspired in this approach by his exposure to Freud's work and saw a direct parallel between philosophical analysis and psychoanalysis (Chessick, 1977). Although the latter works on unconscious beliefs of emotional significance, the former works on unconscious beliefs of cognitive significance. Both lead to a discovery that the initial problem is representative of a different sort of problem at a deeper unconscious (or nonconscious) level. Once this underlying problem is pointed out, the initial problem vanishes. The underlying problem, once raised to the level of awareness, is solvable by recognizing its existence. Rather than an unresolvable conflict, the underlying problem consists of mistaking one context for another. Once the mistake has been made conscious, one can choose to avoid it.

Philosophical analysis is thus consistent with the logical positivist program of doing away with metaphysics and moral philosophy. The problems are pseudoproblems. There are no answers, only cures. As Wittgenstein (1958) said, the purpose of philosophy is to "show the fly the way out of the bottle" (p. 103). People are trapped by language into thinking that there are philosophical questions to be answered. However, there are no answers. Rather, the answer is to reject the questions as pseudoquestions—linguistic errors.

This is a very appealing agenda. It gives philosophy a very clear and precise task that, in a scientific environment, is necessary in order for philosophy to be viewed as a legitimate enterprise. The departments of philosophy at the major universities in the United States, the United Kingdom, Canada, and Australia and New Zealand adopted this approach for nearly 50 years. Unfortunately, or perhaps fortunately for lovers of philosophy, the analytical agenda was never fully realized. Certainly, some philosophical conflicts have yielded to analysis. Language does tend to confuse people when they talk about highly abstract subjects such as reality, freedom, the will, truth, the mind, and so on. (Witness the difficulties with "objective" and "subjective" here). One needs to be aware that there are several different meanings of these words. As one slips in and out of using different meanings without realizing it, confusion or absurd conclusions result. On the other hand, not all philosophical bewilderment is of this sort. When one puzzles over the nature of the mind, Ryle (1949), for example, was correct to point out that many mentalistic terms are really about behavioral dispositions and not about some inner world of experience. On the other hand, there are some expressions (viz., first-person experiential reports) that do not, despite Ryle's assertions to the contrary, appear to be dispositional. They do appear to be about mental contents. The statement "I am terrified" is not equivalent to the statement "I am disposed to run away and/or freeze, and/or vomit, etc." Felt experience and its relationship to the physical self is a legitimate philosophical question that will not disappear (Natsoulas, 1978).

The more serious problem for philosophical analysis has been the unbearable tedium of its literature. Philosophy papers that read like technical scientific reports do not satisfy whatever it is that brings most students to philosophy. Philosophical analysis is dying under the weight of its very substantial collective accomplishments. It is often devoid of life, passion, or commitment, or so it seems to many of its readers. Freud's analytic case studies read like good literature. They are engaging life histories. In fact, Freud's only academic award was the Goethe prize for writing

(Jones, 1955). Philosophical analyses read like legal findings or mathematical derivations—hardly the sort of work to captivate a wide readership.

Another major contribution of this school is its development of the philosophy of science. By examining the logic of scientific theory, evidence, and reasoning, the philosophy of science has stimulated much careful analysis of the process of formulating and confirming hypotheses. The logical positivists maintained that the goal of science is to develop "covering laws" based on one set of empirical observations that explain and predict a much wider range of observable phenomena (Hempel, 1966). From a covering law, one can deduce what observable conditions should be found in a given context, and this leads to the development of a specific experimental hypothesis that can be tested. Theories that either are too vague to permit specific hypotheses to be generated or that consistently lead to hypotheses that fail the test of experimental confirmation are unscientific (Losee, 1972, pp. 158–160).

Criticisms of this approach to science are central to the debate over the nature of psychology and clinical psychology, and many of the articles that follow address this question. Suffice it to say for now that the criticisms have been of two sorts: historical–contextual and logical. The historical argument is that science has not progressed solely by the method of hypothesis testing outlined earlier but also because of social and political forces influencing the formulation of theory (Kuhn, 1970). Second, it has been pointed out that the question of whether data count as supporting or disconfirming a hypothesis is not easily decidable. It is a matter of judgment, perhaps bias, how to interpret the data generated in an experimental study. The data are not some sort of objective arbiter of the hypothesis (Bernstein, 1983). They are, to some extent, theory laden in themselves. This critique of logical positivist and analytical philosophy of science will be encountered as a central tenet of hermeneutical philosophy. Finally, in the nature of friendly criticism, Popper (1959) argued that because theories are universal statements, one can never, theoretically, confirm a theory, only the existence of a specific set of circumstances predicted by the general law.

This is related to the logical fallacy of *affirming the consequent*. In a hypothesis of the form "If A, then B," should *B* turn out to be true, it does not follow that *A* is then true. For *A* to be true as a result of *B* being true, the hypothesis would have to read "If B, then A." For example, one could hypothesize that if the psychodynamic theory of repression *(A)* is true, then lists of words with aggressive or sexual connotations will be more difficult to remember than lists of emotionally neutral words *(B)*. If, in fact, *B* is true and the lists with sexual and aggressive words are more difficult to remember, *A* is not therefore true. If *B* is false and there is no difference in the retention of the words on both lists, then the theory of repression *(B)* is disconfirmed.

If contradictory data are found, one can reject (or falsify) a theory because one counterinstance refutes a universal statement. A theory's openness to disconfirmation is then the hallmark of scientific theory. Confidence grows in those theories that have been subjected to repeated empirical tests but have yet to be falsified or modified in arbitrary ways to sidestep disconfirming data. Popper (1959) switched the criterion of science from verifiability to falsifiability.

Existentialism and Phenomenology

Existentialism and phenomenology are independent philosophical movements in European philosophy that had their clear beginnings in the 19th century and continued to be strong throughout the 20th century as well. Phenomenology is a direct descendant of the rationalism of Kant and the idealism of Hegel. Edmund Husserl (1913/1931, 1936/1970) is credited with being the father of this movement that insisted that philosophy must be a knowledge of the certain and absolute truths of the world. As might be expected, he took mathematical truth as his exemplar of knowledge. To find certain knowledge, people must first understand their own experiential capacity—their own phenomenal world—because it is the filter through which all else that can be known must pass. Husserl wanted to suspend all questions about the relationship between mind and the physical world until the limits and logic of the mind were known. He called this process "bracketing" experience: taking experience on its own terms, separate from all other questions. Philosophy is then to analyze experience as such and determine its content, framework, and logic. It is a deeply introspective, detailed, and at times intuitive process. It must clear away all of the confusions created in philosophy by those who tried to answer these other questions without an adequate understanding of phenomenology. Friedman (1964) wrote of Husserl:

> By the method of "parenthesizing" or phenomenological reduction, which he calls by the Greek word *epoche*, Husserl replaces the detached subject and independent object of older philosophy by a field of knowing in which the phenomena are accented as pure phenomena without questioning their independent existence . . . For, all this Husserl remains an idealist who, if he does not discover universal ideas, like Plato, or universal orderings of knowledge, like Kant, does attain "eidetic" insight into universal essences in the necessary structure of experience. (p. 70)

As literature, phenomenology proper is as forbidding and difficult as the positivist and analytical literature (see chapter 20 for further discussion of Husserl's work).

This cannot be said of much of the existential literature; Kierkegaard, Nietzsche, Camus, Sartre, Dostoevsky, and Kafka all contributed to this movement. Focusing on the dehumanizing effects of the scientific and industrial revolutions on the everyday life of Western men and women, existentialism rejected academic philosophy as a sterile and irrelevant manifestation of this process of dehumanization. Its proponents rejected any suggestion that they were part of a common movement, insisting instead on the importance of the individuality of thought (Kaufmann, 1955). This was a philosophy of emotion, of urgent concern with the anxieties of modern life, the struggle for meaning in a world that was becoming increasingly absurd, and the perplexities of selves cut loose from their moorings. Philosophy was once again a struggle with the question, "How shall we live?" rather than "How can we know?" Its method, however, was compatible with phenomenology in that it was a highly introspective philosophy, although much more personal and less interested in universal truths than individual survival. Chessick (1977) saw these existential philosophies as being the intellectual precursors to modern psychoanalytic theory. For Chessick, the existentialists revived the tradition of moral philosophy begun by Socrates, a tradition he believes is carried on today in psychoanalytic psychotherapy.

The existentialists explored more fully than anyone before them the philosophical implications of human irrationality and human suffering. Freedom, rather than being an abstract category of existence, becomes a torturous dilemma and an overwhelming responsibility, as in Sartre's (1955) famous line, "Man is condemned to be free." People must choose, and not to decide is to decide. The self, no longer directing the body through rational deliberation, becomes a seething cauldron of ambivalent feelings, surprised by unexpected thoughts and emotions, split and divided against itself. The search for certain knowledge is abandoned and replaced by the moral task of learning to live with the reality of unending uncertainty, ambiguity, and ambivalence even over such central questions as "What is life's meaning?" Truth is important, not as certainty but as authenticity. Authenticity is a basic honesty that comes from facing the predicament of life squarely, without blinders on.

There is a more abstract, academic form of existentialism as it appears in the work of Heidegger (1962) and Jaspers (1950). Using Husserl's (1913/1931) phenomenological method but tackling the questions of metaphysics head-on (rather than deferring to Husserl's epistemological agenda), Heidegger confronted *being* itself. Kaplan (1961) summarized Heidegger's existential position in this way:

> Indeed, existentialism is best characterized by its distinctive conception of man's existence . . . When I entertain a concept about anything whatever—a concept of a chair or of an equilateral triangle or of an expanding universe in which entropy is constantly increasing—I have grasped or formulated a certain *essence* . . . In all cases experience may disclose whether there does or does not exist in this world of ours anything having the essence in question. And so with regard to anything in the universe—with one exception, namely, man. With regard to anything else whatsoever, *its essence precedes its existence* . . . Now in the case of the human being the situation is reversed: for man and man alone, his existence precedes his essence. First, a man is; and *what* he is settled in the course of his existence and is not predetermined, not an antecedent condition of his existence . . . This is the special sense that the existentialist gives to the category of existence. We may say that for him things just are while man exists. It is only man who, in Heidegger's phrase, stands in the *openness of being*. Only man exists in the sense that what he is not limited, specified, determined beforehand—in a word, defined prior to his existence. (pp. 102–104)

As his encounters with being proceeded, Heidegger's works took on a mystical, intuitive dimension. He saw the task of philosophy as being more akin to that of poetry than science. One must use one's poetic imagination to read and interpret Heidegger. Yet, Heidegger was concerned with articulating issues similar to the other existentialists. His analysis of being was dominated by the confrontation with being and nothingness—death. People's dread of death is what makes them inauthentic: they refuse to face their own mortality and thus begin a process of denial that takes them away from life as well. Anxiety replaces authentic engagement in life (Bochenski, 1955). Ultimately, this is what dehumanizes people. Only when people can understand their own human form of being (*Dasein*) can they hope to break out of this dehumanizing influence. To do so will require radically different concepts of being than people currently have at their disposal. Heidegger wanted to break through to a new level of consciousness and break out of conventional, commonsense patterns that have contributed to inauthenticity. Scientific or concrete descriptive language that is tied to common sense is of little help here: thus, the need for poetry (Kaufmann, 1955).

The existentialist philosophies just reviewed share a number of constructive features. First, they loosen the stultifying stranglehold that logical positivism has had on philosophy (and psychology). These philosophical works are filled with intensity, moral concern, and commitment. They reach for a deeper and higher understanding of human existence and satisfy, in part, the motive that brings people to philosophy. They speak clearly of the problems of making sense out of 20th-century Western science, art, and culture.

Although the existential philosophies risk inspiring people, they may also infuriate. Their poetic language is too unclear and one may find himself or herself mystified. Most important, they risk the criticism of all philosophies that begin with subjective experience—they appear solipsistic. One is offered a new world of meaning and experience, but how can it be connected to anyone else's world of meaning? People are, philosophically speaking, totally alone.

Another important contribution by Heidegger was his emphasis on the hermeneutic aspect of phenomenology. Hermeneutics—the discovery of the meaning of a text by a process of interpretation—is taken by Heidegger as the process that must be applied to being to reveal what is hidden and obscure (Bochenski, 1955). It is this hermeneutic aspect of Heidegger's work that has stimulated much of the contemporary hermeneutical philosophy to which I now turn (see chapter 19 for further discussion of Heidegger).

Philosophical Hermeneutics

Howard (1982) described the convergence of three philosophical traditions on the theme of hermeneutics: antipositivist analytical philosophers, represented by von Wright (1963, 1971) and Winch (1958); the "Frankfurt" school of German philosophy that includes a neo-Marxist component and is represented by Habermas (1971, 1973); and the ontological hermeneutics of Heidegger's student, Gadamer (1975, 1976). Bernstein (1983) also argued for a convergence of analytical and continental philosophy citing the same three basic trends. Despite their different traditions, each of these approaches shares a belief that human existence is inherently a process of understanding and interpreting the world. Philosophy must come to terms with *understanding* as the basic concept in epistemology. For the analytical philosophers, this focuses on the problem of what it means to understand a language; for the psychosocial school, what it means to understand a social–historical event; and for the ontological school, what it means to understand being itself.

Of central importance in the philosophy of psychology is the question of understanding the behavior of human beings. Here, the problem is doubly hermeneutic in that the observer is trying to understand a being that itself is trying to understand or interpret its world. This distinguishes what Dilthey (1833–1911) called the "human sciences" from the natural sciences. Dilthey was a 19th-century historian–philosopher identified with German Romanticism. He brought into prominence the terms *verstehen* (to understand) as the basic method in the *Geisteswissenschaften* (culture studies or human sciences). Dilthey himself created the term *Weltanschauunglehre* (worldview of a culture) to represent the spirit of a society that must be grasped by understanding. The social scientist–historian must understand the intentions of those being studied, whereas the natural scientist must simply explain phenomena. To understand another human being, one must find a way to know what it is like to live as that person lives, to join in his or her experience of being or life.

In the Frankfurt school and in the work of Habermas (1971, 1973), the emphasis is on the social construction of reality and knowledge. Knowledge claims, including philosophical propositions, are the result of the social, political, and economic forces operating within a particular culture. Social science is the product of these forces. However, Habermas went beyond Marx to not only reject a positivistic view of social science but to provide a model for social science that is critically self-reflective (Howard, 1982). Philosophy itself is grounded in this critical social science, and both must be able to examine and evaluate their own social context. To do this, Habermas focused attention on the language community and on the requirements of discourse: openness, truth, and justice. The conditions of dialogue and discourse form the basic values used to assess the legitimacy of social institutions and forces that produce knowledge claims. Habermas saw both philosophy and social science as being committed to promoting human freedom and liberating humanity from its political and economic subjugation. There is no value-free social science or psychology.

This is the same conclusion reached via a very different route by the analytical philosophers working in the tradition of Wittgenstein. Wittgenstein, in his later postpositivist position, viewed language as a series of social conventions or rules: language games. Understanding language means discovering the social rules in which it is embedded. Applying this method to the social sciences, analytical philosophers argued that the language of social phenomena is fundamentally different from the language of natural phenomena. Social science cannot be unified with physical science without violating the rules of the social science language game. The language of social phenomena (i.e., intentions, goals, purposes, meaning) cannot be written out of the picture without altering the picture and making it incomprehensible. Furthermore, in order to understand the intentions, purposes, or meaning behind an agent's behavior, one needs to be able to understand the social and linguistic contexts of that behavior. There are no guarantees that this will prove possible because the observer may operate in such a different language game that comprehension is impossible. Social purposes, intentions, meanings, and so forth, are best communicated by narrative rather than statistical analysis (Winch, 1958). Explanations in the social sciences are fundamentally different from those in the natural sciences (see chapter 4).

Gadamer's (1975, 1976) ontological hermeneutics shares the disdain for positivist approaches to human behavior. Returning to Heidegger, he viewed hermeneutics as being the essence of being human. Human existence is always open to one's interpretation and cannot be otherwise. People's interpretations are governed by their cultural and personal histories and, again, cannot be otherwise. There is no truth about these matters, or in fact any matter, that is other than interpretation. Truth is not a product of methodology but a feature of being itself. Gadamer maintained that "the truth finds us" and is not just the result of something one wants to find or do. Howard (1982) wrote of Gadamer:

> The flow of existence itself, then, is a disclosure of meanings. It is the fundamental deciphering or hermeneutical agency which then itself requires elucidation. This agency lies prior to such mental acts as issue in theories, hypotheses, and explanations, in the way that being precedes beings, truth precedes truths and the task of philosophical hermeneutics precedes philological hermeneutics or of methodology generally. (p. 126)

For Gadamer, hermeneutics is about ontology before it is about epistemology. An individual's existence is meaning, and so truth is being. Because truth is not a characteristic only of propositions but of reality, it inheres in action and moral judgments as well. The truth finds people as they muddle through the practical dilemmas of surviving. People cannot get beyond or outside of the prejudices of their historical period, but prejudices are simply one set of powerful hermeneutical responses to the world. The challenge is to view these prejudices self-reflexively as prejudices, thus neutralizing what may be untrue in them.

Hermeneutic philosophies have provided an incisive critique of logical positivism as a basis for the philosophy of the social sciences and psychology. This critique is certainly strengthened by its emergence out of two radically disparate traditions that many thought only a few decades ago to be totally irreconcilable. That Heidegger's metaphysics and Wittgenstein's antimetaphysical analytical philosophy would converge with a neo-Marxist epistemology was almost inconceivable, yet it is now a well-documented trend in the current philosophical scene.

There are many philosophers, particularly the more traditional logical positivists, who, of course, remain unimpressed. They see in hermeneutics an unabashed relativism that provides no account of the difference between objective social science and biased ideology. Are all interpretations, or language games, equally true? How can one separate coerced consensus from a true consensus, particularly when subtle forms of coercion are used? How does one know when the truth has found him or her? They see no answers to these questions and see little possibility of any emerging. Neither Heidegger, Gadamer, nor any of the continental hermeneutic theorists have escaped the rationalism and idealism that they had so assiduously labored to escape (see chapter 26 for a neopositivist response to hermeneutics). As for the analytical version of interpretative social science, the unreconstructed positivists hope for the success of a biological psychology that will explain behavior without resorting to social psychological explanation. They hope to see the whole problem of hermeneutics superseded by breakthroughs in the neurosciences, that is, the triumph of central state materialism (Armstrong, 1968; Smart, 1963). On this view all subjective experience is reduced to some state of the central nervous system.

PHILOSOPHY AND THE DISCIPLINE OF CLINICAL PSYCHOLOGY

I hope that even after such cursory review of the problems and development of Western philosophy that readers will realize the extent to which clinical psychology remains a philosophical discipline. One can hardly begin to discuss differing theories of personality, psychopathology, psychotherapy, or research methodology without unearthing at least one thread of the objectivity versus subjectivity dispute. Indeed, it might be argued that it is precisely in the day-to-day world of clinical practice—with its controversies over the use of psychological tests in the schools, the use of medications in the clinics, or the effectiveness of various therapy techniques—that the practical implications of the Western philosophical tradition is most alive. Academic philosophy might benefit as much from a joining of the issue as would clinical psychology, as a number of the chapters in this book demonstrate.

There is the danger, however, that by placing the controversies in contemporary clinical psychology within the context of this philosophical tradition, they are made to seem unsolvable. A cloud of pessimism would then hang over the discipline. If philosophers have been unable to solve these problems for over 2,000 years, how can clinicians have any hope of doing so? There is a kind of nihilism about philosophy: It does not matter because no practical advantage will accrue to those who take its burdens on their shoulders. For such a reader, the relationship between the definition of mental illness and the 2,500-year history of the idealism versus materialism debate is a negative rather than positive discovery. Philosophy is a tradition that should be avoided like a quagmire rather than entered into as ennobling or edifying.

Russell (1945) tackled this objection by noting that these age-old controversies are unavoidable. They will surface in any discussion in which knowledge is sought and if ignored, they will simply serve to muddle any attempt at intelligent discourse. Better to be prepared for the inevitable than unprepared. If one is prepared, one may avoid the pitfalls of past inadequate proferred solutions or occasionally benefit from strategies that have worked for others in clarifying questions and possible answers. At the very least, a knowledge of the history of such dialogues is a bulwark against dogmatic thinking, which is no small accomplishment. Of course, it is not a guarantee against narrow-mindedness, prejudice, and so on. However, it certainly gets harder to maintain a narrow, rigid, or uninformed position as one is exposed to the point and counterpoint of philosophical discourse. Perhaps, as Russell suggested, this process of dialogue is as important as the outcome. Struggling with the deepest and most profound problems of human existence is central to the essence of life itself. One is humbled by the limitations of one's own intellect, awed by the complexity of existence, and enriched by engaging with other people at this level of discourse. It is the journey, not the destination, that is important. For dogmatism, theoretical preciousness, therapeutic chauvinism, and professional schisms are all thereby impeded.

Of course, to participate in the philosophical dialogue, one must be prepared for the issues in question and know the history of the arguments. The chapters that follow show that such a discussion can indeed take place within the discipline of clinical psychology itself; in fact, has been taking place in a sporadic and dispersed manner over the past 30 years. I hope that by putting these writings together in one place and organizing them to make them more accessible to those with little background in philosophy, it will be possible for this discussion to become more central the discipline's development.

REFERENCES

American Psychological Association. (1987). Resolutions approved by the National Conference on Graduate Education in Psychology. *American Psychologist*. 42, 1070–1084.

Armstrong, D. M. (1968). *A materialist theory of mind.* London: Routledge & Kegan Paul.

Ayer, A. J. (1952). *Language, truth, and logic* (2nd ed., rev.). New York: Dover.

Baier, K. (1965). *The moral point of view.* New York: Random House.

Bakan, F. (1969). *On method.* San Francisco: Jossey-Bass.

Bernstein, R. (1983). *Beyond objectivism and relativism.* Philadelphia: University of Pennsylvania Press.

Block, N. (Ed.). (1980). *Readings in philosophy of psychology* (Vol 1). Cambridge, MA: Harvard University Press.

Bochenski, I. M. (1955). *Contemporary European philosophy.* Berkeley: University of California Press.

Buchler, J. (Ed.). (1955). *Philosophical writings of Pierce.* New York: Dover. (Original work published 1940)

Chessick, R. (1977). *Great ideas in psychotherapy.* Northvale, NJ: Jason Aronson.

Chessick, R. (1982). Metaphysics or autistic reverie. *Contemporary Psychoanalysis, 18,* 160–172.

Copleston, F. J. (1962a). *A history of philosophy* (Vol. 1, Pt. 1). New York: Image Books. (Original work published 1946)

Copleston, F. J. (1962b). *A history of philosophy* (Vol. 1, Pt. 2). New York: Image Books. (Original work published 1946)

Cornford, F. M. (1932). *After Socrates.* Cambridge, England: Cambridge University Press.

Descartes, R. (1969). *The philosophical works of Descartes* (Vols. 1 and 2, E. S. Haldane and G. R. T. Ross, Trans.). Cambridge, England: Cambridge University Press.

Freud, S. (1965). New introductory lectures on psychoanalysis. In J. Strachey (Ed. and Trans.), *The standard edition of the complete psychological works of Sigmund Freud* (Vol 22, pp. 139–160). New York: Norton. (Original work published 1933)

Friedman, M. (Ed.). (1964). *The worlds of existentialism: A critical reader.* New York: Random House.

Gadamer, H. G. (1975). *Truth and method* (G. Barden and J. Cumming, Eds. and Trans.). New York: Seabury Press.

Gadamer, H. G. (1976). *Philosophical hermeneutics* (D. Linge, Trans.). Berkeley: University of California Press.

Gardner, H. (1985). *The mind's new science.* New York: Basic Books.

Habermas, J. (1971). *Knowledge and human interests* (J. J. Shapiro, Trans.). Boston: Beacon Press.

Habermas, J. (1973). *Theory and practice* (J. Vertel, Trans.). Boston: Beacon.

Halleck, S. (1971). *Politics of therapy.* New York: Science House Press.

Hare, R. (1963). *Freedom and reason.* London: Oxford University Press.

Heidegger, M. (1962). *Being and time* (J. Macquarrie and E. Robinson, Trans.). London: SCM Press.

Hempel, C. G. (1966). *Philosophy of natural science.* Englewood, NJ: Prentice-Hall.

Howard, R. (1982). *The three faces of hermeneutics: An introduction to current theories of understanding.* Berkeley: University of California Press.

Husserl, E. (1931). *Ideas: General introduction to pure phenomenology.* New York: Macmillan. (Original work published 1913)

Husserl, E. (1970). *The crisis of European sciences and transcendental philosophy.* Evanston, IL: Northwestern University Press. (Original work published 1936)

James, W. (1907). *Pragmatism.* New York: Longman.

Jaspers, K. (1950). *The perennial scope of philosophy* (R. Manheim, Trans.). London: Routledge & Kegan Paul.

Jones, E. (1955). *The life and work of Sigmund Freud* (Vol. 2). New York: Basic Books.

Kant, I. (1929). *The critique of pure reason* (N. Kemp-Smith, Trans.). London: Macmillan. (Original work published 1781)

Kaplan, A. (1961). *The new world of philosophy*. New York: Vintage Books.

Kaufmann, W. (Ed.). (1955). *Existentialism: From Dostoevsky to Sartre*. Cleveland, OH: World Publishing.

Kimble, G. A. (1984). Psychology's two cultures. *American Psychologist, 39*, 833–839.

Koch, S. (1981). A century of psychology qua science. *American Psychologist, 36*, 257–269.

Körner, S. (1955). *Kant*. Baltimore, MD: Penguin Books.

Kuhn, T. (1970). *The structure of scientific revolutions* (2nd ed.). Chicago: University of Chicago Press.

London, P. (1964). *The modes and morals of psychotherapy*. New York: Holt, Rinehart & Winston.

Losee, J. (1972). *A historical introduction to the philosophy of science*. London: Oxford University Press.

Margolis, J. (1966). *Psychotherapy and morality*. New York: Random House.

McKeon, R. (1941). *The basic works of Aristotle*. New York: Random House.

Miller, R. (1983). A call to armchairs. *Psychotherapy: Theory, Research and Practice, 20*, 208–219.

Moore, G. E. (1903). *Principia ethica*. Cambridge, England: Cambridge University Press.

Moore, G. E. (1962). *Some main problems of philosophy*. New York: Macmillan. (Original work published 1953)

Nagel, T. (1986). *The view from nowhere*. New York: Oxford University Press.

Natsoulas, T. (1978). Residual subjectivity. *American Psychologist, 33*, 269–283.

Passmore, J. (1967). Philosophy. In P. Edwards (Ed.), *The encyclopedia of philosophy* (Vol. 6, pp. 217–226). New York: Macmillan.

Popper, K. (1959). *The logic of scientific discovery*. London: Hutchinson.

Rawls, J. (1971). *A theory of justice*. Cambridge, MA: Harvard University Press.

Robinson, D. (1985). *Philosophy of psychology*. New York: Columbia University Press.

Rogers, C. R. (1955). *Client centered therapy: Its current practice, implications and theory*. Boston: Houghton Mifflin.

Rorty, R. (1979). *Philosophy and the mirror of nature*. Princeton, NJ: Princeton University Press.

Russell, B. (1945). *A history of Western philosophy*. New York: Simon & Schuster.

Rychlak, J. F. (1969). *A philosophy of science for personality theory*. Boston: Houghton Mifflin.

Ryle, G. (1949). *The concept of mind*. London: Hutchinson University Library.

Sarason, S. B., Levine, M., Goldenberg, I. I., Cherline, D. L., & Bennett, E. M. (1966). *Psychology in community settings: Clinical, educational, vocational, and social aspects*. New York: Wiley.

Sartre, J. (1955). Existentialism. In W. Kaufmann (Ed.), *Existentialism: From Dostoevsky to Sartre* (pp. 222–311). Cleveland, OH: World Publishing.

Skinner, B. F. (1974). *About behaviorism*. New York: Random House.

Smart, J. J. C. (1963). *Philosophy and scientific realism*. London: Routledge & Kegan Paul.

Stevenson, C. L. (1950). *Ethics and language*. New Haven, CT: Yale University Press.

Toulmin, S. (1958). *Reason in ethics*. Cambridge, England: Cambridge University Press.

Toulmin, S. (1979, September). The cult of empiricism in psychology. In P. F. Secord (chair), *Psychology and philosophy*. Symposium conducted at the 87th Annual Convention of the American Psychological Association, New York.

Urmson, J. (1956). *Philosophical analysis*. London: Oxford University Press.

Valentine, E. (1982). *Conceptual issues in psychology*. London: Allen & Unwin.

Weiss, F. G. (Ed.). (1974). *The essential writings of Hegel*. New York: Harper & Row.

Winch, P. (1958). *The idea of social science and its relation to philosophy*. London: Routledge & Kegan Paul.

Wittgenstein, L. (1958). *Philosophical investigations* (2nd ed.). Oxford, England: Blackwell Scientific.

Wolman, B. (1965). Clinical psychology and the philosophy of science. In B. Wolman (Ed.), *Handbook of clinical psychology* (pp. 3–27). New York: McGraw-Hill.

Wright, G. H. von (1963). *The logic of preference: An essay*. Edinburgh, Scotland: University Press.

Wright, G. H. von (1971). *Explanation and understanding*. Ithaca, NY: Cornell University Press.

I

PHILOSOPHICAL PERSPECTIVES ON GENERAL PSYCHOLOGY

INTRODUCTION: PHILOSOPHICAL PROBLEMS OF PSYCHOLOGY

RONALD B. MILLER

In the introduction I noted that one should be careful not to assume that the philosophical problems of clinical psychology are simply a subset of the philosophical problems of general experimental psychology. The three key philosophical problems of clinical psychology identified in the preceding chapter were (a) the metaphysical question of the nature of psychological reality (mental, physical, behavioral, systemic, or unconscious); (b) the ethical content of theories of psychopathology and psychotherapy, including the definition of mental illness; and (c) the relationship between clinical and scientific knowledge. The first and third of these contain elements that reflect concerns of direct relevance to the philosophy of general experimental psychology. For this reason, and because this is the field in which some of the best philosophical work has been done, the first few chapters are on this more general theme. Although they are more general, they are no less relevant to the philosophy of clinical psychology. One finds, for example, that philosophical disagreements between existential and logical positivist *philosophy* are reflected in disagreements between humanistic and behavioral (or biological) theories of *psychology* and, ultimately, in the schism between humanistic and behavioral (or biologically oriented) *clinical approaches*. Logical positivist criticisms of psychoanalytic theory are echoed in the behaviorist, biological, and systems approach critiques of psychoanalytic treatment. Although the issues remain substantially the same, the quality of the philosophical dialogue tends to erode at each new step in the progression.

Herbert Feigl was one of the earliest members of the Vienna Circle and (with A. E. Blumberg) coined the phrase "logical positivism" to identify their approach to philosophy. His 1959 article (see chapter 2) represents a revised or neo-positivist view of psychology, having been published some 30 years after he left Vienna, Austria, for the United States. Using conceptual analysis, Feigl critiqued the epistemological assumptions of both classical psychoanalysis and radical behaviorism. Consistent with the early position of the logical positivists, he held out physics as the paradigm of scientific methodology, but it is a physics that has come to terms with the implications of quantum theory. Ultimately, scientific propositions must be tied to observations, but there must be room for theoretical constructs that have no direct observability and for lawlike relationships that are predicted as probabilistic rather than necessary truths. Feigl also summarizes his own work that later was published in *The Mental and the Physical* (Feigl, 1967), the outstanding analytic work on the mind–body problem, and suggests that a form of the identity thesis is correct (i.e., the mind and brain are really identical). In his view, mental phenomena constitute real scientific variables because they correspond to neurophysiological brain states.

Michael Polanyi (1946, 1958) began his career as a physical chemist but ended it as a philosopher of science. In chapter 3, he offers an interpretation of science that is grounded in human rationality, aesthetics, and passion. As such, it represents a continuation of the Kantian tradition of rejecting empiricism as the sole basis of science and is in keeping with the existential–phenomenological tradition of emphasizing subjective experience. Polanyi explicitly rejects the positivist principle of verifiability and claims that scientific knowledge is based on three indeterminancies: content, truth criteria, and fact. Polanyi claims, therefore, that human knowledge is always the result of tacit processes akin to those that operate in insight and intuition that cannot be eliminated from the account given of scientific methodology without misrepresenting the reality of science. Polanyi's view has much in common with the work of Kuhn (1970), who is cited often in the psychological literature for his theory of the revolutionary nature of paradigm shifts in the history of science.

Working with this rationalistic model of science, Polanyi also (a) rejects solutions to the mind–body problem that identify mind with body, (b) asserts that knowledge of other people's minds is possible through tacit processes, and (c) judges radical behaviorism as mistaken for eliminating mentalism from psychology.

Charles Taylor (1964, 1985a, 1985b), although trained in Britain in analytical philosophy, is working toward a rapprochement with continental philosophy, particularly in the area of hermeneutics (see chapter 4). He proposes to reconcile the philosophy of science of psychology by arguing that traditional experimental psychology that links psychological experience to neurophysiological function (i.e., research in physiological psychology, sensation, and psychophysics) may be conceived of as being part and parcel of the physical sciences. In these areas scientific theories can be generated and investigated by scientific methods. However, in those areas of psychology that study whole persons rather than part functions (i.e., developmental, social, personality, and clinical psychology), a hermeneutic method is required that recognizes that the subjects being studied, and the scientists doing the research, are interpretative beings. Again, behaviorism is criticized for its failure to recognize the difference between psychological and physical "facts." Taylor's position has found strong support in the work of Margolis (1989), MacIntyre (1981), and Bernstein (1983), among other Anglo-American philosophers.

The last selection in this section is an early work by Joseph Margolis (see chapter 5) and is the only one directly concerned with clinical matters. Although his current work (1989) is heavily influenced by continental hermeneutics, this excerpt from *Psychotherapy and Morality* is an exceptional demonstration of the benefits of the method of conceptual analysis as applied to psychological theory. He examines the issue of whether any theory of psychotherapy, particularly a psychoanalytic theory, can be value-neutral, as claimed by many early analysts and psychotherapists. Is psychological intervention simply a set of techniques for changing people that can be applied willy-nilly to any problem and toward any end? This specifically addresses what I identified earlier as the second basic problem for clinical psychology. Margolis finds that psychotherapy is a moral enterprise in two senses: As a professional practice, like any practice, it can be held up to moral review; and that the problems that it addresses as a profession are in fact problems that have always been regarded as, at least in part, of a moral nature (e.g., interpersonal conflict, parental and marital responsibilities, sexual conduct, etc.). As a moral enterprise, psychotherapy (and, by inference, all clinical work), brings one potentially into conflict with community standards of morality—conflict between what is "right" and what is "good." Margolis then analyzes the logic of moral arguments in which such conflicts are resolved, thus enabling psychologists to avoid adding logical blunders to the already difficult task of resolving moral dilemmas in clinical practice.

REFERENCES

Bernstein, R. (1983). *Beyond objectivism and relativism.* Philadelphia: University of Pennsylvania Press.

Feigl, H. (1967). *The mental and the physical.* Minneapolis: University of Minnesota Press.

Kuhn, T. (1970). *The structure of scientific revolutions* (2nd ed.). Chicago: University of Chicago Press.

MacIntyre, A. (1981). *After virtue.* Notre Dame, IN: University of Notre Dame Press.

Margolis, J. (1989). *Texts without referents: Reconciling science and narrative.* New York: Basil Blackwell.

Polanyi, M. (1946). *Science, faith, and society.* London: Oxford University Press.

Polanyi, M. (1958). *Personal knowledge.* Chicago: University of Chicago Press.

Taylor, C. (1964). *Explanation of behavior.* London: Routledge & Kegan Paul.

Taylor, C. (1985a). *Human agency and language: Philosophical papers.* Cambridge, England: Cambridge University Press.

Taylor, C. (1985b). *Philosophy and the human sciences: Philosophical papers 2.* Cambridge, England: Cambridge University Press.

2

PHILOSOPHICAL EMBARRASSMENTS OF PSYCHOLOGY

HERBERT FEIGL

I appreciate deeply the honor and privilege of being the guest speaker for this distinguished audience. You chose to invite a philosopher, and I can only hope you will not suffer too much from the consequences.

As I am sure you know, philosophers are specialists in generalities. They are usually also somewhat opinionated. Hence, there is the danger that scientists may regard them as unwelcome kibitzers at their game. In this regard their role is similar to that of the literary or the art critic. Physicists, according to my impressions, have in recent years put up a sign: "Philosophers please keep out; reconstruction going on." Small wonder, as the printer's devil once had it: "Nuclear" physics is "unclear" physics. The majority of physicists want to unmuddle themselves without the aid of philosophical clarifiers. But I have found psychologists and social scientists much more hospitable. Just like a certain small minority of physicists, they seem to appreciate a few hints from the philosophers of science. But there is on the one hand the danger of running in open doors, i.e., of laboring the obvious and the trivial; and on the other hand there is the danger of stepping on sensitive toes—especially with as large and diversified an audience as the present one. I shall have to take these risks and hope for the best. The only reassurance I can offer is that I have been concerned with the philosophy of the empirical sciences for a good many years and that, though my original scientific background was that of physics, chemistry, and astronomy, I have had also a long and enduring interest in psychological theory. This dates back at least to the year 1932 when I taught at the University of Iowa. I still remember the day when, with fear and trembling, I approached Dean Carl E. Seashore, that pioneer of American experimental psychology, and asked him whether he would approve of my offering a seminar in Philosophical

Reprinted from the *American Psychologist, 14,* 115–128. (1959). In the public domain.

Problems of Psychology. Seashore was known for the forceful manner in which he discouraged projects that appeared to him as "out of line," "utopian"—or in short, as "so much moonshine." But to my great and pleasant surprise, he slapped my shoulder and said "Feigl, that's *good!*" Well, I have felt encouraged ever since, and in this paper I shall try to review some of the philosophical perplexities and embarrassments of psychology.

Let me say immediately that the embarrassments are mutual, they go both ways. Important philosophical issues keep bothering the psychologists; and many significant developments in psychology have baffled the philosophers. It is true that the same holds also for mathematics, physics, biology, and the social sciences; but the philosophical issues have a very special poignancy in connection with psychology.

Philosophy and psychology, only some 40 or 50 years ago, appeared so intimately related that these two fields were even administratively conjoined in one department in many colleges and universities. But with the development of the experimental techniques in psychology, there came a long series of separations and divorces. The sort of emancipations which had occurred much earlier in all the other fields of science had finally been achieved also by psychology. But, now that the divorce is fully accepted by both parties, and remarriage is clearly out of the question, there are signs that a good friendship may be mutually profitable. This seems all the more possible and hopeful because philosophy itself has thoroughly mended its ways. In fact there are many who speak of a "revolution" in philosophy. (If you should be sensitive to this "subversive" term, I shall call it a "thorough transformation"—avoiding the equally subversive label "radical change of outlook.")

Not without justification has the enterprise of philosophy been regarded with distrust and suspicion by tough-minded scientists. Speculative philosophers throughout the ages have wrestled with the riddles of the universe and have quarreled and argued in a manner that seems to exclude any responsible settlement. There are ways of stating and handling problems that make them 100% guaranteed insoluble. I shall illustrate later on how speculative thinking, usually quite unwittingly, can produce completely unanswerable questions. For the present I want to indicate, only in a general way, that the much greater sophistication of recent philosophical analysis has furnished us with an adequate diagnosis, as well as with "hygienic" and "therapeutic" measures for the prevention and the extermination, of this sort of philosophical malady. (Some colleagues in my profession still resent my defining philosophy as the disease of which it should be the cure.)

More seriously speaking, there is now a fairly generally accepted similarity between philosophical analysis and psychotherapy. Philosophical analysis attempts to make fully explicit the *conceptual* conflicts that underlie the intellectual symptoms of inconsistency or paradox, just as psychotherapy attempts to produce full awareness of the *emotional* conflicts that underlie the behavioral symptoms or maladjustments. I suspect that most philosophical quandaries are ultimately rooted in emotional tensions. I have known professional philosophers who have been so deeply disturbed by their puzzles that both philosophical analysis as well as psychoanalysis might be "interminable" with them. But, fortunately, in many cases the philosophical treatment suffices even though it is much closer to the surface. Some philosophical troubles are the result of simple ambiguities. Let me illustrate this by a perplexity that seems to have exercised lately a few prominent psychologists: the famous issue of free will vs. scientific determinism. I shall not tarry long over this hoary puzzle, but even a brief discussion might persuade you of the cathartic and clarifying power of philosophical analysis.

The perplexity of this ancient issue consists in the apparent logical incompatibility between two beliefs, each of which appears plausible on its own grounds: The assumption of free choice seems borne out by the testimony of introspection; also it seems indispensable as a presupposition for moral responsibility. On the other hand, a great deal of biological and psychological evidence points in the direction of a fairly strict determinism in regard to human behavior. "Nature" and "nurture" (i.e., hereditary constitution and all environmental influences up to the moment of choice or action) are assumed to go a long way toward determining our decisions as well as our conduct. But, so it seems to many thinkers, if we are to be free, we cannot be enmeshed in a strict network of causal relations. Hence, the relief and jubilation in many quarters when the "good tidings" of indeterminacy in basic physics were proclaimed.

But a little critical reflection shows readily that this sort of "absolute chance," far from constituting free choice, would be experienced as a queer kind of compulsion, and thus not serve at all as a basis for moral responsibility (i.e., praisability or blamability). Only if, to a significant extent, we are the choosers of our choices, and the doers of our deeds, can we be held accountable. The entire bafflement is due to a confusion which can be easily dispelled. We must not confuse freedom with indeterminacy (i.e., the absence of causality), and we must not confuse causal determination with compulsion, coercion, or constraint. As already Spinoza essentially saw it, we are free to the degree that our choices and our conduct are determined by our character and personality. The fact that our personality and character in turn may have been completely determined by antecedent conditions does not militate against regarding our actions as a consequence of what we are at the moment of action. Apples are produced by apple trees, even if apple trees themselves are the products of seeds, soil, air, rain, and sunshine. To be unfree means no more than to be under some sort of constraint. To be free means that the chooser or agent is an essential link in the chain of causal events and that no extraneous compulsion—be it physical, biological, or psychological—forces him to act in a direction incompatible with his basic desires or intentions.

It has been asked how one can be held responsible for actions springing from a personality whose structure might have been determined by the initial and boundary conditions long before the infant was born. The answer to this question can be found by a logical analysis of the concept of responsibility. We are responsible to the extent that our behavior is responsive to the usual sanctions of society. Rewards and punishments, encouragements and discouragements of any sort can be successfully applied *only* under the conditions of at least a high degree of causal determinism. The nonresponsibility of the psychotic as well as the responsibility of the normal person can be understood only within the causal scheme of events. (The borderline cases of neurotic compulsion may be intriguing, but have to be dealt with pragmatically and in the light of the nature of the special situation on hand.) Empiricist philosophers have long ago explicated causal necessity in terms of lawfulness and predictability.

Free will, properly understood, "presupposes causal determination (in this sense) and is inconceivable without it" (Hobart, 1934). If human acts to any extent, and through some amplification processes, were a result of basic quantum indeterminacies (i.e., on the microlevel of atomic interactions), then to that extent we could not be held responsible for our conduct. The phrase "I could have acted differently," as used in common parlance, does not imply indeterminacy of this or any other sort. It merely means "If I had been wiser or if I had had different attitudes, I would have acted differently." Under the influence of positive and negative reinforcements (some of which may well be internal to our personalities) we learn how to adjust ourselves for future exigencies and contingencies. The sentiments of regret or remorse can be instrumental in this respect only if they do not hopelessly and exclusively fix the individual's attention upon his past deeds, but rather if they are *prospective* and thus mobilize the resolution to act differently on future similar occasions. Docility, the capacity of modifying both one's beliefs and one's attitudes under the influence of cumulative experience, is of the very essence of freedom.

I hope this brief sketch will have shown that an examination of the meaning of the terms we use can go a long way toward the clarification of deeply puzzling issues. Proper attention to the two questions "What do you mean?" and "How do you know?" quite generally constitutes the most effective strategy in modern philosophical analysis. (It should be noted, however, that this is nothing really new in philosophy. Ever since Socrates conversed with the bright young men of Athens, inquiries into meaning and validity have been an important part of the philosophical endeavor; but this search for clarity has often been overshadowed, if not suppressed, by the extravagancies of speculation concerning absolute truth, reality, or values.)

Let me conclude this introductory discussion by a brief formulation of the aims and procedures of current philosophy of science. As we understand our endeavors nowadays, they are not directed toward a speculative anticipation of future scientific systems or unifying syntheses and integrations. The new emphasis is placed on the quest for a clear understanding of the basic concepts, assumptions, and methods of the sciences. Two philosophical techniques stand out in this enterprise: One is the informal type of logical clarification through linguistic analysis. (My discussion of the free will perplexity may be taken as an example of this technique.) The other approach is that of a more formal (sometimes also quite formalistic, not to say formidable) reconstruction of scientific theories in term of syntactical, semantical, and pragmatic metalanguages. As I see it, these two techniques supplement each other: a higher level of aspiration in regard to logical exactitude requires the first technique to be consolidated by the second one. In what follows I shall, for ease of exposition, restrict myself to the relatively informal type of discourse of the first technique.

I propose now to discuss some of the philosophical embarrassments that attach to fundamental issues of psychology as a science. Since it is not feasible to separate neatly questions of *subject matter* and questions of *method,* I shall treat both of them as they become relevant.

PSYCHOLOGY AMONG THE SCIENCES

It is customary to assign to psychology a place in the system of the sciences, somewhere straddling the fence between the natural and the social sciences. This is to say that, if we first distinguish the formal sciences (i.e., pure logic and mathematics) from the empirical or factual sciences, psychology is clearly one among the latter; and in some of its divisions like psychophysics and psychophysiology, as well as in the behavioristic studies of the learning processes, psychology shares many of the characteristics of the natural sciences; it is in this respect closely akin to, and allied with, biology. But when it comes to clinical psychology, psychoanalysis, the psychology of thought, to social and anthropological psychology, the relation to the social and cultural sciences appears much closer. Possibly under the influence of certain philosophical doctrines, some psychologists (but they are a minority) still insist on a fundamental difference not only in subject matter, but also and especially in *method,* between the natural and the social sciences.

Thus it has been claimed that the natural sciences are "nomothetic" while the social sciences are "idiographic." This means that the natural sciences are supposed to concentrate on the discovery of general laws whereas the social sciences are said to concentrate on unique and individual cases and events. This seems plausible enough if one compares, e.g., theoretical physics with history. But there are idiographic natural sciences—such as descriptive astronomy, physical geography—and even such historical disciplines as paleontology. And there are clearly nomothetic social sciences such as sociology or economics. Even if you question their success in the discovery of reliable laws in these fields, the intent of the research is undeniably nomothetic. I think many of the recurrent disputes in regard to this issue can be settled by a recognition and proper allocation of the nomothetic (generalizing) and the idiographic (individualizing) components in the natural as well as the social sciences. Even if we feel that we do not have very precise and reliable theories of personality in current psychology, the very concepts which have been introduced in this discipline lend themselves to both: the description of the individual case, *and* the formulation of general regularities. These regularities may be only a *statistical* character, but this still does not diminish their difference from individual description.

Cutting a little more deeply, there is the related alleged difference between *explaining* and *understanding*. Various schools of thought—mostly of German descent—have emphasized this as a fundamental distinction between the natural and the social sciences. To come down to specific examples, we are told that the regularities, e.g., concerning negative afterimages or concerning thresholds and limens in psychophysics, are not in any way "understandable" in the manner in which we can understand that frustration engenders aggression, that success leads to greater self-confidence, or that some given premises lead a thinker to draw a special conclusion. The role of the phenomenological approach, the importance of *empathy*, has been stressed by certain representatives of clinical psychology. It had of course also been an important tenet of Gestalt psychology. "Intuition," "insight," "understanding," and "empathy" have been key words in the strife of psychological movements. These terms are used honorifically by one party, but they are suspect (if not on the *index verborum prohibitorum*) with the other party.

But I think the dust and the heat of the disputes now are clearing away. We recognize that, especially in the psychology of human motivation, and in psychodynamics generally, empathy is an often helpful and important heuristic tool. But we realize also that empathetic judgments can go woefully wrong, no matter how strong their intuitive conviction. Empathy may be a *source* of knowledge in that it *suggests* hypotheses. But it is not self-authenticating. Objective tests alone can confirm the correctness of these "hunches." The philosophical embarrassment here arises out of a confusion between the origin and the justification of knowledge-claims. Once we distinguish between the psychological roots and the methodological validation of our judgments, there remains no fundamental difference in the type of justification legitimately applied in the natural and the social sciences. This may be recognized quickly if "understanding" is seen to rest on familiarization. Familiarity breeds intuition; but it is neither a necessary nor a sufficient condition for scientific explanation. In the more advanced physical sciences highly abstract theories possess great explanatory power, but the postulates of those theories are not in the least self-evident or intuitively convincing. They are effective premises for the sort of derivation which constitute scientific explanations. We should not feel constrained to explain the new, the surprising, or the unfamiliar exclusively on the basis of old, customary, and familiar premises. To be sure, it is pleasant if it can be done this way, but, I repeat, this is neither necessary nor sufficient for a good scientific explanation.

The phrase "clinical experience has shown . . ." is sometimes intended to disparage or discourage independent objective tests. Freud, for example, despite his respect for the scientific method and his general naturalistic outlook, was not interested in the experimental confirmation of his doctrines. But though it is admittedly difficult to test psychoanalytic hypotheses, it seems imperative at least to formulate them in such a way that an experimental confirmation or disconfirmation becomes possible. I have no particular partisan axe to grind in regard to psychoanalytic theory or any other school of thought in contemporary psychology. The philosopher of science can afford, and should sincerely attempt, to remain above the battle. After all, we philosophers operate mostly by hindsight anyway. Do not expect us to blaze many new scientific trails—those glorious times are over. Altogether too many philosophers have sold their birthright for a pot of message! (The "prophet motive" operates here! This is part of *our* embarrassment.) In view of the enormous complexity of modern scientific research, we have had to lower our level of aspiration. We are glad if we can provide a clearer understanding of the scientific enterprise. But here, I am confident, we can fulfill a useful auxiliary role; especially in collaboration with productive scientists we can serve as critics and catalysts. This is the sort of thing we have been doing at the Minnesota Center for Philosophy of Science—in connection with psychological as well as with physical theory.

After this modest advertisement I return to the issues of Understanding vs. Explaining: Hardheaded psychologists, especially those of radically behaviorist convictions, usually repudiate psychoanalytic interpretations as so much fantasy or metaphysics. But let us see whether the wheat cannot be separated from the chaff; or, if you permit a horrible shift in metaphors, whether we cannot save the baby while throwing out only the dirty bath water. As is well known, Freud himself considered his theory as "monolithic"; i.e., he did not permit his disciples to pick and choose among its postulates. Only wholesale acceptance or wholesale rejection seemed legitimate to the grand old man. But this is surely not in accordance with Freud's own procedure. On numerous occasions he revised parts of his doctrine—no doubt on the basis of clinical experience! Even from a logical point of view it must be admitted that scientific theories consist of relatively independently testable hypotheses. It is true, and has been stressed ever since Pierre Duhem and Henri Poincaré, that there are no *strictly* crucial experiments. But this is simply a logical triviality, viz., that a particular experimental finding can never establish the truth *or* the falsity of a single hypothesis which is part of a whole set of postulates. But careful experimental or statistical designs can group and regroup the to-be-tested hypotheses in such a way that the probabilities of confirmation or of disconfirmation become so significant as to be practically sufficient for the (always tentative) acceptance or rejection of a given hypothesis. As we empiricist philosophers must never forget to repeat: Scientific truth can be held only "until further notice," such notice to be given when contrary evidence crops up.

Now there are theories (and some of the Freudian doctrines are examples) which are so conceived as to be irrefutable by *any* sort of evidence. But these are the excesses of the psychoanalytic creed. When we consider the Eros-Thanatos doctrine, i.e., the attempts of explaining behavior in terms of life and death instincts, we find that it explains too much, namely, *any* conceivable type of behavior. This, far from being a virtue, vitiates the theory. Theories of this sort—I am tempted to call them manichaean—are (usually unwittingly) made immune against any conceivable test. They are proof against disproof. They constitute a *methodological* embarrassment. The history of scientific and philosophic thought offers many parallel examples. Doctrines of material substance, of an indestructible soul, of absolute space and time, the phlogiston hypothesis in early chemistry, the ether hypothesis in its comatose last ditch stand, the speculation about vital forces or entelechies in biology, etc. have all been defended in a manner that precludes even the most indirect or incomplete confirmations or disconfirmations. Closer logical analysis reveals that the factual content claimed for such doctrines and hypotheses simply does not exist. This may come about in the following ways: Some of the key terms of the doctrine may fail to have empirical significance in that they are completely severed from any and all observation bases. This in turn may be the result either of (implicit or explicit) stipulation, or it may come to pass by a process most aptly described as "whittling away" whatever empirical meaning those key terms may have had to begin with. In the case of Freud's manichaean doctrine, very much like in the case of the older formulations of the pleasure-displeasure principle in British psychology, the factual emptiness results from a slide into tautology. It is like the well known rule for weather prediction: "The weather will either remain the same or it will change." The quest for certainty, the craving for infallibility, has produced the embarrassments of *emptiness* and *circularity*. If behavior is to be explained or be predicted on the basis of Eros or Thanatos, and if the only criterion supplied for deciding which of the two to adduce is the actual conduct, then there can be no explanation or prediction at all.

It would however be grossly unfair to psychoanalytic theory if, in the light of these criticisms, we were to repudiate it altogether. There are much more substantial contributions in the theories concerning the unconscious. The mechanisms of repression and of defense, the interpretation of dreams, the psychopathology of everyday life, the explanations of neurotic behavior, etc. are in principle capable of empirical examination. But here again, tough-minded operationists and radical behaviorists have criticized the theories as metaphysical and have attempted to reduce their tenable core to empirical regularities concerning the positive or negative reinforcement of behavior.

Before I turn to a more general discussion about the nature of, and the need for, theories in psychology, there are a few remarks to be made about the notion of *evidence* in psychological explanation, interpretation, and prediction. Let us take as examples the psychoanalytic view of dreams and of free associations. As I have already mentioned, the intuitive conviction carried by some of these interpretations may by far outrun anything that a scientifically minded psychologist would grant in terms of objective probabilities. The high level of aspiration in experimental science seems to prevent acknowledgment of the cognitive significance of such weak indicators as are at the disposal of the clinical psychologist or psychoanalyst.

But if we reject these indicators as evidence, we would in all consistency have to reject likewise the clues in historical research or in detective work. Straightforward experimental procedures and even explicit statistical designs are here scarcely applicable. This is a matter of stark practical impossibility. But historical and detective methods may be quite scientific in that they consist in a careful scrutiny and critical comparison of the various items of evidence. If the historian ascribes a given painting to an individual artist of the fifteenth century, he utilizes clues of various sorts and of course holds his interpretation open to further confirmation, as well as possibly to disconfirmation, by whatever relevant evidence may be discovered later on. This is not different in principle from such reconstructions of past events as we find in geology or paleontology. To be sure, if we define the scientific character of an hypothesis in terms of a criterion of strict *predictability*, most of what goes on in historical studies of any kind would be relegated to the limbo of the unscientific or the nonscientific endeavors. But surely, this is too narrow a view of the scientific enterprise. The specific and detailed features of an island that arose out of volcanic activities, or of a canyon that was formed by erosion, could not have been predicted before these events happened. The particular shape of the devastation or the shambles produced by an earthquake are unforeseeable. The *particular* structures and functions of plants and animals as they came about in the evolution of the species will very likely remain unexplained. But the ex post facto explanation of the *gross* features of the respective results (i.e., the general features of the island, of the canyon, of the devastation, of the organisms) is perfectly legitimate.

Mutatis mutandis this may be applied to human behavior. The particular manner in which a murder or a suicide was executed would generally not have been predictable on the basis of even a fairly complete knowledge of the antecedent circumstances. Similarly, just which specific images occur in the manifest content of a dream may forever remain unpredictable. But this need not prevent a psychoanalytic interpretation of the manifest image as a symbol. Just what specific free associations will be produced in response to a certain stimulus situation may well remain equally unforeseeable. But this again does not exclude an explanation of the emitted verbal responses on the basis of assumed unconscious mental states as long as these are accessible through other independent avenues of confirmation.

The diffidence with which predictions and explanations of this type are treated by tough-minded scientists may have much to do with a fixation on the well known *deductive* model of inference. But once it is realized that the deductive model fits only some very special cases, and is applicable even to these only by way of considerable idealization, a more liberal attitude may well be accepted. There are perfectly good explanations not only in common life but also in the sciences in which the derivation of the facts or regularities to be explained from the laws and the conditions which provide the explanation is no more than *probabilistic*. Deductive necessity can be had only *more geometrico*. The classical theories of mechanics, thermodynamics, and electromagnetics were deductive systems, owing mainly to the deterministic form in which their postulates were cast. With the intrusion of probabilistic and statistical concepts even in basic physics, the deductive model must now be regarded as an ideal limit case. And in the light of pertinent scientific evidence it is highly precarious to hope for successive approximations which will take us anywhere near this limit. (Perhaps I should remark here that my previous definition of free will does not presuppose a *strict* determinism. A statistical type of causality is perfectly sufficient for the ascription of responsibility.)

The ways and means of behavior, I conclude, may not ever be more accurately predictable than probabilistically. But this is sufficient for an (equally probabilistic) type of explanation. Out of the thousands of images or words that may occur in a given situation one only actually occurs. This specific item has therefore only an extremely low probability. But in the light of psychoanalytic theory (i.e., if we could only fully spell it out) there is always a *class* of responses which is greatly more probable than the class of all alternative responses. The difficult job to be done consists in specifying the first class in terms of its defining characteristics. Here, too, we should not and need not aspire to too much precision. Classes with vague borderlines are used commonly and profitably in many sciences. Perhaps one way of getting at the defining characteristics would be by utilizing the intuitive experiences of empathizers as a first guide. After all, something very similar is done in the construction of personality and other psychological tests. Later validations can correct whatever errors are due to the original "bootstraps" procedure. Prima facie this might seem to re-establish the difference between the social and the natural sciences which I have been at pains to deny. But remembering the helpful distinction between the context of discovery and the context of justification we can recognize that criteria which have their origin in clinical intuition may later be validated objectively and scientifically. We may even be able subsequently to explain the workings of intuition.

Let me illustrate this by a story (no doubt a canard) which appeared in the newspapers a long time ago. A doctor had a dog that would bark a peculiar way when confronted with patients who had an incipient cancer. The cancers were in such an early stage of development that they could not be detected by the usual (x-ray, etc.) methods. Just how the dog managed this marvelous feat was completely obscure. But, if one wanted to be "scientific" about it, the relative frequency of "correct" barkings could be ascertained statistically. Once it is established that this frequency is significantly above change, then the question of how to explain this fact may be tackled. (This is, after all, the attitude many psychologists take in regard to graphology, or in regard to extrasensory perception.) I suggest that the clinical psychologist, and the empathizer generally, is his own diagnosis dog. If and only if a high "batting average" can be established, on the basis of subsequent objective evidence, is he entitled to some confidence in his diagnoses. This way of looking at the matter should satisfy even a rigorous behaviorist.

DEFINITION OF SUBJECT MATTER

This brings me to what is perhaps the most painful philosophical embarrassment of psychology: the definition of its very subject matter. As the well known saying goes: psychology first lost its soul, later its consciousness, and seems now in danger of losing its mind altogether. I know very well that the specification of psychology's subject matter is highly controversial. The disputes concerning it seem to be emotionally highly charged, if, for no other reason, then certainly because of the perennially puzzling mind-body problem. This problem is currently not fashionable, not even in pure philosophy. I think that the behaviorist revolution in psychology has much to do with this state of affairs. According to my own diagnosis, the mind-body problem has been repressed, and all sorts of defense mechanism have been developed to evade this issue which traditionally has been so closely tied up with theology, religion, and metaphysics. Powerful emotions are elicited whenever we touch questions of *Weltanschauung*. I do not flatter myself that I could desensitize many of you in the course of a few brief remarks. But perhaps I can at least suggest to you that repression of the problem merely produces troublesome symptoms—paradoxes and perplexities in this case—and that philosophical analysis can provide a helpful catharsis. Judging by recent publications in theoretical and methodological matters, the issues of introspective vs. behavioristic, of phenomenological vs. neurophysiological psychology crop up again and again, and with remarkable tenacity. The *Zeitgeist* may not be favorable for a revival of these traditional issues, but since I believe there is a genuine possibility for a constructive solution, I shall take the liberty of briefly sketching it out for you. (I must ask you to forgive the somewhat dogmatic tone of my presentation. It took me over a hundred pages in an essay (Feigl, 1958) published earlier this year to deal with the major facets of this badly tangled problem.)

If we extricate the mind-body problem from its traditional theological and metaphysical background, there remain nevertheless a number of questions which are apt to produce intellectual discomfort, if not anxiety. The central issue is this: Can we give a logically consistent and scientifically acceptable account of the relations between subjective immediate experience on the one hand and behavioral or neurophysiological processes on the other? The traditional answers are well known to you. (Psychology textbooks used to mention them at least in the introductory chapter.) They are: dualistic interactionism, psychophysiological parallelism (usually in the form of epiphenomenalism), the double aspect doctrine, and the theory of emergent evolution. The endless disputes between these different attempts at a solution of our "riddle of the universe" have been so discouraging that many thinkers—in the camps of philosophy as well as psychology—have tried to undercut the whole issue. They have tried to show that this is a pseudoproblem which need not trouble us. But, as I hope to show you, these are maneuvers of evasion. Prominent among them are phenomenalism (or neutral monism) and logical behaviorism. Characteristically, the positivist movement in more than a century of vigorous influence upon epistemology and philosophy of science has embraced sometimes the one and at other times the other of these points of view. But both phenomenalism and radical behaviorism must be accused of committing reductive fallacies. The phenomenalists reduce our concepts concerning physical objects to logical constructions out of the data of direct experience. And the logical behaviorists reduce "mentalistic" concepts (including those that refer to direct experience) to logical constructions out of the publicly observable peripheral behavior. (If we are not to spend hours on formal technicalities, I shall have to ask you to let me get by with these rather loose characterizations.) It appeared for a while that we must choose between a reductive view (of either sort) and a metaphysical solution of the mind-body problem. Metaphysical solutions are abhorred by the tough-minded scientists—though they have been tempting to the speculative philosopher. I have called them "seductive" fallacies, because they arise out of wishful thinking.

Is there no *via media* between the philosophies of the "nothing but" and the philosophy of the "something more"? My own way of thinking in these matters was dubbed by my students as "Feigelian dialectics." That is to say that I discern and recommend a constructive *synthesis* of the *thesis* of tender-minded and the *antithesis* of tough-minded thinking. (You will remember that William James, a long time ago, proposed this sort of resolution of philosophical issues. James himself, however, never found a satisfactory equilibrium. He vacillated between radical empiricism and an early form of functionalism. Perhaps I should also remark that my approach has precious little in common with either Hegelian or Marxian dialectics. I do not plead for a new logic. I use the dialectical pattern only as a means of exposition.) In short, I suggest that instead of committing ourselves to either a philosophy of the "nothing but" or of the "something more," we adopt a philosophy of the "*what's what*"! That is to say that we need not impoverish the world by absurd reductions, nor enrich it by unconfirmable projections. We may, instead, follow the lead of the scientific method: ascertaining what there is and attempting to explain and formulate it in a clear, coherent, and parsimonious manner.

More specifically, I plead for a monistic, naturalistic view of the mental and the physical, allowing for a qualified reinstatement of the introspective and phenomenological approaches; and I look to neurophysiological theory for an eventual emendation and supplementation of behavior theories. At first this may sound to you either cheaply eclectic or hopelessly programmatic, if not utopian. But there are increasing indications that such a synthesis is not only logically possible, but that it is a fruitful direction of research. To bring this closer home to you, and to make it more concrete, I would say (even at the risk of shocking part of my audience) that an approach such as Donald Hebb's *Organization of Behavior* may well supplement B. F. Skinner's *Behavior of Organisms.* (I have been wondering whether Hebb had chosen the title of his book in contrast and opposition to that of Skinner's.) Clark Hull's neurophysiological speculations, it is true, were rather idle wheels in the machinery of his system, but his basic methodological orientation at least provided a place for neurophysiological theory. Edward C. Tolman's "intervening variables" may yet turn out to be hypothetical constructs or theoretical concepts which will correspond to neurophysiological concepts in a more complete theory à la Hebb, perhaps in the not-too-distant future. Some of Kurt Lewin's field theoretical and dynamic concepts have been absorbed in Tolman's approach, and would in any case in principle be open to the same neurophysiological specification. This is, of course, in keeping with the original isomorphism doctrine, especially in the form given to it by Wolfgang Köhler. Add to this the promising contributions of Norbert Wiener, Warren McCulloch, and others, along the lines of cybernetics, and we have at least the beginnings of a theory of those intriguing teleological (i.e., goal directed and self-regulating) processes which in earlier times drove some philosophers, and even some psychologists, into a defeatist vitalism.

I realize that there are a great many empirical questions yet to be settled in this highly controversial area. But it does seem to me, at least from the vantage point of my philosophical armchair, that the doctrine of isomorphism has a good deal of experimental evidence in its favor. I think, moreover, that the doctrine has been subjected to unjustifiable criticisms by behaviorists and operationists. The reintroduction of introspection, the new concern with the phenomenal field, the clinical attention to subjective experience, the studies in social perception, etc. seem to me to indicate, not indeed a regression to an obsolete psychology, but rather an advance along the spiral (or should I say "helix"?) of the evolution of the scientific outlook.

The limitations of the introspective and phenomenological approach are realized and admitted. We are aware of the sources of error in introspective description and phenomenological-clinical observation and interpretation; and being aware, we can apply measures to correct these errors. If we refrain from fallaciously reducing subjective experience to response patterns, we may well reinstate the classical distinction between mental states and their behavioral manifestations. It is precisely because we have been cautioned by the behaviorists that we can do this with greater sophistication, and hence with a better intellectual conscience. And thinking the situation through to its logical conclusion, we may go beyond a timid psychophysiological parallelism and hold an identity theory of the mental and the physical. That is to say that the data of subjective experience are identical with certain central states of behavior theory, and thus ultimately with certain neurophysiological states. Let me indicate the logic of these identifications by way of a succinct outline.

As I diagnose one of the main motives of classical behaviorism, it was the problem of our knowledge of other minds which constituted the major philosophical embarrassment. Progressional philosophers have carried on agonizing discussions over this puzzle. The admitted impossibility for one person to inspect another person's mental contents seemed to conflict with the firm beliefs of commonsense. Even if, in ordinary life or in clinical observation, we claim to apprehend fairly directly or intuitively what goes on in the other person, it was rightly maintained that this—by itself—does not constitute a justification for our assertions about other minds. The obvious gambit of using analogy arguments for such a justification seemed excluded because of a fundamental difference between this particular application of analogical reasoning from the ordinary type of analogical argument. In most ordinary cases the conclusion can be independently verified with the same directness and to the same degree of certainty as the premises of the argument. But just this is fundamentally impossible in the case of the inference to other minds. Aided and abetted by the positivists, the behaviorists insisted on a criterion of meaning according to which only objectively verifiable assertions are scientifically meaningful. Introspection as such did not seem to qualify—unless interpreted (as already suggested by John B. Watson) as a response to previous responses. The objectively certifiable behavior of organisms, along with, and in the same sense as, the processes and events in the lifeless or inorganic realm, was considered the only legitimate subject matter of science. No wonder then that behaviorism (as Max Mayer put it so strikingly in the title of his 1921 book) became "the psychology of the other one." (To be sure, there are other facets of behaviorism, such as the emphasis on the experimental method and the faith in environmentalism; but these are irrelevant in the present context.)

You may feel that since the battle of behaviorism was fought some 30 or 40 years ago, that there is no point in reviewing it today. But I surmise we might get a very different picture in a current opinion poll among psychologists. Even the positivists have mended their ways. They have liberalized their erstwhile extremely restrictive meaning criterion. That is the main reason why most of them prefer to label themselves as "logical empiricists" or "scientific empiricists." These new party designations are intended to convey the shift from verifiability to *confirmability*. That is to say that we no longer insist on complete and direct testing, but that we consider any statement as scientifically meaningful if it is at least incompletely and/or indirectly testable.

The problem of other persons' mental states thus appears in a very different light. As long as we conceive of mental states, be they our own or those of others, as part and parcel of a network of lawfully related facts, they are no longer inaccessible to confirmation, i.e., to indirect verification. The phenomenal data of one's own experience are of course susceptible to direct verification, they are open to immediate inspection. And in keeping with our commonsense convictions, we have every reason to identify these directly inspected or inspectable states with mental states imputed to us by others or, after a little scientific refinement, with the central states of modern behavior theories. What will *not* work in this connection is a purely peripheralistic behaviorism. As I have pleaded before, peripheral stimulus situations and response patterns may serve as (probabilistic) indicators of central (i.e., mental) states, but they cannot be identified with them. Even B. F. Skinner—perhaps the most consistent among the behaviorists—now has a place for something like private central states in his conceptual scheme of things. Of course this privacy is not the "absolute" privacy of the metaphysicians. It is the relative, practical privacy familiar from everyday life and admitted by any psychologist who accepts confirmability, but does not insist on direct verifiability.

The embarrassment of unanswerable questions can be avoided if we do not introduce absolutely unconfirmable entities into our theories. Such puzzles as that of the "inverted spectrum" illustrate this vividly. This ancient poser has been revived a great many times and caused innumerable philosophical headaches. The question is: Even if two subjects A and B perform equally well in thorough color discrimination tests, could they not "privately" experience different color qualities? Could there not be a systematic difference between A and B, such that A experiences, e.g., green when B experiences red, and vice versa, throughout the whole circle of pure hues? If it is further assumed that all other behavior tests, and even neurophysiological investigations do not reveal any significant individual differences between A and B, then the scientifically minded psychologist feels he can rest his case and assert that the color experiences are similar in A and B. But the metaphysician insists that there might be differences in the private experiences which remain forever and absolutely incapable of objective test.

Shall we just shrug our shoulders and give up on philosophers who make life so difficult for themselves? Perhaps we can attempt a little philosophical therapy. We might show the philosopher that he has illegitimately extended ordinary or empirical doubt and thus fallen into metaphysical doubt. Ordinary empirical doubt may occasionally be hard to settle. But if it is transformed into metaphysical doubt, then there is no conceivable way of settling it by either logical argument or by empirical demonstration. Will this cure the metaphysician? Not necessarily. He may grant that unanswerable questions should be kept out of science, but that they are a worthy subject of puzzlement for the philosopher. But if the philosopher remains forever puzzled, this is a most frustrating state of affairs even to him. Perhaps we can suggest that the philosopher's mistake consists in conceiving of color experience merely on the basis of his direct acquaintance with the qualities he experiences, that he lifts this concept artificially and arbitrarily out of the rich network of causal relations which constitutes the meaning of the concept in ordinary discourse, and even more fully so in scientific knowledge. Perhaps we can show him that on the basis of all these lawful relations his concepts of mental qualities can be recognized as denoting the very same referents that terms of behavior theory (and ultimately of physiological theory) also denote.

This view of co-reference of different terms, as I have already hinted, may well be the key to the solution of the mind-body problem. And it would thus also solve, or rather *dissolve,* the embarrassing puzzles concerning our knowledge of other minds. As long as, in the spirit of the scientific method, we require that it must in principle be possible to *give reasons* for our knowledge claims, we must never entertain knowledge claims that are entirely and absolutely divorced from, and hence unsupportable by, empirical evidence. Philosophical doubt concerning other minds is in this respect similar to philosophical doubt about the occurrence of past events. There is no logical guarantee—so the skeptic argues—that the laws of nature might not have changed from period to period, and that therefore our inferences of past events are hopelessly precarious. He might even go so far as to say that there was no past at all and that the universe originated with a bang a second ago, with all the so-called remnants (geological strata, fossils, memories, etc.). This is just as irrefutable as is solipsism, but of course just as insanely irrational. A little reflection suffices to show that the very meaning and essence of rational belief, as we understand it in common life and in science, includes most prominently the "normal" procedures of inductive and analogical inference, as well as of the hypothetico-deductive or hypothetico-probabilistic methods of theory construction.

The mind-body problem need no longer be evaded or repressed. Advances in science as well as in logical analysis have helped in freeing us from its metaphysical shudders. An explicit uncovering of the various functions of language and of the corresponding types of significance may break whatever resistance still remains against the sort of identity or co-reference view I am advocating. Language serves all sorts of purposes. It may be used for the sake of the formulation and the communication of information. This is *cognitive* meaning. But it may also express or evoke images, emotions; and it may be used in eliciting action or in the molding of dispositions or attitudes. The alleged gulf between the qualities of the mental and the physical, I submit, are largely due to the images which we connect with the use of *physical* concepts. "How can the processes in central nervous systems or the cortex be identical with mind or subjective experience?" If you conceive the brain as that grayish mass you perceive upon opening a skull, or if you visualize the protein molecules of the nervous tissues in terms of the tinkertoy models chemistry instructors show to their classes, then it is indeed impossible to form any consistent idea of mind-body identity. But this is picture-thinking. Pictures and illustrative models are a help, heuristically or didactically. But even in basic theoretical physics such pictures are now at best regarded as an intellectual scaffolding which is to be removed once the building of knowledge has been erected. "Thou shalt not make graven images unto thee!" The proper factual content of physical theories is strictly speaking unvisualizable. It consists in the abstract conceptual formulation of the postulates which are connected by correspondence rules (usually probabilistic ones) with the observables in various domains of evidence. The description of a neural process in abstract physical terms may therefore be interpreted as referring to the very same events which may be described also in phenomenal language on the basis of introspection.

Psychological theories, such as those of molar behaviorism of those of Freudian psychodynamics, use theoretical concept which, perhaps after some revisions or refinements, may well dovetail with certain concepts of neurophysiology. I can see no objection in principle or from a *logical* point of view against the possibility of such a final identification. Any serious doubts about it must be empirical ones and concern the explicability of behavior on a neurophysiological basis. In this connection both the psychologist and the philosopher had better be cautious and await further evidence. For example, the facts of parapsychology—if indeed they are facts and not due to experimental error, hoax, or fraud—might well force upon us a thorough reconsideration of the very framework of presuppositions in psychophysiology. But there is, as far as I know, not even a glimmer as yet of an acceptable and responsible theory of these curious phenomena. As an empiricist I have at least to go through the motions of an open mind on this topic.

PROBLEMS OF THEORY CONSTRUCTION

Let me conclude this long paper with a few more explicit remarks about the problems of theory construction in psychology. The embarrassment here is a *methodological* one; and to the historian and logician of science it is familiar from parallels in the development of physics and chemistry. There have been proponents as well as opponents of theory construction both in the physical as well as in the behavioral sciences. The philosophical perplexity consists in the question: What do theories enable the scientist to do that he could not do with the aid of straightforward empirical generalizations? The two parties to this dispute are the theoreticians and the radical empiricists (we call them "dustbowl empiricists" at Minnesota). I must leave it to you to diagnose and to explain the temperamental differences between these character types; this is of course a matter for psychological or cultural-anthropological study. I will only suggest that radical empiricism has a good deal to do with the wish for intellectual security, i.e., with the desire to restrict one's extrapolations to the domain in which they have been thoroughly tested; it also has a good deal to do with the fear of the invisible and intangible. Hypothesis-phobia has often been a personality trait of positivists—that is why they are such *negativists*! The theoreticians on the other hand do not mind living dangerously. This seems commendable as long as they keep their theories open to revision. Fixation on theories is of course a frequent weakness. But rivalry, competition, and fierce criticism are the order of the day and help in the avoidance of dogmatism.

But enough of this dilettante psychology. I wish to tackle the question from a *logical* angle. This requires a little reflection upon the aims of science. If we distinguish the applied sciences, with their aims of control and guidance, from the pure or fundamental sciences, then the aim of the latter may be defined as the attainment of adequate descriptions and explanations. Prediction, vitally important in all practical applications of science, enters pure science primarily as a means of checking the adequacy of laws and theoretical assumptions. It should not be necessary to defend the distinction between description and explanation. Explanation always involves inference or derivation, deductive or probabilistic, as the case may be. Among the premises of an explanation we need at least one law-like assumption, deterministic or statistical in character. It is expedient to restrict the meaning of the word "description" to singular statements of specific facts—or to conjunctions or disjunctions thereof. This makes for a clean distinction or explanation and description.

Now, according to the radical empiricist, the cognitive, factual content of science consists in the descriptive facts and in the regularities formulated in empirical laws. Empirical laws are usually conceived as fairly directly testable functional relations (again, either deterministic or statistical) between observables. It is my impression that the radical empiricists confuse "factual content" with "cash value." The term "cash value" is not intended here in a pejorative sense. I use it merely to designate the kind of information which is eminently useful in the practical applications of scientific knowledge. I would argue, however, that in the very interest of obtaining this sort of "cash value," *theories* have become extremely helpful, and in many fields indispensable. But quite apart from the practical applications, theories have the distinct value of helping us to *understand* the world and man's place in it. Man does not live by bigger and better technologies alone! Through a sort of "heterogony of purposes" (Wundt) or through "functional autonomy" (Allport) civilized man has acquired curiosities which can be satisfied only by adequate and comprehensive explanations. Such explanations can be achieved only with the aid of theories. A good theory enables us to *derive* empirical laws—and not only those which we have already attained by simple generalization, but also others which still remain to be certified experimentally. Theories are thus not merely convenient and compendious summaries of empirical laws, they are heuristically fruitful in that they enable us to infer further, as yet untested regularities.

But right here our antitheorists ask: Suppose we had investigated all empirical regularities of a given domain, would a theory then be more than, at best, an equivalent though compressed and possibly elegant formulation of a set of empirical laws? My answer is in the negative—and for the following reasons. First of all, most of the so-called empirical laws of science are not as empirical as they appear to be. The concepts in terms of which they are formulated are rarely open to straightforward operational definition. I am referring here not only to the usual idealizations and simplifications experimental scientists apply in the formulation of empirical laws. I have in mind especially the *ceteris paribus* clauses which are often implicitly taken for granted. This is tantamount to guessing at a functional relation between certain key variables—a functional relation which would manifest itself in measurements and experiments, if it were not camouflaged by certain obfuscating variables which are not sufficiently known and hence largely beyond control. The empirical laws that psychologists confidently incorporate in their textbooks are thus not as directly testable as they are often made out to be.

Operationism, just like behaviorism or other forms of radical positivism, has had an undeniably helpful influence in the development of recent science. Untestable assumptions have been relegated to the limbo of metaphysics. But it is time to recognize that radical operationism would curtail the enterprise of science very severely indeed. Of course, "operationism" is now often understood in the much more liberal sense of a methodological attitude, insisting on clarity in regard to the rules—according to which we use our terms. And if these rules concern the observational-experimental *as well* as the logico-mathematical procedures, then "operationism" simply becomes synonymous with "good scientific method" and loses its distinctive reductionist emphasis. But the earlier more restrictive operationist ideology is not at all in agreement with the actual procedures of science.

I have anticipated the essential point here already in some of my earlier remarks. Radical operationists, very much like the logical positivists of some 20 or 30 years ago, are so fixated on direct verifiability that they never analyze the implications of (indirect and incomplete) confirmability. But just this is the essential feature of all sciences which advance beyond the observational, fact-collecting ("botanizing") stage. The radical operationist maxim "different operations, different concepts" is severely at variance with the actual manner in which the meaning of theoretical concepts is specified. The most important syntheses and unifications in science depend on the introduction of theoretical concepts through convergent avenues of specification, coming from different, often at first very heterogeneous areas of evidence.

I admit that for a while it did seem plausible to view many scientific concepts as dispositional and hence to define them by means of test operation→test result conditionals. For example, habit strength in Hullian psychology, or expectancy in Tolman's, seemed dispositional in the sense that, though direct observation is impossible (just as in the case of magnetic strength in physics), these concepts could be regarded as shorthand for certain stimulus-response or (more generally) certain empirical regularities in the sequence of test operations and test results. This procedure was formalized by R. Carnap (1936–37) in a very influential essay more than 20 years ago by the device of reduction sentences. But Carnap (1958; see also Hempel, 1958) himself has abandoned this approach, mainly for the reason that even open sets of such reduction sentences do not adequately reconstruct the actual role of theoretical concepts and their relations to the observables.

Ever since the incisive article by MacCorquodale and Meehl (1948) we at Minnesota, as well as Carnap, have found it helpful to distinguish between purely empirical dispositional concepts ("intervening variables" in the narrower sense) and hypothetical constructs (or "theoretical concepts," as they had better be called). Theoretical concepts are introduced by postulates which, as it were, define these concepts implicitly. The meaning of theoretical concepts is thus given by their place in the network of laws—the "nomological net" as we label it. The nomological net is what Einstein used to call a matter of relatively "free construction." It is anchored only in a few places in the facts of observation. Or, in less picturesque language, theories are postulate systems which derive their empirical meaning and factual reference through the correspondence rules by which the theoretical concepts are connected with certain concepts in the observation language. This allows for the empirical confirmation (or disconfirmation) of theories; it also provides for the multiple routes from various domains of evidence to the theoretical concepts; and it provides for a legitimate way in which to include statements about unobservable entities in our theories.

Since most correspondence rules are not simply explicit definitions or semantic designation rules, but rather probabilistic indicator relations, it is clear that the cognitive content of theories cannot be translated into observation statements, not even an infinite set of these. Modern physics certainly cannot be interpreted in any other way. The concepts of the atomic and the quantum theories refer to unobservables, but they are related to observables in many various areas of evidence. It seems to me that the situation in psychological theory is quite analogous. Just as in physics, we may begin with the formulation of empirical laws. But empirical laws almost always are severely limited in their range of validity. For more comprehensive integrations we have to ascend to higher levels of explanations. This usually results in corrections to be applied to the empirical laws with which we started. Molar behavior theory—and psychodynamics may be construed as part of it—is in many respects methodologically analogous to classical ("phenomenological") thermodynamics. There is clearly a good measure of explanatory power present in theories of this type. But just as physics had to rise to the next higher level of explanation by introducing the molecular theory of matter and the kinetic theory of heat, so molar behavior theory is now in the initial stages of being reduced to neurophysiology.

I realize that many psychologists feel threatened by this sort of reduction. They think that their own subject matter of research is being supplanted by another one in which they do not feel at home and which they regard as beyond the limits of psychology proper. As a philosopher of science I can afford to view these developments with equanimity. Anyone (like myself) interested in the adventure of the unification of the sciences will even welcome these interdisciplinary transgressions. But the experimental and the clinical psychologists may in any case rest assured that a tremendous amount of work remains to be done on their particular level of research. I would merely plead that neurophysiological theory may yield important fruit much sooner than many molar behaviorists seem to believe.

Space does not permit me to deal with other philosophical perplexities of psychology. There are many other embarrassments, and one can never be sure to have selected the ones that are most poignant to one's readers. The whole area of value judgments and its relations to scientific knowledge is in urgent need of thorough clarification. There are also a number of topics much closer to the issues I did discuss, and which I had to omit from this paper.

By way of an *envoi* let me say that modern psychological research and modern logical and methodological analysis may have much to offer to each other. We have made a promising start in the collaboration between creative science and critical, clarifying methodology. The time has come to emancipate ourselves from the radical empiricism of the operationists and the behaviorists. A more liberal view of the nature of scientific theory will help us more adequately and clearly to assign to psychology its proper place in the uniting sciences and to remove many of the philosophical embarrassments that have stood in the way of scientific progress.

REFERENCES

Carnap, R. Testability and meaning. Parts I–IV. *Phil. Sci.*, 1936, 3, 419–471; 1937, 4, 1–40.

Carnap, R. The methodological character of theoretical concepts. In *Minnesota studies in the philosophy of science.* Vol. I. Minneapolis: Univer. Minnesota Press, 1958. Pp. 38–76.

Feigl, H. The "mental" and the "physical." In *Minnesota studies in the philosophy of science.* Vol. II. *Concepts, theories and the mind-body problem.* Minneapolis: Univer. Minnesota Press, 1958. Pp. 370–497.

Hempel, C. G. The theoretician's dilemma. *In Minnesota studies in the philosophy of science.* Vol. II. *Concepts, theories and the mind-body problem.* Minneapolis: Univer. Minnesota Press, 1958. Pp. 37–98.

Hobart, R. E. Free will as involving determination and inconceivable without it. *Mind,* 1934, 43, 1–26.

MacCorquodale, K., & Meehl, P. E. On a distinction between hypothetical constructs and intervening variables. *Psychol. Rev.*, 1948, 55, 95–107.

3

LOGIC AND PSYCHOLOGY

MICHAEL POLANYI

I am happy to have this opportunity to put before you thoughts about the nature of scientific knowledge which I have pursued for some time past. My starting point dates back to my book, *Science, Faith and Society* (Polanyi, 1946). Upon examining the grounds on which science is pursued, I saw that its progress is determined at every stage by indefinable powers of thought. No rules can account for the way a good idea is found for starting an inquiry, and there are no firm rules either for the verification or the refutation of the proposed solution of a problem.

This speculation may sound similar to much of what is often heard today. We are told that the teachings of science claim only to be probable but also to be merely tentative, ever open to refutation by adverse evidence. But this is not true. We bet our lives on the certainty of science every day, be it in medicine or engineering; in fact, nothing is more certain in our world than the established results of science. My point is that the *absence of strict criteria* on which to base our acceptance of science merely shows that our confidence in scientific knowledge *is based on nonstrict criteria.* Science is grounded, and is firmly grounded, on the kind of indefinable insights which the current view of science regards as mere psychological phenomena, incapable of producing rational inferences.

I believe, therefore, that any attempt to eliminate nonstrict modes of inference—or even to reduce them to insignificance—must be misleading. Such attempts have hampered philosophy and damaged our scientific methods. Later I shall give some examples of such cases.

My main task will be to survey the nonstrict rules of inference—in other words, the informal logic—on which science rests. This nonstrict logic will be seen to rest to some extent on psychological observations not hitherto accepted as the foundations of scientific inference. In these informal elements of science we shall recognize the *indeterminacy of scientific knowledge,* and I shall start by describing *three closely linked kinds of such indeterminacy.* The *first* indeterminacy

Reprinted from the *American Psychologist, 33,* 27–43. (1967). Copyright © 1967 by the American Psychological Association.

lies in the *indeterminate content* of scientific knowledge. We shall find a *second* indeterminacy in the fact that the *coherence* which makes us accept a discovery to be true can be only *vaguely defined,* and a third indeterminacy will be seen when we find that the *data* on which a discovery ultimately rests *are not fully identifiable.*

THREE INDETERMINACIES OF KNOWLEDGE

All knowledge has an indeterminate content whenever it bears on reality. I shall show this to be scientific knowledge. It was Copernicus who claimed for the first time that science can discover new knowledge about fundamental reality, and this claim triumphed in the Copernican revolution. But recently—for the past 80 years or so—the claim of science to know reality has been shaken by a positivist critique which condemned such claims as metaphysical. But I myself agree with Copernicus. In my opinion it is impossible to pursue science without believing that it can discover reality, and I want to reestablish here this belief in reality, although the resurrected idea of reality will, admittedly, look different from its departed ancestor.

It is not easy, of course, to say exactly what Copernicus believed when he persistently maintained, against heavy opposition, that his system was not merely a new computing device, but was a true image of the planets circling the sun. But it will become clear what he meant if we first look at the way successors of Copernicus—for example, Kepler—relied on the reality of the heliocentric system. The three laws discovered by Kepler were based on the reality of the Copernican system: He was able to discover these laws only because he accepted it *as a fact* that the earth goes round the sun.

Whenever we believe in the reality of a thing, we expect that the thing will manifest itself in yet unknown ways in the future. But notice also that the laws by which Kepler confirmed the reality of the heliocentric system were very different from anything Copernicus himself might have expected. The elliptic planetary paths of Kepler conflicted sharply with the basic beliefs of Copernicus. Yet it remains true that Kepler's discoveries confirmed Copernicus' claim that his system was real, which shows that a claim to reality is essentially indeterminate. Affirmations of reality in nature always have a widely indeterminate content.

This fact brings us to our next point, which is the indefinable character of the signs by which we recognize reality in nature. The vagueness of the signs pointing to reality can be seen in the work of Copernicus. Copernicus claimed that his theory was an image of reality because it had a coherence that was lacking in the Ptolemaic system, and the principle of this argument was sound because it is the coherence of a thing that makes us attribute reality to it. We commonly recognize its coherence at a glance by merely looking at a real thing. I look at my right hand as I move it about in front of me, and I see a thousand rapidly changing clues as one single, unchanging object moving about at changing distances, presenting different sides at variable angles and in variable light. The integration of innumerable, rapidly changing particulars makes us see a real object in front of us.

Solid objects are deemed to be real inasmuch as they suggest another side not visible at the moment and also a hidden interior—and, moreover, they promise to last for some time, possibly colliding with other things and affecting them in one of an infinite number of possible ways. Such are the typical indeterminacies of a real thing.

By pointing at coherence as a token of reality, Copernicus made an essential contribution to the method on which empirical science was to be established. Science was to him (like perception) a way of seeing reality, and was what the theory of Copernicus meant to his successors who developed it further up to Newton's day. It is indeed what the body of science is to the scientist to this day: He sees in science an aspect of reality which as such is an inexhaustible source of new and promising problems. Natural science continues to bear fruit, because it offers us an insight into external reality.

These views of science and of its belief in reality were put forward about 20 years ago in my *Science, Faith and Society* (Polanyi, 1946). Since then I found welcome support for regarding science as an extension of perception when I became acquainted with the great work of Whewell (1890), written nearly a century before. Speaking of Kepler's discovery of the elliptic path of the planet Mars, Whewell wrote:

> To hit upon the right conception is a difficult step; and when the step is once made, the facts assume a different aspect from what they had before: that done, they are seen in a new point of view; and the catching of this point of view is a special mental operation, requiring special endowments and habits of thought. Before this, the facts are seen as detached, separate, regular; as parts of a general fact, and thereby possessing new relations, before unseen [p. 254].

Whewell knew well that he was dissenting here from the Baconian theory of induction; he fiercely attacked Mill's development of this theory, which was nevertheless to dominate the conception of scientific theory for many years afterward. Whewell held that Baconian enquiry can succeed only when guided by dawning insight. And in describing the act of insight, he reveals its kinship to the way our eyes, sharpened by native gifts and by special training, make out the true nature of a puzzling spectacle before us.

In the passage here quoted, Whewell also anticipates another part of my theory. He says that, by becoming parts of a comprehensive entity, the facts acquire new relations, hitherto unseen. I think he speaks here of a true coherence in nature, the inexhaustible implications of which are felt in its bearing on reality.

My view of coherence in science owes much to Gestalt psychology, but I go beyond Gestalt when speaking of *true* coherence in nature. A tendency to good closure is only a *clue to coherence*; it does not establish *true coherence*. Take the famous ambiguous picture representing either a vase or two opposing profiles. As we shift from one way of seeing it to the other, we either see the vase as a real body and the rest of the picture as empty background, or we see, on the contrary, the profiles as real bodies and the space between them as empty. We can observe here a sensory quality indicating coherence as well as the reality of coherence. But since this sensory quality can be shifted at will between two mutually exclusive alternatives, it does not *establish* a true coherence.

The way a judgment of true coherence is arrived at can be seen when a jury faces a serious and difficult decision. The jurors may see a pattern of circumstances pointing to the accused. But it is always conceivable that this pattern may be due to chance. How unlikely a chance should they admit to be possible? Or what degree of coincidence should be considered not to be reasonably believable? No rule can decide this. The decision must be arrived at under the discipline of a grim personal responsibility. It must rely on an ultimate power of the mind, on which the scientist too must ultimately rely for establishing a true coherence in nature.

This concludes my sketch of two major indeterminacies introduced by Copernicus into the foundation of science. I pass now to a third kind of indeterminacy that is intrinsic to all empirical knowledge, and hence also to science.

I have spoken of the numberless items that contribute to my seeing my hand in front of me. They are known to us mainly by observing the various deficiencies caused by cutting out these several items. I can cut out marginal clues by looking at my hand through a blackened tube and observing that this makes my hand appear to swell up when brought nearer to my eyes. We can observe that the action of our eye muscles contributes clues to our vision by the application of drugs which increase the effort of contracting the muscles, and hence makes objects look smaller. Afflictions of the inner ear cause the whole spectacle before us to lose its balance; and there is ample evidence that past experiences, which we can hardly recall, affect the way we see things.

Perception thus establishes an observation of external facts without formal argument and even without explicitly stating the result; I hope to eventually show that science, too, is based on such nonexplicit knowing. But first I must set out the general structure of such knowing and expose the new indeterminacies introduced by it into empirical knowledge.

Consider the act of viewing a pair of stereoscopic pictures in the usual way, with one eye on each of the pictures. Their joint image might be regarded as a whole, composed of the two pictures as its parts. But we can get closer to understanding what is going on here if we note that, when looking through a stereo viewer, we see a stereo image at the focus of our attention while we are aware of the two stereo pictures in some peculiar nonfocal way. We seem to look through these two pictures, or past them, while we look straight at their joint image. We are indeed aware of them only as guides to the image on which we focus our attention. I can describe this relationship of the two pictures to the stereo image by saying that the two pictures function as *subsidiaries* to our seeing their *joint* image which is their joint meaning. This is the typical structure of tacit knowing which I shall now describe in some detail.

The grounds of all tacit knowing are items—or particulars—like the stereo pictures of which we are aware in the act of focusing our attention on something else, away from them. This I call the *functional relation* of subsidiaries to the focal target, and we may also call it a *from-to relation.* Moreover, I can say that this relation establishes a *from-to knowledge* of the subsidiaries, as linked to their focus. Tacit knowing is a from-to knowing. Sometimes it will also be called a from-at knowing, but this variation will be only a matter of convenience.

It will not be difficult to demonstrate the indeterminacies inherent in from-to knowledge, but I want first to add some other features to the structure of from-to knowledge. A characteristic aspect of from-to knowledge is exemplified by the change of appearance which occurs when the viewing of a pair of stereo pictures transforms these into a stereo image. A stereo image has a marked depth and also shows firmly shaped objects not present as such in the original stereo pictures. It therefore shows a novel sensory experience created by tacit knowing. Such *phenomenal transformation* is a characteristic feature of from-to knowing. I have already actually mentioned such a case when I spoke of the sensory quality of coherence in nature.

A moment ago I anticipated another feature of from-to knowing when I said that the stereo image is the *joint meaning* of the stereo pictures. The subsidiaries of from-to knowing bear on a focal target; in my view, whatever a thing bears on may be called its meaning. Thus the focal target on which they bear is the meaning of the subsidiaries. We may call this an act of sense giving and recognize it as the *semantic aspect* of from-to knowing.

A few examples will help to make us familiar with these three aspects of tacit knowing: the functional, the phenomenal, and the semantic. I could cite here the cases of visual perception and of scientific discovery, which are my main interest in this exposition, but they have complications which I wish to avoid for a time.

Take, as a simpler case, the from-to structure of the act of reading a printed sentence. The sight of the printed words guides our focal attention away from the print to a focal target that is its meaning. We have here both the *function* of from-to knowing and its *semantic* aspect. Its *phenomenal* aspect is also easy to recognize; it lies in the fact that a word in use *looks different* from what it would be like to someone who met it as a totally foreign word. The familiar use of a word, which is our subsidiary awareness of it, renders it, in a way, bodiless, or, as it is sometimes described, transparent.

Another example—and one that will help us later to understand visual perception—is the case of tactile cognition: of using a probe to explore a cavity, or a stick to feel one's way in the dark. Such exploration is a from-to knowing, for we attend subsidiarily to the feeling of holding the probe in the hand, while the focus of our attention is fixed on the far end of the probe, where it touches an obstacle in its path. This perception is the function of tacit knowing and is accompanied by particularly interesting *phenomenal transformation.* The sensation of the probe pressing on fingers and palm, and of the muscles guiding the probe, is lost, and instead we feel the point of the probe as it touches an object. And, in addition to the functional and the phenomenal, the probing has, of course, a *semantic* aspect. For the information we get by feeling the point of the instrument is its meaning to us: It tells us what it is that we are observing by the use of the probe.

This use of probes may remind us of the fact that all sensation is assisted by some, however slight, skillful performance, the motions of which are performed with our attention focused on the intended action so that our awareness of the motions is subsidiary to the performance. From-to structure includes all skillful performances, from walking the street to walking a tightrope, and from tying a knot to playing a piano. More about this later.

We now have enough material to uncover the indeterminacies inherent in from-to knowing. We have a very obvious indeterminacy before us in the case of stereo vision. The three-dimensional depth of the stereo image has its basis in the differences between the two stereo pictures, that is to say, the differences due to the fact that the pictures are taken at points a few inches apart. These tiny differences are not noticeable by simple inspection, and even if we used powerful methods for measuring them, we would find them difficult to itemize since they extend all over the surface. We see, then, how readily our subsidiary awareness picks up and embodies in the focus of our attention items of evidence that we should never notice directly and might indeed find difficult to identify even if we searched for them. This demonstration should suffice to make it clear that the *grounds* of from-to knowledge may often be *unspecifiable.*

Let me stop here for a moment and recall the indeterminacy of all knowledge bearing on reality and the indeterminacy due to the impossibility of giving a precise rule for establishing true coherence in nature. We have now added, as a third indeterminacy of empirical knowledge, the fact that we may not know on what grounds we hold our knowledge to be true.

But let us realize that we could turn this deficiency into a flourish. Instead of deploring that a statement about external reality has an indeterminate content, we could take pride in the fact that we can thus *see beyond established facts*; instead of regretting that we cannot define the quality of coherence in nature, we could be gratified at the capability of *feeling* such subtle, virtually invisible, signs of reality. Far from being embarrassed by our incapacity to state all the grounds on which empirical knowledge rests, we could insist on the recognition of our powers to *know far more than we can tell.* These faculties are indeed those that we *shall* claim once we have accepted tacit knowing as a legitimate and, in fact, indispensable source of all empirical knowledge. But we must realize the whole depth of our tacit commitments before we can make them so firmly our own. For this, let me show yet further aspects of our tacit knowledge.

THE TACIT TRIAD

The structure of tacit knowledge includes a conjoint pair of constituents. Subsidiaries exist as such by bearing on the focus to which we are attending from them. In other words, the functional structure of from-to knowing includes jointly a subsidiary "from" and a focal "to" (or "at"). But this pair is not linked together of its own accord. The relation of a subsidiary to a focus is formed by the act of a person who integrates one to the other. And so the from-to relation lasts only so long as a person, the knower, sustains this integration.

This is not merely to say that if we no longer look at a thing, we shall cease to see it. There is a specific action involved in dissolving the integration of tacit knowing. Let me describe this action.

We have now seen three centers of tacit knowledge: first, the subsidiary particulars; second, the focal target; and third, the knower who links the first to the second. We can place these three things in the three corners of a triangle. Or we can think of them as forming a triad, controlled by a person, the knower, who causes the subsidiaries to bear on the focus of his attention.

We can then say that the knower integrates the subsidiaries to a focal target—or that the subsidiaries have a meaning to the knower which fills the center of his focal attention, and that hence the knower can dissolve the triad by merely looking differently at the subsidiaries. The triad will disappear if the knower shifts his focal attention away from the focus of the triad and fixes it on the subsidiaries.

For example, if, instead of looking at the stereo pictures through the viewer, we take them out and look at them directly, we lose sight of their joint appearance on which we had focused before. Or if we focus our attention on a spoken word and thus see it as a sequence of sounds, the word loses the meaning to which we had attended before. Or again, we can paralyze the performance of a skill by turning our attention away from its performance and concentrating instead on the several motions that compose the performance.

These facts are common knowledge, but their consequences for the theory of tacit knowledge are remarkable. For the facts confirm our view that we can be aware of certain things in a way that is quite different from focusing our attention on them. They prove the existence of two kinds of awareness that are mutually exclusive, a *from-awareness* and a *focal awareness.* They also confirm that in the from-awareness of a thing we see a meaning of it, a meaning which is wiped out by focusing our attention *on* the thing, which will face us then in itself, in its raw bodily nature. The dual nature of awareness is made manifest here as the sense deprivation involved in substituting one kind of awareness for another.

Suppose, then, that it is possible, at least in principle, to identify all the subsidiaries of a triad; however elusive they may be we would still face the fact that anything serving as a subsidiary ceases to do so when focal attention is directed on it. It turns into a different kind of thing, deprived of the meaning it had in the triad. Thus subsidiaries are—in this important sense—essentially unspecifiable. We must distinguish, then, between two types of the unspecifiability of subsidiaries. One type is due to the difficulty of tracing the subsidiaries—a condition that is widespread but not universal—and the other type is due to a sense deprivation which is logically necessary and in principle absolute. This adds a fourth, and quite fundamental, indeterminacy to the grounds on which empirical knowledge rests.

I hope that if this analysis convinces us of the presence of two very different kinds of awareness in tacit knowing, it will also prevent us from identifying these two different kinds of awareness with a difference between conscious and unconscious awareness. Focal awareness is, of course, always conscious, but subsidiary awareness, or from-awareness, can have all levels of consciousness; it can range from a subliminal level to a fully conscious level. What makes awareness subsidiary is its functional character, and I shall therefore claim the presence of subsidiary awareness even for functions inside our body at levels completely inaccessible to experience by the subject. This claim will be particularly important for the theory of visual perception.[1]

[1]What I call "subsidiaries" include "subceived stimuli" (see Polanyi, 1966, pp. 7–9). Wall and Guthrie (1959, pp. 205–210) have shown that conditioning to shock syllables persists without reinforcement for subliminal presentation, but is extinguished for subliminal presentation when extinguished for supraliminal presentation. They note the parallelism between the subceived stimulus and the Freudian unconscious.

TACIT INFERENCE

Subsidiaries function as such by being integrated to a focus on which they bear. This integration is the tacit act of a person and can be valid or mistaken. Perception can be true or mistaken and so can our judgment of coherence, whether in deciding on the facts of a legal case or when perceiving coherence in nature. To arrive at such conclusions may be called an *act of tacit inference,* but such inferences differ sharply from drawing conclusions by an explicit deduction.

Piaget (1950) has described the contrasts between a sensorimotor act like perception and a process of explicit inference. Explicit inference is reversible: We can go back to its premises and go forward again to its conclusions, and we can rehearse this process as often as we like. This is not true for perception. For example, once we have seen through a visual puzzle, we cannot return to an ignorance of its solution. This holds, with some variations, for all acts of tacit knowing. We can go back to the two pictures of a stereo image by taking them out of the viewer and looking at them directly, but this completely destroys the stereo image. When flying by airplane first started, the traces of ancient sites were revealed in fields over which generations of country folk had walked without noticing them. But once he had landed the airman could no longer see them either.

In some cases sense deprivation is incomplete. Thus we can concentrate on the sound and the action of our lips and tongue in producing a word, and this will cause us to lose the meaning of the word although the loss can be instantly made good by casting the mind forward for using the word once more in saying something. The same is true for a pianist who paralyzes his performance by intensely watching his own fingers: He can promptly recover their skillful use by attending once more to his music. In these instances the path to the integrated relation—which may have originally taken months of labor to establish—is restored from its abeyance in a trice, while at the same moment the sight of the sense-deprived particulars is lost.

Explicit inference is very different; no such breaking up and rediscovery takes place when we recapitulate the deduction of the theorem of Pythagoras. Once this basic distinction between explicit inference and tacit integration is clear, it throws new light on a 100-year-old controversy. In 1867 Helmholtz offered to interpret perception as a process of unconscious inference, but this theory was generally rejected by psychologists, who pointed out that optical illusions are not destroyed by demonstrating their falsity. Psychologists had assumed, quite reasonably, that "unconscious inference" had the same structure as a conscious explicit inference. But if we identify "unconscious inference" with tacit integration, we have a kind of inference that is not damaged by adverse evidence, as explicit inference is. This difference between a deduction and an integration lies in the fact that deduction connects two focal items, the premises and consequents, while integration makes subsidiaries bear on a focus. Admittedly there is a purposive movement in a deduction—which is its essential tacit coefficient—but the deductive operation can be mechanically performed while a tacit integration is intentional throughout and, as such, can be carried out only by a conscious act of the mind. Brentano (1942, orig. publ. 1874) has taught that consciousness necessarily attends to an object, and that *only* a conscious mental act can attend to an object. My analysis of tacit knowing has amplified this view of consciousness. It tells us not only that consciousness is intentional, but also that it always has roots *from which* it attends to its object. It includes a tacit awareness of its subsidiaries.

Such integration cannot be replaced by any explicit mechanical procedure. In the first place, even though one can paraphrase the cognitive content of an integration, the sensory quality which conveys this content cannot be made explicit. I have already illustrated this fact much earlier by pointing to the quality of coherence in nature, but all of my examples of tacit knowing can be used to demonstrate it.

The irreducibility of tacit integration can be observed more fully for practical knowing. I could point to our incapacity to control directly the several motions contributing to a skillful performance—even such a familiar act as using our limbs. But these cases are perhaps too common to impress the imagination. So I shall take instead the example of finding one's way with inverting spectacles. It is virtually impossible to get about while wearing inverting spectacles by following the instruction that what—in the case of right-left inversion—is seen on the right is actually on the left, while, conversely, things seen on the left are on the right. The Austrian psychologist, Heinrich Kottenhoff (1961), however, has shown that continued efforts to move about while wearing inverted spectacles produce a novel quality of feeling and action by integrating the inverted sights to appropriate sensorimotor responses, so that the subject again finds his way about. This reintegration can be performed only subsidiarily; any explicit instruction to reintegrate sights and sensorimotor responses would be quite meaningless.

I have often quoted the case of the cyclist, but it still teaches its lesson here. We cannot learn to keep our balance on a bicycle by taking to heart that, to compensate for an imbalance, we must take a curve of which a radius is proportional to the square of the bicycle's velocity over the angle of imbalance. Such knowledge is totally ineffectual unless it is known tacitly.

The way in which particulars are picked up and assimilated as subsidiaries will be extensively dealt with in the section on scientific discovery. But we may anticipate one of its aspects, pointed out by Konrad Lorenz (1967) who arrived independently at the view that science is based on a gestaltlike integration of particulars. He demonstrated that the speed and complexity of tacit integration far exceeds the operations of any explicit selection of supporting evidence. I have recently (Polanyi, 1967b) developed this idea further by showing that the serial behavior demonstrated by Lashley (1951) in the production of a spoken sentence can be understood by considering that tacit knowing can pick up simultaneously a whole set of data and combine them in a meaningful spoken sequence.

An integration established in this summary manner will often override single items of contrary evidence. It can only be damaged by new contradictory facts if these items are absorbed in an alternative integration which disrupts the one previously established. In Ames's skew-room experiment the illusion of a boy taller than the man persists so long as the evidence of the room's skew shape is slight, but the illusion is instantly destroyed if a shift of the observer's position or a tapping of the ceiling makes the skewness of the room more manifest. This fact effectively competes, then, with the hitherto established integration and destroys it.

David Hume has taught that, when in doubt, we must suspend judgment. This theory might apply to conclusions derived on paper which can be manipulated at will—at least on paper. Our eyes continue to see a little boy taller than a grown man although we know this to be false, so long as no feasible alternative integration is presented to the imagination. But if an alternative is presented, and this perception happens to be true, a new perception will take place and correct our errors. Helmholtz could have answered his opponents on this score, but he would have had to admit that his "unconscious inferences" were very different from conscious inferences.

INDWELLING

There is yet another important aspect of tacit knowing which should be included here. In all examples of tacit knowing that I have given, the focal target which forms the meaning of the subsidiaries is placed some distance away from them. Most striking, perhaps, was the displacement of meaning when the sensations of hand and muscles holding a probe were displaced to the far end of the probe. The displacements of the focal target invariably went in the same direction, namely, away from us. And if one tries to construct a triad, the focus of which points in the opposite direction—so that the meaning of the subsidiaries would lie on our side of them—this proves impossible.

The most important displacement of meaning is found in visual perception; I mention perception here only to explain why meaning produced by tacit knowing is always displaced outward. Our senses point into external space and our actions, too, are, as a rule, projected outward; so the objects of our conscious attention lie predominantly outward from us. Our muscles, our sense organs, our nervous system, are experienced as they perform their functions of noticing and interpreting things outside and manipulating them for our own purposes. One is aware of the body subsidiarily as it performs these functions, while focal observation of one's own body is only superficial. We may look focally at our hands and feet, but even so our subsidiary awareness of them predominates: One still feels them to be a part of the body. This is what the from-knowledge of the body feels like to us: It amounts to awareness of living in one's own body.

Having identified the feeling of being in one's body with from-knowledge of the body, one can look upon all from-knowledge as akin to the sense of being in one's body. *In this sense, then, to make something function subsidiarily is to interiorize it, or else to pour one's body into it.* The fact that we do feel probes and tools to be part of the body bears out this parallelism. Any integration of things which makes them bear on our focal interest can be regarded as an indwelling of these things.

We may say that our own existence, which we experience, and the world that we observe are interwoven here. Bodily being, by participating subsidiarily in one's perceptions and actions, becomes a being in the world, while external observations and projects subsidiarily involving one's own bodily feelings become, up to a point, a self-transformation, an existential choice. And this involves our cultural framework. Every time we rely on our traditional grounds in forming a judgment, we somewhat modify their meaning, and on these lines a creative act can renew our grounds extensively. Copernicus, for example, radically changed the grounds of empirical judgment, and since then the grounds of scientific judgment have been further modified repeatedly.

This adds yet another indeterminacy to the four I have previously mentioned. Applied to science, our fifth indeterminacy consists of the existential choices involved in modifying the grounds of scientific judgment.

But something even more vital follows from formulating tacit knowing as an act of indwelling. It deepens our knowledge of living things. Biology studies the shapes of living things and the way they grow into these shapes from germ cells; it describes the organs of plants and animals and explains the way they function; it explores the motor and sensory capacities of animals and their intelligent performances. These aspects of life are controlled by biological principles. Morphology, embryology, physiology, psychology all study the principles by which living beings form and sustain their coherence and respond in ever new ways to an immense variety of novel circumstances. The ways in which animals, such as cattle or dogs or men, coherently control their bodies form a comprehensively functioning system. Any chemical or physical study of living things that is irrelevant to these workings of the organism forms no part of biology.

We therefore recognize and study the coherence of living things by integrating their motions—and any other normal changes occurring in their parts—into our comprehension of their functions. *We integrate mentally what living beings integrate practically.* Chess players rehearse a master's game to discover what he had in mind. Generally we share the purpose of a mind by indwelling its actions. This is my answer to the great question: How do we know another mind?

SOME SIGNS OF A DEFICIENCY

I shall now show, as I promised, how philosophic thought and the methodological principles of science have been misguided by not having a clear knowledge of tacit knowing. I shall take as my examples, first, the knowledge of other minds; second, universal terms; third, principles of explanation; and fourth, empirical generalization.

Knowledge of Other Minds

Up to a point, Gilbert Ryle (1949) has argued about our knowledge of other minds as I have done here. He strikingly demonstrated that we do not get to know the workings of another mind by a process of inference; we are following them (p. 61), but since he had no conception of tacit knowing, he concluded that body and mind are "not two things [p. 74]," "not tandem operations [p. 46]," and that accordingly "most intelligent performances are not clues to the mind; they are those workings [p. 58]."

This theory I shall reject; the theory of tacit knowing also tells us that we do not know another mind by a process of inference, but nevertheless it retains the dualism of mind and body. It says that the body seen focally is one thing, while the body seen subsidiarily points to another thing; these two different things are the body and the mind. More about this later.

Merleau-Ponty (1962), writing some years before Ryle, anticipated his premises by declaring: "I do not understand the gestures of others by an act of intellectual interpretation . . . [p. 185]," to which he added a little further on: "The act by which I lend myself to these spectacles must be recognized as irreducible to anything else [p. 185]."

This teaching anticipated the existential commitment present in tacit knowledge, but did so without recognizing the triadic structure which determines the functions of this commitment—the way it establishes our knowledge of a valid coherence. The contrast between explicit inference and an existential experience imbued with intentionality is not sufficient for defining the structure and workings of tacit knowing. We are offered an abundance of brilliant flashes without a constructive system.

The philosophy of behaviorism does not contest the duality of body and mind,[2] but it assumes that all mental performances can be fully specified without referring to any mental motives. Could this be true? Consider an analogy. All textbooks of physiology refer to organs and the function of organs, and in spite of frequent solemn declarations that such teleological conceptions are unnecessary and indeed objectionable, no one has yet published a textbook of physiology that does not speak of organs and their functions. For the biological functions of organs can be known only as coherent wholes. This also applies, of course, to the motions forming a skillful performance, or an act of intelligence; these can be identified only as parts of their meaningful combination. To describe, as behaviorists claim to do, workings of the mind without relying on the guidance of mental motives is as impossible as it is to describe physiological events occurring in an organ without being guided by the observation of its coherent physiological functions.

To some extent behaviorism succeeds in claiming the impossible, because our knowledge of the mind's coherence is so stable that any isolated workings of the mind will instantly evoke their underlying mental motives which the isolated workings are supposed to replace. In my book, *Personal Knowledge* (Polanyi, 1958, pp. 370–371) I have described how the behaviorist psychology of learning achieves such a semblance of its program. To begin with, the performance

[2]See, for example, B. F. Skinner (1964, p. 79).

is favored by limiting the enquiry to the crudest forms of learning. These much simplified cases can then be plausibly described in objectivist terms, but even so they can be shown to apply to the actual process of learning only because their meaning is tacitly understood by their bearing on the mental events covertly kept in mind. One thus succeeds in using objectivist terms which are, strictly speaking, meaningless, as effective paraphrases for the mentalistic terms which they are supposed to eliminate.

Noam Chomsky's (1959) critique of B. F. Skinner's (1957) *Verbal Behavior* presents many illustrations of such behaviorist paraphrasing. Apparently objective terms, like stimulus, control, response, and so on, are so used that their ambiguity covers the mental terms which they are supposed to replace. Chomsky shows that either you use these objectivist terms literally—and then what is said is obviously false and absurd—or you use them as substitutes for the terms which they are supposed to eliminate—and then you do not say anything else than what you would have said in mentalist terms.

The same criticism applies to the mechanical simulation of tacit knowing. A tacit integration can only be superficially paraphrased by a computer, and such paraphrases succeed by evoking the mental qualities which they claim to enact.

Universal Terms

The mere fact that biology deals with classes of plants and animals involves indeterminacies which, for centuries past and up to this day, philosophers have tried in vain to eliminate.

Plato and his school were the first to be troubled by the fact that *in applying our conception of a class of things, we keep identifying objects that are different from one another in every particular.* If every man is clearly distinguishable from any other man and we yet recognize each of them as a man, what kind of "man" is the one by reference to whom all these men are recognized? He cannot be both fair and dark, young and old, nor brown, white, black, and yellow all at once; but neither can he have any one of these alternative properties, nor indeed any particular property whatever. Plato concluded that the general idea of man refers to a *perfect man* who has no particular properties, and of whom individual men are imperfect copies, corrupted by having such properties.

The Platonic idea of man, however, embodies the incompatibility of identifying different individuals, instead of eliminating it. An attempt to avoid this fallacy was made about 900 years ago by Roscellinus in the idea of nominalism. According to this doctrine, the word "man" is but the name for a collection of individual men. But the indeterminacy reappears once more, when we ask how to justify the labeling of a collection of different individuals by the same name, and how, moreover, we can continue to label in a constant fashion, as time goes on, any number of further individuals differing in every particular from any individual thus labeled before, and yet can continually exclude a vast number of other individuals as not belonging to the class we have labeled.

Perhaps it is no wonder that another 700 years later Kant (1929) should have declared that the way our intelligence forms and applies the conception of a class of particulars "is a skill so deeply hidden in the human soul that we shall hardly guess the secret trick that Nature here employs [p. A141]."

Yet, in the present age of philosophy, in 1945 F. Waismann attempted to answer the question deemed insoluble by Kant. He pointed out that general terms have an "open texture," which admits differences in the instances to which it applies. But this merely shifts the question, for to ascribe "open texture" to a word is merely to imply that among an indefinitely extending series of different objects the word properly applies to some objects and not to the rest. The question how this is done remains open, exactly as before.

No wonder that the more incisive reappraisal of the old quandary by W. V. O. Quinne[3] (1960, 1967) led him back to the conclusion reached by Kant: that the grounds on which instances are assigned to an empirical category of objects are inscrutable.

Yet the speculations of two and a half millennia, striving to eliminate the indeterminacy involved in subsuming a presumed instance of a class to that class, seem to have been misguided. This indeterminacy is irreducible, but its comprehension is safely controlled by tacit integration.

Tacit knowing commonly integrates groups of particulars to their joint meaning. Members of a class like a species, a family, a language—or members of any other group properly denoted by a single universal term—possess a joint meaning. Moreover, the meaning of a class is an aspect of reality for it points to yet unrevealed joint properties of its members. If the joint appearance of disparate members of a class in the conception of a class should need support by analogy, I would think once more of a binocular sight uniting two slightly different images in a single image of a different sensory character; or of the fact that the way we see an object integrates, among many other events in the body, innumerable memories beyond conscious recollection; or of a metaphor fusing two disparate ideas in a powerful joint meaning or, again, of the way we instantly understand a novel chain of words conveying a joint meaning we have never before encountered.

Principles of Explanation

Once we have fully realized the structure of the tacit triad, the recognition and acceptance of its functions become irresistible. I shall demonstrate this by discussing the way in which we produce a scientific explanation. Our capacity to look for an explanation depends on our propensity to be puzzled. But to be puzzled implies a judgment. For example, most physicists believe today that it is nonsensical to be puzzled by the fact that one radium atom decomposes today and another perhaps 50 years later, since there can be no explanation for this. Some scientists, however, oppose this view and this opposition implies a fundamental difference of opinion. Furthermore, it is useless to be puzzled by events which, although they may be explicable in principle, are not ripe for explanation, or are not worth the trouble of explaining them. There are many variations of the advisability of being puzzled. In any case, a scientific explanation must serve to dispel puzzlement.

Relief from puzzlement, however, may be attained by other means than that of explanation, and such cases throw light on explanation itself. Suppose we are puzzled by the way an intricate piece of machinery is constructed and the way it works, or by the layout of a building in which we keep losing our way. What we are seeking here is an understanding of the machine or the building—an insight into them, but not an explanation. Such insight is a particular type of tacit integration that I have not yet mentioned. Its subsidiary items are the particulars of the complex entity—the machine, or the rooms in the building—and when we integrate these particulars and thus bring out their joint meaning, their puzzling aspect is transformed into a lucid image. This process is the insight that relieves our puzzlement.

Such insight is in general not an image that can be seen on a sheet of paper. For it often serves to illuminate a spatial arrangement of opaque objects, like complex machines and buildings. The anatomy of a complex living thing, or a complex arrangement of geological strata, or a complex atomic arrangement in crystals, may also be baffling and can be understood only by an act of insight. But any plane aspect can give only a fragmentary view of such systems and only by combining such aspects in the imagination can a three-dimensional understanding of

[3]In his contribution to the Symposium on Logic and Psychology at the Convention of the American Psychological Association in 1967, Quine ascribed the identification of specimens of a class to undefined native powers, and also showed that the general features of a class cannot be empirically demonstrated. He regards this as an instance of the inscrutability of the categoricals. Cf Quine (1960, p. 60f).

the aggregate be achieved. Such insight is a purely mental fact, like any other focal target, comprising a large number of subsidiaries. Such insight differs, however, from all the focal targets (like those of stereo vision, reading a sentence, exploration of a cavity, etc.) that I have mentioned before, in that this focal target does not lie away from the subsidiaries, but coincides in our imagination with the spectacle of the aggregate of which it is our insight. It signifies that the imaginative probing of a puzzling aggregate has established in it an intelligible coherence.

If this coherence can be formulated in explicit terms, it can amount to the kind of discovery exemplified by Whewell in the discovery of Kepler's planetary laws. But its area can be extended also in the opposite direction, down to the level of animal intelligence as in the classic experiments of Wolfgang Köhler on the powers of insight in chimpanzees. The chimpanzee, presented with a string slung doubly across a rod, realized that the string could not be disengaged by pulling at its end, but first must be unwound. Returning to human thought, we note that biology frequently starts with the question, "How does it work?" much as we start when we try to understand complex machinery. Furthermore, I have shown previously that we understand living things, the functioning of their organs, and the working of their intelligence, by indwelling them, which is also an act of insight. Similar insight is involved in taxonomy which orders biological specimens much as X-ray crystallography does in establishing the space group to which a crystalline specimen belongs.

Thus the establishment of coherence has many forms, some tacitly known, others explicitly formulated, some in common use and others forming part of science.

This brings us back to the subject of scientific explanation. One possibility for extending the recognition of coherence in nature consists in subsuming a natural law within a more general law of which it is a special case. This procedure has been singled out by modern philosophers from J. S. Mill (1943) to Carl G. Hempel (Hempel, 1964; Hempel & Oppenheim, 1948) and Ernest Nagel (1961) as constituting the scientific explanation of natural phenomena. But thus to limit the study of a wide area to the analysis of a fragment of it obscures the subject. Michael Scriven (1962) has criticized this analysis of explanation, and has suggested that concepts condemned by many logicians "as psychological not logical"—for example, understanding, belief, judgment—might have to be returned to circulation. My account of relief from puzzlement by the spreading of coherence extends Scriven's criticism. To define the explanation of an event as its subsumption under a general law leaves unexplained its capacity to relieve puzzlement and isolates it from numerous other, more fundamental, acts which have this capacity. Explanation must be understood as a particular form of insight.

The consequences of striving for strictness are similar here to those arising in the case of behaviorism. The actual subject matter is restricted to a fragment found suitable for formalization. This formalization, if carried out strictly, would produce a result that has no bearing on the subject matter, but by calling it an "explanation" one imbues it with the memory of that informal act of the mind which it was supposed to replace.

Such a denial of mental powers avoids its ultimate consequences by borrowing the qualities of the very powers it sets out to eliminate. I have called this a pseudosubstitution. A pseudosubstitution is a gesture of intellectual self-destruction that is kept within safe bounds by its inconsistency. I have mentioned this practice in my critique of behaviorism and of the simulation of tacit integration by computers; our culture is pervaded by such false intellectual pretenses.

Empirical Generalization

If the orthodox theory of scientific explanation is misleading, the treatment of empirical generalization is equally so. Without going into detail, I may point out here three major errors which have resulted from the attempt to define empirical validity by strict criteria. First, since no formal procedure could be found for having a good idea from which to start on an enquiry, philosophers virtually abandoned the attempt to understand how this is done. Second, having arrived at the conclusion that no formal rule of inference can establish a valid empirical generalization, it was denied that any such generalization could be derived from experimental data—while ignoring the fact that valid generalizations are commonly arrived at by empirical enquiries based on *informal* procedures. Third, it was claimed that a hypothesis is strictly refutable by a single piece of conflicting evidence—an illusory claim, since one cannot formally identify a contradictory piece of evidence.

I established these mistakes in *Science, Faith and Society* (Polanyi, 1946) and also developed there some ideas about the informal powers which guide the pursuit of science and provide criteria for accepting its results. Underlying these ideas was the assumption that science was based on our powers to discern coherence in nature. This discernment is what sight and other senses do on the physiological level in the act of perception and I generalized these powers to include scientific discovery. I said that "the capacity of scientists to guess the presence of shapes as tokens of reality differs from the capacity of our ordinary perception only by the fact that it can integrate shapes presented to it in terms which the perception of ordinary people cannot readily handle [p. 24]."

Since that was written, I have tried to pursue systematically the kinship of perception and scientific discovery. Among earlier writers I relied for my work on Poincaré (1908), Hadamard (1945), and Polya (1945), and confirmation of my position came later in the works of philosophers criticizing the hypothetico-deductive method. Fuller confirmation was to be found in the admirable *Harvard Case Histories in Experimental Science* directed by J. B. Conant (1957). The work in Thomas S. Kuhn's (1962) book *On the Structure of Scientific Revolutions* brought further confirmation of my views in detail, and the analysis of science by Leonard K. Nash (1963) in *The Nature of the Natural Sciences* has combined my own views with those of other authors in a presentation of science as an insight into the nature of reality. A few years ago I experienced the wonderful surprise of finding my basic assumptions anticipated by Whewell. I have illustrated this previously in a quotation in this paper.

VISUAL PERCEPTION

In my earlier section on "Indwelling" I have moved fast over a wide range of subjects. I have described how meaning is displaced outward because we have no effective focal awareness of the body; next I explained the feeling we have of being in our body and included in this feeling our from-awareness of other subsidiaries, so that finally we arrived at recognizing how we know another mind. Carrying these results forward, we can now undertake to describe visual perception as a case of tacit knowing and then use this result for defining the way the mind controls the body.

Let me spell out first how visual perception is to be interpreted as tacit knowing. Think once more of a beam of light coming from an object and entering my eyes. The responses to the beam occur in my eyes, and in the muscles adjusting my eyes as well as those sustaining the position of my head, and they also include events in my inner ear and the effects of memories, some vivid and others not consciously recalled. These responses function as subsidiaries which I integrate to form the sight of the object; *the object as I see it is the meaning I give to the responses the object evokes in my body.*

There are three points in this theory of perception that may present difficulties, and each of these difficulties will bring up a long-standing problem of visual perception. I hope to resolve these problems by aligning the structure of visual perception with that of other cases of from-to knowledge having very different content.

The first difficulty may be found in the radical transformation of sensory qualities involved in seeing things outside in their colors and shapes as being at a particular distance and in a particular motion, and in seeing them also as a particular kind of object. For these qualities are totally different from those of the internal bodily responses of which they are supposed to be the meaning. But we may answer that such far-reaching transformations are quite common in from-to knowing. For example, the meaning of most spoken words in no way resembles the sound of the words from which we attend to this meaning of them.

Second, we may find it difficult to assume that the meaning of events inside one's body can be seen outside at some distance from one. We have seen, however, other nonvisual displacements of meaning in the case of probes and tools, and there is much experimental material showing that events generated inside the body, not capable of being experienced in themselves, may be made to evoke conscious expectations of events outside the body.

Third, one may think it difficult to accept that we should claim to be subsidiarily aware, in terms of our visual perception, of bodily events—for example, events inside the labyrinth—which we cannot experience in themselves at all. Let me say, therefore, once more that when I speak of my "subsidiary awareness" of something, I do not describe an awareness of it in the usual sense; I merely refer to the *function* of an event in affecting my awareness of its meaning, as observed at the focus of my attention. When understood in this way—which is the way I defined it from the start—subsidiary awareness will be found and accepted at all levels of consciousness.

The three difficulties I mentioned are thus disposed of, but we are still left with an important problem. Just how far should we go in tracing the responses of the body to a beam of light and including them as subsidiaries of our visual perception? For my part I can see no reason for halting our pursuit of the responses affecting visual perception at the point where they generate neural traces entering the cortex. I shall say that we are subsidiarily aware of these neural traces. And this step actually involves no extension of the perceptual mechanism accepted previously, since we can see nothing with our eyes detached from the brain. To integrate extracortical responses of the body to the sight of an object means, therefore, also to integrate their cortical traces to this sight.

Moreover, this completion of our scheme solves an important problem. Cortical traces spread simultaneously along many lines that have no anatomical link to any single point of the brain, and thus the unity of consciousness has no representation in the brain structure. Both Sherrington and Eccles have pointed out this fundamental gap in the equivalence of brain and consciousness. The theory of perception as tacit knowing necessarily ascribes to consciousness such powers of integration which may be taken to secure the unity of conscious experience, in spite of the unconnectedness of its cortical traces.

In my explanation of visual perception as a from-to knowledge of bodily responses to a beam of light, I have relied on experimental data in which such bodily responses were recorded. We must yet ask how these two different aspects of perception—the somatic and the mental—have been established, and this will necessarily raise the problem of body and mind.

We can formulate the mind-body dualism as the disparity between the experience of a subject observing an external object like a cat, and a neurophysiologist observing the bodily mechanisms by which the subject sees the cat. The experience of the two is very different. The subject sees the cat, but does not see the mechanism he uses in seeing the cat, while, on the other hand, the neurophysiologist sees the mechanism used by the subject, but does not share the subject's sight of the cat.

Admittedly, the neurophysiologist is aware of the subject's mind seeing the cat, for up to a point he shares the subject's mind by indwelling its external workings. He sees the subject as a sentient thinking fellow man and can understand his response to the sight of the cat; for example, he can follow the subject's description of the cat. And, of course, on his part, the subject can understand the description of his own neural mechanism, although he himself cannot observe it.

But the fact remains that to see a cat differs sharply from a knowledge of the mechanism of seeing a cat. They are a knowledge of quite different things. The perception of an external thing is a from-to knowledge. It is a subsidiary awareness of bodily responses evoked by external stimuli, seen with a bearing on their meaning situated at the focus of our attention. The neurophysiologist has no experience of this integration, he has an at knowledge of the body with its bodily responses at the focus of his attention. These two experiences have a sharply different content, which represents the viable core of the traditional mind-body dualism. "Dualism" thus becomes merely an instance of the change of subject matter due to shifting one's attention from the direction on which the subsidiaries bear and focusing instead on the subsidiaries themselves.

Current neurophysiology is based on a parallelism of body and mind as two aspects of the same thing. This theory is false; but it is plausible, because body and mind are closely connected. The mind relies for its actions on the body, and since to our modern thinking matter appears more substantial than mind, it seems reasonable to assume that the body altogether determines mental actions.

I must contradict this, however briefly, by defining the actual relation of body and mind. Some principles—for example, those of physics—apply in a variety of circumstances. These circumstances are not determined by the principles in question; they are its boundary conditions, and no principle can determine its own boundary conditions. When there is a principle controlling the boundary conditions of another principle, the two operate jointly. In this relation the first can be called the higher, the second the lower principle.

Mental principles and the principles of physiology form a pair of jointly operating principles. The mind relies for its workings on the continued operation of physiological principles, but it controls the boundary conditions left undetermined by physiology. This lends substance to my conclusion derived from the structure of tacit knowing, that body and mind are profoundly different singly, and not two aspects of the same thing.[4]

This disposes of mechanical determinism. If mind and body were two aspects of the same thing, the mind could not conceivably do anything but what the bodily mechanism prescribed. But the existence of two kinds of awareness—the focal and the subsidiary—distinguishes sharply between the mind as a from-to experience and the subsidiaries of this experience when seen focally as a bodily mechanism. Though rooted in the body, the mind is free in its actions—exactly as our common sense knows it to be free.[5]

THE PURSUIT OF SCIENCE

By now we have collected enough evidence demonstrating the powers of tacit knowing. In returning, therefore, to the foundations of science which were to be the main subject of this

[4]My theory of irreducible levels goes back to my *Personal Knowledge* (Polanyi, 1958) and has since been developed further in a number of stages, a survey of which is to be found in my book, *The Tacit Dimension* (Polanyi, 1966). See also my paper, "Life Transcending Physics and Chemistry" (Polanyi 1967a). An application of the theory to the body-mind relation is to be found in my paper, "The Structure of Consciousness" (Polanyi, 1965).

F. S. Rothschild (1958, 1962) anticipated my conclusion that the mind is the meaning of the body. His writings extend back to 1930. They are summarized in *Das Zentralnervensystem als Symbol des Erlebens,* with a briefer summary in English in 1962 (see references). He has developed this idea widely in neurophysiology and psychiatry, where I am not competent to follow him.

[5]The fact that we cannot predict what a person will do if we tell him what he would have done if we had not told him of our prediction does not disprove the deterministic character of a mechanical model of man. If predictability is to represent our capacity for accounting for the behavior of a system, the system must remain closed until we have verified our prediction.

paper, I shall expand our view of tacit knowing in the direction of its *dynamics*. This will include science in the making, from the sighting of a problem to the claiming of discovery.

I have previously described how we can wipe out the meaning of a word by attending directly to its physical details. Such loss of meaning can be made good by casting the mind forward to the act of saying something in which the word will have to be included with its proper meaning.

This illustrates a basic principle of tacit dynamics. The casting forward of an intention is an act of the imagination. It is only the imagination that can direct our attention to a target that is as yet unsupported by subsidiaries. Although the lost meaning of a word is in recent memory, when our imagination sallies forth seeking to restore it, this meaning is not yet present. But the imagination must feel that this lost meaning is available if it is to start on an action which will require the use of the word in its restored meaning. For only by thrusting in a feasible direction can the imagination succeed in evoking a lost meaning.

I shall now develop further this kind of imaginative action. Our intention of saying something normally evokes our verbal expression of it. Modern linguistics, however, has shown that most of our speech consists of sentences we have never before used; they are composed for the first time on this occasion. Yet when we start uttering such a sentence, we are as a rule confident that we shall find the words we need and bring them out in the order expressing our thought. We can speak as we do because we feel that many thousands of words are available for our novel purposes, and we can trust the powers of our imagination, bent on this purpose, *to evoke from these available resources the implementation of our purpose.*

To listen to speech and understand novel sentences is a similar action. Our imagination moves ahead of a novel text before us, trusting itself to evoke an understanding of it, and it commonly does so by evoking and combining available meanings that will match the meaning of the unprecedented sentences before us.

This is, in essence, also the way the imagination works on its major tasks. It is the way it works in search of discovery. The scientist's imagination does not roam about casting up random hypotheses to be tested by him. He starts by thrusting forward ideas he feels to be promising because he senses the availability of resources that will support them—and his imagination then goes on to hammer away in directions felt to be plausible, bringing up material that has a reasonable chance of confirming these guesses.

The scientific imagination, achieving discovery, passes through a typical life cycle. The claim of Copernicus that his system was real declared a vision of boundless unknown implications. For 60 years this vision remained quiescent. Then Kepler's imagination transformed the vision of Copernicus into a new and dynamic anticipation. He brushed aside as unreal Copernicus's fantastic system of epicycles and set out to find laws reflecting the mechanical foundations of the heliocentric order. His triumph offered a new becalmed vision to the imagination. Thus ended a life cycle.

When the imagination goes into action to start a scientific enquiry, it not only becomes more intense, but also more concrete, more specific. Although the target toward which it thrusts is yet empty, it is seen to lie in a definite direction. It represents a particular problem vaguely pointing but still always pointing to a hidden feature of reality. Once the problem is adopted, its pursuit will rely on a particular range of resources that are felt to be available in a particular direction. These resources will include the amount of labor and money needed for the quest. No problem may be undertaken unless we feel that its possible solution would be worth the probable expense.

These strangely perceptive anticipations are not arrived at either by following rules, or by relying on chance; nor are they guaranteed by a wealth of learning. Yet their practice is common and indeed indispensable; no scientist can survive in his profession unless he can make such anticipations with a reasonable degree of success. For this goal he needs exceptional gifts. But his gifts, although exceptional, are of the same kind as underlie the mere use of speech, and are actually found at work in every deliberate human action. They are intrinsic to the dynamics of all from-to knowledge, down to the simplest acts of tacit knowing.

In science the path from problem to discovery can be lengthy. The enquiry having been launched, the imagination will continue to thrust forward, guided by a sense of potential resources. It batters its path by mobilizing these resources, occasionally consolidating some of them in specific surmises. These surmises will then tentatively fill, up to a point, the hitherto empty frame of the problem.

It is a mistake to think of heuristic surmises as well-defined hypothetical statements which the scientist proceeds to test in a neutral and indeed critical spirit. Hunches often consist essentially in narrowing down the originally wider program of the enquiry. They may be most exciting, and may indeed turn out later to have been crucial, yet they are mostly far more indeterminate than the final discovery will be. The range of their indeterminacy lies at some point between that of the original problem and of its eventual solution.

Besides, the relation of the scientist to his surmises is one of passionate personal commitment. The effort that led to a surmise committed every fiber of his being to the quest; his surmises embody all his hopes.

The current theory that ignores the mechanism of tacit knowing must ignore and indeed deny such commitments. The tentativeness of the scientist's every step is then taken to show that he is uncommitted. But every step made in the pursuit of science is *definitive,* definitive in the vital sense that it definitely disposes of the time, the effort, and the material resources used in making that step. Such investments add up with frightening speed to the whole professional life of the scientist. To think of scientific workers cheerfully trying this and trying that, calmly changing course at each failure, is a caricature of a pursuit consuming a man's whole person. Any questing surmise necessarily seeks its own confirmation.

You might expect me to conclude by showing how a problem is eventually resolved by the discovery of a coherence in nature, the hidden existence of which had first been sighted in a problem and which had become increasingly manifest by its pursuit. I must, however, first introduce another factor, the identification of which we owe to Henri Poincaré. In a classic essay included in *Science et Méthode* (1908) he described two stages in the way we hit upon an idea that promises to solve a scientific problem. The first stage consists in racking one's brains by successive sallies of the imagination, while the second, which may be delayed for hours after one has ceased one's efforts, is the spontaneous appearance of the idea one has struggled for. Poincaré says that this spontaneous process consists in the integration of some of the material mobilized by thrusts of the imagination; he also tells us that these thrusts would be useless but for the fact that they are guided by special anticipatory gifts of the scientist.

It seems plausible to assume, then, that two faculties of the mind are at work jointly from the beginning to the end of an enquiry. One is the deliberately active powers of the imagination, and the other a spontaneous process of integration, which we may call *intuition.* It is intuition that senses the presence of hidden resources for solving a problem and which launches the imagination in its pursuit. And it is intuition that forms there our surmises and which eventually selects from the material mobilized by the imagination the relevant pieces of evidence and integrates them into the solution of the problem.

But, you may ask, what about the measurements, computations, and algebraic formulae used in the pursuit and formulation of science? These are, of course, essential, but I have dealt with them when showing that the use of language is a tacit operation, both in our spoken language and in our understanding of it when spoken by others. The same applies to all other explicit thought; it can be developed and understood only by a tacit operation and it is thus based throughout on tacit knowing. All knowledge is either tacit or rooted in tacit knowing.

To sum up, I call "logic" the rules for reaching valid conclusions from premises assumed to be true. Currently logic seems to be defined instead as the rules for reaching strict conclusions from strict premises. I think we should reject this definition. No strict rules can exist for establishing empirical knowledge. Most people know this, but would urge us to accept strictness as an unattainable ideal for which to strive. But this is to turn a blind eye on tacit knowing, in which alone lies our capacity for acquiring empirical knowledge.

Our age prides itself on its unflinching frankness in calling a spade a spade and worse than that. But for all this bluntness, we are strictly Victorian when it comes to mentioning the mind, acknowledging its autonomous actions and its indeterminate range of knowing—even though all the power and beauty of thought relies on these tacit faculties.

I think we should drop these intellectual fictions, for there are reasonable alternatives that are much nearer the truth.

REFERENCES

Brentano, F. *Psychologie vom empirischem Standpunkt.* (Reprint of 1874 ed.) Leipzig: Oskar Kraus, 1942.

Chomsky, N. Review of B. F. Skinner, *Verbal behavior. Language,* 1959, **35,** 26–58.

Conant, J. B. *Harvard case histories in experimental science.* Cambridge: Harvard University Press, 1957.

Hadamard, J. *The psychology of invention in the mathematical field.* Princeton: Princeton University Press, 1945.

Helmholtz, H. von. *Handbuch der Physiologischen Optik.* Leipzig: L. Voss, 1867.

Hempel, C. G. Scientific explanation. In, *Forum philosophy of science series.* Washington, D. C.: United States Information Agency, Voice of America, 1964. (Pamphlet)

Hempel, C. G., & Oppenheim, P. Studies in the logic of explanation. *Philosophy of Science,* 1948, **15,** 135–178.

Kant, I. *Critique of pure reason.* (Trans. by N. Kemp-Smith) New York: St. Martin's Press, 1929.

Kottenhoff, H. Was ist richtiges Sehen mit Umkehrbrillen und in welchem Sinne stellt sich das Sehen um? In, *Psychologia Universalis.* Vol. 5. Meisenheim am Glan: A. Hain, 1961.

Kuhn, T. S. *The structure of scientific revolutions.* Chicago: University of Chicago Press, 1962.

Lashley, K. S. The problem of serial behavior. In L. A. Jeffress (Ed.), *Cerebral mechanisms in behavior. The Hixon symposium.* New York: Wiley, 1951.

Lorenz, K. Gestalt perception as fundamental to scientific knowledge. *General Systems,* 1967, **7,** 37–56.

Merleau-Ponty, M. *Phenomenology of perception.* London: Routledge, 1962.

Mill, J. S. *System of logic, ratiocinative and inductive.* Vol. 1. London: Parker, 1943. Pp. 450–505.

Nagel, E. *The structure of science.* New York: Harcourt, Brace & World, 1961.

Nash, L. K. *The nature of the natural sciences.* Boston: Little, Brown, 1963.

Piaget, J. *Psychology of intelligence.* New York: Harcourt, Brace, 1950.

Poincaré, H. *Science et méthode.* Paris: Flammarion, 1908.

Polanyi, M. *Science, faith and society.* London: Oxford University Press, 1946. (Reprinted: Chicago: University of Chicago Press, 1964).

Polanyi, M. *Personal knowledge.* Chicago: University of Chicago Press, 1958. (Rev. ed., New York: Harper Torchbooks, 1964.)

Polanyi, M. The structure of consciousness. *Brain,* 1965 (Part 4), 799–810.

Polanyi, M. *The tacit dimension.* New York: Doubleday, 1966. (Reprinted: London: Routledge, 1967.)

Polanyi, M. Life transcending physics and chemistry. *Chemical and Engineering News,* 1967, **45,** No. 35. (a)

Polanyi, M. Sense-giving and sense reading. *Philosophy,* 1967, **42,** 301. (b)

Polya, G. *How to solve it.* Princeton: Princeton University Press, 1945.

Quine, W. V. O. *Word and object.* Cambridge: M.I.T. Press, 1960.

Quine, W. V. O. In S. Koch (Chm.), Logic and psychology. Symposium presented at the meeting of the American Psychological Association, Washington, D. C., September 1967.

Rothschild, F. S. *Das Zentralnervensystem als Symbol des Erlebens.* Basel and New York: S. Karger, 1958.

Rothschild, F. S. Laws of symbolic mediation in the dynamics of self and personality. *Annals of the New York Academy of Sciences,* 1962, **96,** 774.

Ryle, G. *The concept of mind.* London: Hutchinson, 1949.

Scriven, M. Explanation, prediction and laws. In, *Minnesota Studies in the Philosophy of Science.* Vol. 3. Minneapolis, University of Minnesota Press, 1962.

Skinner, B. F. *Verbal behavior.* New York: Appleton-Century-Crofts, 1957.

Skinner, B. F. Behaviorism at fifty. In T. W. Wann (Ed.), *Behaviorism and phenomenology.* Chicago: University of Chicago Press, 1964.

Waismann, F. Verifiability. *Proceedings Aristotelian Society Supplement,* 1945, **19.**

Wall, H. W., & Guthrie, G. M. Extinction responses to subceived stimuli. *Journal of General Psychology,* 1959, **60,** 205–210.

Whewell, W. *Philosophy and discovery.* (Quoted text written in 1856) London: John W. Parker, 1890.

4

PEACEFUL COEXISTENCE IN PSYCHOLOGY

CHARLES TAYLOR

I

Psychology is a vast and ramified discipline. It contains many mansions. But this does not prevent it from being intellectually divided against itself. I would like to discuss in particular one major division in psychology, and in so doing suggest a way of reconciling the two sides. Out of such reconciliation, there might come a new perspective on the discipline.

The deep division in the discipline which I would like to examine concerns basic notions about science and the methods of science. At bottom it is a difference of epistemology. The epistemology which is dominant among experimental psychologists in America is the one which emerged with the scientific revolution in the seventeenth century. There are many ways of characterizing this view of science, but for the purposes of this discussion we can single out two features, because they are the principal sticking points in any confrontation between the two epistemologies.

The first is the principle that science must be grounded in data that are intersubjectively univocal. This point is often put by saying that experiments must be replicable by anyone, and any results must be such that others can check them. Science achieves its impressive show of objectivity through intersubjective agreement. Now this puts a restriction on what can be counted as data of a science. There are many ranges of judgements we make in ordinary life which cannot come close to meeting this requirement of intersubjective univocity. For instance, the judgement I might make about a painting that it reflects a powerful harmony between certain elements, or the judgements we make every day about people's characters and motives—these

Reprinted from *Social Research, 40,* 55–82. (1973). Copyright © 1973 by *Social Research.* Reprinted by permission of the publisher and author.

and others notoriously do not lend themselves to intersubjective agreement, and, what is more important, they do not often lend themselves even to univocal consensus on the meaning of the key terms involved in them. Judgements of this kind cannot be the data statements of a science according to the model we are characterizing here. The phenomena they relate to would have to be identified in a quite different vocabulary in order to be studied scientifically.

This requirement, then, is for what one might call 'brute data'—to coin a term for it, that is, data which are available without any personal discernment or interpretation on the part of the observer.[1] For as long as such an element of discernment is present, there will be unarbitrable differences of judgement between observers. And this should on no account be allowed, according to our model of scientific procedure. Differences of theory will inevitably exist in any domain where the established data allow for more than one, and allegiance to different theories will repose on differences of judgement about plausibility, the importance of certain factors, and so on. But this theoretical Babel which any science may fall prey to must be held within certain bounds by the univocity of its data.

The companion requirement to the need for brute data is that the operations which are carried out on the input data must be similarly interpretation-free. Any science which is more than a list of correlations obtained by enumerative induction must contain a component which is not simply a record of data, but which purports to map in some way the processes or transformations which underlie regularities in observable data. Hypotheses in this domain are ultimately verified by observable data. But if this is to be so, then their links with these data must also be univocal. A proposition about underlying processes can only be intersubjectively verified if its implications for observable data are univocal. If these implications cannot be unambiguously settled, agreement is impossible.

This second requirement—let us call it 'univocal operations'—is what underlay a number of ill-starred formulations of the high days of positivism, such as 'operational definition'. But this requirement is not implicated in the confusions of extreme positivism. It does not call for any kind of reduction of 'theoretical entities' to 'observational' terms, but simply asks that the calculations and transformations carried out on the input data used to map the underlying processes be univocal. For instance, in a paradigm case for this model of science—say, mathematical physics—the operations are expressed in mathematics and hence are thought to be beyond dispute arising out of personal discernment or intuition.[2]

Now these two requirements have been viewed by many psychologists as entailing a third—that of 'physicalism'. This was not always the case; earlier attempts at a rigorous scientific psychology on this model were prepared to include mental states, and the deliverances of introspection among their data. But in American psychology, this approach was swept aside a half century ago by the behaviourist revolution. One may well ask whether introspection was really

[1]Of course, this characterization still needs a lot of refinement. Paradigmatic as brute data are states which are recognized by clear criteria and where the recourse to criteria can continue through indefinitely many stages. Certain physical states meet this condition; e.g., an object's being x metres long: there is no limit to the procedures we can go through to check the measurement, check our yardsticks, apparatus, etc., in order to meet any doubt and objections. Intuitive judgements can always be checked.

But we may also be led to admit as brute data statements certain judgements for which we can give no clear criteria but on which there is in fact no disagreement—e.g., judgements in chicken-sexing, or the data of certain experiments in cognitive psychology where subjects attribute a certain degree of density to sounds. (I owe this latter point to Susan Carey.) This shows the importance that intersubjective agreement plays in our notion of scientific objectivity.

For a further discussion of 'brute data' see my 'Interpretation and the sciences of man', *Review of Metaphysics*, 25:1 (Sept. 1971), pp. 3–51.

[2]Of course, it is very much a debatable question whether mathematics is really interpretation-free in this sense. My point here is just that there is an influential tradition from the seventeenth century that regards it as a paradigm domain in which disputes are intersubjectively arbitrable, and hence as a central guarantee of scientific objectivity.

done away with, or whether it is not still with us in another guise—in, say, sensory threshold experiments and other experiments in cognitive psychology—but there is no doubt that the intent was to do away with it.

The attraction to physicalism on the part of those who accept the two prior requirements stems from more than the obvious consideration that a subject's introspective data are available only to him. Indeed, this is not in itself a very serious obstacle, since replication in introspective experiments can be interpreted to mean that others obtain similar introspective data under the same conditions, and this is how it was interpreted by those who carried on introspective psychology. The more important connection with physicalism lies in the fact that physical parameters can be more reliably identified as brute data. A dispute about a physical parameter can often be settled by observing the object's interactions with other things. Thus we can devise machines, like scales, thermometers, and so on, to increase the accuracy/certainty of our observations.

And so the mainstream of academic psychology in America, which took up the two requirements of the classical model of science, also took up physicalism—first in a behaviourist form; but when the star of behaviourism began to pale, other approaches with a richer theoretical component took over the allegiance to physicalism. Take, for example, the family of computer-inspired theories of mental function. These are based on the two classical requirements: brute input data, and a set of subsequent operations which are specified univocally enough so that they can be run as a program on a machine. Indeed, their expressibility in a machine program is the criterion of their univocity (as Minsky makes clear in his definition of an 'effective procedure').[3] The computer model thus also infers from the two classical requirements the necessity of physicalism.

II

This package of the two classical requirements plus physicalism runs up against an obvious objection in psychology—or indeed any science dealing with human emotion or action—which is that the phenomena of this domain, that is, acts and feelings, are partly characterized in terms of the thoughts, images, intentions, and ways of seeing of the people concerned. How do we identify an action as being of a given kind? By the purpose it aims to achieve. In many cases, of course, we read this purpose easily from the overt action, aided by our knowledge of the context. We see that someone is 'turning off the light' when we see him flip the switch, or 'reaching for a chocolate' when someone proffers the box. But even in these relatively unproblematic cases we can be led to change our mind if the agent tells us credibly that he had some quite different intention—that he wanted to align the switch with others on the wall because it looked better that way, or that he reached out to stop the box from falling. If we believe these explanations of purpose, we re-describe the actions. The purpose is therefore crucial here. And beyond these relatively transparent cases, there are all those where we have to understand the agent's vision of things in order to know what he is doing: is he trying to save face, or is he really expressing indignation? The answer to this takes us deep into the meanings that things have for him, deeper perhaps than he can consciously go or at least admit.

The same point can be made about feeling. What makes a feeling one of shame? That it is occasioned by a sense that something I am or have done or that belongs to me is dishonourable, demeaning, and something that I very much want to hide from others. The emotion is defined by the thoughts and perceptions of the subject individual, by the meanings things have for him.

[3]Marvin Minsky, *Computation* (Englewood Cliffs, NJ, 1967), p. 105.

But if this is so, then the data of psychology are of a peculiar kind, one to which the first requirement of the classical model may not be applicable. This first requirement called for 'brute data', that is, data which were beyond dispute arising from personal interpretation or discernment. But if action and feeling are characterized partly by the way agent or subject sees the situation, then his personal interpretation can enter into the definition of the phenomenon under study. So, far from these being obstacles to the science of psychology, they are essential to the constitution of its objectives.

Thus to return to the example of shame above, we saw that the feeling is identified as such by its object being dishonourable in the eyes of the subject. But what is dishonourable to a man is very much a function of his personal interpretations. Of course, he is using a generally available concept, that of dishonour, or perhaps a more particular characterization of the dishonourable action, such as—let us say—'cowardly'. And there may be widespread or even general agreement on the appropriateness of this description. But still this kind of judgement is similar to the judgement about the painting given above, in that if there is disagreement there are no criteria we can use to settle the dispute which are themselves beyond interpretive dispute. Agreement about dishonour, as about harmony in paintings, reposes on common discernment; once this is lost the only way to regain agreement is to recover the community of insight. There is no way we can reach agreement by finessing insight, as it were, through an appeal to brute data as criteria.

This is far from saying that there are no criteria in this area. If we disagree about harmony in a painting or about the dishonourable nature of an action, there is a lot we can still say to each other. We can point to the balance of strength and weakness in the painting, or depth and movement; we can point to the pusillanimity, or cowardice or pettiness, and so on, of an action. But in both these cases, the concepts we have recourse to—'strength' or 'depth' in the painting, 'pusillanimity' or 'pettiness' in the action—themselves require the same discernment in their application. It is not that dishonour and harmony are without criteria; but rather that the criterial terms demand the same degree of insight. We cannot step outside the circle of interpretations. Thus an argument about harmony or dishonour is not won by pointing to irrecusable data; rather it comes to an end when one side communicates insight to the other, and hence they both come to use the terms in the same way, to 'speak the same language'. But one comes to grasp the language of the other the way we pick up our first language, not through unambiguous explanations, but through hearing it. Hearing the language brings to light what the language is about.

Action and feeling are thus partly defined by judgements and perceptions which are not brute data and cannot be reduced to judgements about brute data. If one takes one's cue from this, then the classical model of science will be seen as inapplicable to the sciences of man. Rather one will opt for a type of science which is partly founded on interpretation—what has been called a 'hermeneutical' approach. This means that instead of trying to build a science grounded on brute data which can be seen as linked together through some underlying processes (or optionally, where these underlying processes can be set aside altogether, as in the extreme, caricatural behaviourism of B. F. Skinner), we strive to define correctly the interpretations of the agent, even those of which he is not aware, and relate these in terms of underlying mechanisms of a quite different sort.

A number of examples could be given of this kind of science of man. In fact, the dispute between the two epistemologies, the classical scientific and the hermeneutical, seems to crop up in all the disciplines which study human behaviour. So in political science, for instance, we have 'behaviouralism' versus an approach founded on political theory;[4] in sociology we have a

[4]For a discussion of the debate in this field, as well as further treatment of the characteristics of a hermeneutical science, see my 'Interpretation and the sciences of man'.

theory like that of Max Weber versus an empiricist approach (although attempts have been made in American sociology to reduce the *verstehen* dimension of Weber's thought and thus recruit him for the opposite school). But in psychology, the most obvious case of a hermeneutical science is that of psychoanalysis and the various approaches which have descended from it, for example, the psycho-history of Erikson, certain personality theories, like that of Rogers, and so on.

This is not universally appreciated, since Freud himself was very much under the spell of the classical scientific epistemology. But in fact psychoanalysis is a science grounded on interpretation. It involves reading, from the patients' symptoms, lapses, associations and the like, what the meaning of his situation is for him, a meaning which he cannot himself disclose—rather, against whose disclosure he fights vigorously. Ricoeur has presented this understanding of psychoanalysis very convincingly in his *De l'Interprétation.*[5]

But it is easy to make a symmetrical mistake about psychoanalysis to that which aligns it with the classical model. This is the view which sees it as purely a science of interpretation, as only concerned with understanding, and not with the causal forces which shape behaviour and feeling. And this is wrong; the metaphors of force and distortion in Freud's vocabulary—'repression', 'condensation', 'displacement', and so on—are to be taken seriously. The meanings which Freud is interested in reading are meanings which have suffered distortion, through having undergone great pressures, as it were. Psychoanalysis is not simply a hermeneutics, but one which is also bound up with a causal theory, as Ricoeur shows.

The fact that it is a causal theory which appeals to underlying forces does not mean that it can be aligned with the classical model. For the operation of these forces is traced not through brute data, but rather through the data of interpretation. The verbal slip reveals the repression and displacement not *qua* physical event, but in terms of its meaning. There is no way of finessing this level of interpretation and observing the forces outside its medium. That is why Freud's underlying force terms are not quantifiable.[6]

Epistemologically, this means that psychoanalysis cannot meet the requirements of the classical model because disputes within it cannot be settled by pointing to brute data. Instead disputes turn on the plausibility of rival interpretations, and the plausibility of an interpretation cannot be reduced to cut and dried criteria. On the contrary, it requires a certain discernment to appreciate it. Hence the grave dissatisfaction, not to say frustration, with psychoanalysis on the part of those who are wedded to the classical model—and there are many of these in academic psychology, to whom psychoanalysis seems almost scandalous when viewed as a putative science.

Let us take the oft-repeated complaint that concepts like 'resistance' enable Freudians to have it both ways: if one admits to an interpretation, this helps confirm it; but if one rejects it, this also may be viewed as confirmation, since the repressed interpretation is one that the patient resists, and indignant rejection is predictable in these circumstances; indeed, the more definite the rejection, the more likely the hypothesis. This seeming 'heads-I-win, tails-you-lose' predicament is thought to make psychoanalytical hypotheses irrefutable; and, by a well-known principle of classical science, what is irrefutable is also devoid of explanatory content.

But this objection appears strong only to those who have assumed beforehand the exclusive validity of the classical model. To start with, it cannot be the intention of those who hold this objection to claim that a phenomenon like resistance is impossible. This would be a bit of wholly gratuitous *a priori* legislation. But if resistance is a feature of human psychology, then there will

[5]Paul Ricoeur, *De l'Interprétation* (Paris, 1965).

[6]Cf. a discussion of 'affective charge' by Judith Winter, 'The concept of energy in psychoanalytic theory', *Inquiry*, 14:12 (1971), pp. 138–47.

be cases where rejection of an interpretation does not weaken it, but rather may help to confirm it. What one can legitimately ask of the analyst is that he be able to distinguish the case where an interpretation is rejected because it is false from that case where it is rejected because it is true and inadmissible to consciousness. Analysts claim to be able to do this (sometimes—but what more can you ask?) from other interpretations made in the analysis and from the manner of the rejection itself. For instance, is the rejection expressed with more than necessary vehemence, and/or with anxiety? So his judgement is not without criteria, nor his hypothesis irrefutable. Of course, the question then arises of how one determines what amount of vehemence is 'more than necessary', or whether there is anxiety. And here the answer is that although these judgements do not lack criteria, they do repose on discernment and cannot be reduced to brute data. Here we get to the nub of the problem. The psychoanalyst cannot avoid interpretation, nor can he ground his interpretations on brute data. He claims to be able to distinguish the two kinds of rejection, but not by brute criteria. But if one accepts no distinctions as scientifically valid except those founded on brute data, then this claim must appear bogus. Hence it appears perfectly arbitrary that some rejections are taken as confirmations, and the analyst appears to be playing a game he cannot lose. But all this is based on the epistemological premise that science requires brute data, that the classical model is the only one allowable. As an attempt to prove the non-scientific nature of psychoanalysis, it therefore fails because it assumes what it intends to prove.

My intention in citing this objection was not to enter this polemic, but just to show that here, too, the key issue comes down to that between two epistemologies, two models of science, one of brute data versus one which admits of interpretation. The same basic issue crops up in other disputes related to psychoanalysis, such as the attempts that have been made to establish a cure rate for psychoanalytic treatment. This raises the necessity of establishing what will count as a cure, and there are no interpretation-free criteria for a psychological 'cure'.

III

So two rival epistemologies confront each other in psychology, as in other sciences of man, in a sort of dialogue of the deaf. The protagonists of one view—let us call them the correlators—argue that the classical model alone offers the kind of intersubjective certainty that deserves the name of science. it does not rely on a form of intuition which can lead to unarbitrable disputes, and all results are fully replicable. To which their adversaries—let us call them the interpreters—reply: Don't blame us, we didn't make the world, and it's not our fault if it contains phenomena which are arguable and thus require interpretation. The point about science is to strive for the degree of certainty of which the domain under study is capable, not to apply an inappropriate model just because such a model would give more satisfactory results *if* it applied. (At this point the interpreters will tell you the anecdote about the drunk looking for his keys under the lamp-post—which is too familiar to bear repetition here.)

But the correlators are not satisfied with this. They stick to their view that only sciences after the classical model deserve the name. They generally believe that human behaviour characterized as action and feeling cannot be treated according to this model, and their response is to seek other levels of description on which to treat human behaviour. The levels chosen have usually been physicalistic in one way or another. The best known such attempt was classical behaviourism, which strove to account for behaviour by correlating stimulus input and movement. With the decline of faith in behaviourism, various theories have been developed which make appeal to central processes linking input and output, including theories modelled on computer programs. But input and output are still identified physicalistically, and the central processes are thought to be ultimately identifiable with operations in the brain and central nervous system. These 'centralist' theories ultimately converge with a third approach which is trying to develop a thoroughgoing neuro-physiological account of behaviour.

Now all these approaches have run into trouble. This form of behaviourism could not cope with the purposeful, intelligent behaviour even of rats, let alone men. When I say 'could not cope', I mean this: that it could not match the regularities of behaviour characterized in terms of purpose and cognition with descriptions of environment and behaviour characterized as stimulus and response. Faced with some of the insightful and innovative behaviour of some mammals in learning situations, behaviourists turned more and more to *ad hoc* hypotheses (such as Hull's 'fractional anticipatory goal responses', or the various 'secondary drives'), which became increasingly difficult to give a clear empirical meaning to, and this indeterminacy of empirical meaning began to invade the key terms of the theory as well. Ritchie makes this point in connection with 'reinforcement' in the S-R treatment of latent learning.[7] Chomsky makes a similar case in his review of Skinner's *Verbal Behaviour*,[8] pointing out the circularity involved in Skinner's use of 'response'.

The key concepts of behaviourism were thus stretched and enlarged to a point of near-vacuity in the attempt to cope with refractory phenomena. And, inevitably, these terms began to incorporate surreptitiously the dimensions of purpose and cognition they were meant to exclude. Thus the 'response' which was meant to be identified *qua* 'colourless movement'—and there would be little point in launching on the behaviourist enterprise if it were not—in fact was almost invariably classified in terms of the end-goal of the action concerned. The unit studied was, for example, 'pressing the bar', where this could be accomplished with left paw, right paw, or teeth. If this discrepancy was noticed at all, it was dismissed with the breezy assurance that any correlation linking such an action category could be further reduced to correlations linking the component movement classes—a not terribly plausible assumption, and a surprising thing to leave as an *assumption* when the whole question at issue between behaviourism and its opponents is whether or not one can do without the dimensions of purpose and cognition. Similarly, on the input side, all sorts of fancy additions were allowed, such as 'relative stimuli' and 'comparative stimuli', which in fact reintroduced the perception of relationship and significance which was meant to be excluded.[9]

Now this is exactly what one would expect if behaviourism were on the wrong track. To be on the wrong track in science, not just in the sense of having a faulty hypothesis, but in the more fundamental sense of trying a wrong approach, is to be incapable of finding explanatory correlations on the level of description one has chosen. After fifty years of life, behaviourism has clearly come up against this barrier. When plausibility can only be attained by stretching categories to near vacuity, and surreptitiously incorporating some key categories of the rival view, we have a pretty clear indication of bankruptcy. Appearances can be kept up only by ignoring the difference between a vacuous general description form and a set of categories with some ontological bite. If 'behaviourism' means merely that behaviour alters with experience, and this in a way related to the positive and negative valence of this experience, it will be hard to find anyone to disagree. If, on the other hand, the claim is made that we can trace this alteration of behaviour by characterizing both environment and behaviour in concepts which make no reference to meaning or purpose, and also employ a similarly physicalistic, interpretation-free notion

[7] B. F. Ritchie, 'Concerning an incurable vagueness in psychological theories', in B. Wollmann and E. Nagel (eds)., *Scientific Psychology* (New York, 1965).

[8] Noam Chomsky, Review of Skinner's 'Verbal Behaviour', *Language*, 35:1 (1959), pp. 26–58.

[9] Cf. Charles Taylor, *Explanation of Behaviour* (London and New York, 1964).

of reinforcement, then 'behaviourism' has real content, but appears unsustainable. The theory can only survive through paralogistic argument, where the sense given to the theory shifts between the loose and the tight interpretations. B. F. Skinner, for instance, excels in this. Old theories, like old soldiers, never die, they just fade into a self-absorbed vacuity.

Behaviourism's inadequacies are now evident to the majority of practising psychologists. And this is part of the reason for the boom in centralist theories, notably those which are inspired by the progress of the digital computer and which try to model human intelligent functions on the Turing machine. But these theories have run into what is at bottom the same difficulty as behaviourism. I say 'at bottom' because on a superficial level the experience of artificial intelligence, seen as a model of human function, and computer simulation run into quite different problems. To start with, the kind of fudging and extending of concepts which behaviourism indulged in is impossible on the level of a computer program. It has precisely to be made entirely explicit in order to be run on a machine. This is why many workers in the field constantly stress the value of computer programming as a test of the coherence of a hypothesis about internal processes. At the same time, Artificial Intelligence and Computer Science also started with human functions, and some difficult ones at that, instead of making things easy by putting rats into the restricted environment of a maze, not to speak of pigeons in a Skinner box.

The result is that this approach has run into evident difficulty a lot faster, and this is all to its credit. The difficulty in matching such behaviour as reaching for an object in space, playing chess, making simple inferences, storing and using vocabulary, and so on, is that approximation to these activities is only possible in a relatively schematic and rigid way, and the task of going beyond this to a fuller matching of the flexible adaption of human performance becomes increasingly difficult. It requires an exponential growth in information storage and program routines which not only exceeds the capacity of existing machines (in itself not a difficulty in principle), but poses seemingly intractable search and selection problems.[10]

But this is exactly what one would expect on the assumption that these computer-modelled theories are on the wrong track. The issue between them and the hermeneutical approach to psychology is whether human functions that on a phenomenological level seem to involve a flexible know-how and perception of things which is not reducible to brute data and an exactly specified procedure can be matched by a machine which does operate on particulate input by just such an exact procedure. If the match were impossible, then one would expect that the programs would be rigid and narrow gauge relative to the live performance, and that they could only meet the full flexibility of the latter by a multiplication of special programs. This is in fact what seems to be occurring. Exponential growth of the *ad hoc* is in general the symptom of a mistaken theory, as can be seen from a classical illustration: the multiplication of epicycles to which the Ptolemaic theory was forced in order to save the phenomena.

As for the development of physiological explanations of human behaviour, this seems an even less likely bet for the moment. Some years ago when our notions of the function of brain and central nervous system were modelled on the reflex arc—or at worst, the telephone exchange—hope seemed possible. But already with Lashley's work, a quarter of a century ago, this perspective began to recede into the middle distance, and everything we have learned about neurophysiological function since has only served to complicate the picture further. Whatever the hope of ultimately achieving a link-up between the explanation of behaviour and neurophysiology, we cannot start with a neurophysiological explanation of mental function and action unless we understand the former better than the latter. But the reverse is the case. A reduction of this kind would be in the cards, if one is possible at all, only after we have achieved further progress on the psychological level. And, in fact, if such a link-up ever comes to pass, it is likely

[10]Cf. discussion in H. L. Dreyfus, *What Computers Can't Do* (New York, 1979).

that it will require a great enrichment of our neurophysiological concepts in order to match the rich variety of self-interpretations which human beings are capable of, only a part of which probably has been manifested so far in the transformations of human cultural history.

IV

The attempt by the correlators to finesse the level of interpretation has not been successful. The indications are rather that they have been barking up the wrong tree. But instead of drawing from this the opposite conclusion—that the interpreters are globally right and the correlators globally wrong—I would like to explore another possibility: that there is a place for both models in the very diversified field which is psychology; that the trouble comes mostly from the limitless imperialism of the correlators. Once they accept their limits, they can coexist with the other school—hence the title of this paper. But this coexistence can be something more than just an arm's length toleration; it could also be very fruitful for psychology, and therein lies the interest in the proposal.

To speak of psychology as a diversified field is an understatement. A field which contains the different standard interests of experimental psychology, learning, motivation, and discrimination experiments, cognitive psychology, personality theory, social psychology, clinical psychology, developmental psychology, psychoanalysis, psycholinguistics, and lots more, obviously cannot be reduced to a single formula. But for the sake of simplification, I would like to single out three kinds of study within the field, a typology which is probably far from exhaustive, but which will enable me to draw some kind of rough dividing line between the two models of science.

When we talk of psychology in general we sometimes think of the science which attempts to explain why people act the way they do—that is, the explanation of motivated behaviour and the exercise of our capacities. But a tremendously important part of experimental psychology is taken up with the study of the necessary or infrastructural conditions for the exercise of these capacities. These are studies on the psychophysical boundary—for instance, the study of physiological psychology, or studies in perception of the conditions in the stimulus array necessary for a certain level of discrimination or a certain perception.

Now the relevant point about such a psycho-physical domain is that here the classical model of science is the appropriate one. The aim of these studies is to discover correlations between physically defined dimensions and certain psychic states or capacities which are unambiguously present or absent, for example between a certain state of body chemistry and feeling hungry, a certain stimulus array and discriminating distance. Of course, it can be said that for one of the terms in these correlations we rely on 'introspection', but we have seen above that this is no real problem. If we have qualms about introspection we can say that the second term is the subject's claim, an overt act of speech.

Secondly, aside from the infrastructure of our capacities, we can study the structure of these capacities, our competences. The most-quoted example these days is the transformational grammar pioneered by Chomsky, but we should also mention Piaget's study of the stages of child development. Here, too, the aim is to discover the structure of competence, the kinds of operations children are capable of at different ages. In both these cases, we have rather sophisticated theories which make appeal to developed formal structures, but the study of competence can be carried out at a more empirical level, such as the correlations involved in intelligence testing.

Both infrastructure studies and competence studies can be distinguished from the study of what is sometimes called performance, that is, actual motivated behaviour, particular exercises of competence toward a given end. What is involved here is the explanation of action and feeling, what we do and the emotions we experience, and this requires more than the understanding of the structure of the competence involved and the identification of the physical infrastructural conditions.

It is in this third domain that the hermeneutic model is appropriate, whereas the classical model invades the domain to its peril. Thus the attempts to develop learning theory—not the identification of physical conditions but the attempt to explain how rats learn to get around an environment or human beings learn a language—carried out according to the classical model have been depressingly sterile. Behaviourism was never anything but an unmitigated disaster in this area, first because it had no place for the notion of the structure of a capacity, the rat's 'map' of space or the speaker's linguistic competence. It was wedded to a unidimensional account, in which there was no possibility of distinguishing between a competence and its multiple uses.

Furthermore, the failure to distinguish competence from performance not only deprived the behaviourists of structural concepts, it also meant that what they were committed to explain was fully motivated behaviour, what the rat does or the man says after the learning period. And its theoretical resources were much too meager for this, for as we saw above, explaining what we do involves an appeal to what we desire and feel and how we see our situation, all of which cannot be identified within the narrow purview of the classical requirements, particularly if these are interpreted as entailing physicalism.

Take the second example above, that of verbal behaviour. On reflection, it must appear very implausible that what I am actually saying on a given occasion in a real-life situation can be explained by operant conditioning, as Skinner's theory would have it; that is, that the sounds I utter are linked to certain stimulus conditions. For as Chomsky and others have shown, the elements of our speech acts cannot be paired with stimulus conditions of the appropriate, physicalistic kind. I may say 'dog' in the presence of a dog (the first obvious candidate for the 'stimulus condition'), but I may utter it also in the course of a philosophical argument, as here, or on the stage, or when thinking of presents for someone's birthday, or in a whole host of cases. The whole conditioning model prescinds from the fact that there are many different kinds of activities that we carry on in speech, and that our words relate differently to reality as a function of this. Behaviourism cannot distinguish between the capacity and its many uses and hence cannot explore the structure of the former. And even if we could analyse verbal behaviour in terms of the meanings of individual words and expressions, these would not always be linked to genuine stimulus classes—what could be the 'stimulus meaning' (to use Quine's term) for 'charismatic', 'romantic' or 'serene'?

Hence it is not surprising that experiments on the verbal conditioning model generally avoid tackling something analogous to real-life speech acts, but rather focus on marginal ones which can be artificially restricted to meet the needs of this approach, for example learning nonsense syllables, or saying individual unrelated words, or speech within a 'declutched' game-like context created by the experiment. Where conditions of normal interchange are approached, the results become more random and contradictory.[11]

As a step towards an account of human linguistic behaviour, verbal conditioning experiments are doomed to frustration. But this is not to say that they cannot give us information about something else. For instance, studying the learning of nonsense syllables contributed, I believe, to certain discoveries about short-term memory. Experiments which thus contribute to enlarging our knowledge of the psycho-physical infrastructure of certain of our standing capacities have an unquestionable value. But experiments whose only *raison d'être* is to provide building

[11]Cf. Kenneth Heller and G. A. Marlatt, 'Verbal conditioning, behavior therapy, and behavior change', in C. M. Frank's (ed.), *Behavior Therapy, Appraisal and Status* (New York, 1969), pp. 576–9.

blocks in a chimeric prospective global explanation of verbal behaviour illuminate nothing at all. In a similar way, the behaviourist treatment of motivation as 'drive' has also proved quite unilluminating, moving from a simple base in a few organic drives to an elaborate superstructure of secondary drives which rapidly showed all the vices of vacuity without beginning to match the richness of motivational phenomena.

Thus the conclusion which most naturally flows from the successes and failures of the classical model is a division of spheres between the two epistemologies: the classical one in its natural place in the first domain, that of psycho-physical or infrastructural studies; the hermeneutic model as the natural approach to the explanation of fully motivated performance. The third domain, that of competences, is intermediate between the two others. It can admit of a high degree of formalization (e.g., Chomsky and Piaget), but the application of these structural concepts may require an interpretation which cannot be reduced to brute criteria.

The point of this typology of domains is not to establish a boundary between the spheres of influence of the two epistemologies, but rather to account for both the powerful attraction of the classical model and the disastrous results that occur when it is used as a universal key to psychology. Correlators cannot believe that the classical model is all wrong because they are well aware of its successes in the first domain. Where they go wrong is in assuming that the whole of psychology is homogeneous with this first domain, that it is simply a matter of proceeding further and adding more correlations of the same sort in order to account for fully motivated behaviour—that what one discovers in this way about the conditions for recall of a list of nonsense syllables is a step on the road to learning about language acquisition. To see the distinction between infrastructure and fully motivated behaviour is to see why the success of the model at one level is no warrant for its appropriateness at the other. If once this point is allowed, coexistence is possible in psychology.

V

But what use is coexistence, beyond the obvious gain in tolerance and harmonious relations? The answer is that this kind of recognition of the limits of the classical model is necessary not only to create a climate of tolerance in which theories of the interpretive kind can develop; it is also necessary to liberate our imagination, without which these theories are sterile. For the myth of the omnicompetence of the classical model not only prevents us from posing the kinds of questions that only interpretive psychologies can answer; it also severely restricts the answers we can come up with when we do pose them.

To see this, let us turn to a range of questions which are of pressing importance nowadays, questions whose urgency makes the issue I am trying to get at here of more than academic interest. It cannot escape anyone, least of all academics, that a large-scale cultural mutation is taking place in our civilization, and one of the major loci of this change is the young, particularly students. It is hard to characterize this change, and the attempt to do so is one of those creative theoretical tasks to which psychology should contribute. But if I may provisionally use some psychological terminology to identify the phenomenon, I would say that certain of the fundamental reference points for the formation of identity in our civilization are being challenged.

The model of maturity under challenge is that of a self-defining subject, that is, one whose defining aspirations, values and loyalties are determined out of himself, and not in reference to anything outside. This idea was so central to American society that even patriotism was seen as owing to a 'way of life', which was defined in terms of individual freedom. Corresponding to this model of the subject is a view of the world surrounding him not as the locus of reference points for his identity, as earlier cultures had viewed it, but rather as raw material for his productive purposes. Thirdly, connected with this purposive transformation of things is an orientation to the future, a negative relation to the past as something to be constantly surpassed, matching the relation to the world as something to be constantly made over to suit even more fully human purposes.

There is a massive crisis in allegiance to this model among the rising generations. Partly this is due to the disastrous consequences, ecological and social, which can be plausibly laid at its door. But the revulsion is not inspired only by these concrete consequences. There is also a sense that the reigning model of maturity is inhuman, that it cuts us off from the sources of community, creativity, and human feeling. In this respect, the present identity crisis resembles the Romantic revolt against the Enlightenment—but there are radically new elements in it and it is incomparably more widespread. There should be a way for the sciences of man to come to grips with this mutation. Not only should there be, there *must* be, if we are to use our best resources of intelligence and reason to face this transition. Without any understanding on our part, this crisis is not in any sense guaranteed a happy outcome. In revulsion against the models of their own civilization, many young people are reaching back to those of earlier unrecoverable cultures or weaving sentimental images of the cultures of the East. And none of this adds up to a viable alternative. What we need above all is an insightful understanding of what is happening to us.

Psychology should, *must,* contribute to this. It is evident that a very important contribution will be made by those disciplines which have been concerned with cultural change, and with the rise of the modern identity, for example anthropology and history. But phenomena of the kind we are concerned with here cannot be tackled by respecting existing disciplinary lines of demarcation. We need to bring all the relevant theoretical resources to bear together on the problem, regardless of their provenance. In this respect, I believe that the work of Erik Erikson has made a very valuable contribution. Unfortunately, the belief in the omnicompetence of the classical model of science helps hold psychology back from contributing in this domain. Not just because it discourages interpretive psychology in general—this is bad enough, since any science which comes to grips with the problems of cultural change must be interpretive, having to deal as it does with differences in self-interpretation—but also because this belief is an integral part of the culture which is under attack, and therefore cannot offer a perspective from which this attack can be understood.

In all the disciplines where the classical model has been dominant, for instance psychology, political science, and sociology, student rebellion against 'the system' has also been directed against this paradigm of science. The rebellion has frequently been confused and sometimes very destructive, an attempted assassination of treason. (This provides another example of how little we can count on a guaranteed happy outcome to the current crisis.) But there is a correct perception underlying this challenge to the reigning 'methodology'.

In the eyes of its protagonists, the correlators, the classical model is a neutral procedure by which any reality can be approached 'scientifically'. It never occurs to them that this procedure weights the dice in favour of certain solutions, certain theories over others. But this it cannot fail to do. For a normative model of science cannot but involve a notion of the subject, and this in two ways: first, the thesis that all reality can be understood in terms of brute data and univocal operations says something by inclusion about man as an object of science, in that he is not to be understood as a self-interpreting being. But in addition, a model of scientific procedure must say something about the subject of this science. And this is the relevant connection here.

The classical model prescribes a certain stance on the part of the subject towards the world he is to understand. He is to look on this world not as a locus of meanings by reference to which he can understand himself and his world, but as a neutral domain of facts, of contingently correlated elements, the tracing of whose correlations will enable greater and greater manipulation and control of the world. This stance, let us call it the objectification of the world, was what the seventeenth-century revolution in science, the revolution of Bacon, Descartes, Newton, won through to, in an epoch-making polemic against the world-view of the Middle Ages and the high Renaissance, with its reliance on final causes and its vision of the universe as a hierarchy of meaning. This vision was among the 'Idols of the Mind' which Bacon castigated. As against this illusory, interpretive view of things, true knowledge brought power.

This is the stance involved in the classical model, and few contemporaries would want to question its validity for natural science. But the ideology of scientism, the belief that this model is omnicompetent, and that man reaches his greatest perfection and his most appropriate relation to things in the scientific stance, claims far more. It claims that human reality as well, our social institutions, the men in relation with whom we live, even our own lives, must be objectified to be understood. It claims that men reach their highest development in achieving the objectification of everything. Scientism is a transposition of the foundational Western tradition that man's vocation is reason, but reason has been drastically reduced from vision to objectification.

Scientism, the belief in the omnicompetence of the classical model, is closely bound up with the norm of maturity against which many young people are rebelling today. It is both one of its expressions and one of its props. For scientism, too, defends the norm of a self-defining subject, relating to his world not as a locus of meaning but as neutral matter, to be shaped according to his purposes. And since this objectification touches the human world as well as that of nature, this subject tends to define himself as an individual. In effect, the ideal subject of scientism is an extreme version of the modern norm of the conscious, autonomous individual: for he would experience none of his possible objects of awareness—not the human world or even his own body—as necessary reference points for his definition of himself or as indispensable interlocutors, but only as the phenomena of a neutral science of nature, some of which might be of use in the furtherance of his purposes.

In other words, scientism is ultimately bound up with the atomist, utilitarian bent in our civilization, whose orientation towards nature is manipulative, and which, where it is not also manipulative towards men, cannot get beyond the ideal of an arm's-length coexistence of independent individuals to any vision of community. Hence it is that an extreme protagonist of scientism, like B. F. Skinner, comes up with the *ne plus ultra* of manipulative nightmares—although in less spectacular form we can see the connection in the work of, say, D. C. McClelland on the achievement motive. Here the individualistic, productive orientation of our civilization is not only affirmed, but it is prescribed universally for developing nations and groups as the specific which will open the road to progress.

For in spite of the fact that McClelland's legend, folk-tale and story content analyses turn up high achievement motivation in cultures at all stages and ages of development, the 'need to achieve' itself is defined in terms which are specific to the modern identity. People with high need to achieve 'behave like successful, rationalizing business entrepreneurs'.[12] As the term 'rationalizing' implies, such people not only set themselves goals which offer some challenge, but are able and willing to look on the world around them as a task zone, a set of obstacles and potential means to these personally chosen goals. The self is the source of autonomously chosen aims, the world is to be scrutinized to discern the means to bring them to fruition. Increasing a man's achievement motivation, as we see in McClelland's 'missionary' work in India, involves increasing 'his sense of personal efficacy—his feeling that he could rely on himself, take initiative,

[12]D. C. McClelland and D. G. Winter, *Motivating Economic Achievement* (New York, 1969), p. 11.

become activity-oriented rather than just "goal-state" oriented, solve problems rather than avoid them'.[13]

It is plain that McClelland strongly believes in the value of this identity. He thinks it is one of the key factors in economic growth, and his research projects in other countries (such as those in India) in fact double up as exercises in proselytization. The trainees are converted to the new gospel by a combination of techniques ranging from the 'prestige suggestion' of the modern world[14] to more traditional methods outlined by Ignatius Loyola, such as the retreat setting and the foundation of a new reference group. All this will find its defenders, those who believe that what the Third World needs is headlong modernization after our model. But it casts no light on the change in identity itself, nor on possible alternatives. For one thing, 'need to achieve' is understood sometimes in an extremely general sense, as when 'scoring' material from ancient Greek literature, where stress on doing well in some competitive activity is a sufficient criterion; whereas for purposes of contemporary study and 'missionary' work, it also contains extremely important modern elements, for example, self-definition (measuring excellence against some *chosen standard*), a modern sense of time, and a faith in the power of science to shape our destiny.[15]

Moreover, this oscillation between a general and a specific category adds no new insight to the important historic question of the rise of the modern identity. Here McClelland only offers a simplifying rewrite of Weber: 'So it seems reasonable enough to interpret Weber's argument for the connection between Protestantism and the rise of capitalism in terms of a revolution in the family, leading to more sons with strong internalized achievement drives.'[16] Weber's historically specific account of Calvinism, of the particular goals and cravings which spurred men to make themselves over into the life-form of rationalizing achievement—all this is washed away; what we are left with is merely the drive to achieve for its own sake, weakly generalized across ages and societies. Such a blunt tool provides little explanatory edge.

And finally, there is no sense of cost or of alternatives. On very superficial evidence (questionnaire answers to questions about beliefs and practices), McClelland seems partly convinced that traditional Hindu beliefs and practices are not undermined by the modern identity. But apart from all other considerations, we have good reason to distinguish the effects of a new identity on a few individuals in a largely unchanged society from its impact once the whole society has been made over. Advanced societies are beginning to show some of the latter, which is why many thoughtful people in developing countries are asking themselves whether it is possible to increase production and yields without acquiring a globally manipulative stance toward nature and eventually toward men as well. Perhaps Tanzania, perhaps China, will help the human race answer this. But they will not be helped by Dr. McClelland and his exaltation of the need to achieve for its own sake; rather they seek an identity in which the desire for achievement is subordinated to human significant purpose.

Just because it is so rooted in one temporally and culturally bound self-interpretation of man, which had its origins in the past and may now be facing its demise, the belief in the omnicompetence of the classical model in science cannot help us understand this transition. It can only serve to entrench us narrowly in one of its terms, precisely that one whose inadequacy

[13] *Ibid.*, p. 334.

[14] *Ibid.*, pp. 66f.

[15] *Ibid.*, p. 378.

[16] Cf. D. C. McClelland, *The Achieving Society* (New York, 1967), p. 49.

is at the origin of the crisis. The only excuse for holding fast to this position would be if it were effectively what it claimed to be, the only viable model of science. But we have seen reason to doubt this. That it is a valid model cannot be questioned; that it has a major role in psychology is also beyond doubt. But only if its imperialist pretensions to englobe the whole field are resisted can psychology make its contribution to understanding the crisis of our civilization. This contribution would then not just be the act of a few inventive outsiders who are out of contact with the mainstream of empirical research, and looked at askance by academic psychology's best researchers. Rather it would be one toward which the many branches of study in this diversified field can converge.

5

PSYCHOTHERAPY VS. MORALITY

JOSEPH MARGOLIS

THE PERTINENCE OF MORAL REVIEW

If we regard psychotherapy as a practice and a practice as a kind of conduct, we are irresistibly led to admit that the profession of psychotherapy cannot logically escape moral scrutiny. The argument is simple and, I think, correct. But it has been strenuously resisted and debated in psychiatric circles for a long time, and one supposes that the antagonists have had some justification that is ignored by oversimplified arguments of the sort just supplied.

Heinz Hartmann, for instance, speaks of "analytic therapy [as] a kind of technology"[1]—by which he means to remind us of Freud's own conception of psychoanalysis as a value-free, scientific endeavor.[2] Psychotherapy is said to have its own appropriate goals which are "not questioned" in the professional setting,[3] and to which professionals address themselves solely in terms of efficacy. They are, therefore, not obliged to concern themselves with moral values in their practice; in fact, as scientists, they are professionally unable to advance moral recommendations. As Hartmann says: "Science cannot decide on what aims one 'ought' to strive for, or what values should be considered supreme. Generally speaking, imperatives cannot logically be deduced from affirmative propositions."[4]

The contrast between the two views above is gratifyingly direct, because it invites us in the clearest way possible to sort out the logical relationships that hold between therapy and morality. The issues are, of course, a good deal more complicated than that of a mere choice between our alternatives. For one thing, Freud and Freudian analysis have, not unsympathetically, often been taken to be heavily committed to certain preferred moral doctrines. Thus Philip Rieff challengingly contends:

Reprinted from *Psychotherapy and Morality: A Study of Two Concepts* (p. 13) by Joseph Margolis, 1966, New York: Random House.

> The genital character is characterized, for Freud, by achieved harmony, efficiently deployed energy, directness, and fully employed libido. So qualitatively different is this final biomoral type from its predecessors [oral-anal-phallic] that "genital" becomes a tendentious term, describing the whole man, the normal man in an abnormal society. Although Freud saw it as the terminal stage, genitality is not so much another stage as the abolition of stages. The genital character is an ideal.[5]

If this is true, it means that psychotherapy, though it be a technology (in Hartmann's sense), presupposes goals that are morally significant and that cannot themselves be supplied (again, in Hartmann's sense) by any scientific endeavor. This not only directly contradicts Freud's view of his own enterprise, but it raises the question of whether psychotherapy can, logically, ever be value-neutral.

The argument by no means depends on an acceptance of Freud's picture of mental health. We may notice that more recent conceptions of psychotherapy, particularly among the neo-Freudians, frankly seek to integrate the values of morality and therapy.[6] Erich Fromm's explicit venture into moral theory, in *Man for Himself,*[7] fixes this development inescapably, with its eudaimonism expressed psychologically in terms of self-love. Existentialist analysis, departing even more strikingly from Freud's original models, quite candidly links medical with non-medical values. Ludwig Binswanger, for instance, asserts that "we must never separate 'anxiety' from 'world,' and we keep in mind that anxiety always emerges when the world becomes shaky or threatens to vanish. The emptier, more simplified, and more constricted the world design to which an existence has committed itself, the sooner will anxiety appear and the more severe will it be."[8] He bridges the medical and the moral by means of the existential category of the Uncanny (*Unheimlichen*).[9] Also, recent contributions to the large and eclectic literature of psychotherapy and values, selected at random, regularly observe that "the study of values in psychotherapy can be handled successfully only if related to the study of values in human life and human development"[10]—which, by its very air of comfortable truth, casually marks the prevailing view.

The problem is set then by debate within professional circles; it is not imposed, for any ulterior reasons, by outside critics. On the one hand, we have a picture of a scientific, value-neutral enterprise, pursuing professionally formulated goals in terms of causal efficacy; on the other, we have a picture of technically qualified workers who, in offering professional advice, are promoting what they conceive to be the good life. One may suspect, as an independent observer, that, given the general nature of debates of this sort, there is a measure of justice on both sides.

We may perhaps best preserve a sense of neutrality here by distinguishing the principal ways in which therapeutic and moral considerations actually impinge on, or remain clearly independent of, one another. These conditions are comparatively easy to identify and serve to explain much (though not all) of the confusion regarding the scientific or moral status of psychiatry and psychotherapy.

Consider once again Hartmann's view of "analytic therapy [as] a kind of technology." He is, of course, correct—in a sense. Psychotherapy is a professional enterprise committed to the goals of mental health. For our present purpose, we may suppose that these goals are clearly defined for professional practitioners. Recruits are regularly instructed in both the goals and the techniques for achieving those goals that constitute the professional tradition of psychotherapy. From this point of view, the goals of the field are, relatively speaking, accepted on face value, unchallenged, an essential part of the training orientation of would-be psychotherapists. And it is precisely this point of view that lends an impression of plausibility to the otherwise somewhat narrowly technological account of Hartmann.

The technological view of psychotherapy draws attention to two important and distinctive features of that practice. First, statements made in the therapeutic setting are professionally competent. Second, such statements are concerned with "causal" matters (that is, with matters of effective change). The contrast with moral discourse could not be more complete. For, moral judgments, we concede, may be competently made by the man in the street and are taken to be evaluative and non-causal by nature. Actually, "causal" considerations are quite relevant in the moral context because, as P. H. Nowell-Smith has argued, moral judgments affect "actions that are caused by characteristics that can be strengthened or inhibited by praise and blame."[11] Still, it is the evaluative element, the element that actually assigns praise and blame, that gives the moral judgment its distinctive character. Also, it is not quite true that professional opinions are never relevant to, or decisive for, the rendering of moral judgments. Sometimes, a psychiatrically competent opinion may establish that a man has acted under compulsion and "could not have acted otherwise"—which clearly affects the moral judgment; even here, however, the presumption is that the moral man-in-the-street may competently judge from the information provided, and that the psychiatrist who reached a moral judgment would not himself be thereby functioning professionally.

One very simple further observation needs to be made about the technological view of psychotherapy. It is logically possible that the therapeutic recommendations made by some practicing physician are eligible for moral review. That is, grant that a therapist prescribes a line of conduct for his patient solely in terms of its probable advantage in promoting healing—for instance, he advises a female client not to reveal her extramarital affairs to her husband, at least through the present interval of therapy (or perhaps he simply conveys a permissive or noncommittal attitude regarding this issue). Subtle difficulties arise here, of course, crucial to both therapy and the accurate description of the therapeutic setting, but they do not affect our present issue.[12] For example, one may disagree about whether a therapist actually does, or ought to, *prescribe* such conduct; one may also disagree about the division, between therapist and patient, of responsibility for truth-telling in a given interval of time. But such matters are themselves always refinements within moral debate and, therefore, implicitly acknowledge the appropriateness of a moral review of the therapist's practices. What we have to see, very simply, is that a therapist's professional practice is, in principle, morally debatable. I do not see how this can be denied; in itself, it is quite sufficient to demonstrate the narrowness and inadequacy, though not, strictly, the falsity, of the technological conception of psychotherapy.

It is also not infrequently argued, citing Freud's own remarks, that, as a practice, psychoanalysis is concerned to bring into consciousness material that has hitherto been unconscious.[13] But even if this were construed in terms other than those of mental health, the eligibility of a moral review of analysis could hardly be denied (and the professional refusal to consider such a review would itself have to count as a decision of a morally significant sort);[14] on the other hand, Freud himself was sometimes inclined to speak of the goals of his practice in terms of the reduction of symptoms.[15]

It is not, however, entirely fair to construe psychiatry's own view of psychotherapy in exclusively technological terms, even if important spokesmen have tended to overstate their case. There is always to be found, for example, some recognition of a professional code of conduct. Hartmann himself pertinently observes:

> . . . in the therapeutic situation something appears that we account for only if we decide to make a distinction between the therapist's general moral codes and the one he is guided by in his therapeutic work, which could be called his "professional code." In his therapeutic work he will keep other values in abeyance and concentrate on the realization of one category of values only: health values. These are given special consideration in his work; they are taken for granted; and every therapist will, in his therapeutic work, consider their realization in his patients as his immediate and overriding concern. Is this an exception to the technical rule I . . . referred to, that the psychoanalyst should, in the analytic situation, try to keep his

> personal system of values in the background? I do not think so. It would be quite erroneous to assume that outside his professional activities the same therapist considers health values as the "highest."[16]

Now, a professional code of conduct is a somewhat paradoxical invention. For professionals are never *professionally* competent to provide their own code, though there is no doubt that they are competent to do so. What I mean is that a code of conduct for professionals, just as for nonprofessionals, is merely a part of a general moral code, adjusted in terms of relevance to the special practices of the group in question. The general presumption in preparing such a code is that the conduct prescribed is not arbitrary—is, rather, reasonably justified in terms of a more comprehensive tradition of acceptable behavior.

Clearly, the profession undertakes to review the moral (the "professional") conduct of any particular therapist. It will do so, and quite rightly, with the same kind of competence that the man in the street may exhibit in making moral judgments about his fellows; the expert factual information that may be required does not affect the issue in the least. A professional code argues the existence of a public moral tradition in terms of which it is itself to be justified; it recognizes the propriety of a moral review of professional practice because it actually makes provision for it; having done so, it cannot in principle deny that professional practice is eligible for such review outside professional circles.

To put the matter more simply, the fact that the goals of therapy are professionally formulated permits the therapist to construe his work primarily in terms of effectiveness (in "causal" terms, if we agree to speak loosely); the fact that the profession formulates for itself a code of acceptable practice enables any practicing therapist to judge his own professional conduct in a clear-cut way. The existence of the goals and their authority incline the therapist to think, not so much of his professional *conduct* as of his professional *facility;* he thinks more in terms of achieving therapeutic goals than in terms of responsibility for his professional decisions. This is not to say that psychotherapists are irresponsible; it is to say only that, in theorizing about their roles, they tend to assimilate what they are doing to the model of scientific explanation rather than to that of moral justification. They manage, however, also to formulate a professional code for themselves, which shows their responsiveness to moral considerations and suggests the source of their assurance that they may confine themselves, in their professional role, solely to therapeutic questions. I am, therefore, criticizing a certain picture of psychotherapy, not psychotherapy itself—not what the therapist does but what a professional, in an informal philosophical moment, may say he does.

The issue at stake is particularly striking in the context of therapeutic practice because of the unusually intimate bearing of professional decisions upon the *conduct of patients.* It is obvious, I think, that no other branch of medicine may be characterized in quite the same way. Other disciplines, usually regarded as sciences, show an even more remote connection between their work and the conduct of men. This is not to say that scientific work produces no changes in behavior; of course it does. But psychotherapy is itself focused primarily on the behavior and conduct of patients, the disorders it treats are themselves located chiefly in the patterns of human behavior, and the treatment it advances is in large measure an adjustment of those patterns.

If psychotherapy were not distinguished in these respects, the insistence on the moral complexities of the profession might well be trite and unnecessary. All professional life raises moral questions; the existence of professional codes attests to this. But the issues that other professionals face usually concern their own conduct, concern whether or not what they do is appropriate in terms of their own code and the traditions of their society. The psychotherapist, on the other hand, must see that he has a particularly direct effect and influence on the judgment and conduct of his client. This cannot be helped, to be sure, since it is in the nature of his practice. In fact, psychotherapy would be pointless if the therapist did not have some ability to facilitate, to encourage, even to direct changes in the lives of his patients.

In a word, psychotherapeutic practice is doubly subject to moral review. For one thing, it is a professional activity. Construed as conduct, it invites the usual moral reflections concerning confidentiality, protection of patient and society, conflicts between professional advice and existing prescriptions of conduct. For another, it is a unique activity that views human behavior itself in terms of health and disease. Consequently, it is directly and professionally concerned with influencing changes in human action and motivation, a matter that ordinarily falls within the domain of morality. The possibility of a conflict between moral and therapeutic values, therefore, is especially noteworthy and significant. The enterprise of psychotherapy, whatever the variety in doctrinal conviction, clearly presupposes a set of values in the name of which the alteration of the lives of patients is undertaken.

The technological view of therapy, we may conclude, altogether fails to provide for the profession's concern with altering behavior and motivation. On the other hand, merely to assert that there is a close connection between therapeutic and moral judgments does not serve to specify the nature of that connection or, indeed, the distinction between the judgments so connected. We have made an advance in establishing the responsibility of psychotherapeutic practice. But we must go on to substantive conflicts between therapy and morality, and the nature of these can be made very much clearer by even the briefest attention to certain linguistic distinctions.

POSSIBLE TERMINOLOGICAL CONFUSIONS

It is a familiar truism that moral values define the highest values of a society; if this is so, then no theoretical conflicts between therapeutic and moral values would seem possible, since the moral would always take precedence over the therapeutic. Also, it would be unintelligible how, if the truism held, psychotherapy could ever, with good conscience, have dealt with the problems of mental health, since to do so inevitably requires a flexible handling of certain moral values and even, at times, their subordination to therapeutic values.

The issue is a clear one and obviously lies at the very heart of all discussions of the moral responsibility of psychotherapy. But though it is the central issue, we cannot afford to come to it unless we first examine some of the terminological peculiarities of "therapy" and "morality." (I shall, incidentally, waive any differences that one might wish to make use of here between the terms "moral" and "ethical." In the Western philosophical tradition, it is perfectly clear that the great classics of moral theory, from Aristotle to G. E. Moore, have not abided by any consistent rule distinguishing the moral from the ethical.)

There is a crucial difference in the usage of such terms as "psychotherapy" and "morality": the first is based on a professional distinction; the second is not. Innocent as it may seem to be, this contrast has far-reaching consequences. We may judge the accuracy and adequacy of a proposed definition of psychotherapy by examining the actual practice of professionals. We cannot, in any parallel way, test a proposed definition of morality. And this is important because it suggests (as may be demonstrated more closely) that the use of such a term as "moral" to mark out the boundaries of a large category of judgments—to allow us to contrast, for instance, the moral, the legal, the political, the aesthetic, the religious, the therapeutic—depends more on decisions that are taken to be useful and convenient than on findings about actual usage.

There is no question that large philosophical terms such as "moral" and "ethical" (not used in such small-scale judgments as "He has no respect for professional ethics," "It wouldn't be ethical for your physician to do that," but rather used to mark out an entire domain of inquiry) have their own distinctive currency. We may characterize very broadly the kinds of interests that, historically, have fallen under the general heading of morality. But what we must take note of is that every new discussant of such an issue as this—the relationship between therapeutic and moral values—will be entitled to draw the line of the "moral" more tightly or more loosely than his predecessors, without risk of simple error. There is no standard division of morality. And though all proposed definitions may be compatible with the shifting moods of moral philosophy, the precise way in which the therapeutic and the moral are contrasted is a matter of reasoned choice and not of discovery. We are entitled to be suspicious, therefore, of all purely verbal quarrels about what is and what is not *really* a moral issue (though these are, of course, altogether different from disagreements, say, about what should be done under these or those circumstances).

Clearly, this affects the truism with which we began. If the use of "moral" and "ethical" is prone to shift in the manner indicated, we cannot possibly have a straightforward answer to the question of the hierarchy of values. I am not suggesting that the term "therapeutic" raises no difficulties. Of course it does. Any canvass of the range of notions of what mental health is[17] will show considerable professional variation regarding models of normality and health. Also, it is not unusual to find the very notion of medical therapy for mental illness challenged as dubious and possibly inappropriate. One influential psychiatrist, for instance, declares flatly:

> It is customary to define psychiatry as a medical speciality concerned with the study, diagnosis, and treatment of mental illnesses. This is a worthless and misleading definition. Mental illness is a myth. Psychiatrists are not concerned with mental illnesses and their treatments. In actual practice they deal with personal, social, and ethical problems in living. . . . The notion of a person "having mental illness" is scientifically crippling. It provides professional assent to a popular rationalization, namely, that problems in human living experienced and expressed in terms of bodily feelings or signs (or in terms of other "psychiatric symptoms") are significantly similar to *diseases of the body*.[18]

This extreme view (which does not quite appreciate the propriety of extending the use of a term—for example, calling a corporation a "person" in law) wishes to collapse the therapeutic into the moral altogether, in order to stress (what is in itself useful) the concept of personal responsibility. It serves to make an interesting contrast with the technological view of psychotherapy, which holds therapeutic values to be independent of moral ones. But it also dramatizes the terminological problem, because it seeks to persuade us that we cannot properly draw the line between psychotherapeutic and ethical values.[19] Thomas Szasz, the psychiatrist just quoted, does provide (in a somewhat pejorative sense) for the psychotherapist as a sort of "social engineer,"[20] so that we may see that what he offers is a persuasive redescription of the entire domain of psychotherapy and morality.

I am attempting here to indicate the importance of distinguishing among the terminological debates regarding the therapeutic and the moral. Difficulties arise with regard to both terms, but they are of different sorts. The boundaries of the "moral" are decided upon rather than found; the boundaries of the "therapeutic" are found rather than decided upon. But whether what therapists do and say is what they ought to do and say is open, apparently, to serious professional dispute; dispute along such lines tends to muddy the kinds of distinctions we require.

Historically, the moral tradition has moved along two grand roads that sometimes have been made to cross and overlap. There are various ways of providing the contrast required, all of which are bound to be somewhat oversimplified. But I think we shall understand reasonably well what the two principal lines of development are if we say that morality covers questions both of justice and duties, on the one hand, and of happiness and well-being, on the other. Schematically, this is sometimes expressed by saying that morality concerns both the "right" and the "good." It lies for instance, at the basis of Kant's distinction between the *summum bonum* and the *supremum bonum,* and it serves to contrast in a rough way the tendencies of Biblical and Greek morality.

Obvious as this historical distinction is, its significance for disputes about therapeutic and moral values has been largely overlooked. When one argues for the separation of these two sorts of values (as Heinz Hartmann does, for instance), one tends to think of morality in terms of duties and obligations; when one argues that therapeutic values are inherently ethical (as Thomas Szasz does, for instance), one tends to think of morality in terms of happiness and well-being. If we add to our appreciation of this confusion a reminder that, within limits, "moral" and "ethical" may fairly be made to cover different ranges for different speakers, we shall have a very clear idea why it is very nearly hopeless to pursue the question of the relative priority of moral and therapeutic values.

The difficulty may be fixed at a stroke if we note that therapeutic values may, given the sense of "moral," themselves be viewed as an important part of moral values. There would, at any rate, be no logical difficulties in such a construction. Marie Jahodá's comprehensive survey of the literature of mental health shows conclusively that therapeutic values are formulated within at least that part of the moral tradition that concerns happiness and well-being. As she observes:

> . . . the absence of disease may constitute a necessary, but not a sufficient, criterion for mental health.[21]
>
> . . . human behavior cannot be understood in terms of isolated symptoms but must rather be viewed in conjunction with the social norms and values of the communities in which the symptoms are observed.[22]
>
> . . . when happiness or well-being are clearly conceived of as personality predispositions, rather than as momentary feeling states depending on circumstances, . . . these criteria appear useful [for the concept of mental health].[23]

I think it is not unfair to say that the great variety of statements she has collected on mental health are predominantly eudaimonistic.[24] This is exactly what one should have expected. But for our present purpose, this means that, in one respect at least, there cannot be a conflict between therapeutic and moral values, though disputes may certainly arise about integration, self-realization, happiness, well-being, adjustment, normality, health and the rest. Questions of that sort lead us in another direction; we shall have to refuse to discuss them here. But what we may see, by way of a kind of subtraction, is that conflicts between therapeutic values and moral values can arise in an interesting way only when we try to deal with obligations and duties, with justice and what is right.

We may put this somewhat more manageably if we say that the problem of a conflict between therapy and morality is simply a special case of the possible conflicts between the two large branches of morality itself—conflicts, that is, between goodness and rightness, utility and justice, pleasure and obligation, and such values as are congruent with these pairs. But this is not surprising. The classic, recurrent cases that both professionals and non-professionals puzzle over, that mark overt conflicts between therapeutic and moral values, regularly single out elements of obligation and justice and rightness. Think, for example, of a physician who deliberately misleads a patient about her imminently fatal disease, on palliative grounds; think of a physician who encourages or advises a patient not to tell her husband about her extra-marital relations, on the grounds of reducing barriers against the recovery of her mental health. These are, without a doubt, paradigms of the moral-therapeutic dilemmas.

I am not concerned here with the resolution of these dilemmas (that is not a professional concern of philosophers), but only with the logical conditions on which they may be resolved.

They are, obviously, resolved in practice all the time. Physicians do mislead patients about fatal diseases under certain circumstances, and feel, not at all arbitrarily, that they have some justification for doing so. Therapists knowingly do allow patients, under certain circumstances, to continue deceiving their mates about extra-marital relations, and they believe themselves to be justified. What we want to know is not so much the justification of this or that policy (ultimately, this must be provided by the persons concerned), but whether and how justification is at all possible.

One further preliminary is in order. The professional code of psychotherapy and the nature of the tradition in which such codes arise make it altogether possible for a physician to assert that it is his obligation to promote the health of his patient. There is, in fact, a good Kantian duty that runs parallel to this. Special problems undoubtedly arise from the admission of a professional ethic. But for our present purpose, it makes little difference whether we consider conflicts between health and obligations or conflicts between obligations to promote health and other obligations. Changes of this sort, in our present context, are largely verbal—which helps to explain, incidentally, the implicit convergence of the most disparate views of psychotherapy—the technological (Hartmann) and the moralistic (Szasz).

THE RESOLUTION OF SUBSTANTIVE CONFLICTS

What we have examined, in the preceding section, are only terminological issues. The substantive question remains: How is it possible to resolve conflicts between therapeutic and moral values? We may, in order to fix the problem less ambiguously, rephrase, in the light of the distinctions already made, the truism with which we began. Thus, moral obligations define the highest values of a society; therefore, therapeutic values (and *a fortiori* the obligation to promote therapeutic values) are always subordinate to our moral obligations. The issue can no longer be sidestepped. We must answer and, in answering, seek to explain why therapists may, in good conscience, take exception to certain well-known and apparently binding moral obligations. Obviously, to answer in this way is to suppose that the alleged truism is not altogether true.

Our strategy will be to select important kinds of counter-instances from the specifically moral domain and to show that the questions that arise in the therapeutic setting are essentially of the same sort.

There is, first of all, the well-known problem of "hard cases." Grant that there exists an injunction against murder: "Thou shalt not kill." Then consider someone who, otherwise blameless and acting presumably in the interests of the well-being of a community, deliberately takes the life of a vicious tyrant. Is he to be condemned for murder? (Think of this, not so much in legal, as in moral, terms.) It is not necessary to decide, however, whether he is or is not to be condemned. The point is that the matter is clearly *debatable.* This is absolutely all that needs to be noted. If it is debatable—and it is—this means that, in "hard cases," in cases in which great *evil* (note: not injustice) follows from holding strictly to what is *right,* we are prepared to consider that the rule of justice may be set aside for the *good* of the community. Sometimes—and it is important to notice that there is no rule to follow—we allow considerations of utility to dispute and to win over considerations of justice.[25] With respect to murder, or the taking of life (the change in terms is not altogether significant, nor is it altogether without significance), we may cite also the question of justifying the killing of a moral monster, the taking of life of a thalidomide baby, the taking of life of a hopelessly ill and suffering person, in order to confirm our view that, at times in "hard cases," we are prepared to allow considerations of mercy, utility, well-being to take precedence over considerations of justice and obligation.

It is not important for our purpose to know what the actual outcome of any such debate is; it is sufficient that, in principle, obligations and justice may be subordinated to the interests of health and happiness, well-being and the reduction of pain. The argument to that effect is itself a *moral* argument and the preference of the therapist's values over, say, obligations of truth-telling (as in the instance of our fatally ill patient) is a perfect parallel to these cases involving the taking of life. I must say again that I am not, at the present moment, concerned with the resolution of any of these dilemmas and nothing that I have said so far would serve to decide any particular issue. Nevertheless, our finding is of the utmost importance. For it shows, by analogy, that the therapist is obliged to make a moral, and not merely a technical, judgment in deciding cases of this sort, and it shows that it is logically possible to defend, in moral terms, his preference of therapeutic values over particular, well-established obligations.

The therapist is understandably embarrassed by the seeming conflict between his professional goals and standard obligations in the society at large. Without a doubt, he himself has been trained to respect those obligations. He learns his professional code without anticipating conflicts of the sort under discussion; when dilemmas arise to face him directly, he is at a loss to supply the defense that his professional good judgment requires. What our counter-instances provide is the assurance that a defense of his preference for therapeutic values is at least logically possible.

There is, relevant to our present question, a second sort of problem that arises in the moral domain, which may also provide us with the counter-instances we are looking for. This is the problem of the conflict of duties or, more accurately, the problem of incompletely formulable duties. A standard case of this sort is already formulated in the opening lines of Plato's *Republic*, though it is merely posited there and not at all analyzed. Cephalus and Socrates are made to discuss the nature of a just life. Cephalus holds that justice consists, among other things, in paying debts back as promised; Socrates then asks:

> Suppose, for example, a friend who had lent us a weapon were to go mad and then ask for it back, surely anyone would say we ought not to return it. It would not be 'right' to do so; nor yet to tell the truth without reserve to a madman.[26]

Cephalus agrees with Socrates but, before any clarification can be made, he must hurry off to sacrifice to the gods. What is crucial here is that there is no quarrel between the two men regarding what would be right *under the circumstances*. Nevertheless, two of the cornerstones of the morality of obligations would seem to have been shaken: there are circumstances under which it would be wrong to repay a debt, and there are circumstances under which it would be wrong to tell the truth.

These are classic problems and, without a doubt, difficult to resolve theoretically. Small wonder that they should prove trying in the therapeutic context. What needs to be emphasized more than their difficulty, however, is the fact that they are of precisely the same sort logically as the therapist's problem about telling the truth to his dying patient (which is not the same as saying that the solution of the one must be the same as the solution of the other).

Now, let us look more closely at a situation in which we have a conflict of duties. One ought to tell the truth, we say, but, on the other hand, one ought not to put another in mortal jeopardy. The logically crucial feature about all such cases is that, though we may formulate seemingly binding rules for each of the separate duties that happen to conflict with one another in some particular circumstance, we cannot hope to formulate an adequate *rule* for the resolution of the conflict—though this does not mean that we cannot actually resolve the conflict itself. If I start with a familiar moral rule like, "One ought to tell the truth," I shall be bound, in cases like those that Cephalus and Socrates were discussing, to introduce a reasonable proviso: "Well, perhaps except when not telling the truth may save or protect a human life." But having entered that exception, I shall find myself bound to make further adjustments; for instance: "That is, if I am not doing harm to the lives of others in saving this particular life," or "if I am not protecting a possible murderer." Once refinements of this sort are allowed, we are bound to see that there is no end to the possible exceptions that will have to be entered. This does not at all mean that moral judgment is hopeless; on the contrary, it merely means that the making of moral judgments cannot possibly be adequately described in terms of the application of rules to cases.[27]

Put another way, we regard the moral order as internally consistent. Nevertheless, conflicts do arise, in particular situations, that call for the weighing of alternative moral claims, each of which is otherwise viewed as binding on our conduct. In order to maintain the internal harmony of the moral world, we are obliged to regard all particular moral rules as *incompletely formulated* and, in fact, as logically incapable of being fully formulated. We may express this schematically in the following way: the rule, "One ought to tell the truth," is an ellipsis for the "rule," "One ought to tell the truth. . . ." By this, I mean to draw attention to two important features of moral rules: one, that a rule is intelligible only in terms of standard cases in which the conduct called for properly applies; two, that in abiding by such a rule, we understand that other somewhat different, but seemingly similar, cases are not bound by this rule, though we cannot in advance exhaustively collect the apparent exceptions.[28]

This means that the moral tradition is primarily a collection of cases of how one ought and ought not to act rather than a collection of rules of conduct. Alternatively stated, the rules of conduct are simply keys to collections of cases. New moral problems are examined in the light of paradigm instances that they most clearly resemble. If, for example, the case before Cephalus and Socrates be admitted as a paradigm instance in which we are not obliged to tell the truth (telling the truth to a madman), we may consider more hopefully the possibility of defending the therapist who deceives a dying patient about her condition, on palliative grounds. Cases of these sorts may still be substantially different. But the genius of moral dispute (and of both legal and therapeutic disputes) lies precisely in the ability of interested parties to arrange sequences of resembling, but increasingly different, cases which move convincingly toward the inclusion of the case in question. Debate and disagreement are still quite possible (how could it be otherwise?), but the procedures involved are clearly not arbitrary, nor, conceding the limitations of a rule-formulated morality, need we hold the testing of moral judgments to be without any rigor at all.

The point of these illustrations, in the present context, is that it is common, even among narrowly moral issues, to advise against a seemingly well-established rule of conduct. The apparent breach of such well-worn rules as "Thou shalt not kill," "One ought to tell the truth," "Debts must be paid," "Promises ought to be kept" is not in itself adequate evidence that the actions involved are to be censured. They may or may not prove to be censurable; the point is that the issue is debatable. But if this is so among full-fledged moral disputes, it is *a fortiori* true of possible disputes between a therapist's obligation to promote his patient's health and other obligations recognized in the community at large.

We may express this somewhat differently. Moral rules tend (though this is admittedly not necessary) to be formulated as tautologies: "One ought not kill," for instance, is to be understood as roughly equivalent to "It is morally wrong to take another's life in a way that is morally reprehensible." In short, dispute rarely centers on the presumed rules of conduct; if they are genuine tautologies, it cannot do so. The serious questions always involve identifying cases that may be appropriately subsumed under this or that rule, and statements specifying these are always contingent and debatable. One may also observe that the tautological translation of the familiar rule about murder makes it clear that the *justifiable* taking of another's life is neither ruled out nor specified by the rule itself.

A dispute between therapeutic and moral values, then, cannot possibly be resolved by the presentation (somewhat in the manner of a traffic ticket) of a standard moral rule. Therapeutic practice may, indeed, be morally censurable and, in fact, censurable on precisely the grounds brought to our attention by the rule cited. But the procedure of recalling a rule must count as an ellipsis for the citing of standard cases of acceptable conduct to which the case in question may be reasonably assimilated. Moral rules are inoperative and, indeed, unintelligible, apart from a context of traditional practice; the substantive debates between therapeutic and moral values must be debates about the details of such practice rather than about the rules themselves. And this is important because *therapeutic practice is itself a recognizable part of the traditional practices of a community.*

In short, if disputes between therapeutic and moral values are to be resolved by consulting acceptable and admissible conduct (not merely conduct that may actually be found in a society, but conduct that will be viewed as justified conduct), it cannot possibly be denied that, *sometimes* at least, the community at large is prepared to accept as morally defensible, both in and out of a professional therapeutic situation, lying to save a life and other similar breaches of accepted moral rules. That is to say, the argument depends on what the facts are about our actual moral tradition. One starts with indubitable instances and gradually approaches the case in question. For instance, I may remind you that we would surely view it as morally acceptable conduct to mislead a child about the truth of some intimate tragedy if we believed that discovery at that moment would have very serious and harmful effects on the child; we would surely justify lying to the enemy in order to save one's country. We thereby force ourselves to recognize that apparent exceptions to rules are neither simply exceptions nor more doubtful than clear instances that fall under the rules. And once we do recognize this, it becomes possible to turn back to the detailed questions of therapeutic practice with a more hopeful eye.

It is plain, I think, that no substantive moral issues are in the least distorted or influenced by the kind of reflections offered here. This is as it should be. I do not wish to deny that moral disputes are responsibly resolved and that, here and there, men appear with a genuine gift for making the required distinctions. But we have deliberately avoided the substantive problems in order to provide an accurate description of their logical features. The truth is that our ability to resolve moral puzzles is itself *presupposed* by our inquiry and, consequently, not affected by it.

The problem we have been examining arises quite spontaneously for professional psychotherapists (counterpart versions arise for all of us). The therapist, in doubting the morality of what he is doing, is not so much weighing the relevant evidence for or against his decisions as asking himself a philosophical question about the possibility of defending therapy at all, when it comes into conflict with standard moral obligations. He tends to paralyze his critical faculties, idling over the theoretical relations between therapy and morality. And, therefore, to explain to him the sense in which what he does is theoretically defensible in moral terms is to throw him into gear once again, so that he may take up his day-to-day problems. In this respect, philosophical inquiry does have its practical contribution to make—not, however, by solving the questions of professional decision, but by undoing our puzzlement about how the professional enterprise is, under the circumstances, possible at all.

Still, these moral issues, important as they are, are addressed not so much to the technical aspects of psychotherapy as to the bearing of these on considerations of acceptable conduct in the community at large. It turns out that, in spite of their being personally and socially pressing, they are rather less useful in providing a philosophical picture of therapeutic judgments than a generous scanning of the range of value judgments would be. We shall, therefore, turn rather abruptly to this more promising inquiry—which will, in fact, facilitate certain final remarks about problems of conduct.

NOTES

[1]Heinz Hartmann, *Psychoanalysis and Moral Values* (New York, 1960), pp. 20–21.

[2]Cf. for example, Sigmund Freud, "A Disturbance of Memory on the Acropolis" (1936), in *Collected Papers,* Vol. V, edited by James Strachey (London, 1950). Nevertheless, in the therapeutic setting, Freud was inclined to express himself in quite sanguine terms; cf. for example, "The Future Prospects of Psychoanalytic Theory" (1910), in *Collected Papers,* Vol. II, edited Joan Rivière (London, 1950); also Gregory Zilboorg, *Mind, Medicine, and Man* (New York, 1943), p. 167.

[3]Hartmann, *op. cit.*, pp. 20–21. Cf. also, Jules H. Masserman (ed.), *Psychoanalysis and Human Values* (New York and London, 1960).

[4]Hartmann, *op. cit.*, p. 51. I add at once a counter-statement that shows how profoundly divergent are the views of psychiatrists on this issue. Karl Menninger, in his *Theory of Psychoanalytic Technique* (New York, 1958), offers the following extraordinary statement: "We cannot ignore the fact that what the psychoanalyst believes, what he lives for, what he loves, what he considers to be the purpose of life and the joy of life, what he considers to be good and what he considers to be evil, become known to the patient and influence him enormously not as 'suggestion' but as inspiration. A degree of identification with the analyst is inevitable, although not necessarily permanent. However, for that longer or shorter post-analytic period during which identification with the analyst is operative, the patient shows forth the analyst—or at least some aspects of him—to the world. No matter how skillful the analyst in certain technical maneuvers, his ultimate product, like Galatea, will reflect not only his handicraft but his character," p. 91. Cf. also, J. C. Flugel, *Man, Morals and Society. A Psychoanalytical Study* (New York, 1945), pp. 28–29.

[5]Philip Rieff, *Freud: The Mind of the Moralist* (New York, 1959), p. 55.

[6]Cf. Martin Birnbach, *Neo-Freudian Social Philosophy* (Stanford, 1961).

[7]Erich Fromm, *Man for Himself* (New York, 1947).

[8]Ludwig Binswanger, "The Existential Analysis School of Thought" (translated by Ernest Angel), in Rollo May *et al.* (eds.), *Existence* (New York, 1958), p. 205.

[9]*Ibid.*, p. 208.

[10]Charlotte Buhler, *Values in Psychotherapy* (New York, 1962), p. ix.

[11]P. H. Nowell-Smith, "Freewill and Moral Responsibility," *Mind,* Vol. LVII (1948), 45–61.

[12]Cf. Hans H. Strupp, "Patient-Doctor Relationships: Psychotherapist in the Therapeutic Process," in Arthur J. Bachrach (ed.), *Experimental Foundations of Clinical Psychology* (New York, 1962).

[13]Cf. for example, Sigmund Freud, "Some Elementary Lessons in Psycho-analysis" (1938), in *Collected Papers,* Vol. V, *op. cit.*

[14]Cf. Leo Stone, *The Psychoanalytic Situation* (New York, 1961), pp. 12–28, especially p. 16, 21–22.

[15]Cf. for example, Sigmund Freud, "Analysis Terminable and Interminable," in *Collected Papers,* Vol. V, *op. cit.*

[16]Hartmann, *op. cit.*, pp. 55–56.

[17]Cf. Marie Jahoda, *Current Concepts of Positive Mental Health* (New York, 1958).

[18]Thomas Szasz, *The Myth of Mental Illness* (New York, 1961), p. 297.

[19]*Ibid.*, pp. 7–8.

[20]*Ibid.*, pp. 292–293.

[21]Jahoda, *op. cit.*, p. 15.

[22]*Ibid.*, p. 14.

[23]*Ibid.*, p. 21.

[24]*Ibid.*, Ch. III. Cf. also, Barbara Wootton, *Social Science and Social Pathology* (New York, 1959), pp. 211–214.

[25]Cf. Jonathan Harrison, "Utilitarianism, Universalization, and Our Duty to be Just," *Proceedings of the Aristotelian Society,* Vol. LIII (1952–1953), 105–134. The point at stake serves also to challenge the interesting and influential position of John Rawls, "Two Concepts of Rules," *Philosophical Review,* Vol. LXIV (1955), 3–22, though Rawls, in a closing footnote (32), tends to restrict his thesis to "legal-like arguments" rather than to moral arguments. Also, his alleged rule-utilitarianism cannot be satisfactorily contrasted with so-called act-utilitarianism, because he himself frankly admits that the required rules "cannot be fully stated." Cf. also, W. D. Ross, *The Right and the Good* (Oxford, 1930).

[26]Socrates, *Republic,* Bk. I (translated by F. M. Cornford) in *The Republic of Plato* (London, 1941).

[27]Cf. Joseph Margolis, " 'Lying is Wrong' and 'Lying is not Always Wrong,' " *Philosophy and Phenomenological Research,* Vol. XXIII (1963), 414–418.

[28]The point here is somewhat related to, though significantly different from, that of H. L. A. Hart, "The Ascription of Rights and Responsibilities," in Antony Flew (ed.), *Logic and Language,* First Series (Oxford, 1951). Hart speaks of the "defeasibility" of legal charges, pointing to standard types of defense against given charges—in which the case in question is construed as an admissible exception, though we cannot, in law, antecedently specify all admissible exceptions. In the moral situation, we are called upon not only to defeat but also to defend a particular way of construing an action.

RECOMMENDED READING

The following is a list of articles and books that discuss topics covered in this section. There are similar lists at the end of each section. Many entries on these lists demand a greater level of philosophical sophistication than the readings reprinted in this book, which serve as preparation for such work. These are not intended to be comprehensive bibliographies on the subjects in question.

Bakan, D. (1969). *On method.* San Francisco: Jossey-Bass.

Block, N. (Ed.). (1980). *Readings in philosophical psychology* (Vol. 1). Cambridge, MA: Harvard University Press.

Brown, S. C. (Ed.). (1979). *Philosophical disputes in the social sciences.* Highland, NJ: Humanities Press.

Drane, J. F. (1982). Ethics and psychotherapy: A philosophical perspective. In M. Rosenbaum (Ed.), *Ethics and values in psychotherapy* (pp. 15–50). New York: Free Press.

Eackes, J. N. (1925). *Problems of philosophy and psychology.* Chicago: Nelson-Hall.

Feigl, H. (1967). *The "mental" and the "physical."* Minneapolis: University of Minnesota Press.

Harre, R. (1981). The philosophical basis of psychiatric ethics. In S. Bloch & P. Chodoff, (Eds.), *Psychiatric ethics.* London: Oxford University Press.

Harre, R., Manicas, P., Margolis, J., & Secord, P. F. (1986). *Psychology: Designing the discipline.* Oxford, England: Basil Blackwell.

Kimble, G. (1989). Psychology from the standpoint of a generalist. *American Psychologist, 44,* 491–499.

Koch, S. (1981). The nature and limits of psychological knowledge: Lessons of a century qua "science." *American Psychologist, 36,* 257–269.

Lessnoff, M. (1974). *The structure of social science: A philosophical introduction.* London: Allen & Unwin.

London, P. (1964). *The modes and morals of psychotherapy.* New York: Holt, Rinehart & Winston.

Margolis, J. (1984). *Philosophy of psychology.* Englewood Cliffs, NJ: Prentice-Hall.

Margolis, J. (1987). *Science without unity: Reconciling the natural and human sciences.* Oxford, England: Basil Blackwell.

Natanson, M. (Ed.). (1963). *Philosophy of the social sciences: A reader.* New York: Random House.

O'Donohue, W. (1989). The (even) bolder model: The clinical psychologist as a metaphysician-scientist-practitioner. *American Psychologist, 44,* 1460–1468.

Polanyi, M. (1962). *Personal knowledge: Towards a post-critical philosophy.* Chicago: University of Chicago Press.

Robinson, D. (1985). *Philosophy of psychology.* New York: Columbia University Press.

Taylor, C. (1971). Interpretation and the sciences of man. *Review of Metaphysics, 25,* 3–51.

Taylor, C. (1985). *Philosophy and the human sciences: Philosophical papers.* Cambridge, England: Cambridge University Press.

Valentine, E. R. (1982). *Conceptual issues in psychology.* London: Allen & Unwin.

II

PHILOSOPHICAL ISSUES OF THE BEHAVIORAL AND COGNITIVE–BEHAVIORAL APPROACHES

INTRODUCTION: PHILOSOPHICAL PROBLEMS OF THE BEHAVIORAL AND COGNITIVE–BEHAVIORAL APPROACHES

RONALD B. MILLER

The tremendous growth in the field of clinical psychology after World War II coincided with the rise to prominence of the behavioral approaches to clinical psychology. Although it is difficult to know the direction of causality, it seems reasonable to assume that the development of assessment and treatment strategies that relied solely on the knowledge base of psychology would boost its standing among the mental health professions. No longer was clinical psychology parasitic on psychiatry or social work for either its theoretical perspective or clinical techniques. Viewing clinical disorders as learned behaviors that could be unlearned via the use of classical, operant, or cognitive learning principles (Bandura, 1969) was an empowering perspective for clinical psychologists to take. Clinical assessment became a process of the functional analysis of specific behaviors that composed the clinical picture, and treatment became specifically designed behavior therapy or modification programs based on a standard set of techniques (systematic desensitization, reinforced practice, time-out, aversive conditioning, shaping desirable alternative responses, token economies, etc.). Clinical progress depended on the further development of research in applied behavioral analysis. Given the tremendous impact that behavior therapy and modification had on the field, the impact of methodological and radical behaviorism on the practice of psychology merits serious attention.

First, it should be noted that these are the clinical approaches most identified with the philosophical outlook of general experimental psychology. In fact, a past president of the Association for the Advancement of Behavior Therapy, Wilson (1982), suggested that the primary commonality that clinicians of this approach share is a commitment, not to a particular substantive learning theory but to the methodology of quantitative, controlled research. Wilson's view was that behavior therapists are committed to practice guided, whenever possible, by a scientific conception of human beings and scientific research. This is the view that is frequently identified as methodological behaviorism (Day, 1976).

Methodological behaviorism is the view that psychology, in order to be a science, must link all of its concepts and hypotheses to some aspect of observable behavior. This is essentially the view espoused by Feigl and the neopositivists. Psychologists must limit their knowledge claims to topics that are amenable to observation by independent observers. Key constructs must be operationalized (i.e., a means of measurement must be specified), and procedures must be replicable. *Operationism* (Stevens, 1939) in psychology is equivalent to methodological behaviorism.

This is to be distinguished from what has been called radical behaviorism. Radical behaviorism is the creation of B. F. Skinner (1938, 1953, 1957, 1974), who many consider to be the most influential American psychologist of the 20th century. Skinner's position, summarized in chapter 6, is that mentalistic terms are superfluous to a scientific account of human behavior and vitiate the usefulness of theories of psychotherapy, as well as cognitive and humanistic psychology. He saw no value in assigning any causal efficacy to mental states whatsoever, even when such references are linked to observable behaviors. He believed that mental events are epiphenomena (having no causal impact on behavior) and that human behavior can be predicted and controlled by theories of behavior that avoid all such explanations.

For Skinner, mentalistic terms such as choosing, deciding, thinking, perceiving, wishing, feeling, wanting, and so on, are all either short-hand terms for complex behavior–environment interactions or labels for physiological processes that go on under the skin. Psychology is an extension of biology, pure and simple. It is assumed that all psychological phenomena are determined and can be explained via the laws of behavior.

It is a great irony of 20th-century psychology that the primary message of America's leading scientific psychologist is a philosophical one. In *About Behaviorism*, Skinner (1974) introduced his book as a work in the philosophy of behaviorism, but his readers will recognize little difference between it and large portions of his earlier classic textbook, *Science and Human Behavior* (Skinner, 1953). Skinner denied that his position is a metaphysical one of reductive materialism: He never addressed the question of whether mental events are distinct from physical ones, only that a scientific psychology must not address mental events and need not as long as it understands the contingencies of reinforcement. This seems to be excessive hair-splitting, for the net effect is to banish mental events from any systematic attempt to explain behavior unless they are reworked as behavioral or physiological variables. For Skinner, if the mental does exist distinct from the physical, it is of little interest because it is just not "where the action is," so to speak.

It may be fairer to categorize Skinner's radical behaviorism with philosophical behaviorism (Ryle, 1949; Wittgenstein, 1958). Day notes in chapter 8 that Skinner's arguments in favor of radical behaviorism are quite similar to the arguments used in the ordinary language approach to analytical philosophy. Skinner (see chapter 6) is arguing that what psychologists *mean* by mentalistic terms is really something about behavior, and so the mental as a separate realm of reality is unnecessary. Particularly if psychologists are trying to *explain* behavior, that is, give a *causal explanation* of behavior, Skinner believes that psychology must adhere to the conceptual framework of natural science and must become fully integrated with biology.

This leads to the question of the philosophy of science or epistemology of behaviorism. Skinner is quite clear that, for him, scientific knowledge is a knowledge that permits the prediction and control of a variable. Other forms of understanding may exist (e.g., poetic, aesthetic, empathic), but they are not scientific understanding and consequently form no part of the science of human behavior. He is just not interested in other kinds of knowledge. This is equally true of the methodological behaviorists, who share with Skinner a veneration of scientific rigor, although methodological behaviorists are more tolerant of nonexperimental quantitative (correlational) research than the Skinnerians.

In chapter 7, Mahoney takes issue with Skinner's claim that the scientific viewpoint requires that psychology subscribe to radical behaviorism. Defending the cognitive revolution in clinical psychology, Mahoney argues that radical behaviorism is wedded to an outmoded logical positivist philosophy of science and is therefore losing its grip on the new generation of behavioral practitioners. It is wedded to a naive commonsense realism in which objective reality and objective knowledge are totally separated from subjective experience. Because this is more "objectivist" than either modern physics or philosophy of science have found defensible, Mahoney labels radical behaviorism *scientistic* rather than *scientific.* He finds methodological behaviorism preferable and much less dogmatic.

Day (see chapter 8) offers a strong defense of radical behaviorism as a philosophical viewpoint and basis for a scientific psychology. He notes the differences between methodological behaviorism and radical behaviorism cited earlier and argues that although methodological behaviorism is strongly wedded to a logical positivist philosophy of science, radical behaviorism is not. He notes that Skinner was willing to acknowledge phenomenological experience as a covert behavior under the control of environmental variables like any other behavior. In Day's writing, the power of radical behaviorism to give a systematic account of human life without recourse to mentalistic concepts is made impressively clear. Behaviorism is an alternative language or conceptual system that permits the behaviorist to say what is really meant and thus avoid the traps set by ordinary talk about the mind. Thus, the integration of psychology with the natural sciences, particularly biology, will be made possible.

It is this very commitment to the objective, scientific viewpoint that is critiqued from a hermeneutical perspective by Woolfolk and Richardson in chapter 9. They argue that behavior therapy typifies exactly what Habermas (1971) and Gadamer (1976) find most objectionable in modern culture (modernity), namely, a preference for technological solutions, overemphasis and dependence on rationality, and amoral theorizing. The modern view holds that values are not the business of science: They are to be left up to each individual to decide. In this way, behavioral ideology is consistent with the ideology of individualism that was so central to the development of liberal Western democracies, and unable to effectively confront the negative consequences for human beings of this form of social organization (e.g., loss of community, meaning and purpose in life).

Kitchener, in chapter 10, adds to this discussion of the moral implications of behavior therapy the perspective of the analytic philosopher. He agrees that the basic moral position endorsed by the behavior therapists is, after Skinner, one of ethical relativism, because "good" is defined as "reinforcing" and what is reinforcing varies with, or is relative to, each individual. On the other hand, in practice, behavior modifiers and therapists must make daily decisions to change behaviors that are currently reinforcing to the client (or at least to someone). To escape this unfortunate consequence of relativism, Skinner was forced to issue a second definition of the "good" as that which promotes survival of the species or culture. Kitchener argues that this evolutionary ethic is of little use because it leads to contradictory advice in actual practice. One still has to decide what kind of society he or she thinks *ought* to survive. Kitchener notes that in practice, despite what the theory has to say about ethical principles, behavior therapists tend to adopt nonrelativist positions. These are regrettably poorly thought out and inconsistent, as one would expect under the circumstances. Kitchener suggests that behavior therapy should abandon ethical relativism and related forms of ethical naturalism (which view ethical principles as laws of nature to be discovered by psychological or social science research) and instead adopt the view that moral principles do govern the practice of therapy and that these principles are governed by human rationality (the "good reasons" approach to ethics).

Krasner (Krasner & Ullman, 1965) was one of the pioneers in behavior modification applications in clinical settings. In chapter 11, Houts and Krasner reply directly to Kitchener's (see chapter 10) analysis by questioning the fact–value dichotomy and suggesting that a naturalistic ethic may be preferable to a rationalistic ethic. Their position is that the basis of ethical beliefs is open to question and that a scientific approach at least has the potential for arriving at an objective view of desirable ends for therapy. They do not accept Kitchener's position that a naturalistic ethic is necessarily relativistic.

As noted in chapter 1, behavioral therapies authorize the therapist to be directive and in control of the therapy process. As such, these therapies have a greater *potential* for permitting far-reaching exploitation of patients by their therapists. (It is, of course, possible for poorly trained clinicians of any theoretical persuasion to seek to manipulate their clients' behavior.) Behavior therapists seek to control their clients' behavior in order to increase adaptive behavior and decrease inappropriate or maladaptive behavior. Halleck (1971) noted how easily this can become self-serving and bolster the social–political status quo. At the same time, behavioral approaches have had a very salutary effect on dispossessed mental patients and on mentally retarded patients who may have been written off as untreatable but who can be motivated using behavioral methods. The behavioral and cognitive–behavioral approaches, because of their ambiguous positions about ethical values, are likely to be used to support the prevailing values of the therapist's culture. In liberal societies, they will be used for liberal ends and in repressive societies for repressive ends. Behavioral theory is of little help in resolving ethical dilemmas, and so the behavioral or cognitive–behavioral clinician must fall back on her or his own personal moral principles as a human being.

REFERENCES

Bandura, A. (1969). *Principles of behavior modification.* New York: Holt, Rinehart & Winston.

Day, W. (1976). Contemporary behaviorism and the concept of intention. In J. Cole (Ed.), *Conceptual foundations of psychology: Nebraska Symposium on Motivation* (pp. 65–131). Lincoln: University of Nebraska Press.

Halleck, S. (1971). *Politics of therapy.* New York: Science House.

Krasner, L., & Ullman, L. P. (Eds.). (1965). *Research in behavior modification.* New York: Holt, Rinehart & Winston.

Ryle, G. (1949). *The concept of mind.* London: Hutchinson's University Library.

Skinner, B. F. (1938). *The behavior of organisms.* New York: Appleton-Century-Crofts.

Skinner, B. F. (1953). *Science and human behavior.* New York: Macmillan.

Skinner, B. F. (1957). *Verbal behavior.* New York: Appleton-Century-Crofts.

Skinner, B. F. (1974). *About behaviorism.* New York: Random House.

Stevens, S. S. (1939). Operationism and logical positivism. *Psychological Bulletin, 36,* 221–263.

Wilson, G. T. (1982). Psychotherapy process and procedure: The behavioral mandate. *Behavior Therapy, 13,* 291–312.

6

WHATEVER HAPPENED TO PSYCHOLOGY AS THE SCIENCE OF BEHAVIOR?

B. F. SKINNER

There can scarcely be anything more familiar than human behavior. We are always in the presence of at least one behaving person. Nor can there be anything more important, whether it is our own behavior or that of those whom we see every day or who are responsible for what is happening in the world at large. Nevertheless it is certainly not the thing we understand best. Granted that it is possibly the most difficult subject ever submitted to scientific analysis, it is still puzzling that so little has been done with the instruments and methods that have been so productive in the other sciences. Perhaps what is wrong is that behavior has seldom been thought of as a subject matter in its own right, but rather has been viewed as the mere expression or symptom of more important happenings inside the behaving person.

The Homeric Greeks thought they knew the very organs. The *thumos,* or heart, was one of them. It was a vital organ (when it stopped, the person died), but for the Greeks it was also the seat of such things as hunger, joy, fear, will, and thought. To be undecided about something, for example, was to have a divided *thumos.* We may smile at that, but we do much the same thing ourselves. Here are some of the definitions of the word *heart* in *Webster's Third New International Dictionary* (1981): *the whole personality* ("deep in one's heart"), *intelligence* ("knowing something by heart"), *character* ("look into the heart of a person"), *compassion* ("have a heart"), *mood* ("a heavy heart"), *opinion* ("a change of heart"), *affection* ("a broken heart"), *goodwill* ("with all my heart"), *courage* ("a stout heart"), and *taste* ("a man after one's own heart"). Of course, we do not mean the real heart, but the Greeks may not have meant that either. The point is that, like them, we appeal to something inside a person to explain what that person does.

Reprinted from the *American Psychologist, 42,* 780–786. (1987).
The author thanks Margaret E. Vaughan and Julie S. Vargas for much needed help in the preparation of this article.

When Galen described human anatomy in greater detail, especially the nerves connecting the brain with sense organs and muscles, it was clear that the Greeks had got the wrong organ. They should have said brain. It was Descartes who showed how the brain and nerves could explain the kind of behavior that was later called reflex. Although the notion of a stimulus suggested an external cause, the search for internal causes did not stop. During the 19th and early 20th centuries, reflexes were studied by physiologists. Sherrington's (1906) book was called *The Integrative Action of the Nervous System,* and Pavlov's (1927) book had the subtitle *The Physiological Activity of the Cerebral Cortex.*

It was hard to find plausible organs for many kinds of behavior, of course, and Plato and others gave up the attempt. Speculation could then be freer. Although we think we see the object we are looking at, for example, it was said that we must see only an internal copy of it, because we can still see it with our eyes closed and even recall it from memory later on. Before we act, moreover, we can merely think of acting; we can have intentions, expectations, or ideas and do nothing more about them. Somewhere inside the body, in short, there seemed to be another person made of a different kind of stuff. For 2,500 years philosophers and psychologists have discussed the nature of that stuff, but for our present purposes we may accept the famous dismissal that appeared in *Punch* in 1855:

What is Matter?—Never mind.
What is Mind?—No matter (quoted in Bartlett, 1968, p. 810A).

Mind or matter, it was something *inside* a person that determined what that person did.

EARLY BEHAVIORISM

The theory of evolution raised a different question about those internal causes. Nonhuman animals had reflexes and organs, but did they have minds? Darwin, committed to the continuity of species, said yes, and he and his contemporaries could cite examples that seemed to prove him right. It was Lloyd Morgan who objected that the examples could be explained in other ways and Watson who took the inevitable next step and contended that the same thing could be said of human animals. An early form of behaviorism was born.

The predilection for internal causes survived, however. Probably as a reaction to the heavily mentalistic psychology of the time, a central issue in early behaviorism was the existence of consciousness. Experiments were designed to show that animals either could or could not do everything traditionally attributed to feelings and states of mind. If they could not, something like a mental life would have to be recognized. Perhaps because Watson first studied instincts, he replaced feelings and states of mind with habits. He may have meant nothing more than the behavior said to show the presence of instincts and habits, but he turned later to conditioned reflexes, and his associate, Lashley, went still further into the nervous system. Later, Tolman restored purpose to the organism and still later installed cognitive maps and hypotheses. Clark Hull built an elaborate system of internal processes that, as in "afferent neural interaction," for example, became increasingly physiological. In short, 3,000 years after the Homeric Greeks, mentalistic and behavioristic psychologists alike were still looking inside the organism for explanations of its behavior. To say that the habit of doing so must have been deeply ingrained would be to give another example.

RADICAL BEHAVIORISM

Behavior seems to have been first accepted as a subject matter in its own right when organisms were studied that were too small, and their behavior too simple, to suggest internal initiating processes. H. S. Jennings's (1906) *The Behavior of the Lower Organisms* was the great classic, of course, but more to the point were the work and theories of Jacques Loeb. Loeb's formulation of tropisms and his emphasis on "forced movement" dispensed with internal explanations. The thing to be studied was the behavior of the "organism as a whole" (Loeb, 1916). (For an excellent account of Loeb's contributions, see Pauly [1987].) And that could be said of larger organisms, as well.

Equally important were new developments in the philosophy of science. Concepts began to be more carefully defined in terms of the operations from which they were inferred. Ernst Mach, especially with his *Science of Mechanics* (Mach, 1915), was an important figure. Later, P. W. Bridgman (1927) took a similar line in his *Logic of Modern Physics.* In *Philosophy* (Russell, 1927), a book said to have been written as a potboiler, Bertrand Russell anticipated the logical positivists by several years and "behavioristically considered" a number of psychological processes. (For a full discussion of behaviorism and logical positivism, see Smith [1986].) My thesis, "The Concept of the Reflex in the Description of Behavior" (Skinner, 1931), was in that tradition. A reflex, I argued, was not something that happened inside the organism; it was a law of behavior. All we actually observed was that a response was a function of a stimulus. It could also be a function of variables in the fields of conditioning, motivation, and emotion, but they too were outside the organism. I called them "third variables," but Tolman later put them back inside and called them "intervening."

It was easy to make my case because reflexes, conditioned or unconditioned, were only a small part of the behavior of more complex organisms. The research I was doing at the time, however, had a broader scope: The environment not only triggered behavior, it selected it. Consequences seemed, indeed, to be more important than antecedents. Their role had, of course, long been recognized—for example, as reward or punishment. It was Thorndike who first studied their effects experimentally. Given several possible ways of solving a problem, a cat eventually took the successful one when incorrect ways, or "errors," dropped out.

I studied the same process in a different way. Prompted by Pavlov's emphasis on the control of conditions, I made sure that all Thorndike's "errors" were eliminated before a successful response could be made. A single "reinforcing" consequence was then enough; the response was immediately and rapidly repeated. I called the process operant conditioning. Thorndike had attributed his effect to feelings of satisfaction and annoyance, which were inside the organism, of course, but I traced the strengthening effect of an operant reinforcer to its survival value in the natural selection of the species.

My first arrangement of setting, response, and consequence was quite simple, but I reported the effects of more complex "contingencies of reinforcement" in *The Behavior of Organisms* (Skinner, 1938). Still more elaborate ones have been studied for more than 50 years in laboratories throughout the world. Most of the work has been done with nonhuman animals in order to cover a wider range of conditions than would be feasible with human subjects and to avoid "verbal contamination."

The contamination has also been studied, however. Verbal behavior differs from nonverbal in certain features of the contingencies of reinforcement. The verbal stimuli we call advice, rules, or laws describe or allude to contingencies of reinforcement. People who have been advised or who follow rules and obey laws behave for either of two very different reasons: Their behavior has been directly reinforced by its consequences, or they are responding to descriptions of contingencies. How and why they respond to descriptions must also be explained by analyzing verbal contingencies of reinforcement.

A better understanding of verbal contingencies has also brought two important fields of psychology within range of an operant analysis. One is self-observation. The analysis neither "ignores consciousness" nor brings it back into a behavioral science; it simply analyzes the way in which verbal contingencies of reinforcement bring *private* events into control of the behavior called introspecting. Only when we are asked about what we have done, are doing, or are about to do, and why, have we any reason to observe or recall our behavior or its controlling variables. All behavior, human and nonhuman, is unconscious; it becomes "conscious" when verbal environments provide the contingencies necessary for self-observation. (It is the person, of course, who is "conscious" or "unconscious," not the behavior.) Other verbal contingencies generate the behavior called self-management or thinking, in which problems are solved by manipulating either contingencies (as in practical problem solving) or rules (as in "reasoning").

Much of this is at the moment only an interpretation, but that is common scientific practice. Astronomers interpret the waves and particles reaching Earth from outer space by using what has been learned under controllable conditions in the laboratory—for example, in high energy physics. In a similar way we use what has been learned from an experimental analysis to explain behavior that cannot, at the moment at least, be brought under experimental control, such as covert behavior or behavior observed casually in daily life.

The traditional preoccupation with internal explanatory agents broke behavior into fragments. Psychophysicists, for example, study the effects of stimuli, but only up to the point at which they are supposedly received by an inner agent. Psycholinguists record changes in the number of words or the length of sentences a child speaks over a period of time, but usually with no record of what happened when the child heard similar words or sentences or of what consequences followed when they spoke them. Psychologists study verbal learning by asking their subjects to memorize and recall nonsense syllables, but the word *nonsense* makes it clear that they are not interested in all of the variables controlling the behavior. Somehow the internal entity or process acts as a starting or stopping place. A bit of sensing is studied by one psychologist, a bit of behaving by another, and a bit of changing by still another. The experimental analysis of behavior puts Humpty Dumpty together again by studying relatively complete episodes, each with a history of reinforcement, a current setting, a response, and a reinforcing consequence.

Many of the facts, and even some of the principles, that psychologists have discovered when they may have thought they were discovering something else are useful. We can accept, for example, what psychophysicists tell us about responses to stimuli without agreeing that they show a mathematical relation between mental and physical worlds. We can accept many of the facts reported by cognitive psychologists without believing that their subjects were processing information or storing representations or rules. We can accept what happens when subjects respond to descriptions of contingencies of reinforcement without believing that they are "subjectively evaluating expected utilities."

The relation between analysis of behavior as such and physiology is no problem. Each of these sciences has instruments and methods appropriate to part of a behavioral episode. There are inevitable gaps in a behavioral account. Stimulus and response are separated in time and space, for example, and so are a reinforcement on one day and stronger behavior on the next. The gaps can be filled only with the instruments and methods of physiology. They cannot be filled by introspection, because there are no sensory nerves going to the right parts of the brain.

For more than half a century the experimental analysis of behavior as a function of environmental variables and the use of that analysis in the interpretation and modification of behavior in the world at large have reached into every field of traditional psychology. Yet they have not *become* psychology, and the question is, Why not? Perhaps answers can be found in looking at three formidable obstacles that have stood in the path of an experimental analysis of behavior.

OBSTACLE 1: HUMANISTIC PSYCHOLOGY

Many people find the implications of a behavioral analysis disturbing. The traditional direction of action of organism and environment seems to be reversed. Instead of saying that the organism sees, attends to, perceives, "processes," or otherwise acts upon stimuli, an operant analysis holds that stimuli acquire control of behavior through the part they play in contingencies of reinforcement. Instead of saying that an organism stores copies of the contingencies to which it is exposed and later retrieves and responds to them again, it says that the organism is changed by the contingencies and later responds as a changed organism, the contingencies having passed into history. The environment takes over the control formerly assigned to an internal, originating agent.

Some long-admired features of human behavior are then threatened. Following the lead of evolutionary theory, an operant analysis replaces creation with variation and selection. There is no longer any need for a creative mind or plan, or for purpose or goal direction. Just as we say that species-specific behavior did not evolve *in order that* a species could adapt to the environment but rather evolved *when* it adapted, so we say that operant behavior is not strengthened by reinforcement *in order that* the individual can adjust to the environment but is strengthened *when* the individual adjusts (where "adapt" and "adjust" mean "behave effectively with respect to").

The disenthronement of a creator seems to threaten personal freedom (Can we be free if the environment is in control?) and personal worth (Can we take credit for our achievements if they are nothing more than the effects of circumstances?). It also seems to threaten ethical, religious, and governmental systems that hold people responsible for their conduct. Who or what is responsible if unethical, immoral, or illegal behavior is due to heredity or personal history? Humanistic psychologists have attacked behavioral science along these lines. Like creationists in their attack on secular humanists (with the humanists on the other side), they often challenge the content or selection of textbooks, the appointment of teachers and administrators, the design of curricula, and the allocation of funds.

OBSTACLE 2: PSYCHOTHERAPY

Certain exigencies of the helping professions are another obstacle in the path of a scientific analysis of behavior. Psychotherapists must talk with their clients and, with rare exceptions, do so in everyday English, which is heavy laden with references to internal causes—"I ate because I was *hungry*," "I could do it because I *knew* how to do it," and so on. All fields of science tend to have two languages, of course. Scientists speak one with casual acquaintances and the other with colleagues. In a relatively young science, such as psychology, the use of the vernacular may be challenged. How often have behaviorists heard, "You just said 'It crossed my mind!' I thought there wasn't supposed to be any mind." It has been a long time since anyone challenged a physicist who said, "That desk is made of solid oak," by protesting, "But I thought you said that matter was mostly empty space."

The two languages of psychology raise a special problem. What we feel when we are hungry or when we know how to do something are states of our bodies. We do not have very good ways of observing them, and those who teach us to observe them usually have no way at all. We were taught to say "I'm hungry," for example, by persons who knew perhaps only that we had not eaten for some time ("You missed your lunch; you must be *hungry*") or had observed something about our behavior ("You are eating ravenously. You must be *hungry*"). Similarly, we were taught to say "I know" by persons who had perhaps only seen us doing something ("Oh, you *know* how to do that!") or had told us how to do something and then said "Now you *know.*" The trouble is that private states are almost always poorly correlated with the public evidence.

References to private events are, nevertheless, often accurate enough to be useful. If we are preparing a meal for a friend, we are not likely to ask, "How long has it been since you last ate?" or "Will you probably eat a great deal?" We simply ask, "How *hungry* are you?" If a friend is driving us to an appointment, we are not likely to ask, "Have you driven there before?" or "Has anyone told you where it is?" Instead we ask, "Do you *know* where it is?" Being hungry and knowing where something is are states of the body resulting from personal histories, and what is said about them may be the only available evidence of those histories. Nevertheless, how much a person eats does depend upon a history of deprivation, not upon how a deprived body feels, and whether a person reaches a given destination does depend upon whether he or she has driven there before or has been told how to get there, not upon introspective evidence of the effects.

Psychotherapists must ask people what has happened to them and how they feel because the confidential relationship of therapist and client prevents direct inquiry. (It is sometimes argued that what a person remembers may be more important than what actually happened, but that is true only if something else has happened, of which it would also be better to have independent evidence.) But although the use of reports of feelings and states of mind can be justified on practical grounds, there is no justification for their use in theory making. The temptation, however, is great. Psychoanalysts, for example, specialize in feelings. Instead of investigating the early lives of their patients or watching them with their families, friends, or business associates, they ask them what has happened and how they feel about it. It is not surprising that they should then construct theories in terms of memories, feelings, and states of mind or that they should say that an analysis of behavior in terms of environmental events lacks "depth."

OBSTACLE 3: COGNITIVE PSYCHOLOGY

A curve showing the appearance of the word *cognitive* in the psychological literature would be interesting. A first rise could probably be seen around 1960; the subsequent acceleration would be exponential. Is there any field of psychology today in which something does not seem to be gained by adding that charming adjective to the occasional noun? The popularity may not be hard to explain. When we became psychologists, we learned new ways of talking about human behavior. If they were "behavioristic," they were not very much like the old ways. The old terms were taboo, and eyebrows were raised when we used them. But when certain developments seemed to show that the old ways might be right after all, everyone could relax. Mind was back.

Information theory was one of those developments, computer technology another. Troublesome problems seemed to vanish like magic. A detailed study of sensation and perception was no longer needed; one could simply speak of processing information. It was no longer necessary to construct settings in which to observe behavior; one could simply describe them. Rather than observe what people actually did, one could simply ask them what they would probably do.

That mentalistic psychologists are uneasy about these uses of introspection is clear from the desperation with which they are turning to brain science, asking it to tell them what perceptions, feelings, ideas, and intentions "really are." And brain scientists are happy to accept the assignment. To complete the account of an episode of behavior (for example, to explain what happens when a reinforcement brings an organism under the control of a given stimulus) is not only beyond the present range of brain science, it would lack the glamour of a revelation about the nature of mind. But psychology may find it dangerous to turn to neurology for help. Once you tell the world that another science will explain what your key terms really mean, you must forgive the world if it decides that the other science is doing the important work.

Cognitive psychologists like to say that "the mind is what the brain does," but surely the rest of the body plays a part. The mind is what the *body* does. It is what the *person* does. In other words, it is behavior, and that is what behaviorists have been saying for more than half a century. To focus on an organ is to rejoin the Homeric Greeks.

Cognitive psychologists and brain scientists have formed a new discipline called cognitive science. It is enormously appealing. From a single page in a book review in the *New York Times* titled "Inside the Thinking Animal" (Restak, 1985), we learn that the separation of mind and brain, as represented by the separation of psychiatry and neurology, is now blurring, that biochemistry will tell us about depression, that in dreams information is processed very differently from in the waking state, that cognitive neuroscientists would not explain forgetting a friend's name as repression but as a breakdown of memory retrieval, that psychoanalysis was a precursor to current developments in the neurosciences, and that quantum physics offers the most satisfying answer to understanding the mind and brain relationship and the nature of reality itself. Very rich fare, indeed, until one counts the calories. The bodily state felt as depression will no doubt *eventually* be understood by biochemists (it is now being changed with the biochemicals we call drugs). Dreaming is no doubt different from the waking state, but whether "information" is "processed" in either state is still a question. Is there any difference between "forgetting" and "failing to retrieve a memory" except the gratuitous metaphor in the latter expression? Is it likely that neurology will eventually find the elaborate "mental apparatus" of psychoanalysis? And must we wait for quantum physics before saying anything useful about the mind–brain relationship, let alone reality itself?

A preference for rule-governed rather than contingency-shaped behavior explains the warmth with which cognitive psychologists have also welcomed artificial intelligence. The artificial organisms that show artificial intelligence are much more complex than the automata that inspired the reflex theory of Descartes, but both do only what they are told to do. Fairly simply models have been built that are changed by the consequences of their behavior, and they are much more like real organisms, but cognitive psychologists naturally prefer those that follow rules, including rules for deriving new rules from old. Logicians and mathematicians have been discovering, composing, and testing rules of the latter sort for centuries. Machines can do some of the work and, like a hand calculator, do it much faster. Mathematicians and logicians have never given very consistent accounts of how they work, in part because they have tried to discover their "thought processes." If an artificial organism can be designed to do what logicians and mathematicians do, or even more than they have ever done, it will be the best evidence we have that intuitive mathematical and logical thinking is only following rules, no matter how obscure. And following a rule is behaving.

DAMAGE AND REPAIR

By their very nature, the antiscience stance of humanistic psychology, the practical exigencies of the helping professions, and the cognitive restoration of the royal House of Mind have worked against the definition of psychology as the science of behavior. Perhaps that could be justified if something more valuable had been achieved, but has that happened? Is there a better conception of psychology? To judge from the psychological literature, there are either many conceptions, largely incompatible, or no clear conception at all. Introductory textbooks do not help because, with an eye on their books' being adopted, the authors call their subject the "science of behavior *and* mental life" and make sure that every field of interest is covered. What the public learns from the media is equally confusing.

Is there a rapidly expanding body of facts and principles? Of our three obstacles, only cognitive psychology offers itself as an experimental science. It usually does so with a certain éclat, but have its promises been kept? When the journal *Psychology Today* celebrated its 15th anniversary, it asked 10 psychologists to name the most important discoveries made during that period of time. As Nicolas Wade (1982) has pointed out, no 2 of the 10 agreed on a single achievement that could properly be called psychology. For more than two years *Science* has not published a single article on psychology, except one on memory citing work on brain-operated and brain-damaged people and one on the neurological basis of memory retrieval. Apparently the editors of *Science* no longer regard psychology itself as a member of the scientific community.

Nor has psychology developed a strong technology. Internal determiners get in the way of effective action. An article on "Energy Conservation Behavior" in the *American Psychologist* (Costanzo, Archer, Aronson, & Pettigrew, 1986), carries the significant subtitle, "The Difficult Path From Information to Action." If you take the "rational-economic" path and tell people about the consequences of what they are doing or of what they might do instead, they are not likely to change. (And for good reason: Information is not enough; people seldom take advice unless taking other advice has been reinforced.) If, on the other hand, you adopt the "attitude-change" approach, people are also not likely to change. Attitudes are inferences from the behavior that is said to show their presence and are not directly accessible. If I turn off unnecessary lights and appliances in my home, it is not because I have a "positive attitude" toward conservation, but because doing so has had some kind of reinforcing consequence. To induce people to conserve energy, one must change contingencies of reinforcement, not attitudes. No one should try to beat a "path from information to action," because action is the problem and contingencies the solution.

Unable to offer a useful conception of its subject matter, psychology has not formed good relations with other sciences. As we have seen, it has given neurologists an impossible assignment, and the search for internal determiners has obscured any help it could give genetics. Once you have formed the noun "ability" from the adjective "able," you are in trouble. Aqua regia has the *ability* to dissolve gold; but chemists will not look for an ability, they will look for atomic and molecular processes. Much of the controversy about the heritability of intelligence, schizophrenia, delinquency, and so on is due to the conceptualization of abilities and traits of character as explanatory entities. Longevity is a "heritable trait," but rather than try to assign it to a gene, geneticists will look at the processes that contribute to a long life. The genetics of behavior can be much more directly studied by interbreeding members of a species that behave in different ways under the controlled conditions of the laboratory.

Psychology gives very little help to the "behavioral sciences"—sociology, anthropology, linguistics, political science, and economics. They have their own technical vocabularies, but beyond them—except for brief flirtations with utilitarianism, Marxism, psychoanalysis, and the like—they use the vernacular, with all its references to internal causes. Their data are usually more objective than those of psychology, but hypothetical explanations still flourish.

Beyond the current reach of all of the sciences lies an issue that cannot be safely neglected by any of them—the future of the world. For a variety of reasons all three of our "obstacles" have had special reasons for neglecting it. Humanistic psychologists are unwilling to sacrifice feelings of freedom and worth for the sake of a future, and when cognitive psychologists turn to feelings and states of mind for theoretical purposes and psychotherapists for practical ones, they emphasize the here and now. Behavior modification, in contrast, is more often preventive than remedial. In both instruction and therapy, current reinforcers (often contrived) are arranged to strengthen behavior that student and client will find useful *in the future*.

When Gandhi was asked, "What are we to do?" he is said to have replied, "Think of the poorest man you have ever met and then ask if what you are doing is of any benefit to him." But he must have meant "of any benefit to the many people who, without your help, will be like him." To feed the hungry and clothe the naked are remedial acts. We can easily see what is wrong and what needs to be done. It is much harder to see and do something about the fact that world agriculture must feed and clothe billions of people, most of them yet unborn. It is not enough to *advise* people how to behave in ways that will make a future possible; they must be given effective reasons for behaving in those ways, and that means effective contingencies of reinforcement now.

Unfortunately, references to feelings and states of mind have an emotional appeal that behavioral alternatives usually lack. Here is an example: "If the world is to be saved, people must learn to be noble without being cruel, to be filled with faith, yet open to truth, to be inspired by great purposes without hating those who thwart them." That is an "inspiring" sentence. We like nobility, faith, truth, and great purposes and dislike cruelty and hatred. But what does it inspire us to *do*? What must be changed if people are to behave in noble rather than cruel ways, to accept the word of others but never without questioning it, to do things that have consequences too remote to serve as reinforcers, and to refrain from attacking those who oppose them? The fault, dear Brutus, is not in our stars *nor in ourselves* that we are underlings. The fault is in the world. It is a world that we have made and one that we must change if the species is to survive.

For at least 2500 years philosophers and psychologists have proceeded on the assumption that because they were themselves behaving organisms, they had privileged access to the causes of their behavior. But has any introspectively observed feeling or state of mind yet been unambiguously identified in either mental or physical terms? Has any ability or trait of character been statistically established to the satisfaction of everyone? Do we know how anxiety changes intention, how memories alter decisions, how intelligence changes emotion, and so on? And, of course, has anyone ever explained how the mind works on the body or the body on the mind?

Questions of that sort should never have been asked. Psychology should confine itself to its accessible subject matter and leave the rest of the story of human behavior to physiology.

REFERENCES

Bartlett, J. (Ed.). (1968). *Bartlett's familiar quotations.* Boston: Little, Brown.

Bridgman, P. W. (1928). *The logic of modern physics.* New York: Macmillan.

Costanzo, M., Archer, D., Aronson, E., & Pettigrew, T. (1986). Energy conservation behavior. The difficult path from information to action. *American Psychologist, 41,* 521–528.

Jennings, H. S. (1906). *The behavior of the lower organisms.* New York: Columbia University Press (Macmillan Co-agents).

Loeb, J. (1916). *The organism as a whole, from a physicochemical viewpoint.* New York: Putnam.

Mach, E. (1915). *Science of mechanics; a critical and historical account of its development.* Chicago: Open Court Publishing.

Pauly, P. J. (1987). *Controlling life: Jacques Loeb and the engineering ideal in biology.* New York: Oxford University Press.

Pavlov, I. P. (1927). *Conditioned reflexes: The physiological activity of the cerebral cortex.* London: Oxford University Press.

Restak, R. M. (1985, January 20). Inside the thinking animal. *New York Times Book Review,* Section 7, p. 1.

Russell, B. (1927). *Philosophy.* New York: Norton.

Sherrington, C. C. (1906). *Integrative action of the nervous system.* New Haven, CT: Yale University Press.

Skinner, B. F. (1931). The concept of the reflex in the description of behavior. *Journal of Genetic Psychology,* 5, 427–458.

Skinner, B. F. (1938). *The behavior of organisms.* New York: Appleton-Century-Crofts.

Smith, L. D. (1986). *Behaviorism and logical positivism.* California: Stanford University Press.

Wade, N. (1982, April 30). Smart apes or dumb? *New York Times,* p. 28.

Webster's third new international dictionary (1981). Springfield, MA: Merriam-Webster.

7

SCIENTIFIC PSYCHOLOGY AND RADICAL BEHAVIORISM: IMPORTANT DISTINCTIONS BASED IN SCIENTISM AND OBJECTIVISM

MICHAEL J. MAHONEY

It is not unusual for historical observers to portray their own time as one of transition, and there is one sense in which all such portrayals are correct: The complex dynamics of the present are necessarily linked to both the past and the future. Even so, some "times" exhibit more change than others, and their pivotal role in later developments often earns them a retrospective title (hence, the Renaissance, the Enlightenment, and the Scientific Revolution). Although it is impossible to predict the scope and trajectory of recent and current events in late 20th-century civilization, it is increasingly clear that some major changes are afoot. Above and beyond (but not necessarily independent of) recent developments in world politics, economics, and the humanities, there are signs of dramatic change in the sciences in general (e.g., Eigen & Winkler, 1981; Gleick, 1987; Prigogine & Stengers, 1984). Some of these changes relate to significant technical and theoretical developments, and others reflect new patterns of inquiry and interdisciplinary collaboration.

Within the science of psychology, one can point to salient examples of both stasis and change over the last century (Altman, 1987, Ash & Woodward, 1988; Hearst, 1979; Hilgard, 1987). Indeed, the number and diversity of analyses of that topic make up a formidable literature of their own (Block, 1980; Fiske & Schweder, 1986; Manicas, 1987; Margolis, 1987; Royce, 1970). Rather than either review such analyses or add to their number, I will provide a brief commentary on a small but significant slice of some distinctions and tensions that are relevant

Reprinted from the *American Psychologist, 44,* 1372–1377. (1989).

to the definition and development of scientific psychology. Specifically, I will address the changing relationship between scientific psychology and radical, or orthodox, behaviorism.

HISTORICAL CONTEXT

My remarks must first be placed in the historical context of the emergence of modern science. Because there are entire libraries devoted to that topic, my contextualization will focus on events and themes that have played an important role in psychology's bid to become a science and radical behaviorism's recurrent claim to be the essence or ideal form of scientific psychology.

To begin with, science as we now know it emerged during and after the Renaissance in the mid-16th and 17th centuries. The density of revolutionary developments in both theory and method during that era was truly extraordinary. In a span of less than 150 years, our view of and posture toward the "natural world" was repeatedly transformed. Copernicus, Brahe, Kepler, and Galileo showed that our planet was not the center of the solar system, let alone the universe. Oughtred invented the slide rule in 1621, Pascal created an adding machine soon thereafter, and the calculus (differential and integral) was introduced by Leibniz and Newton. With Newton's laws of motion and gravitation, Boyle's law of gases, and Huygens's wave theory of light, the external world began to reveal unprecedented order. The microscope was put to use by Hooke and van Leeuwenhoek, and the mysteries of the human body began to be revealed in the careful studies of Vesalius and Harvey. To keep pace with and document this flurry of activity, the first two scientific journals were begun in 1665.

The two most important figures from this era in terms of the present topic, however, were Francis Bacon and Rene Descartes. Bacon's *Novum Organum* (literally, "new method") was published in 1620 and represented the first formal call to systematic observation, experimentation, and inductive inference. It was an explicit attempt to move beyond the dominant scholasticism of Aristotle, which had emphasized rationality and formal logical deduction. Descartes's *Discourse on Method* was published in 1637; in this work, he emphasized the role of systematic doubt in inquiry and proposed that self-aware cognition—with a little supernatural assistance—could form the cornerstone of all rational conjectures about existence (*cogito, ergo sum:* "I think, therefore I am"). Because he was concerned about its reception by the church, Descartes delayed the publication of his mechanistic theory of how the body operates until after his own death.

There is a certain irony in the roles played by Bacon and Descartes in the latter development of behaviorism. An ardent empiricist, Bacon emphasized the importance of observation, and hence sense experience, in the refinement of knowledge. He was clearly *not* a radical behaviorist, however, and can in fact be credited with pioneering insights into how social pressures, tradition, language customs, and the inclinations of the human mind may mitigate against accurate observation and unbiased inference. For example, Bacon was the first to note *confirmatory bias:* the tendency among all humans (including scientists) to distort information and attention toward the perpetuation of prior beliefs (Mahoney, 1974, 1976). Descartes, on the other hand, holds a revered place in the history of behaviorism (e.g., Rachlin, 1970) despite his having been an archetypal rationalist in the tradition of Pythagoras, Plato, and Aristotle. He formalized the mind–body *dualism* of these Greek philosophers and posited that the pineal gland was the seat of the soul. It was his mechanistic theory of bodily action, however, and his anticipation of the reflex arc that won him respect among 20th century behaviorists.

It is not surprising, of course, that radical behaviorists have lauded the environmental determinism and mechanism of such scientists as Pavlov, Thorndike, Watson, and Skinner. For example, in a recent lament that psychology has lost sight of its proper focus as the science of *behavior,* Skinner (1987) applauded Pauly's (1987) "excellent account" of the influential works of the biologist Jacques Loeb, who was one of Watson's teachers at the University of Chicago. In his review of Pauly's biography of Loeb, Servos (1987) noted that Loeb's work set the stage for Skinner's adamant avoidance of the analysis of internal mechanisms, as well as his preoccupation with input–output functions:

> Loeb stands at the fountainhead of a new tradition in the biological sciences—a tradition that places more emphasis upon the control of organisms than on a formal or complete understanding of their nature. Whereas his contemporaries, like Francis Bacon before them, believed that power and knowledge were inextricably linked, Loeb thought it possible to manipulate life without understanding it, to treat the organism as a black box from which all manner of behaviors could be coaxed by environmental cues . . . [He believed] that scientists, rather than searching vainly for true causes, should really be concerned with producing effects. By 1891, Loeb had come to see himself as an engineer of living substance . . . [and his] experiments . . . were attempts to manipulate life processes in the absence of an understanding of mechanisms. (p. 305)

It is thus noteworthy that Pauly's (1987) biography of Loeb, recommended by Skinner, is titled *Controlling Life: Jacques Loeb and the Engineering Ideal in Biology.* Nor, perhaps, should it be surprising that Skinner (1987) has viewed humanistic psychology, psychotherapy, and cognitive psychology—each preoccupied with their own analyses of internal processes—as "three formidable obstacles" to psychology's becoming fully identified with the experimental analysis of behavior qua behavior.

The behaviorists' preoccupation with unmediated functionalism is itself an expression of multiple ideological legacies, the most formative having been evolutionism, associationism, determinism, operationism, pragmatism, positivism, and objectivism. For the sake of brevity, analyses of most of these "isms" can be delegated to other resources. That behaviorism was an outgrowth and expression of post-Darwinian functionalism and pragmatism, for example, has been amply documented (Boakes, 1984; Manicas, 1987; Moore, 1987; O'Donnell, 1985; Richards, 1987). The link between behaviorism and associationism has also been widely noted, and the formal theoretical limits of the latter have been demonstrated (Bever, Fodor, & Garrett, 1968). The close links between radical behaviorism, operationism, and positivism are likewise readily identifiable (Kazdin, 1978; Rachlin, 1970; Skinner, 1971, 1974, 1977, 1987; Smith, 1986). What is noteworthy here, as well as in the case of determinism, is the fact that orthodox behaviorists have continued to adhere to perspectives long since abandoned by their originators. Positivism was soon conceded to be illogical on its own criteria (Munz, 1987; Weimer, 1979); operationism has been thoroughly dismantled by research methodologists (Hudson, 1972; Plutchik, 1963; Scheffler, 1967); and the Newtonian ("billiard ball") form of determinism so stridently emulated by orthodox behaviorists was abandoned by most physical scientists in the decades following the 1927 Copenhagen Interpretation of Quantum Mechanics.

Perhaps because of these anachronisms, one does not find the assumptions or assertions of radical behaviorism to be either primary or foundational in modern texts on scientific methodology within the social sciences (e.g., Cook & Campbell, 1979). In its quest to be rigorously scientific and nonmetaphysical, the most extreme version of behaviorism remained diligently "radical" and "orthodox" (from the Greek *orthos doxa,* "right opinion"). In holding to original assumptions and assertions, however, radical behaviorism isolated itself from and came to lag behind changing perspectives on the nature and practice of optimal scientific inquiry. Then again, radical behaviorists have not been the only aspirants to science who, in turning their backs on the lessons of philosophy, have found themselves unnecessarily tethered by their own first assumptions:

> Few things are more ironic than for a self-styled "empiricist" openly to repudiate philosophy, when he himself has unconsciously adopted the philosophical views of Comte, Mill, Mach,

or Carnap and unconsciously repudiated the scientific *practice* of anti-positivists such as Lavoisier and Dalton in chemistry, Lyell and Darwin in biology, and Galileo, Newton, Planck, and Einstein in physics who *all* assumed the reality of a physical world *beyond* sensory appearances and who thought that the primary task of science was to understand that trans-empirical world (i.e., "elements" and "atoms" were not observable, geological and biological history are not observable, the real motion of the planets is not observable, and the absolute speed of light in a vacuum is a constant whether observable or not). In other words, anti-philosophical empiricists are commonly the victims of the most *anti-scientific* of all philosophies, namely the positivism and subjective idealism of Berkeley and Hume, *who aimed above all else to restrict the scope and importance of science.* (Blackmore, 1979, pp. 130–131)

OBJECTIVISM AND SCIENTISM IN RADICAL BEHAVIORISM

One "ism" that lies at the core of orthodox behaviorism and that is central to the present thesis is objectivism, the contention that (a) an objectively separate "real world" lies beyond the organism and exists independently of being perceived (i.e., the essence of classical realism, see Blackmore, 1979), (b) true or valid knowledge about that world is ultimately rendered through sensory experience (i.e., the essence of classical empiricism), and (c) such knowledge can (and, in the strongest form of objectivism, *must*) be totally separated from the individual knower. Up until the 1980s, objectivism was deemed little more than a formal expression of realism. With recent developments in physics, philosophy, hermeneutics, biology, and the cognitive sciences, however, common-sense objectivism has come under increasingly critical scrutiny (e.g., Bannister, 1987; Johnson, 1987; Lackoff, 1987; Mahoney, in press; Maturana & Varela, 1987; Pattee, 1978; Varela, 1979; Watzlawick, 1984; Weimer, 1982; Wheeler, 1982).

First, there has been a shift away from "justificational" (authority-based) epistemologies and toward nonjustificational (critical) epistemologies. Second, there has been a shift away from passive and predominantly sensory/storage models of cognition and toward proactive and motoric/process models. Third, there has occurred a shift away from presuming a discrete, static boundary between organism and environment in favor of more fluid and dynamic regions and processes of demarcation. Finally, there is an increasing recognition that the knower/observer cannot be removed from either the process or the product of knowing. Given the range and complexity of these issues, I will defer to their elaboration elsewhere (e.g., Mahoney, in press).

What is pertinent here is that the objectivist tradition has created an extreme dualism in scientific inquiry and encouraged an impossible ideal of "absolute" (observer-free) knowledge. In the 19th and early 20th centuries, objectivity became the sine qua non of science. Although it spawned a host of technological advances in instrumentation and measurement, its dogmatic extremes led to serious foreclosures on entire areas and alternate methods of investigation (Baars, 1986; Hilgard, 1987). Hornstein (1986) thus has documented how the nascent field of psychology was shaped and constrained by the requirement for quantification as a demonstration that the discipline was genuinely scientific. Likewise, Bannister (1987) has shown how the quest to be "scientific" in the narrow, objectivist sense of that term played a significant role in the shaping of American sociology. He also pointed out that objectivism has been closely allied with "scientism" in the history of science.

Scientism is a term that has been used by philosophers to refer to dogmatically self-righteous, presumptuous, and exclusionary perspectives on science and scientific method (Bannister, 1987; Hayek, 1952, 1978; Koch, 1959; Koestler, 1967; Weimer, 1979, 1982). As such, a "scientistic" approach is one that (a) proposes a single and exclusive set of assumptions, methods, or legitimate questions as proper to genuine science, (b) ignores or generally discredits all theories and research foreign to its own assumptions, questions, and methods, and/or (c) presumes absolute knowledge about phenomena well beyond current theory and research. Tolerance for other styles or foci of inquiry is minimal, and the famous "demarcation problem" (i.e., the distinction between science and nonscience) is equated with the distinction between sense and nonsense. Contrary to the spirit of openness, exchange, and diversified questioning that lies at the heart of scientific philosophy, advocates of a scientistic outlook tend to talk about "*the* scientific method" (in the singular) and show little interest in or respect for forms of study other than their own.

What I am leading toward here, with conscious reluctance, is the suggestion that radical or orthodox behaviorism may have lost much of its hold on scientific psychology in large part because of its dogmatic objectivism and scientistic intolerance, an intolerance that has become increasingly more evident as that hold has dissipated. Before documenting that suggestion, however, I hasten to add that this assertion applies only to orthodox (radical) behaviorism and not to the more common liberal versions of behavior therapy or to the varieties of methodological behaviorism that encourage creativity and innovation in experimental methods and conceptual models.

THE DECLINE OF RADICAL BEHAVIORISM

Observers within the community of behavioral psychologists have long since noted that significant changes have characterized that group over the last quarter century. Above and beyond the rivalries between adherents of the various learning theories, there have been increasingly robust challenges to some of the foundational assumptions of environmental determinism. The "misbehavior of organisms" and the need to acknowledge complexities beyond the level of discrete and artificial responses began to be increasingly acknowledged by respected scientists who challenged or revised radical behaviorist accounts of learning (e.g., Breland & Breland, 1961; Estes, 1971; Hilgard, 1987; Neuringer, 1969, 1970; Rescorla, 1988). Beginning in the mid-1950s and accelerating into the 1970s, there were signs of increasingly mediational conceptualizations, eventually resulting in the "cognitive revolution" within behavior modification and across the social sciences in general (e.g., Bandura, 1969; Dember, 1974; Mahoney, 1974, in press; McKeachie, 1974). Historians of modern behaviorism have already begun to document the tensions that the cognitive movement appeared to engender within the community.

One example of these tensions is shown in the development and circulation of a list of "banned readings," books that faculty and students in some radical behavioral departments were instructed not to read. In addition, there were recurrent arguments within the Executive Board of the Association for the Advancement of Behavior Therapy (AABT) regarding the acceptability of including articles on "cognitive–behavioral" research and practice in the journal *Behavior Therapy* and providing coverage for this area at annual association meetings. Finally, AABT's most orthodox members have left and have expanded a regional group into the national Association for Behavior Analysis (ABA), partially to protest the liberal welcome granted cognitive researchers within AABT. The ABA was supplemented in 1987 by the establishment of The International Behaviorology Association (TIBA), dedicated explicitly to fostering radical behaviorism and, among other things, striving to require demonstrated knowledge of the "basic laws" of behavior as a prerequisite for graduation at all educational levels (kindergarten through college). In 1987 a special panel was organized at the annual meeting of the AABT to address the question, Why is it so hard to find a radical behaviorist when you really need one? There was no disagreement among the panel members about the scarcity of radical behaviorists, but there was dissension over when and whether they were needed. Data on the growth of the behavioral movement suggest, if anything, that the popularity of behavioral approaches reached a plateau between 1980 and 1986 and that the more liberal (cognitive and clinical) varieties of behavior therapy became increasingly more popular than their radically orthodox counterparts (Mahoney, Norcross, Prochaska, & Missar, 1987; Zaiser, Geire, Knip, & Mertens, 1986). This movement toward more liberal (and explicitly mediational) versions of behavioral theory may have also played a role in the recent appearance of what some have termed "evangelical" behaviorism in the form of major attempts to reconstruct and revive the declining orthodoxy (e.g., Hayes, 1987; Killeen, 1984; Zuriff, 1985, 1986).

Data from a longitudinal study of influential behaviorists and cognitivists are relevant here. In 1977 a sample of 42 influential representatives of these two groups completed a lengthy questionnaire assessing their beliefs about scientific method, the nature of learning, and so on (Mahoney, 1979). In 1985 they were asked to respond again to 12 of the most discriminating questions that they had answered eight years earlier and also to rate how "cognitive" they were (Mahoney & Gabriel, in press). Within ranges of individual variability, respondents clustered into three discernible groupings: (a) extreme behaviorists (hereafter just behaviorists), (b) cognitive–behaviorists, and (c) extreme cognitivists. Differences between groups were both familiar and illuminating. For example, behaviorists granted more credibility to conditioning models and environmental influences than did cognitivists. Self-defined cognitive–behaviorists were midrange on most issues, including the merits of cognitive research, whereas cognitivists were, not surprisingly, most affirming of personal agency and of the promise of cognitive science.

More interesting, however, were changes *within* groups over the eight-year period. Cognitive–behaviorists showed a significant drop in their ratings of the adequacy of conditioning models, and even the behaviorists exhibited a 20% decline on this issue. Consistent with their midline stance, cognitive–behaviorists also showed a significant drop in their estimates of the evidence for a relationship between private events and human adjustment. Both cognitive–behavioral and extreme behavioral respondents showed signs of shifts in the direction of personal agency as an important counterbalance to exclusive environmental determinism. Cognitivists appeared to be going even further in this direction, exhibiting a clear trend toward acknowledging the influence of unconscious processes.

Across the three groups, behaviorists had changed least of all over the eight years of the study. None of their within-group responses over time had changed significantly, and yet their 1985 group variance was significantly greater than that of the other two groups. The impression is one of rumblings of change, with sizable individual variability limiting the utility of central tendency measures. All in all, these data suggest that behaviorism is both changing and static, a situation that demands that its adherents and critics alike concur on what terms they use and which types of behaviorism they are discussing.

Genuinely radical behaviorists are becoming increasingly difficult to find not simply because they are becoming more scarce and not simply because there may be fewer efforts to find them. Rather, the data suggest that such a search is complicated by the fact that the meanings and models of behaviorism are now in the throes of dramatic revision. Such is the case with many other perspectives in late 20th century psychology. It would be a mistake, however, to assume that radical behaviorism is or should be conceptually dead. Genuinely radical behaviorism is still quite alive and energetically faithful to the intellectual traditions of materialism, associationism, functionalism, determinism, and environmentalism. These traditions represent major navigational reference points from which recent theoretical developments have differentiated themselves, and they participate integrally in what Thomas Kuhn (1977) has termed the "essential tensions" between changing and unchanging themes in the uncertain progression of scientific knowledge.

The fundamental issue is not "who is right" in this seemingly eternal debate over internal versus external determinants and analyses of organismic activity. The reciprocity models afforded by "active Darwinian" theories are probably more viable than extreme versions of either brand of determinism. Moreover, our ideological questions help inform us about our assumptions, our conceptual past, and possible trajectories for future theoretical development. The challenge facing behaviorism is thus the same challenge faced by all expressions of the scientific spirit and, indeed, all open, developing systems, namely, the challenge of remaining flexible enough to adapt, yet self-stabilizing enough to protect and preserve systemic integrity. The relevant dimension here is *viability,* not *validity.* In facing that challenge, I would argue that any system that remains open to change while honoring tradition thereby remains a valuable participant in the process of science itself.

CONCLUDING REMARKS

The point, then, is very simple. It is essential that a distinction be drawn between scientific psychology and radical behaviorism if only to respond to and qualify the claims of some radical behaviorists to the effect that their approach represents the *only* scientific psychology: past, present and future (e.g., Skinner, 1974, 1987). It would be a mistake, however, to simply invert the judgment and imply that radical behaviorism is not scientific. Whatever else they may render, future historiographies will need to credit both metaphysical and methodological behaviorism with having played an important role in psychology's earliest attempts to be scientific.

The central thesis of this article is that radical behaviorists, like their ideological rivals, are free to claim to be the only truly scientific students of human experience, but in so doing they jeopardize their warrant for that very claim by demonstrating a failure to appreciate some essential aspects of the "true" science to which they aspire. Naive objectivism is a misguided (and misguiding) ideal in modern science, and scientism is a dogmatic form of myopia "which is decidedly unscientific in the true sense of the word" (Hayek, 1952, p. 15). Thus, in response to the question "Whatever happened to psychology as the science of behavior?" (Skinner, 1987), I concur with Hilgard (1987) that the discipline has matured enough to recognize the limitations of that equation.

There are diverse expressions of scientific psychology beyond the confines of behaviorism, whether metaphysical or methodological. The time has come to transform ideological swords into conceptual plowshares and to risk trusting in the harvest of open dialectical exchange. It will be out of the context of such exchanges that more adequate theories of human experience will most likely emerge and, with them, that we will ultimately develop more optimal means for protecting and facilitating the infinite individuality of human development.

REFERENCES

Altman, I. (1987). Centripetal and centrifugal trends in psychology. *American Psychologist, 42,* 1058–1069.

Ash, M. G., & Woodward, W. R. (Eds.). (1988). *Psychology in twentieth-century thought and society.* Cambridge, England: Cambridge University Press.

Baars, B. J. (1986). *The cognitive revolution in psychology.* New York: Guilford.

Bacon, F. (1905). *Novum organum* [The new method]. London: George Routledge. (Original work published 1620).

Bandura, A. (1969). *Principles of behavior modification.* New York: Holt, Rinehart & Winston.

Bannister, R. C. (1987). *Sociology and scientism: The American quest for objectivity, 1880–1940.* Chapel Hill: University of North Carolina Press.

Bever, T. G., Fodor, J. A., & Garrett, M. (1968). A formal limit of associationism. In T. R. Dixon & D. L. Horton (Eds.), *Verbal behavior and general behavior theory* (pp. 582–585). Englewood Cliffs, NJ: Prentice-Hall.

Blackmore, J. (1979). On the inverted use of the terms "realism" and "idealism" among scientists and historians of science. *British Journal for the Philosophy of Science, 30,* 125–134.

Block, N. (Ed.). (1980) *Readings in philosophy of psychology.* Cambridge, MA: Harvard University Press.

Boakes, R. A. (1984). *From Darwin to behaviourism.* Cambridge, England: Cambridge University Press.

Breland, K., & Breland, M. (1961). The misbehavior of organisms. *American Psychologist, 16,* 681–684.

Cook, T. D., & Campbell, D. T. (1979). *Quasi-experimentation: Design and analysis issues for field settings.* Boston: Houghton Mifflin.

Dember, W. N. (1974). Motivation and the cognitive revolution. *American Psychologist, 29,* 161–168.

Descartes, R. (1946). *Discourse on method.* La Salle, IL: Open Court. (Original work published 1637).

Eigen, M., & Winkler, R. (1981). *Laws of the game.* New York: Harper Colophon.

Estes, W. K. (1971). Reward in human learning: Theoretical issues and strategic choice points. In R. Glaser (Ed.), *The nature of reinforcement* (pp. 16–36). New York: Academic Press.

Fiske, D. W., & Schweder, R. A. (Eds.). (1986). *Metatheory in social science: Pluralisms and subjectivities.* Chicago: University of Chicago Press.

Gleick, J. (1987). *Chaos: Making a new science.* New York: Viking Press.

Hayek, F. A. (1952). *The counter-revolution of science.* Glencoe, IL: Free Press.

Hayek, F. A. (1978). *New studies in philosophy, politics, economics, and the history of ideas.* Chicago: University of Chicago Press.

Hayes, S.C. (1987). A contextual approach to therapeutic change. In N. S. Jacobson (Ed.), *Psychotherapists in clinical practice: Cognitive and behavioral perspectives* (pp. 327–387). New York: Guilford.

Hearst, E. (Ed.). (1979). *The first century of experimental psychology.* Hillsdale, NJ: Erlbaum.

Hilgard, E. R. (1987). *Psychology in America: A historical survey.* New York: Harcourt Brace Jovanovich.

Hornstein, G. A. (1986, October). *The social construction of quantification in American psychology, 1880–1930.* Paper presented at the annual meeting of the Society for the Social Study of Science, Pittsburgh, PA.

Hudson, L. (1972). *The cult of the fact.* New York: Harper & Row.

Johnson, M. (1987). *The body in the mind: The bodily basis of meaning, imagination, and reason.* Chicago: University of Chicago Press.

Kazdin, A. E. (1978). *History of behavior modification.* Baltimore, MD: University Park Press.

Killeen, P. (1984). Emergent behaviorism. *Behaviorism, 12,* 25–39.

Koch, S. (1959). *Psychology: The study of a science.* New York: McGraw-Hill.

Koestler, A. (1967). *The ghost in the machine.* Chicago: H. Regnery.

Kuhn, T. S. (1977). *Essential tensions.* Chicago: University of Chicago Press.

Lackoff, G. (1987). *Women, fire, and dangerous things: What categories reveal about the mind.* Chicago: University of Chicago Press.

Mahoney, M. J. (1974). *Cognition and behavior modification.* Cambridge, MA: Ballinger.

Mahoney, M. J. (1976). *Scientist as subject: The psychological imperative.* Cambridge, MA: Ballinger.

Mahoney, M. J. (1979). Cognitive and non-cognitive views in behavior modification. In P. O. Sjoden, S. Bates, & W. S. Dockens (Eds.), *Trends in behavior therapy* (pp. 39–54). New York: Plenum.

Mahoney, M. J. (in press). *Human change processes.* New York: Basic Books.

Mahoney, M. J., & Gabriel, T. J. (in press). Essential tensions in psychology: Longitudinal data on cognitive and behavioral ideologies. *Journal of Cognitive Psychotherapy: An International Quarterly.*

Mahoney, M. J., Norcross, J. C., Prochaska, J. O., & Missar, C. D. (1987). *Human psychological development and psychotherapy: Convergence among clinical psychologists.* Unpublished manuscript. University of California, Santa Barbara.

Manicas, P. T. (1987). *A history and philosophy of the social sciences.* New York: Basil Blackwell.

Margolis, J. (1987). *Science without unity.* New York: Basil Blackwell.

Maturana, H. R., & Varela, F. J. (1987). *The tree of knowledge: The biological roots of human understanding.* Boston: Shambhala Publications.

McKeachie, W. J. (1974). The decline and fall of the laws of learning. *Educational Researcher, 3,* 7–11.

Moore, J. (1987). The roots of the family tree: A review of four books on the history and nature of behaviorism. *The Psychological Record, 37,* 449–470.

Munz, P. (1987). The unity of science and the dubious credentials of positivism. In G. Radnitzky (Ed.), *Centripetal forces in the sciences* (pp. 13–41). New York: Paragon House.

Neuringer, A. J. (1969). Animals respond for food in the presence of free food. *Science, 166,* 399–401.

Neuringer, A. J. (1970). Many responses per food reward with free food present. *Science, 169,* 503–504.

O'Donnell, J. M. (1985). *The origins of behaviorism: American psychology, 1870–1920.* New York: New York University Press.

Pattee, H. H. (1978). The complementarity principle in biological and social structures. *Journal of Biological and Social Structures, 1,* 191–200.

Pauly, P. J. (1987). *Controlling life: Jacques Loeb and the engineering ideal in biology.* Oxford: Oxford University Press.

Plutchik, R. (1963). Operationism as methodology. *Behavioral Science, 8,* 234–241.

Prigogine, I., & Stengers, I. (1984). *Order out of chaos: Man's new dialogue with nature.* New York: Bantam.

Rachlin, H. (1970). *Introduction to modern behaviorism.* San Francisco: W. H. Freeman.

Rescorla, R. A. (1988). Pavlovian conditioning: It's not what you think it is. *American Psychologist, 43,* 151–160.

Richards, R. J. (1987). *Darwin and the emergence of evolutionary theories of mind and behavior.* Chicago: University of Chicago Press.

Royce, J. R. (Ed.). (1970). *Toward unification in psychology.* Toronto: University of Toronto Press.

Scheffler, I. (1967). *Science and subjectivity.* New York: Bobbs-Merrill.

Servos, J. W. (1987). Biology as power. *Science, 237,* 305.

Skinner, B. F. (1971). *Beyond freedom and dignity.* New York: Knopf.

Skinner, B. F. (1974). *About behaviorism.* New York: Knopf.

Skinner, B. F. (1977). Why I am not a cognitive psychologist. *Behaviorism,, 5,* 1–10.

Skinner, B. F. (1987). Whatever happened to psychology as the science of behavior? *American Psychologist, 42,* 780–786.

Smith, L. D. (1986). *Behaviorism and logical positivism.* Stanford, CA: Stanford University Press.

Varela, F. J. (1979). *Principles of biological autonomy.* New York: Elsevier North Holland.

Watzlawick, P. (Ed.). (1984). *The invented reality: Contributions to constructivism.* New York: Norton.

Weimer, W. B. (1979). *Notes on the methodology of scientific research.* Hillsdale, NJ: Erlbaum.

Weimer, W. B. (1982). Hayek's approach to the problems of complex phenomena: An introduction to the theoretical psychology of *The sensory order.* In W. B. Weimer & D. S. Palermo (Eds.), *Cognition and the symbolic processes* (Vol. 2, pp. 267–311). Hillsdale, NJ: Erlbaum.

Wheeler, J. A. (1982). Bohr, Einstein, and the strange lesson of the quantum. In R. Q. Elvee (Ed.), *Mind in nature* (pp. 1–30). New York: Harper & Row.

Zaiser, A., Geire, S., Knip, D., & Mertens, G. C. (1986). What is the "proper measure" of growth in the behavioral movement? *The Behavior Therapist, 9,* 185–186.

Zuriff, G. E. (1985). *Behaviorism: A conceptual reconstruction.* New York: Columbia University Press.

Zuriff, G. E. (1986). Precis of *Behaviorism: A conceptual reconstruction. The Behavioral and Brain Sciences, 9,* 687–723.

8

RADICAL BEHAVIORISM IN RECONCILIATION WITH PHENOMENOLOGY

WILLARD F. DAY

Much of the material which follows is under partial audience-control of the symposium on behaviorism and phenomenology held in the spring of 1963 at Rice University. The papers presented at this symposium, together with the discussion among the speakers and members of the audience, have been published in a recent book edited by Wann (1964) and entitled *Behaviorism and Phenomenology: Contrasting Bases for Modern Psychology.* Of the six speakers at the symposium two, Sigmund Koch and B. F. Skinner, are acknowledged authorities on the practice of behaviorism: two, R. B. MacLeod and Carl R. Rogers, are widely held to be advocates of phenomenology in psychology; and two, Norman Malcolm and Michael Scriven, are prominent professional philosophers, both known for their interest in the philosophical implications of contemporary psychological thought. The significance of the Rice symposium should not be underestimated by psychologists. The papers presented are instances of professional comment of unusually high quality, and they cast an especially instructive light on the current state of affairs of psychology as a science.

In overview, two significant conclusions appear to have emerged from the Rice symposium. The first of these is that behaviorism, in the sense in which the term is widely used among psychologists, is essentially an unproductive and unrealistic framework within which to pursue psychological research. This is to put the matter as mildly as possible, for the point was pursued with much force and clarity by Koch in his paper, and it was strongly seconded by Scriven, as part of his broader appraisal of the long-range potentialities of professional psychology. In a particularly choice statement, Koch expressed what appears to be to some extent his reaction to

Reprinted from the *Journal of the Experimental Analysis of Behavior, 12,* 315–328. (1969).

the symposium as a whole: "I would be happy to say that what we have been hearing could be characterized as the death rattle of behaviorism, but this would be a rather more dignified statement than I should like to sponsor, because death is, at least, a dignified process" (p. 162).[1] The following is representative of what Scriven had to say on the same topic.

> So I would conclude by saying that Professor Koch's criticisms of behaviorism effectively destroy a specter which was, indeed, haunting and which has continued to haunt the subject. I think of behaviorism, as I know he does, as something which will leave its mark on a generation of graduate students now arising and will thus be with us for thirty or fifty years. I spend my life going around campuses and finding in each new psychology department a new burst of colossal enthusiasm; the leading lights of the graduate student body turn out to be enthusiastic, tough-minded positivists circa 1920. And they are now in their twenty-second year of age and, unfortunately, are likely to live a very long time. Some of them will presumably retain this approach to the subject. This is one reason why I believe that philosophy has an enormous influence on psychology though it has often been very bad. But that is, of course, because it was the wrong philosophy! (pp. 181–182)

Were anyone to search the symposium for disagreement with the conclusion that if conventional behaviorism is not now dead we should certainly all be better off if it were, he would have to content himself, rather remarkably, with certain statements of Carl Rogers. At one point in the discussion Rogers remarks that it had not been his purpose to point out "any theoretical flaw in behaviorism. There is a lot about behaviorism that I accept. I was simply trying to go beyond it" (p. 157). To be sure, Rogers calls attention to what he considers certain weaknesses of behaviorism. "Valuable as have been the contributions of behaviorism, I believe that time will indicate the unfortunate effects of the bounds it has tended to impose. To limit oneself to consideration of externally observable behavior, to rule out consideration of the whole universe of inner meanings, of purposes, of the inner flow of experiencing, seems to me to be closing our eyes to great areas which confront us when we look at the human world" (p. 119). However, the spirit of his paper is essentially conciliatory. "There are without doubt some individuals in this current of thought who maintain the hope that this new point of view will supplant the behaviorist trend, but to me this is both highly undesirable and highly unlikely. Rather it will mean, I believe, that psychology will preserve the advances and contributions that have come from the behaviorist development but will go beyond this" (p. 118). Rogers proceeds to argue for the measurement of new phenomenological variables, employing "thoroughly objective measures, whose results are publicly replicable" (p. 120), "using methods which are strictly operational" (p. 121), *etc.* Such procedures would presumably yield knowledge stemming from only one of the "three ways of knowing" that he differentiates in his paper.

The reader need not look to the paper by B. F. Skinner for a defense of conventional behaviorism. Skinner's radical behaviorism stands sharply in contrast to the more popular varieties of behaviorism criticized so effectively by Koch and defended in part by Rogers. The theme of Skinner's antagonism to conventional behaviorism runs through much of his later work. His objections to the inroads upon behaviorism of logical positivism and of what he calls "the operationism of Boring and Stevens" can be seen explicitly in as early a work as his revolutionary paper on operationism (1945). It is clear that Koch did not intend to exempt Skinner from the force of the attack developed in his paper. Yet it is equally clear that Skinner did not feel that the major points of Koch's argument applied to him. In the discussion following Koch's paper Skinner insisted that he does not "subscribe to any of the stratagems of science" Koch described (p. 42). A member of the audience remarked that what Professor Koch presented did not seem

[1]Where no date is given, references apply to page numbers in Wann (1964).

"truly representative of what Skinner has to say" (p. 42). Even Scriven, in his formal critique of Koch's paper, emphasized the need for keeping clearly in mind the differences between conventional behaviorism and Skinner's views: "We notice that it is characteristic of Skinner's behaviorism that he does not saddle himself with this apparatus of the logic of science, which Koch so rightly criticizes. I would, therefore, put in a plea here for making a very careful distinction between the standard forms of behaviorism, and Skinner's, which really meets only two of Koch's five criteria for behaviorism, and these, in a rather special way" (p. 181). However, Koch was not unaware of the fact that certain differences exist between conventional behaviorism and Skinner's point of view. He seemed, rather, to feel that the Skinnerian position is in some fundamental way internally inconsistent. He referred to the position as "strange and equivocal", "systematically ambiguous", and "Pickwickian" (p. 43). Other more specific objections are mentioned. Although Koch persisted throughout the symposium in his view that Skinner's radical behaviorism is little more than a rather unusual variety of neo-neobehaviorism, in one of the discussions he made the following comment concerning the need to clarify the differences between conventional and radical behaviorism: "[Skinner's formulation in the paper presented was so] extraordinarily libertarian . . . that one begins to wonder what the actual defining characteristics of the behaviorist thesis or the behaviorist method might be in his particular case" (p. 98).

The second general conclusion to emerge from the Rice symposium was that in spite of the patent difficulties of a conservative and conventional behaviorism, there are marked indications of an increasing *rapprochement* between the interests of behaviorism and phenomenology. This conclusion was apparently not expected by those who organized the symposium. Wann appeared surprised to have to conclude that the major trend in the symposium was a "blunting rather than a sharpening of the contrasts between behaviorism and phenomenology", and that "Professors MacLeod, Malcolm, Rogers, and Scriven, in one way or another, suggest the possibility of coexistence" (p. vii). Even Koch was aware of this trend, although he found it deplorable (p. 162). There was little uniformity of opinion concerning the nature of the implied compatibility. MacLeod suggested, with some diffidence, that the phenomenological approach in psychology might lead in part into some kind of "sophisticated behaviorism" (p. 55), and Scriven spoke specifically of the reconciliation of what he called *defensible* forms of phenomenology and behaviorism (p. 180). Malcolm was led to the conclusion "that Skinner had stated here an absolutely decisive objection to introspectionism", and he devoted considerable attention to giving "an account of the hard core of logical truth contained in behaviorism" (p. 149). Malcolm qualified his endorsement by stating that the Achilles' heel of behaviorism lay in its treatment of psychological sentences in the first-person-present tense. Skinner, for his part, thanked Malcolm for his support and suggested that perhaps agreement could be reached, even with respect to first-person statements (p. 155).

However, Wann is not so sure that Skinner's views as presented in the symposium are compatible with the interests of phenomenology. In his introduction, Wann leaves it for the reader to decide whether Skinner joins the majority of the symposium in seeing the possibilities of a reconciliation (p. viii). On the inside flap of the book's jacket it is stated that "only Koch and Skinner dissent from the view that coexistence is possible." Certainly this hesitancy to regard Skinner's position as in any way compatible with phenomenology is characteristic of the attitude maintained by a majority of contemporary psychologists. The purpose of this paper is to show that Skinner's radical behaviorism is indeed capable of encompassing a productive phenomenology. In the material that follows there is first a description of what I shall call the basic dimensions of radical behaviorism. This is partly in response to Koch's request for a statement of the "defining characteristics" of Skinner's position. Next, I shall attempt to illustrate the way in which radical behaviorism might profitably proceed to interact with problems that are often considered phenomenological in nature. Finally, I shall close with a brief discussion of some of the major problems that are faced in bringing about an effective reconciliation of radical behaviorism and phenomenology.

THE BASIC DIMENSIONS OF RADICAL BEHAVIORISM

In this section I shall try to describe what I consider to be the basic dimensions of Skinner's radical behaviorism. I feel that almost all of what I have to say is rigidly under the control of a careful study of Skinner's work in breadth and depth. Nevertheless, I am prepared to accept responsibility if some defense should be necessary of the presentation that I make. I have chosen this course of action largely for reasons of simplicity and convenience. Skinner's work is difficult to understand, and a detailed textual explication of the relevant material scattered throughout his writing would involve a tiresome analysis of specific contexts.

As an example of the problem faced in detailed explication, consider the following two statements by Skinner which bear directly upon the difference between radical and conventional behaviorism. First, in the early symposium on operationism Skinner discusses the difficulties which arise in making a distinction between things that are public and those that are private. He criticizes "the arid philosophy of 'truth by agreement' ", a perspective often adopted by conventional behaviorists who claim that scientific knowledge must somehow be essentially public in nature. Skinner proceeds to state that "the distinction between public and private is by no means the same as that between physical and mental. That is why methodological [or conventional] behaviorism (which adopts the first) is very different from radical behaviorism (which lops off the latter term in the second)" (1945, p. 294). Secondly, in response to a question raised by Scriven in the Rice symposium concerning how he can justify calling himself a radical behaviorist, Skinner replies that, "I am a radical behaviorist simply in the sense that I find no place in the formulation for anything which is mental" (p. 106). These comments by Skinner are likely to appear somewhat cryptic to someone who has not studied Skinner's published work intensively. It is clear that Skinner is objecting here not to things that are private but to things that are mental. It is true that the distinction between radical and conventional behaviorism hinges in a number of ways on the issue of mentalism. It is also true that one of Skinner's most persistent objections to conventional behaviorism is directed at a fundamental mentalism which he sees as all too thinly disguised. Yet actually, the issues involved in what Skinner means by "mentalism" are quite complex. The careful clarification of what Skinner is getting at in such statements as these requires a more detailed analysis than can be given here.

A Focal Interest in the Control of Behavior

Perhaps the most conspicuous characteristic of radical behaviorism is its focal interest in the control of behavior. Radical behaviorists view themselves as essentially engaged in a search for what they call controlling variables, even though the term *variable* is often used in a sense only distantly related to its etymology. Events are considered controlling variables when they are seen, or perceived, to be related to behavior in some way. However, many times the identification of controlling variables does not follow from anything so simple as an observation of the temporal contiguity of phenomenal events. The identification is often likely to be emitted more after the fashion of what might be called a guess, a hunch, or an insight. Verbal behavior describing a relation between behavior and controlling variables is called the statement of a functional relationship, and a more or less systematic attempt to describe functional relationships is called a functional analysis of behavior. In the statement of a functional relationship, the controlling variable is called a stimulus, and that aspect of behavior seen in relationship to the controlling variable is called a response.

In using such words as *seen, perceived, observation, guess, hunch,* and *insight,* as in the preceding paragraph, the radical behaviorist does not feel that he is specifying with very much precision what many psychologists would call either behavioral or mental processes. He is simply talking as best he can—actually, in this case he is not talking as carefully as he might—and he is responding to discriminable events which have not been very consistently differentiated by whatever factors govern the way in which we learn to talk as we do. He calls a stimulus a stimulus for reasons that are presumably similar to those which make people speak of cows as cows, and he can be led to attempt to define a stimulus under circumstances (and with characteristic difficulties) that are much the same as what one might expect to find in being called upon to define a cow. Yet why struggle to define a cow when any child sufficiently exposed to the ordinary verbal community can identify one on sight? Similarly, the capacity to identify a stimulus as such presumably depends largely upon the reinforcing practices of some scientific verbal community.

The practice of looking for functional relationships is obviously similar in certain respects to the effort to find relations between cause and effect. Yet in attempting to discover functional relationships the radical behaviorist does not accept any *a priori* logical assumption of a universe that is orderly in a mechanical sense upon which he feels he must base his scientific work. To be sure, he can easily be led, by appropriate verbal manipulation, to state that he "[assumes] that nature is orderly rather than capricious" (Skinner, 1950, p. 193). However in doing so, nothing of the least systematic significance is asserted. A rancher can undoubtedly be led to state that he assumes cattle are on a particular range where he expects to find them, yet it is absurd to look to a cowboy for profound philosophy.

The interest of the radical behaviorist in the concept of control reflects his conviction that if knowledge is to be trusted it is often likely to lead ultimately to effective action. He is most confident in his statement of a functional relationship if it plays some part in guiding him eventually to the successful manipulation, *i.e.*, control, of specific behavior. Furthermore, a focal interest in the control of behavior does not prejudice the case for the importance in human functioning of genetic or constitutional factors, nor does it lead to any such grandiose hypothesis as that all behavior is controlled by reinforcement.

The Focal Awareness That Any Scientist Is Himself a Behaving Organism

A second basic dimension of radical behaviorism is its insistence that scientists are themselves no more than behaving organisms. Science is at heart either the behavior of scientists or the artifacts of such activity, and scientific behavior is in turn presumably controlled by much the same kind of variables as those which govern any other aspect of complex human behavior.

However, as commonplace as this notion may appear to most psychologists, it leads in the mind of radical behaviorists to conclusions that are likely to seem strange to many persons. The radical behaviorist faces the fact that the ultimate achievement of his scientific activities is for the most part either further verbal behavior on his own part or a new set of acquired behaviors which hopefully enable him to control nature more effectively. Yet in viewing his own verbal and intellectual behavior as significantly controlled in a number of ways, he is led in a sense not to trust it at face value. He is aware, for example, that much of what he says in offering systematic psychology is likely to reflect psychological distinctions that are modeled after linguistic practices uncritically acquired simply in learning to speak the lay vocabulary. He is particularly conscious of the fact that much psychological talk reflects stereotyped conceptions both of the nature of the knowing process and of the relation between our knowledge of things and the structure of whatever it is that is taken to be the object of psychological investigation. For example, he is suspicious of primitive animism, which embodies nature with man-like powers, strengths, and forces, as well as of a facile determinism, which views the aim of research as isolating the fundamental elements of nature which are thought of as existing in some kind of mechanical interrelationship.

His resistance to such hidden epistemology leads at times to an obstinate refusal to think in terms of a particular common-sense theory of what it is to have knowledge about one or another subject matter. This is the notion that whenever we have significant knowledge, this knowledge consists of an at least partial identification of the inherent nature of what it is that is known about. The notion is, in other words, that in knowing about something the expression of our knowledge consists in a comment on the *nature* of the object of knowledge or of a statement of what the object of knowledge *is.* It is as if in verbalizing our knowledge of things we have always to express an identification of one or another aspect of the permanent structure of nature. Yet the radical behaviorist is aware that we may attribute thing-ness to events largely because we are accustomed to speak of the world about us as composed of objects which are felt to possess an inherent constancy or stability. He is reluctant to take for granted that all useful knowledge must be conceptualized in terms of verbal patterns of thought derived simply from our experience with material objects. Consequently, he is led to a position which is peculiarly anti-ontological.

In particular, he objects to speaking of the events associated in a functional relationship as if they were things and objects having a more or less permanent identity as real elements of nature. He does not believe that the functional relations he describes constitute an identification of anything which might be called "true laws of nature", in the sense that the systematic collection of such functional relations can ultimately be expected to fit together into a completed picture of an account of human interaction with the environment. Rather, he is content for the most part simply to describe whatever natural consistency he can actually see, and to hope that the report he makes of his observations will in turn generate ultimately more productive behavior in the control of human affairs. He adopts this course of action out of an interest in increased efficiency and a conviction that only the analysis of behavior will lead some day to a more trustworthy set of guidelines for the acquisition of knowledge.

Consider several illustrations of this point of view. The statement made above that science is the behavior of scientists is not viewed by the radical behaviorists as a reductionist treatment of what might be viewed as an ontological assertion. It is regarded instead as an highly abstract description of what we are probably looking at when we identify events as constituting science. In the Rice symposium Skinner bluntly states that he is not interested in the nature of reinforcement. He comments: "I do not know why [food is reinforcing to a hungry animal] and I do not care" (p. 104). Skinner is also well known for his repudiation of reference theories of meaning (*e.g.*, 1957, p. 7*f.*, p. 114*f.*). Such theories generally assume that words are objects which are somehow attached to other objects or entities which are called meanings. In what Skinner calls mentalism, inner psychological processes are given homuncular power to cause other more behavioral events to come about. It is not so widely recognized that it is possible to "mentalize" environmental events, as where reinforcers are endowed, often in the thinking of avowed Skinnerians, with some sort of demoniacal power to forge the chains of a reified conception of conditioning.

The reader is likely to resist strenuously such an anti-ontological outlook. Consider the following remarks by Koch: "More generally, I think there is something frightening about the way neo-neobehaviorism is treating the newly reclaimed subject-matter. . . . Scientific knowledge is, of course, 'selective'—but when ontology is distorted, denied, or evaded past a certain point, one is no longer in the context of serious scholarship" (p. 32). Similarly, MacLeod has the following to say: "To build a science of psychology one must begin with the phenomenal world, but then one must transcend it. . . . Every scientist is a metaphysician, whether or not he likes to admit it, at least to the extent that he asserts the existence of something which he does not fully understand but which he is determined to investigate" (p. 54).

Still, the force of radical behaviorism presses for the formulation of a radically new epistemology. The most conspicuous characteristic of this new epistemology will be that it will have been obtained by the psychological analysis of the behavior, both public and private, of scientists, scholars, and whatever other persons can reasonably be said to know things. It will involve, more specifically, the analysis of the variables controlling the verbal behavior of whosoever uses the word *knowledge* and related terms in an interesting and significant way. Skinner has called at great length and over a period of many years for the formulation of such an epistemology (*e.g.*, 1945, p. 277; 1957, Ch. 18; 1961, p. 392; 1964, p. 104), but as yet no serious attempt at the requisite behavioral analysis has been undertaken.

Even so, in the last analysis the radical behaviorist is committed to an exceedingly liberal position with respect to the verbal behavior of his professional colleagues. Admittedly, the reliance upon a speculative epistemology is deplorable, especially when unrecognized or unintended, but objection is ultimately to be raised only on pragmatic grounds. Anyone is basically free to speak as he does. A man says what he can say; he says what he *does* say, and all this is in principle acceptable to the radical behaviorist, since whatever is said is as such a manifestation of complex human functioning and is consequently the legitimate object of behavioral investigation. In responding to professional language, the radical behaviorist has his own new course to follow: he must attempt to discover the variables controlling what has been said. Even the most mentalistic language is understandable and valuable in this sense. The meaningfulness of psychological and mental terms provides no insuperable problem, provided the verbal practices of both speaker and hearer have been shaped by overlapping verbal communities. The meaning of such terms can be clarified by an attempt to assess the observable (not necessarily publicly observable) events that act as discriminative stimuli in control of emission of the term. This kind of analysis is what Skinner has in mind when he speaks of "operational definition" (1945, p. 271).

The Focal Interest in Verbal Behavior Controlled by Directly Observed Events

The radical behaviorist is further characterized by the heavy value he places on the consequences of direct observation. In his view, the more he can bring his own verbal behavior under the control of what he has actually observed, the more productive and useful it is likely to be. The control exercised by the observed event may be relatively direct, as in simple description, or rather more complex, as in the identification of controlling variables or in the behavior of deciding which of a variety of potential variables next to manipulate. In the early stages of research, or when an overabundance of theoretical speculation has become involved, there is generally a preference for simple description. The power of simple description as a method for generating knowledge appears to have been grossly underestimated. Of course, nothing in the Skinner system requires that the observer restrict his talk simply to the emission of descriptive statements. Once the observation of behavior has taken place, the observer should be encouraged to talk interpretatively about what he has seen, not necessarily restricting himself to the identification of controlling variables. To be sure, the radical behaviorist recognizes that the particular interpretation that he makes will be a function of his own special history, and clearly interpretation guided by extensive observation of relevant behavior is to be preferred to speculation by the novice. It is, of course, only under very special circumstances that the interpretations that an observer makes of what he has seen should be identified as a contribution to psychological "theory".

This outlook is viewed as markedly in contrast with most popular approaches to psychological research. The standard machinery of experimental method in psychology is seen as yielding results that are much too distantly related to anything directly observable. To be sure, in most psychological studies subjects are required at some point or other to do at least something which is capable of being seen. But how often does the psychologist actually watch his subjects in action, hoping simply that what he sees will lead him to talk more informatively about what he is investigating? All too frequently, the principal investigator of a research project merely surveys an orderly collection of numbers, usually purported to be composite "measures" of something of other. These numbers have in turn been written down by some more fortunate graduate student who presumably had at least the opportunity to observe the relevant behavior as it actually took place. Even in circumstances where the behavior of immediate interest is preserved intact, as in the verbal protocols used in content analysis, how frequently is the experimenter himself in a position to observe the specific stimulating conditions under which the behavior has been emitted? Without the most skillful practices of observation on the part of the experimenter himself, why should one expect a relation between stimulus and response ever to be perceived? It is not that conventional experimental method is incapable of generating the observed functional relationships so much of interest to the radical behaviorist, especially when the method has been purged of statistical over-refinement. The point is only that most psychologists rarely take active advantage of the opportunity to inspect both behavior and its controlling stimulation as closely as they might. Cumulative records are valued by Skinner precisely because he feels they make certain interesting changes in behavior conspicuously *visible.*

However, the interest of the radical behaviorist in the effects of observation is neither complex nor profound. He merely hopes that what he sees will come to exert an increasing influence on what he says. In this he is not unlike the unpedantic clinical psychologist who simply behaves in the therapeutic situation in a way that he regards as the natural outcome of his past experience in treating patients. Usage here of the term *observation* does not imply any special mental or behavioral process. The verbal community teaches us all to distinguish observation from reflection, speculation, wool-gathering, thinking, and other psychological activities, although the extent to which the differential reinforcement involved is consistent has not as yet been described. Neither does the focal interest in observation commit the radical behaviorist to the notion that observation must somehow be essentially public. In fact, most of the time it is easiest to view observation as something private, in the sense that no more than one individual participates in the behavioral event we identify as a single act of observation. Similarly, there is no restriction of interest to events which are considered to be observable "in principle" by someone else. The radical behaviorist feels as free to observe or otherwise respond to his own reactions to a Beethoven sonata as he is to observe those of someone else.

The Focal Awareness of the Importance of Environmental Variables

The radical behaviorist is interested in the environment for a variety of reasons. First of all, it is simply obvious that a great deal of behavior is to some extent under environmental control. However, it is not so obvious that the grain of the environmental control of behavior is much finer than is commonly appreciated: the slightest difference in stimulating conditions (which the experimenter is often not prepared to appreciate) may lead to very gross differences in behavior. For example, in an experimenter's attempt to get a human subject to press a button over and over again in a standard rate of response study, the instruction, "Following your first press, if you wish to continue to press the button, you may do so", is observed to lead some subjects simply to keep the button depressed for as long as 15 minutes, with no environmental change taking place. Similarly, in teaching machine programming, it generally requires very subtle environmental engineering to make it highly likely that the experimental student will emit the desired response.

An interest in the environment also follows from the inherently practical orientation of the radical behaviorist. In so far as he is interested in manipulation and control, he becomes committed to a basic concern with the environment. Whatever is done by way of any manipulation inevitably consists of some change in the environment of the person whose behavior is to be affected, and one has little reason to expect a manipulation to be successful unless it reflects some functional relation between behavior and the relevant environmental change. To precisely the same extent as one is interested in manipulation he becomes concerned with ways in which the environment is related to behavior. However, the radical behaviorist is interested in manipulation not only for its immediate effect upon the behavior he is attempting to control, but also because he wants the manipulation to have some effect upon his own behavior as a scientist. The extent to which he is able to manipulate behavior successfully is perhaps the most important variable that acts to shape his own research activities. He is likely to feel that the most effective means of acquiring knowledge about some aspect of behavior is to attempt to learn how to shape up that very behavior in which he is interested. In speaking of the need for an empirical epistemology, Skinner states that "it is possible that we shall fully understand the nature of knowledge only after having solved the practical problems of imparting it" (1961, p. 392).

The radical behaviorist is interested in the environment for a still more basic reason. He holds the view that *all* verbal behavior, no matter how private its subject matter may appear to be, is to some significant extent controlled by the environment. Although he recognizes that the range of phenomena related to human verbal functioning varies from the most intimately personal to the most spectacularly social, he sees that all meaningful language is shaped into effective form by the action of an environmental verbal community. It is this contact of language with the environment that enables us to respond effectively to it. We know, in other words, what language means because some common environmental contingency controls both our own behavior and that of the speaker whose talk is of interest to us. To be sure, it is only rarely possible for us to perceive directly the relevant environmental variables as they operate to shape the verbal behavior with which we are concerned. Yet the problem here is no different in kind from that faced in attempting to infer the contingencies controlling any aspect of a person's previous history. The verbal community has taught us a variety of practices by which we guess at relevant factors, some more useful than others.

The case is not prejudiced for an interest in what someone has to say about what he considers his own private experience. Verbal behavior constitutes by far the most convenient avenue of access to anything that might be considered a significant aspect of human knowledge, including one's own knowledge of himself. If we want to find out more about what a man is experiencing in a certain situation, one of the simplest things to do is to try to get him to talk. Of course, whether or not we happen to trust the speaker depends upon the nature of the environmental control exercised by him over our own behavior. Yet the radical behaviorist is not basically concerned with whether or not a speaker is telling the truth. What he wants to know is what makes him say the things that he does. This leads him inevitably to a concern, at least in part, with the environmental events that have acted to teach him to talk. It leads also to an interest in possible events in the present and recent environment of the speaker that bear some similarity to the stimulation available to the verbal community in providing initial differential reinforcement. In searching for such influences he will be himself for the most part responding in some way to the environment. It is the belief of the radical behaviorist that by tracing the environmental chain of command over verbal behavior as far as possible, he can extend the range of his effective action as a scientist most profitably. Suppose, for example, that a student begins to suspect that he senses some order of a particular kind in human functioning. What must he do? He must not fail to proceed directly to an explicit verbal description of *what he has seen* that appears to make him think he has found something. This first step involves, of course, an analysis of the environmental control of his own behavior.

There is yet a fourth way in which the radical behaviorist is interested in the environment. He tends to regard explanations as simply incomplete if they do not involve tracing the observable antecedents of behavior back as far as possible into the environment. Many current psychological explanations are thus seen as incomplete, since they often do little more than specify some inner process as the cause of a particular aspect of behavior. Issues of ontology are again involved here, since explanatory inner processes are generally regarded as having a kind of power metaphorically related to primitive animism. However, if the ontological pattern of language is insisted upon, it is only reasonable to ask what makes the inner process work as it does. Since an answer to this question is usually not provided, the radical behaviorist regards such explanations as incomplete.

The case is different if the explanation involves no more than the description of a relation between behavior and some observed private event. Such a relation constitutes a legitimate functional relationship in precisely the same way as does the statement of a relation between behavior and the environment. Here the radical behaviorist asks only that the situation be more closely examined to see if the private event in turn cannot be seen to bear some relation to the environment. If it can, then the functional relation as stated is clearly incomplete as an explanation of the behavior. In those cases where the private event is conspicuously related to the environment, then reference to the private event is likely to be considered irrelevant or unnecessary for purposes of manipulation and control. In those absurd situations where private events are said to control behavior even though they are not themselves directly observable even to a single observer, as in much of Freud and in certain uses of the term *self,* then the explanation is of interest only as a sample of very complexly constructed verbal behavior.

However, the preference for environmental explanation does not mean that it is the only meaningful form of explanation. The radical behaviorist makes no prior epistemological assumption that an explanation is complete only when environmental controlling variables have been identified. Many patters of verbal behavior pass as successful explanation to many people, and indeed common practices of explanation provide an interesting area for empirical investigation. The complex verbal material that composes psychological theory is not to be abhorred on principle. The radical behaviorist simply calls attention, again, to the fact that psychological theory is after all directly observed as verbal behavior on the part of the theorist, and it seems good advice to suggest that the theorist at least attempt to understand the factors that operate to make him generate his theory in the way that he does. Even a fairly casual inspection of most of the verbal material that is considered by many to be psychological theory can be seen to manifest conspicuous control by ordinary language habits, extensive chains of familiar intraverbals, and one or another preconception about the inherent nature of scientific explanation.

RADICAL BEHAVIORISM AND PHENOMENOLOGICAL RESEARCH

It is probably already clear that there is no inherent incompatibility between a robust interest in phenomenology and the basic dimensions of radical behaviorism. Koch himself has stated the terms that must be met before a harmonious coexistence between behaviorism and phenomenology is possible. He argues that psychology has to be a "conceptually heterogeneous" science. He would "no longer have any objection to neo-neobehaviorists" if "even the most libertarian" among them would "permit" such conceptual heterogeneity (p. 186). Clearly these terms are met by radical behaviorism. Any kind of professional language, no matter how esoteric, is of interest to the radical behaviorist as a sample of verbal behavior. What he wants to know is what sort of factors have been involved in leading the speaker to say what he does. Still, it seems natural to protest that when professional psychological talk is viewed simply as a sample of verbal behavior, what the psychologist is really trying to say has not been taken very seriously. Yet such a reaction reflects a misunderstanding of how earnestly the radical behaviorist is prepared to try to understand whatever factors control the emission of any interesting psychological talk. To know thoroughly what has caused a man to say something is to understand the significance of what he has said in its very deepest sense.

It is true that Skinner has not rushed to embrace with star-eyed enthusiasm the sentimental, emotional, common-sensical, or obscure outpourings that often pass as pleas for phenomenology in psychology. Why should he? Skinner has his own row to hoe in attempting to advance an explicit interest in the analysis of behavioral control, which is what many psychologists are basically interested in anyway. He does this in the face of a frankly embarrassing professional shallowness in the interpretation of his work. The popular "Skinnerian" myth that any concern with private experience must be "mentalistic" and is hence unbecoming to the radical behaviorist simply flies in the face of some of Skinner's best thought. Consider the following quotation from Skinner's contribution to the Symposium on Operationism.

> "Science does not consider private data," says Boring. (Just where this leaves my contribution to the present symposium, I do not like to reflect.) But I contend that my toothache is just as physical as my typewriter, though not public, and I see no reason why an objective and operational science cannot consider the processes through which a vocabulary descriptive of a toothache is acquired and maintained. The irony of it is that, while Boring must confine himself to an account of my external behavior, I am still interested in what might be called Boring-from-within. (1945, p. 294)

In the Rice symposium only Scriven seems really to appreciate what Skinner is basically up to, and Scriven is a philosopher. Both Rogers (p. 140) and Koch (p. 186) consider Skinner's verbal behavior as in some way inherently intolerant. But a specialization of interest does not imply intolerance, nor is intolerance implied by a decreasing interest in verbal behavior as its control by observable events becomes more hopelessly obscure.

The radical behaviorist understandably reacts slowly to phenomenological talk that is to some extent too distantly removed from the direct observations that have made the speaker excited to begin with. Even MacLeod, a phenomenologist to whom the radical behaviorist can look squarely with respect, remarks, "To be quite frank, I must confess that I find Heidegger as deadly as Hegel and that many existentialist plays leave me simply uncomfortable" (p. 51). It is easiest, for example, simply to try to swim along with Rogers through the first page of his paper for the Rice symposium, where the composition is heavily controlled by a torpid oceanic metaphor. "Like the flotsam and jetsam which float on each ocean current, certain words and phrases identify, even though they do not define, these separate flowing trends" (p. 109). Or, "Toward what shores, what islands, what vastnesses of the deep is its compelling current carrying us" (p. 100)? With respect to the second of these quotations, it could in fact be helpful, in trying to get an idea of what Rogers must have seen in his relevant therapeutic experience, to know to what extent and in what way the composition of this particular statement of his was under partial control of "The Tyger" by Blake.

However, it is more the purpose of this paper to clarify the possibilities of active reconciliation, rather than mere peaceful coexistence. There are numerous ways in which a flourishing phenomenology and radical behaviorism need each other. Consider first the case of radical behaviorism, whose current situation presses for the more explicit study of phenomenological functional relationships. Skinner's analyses of obviously phenomenological subject matter, as his chapter on "Private Events in a Natural Science" in *Science and Human Behavior* (1953, Ch. 17), or the paper on operationism (1945), or his contribution to the Rice symposium (1964), are clearly under the control of considerable self-observation on the part of Skinner himself. It is not that what Skinner has to say in his material needs "experimental test". What is needed is extensive descriptive analysis of verbal behavior controlled by observable events that are likely to be identified by the speaker as his own conscious experience, his inner subjective feelings, or his private hopes, fears, and aspirations. Without such a behavioral analysis, coverage of the obviously interesting aspects of human functioning will remain incomplete. Perhaps one need not expect to find in the analysis of phenomenological verbal behavior important causes of the social and personal-adjustmental behavior so much of current interest. However, the careful description of such functional relations can be expected to have an ameliorative influence upon the extent to which inner mental processes are called upon in the explanation of behavior. A sound phenomenology is the beat defense against a facile mentalism.

Similarly, radical behaviorism needs to attend to other, more complex aspects of behavior which are coming to be identified as phenomenological in a looser usage of the terms. There is great current interest in questions pertaining to the value, meaningfulness, and significance of a person's experience, and this interest is increasing. Except for want of time, there is no reason for the radical behaviorist to neglect to analyze the complex behavioral situations that are taken to be the signs of these broader phenomenological concerns. In making sense out of this behavior, he has no other recourse than to put himself in a position to make the same kind of observation—often clinical, literary, social, religious, or aesthetic in nature—that gives rise to such phenomenological talk. Extensive observation of the extraordinarily wide range of human functioning, from the contemplative behavior of the mystic through the puzzling behavior of the leather-jacketed cyclist, is urgently needed. How can we expect a viable psychology, when we find that so many psychologists are themselves simply rather narrowly experienced people? At the present time, radical behaviorism rapidly advances to the study of higher intellectual functioning in education, the rehabilitation of juvenile delinquents and criminals, the appreciation of music and art, and the behavior of psychotics and people who seek psychotherapy. In all this, the simple observation and description of the relevant behavior, conspicuously including what the persons involved have to say themselves, becomes of increasing importance. The current work of Murray Sidman (see, *e.g.*, Sidman and Stoddard, 1966) on the rehabilitation of mentally defective children is exemplary of the way in which a radical behaviorist can profitably take advantage many times of analyses which might easily be called phenomenological in nature.

As for the phenomenologist, he is for the most part still grossly unaware of the first lessons to be learned from the experimental analysis of behavior. The ways in which radical behaviorism impinges upon the domain of phenomenology have been delineated to a great extent by Skinner in the works referred to above. This paper has also attempted to clarify the radical behaviorist point of view so that its relevance to phenomenological interests can be appreciated. However, it should perhaps be stressed again, by way of summary, that insofar as the phenomenologist is in any way in contact with human functioning, he is looking at, and responding to, *behavior*, even though it may not be public in nature. Much of both his own behavior and that in which he is interested is under complex control, a control that is likely to be to a considerable extent environmental in nature. The phenomenologist needs greatly to recognize that a little less metaphor and theory, and a lot more simple description of the things that he has actually observed, would be of much help to others in understanding the problems he faces. For example, it is relatively exciting to learn that Rogers suspects some relationship between a patient's "willingness to discover new feelings and new aspects of himself" and "personality change". Yet it is not so interesting to watch him then go out and get a small gun from the arsenal of statistics and victoriously reject the notion of precisely zero correlation between some measure of self-exploration and another measure of personality change (p. 124). Here the perceived functional relation is directly of interest in itself. It is enough that it control verbal behavior. There is no need to use statistics to bolster one's self-confidence or to justify one's right to talk about behavior. The practical value of statistics lies elsewhere than in providing a simple criterion for deciding whether or not one knows anything about behavior.

The phenomenologist should be especially wary of the ways in which his previous experience acts to influence however he happens to talk, particularly in constructing theories, planning research, and reaching explanatory conclusions. He should, at least to some extent, attempt to assess the variables in his own history which affect his professional performance in any of its significant facets. When he places heavy emphasis on a word taken from the lay vocabulary, he must not fail to examine carefully the observable events which control his usage of the term and guarantee its successful effect upon the behavior of others. He should satisfy himself, in making use of a psychological test, that he really wants to regard the elicitation of specific samples of behavior as the "measurement" of some inner "thing", supposedly in part an element of the psychic apparatus. If he happens to prefer practices of explanation in which powers or forces are attributed to entities of any kind, he should try to form some notion of how he has come to acquire this particular preference. In the study of complex mental processes he must be sure he had observable evidence to help him decide what is chicken and what is egg, the prior environment or some inner mental entity presumed to influence behavior. When a mental process is purported to exist, he must know clearly in his own mind precisely to what extent the process is observable, *directly* observable, at least to someone.

Finally, the phenomenologist should recognize that he engages blindly in efforts at manipulation unless he is clearly aware of the pertinent relations between the environment (including his own behavior) and the behavioral change he is interested in making. He should keep in mind that an environmentalistic frontal attack on any problem of control may be considerably more profitable than recourse to verbal interpretations involving mental states. The best way to change a mental condition may be to try to change other, more conspicuous aspects of behavior first; the desired changes in covert behavior may occur as a result. For example, it is one thing to get a subject to respond on a paper-and-pencil test and quite something else again to know what the same Caucasian subject will feel when he first learns that his children will soon have to attend a predominantly non-white school. A particular manipulation may well succeed for rather trivial reasons in changing performance on a paper-and-pencil test; yet clearly much more complex problems of control are involved in shaping vigorous support for integration in the public school system. It is entirely possible that the best way to get a person to feel comfortable inside himself about issues of civil liberties is to attempt *first* to control his overt behavior in relevant social situations. One would possibly then find that the observable covert or overt behaviors taken as evidence of his attitudes on the subject have also changed.

PRACTICAL PROBLEMS IN RECONCILIATION

In closing, let me mention four problems that seem to me to stand particularly in the way of a healthy interaction between radical behaviorism and phenomenology. The first of these is the superficiality with which the profession at large is familiar with Skinner's work. A couple of survey courses in learning theory, possibly a reading of *The Behavior of Organisms*, a glance at *Science and Human Behavior* or *Walden Two*, the isolated study of such papers as "Are Theories of Learning Necessary?", or primary reliance on such digests as Hilgard and Bower's *Theories of Learning* (1966) will not do. If radical behaviorism is to be understood, Skinner's work must be studied by professionals with precisely the same diligence as that we take for granted from our better graduate students. In particular, the paper on operationism (1945), *Verbal Behavior* (1957), the later papers on programmed instruction (*e.g.*, 1961), and the paper for the Rice symposium (1964) must be *mastered*. By way of help, Verplanck's critique of Skinner's views in *Modern Learning Theory* (1954) can be taken as authoritative, in spite of the fact that it is now very much out of date.

The lack of careful study of Skinner's work has led to professional absurdities too numerous to review in detail. Strange blends of Skinner and conventional behaviorism abound. I would rather not identify the even relatively prominent Skinnerians who fail to concede that private events have any place in a natural science. Others view *Science and Human Behavior* as somehow beneath their empirical dignity; the word is passed around that the sticky parts of the book are to be excused because it is, after all, no more than a sophomore level text—this in spite of the fact that in a work as crucial as *Verbal Behavior*, Skinner refers the reader back again to *Science and Human Behavior* for his most thorough analysis of the issue of private experience (1957, p. 130). Mentalism among Skinnerians is rampant, and they are quickly trapped by the operationism of Boring and Stevens. Unfortunately, only very few people have an accurate idea of what Skinner means by operational definition. I have taken the liberty of speaking here directly to some of those who preach most loudly a supposedly Skinnerian line. One hardly knows where to begin to analyze the grossly uninformed verbal material that is generated concerning Skinner's work by the typical psychologist.

A second problem is the failure to distinguish sharply enough between radical and conventional behaviorism, a point much emphasized in this paper. Operationism and the logical positivism of the 1930's operate to influence both points of view but in markedly different ways. Skinner came quickly to detest logical positivism. In the Rice symposium, one would have expected Koch to focus his intelligence on radical rather than on conventional behaviorism at the time. It is much to be hoped that Koch will not long delay in accepting the challenge of a critique of radical behaviorism. The radical behaviorist cannot look profitably for relevant criticism to the painstaking review of *Verbal Behavior* made by Chomsky (1959). Chomsky writes under the misconception that Skinner's work is more or less another form of conventional behaviorism dominated by logical positivism in the usual way. The same misconception leads Malcolm in the Rice symposium (p. 144*f.*) to try to clarify the philosophical implications of Skinner's views by extensive quotations from Carnap and Hempel. We can similarly excuse Malcolm's unfortunate remark that, "In his brilliant review . . . of Skinner's *Verbal Behavior*, Noam Chomsky shows conclusively . . . that Skinner fails to make a case for his belief that 'functional analysis' is able to deal with verbal behavior" (p. 154). The philosophical character of Skinner's work is considerably closer to what is often now called "analytic philosophy" or "ordinary language analysis" than to the narrow forms of logical positivism that have influenced psychological thinking to so great an extent. Koch (p. 23) suspects that behaviorism might try to look to analytic philosophy for its defense, and Scriven (p. 179) associates Skinner's analysis of the language of private experience with the central problem of the *Philosophical Investigations* of Ludwig Wittgenstein (1953). Wittgenstein's later work forms the basis of much of the force of analytic philosophy, and a number of similarities between his views and Skinner's are pointed out in a paper now in press (Day, 1969). The student of radical behaviorism is well advised to read the *Philosophical Investigations* as an antidote to the inroads of logical positivism on psychology. It would also make the reading of Skinner's work somewhat easier.

A third and related problem faced in the effective reconciliation of radical behaviorism and phenomenology is the lack of training among psychologists in contemporary philosophy. The traces of an Oedipal resentment of philosophy by psychology still persist, much to the detriment of effective self-criticism among psychologists. Unfortunate preconceptions about the nature of science are currently under considerable philosophical attack, and this theme runs throughout much of Koch's paper for the Rice symposium. There is presently a new and vigorous excitement about phenomenology in professional philosophy. The relevance of these philosophical interests to practical problems in psychology is coming increasingly to be appreciated. Witness the birth of the new division of philosophical psychology in the American Psychological Association. Scriven's lengthy paper for the Rice symposium is essentially philosophical in nature, yet it will afford an eye-opening experience for any psychologist who takes the time to give it careful study. In two pages Scriven takes the trouble to list no less than 13 "other philosophical topics that have been deeply involved . . . in the course of the symposium" (p. 178*f.*). Yet how many psychologists have learned simply to turn a philosopher off when he starts to say something they do not like to hear? In the discussion following his paper, Scriven bluntly comments that "pure research in social psychology is among the most unproductive fields of human endeavor today" (p. 190). In another context he notes that "steaming somebody up to think that the only way to do psychology is via phenomenology and that all behaviorists are wicked may well turn out to be a good way of getting him to do something worthwhile, but it is certainly an unfortunate comment on psychology if psychologists need to do this. Do we *have* to feed ourselves fibs as fuels for our forward movement" (p. 177)? How many of us psychologists are sufficiently prepared to understand Scriven when he talks?

Finally, a fourth problem lies in certain practical difficulties faced in attempting to carry out explicitly descriptive research. These difficulties stem from the complex set of professional practices that define what is, and what is not, acceptable as psychological research. A simple interest in behavior no longer suffices to lead a man to try to make the relevant observations. He must first justify, often with hypocrisy, and inevitably with great caution, whatever interest in behavior he may have. The justification of research must walk the razor's edge of sufficient but not too much similarity to the research activities of other scientists. What is the hypothesis tested? What possible outcomes are anticipated? Except in those areas where we already have considerable knowledge and consequently need research the least, how can a man be expected to know what he may find in his research? Conspicuously exploratory research is frowned upon; it is tolerated only when the researcher's competence is buttressed by a formidable list of publications, often in some picked-over area. To remonstrate that the very canons of the respected establishment are under attack is to no avail. Who would suspect that simply by looking carefully at whatever one is interested in, no matter how complex the behavior may be, and by trying to push it around a bit, one can come to know a great deal more about the subject?

The profession greatly needs a lot more writing that consists of little more than careful description of what is actually observed by psychologists. One is understandably anxious in research to go beyond the stage of mere description to the statement of significant conclusions concerning behavioral control. It is understandable also that conclusions, rather than descriptions, find themselves the prized commodity in the market of publication. However, conclusions are specimens of verbal behavior that involve a very complex kind of control. Equally profitable in the control of productive professional behavior are the direct observations that presumably govern the published conclusions. The need for simple descriptions of observed behavior is especially great in precisely those areas of psychology where clear-cut conclusions are difficult to draw. Although someone is able to make only the most tentative conclusions—here, of course, he is conditioned to hesitate even to speak, much less to publish—the professional community still needs the benefit of his experience. Similarly, the man who looks but fails to find at all must nonetheless be encouraged to report what he has seen. Without publication, the possibility that his observations may have some more fortunate effect on the behavior of someone else is lost. Unless the beginning psychologist can rely on having access to the direct observations of others, he must face the bleak prospect of a career in research that even he himself may view as trivial, or he must undertake the uphill fight of analyzing behavior essentially by himself, alone.

In short, the hearty interaction of radical behaviorism and phenomenology is hindered only by one or another form of narrowness of outlook. With a deeper and wider scholarship on the part of the interested psychologist, with a considerably enlarged familiarity on his part with the rich spectrum of human activities, and with a greater freedom to make the observations upon which a broader understanding of behavior must depend, then the inherent liberalism of radical behaviorism can find successful reconciliation with the libertarian aspirations of phenomenology.

REFERENCES

Chomsky, N. Review of Skinner's *Verbal Behavior*. *Language*, 1959, 35, 26–58.

Day, W. F. On certain similarities between the *Philosophical Investigations* of Ludwig Wittgenstein and the operationism of B. F. Skinner. *Journal of the Experimental Analysis of Behavior*, 1969 (in press).

Hilgard, E. R. and Bower, G. H. *Theories of learning*. (3rd ed.) New York: Appleton-Century-Crofts, 1956.

Sidman, M. and Stoddard, L. T. Programming perception and learning for retarded children. *International Review of Research in Mental Retardation*, 1966, 2, 151–208.

Skinner, B. F. The operational analysis of psychological terms. *Psychological Review*, 1945, 52, 270–277, 291–294.

Skinner, B. F. Are theories of learning necessary? *Psychological Review*, 1950, 57, 193–216.

Skinner, B. F. *Science and human behavior*. New York: Macmillan, 1953.

Skinner, B. F. *Verbal behavior*. New York: Appleton-Century-Crofts, 1957.

Skinner, B. F. Why we need teaching machines. *Harvard Educational Review*, 1961, 31, 377–398.

Skinner, B. F. Behaviorism at fifty. *Science*, 1963, 140, 951–958, and in T. W. Wann (Ed.). *Behaviorism and phenomenology*. Chicago: University of Chicago Press, 1964. Pp. 79–97.

Verplanck, W. S. In W. K. Estes, S. Koch, K. MacCorquodale, P. E. Meehl, C. G. Mueller, Jr., W. N. Schoenfeld, and W. S. Verplanck. *Modern learning theory*. New York: Appleton-Century-Crofts, 1954. Pp. 267–316.

Wann, T. W. (Ed.) *Behaviorism and phenomenology*. Chicago: University of Chicago Press, 1964.

Wittgenstein, L. *Philosophical investigations*. New York: Macmillan, 1953.

9

BEHAVIOR THERAPY AND THE IDEOLOGY OF MODERNITY

ROBERT L. WOOLFOLK AND FRANK C. RICHARDSON

A lucid and highly regarded textbook on behavior therapy offered the following definition:

> As an applied science, behavior therapy is simply a collection of principles and techniques about how to change behavior; it says nothing about who should modify what behavior, why, or when. (Wilson & O'Leary, 1980, p. 285)

Though behavior therapy has been given many other definitions (Bandura, 1969; Wolpe, 1973), virtually all have conceived of it as a neutral structure, a body of "objective knowledge" verified by experimental test. Behavior therapy's self-image is that of an applied science, devoid of any inherent prescriptive thrust or implicit system of values, the essence of which can be accounted for without reference to any cultural or historical context.

Recent work in the philosophy and history of science, however, has undermined seriously the view of science on which behavior therapy's self-image is based. Attempts to equate scientific knowledge with that which is empirically verifiable or to identify scientific progress with some inflexible standard of verification have proven lacking (Bartley, 1962; Burtt, 1964; Weimer, 1979). The form and content of scientific knowledge are strongly influenced by socio-political factors as well as those related to the attitudes and sensibilities of the community of scientists (Feyerabend, 1975; Kuhn, 1970a, 1970b; Polanyi, 1966). Because their subject matter bears so directly on and is influenced by the human self-image, the social sciences and systems of psychotherapy are even more limited in their ability to remain independent of cultural influence (Buss, 1975; London, 1964; Lowe, 1976; Sampson, 1978, 1981).

Reprinted from the *American Psychologist, 39,* 777–786. (1984).

The notion that all knowledge arises out of a social context and that, hence, a complete account of any system of thought must encompass its cultural and ideological foundations has its roots in the philosophies of Hegel and Marx and has found its most recent expression in three related intellectual movements: the sociology of knowledge, critical theory, and hermeneutic philosophy. Our analysis of behavior therapy draws on all three of these sources. The sociology of knowledge (Berger & Luckman, 1966; Mannheim, 1936; Scheler, 1960) takes the perspective that knowledge is one among the many and various products of culture. Thinkers in this tradition seek to elucidate the relationship between the nature of a given society and the Weltanschauungen to which it gives rise as well as the processes by which definitions of "reality" are socially constructed. Critical theory (Habermas, 1972, 1973; Horkheimer, 1972) has been engaged in the critique of contemporary patterns of intellectual activity and of modern social institutions. One of the main concerns of thinkers in this tradition has been to trace the connection between intellectual and social forms of fragmentation and alienation in modern society, on the one hand, and on the other hand, the increasing rationalization (in the Weberian sense) of the relations of social life in a technically managed society. The interpretive or hermeneutic approach to the study of human society and action (Gadamer, 1975; Ricoeur, 1981; Taylor, 1971) holds that any scientific account of human activity is, of necessity, epistemologically embedded within a world of intersubjective cultural meanings that are constitutive of the conceptual categories within which the science operates. From this perspective, no social science can ever truly stand outside or transcend the social practices and institutions that have served to constitute it in the first place.

From the perspectives of the sociology of knowledge, critical theory, and hermeneutics, behavior therapy is a more interesting and complex phenomenon than it purports to be. In addition to being a scientific account of the alteration of emotional and behavioral problems, behavior therapy is also an intellectual movement, a set of social practices, and a system of thought. In each of these guises it contains not only theoretical and technological aspects but also a prescriptive, ideological component: a favored mode of thinking and implicit criteria for making judgments that guide behavior therapists in their activities and also represent a vision of reality underlying those activities that justify and support them. Our approach to behavior therapy will not be to examine it as a body of techniques and a supporting theory to be compared on the dimensions of technical efficacy or theoretical elegance with some other therapeutic school such as psychoanalysis. Indeed, to do so would leave unexamined those tacit, epistemological biases and value commitments that must be encompassed by any fundamental critique.

Rather, we shall show how behavior therapy is implicitly predicated on modern epistemological and ethical assumptions. We also shall demonstrate how its scientific–technological sensibility is reflected in both its immense and estimable achievements as well as in what appear to be very serious limitations in its capacity to address some aspects of the human situation that are basic to the conduct of psychotherapy in the contemporary world. Our explication of the ideological underpinnings of behavior therapy is closely related to an analysis of modernity and modern modes of thought.

MODERNITY

Modernity refers to the total condition of culture in those societies that have been transformed by science and the application of scientific technology.

> What is involved in modernization is a "total" transformation of a traditional or pre-modern society into the types of technology and associated social organization that characterize the

"advanced," economically prosperous, and relatively politically stable nations of the Western World. (Moore, 1963, p. 89)

Along with the application of scientific technology to the means of production within a society come inevitable changes in the world view of its people (Berger, 1977). This modernization of the consciousness of premodern cultures is a reliable, patterned phenomenon that has been occurring in Western societies since the advent of the Industrial Revolution (Nelson, 1981). Such changes of outlook begin in the intellectual elites and extend to the population at large as education, the absorption of individuals into modern, technocratically managed institutions, and the proliferation of media become more widespread (Parsons, 1971).

The world view of modernity is dominated by science and scientific technology and the modes of thought peculiar to them (Gehlen, 1980). It is rooted in the ideal of progress, a faith in the power of human abilities to be equal to any problem, the quest for certitude, and a devaluation of the traditional past (Shills, 1981). The cognitive style of modern consciousness tends toward the pragmatic and the rational. The focus of evaluation shifts from the ends of activity to means and their efficiency, as technique and technical considerations achieve paramount importance. Utility emerges as a generally agreed upon value (Ellul, 1964). The aims of prediction and control and a style of planning and decision making in which emotional and aesthetic considerations are subservient to the rational and pragmatic are the essential features of modern organizational direction, whether those organizations be communist bureaucracies or capitalist industrial corporations (Berger, Berger, & Kellner, 1973). Science becomes the ultimate source of knowledge and the model for all forms of intellectual activity (Hayek, 1952; Winner, 1977).

Modernization, whether it be of society or of methods of psychotherapy, always cuts two ways. Within society, the same forces that boldly advance human freedom and opportunity also erode those traditional belief systems that confer meaning upon experience and do damage to those social institutions that sustain emotional security, thus creating the heretofore novel human predicaments of loss of meaning, isolation, and alienation (Baumer, 1977). There is a "dark side" to modernity chronicled thoroughly by sociologists from Weber to Berger: the "disenchantment" of the world, the loss of community, the end of a self-evident moral structure and of a meaningful relationship between individual and cosmos. The "modern consciousness" of the industrialized West is a world view beset with dilemmas and malaises not found in primitive and traditional views of reality (Lévi-Strauss, 1966). So, too, the world view of behavior therapy, even in its most complex and sophisticated contemporary variations—for example, cognitive behavior therapy—partakes so fully of the modern perspective on life and living that it is consequently subject to both the advantages and disadvantages of the modern outlook. In this respect, behavior therapy is not unique among systems of therapy, many of which have "modern" thrusts (Bergin, 1980), but is rather a purer and more extreme embodiment of the chief strains of modernity.

THE BEHAVIORAL WELTANSCHAUUNG

Behavior therapy is a quintessentially modern set of activities: the application of a scientifically derived technology to the alteration of behavior. It is, in addition, a system of thought that adopts a radically scientific and technological perspective on human contact and on the enterprise of behavior change. Behavior therapy, in its theory and clinical practice, exemplifies both modern modes of thinking and the values of the modern technological society. The close affinity of the Weltanschauung of behavior therapy and that of modernity can be seen clearly by examining the presence in behavior therapy of four distinct but interrelated aspects of modernity: technicism, rationality, amorality, and humanism.

Technicism

Although virtually every other system of therapy is partially composed of therapeutic activities that could be properly regarded as techniques, none has sought so self-consciously to function as pure psychotechnology as has behavior therapy. None has sought to characterize itself almost entirely in terms of relationships between sets of explicit therapeutic aims and specific methods thought to reliably achieve those aims as "an empirically based technology of behavior change" (Kazdin & Wilson, 1978, p. 178). Most other systems carry what is from a technological vantage point some excess baggage: (1) methods of treatment that lack power, directness, and immediacy; (b) a theory of human functioning that contains rather obvious prescriptive components and, hence, a moral thrust; or (c) a prizing of certain forms of understanding or experiencing simply for their own sake, apart from any measurable, correlated changes in behavior that might ensue.

From its inception, behavior therapy adopted that most modern of sensibilities that has been variously termed the *technological attitude* (Berger & Kellner, 1981), or *technocratic consciousness* (Gouldner, 1976). From the very beginning, behavior therapy avoided the sins of inactivity characteristic of the early insight therapies and placed its emphasis on the refinement of technique and on the achievement of measurable results (Kazdin, 1978). Perhaps the most distinctive feature of behavior therapy's reformulation of psychotherapy theory and practice was its pragmatic temper, its insistence on the demonstrable utility of therapeutic activity, and its attempt to characterize that activity as a body of techniques with specific effects.

The goal of technology is the predictable, rational direction or control of events (Winner, 1977). Not surprisingly, the concept of control is crucial to behavior therapy and permeates its literature. Krasner (1962) wrote that the fundamental aim of behavior therapy research was that of devising "techniques of behavior control" (p. 103). In their classic book, Goldfried and Davison (1976) state, "To begin with, the very fact that the client has sought help is an open admission that he has been unable to adequately control certain aspects of his own life" (p. 9). Similarly, Lazarus (1976) identified the "control" of unpleasant emotions as an important goal of multimodal behavior therapy. Those methods involving the self-administration of behavioral procedures, termed *self-control,* further attest to the technological attitude of the behavior therapist. Here the therapist seeks to train the client to manipulate both self and environment so as to systematically regulate affect, cognition, and behavior. Clients are taught, in essence, how to engineer their own actions and feelings by the use of specific techniques. Krasner (1982) has suggested that all behavior therapy procedures might be properly viewed as methods of self-control.

The technological orientation of behavior therapy without question has enabled it to supply useful methodological and theoretical correctives to the field of psychotherapy and has greatly expanded the range of available therapeutic procedures. Successful technologies, however, carry with them a number of potential drawbacks. One unhappy effect of the proliferation of technology and technological thinking within contemporary society has been to drive out other forms of thinking, often resulting in a triumph of form over content, means over ends, methodology over theory (Barrett, 1978; Stanley, 1978). The ascendance of methodological and technical concerns can divert our attention from those troublesome questions that address the value of the goals achieved by the technology or that ask upon what basis such goals are to be determined.

Rationality

Max Weber (1958) spoke of the premodern world appearing as an "enchanted garden" to its inhabitants. He observed that, in contrast, "the fate of our times is characterized by rationalization and intellectualization and, above all, by the 'disenchantment of the world' " (p. 155). In a similar vein, Habermas (1973) has written that modern technological society prizes rationality above all other values:

> Because this value [rationality] can be legitimized by pointing to the process of scientific investigation and its technical application, and does not have to be justified in terms of pure commitment alone, it has a preferential status as against all other values. (pp. 270–271)

Rationality can be thought of as the cognitive framework within which all forms of modern technological activity are constituted. It involves:

> the imposition of strict means–end criteria . . . the exclusion of all that is purely traditional, charismatic, or ritualistic, all, in short, that is not directly related to the means necessary to efficient realization of a given end. (Nisbet, 1976, p. 111)

Those patterns of thought and action that accompany the application of technology are in close harmony with the values linked to the Apollonian sensibility (Berger et al., 1973; Gehlen, 1980). The Apollonian–Dionysian continuum was first introduced by Nietzsche (1956) and was subsequently employed as a tool of cultural analysis by anthropologists (e.g., Benedict, 1934). The Apollonian emphasizes balance, restraint, order, reason, and sobriety. The Dionysian, on the other hand, values extremism, intensity of experience, spontaneity, emotionality, and passion.

The attitude of behavior therapy toward emotion bespeaks its valuing of the rational, its Apollonian sensibility. The behavior therapist does not "work with" affect in any manner analogous to that of more traditional psychotherapy (Messer & Winokur, 1980). Helping clients "get in touch with," develop, or explore feelings is not a high priority in behavior therapy. Even in those instances in which emotion is purposefully aroused, such as in flooding or implosive therapy, the aim is the extinction rather than the exploration or cultivation of emotional responsiveness or sensitivity (Wilson & Evans, 1977). Mahoney (1980) recently has suggested that current cognitive-behavioral therapists take an overly narrow view of emotion and has written critically of their "strong and pervasive assumption" that feelings are phenomena to be "averted, regulated, or otherwise controlled" (p. 167).

Contemporary behavior therapy clearly does emphasize rationality and logic over intuitive and emotional functions, perhaps to an even greater degree than in its precognitive days (Messer & Winokur, 1984). The cognitive revolution in behavior therapy (Mahoney & Arnkoff, 1978; Meichenbaum, 1977) has seen the rapid assimilation of therapies that stress reason, "logical" thinking, and rational problem solving. Among these recent therapeutic inductees are rational-emotive therapy (Ellis & Grieger, 1977), cognitive therapy (Beck, 1976), and problem-solving therapy (D'Zurilla & Goldfried, 1971).

Many of the methods of behavior therapy require of patients a rather advanced level of maturity, rationality, or ego strength, call it what you will. The ability of clients to achieve clarity about what they want, to trust and collaborate with the therapist, and to then act rationally upon the basis of that information—all of this is presupposed by behavioral interventions, especially those procedures, labeled *instigation therapy* by Kanfer and Phillips (1966), that involve implementation of specific suggestions by the clients in their daily environments. Gurman and Knudson (1978) have suggested that in behavioral marital therapy it is assumed (often incorrectly) that the spouses are two "rational" adults "in large part, directly open to the therapist's suggestions and counsel on how to achieve behavioral change . . . in their own rational self-interest" (p. 125). Yet numerous clients seemingly do not enter therapy able to function at such mature levels. In fact, deficits in "maturity" may be the chief problem. In some clients the capacities to act rationally on their own behalfs first must be developed. How best to do so is a question to which many systems of psychotherapy have proposed many different answers, all of which involve clinical and theoretical incorporation of the irrational, emotion-driven aspects of life. Both the limited power of the "reason-based" methods of cognitive behavior therapy to modify irrational feelings and actions and the shortcomings of the theories of emotion upon which such methods are predicated have been underscored by a number of eminent behavior therapists (Bandura, 1977; Rachman, 1981). In developing its own answer to the dilemmas posed by the resistance, lack of motivation, and seeming self-destructiveness manifested by many clients in therapy, modern behavior therapy probably will need to achieve some improved formulation of the capricious and evanescent realm of affect (Pervin, 1981). Here it may find its Apollonian sensibility to be a hindrance.

Amorality

Amorality, when described as a dimension of modern consciousness, refers to the modern separation of fact and value and the removal of "the good" from the objective order of things (Smith, 1982). This aspect of modernity is related to secularization, the ascendance of science, and the proliferation of technical reason (Habermas, 1973). Within a technological society the real, objective external reality of the world is constituted exclusively by empirically derived "facts." Morality comes to be viewed as subjective and relative (Adams, 1975; MacIntyre, 1981).

Consistent with this axiological stance of modernity, behavior therapists have tended to be ethical skeptics and relativists (Erwin, 1978; Kitchener, 1980). Behavior therapy also has sought a clear demarcation between the realms of fact and value and has attempted to include within its purview only those propositions that could be verified by empirical test. When contrasted with the theoretical foundations of other approaches, the clinical theory that underlies behavior therapy is less normative. Two related developments in the history of behavior therapy help to explain this lack of evaluative content.

The goals of traditional psychotherapy were provided in large measure by theories of personality that supplied some definition of what people ought to be and a picture of optimal human functioning. Numerous commentators have demonstrated the evaluative character of traditional personology (Hogan, 1975; Rieff, 1966; Sampson, 1977), revealing such constructs as "sublimation," "social interest," and "self-actualization" to be moral terms operating in disguise and serving a clear prescriptive function within their respective approaches.

But the kind of personality theory that infused earlier systems of psychotherapy with prescriptive thrust was antithetical to the behavioral approach. In its first years, behavior therapy favored explanations of behavioral dysfunction derived from conditioning theory and emphasized the external, observable determinants of behavior. Mischel's (1968) critique of classical personalogy and psychodiagnosis was widely read and was so frequently cited by behavior therapists that it came to be regarded as a basic text in the field. Behavior therapy rejected trait-based conceptions of human behavior (Craighead, Kazdin, & Mahoney, 1981) in favor of a complex "cognitive social learning theory" (Bandura, 1977; Mischel, 1973) that is neutral with respect to what would constitute a personal ideal or ideal person.

The inherent ethical thrust of behavior therapy's clinical theory was also limited by what has frequently been cited as a defining characteristic of the approach (Kazdin, 1978), that is, its opposition to the medical or disease model of psychological dysfunction. Here again behavior therapy divested itself of a system of global, evaluative labels that defines what kinds of persons are in need of therapeutic attention and in what direction their behavior ought to be changed.

The amorality of behavioral clinical theory is entirely consistent with the proclivities of behavior therapy toward objectivity and facticity. This kind of amorality, however, can serve a higher metamorality. The aspiration to a value-free clinical theory, one that minimally constrains possible therapeutic directions, is entirely consistent with the modern "formal" virtues of freedom, tolerance, and equality (Stanley, 1978) and with an ideology that emphasizes democratic humanism.

Humanism

One of the odd ironies that has emerged from the literature critical of behavioral approaches (e.g., Wheelis, 1973) is the suggestion that behavior therapy is antithetical to humanistic viewpoints. There are at least two versions of humanism reflected in contemporary psychology. The humanistic psychology of Rogers, Perls, and Maslow espouses a kind of "romantic" humanism in its emphasis upon cultivation of the passions, aesthetic and emotional sensitivity, and creativity. Behavior therapy, on the other hand, is imbued with a "classical" humanism. In fact, no other system of psychotherapy can lay such a direct and legitimate claim to the humanistic tradition of the Enlightenment. This is the tradition that, without reservation, commits its allegiance to the primacy of science and reason in intellectual affairs, opposes all irrational authority and arbitrary privilege, and dedicates itself to the active enhancement of human liberty (Brinton, 1963). Contemporary humanistic psychology, with its emphasis on feeling and spontaneity, is certainly antagonistic to the rationality of behavior therapy, just as the Romantic movement of the 19th century was opposed to the Enlightenment's subordination of other human capacities to the dictates of reason. Both behavior therapy and humanistic psychology, however, reflect what is common to all forms of humanism: a dedication to the promotion of human freedom and happiness (Lamont, 1982).

The early years of behavior therapy are appropriately viewed as a kind of psychotherapeutic reformation. The flavor of this reformation is found in such classic works as Bandura's (1969) *Principles of Behavior Modification,* Ullmann and Krasner's (1965) *Case Studies in Behavior Modification,* and Lazarus's (1971) *Behavior Therapy and Beyond.* Behavior therapy was a vigorous, polemical reform movement that sought to hold the feet of dogmatic therapeutic creeds to the fire of empirical test, to challenge irrational authority, and to unleash human capacities for exploration, achievement, and self-determination. Early behavior therapy supplied powerful theoretical and methodological correctives to the field of psychotherapy by its introduction of alternative models of human functioning and its insistence upon rigorous evaluation of therapeutic methods.

But behavior therapy also provided an ethical as well as a scientific corrective to the field of psychotherapy. Behavior therapy was a social movement with an ideological agenda. The ethical motives of its founders, when inferred from their writings, seem clear:

> A behavioral approach to the formulation and treatment of people called abnormal. . . . can only end in the realm called humanism. . . . It is to be hoped that giving up concepts of demons and diseases leads to more accurate observation and more effective responses. The object is to give people not charity but dignity, not tolerance but respect. To the extent that a person can do this, he is a little closer to the realities of his existence, a little freer of his intellectual limitations, a little more a human being. (Ullmann & Krasner, 1969, p. 599)

Even so rigorous and precise a thinker as Bandura, who is always careful to separate the realms of fact and value, showed in himself a bit of the reformer when he spoke out against the potential abuses of traditional psychotherapy:

> More serious from an ethical standpoint is the unilateral redefinition of goals by which psychotherapists often impose insight objectives (which mainly involve subtle belief conversions) upon persons desiring changes in their behavioral functioning . . . behavioral approaches hold much greater promise than traditional methods for the advancement of self-determination and the fulfillment of human capabilities. (Bandura, 1969, p. 112)

The ethical spirit of behavior therapy was iconoclastic, egalitarian, and radically pragmatic. These values functioned as an antithesis to the pronounced strain of scholasticism, indifference to scientific self-scrutiny, and conformity that, at that time, ran through medical psychiatry, much of psychoanalysis, and the mental health movement in general (Franks & Rosenbaum, 1983; Szasz, 1978).

Early behavioral models were advanced in the spirit of reform, within that philosophical context that presupposes that science and hence human abilities are capable of transforming the human situation. Time has left unaltered both the humanistic purposes and the faith in science that were characteristic of the first days of behavior therapy. In his recent presidential address to the Association for Advancement of Behavior Therapy, David Barlow (1980) stated:

> If nothing else behavior therapy is a true, humanistic approach to behavioral and emotional problems . . . [and] at the core of the philosophy of humanism is a supreme faith in human reason and the methods of science to confront and solve the many problems that humans face and to rearrange the world so that human life will prosper. (p. 316)

PSYCHOTHERAPY AS TECHNOLOGY: LIMITATIONS AND ANOMALIES

Values and Psychotechnology

Wilson and O'Leary (1980) provide a concise and illustrative statement on the place of values within the behavioral approach:

> Selecting effective techniques with which to change behavior is an empirical question in which the therapist is presumably an expert; choosing therapeutic objectives is a matter of value judgment and ought to be determined primarily by the client. (p. 285)

The position on values stated here is not unique to these authors but is also found in Bandura (1969) and other major sources on behavior therapy. When this position is pressed to its logical limits, however, certain anomalies emerge.

According to the behavioral view, the therapist ascertains the client's goals and then facilitates the realization of those objectives. Of course, the therapist and client must engage in some kind of communication for the therapeutic aims to emerge. But if behavior therapy is, as it claims to be, "nothing more than an applied science," several questions come to mind. Are there scientifically documented techniques of goal assessment? If not, then what procedures are being employed by the behavior therapist in this sphere of activity? Is the behavioral clinician then thought to be operating outside the bounds of science? What about the statement that the therapeutic objectives ought to be determined by the client? Is this statement itself considered a value judgment or a proposition of science? Suppose the client wants the therapist to choose the objectives. What then?

Because it is necessary for the behavior therapist to get involved in some way in a discussion of objectives with the client, if this dialogue does not derive from controlled laboratory studies, then this important part of behavior therapy is without empirical basis. We have in the behavioral literature thousands of studies of therapeutic technique and a growing literature on behavioral assessment but virtually no attention to what therapists are doing when they assist the client in specifying exactly what it is that the client wants to achieve in therapy.

It is, in fact, inconceivable that a program of laboratory research could dictate a total course of action for the therapist. The propositions of science take the logical form of material implication: If A, then B. In its most elegant and useful configuration, science is made up of testable, falsifiable propositions that specify *predictive* relationships among variables or events (Popper, 1962). Research can tell us only *which* techniques will achieve *what* therapeutic objectives or the achievement of *which* objectives is related to *what* life outcomes. But knowledge of this kind is insufficient to account for the conduct of behavior therapy. The structure of scientific knowledge is such that it describes contingent relations among phenomena. Science can tell us only what events will follow other events. Hence, research can never generate the goals of therapy. Yet the therapist cannot act in the absence of a clear sense of which therapeutic objectives or what life outcomes to promote. The therapist requires a starting point, some basis upon which to make the first move, some rule that channels his or her attention and behavior. These primary directives of any system of psychotherapy derive fundamentally not from research but from an ethical ideal, some vision of what is good and proper in human affairs. Any system of thought, when it enters the realm of application, requires bases for the decisions and choices necessary to that application and, therefore, some value position. Hence, behavior therapy necessarily must contain propositions that do not derive from empirical research. The fundamental premise of clinical behavior therapy is that the client shall decide the goals of therapy. This directive, upon which clinical behavior is predicated, is not a scientific proposition but an ethical axiom, one that is related closely to its modern democratic, humanistic ideological underpinnings described earlier.

We must, however, question a viewpoint that requires that clinical activity be so subservient to the avowed preferences of the client. Perhaps the first years of behavior therapy, with their redoubtable successes, led early practitioners astray and convinced them wrongly that all human difficulties can be treated as straightforwardly as simple phobias, given a proper behavioral assessment. Yet clients do not always know what they want, much less what ails them, in the initial stages of therapy. Presenting complaints often are only tangentially related to the client's fundamental problems (Woolfolk & Lazarus, 1979). Along with various critics of behavior therapy (Gurman & Knudson, 1978; Messer & Winokur, 1980), we see in the behavioral literature an unfortunate tendency to take client behavior dogmatically at face value, as though to do anything else would constitute an implicit endorsement of the kind of psychoanalytic mystification that assumes nothing the client says is ever what it seems on the surface to be.

What we find missing in contemporary behavior therapy is not only the absence of any locus of evaluation external to the therapeutic direction prescribed by the client but also a failure to allow for any basis for such an evaluation. It has been apparent to poets, philosophers, and psychotherapists throughout the ages that an individual's aims in life are often functionally related to that individual's suffering. Inappropriate goals, fantastic goals, or conflict among goals are at the root of many problems of living. The great difficulty for behavior therapists is in remaining faithful to their system while simultaneously managing to encompass client aims within a therapeutic dialectic, to challenge the client's goals, or to view certain of the objectives that people bring into therapy as manifestations or outright causes of their difficulties.

Thus, behavior therapy contains few concepts that allow the therapist to take any perspective on the client external to the client's frame of reference. Freud, at least, could within his system unabashedly advocate the ability to love and the ability to work as universal criteria of competence in living. The behavior therapist has no analogous pronouncement to make. In the absence of such normative concepts as health and sickness, growth and stagnation, which in other systems transcend the preferences of the individual, the behavior therapist has fewer categories with which to evaluate client behavior. Thus, without an independent, therapeutic compass of this sort the behavior therapist is always thrown back upon the preferences of the individual. One might, in fact, argue that this is a principal ideological vector of behavior therapy: to dispense with perspectives that limit the rights of individuals to pursue self-chosen goals in the most expedient manner science can produce.

Meaning and Purpose

Throughout its short history, behavior therapy not only has aspired to the ideals of science but also has sought to exclude from its province all that was not or could not be science. Hence, it falls prey to the difficulties that the modern scientific–technological perspective has in encompassing some essential aspects of the contemporary human dilemma. Behavior therapy seems especially limited in addressing those concerns and discontents that have come to be seen by sociologists and philosophers as inevitable accompaniments of modernity. A chief discontent relates to what is lost in the transition from premodern forms of social organization to modern society.

With the advent of modernity, those institutions that once provided a sense of meaningful identity and belonging—the church, the community, and the family—were weakened and the ties of individuals to them were diminished (Berger & Kellner, 1981). Such entities as religion, art, and ethics, once possessed of an authority equal or superior to that of science, have become debased epistemological currencies. They have lost their status as constituents of an objective external reality, been made relative, and been reduced to subjective elements in the inner lives of individuals (Heller, 1959). The loss of community, the failure of modern institutions to provide durable social support for so many, the relativization of standards of conduct, and the inability of modern consciousness to fashion some intersubjective consensus on metaphysical questions have led to considerable psychosocial stress (Garfield, 1979) and philosophical disorientation (Smith, 1982).

> Modernity has accomplished many far-reaching transformations, but it has not fundamentally changed the finitude, fragility, and mortality of the human condition. What it has accomplished is to seriously weaken those definitions of reality that previously made the human condition easier to bear. (Berger et al., 1973, p. 185)

As Frankl (1969) and numerous philosophers from Kierkegaard (1962) to Sartre (1956) have attested, there are inherent difficulties in any attempt to fashion a meaningful understanding of existence in terms of the moral and epistemological categories provided by scientific culture. Nor is a "sense of meaning" a philosophical frill, an intellectual luxury with import only for those consumed by too much zeal for understanding the ultimate nature of things. Concluding his analysis of an impressive epidemiological data base, Antonovsky (1979) argued that some aspects of physical health and the maintenance of tolerable levels of psychological stress depend upon what he termed a *sense of coherence*. As Antonovsky defined it, a sense of coherence requires that one's coping activities occur within a personally meaningful context of community, tradition, or cosmos that both sets a limit to personal control and makes "affectively comprehensible" the many uncontrollable and tragic aspects of human life. In related research that has confirmed the wisdom of sociologists and existential psychologists, Kobasa and her colleagues (Kobasa, 1979; Kobasa, Maddi, & Courington, 1981; Kobasa, Maddi, & Puccetti, 1982) have shown that the capacity to tolerate life stress is greatly impaired by alienation, lack of purpose, and the absence of commitment.

Behavior therapy has a difficult time conceptualizing and doing justice to questions of meaning and purpose. As we have seen, science and the technology that flows from it are capable of generating means for the achievement of preordained ends, but not the ends themselves. This is because the structure of knowledge within behavior therapy allows it to illuminate only the relationship between means and ends. It cannot adumbrate the wisdom, appropriateness, or desirability of ends except in relation to some standard (some other end) that is generated independently of orthodox behavior therapy procedure. Behavior therapy, as it is presently constituted, is unable to further the search for meaning because success in this endeavor necessitates the discovery or creation of the goals and standards that supply purpose and meaning—the determination of what is worth doing at all rather than the most effective means of doing it.

As one might imagine, behavior therapists have written sparingly on this topic of "existential questions." Kanfer and Saslow (1969) have essentially advocated an abdication by behavior therapy of responsibility for addressing issues involving "dissatisfactions with or uncertainties" about "self-attitudes, or a loss of meaning or purpose" and a reliance on "clergymen, teachers, counsellors, work supervisors, even neighbors and friends" (p. 429). Ullmann and Krasner (1975) quite correctly have pointed out that some self-reports of *angst* mask more conventional clinical problems amenable to straightforward behavioral intervention. But not all existential quandaries can be explained away. And those that cannot do not admit of technical answers. About all behavior therapy can offer here is some technique to control the emotional and behavioral impact of an absence of meaning. And although such palliatives have their place, one doubts that the simple elimination or control of the negative affect and cognitions emanating from our modern existential predicament is either an effective or a worthy solution. Among behavioral clinicians, Goldfried and Davison (1976) manifest the clearest understanding of this point and characterize the handling of existential concerns as a major shortcoming of behavior therapy.

CODA: AN UNCRITICAL POSTSCRIPT

The aim of this writing has been critical. We have sought to uncover the ideological foundations of behavior therapy and subject them to critical scrutiny. We see in this work neither an endorsement nor a repudiation of behavior therapy but rather a delineation of the distinctive features of its assumptive world as they emerge through the critical process. We have found problems with the approach that seem inextricably bound up with essential features of modern consciousness and contemporary Western culture.

As we have mentioned earlier, behavior therapy is not alone among systems of psychotherapy in reflecting modern ideological positions. Behavior therapy is, perhaps, simply the most literal translation into therapy practice of certain facets of modernity. A comparative study of contemporary therapeutic ideologies is, however, a topic for another writing. We are satisfied here to take one step toward developing a model of inquiry for understanding the embeddedness of systems of psychotherapy within history and culture. A hermeneutic analysis of psychotherapy allows us to take an alternative, somewhat more distal perspective—one not so thoroughly informed by the same assumptions as the object of scrutiny. Knowledge so derived is of both intrinsic interest and practical import. It is vital that we frame our understanding of psychotherapy in social and historical terms because the relation between psychotherapy and culture is one of reciprocal influence. Systems of psychotherapy not only reflect culture but shape culture as well. If modern men and women are indeed self-defining animals as Charles Taylor (1975) has suggested, then the values and human image implicit in psychotherapies come to be consequential components in that process of self-definition.

REFERENCES

Adams, E. M. (1975). *Philosophy and the modern mind: A philosophical critique of modern Western civilization.* Chapel Hill: University of North Carolina Press.

Antonovsky, A. (1979). *Health, stress, and coping.* San Francisco: Jossey-Bass.

Bandura, A. (1969). *Principles of behavior modification.* New York: Holt, Rinehart & Winston.

Bandura, A. (1977). *Social learning theory.* Englewood Cliffs, NJ: Prentice-Hall.

Barlow, D. (1980). Behavior therapy: The next decade. *Behavior Therapy, 11,* 315–328.

Barrett, W. (1978). *The illusion of technique.* Garden City, NY: Anchor Press/Doubleday.

Bartley, W. W. (1962) *The retreat to commitment.* New York: A. A. Knopf.

Baumer, F. L. (1977). *Modern European thought: Continuity and change in ideas 1600–1950).* New York: Macmillan.

Beck, A. T. (1976). *Cognitive therapy and the emotional disorders.* New York: International Universities Press.

Benedict, R. (1934). *Patterns of culture.* Boston: Houghton Mifflin.

Berger, P. L. (1977). *Facing up to modernity.* New York: Basic Books.

Berger, P. L., Berger, B., & Kellner, H. (1973). *The homeless mind.* New York: Random House.

Berger, P. L., & Kellner, H. (1981). *Sociology reinterpreted.* Garden City, NY: Anchor Press/Doubleday.

Berger, P. L., & Luckman, T. (1966). *The social construction of reality.* Garden City, NY: Doubleday.

Bergin, A. E. (1980). Psychotherapy and religious values. *Journal of Consulting and Clinical Psychology, 48,* 95–105.

Brinton, C. (1963). *The shaping of modern thought.* Englewood Cliffs, NJ: Prentice-Hall.

Burtt, E. A. (1964). *The metaphysical foundations of modern science.* London: Routledge & Kegan Paul.

Buss, A. R. (1975). The emerging field of the sociology of psychological knowledge. *American Psychologist, 30,* 988–1002.

Craighead, W. E., Kazdin, A. E., & Mahoney, M. J. (1981). *Behavior modification: Principles, issues, and applications.* Boston: Houghton Mifflin.

D'Zurilla, T. J., & Goldfried, M. R. (1971). Problem solving and behavior modification. *Journal of Abnormal Psychology, 78,* 107–126.

Ellis, A., & Grieger, R. (Eds.). (1977). *Handbook of rational-emotive therapy.* New York: Springer.

Ellul, J. (1964). *The technological society.* New York: Random House.

Erwin, E. (1978). *Behavior therapy: Scientific, philosophical, and moral foundations.* Cambridge, England: Cambridge University Press.

Feyerabend, P. (1975). *Against method.* London, NLB.

Frankl, V. E. (1969). *The will to meaning.* New York: New American Library.

Franks, C. M., & Rosenbaum, M. (1983). Behavior therapy: Overview and personal reflections. In M. Rosenbaum, C. M. Franks, & Y. Jaffe (Eds.), *Perspectives on behavior therapy in the eighties.* New York: Springer.

Gadamer, H. (1975). *Truth and method.* New York: Crossroad.

Garfield, C. A. (Ed.). (1979). *Stress and survival: The emotional realities of life-threatening illness.* St. Louis: C. V. Mosby.

Gehlen, A. (1980). *Man in the age of technology.* New York: Columbia University Press.

Goldfried, M. R., & Davison, G. C. (1976). *Clinical behavior therapy.* New York: Holt, Rinehart & Winston.

Gouldner, A. W. (1976). *The dialectic of ideology and technology.* New York: The Seabury Press.

Gurman, A. S., & Knudson, R. M. (1978). Behavioral marriage therapy: I. A psychodynamic-systems analysis and critique. *Family Process, 17*, 121–138.

Habermas, J. (1972). *Knowledge and human interests*. Boston: Beacon Press.

Habermas, J. (1973). *Theory and practice*. Boston: Beacon Press.

Hayek, F. A. (1952). *The counter-revolution of science*. Glencoe, IL: Free Press.

Heller, E. (1959). *The disinherited mind*. New York: Meridian.

Hogan, R. (1975). Theoretical egocentrism and the problem of compliance. *American Psychologist, 30*, 533–540.

Horkheimer, M. (1972) *Critical theory*. New York: The Seabury Press.

Kanfer, F. H., & Phillips, J. S. (1966). Behavior therapy: A panacea for all ills or a passing fancy. *Archives of General Psychiatry, 15*, 114–128.

Kanfer, F. H., & Saslow, G. (1969). Behavioral diagnosis. In C. M. Franks (Ed.), *Behavior therapy: Appraisal and status*. New York: McGraw-Hill.

Kazdin, A. E. (1978). *History of behavior modification: Experimental foundations of contemporary research*. Baltimore: University Park Press.

Kazdin, A. E., & Wilson, G. T. (1978). *Evaluation of behavior therapy: Issues, evidence, and research strategies*. Cambridge, MA: Ballinger.

Kierkegaard, S. (1962). *The present age*. New York: Harper & Row.

Kitchener, R. F. (1980). Ethical relativism and behavior therapy. *Journal of Consulting and Clinical Psychology, 48*, 1–7.

Kobasa, S. C. (1979). Stressful life events, personality and health: An inquiry into hardiness. *Journal of Personality and Social Psychology, 37*, 1–11.

Kobasa, S. C., Maddi, S. R., & Courington, S. (1981). Personality and constitution as mediators in the stress-illness relationship. *Journal of Health and Social Behavior, 22*, 368–378.

Kobasa, S. C., Maddi, S. R., & Puccetti, M. C. (1982). Personality and exercise as buffers in the stress-illness relationship. *Journal of Behavioral Medicine, 5*, 391–404.

Krasner, L. (1962). The therapist's contribution. In H. H. Strupp & L. Luborsky (Eds.), *Research in psychotherapy: Vol. 2*. Washington, DC: American Psychological Association.

Krasner, L. (1982). Behavior therapy: On roots, contexts, and growth. In G. T. Wilson & C. M. Franks (Eds.), *Contemporary behavior therapy*. New York: Guilford Press.

Kuhn, T. S. (1970a). Reflections on my critics. In I. Lakatos & A. Musgrove (Eds.), *Criticism and the growth of knowledge*. Cambridge, England: Cambridge University Press.

Kuhn, T. S. (1970b). *The structure of scientific revolutions* (2nd ed.). Chicago: University of Chicago Press.

Lamont, C. (1982). *The philosophy of humanism*. New York: Frederick Ungar.

Lazarus, A. A. (1971). *Behavior therapy and beyond*. New York: McGraw-Hill.

Lazarus, A. A. (1976). *Multimodal behavior therapy*. New York: Springer.

Lévi-Strauss, C. (1966). *The savage mind*. Chicago: University of Chicago Press.

London, P. (1964). *The modes and morals of psychotherapy*. New York: Holt, Rinehart & Winston.

Lowe, C. M. (1976). *Value orientations in counseling and psychotherapy: The meanings of mental health* (2nd ed.). Cranston, RI: Carroll Press.

MacIntyre, A. (1981). *After virtue: A study in moral theory*. Notre Dame, IN: University of Notre Dame Press.

Mahoney, M. J. (1980). Psychotherapy and the structure of personal revolutions. In M. J. Mahoney (Ed.), *Psychotherapy process*. New York: Plenum.

Mahoney, M. J., & Arnkoff, D. B. (1978). Cognitive and self-control therapies. In S. L. Garfield & A. E. Bergin (Eds.), *Handbook of psychotherapy and behavior change* (2nd ed.). New York: Wiley.

Mannheim, K. (1936). *Ideology and utopia.* New York: Harcourt, Brace & World.

Meichenbaum, D. H. (1977). *Cognitive behavior modification: An integrative approach.* New York: Plenum.

Messer, S. B., & Winokur, M. (1980). Some limits to the integration of psychoanalytic and behavior therapy. *American Psychologist, 35*, 818–827.

Messer, S. B., & Winokur, M. (1984). Ways of knowing and visions of reality in psychoanalytic and behavior therapy. In H. Arkowitz & S. B. Messer (Eds.), *Psychoanalytic therapy and behavior therapy: Is integration possible?* New York: Plenum.

Mischel, W. (1968). *Personality and assessment.* New York: Wiley.

Mischel, W. (1973). Toward a cognitive social learning reconceptualization of personality. *Psychological Review, 80*, 252–283.

Moore, W. E. (1963). *Social change.* Englewood Cliffs, NJ: Prentice-Hall.

Nelson, B. (1981). *On the roads to modernity* (T. E. Huff, Ed.). Totowa, NJ: Rowman and Littlefield.

Nietzsche, F. (1956). *The birth of tragedy and the genealogy of morals.* Garden City, NY: Doubleday/Anchor.

Nisbet, R. (1976). *Sociology as an art form.* London, England: Oxford University Press.

Parsons, T. (1971). *The system of modern societies.* Englewood Cliffs, NJ: Prentice-Hall.

Pervin, L. A. (1981, November). *Conceptual and applied limitations of behavior therapy: A dynamic systems perspective.* Paper presented at the meeting of the Association for Advancement of Behavior Therapy, Toronto, Canada.

Polanyi, M. (1966). *The tacit dimension.* Garden City, NY: Doubleday.

Popper, K. R. (1962). *The logic of scientific discovery.* London, England: Hutchinson.

Rachman, S. (1981). The primacy of affect: Some theoretical implications. *Behaviour Research and Therapy, 19*, 279–290.

Ricoeur, P. (1981). *Hermeneutics and the human sciences* (J. B. Thompson, Ed.). Cambridge, England: Cambridge University Press.

Rieff, P. (1966). *The triumph of the therapeutic.* New York: Harper & Row.

Sampson, E. E. (1977). Psychology and the American ideal. *Journal of Personality and Social Psychology, 35*, 767–782.

Sampson, E. E. (1978). Scientific paradigms and social values: Wanted—A scientific revolution. *Journal of Personality and Social Psychology, 36*, 1332–1343.

Sampson, E. E. (1981). Cognitive psychology as ideology. *American Psychologist, 36*, 730–743.

Sartre, J. (1956). *Being and nothingness.* New York: Philosophical Library.

Scheler, M. (1960). *Die Wissenformen und die Gesellschaft.* Bern: Francke.

Shils, E. A. (1981). *Tradition.* Chicago: University of Chicago Press.

Smith, H. (1982). *Beyond the post-modern mind.* New York: Crossroad.

Stanley, M. (1978). *The technological conscience: Survival and dignity in an age of expertise.* New York: Free Press.

Szasz, T. (1978). *The myth of psychotherapy.* New York: Anchor Press.

Taylor, C. (1971). Interpretation and the sciences of man. *Review of Metaphysics, 25*, 3–51.

Taylor, C. (1975). *Hegel.* Cambridge, England: Cambridge University Press.

Ullmann, L. P., & Krasner, L. (Eds.). (1965). *Case studies in behavior modification.* New York: Holt.

Ullmann, L. P., & Krasner, L. (1969). *A psychological approach to abnormal behavior.* Englewood Cliffs, NJ: Prentice-Hall.

Ullmann, L. P., & Krasner, L. (1975). *A psychological approach to abnormal behavior* (2nd ed.). Englewood Cliffs, NJ: Prentice-Hall.

Weber, M. (1958). *From Max Weber: Essays in sociology*. (H. H. Gerth & C. W. Mills, Eds.). New York: Oxford University Press.

Weimer, W. B. (1979) *Notes on the methodology of scientific research*. Hillsdale, NJ: Erlbaum.

Wheelis, A. (1973) *How people change*. New York: Harper & Row.

Wilson, G. T., & Evans, I. (1977). The therapist-client relationship in behavior therapy. In A. S. Gurman & A. M. Razin (Eds.), *The therapist's contribution to effective psychotherapy: An empirical approach*. New York: Pergamon Press.

Wilson, G. T., & O'Leary, K. D. (1980) *Principles of behavior therapy*. Englewood Cliffs, NJ: Prentice-Hall.

Winner, L. (1977). *Autonomous technology: Technics-out-of-control as a theme in political thought*. Cambridge, MA: MIT Press.

Wolpe, J. (1973). *The practice of behavior therapy* (2nd ed.). New York: Pergamon Press.

Woolfolk, R. L., & Lazarus, A. A. (1979). Between laboratory and clinic: Paving the two-way street. *Cognitive Therapy and Research, 3*, 239–244.

10

ETHICAL RELATIVISM AND BEHAVIOR THERAPY

RICHARD F. KITCHENER

In the past few years behavior therapists have devoted considerable attention to discussing the ethical issues surrounding behavior modification. (For a current summary see Begelman, 1975.) If the behavior therapist is controlling the behavior of his or her client, for example, then which behaviors should be changed? What moral and legal principles should be used to decide this question?

If it is true that the behavior therapist is forced to make value judgments in therapy, then a further issue arises that has not received sufficient attention: When a therapist makes a value judgment (e.g., Behavior X ought to be changed), this judgment must be justifiable. The therapist must be able to defend this judgment rationally and to give adequate reasons in support of what he or she did or decided.

To refuse to justify ethical judgments is to refuse to accept therapeutic responsibility and to claim that no one is accountable for how one uses or misuses behavior modification techniques.

If it is true that therapists must be able to justify their value judgments, then behavior therapy must allow for the possibility of a rational justification. This, in turn, rules out the widespread belief that value judgments are relative and subjective. The remainder of this article attempts to show why this is so.

ETHICAL RELATIVISM

A view commonly held by social and behavioral scientists is that value judgments are relative to the individual and culture. Feldman (1976) for example concluded, "A great many

Reprinted from the *Journal of Consulting and Clinical Psychology, 48,* 1–7. (1980).

The author thanks Karen Strohm Kitchener for reading and commenting on an earlier version of this article. He also thanks the anonymous reviewers of this journal for their suggestions.

other instances could be quoted to support the case that moral beliefs are relative to the persons and situations concerned, and are not absolute and unchanging" (p. 407). Similar remarks are echoed by Krasner and Ullmann (1973) and Krasner (1977). In fact, Skinner (1971) wrote,

> What a given group of people calls good is a fact: it is what members of the group find reinforcing as the result of their genetic endowment and the natural and social contingencies to which they have been exposed. Each culture has its own set of goods, and what is good in one culture may not be good in another. To recognize this is to take the position of "cultural relativism." What is good for the Trobriand Islander is good for the Trobriand Islander, and that is that. (p. 128)

What does it mean to say "moral beliefs are relative to the persons and situations concerned"? Following a customary distinction, let me distinguish two kinds of relativism. *Psychological (cultural) relativism* is the view that, as a matter of empirical fact, different individuals (groups) value different things or have different beliefs about what is valuable. This version of relativism is a straightforward scientific hypothesis, and the evidence for it comes largely from anthropologists, several of whom (Benedict, 1934; Herskovits, 1948) have insisted that cultural relativism is true. It should be pointed out, en passant, that other anthropologists (e.g., Kluckhohn, 1955) believe cultural relativism is false (or at least greatly exaggerated) and that all cultures share the same basic moral beliefs about (at least) some things. Asch (1952) has made the same point about psychological relativism.

A second version of relativism has been called *ethical relativism,* the view that each thing believed to be valuable by the individual (culture) is actually valuable. Not only do individuals have different beliefs about values, but each belief (value judgment), according to this view, is true, and thus the corresponding object of the belief is valuable, worthy, and desirable. Anthropologists such as Benedict (1934) have historically espoused both versions of relativism and have furthermore believed that cultural relativism entails ethical relativism. Many psychologists likewise think that psychological relativism entails ethical relativism.

Psychological relativism could entail ethical relativism only if there were some principle connecting the two claims. Two such principles can be found in the writings of psychologists.

First, if *valuable* referred to some psychological property such as social conformity or to *is reinforcing,* then ethical relativism would follow from psychological relativism.[1] Such a definition would be a form of *ethical naturalism,* which maintains that ethical concepts are definable in terms of naturalistic concepts (Kitchener, in press). Second, ethical relativism might seem to follow from psychological relativism if there were no objective way of adjudicating between different values actually held by different individuals (*ethical skepticism*). In this case, since there would be no objective way to decide (no way to know) which particular value was better, everyone's values would be equally good.[2] Ethical skepticism is perhaps as widespread as ethical relativism (cf. "Who's to say one person's values are better than another person's?") and is often associated with another view, *ethical subjectivism.* Ethical subjectivism maintains that ethical judgments are propositions about the speaker's feelings, attitudes, or behavioral reactions. "Cheating is wrong" therefore means "I have a certain negative feeling about cheating" or "I don't find cheating very reinforcing." Ethical subjectivism is distinct from its cousin *emotivism,*

[1]Actually, the argument is much more complicated than I have suggested. Many arguments in support of ethical relativism do not even require a premise about psychological relativism. Furthermore, most arguments for ethical relativism really take the form of denying that there is any distinction between psychological and ethical relativism.

[2]Again, the situation is more complicated than I suggest. For if there is no way to decide which values are better (or which belief is true), then surely it does not follow that every value is good (every belief is true). On the contrary, what should be concluded is that each belief is neither true nor false (or that one does not know which one is true). Thus ethical relativism should not be thought to follow from ethical skepticism.

which maintains that ethical propositions are not propositions at all and are therefore neither true nor false, since they are the very expressions of emotions, analogous to "Cheating, ugh!!!" (Ayer, 1946; Stevenson, 1944).

In conjunction with either of these assumptions, ethical relativism would result (or rather would seem to result), but there would be no possibility of justifying ethical judgments. Clearly, it would be impossible if one adopted ethical skepticism, but it would also be impossible if one adopted the view that *good* means *positive reinforcer.* Thus, I could not justify giving shock to a nonconsenting homosexual by mentioning what I find reinforcing. Since behavior therapists are concerned with justifying such judgments, we are in a dilemma: Either we give up relativism, or we give up the justifying of value judgments. Since behavior therapists cannot (and should not) give up the possibility of justifying ethical judgments, they must give up relativism. I (Kitchener, 1979, in press; Kitchener, Note 1) have argued that other aspects of radical behaviorism require a reexamination of the possibility of ethical justification because justification is a normative concept presupposing concepts incompatible with a radical behaviorism. The question therefore is whether behavior therapists can give up relativism, and if so, what conceptual changes must be made in their theoretical views?

BEHAVIOR THERAPY AND VALUES

To give up ethical relativism, a behavior therapist would have to give up one of the principles connecting psychological relativism to ethical relativism. I consider both possibilities, point out the problems with each, and then show that behavior therapists cannot give up these principles without modifying other views of theirs in a fundamental way.

What are values? What do *good* and *valuable* mean? The only account of such concepts I have been able to find in the writings of behavior therapists is a view characteristically identified with Skinner and one endorsed by several behavior therapists. According to this view, good is identified with what is positively reinforcing. (For a discussion of the problems surrounding the notion of reinforcement, see Kitchener, 1976.) Skinner equates the two in various places (Skinner, 1971, pp. 103, 107; 1974, p. 204), and such a practice is followed by several behavior therapists (Feldman, 1976; Krasner & Ullmann, 1973). Krasner (1977) for example wrote, "That which leads to positive reinforcement for the individual is good; that which leads to adverse consequences is bad" (p. 631).[3]

If good means positively reinforcing, then psychological relativism and ethical relativism follow. For as Feldman (1976) correctly pointed out, if one translates *desirable* as *positive reinforcer,* then "the problem, of course, is that what is 'good' to one person may be 'bad' to another" (p. 406). What is positively reinforcing to me may not be positively reinforcing to you. As a result, what is good (desirable) to me is not good (desirable) to you; we are back with ethical relativism. The tempting move to translate *what is good* as *what is positively reinforcing* therefore leads to the relativism and to the rejection of the possibility of justifying values in therapy.

A second account of values can also be found among certain behaviorists (notably Skinner), although this account is not explicitly present in the writings of behavior therapists. Since it represents an account in keeping with the theoretical views of behavior theory, however, it is worth considering.

[3]One may object that this is a naive version of what behavior therapists mean, since it is so obviously mistaken. Whether mistaken or not, it is a view seriously advanced by prominent behavior therapists and is apparently intended to be taken in this naive form.

According to this account, what is valuable is that thing that contributes to the survival of the species or culture (Skinner, 1971, p. 136; 1974, pp. 192, 205). Such an evolutionary ethic (championed in a different form by individuals from Herbert Spencer to C. H. Waddington; see Flew, 1967) is deficient, however, and is of questionable value to the therapist. Suppose one has a homosexual for a client and is faced with the question of whether to modify his or her sexual behavior. The evolutionary ethic would seem to dictate modifying the sexual behavior from homosexual to heterosexual, since heterosexual behavior contributes to the survival of the species and our (heterosexual) culture. To do the opposite would be tantamount to claiming that our culture needs changing to allow for homosexual behavior. But this would be to say that our culture as it is should not survive. Does our evolutionary ethic dictate that we ought to act not just to perpetuate the survival of our culture as it is, but to perpetuate the advancement and evolution of our culture to a higher stage, one in which there is more happiness, greater freedom of differing sexual expression, and so on? The issue therefore is not one of mere survival but one of what kind of culture we want; here our evolutionary ethic is of little, if any, help.

The formulation of such an evolutionary ethic by psychologists such as Skinner seriously needs elaboration. For as it stands, as one has just seen, it is riddled with confusing notions. What does *survival* mean? Merely physical survival and propagation of the species? Or survival of a progressing species? What is the relationship between the survival of the species and the survival of a culture? Surely these two goals are not always compatible (e.g., the survival of our culture may require a decrease in birth rate, a point at odds with the standard notion of biological survival), and how we are to decide such cases is not at all clear.

Finally, and most important, if such an evolutionary ethic were elaborated and defended, it (in one form) would be inconsistent with relativism. Although what is reinforcing may be relative, what makes for the survival of a species is presumably not relative. Such biological survival value would apply to any member of such a species; this is part of what is meant in saying that a characteristic has survival value for the species. Food has survival value, for example, whether one is Eskimo or Chinese. Thus, if this approach were developed in the way evolutionary biologists have suggested, relativism could not be entertained, nor could ethical subjectivism.

In sum, then, the view that *good* equals *positive reinforcer* must be abandoned if ethical justification is to be possible. This account of values must be replaced by some other view. An evolutionary ethic might be such a view, but there are serious objections to it, and therefore it does not seem to be very helpful.

ETHICAL SUBJECTIVISM AND ETHICAL SKEPTICISM

Ethical subjectivism and ethical skepticism must also be given up. Ethical skepticism is the view that there is no way to know which values are better (no way to objectively decide which value is better.) No justification would be possible, therefore, since no adequate reasons could be given in support of any ethical conclusion. Often this takes the form of saying that there is no scientific way to determine the truth or falsity of an ethical claim and that therefore ethical judgments cannot be rationally defended but must be construed as personal biases or preferences. This, in turn, naturally leads to ethical subjectivism or emotivism. An ethical subjectivist believes there is nothing to defend because an ethical judgment is a report of an individual's personal feelings and reactions. The reason for ethical subjectivism lies in the fact that ethical disagreements are not disagreements over the nature of objective reality at all, since it is all really a matter of taste. In matters of taste, there can be no rational defense or justification.

Emotivism, in contrast with ethical subjectivism, holds that ethical statements are neither true nor false and that their noncognitive status is the source of their inability to be rationally defended. Emotivism, as elaborated by Hull (1943), for example, would also entail the impossibility of justification and for that reason ought also to be abandoned by behavior therapists.[4]

THE BEHAVIOR OF BEHAVIOR THERAPISTS

Ethical relativism, ethical subjectivism, and ethical skepticism ought to be abandoned by behavior therapists; otherwise the possibility of justification is ruled out. Moreover, behavior therapists themselves seem to abandon these principles when they talk about what moral principles ought to be adopted by therapists. In their very behavior they advance moral principles, rationally defend them, and claim that they should be accepted by others. A recent article by Feldman (1976) aptly illustrates this. At the beginning of his article, Feldman is an explicit relativist, skeptic, and subjectivist:

> Two conclusions follow from the above argument. First, any ethical framework within which is discussed the relationship between behavior therapy and society is personal to the writer. Second, it is not susceptible to one of the crucial features of the scientific method, namely falsifiability by empirical test and its appeal, therefore is *persuasive* and *emotional,* i.e. subjective rather than objective. (Feldman, 1976 p. 408)

Later, however, he arrives at moral principles—egoism, utilitarianism, the Golden Rule—that are not relativistic at all. Now forgetting for the moment that these principles are incompatible with each other, notice how Feldman characterizes the issues; his characterization is the exact opposite of relativism, for in each case the author advances a moral principle that he feels ought to be adopted by other therapists:

> Instead of specifying the content of "goods" and "ills," we might restrict ourselves to the following statement which allows individuals and groups to supply their own content. Therapists *should* act so as (a) to increase the access of their clients to those consequences defined as positive by the client and (b) to remove consequences defined by the client as aversive. (Feldman, 1976, p. 422, italics added)

This is a principle, the author says, all therapists should adopt, but if so, then the principle itself is not relative or subjective. Later this first moral principle is supplemented by a quite different one, a principle of utilitarianism:

> What *should* be the criteria by which the court should decide in cases of dispute between the interested parties? I consider that the court, like therapists, *should* adopt the principles set out earlier, which might be characterized as "maximum benefit" and "least harm," with pride of place going to those interested parties whose lives are most negatively affected by the problem behaviour concerned and who would most benefit from the absence of the problem. (Feldman, 1976, p. 424, italics added)

This same point applies to other behavior therapists (Bandura, 1969; Franks & Wilson, 1973; Goldiamond, 1974; Krasner, 1969, 1977) who have advocated certain principles or criteria that ought to be adopted by behavior therapists. For example, when someone says we ought to adopt the principles of free consent, he or she is obviously no longer a relativist or subjectivist, since in attempting to persuade us that this is a good principle, he or she, in effect, is saying that this is a principle that everyone ought to adopt, that there are good reasons for adopting it, and so

[4]Although ethical subjectivism is a view found among behavior therapists, very few are emotivists, since most psychologists do not distinguish between emotivism and subjectivism. For this reason, I do not deal with emotivism in the remainder of this article.

on. Now, if there are good reasons for adopting a certain moral principle, then how can it all be a matter of personal feeling, taste, reaction, or reinforcement? In supplying good reasons in support of a moral principle, one is advancing a moral argument and one is engaging in moral reasoning that is like any other type of reasoning. Although moral reasoning may not be as compelling as mathematical reasoning, it does have much in common with other forms of reasoning, especially inductive reasoning. In any case, someone who gives a rational defense of his or her moral conclusions, as behavior therapists do, is surely not claiming that such conclusions are subjective and relative.

APPEAL OF RELATIVISM

Why has relativism been so influential and popular among social and behavioral scientists? Why has it seemed to be a logical conclusion that inevitably had to be drawn? I could give several reasons, but an obvious one is the following. In looking around at different individuals and cultures, one of the most striking features is the obvious fact that people value different things; for example, one group favors capital punishment, another one does not. Clearly, what is therefore valued—what behavior is valued, what reinforcers are valued—differs considerably from individual to individual. Even if this were true (and there are reasons to think it is not), it would not show that psychological relativism and cultural relativism are true. It does not follow that what ought to be valued differs from individual to individual (ethical relativism). For it would only follow if the valuable were definable in some way as the valued. But the distinction between what is actually valued by the individual (the valued) and what ought to be valued (the valuable) remains a distinction that cannot be ignored. Behavior therapists often want to say, "Patient A (Therapist A, our society) values X but ought to value Y instead (ought to adopt a certain moral principle such as client consent)," and so forth. Much of the appeal of relativism comes from the ambiguity of the statement "Everyone has different values," which can mean "Everyone actually values different things" or "Everyone's values are valuable" (i.e., what is valuable is different from individual to individual). But once one sees this distinction, much of the value of relativism is undercut.

Why have social scientists tended to ignore this distinction, to discount it, even to be unable to see it once it is pointed out to them? The point that there is a difference between what is and what ought to be, between facts and values, has lucidly been made by psychologists and therapists (Begelman, 1975; Meehl, 1975), and philosophers from David Hume to G. E. Moore have made the point in various ways. Why have some psychologists had this "blind spot," as Meehl put it?

One reason that comes to mind is this: As scientists, psychologists have not known what to do with the realm of values. Not wanting to admit a Platonic, transcendent realm in which values reside—since this seemed antithetical to science—they were forced to identify values with some aspect of the natural world. For a psychologist this aspect could either be some aspect of the mind or some aspect of behavior, and behavior therapists—at least in the operant tradition—have been reluctant to lodge values in the mind (Krasner, 1969, p. 538). The only alternative was to locate them in behavior (Kitchener, 1977); after all, where else could they be for a radical behaviorist.[5]

[5]The problem here is that either alternative—psychological naturalism or Platonism—seems to be inadequate and that what is needed is an additional alternative, one that is consistent with a scientific approach but one that does not turn values into brute facts. What such an approach would be is, of course, very controversial, but the theory of Rawls (1971) might be a likely candidate.

The rationale for equating facts and values therefore comes from a radical naturalism widespread among psychologists and epitomized by Skinner. I have argued elsewhere (Kitchener, 1979; Kitchener, Note 2) that such a view is mistaken, and as I have tried to show in this article, it leads to dangerous confusion in the realm of behavior therapy and values. An even more dangerous consequence of such a view is the belief that moral decisions in therapy do not ever have to be justified because they cannot be justified (Kitchener, in press; Kitchener, Note 1).

If such a view is a consequence of a radical naturalism, then perhaps it is time this position be questioned and psychologists begin looking for an account of values that is scientifically respectable on the one hand and allows them to raise the kind of moral issues that are being raised in behavior therapy now on the other. An absolutely essential part of any such conception of values vis-à-vis psychology would be, as I have argued, the possibility of justifying the ethical decisions made daily by therapists. If behavior therapy's conception of values does not allow this, then it is time that this conception be abandoned and a new one sought.

REFERENCE NOTES

1. Kitchener, R. F. *The role of ethics in behavior modification: Radical naturalism.* Paper presented at the meeting of the International Congress of Behaviour Therapy, Uppsala, Sweden, August 1977.
2. Kitchener, R. F. *Skinner's theory of theories.* Unpublished manuscript, Colorado State University, 1976.

REFERENCES

Asch, S. *Social psychology.* Englewood Cliffs, N.J.: Prentice-Hall, 1952.

Ayer, A. J. *Language, truth and logic* (2nd ed.). New York: Dover, 1946.

Bandura, A. *Principles of behavior modification.* New York: Holt, Rinehart & Winston, 1969.

Begelman, D. A. Ethical and legal issues of behavior modification. In M. Hersen, R. M. Eisler, & P. M. Miller (Eds.), *Progress in behavior modification* (Vol. 1). New York: Academic Press, 1975.

Benedict, R. Anthropology and the abnormal. *Journal of General Psychology,* 1934, *10,* 59–80.

Feldman, M. P. The behaviour therapies and society. In M. P. Feldman & A. Broadhurst (Eds.), *Theoretical and experimental bases of the behaviour therapies.* New York: Wiley, 1976.

Flew, A. G. N. *Evolutionary ethics.* New York: St. Martin's Press, 1967.

Franks, C. M., & Wilson, G. T. *Annual review of behavior therapy: Theory and practice, 1973.* New York: Brunner/Mazel, 1973.

Goldiamond, I. Towards a constructional approach to social problems. *Behaviorism,* 1974, *2,* 1–84.

Herskovits, M. *Man and his works.* New York: Knopf, 1948.

Hull, C. *Principles of behavior.* New York: Appleton-Century-Crofts, 1943.

Kitchener, R. F. Are there molar psychological laws? *Philosophy of the Social Sciences,* 1976, 6, 143–154.

Kitchener, R. F. Behavior and behaviorism. *Behaviorism,* 1977, 5, 11–72.

Kitchener, R. F. A critique of Skinnerian ethical principles. *Counseling and Values,* 1979, *23,* 138–147.

Kitchener, R. F. Radical naturalism and radical behaviorism. *Scientia,* in press.

Kluckhohn, C. M. Ethical relativity. *Journal of Philosophy,* 1955, *52,* 663–677.

Krasner, L. Behavior modification—Values and training. In C. M. Franks (Ed.), *Behavior therapy: Appraisal and status.* New York: McGraw-Hill, 1969.

Krasner, L. Behavior modification: Ethical issues and future trends. In H. Leitenberg (Ed.), *Handbook of behavior modification.* Englewood Cliffs, N.J.: Prentice-Hall, 1977.

Krasner, L., & Ullmann, L. P. *Behavior influence and personality: The social matrix of human action.* New York: Holt, Rinehart & Winston, 1973.

Meehl, P. Control and counter-control: A panel discussion. In T. Thompson & W. S. Dockens III (Eds.), *Applications of behavior modification.* New York: Academic Press, 1975.

Rawls, J. *A theory of justice.* Cambridge, Mass.: Harvard University Press, 1971.

Skinner, B. F. *Beyond freedom and dignity.* New York: Knopf, 1971.

Skinner, B. F. *About behaviorism.* New York: Knopf, 1974.

Stevenson, C. L. *Ethics and language.* New Haven, Conn.: Yale University Press, 1944.

11

SLICING THE ETHICAL GORDIAN KNOT: A RESPONSE TO KITCHENER

ARTHUR C. HOUTS AND LEONARD KRASNER

Kitchener (1980) has raised some important questions about the role of values in the application of behavior science to clinical situations. He has alerted us to the necessity of examining our philosophical commitments (explicit and implied) to certain ethical positions. It is significant that a scientific journal is encouraging the engagement of professional philosophers and psychologists in dialogue on the relationship of behavior therapy to philosophical ethics. Franks and Wilson (1978) have also welcomed Kitchener's contributions to the growing discussion of the ethics of behavior therapy and appear to be in broad agreement with what they interpret as the consequences of Kitchener's attack on ethical relativism.

Several problems, both philosophical and factual, exist, however, with Kitchener's charge that behavior therapists have adopted ethical relativism. Although data from the behavioral sciences (psychology, sociology, anthropology) have been used to advocate ethical relativism, the real source of such a view lies in philosophy and logic. The genesis of ethical relativism is to be found in some philosophers'[1] strict adherence to an unbridgeable hiatus between science and ethics, between *fact* and *value*.

Reprinted from the *Journal of Consulting and Clinical Psychology,* 48, 8–10. (1980).

Aspects of this project were supported by National Science Foundation Grant OSS-7824572 from the NSF Ethics and Values in Science and Technology Program and the National Endowment for the Humanities Science, Technology and Human Values Program.

[1]We refer here to the logical positivists or logical empiricists, who were no doubt the major influencers of the view of science that was adopted by behavior therapists. We recognize that there are alternative views in philosophy of science that would entail a different response to Kitchener's (1980) article.

The logical distinction between fact and value (*is* and *ought*) was historically made possible when scientific thinking abandoned teleological explanations of nature (Dewey, 1939; Heelan, 1972) and stripped from nature its Aristotelean moral purpose. In ordaining a strict logical separation between scientific and ethical discourse, philosophers were able to keep science out of ethics and offered scientists a rationale for claiming the ethical neutrality of science. In this way it became impossible to examine ethics scientifically, and the project of establishing a standard for the good (axiology) or for principles of right action (deontology) was left to speculation.

The problem of ethical relativism is a problem of the indeterminancy of standards, and as long as philosophers maintain a strict separation of value and fact the problem will remain by definition insoluble. In this regard we are sympathetic to the comment of Edel (1955): "But I cannot repress a sense of amazement at the proportions to which a limited logical proposition has been blown up, and the weight of theory it has been made to bear" (p. 75).

Kitchener (1980) charges that behavior therapists have supported ethical relativism because they have approached the problem of ethics from the position of either *ethical naturalism* or *ethical skepticism.* Because he does not cite much evidence that psychologists have advocated ethical skepticism, we concentrate on the arguments regarding ethical naturalism. It should be noted in passing that Kitchener attributes to Hull a position compatible with the "emotivism" of Ayer (1959). This is not necessarily the case, for Hull (1944) clearly stated that he was in search of a scientific ethics based on verifiable definitions of value; this is a naturalist's, not an emotivist's, position.

Kitchener reasons that ethical naturalism necessarily leads to ethical relativism. It is not true, however, that one leads to the other. Faced with the logical gulf between *is* propositions and *ought* propositions, one possible solution to the problem of indeterminancy of standards is a definitional one. Edel (1955) has characterized the situation clearly:

> It is true, roughly speaking, that a categorical assertion containing a given term does not follow validly from premises which do not contain that term. No conclusions about what ought to be or what is good can be drawn from premises solely about what is. No conclusions about colors can be drawn from premises solely about light waves; you have to introduce premises, relating colors and light waves, (p. 75).

Ethical naturalism is an attempt to introduce a premise relating what is to what ought to be. Thus, Skinner (1953) introduced a premise that defines *good* as *positive reinforcer.* The introduction of such a premise is an attempt to overcome that ethical relativism created by the logical paradox that philosophers have erected. One can certainly argue the adequacy or inadequacy (Begelman, 1977; Day, 1977) of such a definition, but they are hardly evidence for psychologists' promotion of ethical relativism.

Kitchener admonishes behavior therapists to abandon radical naturalism so as to avoid ethical relativism and its apparent dangers and to take up an account of values that is "scientifically respectable." It is not at all clear how Kitchener would have the behavior therapist resolve the logical paradox between *is* and *ought,* though he suggests that one solution is to adopt the account of values offered by Rawls (1971). Erwin (1978) has recently offered a similar suggestion. Rawls's deontological account of ethics is in the tradition of Kant and attempts to resolve the is–ought paradox on the side of *ought* by starting from a hypothetical social contract situation and reasoning out what principles of right action logically follow. Rawls's efforts are impressive, and his results are quite appealing, but there is no basis for calling it a more scientifically respectable account of values. Indeed, if fact and value are separated by an insurmountable gulf, as Kitchener seems to contend, then it does not make sense to speak of a scientifically respectable account of values unless one can provide a premise that relates fact to value.

Moreover, Margolis (1966), who argued against solving the is–ought paradox on the naturalistic side, presented an interesting argument against a resolution from the *ought* side of the paradox. Margolis took an ordinary language approach and pointed out that any so-called justification of a norm or standard must be carried out within the confines of our language. However, logical or illogical, such a justification would require being able to step outside of ordinary language to achieve the independent verification of any proposed standard. If by definition, *what is* (facts) cannot be the source of such an independent verification, then one must ask just what sort of nonlanguage verification would be able to support a standard from which could be deduced the principles of right action. Some philosophers have proposed intuition (Moore, 1903), some reason (Kant, 1949), and of course the theologians have proposed revelation (Barth, 1957). Given the alternative solutions to the is–ought paradox, it should not be surprising that the behavior therapists have opted for a tentative solution by introducing hypotheses relating *is* and *ought*.

We are in agreement with Kitchener (1980) on his point that the clinical applications of a science of behavior involve value decisions. Many psychologists and philosophers have pointed out that clinical situations involve both scientific and ethical decisions (Heelan, 1977; Krasner, 1962; 1969; London, 1964; Margolis, 1966). However, not all decisions regarding target behaviors are value judgments in the sense of requiring some ultimate standard. It is possible to recount clinical situations in which such a judgment is not strictly speaking a value judgment, but a scientific judgment. For example, if a phobic client and his therapist agree on eliminating a crippling phobia (perhaps a value judgment), then the therapist's judgment that the client *ought* to approach the fear-eliciting stimuli is not a value judgment in any moral sense. This *ought* is a judgment based on basic scientific research and a resultant theory of what behavior will most likely extinguish fear. It is no more a value judgment than the following: If you want to boil water under normal atmospheric conditions, you ought to generate a thermodynamic movement equivalent to a temperature of 212° on the Fahrenheit scale.

Granted that some of the decisions by a therapist are ethical decisions in the sense of implying a standard, the question remains as to how a therapist committed to a scientific approach to behavior can bridge the philosophical chasm between science and ethics. Given the current lack of an adequate ethics of science and the absence of a scientific ethic, we favor the position of critical dualism (Popper, 1962). As Popper (1962) remarked,

> We may take the idea of an absolute truth—of correspondence to the facts—as a kind of model for the realm of standards, in order to make it clear to ourselves that just as we may *seek* for absolutely true propositions in the realm of facts or at least for propositions that come nearer to the truth, so we may seek for absolutely right or valid proposals in the realm of standards—or at least for better, or more valid, proposals.
>
> However, it would be a mistake, in my opinion, to extend this attitude beyond the *seeking* to the *finding*. For though we should seek for absolutely right or valid proposals, we should never persuade ourselves that we have definitely found them, for clearly, there cannot be a *criterion* of *absolute rightness*—even less than a criterion of absolute truth. (pp. 385–386)

Thus, as scientists and as moralists, behavior therapists can search for ways of reducing the indeterminancy of ethical standards. Given the commitment of behavior therapists to a "scientific approach"[2] to inquiry, it seems reasonable to suggest that they continue to employ the methodology of science to study human ethical behavior. Such a caveat entails propositions

[2]Scientific approach is in quotation marks to reflect our belief that the demarcation between science and nonscience depends on one's philosophy of science.

(premises) relating facts to values, and these may or may not involve ethical naturalism. In any case, it requires a reasonable tentativeness with respect to ethical standards, and if this tentativeness is construed as thoroughgoing relativism, then so be it.

REFERENCES

Ayer, A. J. *Logical positivism.* New York: Free Press of Glencoe, 1959.

Barth, K. *Church dogmatics* (Vol. 2). Edinburgh, Scotland: Clark, 1957.

Begelmen, D. A. Commentary. In J. E. Krapfl & E. A. Vargas (Eds.), *Behaviorism and ethics.* Kalamazoo, Mich.: Behaviordelia, 1977.

Day, W. Ethical philosophy and the thought of B. F. Skinner. In J. E. Krapfl & E. A. Vargas (Eds.), *Behaviorism and ethics.* Kalamazoo, Mich.: Behaviordelia, 1977.

Dewey, J. *Theory of valuation.* Chicago: University of Chicago Press, 1939.

Edel, A. *Ethical judgment: The use of science in ethics.* Chicago: Free Press, 1955.

Erwin, E. *Behavior therapy: Scientific, philosophical, and moral foundations.* Cambridge, England: Cambridge University Press, 1978.

Franks, C. M., & Wilson, G. T. *Annual review of behavior therapy: Theory and practice, 1977.* New York: Brunner Mazel, 1978.

Heelan, P. A. Nature and its transformations. *Theological Studies,* 1972, *33,* 486–502.

Heelan, P. A. The nature of clinical science. *Journal of Medicine and Philosophy,* 1977, *2*(1), 20–32.

Hull, C. L. Value, valuation and natural science methodology. *Philosophy of Science,* 1944, *11,* 125–141.

Kant, I. *Critique of practical reason* (L. W. Beck, Ed. and trans.). Chicago: University of Chicago Press, 1949.

Kitchener, R. F. Ethical relativism and behavior therapy. *Journal of Consulting and Clinical Psychology,* 1980, *48,* 1–7.

Krasner, L. Behavior control and social responsibility. *American Psychologist,* 1961, *17,* 199–204.

Krasner, L. Behavior modification—Values and training: A psychologist's perspective. In C. M. Franks (Ed.), *Behavior therapy: Appraisal and status.* New York: McGraw-Hill, 1969.

London, P. *The modes and morals of psychotherapy.* New York: Holt, Reinhart & Winston, 1964.

Margolis, J. Z. *Psychotherapy and morality: A study of two concepts.* New York: Random House, 1966.

Moore, G. E. *Principia ethica.* London: Cambridge University Press, 1903.

Popper, K. R. *The open society and its enemies.* Princeton, N.J.: Princeton University Press, 1962.

Rawls, J. *A theory of justice.* Cambridge, Mass.: Harvard University Press, 1971.

Skinner, B. F. *Science and human behavior.* New York: Macmillan, 1953.

RECOMMENDED READING

Bandura, A. (1989). Human agency in social cognitive theory. *American Psychologist, 44,* 1175–1184.

Day, W. F. (1976). Contemporary behaviorism and the concept of intention. In W. Arnold (Ed.), *Nebraska Symposium on Motivation* (pp. 65–131). Lincoln: University of Nebraska Press.

Krasner, L., & Houts, A. C. (1984). A study of the "value" systems of behavioral scientists. *American Psychologist, 39,* 840–850.

Krasner, L. (1978). The future and the past in the behaviorism—Humanism dialogue. *American Psychologist, 33,* 799–804.

Kitchener, R. F. (in press). The ethical foundations of behavior therapy. *Ethics and Behavior.*

Mahoney, M. J. (1984). Psychoanalysis and behaviorism: The yin and yang of determinism. In H. Arkowitz & S. Messer (Eds.), *Psychoanalytic and behavior therapy: Is integration possible?* (pp. 303–325). New York: Plenum Press.

Richardson, F. C. (1989). Freedom and commitment in modern psychotherapy. *Journal of Integrative and Eclectic Psychotherapy, 8,* 303–319.

Skinner, B. F. (1974). *About behaviorism.* New York: Random House.

Skinner, B. F. (1990). Can psychology be a science of the mind? *American Psychologist, 45,* 1206–1210.

Smith, L. D. (1986). *Behaviorism and logical positivism: A reassessment of the alliance.* Palo Alto, CA: Stanford University Press.

Wilson, G. T. (1982). Psychotherapy process and procedure: The behavioral mandate. *Behavior Therapy, 13,* 291–312.

Woolfolk, R. L., & Sass, L. A. (1988). Behaviorism and existentialism revisited. *Journal of Humanistic Psychology, 28,* 108–119.

Woolfolk, R. L., & Sass, L. A. (1989). Philosophical foundations of rational-emotive therapy. In M. E. Bernard & R. DiGuiseppe (Eds.), *Inside rational-emotive therapy: A critical appraisal of the theory and therapy of Albert Ellis* (pp. 9–26). San Diego, CA: Academic Press.

Zuriff, G. D. (1986). *Behaviorism: A conceptual reconstruction.* New York: Columbia University Press.

Zuriff, G. D. (1986). Precis of behaviorism: A conceptual reconstruction. *Behavioral and Brain Sciences, 9,* 687–699. (Contains 20 commentaries by other authors.)

III

PHILOSOPHICAL ISSUES OF THE BIOLOGICAL APPROACH

INTRODUCTION: PHILOSOPHICAL PROBLEMS OF THE BIOLOGICAL APPROACH

RONALD B. MILLER

Initially, it would seem that clinical psychologists would have little to gain from a commitment to a biological model of psychopathology or clinical treatment. Not having the authority to prescribe psychotropic medications, or any other invasive biological intervention, they would be putting themselves out of business in short order by promoting this model. However, as clinical researchers or as academic theoreticians, these constraints do not apply. In fact, given the decided shift in funding patterns toward biological and away from social or psychological programs of research at the federal level, there may be an incentive to promote just such a model.

At the same time, given the increasingly biological focus of general psychology (e.g., Gazzaniga, 1988), and the predominance of neopositivist thinking about the mind–body problem (as in Feigl's identity hypothesis), it stands to reason that many psychologists would find this model compatible with their basic assumptions about a scientifically based practice. Furthermore, given the predominance of psychiatry in the mental health professions, and the strength of this model among psychiatrists, the philosophical foundations of the biological model must be of central concern to clinical psychologists.

The major problem encountered by anyone interested in understanding the philosophical assumptions or principles of a biological approach to clinical psychology or psychiatry is the absence of any clearly articulated statement of these assumptions or principles. Biological theorists seem more committed than most to a sort of theoretical preciousness and to the denial of any relevant philosophical issues in their work. In truly positivist fashion, the scientific biological approach to clinical research and practice has no use for philosophical discourse. Its fundamental assumptions and tenets are those of natural science and the scientific method, the success of which seems beyond question. The belief in a deterministic materialism and an operational methodology has become so pervasive in the culture as to qualify as "common sense," not something one would think to question or as in need of defense. The biological approach finds the application of such beliefs to human behavior the only sensible, ethical, and intelligent way to proceed and sees little point in discussing the obvious. Halleck (1978) noted that in practice, biologically oriented psychiatry is even more "derisive" of nonmedical therapies than the textbooks of psychiatry would indicate.

Trimble (1988), in his textbook *Biological Psychiatry*, illustrated this view well:

> The position today is that these psychological theories of pathogenesis have been overtaken by a wealth of neurochemical and neuropathological hypotheses and findings, especially with regards to the major psychoses. Further, in addition to using knowledge accumulated in cooperation with other disciplines, biological psychiatry now seeks an understanding of psychopathology using theories and findings often based on clinical observations of patients and their effective treatment with biological remedies. Hence the importance of the neurochemical era ushered in by psychopharmacological discoveries of the 1950's. These have given us not only a completely new image of the brain to work with, but have allowed a more complete understanding of the underlying functional and structural changes of the brain that accompany psychiatric illness. Functional, a misused word in the clinical neurosciences, once again may be used in its original sense, to designate a physiological disturbance, rather than an epithet for "psychological." Indeed, with our present knowledge the distinction between "organic" and "functional" melts away, stripped of its Cartesian dualism. (p. xii)

Later, Trimble (1988) identified psychological and psychoanalytic theory with abstract metaphysics and approvingly quoted Maudsley's disparaging remarks about metaphysics as being "empty propositions" and a discipline that "has never made any advance." Yet, in the very next statement, Trimble appeared to credit psychoanalysis as a true advance in the understanding of psychopathology, leaving the reader confused. This is a confusion frequently found in the literature of biological psychiatry and clinical psychology. Its proponents are ideologically committed to a reductionist program of biological determinism (i.e., materialism) and believe that real scientific explanations must always be at the biological level, yet they cannot quite bring themselves to dismiss psychological explanation. Even Trimble (1988) suggested that personality disorders might not belong within the purview of psychiatry:

> An alternative argument would be that psychiatrists should deal with illness, not personality problems, for which latter group other agencies in society are readily available as a source of help. (p. xiv)

Rudnick (1990), after reviewing the paucity of serious philosophical thinking in the literature of biological psychiatry, concluded the following:

> The epistemology of contemporary biological psychiatry adopts a mechanistic conception which is simplistically taken from modern biology (which in turn borrowed it from the physicochemical sciences). As this conception is irrelevant (on its own) to the psychobiological domain, it entails simplistic reductionism in biological psychiatry; this suggests that biological psychiatry has not yet come to its own epistemology, i.e., "philosophically." Methodologically, the irrelevance of the mechanistic hypotheses of contemporary biological psychiatry entails the dominance of serendipity (in scientific progress), which is considered a sign of "backward" sciences. From the logical point of view, contemporary biological psychiatry commits the fallacy of aiming at uncovering a *necessary but not sufficient* set of conditions of psychological disturbances, i.e. biochemical disturbances. And as for the goals of biological psychiatry, it follows that the goals of contemporary biological psychiatry are the goals of biochemistry and physiology and not those of psychobiology; that is that are not biological psychiatry's own *true* goals. (p. 87)

It is within the context of the philosophical debate on the adequacy of a reductionistic, mechanistic materialism as an explanatory model for human behavior that one must read Szasz's famous article, "The Myth of Mental Illness" (see chapter 12). His argument, like Skinner's (outlined in Section II), is essentially in the analytic tradition of Wittgenstein, arguing that psychologists use the term *mental illness* to identify individuals whose behavior is problematic either for them or for the patients. Thus, it is an expression of moral values: Psychologists find certain behaviors undesirable and in need of correction. A word's use is its meaning, and thus "mental illness" means "problems in living," not biological disorder or disease.

Szasz then further argues that the problems in living that express themselves in psychiatric symptoms are frequently themselves moral concerns (e.g., manipulations of the weak by the strong, the poor by the wealthy, the young by the old). By medicalizing the problem, psychiatry and clinical psychology respond amorally to a moral dilemma that has the net effect, whether intended or not, of preserving the status quo. This is the sort of argument psychologists have come to expect from the contemporary psychosocial hermeneutic writers such as Habermas, and it is startling to realize that Szasz was offering this sort of critique nearly 30 years ago.

It is unfortunate that so little attention has been paid to the philosophical argument put forward by Szasz, although it is understandable given both clinical psychology and biological psychiatry's general avoidance of philosophical discourse. The focus has instead been on gathering empirical evidence on the biological correlates of mental illness, as if the data could make a philosophical argument for its own interpretation.

Szasz's claim is about what psychologists mean when they say something, or as the ordinary language philosophers would say, how they use the terms of their language. Szasz's argument is that reductionism in psychiatry cannot be right because it reduces a moral condition (socially inappropriate or disturbing behavior) to a physiological disorder or illness. Such a reduction of an "ought" to an "is" is a logical error, an example of how language can "go on holiday" and lead to illogical thinking. It violates the fact–value distinction that G. E. Moore argued is an inherent logical distinction.

Kety's article (see chapter 13) is a response to Szasz and other critics of biological psychiatry and is about as close as anyone adhering to this approach comes to writing philosophically. Kety argues that both the history of medicine and current genetic research suggest that there is a physiological abnormality that underpins the behavior psychologists call mental illness. Medical science is depicted as a part of the enlightenment, offering both a more humane approach to the mentally ill and a more effective one as well. Kety identifies the antipsychiatry movement with prescientific thinking. The 19th century had seen many intellectuals who thought that general paresis of the insane was simply a moral condition and who thought the search for a physical explanation was misguided. However, they were entirely wrong, as are Szasz and his supporters. This argument, that scientific approaches have worked so well in the past that they must be trusted in the future, is a powerful one that recurs in philosophical discussions about behaviorism, biological approaches, and research methodologies.

Kety is a leading researcher on the biological–genetic etiology of schizophrenia. When he began his work, it was common for psychologists to assume that all serious mental disorders were caused by social or psychological factors. At that time, to take the position that these disorders might be, in part, caused by a physiological abnormality was regarded as a radical leap of faith. Over the course of his career, the burden of proof has markedly shifted to those such as Szasz who reject the centrality of physiological causation in these disorders. Kety does not deny the existence of social problems with moral implications that affect the lives of psychiatric patients. He wishes only to deny that these problems are the concern of psychiatry as a medical (read "scientific") specialty. In essence, he invokes the fact–value distinction to protect psychiatry from having to deal with moral (value) issues, thus sidestepping Szasz's point that the primary *meaning* of most psychiatric terms is a moral one.

Karl Pribram is one of the premier neuropsychologists of 20th-century American psychology, although he originally was trained as a physician. Pribram's article (see chapter 14) on the implications of contemporary psychological and physiological research for understanding the mind–body problem demonstrates both a sophisticated approach to biological and philosophical issues. Although Pribram does not specifically address the nature of mental illness, his article has great relevance for that debate. Pribram reviews the philosophical history of the mind–body problem and argues that the mental versus physical dichotomy breaks down in the realm of quantum physics (i.e., at the subatomic level). The mental and the physical are two different conceptualizations of the same process or entity, and neither mode of explanation need be considered more basic or causally efficacious. This amounts to a neutral monist view that shares many features with that put forth by Feigl (although stripped of its remaining positivist features). This is a difficult article, but one well worth the effort of the multiple readings it requires.

Finally, Schacht and Spitzer (see chapters 15 and 16, respectively) engage in a spirited debate as to whether the third edition of the *Diagnostic and Statistical Manual of Mental Disorders (DSM–III)* is a scientific classification system or whether it is, as Szasz and others from the critical hermeneutic tradition would argue, a piece of moral legislation with significant political content and implications. As the chairman of the American Psychiatric Association committee that is responsible for the *DSM–III* and its revisions, Spitzer maintains that it is both a scientific and a political document. Yet, he doubts that its political content is problematic or interferes with its scientific mission to improve the reliability and validity of diagnosis. Schacht, a clinical psychologist, wishes to go further and argues that its political and scientific use and meaning are inseparable. Consequently, clinical psychology and psychiatry must admit moral and political elements in both theory and practice, as well as discuss such issues openly.

It should be noted that the biological position continues to take the neopositivist position that the fact versus value dichotomy holds up under scrutiny in the epistemological realm. Science can give us the facts only. Critics of the biological approach tend to rely on the hermeneutical view that facts and values are fused in such a manner so as to make them inseparable. There are some in the biological school of thought who define the goals of therapy or mental health in terms of average biological functioning (e.g., blood levels of norepinephrine, dopamine, etc.). Paradoxically, this also invites a fusion of facts and values. Values are reduced to facts. This is similar to the argument put forward by Houts and Krasner in chapter 11—a naturalization of ethics. This parallel argument in behavioral and biological circles is not that uncommon. Despite the antipathy often found between behavioral psychologists and biological psychiatrists, their philosophical outlook taken from the natural sciences is very similar on metaphysical, epistemological, and ethical matters. They both lean toward materialism, determinism, empiricism, and either an insistence that facts may be observed in a value neutral context or that values may be reduced to facts in a naturalized ethics.

REFERENCES

Gazzaniga, M. (1988). *Mind matters.* Boston: Houghton Mifflin.

Halleck, S. (1978). *The treatment of emotional disorders.* Northvale, NJ: Jason Aronson.

Rudnick, A. (1990). Towards a rationalization of biological psychiatry: A study in psychobiological epistemology. *Journal of Medicine and Philosophy, 15,* 75–96.

Trimble, M. R. (1988). *Biological psychiatry.* New York: Wiley.

12

THE MYTH OF MENTAL ILLNESS

THOMAS S. SZASZ

My aim in this essay is to raise the question "Is there such a thing as mental illness?" and to argue that there is not. Since the notion of mental illness is extremely widely used nowadays, inquiry into the ways in which this term is employed would seem to be especially indicated. Mental illness, of course, is not literally a "thing"—or physical object—and hence it can "exist" only in the same sort of way in which other theoretical concepts exist. Yet, familiar theories are in the habit of posing, sooner or later—at least to those who come to believe in them—as "objective truths" (or "facts"). During certain historical periods, explanatory conceptions such as deities, witches, and microorganisms appeared not only as theories but as self-evident *causes* of a vast number of events. I submit that today mental illness is widely regarded in a somewhat similar fashion, that is, as the cause of innumerable diverse happenings. As an antidote to the complacent use of the notion of mental illness—whether as a self-evident phenomenon, theory, or cause—let us ask this question: What is meant when it is asserted that someone is mentally ill?

In what follows I shall describe briefly the main uses to which the concept of mental illness has been put. I shall argue that this notion has outlived whatever usefulness it might have had and that it now functions merely as a convenient myth.

MENTAL ILLNESS AS A SIGN OF BRAIN DISEASE

The notion of mental illness derives its main support from such phenomena as syphilis of the brain or delirious conditions—intoxications, for instance—in which persons are known to manifest various peculiarities or disorders of thinking and behavior. Correctly speaking, however,

Reprinted from the *American Psychologist, 15,* 113–118. (1960). In the public domain. Reprinted by permission of the author.

these are diseases of the brain, not of the mind. According to one school of thought, *all* so-called mental illness is of this type. The assumption is made that some neurological defect, perhaps a very subtle one, will ultimately be found for all the disorders of thinking and behavior. Many contemporary psychiatrists, physicians, and other scientists hold this view. This position implies that people *cannot* have troubles—expressed in what are *now called* "mental illnesses"—because of differences in personal needs, opinions, social aspirations, values, and so on. *All problems in living* are attributed to physicochemical processes which in due time will be discovered by medical research.

"Mental illnesses" are thus regarded as basically no different than all other diseases (that is, of the body). The only difference, in this view, between mental and bodily diseases is that the former, affecting the brain, manifest themselves by means of mental symptoms; whereas the latter, affecting other organ systems (for example, the skin, liver, etc.), manifest themselves by means of symptoms referable to those parts of the body. This view rests on and expresses what are, in my opinion, two fundamental errors.

In the first place, what central nervous system symptoms would correspond to a skin eruption or a fracture? It would *not* be some emotion or complex bit of behavior. Rather, it would be blindness or a paralysis of some part of the body. The crux of the matter is that a disease of the brain, analogous to a disease of the skin or bone, is a neurological defect, and not a problem in living. For example, a *defect* in a person's visual field may be satisfactorily explained by correlating it with certain definite lesions in the nervous system. On the other hand, a person's *belief*—whether this be a belief in Christianity, in Communism, or in the idea that his internal organs are "rotting" and that his body is, in fact, already "dead"—cannot be explained by a defect or disease of the nervous system. Explanations of this sort of occurrence—assuming that one is interested in the belief itself and does not regard it simply as a "symptom" or expression of something else that is *more interesting*—must be sought along different lines.

The second error in regarding complex psychosocial behavior, consisting of communications about ourselves and the world about us, as mere symptoms of neurological functioning is *epistemological.* In other words, it is an error pertaining not to any mistakes in observation or reasoning, as such, but rather to the way in which we organize and express our knowledge. In the present case, the error lies in making a symmetrical dualism between mental and physical (or bodily) symptoms, a dualism which is merely a habit of speech and to which no known observations can be found to correspond. Let us see if this is so. In medical practice, when we speak of physical disturbances, we mean either signs (for example, a fever) or symptoms (for example, pain). We speak of mental symptoms, on the other hand, when we refer to a patient's *communications about himself, others, and the world about him.* He might state that he is Napoleon or that he is being persecuted by the Communists. These would be considered mental symptoms *only* if the observer believed that the patient was *not* Napoleon or that he was *not* being persecuted by the Communists. This makes it apparent that the statement that "X is a mental symptom" involves rendering a judgment. The judgment entails, moreover, a covert comparison or matching of the patient's ideas, concepts, or beliefs with those of the observer and the society in which they live. The notion of mental symptom is therefore inextricably tied to the *social* (including *ethical*) *context* in which it is made in much the same way as the notion of bodily symptom is tied to an *anatomical* and *genetic context* (Szasz, 1957a, 1957b).

To sum up what has been said thus far: I have tried to show that for those who regard mental symptoms as signs of brain disease, the concept of mental illness is unnecessary and misleading. For what they mean is that people so labeled suffer from diseases of the brain; and, if that is what they mean, it would seem better for the sake of clarity to say that and not something else.

MENTAL ILLNESS AS A NAME FOR PROBLEMS IN LIVING

The term "mental illness" is widely used to describe something which is very different than a disease of the brain. Many people today take it for granted that living is an arduous process. Its hardship for modern man, moreover, derives not so much from a struggle for biological survival as from the stresses and strains inherent in the social intercourse of complex human personalities. In this context, the notion of mental illness is used to identify or describe some feature of an individual's so-called personality. Mental illness—as a deformity of the personality, so to speak—is then regarded as the *cause* of the human disharmony. It is implicit in this view that social intercourse between people is regarded as something *inherently harmonious,* its disturbance being due solely to the presence of "mental illness" in many people. This is obviously fallacious reasoning, for it makes the abstraction "mental illness" into a *cause,* even though this abstraction was created in the first place to serve only as a shorthand expression for certain types of human behavior. It now becomes necessary to ask: "What kinds of behavior are regarded as indicative of mental illness, and by whom?"

The concept of illness, whether bodily or mental, implies *deviation from some clearly defined norm.* In the case of physical illness, the norm is the structural and functional integrity of the human body. Thus, although the desirability of physical health, as such, is an ethical value, what health *is* can be stated in anatomical and physiological terms. What is the norm deviation from which is regarded as mental illness? This question cannot be easily answered. But whatever this norm might be, we can be certain of only one thing: namely, that it is a norm that must be stated in terms of *psychosocial, ethical,* and *legal* concepts. For example, notions such as "excessive repression" or "acting out an unconscious impulse" illustrate the use of psychological concepts for judging (so-called) mental health and illness. The idea that chronic hostility, vengefulness, or divorce are indicative of mental illness would be illustrations of the use of ethical norms (that is, the desirability of love, kindness, and a stable marriage relationship). Finally, the widespread psychiatric opinion that only a mentally ill person would commit homicide illustrates the use of a legal concept as a norm of mental health. The norm from which deviation is measured whenever one speaks of a mental illness is a *psychosocial and ethical one.* Yet, the remedy is sought in terms of *medical* measures which—it is hoped and assumed—are free from wide differences of ethical value. The definition of the disorder and the terms in which its remedy are sought are therefore at serious odds with one another. The practical significance of this covert conflict between the alleged nature of the defect and the remedy can hardly be exaggerated.

Having identified the norms used to measure deviations in cases of mental illness, we will now turn to the question: "Who defines the norms and hence the deviation?" Two basic answers may be offered: (*a*) It may be the person himself (that is, the patient) who decides that he deviates from a norm. For example, an artist may believe that he suffers from a work inhibition; and he may implement this conclusion by seeking help *for* himself from a psychotherapist. (*b*) It may be someone other than the patient who decides that the latter is deviant (for example, relatives, physicians, legal authorities, society generally, etc.). In such a case a psychiatrist may be hired by others to do something *to* the patient in order to correct the deviation.

These considerations underscore the importance of asking the question "Whose agent is the psychiatrist?" and of giving a candid answer to it (Szasz, 1956, 1958). The psychiatrist (psychologist or nonmedical psychotherapist), it now develops, may be the agent of the patient, of the relatives, of the school, of the military services, of a business organization, of a court of law, and so forth. In speaking of the psychiatrist as the agent of these persons or organizations, it is not implied that his values concerning norms, or his ideas and aims concerning the proper nature of remedial action, need to coincide exactly with those of his employer. For example, a patient in individual psychotherapy may believe that his salvation lies in a new marriage; his psychotherapist need not share this hypothesis. As the patient's agent, however, he must abstain from bringing social or legal force to bear on the patient which would prevent him from putting his beliefs into action. If his *contract* is with the patient, the psychiatrist (psychotherapist) may disagree with him or stop his treatment; but he cannot engage others to obstruct the patient's aspirations. Similarly, if a psychiatrist is engaged by a court to determine the sanity of a criminal, he need not fully share the legal authorities' values and intentions in regard to the criminal and the means available for dealing with him. But the psychiatrist is expressly barred from stating, for example, that it is not the criminal who is "insane" but the men who wrote the law on the basis of which the very actions that are being judged are regarded as "criminal." Such an opinion could be voiced, of course, but not in a courtroom, and not by a psychiatrist who makes it his practice to assist the court in performing its daily work.

To recapitulate: In actual contemporary social usage, the finding of a mental illness is made by establishing a deviance in behavior from certain psychosocial, ethical, or legal norms. The judgment may be made, as in medicine, by the patient, the physician (psychiatrist), or others. Remedial action, finally, tends to be sought in a therapeutic—or covertly medical—framework, thus creating a situation in which *psychosocial, ethical,* and/or *legal deviations* are claimed to be correctible by (so-called) *medical action.* Since medical action is designed to correct only medical deviations, it seems logically absurd to expect that it will help solve problems whose very existence had been defined and established on nonmedical grounds. I think that these considerations may be fruitfully applied to the present use of tranquilizers and, more generally, to what might be expected of drugs of whatever type in regard to the amelioration or solution of problems in human living.

THE ROLE OF ETHICS IN PSYCHIATRY

Anything that people *do*—in contrast to things that *happen* to them (Peters, 1958)—takes place in a context of value. In this broad sense, no human activity is devoid of ethical implications. When the values underlying certain activities are widely shared, those who participate in their pursuit may lose sight of them altogether. The discipline of medicine, both as a pure science (for example, research) and as a technology (for example, therapy), contains many ethical considerations and judgments. Unfortunately, these are often denied, minimized, or merely kept out of focus; for the ideal of the medical profession as well as of the people whom it serves seems to be having a system of medicine (allegedly) free of ethical value. This sentimental notion is expressed by such things as the doctor's willingness to treat and help patients irrespective of their religious or political beliefs, whether they are rich or poor, etc. While there may be some grounds for this belief—albeit it is a view that is not impressively true even in these regards—the fact remains that ethical considerations encompass a vast range of human affairs. By making the practice of medicine neutral in regard to some specific issues of value need not, and cannot, mean that it can be kept free from all such values. The practice of medicine is intimately tied to ethics; and the first thing that we must do, it seems to me, is to try to make this clear and explicit. I shall let this matter rest here, for it does not concern us specifically in this essay. Lest there be any vagueness, however, about how or where ethics and medicine meet, let me remind the reader of such issues as birth control, abortion, suicide, and euthanasia as only a few of the major areas of current ethicomedical controversy.

Psychiatry, I submit, is very much more intimately tied to problems of ethics than is medicine. I use the word "psychiatry" here to refer to that contemporary discipline which is concerned with *problems in living* (and not with diseases of the brain, which are problems for neurology). Problems in human relations can be analyzed, interpreted, and given meaning only within given social and ethical contexts. Accordingly, it *does* make a difference—arguments to the contrary notwithstanding—what the psychiatrist's socioethical orientations happen to be; for these will influence his ideas on what is wrong with the patient, what deserves comment or interpretation, in what possible directions change might be desirable, and so forth. Even in medicine proper, these factors play a role, as for instance, in the divergent orientations which physicians, depending on their religious affiliations, have toward such things as birth control and therapeutic abortion. Can anyone really believe that a psychotherapist's ideas concerning religious belief, slavery, or other similar issues play no role in his practical work? If they do make a difference, what are we to infer from it? Does it not seem reasonable that we ought to have different psychiatric therapies—each expressly recognized for the ethical positions which they embody—for, say, Catholics and Jews, religious persons and agnostics, democrats and communists, white supremacists and Negroes, and so on? Indeed, if we look at how psychiatry is actually practiced today (especially in the United States), we find that people do seek psychiatric help in accordance with their social status and ethical beliefs (Hollingshead & Redlich, 1958). This should really not surprise us more than being told that practicing Catholics rarely frequent birth control clinics.

The foregoing position which holds that contemporary psychotherapists deal with problems in living, rather than with mental illnesses and their cures, stands in opposition to a currently prevalent claim, according to which mental illness is just as "real" and "objective" as bodily illness. This is a confusing claim since it is never known exactly what is meant by such words as "real" and "objective." I suspect, however, that what is intended by the proponents of this view is to create the idea in the popular mind that mental illness is some sort of disease entity, like an infection or a malignancy. If this were true, one could *catch* or *get* a "mental illness," one might *have* or *harbor* it, one might *transmit* it to others, and finally one could get *rid* of it. In my opinion, there is not a shred of evidence to support this idea. To the contrary, all the evidence is the other way and supports the view that what people now call mental illnesses are for the most part *communications* expressing unacceptable ideas, often framed, moreover, in an unusual idiom. The scope of this essay allows me to do no more than mention this alternative theoretical approach to this problem (Szasz, 1957c).

This is not the place to consider in detail the similarities and differences between bodily and mental illnesses. It shall suffice for us here to emphasize only one important difference between them: namely, that whereas bodily disease refers to public, physicochemical occurrences, the notion of mental illness is used to codify relatively more private, sociopsychological happenings of which the observer (diagnostician) forms a part. In other words, the psychiatrist does not stand *apart* from what he observes, but is, in Harry Stack Sullivan's apt words, a "participant observer." This means that he is *committed* to some picture of what he considers reality—and to what he thinks society considers reality—and he observes and judges the patient's behavior in the light of these considerations. This touches on our earlier observation that the notion of mental symptom itself implies a comparison between observer and observed, psychiatrist and patient. This is so obvious that I may be charged with belaboring trivialities. Let me therefore say once more that my aim in presenting this argument was expressly to criticize and counter a prevailing contemporary tendency to deny the moral aspects of psychiatry (and psychotherapy) and to substitute for them allegedly value-free medical considerations. Psychotherapy, for example, is being widely practiced as though it entailed nothing other than restoring the patient from a state of mental sickness to one of mental health. While it is generally accepted that mental illness has something to do with man's social (or interpersonal) relations, it is paradoxically maintained that problems of values (that is, of ethics) do not arise in this process.[1] Yet, in one sense, much of psychotherapy may revolve around nothing other than the elucidation and weighing of goals and values—many of which may be mutually contradictory—and the means whereby they might best be harmonized, realized, or relinquished.

The diversity of human values and the methods by means of which they may be realized is so vast, and many of them remain so unacknowledged, that they cannot fail but lead to conflicts in human relations. Indeed, to say that human relations at all levels—from mother to child, through husband and wife, to nation and nation—are fraught with stress, strain, and disharmony is, once again, making the obvious explicit. Yet, what may be obvious may be also poorly understood. This I think is the case here. For it seems to me that—at least in our scientific theories of behavior—we have failed to *accept* the simple fact that human relations are inherently fraught with difficulties and that to make them even relatively harmonious requires much patience and hard work. I submit that the idea of mental illness is now being put to work to obscure certain difficulties which at present may be inherent—not that they need be unmodifiable—in the social intercourse of persons. If this is true, the concept functions as a disguise; for instead of calling attention to conflicting human needs, aspirations, and values, the notion of mental illness provides an amoral and impersonal "thing" (an "illness") as an explanation for *problems in living* (Szasz, 1959). We may recall in this connection that not so long ago it was devils and witches who were held responsible for men's problems in social living. The belief in mental illness, as something other than man's trouble in getting along with his fellow man, is the proper heir to the belief in demonology and witchcraft. Mental illness exists or is "real" in exactly the same sense in which witches existed or were "real."

CHOICE, RESPONSIBILITY, AND PSYCHIATRY

While I have argued that mental illnesses do not exist, I obviously did not imply that the social and psychological occurrences to which this label is currently being attached also do not exist. Like the personal and social troubles which people had in the Middle Ages, they are real enough. It is the labels we give them that concerns us and, having labelled them, what we do about them. While I cannot go into the ramified implications of this problem here, it is worth noting that a demonologic conception of problems in living gave rise to therapy along theological lines. Today, a belief in mental illness implies—nay, requires—therapy along medical or psychotherapeutic lines.

What is implied in the line of thought set forth here is something quite different. I do not intend to offer a new conception of "psychiatric illness" nor a new form of "therapy." My aim is more modest and yet also more ambitious. It is to suggest that the phenomena now called mental illnesses be looked at afresh and more simply, that they be removed from the category of illnesses, and that they be regarded as the expressions of man's struggle with the problem of *how* he should live. The last mentioned problem is obviously a vast one, its enormity reflecting not only man's inability to cope with his environment, but even more his increasing self-reflectiveness.

By problems in living, then, I refer to that truly explosive chain reaction which began with man's fall from divine grace by partaking of the fruit of the tree of knowledge. Man's awareness of himself and of the world about him seems to be a steadily expanding one, bringing

[1]Freud went so far as to say that: "I consider ethics to be taken for granted. Actually I have never done a mean thing" (Jones, 1957, p. 247). This surely is a strange thing to say for someone who has studied man as a social being as closely as did Freud. I mention it here to show how the notion of "illness" (in the case of psychoanalysis, "psychopathology," or "mental illness") was used by Freud—and by most of his followers—as a means for classifying certain forms of human behavior as falling within the scope of medicine, and hence (by *fiat*) outside that of ethics!

in its wake an ever larger *burden of understanding* (an expression borrowed from Susanne Langer, 1953). *This burden,* then, *is to be expected and must not be misinterpreted.* Our only *rational* means for lightening it is *more understanding,* and appropriate *action* based on such understanding. The main alternative lies in acting as though the burden were not what in fact we perceive it to be and taking refuge in an outmoded theological view of man. In the latter view, man does not fashion his life and much of his world about him, but merely lives out his fate in a world created by superior beings. This may logically lead to pleading nonresponsibility in the face of seemingly unfathomable problems and difficulties. Yet, if man fails to take increasing responsibility for his actions, individually as well as collectively, it seems unlikely that some higher power or being would assume this task and carry this burden for him. Moreover, this seems hardly the proper time in human history for obscuring the issue of man's responsibility for his actions by hiding it behind the skirt of an all-explaining conception of mental illness.

CONCLUSIONS

I have tried to show that the notion of mental illness has outlived whatever usefulness it might have had and that it now functions merely as a convenient myth. As such, it is a true heir to religious myths in general, and to the belief in witchcraft in particular; the role of all these belief-systems was to act as *social tranquilizers,* thus encouraging the hope that mastery of certain specific problems may be achieved by means of substitutive (symbolic-magical) operations. The notion of mental illness thus serves mainly to obscure the everyday fact that life for most people is a continuous struggle, not for biological survival, but for a "place in the sun," "peace of mind," or some other human value. For man aware of himself and of the world about him, once the needs for preserving the body (and perhaps the race) are more or less satisfied, the problem arises as to what he should do with himself. Sustained adherence to the myth of mental illness allows people to avoid facing this problem, believing that mental health, conceived as the absence of mental illness, automatically insures the making of right and safe choices in one's conduct of life. But the facts are all the other way. It is the making of good choices in life that others regard, retrospectively, as good mental health!

The myth of mental illness encourages us, moreover, to believe in its logical corollary: that social intercourse would be harmonious, satisfying, and the secure basis of a "good life" were it not for the disrupting influences of mental illness or "psychopathology." The potentiality for universal human happiness, in this form at least, seems to me but another example of the I-wish-it-were-true type of fantasy. I do not believe that human happiness or well-being on a hitherto unimaginably large scale, and not just for a select few, is possible. This goal could be achieved, however, only at the cost of many men, and not just a few being willing and able to tackle their personal, social, and ethical conflicts. This means having the courage and integrity to forego waging battles on false fronts, finding solutions for substitute problems—for instance, fighting the battle of stomach acid and chronic fatigue instead of facing up to a marital conflict.

Our adversaries are not demons, witches, fate, or mental illness. We have no enemy whom we can fight, exorcise, or dispel by "cure." What we do have are *problems in living*—whether these be biologic, economic, political, or sociopsychological. In this essay I was concerned only with problems belonging in the last mentioned category, and within this group mainly with those pertaining to moral values. The field to which modern psychiatry addresses itself is vast, and I made no effort to encompass it all. My argument was limited to the proposition that mental illness is a myth, whose function it is to disguise and thus render more palatable the bitter pill of moral conflicts in human relations.

REFERENCES

Hollingshead, A. B., & Redlich, F. C. *Social class and mental illness.* New York: Wiley, 1958.

Jones, E. *The life and work of Sigmund Freud.* Vol. III. New York: Basic Books, 1957.

Langer, S. K. *Philosophy in a new key.* New York: Mentor Books, 1953.

Peters, R. S. *The concept of motivation.* London: Routledge & Kegan Paul, 1958.

Szasz, T. S. Malingering: "Diagnosis" or social condemnation? AMA *Arch Neurol. Psychiat.*, 1956, **76,** 432–443.

Szasz, T. S. *Pain and pleasure: A study of bodily feelings.* New York: Basic Books, 1957. (a)

Szasz, T. S. The problem of psychiatric nosology: A contribution to a situational analysis of psychiatric operations. *Amer. J. Psychiat.*, 1957, **114,** 405–413. (b)

Szasz, T. S. On the theory of psychoanalytic treatment. *Int. J. Psycho-Anal.*, 1957, **38,** 166–182. (c)

Szasz, T. S. Psychiatry, ethics and the criminal law. *Columbia Law Rev.*, 1958, **58,** 183–198.

Szasz, T. S. Moral conflict and psychiatry, *Yale Rev.*, 1959, in press.

13

FROM RATIONALIZATION TO REASON

SEYMOUR S. KETY

The attitude of the public toward the insane throughout all of recorded history has rarely been marked by sympathy and understanding. Rather, it has fluctuated among fear, revulsion, violent hostility, or simply isolation and neglect. Among physicians, however, for the past 2,500 years insanity has been thought of as a form of illness with mental, rather than somatic, symptoms.

Hippocrates (c. 460–377 B.C.) argued in a compelling way against the prevailing attribution of insanity to supernatural causes:

> And men ought to know that from nothing else but thence [from the brain] come joys, delights, laughter and sports, and sorrows, griefs, despondency, and lamentations. And by this, in an especial manner, we acquire wisdom and knowledge, and see and hear and know what are foul and what are fair, what are bad and what are good, what are sweet, and what unsavory. . . . And by the same organ we become mad and delirious, and fears and terrors assail us, some by night, and some by day, and dreams and untimely wanderings, and cares that are not suitable, and ignorance of present circumstances, desuetude and unskilfulness. All these things we endure from the brain, when it is not healthy, but is more hot, more cold, more moist, or more dry than natural, or when it suffers from any other preternatural and unusual affection (1, p. 357).

Throughout the Dark Ages in Europe that concept was largely forgotten. It did not reappear until well after the Renaissance. Johann Weyer, early in the 16th century, believed that the insane were sick and could be treated. He was slandered and vilified by the public and the church. Pinel's humanitarian thrust against the atrocious treatment of the insane in 18th-century France was based upon his belief that these patients were suffering from mental illness. He contributed not only to more enlightened attitudes toward the mentally ill but also to the

Reprinted from the *American Journal of Psychiatry, 131,* 957–963. (1974).

characterization and diagnosis of mental illness. Following the French Revolution and through the age of rationalism that accompanied the 19th century in Europe, science blossomed and permeated all of medicine. It brought knowledge and understanding of the infectious diseases that had plagued the world and paved the way toward their eventual treatment and prevention. The medical model of mental illness was generally accepted by physicians and psychiatrists, becoming the basis for differentiating one form of insanity from another, providing the opportunity to characterize two mental disorders that were widespread at that time, pellagrous psychosis and general paresis, and stimulating research to elucidate their causes and eventually to develop rational and effective methods for their treatment and prevention.

Other forms of insanity remained with us, however, and, despite the gratifying and remarkable progress that has been made in the treatment of schizophrenia and the affective disorders, they still affect five to ten percent of the people in this and every country in the world.

CHALLENGES TO THE MEDICAL MODEL

The medical model of mental illness has, in recent times, been seriously challenged. Psychiatric diagnosis has been described as a political judgment, and mental illness has been said to be either a myth or an adaptive and creative response to a hopeless social situation.

Szasz has taken the position that "mental illness is a myth whose function it is to disguise and thus render more palatable the bitter pill of moral conflicts in human relations" (2, p. 53). His arguments to advance that position have been addressed more to the social sequelae of some kinds of psychiatric diagnosis in some places than to the validity of the concept.

Albert Deutsch, a great journalist who worked harder and accomplished more to change the conditions of the mentally ill in the United States than has the whole "antipsychiatry" movement, never found it necessary in doing so to attack psychiatry, science, or the concept of mental illness.

Peter Breggin has undertaken a crusade against biological psychiatry, institutional psychiatry, and behavioral psychiatry, which he likens to Hitler's treatment of the mentally ill. He defined biological psychiatry as: "Both the theory that so-called mental illness is biologic and genetic, and the treatment approach which involves drugs, electroshock and psychosurgery, as well as eugenics" (3). He went on to state: "Clearly, the 'politicalization' of psychiatry is not the responsibility of recent activists, but of traditional biologic, behavioral and institutional psychiatry with their totalitarian politics" (3). I would not previously have believed that admitting a suicidal patient to a mental hospital and prescribing antidepressant drugs or that conducting research on the biochemistry of the brain with the hope of elucidating some of the causes of mental illness could be labeled "totalitarian politics." Dr. Breggin, who seems to be particularly sensitive to criticism against himself, is quite cavalier in his denunciation of entire areas of sober and sincere psychiatric and scientific effort.

The writing of many of the antipsychiatrists is characterized by the broad brushstrokes of diatribe that places blame indiscriminately and inappropriately, by rhetoric and by rationalization rather than by reason. One can apparently do without reason simply by being antiscience. There are valid issues—legal, moral, and public—that are involved in the institutionalization of the mentally ill and that deserve thoughtful discussion and sober adjudication. The complex question of preventive detention is being thoughtfully examined by legal authorities (4), and a distinguished jurist, Judge David Bazelon, has given much thought and substance to the civil rights of the mentally ill as well as their right to treatment (5–7). Each of the drugs that are now highly regarded for the treatment of schizophrenia, mania, or depression has been subjected to the most rigorous kind of critical evaluation in terms of therapeutic benefit and possible risk. Such evidence has not been adduced in support of psychosurgery or megavitamin treatment in the therapy of serious mental illness. The scientific and psychiatric communities have shown themselves sensitive and competent to make such discriminations and are likely to continue to do so without throwing out the baby with the bath water.

What is the nature of the evidence and what are the ethical considerations that permit a physician and psychiatrist to deny to his patients those benefits of medical science which have been critically examined and widely accepted, or to promulgate to the public at large their abandonment in favor of alternatives that are poorly spelled out, untested, or illusory? Those who argue most vehemently for the regulation of clinical trials and restrictions on therapeutic drugs apparently see little need for the evaluation or control of their social panaceas.

Among the antipsychiatry movements that Martin Roth has described as "improbable alliances between groups of sociologists, psychologists, psychoanalysts and Marxist critics of contemporary Western society" (8) are those which make sufficient use of stereotyped revolutionary clichés so as to suggest that the state of psychiatry and the plight of the mentally ill are not their major concern.

I appreciate the opportunity I had last June to visit the People's Republic of China, which afforded me an illuminating and refreshing insight into psychiatry there. I was impressed, as every visitor has been, with the important social changes that have taken place—the equalization of wealth and living standards and the great strides that have been made in the relief of poverty and the eradication of major epidemic disease. I also learned something about mental illness in China and the sensible approach to its treatment taken there.

After a few encounters with a doctrinaire denial of the existence of mental illness on the part of those unfamiliar with the problem, I visited the psychiatric department of a large general hospital and a large psychiatric hospital in two of the largest cities. These were very much like their counterparts in the United States. I saw schizophrenic patients humanely and effectively treated with group therapy and phenothiazine drugs, and I learned that the tricyclic antidepressant drugs were highly regarded in the treatment of depression. Schizophrenia was thought of as a mental illness that has both biological and psychological components. For that reason, its most effective treatment depended upon drugs, which could ameliorate the biological disturbances, and reeducation, which might correct the effects of untoward experience. There were fewer hospital beds devoted to mental illness in the large cities of China than in cities of similar size in the West, but it was not felt that the explanation lay in a reduced incidence of mental illness. Instead, it was suggested that Chinese society is more tolerant of mental illness so that patients can be treated in the community and by periodic visits to an outpatient department.

Laing argued against the medical model of schizophrenia in the following way: "There are no pathological anatomical findings *post mortem.* There are no organic structural changes noted in [the] course of the 'illness.' There are no physiological-pathological changes that can be correlated with these illnesses . . ." (9, p. 352). What he could have said is that none of these has yet been found.

Neither Szasz nor Laing denied the reality and validity of general paresis as a disease of the brain. That raises the interesting question of what it was before that was established. Was it a myth, a political judgment, a creative adaptation to an evil society, or simply a mental illness of unknown origin?

THE MEDICAL MODEL AS A PROCESS

It should be pointed out that according to the medical model, a human illness does not become a specific disease all at once and is not equivalent to it. The medical model is an evolving intellectual process, consonant with the scientific method, which involves long periods of observation and description, increasingly sharper differentiation, and research rather than wishful thinking.

The medical model of an illness is a process that moves from the recognition and palliation of symptoms to the characterization of a specific disease in which the etiology and pathogenesis are known and the treatment is rational and specific. That progress depends upon the acquisition of knowledge and may often take many years or centuries. Numerous medical disorders and one or two mental illnesses have moved to the final stages of understanding, but many are still at various points along the way. After the recognition of symptoms, there comes the realization that some symptoms occur in fairly regular clusters, which are then described as syndromes. These may ultimately turn out to represent one or several etiological and pathogenetic components, the nature of which may be obscure at earlier stages of knowledge.

The syndromes that are described as schizophrenia, manic-depressive psychosis, or unipolar depression have persisted through several generations of psychiatric experience. Their particular designation may change with time or place, but psychiatrists with different types of training will usually recognize and can agree upon the phenomenologic cluster. The reliability of independent diagnoses, once a standard nosology has been agreed upon, is reasonably high. When we realize that these syndromes have no objective features but are based on subjective evaluation, the reliability becomes even more impressive.

The syndrome too evolves, sometimes breaking up into various subtypes on the basis of new clinical or laboratory information. These may eventually be designated "diseases" when a common pathogenesis or underlying pathology is discovered. Hodgkin's disease and multiple sclerosis are examples of diagnoses based upon recognizable pathology, even though their etiology is obscure, while Parkinson's disease has two quite distinct etiologies. Psychiatrists do not like the term "disease," since it improperly assumes something internal. Instead, they prefer the term "reaction" (which unwarrantedly assumes something external). Of this, Gruenberg wrote:

> The routinizing of the word "reaction" in our standard nomenclature has accomplished little that is positive—it has given many psychiatrists the false notion that mental disorders are reactions of the organism to circumstances, but that tuberculosis and diabetes and nephritis and measles and mumps are "things" independent of the patient's nature. For all medical diseases are also reactions of the organism to certain life circumstances and do not exist independently of the people who are sick (10, p. 368).

The evolution of a medical model from symptoms through syndromes to diseases with specific pathology and, ultimately, with definitive etiologies and rational treatment is an excellent example of the scientific method applied to the alleviation of human suffering. It involves careful observation and study, the generation, sharpening, and testing of hypotheses, and the elucidation of underlying mechanisms, all pointing toward prevention and effective treatment. In many instances throughout medicine, this process has been successful, and there is justifiable concern that the fruits of this knowledge are not available to all the population.

Sometimes the suffering is so great, our understanding so fragile, and the delays in the acquisition of new knowledge so long that we become impatient. Then, not only do we treat with what seems plausible or what we feel offers relief, but we attribute to the treatment more effectiveness and value than we can rigorously demonstrate. Instead of developing hypotheses we adopt doctrines, and instead of testing them we rationalize them. Both psychoanalysis and community psychiatry were thus given more confidence than they have been able to justify and permitted more complacency than was reasonable for their ability to treat or prevent serious mental illness. The extravagant claims of those who treat schizophrenia with extraordinary doses of vitamins do not stand up to critical evaluation. Mental illness is indeed different from infectious disease, and the important need is not in the delivery or promulgation of our ignorance regarding its causes, specific treatment, or prevention. Nor does denying the reality of mental illness or calling it a creative and adaptive experience make it disappear. Insofar as any of these beliefs diminish our perception of the problem and placate our need to understand it better, they retard progress.

The medical model of mental illness has been attacked not only on the basis that the underlying mechanisms of mental illness have not been discovered but also that even the syndromes are illusory. Rosenhan (11) felt that he demonstrated this by having eight normal individuals feign hallucinations and thus gain admission to mental hospitals, where they then behaved "normally" (like taking notes on the ward and not insisting on discharge). He also described a follow-up study in which the threat of sending other pseudopatients to various mental hospitals resulted in ten percent of the actual patients admitted being *suspected* by a psychiatrist of feigning symptoms. There is no indication that any of these suspicions was strong enough to prevent the admission of an actual patient. Although Rosenhan drew many conclusions from his experiment, this one stands out: "The facts of the matter are that we have known for a long time that diagnoses are often not useful or reliable, but we have nevertheless continued to use them. We now know that we cannot distinguish insanity from sanity" (11).

If I were to drink a quart of blood and, concealing what I had done, come to the emergency room of any hospital vomiting blood, the behavior of the staff would be quite predictable. If they labeled and treated me as having a bleeding peptic ulcer, I doubt that I could argue convincingly that medical science does not know how to diagnose that condition. Rosenhan's pseudopatients received a diagnosis of schizophrenia on admission and schizophrenia in remission on discharge, although we are not told the qualifications that must have accompanied those diagnoses in at least some of the cases. Although that may not justify his rather far-flung conclusions, it could be used to support a statement made some years earlier by another psychologist, Paul Meehl, who has spent many years studying schizophrenia: "Rather than decrying nosology, we should become masters of it, recognizing that some of our psychiatric colleagues have in recent times become careless, and even unskilled in the art of formal diagnosis" (12).

SCHIZOPHRENIA: MYTH OR ILLNESS?

My colleagues David Rosenthal, Paul Wender, Fini Schulsinger, Bjørn Jacobsen, and I have recently obtained some results (13) that bear rather directly on the claims of Szasz, Laing, and Rosenhan that schizophrenia is a myth, that it has no biological substrate, and that it cannot be diagnosed reliably. Interestingly enough, we did not carry out the work in order to refute those arguments, since when it began we were either unaware of them or did not take them seriously. Our purpose was to obtain evidence, as free from selective and subjective bias as we could make it, regarding the operation of genetic and environmental factors in the transmission of schizophrenia.

We had surveyed a sample of nearly 5,500 adults who had been adopted early in life by people not biologically related to them and then identified 33 among them who had been admitted to mental hospitals and on whom we could agree in a diagnosis of definite schizophrenia: severe and chronic, mild or latent, or acute schizophrenic reaction. We then picked matching controls for each schizophrenic index patient from adopted individuals who had never been admitted to a mental hospital. The biological and adoptive relatives were then identified: parents, siblings, and half-siblings of the schizophrenic index cases and of their controls—a total of 512 relatives. Of these, 119 had died and 29 had emigrated or disappeared. Of the remainder, more than 90 percent participated in an exhaustive psychiatric interview conducted by Dr. Jacobsen, who had not known the relationship of any subject to a proband. In practically all of the biological relatives, the subject himself did not know of that relationship or did not inform Dr. Jacobsen.

Extensive summaries of these interviews were then prepared, edited to remove any clues that would permit a guess of the relationship of the subject to a proband, and then read independently by each of three raters who were, by training, a clinical psychologist, a psychiatrist, and a physician who had spent a number of years in psychiatric research. Each rater independently recorded his best psychiatric diagnosis for each subject from the transcribed interview. The possible diagnosis covered the entire range listed in the APA diagnostic manual (*DSM-II*) (14) and ranged from no mental disorder to chronic schizophrenia. Since the subject of the study was schizophrenia, the three raters had previously discussed and reached some agreement on the criteria for a diagnosis of the three types of definite schizophrenia employed in the selection of the index cases as well as a diagnosis of uncertain schizophrenia when schizophrenia seemed to be the most likely diagnosis although some doubt existed. A diagnosis of schizoid or inadequate personality, with some schizoid features, was included in what we termed the "schizophrenia spectrum" as being possibly related to schizophrenia.

In all, 365 interviews[1] on as many subjects were independently read and diagnosed by the three raters with the following results:

1. In 324 subjects (89 percent) *no* rater made a primary diagnosis of schizophrenia or uncertain schizophrenia.
2. On the other hand, in 7 subjects (2 percent), at least one rater made a primary diagnosis of chronic schizophrenia and, in every instance, each of the other raters made a primary diagnosis of definite schizophrenia, usually chronic, sometimes latent, and, in one instance, acute. It is not difficult to recognize independently and reliably the syndrome that Kraepelin described 80 years ago, although there may be disagreement on the severity of the symptoms and the degree of incapacity.
3. In 17 subjects (5 percent), at least one rater made a primary diagnosis of definite schizophrenia, but latent or acute rather than chronic. In all but one of these, the two other raters made diagnoses within the schizophrenia spectrum.

The kappa value for agreement by all three raters on definite schizophrenia in this study was 0.67 and shows a high degree of reliability even when compared with the interrater reliability of only two diagnosticians (15). The kappa values are somewhat lower (0.61 and 0.58, respectively) for definite and uncertain schizophrenia or for the total schizophrenia spectrum. Although the values indicate a satisfactory degree of agreement among these more recent accretions to the original schizophrenia syndrome, there is clearly a need and a basis for sharpening these concepts. The results, however, do indicate that it is possible to distinguish insanity quite readily from sanity, and, in fact, to distinguish a particular form of insanity called schizophrenia.

One could argue that the ability of three raters to agree upon a diagnosis does not give it validity, which can only be derived by reference to some independent criterion. The subjects who have been lumped together thus far are actually divisible into four different populations: the biological and adoptive relatives of schizophrenic adoptees and the biological and adoptive relatives of control adoptees. Of these four populations, one is different from the rest in being genetically related to a person with schizophrenia (with whom they have not lived), i.e., the biological relatives of the index cases. With regard to mental illness other than schizophrenia, these relatives do not differ from the rest (see table 1).

[1]This included 26 interviews with control adoptees which had been randomly distributed among the pool of relatives.

TABLE 1
Consensus Diagnoses Outside the Schizophrenia Spectrum in Biological and Adoptive Relatives

	Interviewed Relatives, in Percents*			
	Index Group		Control Group	
Diagnosis	Biological (N = 81)	Adoptive (N = 31)	Biological (N = 121)	Adoptive (N = 41)
Psychiatrically normal	37	36	41	27
Organic illness	9	16	5	15
Neurotic illness	5	10	5	5
Affective illness	2	3	9	7
Personality disorder	33	26	32	37
All nonschizophrenic diagnoses	49	55	51	63

*The Ns represent interviewed relatives whose consensus diagnoses were outside the schizophrenia spectrum.

In the case of the schizophrenia spectrum of disorders and for chronic, latent, and uncertain schizophrenia, however, there is a significant concentration in the biological relatives of index cases in contrast to the persons who are not genetically related to a schizophrenic. For chronic schizophrenia, the prevalence in the biological relatives of index cases is 2.9 percent, compared with 0.6 percent in the others; for latent schizophrenia it is 3.5 percent compared with 1.2 percent; and for uncertain schizophrenia it is 7.5 percent compared with 2 percent. For any of these diagnoses of schizophrenic illness, the prevalence in those genetically related to the schizophrenic index cases is 13.9 percent compared to 2.7 percent in their adoptive relatives or 3.8 percent in all subjects not genetically related to an index case (see table 2). These differences between the group genetically related to the schizophrenic index cases and those not so related are highly significant statistically and speak for the operation of genetic factors in the transmission of schizophrenia.

The evidence presented thus far is compatible with a genetic transmission in schizophrenia, but it is not entirely conclusive, since there are possible environmental factors such as in utero influences, birth trauma, and early mothering experiences; these have not been ruled out. However, there are 127 biological paternal half-siblings of index cases and controls among these relatives who can help to settle that question, since the biological paternal half-siblings did not share the same mother, neonatal mothering experience, or postnatal environment with their adopted half-sibling. The only thing they shared was the same father and a certain amount of genetic overlap. The number of paternal half-siblings is almost identical for index cases and the controls, but the number of those who were diagnosed as having definite or uncertain schizophrenia is markedly different, with 14 among the half-siblings of the index cases and only 2 among the controls ($p = .001$). There is a similar concentration if we restrict the diagnosis to definite schizophrenia (see table 3). We regard this as compelling evidence that genetic factors operate significantly in the transmission of schizophrenia.

These data do not permit the conclusion that schizophrenia is a unitary disorder, since they are equally compatible with a syndrome of multiple etiologies and different modes of genetic transmission. They make it difficult, however, to deny the existence of a syndrome that indepen-

TABLE 2
Prevalence of Schizophrenia Spectrum Disorders in the Biological and Adoptive Relatives of Schizophrenic Index and Control Subjects, from Consensus Diagnosis on Interview

Type of Relative	Number of Relatives Identified	Diagnosis of Schizophrenia in Relatives							
		Chronic		Latent		Uncertain		Total	
		Number	Percent	Number	Percent	Number	Percent	Number	Percent
Biological relatives of schizophrenic adoptees	173	5*	2.9	6	3.5	13**	7.5	24***	13.9
Biological relatives of control adoptees	174	0	—	3	1.7	3	1.7	6	3.4
Adoptive relatives of schizophrenic adoptees	74	1	1.4	0	—	1	1.4	2	2.7
Adoptive relatives of control adoptees	91	1	1.1	1	1.1	3	3.3	5	5.5

*$p < .05$ (significances apply to differences between biological relatives of schizophrenic adoptees and controls; other differences were not significant).
**$p < .01$.
***$p < .001$.

TABLE 3
Schizophrenic Illness in the Biological Paternal Half-Siblings of Index and Control Groups

	Biological Paternal Half-Siblings of			
	Index Group (N = 63)		Control Group (N = 64)	
Diagnosis	Number	Percent	Number	Percent
Definite schizophrenia	8	13*	1	1.6
Definite or uncertain schizophrenia	14	22**	2	3.0

*p = .015 (significances apply to differences between index and control groups, by Fisher's exact probability test).
**p = .001.

dent raters can agree upon quite reliably and that each rater without knowledge of the relationship finds significantly concentrated only in the biological relatives of schizophrenics. If schizophrenia is a myth, it is a myth with a strong genetic component!

These data do not imply, nor do I believe, that genetic factors and the biological processes involved in their expression are the only important influences in the etiology and pathogenesis of schizophrenia; in fact, we are currently engaged in analyzing these interviews with respect to how experiential factors and their interaction with biological vulnerability make possible or prevent the development of schizophrenia. Environmental factors have always been an important part of medical models of illness, and, in the case of disorders of thought, mood, and behavior, one recognizes the operation of psychological processes and social influences that cannot be described or examined in physicochemical terms (16). They can still be studied scientifically, however, and there are important scientific disciplines devoted to that pursuit.

Diabetes mellitus is analogous to schizophrenia in many ways. Both are symptom clusters or syndromes, one described by somatic and biochemical abnormalities, the other by psychological. Each may have many etiologies and shows a range of intensity from severe and debilitating to latent or borderline. There is also evidence that genetic and environmental influences operate in the development of both. The medical model seems to be quite as appropriate for the one as for the other.

CONCLUSIONS

The medical model of mental illness has been criticized for the unnecessary and unfortunate social consequences that sometimes accrue to the mentally ill (and that have occurred throughout history, long before there was ever a concept of mental illness). Good sense and logic would require that we address ourselves to the problem of social attitudes. Meanwhile, let us not forget the salutary consequences that are an inherent part of the medical model: the requirements to relieve suffering; to observe, to study, to try to understand the underlying mechanisms of the disorder; to carry out research so that someday we will be able to prevent it and treat it effectively.

The psychiatrist is best equipped to carry out these responsibilities toward the mentally ill on the basis of his broad background in medicine, in clinical psychology and psychopathology, and in the scientific method as it is applied to medicine. Yet psychiatry is in an identity crisis precisely because it has branched out well beyond mental illness into problems it is not especially qualified to handle—community, national, and international affairs; poverty, politics, and criminality. In each of these areas, we have responsibilities as citizens and human beings; we have yet to demonstrate any special competence as psychiatrists. Sir Aubrey Lewis commented on the state of psychiatry thus, "It may be that there is no form of social deviation in an individual which psychiatrists will not claim to treat or prevent—the pretentions of some psychiatrists are extreme" (17, p. 189). I am also reminded of a little poem for which I am indebted to Dana Farnsworth:

> There was a man named Dr. Peck,
> Who fell in a well and broke his neck.
> People said he should have known,
> To treat the sick and leave the well alone.

The medical model led in another era to the conquest of the psychoses of paresis and pellagra, which were major mental illnesses of their time; for these disorders our efforts today must be applied to the delivery and utilization of the knowledge we have. But there are several million people in our society, and a comparable fraction in every human society that has been examined, who suffer from various forms of serious mental illness that we do not yet understand. The mentally ill do not disappear under the most drastic of social changes; their number remains unhappily large under democracy or monarchy, fascism or communism, tyranny or benevolence. Psychiatry has learned to describe their illnesses and to differentiate them into diagnostic categories for the purpose of treatment, which it can sometimes carry out effectively. They suffer from illnesses whose etiology and pathogenesis at the biological, psychological, and sociological levels are still obscure and we have only unsubstantiated hypotheses of how to prevent them. Only research can give us these answers (18). Rationalizations that retard research can only make that goal more difficult to attain.

REFERENCES

1. Hippocrates: On the sacred disease, in The Genuine Works of Hippocrates. Translated by Adams F. Baltimore, Williams & Wilkins Co, 1939, pp 347–360
2. Szasz TS: Repudiation of the medical model, in Psychopathology Today. Edited by Sahakian WS. Itasca, Ill, FE Peacock, 1970, pp 47–53
3. Breggin PR: Psychiatric totalitarianism: Nazi Germany and today. Freedom (independent journal published by the Church of Scientology), May–July 1974 (whole issue)
4. Dershowitz A: Preventive confinement: a suggested framework for Constitutional analysis. Texas Law Review 151:1277–1324, 1973
5. US v Brawner, 471 F 2d 969 (1972)
6. Rouse v Cameron, 373 F 2d 451 (1966)
7. Lake v Cameron, 331 F 2d 771 (1964)
8. Roth M: Presidential address: psychiatry and its critics. Can Psychiatr Assoc J 17:343–350, 1972
9. Laing RD: Phenomenological approach to schizophrenia, in Psychopathology Today. Edited by Sahakian WS. Itasca, Ill, FE Peacock, 1970, pp 351–358
10. Gruenberg E: How can the new diagnostic manual help? Int J Psy-
11. Rosenhan DL: On being sane in insane places. Science 179:250–258, 1973
12. Meehl PE: Some ruminations on the validation of clinical procedures. Am J Psychol 13:102–128, 1959
13. Kety SS, Rosenthal D, Wender PH, et al: Mental illness in the biological and adoptive families of adopted individuals who have become schizophrenic: a preliminary report based upon psychiatric

interviews, in Genetics and Psychopathology. Edited by Fieve R, Brill H, Rosenthal D. Baltimore, Johns Hopkins Press (in press)

14. American Psychiatric Association: Diagnostic and Statistical Manual of Mental Disorders, 2nd ed. Washington, DC, APA, 1968
15. Spitzer RL, Fleiss JL: Unpublished statement cited in Spitzer RL, Wilson PT: Classification and nosology in psychiatry and the Diagnostic and Statistical Manual of the American Psychiatric Association, in Comprehensive Textbook of Psychiatry, 2nd ed. Edited by Freedman AM, Kaplan HI, Sadock BJ. Baltimore, Williams & Wilkins Co (in press)
16. Kety SS: A biologist examines the mind and behavior: many disciplines contribute to understanding human behavior, each with peculiar virtues and limitations. Science 132:1861–1870, 1960
17. Lewis A: The State of Psychiatry. New York, Science House, 1967
18. Kety SS: The academic lecture: the heuristic aspect of psychiatry. Am J Psychiatry 118:385–397, 1961

14

THE COGNITIVE REVOLUTION AND MIND/BRAIN ISSUES

KARL H. PRIBRAM

Interest in the relationship between mind and brain has become invigorated by the surge of activity in the neurosciences and in what has come to be called "cognitive science." The time is therefore ripe to take a new look at this age-old problem, but now from the standpoint of the scientist as well as from that of the philosopher. Today, we are in a position not only to reevaluate major philosophical stances but also to develop more limited and precise theories and models of mind/brain relationships that subsume a restricted database.

The surge of interest in mind/brain issues has come in various guises. Cognitive scientists have argued whether "representations" or "computations" characterize the relationship (see, e.g., Gardner, 1985; "Special Issue" in *The Behavioral and Brain Sciences,* 1980). A philosopher and a neuroscientist have banded together only to find themselves maintaining an interactive separateness of mind and brain (Popper & Eccles, 1977). And a neuroscientist (Sperry, 1952, 1969, 1976), as well as a philosopher (Searle, 1979) have declared themselves solidly on the side of mind (Sperry, 1980), whereas a psychologist (Skinner, 1971, 1976) has given up hope that a "science of mental life" as William James (1901), and more recently George Miller (1962), have dubbed it, is possible at all because such a science would depend on verbal communications, which are notoriously ambiguous.

It is this variety in the attempts to deal with mind/brain relations that calls forth my reevaluation. I know most of the protagonists personally and have high regard for all of them, as I have for much of the philosophical discourse that bears on the issues. It seems to me that these intelligent scholars cannot all be wrong despite the fact that their respective contributions

Reprinted from the *American Psychologist, 41,* 507–520. (1986).

are at variance with one another. Could it then be that they are all correct, in some nontrivial sense? If so, how?

My suggestion, to be developed here, is that each of these espoused philosophical positions has captured a part of the domain of issues and that what is necessary is to determine the database on which the position rests. The failure of philosophy to resolve the issues comes when a position is maintained beyond the confines of its relevant database to a point where another position is more appropriate.

The danger of such an eclectic approach is that one may end up with an "any worlds" or at least with a "many worlds" relativist viewpoint, which is fine if one wishes to show merely that there are many different answers to the questions posed. But I am not satisfied with such a result. I hope to be able to show that the several databased theoretical frames fit different agendas in philosophy and that a unified view can be constructed out of the diversity of theories.

I will provide one caveat: The approach taken here is new and must therefore of necessity be inadequate and even "wrong" in detail. The important consideration is that the approach is a viable one and that it can be progressively sharpened by recourse to experimental disconfirmation (see Popper, 1968a, 1968b). The approach is essentially scientific but heeds the questions so carefully honed by philosophical inquiry.

The approach taken here leads to some apparent paradoxes: Dualism, pluralism, monism, constructivism, realism, and even idealism all find a place in the metaphysical scheme. Inferences from reaction time data, recordings of event-related brain potentials, and other results of experimental observations have led to the acceptance of the idea that cognitive operations are taking place in the brains of sensing and behaving organisms. As I hope to make clear, this epistemological acceptance leads to a pluralistic realism that is comfortable with dualism at the ordinary level experienced by behaving organisms.

In contrast, the reliance of cognitive science on computers and programs and of neuroscience on "information processing" interpretations, is constructivist and leads us close to idealism: an "informational" monisn as seen from the identity vantage. Codes and transforms are shown to be the vehicles by means of which informational structures remain invariant over a variety of embodiments, a variety of realizations.

Finally, an ontological neutral origin is shown to resolve the apparent paradox of invariance of informational structure and a plurality of realities. It is shown that to identify invariance solely as mental leads to awkward interpretations such as those that would hold that computers have "minds" and "feelings." Instead, a plausible case is made that what remains invariant across transformations is neutral to the mind/brain, mental-material duality and is captured by physicists' definitions of energy and the amount of its structure: entropy, and its converse, negentropy (i.e., information). Such information can be realized mentally as well as materially, an idea captured by the aphorism that, on occasion, the pen can be mightier than the sword.

METAPHYSICS

Some Recent History

The story of current thinking on the mind/brain issue begins with Ernst Mach (1914) and the positivist approach. Mach was a dualist and a parallelist; mind and brain for him had identical structures but were forever separate entities. Mach's position gave rise to two major approaches, each centered on a particular problem. The first of these approaches accepted Mach's dualism but noted that mind and brain do interact, that is, influence each other. The question arose as to how that interaction might take place. Popper and Eccles (1977) answered this question by suggesting that mental processes create a "World 3" of language and culture that in turn feeds back, through the senses, to influence brain mechanisms. Mind itself was noted to be an emergent of this interaction, an emergent immersed in the sensory (and motor) processes that relate the brain to the organism's environment.

The Vienna Circle, and especially Feigl (1960), addressed a different problem in Mach's formulation. If indeed identical structures characterize brain and mind, what is it that is structurally identical? Feigl, in keeping with positivist tradition, focused on language and suggested that mind talk and brain talk were different aspects of some underlying Machian structure. In his identity theory, Feigl gave up dualism and opted for the monistic emphasis on basic structure.

Both Popper's and Feigl's programs have much merit, but each also poses new questions, questions that can lead to further insights. Just what is it that makes up World 3? What is the essence of language and culture that can so readily influence the brain? In the multiple aspects view, what is it that the aspects refer to? My answer to these questions is presented in scientific rather than philosophical terms. By this I mean that I am to identify the data set that each of the philosophic programs addresses rather than to push each program to its logical limit. The result of this approach is a neutral monism, neutral to the mind/brain duality, with the potential for multiple realizations. Feigl's linguistic dual aspects (e.g., mind talk and brain talk) are replaced by a plurality of realizations. A new duality is discovered: the duality between potential orders and their realizations.

Behavior and Experience

In contrast to philosophers, psychologists, under the banner of a realist radical behaviorism, eschewed any scientific reference to mind. As noted, the reasons for this are not arbitrary. Rather, as both Skinner (1971, 1976) and Quine (1960) have pointed out, the issue is that no two people mean exactly the same thing when they use a particular word or phrase. Furthermore, we can never be sure that even when we use a word such as *green* that it denotes the same experience to each person using it. But this is an issue common to all of science and indeed to all cognition, as Berkeley (1904) so persuasively argued. Are we therefore to give up, hang our heads, and sit in isolation in our respective corners? Of course not. Nor does it mean that in constructing a science we *must* exclude reference to our conscious experience. A common alternative is to make inferences and to proceed to deal with them. Cognitive science can and does proceed in just this fashion (see, e.g., Johnson-Laird & Johnson-Laird, 1983).

The issue is not just a philosophical one. When patients with occipital lobectomies say that they are blind even though they are able to respond correctly to the location and configuration of visual cues (Weiskrantz, 1974; Weiskrantz, Warrington, Sanders, & Marshall, 1974), how are we to deal with their "blind-sight" except to distinguish their instrumental responses from their verbal reports of introspection? A radical behaviorist would want to discount the introspective report as not "real"; in fact, several died-in-the-wool behaviorists have told me that they are certain that either the patients or the experimenters were lying. But this type of patient is not unique. Brenda Milner's (1966) famous subject, H.M., who had sustained a bilateral medical temporal lobe resection, has a similar difficulty: He cannot consciously remember Brenda even after some 30 years of repeated testing while at the same time be performs perfectly in an operant situation that he learned many months before (Sidman, Stoddard, & Mohr, 1968).

The alternative is to ascertain to the best of our ability that we can accept at face value both the instrumental behavior and the verbal report and to go about the search for the neural mechanism that, when injured, can account for the dissociation. We accept the inference that the subject has a "mental life," that his or her psychological processes are accessible by way of his or her verbal reports and instrumental behaviors, and furthermore, that these different forms of behavior may reflect different processes.

Philosophers and psychologists of a nonbehaviorist persuasion may counter that any argument about mental phenomena derived from behavior is spurious. They would rather begin with "the phenomenon itself existentially experienced." But there is little that can be done with such experiences except to attempt to describe them (behaviorally) and to organize the descriptions (structurally). Thus, Maurice Merleau-Ponty (1963), an existentialist philosopher, has authored a book entitled *The Structure of Behavior,* which in both spirit and content shows remarkable resemblances to our *Plans and the Structure of Behavior* (Miller, Galanter, & Pribram, 1960; see also Pribram, 1965), which tackles the issues from a behavioral and information-processing vantage. I do not mean to convey here that there is no distinction between a behavioristic and an existential-phenomenalistic approach to mind. Elsewhere I detail this distinction in terms of a search for causes by behaviorists and a search for informational structure reasonably (meaningfully) composed by phenomenologists (Pribram, 1979). What I do want to emphasize here is that both approaches lead to conceptualizations that cannot be classified readily as either mental or material. In their search for causes, behaviorists rely on drives, incentives, reinforcers, and other "force-like" concepts that deliberately have a Newtonian ring. In their quest for understanding mental experience, existentialists come up with structure much as do anthropologists and linguists when they are tackling other complex organizations. And structural concepts are akin to those of modern physics where particles arise from the interactions and relationships among processes. The view to be developed here is that in neither case can this resultant of inquiry be characterized as mental or material unless one wishes simply to state a bias in favor of one or the other as being more meaningful to oneself.

Hierarchy, Reciprocal Causation, and Mind/Brain Identity

Let us look at this issue of structure in terms of computers, programs, and the processing of information in some detail because in many respects these artifacts so clearly portray some of the problems involved in the mind/brain issue. As has been repeatedly noted (see, e.g., Searle, 1984), the computer is not a brain, but its programs are constructed by people who do have brains. Nonetheless, computers and their programs provide a useful metaphor in the analysis of the mind/brain issue in which the distinction between brain, mind, and spirit can be seen as similar to the distinction between machine (hardware), low-level programs (e.g., operating systems), and high-level programs (e.g., word processing programs). Low-level programs such as machine languages and assemblers are not only idiosyncratic to particular types of computer hardware, but there is also considerable similarity between the logic of these languages and the logic operations of the machines in which they operate. In a similar vein, to some extent, perceptual processes can be expected to share some similarity to brain processes. On the other hand, high-level languages such as Fortran, Algol, and Pascal are more universal in their application, and there is less obvious similarity between their implicit logic and the logic of machines. At the highest level, in languages such as English, with which I address my computer in order to use it as a word processor, the relation between the logos of English (word, concept, logic) and that of the machine is still more remote. However, English relates me to a sizable chunk of the human social order. To complete the analogy, humanity's spiritual nature strives to make contact with more encompassing orders whether they be social, physical, cosmological, or symbolic.

Understanding how computer programs are composed helps to tease apart some of the issues involved in the "identity" approach in dealing with the mind/brain relationship. Because our introspections provide no apparent connection to the functions of the neural tissues that comprise the brain, it has not been easy to understand what theorists are talking about when they claim that mental and brain processes are identical. Now, because of the computer/program analogy, we can suggest that what is common to mental operations and the brain "wetware" in which the operation is realized, is some order that remains invariant across transformations. The terms *information* (in the brain and cognitive sciences) and *structure* (in linguistics and in music) are most commonly used to describe such identities across transformations.

Order invariance across transformations is not limited to computers and computer programming. In music we recognize a Beethoven sonata or a Berlioz symphony irrespective of whether it is presented to us as a score on sheets of paper, in a live concert, over our high fidelity music system, and even in our automobiles when distorted and muffled by noise and poor reproduction. The information (form within) and the structure (arrangement) is recognizable in many embodiments. The materials that make the embodiments possible differ considerably from each other, but these differences are not part of the essential property of the musical form. In this sense, the identity approach to the mind/brain relationship, despite the realism of its embodiments, partakes of Platonic universals, that is, ideal orderings that are liable to becoming flawed in their realization.

In the construction of computer languages (by humans) we gain insight into how information or structure is realized in a machine. The essence of biological as well as of computational hierarchies is that higher levels of organization take control over, as well as being controlled by, lower levels. Such reciprocal causation is ubiquitous in living systems: Thus, the level of tissue carbon dioxide not only controls the neural respiratory mechanism but is controlled by it. Discovered originally as a regulatory principle that maintains a constant environment, reciprocal causation is termed *homeostasis*. Research over the past few decades has established that such (negative) *feedback* mechanisms are ubiquitous, involving sensory, motor, and all sorts of central processes. When feedback organizations are hooked up into parallel arrays, they become feedforward control mechanisms that operate much as do the words (of bit and byte length) in computer languages (Miller et al., 1960; Pribram, 1971a).

Equally important, programming allows an analysis to be made of the evolution of linguistic tools that relate the various levels of programming languages. Digital computers with binary logic require a low-level language (coded in the numerals 0 or 1) that sets a series of binary switches. At the next level, switch settings can be grouped so that the binary digits (bits) are converted into a more complex code consisting of bytes, each of which is given an alphanumerical label. Thus, for example, the switch setting 001 becomes 1, the setting 010 becomes 2, and the setting 100 becomes 4.

Given that 000 is 0, there are now eight possible combinations, each of which is an octal byte.

This process is repeated at the next level by grouping bytes into recognizable words. Thus 1734 becomes ADD; 2051 becomes SKIP, and so forth. In high-level languages, *groups* of words are integrated into whole routines that can be executed by one command.

It is likely that some type of hierarchical integration is involved in relating mental processes to the brain. Sensory mechanisms transduce patterns of physical energy into patterns of neural energy. Because sensory receptors such as the retina and the cochlea operate in an analog rather than a digital mode, the transduction is considerably more complex than the coding operations described above. Nonetheless, much of neurophysiological investigation is concerned with discovering the correspondence between the pattern of physical input and the pattern of neural response. As more complex inputs are considered, the issue becomes one of comparing the physically determined patterns with subjective experience (psychophysics) and recording the patterns of response of sensory stations in the brain.

These comparisons have shown that a number of transformations occur between sensory receptor surfaces and the brain cortex. These transformations are expressed mathematically as transfer functions. When the transfer functions reflect identical patterns at the input and output of a sensory station, the patterns are considered to be geometrically isomorphic (*iso* means same; *morph* means form), that is, of the same form. When the transfer functions are linear (i.e., superposable and invertible, reversible), the patterns are considered to be secondarily or algebraically isomorphic (Shepard & Chipman, 1970). Thus, as in the case of computer programming, levels of processing are recognized, each cascade in the level producing transformations that progressively alter the form of the pattern while maintaining intact some basic order, an informational structure.

In short, holding the identity "position" with regard to the mind/brain issue involves specifying what it is that remains identical. Unless something remains constant across all of the coding operations that convert English to binary machine code and back to English, my word processing procedures would not work. Identity implies reciprocal stepwise causation among structural levels. Contrary to the usually held philosophical position, identity does not necessarily mean geometrical or even algebraic isomorphism. Transformations, coding operations, occur that hierarchically relate levels of complexity with one another. A level is defined by the fact that its description, that is, its code, is in some nontrivial sense more efficient (i.e., requires less work, less expenditure of energy) than use of the code of the components that compose it. In the case of the word processor, the coding is arbitrary, and the arbitrariness is stored on a diskette and copyrighted. In the case of the mind/brain relationship, the nature of the coding operations is more universal and the efforts of a century and a half of psychophysical, neuropsychological, and cognitive research have provided knowledge concerning at least some of the coding operations involved.

I am belaboring these findings of scientific research to indicate that, contrary to what some philosophers hold (see, e.g., Dewan et al., 1976), they have relevance to philosophical issues. If the mind/brain problem arises from a distinction between the mental and the material and we find that at a certain level of analysis we no longer can clearly make such a separation, then the very assumptions upon which the issue is joined may be found wanting.

Within the framework of these considerations, let us now look at some specific dualistic and mentalistic proposals that have been forwarded recently and place them within a perspective that states that the material-mental dichotomy holds only for the ordinary Euclidean-Newtonian world of appearances.

DO EXPERIENCES MATTER OR DOES MATTER BECOME EXPERIENCED?

In the ordinary world of appearances there is no question but that human mental experiencing can be distinguished sharply from the contents of the experience. The issue has been labeled "intentionality" (or intentional inexistence) by Franz Clemens Brentano and has given rise to inferences about the nature of reality (Brentano, 1973; Chisholm, 1960). The question is often phrased: Are my perceptions (my phenomenal experiences) the "real," or does the content of those perceptions make up the "real" world? My phenomenal experiences are mental; the world as it appears to me is material. I can give primacy to my experience and become a phenomologist, or I can give primacy to the contents of the experience and become a materialist. But I can also give primacy to neither and attest to the dual nature of reality.

Materialism and phenomenology run into difficulty only when each attempts to deny the other. As long as only primacy is at stake, either view can be made consistent. After all, our experiences are primary, and empiricism is not inimical to a real material world. And we do appear to be experiencing something(s), so our experiences may well become organized by those real (material) somethings (see Bunge, 1980, for a persuasive development of this position).

However, by accepting such a moderate position with regard to mind and matter we immediately come up against a set of dualist problems. Are the contents of perception "really" organized by the experience of the perceiver? Is that experience in turn organized by brain function, sensory input, and the energies impinging on the senses? Would a complete description of brain function of an organism also be a description of the experience of that organism? If so, are not the material descriptions of brain, senses, and energies sufficient? Or at least do the descriptions of experience add anything to the material descriptions? Cannot the inverse be equally true? What do the descriptions of brain, senses, and energies materially add to what we so richly experience?

EPISTEMOLOGY

Transcending Dualisms Without Denying Them

I believe that today there are answers to these questions where only a few years ago there were none. These answers come from "unpacking" conceptual confusions and demonstrating where each conceptualization captures a part of a truthful whole.

A semantic analysis shows that descriptors of brain, senses, and energy sources are derived from an analysis of experience into components. The components are organismic and environmental (biological and physical or social), and each component can be subdivided further into subcomponents until the quantum and nuclear levels of analysis are reached. This procedure of analysis downward in a hierarchy of systems is the ordinary way of descriptive science. Within systems, causes and effects are traced. When discrepancies are found, statistical principles are adduced and probabilities invoked. Scientists have become adept and comfortable with such procedures.

Mental language stems from different considerations. As in the case of descriptive science, mental terms take their origin in experience. Now, however, experience is validated consensually. Experience in one sensory mode is compared with that obtained in another. Then validation proceeds by comparison of one's experience with that of another. A little girl points to a horse. Up to now, her mother has allowed her to say "cow" whenever any animal is pointed to. But the time has come to be more precise, and the experience of horse becomes validly different from that of a cow. Mental language is derived from such upward validations in a hierarchy of systems.

Elsewhere I detail the differences in scientific approach that this upward—or outward—look entails (Pribram, 1965). It is certainly not limited to psychology. When Albert Einstein enunciated his special and general theories of relativity, he was looking upward in the set of hierarchically arranged physical systems. The resultant relativistic views are as applicable to mental conceptualizations as they are to physical ones. It is these relativisms that existentialists and phenomenologists constantly struggle to formulate into some coherent principles. My own belief is that they will be successful only to the extent that they develop the techniques of structural analysis. But structured analyses often depend on enactment to clarify the complexities involved. Abhorrent as the computer and other engineering devices may be to philosophers and psychologists of the existential–phenomenal persuasion, these tools may turn out to be of great service to their mode of inquiry.

If the above analysis is correct, then a dualism of sorts can be entertained as valid. First, however, let me provide a cautionary note. This form of dualism is concerned with the everyday domain of appearances—or ordinary experiences. Commencing with such ordinary experiences, two modes of conceptualization have developed. One mode operates downward in a hierarchy of systems, analyzing experience into components and establishing hierarchical and cause–effect relationships between these components. The other operates upward toward other organisms to attain consensual validation of experiences by comparing and sharing them.

Thus two mirror images—two optical isomers, as it were—are constructed from experience. One we call material and the other mental. Just as optical isomers in chemistry have differing biological properties, although they have identical components and arrangements, so the mental and material conceptualizations have different properties even though they initially arise from the self-same experiences.

I suggest that this is the origin of dualism and accounts for it. The duality expressed is of conceptual procedures, not of any basic duality in nature. As we will see, there are other dualities that are more basic, but these are not the ones that have become the staple of those arguing for dualism.

Mind as Emergent and as Actor

The views expressed thus far have provided a coherent theory that accounts for dualistic views but transcends them by showing them to arise from procedural differences that separately realize a common structure. That structure is neutrally described in mathematical and information-processing (or similar) terms—terms that cannot readily be characterized as either material or mental.

This theory is considerably different from more classical dualistic views that hold to a fundamental separation between the mental and material. This separation has also been ameliorated recently by the proposal (Popper & Eccles, 1977) that interaction between the mental and material takes place by way of a material-like cultural domain that feeds back through the material senses to the material brain. Mental processes are then the emergents that result from this interaction. However, I have argued elsewhere that the way Popper—and Eccles—defined mind in terms of such interactions is akin to a colloquial use of the concept "force" (Pribram, 1976). We say, for instance, that gravitational force, "gravity," pulls us to the earth. However, the concept of gravity was derived from studying the interactions of masses in motion. Gravity is thus by definition an interaction term; gravity would not "exist" were there no "us" to be attracted to the earth (and other bodies). We would reify gravity and have it pull us; and appearances certainly confirm this way of conceiving forces: that they are being "produced" by one body and operating on another. Popper developed his thesis of World 3 being "produced" by World 2 in this spirit.

What I see as helpful in the World 2–World 3 division is the attempt to portray the same issue that I discuss in terms of structure and its realization. In a sense, what I call "structure" is what Popper and Eccles called "mind." The difference is, however, that my "structures," also derived from sensory and behavioral interactions, are realized in material, physical environments (such as the structure of a symphony being embodied in a printed score or a magnetic tape). If these structures are to be identified as mental, my formulation would be akin to those of Alfred North Whitehead (1925), Roger Sperry (1980), John Searle (1983), and Eugene Wigner (1969)—a form of mentalism. But, I am not willing to go that far. Rather, I prefer to hold the line by stating that structures transcend both the physical and mental realities in which they become realized.

As noted, strictly speaking mentalism per se implies dualism because there is no need for mentalism if there were no materialism. There is no up without a down. Further, Sperry and Searle attempted to limit their mentalism to those structures that are organized by and in turn organize the brain. But it is not clear whether they would be willing to go to the epistemological limit that holds that mind interacts with the elementary components making up the brain. Intuition regarding the biological roots of mentality is certainly accurate. To confuse the analogy of the computer with the historically based homologies that have given rise to psychological processes is akin to calling a whale a fish. By the same token, however, Sperry and Searle are adamantly opposed to an "independent existence of conscious mind apart from the functioning brain" (Sperry, 1980, p. 195); their mentalism does not stretch to cover the very essence of what motivates mentalism in the hands of those who oppose it to materialism; that is, the *primacy* and independence of mental structures.

Constructional Realism: A Pluralistic Monism

Before I proceed with a precise delineation of the experimental and theoretical basis for the approach taken here, it may be helpful to summarize what has been proposed thus far: a "monism," which states simply that the truly basic components of the universe are neither material nor mental, but neutral. The dematerialization of matter at the level of analysis that concerns modern physics (which I will review later in this article) supports such a "neutral monism" (James, 1909; Russell, 1948). Critical philosophers (e.g., Herbert Feigl, 1960), who were steeped in linguistic analysis, developed this monistic view by suggesting that the "mental" and "material" are simply different ways of talking about the same processes. Thus "mind" and "brain" come to stand for separate linguistic systems, covering different aspects of a commonality. The problem has been to find a neutral language to describe the commonality without being either mental or material in its connotations.

I have taken this "dual aspects" view a step further by proposing that each aspect not only is characterized linguistically but in fact is a separate "realization" or "embodiment" (Pribram, 1971b). As noted, I have further proposed that what becomes embodied is informational "structure." Thus, in essence I have stood the critical philosopher's approach on its head: The enduring "neutral" component of the universe is informational structure, the negentropic organization of energy. In a sense, this structure can be characterized as linguistic—or mathematical, musical, cultural, and so on. Dual aspects become dual realizations—which in fact may be multiple—of the fundamental informational structure. Thus, a symphony can be realized in the playing at a concert, in the musical score, on a record or on a tape, and thence through a high-fidelity audio system at home.

Mind and brain stand for two such classes of realization, each achieved, as described earlier, by proceeding in a different direction in the hierarchy of conceptual and realized systems. Both mental phenomena and material objects are realizations and therefore realities. Both classes of reality are constructions from underlying "structures," which it is the task of science to specify in as neutral a language as possible (neutral, i.e., with respect to connotations that would suggest that the "structures" belong in one or the other class). I note elsewhere the relationship of such a constructional realism to critical realism, pragmatism, and neo-Kantian rationalism (Pribram, 1971a).

There is thus an important difference between a constructional realism such as I propose and mentalist, dualist, and triadic interactionisms. In a constructional scheme the precise place of brain mechanisms can be specified. The sensory and brain perceptual mechanisms that are used to construct the Newtonian reality of appearances; the cognitive, "intrinsic" (my term for Eccles's "liaison") brain mechanisms that are necessary to the formulation of quantum and nuclear physics; the conative, motor brain mechanisms that organize intention and plan; the emergence of feelings from the neurochemical organizations of the brain—all can be fitted into their precise and proper place in the scheme. There is no global "mind" that has to make mysterious contact with global "brain." Many mysteries are still there—to name only one, for example, how emergents come about and why they are so utterly different from their substrate. But issues become scientific and manageable within the broader context of philosophic enquiry.

The Neural Microstructure

One example is in the order of such manageability and the precision with which the problems can be stated. I take this example from my own work because Eccles reviewed it and criticized it in his part of the book, *The Self and Its Brain* (Popper & Eccles, 1977). The problem relates to both perception and memory. The issue is how sensory input becomes encoded in the brain cortex. Eccles put the problem in the following way:

> What neural events are in liaison with the self-conscious mind both for giving and receiving. . . . We reject the hypothesis that the agent is the field potential generated by the neural events. The original postulate of the gestalt school was based on finding that a massive visual input such as a large illuminated circle resulted in some topologically equivalent potential field in the visual cortex, even a closed loop! This crude hypothesis need not be further considered. However a more refined version has recently been proposed by Pribram (1971a) in his postulate of micro-potential fields. It is assumed that these fields provide a more subtle cortical response than the impulse generation by neurones. However, this field potential theory involves a tremendous loss of information because hundreds of thousands of neurones would be contributing to a micropotential field across a small zone of the cerebral cortex. All the finer grain of neuronal activity would be lost in this most inefficient task of generating a minute electrical potential by current flow in the ohmic resistance provided by the extracellular medium. In addition we have the further problem that there would have to be some homunculus to read out the potentials in all their patterned array! The assumed feedback from micro-potential fields onto the firing frequencies of neurones would be of negligible influence because the currents would be extremely small.
>
> We must believe that there is an essential functional meaning in all the discrete neuronal interactions in spatiotemporal patterns, otherwise there would be a great loss of information. In this context, we must consider the organization of the cortical neurones in the anatomical and physiological entity that is called a module . . . In the first place it is inconceivable that the self-conscious mind is in liaison with single nerve cells or single nerve fibers. These neuronal units as individuals are far too unreliable and ineffective. In our present understanding of the mode of operation of neural machinery we emphasize ensembles of neurones (many hundreds) acting in some collusive patterned array. Only in such assemblages can there be reliability and effectiveness . . . the modules of the cerebral cortex . . . are such ensembles of neurones. The module has to some degree a collective life of its own with as many as 10,000 neurones of diverse types and with a functional arrangement of feed-forward and feedback excitation and inhibition. As yet we have little knowledge of the inner dynamic of life of a module, but we may conjecture that, with its complexly organized and intensely active properties, it could be a component of the physical world (World 1) that is open to the self-conscious mind (World 2) both for receiving from and for giving to. We can further propose that not all modules in the cerebral cortex have this transcendent property of being "open" to World 2, and thus being the World 1 components of the interface. By definition there would be restriction to the modules of the liaison brain, and only then when they are in the correct level of activity. Each module may be likened to a radio transmitter-receiver unit . . . the module may be thought of as an integrated microcircuit of electronics, only vastly more complicated. (Popper & Eccles, 1977, pp. 365–366)

Although Eccles quoted my book *Languages of the Brain: Experimental Paradoxes and Principles in Neuropsychology* (Pribram, 1971a), he ignored in the above account whole sections (e.g., pp. 126–131, 324–327) devoted to what I labeled "logic modules" (Pribram, 1971a). The structure of such modules is presented in much greater detail than Eccles has done in *The Self and Its Brain* or anywhere else. Furthermore, the precise operation of the modules has been simulated by computer on several occasions in my laboratory (Bridgeman, 1971; Phelps, 1974; Pribram, Nuwer, & Baron, 1974; Spinelli, 1966).

But there is more. Eccles criticized me in the first paragraph quoted earlier: "The assumed feedback from micropotential fields onto the firing frequencies of neurones would be of negligible influence because the currents would be extremely small." However, further on he used these same currents (which, as clearly defined in *Languages of the Brain,* are the depolarizations and especially the hyperpolarizations that occur at synapses and within dendritic fields) to "emphasize ensembles of neurones (many hundreds) acting in some collusive patterned array . . . with as many as 10,000 neurones of diverse types and with a functional arrangement of feed-forward and feedback excitation and inhibition." Excitation and inhibition for the most part are carried out in axonless (Golgi type 2) "local circuit" neurons that depend on the very micropotentials that Eccles criticized in the first paragraph (Rakic, 1976). It is becoming clearer that processing in the brain—processing within local neuronal circuits—is proceeding by way of local electrotronic and chemical communications that characterize dendrodendritic interactions rather than via the action potential made so characteristic of long sensory and motor pathways (see, e.g., Schmitt, Dev, & Smith, 1976).

G. M. Shepherd and W. Rall have presented voluminous neurophysiological evidence on the functional organization of these local microcircuits—evidence on which I based by proposal of microstructures (Rall, 1970; Shepherd, 1976). What then is the actual difference between Eccles's microcircuits and my microstructures except that I clearly specify the graded response characteristics of the patterning of electrical potentials that produces the functional arrangements within microstructures (or microcircuits) whereas Eccles failed to do so and took umbrage at the self and its mind operating a "radio transmitter-receiver" (the brain modules).

So much for the neurophysiology. The question is of course: What does this neurophysiology gain us with respect to the mind–body problem? I have suggested that the neuronal microstructure, the microcircuitry, is encoding periodic activity and that sensory transduction of environmental energy results in patterns of neuronal activation in the spectral domain. Eccles was not averse to this when he suggested that microcircuits act much as radio transmitters-receivers. Radios operate on periodic information; they are tuned to transmit and receive spectral codes.

The initial evidence for neural encoding in the spectral domain was presented in *Languages of the Brain* (Pribram, 1971a, chap. 8). Since its publication, evidence continues to pour in. Originally, G. S. Ohm and Hermann von Helmholtz suggested that the auditory system operates as a spectral analyzer (Helmholtz, 1863; Ohm, 1843). Georg von Bekesy (1957) showed that the skin and the somatosensory mechanism behave in a similar fashion. But the most dramatic evidence concerns the visual system. More and more evidence is accumulating to show that visual–spatial processing is accomplished in the spectral domain. The visual system analyzes the periodic fluctuations of the intensity of light over space (Campbell & Robson, 1968; DeValois, Albrecht, & Thorell, 1978a, 1978b; Movshon, Thompson & Tolhurst, 1978a, 1978b, 1978c; Pribram, Lassonde, & Ptito, 1981).

In the engineering sciences, such processing in the spectral domain is called optical information processing (if done with lens systems) or image processing (if performed with computers) or holography (if storage on photographic film is employed). It is holography that first called my attention to the attributes of the spectral domain and their relevance for understanding the mind/brain (Pribram, 1966). In a hologram (the photographic film that stores the microstructure of periodic changes of light and dark over space) the information about forms in space becomes distributed. This sheds light on one of the most difficult problems of neuroscience, namely, how to explain the fact that local lesions in the brain do not selectively impair one or another memory trace. In a hologram, restricted damage does not disrupt the stored information because it has become distributed.

In essence, the information becomes blurred over the entire extent of the holographic film but in such a precise fashion that it can be deblurred by performing the inverse procedure. Thus, image reconstruction (or construction) from the stored spectral domain is simple; applying the same transform that produced the store will also decode it into an image. In short, contrary to what Eccles stated to be a problem with my theory, the evidence that the brain encodes information in the spectral domain indicates that no "homunculus" is needed to read out the memory trace. Either an input from the senses or from central source (such as Popper's suggestion that the pain–pleasure expectation and attention mechanisms might be responsible; see also Pribram & McGuinness, 1975) will activate the spectrally encoded memory trace to produce an image. No "self-conscious mind" is sitting there, biasing the functions of the association cortex, as Eccles suggested. Rather, as Popper claimed, self-conscious mind is conceived best as an emergent property of a specifiable brain organization.

This mechanism has direct relevance for the mind/brain problem. Note that storage takes place in the spectral domain. Images and other mental contents as such are not stored, nor are they "localized" in the brain. Rather, by virtue of the operation of the local brain circuitry, usually with the aid of sensory input from the environment, images and mental events emerge and are constructed. The images *are* Gilbert Ryle's (1949) ghosts resulting from the operations of the "machine" (brain). But, when implemented (i.e., realized, materialized) through action (i.e., in the organism's environment), these ghosts *can* causally influence, through the senses, the subsequent operations of the brain.

A similar mechanism involving the motor mechanisms of the brain can account for intentional, planned behavior. The evidence that such a mechanism exists is presented in *Languages of the Brain* and elsewhere (Pribram, 1971a, 1976; Pribram et al., 1981). Much of my laboratory research has been involved in demonstrating that brain function is active, not passive, in its interactions with environment, and in elucidating the processes operative in this active aspect of mind. This research has shown that the intrinsic cortex and the limbic formations of the forebrain actively organize sensory input (see review by Pribram, 1980).

I have belabored this neurophysiology because the discovery that certain operations of the brain can be understood best in terms of processing in the spectral domain is directly related to the discovery in quantum and nuclear physics that ultimately the appearances of matter may be immaterial. We must take a close look at this database so fundamental to a materialist view.

ONTOLOGY

The Dematerialization of Energy

The fundamental assumption that has given rise to the mind/brain problem is that mental phenomena and the material universe are in some essential fashion different from each other. As we have seen, in the ordinary domain of appearances, at the Euclidean–Newtonian level of analysis, this view is certainly tenable. But at the levels of the macro- and microphysical universes dualism becomes awkward. Niels Bohr's complementarity and Werner Heisenberg's uncertainty principle emphasize the importance of the observer in any understanding of what presumably is observed (Bohr, 1966; Heisenberg, 1959). Eugene P. Wigner (1969) stated the issue succinctly: Modern microphysics and macrophysics no longer deal with relations among observables but only with relations among observations.

An objection can be entered that such difficulties of distinguishing observables from observations encountered today by physicists are temporary, superficial, and of no concern to philosophers interested in the eternal verities. But that is not the message these thoughtful pioneers in physics are attempting to convey. They have been exploring universes where the everyday distinction between material and mental becomes disturbingly untenable at a very fundamental level. As I proceed, I shall tender some explanations that may help account for their views.

The dematerialization of matter can be traced in some sense to earlier formulations. For instance, physics was conceptually understandable in James Clerk Maxwell's day when light waves were propagated in the "ether." But then physicists did away with the "ether." Still, they did not rid themselves of Maxwell's wave equations or the more recent ones of Erwin Schroedinger (1928) or Louis Victor Prince de Broglie (1964). One readily can conceptualize waves traveling in a medium, such as when sound waves travel in air, but what can be the meaning of light or other electromagnetic waves "traveling" in a vacuum? Currently physicists are beginning to fill that vacuum with dense concentrations of energy, potentials for doing work when interfaced with matter. It is this potential that, I propose, is neutral to the mental–material duality.

Energy and Entropy (Informational Structure) as the Neutral Potential

In science, such potentials are defined in terms of the actual or possible work that is necessary for realization to occur and are labeled *energy.* Thus, multiple realizations imply a neutral monism in which the neutral essence, the potential for realization, is energy. And, as stated in the second law of thermodynamics, energy is entropic, that is, it has structure.

Heisenberg (1959) developed a matrix approach to understanding the organization of energy potentials. Currently, this approach is used in s-matrix, bootstrap theories of quantum and nuclear physics by Henry Stapp (1965) and Geoffry Chew (1966). These investigators (among others, i.e., Dirac, 1951) have pointed out that measures of energy potential are related to measures of location in space–time by a way of Fourier transform. The Fourier theorem states that any pattern of organization can be analyzed into, and represented by, a series of regular waveforms of different amplitudes and frequencies. These regular waveforms can in turn be superimposed, convolved, with one another and, by way of the inverse Fourier procedure, can be transformed to obtain correlations in the original space–time configuration. Thus, the Fourier transform of a set of patterns displays a spectral organization that is, of course, different from that which is displayed after the inverse Fourier transform has again converted the pattern into the space–time order.

In terms of the proposition put forward by Stapp and Chew, this means that the organization of energy potentials is considerably different from the space–time organization of our ordinary perceptions that can be expressed in Euclidean, Cartesian, and Newtonian terms. David Bohm (1971, 1973, 1976) has identified these nonclassical organizations of energy potentials as "implicate," that is, enfolded, and has used the hologram as an example of such enfolded orders. Dennis Gabor (1946, 1948), the inventor of the hologram, based his discovery on the fact that one can store interference patterns of waveforms produced by the reflection or refraction of light from an object on a photographic film and reconstruct from such a film the image of the object. The description of the enfolded organization of the stored potential for reconstruction is related to the unfolded space–time description of the object by a Fourier transform.

More Neuroscience

The Fourier theorem has also played an important role in the recent discoveries in the brain sciences that were reviewed in part in the section on the neural microstructure. In the late 1960s, several groups of investigators found that they could explain their findings in visual research when they realized that their results indicated that encoding of spatial patterns in the visual system involved what they called *spatial frequency*. This term describes the spectral domain that results when a Fourier transform is performed on space–time and was coined by Fergus Campbell and John Robson (1968) of Cambridge University when they discovered unexpected regularities in their data. Responses to gratings of different widths and spacings adapted not only to the particular grating shown but also at other data points. These additional adaptations could be understood by describing the gratings as composed of regular waveforms with a given frequency and the regularities in terms of harmonics. The spectral frequency was determined by the spacings of the grating, and thus the term spatial frequency. Spatial and temporal frequencies are related of course: Scanning by a steadily moving beam would describe the grating's temporal frequency. Physicists therefore use the term *wave number* to denote the spectral form of description of patterns.

In the late 1950s and 1960s, David Hubel and Thorsten Wiesel (1959, 1968) had discovered that single cells in the visual cortex responded best when the visual system was stimulated with lines at a certain orientation. In the early and mid 1970s, Daniel Pollen and his colleagues (Pollen, Lee, & Taylor, 1971; Pollen & Taylor, 1974) noted that when such lines were drifted across the visual field, the response of the cell was not uniform but described a waveform similar to that which described the gratings used by Fergus Campbell. Campbell (1974) meanwhile showed that the responses of single cells in the visual cortex also adapted to the harmonics of the gratings that were presented, much as did the organism as a whole. Finally, Russell and Karen DeValois and their collaborators, (DeValois, Albrecht, & Thorell, 1978a, 1978b; DeValois & DeValois, 1980; DeValois, DeValois, & Yund, 1979) demonstrated that the response of these visual cortical cells is only poorly described by the orientation of a line, whereas it is accurately described in terms of the orientation and spatial frequency of a grating, that is, the cell is tuned to a spatial frequency range of approximately one-half to one octave. Furthermore, these investigators showed that when checkerboards and plaids were used to stimulate the visual system, the cells responded maximally to the Fourier transform of the space–time patterns, as determined by computer display, and that the cells were essentially unresponsive to the orientation of the individual lines that composed the checkerboards and plaids. In short, it appears that the visual system performs a Fourier transform on the retinal image produced by the lens of the eye.

What this means is that the optical image is decomposed into its Fourier components: regular waveforms of different frequencies and amplitudes. Cells in the visual system respond to one or another of these components and thus, in aggregate, comprise an optical image processing filter or resonator that has characteristics similar to the photographic filter comprising a hologram, from which images can be reconstructed by implementing the inverse transform.

There are, however, important differences between ordinary photographic holograms and the visual nervous system. Ordinary holograms are composed by a global Fourier transform that distributes the information contained in a space–time image throughout the transform domain. In the visual nervous system, distribution is limited anatomically to the input channeled to a particular cortical cell. There are, however, holographic techniques that use similar "patch" or multiplex constructions. Bracewell (1965) at Stanford University pioneered these techniques in radioastronomy by stripping together the holographic transformations of limited sectors of the heavens as viewed by radiotelescope. When the inverse transform is applied, space–time images of the whole composite can be viewed in three dimensions.

Furthermore, the transform that best describes the process in the visual system is a Gabor, not a Fourier. The Gabor transform (1946, 1948; Daugman, 1985; Marcelja, 1980) is formed by placing a Gaussian envelope on the otherwise unlimited Fourier transform. This is another way of stating that the transformation is not global, and it gives mathematical precision to the limits involved.

Finally, the arrangement of the visual channels and the cortical cells is not haphazard with regard to one another. A clear retinotopic to cortical spatial arrangement is maintained. Thus the gross grain of the visual filter determines space–time coordinates, whereas its fine grain describes the Fourier components.

What advantage is gained by this fine-grain holographic-like organization? Recall that in the transform domain correlations among patterns are readily performed. This is why the Fast Fourier Transform (FFT) as performed by computer is such a powerful tool in statistical analysis and in computerized tomography (CT scans). The brain is an excellent correlator by virtue of its fine-grain processing potential.

The dual properties of an enfolded fine-grain (technically, the receptive field organization) and a gross-grain space-time organization applies to other sense modalities as well, although the experimental evidence is not as complete. Georg von Bekesy (1967) performed critical studies in the auditory and somasthetic modalities, Walter Freeman (1960) conducted studies in the olfactory, and Pribram, Sharafat, and Beekman (1984) have shown that cells in the sensorimotor cortex are tuned to specific frequencies of movement. At the same time, in all these sensory systems the spatial organization of the receptor surface is topographically represented in the gross-grain arrangement of the cortical cells that receive the sensory input.

In summary, there is good evidence that another class of orders lies behind the ordinary classical level of organization, which we perceive and which can be described in terms of Euclidean and Newtonian views and mapped in Cartesian space–time coordinates. This other class of orders is constituted of fine-grain organizations that describe potentials that had been poorly understood because of the radical changes that occur in the transformational process of realization. When a potential is realized, information becomes unfolded into its ordinary space–time appearance; in the other direction, the transformation enfolds and distributes information as this is done by the holographic process. Because work is involved in transforming, descriptions in terms of energy are suitable, and as the structure of information is what is transformed, descriptions in terms of entropy (and negentropy) are also suitable. Thus, complete understanding involves at least a duality: On the one hand, there are enfolded orders manifested as energy potential; on the other; there are unfolded orders manifested in negentropic space–time.

Is Information Material or Mental?

Furthermore, when forces are postulated to exist between material bodies, the forces are often conceptualized as "material" even though they themselves are not constituted of matter. When matter and energy are related by the equation $E = mc^2$, energy is commonly assumed to be "material." But this is a misreading of the equal sign. The equal sign does not indicate sameness: For instance, $2 + 2 = 4$ and $2 \times 2 = 4$. If the equal sign indicated sameness, "$\times$" and "$+$" would be the same, but they are not: $2 + 2 = 2 \times 2$ because they are equal though different. This is a point I have had to make repeatedly when I present evidence that men and women are biologically and psychologically different. I am *not* arguing, therefore, that they are unequal.

Energy is not material, only transformable into matter. It is measured by the amount of work that can be accomplished by using it and the efficiency of its use depends on its organization as measured by its entropy. The invention of the vacuum tube and subsequent devices have shown that properly configured minute amounts of energy can control large expenditures and that these minute organizations provide "information," that is, they inform and organize energy. Measures of information and entropy thus were seen as related (see, e.g., Brillouin, 1962; von Weizsacker, 1974). Computers were constructed to process information, and programs were written to organize the operations of computers. Is the information contained in a program "material" or "mental"? If it is either, what then of the information in a book? Or the entropy that describes the behavior of a heat engine or of a warm-blooded mammal? Clearly, we have come to the limit of usefulness of a distinction between the material and the mental.

CONCLUSIONS

A New Duality: The World of Appearances Versus the World of Potentiality

The point was made earlier in this essay that the dualism of mental versus material holds only for the ordinary world of appearances—the world described in Euclidean geometry and Newtonian mechanics. An explanation of dualism was given in terms of procedural differences in approaching the hierarchy of systems that can be discerned in this world of appearances. This explanation was developed into a theory, a constructional realism. But it was also stated that certain questions raised by a more classical dualistic position were left unanswered by the explanations given in terms of a constructional realism.

What are these questions? Recall that Popper and Eccles proposed entirely different—and, in a fundamental sense, opposite—views of how mind and brain interact. In Popper's view, mind is an emergent from brain functioning; according to Eccles, mind operates on the intrinsic "liaison" formations of brain cortex. Still, these authors managed to publish a book together. Each must have felt some affinity for the other's views. What is it that they may have sensed to be in common? What deep feeling did they fail to articulate adequately in their book?

I believe that the analysis provided earlier in this essay may help clear up this issue. Note that when one looks downward in the hierarchy of systems that compose the ordinary world of appearances, essentially reductive analyses are engaged. To take account of new properties that arise, when components become organized into higher order, more complex structures, "emergence" is proposed; the proposal is essentially descriptive of what is observed. The upward look in the hierarchy, as in the phenomenal and existential approaches, simply takes these "emergents" as the fundamental achievements of observations. Constructional realism is compatible with such views of emergence, and as noted earlier, I believe Popper was attempting to achieve a similar end by his construction of World 3.

Eccles by contrast was holding out for a very different sort of formulation. He insisted that mind transcends brain function in that mind operates upon brain, not because mind emerges from the functioning of the brain. As noted above, articulated in this fashion, Eccles's formulation makes no scientific sense.

But now consider the brain as a spectral analyzer and the general characteristics of the transforms that occur. These characteristics have been appreciated fully only recently. The recording of spectral patterns by holography has provided a visible artifact whose properties can be readily conceptualized.

Essentially, space and time become enfolded in the holographic domain. This accounts for translational invariance, the fact that transformation into the ordinary domain can be accomplished from any part of the encoded record. In the holographic record, information becomes distributed, spread over the entire surface of a photographic film, or brain module, much as the waves produced by throwing a pebble into a pond spread to its edges. Several such waves initiated by several pebbles will interact or "interfere," and the record of these interference patterns constitutes the hologram. If a moving picture were made of the origin and development of the interference patterns, the movie could be reversed and the image of the pebbles striking the pond could be recovered. Image reconstruction by holography accomplishes much the same effect by an operation that performs an inverse transform on the record. Thus image (and object) and holographic record are transforms of each other, and the transformations involved are readily reversible.

Consider further the fact that in the holographic domain space and time are enfolded. Only the density of occurrences is manifest. These densities can be recorded as wave number or in scattering matrices representing n-dimensional (Hilbert) domains such as have been used in quantum physics. Holography has become a window through which we are able to conceptualize a universe totally different from that which characterizes the world of appearances. David Bohm (1971, 1973) pointed out that most of our conceptions of the physical world depend on what we can observe through lenses. Lenses focus, objectify, and draw boundaries between parts. Lenses particularize. Holograms by contrast are distributive, unbounded, and holistic. Bohm referred to our lens-given ordinary perceptions and conceptions as explicate and those that are holographic as implicate. Thus, there are at least two discernible orders in the universe: an explicate and an implicate. The explicate order gives an account in terms of particles, objects, and images. The implicate order, still poorly cognized, begins with densities of the fluctuating properties of waveforms.

Bohm and other physicists have become excited by the similarity of conceptualizations of the implicate order and those described by mystics who have experienced a variety of religious and other "paranormal" phenomena (Bohm, 1976; Capra, 1975). The lack of spatial and temporal boundaries, the holographic characteristic that the whole is represented in every part, and the transformational character of shifting from explicate to implicate order are all beyond ordinary human experiencing, which apparently is limited to the everyday, explicate, Euclidean–Newtonian universe to which we have become accustomed.

It is probably no accident that holograms were a mathematical invention (by Dennis Gabor) that used a form of mathematics, the integral calculus, invented by Gottfried Wilhelm Leibniz, who also came to a vision of the implicate order. Leibniz's monadology (1714/1951) is holographic; his monads are distributed, windowless forms each of which is representative of the whole. Substitute the term *lensless* for windowless, and the description of a monad and a hologram is identical.

The fact that the brain is, among other things, a spectral analyzer, that it encodes information in a distributed fashion akin to that which characterizes a hologram, also means that the structural boundaries that characterize the ordinary limits of "brain" and "body" can, on occasion, appear to be transcended. Take as an example our current-day world in a large city. The space surrounding us is filled with spectral forms generated by radio and television stations. We are insensitive to these spectral forms unless we obtain the use of a receiver tunable to one or another of the spectral forms. Only then do we "explicate" into the everyday domain the spectral forms broadcast and enfolded in the space about us. The "mystery" of mind is resolved not by holding to the neo-Cartesian view that Eccles has taken, which is inappropriate to Popper's formulation, nor by adhering to either the materialist or the mentalist stance. Rather, we must recognize the transformational and potential nature of the implicate domain and the fact that our sense organs "make sense" by tuning in (and out) selective portions of this domain.

Summary

In concluding, I will attempt to summarize my position as developed in this article. I began by accepting a dualistic view of everyday experience: We humans can distinguish clearly between the process of experiencing and the contents of that experience. In the centuries since Descartes, this led to the view that the process of experiencing is mental whereas the components of experience, if not themselves material, are at least indicators of a material, physical world. I then went on to show that modern physicists, working both at the microphysical quantum and nuclear level and at the macrophysical "universe" level, have called into question the material basis of matter. Matter is constituted of energy, which in several forms interacts to produce that which we normally experience in ordinary perception. Normal experience is characterized by Euclidean geometry and Newtonian mechanics. Thus, the material nature of matter is limited to the ordinary world or experience, unless one wants to adopt the bias that energy is material because it can be converted to matter as indicated by Einstein's equation, $E = mc^2$. But then why would we have to call such a transformation a conversion? Does not such a materialist bias cloud rather than clarify the fact that, as yet, we do not know how to properly characterize such energy forms? And by this question I do not wish to suggest that they be characterized as mental.

Beginning from the other end of the mental–material dichotomy, we run into a similar limitation on its usefulness. Information and information processing, as when a computer is programmed or a brain is informed by sensory signals, are shown to involve minute amounts of energy that can organize or reorganize large-scale systems. The configurations that energy systems display rather than their raw amount are shown to be critical. Are such figural changes to be conceived as mental or material when they involve languages, cultures, and so on? Once again, a limit is reached where the mental–material distinction becomes useless.

Next I analyzed the issue of dualism on its own ground, that is, within the purview of ordinary experience. Here dualism is found to be based on mirror-image views constituted by different analytic procedures. The reductive materialistic view held by most scientists is found by looking downward from one's experience into the hierarchy of components that constitute that experience. This reductive view is balanced ordinarily by the recognition that novel properties "emerge" when specific configurations of components are formed.

Looking upward from one's experiences involves validating the experience with that of others. Experienced "phenomena" are described and compared. Emphasis is on the existence of the experience per se, its existential nature, and when precision is attempted the emphasis is on the structural relationships among phenomena. Consensual validation, enactment, and structural analysis of relationships constitute the tool of enquiry, not separation into parts causally related to one another as in the reductive sciences. Thus, the language of phenomenology, existentialism, and structuralism is "mental" because it is experience per se that constitutes the focus of interest.

Recognition of the procedural difference that is responsible for dualism in the ordinary world of experience allows one to transcend this dualism without denying its usefulness to deal with the problems of that ordinary world. I propose that dualism can be transcended by carefully combining the techniques and results of both the reductive and phenomenal approaches to enquiry. Structure having been made the central, enduring, single quality of a pluralistic monism, both reductive entities and phenomena are seen as realizations of identical structures derived from a more basic existential given.

Once this constructional realism is formulated, however, it has to face another issue. True, dualism is not denied; it simply is shown to operate in a limited sphere. But transcending dualism with a structural monism violates the very spirit of what dualists and mentalists believe in and are trying to articulate: the unique character of mental processes and their contents.

My final proposal meets the requirement of this aspect of dualism. Brain physiologists have shown the nervous system to be, among other things, a spectral analyzer. Furthermore, input apparently becomes distributed and stored in the transform domain in the manner of a holographic record. And physicists have suggested that a holographic-like order may well characterize the microstructure of the physical world. In this domain, space and time become enfolded; only density of occurrences is represented.

Descriptions of this domain and other similar orders that account for the observations of modern physics seem to be remarkably similar to mystics' descriptions of paranormal and religious experiences. I propose, therefore, that the duality between the normal, everyday domain of appearances and the transform domain captures the concerns of mentalists and dualists and accounts in a specific and precise mathematical fashion for what hitherto has been incomprehensible.

Structural realism is thus primarily a neutral monism that deals with a number of dualities of which two are especially significant for unpacking the issues involved in a mind/brain dualism: (a) a procedural duality that faces upward and downward in the hierarchy of systems discerned in the ordinary world of appearances and (b) a transformational duality that apposes the ordinary world of appearances to that viewed through the window of the spectral transform domain characterized by descriptions akin to those of the experiences of mystics that provide the basis for some important insights in various religious traditions.

Other dualities may well be discovered to underlie as yet unarticulated premises of dualism. What appears clear at the moment is that a dualism based on the distinction between mental and material is too limited to deal with the very issues that it poses. Other dualities can articulate answers to the problems raised by these issues and can deal not only with their substance but also with their spirit. Furthermore, these dualities can be specified by scientifically sound procedures and mathematically precise formulations that are encompassed by an ontological neutral monism from which an epistemological plurality of duals are constructed. Finally, their constructions are known to stem directly from discoveries in the physical, information, and behavioral sciences. Thus the often-made argument that the results of scientific research have no bearing on philosophically framed issues has been shown to be wrong. In fact, what has been shown is that only through the results of scientific research can philosophical issues, even at the ontological level, be refreshed.

REFERENCES

Bekesy, G. von (1957). Neural volleys and the similarity between some sensations produced by tones and by skin vibrations. *Journal of the Acoustical Society of America, 29,* 1059–1069.

Bekesy, G. von (1967). *Sensory inhibition.* Princeton, NJ: Princeton University Press.

Berkeley, G. (1904). *Three dialogues between Hylas and Philonous.* Chicago: Open Court.

Bohm, D. (1971). Quantum theory as an indication of a new order in physics. Part A. The development of new orders as shown through the history of physics. *Foundations of Physics, 1,* 359–381.

Bohn, D. (1973). Quantum theory as an indication of a new order in physics. Part B. Implicate and explicate order in physical law. *Foundations of Physics, 3,* 139–168.

Bohm, D. (1976). *Fragmentation and wholeness.* Jerusalem: VanLeer Jerusalem Foundation.

Bohr, N. (1966). *Atomic physics and human knowledge.* New York: Vintage.

Bracewell, R. N. (1965). *The Fourier transform and its application.* New York: McGraw-Hill.

Brentano, F. C. (1973). *Psychology from an empirical standpoint* (A. C. Rancmello, D. B. Terrell, & L. L. McAlister, Trans.). London: Routledge & Kegan Paul.

Bridgman, B. (1971). Metacontrast and lateral inhibition. *Psychological Review, 78,* 528–539.

Brillouin, L. (1962). *Science and information theory* (2nd ed.). New York: Academic Press.

Bunge, M. (1980). *The mind-body problem.* Oxford, England: Pergamon Press.

Campbell, F. W. (1974). The transmission of spatial information through the visual system. In F. O. Schmitt & F. G. Worden (Eds.), *The neurosciences third study program* (pp. 95–103). Cambridge, MA: MIT Press.

Campbell, F. W., & Robson, J. G. (1968). Application of Fourier analysis to the visibility of gratings. *Journal of Physiology, 197,* 551–566.

Capra, F. (1975). *The tao of physics.* Berkeley, CA: Shambhala.

Chew, G. S. (1966). *The analytic s-matrix: A basis for nuclear democracy.* New York: Benjamin.

Chisolm, R. M. (1960). *Realism and the background for phenomenology.* New York: Free Press.

Daugman, J. G. (1985, July). Uncertainty relation for resolution in space, spatial frequency, and orientation optimized by two dimensional visual cortical filters. *Journal of the Optical Society of America, 2* (7), 1160–1169.

DeValois, R. L., Albrecht, D. G., & Thorell, L. G. (1978a). Spatial tuning of LGN and cortical cells in monkey visual system. In H. Spekreijse (Ed.), *Spatial contrast.* Amsterdam: Royal Netherlands Academy of Sciences.

DeValois, R. L., Albrecht, D. G., & Thorell, L. G. (1978b). Cortical cells: Line and edge detectors, or spatial frequency filters? In S. Cool & E. L. Smith (Eds.), *Frontiers of visual science* (pp. 544–556). New York: Springer-Verlag.

DeValois, R. L., & DeValois, K. K. (1980). Spatial vision. *Annual Review of Psychology, 31,* 309.

DeValois, K. K., DeValois, R. L., & Yund, E. W. (1979). Responses of striate cortex cells to grating and checkerboard patterns. *Journal of Physiology, 291,* 483–505.

Dewan, E. M., Eccles, J. C., Globus, G. G., Gunderson, K., Knapp, P. H., Maxwell, G., Pribram, K. H., Savage, C. W., Savodnik, I., Scriven, M., Sperry, R. W., Weimer, W. B., & Wimsatt, W. C. (1976). The role of scientific results in theories of mind and brain: A conversation among philosophers and scientists. In G. G. Globus & G. Maxwell (Eds.), *Consciousness and the brain* (pp. 317–328). New York: Plenum Press.

Dirac, P. A. M. (1951). Is there an aether? *Nature, 168,* 906.

Feigl, H. (1960). Mind-body, not a pseudoproblem. In S. Hook (Ed.), *Dimensions of mind* (pp. 33–44). New York: Collier.

Freeman, W. J. (1960). Correlation of electrical activity of prepyriform cortex and behavior in cat. *Journal of Neurophysiology, 23,* 111–131.

Gabor, D. (1946). Theory of communication. *Journal of the Institute of Electrical Engineers, 93,* 429.

Gabor, D. (1948). A new microscopic principle, *Nature, 161,* 777–778.

Gardner, H. (1985). *The mind's new science.* New York: Basic Books.

Heisenberg, W. (1959). *Physics and philosophy.* London: Allen & Unwin.

Helmholtz, H. von (1863). *Lehre von den Tonempfindungen* [Sensations of tone]. Braunschweig, Germany: Vieweg.

Hubel, D. H., & Wiesel, T. (1959). Receptive fields of single neurones in the cat's striate cortex. *Journal of Physiology, 148,* 475–591.

Hubel, D. H., & Wiesel, T. (1968). Receptive fields and functional architecture of monkey striate cortex. *Journal of Physiology, 195,* 215–243.

James, W. (1901). *Principles of psychology.* London: McMillan.

James, W. (1909). *A pluralistic universe.* London: Longman's, Green & Co.

Johnson-Laird, A., & Johnson-Laird, P. (1983). *Mental models.* Berkeley, CA: Osborne/McGraw Hill.

Leibniz, G. W. (1951). *The Monadology and other philosophical writings.* London, England: Oxford University Press. (Original work published 1714)

Mach, E. (1914). *The analysis of sensations and the relation of the physical to the psychical.* Chicago: Open Court.

Mercelja, S. (1980). Mathematical description of the responses of simple cortical cells. *Journal of the Optical Society of America, 70,* 1297–1300.

Merleau-Ponty, M. (1963). *The structure of behavior* (A. L. Fisher, Trans.). Boston: Beacon Press.

Miller, G. A. (1962). *Psychology: The science of mental life.* New York: Harper & Row.

Miller, G. A., Galanter, E., & Pribram, K. H. (1960). *Plans and the structure of behavior.* New York: Holt.

Milner, B. (1966). Amnesia following operation on the temporal lobes. In C. W. M. Witty & O. L. Zangwill (Eds.), *Amnesia* (pp. 109–133). Montreal: Butterworths.

Movshon, J. A., Thompson, I. D., & Tolhurst, D. J. (1978a). Spatial summation in the receptive fields of simple cells in the cat's striate cortex. *Journal of Physiology, 283,* 53–77.

Movshon, J. A., Thompson, I. D., & Tolhurst, D. J. (1978b). Receptive field organization of complex cells in the cat's striate cortex. *Journal of Physiology, 283,* 79–99.

Movshon, J. A., Thompson, I. D., & Tolhurst, D. J. (1978c). Spatial and temporal contrast sensitivity of neurones in areas 17 and 18 of the cat's visual cortex. *Journal of Physiology, 283,* 101–120.

Ohm, G. S. (1843). Uber die Definition des Tones [On the definition of tone]. *Annale der Physikalischen Chemie, 59,* 513–565.

Phelps, R. W. (1974). Effects of interactions of two moving lines on single unit responses in the cat's visual cortex. *Psychological Review, 78,* 1371–1375.

Pollen, D. A., Lee, J. R. & Taylor, J. H. (1971). How does the striate cortex begin the reconstruction of the visual world? *Science, 173,* 74–77.

Pollen, D. A., & Taylor, J. H. (1974). The striate cortex and the spatial analysis of visual space. In F. O. Schmitt, & F. G. Worden (Eds.), *The neurosciences third study program* (pp. 239–247). Cambridge, MA: MIT Press.

Popper, K. R. (1968a). *The logic of scientific discovery.* New York: Harper & Row.

Popper, K. R. (1968b). Epistemology without a knowing subject. In van Rootselaar & Stoal (Eds.), *Logic, methodology and philosophy of sciences III* (pp. 333–373). Amsterdam: North-Holland.

Popper, K. R., & Eccles, J. C. (1977). *The self and its brain.* Berlin: Springer-Verlag.

Pribram, K. H. (1965). Proposal for a structural pragmatism: Some neuropsychological considerations of problems in philosophy. In B. Wolman & E. Nagle (Eds.), *Scientific psychology: Principles and approaches* (pp. 426–459). New York: Basic Books.

Pribram, K. H. (1966). Some dimensions of remembering: Steps toward a neuropsychological model of memory. In I. J. Gaito (Ed.), *Macro molecules and behavior* (pp. 165–187). New York: Academic Press.

Pribram, K. H. (1971a). *Languages of the brain: Experimental paradoxes and principles in neuropsychology* (3rd ed.). New York: Brandon House.

Pribram, K. H. (1971b). The realization of mind. *Synthese, 22,* 313–322.

Pribram, K. H. (1976). Problems concerning the structure of consciousness. In G. G. Globus, G. Maxwell, & I. Savodnik (Eds.), *Consciousness and the brain: A scientific and philosophical inquiry* (pp. 798–809). New York: Plenum Press.

Pribram, K. H. (1979). Behaviorism, phenomenology and holism in psychology: A scientific analysis. *Journal of Social and Biological Structures, 2,* 65–72.

Pribram, K. H. (1980). Cognition and performance: The relation to neural mechanisms of consequence, confidence, and competence. In A. Routtenberg (Ed.), *Biology of reinforcement: Facets of brain stimulation reward* (pp. 11–36). New York: Academic Press.

Pribram, K. H., Lassonde, M. C., & Ptito, M. (1981). Classification of receptive field properties in cat visual cortex. *Experimental Brain Research, 43,* 119–130.

Pribram, K. H., & McGuinness, D. (1975). Arousal, activation, and effort in the control of attention. *Psychological Review, 82,* 116–149.

Pribram, K. H., Nuwer, M., & Baron, R. (1974). The holographic hypothesis of memory structure in brain function and perception. In R. C. Atkinson, B. H. Krantz, R. C. Atkinson, R. D. Luce, & P. Suppes (Eds.), *Contemporary developments in mathematical psychology* (pp. 416–467). San Francisco, CA: Freeman.

Pribram, K. H., Sharafat, A., & Beekman, G. J. (1984). Frequency encoding in motor systems. In H. T. A. Whiting (Ed.), *Human motor actions: Bernstein reassessed* (pp. 121–156). Amsterdam: North-Holand/Elsevier.

Prince de Broglie, L. V. (1964). *The current interpretation of wave mechanisms: A critical study.* (Express Transaction Service, Trans.) Amsterdam: Elsevier.

Quine, W. V. (1960). *Word and object.* Cambridge, MA: M.I.T. Press.

Rakic, P. (1976). *Local circuit neurons.* Cambridge, MA: MIT Press.

Rall, W. (1970). Dendritic neuron theory and dendrodendritic synapses in a simple cortical system. In F. O. Schmitt (Ed.), *The neurosciences: Second study program* (pp. 552–565). New York: Rockefeller University Press.

Russell, B. (1948). *Human knowledge, its scope and limits.* New York: Simon & Schuster.

Ryle, G. (1949). *The concept of mind.* New York: Barnes & Noble.

Schmitt, F. O., Dev, P., & Smith, B. H. (1976). Electronic processing of information by brain cells. *Science, 193,* 114–120.

Schroedinger, E. (1928) Quantization as a problem of proper values. In J. F. Shearer & W. M. Deans (Eds.), *Collected papers on wave mechanics.* London: Blackie.

Serle, J. R. (1979). *Expression and meaning.* London, England: Cambridge University Press.

Searle, J. R. (1983). *Intentionality, an essay on the philosophy of mind.* London, England: Cambridge University Press.

Searle, J. R. (1984). *Minds, brains and science.* Cambridge, MA: Harvard University Press.

Shepard, R. N., & Chipman, S. (1970). Second-order isomorphism of internal representations: Shapes of states. *Cognitive Psychology, 1,* 1–17.

Shepherd, G. M. (1976). *The synaptic organization of the brain: An introduction.* New York: Oxford University Press.

Sidman, M., Stoddard, L. T., & Mohr, J. P. (1968). Some additional quantitative observations of immediate memory in a patient with bilateral hippocampal lesions. *Neuropsychologia, 6,* 245–254.

Skinner, B. F. (1971). *Beyond freedom and dignity.* New York: Knopf.

Skinner, B. F. (1976). *About behaviorism.* New York: Vintage.

[Special issue on the foundations of cognitive science]. (1980). *The Behavioral and Brain Sciences, 3*(1).

Sperry, R. W. (1952). Neurology and the mind-brain problem. *American Scientist, 40,* 291–312.

Sperry, R. W. (1969). A modified concept of consciousness. *Psychological Review, 76,* 532–636.

Sperry, R. W. (1976). Mental phenomena as causal determinants in brain function. In G. G. Globus, G. Maxwell, & I. Savodnick (Eds.), *Consciousness and the brain* (pp. 163–177). New York: Plenum Press.

Sperry, R. W. (1980). Mind/brain interaction—Mentalism, yes—Dualism, no. *Neuroscience, 2,* 195–206.

Spinelli, D. N. (1966). Visual receptive fields in the cat's retina: Complications. *Science, 152,* 1768–1769.

Stapp, H. P. (1965). Space and time in s-matrix theory. *Physiological Review, 135B,* 257–270.

Weiskrantz, L. (1974). The interaction between occipital and temporal cortex in vision: An overview. In F. O. Schmitt & F. G. Worden (Eds.), *The neurosciences third study program* (pp. 189–204). Cambridge, MA: MIT Press.

Weiskrantz, L., Warrington, E. K., Sanders, M. D., & Marshall, J. (1974). Visual capacity in the hemianopic field following a restricted occipital ablation. *Brain, 97,* 709–728.

Weizsacker, E. von (1974). *Offene systems I.* Stuttgart, F. R. Germany: Verlag.

Whitehead, A. N. (1925). *Science and the modern world.* New York: Macmillan.

Wigner, E. P. (1969). Epistemology of quantum mechanics: Its appraisals and demands. In M. Grene (Ed.), *The anatomy of knowledge* (pp. 31–45). London: Routledge & Kegan Paul.

15

DSM-III AND THE POLITICS OF TRUTH

THOMAS E. SCHACHT

If an angel were sent by God to drive out of the temple of science all those people [in it for reasons other than their love of truth] it would become embarrassingly empty.
—Albert Einstein, quoted in *Society for Social Responsibility in Science Newsletter,* 1953, p. 8

All really great lies are half true.
—John Funder, 1979, p. 1139

The third edition of the American Psychiatric Association's *Diagnostic and Statistical Manual of Mental Disorders* (DSM-III; American Psychiatric Association, 1980) ranks high on any list of controversial topics in the interdisciplinary field of mental health. Divergent viewpoints became evident even before its official completion, adoption, and publication in 1980 (Garmezy, 1978; McLemore & Benjamin, 1979; McReynolds, 1979; Schacht & Nathan, 1977; Zubin, 1978), and subsequent evaluations further sharpened conflicting positions (e.g., Foltz, 1980; Hoffman La Roche, Inc., 1981; Kaplan, 1983; Miller, Bergstrom, Cross, & Grube, 1981; Singerman, 1981; Spitzer, 1981; Williams & Spitzer, 1983). This article returns to a central topic of my 1977 appraisal of DSM-III (Schacht & Nathan, 1977); namely, the relationship between science and politics and what that relationship means for our understanding of and response to DSM-III.

More specifically, I argue that our views of DSM-III are frequently shaped by assumptions (often tacit) about the nature and proper relationship of science and politics. Examples will be offered illustrating how these assumptions about science and politics (constituting a kind of epistemopathy or cognitive pathology; Koch, 1981) may foster a peculiar kind of double-talk

Reprinted from the *American Psychologist,* 40, 513–521. (1985)
Preparation of this article was supported in part by National Institute of Mental Health Grant MH 16247.

about DSM-III. A further effect of these assumptions may be to emotionalize discussions of political aspects of DSM-III by causing any mention of politics to seem like an attack. Because of the substantial risk of being misunderstood on this very point, it is important to state at the outset that the purpose of the present article is not to attack DSM-III. Rather, the goal is to examine certain self-defeating consequences of some ways we think about DSM-III, regardless of our stance as proponents or opponents of particular substantive aspects of the taxonomy.

POLITICS AND MENTAL HEALTH PROFESSIONS

Acquisition, exercise, and preservation of social power are the defining activities of politics. Social power is expressed in a fabric of authorities, rights, liberties, participations, protections, and opportunities that collectively legitimize a pattern of asymmetric interactions between persons or groups. Although negative reactions to politics may be fashionable, it is important to remember that this fabric of social power provides a supporting matrix for most useful and important institutions and programs. The ordinary exercise of social power, although classically coercive and even brutal, has commonly softened in modern times. Nisbet (1975), for example, observed that contemporary social power as compared to historical versions may be blander, more indirect, and more likely to be engaged in "immobilization of the human mind" via "organization, technology, social work, psychiatry, [etc.]" (p. 223). This softened power decreases individuals' experience of political impact on their lives and thought, promoting uncritical internalization of prevailing ideologies and anesthetizing persons to the ways in which they are being led, influenced, or controlled. Softened power circumscribes their consciousness, allowing illusions of free choice to persist while available choices are curtailed through a subtle foreshortening of their imagination.

Mental health professionals exert enormous social power, of both the coercive and softened varieties (cf. Halleck, 1971). For example, under certain circumstances, the power of the mental health professional influences actions under both civil and criminal law, as in issues of competence to make a contract or to stand trial. As partial custodians of the state's police power, mental health professionals may separate parents from their children through expert testimony in custody hearings or may deprive persons of physical liberty through the process of involuntary commitment. As their "special language" for communicating about mental disorders (Kline, cited in Bayer & Spitzer, 1982, p. 47), the DSM-III also confers upon professionals the power of linguistic dominance, serving as a private communication mode that helps to preserve and promote acceptance of their beliefs and value systems.

These social powers (and others) derive partly from psychodynamics associated with society's increasing reliance on scientific experts for the management of uncertainty (cf. Benveniste, 1977; Illich, 1976) and partly from legislators' corresponding willingness to grant the various quasi-monopolies conveyed by professional licensure. Mental disorders are among life's most frightening vicissitudes, and the privilege to reduce their associated uncertainties by defining and naming the boundaries of "illness" confers tremendous social power upon the diagnosing professions. Furthermore, in addition to gaining power via reduction of naturally occurring uncertainties, social agents may also accrue power through their manipulation of the occasions for uncertainty (Benveniste, 1977). Thus, psychiatry, which has been losing social power both to allied professions and as part of a more general decline in the "golden age of medicine" (Burnham, 1982), may stand to regain power first by agreeing with its critics and declaring DSM-II obsolete, thereby generating uncertainty over nosological issues, and second, by then reducing this created uncertainty through publication of a new, official, and "more scientific"

DSM-III. This gaining of power may occur entirely independently from any intent to do so—it is intrinsic to the sociological situation.

These aforementioned extraordinary social powers accorded to mental health professions are designed to operate in the service of humanitarian interests. These powers also possess a darker potential, however, that has prompted critics such as Szasz (1982) to refer somewhat cynically to the mental health establishment as a "therapeutic state" (p. 768). In this sinister bureaucracy, as Zimbardo (1984) put it, "control is cloaked as cure, surveillance as a security service and repression as a rehabilitation program" (p. 71). Whether one views the political aspects of psychodiagnosis as dangerous or as desirable, DSM-III, perhaps more than any other document, functions as a "constitution" for this clinical body-politic. In its political incarnation, the DSM-III becomes an instrument of social organization, an official document that participates in the organization and distribution of social and economic power. More specifically, from within this political perspective the following conclusions can be drawn:

1. DSM-III serves to validate and reinforce the mechanisms by which we draw politically important distinctions between persons. Although DSM-III is a "mixed model," embodying both categorical and dimensional approaches to classification, the final outcome of the diagnostic process involves assigning a person to a diagnostic category.[1] These category assignments may lead to concomitant changes in status, benefits, opportunities, self-image, and reputation. The alternative dimensional approach involves placing persons on various continua with both healthy and unhealthy poles (cf. McLemore & Benjamin, 1979; Widiger & Kelso, 1983). Although the choice to use a categorical approach is ostensibly a scientific matter, the categorical approach also supports the isolation (Foucault, 1965) of the "mentally ill" by making it conceptually and emotionally easier to view them as different rather than as like us except in degree (Widiger & Kelso, 1983). The social isolations potentially associated with assignment of a DSM-III diagnostic label include loss of physical liberty (involuntary commitment), employment handicaps, problems in purchasing health or life insurance, and discriminatory treatment in the educational, military, and correctional systems.

2. DSM-III participates in the social regulation of both clients' and professionals' access to social resources. DSM-III diagnoses are frequently involved in the processes of awarding insurance reimbursements, in disability determinations, in assessing professional accountability, in determining eligibility for special programs, and so on. For example, insurers may require a DSM-III diagnosis before paying for treatment, and they may restrict reimbursement to selected DSM-III categories (e.g., schizophrenia may be reimbursable, but uncomplicated marital difficulties may not.)

3. DSM-III helps to establish and validate boundaries for restrictive professional guilds. Claims to possession of unique and specialized knowledge are central to the establishment and maintenance of professional boundaries (cf. Gross, 1978). In its status as an official document, the DSM-III implies the existence of a world in which control, clarity, and certainty about classifying mental disorders appear possible (and hence, expertise about these matters is also possible). Furthermore, the DSM-III itself becomes a topic to be knowledgeable about, thereby substantiating professionals'

[1]There has been substantial argument regarding the question of whether DSM-III classifies "persons" (the basic unit of most sociopolitical structures) or "patterns of behavior," "syndromes," and so on. It is not mandatory that one of these alternatives be selected to the exclusion of the other. In describing DSM-III as a document for classifying persons, I am emphasizing (at this point in the discussion) the central role that classifying persons plays in the political domain.

roles as experts and their claims to unique and specialized knowledge. Although DSM-III is frequently described as neutral with respect to the professional qualifications of its users (a point that will be returned to) it is clearly not intended to be a publicly accessible document usable by consumers as a self-help manual. Furthermore, despite the claims to neutrality, some DSM-III classifications correlate highly with the professional identity of the individuals applying the label. For example, psychologists are almost always involved with the diagnosis of mental retardation because of the common requirement for standardized intellectual assessment (Grossman, 1973). Likewise, physicians are almost always associated with labeling mental disorders related to acute organic brain syndromes.

SCIENCE IN DSM-III'S POLITICS

Traditional wisdom holds that scientific psychiatry and professional politics are separate and discrete domains. This conceptual separation of science and politics has a long history, traceable at least to the ancient Greek distinction between philosophy (love of knowledge) and rhetoric (the craft of persuasion). Idealized modern science represents objectivity and stresses the value of the empirical and the rational. This ideal science seeks after truth and seeks to control phenomena only as a means to further understanding of their essential nature. Politics, in contrast, represents subjectivity and special interest; it values the demagogic and emotional as well as the empirical and rational. Rather than seeking knowledge for its own sake, politics seeks power and seeks knowledge primarily as a practical means to power. Politics seeks control of events not as a means to understanding but as an end in itself.

In its strongest form, the belief that science and politics should (or can) be clearly discrete and separable may support diametrically opposite (and oversimplified) claims about DSM-III.

1. DSM-III is a *scientific* document. It is simply a public repository of knowledge, a common language for research and theorizing that was created as a work of joint scholarship and is owned by no one. In this view, DSM-III is part of an apolitical knowledge-seeking enterprise that has no aim beyond learning about the processes and structures of abnormal behavior and experience. Differences of opinion engendered by DSM-III are, in principle, resolvable by appeal to the impersonal authority of "objective" data and rational argument. Any legitimate political connections are limited to adjunctive nonscientific matters such as using diagnostic categories to determine eligibility for services or benefits. From this perspective, more intimate involvement of political concerns appears as a misuse or abuse that is external to DSM-III per se. Appelbaum (1977), for example, characterized the confounding of diagnostic science with politics as an avoidable sin, claiming that presence of "political" features constituted a "subversion" of "genuine clinical diagnosis," and warning diagnosticians to beware of "insidious contamination of technical procedures with social and political values" (pp. 162–163). A similar example is provided by Millon's (1983, p. 813) reaffirmation of Zigler and Phillips's (1961) assertion that "systems of classification must be treated as tools for further discovery, not bases for polemic disputation."
2. DSM-III is a *political* document. In line with previous discussion of politics and mental health professions, DSM-III in this view is seen primarily as a strategic resource, an example of knowledge as real estate (Keatley, 1983), central to major

social and professional imperatives and as valuable to its owners as is oil to OPEC.[2] DSM-III, in this view, is a tool for organizing advocacy, a source of authority behind answers to socially important questions (such as who is entitled to treatment, to benefits, etc.). It pays lip service to science so that various special interests may acquire a guise of respectability, and its major purpose is to reinforce and expand the health–industrial complex in general, and various forms of professional hegemony in particular. To borrow from Goldfried (1980), the political view emphasizes "*who* is correct, not *what* is correct," so that the question "How do you know?" becomes equivalent to "Who says?" (p. 991). As an example, consider psychiatrist Bursten's (1981, p. 371) claim that the phrase "medical model," with its freight of scientific connotations, is useful "to rally the troops . . . and to thwart the (psychologist, etc.) attackers. Economics demands that we be medical . . . we use the term to rout the enemy within" (cited in Smith & Kraft, 1983, p. 780).

AN INTEGRATED ALTERNATIVE

The foregoing opposing positions reflect a universe in which science and politics are discrete or even mutually exclusive. Correspondingly, DSM-III becomes *either* scientific *or* political: It cannot be conceived as both. The present article, in contrast, concurs with alternate views that science and politics cannot be discrete, that to confound them is inevitable, and that to insist otherwise is at best an idealistic fiction. In this context, an either/or dichotomy between science and politics is not a philosophical or ideological necessity so much as a convenient rhetorical custom. Furthermore, as will be illustrated later, assumption of an either/or dichotomy between science and politics may be a kind of cognitive pathology or epistemopathy (Koch, 1981) that promotes error, confusion, and double-talk. In all published discussions of DSM-III of which I am aware, the conventional science–politics dichotomy, although often invoked, has itself remained unexamined. The dichotomy is so taken for granted that it has acquired many characteristics of an unconscious organizing principle that shapes our views but itself remains transparent. We do not look at the science–politics dichotomy because we are forever looking through it. This article is written in the belief that to look only through the science–politics dichotomy, and not also to look at it, may contribute substantially to inter- and intraprofessional misunderstanding and conflict about DSM-III.[3]

There is considerable reluctance among scientists to accept or even acknowledge the influence of political forces upon scientific thought (and upon the form of scientists' academic and social roles). Bevan (1980), for example, lamented that "science is no longer simply a way of satisfying the curiosity of the individual scientist: It has become a means of accumulating political power by particular interest groups" (p. 782). Such attitudes often stem from an idealistic insistence upon the supposed autonomy and objectivity of science. Without such autonomous objectivity we must acknowledge that subjective, ideological, and political forces are an integral part of the rational–scientific knowledge-producing process—a conclusion that is almost automatically rejected by those who insist on a clear separation of science and politics. To indicate

[2]The question of ownership of DSM-III is of crucial importance. Although psychiatry unilaterally controlled the creation and dissemination of DSM-III (a crucial test of ownership), there are nevertheless efforts to avoid the political implications of this ownership. Thus there are frequent references to the interprofessional and multidisciplinary nature of the DSM-III (cf. Spitzer, 1981). The failed effort by psychologists to develop a "competing" system for behavioral classification (and the failure to include other professions in the tentative efforts that were made) further reflects the importance of this ownership dimension.

[3]The same point may be made about many other "scientific" topics (e.g., psychotherapy research) that, like DSM-III, have significant political aspects.

the need for this strong form of separating science and politics, critics justifiably point to such travesties as Lysenkoism (the once "official" Soviet genetic theory), to the American cigarette industry's self-serving interpretations of the evidence for a tobacco–cancer link, to incidents such as the firing of a scientist for attempting to report politically sensitive and unpopular environmental data (Holden, 1980), or to the notorious exploitations of "psychiatric" diagnosis and confinement by repressive governments.

We should not ignore abuses of social power. However, adhering to a rigid science–politics conceptual dichotomy that closes our eyes to the political dimension will not make us immune to abuses, nor will it keep our science pristine. Rather, as I will argue, the dichotomous thinking that accompanies a naive or simplistic separation of science and politics may ironically foster problems similar to those it is intended to prevent.

A contemporary philosophical alternative views science and politics nondichotomously as inherently and inseparably integral. This integrated philosophical view reflects Kuhn's (1962) emphasis on the importance to science of nonrational factors such as the historical context and the psychology of the individual scientist (see also Blum, 1978; Mahoney, 1976; Stolorow & Atwood, 1979). In this vein, Weizenbaum (1975, p. 279) admonished scientists to "resist the temptation to arrogance" inherent in granting "imperial rights" to an impersonal, virginal, apolitical vision of science. D. L. Watson plainly asserted that "the task of the scientific theorist who wishes to be recognized in his lifetime is as much a matter of weighing the likes, dislikes, prejudices, and intellectual honesty of office holders as it is of questioning phenomena" (cited in Mahoney, 1976, p. 108). Perhaps the strongest representative of this position is Feyerabend (1970), who argued vociferously that real science, as opposed to some unattainable ideal, is a thorough mix of rational argument and power tactics of subterfuge, rhetoric, and propaganda. Feyerabend asserted that because no theory ever accounts for all the evidence, and because there is no single approach to science, political power and techniques of persuasion must ultimately determine what is regarded as a fact, what shape a theory will assume, and which theory will prevail. In his word, "An argument is not a confession. . . . It is an instrument designed to make an opponent change his mind" (cited in Broad, 1979, p. 534). This claim may be equally true of DSM-III and of this article's present remarks.

Sentiments about the integral relationship of science and politics are not new. Perry (1966), for example, observed that naive ideologies of scientific purity have been subjected to numerous attacks over the last century; yet, as he also noted, the purity myth remains a "common and sturdy misapprehension about science" (p. xiv). Why, one might wonder, does a philosophically and epistemologically suspect vision of science persist so tenaciously? Fully considered answers to this question would require excursions into the sociology and psychology of knowledge that are beyond the present discussion. In the context of DSM-III, however, it can be argued that certain factors underlying retention of the myth of a clear science-politics dichotomy are themselves ideological and political. The vision of an untainted "pure" science is asserted, in part, because it affords an automatic veneer of legitimacy and thereby represents a politically useful simplification. There is a central ironic element to this process, because in order to invoke the name of "pure" science for political purposes, it becomes necessary to ignore or deny the fact that one is acting or thinking politically.

An almost incredible example of such double-think and double-talk occurred in the recent case of a federal agency that used Federal Bureau of Investigation (FBI) reports to screen scientists for "political compatibility" before inviting them to sit on peer research review panels (Marshall, 1982). The technocrats who confessed to using political orientation as a criterion for selecting peer reviewers nevertheless maintained a steadfast philosophic dichotomy between science and politics, insisting that anyone who claimed the government was trying to "politicize" the review panels must himself or herself be (politically) trying to embarrass the Administration by misrepresenting its commitment to (pure?) science! Although the ostensible content of the officials' communication denied political motives, the dynamic function of the communication was to provide a manifestly political defense. When such disavowals occur in discussions of DSM-III, the resulting communications may simultaneously deny and affirm their political aspects (see illustrations to follow). As with any incongruent communication, one result may be amplification of mistrust—in this case both intra- and interprofessionally.

The integral nature of science and politics (and hence the risk of double-talk and double-think when they are rigidly separated) becomes especially apparent when an ostensibly scientific document becomes "official" (i.e., is voted on by quasi-political organizations such as the American Psychiatric Association and the American Psychological Association; cf. Foltz, 1980) or when a prominent scientific or clinical expert is also visibly active in such a professional–political organization. In this latter situation, the impersonal authority of research data and the personal authority of political office become blended. Data may become tacitly interchangeable with rhetoric, and scientific discussions may become subtly hybridized with political arguments. Because the myth of scientific purity suppresses acknowledgment of this data–rhetoric homogenization, professionally active scientists may be forced to speak half-truths lest they risk appearing to challenge the sacred separation of science and politics.

SOME ILLUSTRATIONS

Mental Versus Medical Disorders

The following dilemma faced by Robert Spitzer seems prototypic of the kind of problem engendered by a strong science–politics dichotomy. Spitzer is the respected and knowledgeable psychiatric researcher who also served as chair of the American Psychiatric Association's DSM-III task force. As Millon (1983) reported, Spitzer and colleague Jean Endicott developed a definition of mental disorders that included the controversial phrase "mental disorders are a subset of medical disorders" (p. 805). According to Millon, this phrase appeared in a scientific article that was not an official document of the DSM-III task force. However, because of Spitzer's intimate association with the task force this distinction went unappreciated by critics. Millon reported that Spitzer and Endicott's scholarly effort to grapple with the difficult problem of defining mental disorders was misunderstood by colleagues who incorrectly perceived Spitzer as acting not in the capacity of scholar or scientist, but rather as chair of a professionally partisan committee. In this situation, any efforts on Spitzer's part to disavow political motivation could be readily interpreted as politically motivated denial (and, indeed, would be phenotypically indistinguishable from such denial). The sacredness of the science–politics dichotomy makes it necessary to deny political influences in science, but each denial risks, in its effect, an ironic affirmation of what is ostensibly being renounced.

Homosexuality

In December 1973, the Board of Trustees of the American Psychiatric Association voted to remove homosexuality from the then-official DSM-III (American Psychiatric Association, 1968) nomenclature. This action followed bitter political debates that had spread beyond the professional association to the media and to gay rights' organizations. The controversies over this action are documented in *Homosexuality and American Psychiatry: The Politics of Diagnosis* (Bayer, 1981).

The American Psychiatric Association Task Force on Nomenclature that oversaw development of DSM-III sought to avoid a repetition of the 1973 scenario, in which gay activist groups had used techniques of social protest to press for diagnostic change. A counterstrategy was employed that restricted the struggle almost exclusively to psychiatrists directly involved in the drafting of DSM-III. An article published in the *Journal of the History of the Behavioral Sciences* (Baker & Spitzer, 1982) described this counterstrategy:

> There was a moment when some participants entertained the thought of broadening the dispute to the general APA membership and even the gay community. Both Richard Green and Richard Pillard, the major proponents of this strategy sought to intimidate Robert Spitzer with such threats. Careful consideration of the potential impact of so politicizing the dispute resulted, however, in an explicit decision to confine the conflict to a narrow band of professionals. (p. 34)

Although it is fallacious to assume that political aspects of science can be avoided via simply excluding certain persons from a debate (that itself is a political action!), by thus limiting the debate to selected "experts" it was hoped that the task force could avoid politicizing the issue. However, the actual written correspondence between task force members, partially reproduced in the Bayer and Spitzer (1982) article, illustrates how views on the relationship between science and politics infused the task force dialogue.

Opponents to inclusion of homosexuality in the DSM-III (or proposed newer versions, such as "dyshomophilia") stressed the lack of scientific support for such a category. Thus, in a letter to several task force members dated April 6, 1977, Richard Green, professor of psychiatry at the State University of New York (SUNY) stated that "psychiatry must move forward in the 1970's and 1980's into the arena of scientific, objective respectability. Psychiatry alone stands as the last bailiwick other than some church groups, plus Eastern European and Arabic countries, in condemning homosexuality as a mental illness or a sin" (in Bayer & Spitzer, 1982, p. 39). This call to science was echoed in a letter dated May 12, 1977 from Judd Marmor of the UCLA School of Medicine to Robert Spitzer: "Clearly the crucial distinction here is an unconscious homophobia which persists in so many of our generation and the origins of which are basically moral and judgmental rather than scientific" (in Bayer & Spitzer, 1982, p. 40). Task force member Richard Pillard from Boston University pithily summarized this appeal to science by quoting George Winokur, who reportedly said, "No new words without new data!" (in Bayer & Spitzer, 1982, p. 39). It is worthwhile to note that, despite this rhetoric, none of the published correspondence deals meaningfully with anything that might be called research data.

Robert Spitzer, as task force chair and proponent of including the category "dyshomophilia" in DSM-III, responded to these allegations of nonscientific motivation with arguments based on an implicit science-politics dichotomy. However, these arguments ironically introduced political elements, undermining the very points they were intended to support. For example, in a reply to Pillard dated May 10, 1977, Spitzer asserted "that to remove the category [of dyshomophilia] entirely from the classification would be a way of removing the *legitimization* of therapeutic efforts to study its etiology" (in Bayer & Spitzer, 1982, p. 39, emphasis added). This reference to research "legitimacy" ironically underscores the political dimension, by acknowledging that inclusion in DSM-III confers legitimacy on a subject of study even prior to obtaining research data that might subsequently support claims to a more objective validity. In later correspondence (dated July 8, 1977) to task force members, Spitzer argued that "in our current state of ignorance [the concept of dyshomophilia] is a scientifically defensible position. I believe that if we removed dyshomophilia from DSM-III we could be justifiably accused of responding to political pressure" (in Bayer & Spitzer, 1982, p. 42). In this argument, Spitzer tried to support science not by citing research data but by denigrating its assumed opposite, politics. His comment implied the dichotomous belief that to be scientific one must avoid all appearance of political involvement. The irony, of course, is that such efforts to avoid the appearance of responding to political pressure themselves gave the appearance of being politically motivated. Without ever citing research data (or otherwise resolving the aforementioned "state of ignorance") Spitzer later lamented to the task force, in a letter dated October 5, 1977, that "there appears to be little enthusiasm for the term *dyshomophilia*" and that this state of affairs constituted "an example of how breakthroughs in science can be ignored" (p. 46).

Politics and DSM-III

In addition to the foregoing examples, many other politically relevant topics could be examined in a similar manner (psychoanalysis, women, alternate "behavioral" taxonomies, etc.). Perhaps most pertinent, however, are discussions that address politics in DSM-III directly. An illuminating example is provided by Spitzer's (1981) *APA Monitor* defense of DSM-III, entitled "Nonmedical Myths and the DSM-III." This brief article was intended to clarify and rebut some alleged common "misunderstandings" of DSM-III by various critics who have focused on its political dimensions. However, a close analysis of Spitzer's (1981) remarks demonstrates the familiar pattern of ironic support for the very positions that are being opposed.

1. *Critic's claim.* The DSM-III was created for political reasons, such as "psychiatry's wish to establish hegemony over the mental health professions" (p. 3).

Spitzer's defense. Spitzer explicitly denied the claim that DSM-III was created for political reasons. He argued that creation of DSM-III was simply scheduled to coincide with the ninth revision of the World Health Organization's International Classification of Diseases (ICD-9).

Analysis. In denying a political basis for DSM-III's creation (indeed, he labeled such assertions "nonsense"), Spitzer might seem to be embracing a scientific one. But the argument does not refer to any compelling scientific reasons for production of DSM-III, although such reasons could easily have been invoked. Instead, the defense resorts to an explanation cast entirely within a (political) epistemology of authority. By arguing that DSM-III's creation was simply scheduled to coincide with the revision of ICD-9, Spitzer overlooked an obvious political connection. Because the World Health Organization is a "bigger" authority than the American Psychiatric Association, to link the DSM-III to the ICD-9 is to acquire more "authority" and hence more "validity" and more social power by sheer strength of political bedfellowship. Regardless of the actual motivations for creation of DSM-III, Spitzer's implicit adherence to a science–politics dichotomy forces a strong denial of political motives in his reading of the history. This denial ironically reinforces the very political implications it seeks to disavow.

2. *Critics' claim.* Scientific values were bent to suit political needs in the development of DSM-III.

Spitzer's defense. Spitzer's reply is worth quoting in full:

> One would have to know the over 100 members of the task force and the various advisory committees (primarily academic and research psychiatrists and several distinguished psychologists) and recall the countless debates over how to classify, describe and define the various mental disorders, to appreciate how absurd is this charge. The only instance that I can recall in which "economic" considerations influenced DSM-III was our reluctant decision to drop the term "chronic minor affective disorders" because a group of clinicians insisted that insurance companies would not want to reimburse for the treatment of a condition that appeared to be both incurable and trivial. (p. 3)

Analysis. Spitzer's defense is faulty on at least two counts. First, as illustrated by the aforementioned quotations from the correspondence debate on homosexuality (Bayer & Spitzer,

1982), there is clear evidence that political concerns were explicitly involved in formulating at least one other classification besides "chronic minor affective disorders." More important, Spitzer's rebuttal assumes that political aspects of DSM-III, to be recognizable, must be overt and explicit. As the concept of "softened power" and the philosophy of science–politics integration suggest, however, it is entirely possible for data and rhetoric to subtly merge, and consequently it is possible to conduct a phenotypically "scientific" debate that is nevertheless highly politicized.

3. *Critics' claim.* DSM-III adheres to a medical model that is inappropriate for psychologists (as exemplified in abandoned plans to include a statement that mental disorders are a subset of medical disorders).

Spitzer's defense. In discussing the rationale for excluding the medical disorders statement from the final DSM-III draft, Spitzer cited no scientific arguments, but rather noted a task force consensus that inclusion of the statement "would not convince any Szaszians that psychiatry was a legitimate branch of medicine (our motivation for having such a statement), and . . . would only alienate our psychology colleagues" (p. 3).

Analysis. Here again, in an article attempting to deny charges that political considerations influenced the creation and structure of the DSM-III, Spitzer named only political and not scientific disadvantages among the reasons for the statement's ultimate exclusion.

4. *Critics' claim.* DSM-III labels people instead of behavior and assumes that psychiatrists are the only mental health professionals competent to use it. (Although these are somewhat separate criticisms, they will be treated together because of shared arguments in Spitzer's rebuttal).

Spitzer's defense. Spitzer's rebuttal draws attention to DSM-III's careful selection of words to suggest neutrality on these issues. He pointed out, for example, that DSM-III never refers to "schizophrenics" or "depressives," but always to individuals that have "schizophrenia" or "depression." Likewise, DSM-III avoids discussion about the professional qualifications necessary for its use. Thus, the word *psychiatrist* is never used, and the terms *clinician* and *mental health professional* appear instead.

Analysis. With this argument, Spitzer would have critics believe that political phenomena cease to exist simply because they are not reflected in the DSM-III's choice of words. Ironically, of course, manipulation of linguistic forms is one of the most subtle manifestations of softened social power. Indeed, by making word choice central to the defense against perceiving DSM-III as a political document, Spitzer's argument implicitly concedes that the DSM-III is so politically important (i.e., likely to be disputed or litigated by opposing interest groups) that word choice becomes crucial. The role of DSM-III as an instrument of social power should not be evaluated solely on the basis of vocabulary. A more reasonable approach might involve empirical sociopsychological investigation of how the DSM-III is actually perceived. What percentage of people (legislators, consumers, etc.) actually infer that psychiatrists are especially qualified users of DSM-III because it is an official document of the American Psychiatric Association? How many people know (or care) that the word *psychiatrist* does not appear in DSM-III? Even though DSM-III itself chooses words that refer to behavior patterns and not to people, how often are the actual uses of the DSM-III consistent with this distinction?

5. *Critics' claim.* No proper study of DSM-III's reliability or validity has been published.

Spitzer's defense. Spitzer referred to validity data extrapolated from prior literature (that was used to formulate the DSM-III categories) and to reliability data from extensive field testing by over 800 clinicians, "many of them psychologists" (p. 33).

Analysis. Although citation of data is laudable, the reference to the professional affiliation of the clinicians appears to have no relevance to the scientific quality of the studies. Instead, this phrase seems clearly cast in the "who says?" metaphor of an authority–epistemology (i.e., psychologists should have faith in the data because their colleagues participated in its collection). Spitzer's subtly political point invites psychologists to emphasize an interprofessional perspective on DSM-III and to feel free to count themselves among the "who's who" in "who says."

CONCLUSIONS

Although heuristically valuable, dichotomies also easily capture our imaginations. By dividing a complex phenomenon into conceptually distinct but inclusive categories, we may succumb to an illusion of mastery, a false belief that complexity has yielded to simple, clear understanding (cf. Butler & Strupp, 1984). Such illusions of simplicity and mastery underlie dichotomization of science and politics in discussions of DSM-III. Dichotomization of science and politics thus serves two main and overlapping purposes: (a) it provides a refuge for those who might wish to simplify their lives by denying inescapably political aspects of their work and thought and (b) it provides a source of "transitive validity" for scientist-politicians who seek to further legitimize their social power by referring to its putative "scientifically valid" underpinnings.

Following the lead of modern philosophers of science, I have argued against simplistic dichotomization of science and politics and have claimed them to be deeply integral aspects of DSM-III and of our academic and clinical existence. With this argument I am not attempting to establish yet another dichotomy—namely that science and politics either are integral or they are not. Rather, I am arguing for a step beyond the dichotomies of science and politics toward a position that permits fuller recognition of the scientific and political complexities of diagnostic taxonomies.

DSM-III is both a tool for the production of scientific knowledge and an instrument of rhetoric, social organization, and power distribution. If we assume that science and politics are rigidly dichotomous and therefore insist that DSM-III cannot serve multiple functions simultaneously, our dialogue risks degenerating into double-talk and stereotyped mistrustfulness. However pure their motives and ideals may be, once in the public arena there are no scientists who are not also politicians (Edsall, 1981). By encouraging a science–politics dichotomy, the myth of scientific purity also encourages students of abnormal behavior to adopt correspondingly polarized role definitions for themselves and others, as either objective scientists or as partisan politicians. These oversimplifications, in turn, provoke compensatory reactions and engender adversarial rather than cooperative relationships by making it difficult to see how the activities may blend, or how persons must often occupy multiple roles simultaneously. Belief in the possibility of scientific purity thus ironically enhances our ability to perceive the DSM-III as a purely political document.

The following points comprise a more realistically complex and integrated stance:

1. DSM-III, its uses, and its users form integrated contextual units. The political dimension is not an objective or stable aspect of DSM-III. Rather, it varies with the historical context (cf. Blum, 1978) and with the special interests and differential sensitivities of various individuals and social groups such as homosexuals, women, nonphysicians, insurance companies, and so on. The DSM-III in the hands of an insurance executive making reimbursement policy is not the same document as the DSM-III used by a researcher in a laboratory. What seems like "objective science" to one person in one setting may be of great political importance to other persons in other settings. The political dimension is thus not an invariant facet of DSM-III, but rather depends crucially on the goals, purposes, interests, and focus of various individuals or groups.

2. Attention to underlying science–politics dichotomization will not, by itself, reduce controversy. However, such rethinking of the roles and boundaries of science and politics may help us to redirect dialogues away from pointless questions such as "Is it science or politics?" and toward more substantive and differentiated issues. The tension between science and politics will not disappear because of intellectual recognition that they may be inseparable. However, by abandoning the antiquated rhetoric of science *or* politics we may reduce the tendency to rigidly defend one aspect of DSM-III to the exclusion of the other, and we may become able to choose our emphases in a more rational manner. We may endeavor to avoid making political statements that pretend to be (apolitical) science, or scientific statements that pretend they are not political. It is not philosophically mandatory that our positions on the relationship of science and politics in DSM-III be informed by a rigid ideology of dichotomy. By recognizing the integral nature of science and politics we are freed to think about DSM-III in a more complex way—a way that transcends dichotomy and permits elective focus on science or politics, while maintaining awareness that one or the other aspect is, at the moment, implicit and not mandatorily absent.

REFERENCES

American Psychiatric Association, (1968). *Diagnostic and statistical manual of mental disorders* (2nd ed.). Washington, DC: Author.

American Psychiatric Association, (1980). *Diagnostic and statistical manual of mental disorders* (3rd ed.). Washington, DC: Author.

Appelbaum, S. (1977). Objections to diagnosis and diagnostic psychological testing diagnosed. In P. W. Pruyser (Ed.), *Diagnosis and the difference it makes* (pp. 161–166). New York: Jason Aronson.

Bayer, G. (1981). *Homosexuality and American psychiatry: The politics of diagnosis.* New York: Basic Books.

Bayer, G., & Spitzer, R. L. (1982). Edited correspondence on the status of homosexuality in DSM-III. *Journal of the History of the Behavioral Sciences, 18,* 32–52.

Benveniste, G. (1977). *The politics of expertise* (2nd ed.). San Francisco: Boyd & Fraser.

Bevan, W. (1980). On getting in bed with a lion. *American Psychologist, 35,* 779–789.

Blum, J. D. (1978). On changes in psychiatric diagnosis over time. *American Psychologist, 33,* 1017–1031.

Broad, W. J. (1979). Paul Feyerabend: Science and the anarchist. *Science, 206,* 534–537.

Burnham, J. C. (1982). American medicine's golden age: What happened to it? *Science, 215,* 1474–1479.

Bursten, B. (1981). Rallying 'round the medical model. *Hospital and Community Psychiatry; 32,* 371.

Butler, S. F., & Strupp, H. H. (1984). *A reconsideration of "specific" and "nonspecific" factors in psychotherapy: Implications for theory, research, and training.* Unpublished manuscript, Center for Psychotherapy Research, Vanderbilt University, Nashville, TN.

Edsall, J. T. (1981). Two aspects of scientific responsibility. *Science, 212,* 11–14.

Feyerabend, P. (1970). Against method: An outline of an anarchic theory of knowledge. In M. Radner & S. Winokur (Eds.), *Minnesota studies in the philosophy of science (Vol. 4).* Minneapolis: University of Minnesota Press.

Foucault, M. (1965). *Madness and civilization.* New York: Pantheon.

Foltz, D. (1980, January). Judgment withheld on DSM-III. *APA Monitor,* p. 33

Funder, J. (1979, December 7). Editorial. *Science,* p. 1139.

Garmezy, N. (1978). Never mind the psychologists: Is it good for the children? *Clinical Psychologist, 31*(3–4), 1–6.

Goldfried, M. R. (1980). Toward the delineation of therapeutic change principles. *American Psychologist, 35,* 991–999.

Gross, S. J. (1978). The myth of professional licensing. *American Psychologist, 33,* 1009–1016.

Grossman, H. J. (1973). *Manual on terminology and classification in mental retardation* (rev. ed.). Baltimore: Garamond/Pridemark Press.

Halleck. S. (1971). *The politics of therapy.* New York: Science House.

Hoffman La Roche, Inc. (1981). DSM-III one year later: Are we seeing eye-to-eye? *Roche Report, 11*(1), 6, 11.

Holden, C. (1980). Scientist with unpopular data loses job. *Science, 210,* 749–750.

Illich, I. (1976). *Medical nemesis: The expropriation of health.* New York: Random House.

Kaplan, M. (1983). A woman's view of DSM-III. *American psychologist, 38,* 786–792.

Keatley, A. (1983). Knowledge as real estate, *Science, 222,* 717.

Koch, S. (1981). The nature and limits of psychological knowledge: Lessons of a century qua "science." *American Psychologist, 36,* 257–269.

Kuhn, T. (1962). *The structure of scientific revolutions.* Chicago: University of Chicago Press.

Mahoney, M. (1976). *Scientist as subject: The psychological imperative.* Cambridge MA: Ballinger.

Marshall, E. (1982). Security checks on USDA peer reviewers. *Science, 216,* 600.

McLemore, C. W., & Benjamin, L. S. (1979). Whatever happened to interpersonal diagnosis? A psychosocial alternative to DSM-III. *American Psychologist, 34,* 17–34.

McReynolds, W. T. (1979). DSM-III and the future of applied social science. *Professional Psychology, 10,* 123–132.

Miller, L. S., Bergstrom, D. A., Cross, H. J., & Grube, J. W. (1981). Opinions and use of the DSM system. *Professional Psychology, 12,* 385–390.

Millon, T. (1983). The DSM-III: An insider's perspective. *American Psychologist, 38,* 804–814.

Nisbet, R. A. (1975). *Twilight of authority.* New York: Oxford University Press.

Perry, S. E. (1966). *The human nature of science: Researchers at work in psychiatry.* New York: Free Press.

Schacht, T. E., & Nathan, P. E. (1977). But is it good for the psychologists? Appraisal and status of DSM-III. *American Psychologist, 32,* 1017–1025.

Singerman, B. (1981). DSM-III: Historical antecedents and present significance. *Journal of Clinical Psychiatry, 42,* 409–410.

Smith, D., & Kraft, W. A. (1983). DSM-III: Do psychologists really want an alternative? *American Psychologist, 38,* 777–785.

Society for Social Responsibility Newsletter. (1953, January). p. 8.

Spitzer, R. L. (1981, October). Nonmedical myths and the DSM-III. *APA Monitor,* pp. 3, 33.

Stolorow, R., & Atwood, G. (1979). *Faces in a cloud: Subjectivity in personality theory.* New York: Jason Aronson.

Szasz, T. S. (1982). The psychiatric will: A new mechanism for protecting persons against "psychosis" *and* psychiatry. *American Psychologist, 37,* 762–770.

Weizenbaum, J. (1975). *Computer power and human reason: From judgment to calculation.* San Francisco: W. H. Freeman.

Widiger, T. A., & Kelso, K. (1983). Psychodiagnosis of Axis II. *Clinical Psychology Review, 3,* 491–510.

Williams, J. B. W., & Spitzer, R. L. (1983). The issue of sex bias in DSM-III: A critique of "A woman's view of DSM-III" by Marcie Kaplan. *American Psychologist, 38,* 793–798.

Zigler, E., & Phillips, L. (1961). Psychiatric diagnoses and symptomatology. *Journal of Abnormal and Social Psychology, 63,* 69–75.

Zimbardo, P. (1984). Mind control in 1984. *Psychology Today, 18*(1), 68–72.

Zubin, J. (1978). But is it good for science? *Clinical Psychologist, 31*(2), 1–7.

16

DSM-III AND THE POLITICS–SCIENCE DICHOTOMY SYNDROME: A RESPONSE TO THOMAS E. SCHACHT'S "DSM-III AND THE POLITICS OF TRUTH"

ROBERT L. SPITZER

In his article, "DSM-III and the Politics of Truth" (*American Psychologist, 40,* pp. 513–521), Thomas Schacht presents the original hypothesis that the traditional view of science and politics as mutually exclusive domains has limited discussion and understanding about DSM-III (American Psychiatric Association, 1980) and has led to "half-truths" and "double-talk" by those defending DSM-III. If one adopts Schacht's remarkably broad concept of *politics,* it is clear that his analysis does not go far enough. I will show that Schacht has failed to list a number of important political elements of DSM-III, some of which have been extensively discussed in the literature, but others of which have not.

Next, I will draw attention to a less than trivial flaw in Schacht's article: the methodology that he employs to determine that an individual suffers from the politics–science dichotomy (what I term the politics–science dichotomy syndrome or PSDS). Employing a rigorous definition of PSDS, I will show that the illustrations Schacht presents as evidence that I suffer from the syndrome are far from convincing.

SCHACHT'S CONCEPT OF POLITICS

Central to Schacht's analysis is his broad concept of what constitutes politics. His definition includes as political all those activities that are motivated by or have consequences for the

Reprinted from the *American Psychologist, 40,* 522–526. (1985).

The author gratefully acknowledges Ronald Bayer's help in reviewing a draft of the manuscript.

"acquisition, exercise, and preservation of social power" (p. 513). Also included are the reliance on "power tactics" and "rhetoric," the importance of "subjectivity" and "self-interest," the presence of "ideology," and the impact of "economics." In contrast to this definition, which would seem to embrace virtually all human activities, Schacht characterizes the prototype of pure science as rational, empirical, and objective. Scientists, in this hypothetical world, are motivated only by "curiosity" and "love of knowledge" (p. 515). Whereas political disputes are resolved by rhetoric and power tactics, in science "differences of opinion . . . are . . . resolvable by appeal to 'objective' data" (p. 515).

Given Schacht's definition of politics, it is curious that he has overlooked so many aspects of DSM-III that display political dimensions. Schacht's terminology is used below for purposes of organizing the discussion only. "Power tactics" is not the most useful way of examining the politics of intraprofessional controversy, nor is "subjective judgments" a useful rubric for distinguishing between fanciful and considered clinical judgment.

POLITICAL ASPECTS OF DSM-III OVERLOOKED BY SCHACHT

Ideological Considerations

Although DSM-III is generally atheoretical with regard to the etiology of mental disorders, clearly DSM-III embraces an ideology or body of concepts in its approach to the classification of mental disorders. The DSM-III descriptive approach emphasizes classification on the basis of shared descriptive clinical features rather than on presumed etiology, and emphasizes the importance of specified diagnostic criteria for improving diagnostic reliability rather than the use of highly inferential clinical concepts for making a diagnosis.

The DSM-III descriptive approach led logically to eliminating neurosis as a basis for classification. The abandonment of this traditional classificatory principle led to an extremely bitter political struggle between the DSM-III task force and a large number of psychiatrists within the American Psychiatric Association who believed that the task force was not representative of American psychiatry and was using DSM-III to expunge Freud's valuable contributions to the understanding of psychopathology. Elsewhere I have described the details of this struggle (Bayer & Spitzer, 1985) in which appeals to "objective data" played no significant role.

The Importance of Subjective Judgments in Developing DSM-III

The developers of DSM-III attempted, whenever possible, to base the new classification on data that had emerged from a large body of diagnostic studies published in the scientific literature. However, as noted in the introduction to DSM-III, "It should come as no surprise to the reader that even when data were available from relevant research studies, Task Force members often differed in their interpretations of the findings" (p. 3). Furthermore, although for a small number of diagnostic categories prior research had shown the utility of specified diagnostic criteria (Feighner et al., 1972), as also noted in the introduction to DSM-III, "most of the diagnostic criteria are based on clinical judgment, and have not yet been fully validated by data" (p. 8). Thus, the subjective judgment of the members of the task force that guided the development of DSM-III and of the members of the various advisory committees played a crucial role in the development of DSM-III, and differences of opinion could only rarely be resolved by appeal to objective data.

Rhetoric in Resolving Nosologic Controversies

Because appeals to objective data for resolving nosologic controversies were relatively rare, speaking and writing skills (rhetoric) played an important role in resolving controversies. This was particularly true in my case because, as chair, I had the responsibility of guiding the task force in its efforts to oversee the ongoing work, balance sometimes competing goals, and resolve such sensitive issues as the consequences of including a statement in DSM-III that mental disorders are medical disorders. I also chaired virtually all of the advisory committees, and in this position (of great political power!) employed rhetorical skills to focus the discussion and to achieve, whenever possible, a group consensus.

The Use of Power Tactics

The DSM-III task force and the various advisory committees spent almost all of their time considering the content of DSM-III. However, I spent a considerable amount of time representing the task force and interfacing with the various components of the American Psychiatric Association whose approval, either formal or informal, was necessary before DSM-III could be adopted. The introduction to DSM-III lists these groups, but the full story of the complicated and frequently heated interactions between myself and these groups and between the groups themselves has never been told.

As this article was being written, the process of revising DSM-III to produce DSM-III-R was well underway. From this vantage point it is not expected that DSM-III-R will be nearly as controversial as was DSM-III. Nevertheless, it is clear that different groups within the American Psychiatric Association have very different perspectives on the wisdom of revising DSM-III at the present time, how extensive the revision should be, and the timetable for DSM-III-R's birth. The ultimate outcome will be determined by a political process involving rhetoric and negotiation among groups with different goals and perspectives, as was the case with DSM-III.

Enhanced Self-Interest in Being, Associated with DSM-III

The careers of many individuals (psychiatrists as well as psychologists) were furthered by association with DSM-III (as was certainly true in my case). Authors of textbooks of psychiatry and abnormal psychology and of self-report inventories have much to gain by using the official terminology of DSM-III. Publishing an article critical of DSM-III in a prestigious journal can also further the author's career.

Economic Value of DSM-III as a Commodity

The American Psychiatric Association had no idea of the economic value of DSM-III when it was being developed, because sales of DSM-I and DSM-II had provided only a modest revenue. In contrast, sales of DSM-III (primarily to nonpsychiatrists) have been enormous and sustained and within the Association have been widely credited for making it possible to avoid an increase in annual dues for the membership. The large sales of DSM-III are also credited with being the stimulus for the initiation of the American Psychiatric Press, the publishing house of the American Psychiatric Association and an important source of revenue to the organization.

Other Political Aspects of DSM-III

Many other political aspects of DSM-III that Schacht fails to note have already been discussed in the literature, such as the impact of DSM-III on contemporary American schools of psychiatry (Klerman, 1983), world psychiatry (Spitzer, Williams, & Skodol, 1983) and the development of the World Health Organization's 10th revision of the International Classification of Diseases (Kendell, 1984; Spitzer, 1984).

THE POLITICS–SCIENCE DICHOTOMY SYNDROME

Failure to acknowledge both the political and scientific dimensions of DSM-III is, according to Schacht, evidence of a politics–science dichotomy that leads to misunderstanding and double-talk about DSM-III. Schacht cites Koch (1981) in using the phrase "cognitive pathology" for this kind of dichotomy. Consistent with this nosologic terminology, I suggest the term, politics–science dichotomy syndrome, or PSDS for short.

A central problem in Schacht's article is his failure to employ a rigorous case-finding technique when diagnosing PSDS. Clearly, denial of one or more specific political aspects of DSM-III is not sufficient for making the diagnosis. What is needed is a denial of *all* political dimensions. Similarly, failure to discuss the political dimension of DSM-III on a particular occasion, such as when presenting its scientific aspects, is not sufficient for making the diagnosis.

Examination of Schacht's illustrations of PSDS reveals that they all involve my activities or statements. (Apparently the critics of DSM-III do not suffer from PSDS, or if they do, they suffer from a less virulent form of the disorder). Close examination of each of these illustrations (taking my remarks in context) shows that I did not deny all political dimensions of DSM-III. I only denied certain specific allegations, such as that the politics of DSM-III compromised its scientific values for professional or economic gain.

Motivation for DSM-III

According to Schacht,

> Spitzer explicitly denied the claim that DSM-III was created for political reasons. He [Spitzer] argued that creation of DSM-III was simply scheduled to coincide with the ninth revision of the World Health Organization's International Classification of Diseases (ICD-9). . . . [His] argument does not refer to any compelling scientific reasons for production of DSM-III, although such reasons could easily have been invoked. . . . This denial [of political motivation] ironically reinforces the very political implications it seeks to disavow. (p. 518–519)

However, Schacht did not include the context in which I discussed the timing of the publication of DSM-III.

In the *APA Monitor* article (Spitzer, 1981b), I discussed several myths about DSM-III. (The other "illustrations" of my "denial" of the political dimensions of DSM-III discussed below are also taken from that article.) The first myth was stated as follows: "The motivation for DSM-III at this time was organized psychiatry's wish to establish hegemony over the mental health professions because of the diminishing mental health dollar" (Spitzer, 1981b, p. 3). In refuting this myth, I wrote:

> Nonsense. In the 1960s, the American Psychiatric Association decided to have future revisions of its diagnostic manual compatible with revisions in the World Health Organization's International Classification of Disease (ICD) which is revised every decade. DSM-III was scheduled to coincide with the publication of the ninth revision of ICD which rendered DSM-II obsolete. (p. 3)

Clearly, all I was asserting was that the decision to introduce DSM-III in 1980 (rather than 1975 or 1985) was a consequence of a decision made by the American Psychiatric Association in the 1960s and therefore could not be attributed to a sudden wish to capture the diminishing mental health dollar. In this context I was addressing the *timing* of DSM-III, and therefore I did not discuss any of the compelling scientific reasons for revising DSM-II (a topic on which the readers of the *APA Monitor* needed no education).

Scientific Values and Economic Needs

In denying the myth that in developing DSM-III scientific values were bent for the needs of third party payment, I wrote,

> The only instance that I can recall in which "economic" considerations influenced DSM-III was our reluctant decision to drop the term "chronic minor affective disorders" because a group of clinicians insisted that insurance companies would not want to reimburse for the treatment of a condition that appeared to be both incurable and trivial. (p. 3)

According to Schacht,

> Spitzer's-defense is faulty. . . . First, as illustrated by the aforementioned quotations from the correspondence debate on homosexuality . . . there is clear evidence that political concerns were explicitly involved in formulating at least one other classification besides "chronic minor affective disorders." (p. 519)

Political concerns were certainly an important part of the DSM-III controversy about Ego-dystonic Homosexuality, as will be discussed below. However economic concerns were never a part of the controversy, and I was only denying that economic concerns were involved in the formulation of specific DSM-III categories.

DSM-III's Use of Neutral Language

Schacht is unimpressed with my account of how DSM-III carefully avoided the use of the terms *psychiatrist* and *physician* so as to avoid the implication that only they have the professional skills needed to use DSM-III. According to Schacht, the real issue is not what words are used in DSM-III but rather,

> what percentage of people (legislators, consumers, etc.) actually infer that psychiatrists are especially qualified users of DSM-III because it is an official document of the American Psychiatric Association. How many people know (or care) that the word *psychiatrist* does not appear in DSM-III? (p. 519)

Many people may not know that the words *psychiatrist* and *physician* do not appear in DSM-III, but Schacht and other psychologists would certainly have loudly spread the word and with justification complained if DSM-III *had* used these words instead of the neutral term *clinician.* Some readers might even conclude that the developers of DSM-III and the American Psychiatric Association should get some credit for not using DSM-III in this particular way to seek political advantage. (Actually, a small group of psychiatrists concerned with turf issues vis-à-vis psychology did complain when, shortly after the publication of DSM-III, they realized that the words *psychiatrist* and *physician* were never used in DSM-III.)

DSM-III Reliability Studies and Psychologists

In describing the DSM-III field trials I noted that of the 800 clinicians who participated, "many of them [were] psychologists" (Spitzer, 1981b, p. 33). According to Schacht,

> the reference to the professional affiliation of the clinicians appears to have no relevance to the scientific quality of the studies. . . . Spitzer's subtly political point invites psychologists to emphasize an interprofessional perspective on DSM-III and to feel free to count themselves among the "who's who" in "who says." (p. 520)

My major purpose in writing the *APA Monitor* article was to encourage psychologists to use DSM-III and diminish barriers between psychiatry and psychology. In this context, of course, I wished to emphasize that psychologists had taken part in the field trials. Schacht's reference to "Spitzer's subtly political point" suggests a deviousness on my part that needs defending (and of course, that is precisely what I have been forced to do!).

Schacht clearly would have noted as "political" a decision to exclude psychologists from participating in the field trials. His charge that my reference to their inclusion was "political" suggests that his own analysis might appropriately be described as "double-talk."

Mental Versus Medical Disorders

The DSM-III task force did consider my proposal that DSM-III assert that mental disorders are medical disorders. The motivation for considering such a statement was to deny the claim of Szasz (1961) that mental illness is a myth and has nothing to do with medicine. This proposal understandably alarmed psychologists (Schacht & Nathan, 1977; Zubin 1978), and after an agonizing reappraisal, the task force decided not to include such a statement. When I first presented my complicated and cumbersome definition of mental disorder as a subset of medical disorder (Spitzer & Endicott, 1978) I acknowledged the political advantages of having such a definition (e.g., justifying the professional activities of psychiatry as a branch of medicine). Elsewhere (Spitzer & Williams, 1982) I discussed the political reasons that the task force decided not to include the statement. The task force concluded that such a statement would only fan the fires of interprofessional rivalry and would be counterproductive.

Based on the above, Schacht's reference to my "efforts to disavow political motivation" (p. 517) is puzzling, as I have never denied the political aspects of this issue.

Homosexuality

Schacht's account of the DSM-III controversy over homosexuality is inaccurate. First of all, the controversy was not about including homosexuality in DSM-III. That issue was resolved in 1973 by a political and scientific compromise between those who argued that homosexuality always represented psychopathology and those who claimed that homosexuality was merely a normal variant and never by itself represented psychopathology (Bayer, 1981). The compromise resulted in the deletion of homosexuality itself from the classification. In its place a new category was added for those homosexuals who were distressed by their inability to have a heterosexual arousal pattern. The controversy during the development of DSM-III was whether this compromise category (called Sexual Orientation Disturbance in DSM-II and Ego-dystonic Homosexuality in DSM-III) should be removed from the classification.

The second inaccuracy in Schacht's account is that the strategy of restricting the controversy to those involved in the DSM-III deliberations was not made by the task force. It was made by those outside of the task force (such as Richard Pillard, who was *not* a task force member) who wished to eliminate the compromise category, thus deleting any reference to homosexuality in DSM-III. This strategy was employed because of a politically realistic concern that if the general membership of the American Psychiatric Association were involved in the decision, homosexuality itself might be returned to the classification.

When I tried to convince the task force that removing any reference to homosexuality in DSM-III would give the impression of bowing to the "political pressure" of those sympathetic to homosexuals, I was merely acknowledging the political reality of the controversy and was not engaging in double-talk. In fact, elsewhere (Spitzer, 1981a) I have acknowledged that the controversy over the diagnostic status of homosexuality did not involve disputes about facts but rather about basic values (which Schacht would certainly classify as political). Examination of the DSM-III correspondence about removing the 1973 compromise category (Bayer & Spitzer, 1982) shows that my main argument was that the profession was still unable to reach a consensus on the diagnostic status of homosexuality itself. Therefore, the 1973 compromise of having a category for homosexuals distressed by their inability to have a heterosexual arousal pattern was still the most responsible way of dealing with the complexities of the issue.

CONCLUSIONS

Schacht has clearly made an original contribution in describing the dangers of a politics–science dichotomy, or what I have termed PSDS. As this article shows, however, I clearly do not suffer from the disorder. Furthermore, Schacht's concept of politics is so broad that it is hard to see how anyone could deny that there were political dimensions to DSM-III or any other scientific activity. Thus, PSDS may be an extremely virulent disorder in search of a victim.

Schacht's article has unfortunately obscured discussion of the real issue of politics and DSM-III: whether the blend of politics and science has been professionally responsible or irresponsible. For Schacht the acknowledgment of politics is the end of the analysis; it should be the beginning.

REFERENCES

American Psychiatric Association. (1980). *Diagnostic and statistical manual of mental disorders* (3rd ed.). Washington, DC: Author.

Bayer, R. (1981). *Homosexuality and American psychiatry: The politics of diagnosis.* New York: Basic Books.

Bayer, R., & Spitzer, R. L. (1982). Edited correspondence on the status of homosexuality in DSM-III. *Journal of the History of the Behavioral Sciences, 18,* 32–52.

Bayer, R., & Spitzer, R. L. (1985). Neurosis, psychodynamics and DSM-III: A history of the controversy. *Archives of General Psychiatry, 42,* 187–196.

Feighner, J. P., Robins, E., Guze, R. A., Woodruff, R. A., Winokur, G., & Munoz, R. (1972). Diagnostic criteria for use in psychiatry research. *Archives of General Psychiatry* 26(1), 57–63.

Kendell, R. E. (1984). Reflection on psychiatric classification for the architects of DSM-IV and ICD-10. *Integrative Psychiatry* 2(2), 43–47.

Klerman, G. L. (1983). The significance of DSM-III in American psychiatry. In R. L. Spitzer, J. B. Williams, & A. Skodol (Eds.), *International perspectives on DSM-III* (pp. 3–25). Washington, DC: American Psychiatric Press.

Koch, S. (1981). The nature and limits of psychological knowledge: Lessons of a century qua "science." *American Psychologist, 36,* 257–269.

Schacht, T. E. (1985). DSM-III and the politics of truth. *American Psychologist, 40,* 513–521.

Schacht, T. E. & Nathan, P. E. (1977). But is it good for the psychologists? Appraisal and status of DSM-III. *American Psychologist, 32,* 1017–1025.

Spitzer, R. L. (1981a). The diagnostic status of homosexuality in DSM-III: A reformulation of the issues. *American Journal of Psychiatry, 138*(2), 210–215.

Spitzer, R. L. (1981b, October). Nonmedical myths and the DSM-III. *APA Monitor,* pp. 3, 33.

Spitzer, R. L. (1984). Rapprochement between ICD-10 and DSM-IV: Some thorny issues. *Integrative Psychiatry 2*(2), 48–49.

Spitzer, R. L., & Endicott, J. (1978). Medical and mental disorder: Proposed definition and criteria. In R. L. Spitzer & D. F. Klein (Eds.), *Critical issues in psychiatric diagnosis* (pp. 15–39). New York: Raven.

Spitzer, R., & Williams, J. B. (1982). The definition and diagnosis of mental disorder. In W. R. Gove (Ed.), *Deviance and mental illness* (pp. 15–32). Beverly Hills, CA: Sage.

Spitzer, R., Williams, J. B., & Skodol, A. (1983). *International perspectives on DSM-III.* Washington, DC: American Psychiatric Press.

Szasz. T. S. (1961). *The myth of mental illness.* New York: Harper & Row.

Zubin, J (1978). But is it good for science? *Clinical Psychologist, 31*(2), 1–7.

RECOMMENDED READING

Dennett, D. C. (1978). Current issues in the philosophy of mind. *American Philosophical Quarterly, 15,* 249–261.

Edelson, M. (1986). The convergence of psychoanalysis and neuroscience. *Contemporary Psychoanalysis, 22,* 479–519.

Fodor, J. (1981). The mind-body problem. *Scientific American, 244,* 144–123.

Gorenstein, E. (1984). Debating mental illness. *American Psychologist, 39,* 50–56.

Kety, S. S. (1961). A biologist examines the mind and behavior: Many disciplines contribute to understanding human behavior, each with its peculiar virtues and limitations. *Science, 132,* 1861–1870.

Kety, S. S. (1979). The metamorphosis of a psychobiologist. *Annual Review of Neuroscience, 2,* 1–15.

Peele, S. (1981). Reductionism in the psychology of the eighties. *American Psychologist, 36,* 807–818.

Popper, K. R., & Eccles, J. C. (1977). *The self and its brain.* Berlin, Federal Republic of Germany: Springer-Verlag.

Praag, H. M. van. (1977). Satisfaction and disappointment: Reflections at an anniversary. In H. M. Praag & J. Bruinvels (Eds.), *Neurotransmission and disturbed behavior.* Utrecht, the Netherlands: Bohn, Scheltema, & Holkema, 1–5.

Rudnick, A. (1990). Towards a rationalization of biological psychiatry: A study in psychobiological epistemology. *Journal of Philosophy and Medicine, 15,* 75–96.

Schacht, T. E. (1985). Reply to Spitzer's "Politics–science dichotomy syndrome." *American Psychologist, 40,* 562–563.

Sperry, R. W. (1988). Psychology's mentalist paradigm and the religion–science tension. *American Psychologist, 43,* 607–613.

Stent, G. S. (1990). The poverty of neurophilosophy. *Journal of Medicine and Philosophy, 15,* 539–557.

Szasz, T. (1974). *The myth of mental illness: Foundations of a theory of personal conduct* (rev. ed.). New York: Harper & Row. (Originally published 1961)

Szasz, T. (1987) *Insanity: The idea and its consequences.* New York: Wiley.

Szasz, T. (1988). *The theology of medicine: The political-philosophical foundations of medical ethics* (rev. ed.) Syracuse, NY: Syracuse University Press. (Originally publilshed 1977)

IV

PHILOSOPHICAL ISSUES OF THE PHENOMENOLOGICAL AND EXISTENTIAL APPROACHES

INTRODUCTION: THE PHILOSOPHY OF HUMANISTIC APPROACHES

RONALD B. MILLER

Existential–phenomenological approaches to clinical psychology are as diverse and unique as the representatives of the philosophical school from which they draw their name. There are nonetheless certain commonalities that most share: a concern with the quality and content of conscious experience; an insistence on the legitimacy of introspective, empathic, and intuitive knowledge; a nondeterministic view of human behavior; and a deep concern with the dehumanizing aspects of a technology and science in American culture. This approach tends to see psychopathological states as resulting from avoiding authenticity in daily life. As people avoid their anxieties about death, or their responsibilities to choose a life for themselves, people become vulnerable to the development of symptoms. Psychological assessment and nosology are shunned by existential–phenomenological psychologists for the most part, and the therapeutic relationship itself is seen as the curative factor (May, 1979). The therapist must offer an opportunity for the client to experience himself or herself in a new way by offering a relationship that is healthier than those experienced in the past.

Existential–phenomenological, or humanistic, approaches to clinical psychology have been avowedly interested in the philosophy of clinical psychology since their inception. Representing as they do a challenge to the prevailing *weltanschauung,* they have a vested interest in pointing out the implicit philosophical positions embedded in mainstream thinking, hoping thereby to open that thinking up to critical review. (The questioning of accepted values and wisdom was, of course, the central message of Socrates, as immortalized in Plato's dialogues.) There is such a wealth of material to draw on here that one might rightfully feel that the selections are too restrictive and that important works and writers have been overlooked.

The selections included in this section were made in order to emphasize the basic philosophical rather than directly applied psychological aspects of existential–phenomenological thought, although the two are obviously intertwined, and the connection of the philosophy to the psychology is of great interest to the purposes of this reader.

Carl Rogers's (1955, 1961; Rogers, Gendlin, Kiesler, & Traux, 1967) contributions to American psychology rival those of B. F. Skinner. Just as the behavioral approaches offered clinical psychology an intellectual autonomy in the 1960s, Rogers's work on client-centered psychotherapy a generation earlier offered clinical and counseling psychologists an intellectual autonomy from psychoanalysis, psychiatry, and experimental psychology. His work gave an early impetus and legitimacy to the independence of clinical psychology as a profession and prepared the way, paradoxically, for the later claims of the behaviorally oriented clinicians that clinical psychologists were entitled to a completely autonomous practice because they had an autonomous and exclusive knowledge base.

Where Skinner was convinced that the starting point of a psychological account had to be the interaction of behavior and environment, Rogers maintained that his point of departure was the self–subjective consciousness and empathic understanding in a dyadic relationship. Rogers was extremely active in pursuing a dialogue with continental philosophy (see Coulson & Rogers, 1968) that would help to provide a foundation to the ideas he had conceived in his own clinical experience. In his classic article, "Persons or Science? A Philosophical Question" (see chapter 17), Rogers formulates the dilemma he experienced in reconciling the understanding of human beings that grew out of his clinical work with that obtained by use of the empirical research methodology of American psychology, which he also used and trusted. He raised a question that had been little discussed in psychology to that point and has had little attention since: How do psychologists relate their empathetic knowing of other people to the knowledge they gain about them through empirical observation and experiment? This is the problem of the nature of clinical knowledge. Rogers's solution was to adopt a view of science very similar to Polanyi's (see chapter 3) interpretation of scientific knowledge as *tacit knowledge* and so to collapse objective and subjective forms of knowing into one category of experience.

Having formulated this alternative view of science as a corollary to his alternative view of personality and psychotherapy, Rogers entered into a series of debates with Skinner on the future of psychology and behavioral control (Wann, 1964). Willard Day's article (see chapter 8) was in response to one of these debates, and readers may wish to consult it again in the context of Rogers's paper. Although Day is most critical of Rogers's attempts to reconcile behaviorism and phenomenological psychology, Day does believe such a reconciliation is possible and desirable. He turns the tables on Rogers's solution to the dilemma and endorses Skinner's solution that phenomenological self-reports be viewed as behaviors that are partially under the control of stimuli only observable to the speaker. These self-reports are also under the control of environmental stimuli and contingencies, as are any verbalizations, and thus may be a part of a scientific account of behavior.

Rychlak (1968, 1981, 1988), who has been a pioneer in the philosophical approach to theoretical differences in clinical psychology, argues in chapter 18 that humanistic and behavioral approaches to clinical problems are founded on fundamentally opposing epistemologies (i.e., the Lockean vs. Kantian models of knowledge). These are essentially what I have called the objective vs. subjective theories of knowledge. Rychlak argues that both perspectives are necessary and that rather than collapsing them into one another, one kind of knowledge needs to be supplemented with the other. He cites Aristotle's metaphysical theory of four types of causation as a basis for this integration. Behavior is moved from without or behind by *material* or *efficient* causation, but from within and ahead by *final* and *formal* causation. Rychlak claims that without all four perspectives on behavior, any theory will be incomplete and less powerful. Rychlak insists that psychologists cannot avoid the metaphysical and epistemological issues that divide the field.

A strict materialism, empiricism, and determinism is counterproductive in psychology because it takes psychologists away from the psychological reality of human purpose and freedom.

Although much is often made of the phenomenological basis of humanistic psychology, Jennings (see chapter 20) proposes that this is often based on a misinterpretation of Husserl's (1913/1931) phenomenology. Husserl's phenomenology was intended not as a method of research but as a method of discovering the logical preconditions of any scientific knowledge. Its goal is to set a conceptual framework that is conducive to valid psychological investigation. It is an analysis, not just a report, of subjective experience that is seen as offering a view of the universal truths of phenomenology. How different this is indeed from the typical use of the term *phenomenology* in most psychological or psychiatric contexts. Some use it to refer to any subjective experience, whereas others use it to refer to any descriptive but not explanatory view of psychopathology, even when all of the descriptions are of behavior or other observable phenomena. It would seem that Rogers's analysis of the conditions of growth in therapy, and the related work of Gendlin (1962), comes closest to capturing the true spirit of Husserl's phenomenology in clinical psychology.

In chapter 19, Packer documents the importance of Husserl's student, Heidegger, to the hermeneutic turn in contemporary humanistic approaches to clinical psychology. By contrasting rationalist and empiricist traditions in general psychology with a hermeneutical approach, Packer illustrates how Heidegger's concept of knowledge that is *ready-to-hand* may be used to guide field research. He agrees with Heidegger that this methodology allows the researcher greater access to psychological reality. It should be noted that Heidegger rejected the absolutist aspects of Husserl's epistemology, and so there is tension within the humanistic approach as to whether to adopt the hermeneutic position. Many of the earlier humanists, for example, A. Maslow or R. D. Laing, wrote as though their position were universally true and not relative to a particular cultural configuration. Self-actualization is good for everyone, everywhere, for all time. By the end of his career, Rogers (1985) endorsed the hermeneutic approach to research as a more adequate solution than the one he had originally offered to the "person versus science" dilemma 30 years earlier.

Not only have the humanists been willing to debate epistemology and metaphysics, but ethics as well. The exchange between Rollo May (see chapter 21) and Carl Rogers (see chapter 22) on the question of evil in human nature is indicative of the openness of the dialogue on values in humanistic psychology. May (1969, 1975) is one of the outstanding figures in 20th-century humanistic psychology. He is also one of the leading advocates of the relevance of existential and phenomenological approaches to philosophy to clinical psychology. His writings in existential psychoanalytic psychology have been popular with professionals and the general reading public alike. In chapter 21, May argues that Rogers has been myopic in identifying only a positive growth potential as being inherent to human nature: May would prefer a dynamic bipolar conceptualization of what he calls the *daimonic* in human nature (i.e., the urge to affirm, assert, perpetuate, and increase oneself). This may result in either constructive or destructive behavior depending on how it is integrated into the personality. May objects to assigning the etiology of evil to cultural factors, for it is people who create their own cultures. May suggests that Rogers inhibits the expression of healthy independence in his clients by not attending sufficiently to their aggressive, hateful, evil, feelings.

In his response, Rogers, for his part, seems to move closer to May's position. There is no question that humans are capable of evil; there are only questions about its origins. Rogers insists that evil originates in social conditions that he sees as moral failures of humankind. If people were more successful moral agents, evil could be eliminated from the world. This is something that all people must choose to dedicate themselves to do. Otherwise, there is no solution.

In chapter 23, Wertheimer presents a critique of humanistic methodologies from the perspective of a more traditional experimental psychology. He argues that humanistic goals are admirable but that the methodology adopted in pursuit of these goals has been sloppy, vague, subjective, and ideological. He, too, argues that science is humanity's best hope and therefore experimental psychology is the true humanistic psychology. Although one may argue as to whether Wertheimer has responded adequately to the existential–phenomenological critique of traditional experimental methodology, it is to his credit as an experimentalist that he is willing, in chapter 23, as he has been throughout his career, to confront the philosophical issues and engage in philosophical discourse.

Finally, Bergin, in chapter 24, joins the critique of humanistic values, which he sees as running counter to the Judeo-Christian heritage. He argues that traditional values offer a better basis for mental health than humanistic psychology. However, rather than basing his value preferences on the reasons he holds these values, he argues that scientific empirical research can prove the superiority of traditional theological values. He fails to see this could only be true if that research tradition implicitly already represented or embodied this values orientation. His view is an odd mixture of deonotological and utilitarian normative ethics in which what is holy is also what makes people happy. One cannot fault him, however, for his courageous insistence that value issues are central to the functioning of both the clinical practitioner and the researcher.

Bergin's critique of humanistic values in clinical psychology triggered a barrage of critical response that, because of space constraints, could not be included here (see chapter 28 for one such response). It is of some significance, though, that a meaningful philosophical discussion in a mainstream clinical psychology journal was abruptly terminated by the editor's decision that it was "sufficient" to publish only two short comments on Bergin's piece, and a short reply by Bergin to those comments in less than 12 pages of discussion. A better case of terminal philosophical ambivalence can hardly be found. The critiques of Bergin's article (see the recommended reading list at the end of this section) focused on two issues: (a) that he had made theological ethics seem a good deal more rational and benign than often experienced by those receiving a religious education and (b) he had made humanistic ethics seem a good deal less rational and a good deal more egoistic than was necessarily the case.

It is one of the ironies of contemporary psychology that the humanistic writers have had much greater success getting a foothold in the general reading public's psyche than they have gaining acceptance in academic psychology. Their viewpoint is so inconsistent with the prevailing scientific *zeitgeist* that their work is rejected out of hand as not being "real" psychology. By now, it should be clear that this is actually an indication of (a) a metaphysical dispute about what the real subject matter of psychology ought to be (material reality or subjective experience); (b) an epistemological dispute concerning what constitutes an appropriate research methodology for whatever "stuff" is central to the discipline; or (c) a dispute over what behaviors are considered most healthy or appropriate for members of the society to engage in. In these readings, one finds evidence of all three kinds of objections to the existential–phenomenological viewpoint.

REFERENCES

Coulson, W. R., & Rogers, C. R. (Eds). (1968). *Man and the science of man.* Columbus, OH: Charles E. Merrill.

Gendlin, E. (1962). *Experiencing and the creation of meaning: A philosophical and psychological approach to the subjective.* New York: Macmillan.

Husserl, E. (1931). *Ideas: General introduction to pure phenomenology.* New York: Macmillan. (Original work published 1913)

May, R. (1969). *Love and will.* New York: Norton.

May, R. (1975). *The courage to create.* New York: Norton.

May, R. (1979). *Psychology and the human condition.* New York: Norton.

Rogers, C. R. (1955). *Client-centered therapy: Its current practice, implications, and theory.* Boston: Houghton Mifflin.

Rogers. C. R. (1961). *On becoming a person.* Boston: Houghton Mifflin.

Rogers, C. R. (1985). Toward a more human science of the person. *Journal of Humanistic Psychology, 25,* 7–24.

Rogers, C. R., Gendlin, E. T., Kiesler, D. J., & Truax, C. B. (1967). *The therapeutic relationship and its impact: A study of psychotherapy with schizophrenics.* Madison: University of Wisconsin Press.

Rychlak, J. F. (1968). *A philosophy of science for personality theory.* Boston: Houghton Mifflin.

Rychlak, J. F. (1981). *Introduction to personality and psychotherapy: A theory construction approach* (2nd ed.). Boston: Houghton Mifflin.

Rychlak, J. F., (1988). *The psychology of rigorous humanism* (2nd ed.). New York: New York University Press.

Wann, T. W. (Ed.). (1964). *Behaviorism and phenomenology.* Chicago: University of Chicago Press.

17

PERSONS OR SCIENCE? A PHILOSOPHICAL QUESTION

CARL R. ROGERS

This is a highly personal document, written primarily for myself, to clarify an issue which has become increasingly puzzling. It will be of interest to others only to the extent that the issue exists for them. I shall therefore describe first something of the way in which the paper grew.

As I have acquired experience as a therapist, carrying on the exciting, rewarding experience of psychotherapy, and as I have worked as a scientific investigator to ferret out some of the truth about therapy, I have become increasingly conscious of the gap between these two roles. The better therapist I have become (as I believe I have), the more I have been vaguely aware of my complete subjectivity when I am at my best in this function. And as I have become a better investigator, more "hardheaded" and more scientific (as I believe I have) I have felt an increasing discomfort at the distance between the rigorous objectivity of myself as scientist and the almost mystical subjectivity of myself as therapist. This paper is the result.

What I did first was to let myself go as therapist, and describe, as well as I could do in a brief space, what is the essential nature of psychotherapy as I have lived it with many clients. I would stress the fact that this is a very fluid and personal formulation, and that if it were written by another person, or if it were written by me two years ago, or two years hence, it would be different in some respects. Then I let myself go as scientist—as toughminded fact-finder in this psychological realm—and endeavored to picture the meaning which science can give to therapy. Following this I carried on the debate which existed in me, raising the questions which each point of view legitimately asks the other.

When I had carried my efforts this far I found that I had only sharpened the conflict. The two points of view seemed more than ever irreconcilable. I discussed the material with a seminar

Reprinted from the *American Psychologist, 10,* 267–278. (1955). In the public domain.

of faculty and students, and found their comments very helpful. During the following year I continued to mull over the problem until I began to feel an integration of the two views arising in me. More than a year after the first sections were written I tried to express this tentative and perhaps temporary integration in words.

Thus the reader who cares to follow my struggles in this matter will find that it has quite unconsciously assumed a dramatic form—all of the dramatis personae being contained within myself; First Protagonist, Second Protagonist, The Conflict; and finally, The Resolution. Without more ado let me introduce the first protagonist, myself as therapist, portraying as well as I can, what the *experience* of therapy seems to be.

THE ESSENCE OF THERAPY IN TERMS OF ITS EXPERIENCE

I launch myself into the therapeutic relationship having a hypothesis, or a faith, that my liking, my confidence, and my understanding of the other person's inner world, will lead to a significant process of becoming. I enter the relationship not as a scientist, not as a physician who can accurately diagnose and cure, but as a person, entering into a personal relationship. Insofar as I see him only as an object, the client will tend to become only an object.

I risk myself, because if, as the relationship deepens, what develops is a failure, a regression, a repudiation of me and the relationship by the client, then I sense that I will lose myself, or a part of myself. At times this risk is very real, and is very keenly experienced.

I let myself go into the immediacy of the relationship where it is my total organism which takes over and is sensitive to the relationship, not simply my consciousness. I am not consciously responding in a planful or analytic way, but simply in an unreflective way to the other individual, my reaction being based (but not consciously) on my total organismic sensitivity to this other person. I live the relationship on this basis.

The essence of some of the deepest parts of therapy seems to be a unity of experiencing. The client is freely able to experience his feeling in its complete intensity, as a "pure culture," without intellectual inhibitions or cautions, without having it bounded by knowledge of contradictory feelings; and I am able with equal freedom to experience my understanding of this feeling, without any conscious thought about it, without any apprehension or concern as to where this will lead, without any type of diagnostic or analytic thinking, without any cognitive or emotional barriers to a complete "letting go" in understanding. When there is this complete unity, singleness, fullness of experiencing in the relationship, then it acquires the "out-of-this-world" quality which many therapists have remarked upon, a sort of trance-like feeling in the relationship from which both the client and I emerge at the end of the hour, as if from a deep well or tunnel. In these moments there is, to borrow from Buber's phrase, a real "I-Thou" relationship, a timeless living in the experience which is *between* the client and me. It is at the opposite pole from seeing the client, or myself, as an object. It is the height of personal subjectivity.

I am often aware of the fact that I do not *know*, cognitively, where this immediate relationship is leading. It is as though both I and the client, often fearfully, let ourselves slip into the stream of becoming, a stream or process which carries us along. It is the fact that the therapist has let himself float in this stream of experience or life previously, and found it rewarding, that makes him each time less fearful of taking the plunge. It is my confidence that makes it easier for the client to embark also, a little bit at a time. It often seems as though this stream of experience leads to some goal. Probably the truer statement, however, is that its rewarding character lies within the process itself, and that its major reward is that it enables both the client and me, later, independently, to let ourselves go in the process of becoming.

As to the client, as therapy proceeds, he finds that he is daring to become himself, in spite of all the dread consequences which he is sure will befall him if he permits himself to become himself. What does this becoming one's self mean? It appears to mean less fear of the organismic, nonreflective reactions which one has, a gradual growth of trust in and even affection for the complex, varied, rich assortment of feelings and tendencies which exist in one at the organic or organismic level. Consciousness, instead of being the watchman over a dangerous and unpredictable lot of impulses, of which few can be permitted to see the light of day, becomes the comfortable inhabitant of a richly varied society of impulses and feelings and thoughts, which prove to be very satisfactorily self-governing when not fearfully or authoritatively guarded.

Involved in this process of becoming himself is a profound experience of personal choice. He realizes that he can choose to continue to hide behind a facade, or that he can take the risks involved in being himself; that he is a free agent who has it within his power to destroy another, or himself, and also the power to enhance himself and others. Faced with this naked reality of decision, he chooses to move in the direction of being himself.

But being himself doesn't "solve problems." It simply opens up a new way of living in which there is more depth and more height in the experience of his feelings, more breadth and more range. He feels more unique and hence more alone, but he is so much more real that his relationships with others lose their artificial quality, become deeper, more satisfying, and draw more of the realness of the other person into the relationship.

Another way of looking at this process, this relationship, is that it is a learning by the client (and by the therapist, to a lesser extent). But it is a strange type of learning. Almost never is the learning notable by its complexity, and at its deepest the learnings never seem to fit well into verbal symbols. Often the learnings take such simple forms as "I *am* different from others"; "I do feel hatred for him"; "I *am* fearful of feeling dependent"; "I do feel sorry for myself"; "I am self-centered"; "I do have tender and loving feelings"; "I could be what I want to be"; etc. But in spite of their seeming simplicity these learnings are vastly significant in some new way which is very difficult to define. We can think of it in various ways. They are self-appropriated learnings, for one thing, based somehow in experience, not in symbols. They are analogous to the learning of the child who knows that "two and two make four" and who one day playing with two objects and two objects, suddenly realizes in *experience* a totally new learning, that "two and two *do* make four."

Another manner of understanding these learnings is that they are a belated attempt to match symbols with meanings in the world of feelings, an undertaking long since achieved in the cognitive realm. Intellectually, we match carefully the symbol we select with the meaning which an experience has for us. Thus I say something happened "gradually," having quickly (and largely unconsciously) reviewed such terms as "slowly," "imperceptively," "step-by-step," etc., and rejected them as not carrying the precise shade of meaning of the experience. But in the realm of feelings, we have never learned to attach symbols to experience with any accuracy of meaning. This something which I feel welling up in myself, in the safety of an acceptant relationship—what is it? Is it sadness, is it anger, is it regret, is it sorrow for myself, is it anger at lost opportunities—I stumble around trying out a wide range of symbols, until one "fits," "feels right, " seems really to match the organismic experience. In doing this type of thing the client discovers that he has to learn the language of feeling and emotion as if he were an infant learning to speak; often, even worse, he finds he must unlearn a false language before learning the true one.

Let us try still one more way of defining this type of learning, this time by describing what it is not. It is a type of learning which cannot be taught. The essence of it is the aspect of self-discovery. With "knowledge" as we are accustomed to think of it, one person can teach it to another, providing each has adequate motivation and ability. But in the significant learning which takes place in therapy, one person *cannot* teach another. The teaching would destroy the learning. Thus I might teach a client that it is safe for him to be himself, that freely to realize his feelings is not dangerous, etc. The more he learned this, the less he would have learned it in the significant, experiential, self-appropriating way. Kierkegaard regards this latter type of learning as true subjectivity, and makes the valid point that there can be no direct communication of it, or even about it. The most that one person can do to further it in another is to create certain conditions which make this type of learning *possible.* It cannot be compelled.

A final way of trying to describe this learning is that the client gradually learns to symbolize a total and unified state, in which the state of the organism, in experience, feeling, and cognition may all be described in one unified way. To make the matter even more vague and unsatisfactory, it seems quite unnecessary that this symbolization should be expressed. It usually does occur, because the client wishes to communicate at least a portion of himself to the therapist, but it is probably not essential. The only necessary aspect is the inward realization of the total, unified, immediate, "at-this-instant," state of the organism which is me. For example, to realize fully that at this moment the oneness in me is simply that "I am deeply frightened at the possibility of becoming something different" is of the essence of therapy. The client who realizes this will be quite certain to recognize and realize this state of his being when it recurs in somewhat similar form. He will also, in all probability, recognize and realize more fully some of the other existential feelings which occur in him. Thus he will be moving toward a state in which he is more truly himself. He will *be,* in more unified fashion, what he organismically *is,* and this seems to be the essence of therapy.

THE ESSENCE OF THERAPY IN TERMS OF SCIENCE

I shall now let the second protagonist, myself as scientist, take over and give his view of this same field.

In approaching the complex phenomena of therapy with the logic and methods of science, the aim is to work toward an *understanding* of the phenomena. In science this means an objective knowledge of events and of functional relationships between events. Science may also give the possibility of increased prediction of and control over these events, but this is not a necessary outcome of scientific endeavor. If the scientific aim were fully achieved in this realm, we would presumably know that, in therapy, certain elements were associated with certain types of outcomes. Knowing this it is likely that we would be able to predict that a particular instance of a therapeutic relationship would have a certain outcome (within certain probability limits) because it involved certain elements. We could then very likely control outcomes of therapy by our manipulation of the elements contained in the therapeutic relationship.

It should be clear that no matter how profound our scientific investigation, we could never by means of it discover any absolute truth, but could only describe relationships which had an increasingly high probability of occurrence. Nor could we discover any underlying reality in regard to persons, interpersonal relationships, or the universe. We could only describe relationships between observable events. If science in this field followed the course of science in other fields, the working models of reality which would emerge (in the course of theory building) would be increasingly removed from the reality perceived by the senses. The scientific description of therapy and therapeutic relationships would become increasingly *unlike* these phenomena as they are experienced.

It is evident at the outset that since therapy is a complex phenomenon, measurement will be difficult. Nevertheless "anything that exists can be measured," and since therapy is judged to be a significant relationship, with implications extending far beyond itself, the difficulties may prove to be worth surmounting in order to discover laws of personality and interpersonal relationships.

Since, in client-centered therapy, there already exists a crude theory (though not a theory in the strictly scientific sense), we have a starting point for the selection of hypotheses. For purposes of this discussion, let us take some of the crude hypotheses which can be drawn from this theory, and see what a scientific approach will do with them. We will, for the time being, omit the translation of the total theory into a formal logic which would be acceptable, and consider only a few of the hypotheses.

Let us first state three of these in their crude form.

1. Acceptance of the client by the therapist leads to an increased acceptance of self by the client.
2. The more the therapist perceives the client as a person rather than as an object, the more the client will come to perceive himself as a person rather than an object.
3. In the course of therapy an experiential and effective type of learning about self takes place in the client.

How would we go about translating each of these[1] into operational terms and how would we test the hypotheses? What would be the general outcomes of such testing?

This paper is not the place for a detailed answer to these questions, but research already carried on supplies the answers in a general way. In the case of the first hypothesis, certain devices for measuring acceptance would be selected or devised. These might be attitude tests, objective or projective, Q technique or the like. Presumably the same instruments, with slightly different instructions or mind set, could be used to measure the therapist's acceptance of the client, and the client's acceptance of self. Operationally then, the degree of therapist acceptance would be equated to a certain score on this instrument. Whether client self-acceptance changed during therapy would be indicated by pre- and post-measurements. The relationship of any change to therapy would be determined by comparison of changes in therapy to changes during a control period or in a control group. We would finally be able to say whether a relationship existed between therapist acceptance and client self-acceptance, as operationally defined, and the correlation between the two.

The second and third hypotheses involve real difficulty in measurement, but there is no reason to suppose that they could not be objectively studied, as our sophistication in psychological measurement increases. Some type of attitude test or Q sort might be the instrument for the second hypothesis, measuring the attitude of therapist toward client, and of client toward self. In this case the continuum would be from objective regard of an external object to a personal and subjective experiencing. The instrumentation for hypothesis three might be physiological, since it seems likely that experiential learning has physiologically measurable concomitants. Another possibility would be to infer experiential learning from its effectiveness, and thus measure the effectiveness of learning in different areas. At the present stage of our methodology hypothesis three might be beyond us, but certainly within the foreseeable future, it too could be given operational definition and tested.

The findings from these studies would be of this order. Let us become suppositious, in order to illustrate more concretely. Suppose we find that therapist acceptance leads to client self-acceptance, and that the correlation is in the neighborhood of .70 between the two variables.

[1]I believe it is now commonly accepted that the most subjective feelings, apprehensions, tensions, satisfactions, or reactions, may be dealt with scientifically, providing only that they may be given clear-cut operational definition. William Stephenson, among others, presents this point of view forcefully (in his *Postulates of Behaviorism*) and through his Q technique, has contributed importantly to the objectification of such subjective materials for scientific study.

In hypothesis two we might find the hypothesis unsupported, but find that the more the therapist regarded the client as a person, the more the client's self-acceptance increased. Thus we would have learned that person-centeredness is an element of acceptance, but that it has little to do with the client becoming more of a person to himself. Let us also suppose hypothesis three upheld with experiential learning of certain describable sorts taking place much more in therapy than in the control subjects.

Glossing over all the qualifications and ramifications which would be present in the findings, and omitting reference to the unexpected leads into personality dynamics which would crop up (since these are hard to imagine in advance), the preceding paragraph gives us some notion of what science can offer in this field. It can give us a more exact description of the events of therapy and the changes which take place. It can begin to formulate some tentative laws of the dynamics of human relationships. It can offer public and replicable statements, that if certain operationally definable conditions exist in the therapist or in the relationship, then certain client behaviors may be expected with a known degree of probability. It can presumably do this for the field of therapy and personality change as it is in the process of doing for such fields as perception and learning. Eventually theoretical formulations should draw together these different areas, enunciating the laws which appear to govern alteration in human behavior, whether in the situations we classify as perception, those we classify as learning, or the more global and molar changes which occur in therapy, involving both perception and learning.

SOME ISSUES

Here are two different methods of perceiving the essential aspects of psychotherapy, two different approaches to forging ahead into new territory in this field. As presented here, and as they frequently exist, there seems almost no common meeting ground between the two descriptions. Each represents a vigorous way of seeing therapy. Each seems to be an avenue to the significant truths of therapy. When each of these is held by a different individual or group, it constitutes a basis of sharp disagreement. When each of these approaches seems true to one individual, like myself, then he feels himself conflicted by these two views. Though they may superficially be reconciled, or regarded as complementary to each other, they seem to me to be basically antagonistic in many ways. I should like to raise certain issues which these two viewpoints pose for me.

The Scientist's Questions

First let me pose some of the questions which the scientific viewpoint asks of the experiential (using scientific and experiential simply as loose labels to indicate the two views). The hardheaded scientist listens to the experiential account, and raises several searching questions.

1. First of all he wants to know, "How can you know that this account, or any account given at a previous or later time, is true? How do you know that it has any relationship to reality? If we are to rely on this inner and subjective experience as being the truth about human relationships or about ways of altering personality, then Yogi, Christian Science, dianetics, and the delusions of a psychotic individual who believes himself to be Jesus Christ, are all true, just as true as this account. Each of them represents the truth as perceived inwardly by some individual or group of individuals. If we are to avoid this morass of multiple and contradictory truths, we must fall back on the

only method we know for achieving an ever-closer approximation to reality, the scientific method."

2. "In the second place, this experiential approach shuts one off from improving his therapeutic skill, or discovering the less than satisfactory elements in the relationship. Unless one regards the present description as a perfect one, which is unlikely, or the present level of experience in the therapeutic relationship as being the most effective possible, which is equally unlikely, then there are unknown flaws, imperfections, blind spots, in the account as given. How are these to be discovered and corrected? The experiential approach can offer nothing but a trial-and-error process for achieving this, a process which is slow and which offers no real guarantee of achieving this goal. Even the criticisms or suggestions of others are of little help, since they do not arise from within the experience and hence do not have the vital authority of the relationship itself. But the scientific method, and the procedures of a modern logical positivism, have much to offer here. Any experience which can be described at all can be described in operational terms. Hypotheses can be formulated and put to test, and the sheep of truth can thus be separated from the goats of error. This seems the only sure road to improvement, self-correction, growth in knowledge."
3. The scientist has another comment to make. "Implicit in your description of the therapeutic experience seems to be the notion that there are elements in it which *cannot* be predicted—that there is some type of spontaneity or (excuse the term) free will operative here. You speak as though some of the client's behavior—and perhaps some of the therapist's—is not caused, is not a link in a sequence of cause and effect. Without desiring to become metaphysical, may I raise the question as to whether this is defeatism? Since surely we can discover what causes *much* of the behavior—you yourself speak of creating the conditions where certain behavioral results follow—then why give up at any point? Why not at least *aim* toward uncovering the causes of *all* behavior? This does not mean that the individual must regard himself as an automaton, but in our search for the facts we shall not be hampered by a belief that some doors are closed to us."
4. Finally, the scientist cannot understand why the therapist, the experientialist, should challenge the one tool and method which is responsible for almost all the advances which we value. "In the curing of disease, in the prevention of infant mortality, in the growing of larger crops, in the preservation of food, in the manufacture of all the things that make life comfortable, from books to nylon, in the understanding of the universe, what is the foundation stone? It is the method of science, applied to each of these, and to many other problems. It is true that it has improved methods of warfare, too, serving man's destructive as well as his constructive purposes, but even here the potentiality for social usefulness is very great. So why should we doubt this same approach in the social science field? To be sure advances here have been slow, and no law as fundamental as the law of gravity has as yet been demonstrated, but are we to give up this approach out of impatience? What possible alternative offers equal hope? If we are agreed that the social problems of the world are very pressing indeed, if psychotherapy offers a window into the most crucial and significant dynamics of change in human behavior, then surely the course of action is to apply to psychotherapy the most rigorous canons of scientific method, on as broad a scale as possible, in order that we may most rapidly approach a tentative knowledge of the laws of individual behavior and of attitudinal change."

The Questions of the Experientialist

While the scientist's questions may seem to some to settle the matter, his comments are far from being entirely satisfying to the therapist who has lived the experience of therapy. Such an individual has several points to make in regard to the scientific view.

1. "In the first place," this "experientalist" points out, "science always has to do with the other, the object. Various logicians of science, including Stevens, show that it is a basic element of science that it always has to do with the observable object, the observable other. This is true, even if the scientist is experimenting on himself, for to that degree he treats himself as the observable other. It never has anything to do with the experiencing me. Now does not this quality of science mean that it must forever be irrelevant to an experience such as therapy, which is intensely personal, highly subjective in its inwardness, and dependent entirely on the relationship of two individuals each of whom is an experiencing me? Science can of course study the events which occur, but always in a way which is irrelevant to what is occurring. An analogy would be to say that science can conduct an autopsy of the dead events of therapy, but by its very nature it can never enter into the living physiology of therapy. It is for this reason that therapists recognize—usually intuitively—that any advance in therapy, any fresh knowledge of it, any significant new hypotheses in regard to it must come from the experience of the therapists and clients, and can never come from science. Again, to use an analogy, certain heavenly bodies were discovered solely from examination of the scientific measurements of the courses of the stars. Then the astronomers searched for these hypothesized bodies and found them. It seems decidedly unlikely that there will ever be a similar outcome in therapy, since science has nothing to say about the internal personal experience which 'I' have in therapy. It can only speak of the events which occur in 'him.' "

2. "Because science has as its field the 'other,' the 'object,' it means that everything it touches is transformed into an object. This has never presented a problem in the physical sciences. In the biological sciences it has caused certain difficulties. A number of medical men feel some concern as to whether the increasing tendency to view the human organism as an object, in spite of its scientific efficacy, may not be unfortunate for the patient. They would prefer to see him again regarded as a person. It is in the social sciences, however, that this becomes a genuinely serious issue. It means that the people studied by the social scientist are always objects. In therapy, both client and therapist become objects for dissection, but not persons with whom one enters a living relationship. At first glance, this may not seem important. We may say that only in his role as scientist does the individual regard others as objects. He can also step out of this role and become a person. But if we look a little further we will see that this is a superficial answer. If we project ourselves into the future, and suppose that we had the answers to most of the questions which psychology investigates today, what then? Then we would find ourselves increasingly impelled to treat all others, and even ourselves, as objects. The knowledge of all human relationships would be so great that we would know it rather than live the relationships unreflectively. We see some foretaste of this in the attitude of sophisticated parents who know that affection 'is good for the child.' This knowledge frequently stands in the way of their being themselves, freely, unreflectively, affectionate or not. Thus the development of science in a field like therapy is either irrelevant to the experience,

or may actually make it more difficult to live the relationship as a personal, experiential event."

3. The experientialist has a further concern. "When science transforms people into objects, as mentioned above, it has another effect. The end result of science is to lead toward manipulation. This is less true in fields like astronomy, but in the physical and social sciences, the knowledge of the events and their relationships leads to manipulation of some of the elements of the equation. This is unquestionably true in psychology, and would be true in therapy. If we know all about how learning takes place, we use that knowledge to manipulate persons as objects. This statement places no value judgment on manipulation. It may be done in highly ethical fashion. We may even manipulate ourselves as objects, using such knowledge. Thus, knowing that learning takes place more rapidly with repeated review rather than long periods of concentration of one lesson, I may use this knowledge to manipulate my learning of Spanish. But knowledge is power. As I learn the laws of learning I use them to manipulate others through advertisements, through propaganda, through prediction of their responses, and the control of those responses. It is not too strong a statement to say that the growth of knowledge in the social sciences contains within itself a powerful tendency toward social control, toward control of the many by the few. An equally strong tendency is toward the weakening or destruction of the existential person. When all are regarded as objects, the subjective individual, the inner self, the person in the process of becoming, the unreflective consciousness of being, the whole inward side of living life, is weakened, devalued, or destroyed. Perhaps this is best exemplified by two books. Skinner's *Walden Two* is a psychologist's picture of paradise. To Skinner it must have seemed desirable, unless he wrote it as a tremendous satire. At any rate it is a paradise of manipulation, in which the extent to which one can be a person is greatly reduced, unless one can be a member of the ruling council. Huxley's *Brave New World* is frankly satire, but portrays vividly the loss of personhood which he sees as associated with increasing psychological and biological knowledge. Thus, to put it bluntly, it seems that a developing social science (as now conceived and pursued) leads to social dictatorship and individual loss of personhood. The dangers perceived by Kierkegaard a century ago in this respect seem much more real now, with the increase of knowledge, than they could have then."

4. "Finally," says the experientialist, "doesn't all this point to the fact that ethics is a more basic consideration than science? I am not blind to the value of science as a tool, and am aware that it can be a very valuable tool. But unless it is the tool of ethical *persons,* with all that the term persons implies, may it not become a Juggernaut? We have been a long time recognizing this issue, because in physical science it took centuries for the ethical issue to become crucial, but it has at last become so. In the social sciences the ethical issues arise much more quickly, because persons are involved. But in psychotherapy the issue arises most quickly and most deeply. Here is the maximizing of all that is subjective, inward, personal: here a relationship is lived, not examined, and a person, not an object, emerges; a person who feels, chooses, believes, acts, not as an automaton, but as a person. And here too is the ultimate in science—the objective exploration of the most subjective aspects of life; the reduction to hypotheses, and eventually to theorems, of all that has been regarded as most personal, most completely inward, most thoroughly a private world. And because these two views come so sharply into focus here, we must make a choice—an ethical personal choice of values. We may do it by default, by not raising the

question. We may be able to make a choice which will somehow conserve both values—but choose we must. And I am asking that we think long and hard before we give up the values that pertain to being a person, to experiencing, to living a relationship, to becoming, that pertain to one's self as a process, to one's self in the existential moment, to the inward subjective self that lives."

The Dilemma

There you have the contrary views as they occur sometimes explicitly, more often implicitly, in current psychological thinking. There you have the debate as it exists in me. Where do we go? What direction do we take? Has the problem been correctly described or is it fallacious? What are the errors of perception? Or if it is essentially as described, must we choose one or the other? And if so, which one? Or is there some broader, more inclusive formulation which can happily encompass both of these views without damage to either?

A CHANGED VIEW OF SCIENCE

In the year which has elapsed since the foregoing material was written, I have from time to time discussed the issues with students, colleagues, and friends. To some of them I am particularly indebted for ideas which have taken root in me.[2] Gradually I have come to believe that the most basic error in the original formulation was in the description of science. I should like, in this section, to attempt to correct that error, and in the following section to reconcile the revised points of view.

The major shortcoming was, I believe, in viewing science as something "out there," something spelled with a capital S, a "body of knowledge," existing somewhere in space and time. In common with many psychologists I thought of science as a systematized and organized collection of tentatively verified fact, and saw the methodology of science as the socially approved means of accumulating this body of knowledge, and continuing its verification. It has seemed somewhat like a reservoir into which all and sundry may dip their buckets to obtain water—with a guarantee of 99% purity. When viewed in this external and impersonal fashion, it seems not unreasonable to see Science not only as discovering knowledge in lofty fashion, but as involving depersonalization, a tendency to manipulate, a denial of the basic freedom of choice which I have met experientially in therapy. I should like now to view the scientific approach from a different, and I hope, a more accurate perspective.

Science in Persons

Science exists only in people. Each scientific project has its creative inception, its process, and its tentative conclusion, in a person or persons. Knowledge—even scientific knowledge—is that which is subjectively acceptable. Scientific knowledge can be communicated only to those who are subjectively ready to receive its communication. The utilization of science also occurs only through people who are in pursuit of values which have meaning for them. These statements

[2]I would like to mention my special debt to discussions with, and published and unpublished papers by Robert M. Lipgar, Ross L. Mooney, David A. Rodgers, and Eugene Streich. My own thinking has fed so deeply on theirs, and become so intertwined with theirs, that I would be at a loss to acknowledge specific obligations. I only know that in what follows there is much which springs from them, through me. I have also profited from correspondence regarding the paper with Anne Roe and Walter Smet.

summarize very briefly something of the change in emphasis which I would like to make in my description of science. Let me follow through the various phases of science from this point of view.

The Creative Phases

Science has its inception in a particular person who is pursuing aims, values, purposes, which have personal and subjective meaning for him. As a part of this pursuit, he, in some area, "wants to find out." Consequently, if he is to be a good scientist, he immerses himself in the relevant experience, whether that be the physics laboratory, the world of plant or animal life, the hospital, the psychological laboratory or clinic, or whatever. This immersion is complete and subjective, similar to the immersion of the therapist in therapy, described previously. He senses the field in which he is interested. He lives it. He does more than "think" about it—he lets his organism take over and react to it, both on a knowing and on an unknowing level. He comes to sense more than he could possibly verbalize about his field, and reacts organismically in terms of relationships which are not present in his awareness.

Out of this complete subjective immersion comes a creative forming, a sense of direction, a vague formulation of relationships hitherto unrecognized. Whittled down, sharpened, formulated in clearer terms, this creative forming becomes a hypothesis—a statement of a tentative, personal, subjective faith. The scientist is saying, drawing upon all his known and unknown experience, that "I have a hunch that such and such a relationship exists, and the existence of this phenomenon has relevance to my personal values."

What I am describing is the initial phase of science, probably its most important phase, but one which American scientists, particularly psychologists, have been prone to minimize or ignore. It is not so much that it has been denied as that it has been quickly brushed off. Kenneth Spence has said that this aspect of science is "simply taken for granted."[3] Like many experiences taken for granted, it also tends to be forgotten. It is indeed in the matrix of immediate personal, subjective experience that all science, and each individual scientific research, has its origin.

Checking with Reality

The scientist has then creatively achieved his hypothesis, his tentative faith. But does it check with reality? Experience has shown each one of us that it is very easy to deceive himself, to believe something which later experience shows is not so. How can I tell whether this tentative belief has some real relationship to observed facts? I can use, not one line of evidence only, but several. I can surround my observation of the facts with various precautions to make sure I am not deceiving myself. I can consult with others who have also been concerned with avoiding self-deception, and learn useful ways of catching myself in unwarranted beliefs, based on misinterpretation of observations. I can, in short, begin to use all the elaborate methodology which science has accumulated. I discover that stating my hypothesis in operational terms will avoid many blind alleys and false conclusions. I learn that control groups can help me to avoid drawing false inferences. I learn that correlations, and t tests and critical ratios and a whole array of statistical procedures can likewise aid me in drawing only reasonable inferences.

[3]It may be pertinent to quote the sentences from which this phrase is taken. ". . . the data of all sciences have the same origin—namely, the immediate experience of an observing person, the scientist himself. That is to say, immediate experience, the initial matrix out of which all sciences develop, is no longer considered a matter of concern for the scientist. He simply takes it for granted and then proceeds to the task of describing the events occurring in it and discovering and formulating the nature of the relationships holding among them." Kenneth W. Spence, in *Psychological Theory*, M. H. Marx (Ed.), Macmillan, 1951, p. 173.

Thus scientific methodology is seen for what it truly is—a way of preventing me from deceiving myself in regard to my creatively formed subjective hunches which have developed out of the relationship between me and my material. It is in this context, and perhaps only in this context, that the vast structure of operationism, logical positivism, research design, tests of significance, etc., have their place. They exist, not for themselves, but as servants in the attempt to check the subjective feeling or hunch or hypothesis of a person with the objective fact.

And even throughout the use of such rigorous and impersonal methods, the important choices are all made subjectively by the scientist. To which of a number of hypotheses shall I devote time? What kind of control group is most suitable for avoiding self-deception in this particular research? How far shall I carry the statistical analysis? How much credence may I place in the findings? Each of these is necessarily a subjective personal judgment, emphasizing that the splendid structure of science rests basically upon its subjective use by persons. It is the best instrument we have yet been able to devise to check upon our organismic sensing of the universe.

The Findings

If, as scientist, I like the way I have gone about my investigation, if I have been open to all the evidence, if I have selected and used intelligently all the precautions against self-deception which I have been able to assimilate from others or to devise myself, then I will give my tentative belief to the findings which have emerged. I will regard them as a springboard for further investigation and further seeking.

It seems to me that in the best of science, the primary purpose is to provide a more satisfactory and dependable hypothesis, belief, faith, for the investigator himself. To the extent that the scientist is endeavoring to prove something to someone else—an error into which I have fallen more than once—then I believe he is using science to bolster a personal insecurity, and is keeping it from its truly creative role in the service of the person.

In regard to the findings of science, the subjective foundation is well shown in the fact that at times the scientist may refuse to believe his own findings. "The experiment showed thus and so but I believe it is wrong," is a theme which every scientist has experienced at some time or other. Some very fruitful scientific discoveries have grown out of the persistent *disbelief,* by a scientist, in his own findings and those of others. In the last analysis he may place more trust in his total organismic reactions than in the methods of science. There is no doubt that this can result in serious error as well as in scientific discoveries, but it indicates again the leading place of the subjective in the use of science.

Communication of Scientific Findings

Wading along a coral reef in the Caribbean this morning, I saw a blue fish—I think. If you, quite independently, saw it too, then I feel more confidence in my own observation. This is what is known as intersubjective verification, and it plays an important part in our understanding of science. If I take you (whether in conversation or in print or behaviorally) through the steps I have taken in an investigation, and it seems to you too that I have not deceived myself, and that I have indeed come across a new relationship which is relevant to my values, and that I am justified in having a tentative faith in this relationship, then we have the beginnings of Science with a capital S. It is at this point that we are likely to think we have created a body of scientific knowledge. Actually there is no such body of knowledge. There are only tentative beliefs, existing subjectively, in a number of different persons. If these beliefs are not tentative, then what exists is dogma, not science. If on the other hand, no one but the investigator believes the finding, then this finding is either a personal and deviant matter, an instance of psychopathology, or else it is an unusual truth discovered by a genius, which as yet no one is subjectively ready to believe. This leads me to comment on the group which can put tentative faith in any given scientific finding.

Communication to Whom?

It is clear that scientific findings can be communicated only to those who have agreed to the same ground rules of investigation. The Australian bushman will be quite unimpressed with the findings of science regarding bacterial infection. He knows that illness truly is caused by evil spirits. It is only when he too agrees to scientific method as a good means of preventing self-deception, that he will be likely to accept its findings.

But even among those who have adopted the ground rules of science, tentative belief in the findings of a scientific research can only occur where there is a subjective readiness to believe. One could find many examples. Most psychologists are quite ready to believe evidence showing that the lecture system produces significant increments of learning, and quite unready to believe that the turn of an unseen card may be called through an ability labeled extrasensory perception. Yet the scientific evidence for the latter is considerably more impeccable than for the former. Likewise when the so-called "Iowa studies" first came out, indicating that intelligence might be considerably altered by environmental conditions, there was great disbelief among psychologists, and many attacks on the imperfect scientific methods used. The scientific evidence for this finding is not much better today than it was when the Iowa studies first appeared, but the subjective readiness of psychologists to believe such a finding has altered greatly. A historian of science has noted that empiricists, had they existed at the time, would have been the first to disbelieve the findings of Copernicus.

It appears then that whether I believe the scientific findings of others, or those of my own studies, depends in part on my readiness to put a tentative belief in such findings.[4] One reason we are not particularly aware of this subjective fact is that in the physical sciences particularly, we have gradually agreed that in a very large area of experience we are ready to believe any finding which can be shown to rest upon the rules of the scientific game, properly played.

The Use of Science

But not only is the origin, process, and conclusion of science something which exists only in the subjective experience of persons—so also is its utilization. "Science" will never depersonalize, or manipulate, or control individuals. It is only persons who can and will do that. This is surely a most obvious and trite observation, yet a deep realization of it has had much meaning for me. It means that the use which will be made of scientific findings in the field of personality is and will be a matter of subjective personal choice—the same type of choice as a person makes

[4]One example from my own experience may suffice. In 1941 a research study done under my supervision showed that the future adjustment of delinquent adolescents was best predicted by a measure of their realistic self-understanding and self-acceptance. The instrument was a crude one, but it was a better predictor than measures of family environment, hereditary capacities, social milieu, and the like. At that time I was simply not ready to believe such a finding, because my own belief, like that of most psychologists, was that such factors as the emotional climate in the family and the influence of the peer group were the real determinants of future delinquency and nondelinquency. Only gradually, as my experience with psychotherapy continued and deepened, was it possible for me to give my tentative belief to the findings of this study and of a later one (1944) which confirmed it. (For a report of these two studies see "The role of self understanding in the prediction of behavior" by C. R. Rogers, B. L. Kell, and H. McNeil, *J. consult. Psychol.*, 1948, **12,** 174–186.)

in therapy. To the extent that he has defensively closed off areas of his experience from awareness, the person is more likely to make choices which are socially destructive. To the extent that he is open to all phases of his experience we may be sure that this person will be more likely to use the findings and methods of science (or any other tool or capacity) in a manner which is personally and socially constructive.[5] There is, in actuality then, no threatening entity of "Science" which can in any way affect our destiny. There are only people. While many of them are indeed threatening and dangerous in their defensiveness, and modern scientific knowledge multiplies the social threat and danger, this is not the whole picture. There are two other significant facets. (*a*) There are many other persons who are relatively open to their experience and hence likely to be socially constructive. (*b*) Both the subjective experience of psychotherapy and the scientific findings regarding it indicate that individuals are motivated to change, and may be helped to change, in the direction of greater openness to experience, and hence in the direction of behavior which is enhancing of self and society, rather than destructive.

To put it briefly, Science can never threaten us. Only persons can do that. And while individuals can be vastly destructive with the tools placed in their hands by scientific knowledge, this is only one side of the picture. We already have subjective and objective knowledge of the basic principles by which individuals may achieve the more constructive social behavior which is natural to their organismic process of becoming.

A NEW INTEGRATION

What this line of thought has achieved for me is a fresh integration in which the conflict between the "experientialist" and the "scientific" tends to disappear. This particular integration may not be acceptable to others, but it does have meaning to me. Its major tenets have been largely implicit in the preceding section, but I will try to state them here in a way which takes cognizance of the arguments between the opposing points of view.

Science, as well as therapy, as well as all other aspects of living, is rooted in and based upon the immediate, subjective experience of a person. It springs from the inner, total, organismic experiencing which is only partially and imperfectly communicable. It is one phase of subjective living.

It is because I find value and reward in human relationships that I enter into a relationship known as therapeutic, where feelings and cognition merge into one unitary experience which is lived rather than examined, in which awareness is nonreflective, and where I am participant rather than observer. But because I am curious about the exquisite orderliness which appears to exist in the universe and in this relationship I can abstract myself from the experience and look upon it as an observer, making myself and/or others the objects of that observation. As observer I use all of the hunches which grow out of the living experience. To avoid deceiving myself as observer. to gain a more accurate picture of the order which exists, I make use of all the canons of science. Science is not an impersonal something, but simply a person living subjectively another phase of himself. A deeper understanding of therapy (or of any other problem) may come from living it, or from observing it in accordance with the rules of science, or from the communication within the self between the two types of experience. As to the subjective experience of choice, it is not only primary in therapy, but it is also primary in the use of scientific method by a person. I have even come to see that freedom of choice is not necessarily antithetical

[5]I have spelled out much more fully the rationale for this view in two recent papers: "The concept of the fully functioning person" (unpublished manuscript), and "Toward a theory of creativity," *ETC*, 1954, **11**, 249–260.

to the determinism which is a part of our framework for thinking scientifically. Since I have recently tried to spell out this relationship elsewhere,[6] I will not take the space to do so here.

What I will do with the knowledge gained through scientific method—whether I will use it to understand, enhance, enrich, or use it to control, manipulate, and destroy—is a matter of subjective choice dependent on the values which have personal meaning for me. If, out of fright and defensiveness, I block out from my awareness large areas of experience—if I can see only those facts which support my present beliefs, and am blind to all others—if I can see only the objective aspects of life, and cannot perceive the subjective—if in any way I cut off my perception from the full range of its actual sensitivity—then I am likely to be socially destructive, whether I use as tool the knowledge and instruments of science, or the power and emotional strength of a subjective relationship. And on the other hand if I am open to my experience, and can permit all of the sensings of my intricate organism to be available to my awareness, then I am likely to use myself, my subjective experience, *and* my scientific knowledge, in ways which are realistically constructive.

This, then, is the degree of integration I have currently been able to achieve between two approaches first experienced as conflicting. It does not completely resolve all the issues posed in the earlier section, but it seems to point toward a resolution. It rewrites the problem or reperceives the issue, by putting the subjective, existential person, with the values which he holds, at the foundation and the root of the therapeutic relationship and of the scientific relationship. For science too, at its inception, is an "I-Thou" relationship with the world of perceived objects, just as therapy at its deepest is an "I-Thou" relationship with a person or persons. And only as a subjective person can I enter either of these relationships.

[6]In my paper on "The concept of the fully functioning person."

18

LOCKEAN VS. KANTIAN THEORETICAL MODELS AND THE "CAUSE" OF THERAPEUTIC CHANGE

JOSEPH F. RYCHLAK

One cannot be sincerely drawn to the field of psychotherapy without feeling a certain uneasiness concerning the state of our specialty these days. We refer here to the embarrassing rift between the so-called "humanistic" and the "behavior" psychotherapists. The writer has argued that at least three motives prompt therapists and clients alike to the consulting room contact, and he frankly admits that his personal predilections have always been of the "scholarly" as opposed to the "ethical" or the "curative" motives (Rychlak, 1965). It was the attraction to "what makes *people* behave as they do?" which prompted him to enter the profession of psychology. Many of us are therefore disturbed over the "unhuman-like" or "mechanistic" image of man being projected—however unintentionally—by the behavior therapists. At the same time, only a fool would go on denying or haggling over the obvious benefits which accrue to clients in the behavior therapies. Though he has a decided "humanistic" bent, the writer is frank to admit that he would personally gravitate to a behavior therapist for any of a number of neurotic disabilities if such were to present themselves. Psychotherapy need *not* affect one's philosophical outlook on life in order for it to be effective. One might hold to Freudian theory yet gain considerably from a series of desensitization sessions regarding a phobia, let us say.

But on the other hand, one's philosophical outlook *could* be changed by the kind of therapy he finds himself committed to as practitioner, and this possibility is predicated on the fact that varying systems of therapy surely *do* make diverse philosophical assumptions concerning the objects of their cures. There are some decidedly antithetical views underlying the *formal* positions

Reprinted from *Psychotherapy: Theory, Research and Practice*, 6, 214–222. (1969).

of a behaviorist as opposed to a psychoanalyst, even though *informally* one man can eat in the other man's kitchen. But, as must inevitably occur, when our cooks write down their recipes of cure for posterity, embarrassments emerge. How important is the "relationship" between client and therapist? Is it demeaning to human nature to treat people as if they were cybernetics machines? Does man really "know" what happens to him in the therapeutic situation? Does he—or need we assume that he might—have a mind at all? These and other issues press upon us and form the nucleus of polite jocularity or worse.

As a declared humanist who has great admiration for the behavioristic approach it will be the writer's aim to show that: (1) the fundamental schism which divides our two camps issues from the use of two historically derived theoretical models: Lockean vs. Kantian; (2) the Lockean model adapts itself to so-called mechanistic efficient and material cause explanations, whereas the Kantian model invites the additional application of the more humanizing formal and final cause descriptive devices; and (3) holding to a strict behavioristic theoretical explanation, based upon the Lockean image of man, is *insufficient* to account for the facts which emerge in the consulting room and are being reported in our research literature.

We will first present the two models and discuss causation in the history of science. Then we will take up the kinds of changes specific to the psychotherapeutic contact.

LOCKEAN VS. KANTIAN MODELS

Although we will not be able to go into the matter too deeply, and the reader is referred elsewhere for a more thorough account (Rychlak, 1968), it should be possible to sketch in our two models and underscore their major differences as regards the role of mental functioning and particularly their theory of "ideas." Turning to the *Lockean* model first, we draw on the philosophical antecedents of Bacon and Hobbes in addition to Locke, all of whom may be counted as representatives of British Empiricism. This tradition is realistic in outlook, and the "hard-headed" academic brand of psychology now practiced in America is framed within it. Locke believed that the contents of mind could only be those which came in from the outside. Each mental content (or "meaning") was embodied in its own discrete unit or a combination of such "idea units." At the base of experience we have the "simple ideas" which embody inputs from an independent reality and etch a mental imprint upon the *tabula rasa* intellect with which we are all born.

These simple ideas are analogical to the lowest whole numbers in mathematics, except that a simple idea cannot itself be further subdivided. In other words, at the base of experience an idea is a discrete unit having an "either-or" characteristic, mapping reality accurately or inaccurately by way of sensory inputs. The mind itself is passive, storing and combining such inputs in a pseudo-mathematical fashion, but never imposing structure onto the world of experience. Simple ideas are like "atomistic building blocks" which combine *in the beginnings* of thought and "add up to" what Locke called "complex ideas." The more abstract complex ideas are reducible to lower level complex ideas, which in turn are reducible to the simple ideas at their base in the same way that halving "eight" gives "four" and halving again gives "two," which in turn dissolves into two "ones" (the indivisible "givens" at the base of all meaning-inputs). There is absolutely nothing which mind *qua* mind can do about the fact that all meanings issue "from below," for, as Locke said: "it is not in the power of the most exalted wit, or enlarged understanding, by any quickness or variety of thought, to *invent* or *frame* one new simple idea in the mind . . . nor can any force of the understanding *destroy* those that are there" (Locke, 1952, p. 128). All of those subjectively felt experiences which we take to be operations of mental cognition like belief, doubt, conjecture, wavering, distrust, or disbelief are actually the relative frequencies of input information which have been fed into the mind by past experience. Considerable input on "this" side of a question is felt as belief or conviction; fairly equal inputs on both "this" and "that" side of a question result in doubt or indecision, and so forth (*Ibid,* p. 369).

Over against this view of how man operates mentally we can place the Kantian model, which is in the Continental line of philosophical descent. We are more likely to find this model in use among psychologists who have a stake in the applied fields, though this is by no means a clear-cut relationship. Though he declared himself a "critical realist" it is not difficult to show that Kantian philosophy sounds a note for the idealistic theoretical predilection. Kant viewed ideas as conceptions of reason which *transcended* experience (Kant, 1952, p. 115). He proposed certain "givens" in thought which generated meaning "from above," framed in by the understanding. These are not inherited ideas so much as they are propensities for viewing and coming to know experience by way of an active intellect. Man's mentality never senses reality directly, "things in themselves" (noumena), but deals only with sensory representations (phenomena) mediated by the understanding. The Kantian categories (unity, plurality, totality, causality, etc.) are not the essential aspects of this model. What *is* vital to the Kantian conception is his view of mind as an active process, as having the means for imposing meaning by way of organizing experience in a certain way. Sensation may be passive, Kant believed, but mental activity (thought) is not.

Thus it is that on the Kantian view of man a certain prerogative is given to the actor. Kant did not advocate distorting the empirical facts, but his view of mentality is partly creative. What if ideas generated by the speculative intellect were subsequently found to be true in the world of events? Then we would have that act of creation which is impossible on the Lockean model. Before we can explicate this more fully it is necessary to turn to another feature of theoretical description—that having to do with the "cause" of anything.

ARISTOTELIAN CAUSES AND MODERN THEORY

If the reader were asked, "what do you mean by the cause of anything?" he would probably respond with something like "Well, it's whatever made it or created it or brought it about." The idea of cause is so firmly identified with its contrasting opposite, "effect," that we presume that causes are always agents which literally bring about effects; they are the something (A) coming before something else (B) which brings about the something else (A to B, or cause to effect). But actually Aristotle, who was the author of the theory of knowledge to which we now refer (taking his thinking from Plato and others), never used the term "cause" in such a restricted sense. Aristotle formulated a theory of knowledge to explicate the meanings being used by men who claimed to know something scientifically. He wanted to clarify their explanations, we might say, to bring out as boldly as possible all that was involved in describing anything. As he phrased it: "We think we have scientific knowledge when we know the cause, and there are *four* causes . . . [Italics added] (Aristotle, *Posterior Analytics,* 1952, p. 128). Aristotle felt that if a man could not cite the causes of some phenomenon under description he was merely stating opinions and thus could not claim to be giving us (scientific) knowledge.

These four causes have been succinctly referred to as the (1) material, (2) formal, (3) efficient, and (4) final (Aristotle, *Physics,* 1952, p. 270). To get these terms clearly in mind, suppose that we wanted to explain the complete nature of a stereophonic hi-fi system which we had built. Following Aristotle's prescription, we could say that the metals and plastics going into the components of the set define a *material* cause of the finished product. The *formal* cause is the blueprint we used in organizing the components into a finished product which matched the standard form or pattern of such electrical equipment. The ways in which we manipulated our eyes and hands in reading the blueprint and in building the set act as the *efficient* causes of the finished product. And finally, the reason we went through all of this work in the first place ("that for the sake of which" it was built)—our love of music or interest in mechanical gadgets—constituted the *final* cause of the completed stereophonic system.

Now, Aristotle felt that anything which could be described might involve these four causes. The more causes we could bring to bear in describing the nature of anything, the *more complex* was our explanation, the more thorough and complete our description. Parsimony (Ockham's Razor) was not valued as it is today. There was no reason for feeling embarrassed about using all four cases in describing things scientifically until the theologians of the Middle Ages had drawn excessive conclusions from theories spun largely on the formal and final causes.

With the advent of what we now call "natural science" or modern physical science, the legitimacy of using formal and final causes to explain physical phenomena was first questioned, then denied. Bacon was very influential in pointing out that "to inquire the form of a lion, of an oak, or gold; nay, of water, of air, is a vain pursuit. . . . If the cause of whiteness in snow or froth be inquired, and it be rendered thus, that the subtile intermixture of air and water is the cause, it is well rendered; but nevertheless is this the form of whiteness? No; but it is the efficient [cause], which is ever the *vehiculum formae*" (Bacon, 1952, p. 44). It is even more important to observe that final causes were considered far less acceptable to natural science explanation than formal causes. Since final causes deal with "that for the sake of which" something exists (a stereo system, or an "act" of behavior), there is an implication here of intentions, purposes, or goals toward which the item being described is moving, striving, or trying to fulfill. In his *Physics,* for example, Aristotle theorized that leaves exist for the purpose of providing shade for the fruit on trees, and he concluded thereby: "that nature is a cause, a cause that operates for a purpose" (1952, pp. 276–277).

Bacon argued that one settles for nonscientific explanations when he tries to find the "goal" (final cause) of natural structures: for example, if one were to claim that "the bones are for [have the goal of] the columns or beams, whereupon the frames of the bodies of living creatures are built . . ." (Bacon, 1952, p. 45). Bones do not have it as their "aim" to hold up the muscles and flesh of our bodies and it adds nothing to our knowledge of bones to claim that they do. This form of teleological or intentional analysis of nature had become customary in the Middle Ages, due to the tendency for theologians (scholastics) to ascribe intentions to physical matter by way of showing God's hand at play in nature (deity teleology). Thus, it was *God's* intention that the bones provide a structure for the frame of the body. Bacon was in revolt against such *proofs* of a deity and such use of final cause arguments, as was Voltaire in a more satirical vein, when he had the "meta-physico-theologo-cosmolo-nigologist" *Pangloss* teach his young charge, *Candide,* that: "everything is made for an end . . . noses were made to wear spectacles; and so we have spectacles" (Voltaire, 1930, p. 14).

Bacon feared that if men of science accepted formal and final causes as explanatory they would not go forth and actively seek empirical knowledge through experimentation. To experiment is to ask a question different from "What is the form or the purpose of this object?" To experiment is to ask, "What brings about this state of affairs?" The latter is a question best answered in efficient cause terms, and this is the attitude which Bacon and the other British Empiricists helped fix as the proper one for a natural science. They limited theoretical explanation to material and efficient causes, and natural science has continued in this vein. Formal and final cause explanations were to be used only in ethical and/or metaphysical argument, in itself a legitimate and worthwhile activity though not suited to science. This is at least one of the reasons scientists have always contended that their form of study was not involved with ethical matters. Ethics went to final causes in getting at purposes. Science must content itself with efficient (and material) causes.

THE HUMANIST'S PROBLEM

The reader can now easily see how the Lockean model and the efficient cause in modern natural science evolved an impossible situation for those theorists who wish to describe man in "humanistic" terms. Whether the humanist makes it clear or not, his argument is against the complete reliance on material and efficient causes in the description of man the actor. He wants to re-introduce the meanings included in formal and final causality. He agrees that it is wrong to "anthropomorphize" inanimate nature (deity teleology) or the behavior of lower animals, but he can find little rationale for fearing to anthropomorphize the "anthro" (human teleology). The Kantian model of an active intellect making use of certain categories and ideas of reason (formal and final causes) organizes rationality and thereby influences behavior and is much preferred as a model for man.

The psychologist who seeks a "natural science" explanation of man hopes to account for all of man's behavior in terms of efficient causes, among which, of course, the S-R conceptualization is the most eminent example. The strategy of theoretical explanation is therefore to cite the "frequency of occurrence" of *this* form of reinforcement over *that* form of reinforcement. There is some difficulty here in defining just what "reinforcement" means—whether it can be reduced further to some physical satisfaction or can operate empirically on its own weight—but a mathematical frequency explanation is the typical gambit settled for. As Margaret Floy Washburn early noted in her Presidential Address to the APA: "The whole behavioristic theory of learning rests . . . upon kinaesthesis. . . . It reduces all forms of association to habit, and habit means such a linking of nervous pathways that the performance of one movement stimulates . . . the next movement in the series" (1922, p. 110). This "series" of discrete units which can be mathematically estimated is the modern counterpart of Locke's simple ideas, flowing along in efficient cause-to-effect fashion.

There is also an attempt among physiological-medical psychologists to reduce behavior to a substrate of material causes. These theorists would argue that a physical "something" must be shown to exist in behavior before a truly scientific account has been rendered. Of course, pushed another step, we return to the efficient cause reliance because as both Wundt and Helmholtz helped establish in psychology, ultimately matter breaks down into energy, simple forces, and motion (Rychlak, 1968, p. 222). This is why our physiological behavioristic psychologists find it easy to live with one another: They both rely on a fundamental Lockean model and accept only material and efficient cause explanation.

In this game of science the humanist stands on the sidelines. He tries to capture such "mystical" and supposedly irrelevant "mental" qualities of human behavior as choice, hypothesis, aspiration, creativity, and transcendence. How is he to do this in a game written on Lockean rules and limited to the moves of efficient and material causation?

THE BEHAVIORIST'S PROBLEM

Fortunately enough, the behaviorist theorist is not without some problems of his own. In attempting to subsume the four meanings of the Aristotelian causes, or at least three of the four under *one* term (efficient cause), he must inevitably put up with an annoying circularity in explaining how he changes behavior. In psychotherapy, for example, if the client improves it is the result of positive reinforcement (or its converse, the removal of a negative reinforcement) engendered by the therapist. But if the client *does not* improve, then here, too, according to the theory it is a positive reinforcement which keeps him neurotic, one which the therapist is unable to circumvent or "extinguish." In his *formal theory*, therefore, whether a person improves or does not improve is explained in identical fashion. In order to make explicit just why some clients actually *do* improve, the behaviorist must invoke all manner of *informal* meaningful comments outside his formal theory, meanings which historically have accrued to the causal constructs no longer in vogue. For example, what makes a therapist's "reinforcements" more positive or "better" than the reinforcements which sustain the neurotic condition? Can frequency of sessions (reinforcements) alone account for the procedure which we actually see taking place in the consulting room? We doubt it, and now wish to make our point in various ways by turning to the behaviorist's theory of cure.

THE EFFICIENT CAUSE THEORY OF CURE

In reading a "behavior therapy" case history, one is struck by just how much goes unsaid in the theory of cure actually advanced. A typical case of this sort might be as follows: a young boy who refuses to speak is brought to a behavior therapist. The latter explains to the child (though he may not) that they will be spending an hour together two or more times per week, either in a play room or simply "hanging around" his office. The child is not pressured in any way to speak, but with each slight move in this direction, he is slipped a piece of candy, or possibly a white-colored plastic chip which he learns at the end of the hour can be exchanged for candy. One grunt or one throat clearing brings one white chip. At the end of the hour, the accrued wealth (reinforcements) is carted off. The next session brings a repetition of this process (mounting frequency of reinforcement), and if perchance there is a word mentioned two or three white chips are presented (increasing level of reinforcement). Often, a method of turning ten white chips in for one red chip is worked out, and five red chips bring a model airplane at the end of that wonderful hour when real change has taken place. And so it goes, until with a little luck and perseverance the child comes away from his supposedly efficiently caused cure a veritable chatter-box.

One more example: an adult comes to the behavior therapist complaining of a fear he has. He is struck with terror each time he must enter a reasonably crowded room. He has avoided seeing anyone about his fear, even though it has probably nagged him to a greater or lesser extent for years, but now it is so unbearable that he is prepared to risk the label of "neurotic" or worse to have relief. The therapist reassures him that he can be helped if he cooperates, asks him some general questions, and then in time establishes the fact that his fears are not limited to this one situation. It is shown that, actually, he has a hierarchy of such feared situations, stretching from most to least severe. Together, therapist and client work out a schedule for relaxation exercises, and after some practice in how to relax (positive response which acts like a positive reinforcement when it gets substituted for an anxiety response), they begin ascending this hierarchy of fear-provoking situations. Gradually, with the help of hypnosis or merely client imagination to put him in the various situations, a progressively favorable outcome is effected as the client learns to substitute this relaxation-response for his anxiety response (Wolpe, 1958). If this client had gone to another type of behavior therapist, he might have found himself—rather than being relaxed up to the worst possible life situation gradually—being plunged into this situation from the outset with the help of a descriptive rendering from the therapist on the belief that an extinction of negative reinforcement was being accomplished, which is the other side of the coin to being positively reinforced. (Stampfl, 1967).

Whether through the direct effect of a positive reinforcement in the child's therapy (Skinnerian), the substitution of a positively sensed response for a negatively sensed response in the adult's fear hierarchy (Wolpian), or conversely, the extinction of a fear response by going directly to the maximum fear-producing situation (Stampflian), all of our clients do in fact show a "cure." Something has changed their "pattern of behavior," and the behavioral therapist characteristically expresses this in efficient cause terms. It all depends upon getting the right kind of reinforcement alignment in the flow of discrete "cause-effect" habit sequences. Behavior "for the sake" of some personal-identity factor is presumably not in the picture. The humanist is often steeped in Freudian, Jungian, or Rogerian concepts, but as theoreticians we must surely grasp that a more *fundamental* confrontation is at play here.

The writer would contend that the *real* issue centers upon whether or not formal and final cause analysis of the client's behavior would add anything to the theories of cure now being advanced by the behavior therapists. The "facts" of supposed white-chip reinforcements, or so-called "hierarchies of response" or "implosions" are not forced on us as the *necessary* explanations of what is actually occurring. Indeed, as we know from other sciences and the philosophy of science, for any fact pattern at play before our eyes there are in principle "N" potential explanations (Rychlak, 1968, p. 118).

Since the advent of Dollard & Miller (1950) it has been fashionable in psychology to translate the more conventional personality constructs of Freud and others into "S-R terms." Psychologists actually believe that in doing so the meanings of Freud's (formal and final cause) constructs are retained in the translation. We would now like to reverse the process, in a sense, and argue that S-R therapies are unable to capture the full meaning of why people get "changed" or "cured." We accuse them of making *informal* use of constructs having the meanings subsumed in formal and final cause terms, while appearing to remain in an efficient cause type of description. We thus now invoke a theory of four causes, subsuming S-R logic under one of these four, and wish to show how it is not only profitable but scientifically necessary to begin thinking of human behavior as something more rich and complex than can be conceived of on the Lockean-efficient cause tandem now in academic vogue.

Now, though our behavior therapist does not include such features in his formal theory, what are we to make of the planned schedules, the hierarchies, and the great stress he places on the future in his technique of treatment?

Though admirably parsimonious, this theoretical strategy has been found wanting in certain pseudo-therapeutic research strategies. Choosing just one area—of verbal conditioning—and though we recognize that not all of the findings are in line, surely the preponderance of the evidence now being cited implies that learning (supposed "control" by the experimenter) either does not take place, or else it is greatly hindered when the subject cannot voice the response-reinforcement contingency (Dulany, 1961, 1962; DeNike, 1964; DeNike and Spielberger, 1963).

If we can assume that the child is like the verbal learning subject—i.e., that he is seeking to find the major ground rule on the basis of which his therapist is giving him candies or white chips—then what is being learned may be more akin to a Kantian formal cause (the therapist's "plan" of reinforcements) than a Lockean efficient cause. Teaching a child that ten white chips can bring one red chip, and five red chips can bring an airplane may seem marvelously efficient from the therapist's extraspective perspective, but introspectively this is the sort of goal setting and life aspiring strategy that all manner of classical psychotherapies have tried to encourage clients to engage in. It is instruction along a final and not along an efficient cause dimension of behavior. And how is it possible for an intellect which merely retains past responses to erect a *hierarchy* of (feared or otherwise) situations? It takes an *evaluating intellect* to array a hierarchy, does it not? Bacon wanted man's evaluating intellect diverted somewhat to ethics and aesthetics, but he never denied that man did, after all, have such an ability to frame a principle (formal cause) "for the sake of which" (final cause) it could evaluate "good" vs. "bad" or "most" vs. "least." It is not even essential that the behavior therapist establish in third person (extraspective) form that this hierarchy is *really* arrayed properly. Just so this hierarchy is what the client *thinks* is the proper rank-ordering, therapy can proceed to take him through the successively difficult tasks. He works for a self-created goal, builds for his future with the help of an effective, didactic technique.

One of the clearest indications of a final cause meaning in any theory emerges when we begin to speak of an orientation toward the future (hypotheses, intentions, etc.). An animal which can extend its life into the future, or which can immerse its identity in a "possibility" of the Stampflian variety is surely not to be circumscribed in solely efficient cause terms. It seems to the writer that the major success of behavior therapy stems from this pragmatic approach it takes to the future. The client, who already has initiated the process when he decided to take the first step to a therapist's door, is brought along methodically to achieve the desired goal with planning, persistent effort, and self-conscious direction.

If the humanistic psychologist could see in behavior therapy a hidden *affirmation* rather than a negation of the image of man he supports, then some of his more unreasoned rejections of behavior therapy would be mitigated. He has to recognize that Wolpe and the Skinnerians teach their clients that plans can be put into effect, that neurotic behavior is not immutable, and that persistence pays off. Stampfl brings his clients up short with "What's the worst that can possibly happen?" and in this examination of future alternatives, extracts the affective over-evaluation which the client has been running away from.

Freud (1963) had taught his clients that their present behaviors were re-enactments (prototypes, formal causes) of their childhood, and thereby indirectly challenged them to live by altered patterns in the present ("insight" via formal-final causes). Today, we see Ellis attacking his clients' major premises, coming more directly to the point of "that for the sake of which" they approach life on daily (Ellis, 1964, p. 304). Kelly advocated the same tactic, except that he referred to his Kantian-like premises as "personal constructs" (1955). It is the same strategy in Adlerian life style terms (1964), or in the Jungian teleological challenge to balance the four points of our psychic compass (1954). And we need not dwell on the self-directing, phenomenological qualities of Rogerian therapy (1951). Attack the categories of reason, major premises, life plan or style; experience the "self-image" (formal cause) in a new way; or, create for the first time a solid basis on which to confront life, and you will effect a satisfying state of affairs for the human identity within which a life is being acted out.

We might observe at this point that modern theories which view abnormality in terms of value disruption (Frankl, 1963), ethico-religious involvement (Mowrer, 1961), or even "rules of the game" deterioration (Szasz, 1961) are all in the spirit of formal and final causation. Mental illness is properly seen as a failure to find one's way in life, a failure to come up onto the future (teleology), rather than being a mechanistic preservation of the unhappy experiences of the past. It is impossible fully to theorize in such ways if we limit our meanings to the material and efficient cause tactic of the Lockean model. Such limits came to the physical sciences for good reasons, but are presently retained in the social sciences for bad reasons.

The writer is fully cognizant of the charges levelled against those who wish to add the formal and final to the material and efficient causes now in scientific vogue. At the very least, we are called muddleheaded by our critics. Yet, once out of the laboratory, the very same critic often speaks informally about how things meet his reinforcement history, or how he would like to gain more positive reinforcements in life (more "cookies" is the usual term). In one debate he carried on with a prominent behavior therapist, the writer advanced the causation arguments already reviewed above, to no great success as the audience was apparently behavioristic in outlook (or so it seemed, based upon the "cookies" sent the writer's way in the form of applause). After the debate, the behavior therapist engaged the writer in a few off-hand remarks to the effect: "You seem to be wanting to bring back superstitions that we were able to remove from psychology, with good riddance, a few generations back." This reference to teleology (free will, and no doubt gods and goblins) was taken with the greatest effort at personal equanimity, but the writer could not help pointing out that the behaviorist was ascribing final causes to his opponent informally which he had denied in all men formally during the debate. This sort of "winking" at language usage outside the laboratory or off the lectern is a favorite sport among the extraspective behaviorist camp (see Skinner, 1957, p. 460). But in all honesty: *how scientifically unbiased is it?*

It is only the press of experimental *and* clinical experience over time which can be said to alter theoretical vogues. This is a *theoretical* issue fundamentally, but it is responsive to the demands of long-standing experience. We have tried to show in this paper that the reason we wish to once again apply the full range of Aristotle's theory of knowledge is because it does meet with our growing understanding of *human* behavior. The challenge now is for the humanist to spell out in experimental terms all of those features of human behavior which are to him important, and which do not lend themselves to a Lockean, frequency interpretation. It is folly simply to re-interpret the findings of others. For the lover of truth, for those psychotherapists who want to come up to the standards of scientific validation yet study the "person" they know themselves to be, the theoretical tools are now available as they have been for centuries. The need is here. Let us not balk at the jibes of those who "do" much but understand little.

REFERENCES

Adler, A. *Problems of neurosis* (edited by Philippe Mairet). New York: Harper & Row, 1964.

Aristotle. In Vol. 8 of R. M. Hutchins (Ed.), *Great books of the western world.* Chicago: Encyclopedia Britannica, 1952.

Physics, Pp. 257–355.

Posterior analytics, Pp. 95–137.

Bacon, F. *Advancement of learning.* In. Vol. 30 of R. M. Hutchins (Ed.), *Great books of the western world.* Chicago: Encyclopedia Britannica, 1952. Pp. 1–101.

DeNike, L. The temporal relationship between awareness and performance in verbal conditioning. *Journal of Experimental Psychology,* 1964, **68,** 521–529.

DeNike, L. & Spielberger, C. Induced mediating states in verbal conditioning. *Journal of Verbal Learning and Verbal Behavior,* 1963, **1,** 339–345.

Dollard, J. & Miller, N.E. *Personality and psychotherapy: An analysis in terms of learning, thinking, and culture.* New York: McGraw-Hill, 1950.

Dulany, D. E., Jr. Hypotheses and habits in verbal "operant conditioning." *Journal of Abnormal and Social Psychology,* 1961, **63,** 251–263.

Dulany, D. E., Jr. The place of hypotheses and intentions: An analysis of verbal control in verbal conditioning. In C. W. Eriksen (Ed.), *Behavior and awareness.* Durham: Duke University Press, 1962, Pp. 102–129.

Ellis, A. Rational psychotherapy. In H. J. Eysenck (Ed.), *Experiments in behavior therapy.* New York, The Macmillan Co., 1964. Pp. 287–323.

Frankl, V. E. *Man's search for meaning: An introduction to logotherapy.* New York: Washington Square Press, 1963.

Freud, S. *Introductory lectures on psycho-analysis.* Part III: *General theory of the neuroses* (1915–1917). Vol. XVI of J. Strachey (Ed.), *The standard edition of the complete psychological works of Sigmund Freud.* London: The Hogarth Press, 1963.

Jung, C. G. *The practice of psychotherapy.* Vol. 16 of H. Read, M. Fordham, and G. Adler (Eds.), *The collected works of* C. G. *Jung.* Bollingen Series XX, 16, New York: Pantheon Books, London: Routledge & Kegan Paul, 1954.

Kant, I. *The critique of pure reason.* In Vol. 42 of R. M. Hutchins (Ed.), *Great books of the western world.* Chicago: Encyclopedia Britannica, 1952. Pp. 1–250.

Kelly, G. A. *The psychology of personal constructs.* Vol. 1. *A theory of personality.* New York: W. W. Norton, 1955.

Locke, J. *An essay concerning human understanding.* In Vol. 35 of R. M. Hutchins (Ed.), *Great Books of the western world.* Chicago: Encyclopedia Britannica, 1952. Pp. 85–395.

Mowrer, O. H. *The crisis in psychiatry and religion.* New York: D. Van Nostrand, 1961.

Rogers, C. R. *Client-centered therapy.* Boston: Houghton Mifflin Co., 1951.

Rychlak, J. F. The motives to psychotherapy. *Psychotherapy,* 1965, **2,** 151–157.

Rychlak, J. F. *A philosophy of science for personality theory.* Boston: Houghton Mifflin Co., 1968.

Skinner, B. F. *Verbal behavior.* New York: Appleton-Century-Crofts, 1957.

Stampfl, T. G., & Levis, D. J. Essentials of implosive therapy: A learning-theory-based psychodynamic behavioral therapy. *Journal of Abnormal Psychology,* 1967, 496–503.

Szasz, T. S. *The myth of mental illness.* New York: Hoeber-Harper, 1961.

Voltaire, F. M. A. *Candide.* New York: J. J. Little & Ives, 1930.

Washburn, Margaret Floy. Introspection as an objective method. *Psychological Review,* 1922, **29,** 89–112.

Wolpe, J. *Psychotherapy by reciprocal inhibition.* Stanford, Calif.: Stanford University Press, 1958.

19

HERMENEUTIC INQUIRY IN THE STUDY OF HUMAN CONDUCT

MARTIN J. PACKER

In recent years there has been increased questioning of the notion that research in psychology is, or can be, value free. More specifically, there is a growing interest in and curiosity about interpretive or hermeneutic research (e.g., Giddens, 1976; Hookway & Pettit, 1978; Rabinow & Sullivan, 1979). Psychologists are showing a growing appreciation of the limitations of both causal empiricist and formal rationalist types of explanation, and hermeneutic theory and methodology can make significant contributions as an alternative paradigm (cf. Bernstein, 1983). My purpose here is to explicate the conceptual background of the hermeneutic approach.

Although hermeneutics is an ancient discipline (Palmer, 1969), its relevance to the human sciences in general, and to psychology in particular, stems largely from the work of Martin Heidegger. In his seminal work, *Being and Time,* Heidegger (1927/1962) proposed that the hermeneutic method is the appropriate approach for the study of human action. Many recent commentators on hermeneutics have relied on the writings of Hans-Georg Gadamer (1975). Gadamer was a student of Heidegger but differed from his mentor in significant ways. Most important, Gadamer failed to maintain Heidegger's distinctions among the practical, reflective, and theoretical modes of engagement. (Heidegger called them the ready-to-hand, unready-to-hand, and present-at-hand). As a consequence, some of the critiques of hermeneutics that have taken Gadamer's work as definitive (e.g., Habermas, 1977) cannot be regarded as final, nor can the claims by essentially rationalist psychologists that they are doing hermeneutics (e.g.,

Reprinted from the *American Psychologist, 40,* 1081–1093. (1985).

The author gratefully acknowledges helpful comments and suggestions made on a draft of this article by three anonymous reviewers.

Kohlberg, Levine, & Hewer, 1983). To understand hermeneutics, even if then to critique it, requires some familiarity with Heidegger's work.

Recent writers (Blasi, 1980; Locke, 1983) have noted that psychology lacks a method for studying the structure or organization of human action. As Locke (1983) wrote, "It is quite unclear how physical behavior, as such, can have a cognitive structure" (p. 14). The hermeneutic approach can make a particularly valuable contribution because it provides a way of understanding and studying action that is grounded in considering such action as having a semantic rather than a logical or causal organization. Human action is a complex and ambiguous phenomenon. An observer of a social interaction does not have direct, unproblematic access to the unambiguous "meaning" of the acts taking place, because people act in a situation that an observer does not share fully; furthermore they themselves do not comprehend all the pertinent aspects of their own actions. Any act, looked at in isolation from its situation, is likely to be ambiguous to the point of opacity or obscurity. For these reasons, a methodology for the study of action must be specifically tailored to its intricacies and peculiarities. The hermeneutic paradigm takes as its starting point the fact that, despite the ambiguities, any observer has a preliminary practical understanding of what the people studied are "up to." The broad outlines and the theoretical justification of such a methodology have been discussed recently by many writers, though the particular conception I shall describe here cannot be attributed to any specific writer (e.g., Bleicher, 1980; de Rivera, 1981; Gauld & Shotter, 1977; Giddens, 1976; Hookway & Pettit, 1978; McCarthy, 1978; Palmer, 1969; Polkinghorne, 1983; Rabinow & Sullivan, 1979; Ricoeur, 1976; E. V. Sullivan, n.d.).

WHAT IS HERMENEUTICS?

Heidegger proposed that hermeneutic phenomenology is the method of investigation most appropriate to the study of human action. This method is an innovative development of the phenomenology of Edmund Husserl (e.g., 1931). Hermeneutics involves an attempt to describe and study meaningful human phenomena in a careful and detailed manner as free as possible from prior theoretical assumptions, based instead on practical understanding. What is meant by practical understanding will become clearer later. Heidegger's method is "hermeneutic" because there is a need for interpretation when one is explicating experience. Hermeneutics was originally a set of techniques for interpreting written texts. Initially it was developed for the examination of biblical texts, carried out to uncover and reconstruct the message from God that it was believed the texts contained but that had become hidden (the term refers to Hermes, messenger of the Greek gods, and himself god of eloquence and cunning as well as of roads and theft). Later it became generalized to a method of textual interpretation that was not restricted to religious works. With Schleiermacher and Dilthey, it was generalized still further to apply also to human action (cf. Palmer, 1969). When we adopt a hermeneutic approach to human action, we essentially treat the action as though it has a semantic and "textual" structure. This different understanding of the nature of the "object" of inquiry is one of several differences between hermeneutics and the two currently dominant paradigms of investigation and explanation in the social sciences and in psychology in particular: the rationalist and the empiricist approaches. These differences are the topic of the body of this article.

We can best appreciate the character of the hermeneutic approach by comparing and contrasting it with these two other paradigms. Within rationalism lie structuralism and much of cognitive science; empiricism includes behaviorism and positivist experimentalism. I will contrast these three paradigms in three areas: their assumptions about the nature and origin of knowledge, the kind of object they set out to study, and the type of explanation they seek.

THE ORIGIN OF KNOWLEDGE

Rationalism

The various forms of rationalist inquiry have a common view of the nature and source of knowledge: one that applies to both scientific research and ordinary activity. "Theorizing" is taken as primary for the generation of knowledge: An individual comes to know and act in the world through hypothesis generation and hypothesis testing. This is a central tenet of Piaget's genetic epistemology, for example. Even the sensorimotor intelligence of infancy, which precedes and grounds later operational and theoretical intelligence, proceeds, according to Piaget, by forms of trial and error that are equivalent to scientific experimentation in their basic motivation: the instrumental control of the environment.

Although this has a prima facie validity for logicomathematical knowledge, stucturalists generally consider that the social world becomes known in the same way. For example, Turiel (1983) maintained that

> social development is a process by which individuals generate understandings of the social world, by *making inferences and forming theories* about experienced social events. . . . The starting point [for cognitive–developmental research] is the premise that through their social experiences children develop ways of thinking, or *theories,* about the social world. . . . In coming to understand social systems, *people act like social scientists, attempting to observe regularities and explain their existence.* (pp. 1–2, emphasis added)

This position has its origins with Kant's transcendental idealism. Kant argued that human knowledge is governed by a set of a priori conditions that determine what can count as an "object" for the human mind. This conception that there are transcendental conditions that structure experience had its influences on Heidegger, but Kant adopted the additional, unargued claim that the a priori structures, the forms of representation, are essentially logical ones: categories, rules, concepts, and principles. For example, according to Kant (1977), "This thought space [i.e., the propositions of geometry] renders possible the physical space [of everyday experience]" (p. 32).

Not only is knowledge essentially deductive in the rationalist paradigm, but an increase or development of knowledge is viewed as proceeding in a logical manner. Both Chomsky (1959) and Piaget (1970) theorized that invariant developmental sequences stem from the inherent logic of the structures guiding theorizing activity, whether they are conceptualized as logicomathematical schemes or as grammar-acquisition devices. The cognitivist notion of "learning procedures" similarly postulates formal procedures that, through information exchange with the environment, generate new internal structures corresponding to a new organization of knowledge. On such an account, knowledge is procedural and is arrived at through processes of theorizing or logical analysis.

Empiricism

According to the empiricist paradigm, in contrast, the grounding of knowledge for both investigator and human subject is provided by "brute data" observables. These "data" are considered to be facts about the world that can be identified and recorded in a manner free from interpretation. Within this paradigm, a key component of scientific inquiry is theory-free "data collection," which is considered prior to and logically independent of theory construction. In the human subject, a similar passive accretion of knowledge is held to take place. This passive view of knowledge is now commonly rejected as a model of an organism's functioning, but it continues to have an underground currency nonetheless, in an odd partnership with a version of rationalism. Computer models of human thought and behavior rely on the notion that there are atomistic "facts" about the world ("bits" of information and features and elements of categories) together with the view that knowledge is produced by means of formal processes. In information-processing models of speech, memory, and perception, context-free information is retrieved from storage or collected from input transducers and then is combined and manipulated by formal procedures.

Hermeneutics

In hermeneutic inquiry and the ontology that grounds it, the primary origin of knowledge is taken to be practical activity: direct, everyday practical involvement with tools, artifacts, and people. Such activity exists prior to any theorizing and has a character distinct from the latter. Most notably, it involves no context-free elements definable in the absence of interpretation. Practical activity also need not be (though it often is) instrumentally motivated. To lay out the hermeneutic interpretation of practical activity more fully—and it is a crucial aspect of interpretive inquiry—I will introduce Heidegger's notion of modes of engagement.

The modes of engagement. Heidegger distinguished three distinct, though interrelated, modes of engagement or involvement that people have with their surroundings: the ready-to-hand, the unready-to-hand, and the present-at-hand modes.

The *ready-to-hand* mode of engagement is, for Heidegger, the basic one. This is the mode we are in when we are actively engaged in practical projects in the world, such as mailing a letter, talking to a friend, or, to use Heidegger's favorite example, using a hammer. When we carry out such activities, our awareness is essentially holistic: We are aware of the situation we find ourselves in, not as an arrangement of discrete physical objects and not as a portion of the physical universe, but globally, as a whole network of interrelated projects, possible tasks, thwarted potentialities, and so forth. This network is not laid out explicitly, but it is present as a "background" to the project we are concerned with, and we can turn to aspects of the network and bring them into focus. There is no deliberate means–ends planning in this mode; indeed, any tools we may be using (and our own body) are not experienced as distinct entities that could be set into a means–ends framework: They "withdraw" in a special manner. When we are involved in ongoing practical activity, we have no need for focal awareness of ourselves and our tools: Both become fused into the activity. Our experience is not of the hammer, nor of the wood and nails as independent entities, but of the hammering, the raising of the wall, the constructing of a home.

The manner in which these aspects of a project are experienced is in turn structured by the personal and historical situation they are part of, so they are not "objectified," either. Our experience alters as our needs change, and as our emotions structure and restructure our activity in the ready-to-hand mode. It is characteristic of practical activity that we are always already in a situation that, in turn, is structured by the concerns our action expresses. This relationship is not circular so much as it is a tailored fit: If my concern is to catch a train, my situation is organized so that aspects relevant to my concern stand out. The train station becomes salient, as does the time; trains run according to a schedule. Means of transportation stand forth, and I may start to experience the town in which I live in terms of shortest routes, one-way streets, blocks, and free-flowing traffic. My action, also, will manifest my concern in obvious ways: I will be searching for timetables, packing my suitcase, and checking my tickets. My emotion fits, too: I may be flustered and rushed, sad at the prospect of leaving, or excited at what is to come. My action and my situation fit each other, structured on the one hand by my concerns and on the other hand by social and personal styles and habitual practices.

The skills and practices we bring to our everyday activity are, for the most part, so overpracticed and familiar to us, so taken for granted, that we are simply unaware of their existence. We act within them, and they rarely, if ever, become problematic. We are not even aware of our ignorance of them. Indeed, if we *were* aware of them we would be overwhelmed and unable to continue to act. When driving a car, one very occasionally becomes explicitly aware of the various skills one is putting into practice: shifting gears, engaging and disengaging the clutch, glancing in the mirror, and so on. When this happens, one's performance deteriorates rapidly. Generally, it is only when we reflect on what we are doing, prompted usually by confronting a problem, that we begin to see the network of interrelated practices, skills, and habits that supports all our apparently simple everyday actions.

The *unready-to-hand* mode is entered when we encounter some problem or upset in our practical activity. Perhaps we try to mail a letter and discover that the mailbox has been knocked down, or we have to struggle for the appropriate phrase in a conversation. Our experience changes as we become aware that there is a problem and then recognize something of its nature. The source of the breakdown of action now suddenly becomes salient, in a way it was not in the ready-to-hand mode. This source is still seen, however, as an aspect of the project we are involved in, rather than as a context-free object. For example, my hammer may prove too heavy for the task I am engaged in. Its "weightiness" becomes salient whereas before it was transparent; but I am not aware of the objective "weight" of the hammer (so many pounds), only that it is "too heavy" to do its appointed job successfully. Experience in the unready-to-hand mode has a structure analogous to the figure–ground structure the Gestalt school found in visual experience: Particular aspects of the whole situation stand out but only against a background provided by the project we are engaged in and the interests and involvements guiding it (cf. de Rivera, 1976).

The *present-at-hand* mode is entered only when we detach ourselves from ongoing practical involvement in a project at hand, usually because we have been unable to find a direct and circumspect way of dealing with a problem that arose. On such occasions we have to "step back," reflect, and turn to more general and abstract (i.e., situation-independent) tools such as logical analysis and calculation in order to solve the problem. At this point our experience changes its character yet again, and we now become aware of, for example, the hammer as an independent entity, removed from all tasks we might pursue by its means, and as endowed with discrete and definite measurable properties, such as a mass, a weight, and a material. These properties are distinct from the situated aspects that characterize the unready-to-hand level, such as the hammer's heaviness.

The ready-to-hand mode, then, gives us the most primordial and direct access to human phenomena. The kind of access of the ready-to-hand mode—emotions, habitual practices, and skills—is radically distinct from the access to phenomena provided by theoretical reflection: "The ready-to-hand is not grasped theoretically at all" (Heidegger, 1927/1962, p. 99). People both constitute and are constituted by cultural and bodily skills and practices with which they make tacit connection in their everyday activities. Heidegger devoted much of his energy in *Being and Time* to beginning a positive account (a hermeneutic interpretation) of the ready-to-hand mode. Because this is the mode of direct practical engagement in which we actually do much of our everyday living, this task amounts, for him, to the same as describing *human being*; and this being is itself a practical activity, rather than a special kind of entity or a formal predicate. This leads us to the question of what the character is of the proper object of inquiry in the study of action.

THE NATURE OF THE OBJECT OF STUDY

Rationalism

Structuralist inquiry explicitly isolates a special object of investigation. For example, de Saussure (1966) declared that language as an abstract system (*la langue*) was the focus of interest, not the speech of individuals in actual settings (*la parole*). Chomsky and Piaget have made equivalent moves; Chomsky (1957) distinguished the linguistic competence of an idealized speaker-hearer from actual language performance and identified the former as the proper object of study. Piaget (1970) traced intelligence as the construction of structures of growing abstraction and reversibility.

These research programs began with a deliberate neglect of the role and relevance of the context of occasions of actual performance. Much effort has been spent since then in trying to reconnect the abstract structures with actual speech and action, with little success. Structuralist linguists have tried to say how syntactic and semantic rules actually work in practice. Cognitive scientists have tried to mimic everyday understanding with rules and "scripts" (Schank & Abelson, 1970; Winograd, 1972). Both have been singularly lacking in success. Specific talk and action evade the rationalist approach, because once the methodological move is made of abstracting a system of formal rules from human action, an unbridgeable and artificial gulf appears between the two. The distinction between competence and performance is an artificial but inevitable consequence of the structuralist approach, and so it cannot be investigated from within that paradigm.

Empiricism

Behaviorism and experimentalism do, on the other hand, focus directly on the interaction of organism and environment, but this interaction is regarded merely as the mechanical interplay of causal forces. The object of study here is a physical system, which operates through relations of cause and effect. Underlying this assumption is in turn a view that phenomena are constituted of isolable elements, which mingle and impinge upon each other but which can in principle be observed in isolation. *Variables* can be independently manipulated; *stimuli* are organism-independent properties of the physical environment, and so forth.

These two sets of presuppositions about the object of inquiry can be clearly seen in the way action has been regarded in the moral development literature. Blasi (1980) recently reviewed research on moral action and in doing so distinguished two conceptions, that acts have *material causes* and that they have *formal reasons*. These two correspond to behaviorist and social-learning approaches on the one hand, and cognitivist and constructivist approaches on the other. The first of the two—the behaviorist, empiricist paradigm—holds that action (actually *behavior*, for human action and physical movement are barely distinguished here) is the immediate result of causal forces. Causal entities (such as habits) and traits (such as personality variables and IQ) are assumed to operate in such a way that the resulting action is automatic and objectively determined. An act is the causal outcome of the mechanistic interaction of elemental, objective properties of the setting and the person. It is arational, the automatically caused outcome of mechanistic processes. The stimulus and response account of classical behaviorism is the most obvious version of such a theory, but a similar view is found in the classical work on moral character by Hartshorne and May (1928), as well as in more recent research, such as that by Mischel and Mischel (1976).

The cognitive, rationalist paradigm, on the other hand, maintains that action is the result of rational and logical procedures. Action is mediated by cognitive processes such as reasoning, categorization, and evaluation, and cognition is necessarily involved behind and before action in the creation of meaning and the determination of truth. Action itself is essentially rational: Meanings are constructed by the logical evaluation of means and ends, based on information about the truth or falsehood of statements about the world. Action is determined, in the same way that a conclusion is determined from a set of premises, or a sentence from a set of grammatical and semantic rules. Situations are evaluated by the application of rules and principles, and the outcome of this process of appraisal determines the action to be performed. Piaget's account of action is of this general form; Broughton (1981) summarized it in the following terms: "Action [is] the rational outcome of truth-oriented and reality-oriented judgments of facts and means/ends relationships" (p. 275).

Kohlberg's latest account of moral action is essentially the same:

> Moral action results from a three-step process. The first step is the making of a deontic judgment of rightness or justice in the situation. The second step is the making of a judgment that the self is responsible or accountable for carrying out this deontic judgment in the moral situation. The third step is carrying it out. (Kohlberg, Levine, & Hewer, 1983, p. 48)

Here again, theoretical judgments, based on rational assessments, are assumed to underly action that is simply "carried out" after its formal character has been planned.

Both the empiricist and the rationalist views can be criticized on three counts. First, they fail to provide a convincing description of more than a small number of actions; they represent extreme cases. Although we might all prefer to think that we always reflect and act rationally and logically, evaluating each situation that confronts us in a principled manner, this is only sometimes the case. It happens only when we have the time and ability to sit back and evaluate with detachment our situation and alternate courses of action. But when we do this, we have the special kind of involvement characteristic of the present-at-hand mode. And equally, we infrequently find our behavior caused simply by objective features of the environment: Sneezes, yawns, and other reflexes seem to exhaust this category. Again, it is possible to see everyday action this way only when one removes oneself from it as an active agent. The vast majority of our actions—all the interesting cases, I think—are characterized by the ready-to-hand and unready-to-hand modes rather than by the physical causation and logical determination that reflect the present-at-hand way of seeing things.

Second, both accounts misrepresent and over-simplify the relations that exist among an agent, his or her action, and an observer of that action. Behaviorism proceeds as though an observer has direct, transparent, and unproblematic perception of elements of behavior and can identify and record them objectively, without interpretation. Cognitivists have rightly criticized this view, but they make an equivalent mistake. Chomsky (1959) argued against the possibility of any simple, objective identification of behavior, because "one would naturally expect that prediction of the behavior of a complex organism (or machine) would require . . . knowledge of the internal structure of the organism, the ways in which it processes input information and organizes its own behavior" (p. 13). However, when Chomsky discussed grammars and the rules that *generate* behavior, he assumed that action is a direct and transparent manifestation of an underlying conceptualization or representation: a "deep structure" in the case of transformational theories of language behavior. So, although Chomsky granted that an observer must make inferences about hidden structure in order to study behavior, the agent's knowledge itself is taken to be organized in a formal, transparent, and unambiguous manner, like a computer program. Such an account has no place for all the peculiar phenomena having to do with agents' knowledge of their own actions: phenomena as complex as weakness of the will, self-deception, and akrasia, and as simple and commonplace as the ambiguity and polysemy to interpretation that every action shows.

Third, behaviorism and cognitivism have a common, inadequate conception of the nature of the world, of how reality is given to us. Dreyfus (1979) summarized this ontological assumption as follows:

> It has proved profitable to think of the *physical universe* as a set of independent interacting elements. The ontological assumption that the human world too can be treated in terms of a set of elements gains plausibility when one fails to distinguish between world and universe, or

what comes to the same thing, between the human situation and the state of a physical system. (p. 213)

Both the stimuli and responses of behaviorism and the features and categories of cognitivism are expressions of a view that reality—the human world as well as the physical universe—is composed of context-independent, interpretation-free elements that are only later combined, compared, contrasted, and collated by logical, formal, context-free rules of inference, deduction, calculation, and generation—or, more simply, that interact according to causal forces that can be described in terms of such rules (Shweder, 1982). For example, sociobiologist Edmund Wilson (Lumsden & Wilson, 1983) has talked recently of "culturegens" of behavior, which are supposedly independent of one another, can be studied individually, and are biologically based.

Hermeneutics

The object of study in hermeneutic inquiry is neither an abstract system of relations nor a mechanical system of forces but rather the semantic or textual structure of everyday practical activity. The ready-to-hand mode of engagement is the starting place for hermeneutic inquiry.

What the hermeneutic investigator studies, then, is what people actually do when they are engaged in the everyday practical tasks of life rather than in the detached contemplation that characterizes pencil-and-paper tasks and most interview situations. Interviewing tells us primarily about the present-at-hand mode, because an interviewee is encouraged to adopt a reflective, disengaged attitude to the topic of discussion. If we are to gain understanding of everyday practical activity, we must examine what people actually do in practical circumstances, not what they speculate that they, or fictional others, might do in a hypothetical situation. Such a methodological stance is not restricted only to hermeneutics; as Broughton (1982) pointed out, Piaget's conception of the relationship between thought and action, though different from Heidegger's, logically calls for action rather than judgments about hypothetical stories as the object of inquiry. Yet the clinical interview, often about hypothetical situations, has become the staple of structuralist practice. Although Piaget used hypothetical interviews himself, he was aware of their limitations ("[When a child] simply has stories told to him, he will be led to make judgements devoid of pity and lacking in psychological insight . . . whereas in real life he would undoubtedly sympathize with those who from afar he regards as the greatest sinners" [Piaget, 1965, p. 185]).

What *is* unique to hermeneutics is the character that practical action is taken to have. I have said that it is semantic or textual, rather than abstract or causal. As social agents ourselves, we always find meaning in a course of action, not by abstracting from it a logical structure but by understanding what human purposes and interests the action serves. Hermeneutics is concerned with meaning, as a sensibleness that can be found to be present or absent in a course of action or in an account of that action. This explication of meaning has several distinct characteristics.

The first characteristic of practical activity, in the hermeneutic account, is that it is perspectival: From one point of view it may seem sensible, whereas from another it may not. From one perspective an action has one meaning, from a different perspective it has another. Social action is understood by people in a manner that is influenced by their own interests and projects and is just not available in the same way to an objective, detached, and disinterested observer (indeed, from the hermeneutic point of view, such a stance is not possible). This plurivocity, this openness to several interpretations, does not lead into total subjectivism, however; there is not a total lack of constraint on the alternative ways of understanding a given act. Our understanding of action seems rather like our perception of multistable visual figures: Each act is seen predominantly in only a few alternative ways, corresponding to the typical contexts of its occurrence. The action of handing a woman a flower may be a peace offering, a bribe, or a gesture of appreciation, but not (or not usually) a threat, the giving of advice, or the making of a dental appointment.

Second, practical activity has a holistic character: Understanding a particular act is not possible without understanding the context within which it occurs. The ready-to-hand mode involves a complexly woven network that Heidegger called the *referential totality.* Action and situation fit together hand in glove in this mode: A situation is experienced primarily as the actual, possible, and thwarted relevant actions, and action in turn is experienced in terms of its fittingness and appropriateness to the task at hand (de Rivera, 1976). Heidegger used the example of the workshop. When we sit at the workbench with a project before us, we find ourselves in a gestalt of courses of action: cutting a wire, drilling a board, soldering a joint. If we do not own an electric drill, certain actions are blocked, although alternatives are possible. We have a constant sense of where we have brought the project and where we are taking it, with a consequent feeling of pride and satisfaction or frustration. This network of actions melds into a background of diffuse cultural and bodily practices that are taken for granted and as a consequence ordinarily go unnoticed. There are conventions for making electric connections; screws and bolts ordinarily have threads with an orientation derived from the common practices of handedness; we have practiced ways of orienting and comporting ourselves as we work that are taken for granted until they break down (fatigue develops or an injury occurs). Any single act that is performed in the workshop— soldering a resistor into a stereo amplifier, for example—is understood in terms of all these layers.

This dependence of the "facts" of human phenomena on their setting is covered up by the empiricist and rationalist approaches, both of which attempt to study objective elements of human action and social relations, refusing to acknowledge their historically situated character (cf. Taylor, 1979) and their alteration with changing social and historical conditions. An example can be drawn from recent theorizing about speech acts (Searle, 1969). We tend to talk about speech acts as though they are objectively identifiable entities, but in practice, identifying an utterance as being a speech act of a particular kind (a promise, an order, etc.) is dependent upon the circumstances of its utterance; there is no fixed mapping between grammatical form and speech act type. Consequently, an utterance removed from its context cannot be identified as a specific speech act; and even when context is considered, there will always be ambiguity to the identification. The utterance "open the door" seems at first glance unambiguously an order, but we can imagine contexts where it might be the answer to a question, a question itself, a threat (the door opens upon a hungry lion), or a challenge or promise (spoken by a game-show host).

The analogy between human action and written text has been developed by some writers (most notably Ricoeur, 1979; cf. Bleicher, 1980; Hekman, 1984; Ihde, 1971). It can be helpful in appreciating the structure of the ready-to-hand mode, but the force of the analogy depends on an appropriate account of just what a text is, and I have argued elsewhere that Ricoeur was not entirely right on that point. There are certain significant ways in which human actions, projects, and experiences resemble the way a written text appears to a reader. Most important, there is a temporal structure to both acting and reading. The reader finds that plot lines set up by what has been read so far are constantly in need of revision and reworking in the present. The plot is projected into the future, as anticipations of what is to come. What has been read and what is yet to be read are in an asymmetrical relationship: The past is known and provides a basis for anticipating the future, which is known only as possibilities. An agent also has a past, which forms a context or background to action in the present. This background provides ways of understanding the present and projects possibilities for forms of conduct in the future. This temporal character of action, and the consequent importance of forms of explanation that preserve and describe that temporality, has been recognized recently by life span psychologists (e.g., Freeman, 1984).

Earlier, I discussed the fact that when we sit back and idly contemplate the world, our experience is structured in a manner characteristic of the present-at-hand mode of engagement. Both philosophers and scientists have typically cultivated this mode, believing that its access is a privileged one. In the present-at-hand mode, our experience is of detached, object-like entities, removed from the activities they were part of and from the people who were involved with them. Such entities may be material things: Tools such as the hammer become mere physical objects. They may be characteristics of the world: Valencies and directions around us become reduced to metric, measurable dimensions. They may be facets of people: Situated responsibilities such as the cares and concerns a man has for his son get reified and rigidified into "roles," where "father" and "son" possess prescribed and explicit values and characteristics that are seen as though they can be isolated from the person's concrete circumstances and from the culture in which that person lives. Heidegger proposed that it is the structure of experience in the present-at-hand mode that is behind the ontological assumption common to both empiricism and rationalism. Both of these paradigms give priority to detached theoretical reflection, and it is when we give credence only to the present-at-hand mode that we mistakenly identify the human world with the physical universe, human action with mechanical processes, and knowledge with formal procedures.

If Heidegger's view is correct, we understand human action— and act ourselves—within a background of practices (bodily, personal, and cultural) that is always present, although it can never be made fully explicit. To attempt analytically to do away with this background and treat human acts as though they are object-like entities is a methodological error, because it would be to remove the conditions for genuine comprehension of the phenomena being studied. Our interests and involvements, our habits and our cultural practices, play a constitutive role for the entities and events that we create and experience around us. In practice, researchers working within the rationalist and empiricist paradigms also employ practical understanding of what they study, but they do so uncritically and unsystematically, because their respective schools of thought minimize the importance of this form of knowledge. Heidegger's argument implies that a structuralist researcher can develop so-called objective knowledge only by employing involved practical understanding, but at the same time, the researcher views this understanding as secondary and unreliable or as irrelevant to the goals of scientific inquiry. The hermeneutic paradigm provides an alternative to the objectivist epistemology common to both empiricist and rationalist paradigms and at the same time gives an account of the origin of that epistemology and the distortions inherent in it.

TYPE OF EXPLANATION

Each of the three paradigms seeks a particular type of explanation that fits its conception of that object of inquiry and of the origin of knowledge.

Rationalism

The type of explanation that rationalist approaches seek is one of formal characterization. Structuralism, for example, comprises two main camps differing primarily in the kind of formalism employed. The first is the original de Saussurian version, in which binary oppositions and systems of differences are sought (Pettit, 1975). For example, phonemes are defined in terms of minimal differences between sound pairs: [*p*] and [*b*] differ in their voicing but have identical places of articulation. By extension, semantic units are sought in terms of conceptual differences between terms: *sister* and *mother* differ in their family relations but are identical in gender. The second form of structuralism is the Piagetian kind where mathematical and logical structures (groups, rings, etc., characterized primarily by operations of transformation) are the model of explanation (Piaget, 1970). In either case the aim is to characterize human phenomena (language; logicomathematical knowledge) as formal structures, where logical rules operate on abstract elements whose only "context" is the formal system they define. All reference to the occasions of actual use or occurrence is deemed irrelevant to the definition of these elements and to the explanations that make use of them.

Chomsky's structuralist linguistics has the same fundamental aims and is a development from de Saussure's beginnings (Pettit, 1975). A generative grammar is a set of recursive syntactic rules that operate on linguistic elements, defined in terms of their abstract features. Even when constructing the semantic component of a transformational grammar, the linguist attempts to analyze word meaning into a combination of elements and features that are independent of the context of actual speech—indeed, that are often intended to be culture independent. The attempt is made to reduce "meaning" to isolable, interpretation-free elements and formal rules.

Similarly, cognitive science (artificial intelligence, cognitive psychology) generally seeks explanations that take the form of algorithms or procedures that "model" phenomena. Computer programs are rationalist in the form of their operation: Logical rules (ultimately, rules of binary addition) operate upon abstract elements ("bits" or "variables," depending on the level of description).

Empiricism

The empiricist approach to explanation is, in contrast, to seek covering laws that reflect the regularities of co-occurrence of observables. The laws are not logical rules but statements that express causal and empirical contingencies. In behaviorism, for example, laws are sought that link observed "stimuli" and "responses" in a straightforward causal manner. Those psychologists who work within this paradigm have adopted one of the tenets of positivism that "an explanation is not fully adequate unless its explanans [what is doing the explaining], if taken account of in time, could have served as a basis for *predicting* the phenomenon under consideration" Hempel & Oppenheim, 1948, p. 138, emphasis added). That is to say, "the goals of inquiry—explanation and prediction—are identical, as is the form in which they are realized: the subsumption of individual cases under hypothetically proposed general laws'" (McCarthy, 1978, p. 138). These general laws, which take the form of statements that certain events would occur given the existence of specified necessary initial conditions, should allow both explanation of the occurrence of a past event (working backward to argue that the initial conditions must have been present) and also prediction of future occurrences (working forward to argue from observing the presence of the causal or predisposing initial conditions). This search for prediction has been traced back to our instrumental interest in bringing phenomena under control in order to understand them (Habermas, 1971).

Another version of the positivist form of explanation underlies experimental design and statistical analysis. The appeal to manipulable variables and dependent measures assumes a network of connections that are causal and predictable. It is designed to generate an empiricist kind of explanation. Statistical correlation and probabilistic association replace the rigid causal laws of classical physics, but the overall goals for explanation are unchanged. Although we teach that "correlation is not the same as causation," we do this to stress that inference about the presence of causal relationships must proceed with care, not that correlational connections are epistemologically distinct from causal ones.

Hermeneutics

In contrast to both formal structures and causal laws, the hermeneutic approach seeks to elucidate and make explicit our practical understanding of human actions by providing an interpretation of them. It is a historically situated approach, regarding explanation as first and foremost the giving of an account that is sensible in the way it addresses current interests and concerns, not a search for timeless and ahistorical laws and formal structures.

In an interpretation, accounts are given of events and actions, principally in narrative, natural language form. There is an architectonic, a structure, to such accounts, but it is one whose elements are not context free in their identification and definition. The hermeneutic approach recognizes that issues of understanding and interpretation arise in the very observation and identification of "data" (McCarthy, 1978) and that there is more to this than a simple statement that data are "theory laden" (Dreyfus, 1980). The structure of a hermeneutic characterization is a semantic one, not a logical or causal one: Its relationships are meaningful ones, sensible and necessary, but only in terms of the particular historical and cultural situation under investigation.

The character of hermeneutic accounts. Developing an interpretation has a well-defined relationship with the three modes of engagement. In the ready-to-hand mode, we have an ongoing understanding of a situation. (More accurately, we have an understanding of ourselves and a disclosure of the situation, but I am glossing over this and several other Heideggerian distinctions here. Human agents are reflexive: Our acts reflect and express a grasp of the situation we find ourselves in, together with a tacit understanding of what we *are* as we act.) This ready-to-hand understanding is ontologically fundamental, prior to, and distinct from explicit propositional knowledge. It is the grounding for all interpretation. When we begin circumspection in the unready-to-hand mode, then we begin interpreting. There is not enough space here to give a full account of the several characteristics of interpretation that Heidegger described. Such an account would need to lay out in detail the relationship of interpretation to understanding; it must suffice here simply to state that interpretation is "the working-out of possibilities projected in understanding" (Heidegger, 1927/1962, p. 189). Heidegger further argued that "the 'world' which has already been understood comes to be interpreted. The ready-to-hand comes *explicitly* into . . . sight" (p. 189). However, if we push interpretation into the present-at-hand mode, we find ourselves left with "assertions": context-free propositions about abstract objects and their predicates. Our understanding in the ready-to-hand mode is prepredicative, and assertion is a derivative and privative form of interpretation. Interpretation continues to make reference to the historical and personal background, whereas assertion ignores it. "The ready-to-hand is always understood in terms of a totality of involvements" (Heidegger, 1927/1962, p. 191).

The ready-to-hand mode is in two respects actually the starting point for the hermeneutic investigation of human action. First, the ready-to-hand mode is the proper object of inquiry for such an investigation. Second, it is the primary source of a researcher's understanding of whatever he or she is studying. Our skillful recognition of social acts, our emotional evaluations, inform us when we observe and study people and their actions. Dreyfus (1979) put it in the following terms: "In general, we have an implicit understanding of the human situation which provides the context in which we encounter specific facts and make them explicit." The hermeneutic method aims at a progressive uncovering and explication (which is, of course, never fully completed) of the researcher's practical understanding of what is being studied. This in turn involves becoming more aware of some of the interests, habits, and practices that form the background against which the phenomena appear and take form.

The hermeneutic method, then, employs a detailed, progressive description of episodes of social interchange and gradually articulates more and more of their organization. The grounding of interpretation in ready-to-hand understanding should not suggest that such an understanding is fully trustworthy (free from contradictions or from personal bias), but simply that there is no place to begin an inquiry other than with this practical, everyday understanding. However, everyday action is generally taken for granted and goes unexamined. We understand people so facilely, ordinarily, that we fail to appreciate the complexity of what we understand, its implications for psychology, or what concerns we have when we interact with others. One task of the hermeneutic method is to push this understanding into the unready-to-hand mode and thereby make it accessible to thematic description. One way in which this is done is by attending to what is *problematic* in the original understanding: the lacunae, the gaps, and the contradictions that, in our everyday practice, we habitually gloss over (cf. Cicourel, 1964). Focusing on these has the consequence of bringing to light those aspects of the interaction that we *do* understand: Significant details of the events being interpreted become "lit up." When we do this, we frequently find that practical activity is confusing, ambiguous, and contradictory and requires some kind of work to be understood, some kind of clarification and elucidation. Our understanding of a person's action (like a written text) is never comprehensive or straightforward at the outset. Some sort of articulation and correction of our understanding is necessary, and a hermeneutic inquiry undertakes this in a systematic and coherent manner.

The resulting interpretation has the potential to be what Giddens (1976) called "revelatory": It can go beyond what our original, unreflective understanding showed us and also beyond what the agents report they were doing. At the same time, it must attempt to explain *why* agent and observer initially failed to grasp certain aspects of what occurred. Hermeneutics thus avoids the subjectivism that could result from building an explanation entirely upon agents' own accounts of their actions (though it has to face some equally complex issues). This is because reflection—even by agents themselves—is never considered incorrigible or complete. Understanding is not seen as a "searchlight" that scans over a field of potential knowledge but rather as a kind of appreciation that is necessarily partial (in both senses of the word: incomplete and with its own point of view).

I have said that a hermeneutic explanation will be neither causally predictive nor formally generative, and the reason for this should now be clear: Causal laws and formal logic characterize our knowledge in the present-at-hand mode, whereas interpretation is an articulation of ready-to-hand practical understanding. The structures of action and ready-to-hand experience are not formal or causal ones but meaningful ones. In their most unproblematic character, prior to reflection, they are holistic and dynamic. For example, emotions, as we experience them, are holistic gestalts that move us to action and restructure our entire situation (Sartre, 1948; Solomon, 1980). When we reflect upon them in the unready-to-hand mode, we can distinguish different regions of movement and interrelations among families of emotion (de Rivera, 1977). We can proceed further still and strip away the flesh of experienced emotions and consider them theoretically, as caused and causal "states", as sets of "components"—physiological processes, facial expressions, and so on—as have many theorists, from James (1890) to Arnold (1968) and Ekman (1980). These formal and mechanical accounts are not without utility, but they would not be possible at all if we did not all have a prereflective understanding of emotion. Without the direct experience of emotions, we could have no theoretical structuralist or causal account of affect, yet the structure of this practical experience itself is neither a formal nor a causal one (Zajonc, 1980).

I recently conducted an interpretive study of moral conflicts between young adults, and an account of this study can serve to illustrate some aspects of hermeneutic methodology. The research is described in detail elsewhere (Packer, 1985), and here I necessarily summarize and condense the course of the interpretive work. The conflicts were ones that developed between college students—groups of friends—as they took part in a modified version of the Prisoners' Dilemma Game (Luce & Raiffa, 1957).

I wanted to look at the details of the students' social interaction during the conflicts in a manner as free as possible from both causal and rational preconceptions. But any hermeneutic inquiry begins with a preliminary and tentative preunderstanding of what is to be studied, of the question being asked, and of what will count as an answer to this question. I needed, then, some preliminary path that would grant me access to their interaction as ready-to-hand practical activity, and to this end I borrowed from recent phenomenological studies of emotion (especially de Rivera, 1977; and Solomon, 1983), from Aristotle's analysis of the rhetorical or persuasive character of discourse (Aristotle, 1954), and from Heidegger's description of emotion and mood as forms of disclosure in the ready-to-hand mode. Together, these pointed to three different aspects of social interaction: the moral status people ascribed to themselves and others as they acted, the kind of interpersonal intimacy their actions produced or maintained, and the "mythology" of their talk—what it was about.

I now had a threefold scheme to guide my study of the conflicts. Using video recordings, I followed these three aspects, trying to understand why people acted as they did, if, as I assumed, they were neither caused to do so nor were they following logical principles or scripts. The young people I was trying to understand typically made an agreement to cooperate, broke the agreement, responded to this "burning" with amusement and pleasure on the one hand, and outrage and withdrawal on the other, and found themselves faced with a protracted breakdown of joint action. In the course of describing as fully as possible the way I understood (or failed to understand) this breakdown, I came to see a distinction between the *concerns* that underlay interpersonal action in its moral status and intimacy aspects, and the *issues* that the young adults were ostensibly talking—and disagreeing—about. Whereas the concerns—over trust and responsibility—were moral and valuative, the issues—generally the number of game points won and lost during the burning—were on the face of it factual and pragmatic. The concerns were acted upon but not voiced. They played a central role in the ready-to-hand activity of the conflict but were not at first articulated in the accounts people gave one another. The following transcript, for example, is of a heated conversation between Len (on the losing, and burned, team) and Bob (one of the burners). The issue they talked about was how many points should be paid back, but concerns of status and responsibility were evident throughout the exchange:

Len: No! We *want* . . . [He raises his index finger in emphasis.]
Bob: You *want*? [He is incredulous. His teammates laugh.]
Len: No, listen . . .
Bob: [Interrupting] You're not in much of a position to *demand*. . . .
Len: [Interrupting] No, listen, listen. We want four rounds where we get to use four and you guys go zero. That's the first four. And then the fifth one, we'll, we're willing to go zero, zero every time. You guys violated the trust, not us.
Bob: That's pretty stupid.
Len: Right now we'll just to four, four every time . . .

Terms like "a position to demand," "violation of trust," and "stupid" point up the concerns, but the issue the two men squabbled over was one of points owed and lost. Though they talked of "trust," this concern was reduced to a pragmatic and factual issue: the number of times competitive play occurred.

An incommensurability in ways of understandings the conflict also became apparent; this too can be seen in the example above. The two teams in the conflict, the burned and the burners, understood events very differently, but they were not themselves aware that their understanding was not shared; it was so self-evident that it could not be doubted. I gradually came to see that these ways of understanding were grounded, first, in the emotions that followed the burning and, more deeply, in the situation people found themselves in at the start of the session, as well as in the background of their friendships. At the beginning of each session, the two teams had, essentially randomly, found themselves "winners" and "losers," with a large disparity in points. This gave the teams different interests and aims, and these in turn led first to the burning, then to different ways of understanding "the facts" of what had happened.

Next, I began to see people deliberating about the events of the burning and giving fresh accounts of "the facts." Their deliberation was motivated by the practical need to influence recalcitrant others. The accounts developed from global, undifferentiated reports ("you blew it," "you're so illogical") to more articulated accounts of the circumstances of the burning (rather than of principles justifying or denouncing it). Three phases were distinguishable here, although groups differed in how far they went. As they negotiated, the young adults eventually came to recognize that theirs was not the only way to understand events. Their accounts began to take a conditional form ("We were going to . . ."). Then they began to articulate the grounds for their understanding, no longer able to leave it unquestioned. One team went so far as to bring up the disparity in points, the breaking of trust, and the teams' different aims. Their own accounts were of topics that I could also identify as concerns at work in their action.

What differences are there, then, between this investigation and what a structuralist or behaviorist would do with the same subject matter? Most obviously, I used no fixed and precisely defined categories of events: The identification of aspects of the interaction was allowed to develop as they were studied. Second, the relationships I uncovered among these aspects were not quantified co-occurrences or logical links. I ended up unable to predict the precise form future conflicts might take (the conflicts differed in ways I did not seek causes for) and unable to "model" such conflicts with a computer program. I had, however, a greatly increased and differentiated sensitivity to the concerns at work in such conflicts.

Several more specific differences can be seen. First is the treatment of the distinction between unreflective activity (and its attendant concerns) and more or less deliberated accounts (with their issues). The distinction seems rarely to be made by behaviorists; if it is, the accounts are typically seen as mere rationalization. Although structuralists may distinguish between the form and function of an act, between semantics and pragmatics, they attempt to describe each in formal terms, whereas I tried to spell out the relation between action and reflection as a socially motivated articulation of one's grounds for acting—an articulation that requires a certain suspension and questioning of those grounds.

The hermeneutic approach is sensitive to both purposive and unintended covering up; interpretation will on occasion identify disavowed motivational elements of action (Fingarette, 1969). It also attends to discrepancies between intended and unintended consequences of action: What we intend when we act is often not what actually happens, because of mistakes on our part, misunderstandings on the part of others, and unanticipated or ambiguous aspects of the situation. Awareness of such characteristics of human action requires a willingness to take emotion seriously as a mode of understanding and as a structuring of action, which is also, I believe, unique to hermeneutically oriented approaches.

A further unique characteristic of hermeneutic inquiry is its openly dialogical nature: the returning to the object of inquiry again and again, each time with an increased understanding and a more complete interpretive account. An initial understanding becomes refined and corrected by the work of interpretation; fresh questions are raised that can be answered only by returning to the events studied and revising the interpretation. This dialogical character means that we must generally employ some way of recording what we are studying—audio- or video-recording it, or at least making detailed field notes—so we can return to it to check out and correct our interpretations. Developing a new interpretation will often change the very form of the "facts" we are dealing with; we shall view our recording in a new way, as fresh aspects of the conduct leap to the foreground. We must be willing to go through experiences much like the young adults I have described, suddenly discovering that our taken-for-granted way of understanding is only one partial way among many. Both rationalism and behaviorism, in contrast, so constrain the way their data is approached that, although formal and causal explanations can be attempted after the fact to explain the various phenomena in the moral conflicts that I have briefly described here, the actual discovery of these phenomena is unlikely, perhaps impossible, within their objectivist frameworks.

The difference between a rationalist or empiricist explanation and a hermeneutic interpretation is a little like the difference between a map of a city and an account of that city by someone who lives in it and walks its streets. The map is the product of detached description (though the description relies on kinds of direct practical involvement, guided by specialized tools and instruments—measuring rods, theodolites—whose role is covered up when the map is finally drawn). Different maps will emphasize different aspects of the city: its street layout, its transportation, or its phone lines. However, all these maps are abstract formalizations, capturing only those features of the place that would be unchanged if no one lived there. They are designed to serve a stranger to the city as much as—perhaps more than—a resident. The account one would give of living in a city on a daily basis, on the other hand, is likely to be personal, incomplete, and prejudiced. Therein lies its usefulness to a newcomer who has come to stay or (to make the simile more accurate) to someone who already lives in the city, but now wishes to get to know it better and to live it more fully. The professional mapmaker must regard a city as merely a juxtaposition of physical objects. For its inhabitants, it is a system of possibilities and resources, frustrations and obstacles, and two people will find both commonalities and differences in their accounts of it.

CONCLUSION

I have tried to show, by argument and by illustration, how psychologists can profitably use a hermeneutic approach in their study of human conduct. Such an approach considers action and social interchange in the rich complexity that we all, in our everyday dealings, know them to have. It does not provide the forms or explanation that we have been taught to consider characteristic of scientific rigor, and some will reject it on this basis. The end product of a hermeneutic inquiry—an interpretive account—is more modest in its aims than is a formal set of rules or a causal law, but at the same time it is, I believe, subtle and complex, intellectually satisfying, and more appropriate to human action, embracing the historical openness, the ambiguity and opacity, the deceptions, dangers, and delights that action manifests.

I know I have not done justice to hermeneutics in this brief summary; its philosophy is an involved one, and I have dealt briefly with complex issues in comparing it with the currently dominant paradigms of inquiry. It is also barely possible to give a flavor of the practice of interpretation by merely discussing an example excerpted from a much larger analysis and presented in isolation. I hope, however, that I have been able to convey a little of the fascination and satisfaction that I have found in this new approach and that my discussion will encourage others to explore the growing literature on hermeneutic methodology.

REFERENCES

Aristotle. (1954). *Rhetoric.* (W. R. Roberts, Trans.). New York: Random House.

Arnold, M. (1968). *The nature of emotion.* Baltimore: Penguin Books.

Bernstein, R. (1983). *Beyond objectivism and relativism.* Philadelphia: University of Pennsylvania Press.

Blasi, A. (1980). Bridging moral cognition and moral action: A critical review of the literature. *Psychological Bulletin, 88,* 1–45.

Bleicher, J. (1980). *Contemporary hermeneutics: Hermeneutics as method, philosophy and critique.* London: Routledge & Kegan Paul.

Broughton, J. M. (1981). Piaget's structural developmental psychology: III. Function and the problem of knowledge. *Human Development, 24,* 257–285.

Broughton, J. M. (1982). Cognitive interaction and the development of sociality: A commentary on Damon and Killen. *Merrill-Palmer Quarterly, 28,* 369–378.

Chomsky, N. (1957). *Syntactic structures.* The Hague: Mouton.

Chomsky, N. (1959). Review of *Verbal behavior* by B. F. Skinner. *Language, 35,* 26–58.

Cicourel, A. V. (1964). *Method and measurement in sociology.* New York: Macmillan.

de Rivera, J. (Ed.). (1976). *Field theory as human science.* New York: Gardner Press.

de Rivera, J. (1977). A structural theory of the emotions. *Psychological Issues, 10* (Whole No. 40).

de Rivera, J. (Ed.). (1981). *Conceptual encounter: A method for the exploration of human experience.* Washington, DC: University Press of America.

de Saussure, F. (1966). *Course in general linguistics.* London: McGraw Hill.

Dreyfus, H. (1979). *What computers can't do: The limits of artificial intelligence* (Rev. edition). New York: Harper & Row.

Dreyfus, H. (1980). Holism and hermeneutics. *Review of Metaphysics, 34,* 3–23.

Ekman, P. (1980). Biological and cultural contributions to body and facial movement in the expression of emotions. In A. Rorty (Ed.). *Explaining emotions* (pp. 73–101). Berkeley: University of California Press.

Fingarette, H. (1969). *Self-deception.* London: Routledge & Kegan Paul.

Freeman, M. (1984). History, narrative, and life-span developmental knowledge. *Human Development, 27,* 1–19.

Gadamer, H. (1975). *Truth and method* (D. E. Linge, Trans.). Berkeley: University of California Press.

Gauld, A., & Shotter, J. (1977). *Human action and its psychological investigation.* London: Routledge & Kegan Paul.

Giddens, A. (1976). *New rules of sociological method.* New York: Basic Books.

Habermas, J. (1971). *Knowledge and human interests* (J. Shapiro, Trans.). Boston: Beacon Press.

Habermas, J. (1977). A review of Gadamer's *Truth and method.* In F. R. Dallmayr & T. McCarthy (Eds.), *Understanding and social inquiry* (pp. 335–363). Notre Dame, IN: University of Notre Dame Press.

Hartshorne, H., & May, M. A. (1928). *Studies in the nature of character. Vol. 1: Studies in deceit.* New York: Macmillan.

Heidegger, M. (1962) *Being and time* (J. Macquarrie & E. Robinson, Trans.). New York: Harper & Row. (Original work published 1927)

Hekman, S. (1984). Action as text: Gadamer's hermeneutics and the social scientific analysis of action. *Journal for the Theory of Social Behavior, 14*, 333–354.

Hempel, C. G., & Oppenheim, P. (1948). The logic of explanation. *Philosophy of Science, 15*, 135–175.

Hookway, C., & Pettit, P. (Eds.) (1978). *Action and interpretation: Studies in the philosophy of the social sciences.* Cambridge, England: Cambridge University Press.

Husserl, E. (1931). *Ideas: General introduction to pure phenomenology.* (W. R. B. Gibson, Trans.). New York: Macmillan.

Ihde, D. (1971). *Hermeneutic phenomenology: The philosophy of Paul Ricoeur.* Evanston, IL: Northwestern University Press.

James, W. (1890). *The principles of psychology* (Vol. 2). New York: Dover.

Kant, I. (1977). *Prolegomena to any future metaphysics* (P. Carus & J. Ellington, Trans.). Indianapolis, IN: Hackett.

Kohlberg, L., Levine, C., & Hewer, A. (1983). Moral stages: A current formulation and a response to critics. *Contributions to Human Development, 10* (entire issue).

Locke, D. (1983). Doing what comes morally: The relation between behavior and stages of moral reasoning. *Human Development, 26*, 11–25.

Luce, R. D., & Raiffa, H. (1957). *Games and decisions.* New York: Wiley.

Lumsden, C. J., & Wilson, E. O. (1983). *Promethean fire: Reflections on the origin of mind.* Cambridge, MA: Harvard University Press.

McCarthy, T. (1978). *The critical theory of Jurgen Habermas.* Cambridge, MA: MIT Press.

Mischel, W., & Mischel, H. N. (1976). A cognitive social-learning approach to morality and self-regulation. In T. Lickona (Ed.), *Moral development and behavior.* New York: Holt, Rinehart & Winston.

Packer, M. J. (1985). The structure of moral action: A hermeneutic study of moral conduct. *Contributions to Human Development, 13* (entire issue).

Palmer, R. E. (1969). *Hermeneutics: Interpretation theory in Schleiermacher, Dilthey, Heidegger and Gadamer.* Evanston, IL: Northwestern University Press.

Pettit, P. (1975). *The concept of structuralism: A critical analysis.* Berkeley: University of California Press.

Piaget, J. (1965). *The moral judgment of the child* (M. Gabain, Trans.). New York: Free Press.

Piaget, J. (1970). *Structuralism* (C. Maschler, Trans.). New York: Harper & Row.

Polkinghorne, D. (1983). *Methodology for the human sciences: Systems of inquiry.* Albany: State University of New York Press.

Rabinow, P., & Sullivan, W. M. (Eds.). (1979). *Interpretive social science: A reader.* Berkeley: University of California Press.

Ricoeur, P. (1976). *Interpretation theory: Discourse and the surplus of meaning.* Fort Worth: Texas Christian University Press.

Ricoeur, P. (1979). The model of the text: Meaningful action considered as a text. In P. Rabinow & W. M. Sullivan (Eds.), *Interpretive social science: A reader* (pp. 73–101). Berkeley: University of California Press.

Sartre, J. (1948). *The emotions: Outline of a theory* (B. Frechtman, Trans.). Secaucus, NJ: Citadel Press.

Schank, R. C., & Abelson, R. P. (1970). *Scripts, plans, goals and understanding.* Hillsdale, NJ: Erlbaum.

Searle, J. (1969). *Speech acts: An essay in the philosophy of language.* Cambridge, England: Cambridge University Press.

Schweder, R. A. (1982). Beyond self-constructed knowledge: the study of culture and morality. *Merrill-Palmer Quarterly, 28*, 41–70.

Solomon, R. C. (1980). Emotions and choice. In A. Rorty (Ed.), *Explaining emotions* (pp. 251–281). Berkeley: University of California Press.

Solomon, R. C. (1983). *The passions: The myth and nature of human emotion.* Notre Dame, IN: University of Notre Dame Press.

Sullivan, E. V. (n.d.). *Psychology as an interpretive activity* (Informal Series No. 18). Ontario, Canada: The Ontario Institute for Studies in Education.

Taylor, C. (1979). Interpretation and the science of man. In P. Rabinow & W. Sullivan (Eds.), *Interpretive social science: A reader* (pp. 25–72). Berkeley: University of California Press.

Turiel, E. (1983). *The development of social knowledge: Morality and convention.* Cambridge, MA: Cambridge University Press.

Winograd, T. (1972). Understanding natural language. *Cognitive Psychology, 3,* 8–11.

Zajonc, R. B. (1980). Feeling and thinking: Preferences need no inferences. *American Psychologist, 35,* 151–175.

20

HUSSERL REVISITED: THE FORGOTTEN DISTINCTION BETWEEN PSYCHOLOGY AND PHENOMENOLOGY

JERRY L. JENNINGS

In recent years, there has been an ever-increasing interest in phenomenology and phenomenological approaches, both in psychology (Faulconer & Williams, 1985; Packer, 1985) and other related disciplines, such as psychoanalysis (Atwood & Stolorow, 1984) and sociology (Giddens, 1976). Therefore, it is increasingly important for psychologists to have a clear, informed, and serviceable understanding of the nature and methods of phenomenology. Unfortunately, most psychologists have a very limited knowledge of phenomenology. For example, in psychology today the term *phenomenological* is typically used as an interchangeable word for *subjective.* Indeed, most psychologists conceive of phenomenology as the study of private subjective responses to a given situation. However, phenomenology certainly encompasses much more than the simplistic notion of studying the individual's "unique point of view."

For experimental psychologists, in particular, the phenomenological approach often means merely paying lip service to information directly obtained from subjects regarding their individual experiences of the experimental situation. In fact, some psychologists use the term phenomenological in a distinctly pejorative sense, signifying the basic "unreliable" nature of subjective self-report data (e.g., Nisbett & Wilson, 1977). Such psychologists often regard consciousness as a will-o'-the-wisp phenomenon that cannot be directly studied in a scientific manner. Or they treat it as a troublesome source of unreliability that needs to be controlled and overcome by objective scientific methods.

Reprinted from the *American Psychologist, 41,* 1231–1240. (1986).

The author expresses special thanks to Robert C. Scharff for his scholarly comments and criticisms. Conversations with Amedeo Giorgi and William Woodward also helped clarify important points.

On the contrary, the so-called founder of phenomenology, Edmund Husserl (1859–1938), actually conceived of phenomenology as the foundation for a rigorous science of absolute knowledge. Husserl's positive program for phenomenology far exceeded the simplistic idea of valuing the individual's subjective point of view. This article revisits Husserl's original guiding aim for phenomenology in an effort to enlighten psychologists about the meaning of phenomenology. As a brief introduction to Husserl's work,[1] the article is intended to better educate contemporary psychologists about the phenomenological approach.

At the same time, the topic of phenomenology is extremely relevant to the recent "crisis of psychology," which has stimulated disputes regarding the methods, concepts, and subject matter proper to psychology, and debates about its status as a science (e.g., Gergen, 1973; Schlenker, 1974; Strickland, Aboud, & Gergen, 1976). In this regard, Giorgi (1981) has explained how the crisis of psychology is actually a "crisis of foundations," which originated in the vigorous debates among psychologists and philosophers at the turn of the century as the "new psychology" sought to establish itself as an independent science. Actually, both William James and Edmund Husserl viewed the confusion between the domains of psychology and phenomenology as one of the central problems for "the new scientific psychology." In fact, as Giorgi (1981) has shown, "a confusion between the two disciplines . . . still persists" (p. 84)! Consequently, an exposition of Husserl's original ideas about phenomenology offers a needed and valuable clarification of the crucial but forgotten distinction between psychology and phenomenology.

The article will address four main interrelated issues in four respective sections. The first section describes the general historical context and philosophical goals that motivated Husserl to develop phenomenology. The second section outlines Husserl's critique of "naturalism," which was a philosophy that heavily influenced the experimental psychology of his time. The third section continues with Husserl's criticisms of experimental psychology as the only viable method for the scientific study of consciousness and explains his alternative positive program for phenomenology. The final section contrasts the phenomenological approach to the study of consciousness with the psychological approach and explains the importance of the "phenomenological reduction" as the basic method of phenomenology.

THE HISTORICAL CONTEXT OF HUSSERL'S GUIDING PHILOSOPHICAL AIMS

When Husserl began his university career in 1887, the field of philosophy was suffering from a crisis of stagnation and insignificance. In fact, throughout his career, Husserl was seriously concerned with the ineffectual, almost embarrassing, position of philosophy among the sciences. In Greek antiquity, philosophy had been "the loftiest and most rigorous of all sciences," and ruled supreme in humanity's enthusiastic pursuit of knowledge (Husserl, 1910–1911/1965, p. 72). However, in the course of 2,000 years, philosophy had fallen from its "royal" position in Greek times to the level of a despondent outcast in an age of experimentalism. Husserl claimed that, over the centuries, philosophy's possessions had been steadily and irreversibly stolen away by new emergent disciplines. The ascendance of the physical sciences and the more recent emergence of the specialized social sciences, such as psychology, had gradually stripped philosophy of its original proud domain and had rendered philosophy a pitiable wanderer in search of a purposeful task. In other words, now that "the world" had been divided up among the various sciences, philosophy found itself dispossessed of a significant area of study.

[1]Because this is merely an introduction to Husserl's thought, it is possible only to acknowledge the fact that there were many revisions in his thinking during the course of his career. In fact, many commentators insist on distinguishing different "periods" in his philosophical work (Spiegelberg, 1960). As noted by Ricoeur (1967), "Husserl abandoned along the way as many routes as he took . . . In a broad sense phenomenology is both the sum of Husserl's work and the heresies issuing from it" (p. 4).

At the same time, Husserl was even more concerned with the growing authority of *Weltanschauung* (world view) philosophy, which he believed further threatened the weakening position of philosophy. World view philosophy had risen to dominance following Hegel and basically held that all knowledge is relative to its historical age.[2] For example, Dilthey (1833–1911) regarded various historical "epochs" as radically distinct from one another, and therefore the knowledge of each epoch has a special character unique to its era (Dilthey, 1961).[3] For Husserl, the presumption that all knowledge is relative to its historical age presented the greatest threat of all to philosophy: the danger of willingly surrendering its last remaining and most previous birthright, which was "humanity's imperishable demand for pure and absolute knowledge" (Husserl, 1910–1911/1965, p. 72). Basically, if philosophy accepted the Weltanschauung presumption of relative knowledge, it would necessarily relinquish its ancient ideal of seeking absolute knowledge and would become a self-committed exile from its own land.[4]

Thus, historically, Husserl's principal mission was to save philosophy from its immediate "crisis," and to restore its kingdom by reviving philosophy's original, and yet unfulfilled, ideal of "rigorous science" in pursuit of absolute knowledge of the world. Hence, like the ancient Greek philosophers, Husserl believed that philosophy should be concerned with "essence," and its goal must be the clear comprehension of the essential nature of reality. By definition, an essence must be a fact or entity that is universal, eternally unchanging over time, and absolute. Conversely, an essence is not relative to a given culture or historical age, is not restricted to personal opinion, and is not dependent on logical arguments.

Because Husserl (1891/1970b) was originally a mathematician, his favorite and perhaps most illuminating example of essence was mathematical axioms and numbers (Spiegelberg, 1960).[5] Mathematical axioms are universal, have no exceptions, are not derived from logical construction, and constitute realities that can be "grasped" in their essence. Thus, for example, $2 + 2 = 4$ and "the sum of the angles of a triangle is 180°" are essences that are eternally the same in all cultures and historical eras and are not dependent on personal opinion or logical reasoning. Essences such as these are neither perceivable through the senses (i.e., "touched" by the hand, or "seen" with the eyes), nor revealed by induction or abstraction (i.e., educational experiences). Yet, an essence, such as a mathematical axiom, is a real form of *being* that has a definite reality. For example, $2 + 2 = 4$ is an absolute essence that has an eternal unchanging kind of "being" in reality whether or not any given person in any given time or place in history actually "thinks" the fact. At the same time, however, essences do not "exist" apart from the conscious experience of beholding them. In other words, essences do not "float around," so to speak, waiting for a mind to behold them and thereby actualize them as real "being." Rather, essences are *immanent*, meaning that they are grasped *in* an act of reflective consciousness. For this reason, consciousness commands the fundamental position as the special medium that constitutes *all* forms of "being" in the world. In turn, as we shall see, Husserl's phenomenology

---

[2]Some of the foremost examples of adherents to this philosophical historicism were Herder, Lotze, Rickert, Meinecke, Windelband, and Dilthey.

[3]Biemel (1970, p. 165) argued that Husserl's critique of Weltanschauung philosophy is actually that of Dilthey and led to an important correspondence between them.

[4]DeBoer (1978) demonstrated that both Husserl and his early mentor Brentano (1838–1917) were concerned with the "rising tide of relativism and historicism," and both advocated a "radical reformation and renewal of philosophy as it then existed" (p. 494).

[5]Biemel (1970) asserted that the "origin" of Husserl's phenomenology can be traced to an early working of *Philosophie der Arithmetik* (1891/1970b), in which Husserl was writing his inaugural dissertation under Carl Stumpf to qualify as a university lecturer. Biemel noted that certain fundamental elements of this early work—such as the emphasis on reflective acts, and the distinction between the physical and psychical—became vital aspects of Husserl's later phenomenology.

provides the methodological guidelines that prepare consciousness to behold "essences," but in a "pure" form that yields clear perception, understanding, and analysis of essences.

At the same time, Husserl stressed that perceiving an "essence" is no more difficult or mysterious than ordinary perception. "Husserl proposed to show that knowledge of essences is altogether experiential, that it does not involve any kind of supersensible faculty" (Merleau-Ponty, 1964, p. 72). Unfortunately, Husserl's (1910–1911/1965) point that everyone is "constantly seeing essences" (p. 110) and using them in daily cognitive operations is frequently lost in the complex explanations and sophisticated philosophical terminology that characterize the phenomenological literature. Consequently, for the unfamiliar reader, phenomenology appears to be some sort of abstruse or idealistic "supersensible faculty."

HUSSERL'S CRITIQUE OF NATURALISM AND THE NATURALISTIC IMPACT ON PSYCHOLOGY

In light of his overall plan to reestablish philosophy as a central discipline, Husserl was greatly concerned with the general philosophy of "naturalism," which thoroughly dominated thinking in the physical and social sciences, particularly psychology. Husserl used the term *naturalism* to identify a specific, often implicit, philosophical viewpoint that reality ultimately consists entirely of "physical being." For this reason, naturalism represents a serious enemy to "the scientific impulse of philosophy" because it conceives of reality in a way that excludes, or fails to incorporate, entire realms of essences, such as mathematical being. In brief, Husserl rejected naturalism because it is *not* a complete and accurate picture of reality. Rather, naturalism is only a perspective on reality that pervades scientific inquiry in the sciences. However, naturalism forgets that it is merely a perspective on reality because it believes that its experimental methods generate true statements about the nature of reality.

Stated simply, naturalism argues that reality ultimately consists of "the natural." The natural may be defined broadly, narrowly, or in a variety of ways by the particular science.[6] However, whatever its particular definition, "natural being" is basically conceived of as some sort of "physical" stuff, which can be studied using the experimental method. Thus natural being essentially has the properties of physical material: It is necessarily ruled by the laws of space, time, and causality, within the totality of one unifying corporeal world.

Husserl recognized the enormous problems caused when naturalism relegates *all* possible phenomena in the world, including and especially human consciousness, to experimentally manipulable events of physical nature. Naturalism ignores the fact that consciousness, mathematical being, and other forms of essences, do not have the same kind of being as "the natural," and therefore they are not subject to the laws of time, space, and causality. For example, a mathematical axiom is not a material thing that is directly affected by physical events and it does not "exist" in a given time and place. Above all, Husserl realized the serious consequences of naturalism for the budding scientific psychology of his time. For instance, Wilhelm Wundt and other early experimental psychologists conducted psychophysical experiments that sought to study consciousness experimentally by first assuming a functional relation between intangible mental events and tangible, directly observable physical events (Boring, 1950). The occurrence of a subjective mental event was measured in terms of its effects in observable physical events.

[6]For example, as a philosophy, naturalism could manifest itself in various forms, such as the mechanical approach of Helmholtz or Faraday; the organic approach of Ostwald; the evolutionism of Darwin or Haeckel; or even the descriptive psychology of Brentano. Husserl specifically criticized Haeckel, Ostwald, and Brentano for "naturalizing consciousness" by applying the wrong method for studying consciousness (DeBoer, 1978, pp. 388, 496).

Thus, for example, the person's mental experience of the color red was measured in terms of finger movement (reaction time) or introspective verbal report (paper-and-pencil responses). The point is that the private mental event was relegated to the status of a "physical" thing, which is in some way dependent on or related to physical events that *can* be manipulated and measured using the experimental method.

Stated differently, the "naturalistic" researcher makes a series of assumptions about the "being" of consciousness. The experimental psychologist first assumes that consciousness is an event "in" nature. Second, the psychologist insists that consciousness *must* be studied using the experimental method because this is believed to be the only reliable way to gain knowledge of reality. Third, because the experimental method is based on the measurement and systematic manipulation of concretely observable events, the psychologist must assume that consciousness is in some way dependent on other existing physical events. Therefore, consciousness must be subject to the same causal laws as everything else that exists as physical material in space and time. Hence, if the psychologist assumes all this, then consciousness must have the same kind of "being" as physical being.

Obviously, Husserl detected a fundamental problem in the new experimental psychology with far-reaching implications that continue to be extremely relevant to modern psychology. Psychology is rooted in the "naturalistic" perspective, which first regards the world as consisting entirely of "natural being," and then treats the mind as something connected with the body as part of that physical world. As a result, psychology commits the dangerous error of *naturalizing consciousness*: treating consciousness as if it is part of the physical world and obeys the laws of physical nature. Natanson (1973) outlined three distinct ways in which psychology naturalizes consciousness.

> First, the "history" of consciousness becomes an evolutionary process in which mind comes into being as a biological event and in which ideas are generated out of contingent neurological circumstances. Second, the logic of mind—the laws of reasoning, for example—is founded on material conditions in nature. Strictly speaking, there is no longer a logic of reason but a physics of brain. Third, consciousness naturalized is consciousness relativized. Since every event in nature is contingent on the circumstances in which it is actualized, . . . meaning, purpose, and value become functions of individual or historical fortuities. (p. 46)

Husserl was acutely aware of the philosophical dangers of "naturalizing consciousness," and he actively challenged *psychologism* as one of the most pernicious forms of this problem. Husserl introduced the term psychologism to characterize the mistake of making all logical reasoning synonymous with thinking, where thinking is conceived of as a neurophysical activity in the brain. In his now-famous critique of psychologism, Husserl argued convincingly that logic has an a priori status that is independent of particular empirical content. In fact, it was Husserl's masterly refutation of psychologism in his *Logical Investigations* (1900–1901/1970a) that first brought major attention to the then-unknown professor.

First, Husserl attacked psychologism as a form of relativism because psychologism reduces every instance of logical reasoning to the specific circumstances of an individual person's learning history and brain tissue. This denies the fact of essential, a priori laws of logic that transcend individual biology and experience. For this reason, psychologism endangered Husserl's primary philosophical ideal of absolute knowledge that is not relative to a particular culture or historical epoch. Second, Husserl refuted psychologism because it threatened to make psychology the foundation of philosophy. If all products of human thought (such as values, purpose, esthetics, and logic) are reducible to basic psychological processes (such as sensation, language, association, or concept formation), then psychology becomes the most fundamental science rather than philosophy.

Clearly then, naturalism was centrally important to Husserl in his program to restore philosophy as the principal discipline among the sciences. On one hand, the merit of naturalism was that it had *not* forsaken the ancient Greek ideal of establishing pure and absolute knowledge. Naturalism actively upheld Husserl's ideal because it claimed the ultimate capacity to generate a true and complete picture of reality. On the other hand, reality consists of much more than just natural being, as falsely presumed by naturalism. For Husserl, reality is comprised of a rich variety of forms of being, including the essences of mathematical being, logical being, animal being, valuational being, divine being, conscious being, and so on, alongside with natural being. Therefore, there are many kinds of phenomena, such as numbers, logical rules, and mathematical axioms, which are fully real although they are not "natural."

Naturalism not only assumes that all reality is ultimately natural, but that to know what is real, one must study it experimentally as material-like "stuff." Consequently, because the realm of conscious being is essentially different from the realm of natural being, there is a basic problem when consciousness is treated as having the same kind of being as physical matter. Using the experimental method, the psychologist tries to study consciousness, which is *not* natural, *as if* it is natural, or tries to translate private mental events into functional relations to physically observable events.

Historically, psychology adopted the experimental methods used by the physical sciences (despite the fact that mental events lack the physical tangibility of "natural" events) because it hoped to claim the same authoritative knowledge enjoyed by the physical sciences (Giorgi, 1970). However, psychology could not simply adopt the experimental method without also adopting its implicit naturalistic perspective and the philosophical problems inherent in that belief system. First, the new scientific psychology actively disallowed any study of consciousness by direct "seeing" of what consciousness is like because such a procedure was regarded as unscientific "introspection."[7] Second, and more important, psychologists were forced to ground the nonnatural phenomena of consciousness in physical events that could be studied experimentally. This problem is analogous to a fool who tries putting 12 oranges into an egg carton because the egg carton did such a great job of neatly ordering eggs. Instead of finding a new container suitable for holding oranges (the phenomenological study of consciousness), the fool cuts and tapes the egg carton until the oranges will fit. Or worse yet, the fool mangles the oranges themselves in a misguided effort to force them into the egg carton (the experimental study of consciousness).

An absurd state of affairs is thus created by psychology's excessive faith in the experimental method and psychology's determination to apply it carte blanche to the nonnatural phenomena of consciousness. For example, in the psychophysical psychology of Husserl's time, psychologists believed that they were studying consciousness itself using the experimental method. But they were actually studying the physical events, such as finger movement and verbal reports, that had been systematically correlated with the mental phenomena.[8] In the words of Husserl (1910–1911/1965), "the fundamental trait of this psychology is to set aside any direct and pure analysis of consciousness . . . in favor of indirect fixations of all psychological facts" (p. 92). "Indirect fixations" refers to the strategy of transforming conscious phenomena into physical events that *can* be handled by experimentation. The absurd outcome is that experimental psychology "expends its energy in trying to overcome the defects of the experimental method itself" (Husserl, 1910–1911/1965, p. 93).

[7]Psychologists who attempted to analyze the "essence" of conscious experience, such as Stumpf, Lipps, and Brentano, were dismissed as armchair scholastics.

[8]It is significant that this problem happened less often as the new behaviorist psychology disavowed itself as the scientific study of consciousness and the mind and insisted instead on making psychology the experimental study of *behavior*.

However, there is an important distinction between (a) the psychophysical science of psychology, which merely *correlates* mental events with physical events and (b) the naturalistic perspective, which *equates* consciousness with physical nature. Husserl only criticized the former as "defective" because psychophysics lacked an appreciation for a more direct (phenomenological) analysis of consciousness. Therefore, he believed that psychophysical psychology could not clarify its preunderstanding of what consciousness is essentially like. In contrast, Husserl condemned the philosophy of naturalism, which takes the exact scientific procedures of psychophysics too seriously and actually equates mental experience with the physical events. This is both absurd and dangerous. For example, in their avid determination to apply the experimental method, psychologists might equate the physical objective measure of rapid eye movements (REM) with the subjective mental experience of dreaming. Obviously, to claim that dreaming *is* REM is self-contradictory and absurd because it denies the very reality of the experience of dreaming, which provides the only possible assurance that REM "means" anything! Husserl himself (1912–1928/1952) offered a similar example of the error of "naturalizing consciousness": The phenomenon of "sound" can be explained by the theoretical concepts of "air vibration" and "stimulation of the auditory sense" (in DeBoer, 1978, p. 205). Such an explanation by itself is unobjectionable. But to maintain that the experience of sound *is* only air vibration is absurd.

HUSSERL'S POSITIVE ALTERNATIVE TO THE EXPERIMENTAL STUDY OF CONSCIOUSNESS

Regardless of his refutation of naturalism, Husserl realized that most psychologists would quietly ignore the problems caused by naturalizing consciousness. He knew that criticizing naturalism on the basis of absurd consequences was unlikely to have any practical impact on the rising tide of positivism and experimentalism for two reasons. First, if researchers are achieving productive results from experimentation, then they probably do not care whether those results are absurd, self-contradictory, or phenomenologically unclear. Second, most naturalists would grant that knowledge gained from experimentation is tentative and subject to further verification and improvement. Hence they would admit that their empirical conclusions are not absolute statements about reality (although naturalists are absolute in asserting the principle of naturalism).

Therefore, Husserl needed a cogent positive alternative to the naturalists' experimental approach to consciousness. He needed a new method that could be used to study conscious phenomena in a rigorously scientific manner, but without committing the error of naturalizing consciousness. Thus, with his new discipline of phenomenology, Husserl hoped to achieve his overall philosophical ideal of "rigorous science" by providing a method for establishing "absolute" essential knowledge of conscious phenomena, that is, universal, unchanging laws or facts of mental being. Husserl envisioned phenomenology as a rigorous science in the classical sense of establishing indubitable universal facts about the nature of consciousness and the world. He intended phenomenology to be an alternative "scientific" approach to the study of consciousness, but not in the modern sense of "scientific" by virtue of using the experimental method.

According to Husserl, empirical psychology in its experimental form was incapable of discerning and clarifying the essential nature of consciousness. It is important to understand, however, that Husserl did *not* flatly reject the experimental investigations of psychology, but he emphasized that an enormous amount of careful phenomenological groundwork was necessary *before* these experimental studies could be justified. For example, the psychologist should not conduct experiments about the relation between a stimulus and perception without first knowing clearly what a "perception" is, that is, without first precisely describing the essential characteristics of perception as an act of consciousness. This was the proper task of phenomenology—to clearly apprehend and delineate the basic essential acts of consciousness.

Nevertheless, Husserl pointed out that there are occasions when experimental psychology closely approximates phenomenology. This occurs when the experimental data are derived from straightforward, immediate self-reports of internal sensory experiences. In other words, psychology is closest to actually directly studying consciousness itself (as it is immediately given in experience) when the experimental procedures allow for immediate descriptions of what consciousness is like, without any additional elaboration of that experience. Unfortunately, from Husserl's point of view, this "naive phenomenological approach" occurs only when "the compulsion of physical facts" is so strong that the experimentalist allows direct descriptions of consciousness to be made (Husserl, 1910–1911/1965, p. 93).

Inevitably, by lacking a comprehensive understanding of the essential acts of consciousness (which could be provided by phenomenology), psychology remains blind to how its descriptions of psychological experience are already pervaded by "a fund of concepts" (Husserl 1910–1911/1965, p. 98). In other words, psychology fails to see how its scientific investigations are based on unrecognized preconceptions of that which is being studied. But the essential "pure" acts of consciousness have still not been studied in themselves. For example, psychologists might employ concepts such as expectation, fantasy, judgment, or recollection to describe the mental experiences of subjects being tested. However, psychologists should first clarify the essence of expectation, judgment, or recollection as universal conscious acts for all persons in all cultures (DeBoer, 1978, p. 478).

Husserl's asserted that psychology improves many components on the pure conscious phenomenon that are *not* found when its essence is grasped in acts of immediate "seeing" (by virtue of the phenomenological method). The preconceptions carried into the psychological analysis not only contaminate descriptions of "pure" consciousness in the first place, but these implicit concepts also remain untouched by the experimental method, and then enter into the final, supposedly objectively true, empirical statements about consciousness (Husserl, 1910–1911/1965, p. 98). Therefore, because psychology does not realize how its preconceptions can influence its analyses of consciousness, Husserl claimed that psychology is likely to remain phenomenologically "naive." Clearly then, it is crucial to understand that Husserl's criticisms of psychology were *not* meant "to undermine empirical psychology but to give it a foundation, to elevate it to a science" (DeBoer, 1978, p. 479).

It was precisely here that Husserl believed phenomenology could contribute to empirical–experimental psychology. Due to its contrasting treatment of consciousness, phenomenology could help psychology clarify what it already knows, so to speak. Basically, phenomenology could help psychology make the *implicit* assumptions and preconceptions that guide its investigations explicitly clear. Husserl argued that psychology's preunderstanding of the essential acts of consciousness should first be rigorously clarified (through phenomenological analyses) prior to any empirical psychological work, such as psychophysics.

Undoubtedly, Husserl's critical analysis of this problem remains just as important today as it was during the formative decades of experimental psychology. In its short history as a science, psychology has generated masses and masses of experimental data, yet its overall progress has been convoluted and comparatively limited. By better utilizing the methods of phenomenology to first clarify their guiding preconceptions about what is being studied, psychologists might have saved themselves untold time and resources in their enthusiastic application of experimentation. For example, social psychologists spent years conducting experiments to specify the exact parameters of a hypothetical motivational state called "cognitive dissonance" (Festinger, 1957). Certainly, an enormous amount of unproductive work could have been saved if phenomenological analyses were first performed to "see" if this supposed psychological state actually existed! Potentially, phenomenology could be used to ground experimental investigations in any given area of human psychology (Giorgi, 1970). Indeed, the final section includes a more detailed description of how one researcher used phenomenology to improve experimental studies of psychotherapy (Gendlin, 1962, 1964).

In summary, then, Husserl's overall program of phenomenology sought to clarify our implicit preunderstandings of the world. Husserl himself began this original enterprise with perhaps his most brilliant insight: He recognized that the quintessential property of consciousness is *intentionality.*[9] In fact, he once said, "The title of the problem which in its scope covers phenomenology in its entirety is intentionality" (Husserl, 1913/1931, p. 373). Husserl demonstrated that every act of consciousness is necessarily "intentional," which is to say, it is always directed toward, or pointing toward some "object." Thus the preeminent feature of human consciousness is its essential *directionality.* Consciousness is always "consciousness-of" something; it always "intends" something, or is "about" something. Hence, all imagining is imagining of something; all perception is perceiving of something; all thinking is thinking of something; all desiring is desiring of something. Moreover, in the same way that consciousness can "intend" a physical object, a mathematical axiom, a cultural value, or an idea, consciousness can also serve as an "object" for itself. Hence, one can be conscious of consciousness itself, "intending" emotions, desires, and other states of conscious experience.

For Husserl, consciousness commanded a fundamental position of "ontological priority" over the world because it is "the supporting ground of reality" (Husserl, 1912–1928/1952). By "ontological priority," Husserl meant that *all* the forms of being that comprise reality (including natural being, logical being, animal being, mathematical being, divine being, conscious being, and so on) are constituted *by* consciousness. In other words, in addition to being *one* special "region" or form of being in reality, consciousness is also the "primordial region," which "makes possible" the appreciation of all the other forms of being that compose reality (DeBoer, 1978, p. 201).

In this regard, Husserl again criticized "naturalism" for its one-sided conception of reality. Basically, naturalism failed to appreciate that a complete account of reality consists of *both* "experimentally informed knowledge" of the world and the knower's preunderstanding of the world as that which is studied with experimentation (i.e., "essential knowledge"). A complete account of reality must include not only that which is knowable and attracts inquiry (encompassing anything from rock formations to antibodies to religious attitudes), but also the act of knowing itself, the knower's knowing (how such entities come to be known). Husserl (1936/1970c) called this "the paradox of human subjectivity," referring to the fact that human consciousness is both *in* the world and *before* the world. On the one hand, human beings are a part of nature by virtue of their physical bodies. On the other hand, the world "exists" owing to human consciousness, which can behold and study that world.

Hence, recognizing the basic "intentional" character of consciousness and its foundational position as the "point of access" to knowledge of the world, Husserl sought a new method that could transform the various forms of being comprising reality into objectivities *for* consciousness. In the main, he had to create a new phenomenological approach to consciousness that offered a valid alternative to psychology's experimental approach.

A COMPARISON OF THE PHENOMENOLOGICAL AND PSYCHOLOGICAL APPROACHES TO CONSCIOUSNESS

The very essence of the phenomenological approach is contained in its method, which is termed "the phenomenological reduction." Therefore, understanding the principle of "the reduc-

[9]Husserl derived the notion of "intentionality" from his mentor Brentano. Spiegelberg (1960) asserted that the idea of intentionality was "completely original with Brentano" (p. 41).

tion" is indispensable for understanding what phenomenology is all about and how it is distinguished from psychology. The primary importance of the reduction is demonstrated, for example, by Fink's (1970) assertion that "the 'phenomenological reduction' alone is the basic method of Husserl's phenomenological philosophy" (p. 75) and Biemel's (1970) claim that the reduction is "the guiding motif of Husserl's thought" (p. 160). However, before describing the nature of the phenomenological reduction, two cautionary remarks are in order. First, although Husserl wrote extensively about it, he never systematically set down the complete problem and procedure of the reduction (Natanson, 1973, p. 75). Second, the meaning of the reduction can be distorted if it is thought of as procedural steps in a routine.

The so-called first move in the phenomenological reduction entails *bracketing the natural attitude*. The natural attitude refers to our everyday acceptance of the world as being something "out there" for us to experience. It is the pervasive unquestioned assumption that our everyday surroundings are real and provide the same reality for others. For example, the natural attitude is evidenced by my indubitable beliefs that I am sitting in this chair, in this place, reading this paper, on this day of this year, and that all these facts are a shared reality for other people. I assume the reality of all these "facts" without question. Thus, the natural attitude is what Natanson (1973) called "the primordial acceptance of everydayness" (p. 26). The natural attitude refers to our tendency to immediately accept the surrounding environment as something that really exists out there and that provides a fixed reality shared by others. However, it is necessary to understand that the natural attitude "is not . . . a particular or explicit act of consciousness; it is something which pervades, and is implicit in, all mental processes which are directed toward the world" (McKenna, 1982, p. 34).

Husserl made the insightful observation that an entire complex of implicit meanings is embedded in the taken-for-granted everydayness of the natural attitude. Chiefly, the natural attitude assumes the material existence of the surrounding environment, that the world operates according to the laws of physical causation; that there is a history behind all these events, and that belief in the true existence of these things is shared by other people. For instance, a community of citizens shares a belief in the existence of the White House as a building constructed in Washington, white in color, symbolizing the seat of government, and having a particular history as part of the nation's capital.

As stated, the phenomenological reduction begins with the bracketing or suspension of the natural attitude, which is termed "the epoché." "Bracketing" means only to *suspend* the everyday believing-in-the-world of the natural attitude for the methodological purpose of "purifying" consciousness. For Husserl, purity has only an artificial methodological meaning (DeBoer, 1978). Husserl emphatically insisted that the actual *existence* of the world is not bracketed during the reduction, only the natural attitude, which absolutizes everything in the world as material and as obeying the spatiotemporal laws of physical causation. Hence, the reduction is *not* like Descartes's famous systematic denial of the existence of accepted reality (Jennings, 1985).[10] The reduction is strictly a *methodological move* to temporarily strip the world of the multitude of implicit presumptions about its existence as "real," thereby allowing aspects of the world to recur as "pure phenomena" for consciousness.

> [Bracketing] means refraining from positing the existence or non-existence of some object or event in experience. It does not mean thinking or saying that the object or event is or may

[10]Although Husserl's indebtedness to Descartes is revealed in his choice of the title, *Cartesian Meditations* (1931/1960), Husserl was carefully aware of how his phenomenological method for establishing "pure and absolute knowledge" differed from Descartes's method. Descartes systematically doubted the very existence of the world in a methodological procedure to obtain absolutely certain knowledge, which he could no longer doubt (Berger, 1972). In contrast, Husserl's (1913/1931, Section 31) procedure only *suspends belief* in the existence of the world, and thereby avoids the problems caused by Descartes's "denial of being" (Jennings, 1985).

> be real or illusory, true or false. With the performance of the epoché, the real world does not change in any way, nor does the phenomenologist undergo any type of transformation. Everything continues as it did before, with the decisive exception that the world which hitherto had been straight-forwardly accepted as real is no longer viewed *in terms of* or *on the basis of* . . . the natural attitude. (Natanson, 1973, p. 58)

Thus, nothing is "lost" or "subtracted" in the reduction. This is a common misunderstanding of the phenomenological reduction. The point is that the reduction is not performed to create cold, lifeless "pure" phenomena from real existing events. Instead, the reduction is designed to transform the essential acts of consciousness themselves into the subject of rigorous analysis. In order to study how consciousness "intends" the features of the world, all potential things-for-consciousness (whether they be mathematical axioms, emotional states, the White House, or whatever) must be treated as phenomena-for-consciousness.[11] Hence, in the reduction, there is only a shift of focus from studying the specific objects of a given conscious experience to studying the essential character of the acts of consciousness, which "intend" or "give meaning to" various events or objects. In other words, the purpose of the reduction is to transform the field of study from "psychological consciousness," which is concerned with the empirical facts of experience, into "pure consciousness," which is the field where essences can be grasped.

Husserl recognized that the pervasive and compelling power of the natural attitude stood in the way of a rigorous analysis of the essence of conscious acts. It will be recalled that Husserl's primary philosophic goal was to reestablish the pursuit of absolute essential knowledge; that is, knowledge that is not relative to a culture, historical age, personal opinion, or individual experience. On the contrary, the assumptions inherent in the natural attitude are always relative and continually subject to situational change.

Consider this example to illustrate the fundamentally different ways that psychology and phenomenology approach the study of consciousness. A social psychologist who is interested in the problem of racial prejudice decides to study the experiences and attitudes of white residents in Middletown U.S. after a black family moves into their exclusively white neighborhood. So the empirical psychologist interviews a sample of white residents, obtaining each individual's subjective reactions to the entry of the new black family. Basically, the psychologist records various empirical data as each subject "reads off" the objects, events, feelings, fantasies, and sensations experienced in reaction to the event. In addition to collecting open-ended descriptive material, such as "I feel intruded upon," the psychologist administers a sequence of rating scales pertaining to attitudes of racial prejudice.

With the exception of the rating scales, most psychologists would mistakenly consider such material to be "phenomenological data" because the information was directly obtained from individual descriptions of subjective experience. However, such data are not at all what Husserl regarded as phenomenological. Rather, these are empirical psychological data dealing with the facts of experience. Embedded in the natural attitude, psychology studies the individual correspondence between actual existent things and events and the mental experience of those existent events. In this example, the psychologist studied the actual real event of a black family moving into a white neighborhood and how that event was subjectively experienced by the individual subjects.

The phenomenologist is not interested in studying the specific contents of each respondent's subjective reaction to the arrival of a black family. In contrast, the phenomenologist wants to analyse the typical character of consciousness (its essence) in meaning-conferring acts. The

[11]Actually, the term phenomenology derives from the general meaning of phenomena as it is used here: It is the study of "pure" phenomena as they present themselves to consciousness, but with any assumptions about nature, existence, and value temporarily set aside.

meaning-conferring act is an essence that transcends (i.e., is not relative to) historical age, culture, individual opinion, personal experience, and so on. But the study of white prejudicial responses to the arrival of a black family in Middletown U.S. in 1986 is *strictly relative* to the specific time, place, participants, circumstances, culture, and personal experiences of the respondents. One would probably obtain very different results if the same study was conducted 20 years ago or 20 years hence, or if it was done in another community. Empirical content such as this is *not* essential because the same content does not occur in all such acts of prejudicial thinking.

Nevertheless, there *is* an essential way in which consciousness "intends" and confers meaning to different classes of events. This is the proper subject of study for phenomenology. In this case, the phenomenologist is interested in analyzing, identifying, and clarifying the essential characteristics of "prejudicial perception" itself: Exactly what implicit and explicit assumptions are contained in any given act of prejudicial perception? What are the basic essential ingredients that constitute such an act of consciousness?[12] This essential way of perceiving transcends the actual content of any given individual prejudicial perception. For example, there is a universal essential way that an ancient Egyptian, a medieval German, or a modern Arab each would perceive persons of different race or background. However, to reach the essence of the conscious act of prejudicial perception, the phenomenologist must first perform the "reduction." The phenomenologist begins by bracketing the natural attitude so that he or she is no longer concerned with actual empirical content (i.e., the actual real existence of the persons, place, time, and circumstances) but with the pure conscious act of perception. In the realm of pure consciousness, it does not matter whether the content of the perceptual act is Caucasian, Chinese, or German. Instead of analyzing the content of actual reactions to an actual object of perception (in this example, a new black family in Middletown U.S.), the phenomenologist analyzes the *directedness* of consciousness to this class of objects in general (i.e., intentionality).

Consider a second example from the area of psychotherapy, which illustrates the crucial distinction between psychology's concern with "empirical consciousness" and phenomenology's contrasting concern with "pure consciousness." Gendlin's (1962, 1964) extensive phenomenological work has revealed that any given instant of conscious awareness is characterized by a global, bodily felt experiential sense, and that this bodily felt aura of *experiencing* constitutes the originating ground for all our explicit words, ideas, and thoughts (Jennings, 1984). Gendlin has shown that our mental images, ideas, thoughts, perceptions, and so on (that which psychology regards as immediate consciousness) are *not* the same as our immediate experiencing of the world. More accurately, our words, concepts, and ideas are *mediate* formulations arising from our *immediate* bodily felt experiencing of the world. Thus, for any given individual, the particular "objects" for conscious attention are ever changing and incredibly diverse, constantly changing in content depending on the specific environmental circumstances of time, place, situation, and personal history (i.e., *relative* empirical fact knowledge). But when consciousness itself is taken as it immediately presents itself to awareness (in any given moment and in any circumstance), we always find that the essential quality and characteristic of consciousness is ongoing bodily felt "experiencing" (an essence).

This essential characteristic of consciousness is easily demonstrated in psychotherapy by the phenomenon that Gendlin (1962) has termed *direct reference.* During therapy, it is often observed that a client is distinctly aware of an important inner feeling experience, but the client does not yet possess the "words" or ideas to formulate an understanding of just what that

[12]A so-called "prejudicial perception" is certainly not a recognized essential act of consciousness that has received phenomenological analysis. Rather the term prejudicial perception is merely suggested as an illustrative example of how a phenomenologist might view a common theme of psychological study.

experiential feeling is about. The client may say things like, "I can really feel it," or "That doesn't quite describe what it is," or "This feeling that I have now puzzles me," even though the client does not yet know what "it" *is*. Hence, in direct reference, a client can focus on (i.e., direct attention toward) an inner-sensed experiential datum without having articulated that datum into words. Although the client may puzzle over what sort of a "this" or "it" he or she is aware of, there is nothing at all vague about the definite way that he or she *feels* "it" and attends to "it." The "it" is only vague conceptually because the client can clearly attend to it, talk about it, point to it, sense its special tonal qualities, and feel it change in response to various conceptualizations or therapeutic events. The inwardly felt datum is entirely meaningful even though it is not yet labeled or formulated into an explicit conceptualization.

Obviously, therapists of all orientations have observed this common phenomenon of direct reference. Some may ignore its significance, and others may explain it in terms of their differing psychological theories, but certainly many psychotherapists already "know" about this important phenomenon. As such, this is a good example of how phenomenology can help psychology to clarify what it already knows. In other words, phenomenology can provide a pretheoretical descriptive account of the essential conscious act by which clients attend to inner data before or without explicit formulation into words or concepts. It is pretheoretical in the sense that there are many different ways of conceptualizing a given moment of experiencing and there are many different theoretical concepts that can "bring out" aspects of experiencing that are already there to be conceptualized. However, at no time does any particular concept itself constitute the actual structure of human experiencing. No formulation can capture all of what one means to say, why one says it, and the context in which it is being said. For example, a moment of experiencing may be conceptualized as a "drive," "trait," "infantile fixation," "S–R bond," "inferiority complex," "self-concept," "animus projection," "experience," and so on, but the actual moment of conscious experiencing is never just that single fixed entity. "Felt experiencing" (or what Heidegger (1927/1962) termed *Befindlichkeit*) is a much richer sense encompassing a multitude of potential meanings, one aspect of which may be formulated in terms of this or that concept or statement (Gendlin, 1978–79).[13]

In the same way, perceiving can be contrasted with a perception. For instance, at this moment, this page of writing is one aspect of the phenomenal field of your ongoing process of perceiving. To think that "this is English printing" formulates one aspect of this complex ongoing process of perceiving into content, a perception. This formulated object of perception, or content, is not the same as the process of perceiving, which may or may not be formulated into any particular perception(s).

The crucial point is that when consciousness is "seen" as it immediately presents itself, we find a bodily felt aura of implicitly meaningful felt experiencing—not explicit words, concepts, or experiences. In other words, at any given moment in therapy, a person has a complex aura of felt experiencing that encompasses many potential meanings. Within a given moment, this inwardly sensed experiential datum might encompass, say, a sense of inferiority, a history of paternal domination, a revengeful fantasy, a wish for autonomy, and many other meanings. However, it is the bodily sensed experiential aura that is *immediately* experienced in awareness, rather than any one of these potentially conceptualizable experiences. Although the particular conceptualized contents may vary greatly, it is the quality of implicitly meaningful "felt experiencing" that is essential: This characteristic of consciousness, like intentionality, is an essence in that it is eternally the same for persons in all cultures and historical ages.

[13]It is well known that the famous philosopher Martin Heidegger (1889–1976) studied under Husserl and was profoundly influenced by Husserl's thinking. One could argue that Chapter 5 of Heidegger's *Being and Time* (1927/1962) and Husserl's *Logical Investigations* (1900–1901/1970a) and *Ideas* (1913/1931) dealt precisely with the basic relationship between experience and the words and various kinds of formulations of experience.

This example also illustrates how, according to Husserl (1910–1911/1965), psychology imposes many components on the pure conscious phenomenon. He was referring to the way that psychologists employ concepts and constructs, like inferiority complex and anxiety, that are presumed to describe the actual immediately given nature of consciousness. As we have seen, directly felt experiencing is that which is immediately given, and words and concepts are mediate formulations of experiencing. Again, by performing the phenomenological reduction, the investigator is no longer focused on the particular conceptualized content of mental activity and its correspondence with actual existent things and events (i.e., psychological consciousness). Instead he or she analyzes the essential conscious act itself (i.e., pure consciousness). For example, the phenomenologist might study the essential act of "direct reference" to subjective experiential data, and the ways clients formulate inner experiencing into explicit words, thoughts, and concepts—regardless of the particular content and concepts used by the client (which may vary considerably depending on the theoretical bent of the psychologist).

Gendlin (1962) was able to clarify and improve experimental research on psychotherapy because he understood the need for new theoretical terms that refer directly to immediate felt experiencing, that is, terms that refer directly to the ever-present inwardly sensed experiential aura, which serves as the ground for our formulations (Jennings, 1984). In contrast, Gendlin (1962) recognized that standard psychological theories consist of a mixture of (a) theoretical constructs lacking immediately observable experiential referents, (b) terms defined by objective external observations, and (c) imprecise commonsense descriptive language that refers to experiencing in a vague manner. More recently, Gendlin (1986) again used phenomenological insights to critique the field of psychotherapy research.

CONCLUSION

In summary, we have seen that Husserl's primary motivation was to restore and revitalize philosophy as a central discipline. Threatened by the relativism of Weltanschauung philosophy and the ascendancy of the experimental sciences, he advocated a return to philosophy's original ideal as the pursuit of absolute knowledge. Husserl specifically attacked the pervasive philosophy of naturalism, which claimed that all facts about reality must be based on objective experimental data. He was especially concerned with the impact of naturalism on the new scientific psychology of his time, which committed the serious error of treating consciousness as if it was a physical event.

At the same time, Husserl's criticisms of naturalism and the new psychology included a positive alternative to the experimental study of consciousness. Husserl believed that phenomenology could "ground" psychology by first performing the foundational task of clarifying the implicit preunderstandings and preconceptions of mental phenomena that guide psychology's empirical investigations. However, Husserl's original foundational function of phenomenology has been overlooked by modern psychologists, who, for the most part, mistakenly consider personal reports of subjective experiences as phenomenological studies. Basically, the forgotten distinction between phenomenology and psychology is that the former analyzes the essential character of various types of conscious acts, whereas the latter studies the empirical contents of actual subjective experiences corresponding to actual existent environmental events (i.e., subjectivized objects in the natural attitude). Examples are used to illustrate this vital difference between the phenomenological and psychological approaches to the study of consciousness. It is hoped that by elucidating the special sort of knowledge that phenomenology can offer to psychology, this article may encourage a more fruitful dialogue between the disciplines.

REFERENCES

Atwood, G., & Stolorow, R. (1984). *Structures of subjectivity: Explorations in psychoanalytic phenomenology.* Hillsdale, NJ: Erlbaum.

Berger, G. (1972). *The cogito in Husserl's philosophy.* Evanston, IL: Northwestern University Press.

Biemel, W. (1970). Decisive phases in the development of Husserl's philosophy. In R. Elveton (Ed.), *The phenomenology of Husserl* (pp. 148–173). Chicago: Quadrangle.

Boring, E. (1950). *A history of experimental psychology.* Englewood Cliffs, NJ: Prentice-Hall.

DeBoer, T. (1978). *The development of Husserl's thought.* The Hague: Nijhoff.

Dilthey, W. (1961). *Gesammette Schriften* [Complete writings]. Stuttgart: Teubner.

Faulconer, J., & Williams, R. (1985). Temporality in human action: An alternative to positivism and historicism. *American Psychologist, 40,* 1179–1188.

Festinger, L. (1957). *A theory of cognitive dissonance.* Stanford: Stanford University Press.

Fink, E. (1970). The phenomenological philosophy of Edmund Husserl and contemporary criticism. In R. Elveton (Ed.), *The phenomenology of Husserl* (pp. 73–147). Chicago: Quadrangle.

Gendlin, E. (1962). *Experiencing and the creation of meaning: A philosophical and psychological approach to the subjective.* New York: Macmillan.

Gendlin, E. (1964). A theory of personality change. In P. Worchel & D. Byrne (Eds.), *Personality change* (pp. 102–148). New York: Wiley.

Gendlin, E. (1978–1979). Befindlichkeit: Heidegger and the philosophy of psychology. *Review of Existential Psychology and Psychiatry, 16,* 43–71.

Gendlin, E. (1986). What comes after psychotherapy research? *American Psychologist, 41,* 131–136.

Gergen, K. (1973). Social psychology as history. *Journal of Personality and Social Psychology, 26,* 309–320.

Giddens, A. (1976). *New rules of sociological method.* New York: Basic Books.

Giorgi, A. (1970). *Psychology as a human science: A phenomenologically based approach.* New York: Harper & Row.

Giorgi, A. (1981). On the relationship among the psychologist's fallacy, psychologism, and the phenomenological reduction. *Journal of Phenomenological Psychology, 12,* 75–86.

Heidegger, M. (1962). *Being and time.* New York: Harper & Row. (Original work published 1927).

Husserl, E. (1931). *Ideas: General introduction to pure phenomenology.* New York: Macmillan. (Original work published 1913).

Husserl, E. (1952). *Ideen zu einer reinen Phänomenologie und phänomenologischen Philosophie, II.* [Ideas toward a pure phenomenology and phenomenological philosophy] The Hague: Nijhoff. (Original work published 1912–1928).

Husserl, E. (1960). *Cartesian meditations: An introduction to phenomenology.* The Hague: Nijhoff. (Original work published 1931).

Husserl, E. (1965). Philosophy as rigorous science. In E. Husserl, *Phenomenology and the crisis of philosophy* (Q. Lauer, Trans., pp. 71–147). New York: Harper & Row. (Original work published 1910–1911).

Husserl, E. (1970a). *Logical investigations.* New York: Humanities Press. (Original work published 1900–1901).

Husserl, E. (1970b). *Philosophie der Arithmetik.* The Hague: Nijhoff. (Original work published 1891).

Husserl, E. (1970c). *The crisis of European sciences and transcendental philosophy.* Evanston, IL: Northwestern University Press. (Original work published 1936).

Jennings, J. L. (1984). *Experiential psychotherapy: Its theory, research, clinical practice, and historical development.* Unpublished doctoral dissertation, University of New Hampshire, Durham.

Jennings, J. L. (1985). The fallacious origin of the mind–body problem: A reconsideration of Descartes' method and results. *The Journal of Mind and Behavior, 6,* 357–372.

McKenna, W. (1982). *Husserl's "Introductions to phenomenology": Interpretation and critique.* The Hague: Nijhoff.

Merleau-Ponty, M. (1964). *The primacy of perception.* Evanston, IL: Northwestern University Press.

Natanson, M. (1973). *Edmund Husserl: Philosopher of infinite tasks.* Evanston, IL: Northwestern University Press.

Nisbett, R., & Wilson, T. (1977). Telling more than we can know: Verbal reports on mental processes. *Psychological Review, 84,* 231–259.

Packer, H. (1985). Hermeneutic inquiry in the study of human conduct. *American Psychologist, 40,* 1081–1093.

Ricoeur, P. (1967). *Husserl: An analysis of his phenomenology.* Evanston, IL: Northwestern University Press.

Schlenker, B. (1974). Social psychology and science. *Journal of Personality and Social Psychology, 29,* 1–15.

Spiegelberg, H. (1960). *The phenomenological movement.* The Hague: Nijhoff.

Strickland, L., Aboud, F., & Gergen, K. (1976). *Social psychology in transition.* New York: Plenum Press.

21

THE PROBLEM OF EVIL: AN OPEN LETTER TO CARL ROGERS

ROLLO MAY

Dear Carl:

Your letter published in the special issue of *Perspectives* (Rogers, 1981) discussed my contribution to humanistic psychology, and I very much appreciate what you wrote. You do me honor in many ways.

You also went on to point out your major differences with me concerning the problem of evil.

As you rightly say, "The presence of terrorism, hostility, and aggression are urgent in our day." I would add that the importance of our confronting these issues is crucial. Central among these destructive forces is the possibility—or probability, as many people believe—of nuclear war and the related threat of nuclear radiation. A recent Gallup poll shows that seven out of ten people in this country believe a nuclear war will actually occur, or that there is a good chance that it will occur, within the next ten years (Newsweek, October 5, 1981, p. 35). It seems obvious that if we cannot deal constructively with the threat in atomic power and the terrorism that goes with it, our civilization will die like those of the ancient Romans, Assyrians, Egyptians, and Greeks.

You wrote, Rollo "sees the demonic as a basic element in the human makeup and dwells upon this in his writing." You contrasted this with your own view, "that it is cultural influences which are the major factor in our evil behaviors. . . . So I see members of the human species . . . as *essentially* constructive in their fundamental nature, but damaged by their experience" (Rogers, 1981, p. 16).

Reprinted from the *Journal of Humanistic Psychology, 22,* 10–21. (1982). Copyright © 1982 by Sage Publications. Reprinted by permission of the publisher and author.

It is difficult to write this letter because of my affection for you and our long friendship. But the problem of evil is so crucial that it is imperative that we see it clearly. I shall therefore try to clarify my own position not only for our personal purposes but to help readers confront these problems themselves, for the sake not only of ourselves but our children and our future world. I agree with the statement of Edmund Burke: "The only thing necessary for the triumph of evil is for good men to do nothing."

1

In the first place, I never use the word *demonic,* except to say that this is *not* what I mean. My term is *daimonic,* which is critically different. I quote from *Love and Will,* the book in which I write most on this topic:

> The daimonic is the urge in every being to affirm itself, assert itself, perpetuate and increase itself . . . [the reverse side] of the same affirmation is what empowers our creativity [May, 1969, p. 123].

Thus I am stating that I see the human being as an organized bundle of potentialities. These potentialities, driven by the daimonic urge, are the source *both* of our constructive and our destructive impulses. If the daimonic urge is integrated into the personality (which is, to my mind, the purpose of psychotherapy) it results in creativity, that is, it is constructive. If the daimonic is not integrated, it can take over the total personality, as it does in violent rage or collective paranoia in time of war or compulsive sex or oppressive behavior. Destructive activity is then the result.

You and I have seen many cases in therapy with adolescents who are accused by their parents of being destructive when they are really only trying to establish their own independence, their own self-assertion, and indeed their own right. If we undercut the daimonic, as many therapists do, we do a disservice to our clients. I believe Rilke was right when he wrote, "If my devils are to leave me, I am afraid my angels will take flight as well."

It is true that the concept of the daimonic gives a rationale for demonic activity just as it gives a rationale for creativity. This may be why you describe me (I think wrongly) as writing about the demonic.

2

In your letter you acknowledge the evil surrounding us. You say, "I am very well aware of the incredible amount of destructive, cruel, malevolent behavior in today's world—from the threats of war to the senseless violence in the streets." But you say that you "believe that it is cultural influences which are the major factor in our evil behaviors."

This makes culture the enemy. But who makes up the culture except persons like you and me? You write about "the destructive influence of our educational system, the injustice of our distribution of wealth." But who is responsible for this destructive influence and injustice, except you and me and people like us? The culture is not something made by fate and foisted upon us.

Obviously the culture is a great boon as well as a source of evil. We could say, as well, that the fact that we have an educational system at all and the fact that we have an economic system at all are themselves results of our culture. It takes culture to create self and self to create culture; they are the yin and yang of being human. There is no self except in interaction with a culture, and no culture that is not made up of selves.

True, any group does exert a conformist tendency toward those within it by virtue of the mutual expectations it establishes that make it a group. But this is only one element and it cannot account for the fact that human beings individually and en masse are able to turn into warmongers and individual or collective assassins. I propose that the evil in our culture is also the reflection of evil in ourselves, and vice versa.

You also write, in another context but on the same theme: "The persons of tomorrow . . . will be the ones capable of living in this new world, the outlines of which are still only dimly visible. But unless we blow ourselves up, that new world is inevitably coming, transforming our culture" (Rogers, 1980). But this very culture which you see as being "transformed" is what you also say may blow us up. The 7 out of 10 people who believe in the likelihood of a nuclear war are also the "persons of tomorrow," but they have a quite different point of view. They obviously do not believe in a new world "inevitably" coming, "transforming our culture." They see other facts: Some of them are aware that a single nuclear bomb dropped on Chicago would result in the deaths of 200,000 people. The United States at the end of this year will have approximately 2,400 more nuclear explosives than it did at the beginning of the year, at a cost of billions of dollars. Norman Cousins (1981), reviewing these facts, states: "A mammoth and deadly illiteracy has seized us." I would call it a collective psychosis, which has got us all in its lethal grip, and we find it attractive enough to participate in it. There is no preordained reason our society should "inevitably" survive or disintegrate as did Rome and Greece and Egypt. What about the "good" in their members? Whether we survive or not depends upon whether you and I and millions like us can and will act to change our destructive directions.

The culture is evil as well as good because we, the human beings who constitute it, are evil as well as good. Our culture is partially destructive because we, as human beings who live in it, are partially destructive, whether we be Russians or Japanese or Germans or Americans.

You have also written on the new world toward which you believe we are moving:

> This new world will be more human and humane. It will explore and develop the richness and capacities of the human mind and spirit. It will produce individuals who are more integrated and whole. . . . It will be a more natural world, with a renewed love and respect for nature. . . . Its technology will be aimed at the enhancing, rather than the exploitation, of persons and nature. It will release creativity, as individuals sense their power, their capacities, their freedom.
>
> The winds of scientific, social and cultural change are blowing strongly. They will envelop us in this new world. . . . We may choose it, but whether we choose it or not, it appears that to some degree it is inexorably moving to change our culture [Rogers, 1980, p. 356].

You paint a seductive and enticing picture, and anyone would like to believe it. But I recall the words of Warren Bennis in the film of you and him, when he characterized your viewpoint as "devilishly innocent."

How do you square this "human and humane" world you predict with the fact (Yankelovich, 1981, p. 184) that the suicide rate in this country has gone up 171% in the last 30 years? Most of this great increase is among young people in their teens and early 20s; how can one tell them that their world explores "the richness and capacities of the human mind and spirit"? What about the fact (Yankelovich, 1981, p. 182) that major opinion polls, which showed in the early 1970s that only 1 in 5 Americans believed that "next year will be worse than this year," reveal now that a 55% majority has been forced into this pessimistic position? How can one talk to those people about releasing "creativity as individuals sense their power, their capacities, their freedom"?

In the 1950s and up to the late 1960s, most Americans believed that the present was superior to the past and that the future would improve on the present. By 1978 this pattern had wholly reversed itself, a "truly historic shift away from optimism to bleakness" (Yankelovich,

1981, p. 183). These "people of tomorrow" do not find the world "enhancing" their "persons and nature."

I wonder also how you square your statements with the famous Milgram (1969) experiments at Yale? You recall that Milgram took subjects from every walk of life (they answered an ad and were paid $4.00 an hour). The purpose of the experiment, as stated to each subject, was to teach the "learner" behind a glass partition by means of giving him electric shocks when he gave the wrong response. But the experiment was actually designed to see how far human beings would go in increasing the voltage to punish the learner for his mistakes. Subjects were told by Milgram to increase the voltage as they went through the experiment.

The results, which shocked Milgram as well as the rest of us who read about them, were that over 60% of the people willingly turned the electric current up to a voltage that they knew would kill the person on the other side of the glass partition. Milgram (1969, p. 178) writes that his studies "are principally concerned with ordinary and routine destruction carried out by everyday people following orders." Milgram points out that his results are similar to the phenomena uncovered in the trial of Lt. Calley for his actions at My Lai in the Vietnam war, when women, children, and old men were slaughtered in cold blood by American soldiers when commanded to do so by Lt. Calley.

How also do you deal with Philip Zimbardo's (1971) "prison" experiment at Stanford? You will remember that Zimbardo and his associates divided his psychology class of students into "guards" and "inmates" and had them go through a prison period, planned to last two weeks, in the basement of a building. He found that the "prisoners" began to taunt the "guards" and that the guards would taunt back, and soon the guards were striking the prisoners with clubs. The real violence became so destructive that Zimbardo, to his surprise and chagrin, had to stop the experiments after one week.

These students had no particular enmity toward each other to begin with. They were middle-class persons like you and me and our colleagues, and they certainly would have fit your category of "people of tomorrow." But they had a capacity for destructiveness that became, without much provocation, an evil acted out in reality. The evil possibilities were just beneath the surface. Philip Zimbardo, like Stanley Milgram, is a psychologist of stature who was simply trying to find out the possibilities in human beings for destructiveness and self-control.

Yes, the culture admittedly has powerful effects upon us. But it could not have these effects were these tendencies not already present in us, for, I repeat, we constitute the culture. When we project our tendencies toward evil on the culture—as we do when we repress the daimonic—the evil becomes the culture's fault, not ours. Then we don't experience the blow to our narcissism that owning our own evil would entail.

If you conclude that the trouble lies in the fact that human beings are so susceptible to influence by their culture, so obedient to orders they are given, so pliable to their environment, then you are making the most devastating of all judgments on evil in human beings. In such a case we are all sheep, dependent upon whoever is the shepherd; and Fred Skinner is right. But I do not think you believe that and neither do I.

True, I could cite as many incidents of heroic and altruistic behavior, as after the recent plane crash in Washington, D.C. I am not arguing that we human beings are only evil. I am arguing that we are bundles of both evil and good potentialities.

4

Let us turn to the question of evil as we experience it in our own field, that of psychotherapy. You will recall your own important experiment, continuing over three years, on client-centered therapy with schizophrenics at the Veterans Administration Hospital in Madison, Wisconsin, some twenty years ago (Rogers, Gendlin, Kiesler, & Truax, 1967). You will also recall that I was chosen as one of the twelve judges, who were experienced and practicing therapists, to assess that therapy.

After listening to the tapes you sent me, I reported that, while I felt the therapy was good on the whole, there was one glaring omission. This was that the client-centered therapists did not (or could not) deal with the angry, hostile, negative—that is, evil—feelings of the clients. It turned out that the other judges, by and large, pointed out the same thing. I quote from the summary written by you and your colleagues of this whole experiment:

> Particularly striking was the observation by all the theorists that the client-centered process of therapy somehow avoids the expected and usual patient expressions of negative, hostile, or aggressive feelings. The clear implication is that the client-centered therapist for some reason seems less open to receiving negative, hostile, or aggressive feelings. Is it that the therapists have little respect for, or understanding of their own negative, hostile, or aggressive feelings, and are thus unable to receive these feelings from the patient? Do they simply 'not believe in' the importance of negative feelings [Rogers et al., 1967, p. 503]?

One of your students, Nathaniel Raskin (1978, p. 367), quotes my report as it was discussed in that book:

> Rollo May, as one of the outside experts in the Wisconsin study, "sometimes got the feeling there were not two people in the room. . . . A consequence of a misuse of the reflecting techniques . . . [is] that we get only an amorphous kind of identity rather than two subjects interacting *in a world in which both participate, and in which love and hate, trust and doubt, conflicts and dependence, come out and can be understood and assimilated.*" May was concerned that the therapist's over-identification with the patient could "take away the patient's opportunity to experience himself as a subject in his own right, to take a stand against the therapist, to experience being in an interpersonal world."

In spite of the fact that "client-centered therapists, both individually and collectively, have advocated openness and freedom in the therapeutic relationship," the outside judges focused "upon what they perceive as the therapist's rigid and controlling nature which closes him off to many of his own as well as to the patients experiences" (Rogers et al., 1967, p. 503).

This same student, who has since become a therapist in his own right, adds some notes about his own experience. I realize that our students develop in their own way, and you and I cannot be responsible for them. But Raskin's (1978, p. 366) comments on his own experience are so relevant to the issues here that I ask your permission to quote it:

> I used the early concept of the client-centered therapist to bolster the inhibition of my anger, my aggression etc. I got some feedback at that time that it was difficult for people, because I was so nice, to tell me things that were *not* nice, and that it was hard for people to get angry at *me*.

He then goes on to say that he needed to find some new ways within the client-centered approach to take in other phenomena, which I have called the "negative, hostile and aggressive feelings."

I find it important in therapy that the patient be able to take a stand against me, the therapist. This is in accord with what Raskin said, that he realized he was taking something away from the patient when he was "too nice, too much identifying with the other person." What he was taking away was the patient's possibility of becoming independent. Patients' anger is an essential part of their motivation in their assertion of individual steps toward psychological health. The anger of the therapist can also be a powerful aid in helping patients experience what effect their behavior has on their relationships in general.

This means that aspects of evil—anger, hostility against the therapist, destructiveness—need to be brought out in therapy. Personal autonomy occurs not by avoiding evil, but by directly confronting it. Therapists need to be able to perceive and admit their own evil—hostility, aggression, anger—if they are to be able to see and accept these experiences in clients.

I am quite ready to believe that it would be impossible for anybody to sit down in a therapeutic hour with you and not be affected for good by it. But every patient does have the possibility to destroy himself or herself, and some patients will destroy themselves no matter how much or how well you and I work with them. You illustrate this when you speak of the trouble you had with a schizophrenic woman in Chicago.

5

I want to return to the question of inevitable cultural transformation. You write that this "new world" that you describe is "inevitably coming," and later you remark that the new world is "inexorably moving to change our culture." How can you be so certain? There are countless scenarios that can be written as predictions of our future. The persons who committed suicide, mentioned above, lived and died in entirely different scenarios from yours, and the polls indicate that the majority of citizens in our country would also write very different predictions. The scenarios I take seriously are those that see the evil in humankind's development as well as the good.

You also write that "we may choose [this cultural change], but whether we choose it or not, it will still happen." Do you mean it will take place regardless of whether we do anything about it? This sounds like Fred Skinner again: The environment will force us into this brave new world whether we want it or not!

As with Skinner's viewpoint, your statement that it will come regardless of what we humans do about it cuts the nerve of social action. A danger of which I am very aware is that people, hypnotically seduced by rosy predictions of the future, will conclude that it requires no effort from them and will sit back and do nothing. This, as Edmund Burke said so well, is the quickest way for evil to triumph.

There are innumerable issues that cry out for our awareness and our energies, quite in addition to the imminence of nuclear war. There is, for one, the food crunch and the problem of hunger. The President's Commission on World Hunger, 1980, stated that there are more ill-fed people on our planet than ever before, amounting to 800,000,000 (not counting the communist countries). The number is growing and, as the available food lessens, will approach panic proportions by the year 2000. This includes hundreds of thousands of children who are starving and millions more who go to bed every night hungry. This includes fathers who walk the streets, their self-esteem eroded because they are unable to find work. It also includes despairing mothers who can do nothing but watch their children starve.

If we do get to a new world, it will only be by solving these problems first. If we don't, we will not have the new world you see coming: The price in human suffering will be too high.

6

In *Love and Will* I also wrote:

> It [the daimonic] constitutes a profound blow to our narcissism. We are the "nice" people and, like the cultivated citizens of Athens in Socrates' time, we don't like to be publicly reminded,

> whether we secretely admit it to ourselves or not, that we are motivated even in our love by lust for power, anger, and revenge. While the daimonic cannot be said to be evil in itself, it confronts us with the troublesome dilemma of whether it is to be used with awareness, a sense of responsibility and the significance of life, or blindly and rashly. . . . When the daimonic is repressed, it tends to *erupt* in some form—its extreme forms being assassination, the psychopathological tortures of the murders on the moors and other horrors we know only too well in this century.
>
> "Although we may recoil in horror," writes the British psychiatrist Anthony Storr, "when we read in newspapers or history books of the atrocities committed by man upon man, we know in our hearts that each one of us harbors within himself those same savage impulses which lead to murder, to torture and to war" [May, 1969, p. 129].

I am pleading for a realistic approach to human evil. A colleague tells me that when you had the discussion with Martin Buber in Michigan you said, "Man is basically good," and Buber answered, "Man is basically good—and evil." I am arguing that we must include a view of the evil in our world and in ourselves no matter how much that evil offends our narcissism. When we can deal with this evil, then and only then what we say about goodness will have power and cogency. Then we can speak in ways that will genuinely affect our culture, in contrast to the miniscule number of people we see in our therapeutic offices.

You and I have often affirmed the capacities of human beings to be autonomous to some extent, to make decisions, to assert some freedom of choice in interrelationship with their destiny and their culture. These capacities put an added responsibility upon us to affirm realistically the anxiety involved, the precarious and limited nature of this freedom, and the fact that our belief in the human being can work for good only when the individual can face the world with all its inner and outer cruelty, its failure, and its tragedy.

The issue of evil—or rather, the issue of not confronting evil—has profound, and to my mind adverse, effects on humanistic psychology. I believe it is the most important error in the humanistic movement. Thus Yankelovich (1981) can say, in his book *New Rules* (which is concerned, as you and I are, with the persons of tomorrow), that humanistic psychology is the narcissism of our culture. I believe he is right. The narcissists are persons who are turned inward rather than outward, who are so lost in self-love that they cannot see and relate to the reality outside themselves, including other human beings. Some people who join and lead the humanistic movement do so in order to find a haven, a port in the storm, a community of like-minded persons who also are playing possum to the evils about us. I, for one, choose to be part of the minority that seeks to make the Association for Humanistic Psychology an organization that commits itself actively to confronting the issues of evil and good in our selves, our society, and our world.

In my experience, our human adventures from cradle to grave take on a zest, a challenge, an attractiveness when we see and affirm this human potentiality of both good and evil. The joy we experience will have, as its other pole, the self-assertion, the hostility, the negative possibilities that I have been talking about. In my experience it is this polarity, this dialectical interaction, this oscillation between positive and negative that gives the dynamic and the depth to human life. Life, to me is not a requirement to live out a preordained pattern of goodness, but a challenge coming down through the centuries out of the fact that each of us can throw the lever toward good or toward evil. This seems to me to require the age-old religious truths of mercy and forgiveness and (here I am sure you would agree with me) it leaves no place for moral superiority or self-righteousness.

I recall that in my younger days in the middle 1930s I had a position as counselor at a midwestern college. The vocal portion of the students at this college were pacifists. We believed in the League of Nations and we felt certain that we needed only to outlaw war for the world to have peace. I remember looking at a professor who said there would be another war as though he were a pariah. How wrong my colleagues and I were! We could not even believe what we read in the papers about the persecution of the Jews in Germany, just as people nowadays cannot believe what they read in the newspapers about nuclear bombs. The important point of this story is that Hitler capitalized on our noble but unrealistic ideals, and this, I believe, contributed to or at least hastened World War II. This is why I wrote in *Love and Will*:

> Not to recognize the daimonic itself turns out to be daimonic; it makes us accomplices on the side of the destructive possession [May, 1969, p. 131].

I am not predicting doom. But I am stating that if we ignore evil, we will move closer to doom, and the growth and triumph of evil may well result.

I am not a pessimist. Yes, I believe in tragedy, as Shakespeare's dramas and Eugene O'Neill and others portray it, because I perceive tragedy as showing the nobility of human existence. Without it life would be pallid, uninteresting, and flat. I smile when I note, in conversations with some of my so-called optimistic friends, that when we get down to fundamental issues such as the possibilities of atomic war or the coming food crunch, or the fact that this planet itself will in all probability be wiped out in a finite number of years, their optimism turns out to be a reaction formation to their hopelessness; and I turn out to be more hopeful than they. This is because, it seems to me, one needs a philosophy for oneself that can stand regardless of failure in our actions or temporary despair.

All of this goes to demonstrate again that the terms "optimism" and "pessimism" refer to the state of one's digestion, and having nothing whatever to do with truth.

I write this letter, dear Carl, with profound respect for you and your contribution in the past to all of us. If I speak strongly, it is because I believe strongly.

Yours,

Rollo May

REFERENCES

Cousins, N. Thoughts at year's end. *Saturday Review,* December 1981, p. 12.

May, R. *Love and will.* New York: Norton, 1969.

Milgram, S. *Obedience to authority.* New York: Harper & Row, 1969.

Raskin, N. Becoming—a therapist, a person, a partner, a parent. *Psychotherapy: Theory Research and Practice,* 1978, **15(4).**

Rogers, C. *A way of being.* Boston: Houghton Mifflin, 1980.

Rogers, C. Notes on Rollo May. *Perspectives,* 1981, 2(1).

Rogers, C., Gendlin, E., Kiesler, D., & Truax, C. *The therapeutic relationship with schizophrenics.* Madison: University of Wisconsin Press, 1967.

Yankelovich, D. *New rules.* New York: Random House, 1981.

Zimbardo, P. G., Banks, W. C., Haney, C., & Jaffee, D. The mind is a formidable jailor: A Pirandellian prison. *New York Times Magazine,* April 8, 1973, p. 38ff.

22

REPLY TO ROLLO MAY'S LETTER TO CARL ROGERS

CARL R. ROGERS

Dear Rollo:

Tom Greening has sent me your eloquent and scholarly letter dealing with the problem of evil and evil behavior. Your thoughtful analyses and arguments will provoke a lot of good thinking and I appreciate that.

Unfortunately, your material arrives on the eve of my departure for Europe and by the time I return, the editor's deadline will be at hand. Consequently, this must be a hasty reply, which I regret. I cannot possibly touch on all the issues that you raised.

I would like first to deal with a couple of lesser points in your letter, ones on which my feelings are clear.

When you speak of the narcissism that has been fostered by humanistic psychology and how many individuals are "lost in self-love," I feel like speaking up and saying, "That's not true!" Then I realize that what I am saying is that it is not true in my experience, but my experience is limited to clients and groups dealt with by my particular brand of humanistic psychology and philosophy. In those groups I simply have not seen the development of a harmful narcissism and certainly not of an excessive self-love. If these characteristics have emerged in other facets of the humanistic movement, I have not been in contact with them. I realize this is quite possible because I am not closely in touch with other aspects of the humanistic movement.

In the groups with which I've had contact, the truth is quite the contrary. Such groups lead to social action of a realistic nature. Individuals who come in as social fanatics become much more socially realistic, but they still want to take action. People who have not been very

Reprinted from the *Journal of Humanistic Psychology, 22,* 85–89. (1982). Copyright © 1982 by Sage Publications. Reprinted by permission of the publisher.

aware of social issues become more aware and, again, opt for realistic actions on those issues. We have had plenty of evidence of this in our encounter groups and workshops. Irrational anger and violence are sometimes defused, but action of a more realistic sort increases.

One amusing bit of personal evidence on this. When I received the copy of your open letter, I was putting the finishing touches on a very strong statement about nuclear war and what might be done to prevent it. I am taking a stand against the policies of our government, which I feel are making nuclear war more likely. This is but one example of the fact that we agree in so many ways it is difficult to be exactly certain where we differ. I am sure that you and I are both acting to do what we can to prevent this monstrous evil of nuclear war.

You speak at length of the failure of people like myself and client-centered therapy to recognize, accept, and respond to feelings of anger, hostility, and negative feelings in general, perhaps especially those directed toward the therapist. I think that to some extent this was definitely true of me in the distant past, although I have also published examples of the way in which I dealt with bitter hostility toward me in therapy. I have never quite agreed with the opinion of the outside evaluators in our schizophrenic research, that we as a group dodged or evaded the negative or hostile reactions. I have to recognize that possibly the evaluators were correct. Certainly in recent years I feel that I have responded much more adequately to such attitudes. The film, "Carl Rogers Counsels an Individual: Anger and Hurt," of which considerable portions are published in *The Comprehensive Textbook of Psychiatry/III* (1980), show that I was responsive to both anger and to the pain that was discovered to be underlying it. I believe I have learned to be acceptant of anger toward me and toward others. There may be truth in what you say, that client-centered therapists have a tendency not to accept or respond to such feelings. If so, I regret this as much as you.

Now I would like to turn to the more fundamental issue. You have never seemed to care whether the evil impulses in many are genetic and inherent or whether they are acquired after birth. For you they are just there. For me their origin makes a great deal of difference philosophically. I would like to try to clarify my reasons. I feel that the tendency toward actualization is inherent. In this, man is like all other organisms. I can count on it being present. It may take bizarre and futile forms. I have given an example of the potatoes in a basement bin, sending their feeble white sprouts upward in a futile effort to reach the light. I feel similarly about the deprived ghetto youth whose only path to ego enhancement is to be the best mugger or the most daring burglar in his gang. My attitude is similar toward the psychotic in a back ward who is Jesus Christ. But the basic, actualizing tendency operates toward fulfillment.

I find in my experience no such innate tendency toward destructiveness, toward evil. I cannot count on the certainty that this individual is striving consciously or unconsciously to fulfill an evil nature. I do not find this in animals either. There is, however, one rare exception which has stuck in my mind. I saw a television show of African wild dogs. There was one female who was jealous of another. When the second female was absent from her den, the first would go into the den, remove one of the cubs, and kill it. This went on day after day until the litter was totally destroyed. I can still remember my shock at that, because it is so uncharacteristic of animals. They kill, but normally only in the interest of actualizing themselves. I gather that you feel the central tendency in human nature is a dual one, aiming both toward creative growth and destructive evil. With the exception I have just mentioned, I don't find that describes animal behavior, or plant behavior, or human behavior. If the elements making for growth are present, the actualizing tendency develops in positive ways. In the human these elements for growth are not only proper nutrition, etc., but a climate of psychological attitudes.

So, how do I account for the evil behavior that is so obviously present in our world? In my experience, every person has the capacity for evil behavior. I, and others, have had murderous and cruel impulses, desires to hurt, feelings of anger and rage, desires to impose our wills on others. It is well to bear in mind that I also have a capacity to vomit, for example. Whether I, or anyone, will translate these impulses into behavior depends, it seems to me, on two elements: social conditioning and voluntary choice. Perhaps we can use Hitler as an example. His early personal life and social circumstances certainly made it natural that he would try to fulfill himself by being a big-shot, a leader full of hatred toward those he perceived as responsible for his humiliation. But beyond that, in acts like the decision to exterminate the Jews, a personal choice for which he was responsible was also a very real factor.

I believe that, theoretically at least, every evil behavior is brought about by varying degrees of these elements.

I will admit that there is much I don't understand about some evil behaviors. The experiments by Milgram and Zimbardo are a shocking puzzle to me, as they were to the experimenters. Certainly Milgram's subjects were influenced by our education for conformity and Zimbardo's subjects by our training in prejudice. But I would agree with you that those scarcely seem like adequate explanations.

It is interesting that in our decisions about what to do about evil behavior and evil situations, we seem remarkably similar. We take the best action we can see to oppose evil, to destroy the causes, to try to reach people who are acting in hurtful ways. I am pleased that I had the opportunity to work with groups composed of hostile and feuding individuals whose evil intentions toward one another were very evident. In a group we worked with from Belfast, which included both Catholic and Protestant extremists as well as moderates, a Protestant young woman said in one of the early sessions, "If a wounded IRA man were lying before me on the street, I would *step* on him"! This was typical of some of the bitter feelings expressed. Yet in a climate of understanding and acceptance those people changed so much in attitudes in a short sixteen hours of contact that when they went back to Belfast they worked in teams of two to show the film to groups in the interest of reconciliation. So I don't for one minute agree that humanistic psychology, at least my kind of humanistic psychology, "cuts the nerve of social action." It enhances social action.

You talk at some length about the transformation that I believe is coming to our world. Here I am much influenced by the thinking of men like Prigogine. The current perturbations in our society and in our world do seem to me to predict that there is an inevitable social transformation coming. In chemistry, and I believe in our culture, these extremes of perturbation lead to a reorganization, to a higher level of order. As to the person of tomorrow, I think you quite misunderstand my description of that person. I was speaking of the person who would be fit to live in the transformed world, not the average person, and though I believe a transformation is inevitable, it certainly will not be a socially constructive transformation unless we all give it every effort. There I think we can agree.

Curiously enough there is one minor point on which I think you are much too optimistic. You speak twice of our culture deteriorating or disintegrating like the cultures of Greece and Rome. I think that is a possible scenario, but it is not what will happen if we have a nuclear war. In that case, our culture will be utterly obliterated. It will not simply deteriorate or disintegrate.

Rollo, you have raised many profound points and this is, I am well aware, a hasty and inadequate reply. Yet I hope that between the two documents people will be stirred to constructive thought. As I said in my earlier published remarks about you, you have been a great contributor to humanistic psychology and I value you very much for that. I hold you in affectionate regard.

Sincerely,

Carl Rogers

23

HUMANISTIC PSYCHOLOGY AND THE HUMANE BUT TOUGH-MINDED PSYCHOLOGIST

MICHAEL WERTHEIMER

Humanistic psychology appears to be gaining the enthusiastic support of many thoughtful people these days. The following pages attempt to address possible problems with humanistic psychology; clearly, it may well also have some virtues, and there may be various dangers associated with some "nonhumanistic" approaches to psychology. But an informed examination of humanistic psychology is likely to lead to more rational evaluations of its merits than would an uncritical, emotional, impulsive endorsement.

WHAT IS HUMANISTIC PSYCHOLOGY?

It is hard to quarrel with such goals as authenticity, actualizing the potential inherent in every human being, creating truly meaningful human relationships, being fully in touch with our innermost feelings, and expanding our awareness. But what, really, is humanistic psychology? To paraphrase an old Jewish joke, if you ask two humanists what humanistic psychology is, you are likely to get at least three mutually incompatible definitions. Indeed, a first glance at the myriad uses of the term *humanistic* gives the disquieting impression that it is used much like the word *dynamic,* as in "a dynamic personality" or in "dynamic psychology." All too often this use

Reprinted from the *American Psychologist, 33,* 739–746. (1978).

The author acknowledges with thanks the helpful comments and bibliographical sleuthing of Sarla Sujan, from Bombay, India, and more recently Perth, Australia, who spent a few months in 1977 with the author in Boulder, Colorado.

is woefully vague and almost purely evaluative rather than substantive. Maybe *humanistic*, like *dynamic*, is just another adjectival equivalent of "correct," "desirable," or "good," or of "my (obviously correct) view, as opposed to the (obviously wrong) views of all those imbeciles who don't agree with me." R. S. Woodworth (1918), Wolfgang Köhler (1940), and various depth psychologists (e.g., Munroe, 1955) have used the word *dynamic* to mean very different things, ranging from a concern with motivation, to physical equilibrium, to psychoanalytic notions about the unconscious. Has the word *humanistic* suffered a similar dilution? I fear it has, and probably even more so than the overworked *dynamic*.

The words *humanism* and *humanistic* have been around for a long time. In the late medieval period and the early Renaissance, they had a particular technical religious meaning within organized Christianity, especially in Italy. During the 18th and 19th centuries they referred, among other things, to classical Greek and Roman scholarship and were also clearly associated with the German romantic movement. And William James even used *humanism* almost synonymously with *pragmatism* as a name for his own philosophy (Dooley, 1975).

But how about the phrase *humanistic psychology* itself? An inspiring, succinct characterization was presented in the exhibitors' directory at the front of the 1977 APA convention program book under Association for Humanistic Psychology. "We are a worldwide network organized to develop the human sciences in ways that recognize our distinctively human qualities. The Association links for support and stimulation people who have a humanistic vision of the person, it encourages others to share this view, and it shows how this vision can be realized." Inspiring, yes; succinct, almost; explicit and unambiguous, no. Where can we find a fuller definition?

DEFINITIONS IN THE *JOURNAL OF HUMANISTIC PSYCHOLOGY*

An obvious place to look is in the original documents that launched the Association for Humanistic Psychology, and its journal, which actually was born before the Association. The Association originally was called the American Association for Humanistic Psychology (AAHP). Anthony J. Sutich, Editor of the *Journal of Humanistic Psychology*, introduced its first issue in part as follows:

> After years of intensive effort, we can say that the "Third Force"—Humanistic Psychology—has taken root and is becoming an acceptable and vital part of the general field of psychology. . . . Drs. Abraham H. Maslow, Erich Fromm, Kurt Goldstein, Carl Rogers, Karen Horney and Gordon Allport have made outstanding contributions to this prolonged effort. . . .
>
> It . . . became apparent that a great contribution could be made to human welfare in the science and profession of psychology if the monopoly of the two main developed forces [meaning behaviorism and psychoanalysis] could be by-passed or circumvented. Existentialist Psychology and Phenomenological Psychology, among others, sprang up in the course of new attempts to open up the vast and crucial inner life of humans with a view to releasing their potentials for maximum self-fulfillment.
>
> In this country "official" organizations, policies, and journals have been rather inhospitable, to say the least, to the publication of findings along the above broadly stated lines of scientific inquiry. . . .
>
> The *Journal of Humanistic Psychology* is being founded by a group of psychologists and professional men and women from other fields who are interested in those human capacities and potentialities that have no systematic place either in positivistic or behavioristic theory or in classical psychoanalytic theory, e.g., creativity, love, self, growth, organism, basic need-gratification, self-actualization, higher values, ego-transcendence, objectivity, autonomy, identity, responsibility, psychological health, etc. This approach can also be characterized by the writings of Goldstein, Fromm, Horney, Rogers, Maslow, Allport, Angyal , Bühler, Moustakas,

> etc., as well as by certain aspects of the writings of Jung, Adler, and the psychoanalytic ego-psychologists. (Sutich, 1961, pp. vii–ix)

Thus, the *Journal of Humanistic Psychology* was begun in protest against behaviorism and psychoanalysis, explicitly as a third force. "Humanistic psychology" was defined as related to existentialism and to phenomenology, as concerned with "neglected" areas such as creativity, love, and identity, and also by the individuals seen as representing the third force: Maslow, some neo-Freudian writers, Rogers, and others. Some people identified with the first two forces might have felt surprised that they weren't supposed to be interested in creativity, love, and so on.

The Articles of Association for the AAHP (*Journal of Humanistic Psychology*, 1962, pp. 96–98) contain a "definition" that is almost identical to the material in Sutich's introduction to the first issue of the *Journal*. The list of capacities and potentialities loses the term *identity* and gains the terms "being, becoming, spontaneity, play, humor, affection, naturalness, [and] warmth." The list of names of those whose writings are characteristic of the approach is the same, although the phrase "existential and phenomenological psychologists" is added at the end. Incidentally, the *Review of Existential Psychology and Psychiatry* was started in the same year as the *Journal of Humanistic Psychology*—1961. Curiously, there has been very little overlap of authors of articles between the two periodicals.

The *Journal of Humanistic Psychology* initially appeared twice a year and since 1973 has been published quarterly. The early Editorial Board included, among others, J. F. T. Bugental, Charlotte Bühler, Hadley Cantril, Kurt Goldstein, S. I. Hayakawa, Sidney M. Jourard, Abraham H. Maslow, Rollo May, Clark Moustakas, Ira Progoff, David Riesman, Carl R. Rogers, and Ernest G. Schachtel. Most of the editors' degrees were indicated as being PhDs, but Schachtel's was changed in the third issue from a PhD to an LID and in the next issue to the LLD; all degrees were dropped from the masthead after that.

The masthead of the second issue was briefer than earlier statements, indicating that

> *The Journal of Humanistic Psychology* is concerned with the publication of theoretical and applied research, original contributions, papers, articles and studies in values, autonomy, being, self, love, creativity, identity, growth, psychological health, organism, self-actualization, basic need-gratification and related concepts.

This statement remained unchanged for many years.

The current editor of the journal is Thomas Greening, and his masthead reads in part as follows:

> *The Journal of Humanistic Psychology* . . . publishes experiential reports, theoretical papers, personal essays, research studies, applications of humanistic psychology, humanistic analyses of contemporary culture, and occasional poems. Topics of special interest are authenticity, encounter, self-actualization, self-transcendence, search for meaning, creativity, personal growth, psychological health, being-motivation, values, identity and love. The *Journal* is a forum for diverse statements about humanistic psychology, including criticisms.

Clearly the focus has changed a bit; the methodology is more permissive; some of the old topics are gone, and there are some new ones. The meaning of some of the new ones is not self-evident—among them being-motivation, self-transcendence, and encounter.

Early issues of the *Journal of Humanistic Psychology* carried articles by such people as Mary Henle on "A Humanistic Research Course in Personality"; by Ronald E. Shor on "A Survey of Representative Literature on Freud's Death-Instinct Hypothesis"; by Richard W. Kilby on "Personal Values of Indian and American University Students"; and many contributions by members of the Editorial Board, especially Maslow, Bühler, and Moustakas. A lot of them, I believe, could easily have made it through the review process for then-existing APA journals.

None of the authors of articles in the first two issues of 1977 were the same as those in the first 3 years or so of the *Journal*'s existence; representative recent paper titles are "On Escaping Death," "Is Gestalt Therapy a Humanistic Form of Psychotherapy?" (incidentally, the author, Len Bergantino, concludes that it is not), "Competence as a Facilitator of Personal Growth Groups," and "Transpersonal Perspectives in Psychotherapy." The type of article, as well as the masthead statement, seems to have changed a bit in a decade and a half.

DEFINITIONS IN BOOKS

Is it clear now what humanistic psychology is? No? Let's look at another potential source of definition of the field—books about it. In recent years, there has been quite a flurry of them, of which I shall mention only a few. An early one was Frank Severin's (1965) book of readings, *Humanistic Viewpoints in Psychology*. He divided his anthology into three parts. Part 1, "The Nature of Man," has sections entitled "The Whole is Greater than the Part," "Living or Being Lived," "The Unique Animal," and "Minding the Body." Part 2, "Science and the Study of Man," is broken down into "The Human Dimensions of Science," "The Influence of Physics on Psychology," "Operationalism," and "Broadening Methodological Horizons." Part 3, "Psychology and Human Values," contains articles on "Cognitive Maps," "Wholesome Personality," "Value Orientation in Counseling," and "Future Man." Among the authors of articles reprinted or excerpted in Severin's book are, of course, Maslow, Bugental, May, Moustakas, and Rogers, but also Gustav Bergmann, P. W. Bridgman, James B. Conant, D. O. Hebb, David C. McClelland, and M. Brewster Smith. Severin (1965, p. xvii) quotes Joseph Wood Krutch as follows, with approval:

> A humanist is anyone who rejects the attempt to describe or account for man wholly on the basis of physics, chemistry, and animal behavior. He is anyone who believes that will, reason, and purpose are real and significant; that value and justice are aspects of a reality called good and evil and rest upon some foundation other than custom; that consciousness is so far from being a mere epiphenomenon that it is the most tremendous of actualities; that the unmeasurable may be significant.

Incidentally, in this book, the names of S. E. Asch and Max Wertheimer are added to the list of persons in whose writings the humanistic approach finds expression.

Sutich and Vich published *Readings in Humanistic Psychology*, another anthology, largely of articles from the *Journal of Humanistic Psychology*, in 1969. This book's three parts are simply called "Theory," "Survey and Research," and "Applications." The first part contains selections by Maslow, Rogers, Bühler and others; the second, by Alan Watts, Rollo May, and others; and the third, by Bugental and Tannenbaum on "Sensitivity Training and Being Motivation," Sidney M. Jourard on "Sex in Marriage," Ronald P. Hattis on "Love Feelings in Courtship Couples: An Analysis," and others. Like the preceding Severin book, this anthology uses the early masthead characterization from the *Journal of Humanistic Psychology* in the introduction in an attempt to define the field. The growing breadth (dare I say vagueness?) of the definition of the approach is acknowledged in such further sentences in the introduction as the following:

> Any attempt at a conclusive definition of humanistic psychology would be premature. Moreover, the original problem of definition continues as a problem of reflecting the powerful thrust of an ongoing, continuously evolving, vital development. . . . It is this perspective which makes it unnecessary, perhaps even impossible for humanistic psychology to be a definite, distinct doctrine or school in psychology. (Sutich & Vich, 1969, pp. 7–8)

How about books about humanistic psychology as such? Maddi and Costa (1972) wrote a book, *Humanism in Personology: Allport, Maslow, and Murray,* whose title at least by implication makes it clear that Gordon Allport and Henry A. Murray are to be considered humanists just as Maslow is. Ralph Heine's foreword (p. xii) says that "The three theorists whose work is described in this volume never let their science come between them and their interest in behaving, intact, self-governing humans, and as a consequence their science was enriched." Maddi and Costa's own introductory chapter once again refers to humanism as the third force, opposed to behaviorism and psychoanalysis, and says it is especially focused on the human *individual* and is positive and optimistic about human nature. In the next chapter, people are characterized as proactive, psychologically complex, rational, psychologically unique, future oriented, and as possessing "psychological organization."

The distinguished Yale social psychologist Irvin L. Child in 1973 published a somewhat curious, but clearly thoughtful, book entitled *Humanistic Psychology and the Research Tradition: Their Several Virtues.* In it (like Senders, 1978), he argues that a truly viable modern psychology fuses the two. By "the research tradition" he means scientific psychology as exemplified by APA's Division 3 and a few others. But in characterizing humanistic psychology, he refers to the humanities and their effort for centuries to understand the human condition and to promote personal welfare and growth.

> Humanistic psychology is defined by its model of man, by its insistence that the body of scientific knowledge about man will develop most usefully if it is guided by a conception of man as he knows himself rather than by some nonhuman analogy. (Child, 1973, p. 13).

Child (1973) accuses many humanistic psychologists of neglecting "the systematic observational side of science" (p. 13), of forgetting that an understanding of people "cannot go far until it is adequately related to the test of observation" (p. 14), of "a frequent vagueness" (p. 19), of "smugness" (p. 21), and of "a trend toward sentimentality" (p. 21). But among their virtues Child finds "respect for individual initiative and freedom, and the desire to expand them" (p. 16), "a regard for individual responsibility" (p. 17), "attention to the person as a whole and to his understanding of the context of his action" (p. 15), their "openness" (p. 18), and especially their "intuitive rightness" (p. 18), their "fit with the general evidence of everyone's personal experience" (p. 19).

Henryk Misiak and Virginia Sexton have a chapter on humanistic psychology in their 1973 book entitled *Phenomenological, Existential and Humanistic Psychologies: A Historical Survey.* Concerning a definition of the field, they write (pp. 115–116),

> There is no conclusive definition of humanistic psychology. The movement can be viewed as both a protest and a new program, even as a new school and a system. Its protest is directed against the entire orientation of psychology since Hobbes and Locke, against its Newtonian and Darwinian models of man, and against its mechanistic, deterministic, and reductionist character. While both Freudism and behaviorism emphasize man's continuity with the animal world, humanistic psychology pays special attention to characteristics and capacities which make man uniquely different from the animals. It is the protest more than specific theories that has attracted, under the banner of humanistic psychology, psychologists who are loosely connected ideologically.

A perceptive description, I believe. Incidentally, Misiak and Sexton's chapter on humanistic psychology contains a substantial section on "the encounter group movement."

Joseph Rychlak's *The Psychology of Rigorous Humanism* was published in 1977. It is a substantial work, half a thousand pages long, riddled with neologisms, and to say only a few words about it is inevitably to do it an injustice. Much of his theme contrasts a Lockean with a Kantian view of psychology, with the latter, the core of which is teleological, having undergone defeat in American psychology at the hands of the Lockean view. A teleological emphasis has, however, reappeared in recent years, as exemplified by Carl Rogers; this is a Kuhnian scientific revolution. Rychlak identifies humanism with a theoretical stance that seeks descriptions in terms of formal and final causes and claims that this can indeed be done rigorously. He provides a detailed example in his "logical learning theory." Rychlak ends his book with 10 "tenets of rigorous humanism" (pp. 492–498), in which he argues that it is impossible in principle to attain theory from method, that external methods are compatible with introspective theories, that any descriptive formulation applicable to an experimenter must be applicable to the subject and vice versa, that any observed factual pattern—experimental or otherwise—has *N* possible explanations, that the word *control* in the phrase "control and prediction" refers to both the logic of experimental design and the subsequent manipulation carried out in the experimental context, that "the line of development from theory to methodological test" should be made more explicit, that the word *variable* should be confined to methodological discussion and removed entirely from theoretical discussion, that formal final-cause constructions should be readmitted in the realm of theory as legitimate explanations in their own right, and that humanistic and humanitarian approaches in psychology should be sharply distinguished. For Rychlak, humanism means using teleology in the description of people's behavior, while humanitarianism means striving to improve the human lot.

OTHER SOURCES OF DEFINITION

For that matter, I have not yet addressed the encounter movement, sensitivity training, the "humanistic psychotherapies," or "humanistic education." This is what "humanistic psychology" means for many people. Typical of many similar agencies on many campuses, the University of Colorado Counseling Center offered free "workshops" during the summer of 1977 on "Creative Anger," "Assertiveness Training," "Developing Intimacy," and other analogous topics. Werner Erhard in 1971 started the Erhard Seminars Training, or "est," which exemplifies the popular human potential movement and provides a variety of large group encounter experiences (Rhinehart, 1976). Albert Ellis's (1973) rational-emotive approach has been called a "humanistic psychotherapy." Richard and Patricia Schmuck (1974) recently published a book entitled *A Humanistic Psychology of Education: Making the School Everybody's House.*

Douglas Heath has written *Growing Up in College* (1968) and *Humanizing Schools* (1971). Heath (1971) believes that children should develop more wholly. Learning should be highly experiential, exercising mental, physical, and emotional energies. He argues that in an atmosphere of mutuality and cooperation, real choices and experiences will foster "skills of being," through which students learn to assess and change themselves as well as their social institutions. All of us, recommends Heath, should free ourselves to become more mature persons open to venturing and risking.

Heath (1968) claims that we develop or mature in five interrelated ways. Maturing people become *more aware* persons, able to reflect on their experience and to bring memories and knowledge readily into awareness. They become *more autonomous,* for they are not so readily determined by unconscious motives, or earlier childhood conflicts, or "hang-ups" and are not so easily coerced by outside influences. They become *more allocentric,* other-centered, in respect to the internalization of their culture, and more socialized by developing out of their egocentric shells to identify with others, to "care" for others, to be sympathetic and loving. Maturing persons become progressively *more integrated* and consistent persons, seeking new experiences, keeping themselves open to new experiences and information, making active attempts to order their experiences and make their values and actions more consistent. They become *more stable* persons with a firm sense of identity, with reasonably stable motives and values that persist over time, with the capacity to "center down," to "bounce back" in difficult times (paraphrased from Heath, 1968). All clearly laudable goals. But how do you know when you have attained them?

Let's try one last source of definition, by example. To what did Division 32, the Division of Humanistic Psychology, devote program time at the 1977 APA convention? Here's a sample: creation of community; intimacy in psychotherapy; meditation, theater, and psychotherapy; Carl Rogers's contributions to humanistic education and to other fields; innovative group approaches to the treatment of sexual dysfunction; a blueprint for the humanistic educations and therapies of the future; clinical and theoretical issues in therapist-patient erotic contact.

THREE POSSIBLE MEANINGS OF "HUMANISTIC PSYCHOLOGY"

Now where does all this leave us, with respect to a definition of humanistic psychology? Hopelessly lost, I fear. "Humanistic psychology" is a phrase that has been used with so many different, and such vague, meanings that it is highly unlikely that an explicit definition of it could be written that would satisfy even a small fraction of the people who call themselves "humanistic psychologists." And yet, one can barely discern some shimmering apparitions in the swirling, misty murk. Although they in no sense cover all of the uses of the phrase, there seem to be at least three distinguishable meanings. Let us tentatively identify them as psychology among the liberal arts, the human potential movement, and antimechanism.

It is hard to see how anyone could quarrel with the old tried-and-true ideal of a liberal education for someone who aspires to become a psychologist—indeed, for anybody. Psychologists do not have exclusive possession of human nature. Dostoevski, Lao-tse, Shakespeare, Beethoven, Goethe, Frank Lloyd Wright, the early Ingmar Bergman, and thousands of other nonpsychologists have contributed mightily to the richness of our understanding of the human condition. Anthropology, drama, biology, political science, sociology, psychiatry, history, the novel, economics, and on and on—there are many endeavors focused on unraveling the human riddle. A proper liberal education can provide a valuable perspective for anyone, including any psychologist. And yet it is doubtful that such a background will have a very profound or direct effect on the day-to-day activities of many psychologists.

The second meaning, associated with human enhancement and closely tied to clinical psychology, seems to have gained adherents in rapidly growing numbers in the last couple of decades. From a "tough-minded" or detached, hopefully dispassionate stance, this development, frankly, makes one uneasy. It has the earmarks of a burgeoning religion. It has a tremendous popular following. It is making huge sums of money for gurus, some with questionable credentials. It is capturing the allegiance of many innocents who don't have the sense to ask for evidence that the magic treatments, experiences, or encounters do indeed result in the idyllic consequences they are supposed to. Uncritical testimonials take the place of hard-nosed data.

Incidentally, I asked a number of my clinical colleagues for literature on the effectiveness of what have been called "the humanistic psychotherapies," "the encounter experiences," "consciousness-raising workshops," and the like. Their responses have generally confirmed my fears. In the first place, and perhaps most disturbing, these approaches are typically inimical to solid data: It is almost heretical, "dehumanizing," to raise a question about the effectiveness of these procedures. And to the extent that there *is* a small literature on their effectiveness, the data appear to be somewhat equivocal. Psychotherapy outcome research is methodologically among the most difficult research areas, although a few reasonably well-designed investigations do exist. Smith and Glass (1977) recently surveyed the approximately 400 controlled evaluations of psychotherapy and counseling extant to date. What is a reasonable conclusion at this stage? That there is, overall, no difference between "behavioral" and "nonbehavioral" therapies, and that, on the average, both have a slight positive effect: The typical therapy client is better off than 75% of untreated controls.

But there is no documentation that any of these forms of treatment—"humanistic" or otherwise—produces results that cannot readily be explained as due to self-fulfilling prophecies. That is, client expectation, socially facilitated by other clients and by the therapist, could be all that is needed to account for the barely positive results. Improvements, if any, might be due to nothing more than a placebo effect. And there also are disconcerting occasional reports that the "therapeutic" procedures may be damaging some clients. All in all, it appears that prudence would dictate caution in the use of such procedures, at least unless and until credible data are available to show that they work, and work in a desirable fashion.

Finally, there is the wholistic, antimechanical concern with human beings as systems, as integrated units, as something other than a sum total of traits or a bundle of conditioned reflexes. This movement can be traced back several thousand years and was one of the rallying slogans of gestalt theory in the first half of the present century. All too often one hears some such cry as "the whole is more than the sum of the parts" which, of course, misses the gestalt point that most wholes are dynamic units in which the nature of the whole determines the nature of the parts; the systemic, integrated gestalt idea is captured better in a phrase like "the whole is *different from* the sum of its parts."

Relatively few theorists these days espouse a simplistic mechanical view of behavior as a sum of reflexes; to that extent, perhaps, a gestalt approach is widely accepted in the field, and a "third force" may no longer be necessary. Indeed, gestalt ideas are now commonplace in the experimental psychology of information processing, learning, perception, problem solving, and memory. A recent issue of the *Journal of Experimental Psychology: Human Perception and Performance,* for instance, includes a study by Pomerantz, Sager, and Stoever (1977) which shows that simple parts of some visually presented geometric figures are easier to discriminate if they are component segments of certain larger wholes than if they are presented in isolation.

Let me summarize. First, the humanities and the other liberal arts are a proper and useful background for a reasonably well-educated psychologist—but this should not blind us to the virtues of psychology as a natural science. A humanist background can be a source of inspiration, and of perspective, but it should not be seen as a license for vague or vapid thought.

Second, the value of humanistic therapies and education remains to be demonstrated; the hope and promise of encounter experience, humanistic education, self-enhancement, and growth groups have not been convincingly fulfilled; indeed it might well be wise to remain cautious about engaging in any such practices. Let us have not just compassion, but enlightenment too (cf. Senders, 1978).

Third, there is no harm in reaffirming the old interactive, trans-summative, systemic view of the nature of the world, including humanity; but there is little point in renaming this view "humanistic psychology" when there are already plenty of good words to refer to it.

THE HUMANISTIC VIRTUE OF BEHAVIORAL SCIENCE

I would like to close by paraphrasing a credo that was published in *A Brief History of Psychology* (Wertheimer, 1970), in which I wrote about the 20th-century revolution in the behavioral sciences: Before the turn of the century, ineffable, rich human nature was safe from the probings of the aseptic scientist; everybody knew that science could never penetrate the peculiarly human characteristics of human beings and degrade them to nothing more than just another inert part of the world of the microscope and the slide rule. The revolution brought about a new view, that there is nothing about human beings to which the cold, dispassionate empirical approach cannot be applied. Modern behavioral scientists claim that there is nothing human that is alien to them: They can study virtually any aspect of human beings that they wish to.

This revolution has not occurred without strong opposition. Some skeptics come up with the vague but strong feeling that this does not really get at the essence of humanity, that it may all be quite interesting, but somehow tangential, irrelevant to an understanding of human nature. Behavioral scientists reply that they would like to know what it is about humanity that this approach misses. Specify what is lacking, they say, and we can get to work on it. As soon as it is specified, it becomes accessible to scientific investigation, that is, to rational, empirical, and eventually pragmatic and utilitarian study.

Paradoxical as it may seem at first glance, a dispassionate scientific approach is, in the last analysis, also the most humanitarian one. We will be in the best position to help people if we know what works, what effects something has when we are trying to help troubled souls get along in this world. Tough-minded, humane science is apt to be more helpful in this endeavor than are magic, wishful thinking, nonempirical speculation, blind faith, or dogma.

REFERENCES

Child, I. L. *Humanistic psychology and the research tradition: Their several virtues.* New York: Wiley, 1973.

Dooley, P. K. *Pragmatism as humanism: The philosophy of William James.* Totowa, N.J.: Littlefield, Adams, 1975.

Ellis, A. *Humanistic psychotherapy: The rational-emotive approach* (E. Sagarin, Ed.). New York: Julian, 1973.

Greening, T. Masthead for *Journal of Humanistic Psychology,* 1977.

Heath, D. H. *Growing up in college.* San Francisco: Jossey-Bass, 1968.

Heath, D. H. *Humanizing schools: New directions, new decisions.* New York: Hayden, 1971.

Köhler, W. *Dynamics in psychology.* New York: Liveright, 1940.

Maddi, S. R., & Costa, P. T. *Humanism in personology: Allport, Maslow and Murray.* Chicago: Aldine, Atherton, 1972.

Misiak, H., & Sexton, V. S. *Phenomenological, existential, and humanistic psychologies: A historical survey.* New York: Grune & Stratton, 1973.

Munroe, R. L. *Schools of psychoanalytic thought.* New York: Dryden, 1955.

Pomerantz, J. R., Sager, L. C., & Stoever, R. J. Perception of wholes and their component parts: Some configural superiority effects. *Journal of Experimental Psychology: Human Perception and Performance,* 1977, *3,* 422–435.

Rhinehart, L. *The book of est.* New York: Holt, Rinehart & Winston, 1976.

Rychlak, J. F. *The psychology of rigorous humanism.* New York: Wiley, 1977.

Schmuck, R. A., & Schmuck, P. A. *A humanistic psychology of education: Making the school everybody's house.* Palo Alto, Calif.: National Press Books, 1974.

Senders, V. L. The future of psychology and the psychology of the future. In M. Wertheimer & L. Rappoport (Eds.), *Psychology and the problems of today.* Glenview, Ill.: Scott, Foresman, 1978.

Severin, F. T. (Ed.). *Humanistic viewpoints in psychology: A book of readings.* New York: McGraw-Hill, 1965.

Smith, M. L., & Glass, G. V. Meta-analysis of psychotherapy outcome studies. *American Psychologist,* 1977, *32,* 752–760.

Sutich, A. J. Introduction. *Journal of Humanistic Psychology,* 1961, *1,* vii–ix.

Sutich, A. J., & Vich, M. A. (Eds.). *Readings in humanistic psychology.* New York: Free Press, 1969.

Wertheimer, M. A brief history of psychology. New York: Holt, Rinehart & Winston, 1970.

Woodworth, R. S. *Dynamic psychology.* New York: Columbia University Press, 1918.

24

PSYCHOTHERAPY AND RELIGIOUS VALUES

ALLEN E. BERGIN

The importance of values, particularly religious ones, has recently become a more salient issue in psychology. The pendulum is swinging away from the naturalism, agnosticism, and humanism that have dominated the field for most of this century. There are more reasons for this than can be documented here, but a sampling illustrates the point:

1. Science has lost its authority as the dominating source of truth it once was. This change is both reflected in and stimulated by analyses that reveal science to be an intuitive and value-laden cultural form (Kuhn, 1970; Polanyi, 1962). The ecological, social, and political consequences of science and technology are no longer necessarily viewed as progress. Although a belief in the value of the scientific method appropriately persists, there is widespread disillusionment with the way it has been used and a loss of faith in it as the cure for human ills.

2. Psychology in particular has been dealt blows to its status as a source of authority for human action because of its obsession with "methodolatry" (Bakan, 1972), its limited effectiveness in producing practical results, its conceptual incoherence, and its alienation from the mainstreams of the culture (Campbell, 1975; Hogan, 1979).

During a long period of religious indifference in Western civilization, the behavioral sciences rose to a crest of prominence as a potential alternative source of answers to basic life questions (London, 1964). Enrollments in psychology classes reached an unparalleled peak, but our promises were defeated by our premises. A psychology dominated by mechanistic thought and ethical naturalism has proved insufficient, and interest is declining. A corollary of this trend

Reprinted from the *American Psychologist, 48,* 95–105. (1980).

The author is grateful to Victor Brown, Truman Madsen, Spencer Palmer, Jeff Bradshaw, and Karl White for their helpful suggestions.

is the series of searing professional critiques of the assumptions on which the field rests (Braginsky & Braginsky, 1974; Collins, 1977; Kitchener, 1980; Myers, 1978).

3. Modern times have spawned anxiety, alienation, violence, selfishness (Kanfer, 1979), and depression (Klerman, 1979); but the human spirit appears irrepressible. People want something more. The spiritual and social failures of many organized religious systems have been followed by the failures of nonreligious approaches. This seems to have stimulated renewed hope in spiritual phenomena. Some of this, as manifested in the proliferation of cults, magic, superstitions, coercive practices, and emotionalism, indicates the negative possibilities in the trend; but the rising prominence of thoughtful and rigorous attempts to restore a spiritual perspective to analyses of personality, the human condition, and even science itself represents the positive possibilities (Collins, 1977; Myers, 1978; Tart, 1977).

4. Psychologists are being influenced by the forces of this developing zeitgeist and are part of it. The emergence of studies of consciousness and cognition, which grew out of disillusionment with mechanistic behaviorism and the growth of humanistic psychology, has set the stage for a new examination of the possibility that presently unobservable realities—namely, spiritual forces—are at work in human behavior.

Rogers (1973) posed this radical development as follows:

> There may be a few who will dare to investigate the possibility that there is a lawful reality which is not open to our five senses; a reality in which present, past, and future are intermingled, in which space is not a barrier and time has disappeared. . . . It is one of the most exciting challenges posed to psychology. (p. 386)

Although there has always been a keen interest in such matters among a minority of thinkers and practitioners (Allport, 1950; James, 1902; Jung, 1958; the pastoral counseling field, etc.), they have not substantially influenced mainstream psychology. But the present phenomenon has all the aspects of a broad-based movement with a building momentum. This is indicated by an explosion of rigorous transcendental meditation research, the organization and rapid growth of the American Psychological Association's Division 36 (Psychologists Interested in Religious Issues, which sponsored nearly 70 papers at the 1979 national convention), the publication of new journals with overtly spiritual contents, such as the journal of *Judaism and Psychology* and the *Journal of Theology and Psychology,* and the emergence of new specialized, religious professional foci, such as the Association of Mormon Counselors and Psychotherapists, the Christian Association for Psychological Studies, and so on.

These developments build in part on the long-standing but insufficiently recognized work in the psychology of religion represented by various organizations (e.g., Society for the Scientific Study of Religion, American Catholic Psychological Association), journals (e.g., *Review of Religious Research*), and individuals like Clark, Dittes, Spilka, Strunk, and others (cf. Feifel, 1958; Maloney, 1977; Strommen, 1971); however, the newer positions are more explicitly pro-religious and are not deferent to mainstream psychology.

The trend is therefore also manifested by the publication of straightforward religious psychologies by academicians such as Jeeves (1976), Collins (1977), Peck (1978), Vitz (1977), and Myers (1978) and by more wide-open values analyses (Feinstein, 1979; Frank, 1977). Even textbooks are slowly beginning to introduce these formerly taboo considerations. In previous years basic psychology texts rarely mentioned religious phenomena, as though the psychology and sociology of religion literature did not exist. But the new edition of the leading introductory text (Hilgard, Atkinson, & Atkinson, 1979) contains a small section called "The Miraculous." Although the subject is still interpreted naturalistically, its inclusion does mark a change in response to changing views.

These shifting conceptual orientations are especially manifest in the field of psychotherapy, in which the value of therapy and the values that pervade its processes have become topics of scrutiny by both professionals (Lowe, 1976; Smith, Glass, & Miller, in press; Szasz, 1978) and the public (Gross, 1978).

In what follows, these issues are analyzed, as they pertain to spiritual values, in terms of six theses.

Thesis 1: Values are an inevitable and pervasive part of psychotherapy. As an applied field, psychotherapy is directed toward practical goals that are selected in value terms. It is even necessary when establishing criteria for measuring therapeutic change to decide, on a value basis, what changes are desirable. This necessarily requires a philosophy of human nature that guides the selection of measurements and the setting of priorities regarding change. Strupp, Hadley, and Gomes-Schwartz (1977) argued that there are at least three possibly divergent value systems at play in such decisions—those of the client, the clinician, and the community at large. They stated that though there is no consensus regarding conceptions of mental health, a judgment must always be made in relation to some implicit or explicit standard, which presupposes a definition of what is better or worse. They asked that we consider the following:

> If, following psychotherapy, a patient manifests increased self-assertion coupled with abrasiveness, is this good or a poor therapy outcome? . . . If . . . a patient obtains a divorce, is this to be regarded as a desirable or an undesirable change? A patient may turn from homosexuality to heterosexuality or he may become more accepting of either; an ambitious, striving person may abandon previously valued goals and become more placid (e.g., in primal therapy). How are such changes to be evaluated? (Strupp et al., 1977, pp. 92–93)

Equally important is the fact that

> in increasing number, patients enter psychotherapy not for the cure of traditional "symptoms" but (at least ostensibly) for the purpose of finding meaning in their lives, for actualizing themselves, or for maximizing their potential. (Strupp et al., 1977, p. 93)

Consequently, "every aspect of psychotherapy presupposes some implicit moral doctrine" (London, 1964, p. 6). Lowe's (1976) treatise on value orientations in counseling and psychotherapy reveals with painstaking clarity the philosophical choices on which the widely divergent approaches to intervention hinge. He argued cogently that everything from behavioral technology to community consultation is intricately interwoven with secularized moral systems, and he supported London's (1964) thesis that psychotherapists constitute a secular priesthood that purports to establish standards of good living.

Techniques are thus a means for mediating the value influence intended by the therapist. It is inevitable that the therapist be such a moral agent. The danger is in ignoring the reality that we do this, for then patient, therapist, and community neither agree on goals nor efficiently work toward them. A correlated danger is that therapists, as secular moralists, may promote changes not valued by the client or the community, and in this sense, if there is not some consensus and openness about what is being done, the therapists may be unethical or subversive.

The impossibility of a value-free therapy is demonstrated by certain data. I allude to just one of many illustrations that might be cited. Carl Rogers personally values the freedom of the individual and attempts to promote the free expression of each client. However, two independent studies done a decade apart (Murray, 1956; Truax, 1966) showed that Carl Rogers systematically rewarded and punished expressions that he liked and did not like in the verbal behavior of clients.

His values significantly regulated the structure and content of therapeutic sessions as well as their outcomes (cf. Bergin, 1971). If a person who intends to be nondirective cannot be, then it is likely that the rest of us cannot either.

Similarly, when we do research with so-called objective criteria, we select them in terms of subjective value judgments, which is one reason we have so much difficulty in agreeing on the results of psychotherapy outcome studies. If neither practitioners nor researchers can be nondirective, then they must accept certain realities about the influence they have. A value-free approach is impossible.

Thesis 2: Not only do theories, techniques, and criteria reveal pervasive value judgments, but outcome data comparing the effects of diverse techniques show that non-technical, value-laden factors pervade professional change processes. Comparative studies reveal few differences across techniques, thus suggesting that nontechnical or personal variables account for much of the change, Smith et al. (in press), in analyzing 475 outcome studies, were able to attribute only a small percentage of outcome variance to technique factors. Among these 475 studies were many that included supposedly technical behavior therapy procedures. The lack of technique differences thrusts value questions upon us because change appears to be a function of common human interactions, including personal and belief factors—the so-called nonspecific or common ingredients that cut across therapies and that may be the core of therapeutic change (Bergin & Lambert, 19778; Frank, 1961, 1973).

Thesis 3: Two broad classes of values are dominant in the mental health professions. Both exclude religious values, and both establish goals for change that frequently clash with theistic systems of belief. The first of these can be called clinical pragmatism. Clinical pragmatism is espoused particularly by psychiatrists, nurses, behavior therapists, and public agencies. It consists of straightforward implementation of the values of the dominant social system. In other words, the clinical operation functions within the system. It does not ordinarily question the system, but tries to make the system work. It is centered, then, on diminishing pathologies or disturbances, as defined by the clinician as an agent of the culture. This means adherence to such objectives as reducing anxiety, relieving depression, resolving guilt, suppressing deviation, controlling bizarreness, smoothing conflict, diluting obsessiveness, and so forth. The medical origins of this system are clear. It is pathology oriented. Health is defined as the absence of pathology. Pathology is that which disturbs the person or those in the environment. The clinician then forms an alliance with the person and society to eliminate the disturbing behavior.

The second major value system can be called humanistic idealism. It is espoused particularly by clinicians with interests in philosophy and social reform such as Erich Fromm, Carl Rogers, Rollo May, and various group and community interventionists. Vaughan's (1971) study of this approach identified quantifiable themes that define the goals of positive change within this frame of reference. They are flexibility and self-exploration; independence; active goal orientation with self-actualization as a core goal; human dignity and self-worth; interpersonal involvement; truth and honesty; happiness; and a frame of orientation or philosophy by which one guides one's life. This is different from clinical pragmatism in that it appeals to idealists, reformers, creative persons, and sophisticated clients who have significant ego strength. It is less practical, less conforming, and harder to measure than clinical pathology themes because it addresses more directly broad issues such as what is good and how life should be lived. It embraces a social value agenda and is often critical of traditional systems of religious values that influence child rearing, social standards, and ultimately, criteria of positive therapeutic change. Its influence is more prevalent in private therapy, universities, and independent clinical centers or research institutes, and among theologians and clinicians who espouse spiritual humanism (Fromm, 1950).

Though clinical pragmatism and humanistic idealism have appropriate places as guiding structures for clinical intervention and though I personally endorse much of their content, they are not sufficient to cover the spectrum of values pertinent to human beings and the frameworks within which they function. Noticeably absent are theistically based values.

Pragmatic and humanistic views manifest a relative indifference to God, the relationship of human beings to God, and the possibility that spiritual factors influence behavior. A survey of the leading reference sources in the clinical field reveals little literature on such subjects, except for naturalistic accounts. An examination of 30 introductory psychology texts turned up no references to the possible reality of spiritual factors. Most did not have the words *God* or *religion* in their indexes.

Psychological writers have a tendency to censor or taboo in a casual and sometimes arrogant way something that is sensitive and precious to most human beings (Campbell, 1975).

As Robert Hogan, a new section editor of the *Journal of Personality and Social Psychology,* stated in a recent *APA Monitor* interview,

> Religion is the most important social force in the history of man. . . . But in psychology, anyone who gets involved in or tries to talk in an analytic, careful way about religion is immediately branded a meathead; a mystic; an intuitive, touchy-feely sort of moron. (Hogan, 1979, p. 4).

Clinical pragmatism and humanistic idealism thus exclude what is one of the largest sub-ideologies, namely, religious or theistic approaches espoused by people who believe in God and try to guide their behavior in terms of their perception of his will.

Other alternatives are thus needed. Just as psychotherapy has been enhanced by the adoption of multiple techniques, so also in the values realm, our frameworks can be improved by the use of additional perspectives.

The alternative I wish to put forward is a spiritual one. It might be called theistic realism. I propose to show that this alternative is necessary for ethical and effective help among religious people, who constitute 30% to 90% of the U.S. population (more than 90% expressed belief, while about 30% expressed strong conviction about their belief: American Institute of Public Opinion, 1978). I also argue that the values on which this alternative is based are important ingredients in reforming and rejuvenating our society. Pragmatic and humanistic values alone, although they have substantial virtues, are often part of the problem of our deteriorating society.

What are the alternative values? The first and most important axiom is that God exists, that human beings are the creations of God, and that there are unseen spiritual processes by which the link between God and humanity is maintained. As stated in the Book of Job (32:8),

> There is a spirit in man and the inspiration of the Almighty giveth them understanding.

This approach, beginning with faith in God, assumes that spiritual conviction gives values an added power to influence life.

With respect to such belief, Max Born, the physicist, said, "There are two objectionable kinds of believers. Those who believe the incredible and those who believe that belief must be discarded in favor of the scientific method" (cited in Menninger, 1963, p. 374). I stand in opposition to placing the scientific method in the place of God, an attitude akin to Bakan's (1972) notion of "methodolatry" that has become common in our culture.

Abraham Maslow, though viewed as a humanist, expressed concepts in harmony with the views presented here. He said, "It looks as if there is a single, ultimate value for mankind—a far goal toward which men strive" (cited in Goble, 1971, p. 92). He believed that to study human behavior means never to ignore concepts of right and wrong:

> If behavioral scientists are to solve human problems, the question of right and wrong behavior is essential. It is the very essence of behavioral science. Psychologists who advocate moral and cultural relativism are not coming to grips with the real problem. Too many behavioral

> scientists have rejected not only the methods of religion but the values as well. (Maslow, cited in Goble, 1971, p. 92)

To quote further, "Instead of cultural relativity, I am implying that there are basic underlying human standards that are cross cultural" (Maslow, cited in Goble, 1971, p. 92). Maslow advocated the notion of a synergistic culture in which the values of the group make demands on the individual that are self-fulfilling. The values of such a culture are considered transcendent and not relative.

Maslow's views are consistent with the notion that there are laws of human behavior. If such laws exist, they do not sustain notions of ethical relativism. Kitchener (1980) has shown, for example, that behavioristic, evolutionary, and naturalistic ethical concepts are not relativistic (cf. Bergin, 1980). He makes the important point that ethical relativism is not a logical derivative of cultural relativism. Such views are consistent with the axiom of theistic systems that human growth is regulated by moral principles comparable in exactness with physical laws. The possible lawfulness of these moral traditions has been argued persuasively by Campbell (1975). Some comparative religionists (Palmer, Note 1) and anthropologists (Gusdorf, 1976) also recognize common religious value themes across dominant world cultures. Palmer in particular has stated that 80% of the world population adhere to common value themes consistent with the theses argued here (cf. Bergin, in press). Conceivably, these moral themes reflect something lawful in human behavior.

In light of the foregoing, it is possible to draw contrasts between theistic and clinical humanistic values as they pertain to personality and change. These are my own constructions based on clinical and religious experience and are not intended to support organized religion in general. History demonstrates that religions and religious values can be destructive, just as psychotherapy can be if not properly practiced. I therefore am not endorsing all religion, I am simply extracting from religious traditions prominent themes I hypothesize may be positive additions to clinical thinking. These are depicted in Table 1 alongside the contrasting views.

It should be noted that the theistic values do not come ex nihilo, but are consistent with a substantial psychological literature concerning responsibility (Glasser, 1965; Menninger, 1973), moral agency (Rychlak, 1979), guilt (Mowrer, 1961, 1967), and self-transcendence (Frankl, Note 2).

The comparisons outlined in the table highlight differences for the sake of making the point. It is taken for granted, however, that there are also domains of significant agreement, such as many of the humanistic values outlined by Vaughan (1971) that are fundamental to personal growth. Fromm's brilliant essays on love (1956) and independence (1947), for example, illustrate value themes that must be given prominence in any comprehensive system. The point of difference is their relative position or emphasis in the values hierarchy. Mutual commitment to fundamental human rights is also assumed, for example, to those rights pertaining to life, liberty, and the pursuit of happiness specified in the Declaration of Independence. Both theistic and atheistic totalitarianism deprive people of the basic freedoms necessary to fully implement any of the value systems outlined here; therefore, clinical humanists, pragmatists, and theists all reject coercion and value freedom of choice. This basic common premise is a uniting thesis. Without it, theories of mental health would have little meaning.

Substantial harmony can thus be achieved among the views outlined, but there is a tendency for clinical pragmatism and humanistic idealism to exclude the theistic position. On the other hand, religionists have tended to be unempirical and need to adopt the value of rigorous empiricism advocated by humanists and pragmatists. My view then would be to posit what each tradition can learn from the other rather than to create an artificial battle in which one side purports to win and the other to lose. Thus, the religion-based hypotheses stated later in Thesis 6 are an open invitation to think about and test these ideas.

TABLE 1
Theistic Versus Clinical and Humanistic Values

Theistic	Clinical–Humanistic
God is supreme. Humility, acceptance of (divine) authority, and obedience (to the will of God) are virtues.	Humans are supreme. The self is aggrandized. Autonomy and rejection of external authority are virtues.
Personal identity is eternal and derived from the divine.Relationship with God defines self-worth.	Identity is ephemeral and mortal. Relationships with others define self-worth.
Self-control in terms of absolute values. Strict mortality. Universal ethics.	Self-expression in terms of relative values. Flexible mortality. Situation ethics.
Love, affection, and self-transcedence are primary. Service and self-sacrifice are central to personal growth.	Personal needs and self-actualization are primary. Self-satisfaction is central to personal growth.
Committed to marriage, fidelity, and loyalty. Emphasis on procreation and family life as integrative factors.	Open marriage or no marriage. Emphasis on self-gratification or recreational sex without long-term responsibilities.
Personal responsibility for own harmful actions and changes in them. Acceptance of guilt, suffering, and contrition as keys to change. Restitution for harmful effects.	Others are responsible for our problems and changes. Minimizing guilt and relieving suffering before experiencing its meaning. Apology for harmful effects.
Forgiveness of others who cause distress (including parents) completes the therapeutic restoration of self.	Acceptance and expression of accusatory feelings are sufficient.
Knowledge by faith and self-effort. Meaning and purpose derived from spiritual insight. Intellectual knowledge inseparable from the emotional and spiritual. Ecology of knowledge.	Knowledge by self-effort alone. Meaning and purpose derived from reason and intellect. Intellectual knowledge for itself. Isolation of the mind from the rest of life.

Thesis 4: There is a significant contrast between the values of mental health professionals and those of a large proportion of clients. Whether or not one agrees with the values I have described above, one must admit that they are commonplace. Therapists therefore need to take into account possible discrepancies between their values and those of the average client. Four studies document this point. Lilienfeld (1966) found at the Metropolitan Hospital in New York City large discrepancies between the values of the mental health staff members and their clients, who were largely of Puerto Rican, Catholic background. With respect to topics like sex, aggression, and authority, the differences were dramatic. For example, in reply to one statement, "Some sex before marriage is good," all 19 mental health professionals agreed but only half the patients agreed. Vaughan (1971), in his study of various samples of patients, students, and professionals in the Philadelphia area, found discrepancies similar to those Lilienfeld obtained. Henry, Sims, and Spray (1971), in their study of several thousand psychotherapists in New York, Chicago, and Los Angeles, found the values of therapists to be religiously liberal relative to those of the population at large. Ragan, Malony, and Beit-Hallahmi (Note 3) reported that of a random sample of psychologists from the American Psychological Association, 50% believed in God. This is about 40% lower than the population at large, though higher than one would expect on the basis of the impression created in the literature and at convention presentations. This study also indicated that 10% of

the psychologists held positions in their various congregations, which also indicates more involvement than is predictable from the public statements of psychologists. Nevertheless, the main findings show that the beliefs of mental health professionals are not very harmonious with those of the subcultures with which they deal, especially as they pertain to definitions of moral behavior and the relevance of moral behavior to societal integration, familial functioning, prevention of pathology, and development of the self.

Thesis 5: In light of the foregoing, it would be honest and ethical to acknowledge that we are implementing our own value systems via our professional work and to be more explicit about what we believe while also respecting the value systems of others. If values are pervasive, if our values tend to be on the whole discrepant from those of the community or the client population, it would be ethical to publicize where we stand. Then people would have a better choice of what they want to get into, and we would avoid deception.

Hans Strupp and I (Bergin & Strupp, 1972) had an interesting conversation with Carl Rogers on this subject in La Jolla a few years ago, in which Carl said,

> Yes, it is true, psychotherapy is subversive. I don't really mean it to be, but some people get involved with me who don't know what they are getting into. Therapy theories and techniques promote a new model of man contrary to that which has been traditionally acceptable. (Paraphrase cited in Bergin & Strupp, 1972, pp. 318–319)

Sometimes, as professionals, we follow the leaders of our profession or our graduate professors in assuming that what we are doing is professional without recognizing that we are purveying under the guise of professionalism and science our own personal value systems (Smith, 1961), whether the system be psychodynamic, behavioral, humanistic, cognitive, or whatever.

During my graduate and postdoctoral training, I had the fortunate experience of working with several leaders in psychology, such as Albert Bandura, Carl Rogers, and Robert Sears. (Later, I had opportunities for substantial discussions with Joseph Wolpe, B. F. Skinner, and many others). These were good experiences with great men for whom I continue to have deep respect and warmth; but I gradually found our views on values issues to be quite different. I had expected their work to be "objective" science, but it became clear that these leaders' research, theories, and techniques were implicit expressions of humanistic and naturalistic belief systems that dominated both psychology and American universities generally. Since their professional work was an expression of such views, I felt constrained from full expression of my values by their assumptions or faiths and the prevailing, sometimes coercive, ideologies of secular universities.

Like others, I too have not always overtly harmonized my values and professional work. By now exercising the right to integrate religious themes into mainstream clinical theory, research, and practice, I hope to achieve this. By being explicit about what I value and how it articulates with a professional role, I hope to avoid unknowingly drawing clients or students into my system. I hope that, together, many of us will succeed in demonstrating how this can be healthy and fruitful.

If we are unable to face our own values openly, it means we are unable to face ourselves, which violates a primary principle of professional conduct in our field. Since we expect our clients to examine their perceptions and value constructs, we ought to do likewise. The result will be improved capacity to understand and help people, because self-deceptions and role playing will decrease and personal congruence will increase.

Thesis 6: It is our obligation as professionals to translate what we perceive and value intuitively into something that can be openly tested and evaluated. I do not expect anyone to accept my values simply because I have asserted them. I only ask that we accept the notion that our values arise out of a personal milieu of experience and private intuition or inspiration. Since they are personal and subjective and are shaped by the culture with which we are most familiar, they should influence professional work only to the extent that we can openly justify them. As a general standard, I would advocate that we (a) examine our values within our idiosyncratic personal milieus; (b) acknowledge that our value commitments are subjective; (c) be clear; (d) be open; (e) state the values in a professional context without fear, as hypotheses for testing and common consideration by the pluralistic groups with which we work; and (f) subject them to test, criticism, and verification.

On this basis, I would like to offer a few testable hypotheses.[1] These are some of the possibilities that derive from my personal experience.

1. Religious communities that provide the combination of a viable belief structure and a network of loving, emotional support should manifest lower rates of emotional and social pathology and physical disease. To some extent this can already be documented (cf. Lynch, 1977).

2. Those who endorse high standards of impulse control (or strict moral standards) have lower than average rates of alcoholism, addiction, divorce, emotional instability, and associated interpersonal difficulties. For example, Masters and Johnson (1975, p. 185) found that "swingers" at a 1-year follow-up had reduced their sexual activity and had stopped swinging. They apparently found that low impulse control increased the subjects' problems, and all but one couple said they were looking for an improved sense of social and personal security.

3. Disturbances in clinical cases will diminish as these individuals are encouraged to adopt forgiving attitudes toward parents and others who may have had a part in the development of their symptoms.

4. Infidelity or disloyalty to any interpersonal commitment, especially marriage, leads to harmful consequences—both interpersonally and intrapsychically.

5. Teaching clients love, commitment, service, and sacrifice for others will help heal interpersonal difficulties and reduce intrapsychic distress.

6. Improving male commitment, caring, and responsibility in families will reduce marital and familial conflict and associated psychological disorders. A correlated hypothesis is that father and husband absence, aloofness, disinterest, rejection, and abuse are major factors and possibly *the* major factors in familial and interpersonal disorganization. This is based on the assumption that the divine laws of love, nurturance, and self-sacrifice apply as much to men as to women but that men have traditionally ignored them more than women.

7. A good marriage and family life constitute a psychologically and socially benevolent state. As the percentage of persons in a community who live in such circumstances increases, social pathologies will decrease and vice versa.

8. Properly understood, personal suffering can increase one's compassion and potential for helping others.

9. The kinds of values described herein have social consequences. There is a social ecology, and the viability of this social ecology varies as a function of personal conviction, morality, and the quality of the social support network in which we exist. If one considers the 50 billion dollars a year we spend on social disorders like venereal disease, alcoholism, drug abuse, and so on, these are major symptoms or social problems. Their roots, I assume, lie in values, personal conduct, morality, and social philosophy. There are some eloquent spokesmen in favor of this point (Campbell, 1975; Lasch, 1978; and others). I quote only one, Alexander Solzhenitsyn, who said,

> A fact which cannot be disputed is the weakening of human personality in the West while in the East it has become firmer and stronger. How did the West decline? . . . I am referring to

[1]Hypotheses like these have been tested, with ambiguous results (Argyle & Beit-Hallahmi, 1975). The reasons for the ambiguous results are analyzed in a forthcoming paper by our research group.

> the calamity of an autonomous, irreligious, humanistic consciousness. It has made man the measure of all things on earth. . . . Is it true that man is above everything? Is there no superior spirit above him? Is it right that man's life . . . should be ruled by material expansion above all? . . . The world . . . has reached a major watershed in history. . . . It will demand from us a spiritual blaze, we shall have to rise to a new height of vision . . . where . . . our spiritual being will not be trampled upon as in the Modern Era. (Solzhenitsyn, 1978, pp. 681–684)

CONCLUSION

Although numerous points of practical contact can be made between religious and other value approaches, it is my view that the religious ones offer a distinctive challenge to our theories, inquiries, and clinical methods. This challenge has not fully been understood or dealt with.

Religion is at the fringe of clinical psychology when it should be at the center. Value questions pervade the field, but discussion of them is dominated by viewpoints that are alien to the religious subcultures of most of the people whose behavior we try to explain and influence. Basic conflicts between value systems of clinical professionals, clients, and the public are dealt with unsystematically or not at all. Too often, we opt for the comforting role of experts applying technologies and obscure our role as moral agents, yet our code of ethics declares that we should show a "sensible regard for the social codes and moral expectations of the community" (American Psychological Association, 1972, p. 2).

I realize that there are difficulties in applying the notion of a particular spiritual value perspective in a pluralistic and secular society. I think it should be done on the basis of some evidence that supports doing it as opposed to the basis of the current format, which is to implement one's values without the benefit of either a public declaration or an effort to gather data on the consequences of doing so.

It is my hope that the theses I have proposed will be contemplated with deliberation and not emotional dismissal. They have been presented in sincerity, with passion tempered by reason, and with a hope that our profession will become more comprehensive and effective in its capacity to help all of the human family.

REFERENCE NOTES

1. Palmer, S. Personal communication, April 1977.
2. Frankl, V. Honors seminar lecture, Brigham Young University, November 3, 1978.
3. Ragan, C. P., Malony, H. N., & Beit-Hallahmi, B. *Psychologists and religion: Professional factors related to personal religiosity.* Paper presented at the meeting of the American Psychological Association, Washington, D.C., September 1976.

REFERENCES

Allport, G. W. *The individual and his religion: A psychological interpretation.* New York: Macmillan, 1950.

American Institute of Public Opinion. Religion in America, 1977–78. *Gallup opinion index,* Report No. 145. Princeton, N.J.: Author, 1978.

American Psychological Association. *Ethical standards of psychologists.* Washington, D.C.: Author, 1972.

Argyle, M., & Beit-Hallahmi, B. *The social psychology of religion.* London: Routledge & Kegan Paul, 1975.

Bakan, C. Interview. In A. E. Bergin & H. H. Strupp (Eds.), *Changing frontiers in the science of psychotherapy.* Chicago: Aldine, 1972.

Bergin, A. E. Carl Rogers' contribution to a fully functioning psychology. In A. R. Mahrer & L. Pearson (Eds.), *Creative developments in psychotherapy* (Vol. 1). Cleveland, Ohio: Case Western Reserve University Press, 1971.

Bergin, A. E. Behavior therapy and ethical relativism: Time for clarity. *Journal of Consulting and Clinical Psychology,* 1980, *48,* 11–13.

Bergin, A. E. Conceptual basis for a religious approach to psychotherapy. In K. S. Larsen (Ed.), *Psychology and ideology* (Vol. 3). Monmouth, Oreg.: Institute for Theoretical History, in press.

Bergin, A. E., & Lambert, M. J. The evaluation of therapeutic outcomes. In S. L. Garfield & A. E. Bergin (Eds.), *Handbook of psychotherapy and behavior change* (2nd ed.). New York: Wiley, 1978.

Bergin, A. E., & Strupp, H. H. *Changing frontiers in the science of psychotherapy.* Chicago: Aldine, 1972.

Braginsky, D., & Braginsky, B. *Mainstream psychology: A critique.* New York: Holt, Rinehart & Winston, 1974.

Campbell, D. T. On the conflicts between biological and social evolution and between psychology and moral tradition. *American Psychologist,* 1975, *30,* 1103–1120.

Collins, G. R. *The rebuilding of psychology: An integration of psychology and Christianity.* Wheaton, Ill.: Tyndale House, 1977.

Feifel, H. Symposium on relationships between religion and mental health. *American Psychologist,* 1958, *13,* 565–579.

Feinstein, A. D. Personal mythology as a paradigm for a holistic psychology. *American Journal of Orthopsychiatry,* 1979, *49,* 198–217.

Frank, J. D. *Persuasion and healing.* Baltimore, Md.: Johns Hopkins University Press, 1961.

Frank, J. D. *Persuasion and healing* (2nd ed.). Baltimore, Md.: Johns Hopkins University Press, 1973.

Frank, J. D. Nature and functions of belief systems: Humanism and transcendental religion. *American Psychologist,* 1977, *32,* 555–559.

Fromm, E. *Man for himself.* New York: Rinehart, 1947.

Fromm, E. *Psychoanalysis and religion.* New Haven, Conn.: Yale University Press, 1950.

Fromm, E. *The art of loving.* New York: Harper & Row, 1956.

Glasser, W. *Reality therapy.* New York: Harper & Row, 1965.

Goble, F. G. *The third force: The psychology of Abraham Maslow.* New York: Pocket Books, 1971.

Gross, M. L. *The psychological society.* New York: Random House, 1978.

Gusdorf, G. P. Philosophical anthropology. *Encyclopedia Brittanica,* 1976, *1,* 975–985.

Henry, W. E., Sims, J. H., & Spray, S. L. *The fifth profession: Becoming a psychotherapist.* San Francisco: Jossey-Bass, 1971.

Hilgard, E. R., Atkinson, R. L., & Atkinson, R. C. *Introduction to psychology* (7th ed.). New York: Harcourt Brace Jovanovich, 1979.

Hogan, R. Interview. *APA Monitor,* April 1979, pp. 4–5.

James, W. *The varieties of religious experience.* Garden City, N.Y.: Doubleday, 1902.

Jeeves, M. A. *Psychology and Christianity: The view both ways.* Leicester, England: Inter-Varsity Press, 1976.

Jung, C. G. *The collected works: Vol. 11, Psychology and religion: West and East.* New York: Pantheon Books, 1958.

Kanfer, F. H. Personal control, social control, and altruism: Can society survive the age of individualism? *American Psychologist,* 1979, *34,* 231–239.

Kitchener, R. F. Ethical relativism and behavior therapy. *Journal of Consulting and Clinical psychology,* 1980, *48,* 1–7.

Klerman, G. L. The age of melancholy? *Psychology Today,* April 1979, pp. 36–42: 88–90.

Kuhn, T. S. *The structure of scientific revolutions* (2nd ed.). Chicago: University of Chicago Press, 1970.

Lasch, C. *The culture of narcissism.* New York: Norton, 1978.

Lilienfeld, D. M. The relationship between mental health information and moral values of lower class psychiatric clinic patients and psychiatric evaluation and disposition (Doctoral dissertation, Columbia University, 1965). *Dissertation Abstracts,* 1966, *27,* 610B–611B. (University Microfilms No. 66-6941).

London, P. *The modes and morals of psychotherapy.* New York: Holt, Rinehart & Winston, 1964.

Lowe, C. M. *Value orientations in counseling and psychotherapy: The meanings of mental health* (2nd ed.). Cranston, R.I.: Carroll Press, 1976.

Lynch, J. J. *The broken heart: The medical consequences of loneliness.* New York: Basic Books, 1977.

Malony, H. N. (Ed.). *Current perspectives in the psychology of religion.* Grand Rapids, Mich.: Eerdmans, 1977.

Masters, W. H., & Johnson, V. E. *The pleasure bond.* New York: Bantam Books, 1975.

Menninger, K. *The vital balance: The life process in mental health and illness.* New York: Viking Press, 1963.

Menninger, K. *Whatever became of sin?* New York: Hawthorn Books, 1973.

Mowrer, O. H. *The crisis in psychiatry and religion.* Princeton, N.J.: Van Nostrand, 1961.

Mowrer, O. H. (Ed.). *Morality and mental health.* Chicago: Rand McNally, 1967.

Murray, E. J. A content-analysis method for studying psychotherapy. *Psychological Monographs,* 1956, *70* (13, Whole No. 420).

Myers, D. G. *The human puzzle: Psychological research and Christian belief.* New York: Harper & Row, 1978.

Peck, M. S. *The road less traveled: A new psychology of love, traditional values, and spiritual growth.* New York: Simon & Schuster, 1978.

Polanyi, M. *Personal knowledge: Towards a post-critical philosophy.* Chicago: University of Chicago Press, 1962.

Rogers, C. R. Some new challenges. *American Psychologist,* 1973, *28,* 379–387.

Rychlak, J. F. *Discovering free will and personal responsibility.* New York: Oxford University Press, 1979.

Smith, M. B. "Mental health" reconsidered: A special case of the problem of values in psychology. *American Psychologist,* 1961, *16,* 299–306.

Smith, M. L., Glass, G. V., & Miller, T. I. *The benefits of psychotherapy.* Baltimore, Md.: Johns Hopkins University Press, in press.

Solzhenitsyn, A. A world split apart: The world demands from us a spiritual blaze. *Vital Speeches of the Day,* 1978, *45,* 678–684.

Strommen, M. P. *Research on religious development: A comprehensive handbook.* New York: Hawthorn Books, 1971.

Strupp, H. H., Hadley, S. W., & Gomes-Schwartz, B. *Psychotherapy for better or worse: The problem of negative effects.* New York: Aronson, 1977.

Szasz, T. S. *The myth of psychotherapy: Mental healing as religion, rhetoric, and repression.* Garden City, N.Y.: Doubleday, 1978.

Tart, C. *Transpersonal psychologies.* New York: Harper & Row, 1977.

Truax, C. B. Reinforcement and nonreinforcement in Rogerian psychotherapy. *Journal of Abnormal Psychology,* 1966, *71,* 1–9.

Vaughan, J. L. Measurement and analysis of values pertaining to psychotherapy and mental health (Doctoral dissertation, Columbia University, 1971). *Dissertation Abstracts International,* 1971, *32,* 3655B–3656B. (University Microfilms No. 72-1394).

Vitz, P. C. *Psychology as religion: The cult of self-worship.* Grand Rapids, Mich.: Eerdmans, 1977.

RECOMMENDED READING

Bakan, D. (1956). Clinical psychology and logic. *American Psychologist, 11,* 655–662.

Barratt, B. B., & Sloan, T. S. (1988). Critical note on Packer's "hermeneutic inquiry." *American Psychologist, 43,* 131–132.

Bauman, Z. (1978). *Hermeneutics and social science.* New York: Columbia University Press.

Bergin, A. E. (1980). Religion and humanistic values: A reply to Ellis and Walls. *Journal of Consulting and Clinical Psychology, 48,* 642–645.

Bergin, A. E. (1991). Values and religious issues in psychotherapy and mental health. *American Psychologist, 46,* 394–403.

Brewster Smith, M. (1950). The phenomenological approach in personality theory: Some critical remarks. *Journal of Abnormal and Social Psychology, 45,* 516–522.

Child, I. (1973). *Humanistic psychology and the research tradition: Their several virtues.* New York: Wiley.

Coulson, W. R., & Rogers, C. R. (Eds.). (1968). *Man and the science of man.* Columbus, OH: Charles E. Merrill.

Day, W. (1988). Hermeneutics and behaviorism. *American Psychologist, 43,* 129–130.

Ellis, A. (1980). Psychotherapy and aesthetic values: A response to A. E. Bergin's "Psychotherapy and Religious Values." *Journal of Consulting and Clinical Psychology, 48,* 635–639.

Gendlin, E. (1973). Experiential phenomenology. In M. Natanson (Ed.), *Phenomenology and the social sciences* (Vol. 1, pp. 281–319). Evanston, IL: Northwestern University Press.

Henley, T. B. (1988). Beyond Husserl. *American Psychologist, 43,* 402–403.

Jennings, J., & Lucca, C. A. (1989). Is the "forgotten distinction" between psychology and phenomenology still forgotten? Reply to comments. *American Psychologist, 44,* 1551–1553.

Laing, R. D. (1969). *The divided self* (pp. 17–38). New York: Penguin Books. (Original work published 1965).

May, R. (1967). *Psychology and the human dilemma* (pp. 111–127). New York: Norton.

May, R. (1958). The origins and significance of the existential movement in psychology. In R. May, E. Angel, & H. F. Ellenberger (Eds.), *Existence* (pp. 3–36). New York: Basic Books.

Packer, M. J. (1988). Hermeneutic inquiry: A response to criticisms. *American Psychologist, 43,* 133–136.

Packer, M. J., & Addison, R. B. (Eds.). (1989). *Entering the circle: Hermeneutic investigation in psychology.* Albany: State University of New York Press.

Rogers, C. R. (1985). Toward a more human science of the person. *Journal of Humanistic Psychology, 25,* 7–24.

Russell, R. L. (1988). A critical interpretation of Packer's "Hermeneutic Inquiry in the Study of Human Conduct." *American Psychologist, 43,* 130–131.

Rychlak, J. F. (1981). *A philosophy of science for personality theory* (2nd ed.). Malabar, FL: Krieger Publishing.

Rychlak, J. F. (1984). Newtonianism and the professional responsibility of psychologists: Who speaks for humanity? *Professional Psychology: Research and Practice, 15,* 82–95.

Snyder, D. M. (1988). Comment on Jennings. *American Psychologist, 43,* 403–404.

Walls, G. B. (1980). Values and psychotherapy: A comment on "Psychotherapy and Religious Values." *Journal of Consulting and Clinical Psychology, 48,* 640–641.

Wertheimer, M. (1988). Obstacles to the integration of competing theories of psychology. *Philosophical Psychology, 1,* 129–135.

V

PHILOSOPHICAL ISSUES OF THE PSYCHOANALYTIC APPROACH

INTRODUCTION: PHILOSOPHICAL PROBLEMS OF THE PSYCHOANALYTIC APPROACH

RONALD B. MILLER

Philosophy and psychoanalysis have had a longstanding love–hate relationship. Freud, despite his own proclivity for metapsychological theorizing that comes perilously close to metaphysical speculation, always disavowed the relevance of philosophy to psychoanalysis. Chessick (1982) noted that Freud would probably have agreed with Fenichel, his loyal follower, who classified metaphysics as a form of autistic thinking. Freud also denied that psychoanalytic theory was value laden and asserted that it was a value-neutral scientific process of inquiry and theory. Despite his own assertions that psychoanalysis was a deterministic science, critics have been skeptical. Freud insisted that psychic reality was determined by causal forces and that laws of psychic functioning could be formulated and tested on the couch in a manner exactly parallel to the laws and methods of physical science. The instincts were the link between physical and psychic reality, although how the physical becomes mental is as mysterious in Freud's writings as in any dualistic theory. However, dualism is not the primary metaphysical problem for Freudian theory; determinism holds that honor. Freudian theory attributes a purposive role to the unconscious. It is a source of wishes, hopes, desired outcomes, and so on. This force that is so closely linked to the deterministic forces of the natural sciences is, as Rychlak (1981) has well pointed out, purposive. As Erikson (1963) suggested, the goal of psychoanalysis is to give people freedom to make choices rationally, to be free of irrational forces dominating their lives. Freud's clinical theory seems to be going in the direction of free will, whereas his metapsychology is clearly deterministic.

With the exception of philosophical critique emanating from the existential tradition, the primary focus of philosophical interest in Freudian theory in recent years has been of an epistemological nature, specifically concerning Freud's claim to scientific status. Anglo-American analytic philosophers have been most critical of Freud's claims that his theories were legitimate scientific theories and that he was doing scientific research with his patients on the couch.

Despite Wittgenstein's fascination with the psychoanalytic method, the logical positivists and neopositivists have been disparaging of Freudian psychology, although Wisdom (1953) also showed an interest in the similarities between these two forms of "analysis." Popper (1959), for example, cited psychoanalysis as an example of a theory that does not permit disconfirmation because it contains so many corollary hypotheses that the "data" can always be made to fit the preexisting theory. So Popper would argue, a Freudian would respond that when one says "I hate you," it proves the basic aggressive drive, but if one says, "I don't hate you," it proves that the basic aggressive drive is so strong that one has to defend against or deny it. Consequently, Popper claims, there is no way to truly test the theory because anything one says will count as supporting it. Thus, psychoanalysis fails the basic test of a scientific theory.

The European continental philosophical tradition has been much more open to Freudian theory, perhaps sensing, despite Freud's denials, that he was deeply but indirectly influenced by German philosophy and its rationalist presuppositions. Habermas and Ricoeur have both found Freud's work to be consistent with, if not an exemplar of, hermeneutics. In chapter 25, Ricoeur argues that Freud presented a mixed model of human motivation—using both material and final causation (to use, with Rychlak, the Aristotelian framework)—and that this is necessary because in the self-alienated state of neurosis, a person is reduced to a thing.

In chapter 26, Grünbaum is extremely critical of this hermeneutic interpretation of Freudian theory. He found Freud to be a self-conscious scientist, well aware of the requirements of scientific methodology. Grünbaum observed that many of Freud's theories are testable scientific hypotheses but that Freud's research methods were systematically biased and unreliable. Grünbaum's work has brought psychoanalysis into the center stage of contemporary philosophy of science. No one in the analytic tradition has given such a detailed, sustained, and in-depth examination of the epistemological or logical features of Freudian theory.

Chessick (see chapter 27), who has been a pioneer in reawakening clinical psychiatry to its philosophical roots, and whose *Great Ideas in Psychotherapy* (1977) is a masterful exposition of the philosophical origins of both existential and psychoanalytic forms of psychotherapy, examines the parallels between Kant's theories of the self and the work of Kohut (1971). Kohut's self psychology is a key contemporary variant of psychoanalysis. Chessick argues that in the latter development of both Kant's and Kohut's thinking, the self becomes a moral agent, capable of initiating action, free of prior determining influence. The self is existential for Kohut, a source of human freedom, choice, and responsibility.

Erikson (1963, p. 419; 1976) has long held that psychoanalysis is a part of the liberal Western moral tradition, relying on human powers of rationality to increase respect for the individual, lessen human suffering, and encourage human freedom. This is why psychoanalysis was forbidden in Nazi Germany, Communist Russia, and the Eastern European bloc. In chapter 5, Margolis demonstrated that the traditional Freudian claim of theoretical moral neutrality is mistaken. Although technically psychoanalytic procedure may prohibit therapists from moralizing or giving direction to the moral actions of patients, this does not obviate the moral context or impact of the theory.

Writing in response to Bergin's article on humanistic values in psychotherapy (see chapter 24), Strupp outlines in chapter 28 the normative position of interpersonally oriented psychoanalytic therapy, which, after Fromm (1941), Strupp also considers to be humanistic. For Strupp, the essential values of psychoanalytic therapy are the promotion of human freedom and relatedness. One uses one's technical understanding of unconscious processes toward these ends, but it can never be just a technical set of procedures. There must be a commitment to these values as well. Strupp does not deal with the hermeneutic critique of technology that would argue that because the ethical relationship between patient and therapist provides the framework for the understanding of the unconscious, the understanding of the unconscious itself is a moral concept.

He still maintains the fact–value distinction of the empiricist tradition, as one would expect of a pioneer in empirical psychotherapy research.

Just as other approaches that aspire to scientific legitimacy are open to the criticism that they are likely to support conservative moral and political influences while they assiduously deny any moral message whatsoever, psychoanalysis has been similarly critiqued. Political activists of many types have criticized the Freudian model of personality and individual intensive psychotherapy or psychoanalysis as elitist (Halleck, 1971) and insensitive to the needs of women (Schafer, 1974), homosexuals (Bell & Weinberg, 1978), and other oppressed minorities. Freud saw himself as a social–political outcast for daring to criticize established religious institutions and aggressive nationalism. A son of the Enlightenment, Freud thought of science as liberating humankind from the prejudices and conformity pressures of the Middle Ages by extending the role of reason in the conduct of human affairs ("Where id was, there shall ego be"). Yet, Freud was an upper-middle-class professional in an essentially capitalistic Austrian society, and he never challenged the economic institutions that supported him. Neo-Marxist and socialist philosophers were quite critical of psychoanalysis until the development of psychosocial hermeneutic theory in which Freud was viewed as a great resource for illustrating interpretative social science (Ingleby, 1980).

It is possible by focusing on different aspects of psychoanalysis to make a legitimate case for the conservative or the radical implications of Freud's theories. Strupp's (see chapter 28) interpretation is weighted toward the radical because it takes into account the evolution of psychodynamic thinking that followed the development of the interpersonal school of psychoanalysis. One can make the best case for the conservative nature of psychoanalytic values if one focuses on the practice of classical psychoanalysis as a treatment procedure, as opposed to a general theory of psychology.

In chapter 29, Messer and Winokur take up the suggestion by Wachtel (1977) that psychoanalytic and behavioral techniques can be integrated to benefit therapeutic change. They argue that there are fundamental philosophical obstacles to such an integration in that psychoanalysis operates in primarily an idealist view of reality, whereas behavior therapy operates in a materialist view. Furthermore, psychoanalysis views the "good life" as being necessarily conflicted and tragic, whereas behavior therapists believe that the "good life" can be straightforwardly happy. This may lead to very different expectations as to what constitutes a positive therapeutic outcome.

Wachtel, in chapter 30, responds with a review of contemporary variants of psychodynamic and behavior therapy in order to show that the incompatibility of these two approaches depends on what is meant by the terms *psychoanalytic* and *behavior therapy.* This is an outstanding illustration of the benefits to psychology of the application of conceptual analysis to psychological terms. It shows that certain aspects of psychoanalytic clinical theory and certain aspects of a cognitive–behavioral approach are compatible in theory and practice. Wachtel acknowledges that there may be epistemological differences that are difficult if not impossible to bridge, but we will know for sure only by pursuing theoretical and conceptual integration.

Integration that is philosophically well thought out is very different from eclecticism. Wachtel's work has stimulated a movement toward psychotherapy integration that he acknowledges is still more focused on technical integration than theoretical integration, yet he argues that theoretical integration is also required for the movement to become mature.

REFERENCES

Bell, A. P., & Weinberg, M. A. (1978). *Homosexualities: A study of diversity in men and women.* New York: Simon & Schuster.

Chessick, R. (1977). *Great ideas in psychotherapy.* Northvale, NJ: Jason Aronson.

Chessick, R. (1982). Metaphysics or autistic reverie. *Contemporary Psychoanalysis, 18,* 160–172.

Erikson, E. (1963). *Childhood and society.* New York: Norton.

Erikson, E. (1976). Psychoanalysis and ethics—Avowed and unavowed. *International Review of Psychoanalysis, 3,* 409–415.

Fromm, E. (1941). *Escape from freedom.* New York: Holt, Rinehart & Winston.

Ingleby, D. (1980). *Critical psychiatry: The politics of mental health.* New York: Pantheon Books.

Kohut, H. (1971). *The analysis of the self.* New York: International Universities Press.

Popper, K. (1959). *The logic of scientific discovery.* London: Hutchinson.

Rychlak, J. F. (1981). *Introduction to personality and psychotherapy: A theory construction approach* (2nd ed.). Boston: Houghton Mifflin.

Schafer, R. (1974). Problems in Freud's psychology of women. *Journal of the American Psychoanalytic Association, 22,* 459–485.

Wachtel, P. (1977). *Psychoanalysis and behavior therapy.* New York: Basic Books.

Wisdom, J. O. (1953). *Philosophy and psychoanalysis.* New York: Oxford University Press.

25

THE QUESTION OF PROOF IN FREUD'S PSYCHOANALYTIC WRITINGS

PAUL RICOEUR

The question of proof in psychoanalysis is as old as psychoanalysis itself. The 1895 "Project" aims at being a project of scientific psychology. The "Interpretation of Dreams" purports to be a science and not a fantastic construction, a "fine fairy tale," to use Krafft-Ebing's remark, hurled at Freud at the close of one public presentation. Each of Freud's didactic works—the Introductory Lectures, the New Introductory Lectures, and the Outline—represent a new effort to communicate to the layman the conviction that psychoanalysis is genuinely related to what is intelligible and what claims to be true. And yet, psychoanalysis has never quite succeeded in stating how its assertions are justified, how its interpretations are authenticated, how its theory is verified. This relative failure of psychoanalysis to be recognized as a science results, I think, from a failure to ask certain preliminary questions to which I devote the first two parts of my paper; the third part is an attempt to reply directly to the original question.

THE CRITERIA FOR "FACTS" IN PSYCHOANALYSIS

The first question concerns what is relevant as a *fact* in psychoanalysis. We may begin by noting that traditional discussions about the epistemological status of analytic theory take it for granted that theories consist of propositions whose role is to systemize, explain, and predict phenomena comparable to those which verify or falsify theories in the natural sciences or in human sciences which, like academic psychology, themselves adopt the epistemology of the

Reprinted from the *Journal of the American Psychoanalytic Association, 25,* 835–871. (1977).

natural sciences. Even when we are not dealing with a narrow empiricism which does not require a theory to be directly validated by observables, we nevertheless continue to ask the same questions we would put to an observational science. In this way, we ask by what specific procedures psychoanalysis connects this or that theoretical notion to definite and unambiguous facts. However indirect the verification process may be, definitions must become operational, that is, they must be shown to generate procedures for verification and falsification. And this is precisely what is in question: what in psychoanalysis merits being considered as a verifiable fact?

My thesis is that psychoanalytic theory—in a certain sense which will be described in the second part of this paper—is the codification of what takes place in the analytic situation and, more precisely, in the analytic relationship. It is there that something happens which merits being called the *analytic experience.* In other words, the equivalent of what the epistemology of logical empiricism calls "observables" is to be sought first in the analytic situation, in the analytic relationship.

Our first task, therefore, will be to show in what way the analytic relationship brings about a selection among the facts that are likely to be taken into account by the theory. I propose four criteria of this process of selection as useful for our discussion.

First criterion: To begin, there enters into the field of investigation and treatment only that part of experience which is capable of *being said.* There is no need to insist here on the *talk-cure* character of psychoanalysis. This restriction of language is first of all an inherent restriction on the analytic technique; it is the particular context of uninvolvement with reality belonging to the analytic situation that forces desire to speak, to pass through the defile of words, excluding substitute satisfactions as well as any regression toward acting out. This screening through speech in the analytic situation also functions as a criterion for what will be held to be the object of this science: not instinct as a physiological phenomenon, not even desire as energy, but desire as a meaning capable of being deciphered, translated, and interpreted. Hence the theory necessarily has to account for what we may call the semantic dimension of desire.

We can already see the misunderstanding that prevails in ordinary epistemological discussions: facts in psychoanalysis are in no way facts of observable behavior. They are "reports." We know dreams only as told upon awakening; and even symptoms, although they are partially observable, enter into the field of analysis only in relation to other factors verbalized in the "report." It is this selective restriction which forces us to situate the facts of psychoanalysis inside a sphere of motivation and meaning.

Second criterion: The analytic situation singles out not only what is sayable, but what is said *to another person.* Here again, the epistemological criterion is guided by something absolutely central to the analytic technique. The transference stage, in this regard, is highly significant, for we might be tempted to confine the discussion of transference to the sphere of psychoanalytic technique and thereby overlook its epistemological implications in our search for relevant criteria. To see this, let us consider just one text crucial for analytic technique, the 1914 essay entitled "Remembering, Repeating, and Working Through."

In this essay Freud begins with the precise moment in the cure when the memory of traumatic events is replaced by the compulsion to repeat which blocks remembering. Focusing on the relation between this compulsion to repeat, resistance, and transference, he writes, "The greater the resistance, the more extensively will acting out (repetition) replace remembering." And he adds, "the patient repeats instead of remembering and repeats under the conditions of resistance" (p. 151). Then he introduces transference, which he describes as "the main instrument . . . for curbing the patient's compulsion to repeat and for turning it into a motive for remembering" (p. 154). Why does transference have this effect? The reply leads to epistemological considerations directly grafted onto what appears to be a strictly technical matter. If the resistance can be cleared away and remembering made free to occur, it is because the transference constitutes something like "a playground in which [the patient's compulsion to repeat] is allowed to expand in almost complete freedom" (p. 154). Extending this analogy of the playground, Freud more specifically says: "The transference thus creates an intermediate region between illness and real life through which the transition from one to the other is made" (p. 154).

It is this notion of transference as a "playground" or "intermediate region" that guides my remarks on the second criterion for what is psychoanalytically relevant as a fact. *In this "playground," this "intermediate region," in effect, we can read the relationship with the other as constituting an erotic demand addressed to another person.* It is in this regard that "transference" has its place not only in a study of analytic technique, but also in an epistemological inquiry about criteria. It reveals this constitutive trait of human desire: not only is it able to be spoken, to be brought to language, but it is addressed to another; more specifically, it is addressed to another desire which is capable of denying its request. What is thereby singled out or sifted out from human experience is the immediately intersubjective dimension of desire.

We should therefore not overlook the fact that if we speak of objects, of "wish objects"—and we cannot fail to speak of them in such contexts as the object-choice, the lost object, and the substitute object, which we will return to below—this object is another desire. In other words, the relationship to the other is not something added on to desire. And in this respect Freud's discovery of the Oedipus complex in the course of his self-analysis is to be included within the very structure of desire seen as a triangular structure bringing into play two sexes and three persons. It follows from this that what the theory will articulate as symbolic castration is not an additional, extrinsic factor, but something which attests to the initial relation of desire to an agency of prohibition and imposition of standards lived out in fantasies by the child as a paternal threat directed against his sexual activities. Therefore, from the outset, all that might be considered a solipsism of desire is eliminated, in spite of what a definition of desire simply in terms of energy as tension and release might lead us to believe. The mediation of the other is constitutive of human desire as addressed to. . . . This other can be someone who responds or who refuses to respond, someone who gratifies, or someone who threatens. He may be, above all, real or a fantasy, present or lost, a source of anguish, or the object of a successful mourning. Through transference, psychoanalysis controls and examines these alternative possibilities by transposing the drama involving several actors which generated the neurotic situation onto a sort of miniature artificial stage. Thus it is analytic experience itself that forces the theory to include intersubjectively within the very constitution of the libido and to conceive of it less as a need than as an other-directed wish.

Third criterion: The third criterion introduced by the analytic situation concerns the coherence and the resistance of certain manifestations of the unconscious which led Freud to speak of "*psychical reality*" in contrast to material reality. It is the distinctive traits of this psychical reality which are psychoanalytically relevant. And this criterion is paradoxical to the extent that what common sense sets in opposition to reality is what constitutes this psychical reality.

In 1917, for example, Freud writes, ". . . phantasies possess *psychical* as contrasted with *material* reality . . . ; *in the world of the neuroses it is psychical reality which is the decisive kind*" (1916–1917, pp. 368). Symptoms and fantasies "abstract from the object and thus renounce every relation with external reality." He then goes on to refer to infantile scenes which themselves "are not always true." This is an especially important admission when we remember how difficult it was for Freud to give up his initial hypothesis of the father's real seduction of the child. More than fifteen years later he remarked how disturbing this discovery remained for him. What is so disturbing about it? Precisely that it is not clinically relevant whether the infantile scenes are true or false. And it does not matter, therefore, from an epistemological point of view, either. This is what is expressed by the phrase "psychical reality."

What is important here is that it is the analytic experience itself that necessitates the use of "psychical reality" to designate certain productions which fall under the opposition of the imaginary and the real, not just according to common sense, but also, in a way, in apparent contradiction to the fundamental opposition in psychoanalysis between the pleasure principle to which the fantasy affixes itself and the reality principle. This is why this concept meets resistance not only as induced by common sense or the attitude formed by the observational sciences, but also from psychoanalytic theory itself and its tenacious dichotomy between the imaginary and the real.

The epistemological consequences of this paradox from analytic experience are considerable: while academic psychology does not question the difference between the real and the imaginary, inasmuch as its theoretical entities are all said to refer to observable facts and ultimately to real movements in space and time, psychoanalysis deals with psychical reality and not with material reality. So the criterion for this reality is no longer that it is observable, but that it presents a coherence and a resistance comparable to that of material reality.

The range of phenomena satisfying this criterion is wide. Fantasies deriving from infantile scenes (observing the parents' sexual relations, seduction, and above all castration) constitute the paradigmatic case to the extent that, in spite of their fragile basis in the real history of the subject, they present a highly structured organization and are inscribed in scenarios which are both typical and limited in number.

The notion of psychical reality is not exhausted by that of fantasy understood in terms of such archaic scenarios, however. The imaginary, in a broader sense, covers all the kinds of mediations implied in the unfolding of desire.

Close to the infantile scene, for example, we may put the whole domain of abandoned objects which continue to be represented as fantasies. Freud introduces this notion in connection with the problem of symptom formation. Objects abandoned by the libido provide the missing link between the libido and its points of fixation in the symptom.

And from the notion of abandoned objects the transition to that of the substituted object, which places us at the very heart of the analytic experience, is easy. The "Three Essays on the Theory of Sexuality" (1905) start from the variability of the object in contrast to the stability of the aim or goal of the libido and derive from this the substitutability of love objects. And in "Instincts and their Vicissitudes" (1915a), Freud goes on to construe on this basis in a systematic fashion the typical configurations arising from the crisscrossing of substitutions—through inversion, reversal, etc., the ego is capable of putting itself in the place of the object, as in the case of narcissism.

Substitutability, in turn, is the key to still another set of phenomena central to the analytic experience. From the time of "The Interpretation of Dreams," Freud perceived the remarkable feature of dreams that they could be substituted for a myth, a folktale theme, or for a symptom, a hallucination, or an illusion. In effect, the entire reality of these psychic formations consists in the thematic unity which serves as a basis for the interplay of their substitutions. Their reality is their meaning, and their meaning is their capability of mutually replacing one another. It is in this sense that the notions of the lost object and the substitute object—cardinal notions for analytic experience—deserve to occupy a key position in the epistemological discussion as well. Put quite simply, they forbid our speaking of a "fact" in psychoanalysis in the same way as in the observational sciences.

I do not want to leave this criterion of psychical reality without adding a final link to the chain of examples which has led us from fantasy to the lost object, then to the substitute object. This final link will assure us that the entire chain is placed fully within analytic experience. This example is the work of mourning.

Mourning, as such, is a remarkable case of reacting to the loss of an object (Freud, 1917, p. 243). It is, of course, reality which imposes the work of mourning, but a reality which includes the loss of the object, therefore a reality signified as the verdict of absence (Freud, 1917). Consequently, mourning consists in "the step by step realization of each of the orders proclaimed by reality." But this realization consists precisely in the interiorization of the lost object, concerning which Freud says, "its existence continues psychically."

If I conclude this examination of the criterion of psychical reality with the work of mourning, it is not only to emphasize the wide range of phenomena arising out of the abandonment of the object, but to show at what point the phenomenon of mourning is close to the very core of psychoanalysis. Psychoanalysis begins by acknowledging the fantasy as the paradigm of what for it represents psychical reality, but it continues by means of a labor that may itself be understood as a work of mourning, that is, as an internalization of the lost objects of instinctual desires. Far from restricting itself to vanquishing the fantasy to the benefit of reality, the cure also recovers it as fantasy in order to situate it, without confusing it with what is real, on the level of the imaginary. This kinship between the cure and the work of mourning confirms, if any further confirmation is required, that it is the analytic experience which requires that we add the reference to fantasies to the two preceding criteria; for what has been said (the first criterion) and what is demanded of the other person (the second criterion) bear the mark of the particular imaginary formations which Freud brings together under the term *phantasieren.* It follows that what is relevant for the analyst is not observable facts or observable reactions to environmental variables, but the meaning which the same events that the behavioral psychologist considers as an observer assume for a subject. I will venture to say, in summation, that *what is psychoanalytically relevant is what a subject makes of his fantasies.*

Fourth criterion: The analytic situation selects from a subject's experience what is capable of entering into a story or narrative. In this sense, "case histories" as histories constitute the primary texts of psychoanalysis. This "narrative" character of the psychoanalytic experience is never directly discussed by Freud, at least to my knowledge. But he refers to it indirectly in his considerations about memory. We may recall the famous declaration (Breuer and Freud, 1893–1895) that "hysterical patients suffer principally from reminiscences." Of course memories will appear to be merely screen-memories and fantasies rather than real memories when Freud seeks the real origin of neurotic suffering, but such fantasies in turn will always be considered in their relation to forgetting and remembering due to their relation to resistance and the connection between resistance and repetition. Remembering, then, is what has to replace repetition. The struggle against resistance—which Freud calls "working through"—has no other aim than to reopen the path of memory.

But what is it to remember? It is not just to recall certain isolated events, but to become capable of forming meaningful sequences and ordered connections. In short, it is to be able to constitute one's own existence in the form of a story where a memory as such is only a fragment of the story. It is the narrative structure of such life stories that makes a case a case history.

That such an ordering of one's life episodes in the form of a story constitutes a kind of work—and even a "working through"—is attested by the role of one fundamental phenomenon of fantasy life, namely the after-the-event phenomenon (*Nachträglichkeit*) which Lacan (1966, pp. 256, 839) has brought out so well. It is the fact that "expressions, impressions, mnesic traces, are recast later in function of new experience, of the access to a new stage of development and that they may assume, not only a new meaning, but a new efficiency" (Laplanche and Pontalis, p. 33). Before raising a theoretical problem, this phenomenon is implied in the work of psychoanalysis itself. It is in the process of working through just mentioned that Freud discovers that the subject's history does not conform to a linear determinism which would place the present in the firm grasp of the past in a univocal fashion. On the contrary, recovering traumatic events through the work of analysis reveals that at the time they were experiences they could not be fully integrated in a meaningful context. It is only the arrival of new events and new situations that precipitates the subsequent reworking of these earlier events. Thus in the Wolf Man, it is a second sexually significant scene which after the event confers upon the first scene its effectiveness. And generally speaking, numerous repressed memories only become traumas after the event. It is a question of more than just a delay or a deferred action. Here we see that we are far removed from the notion of a memory which would simply reproduce real events in a sort of perception of the past; this is instead a work which goes over and over extremely complex structuralizations. It is this work of memory that is implied, among other things, by the notion of the story or narrative structure of existence.

For the fourth time, then, a vicissitude of the analytic experience reveals a pertinent trait of what, psychoanalytically, counts as a "fact."

INVESTIGATORY PROCEDURE, METHOD OF TREATMENT, AND THEORETICAL TERMS

The second preliminary question concerning proof in psychoanalysis is that of the nature of the *relation* which can be found between theory and what counts as a fact in psychoanalysis.

From the perspective of operational analysis, the theoretical terms of an observational science must be capable of being connected to observables by way of rules of interpretation or translation which assure the indirect verification of these terms. The question here is to know whether the operative procedures which allow the transition from the level of theoretical entities to that of facts have the same structure and the same meaning in psychoanalysis as in the observational sciences. To reply to this question, I would like to return to one of Freud's statements which deals precisely with the epistemological status of theory in psychoanalysis. We read that "Psychoanalysis is the name (1) of a procedure for the investigation of mental processes . . . (2) of a method (based upon that investigation) for the treatment of neurotic disorders and (3) of a collection of psychological information obtained along those lines, which is gradually being accumulated into a new scientific discipline" (1922, p. 235). It is this triangular relation between a procedure of investigation, a method of treatment, and a theory which will hold our attention because it takes the place of the theory-fact relation in the observational sciences. Not only does psychoanalysis deal with "facts" of a special nature, as has just been stated, but what takes the place of the operative procedures at work in the natural sciences is a unique type of relation between the investigatory procedure and the method of treatment. It is this relation that mediates between the theory and the facts.

Now, before anything can be said about the role of the third term, theory, in relation to the other two terms, the relation between the investigatory procedure and the method of treatment is itself not easy to grasp. Broadly speaking, we may say that the investigatory procedure tends to give preference to relations of *meaning* between mental productions, while the method of treatment tends to give preference to relations of *force* between systems. The function of the theory will be precisely to integrate these two aspects of psychical reality.

The investigatory procedure has, in effect, a strong affinity with the disciplines of textual interpretation. We read, for example: "The aim which I have set before myself is to show that dreams are capable of being interpreted. . . . My presumption that dreams can be interpreted at once puts me in opposition to the ruling theory of dreams and in fact to every theory of dreams with the exception of Scherner's; for 'interpreting' a dream implies assigning a 'meaning' to it—

that is, replacing it by something which fits into the chain of our mental acts as a link having a validity and importance equal to the rest" (1900, p. 96).

In this regard, interpretation is often compared to the translation from one language into another or to the solution of a rebus (see, for example, Freud, 1900, pp. 277–278; 1913, p. 176; 1915b, p. 166; 1937, p. 236). Freud never doubted that however inaccessible the unconscious might be, it still participates in the same psychic structures as does consciousness. It is this common structure which allows us "to interpolate" unconscious acts into the text of conscious acts. This trait belonging to the method of investigation coheres with the criteria for "facts" in psychoanalysis discussed above, in particular with the criteria of sayability and substitutability. If the investigatory procedure may be applied to both neurotic symptoms and dreams, it may be done because "dream-formation *(Traumbildung)* and symptom-formation *(Symptombildung)* are homogeneous and substitutable" (1900, pp. 605–608). This was recognized as early as 1893, where the "Preliminary Communication" already treats the relation between the determining cause and the hysterical symptom as a "symbolic tie," akin to the dream process. *This deep kinship among all the compromise formations allows us to speak of the psyche as a text to be deciphered.*

This broadly inclusive notion of a text encompasses the profound unity not only of dreams and symptoms, but of these two taken together with daydreams, myths, folktales, sayings, proverbs, puns, and jokes. And the gradual extension of this method of investigation is assured by the special kinship that exists between, on the one hand, the group of fantasies referred to earlier as infantile scenes (classed in "The Interpretation of Dreams" along with typical dreams: dreams of nudity, of death of someone dear, etc.), and, on the other hand, the most highly organized and most permanent mythical structures of humanity. Under the same investigatory procedure comes most notably the "textual" structure common to the Oedipus complex discovered by Freud in his self-analysis and the Greek tragedy Oedipus carried down to us in literature. There is thus a correspondence between the extension of the investigatory procedure and what could be termed *the space of fantasy in general,* in which psychic productions as diverse as daydreams, children's games, psychological novels, and other poetic creations are set out. In the same way, the psychic conflicts portrayed in stone by Michaelangelo's Moses lend themselves to interpretation by virtue of the figurable and substitutable nature of all the sign systems which are included within the same investigatory procedure.

But if we were only to follow the suggestion of the concepts of the text and interpretation, we would arrive at an entirely erroneous notion of psychoanalysis. Psychoanalysis would be purely and simply subsumed under the aegis of the historico-hermeneutical sciences, alongside philology and exegesis. And we would overlook the very features of interpretation that are grasped only when the investigatory procedure is joined to the method of treatment. The meaning of the symptom and of the dream are so difficult to decipher, because of the interposed distortion mechanisms between the manifest and the hidden meaning—the mechanisms Freud listed under the term dream work.

This "distortion" is indeed a strange sort of phenomenon, and Freud employs all sorts of quasi-physical metaphors to render this transformation, which he says, "does not think, calculate, or judge in any way at all" (1900, p. 507). Condensation and displacement are quasi-physical metaphors for the dream work. But it is the central metaphor of *repression* that orders all the others to the point of becoming a theoretical concept whose metaphorical origin is forgotten (as, moreover, is that of the concept of distortion itself, which literally signifies a violent displacement as well as a deformation). And the semi-metaphor of regression belongs to the same cycle.

Another quasi-physical metaphor of equal importance is that of *cathexis,* concerning which Freud does not conceal the kinship with the operation of a capitalist entrepreneur who invests his money in something. This metaphor allows regression to acquire not only a topographic signification, but also a dynamic one, to the extent that regression to an image proceeds from "changes in the cathexes of energy attaching to the different systems" (1900, p. 543). This play of metaphors becomes extremely complex because Freud goes on to interweave textual metaphors (translation, substitution, overdetermination, etc.) and energy metaphors, producing mixed metaphors such as disguise, censorship, etc.

Now, why does Freud get himself into such difficult straits with concepts which remain semi-metaphors and, in particular, with inconsistent metaphors which tend toward the polarity of, on the one hand, the *textual* concept of translation and, on the other hand, the *mechanical* concept of compromise, itself understood in the sense of a result of various forces interacting?

I suggest that it is the conjunction of the investigatory procedure with the method of treatment that compels the theory to operate in this way, using semi-metaphorical concepts which lack coherence.

I would like to pause here to consider the word "treatment," which we earlier distinguished from the method of investigation. The notion of a method of treatment must be understood in a sense that extends far beyond its strictly medical sense of "cure," to designate the whole analytic procedure insofar as analysis itself is a sort of work. This work is both the inverse of what we just described as the dream work and the correlative of what earlier was termed the work of mourning. To the question of how analysis is a work, Freud gives a constant reply: Psychoanalysis is essentially *a struggle against resistances.* And it is this notion of resistance that prevents us from identifying the investigatory procedure with a simple interpretation, with an entirely intellectual understanding of the meaning of symptoms. Interpretation, seen as translation or a deciphering, as the substitution of an intelligible meaning for an absurd one, is only the intellectual segment of the analytic procedure. Even transference (which appeared earlier as an intersubjective criterion of desire) must be treated as one aspect of the handling of resistances (as is apparent in "Remembering, Repeating and Working-Through" [1914]). Hence the three themes of compulsion to repeat, transference, and resistance are found to be connected at the level of analytic praxis.

What does this mean for our epistemological inquiry? Essentially the following: the pair formed by the investigatory procedure and the method of treatment takes exactly the same place as the operative procedures in the observational sciences which connect the level of theoretical entities to that of observable data. This pair constitutes the specific mediation between theory and fact in psychoanalysis. And this mediation operates in the following manner: by coordinating interpretation and the handling of resistances, analytic praxis calls for a theory in which the psyche will be represented both as a text to be interpreted and as a system of forces to be manipulated. In other words, it is the complex character of actual practice which requires the theory to overcome the apparent contradiction between the metaphor of the *text* to be interpreted and that of the *forces* to be regulated; in short, practice forces us to think of meaning and force together in a comprehensive theory. It is through the practical coordination of interpretation and the handling of resistances that the theory is given the task of forming a model capable of articulating the facts acknowledged as relevant in analytic experience. It is in this way that the relation between the investigatory procedure and the method of treatment constitutes the necessary mediation between theory and facts.

Now, does psychoanalysis possess a *theory* that satisfies these requirements? It seems to me that Freud's metapsychology should be examined in the light of the questions just raised. If Freud's metapsychology has been turned into a fetish by some and scorned as marginal by others, it is because it was treated as an independent construction. Too many epistemological works examine the great theoretical texts outside the total context of experience and practice. Isolated in this way, the body of doctrine can only lead to premature and truncated evaluations. The theory must therefore be relativized, by which I mean it must be placed back into the complex network of relations that encompass it.

For my part, I should like to submit two theses, apparently opposed to each other, but which, taken together in their unstable equilibrium, attempt to consider Freud's theoretical work as the imperfect yet indispensable starting point for any reformulation of this theory.

On the other hand, I am prepared to acknowledge that Freud's theoretical model (or models) is (or are) not adequate to analytic experience and practice as these are formulated in his other writings (the case histories, the writings on technique, and on applied psychoanalysis). More specifically, Freud's metapsychology does not succeed in codifying and integrating into a single unified structure meaning and force, textual interpretation, and the handling of resistances.

In the first place, Freud always tends to reverse the relations between theory, on the one hand, and experience and practice, on the other, and to reconstruct the work of interpretation on the basis of theoretical models that have become autonomous. He thus loses sight of the fact that the language of the theory is narrower than that in which the technique is described. Next, he tends to construct his theoretical models in the positivist, naturalistic, and materialist spirit of the sciences of his day. Many texts assert the exclusive kinship of psychoanalysis with the natural sciences and even with physics, or announce that in the future psychoanalysis will be replaced by a more refined pharmacology.

In this respect, Habermas (1971) is correct in speaking of the "self-misunderstanding of psychoanalysis as a natural science" (p. 247). According to Habermas, technique and experience call for a structural model which is betrayed by the preferred model of energy distribution. This latter model is superimposed upon analytic experience, ignoring its derivation from the work of reconstructing an individual history on the basis of scattered fragments. Most seriously, this model is in many ways antecedent to analytic experience, as we see in the Project, and it imposes its reference system on this experience: quantifiable energy, stimulation, tension, discharge, inhibitions, cathexis, etc. Even when the psychical apparatus includes only "psychical localities" which are not anatomically localizable, the spatial arrangement and the temporal sequence of the systems continue to lend support to the energy-distribution model. The great article on "The Unconscious" is the principal witness to its sovereignty.

What is lost from sight in a model like this, however, is the very specificity of the psychoanalytic "fact," with its fourfold nature of being able to be said, to be addressed to another person, to be fantasized, figured, or symbolized, and to be recounted in the story of a life. This set of criteria requires that elements be introduced at the theoretical level in a suitable manner so that they are capable of accounting for what occurs in the analytic relation. This is why I can adopt up to a certain point the suggestions Habermas offers in light of the work of Lorenzer (1973).

These authors assume as their frame of reference the symbolizing process at work in human communication and in human interaction generally. The disturbances that give rise to psychoanalytic interventions are then considered as the pathology of our linguistic competence and are placed alongside the distortions uncovered, on another level, by the Marxist and post-Marxist critique of ideologies. psychoanalysis and the critique of ideologies, in effect, share a common obligation to explain and interpret these distortions, which are not accidental, but systematic in the sense that they are organized systematically in the text of interhuman communication. These distortions are the occasion of a subject's self-misunderstanding. In order to account for this, we need a theory that is not limited to restoring the integral, unmutilated, and unfalsified text, but one that takes as its object the very mechanisms that distort the text. And this explains why, in turn, the interpretive decoding of symptoms and dreams goes beyond a simply philological hermeneutic, insofar as it is the very meaning of the mechanisms distorting the texts that requires explanation. This is also why the economic metaphors (resistance, repression, compromise, etc.) cannot be replaced by the philological metaphors (text, meaning, interpretation, etc.).

But the opposite is no less true: neither can the economic metaphors replace their complements. They cannot lose their metaphorical character and set themselves up as an energic theory to be taken literally. It is basically against this reduction to the literal nature of the energy-distribution model that our authors formulate their own theories in terms of communication and symbolic interaction. According to these alternative models, the mechanisms of the unconscious are no longer held to be things, they are "split-off symbols," "delinguisticized" or "degrammaticized motives." Like banishment or political ostracism, repression banishes a part of language from the public sphere of communication and condemns it to the exile of a "privatized" language. This is how mental functioning simulates a natural process. But only to the extent that it has been objectified and reified. If we forget that this reification results from a process of desymbolization, hence from *a specific self-alienation,* we end up constructing a model wherein the unconscious is literally a thing. But at the same time, we are then unable to understand how resymbolization is possible, that is, how analytic experience itself is possible. We can understand this only if we interpret the phenomena revealed by this experience in terms of *communication disturbances,* and analytic experience as a reappropriation that *inverts the process of splitting off symbols.*

To the extent that I take up this critique of the energic model of Freudian metapsychology, I accept classing psychoanalysis along with the critical social sciences, which are guided by the interest in emancipation and motivated in the final analysis by the wish to recover the force of *Selbstreflexion.*

Yet, in return, I would not want this rapprochement with the critical social sciences and this ultimate reference to self-reflection to go beyond the goal of placing the theory back into the complex network of psychoanalytic experience and practice. This is why I want to defend with equal vigor the complementary thesis, which holds that we must always start from the Freudian system in spite of its faults, even—I would venture to say—because of its deficiencies. Indeed, as Habermas himself has remarked, the self-misunderstanding of psychoanalysis is not entirely unfounded. The economic model, in particular, preserves something essential, which a theorizing introduced from outside the system is always in danger of losing sight of, namely, that man's alienation from himself is such that mental functioning does actually resemble the functioning of a thing. This simulation keeps psychoanalysis from constituting itself as a province of the exegetical disciplines applied to texts—as a hermeneutic, in other words—and requires that psychoanalysis include in the process of self-understanding operations that were originally reserved for the natural sciences.

This requirement may be illustrated through a brief critique of those efforts at reformulating the theory which immediately exclude in principle this simulation of the thing. I am thinking here especially of those reformulations which borrow from phenomenology, from ordinary language analysis, or from linguistics. All these reformulations omit the task of integrating an explanatory stage into the process of desymbolization and resymbolization.

I will limit myself here to those efforts which arise from consideration of the semantics of action in the school of linguistic analysis. (For a discussion of the phenomenological interpretation at length, see Ricoeur, 1970, pp. 375ff.; for a discussion of the properly linguistic reformulations, see Ricoeur, in press.)

Under the name of the philosophy of action, an autonomous discipline has been constituted, one influenced by Austin, Wittgenstein, and the philosophy of ordinary language, which assigns itself the task of describing the logic implicit in our discourse on action when it uses terms designating actions, intentions, motives, individual or collective agents, etc. Some of the analysts who practice this discipline—although less numerous today, it is true, and subjected to increasingly rigorous criticism by other semanticists—have maintained that discourse on action brings into play criteria of intelligibility distinct from and different from the criteria for physical movement or observable behavior. One of the implications of this dichotomy between the two "language games" of action and movement bears directly on the point at issue in our discussion: according to these analysts, our motives for acting can in no way be assimilated to the causes by which we explain natural events. Motives are reasons for our action, while causes are the constant antecedents of other events from which they are logically distinct.

Can psychoanalytic theory be reformulated on the basis of this distinction? Some authors have thought so and have interpreted psychoanalysis as an extension of the vocabulary of action (intention, motives, etc.) beyond the sphere where we are aware of what we do. Psychoanalysis, according to this interpretation, adds nothing to ordinary conceptuality except the use of the same concepts of ordinary language in a new domain characterized as "unconscious." In this way, for example, it is said of the Rat Man that he experienced a feeling of hostility toward his father without being aware of it. Understanding this assertion rests on the ordinary meaning we give to this sort of hostility in situations where the agent is able to recognize such a feeling as his own. The only novelty here is the use of clauses such as "without being aware," "unknowingly," "unconsciously," etc.

In a sense this is true. Freud himself declares that in the unconscious we do find representations and affects to which we can give the same name as their conscious counterparts and which lack only the property of being conscious. But what is completely omitted in this reformulation is the very paradox of psychoanalytic theory, namely, that it is the becoming unconscious as such that requires a specific explanation so that the kinship of meaning between conscious and unconscious contents may be recognized. Now, the explanatory schema capable of accounting for the mechanisms of exclusion, banishment, reification, etc. completely challenges the separation of the domains of action and movement, along with the dichotomy between motive and cause. And in this regard, Michael Sherwood's demonstration in the critical part of his *The Logic of Explanation in Psychoanalysis* (1969) is entirely convincing. What is remarkable about psychoanalytic explanation is that it brings into view motives which are causes and which require an explanation of their autonomous functioning. Besides, Freud could not oppose motive to cause by giving motives the sense of "reason for," inasmuch as rationalization (a term he borrowed from Ernest Jones) is itself a process that calls for an explanation and, by this very fact, does not permit us to accept an alleged reason as the true one.

As a result, Freud is correct in completely ignoring the distinction between motive and cause and in making even its theoretical formulation impossible. In many ways his explanation refers to "causally relevant" factors, whether this is in terms of the initial phenomenon (e.g., the *origin* of a neurosis), the intermediate stages (e.g., the *genesis* of a symptom, of a libidinal structure), its *function* (e.g., compromise formation), or, finally, its "*significance*" (e.g., substitution or symbolic value). These are the four modes of explanation retained by Sherwood, not only in Freud, but in general as well. Freud's use of the idea of cause and of causal explanation is perhaps both complex and flexible—Sherwood (p. 172) quotes a text from Freud which also distinguishes between preconditions, specific causes, and concurrent causes—but he leaves no room for an opposition between cause and motive. All that is important to him is to explain through one or another of the explanatory modes just mentioned, or through an "overdetermined" use of several of them, what in behavior are "the incongruities" in relation to the expected course of a human agent's action.

It is the attempt to reduce these "incongruities" that forbids distinguishing between motives and causes because it calls for an *explanation* by means of causes in order to reach an *understanding* in terms of motives. And this is what I try to express in my own terms by saying that the facts of psychoanalysis arise both from the category of the text, and hence of meaning, and from the categories of energy and resistance, and hence of force. To say, for example, that a feeling is unconscious is not just to say that it resembles conscious motives occurring in other circumstances; rather it is to say that it is to be inserted as a causally relevant factor in order to explain the incongruities of an act of behavior, and that this explanation is itself a causally relevant factor in the work—the working through—of analysis.

From this brief discussion it follows that psychoanalytic theory cannot be reformulated from the outside, on the basis of an alien conceptuality, without mistaking the initial situation in psychoanalysis, namely, that the human psyche under certain conditions of self-alienation is unable to understand itself by simply expanding its immediate interpretive capacities, but instead requires that the hermeneutics of self-understanding take the detour of causal explanation.

If Freud's economic model can therefore legitimately be accused of generating misunderstanding concerning the relation between theory and the analytic situation, it must also be said with equal force and in the opposite direction, that a model of understanding—be it phenomenological, linguistic, or symbolic—that does not integrate some explanatory segment, some economic phase, misunderstands the very facts that are brought to light by analytic experience.

This is why today we can neither be satisfied with the Freudian metapsychology, nor find another starting point to rectify and enrich the theoretical model to the extent that it is true that "the misunderstanding of psychoanalysis as a natural science is not without basis."

TRUTH AND VERIFICATION

Having considered two preliminary questions of the criteria that determine what counts as a *fact* in psychoanalysis, and of the relation which is established between the theory and analytic experience through the *double mediation* of the investigatory procedure and the method of treatment, I shall now attempt to deal directly with the specific question of proof in Freud's psychoanalytic writings.

To inquire about proof in psychoanalysis is to ask two separate questions: (1) What truth-claim is made by the statements of psychoanalysis? and (2) What sort of verification or falsification are these statements capable of?

What truth claim is made by psychoanalytic statements? This question is not only one of degree, but also of the nature of truth, not only a question of quantity, but also of the quality of truth. Or to put it another way, the degree of exactitude that can be expected of psychoanalytic statements depends on the sort of truth that can be expected in this domain. For lack of an exact view of the qualitative diversity of the types of truth in relation to the types of facts, verificational criteria appropriate to the sciences, in which facts are empirically given to one or more external observers, have been repeatedly applied to psychoanalysis. The conclusion has then been either that psychoanalysis does not in any way satisfy these criteria or that it satisfies them only if they are weakened. Now, the question is not how to use strict criteria loosely and so place psychoanalysis higher or lower on a single scale of verifiability (and undoubtedly quite low on the scale), but how to specify the truth claim appropriate to the facts in the psychoanalytic domain.

Let us return to our enumeration of the criteria for facts in psychoanalysis and ask ourselves what sort of adequation of statements is appropriate to them.

First, if analytic experience is desire coming to discourse, the sort of truth that best answers to it is that of a saying-true rather than a being-true. This saying-true is negatively intended in the characterization of the mechanisms of distortion as disguise, falsification, illusion, and in general as forms of misunderstanding. Truth here is closer to that of Greek tragedy than to that of modern physics. *Pathei-mathos,* learn through suffering, says the chorus in Aeschuylus' *Agamemnon.* And what, indeed, is truth for Oedipus, if not the recognition of himself as one who has already killed his father and married his mother? Recognition is accepting instead of denigrating and accusing oneself, and this is the truth befitting saying-true, according to Sophocles.

This movement from misunderstanding to recognition is also the standard itinerary of analytic experience, and it designates what might be called the veracity threshold of truth in psychoanalysis (see Ricoeur, 1974a). And with certain reservations, which will be introduced below, we may say along with Habermas, that this sort of truth involves above all the subject's capacity for *Selbstreflexion.* The truth claim of psychoanalysis is primarily its claim to increase this capacity by helping the subject to overcome the distortions which are the source of self-misunderstanding.

Second, if the analytic situation elicits—principally by means of transference—what is said *to the other,* the truth claim of psychoanalysis can legitimately be placed within the field of intersubjective communication. Everything Freud says about self-misunderstanding can in fact be carried over into misunderstanding the other. All his analyses concerning the object choice, the lost object, substitutions for the lost object, mourning, and melancholia suggest that the place of misunderstanding is the other person.

This second feature of the truth claim of psychoanalytic statements is thereby characterized in a negative manner, namely, that of pursuing self-recognition through the restoration and extension of the symbolic process in the public sphere of communication. In this sense, psychoanalysis pursues in its own way the project of recognition that Hegel placed at the summit of ethical life in his Jena philosophy. This thesis will seem less banal if we see its critical point in relation to the danger of manipulation, which seems to me implicit in any reduction of the historical sphere of communication to the empirical sphere of observable facts. If it is true that the sphere of empirically verifiable statements coincides with what governs our interest for control and domination, then reducing the historical to the empirical would entail the danger of placing the order of symbolic communication under the same system for controlling results as our instrumental action. This warning is not empty in light of a certain tendency of psychoanalysis to take the process of self-recognition and of recognizing the other as an "adjustment" to the objective conditions of a society which is itself diseased.

With the third criterion for psychoanalytic facts, we encounter the major difficulty facing the truth claims of psychoanalysis. We concluded from the study of the third criterion that what is psychoanalytically relevant is what a subject makes of his fantasies. What becomes of the truth claim of psychoanalysis when it is set within the framework of a more positive recognition of fantasy than Freud himself allowed? By losing its reference to actual reality and by giving wider rein to the liberation of fantasizing, to emotional development, and to enjoyment than Freud wanted to do, are we not breaking the bond between veracity and truth? This is undoubtedly so. Nevertheless, I think that there is still something to be sought in the truth claim made from the perspective of the proper use of fantasies. I base this thinking on Freud himself (1924, 1937) wherein arises the notion that the analytic cure may be understood as a work of mourning, which, far from striking down the fantasy, recovers it as a fantasy in order to situate it clearly with the real on the plane of the imaginary in the strong sense of *Einbildungskraft* used by Kant and the great post-Kantians. And in the same sense, I suggested (1970, pp. 372–373) that analytic experience aims at articulating several prime signifiers of existence (phallus, father, mother, death, etc.) in order to make their structuring function appear.

Here the truth claim would concern the passage from the fantasy as alienating to the symbolic as founding both individual and collective identity (see Ricoeur, 1974b).

The fourth criterion for psychoanalytic facts—the criterion of narrativity—will perhaps rid us of some of the difficulties raised by the preceding criterion. One could, in effect, raise the objection to the preceding analysis that by introducing something like a "reasoned mythology" in the recognition process—self-recognition as well as the recognition of the other—we also introduce fiction into the circumference of truth. How can *Dichtung und Wahrheit* be reconciled, to borrow Goethe's title? If we remember that fiction is pretending and that pretending is doing, are we not substituting doing-true, i.e., make-believe, for saying-true? Perhaps. But are not saying-true and doing-true reconciled in the idea of constructing or reconstructing a *coherent story or account* from the tattered remains of our experience? Let us follow this pathway opened up by the narrative character of psychoanalytic facts. Here the truth claim is tied to what Sherwood calls the "narrative commitment of psychoanalytic explanation." It seems to me that this author has shown in a clearly relevant manner that ultimately what is at issue in psychoanalysis is giving "a single extended explanation of an individual patient's entire case history" (1969, p. 4). Hence to explain here is to reorganize facts into a meaningful whole which constitutes a single and continuous history (even if it does not cover an entire life span).

I think it is wise to approach things in this way, for the narrative interest or involvement at issue here has no parallel in an observational science where we speak of "cases" but not of "case histories." The psychoanalytic explanation of a case is a narrative explanation in the sense that the generalizations or law-like statements which are implied by the explanatory segments referred to in the second part of our study contribute to the *understandable narrative* toward which each individual case study leads. If we stated earlier that causal connections are explanatory segments in a process of understanding, even of self-reflection in Habermas' sense, this is because understanding is narrative and because the partial explanatory segments of this or that fragment of behavior are integrated in a narrative structure. So the validation of analytic statements draws its specific nature from this ultimate reference to a *narrative commitment* in the name of which we try to integrate isolated or alien phenomena in "a single unified process or sequence of events" (1969, p. 169).

We are thus invited to reflect upon the concept of narrative intelligibility which psychoanalysis has in common with the historical sciences. Now it is difficult to define this concept inasmuch as the criteria for adequation are difficult to handle on this level. Indeed, it is precisely in psychoanalysis that reduction of the "incongruities" raises the question of knowing what is meant by an intelligible account. A history that would remain inconsistent, incoherent, or incomplete would clearly resemble what we know of the course of life in ordinary experience, namely, that a human life as a whole remains strange, disconnected, incomplete, and fragmented.

We might be tempted therefore to give up any attempt to tie a truth claim to the idea of the intelligible accounts of an existence. But I do not think it would be correct to give in to this epistemological defeatism, for we would thereby turn psychoanalytic statements into the rhetoric of persuasion under the pretext that it is the account's acceptability to the patient that is therapeutically effective. Then, besides the renewed suspicion of suggestion by the analyst—which Freud never ceased to combat—a more serious suspicion is insinuated, namely, that the criterion of therapeutic success is exclusively the patient's ability to adapt to a given social milieu. And this suspicion leads in turn to the suspicion that the psychoanalyst finally represents, with regard to the patient, only the point of view of society, and that he imposes this on his patient by subtly involving him in a strategy of capitulation to which he alone holds the key. This is why we must not give up our efforts to link a truth claim with the narrativity criterion, even if this claim is validated on a basis other than that of narrativity itself. In other words, we must maintain the critical dimension of narrativity, which is just that of self-recognition, of recognition of the other, and of recognition of the fantasy. We may even say, then, that the patient is both the actor and the critic of a history which he is at first unable to recount. The problem of recognizing oneself is the problem of recovering the ability to recount one's own history, to endlessly continue to give the form of a story to reflections on oneself. And working-through is nothing other than this continuous narration.

We can now turn to the second half of our question: what sort of verification or falsification are the statements of psychoanalysis capable of? To ask about the procedures of verification and falsification is to ask which *means of proof* are appropriate to the truth claims of psychoanalysis? My thesis here is as follows: *if the ultimate truth claim resides in the case histories, the means of proof reside in the articulation of the entire network: theory, hermeneutics, therapeutics, and narration.*

The preceding discussion on narrativity is a good introduction to this final stage of our investigation. We have assumed that all truth claims of psychoanalysis are ultimately summed up in the narrative structure of psychoanalytic facts. But it does not follow that the means of proof are contained in the narrative structure itself; and the question remains whether the means of truth relevant to narrative explanation are not carried by the non-narrative statements of psychoanalysis.

To prove this point it will suffice to think about what makes a narration an explanation in the psychoanalytic sense of the term. It is the possibility of inserting several stages of causal explanation into the process of self-understanding in narrative terms. And it is this explanatory detour that entails recourse to non-narrative means of proof. These are spread over three levels: (1) the level of generalizations resulting from comparison with the rest of the clinical explanation; (2) the level of lawlike propositions applied to typical segments of behavior (symptoms, for example), which are, as Sherwood has shown, themselves divided into explanations in terms of origin, explanations in terms of genesis, others in terms of function, and still others in terms of significance; finally (3) the level of *very general hypotheses* concerning the functioning of the psychic apparatus, which could be considered as axiomatic. This last level is divided into the topography, the theory of agencies, and the successive theories of instinctual drives, including the death instinct. Generalizations, laws, and axioms, therefore, constitute the non-narrative structure of psychoanalytic explanation.

At its first level, that of generalizations, this non-narrative structure of explanation is already present in the ordinary explanations of individual behavior; alleged motives—for example, hate or jealousy—are not particular events, but classes of inclinations under which a particular action is placed in order to make it intelligible. To say that someone acted out of jealousy is to invoke in the case of his particular action a feature which is grasped from the outset as repeatable and common to an indeterminate variety of individuals. Such a motive draws its explanatory value from its power to place a particular action in a meaningful context characterized from the start by a certain universality of significance. So to explain is to characterize a given action by ascribing to it as its cause a motive which exemplifies a class. This is all the more true when we are dealing not with classes of motives, identifiable as the general features of human experience, but with fantasies which present organized, stable, and eminently typical scenes, or with stages—oral, anal, genital, etc.—which themselves are also typical organizations of libidinal development. And taking the next step, we are ready to understand that excommunication, on the basis of which an unconscious ensemble is autonomously structured, tends to produce the stereotyped incongruities which are the very object of analytic explanation.

The transition from generalities to lawlike statements broadly corresponds to the explanation not only in terms of unconscious motives but in terms of the mechanisms of distortion which render the motivational process unrecognizable. And above these lawlike statements we still have the propositions concerning the theoretical entities posed by psychoanalysis; these statements constitute the metapsychology as such, which can be considered from the point of view of the structure of these statements as the metalanguage of psychoanalysis—all that can be said regarding instinct, the representatives of instinct, the destiny of instinct, etc. At this level, every narrative feature, by which I mean the reference to a case history, is erased, at least at the manifest level of the statements.

This style of explanation has as its consequence that in Freud what Sherwood calls *narrative commitment* and *explanatory commitment* continually split apart, only to merge together again in the case histories—again we must note that even in the case histories, including the Rat Man, Freud juxtaposes the case study as such and theoretical considerations. In the other writings, which are far more numerous, however, they diverge again. We could even say that in these writings the relation between "narrative commitment" and "explanatory commitment" is reversed. Thus, case histories constitute just one pole of a very wide range of writings for which the essays on metapsychology constitute the other pole, which is basically non-narrative.

Such is the way in which it may be said that in psychoanalysis the means of proof reside in the very articulation of the entire network constituted by the theory, the interpretive procedures, the therapeutic treatment, and the narrative structure of the analytic experience.

I am not unaware that this assertion leads to the most formidable objection of all against psychoanalysis, namely, that these statements are irrefutable and therefore unverifiable if the theory, method, treatment, and interpretation of a particular case are all to be verified at once. If this entire investigation of mine does nothing more than formulate this objection correctly and assemble the means to reply to it, it will have attained its goal.

I will leave aside the crude form of this objection, namely, that the analyst *suggests* to his patient that he accept the interpretation which verifies the theory. I am taking for granted the replies which Freud opposes to this accusation of suggestibility. They are worth what the measures taken at the level of the professional code and the analytic technique itself against the suspicion of suggestion are worth. I grant that these measures define a good analyst and that there are good analysts.

It is more interesting to take Freud at his word and to contend with a subtler form of the accusation of self-confirmation, that is, that validation in psychoanalysis is condemned to remain circular since everything is verified at once. It is all the more important to consider this argument since the notion of a circle is not foreign to all the historico-interpretive disciplines, in which a "case" is not only an example to be placed under a law, but something which possesses its own dramatic structure which makes it a "case history." The problem, Heidegger says with reference to the hermeneutic circle, is not avoiding the circle but properly entering into it. This means: taking measures so that the circle is not a vicious circle. Now a circle is vicious if it takes the form of begging the question, that is, if the verification in each of the areas considered is the condition for verification in another area. The circle of verification will not be vicious, however, if validation proceeds in a cumulative fashion through the mutual reinforcement of criteria which taken in isolation would not be decisive, but whose convergence makes them plausible and, in the best cases, probable and even convincing.

I will say, therefore, that the validation apt to confirm the truth claim belonging to the domain of psychoanalytic facts is an extremely complex process which is based on the synergy of partial and heterogeneous criteria. If we take as our guideline the idea of a constellation formed by the theory, the investigatory procedure, the treatment technique, and the reconstruction of a case history, we can then say the following: (1) a good psychoanalytic explanation must be coherent with the theory, or, if one prefers, it must conform to Freud's psychoanalytic system, or to the system by which this or that school claiming his name is identified—recall, however, that I have limited my consideration in this essay to Freud's writings.

This first criterion is not peculiar to psychoanalysis. In every field of inquiry explanation establishes a connection of this kind between a theoretical apparatus of concepts and an array of facts relevant to this theoretical style. In this sense, all explanations are limited by their own conceptual framework. Their validity extends as far as the correlation between theory and facts works. For the same reason, any theory is questionable. A new theory is required, as Kuhn (1962) has argued, as soon as new facts are recognized which can no longer be "covered" by the ruling paradigm. And something like this is happening today in psychoanalysis, perhaps. The theoretical model of energy distribution appears more and more inadequate, but no alternative model seems to be powerful enough to "cover" all the accepted facts relevant to psychoanalysis or their paradoxical nature.

(2) A good psychoanalytic explanation must satisfy the universalizable rules set up by the procedures of interpretation for the sake of decoding the text of the unconscious. This second criterion is relatively independent of the preceding one to the extent that it relies on the *inner* consistency of the new text substituted by means of translation for the unreadable text of symptoms and dreams. In this respect, the model of the rebus is quite appropriate. It shows that the character of intelligibility of the substituted text resides in its capacity to take into account as many scattered elements as possible from those provided by the analytic process itself, especially as a result of the technique of free association.

A corollary of this second criterion deserves attention. It concerns the expansion of the procedures of interpretation beyond the native domain of psychoanalysis, i.e., symptoms and dreams, along the analogical lines that connect tales, puns, jokes, etc. to the first analogon of this series, the dream. A new kind of coherence is implied here which concerns not only the inner intelligibility of the translated text, but also the analogy of structure which obtains between all the members of the series of psychic productions. This second criterion of validation may be formulated accordingly in two complementary ways as a criterion of intratextual consistency and a criterion of intertextual consistency. The second formulation may even be the more decisive one to the extent that the universalization of the rules of decoding relies on the soundness of the analogical extrapolation from symptoms and dreams to other cultural expressions. At the same time, the merely analogical character of this extrapolation reminds us of the problematic value of this means of proof. But even the limitation resulting from the analogical structure of this criterion of validation proceeds from structural reasons distinct from those which impose a limitation on the first criterion. The second criterion is not only relatively independent of the first one, but it may correct and even shatter it, inasmuch as it is under the guidance of these procedures of investigation that new facts are released which may defeat the claim of the theoretical framework to "cover" them. This is what happens, for example, to the energy-distribution model when it is confronted with the facts yielded by the procedures of interpretation in conjunction with the methods of treatment.

(3) A good psychoanalytic explanation must be satisfactory in economic terms; in other words, it must be able to be incorporated into the work of the analysand, into his "working-through," and so become a therapeutic factor of amelioration. This third criterion, too, is relatively independent of the first one since it implies something which *happens to* the analysand under the condition of his own "work" (hence the substitution of the term analysand for that of patient and even of client). And it is relatively independent of the second one, to the extent that an interpretation which is only understood, i.e., intellectually grasped, remains ineffective and may even be harmful so long as a new pattern of energies has not emerged from the "handling" of resistances. The therapeutic success resulting from this new energetical configuration constitutes in this way an autonomous criterion of validation.

(4) Finally, a good psychoanalytic explanation must raise a particular case history to the sort of narrative intelligibility we ordinarily expect from a story. This fourth criterion should not be overemphasized as would be the case in a purely "narrative" account of psychoanalytic theory. But the relative autonomy of this criterion must not be overlooked either, because narrative intelligibility implies something more than the subjective acceptability of one's own life story. It comes to terms with the general condition of acceptability that we apply when we read any story, be it historical or fictional. In the terms of W. B. Gallie (1968), a story has to be "followable," and in this sense, "self-explanatory." We interpolate explanation when the narrative process is

blocked and in order to "follow-further." These explanations are acceptable to the extent that they may be grafted upon the archetypes of storytelling which have been culturally developed and which rule our actual competence to follow new stories. Here psychoanalysis is not an exception. Psychoanalytic reports are kinds of biographies and autobiographies whose literary history is a part of the long tradition emerging from the oral epic tradition of the Greeks, the Celts, and the Germans. It is this whole tradition of storytelling that provides a relative autonomy to the criterion of narrative intelligibility as regards, not only the consistency of the interpretive procedures, but also the efficacity of the change in the balance of libidinal energies.

Consequently, when these criteria of validation do not derive from one another, but mutually reinforce one another, they constitute the proof apparatus in psychoanalysis. It may be granted that this apparatus is extremely complex, very difficult to handle, and highly problematical. But it can at least be assumed that this cumulative character of the validation criteria is the only one suited to both the criteria for psychoanalytic facts that specify the truth claim in psychoanalysis and the complex relations between the theory, the investigatory procedure, and the method of treatment that govern the means of proof in psychoanalysis.

REFERENCES

Breuer, J. & Freud, S. (1893–1895). Studies on hysteria. *Standard Edition,* 2. London: Hogarth Press. 1955.

Freud, S. (1895). Project for a scientific psychology. *Standard Edition,* 1:283–387. London: Hogarth Press, 1966.

________ (1900). The interpretation of dreams. *Standard Edition,* 4, 5. London: Hogarth Press, 1953.

________ (1905). Three essays on the theory of sexuality. *Standard Edition,* 7:130–243. London: Hogarth Press, 1953.

________ (1913). Claims of psycho-analysis to scientific interest. *Standard Edition,* 13:165–190. London: Hogarth Press, 1955.

________ (1914). Remembering, repeating and working through. *Standard Edition,* 12:147–156. London: Hogarth Press, 1958.

________ (1915a). Instincts and their vicissitudes. *Standard Edition,* 14:117–140. London: Hogarth Press, 1957.

________ (1915b). The unconscious. *Standard Edition,* 14:166–215. London: Hogarth Press, 1957.

________ (1916–1917). Introductory lectures on psycho-analysis. *Standard Edition,* 15, 16. London: Hogarth Press, 1969.

________ (1917). Mourning and melancholia. *Standard Edition,* 14:242–258. London: Hogarth Press, 1957.

________ (1922). Psycho-analysis and the libido theory. *Standard Edition,* 18:235–259. London: Hogarth Press, 1955.

________ (1924). The dissolution of the Oedipus complex. *Standard Edition,* 19:173–179. London: Hogarth Press, 1961.

________ (1937). Analysis, terminable and interminable. *Standard Edition,* 23:209–253. London: Hogarth Press, 1964.

Gallie, W. B. (1968). *Philosophy and the Historical Understanding.* New York: Schocken Books.

Habermas, J. (1971). *Knowledge and Human Interests.* Boston: Beacon Press.

Kuhn, T. (1962). *The Structure of Scientific Revolutions.* Chicago: University of Chicago Press.

Lacan, J. (1966). *Ecrits.* Paris: Seuil.

Laplanche, J. & Pontalis, J. B. (1967). *Vocabulaire de la psychoanalyse.* Paris: Presses Universitaires de France.

Lorenzer, A. (1973). *Ueber den Gegenstand der Psychoanalyse.* Frankfurt: Suhrkamp.

Ricoeur, P. (1970). *Freud and Philosophy.* New Haven: Yale University Press.

——— (1974a). Psychiatry and moral values. In: *American Handbook of Psychiatry,* ed. S. Arieti et al., Vol. 1, 2nd ed. New York: Basic Books, pp. 976–990.

——— (1974b). Fatherhood—from phantasm to symbol. In: *The Conflicts of Interpretation.* Evanston, Ill.: Northwestern University Press, pp. 468–497.

——— (in press). Language and image in psychoanalysis. In: *Psychiatry and the Humanities,* Vol. III, ed. J. H. Smith. New Haven: Yale University Press.

Sherwood, M. (1969). *The Logic of Explanation in Psychoanalysis.* New York: Academic Press.

26

FREUD'S THEORY: THE PERSPECTIVE OF A PHILOSOPHER OF SCIENCE

ADOLF GRÜNBAUM

1. FREUD'S NOTION OF SCIENTIFIC STATUS

Throughout his long career, Freud insisted that the psychoanalytic enterprise has the status of a natural science. As he told us at the very end of his life, the explanatory gains from positing unconscious mental processes "enabled psychology to take its place as a natural science like any other"[1] (S.E. 1940, 23:158). Then he went on to declare: "Psycho-analysis is a part of the mental science of psychology. . . . Psychology too, is a natural science" (S.E. 1940, 23:282). Earlier, Freud had firmly rebuffed the anti-naturalism and methodological separatism that was championed by the *Geisteswissenschaften* movement as a framework for psychology and the social sciences. Its votaries deemed causal explanations to be endemic to the natural sciences in view of the law-like causal connections featured by these disciplines. And they rejected such nomothetic causal explanations as generically alien to the humanistic sciences. For as they saw it, the aim of the study of man ought to be the "hermeneutic" quest for idiographic understanding by such methods as empathy and intuitive self-evidence (Möller 1976, chap. 2; Möller 1978, chap. 2). In diametrical opposition to this view of the task of psychology, Freud proclaimed:

> . . . the intellect and the mind are objects for scientific research in exactly the same way as any non-human things. Psychoanalysis has a special right to speak for the scientific *Weltanschauung* . . . If . . . the investigation of the intellectual and emotional functions of men (and of animals) is included in science, then it will be seen that . . . no new sources of knowledge or methods of research have come into being (S.E. 1933, 22:159).

Reprinted from the *American Philosophical Association Proceedings, 57,* 5–31. (1983).

Minor modifications were made to the original article at the author's request.

In 1895, the psychoanalytic method of clinical investigation by means of free association was only a fledgling mode of inquiry. Likewise, Freud's clinical theory of psychopathology was still nascent. At that very early juncture, he gave a neurophysiological twist to the notion of a scientific psychology. And he couched his then vision of a neurological underpinning for psychic processes in the reductionistic physical idiom of material particles. This biophysical notion animated his 1895 manuscript "Project for a Scientific Psychology" (S.E. 1950, 1:295). Yet Freud abandoned his reductionistic program within only two years of having enunciated it. As he wrote in retrospect:

> . . . every attempt . . . to discover a [brain] localization of mental processes, every endeavor to think of ideas as stored up in nerve-cells and of excitations as travelling along nerve-fibres, has miscarried completely (S.E. 1915, 14:174).

By 1900, the legacy of the abandoned neurological model had become the postulation of a bipartite structure of the mind whose principal component systems were the unconscious and the so-called preconscious (S.E. 1900, 5: chap. vii). The contents of the preconscious system, if not actually conscious, are deemed readily accessible to consciousness. But only the clinical techniques of psychoanalysis are held able to unlock the gates to the unconscious system. Freud now pointedly eschewed the original neurological connotations of the technical vocabulary he had introduced in the 1895 Project. Yet he retained this terminology for use in a purely mentalistic sense. Thus, the erstwhile excitation or "cathexis" of a *neuron* has now become the cathected state of an *idea* or *memory*. Likewise, a train of thought is now held to involve the *flow* of cathexes from one *idea* to another, so that *psychic energy* is invested in the mental representations of objects. And the two component systems of the mind were assumed to differ in regard to permitting the flow of psychic energy towards tension discharge. Later, Freud modified his bipartite structural model of the unconscious and the preconscious, when he replaced it by *three* agencies whose functions need not detain us (S.E. 1923, 19:12–59; 1933, 22:57–80).

These successive models of the structure and function of the psychic apparatus are often denominated as the "metapsychology" of the psychoanalytic edifice (Laplanche & Pontalis 1973, p. 250). The separation of the clinical theory of repression from that metapsychology within the edifice is not always sharp. Yet it is vital to appreciate to what marginal epistemic status Freud relegated its metapsychological part, amid steadfastly claiming natural science status for his construction overall. The metapsychological models, he tells us, are "a speculative superstructure of psychoanalysis, any portion of which can be abandoned or changed without loss or regret the moment its inadequacy has been proved" (S.E. 1925, 20:32–33; see also S.E. 1914, 14:77). And he added pointedly: "But there is still plenty to be described that lies closer to actual experience." The "plenty . . . that lies closer to actual experience" is, of course, none other than his *clinically*-based theory of personality, psychopathology and therapy. The centerpiece of that corpus of hypotheses is the theory of repression, which features his compromise-model of neurotic symptoms, as well as of manifest dream content and of various sorts of slips. These various phenomena are deemed to be "compromises" in the sense of being *substitutive gratifications* or outlets. For they are held to be conatively vicarious surrogates. Moreover, the clinical theory of repression is often couched in personalist language.

But in conspicuous contrast to his depiction of the metapsychology as "a speculative superstructure" which can be sloughed off, if need be, "without loss or regret," Freud explicitly deemed his clinical theory to be "the most essential part" of what he had wrought. For, as he told us, "the theory of repression is the cornerstone on which the whole structure of psychoanalysis rests. It is the most essential part of it" (S.E. 1914, 14:16).

Thus, when Freud unswervingly claimed natural science status for his theoretical constructions throughout his life, he did so first and foremost for his evolving clinical theory of personality and therapy, rather than for the metapsychology of psychic energy flow. After all, he had been chastened in his early reductionistic exuberance by the speedy demise of his neurobiological model in 1896. Thereafter, he never made the scientific status of the clinical theory parasitic on its would-be subsumption under a primordially scientific metapsychology! Instead, he then perennially claimed his theory of personality and therapy to be authenticated by *direct* and cogent evidential support originating on his office couch and in his self-analysis. In brief, during all but the first few years of his career, Freud's criterion of scientificity was methodological and not ontologically reductive.

2. CRITIQUE OF HABERMAS' CHARGE OF "SCIENTISTIC SELF-MISUNDERSTANDING"

The leading spokesmen for the so-called "hermeneutic" construal of Freud's clinical theory have given wide currency to an exegetical thesis that I have just shown to be a myth. This is ironic, since the hermeneuticians see themselves as guardians of the faithful exegesis of texts. According to the philosophers Jürgen Habermas and Paul Ricoeur, and the late psychoanalyst George Klein, Freud attributed natural science status to the clinical theory by *misextrapolation* from its would-be reduction to the primordially scientific metapsychology. Indeed, Habermas (1971) chides Freud for having fallen prey to a far-reaching "scientistic self-misunderstanding" (pp. 246–252). According to this complaint, Freud's misunderstanding was "scientistic," because he idolatrously endowed the clinical theory with natural science status under the ideological aegis of the metapsychology. Furthermore, Freud's view was purportedly a *self*-misunderstanding, because it issued in a philosophical misconception of the very nature of his own clinical theory. Finally, Freud's alleged misconstrual of the clinical theory was far-reaching, if only because it thwarted the recognition of psychoanalysis as a paradigmatically depth-hermeneutic mode of inquiry, as the only tangible example of a science incorporating methodical self-reflection, and as potentially prototypic for the other sciences of man (Habermas 1971, chap. 10).

As recently as 1981, Ricoeur again endorsed Habermas' allegation of "scientistic self-misunderstanding" (Ricoeur 1981, p. 259). And, in an earlier work, Ricoeur hailed the *failure* of Freud's clinical theory to qualify as an empirical or natural science by the received standards as the basis for "a counterattack" against those who deplore this failure (Ricoeur 1970, p. 358).

Habermas, Ricoeur and Klein each give more or less detailed *arguments* for actually denying natural science status to Freud's clinical theory in principle. Here I need to confine myself largely to Habermas, whose views have become influential not only in philosophy but also in some of the social sciences. And I concentrate mainly on his arguments in the conviction that they are quite representative of the mode of reasoning offered by the others.

It is to be clearly understood that far from questioning the etiologic and therapeutic hypotheses of Freud's clinical theory, these hermeneuticians claim to take them for granted without ado. What they purportedly tried to controvert are rather the philosophical tenets that, as they see it, Freud had misguidedly grafted onto those hypotheses. Hence in my appraisal of their views, I shall refrain from challenging the credentials of Freud's clinical hypotheses. But, as we shall see thereafter, there are ample grounds for such a challenge.

It is one of Habermas' cardinal theses that the *law-like* causal nexus present in the causality of nature does *not* inhere in the therapeutic dynamics of the psychoanalytic process of "self-reflection." He presents this denial by reference to a patient's conquest of a neurosis whose salient manifestation is rigidly *repetitive* behavior. And Habermas' astonishing pivotal contention is that the etiologic causal connection which was operative in the pathogenesis of the neurosis is itself "dissolved" when the patient overcomes his affliction in therapy (Habermas 1971, pp. 256–257 *and* 271; 1970, pp. 302, 304). More explicitly, as Habermas would have it, whenever a neurotic overcomes the repetition compulsion by the lifting of his pathogenic repressions, this psychoanalytic self-reflection has actually "dissolved" and "overcome" the very *causal connection* that had previously linked the pathogen to the neurotic behavior (Habermas 1971, p. 271). Yet, in the domain of the laws of nature, there is no counterpart to this alleged overcoming of a causal connection "as such." Hence Habermas uses the Hegelian term "causality of fate" to refer to the sort of fragile causal linkage that, he tells us, is "dissolvable," because it can purportedly be "subdued" by the therapeutic "power of reflection."

But, regrettably, the reasoning he uses to establish this "causality of fate" is a mere tissue of errors. The most damaging of these mistakes becomes clear from the rationale used by Breuer and Freud, when they founded psychoanalysis. In 1893, they enunciated the following epoch-making etiologic hypothesis: In the pathogenesis of a psychoneurosis, repression plays the generic causal role of a *sine qua non* (S.E. 1893, 2:6–7; 1893, 3:29–30). The impetus for this assumption avowedly came from their belief that the therapeutic gains from their method of treatment were causally attributable to the cathartic retrieval of traumatic memories, which their patients had repressed. Once they had decided that such lifting of repressions is therapeutic, they wished to *explain* its remedial efficacy. And, as they soon realized, the desired explanation could be given deductively by the etiologic postulate that repression is causally necessary not only for the initial development of a neurotic disorder, but also for its maintenance. Clearly, if a repression of type *R* is indeed the causal *sine qua non* for the presence of a neurosis of kind *N*, then it follows that the removal of *R* will actually issue in the obliteration of *N*. Hence any patient who rids himself of *R* and thereupon becomes emancipated from *N* plainly *instantiates* that *R* is the causal *sine qua non* for the presence of *N*. Amazingly enough, Habermas claims that this very causal linkage itself is dissolved by the patient's therapeutic achievement. But surely the instantiation of a causal connection cannot possibly also qualify as the dissolution of this linkage! Hence Habermas' notion that a therapeutic achievement can "overcome" an etiologic linkage by dissolving it is deplorably incoherent.

What the patient has indeed overcome is his pathogenic repression as well as his neurosis, but hardly the causal connection between them. To terminate an *effect* by undercutting the cause required for its production is patently *not* tantamount to overcoming the causal connection that links them. On the contrary, it is to *illustrate* it. Hence in Freud's clinical theory, just as in physics, there can be no question at all of "dissolving" a causal linkage between an antecedent C and its effect *E* on the strength of terminating the recurrence of *E* by preventing the further realization of C. Far from having elucidated the role of causality in psychoanalysis, Habermas' importation of the causality of fate has only obfuscated it.[2]

The causality of fate is not the only major causal doctrine enlisted by Habermas to contrast psychoanalysis with the natural sciences. He considers the application of psychoanalytic generalizations, which he calls "general interpretations" (1971, p. 259), to the life history of a particular analysand. Such application generates particular interpretations that combine into a personalized narrative. When offered to the individual patient by the analyst, particular interpretations are presumed to be stated in the "*intentional*" clinical language of desires, affects, fantasies, sensations, memories and the like (1971, p. 272). Since these interpretations are couched in such motivational language, Habermas speaks of them as deriving from the "hermeneutic application" of general interpretations to the life of a particular analysand.

Now, he is concerned to contrast the logic of such hermeneutic utilization with the corresponding application of law-like principles in the nomothetic empirical sciences to particular cases. And his paradigm for the latter sort of instantiation of the antecedent of a physical law is given by " 'this stone' is considered, for example, as 'mass' " (1971, p. 265). Claiming that "this subsumption is unproblematic" (p. 265), he proposes to *contrast* it logically with an instantiation of a general interpretation in psychoanalytic practice. In the empirical sciences, he tells us "we can base explanations on context-free laws. In the case of hermeneutic application, however, theoretical propositions are translated into the narrative presentation of an individual history in such a way that a causal statement does not come into being without this context" (pp. 272–273). Hence he maintains that "general interpretations do not make possible context-free explanation" (p. 273). In brief, his thesis is that—in contrast to psychoanalysis—explanations in physics are generically based on context-free, ahistorical laws. And its enunciation concludes the chapter he entitled "The Scientistic Self-Misunderstanding of Metapsychology," with the subtitle "On the Logic of General Interpretation" (chap. 11).

But to the serious detriment of this further dichotomy of his, there are telling counterexamples to it from venerable principles of physics. And these counterexamples likewise will be seen to redound to the utter discredit of the following equally grandiose assertions by the hermeneutician H. G. Gadamer (1975), who wrote: "It is the aim of science to so objectify experience that it no longer contains any historical element. The scientific experiment does this by its methodical procedure" (p. 311). But how, one asks, does the scientific experiment have this ahistorical import? Gadamer reasons that the experimental method of science predicates confirmation on *repeatability to such a degree* that he feels entitled to conclude: "Hence no place can be left for the historicality of experience in science" (p. 311).

As shown by the laws of classical electrodynamics, Habermas and Gadamer have drawn a *pseudo*-contrast between the nomothetic and human sciences. For a number of these laws embody a fundamental dependence on the history and/or context of the object of knowledge. Indeed, in some of the basic laws of electromagnetism, context-dependence is far greater than was ever contemplated in even the most exhaustive of psychoanalytic explanatory narratives, or in any recapitulation of human history.

Consider an electrically charged particle having an arbitrary velocity and acceleration. We are concerned with the laws governing the electric and magnetic fields produced by this point charge throughout space *at any one fixed time t.* In this theory, the influence of the charge on any other test charge in space is postulated to be propagated with the finite velocity of light, in contrast to the instantaneous propagation familiar from Newton's action-at-a-distance theory of gravitation. But the *non*-instantaneous feature of the propagation of the electrodynamic influence contributes to an important consequence as follows: At any space point *P*, the electric and magnetic fields at a given time *t* depend on the position, velocity and acceleration that the field-producing charge had at an *earlier* time. That earlier time depends, in part, on the distance traversed by the influence arriving at *P* at time *t* after having traveled from the charge to *P* with the velocity of light.

Clearly, the greater the distance that was traversed by the influence by the time *t* of its arrival at point *P*, the earlier its origination time. Thus, for space points at ever larger such distances in infinite space, the origination time will be ever more remotely past. In short, as the distance of a field point becomes infinitely large, the origination time of the influence determining the electric and magnetic field intensities at that point at the fixed time *t* goes to past infinity.

It thus turns out that at ANY ONE INSTANT *t*, the electric and magnetic fields produced throughout infinite space by a charge moving with arbitrary acceleration depend lawfully on its own PARTICULAR ENTIRE INFINITE PAST KINEMATIC HISTORY! The pertinent law-like equations specify the fields as functions of the aforestated kinematic attributes possessed by the charge at the appropriate earlier times (Page & Adams 1940, p. 144, equations (48–7) and (48–8)). Pertinently enough, the authors of one classic treatise state the relevant upshot of these electro-dynamic laws as follows: "expressions for the complete field of an element of charge [throughout space at any one time] involve . . . its entire [infinite] past history" (Page & Adams 1940, p. 161).

Though the individual histories of each of two or more charged particles can be very different indeed, the electrodynamic laws accommodate these differences amid being general. The generality derives from the form of the law-like functional dependencies of the electric and magnetic field intensities on the earlier accelerations, velocities, and positions of the field-producing charge. But the latter's individual history consists of the infinite temporal series of the particular values of these kinematic attributes (variables).

As against Habermas, I submit that these electrodynamic laws exhibit context-dependence with a vengeance by making the field produced by a charge for any one time dependent on the particular entire past history of the charge. And, to the detriment of Gadamer, these delayed action laws are based on replicable experiments but resoundingly belie his thesis that "no place can be left for the historicality of experience in science." Indeed, by being a special case of one of these laws, even Coulomb's simple inverse square law for the electric field is highly history-dependent by holding only if the field-producing charge has been at rest *for all past time* (Page & Adams 1940, p. 161).

There are other instructive cases of context-dependence of laws of physics that reveal further the poverty of Habermas' supposed paradigmatic example of " 'this stone' is considered . . . as 'mass' " (1971, p. 265). These further cases exhibit so-called "hysteresis" in the sense that a property of a physical system, induced by a given present influence upon it, depends not only on that present influence, but also on the *past history* of variation of that influence (Considine 1976, p. 1335). One such case is the hysteresis behavior of highly magnetizable metals (e.g., iron, cobalt, nickel, etc.), which are known as "ferromagnetic." Thus, the present response of the ferromagnetic material to one and the same external magnetic influence will depend on the prior magnetization *history* of the given sample. More generally, suppose that such material is subjected to a cycle of magnetization and demagnetization by a suitable alternation in the external magnetic influence. And let that cycle be depicted graphically by plotting the induced internal magnetization against the external magnetizing field. Then the one complete initial cycle of magnetization and demagnetization will be represented by a closed curve ("hysteresis loop"). Significantly, the dependence of the behavior of the ferromagnetic sample on its *history* then makes itself felt *overall* as follows: The closed curve representing the initial cycle will *never* be retraced by subsequent cycles of demagnetization and remagnetization (Efron 1967, p. 694). Other examples in physics in which the response of materials to current influences is sensitive to the history of their prior exposure to like influences are furnished by solids that exhibit *elastic* hysteresis. Even rubber bands display a like behavior.

The array of context-dependent physical laws that I have adduced seem tailor-made as insuperable difficulties for the second of Habermas' alleged causal dichotomies. And I trust that the context-dependence of the physical cases I have developed either matches or surpasses the degree of any such dependence encountered when general clinical hypotheses are applied to particular patient histories. Habermas' paradigm of the stone that has mass epitomizes the generic notion of a situation in physics on which he relied to buttress his purported dichotomy. Thus, he and Gadamer have managed to parlay the severe limitations of their own personal scientific horizons into a *pseudo*-contrast between the humanistic disciplines and the natural sciences. Indeed, it is a sad commentary on our intellectual culture that by trading on their stone age notions of physics, they have been able to gain adherents to their view.

Habermas likewise makes several *epistemic* allegations to vindicate his reproach of "scientistic self-misunderstanding" against Freud's own construal of the clinical theory. Here I can deal with only one of these contentions.[3]

The logic of validating the general hypotheses of Freud's clinical theory is one of the major themes of Habermas' hermeneutic epistemology. And the pivotal claim of his account is that the patient is the ultimate epistemic arbiter of these general psychoanalytic postulates, which he calls "general interpretations" (1971, p. 261). Within the confines of analytic therapy, these universal hypotheses are used to generate *particular* interpretations pertaining to the individual lives of specific patients. For example, the analyst employs psychoanalytic generalizations retrodictively to construct an etiologic scenario for the pathogenesis of a patient's disorder.

In the context of the clinical setting, Habermas downgrades the doctor cognitively vis-à-vis his patient by endowing the analysand with an epistemic *monopoly* in the testing of the *particular* interpretations pertaining to his own life history. As he puts it, "analytic insights possess validity for the analyst only after they have been accepted as knowledge by the analysand himself" (1971, p. 261). Having claimed that the patient is thus cognitively preeminent, Habermas infers that "the success and failure [of a psychoanalytic construction] cannot be intersubjectively established" (p. 266). Thereupon he assumes that induction from just such particular interpretations is the *sole* means for *validating* Freud's universal hypotheses, and not merely for elaborating these generalizations heuristically (p. 259). Hence he concludes that patients enjoy privileged epistemic access as follows: "the validity of general interpretations depends directly on statements about the object domain being applied by the 'objects,' that is the persons concerned, to themselves" (p. 261). Habermas then relies on this contention, in turn, to arrive at the methodological dichotomy that general interpretations are not governed by the same criteria of validation as the universal hypotheses of the empirical sciences (pp. 261–266).

It appears that the tenability of this dichotomy depends on the merits of Habermas' cognitive tribute to the patient. Note that if the analysand were actually the ultimate epistemic arbiter, as depicted by Habermas, then the patients treated by psychoanalysts would have truly formidable cognitive powers. Each patient would then be not only the best judge, but ultimately the *sole* judge of what was in fact the cause of his neurotic disorder, what engendered his sundry dreams, and what induced his lapses of memory, various slips of the tongue and other bungled actions. Moreover, in Habermas' account, the cognitive monopoly of patients, taken collectively, likewise extends to *universal* psychoanalytic hypotheses. Hence the validation of Freud's etiology of paranoia, for example, would then ultimately rest entirely on the collective verdicts of those treated for this delusional affliction.

I contend that this epistemic thesis is a house of cards, no less than Habermas' two alleged causal dichotomies. One important reason will have to suffice here.[4] As background for it, note that Habermas tacitly and peremptorily banished all *extra*-clinical testing of general psychoanalytic hypotheses from consideration. For he simply took it for granted that the treatment setting is the sole arena for any and all validation or disconfirmation of these universal propositions. Just for argument's sake, let me assume that if one were to confine all testing to the clinical investigations carried out by the doctor-patient dyad, then the analyst can confirm an interpretation only on the authority of his patient's prior certification of its validity.

Even then, it would hardly follow that the clinical setting is the principal arena for the well-designed testing of general psychoanalytic hypotheses, let alone the sole arena.[5] But if extra-clinical tests of at least some of these hypotheses are feasible, as indeed they are, then patients in analysis surely do not have the cognitive monopoly that Habermas conferred on them. In fact, as I shall now show by an example I have developed elsewhere (Grünbaum 1983, chap. 1, sec. B), some important psychoanalytic postulates are testable by *epidemiologic* findings, *without* any recourse at all to data from the analytic treatment setting, let alone to the experiences had by patients when their repressions are being undone in that clinical milieu.

Freud's etiology of paranoia postulates that *repressed* homosexual love is *causally necessary* for being afflicted by paranoid delusions (S.E. 1915, 14:265–266). And when the pathogenically required intensity of repression exists, it is largely engendered by the strong social taboo on homosexuality. Thus, the detailed pathogenesis of paranoia envisioned by Freud warrants the following prediction: a significant decline in the social sanctions against this atypical sexual orientation should issue in a marked decrease in the incidence of paranoia. Incidentally, this prediction alone refutes Karl Popper's claim that psychoanalytic theory is not testable (Grünbaum 1983, chap. 1, sec. B).

It was revealed only very recently that in 1893, Tchaikovsky was very probably blackmailed into suicide under threat of exposure of a homosexual liaison (Brown 1980: 626–628). This tragic episode is a measure of the lethal power possessed by the ban on homosexuality in the Christian world less than a century ago. Tchaikovsky's suicide occurred at the pinnacle of his career, less than a week after the St. Petersburg premiere of his celebrated Pathétique symphony. Yet for the past nine decades, the standard biographies of him listed cholera as the cause of his death at the age of fifty-three (Dorian 1981:224–227). During that time, there has been a marked decline in the taboo on homosexuality, despite the best efforts of Anita Bryant. Perhaps it is therefore not too early now to begin garnering appropriate statistics on the incidence of paranoia, with a view to ascertaining in due course whether these epidemiologic data bear out the psychoanalytically expected decline or disconfirm it. In either case, the testing of this Freudian etiology will be clearly intersubjective, in salient contravention of Habermas' thesis.

What then is the merit of the reproach by Habermas and Ricoeur that Freud fell prey to a "scientistic self-misunderstanding"? I submit that it was not Freud, but these hermeneuticians themselves, who forced the clinical theory of psychoanalysis onto the Procrustean bed of a philosophical ideology demonstrably alien to it. For, as I have argued, they first trumped up a mythic exegesis of his own perennial notion of scientificity, and then used an ante-diluvian paradigm of the natural sciences to boot. So much for the unjustified demand of the hermeneuticians that we abjure the very standards of validation by which Freud himself wanted his theory to be judged.

3. APPRAISAL OF FREUD'S ARGUMENTS FOR THE PSYCHOANALYTIC THEORY OF REPRESSION

Avowedly, his criteria of validation are essentially those of hypothetico-deductive inductivism (S.E. 1914, 14:77; 1915, 14:117, 1925, 20:32). And he took adherence to them to be the hallmark of the scientific probity that he claimed for his theory. Hence it behooves me to appraise Freud's *arguments* for his monumental clinical theory of personality and therapy by his own standards. Thus the verdict that I shall reach on this basis is hardly predicated on the imposition of some extraneous methodological purism. Nor does my application of his avowed norm of scientific rationality to psychoanalysis imply that I deem this touchstone to be *the* criterion of demarcation between science and non-science. In short, I shall grant Freud his own canon of scientific status in addressing the following key question: Did his clinical arguments vindicate the knowledge claims he made for his evolving theory by labeling it "scientific"?

My answer will be two-fold: The reasoning on which Freud rested the major hypotheses of his edifice was fundamentally flawed, even if the probity of the clinical observations he adduced were not in question. Moreover, far from deserving to be taken at face value, clinical data from the psychoanalytic treatment setting are themselves epistemically quite suspect.

The central causal and explanatory significance enjoyed by unconscious ideation in the entire clinical theory rests, I submit, on two cardinal inductive inferences drawn by Breuer and Freud. As we are told in their joint "Preliminary Communication" of 1893 (S.E. 1893, 2:6–7), they began with an observation made after having administered their cathartic treatment to patients suffering from various symptoms of hysteria. In the course of such treatment, it had turned out that, for each distinct symptom S afflicting such a neurotic, the victim had *repressed* the memory of a trauma that had closely preceded the onset of *S* and was thematically cognate to this particular symptom. Besides repressing this traumatic memory, the patient had also strangulated the affect induced by the trauma. In the case of each symptom, our two therapists tried to lift the ongoing repression of the pertinent traumatic experience, and to effect a release of the pent-up affect. When their technique succeeded in implementing this twin objective, they reportedly observed the dramatic disappearance of the given symptom. Furthermore, the symptom removal *seemed* to be durable.

Impressed by this treatment outcome, Breuer and Freud drew their first momentous *causal* inference. Thus they enunciated the following fundamental therapeutic hypothesis: The dramatic improvements observed after treatment were produced by none other than the cathartic lifting of the pertinent repressions. But before the founders of psychoanalysis credited the undoing of repressions with remedial efficacy, they had been keenly alert to a rival hypothesis, which derived at least prima facie credibility from the known achievements of the admittedly suggestive therapies. On that alternative explanation of the positive outcome after cathartic treatment, that benefit was actually wrought by the patient's credulous expectation of symptom relief, not by the particular treatment ritual employed to fortify his or her optimistic anticipation. Breuer and Freud believed that they could rule out such an account of the treatment gains, an account to which I shall refer as "the hypothesis of *placebo effect*" (Grünbaum 1981). In an attempt to counter this challenge, they pointed out that the distinct symptoms had been removed *separately*, such that any one symptom disappeared only after lifting a *particular* repression (S.E. 1893, 2:7).

And they saw very clearly that the threat posed by the rival hypothesis of placebo effect could be ominous. For, unless they could meet it convincingly, it would totally abort their inference of a bold and, in fact, historic *etiological* postulate from their fundamental therapeutic tribute to the undoing of repressions. Indeed, I shall argue that, to this day, the *whole* of the clinical psychoanalytic enterprise is haunted by the mortal threat from the very live possibility of placebo effect. As will emerge, the continuing failure of psychoanalytic research to discredit this altogether reasonable challenge gravely jeopardizes the very foundations of Freud's entire clinical theory. Mind you, the clinical hypotheses comprise not only the asserted therapeutic efficacy of lifting repressions, but also the repression-etiologies of the psychoneuroses, as well as the compromise-models of manifest dream content and of sundry sorts of "Freudian slips".

In any case, at the time, Breuer and Freud believed that their therapeutic results had ruled out the dangerous rival hypothesis of placebo effect. Having inferred the remedial efficacy of undoing repressions, they thought furthermore that this posited therapeutic potency inductively spelled a paramount *etiologic* moral as follows: A coexisting ongoing repression is *causally necessary* for the *maintenance* of a neurosis *N*, and an original act of repression was the causal *sine qua non* for the origination of *N*. This second ground-breaking causal inference was animated by their supposition that the repressed traumatic memory "acts [pathogenically] like a foreign body which long after its entry must continue to be regarded as an agent that is still at work" (S.E. 1893, 2:6). The heuristic value of adopting this analogy becomes patent upon recalling that the inferred etiology yielded a *deductive* explanation of the supposed remedial efficacy of lifting repressions. For, as I noted, if an ongoing repression *R* is causally *necessary* for the pathogenesis *and* persistence of a neurosis *N*, then the removal of *R* must issue in the eradication of *N*.

Note that the affect attached to a traumatic experience *E* can be *suppressed* (strangulated) but such that there is still conscious awareness of this pent-up affect. Thus the affect attached to *E* can be suppressed without also being repressed. For example, Breuer's pioneering patient Anna O. felt disgust at the sight of seeing a dog drinking water from a glass, but she "said nothing as she wanted to be polite" toward the dog's owner (S.E. 1895, 2:34).

But the cognitive repression of *E* can be *lifted without* undoing *E*'s affective *suppression*. Indeed, as Breuer and Freud report, the implementation of just this latter scenario was almost always therapeutically unavailing: "Recollection without [release of the attached pent-up] affect almost invariably produces no [therapeutic] result" (S.E. 1893, 2:6). Thus, it would be empirically false to deem the *mere* lifting of the cognitive repression of *E* *without* catharsis causally sufficient for the removal of the symptom *S*.

Hence we must endeavor to construe the Breuer-Freud etiology of psychoneurosis such that it does *not* entail this empirical falsehood. Yet it would have this untoward consequence if it were taken to assert that *both* cognitive repression *and* affective suppression of *E* are causally *necessary* for neurosogenesis.

On the other hand, just the undesirable false consequence is averted—as Carl Hempel and Morris Eagle have each remarked to me—by articulating the founding etiology of psychoanalysis as follows: Either cognitive repression or affective suppression of *E*, i.e., *at least one* of the two, is causally necessary for neuroso genesis, rather than both. And this version of the etiology would explain the reported therapeutic finding that the *cathartic* lifting of the repression—i.e., the undoing of the affective suppression as well as of the cognitive repression—is causally sufficient for symptom-removal. Yet this same version would *not explain*, but only allow the observation, made by Breuer and Freud, that mere recall without release of pent-up affect is "almost invariably" unavailing therapeutically.

Though the discharge of pent-up affect is thus deemed *therapeutically* essential, to accompany the cognitive retrieval of the repressed memory of *E*, it would be cumbersome to say so whenever one speaks of the presumed therapeutic role of lifting repressions. Therefore, brevity is served by the expository practice of simply crediting the therapeutic gain to the restoration of repressed memories, but with the understanding that affect-release is to be co-present.

It is essential to bear in mind that the posited *therapeutic* efficacy of retrieving repressed memories had provided the *sole* epistemic warrant for the cardinal etiologic postulate. And clearly, this cognitive dependence was hardly lessened when Freud replaced Breuer's hypnotic technique by the innovative method of free association as the means for uncovering repressed mentation. In fact, though it is widely overlooked, *the attribution of therapeutic success to the removal of repressions not only was but, to this day, remains the sole epistemic underwriter of the purported ability of the patient's free associations to certify causes.* Thus, these associations were deemed to be a reliable *investigative* avenue leading to the detection of the pathogens of neuroses. Analysts such as Strachey (S.E. 1955, 2:xvi) and Eissler (1969, p. 461) have hailed free association as an instrument comparable to the microscope and the telescope. And it is asserted to be a trustworthy means of etiologic inquiry in the sense of licensing the following *causal inference:* Let a causal chain of the analysand's free associations be initiated by his neurotic symptoms and issue in the emergence of previously repressed memories; then, we are told, this emergence qualifies as *good evidence* that the prior ongoing repression of these memories was actually the *pathogen* of the given neurosis.

Whereas all Freudians champion this causal inference, a number of influential ones have *explicitly renounced its legitimation* by the presumed *therapeutic dynamics* of undoing repressions. To *them* I say: *Without* this vindication, or some as yet unknown other warrant, not even the tortures of the thumbscrew or of the rack should persuade a rational being that free associations can *certify* pathogens or other causes! For *without* the stated *therapeutic* foundation, this epistemic tribute to free associations rests on nothing to date but a glaring causal fallacy. And even that foundation will turn out to be quite flimsy. Therefore, it is unavailing to extol the method of clinical investigation by free association as a trustworthy resource of etiologic inquiry, while issuing a modest disclaimer as to the therapeutic efficacy of psychoanalytic treatment. And one is dumbfounded to find that noted psychoanalysts such as George S. Klein have done just that (1976, pp. 36–38). Also amazingly, the renowned analyst Judd Marmor (1968) conjectured that it was the accidental need to earn his livelihood as a psychiatric practitioner which drove Freud "to utilize his investigative tool [of free association] simultaneously as a therapeutic instrument" (p. 6). In brief, those who have made it fashionable nowadays to dissociate the credentials of Freud's theory of personality—the so-called "science"—from the merits of psychoanalytic therapy are stepping on thin ice indeed. How very thin will shortly become clear from our scrutiny of the arguments put forward by the mature Freud, in place of those he had championed while he was still Breuer's junior collaborator.

Soon after Freud had begun to practice without Breuer, it became devastatingly plain that they had been all too hasty in rejecting the rival hypothesis of placebo effect. The remissions achieved by additional patients whom Freud himself treated cathartically turned out *not* to be durable. Indeed, the ensuing pattern of relapses, additional treatment, ephemeral remissions and further relapses gainsaid the attribution of therapeutic credit to the lifting of those repressions that Freud had uncovered. Ironically, he began to be haunted by the triumph of the hypothesis of placebo effect over the fundamental therapeutic tenet that Breuer and he had originally enunciated. For he recognized that the vicissitudes of his personal relations to the patient were highly correlated with the pattern of symptom relapses and intermittent remissions. And, in his own view, this correlation "proved that the personal emotional relation between doctor and patient was after all stronger than the whole cathartic process" (S.E. 1925, 20:27). But, once the repression etiology was thus bereft of therapeutic support, the very cornerstone of psychoanalysis was completely undermined. Hence at that point, the new clinical psychoanalytic structure tumbled down and lay in shambles.

Nonetheless, Freud was undaunted. Although the excavation of *adult* repressions had been a therapeutic failure, he conjectured that the uncovering of much earlier ones dating from childhood and sexual in content might well eradicate the neurosis. And he hypothesized further that the patient's free associations would lead to the certification of the early pathogen required for the existence of the affliction (S.E. 1896, 3:194–199). As he reports, the very early repressions that then emerged were in fact thematically sexual. But when his patients improved and he gave therapeutic credit to the lifting of these childhood repressions, he was apparently no longer able to adduce the *separate* symptom removals invoked earlier to hold the rival hypothesis of placebo effect at bay. At this stage (1896), his attribution of remedial efficacy to the disclosure of hidden affect-laden mentation took the form of declaring such insight to be at least causally *necessary* for a cure. Furthermore, Freud's rehabilitation of the generic repression etiology in a new sexual version was now directly built into this newly avowed therapeutic role of insight as follows: Insight could extirpate a neurosis *only if* it afforded the victim conscious mastery of the particular repression causally required by the pathogenesis of his disorder.

In fact, as I have documented elsewhere (Grünbaum 1983, chap. 2, sec. B), from 1896 onward through at least 1917, Freud thought he could claim clinical support for the following extraordinarily strong conjunction of clinical propositions (S.E. 1909, 10:140; S.E. 1914, 12:155–56; 1917, 16:452): A neurosis can be dependably eradicated *only* by the conscious mastery of the repressions that are causally required for its pathogenesis, *and* only the therapeutic techniques of psychoanalysis can generate this requisite insight into the specific pathogen. I shall designate this conjunction of two causally necessary conditions as "Freud's Master Proposition." And I am concerned to point out that once he had equipped himself with the intellectual arsenal contained in it, he was entitled to make a whole series of claims that are each of the first importance for the validation of his enterprise. I shall now develop the ensuing cardinal theses.

1. If a patient has been cured, then the etiologic interpretations that his doctor gave him, at least in the later stages of the analysis, must have been correct or close to the mark. By the same token, insofar as the substantial remission of symptoms can bespeak a genuine cure, this treatment outcome confirms that the analyst has correctly identified the specific pathogen via

the patient's free associations. Hence, collectively the successes achieved by psychoanalytic treatment vouch for the truth of the Freudian theory of personality, including its specific etiologies of the psychoneuroses, and even its general hypotheses about psychosexual development.

As a further corollary, the psychoanalytic probing of the unconscious is vindicated as a method of etiologic investigation by its therapeutic achievements. Thus, this method has the remarkable capacity to validate major causal claims by essentially retrospective inquiries, *without* the burdens of prospective longitudinal studies employing experimental controls. Yet these causal inferences are not vitiated by *post hoc ergo propter hoc.* Magnificent, if true!

2. The clinical data furnished by successfully treated neurotics do not result from self-fulfilling predictions. Thus, these data are exonerated from the charge that they forfeit their probative value. According to this reproach, even a patient who engages in frequent emotional outbursts against his analyst will comply with him doctrinally, like a pupil, despite the doctor's best efforts to forego overt or covert communication of his theoretical expectations. Such epistemic contamination of the patient's sundry responses will occur willy-nilly, it is charged, because the psychoanalyst will unconsciously yet persuasively insinuate his anticipations in a myriad of subtle ways. And since the analysand has sought out an avowedly Freudian therapist for help, he will want to please the authority-figure on whom he now so greatly depends. The ensuing intellectual deference thus makes for *self-fulfillment* of the analyst's theoretical expectations, and thereby for the *spuriousness* of the vauntedly abundant clinical confirmations.

Freud (1954, pp. 334–337) had been stung when even his long-time confrère Wilhelm Fliess dropped this sceptical bombshell, which rankled. Yet to his great credit, Freud eloquently came to grips with its grave challenge, emphasizing that it "is uncommonly interesting and must be answered" (S.E. 1917, 16:447). And he then met it head-on by enlisting his Master Proposition in his 1917 lecture on "Analytic Therapy" (S.E. 1917, 16:452) to authenticate clinical data as probatively legitimate. Thus, if the patient's assent to his analyst's interpretations is epistemically reliable after all, credence may be reasonably given to the patient's introspective *self*-observations, once his repressions no longer hold his motives in distorting and obfuscating thrall.

3. *Only* psychoanalytic treatment can effect genuine cures of neuroses (S.E. 1917, 16:458). But *if* Freud's therapy does enjoy such pre-eminence, then it can warrantedly take credit for the recoveries of its patients *without* statistical comparisons with the results from untreated control groups, or from controls treated by rival modalities (cf. S.E. 1917; 16:461–462). Moreover, when analytic therapy does score remedial triumphs, these gains are *not* placebo effects. For if the first conjunct of the Master Proposition is to be believed, the working through of the patient's unconscious conflicts is the decisive therapeutic factor, although the analyst's role as a parent-surrogate to him serves as an ice-breaker. Freud did recognize that the analysand's so-called "transference" attachment to his doctor plays such a catalytic role in the earlier stages of treatment (S.E. 1926, 20:190). Yet he evidently singled out the patient's correct etiological insight as the one quintessential ingredient "which distinguishes [the therapeutic dynamics of] analytic treatment from any kind of treatment by suggestion" (S.E. 1914, 12:155–156; cf. also 1917, 16:450–452).

As long as Freud felt entitled to champion his Master Proposition, he could have confidence in the three sets of remarkable theses I have just formulated. Thus, with one stroke, he had redeemed his 1917 promise (S.E. 1917, 16:446–447) to nullify the two-fold indictment that suggestion is at once the decisive agent in his therapy and the cognitive bane of the psychoanalytic method of investigation. And, in this way, etiologic hypotheses—which do not themselves pertain at all to either the dynamics or the outcome of analytic therapy—nonetheless were *epistemically parasitic* on therapeutic results, if only to legitimate the probity of the clinical data on which they were predicated. Yet new evidence then severed the dazzling link that Freud had forged in the Master Proposition between the conquest of a neurosis and the patient's discernment of its pathogens.

Indeed, by 1926, he himself repudiated the therapeutic indispensability of his type of treatment. And he demoted the psychoanalytic conquest of the analysand's resistances to the status of a mere expeditor of recoveries that were in the offing anyway. As he put it modestly: "as a rule our therapy must be content with bringing about more quickly, more reliably and with less expenditure of energy than would otherwise be the case the good result which in favourable circumstances would have occurred of itself" (S.E. 1926, 20:154). But just such spontaneous remission *belies* the Master Proposition. And once the latter became defunct, even spectacular therapeutic successes became probatively unavailing for the validation of the generic repression etiology by means of that Proposition. To boot, in 1937, Freud reported ruefully that a satisfactory psychoanalysis is not even prophylactic against the recurrence of the affliction for which the analysand was treated, let alone does it immunize him against the outbreak of a different neurosis (S.E. 1937, 23:216–253). Thus, far from holding out hope fur cures, Freud essentially confined the prospects to palliation. But the import of this therapeutic pessimism is shattering. For, even if the Master Proposition were true, it would need the existential premise of documented cures in order to vouch for the etiologies inferred by means of free association.

As if this were not enough, in recent decades, comparative studies of treatment outcome from rival therapies have failed to reveal any sort of superiority of psychoanalysis within the class of therapeutic modalities that exceed the spontaneous remission rate, gleaned from the (quasi-)untreated controls.[6] This result further impugns the Master Proposition, which entails that only analytic therapy can effect genuine cures of psychoneuroses.

But if analytic treatment is not superior to its rivals in the pertinent diagnostic categories, it becomes quite reasonable—though *not* compelling—to interpret its therapeutic achievements as placebo effects. And, if so, then the therapeutic successes of psychoanalysis are *not* wrought after all by the patient's acquisition of self-knowledge, much to Socrates' sorrow. In this vein, the psychiatrist Jerome Frank has contended that the analyst, no less than his competitor, heals neurotics by supportively counteracting their demoralization, not by excavating their repressions. Indeed, Frank's hypothesis even allows rival therapies to have differential effects in virtue of their differential abilities to mobilize agencies common to all of them. The shared techniques for such mobilization usually include well-practiced rituals, a special vocabulary, a knowledgeable manner, and the therapist's charisma (Grünbaum 1980, pp. 341–351). To be sure, it is still arguable that psychoanalytic treatment-gains are *not* placebogenic. But, as some noted analysts have conceded, the following damaging fact remains: "All-pervading" psychic improvements or even cures can be effected by such rival modalities as behavior therapy, and also by extra-clinical life events (Malan 1976, pp. 172–173, 269, 147). Hence Freud's Master Proposition became untenable.

It emerges that this collapse completely undercuts the pivotal therapeutic argument given by the mature Freud to validate his repression-etiology of the psychoneuroses, *and* to authenticate the probative value of the clinical data generated by the psychoanalytic method. Thus, the ominous reproach that epistemic contamination by suggestion makes for bogus confirmations bedevils clinical validation after all. Moreover, no empirically viable surrogate for the discredited Master Proposition capable of yielding Freud's desired conclusions even seems to be remotely in sight.

But it may well be asked impatiently: Why could Freud not dispense with therapeutic arguments altogether, and rely instead on other sorts of clinical evidence to furnish support for his specific etiologies? In reply, I contend that the genuine confirmation of his etiologies by intra-clinical observations is epistemically quite hopeless. And I am concerned to give the main reasons that, in my view, collectively warrant this dismal conclusion.[7]

1. Freud conjectured that the development of a neurosis N by an individual I depended not only on I's exposure to pathogenic experiences P, but also on I's hereditary vulnerability. Thus, his universal etiological hypotheses typically asserted that exposure to P is causally necessary for the pathogenesis of N, *not* that it is causally sufficient. Any such hypothesis entails the universal *retrodiction* that all those afflicted by N had suffered P.

In the context of this entailment, Freud's Rat Man case has been invoked to maintain that the psychoanalytic etiology of obsessional neurosis would have been confirmed by clinical evidence corroborating the occurrence of the pertinent retrodicted experience P during the Rat Man's early childhood (Glymour 1980, p. 272).

Now suppose, for argument's sake, that in his analysis, the Rat Man had reported having retrieved the distant memory of the traumatic sexual event retrodicted by Freud. And assume further for now that credence can be given to so early a memory under the suggestive conditions of a psychoanalysis. Then it is vital to appreciate that the mere retrospective authentication of the bare occurrence of the early trauma hardly bespeaks the *causal relevance* of this event to the pathogenesis of the Rat Man's obsessions. Surely the mere traumaticity of an event does not itself attest to its etiologic relevance. The human condition would be much worse than it already is, if every psychic blow became the specific pathogen of a neurosis. Yet prominent psychoanalysts have reasoned that the causal relevance of an experience P to a neurosis N is supported by the mere fact that anyone beset by N who suffered P instantiates the retrodiction entailed by Freud's etiology (Waelder 1962, pp. 625–626). Such an inference is no better than *post hoc ergo propter hoc*.

But what if we could assume that the clinical setting has the epistemic resources to certify *retrospectively* that all available victims of neuroses *other than* N had been *spared* the experience P? Even under this sanguine assumption, the envisaged retrospective clinical testing design is *confined* to the class of neurotics. And as Blake Barley has observed, this confinement restricts the probative import of the putative findings as follows: At best, they might bespeak the etiologic relevance of the experience P to N *within* the class of neurotics, but would *not* lend credence to the Freudian claim of pathogenic relevance in the wider class of *persons*.

2. Some analysts have told us that the patient himself is able to determine by *introspection* whether the repressed P was in fact the pathogen of his disorder, once he no longer represses the memory of this episode (Waelder 1962, pp. 628–629). But this thesis of privileged epistemic access to the causes of psychopathology does not bear scrutiny.

Substantial evidence recently marshaled by cognitive psychologists has shown that even in the case of *consciously* motivated behavior, a subject does not enjoy special cognitive access to the discernment of the motivational causes of his various actions (Grünbaum 1980, sec. 3, pp. 354–367). Though the subject often does have direct access to the individual conscious contents of his mental states, he has only *inferential* access—just like outside observers—to such causal linkages as actually connect some of his own mental states. The possession of direct access to the content of momentary states of attention or felt affect is a far cry indeed from being uniquely privy to the actual existence of a hypothesized causal nexus between, say, certain infantile experiences and specified adult personality dispositions. No less than in the case of causal hypotheses pertaining to physical states, the subject's avowal of causal connections between his own mental states is based either on the fallible inferences drawn by himself, or on those carried out by members of his subculture to whom he gives credence. Hence these avowed causal linkages may be fancied or actual. In short, when a subject attributes a causal relation to some of his own mental states, he does so—just like outside observers—by invoking theory-based causal schemata endorsed by the prevailing belief-system.

More often than not, a patient who sought treatment from a Freudian doctor already brings some psychoanalytic beliefs into the therapy, or is at least receptive to etiologic interpretations of his conduct based on the analyst's theoretical stance. No wonder that analytic patients then find the rationale offered to them credible. But this credulity is hardly tantamount to privileged cognitive access to the validity of the ambitious causal claims central to the etiologic reconstruction of the given dysfunction. And, as we saw earlier, the same gullibility may also be responsible for the analysand's therapeutic gains. For these may be due to his *belief* in his doctor's etiologic reconstruction, rather than to the undoing of his repressions. But just as the patient has no direct introspective access to the pathogenesis of his affliction, so also his introspections do not afford him privileged epistemic access to the cause of his therapeutic progress. Thus, he is surely not in a better position to make such a causal attribution than his analyst. And recently, two Freudian investigators of the dynamics of psychotherapies have issued the following agnostic disclaimer: "Psychoanalysts, like other psychotherapists, literally *do not know* how they achieve their [remedial] results" (Luborsky & Spence 1978, p. 360).

3. Freud himself emphasized that the patient's poor mnemic performance often simply fails to authenticate the childhood event retrodicted via his etiology (S.E. 1920, 18:18; 1937, 23:265–266). And, as I have documented elsewhere (1980, p. 353), his writings also multiply attest to the *unreliability* of purported adult memories of early childhood episodes that had presumably been retrieved by the analysis after being repressed. More recently, research on memory has furnished telling empirical evidence that the patient's supposed ability to achieve non-inferential veridical recall of very early repressed experiences is largely a myth.

Experimental studies acknowledged by analysts themselves (Marmor 1970) have borne out the therapist's contaminating regimentation of purported memories recovered by free association. It can be granted, of course, that requirements of consistency or at least overall coherence do afford the analyst *some* check on what the patient alleges to be bona fide memories. And it is to be understood that the epistemic discounting of early childhood memories purportedly retrieved by the adult patient is not a wholesale derogation of adult memories in daily life. But the malleability of adult memories from childhood by suggestion is epitomized by a report from Jean Piaget (Loftus 1980, pp. 119–121), who thought he vividly remembered an attempt to kidnap him from his baby carriage along the Champs Elysées. He recalled the gathered crowd, the scratches on the face of the heroic nurse who saved him, the policeman's white baton, the assailant running away. However vivid, Piaget's recollections were false. Years later his nurse confessed that she had made up the entire story, which he then internalized as a presumed experience under the influence of an authority-figure.

That psychoanalytic treatment ought not to be regarded as a bona fide *memory-jogging* device emerges more generally as a corollary of at least three sets of recent research findings elaborated by Loftus (1980): (1) the remarkable extent to which human memory is malleable, (2) the interpolative reconstruction and bending of memories by theoretical beliefs or expectations, and (3) the penchant, under the influence of leading questions, to fill amnesiac gaps by confabulated material. Earlier we saw that theoretical beliefs rather than direct introspection determine the subject's verdicts on causal relations between his own mental states. Similarly, the interpolative reconstruction and bending of memories by theoretical beliefs combine with the malleability of memory by suggestion to generate pseudo-memories of events that never occurred, especially when they are temporally remote. In short, the retrospective testing design of the psychoanalytic setting cannot even reliably authenticate the bare occurrence of the retrodicted childhood experience *P*, let alone its pathogenic role.

It emerges that the proposed clinical vindication of the repression-etiology *without* reliance on the dynamics of Freud's therapy is no less a fiasco than his attempted therapeutic validation. I gave two main reasons for this additional failure: (i) The testing design of the analytic setting appears incompetent to warrant that the retrodicted childhood experience *P* was, if actual, also pathogenic, and (ii) the retrospective methods of this clinical inquiry cannot even reliably authenticate the bare occurrence of *P.* To my knowledge, besides the sorts of arguments I have canvassed, there are no other *clinical* defenses of Freud's sexual repression-etiology of the neuroses.

Hence I draw the following major conclusions: His sexual version of this generic etiology is now devoid of cogent clinical support, just as Breuer's non-sexual cathartic etiologies, which Freud has disavowed as clinically ill-founded. Furthermore, this collapse of the psychoanalytic etiology, I maintain, basically impugns the *investigative cogency* of free associations in the conduct of etiologic inquiry. For Freud has enunciated his fundamental rule of free association as a maxim of clinical research, because he thought that associations governed by it had reliably *certified* the unconscious pathogens of the neuroses. Yet just this epistemic tribute is now seen to be gratuitous. Finally, Freud is left helpless to rebut the charge that clinical data forfeit their probative value by epistemic contamination through suggestion, a complaint for which there is good evidence. But, for the sake of argument, assume nonetheless that there is no such forfeiture of probative value, and that the patient's clinical responses can be taken at face value after all. It is of fundamental importance to appreciate that even if the clinical data were thus uncontaminated, they would still utterly fail to sustain the causal hypotheses of the psychoanalytic clinical theory of psychopathology, as I have argued.

I must emphasize that these bleak results are equally devastating to the currently fashionable revisionist versions of psychoanalysis that go under the names of Kohutian "self-psychology" and of "object relations theory." Insofar as these post-Freudian theories are indeed recognizably psychoanalytic, they do of course embrace some version of the repression-etiology. And, furthermore, they rely epistemically on free association in the clinical investigation of purported pathogens and other unconscious determinants of behavior, while lifting repressions as one means to effect therapy (Eagle 1983).[8] But, I submit, precisely to the extent that these outgrowths of Freud's ideas are thus recognizably psychoanalytic in content as well as in method of inquiry and therapy, my epistemic critique of Freud's original hypotheses applies with equal force to the etiologic, developmental and therapeutic tenets of these successors (Eagle 1983a; Grünbaum 1983b).

As a direct corollary, we are now able to appraise the psychoanalytic theory of dreams as well as Freud's account of sundry sorts of slips or "parapraxes." Both of these renowned hypotheses attribute a decisive *causal* role to repressed ideation. These two causal attributions were and have remained audacious, if not foolhardy extrapolations from the etiologic function that Freud had ascribed to repression in his explanation of psychopathology. For whereas he claimed to have therapeutic evidence for postulating this pathogenic role, he never produced any independent clinical support for these two momentous extrapolations (Grünbaum 1983, chaps. 4 & 5). As we learn in the opening pages on his method of dream interpretation, the first extrapolation consisted of simply enlarging the epistemic role of free association from being only a method of etiologic inquiry aimed at therapy, to serving likewise as an avenue for finding the purported unconscious causes of dreams (S.E. 1900, 4:100–101).

Thus, having found that his patients reported their dreams while freely associating to their neurotic symptoms, he drew the following inference: "a dream can be inserted into the psychical chain that has to be traced backwards in the memory from a pathological idea. It was then only a short step to treating the dream itself as a symptom and to applying to dreams the method of interpretation that had been worked out for symptoms" (p. 101). Yet, far from being only heuristic in Freud's view, this cavalier *extrapolative* adoption of the symptom-model for manifest dream content was avowedly also probative. As he argued: "We might also point out in our defense that our procedure in interpreting dreams [by means of free association] is identical with the procedure by which we resolve hysterical symptoms; and there the correctness of our method is warranted by the coincident emergence and disappearance of the symptoms" (S.E. 1900, 5:528). *Mutatis mutandis,* the same remarks apply to the further extrapolation that slips are likewise mini-neurotic symptoms. Therefore, the claim that the method of free association can reliably certify the unconscious motives of dream-formation and of parapraxes is cognitively parasitic on the prior thesis that this method can certify repressions to be the pathogens of neuroses.[9]

But in virtue of the extrapolative justification given for the repression-models of dreams and of parapraxes, their epistemic fortunes are dependent on those of Freud's theory of *psychopathology* (S.E. 1925, 20:45; 1900, 4:149). As a consequence of just this epistemic dependence, the ravages from the demise of Freudian psychopathology and of free association as a tool of etiologic certification extend, with a vengeance, to the psychoanalytic theory of dreams and of sundry sorts of "slips."

Originally, Freud had claimed that free association, like Breuer's cathartic method, can certify the required cause of a neurosis in virtue of the method's ability to cure the illness. As Freud put it, "Breuer learnt from his first patient that the attempt at discovering the determining cause of a symptom was at the same time a therapeutic manoeuvre" (S.E. 1893, 3:35). But, as we saw, the arguments for deeming free association capable of certifying pathogens were not viable. And in the wake of their collapse, Freud's extrapolation does not furnish even the *shadow* of a good reason for supposing that associations governed by this "fundamental rule" can reliably certify the unconscious causes of dreams and of parapraxes.

Indeed, as far as I know, Freud's disciples, either orthodox or revisionist, have yet to produce any sound reason for crediting free association with the ability to pick out the causes of dream formation. Hence I claim that the emergence of repressed infantile wishes via free associations triggered by the recall of anxiety dreams and nightmares cannot warrant the hypothesis that these dreams are engendered by such wishes. Indeed, whatever evidence there may be from commonsense psychology that certain particular dreams were generated by unfulfilled wishes, it has now turned out that free association does not have the probative power to *underwrite* this verdict.

4. THE FUTILITY OF HERMENEUTICS WITHOUT CAUSATION

Faced with the bleak import of such a sceptical indictment, psychoanalysts will be intent on salvaging their legacy in some form. And some of them will then be understandably receptive to a rationale that promises them absolution from their failure to validate the cardinal hypotheses of their clinical theory. Be of stout heart, they are told, and take the *hermeneutic* turn. Freud, they learn, brought the incubus of validation on himself by his scientistic pretensions. Abjure his program of causal explanation, some hermeneuticians beckon them, and you will no longer be saddled with the harassing demand to justify Freud's causal hypotheses. One such hermeneutic advocate illustrated this repudiation of causation as follows: "the meaning of a dream does not reside in some prior latent dream [content], but in the manifest dream and the analysand's associations to it" (Steele 1979, p. 400). Thus, the blandishments of this renunciatory stance include the comforting assurance that the practicing analyst is immune to the taunts from critics who dispute the cost-effectiveness of his therapy. And even for the Freudian psychohistorians, the hermeneutician has the glad tidings that henceforth they can hold their heads high as protagonists of a newly legitimated kind of humanistic discipline. In short, the claim is that the challenge to provide validation of the causal propositions has been obviated, and that the continuing demand for it has therefore become an anachronism.

But as against the generic disavowal of causal attributions advocated by some hermeneuticians, I maintain that it is a nihilistic, if not frivolous, trivialization of Freud's entire clinical theory. Far from serving as a new citadel for psychoanalytic apologetics, the embrace of such hermeneuticians is, I submit, the kiss of death for the legacy that was to be saved. On the other hand, insofar as other hermeneuticians, Paul Ricoeur (1981, chap. 10) for example, do countenance the retention of causal hypotheses in psychoanalytic explanations, they are no less obligated to substantiate these hypotheses by cogent evidence than the orthodox Freudians, whom they pilloried as scientistically addicted.

Let me illustrate my case against the stated acausal hermeneutic construal of psychoanalytic significance by reference to an allegedly Freudian lapse of memory that has figured as a paradigmatic instance in the literature. To say that a slip of the tongue, pen, ear, eye or of memory is genuinely "Freudian" is to say that it was engendered by a *repressed* motive. Thus Freud assimilated a seemingly insignificant slip of the tongue to the status of a mini-neurotic symptom by regarding this lapse as a *compromise* between a repressed motive that crops out in the form of a disturbance, on the one hand, and the conscious intention to make a certain utterance, on the other.

The pertinent paradigmatic instance of a lapse of memory involves the forgetting of the Latin pronoun *aliquis* (someone), which a young man omitted when reciting a line from Virgil's *Aeneid* (S.E. 1901, 6:chap. II). Freud supplied the missing word and enjoined Y to use the restored word as the point of departure for free associations. After a tortuous chain of such associations, punctuated by some interjections from Freud, it emerged that Y had been harboring a presumably repressed fear. An Italian girlfriend, he suspected apprehensively, had become pregnant by him. Freud then told him that this repressed anxiety had undeniably produced his *aliquis* lapse. But Y doubted any such causal nexus, although he was fully aware that his worry was genuine.

Now let me contrast Freud's account of this lapse with the hermeneutic claim that Y's slip lends itself to acausal and yet psychoanalytic interpretation.

The orthodox rationale for calling on Y to let the restored word initiate his free associations was clear. Having deemed the lapse to be a mini-neurotic symptom, Freud attributed its occurrence *causally* to the operation of some repression. And when Y asked him to *explain* how the forgetting of the pronoun had been brought about, Freud promised to identify the causally relevant repression by winnowing the free associations triggered in Y by the restored word "*aliquis*" (S.E. 1901, 6:9). Hence, he then used the surfacing of Y's previously repressed pregnancy worry from these particular associations as grounds for concluding that this very fear—while as yet being repressed before the memory lapse—had caused Y to forget that word. And Freud held this inference to be licensed by the principle that a repression *R* present before the commission of a parapraxis by a person *X* qualifies as its cause, if *R* emerges into *X*'s consciousness in the wake of free associations triggered by his awareness of the content of his error (Grünbaum 1983c, sec. 3).

I do not profess to know at all what did cause Y's slip. But, as an immediate corollary of my earlier arguments, I claim that if Y's repressed worry did cause him to forget *aliquis,* Freud has completely failed to supply cogent evidence for this causal nexus. And this failure to justify his causal inference deserves censure, even if one could grant him quite generally that the analyst does not inject epistemically contaminating influences into the sequence of the associations, as he contended (S.E. 1923, 18:238). Seriously flawed though it is, Freud's account nonetheless does offer an explanation of slips *qua slips* by purporting to have identified unconscious motives *for their occurrence.*

But I submit that the alleged interpretive meaning furnished by the acausal hermeneutic rationale is altogether insensitive to the fact that the word "*aliquis*" figured in a *lapse* of memory. Whatever that hermeneutic meaning, I claim that it is *not* the meaning *of a slip qua slip* at all! To be sure, the aforecited hermeneutician, no less than the orthodox analyst, sifts the free associations elicited from Y by the restoration of the forgotten word to his awareness. Yet the hermeneutic view now at issue demurely disclaims the postulation of causes (Steele 1979,

p. 400), and thus forsakes the causal import of treating a slip as a mini-neurotic symptom. Hence, according to this construal, the interpretive meaning which is to be revealed by the winnowing of Y's associations avowedly has no *causal* relevance to the fact that "*aliquis*" did figure in a lapse. How then can the interpretive meaning revealed by the associative content of "*aliquis*" be held to be the significance of the *forgetting* of *aliquis*, rather than simply the associative import of that word per se, regardless of whether it had been forgotten or not? Indeed, on the acausal hermeneutic rationale, why should Y be asked to associate to the word "*aliquis*" rather than to one of the words in the line from Virgil that he had *not* forgotten? Since the emerging meaning is not the meaning of a slip *qua* slip, how can this causal rationale provide a reason for supposing that the associations to a *forgotten* word are richer in interpretive meaning—whatever that is—than the associations to nonforgotten words, or to other associatively evocative items in the subject's life? How then can the hermeneutician see himself as having given any reconstruction at all of Freud's theory of slips *qua* slips?

What of the reply that, though the associations do not bespeak a cause of a slip, they reveal a great deal about the current psychological make-up of the person who has them? I retort by asking: On what basis does the advocate of *acausal* hermeneutics infer the psychological make-up of a person from the latter's free associations? Does the inference rely tacitly on presumed causal linkages between personality structure and associational output? If so, the acausalist is not entitled to invoke them, if only because the validation of causal connections would require non-hermeneutic methods that he is unwilling to license. But let us suppose that the generalizations used to draw the requisite inferences as to the associating person's make-up are not causal. Even then, it is at best unclear how they can be validated short of adopting the very methods that the hermeneutician rejects as "scientistic."

Similar considerations warrant the conclusion that the acausal hermeneutic rationale so truncates the repression-etiology of the psychoneuroses as to trivialize that etiology *qua* theory of psychopathology. And a like verdict serves to convict the stated acausal version of the received theory of dreams, as Michael Moore has argued in his telling critique of hermeneutic "rationalization without causation" (Moore 1983, pp. 32–34).

In a recent book, Esther Menaker (1982) has argued that Freud's one-time disciple Otto Rank repudiated his erstwhile search for *causes* of personality development, thereby abandoning his own thesis of the role of the birth trauma. Instead, Rank claimed an acausal creative role for an individuating will, a notion that is *not* explanatory.

5. CONCLUSIONS

I set out to appraise Freud's principal *arguments* for his monumental clinical theory of personality and therapy. This scrutiny was based on his own avowed inductive standards. By design, I made no mention of any *experimental* findings, either supportive or adverse. For even toward the end of his life, Freud dismissed purported *experimental* support for his theory of repression as superfluous, because of an alleged superabundance of clinical confirmations (MacKinnon & Dukes 1964, pp. 702–703). This epistemic tribute to clinical findings vis-à-vis experimental ones has recently been largely reaffirmed by recognized analysts (Luborsky & Spence 1978, pp. 350, 356–357). And, as Ernest Jones (1959, vol. 1, p. 3) has reminded everyone, the results from the psychoanalytic treatment setting are "the real basis of Psychoanalysis. All of Professor Freud's other works and theories are essentially founded on the clinical investigations."

Several conclusions issue from my appraisal of the arguments that Freud and his disciples have rested on their observations:

1. Insofar as the evidence for the psychoanalytic corpus is now held to derive from the productions of patients in analysis, this warrant is remarkably weak.

2. Despite the poverty of the clinical credentials, it may still turn out that Freud's brilliant theoretical imagination was actually quite serendipitous for psychopathology or the understanding of some subclass of slips.

   Thus, very recently a psychologist claimed to have found genuine *experimental* support for the psychoanalytic theory of speech errors (Motley 1980). He did indeed furnish telling laboratory evidence for the causal relevance of cognitive-affective mental sets, and even of personality dispositions to oral misreadings consisting of phoneme-switchings. And, in this way, the experimenter showed that *semantic* influences produced by the speaker's mental sets, and external to the intended utterance, effected a prearticulatory semantic editing of the words to be pronounced.

   Valuable though they were, the results from these ingenious experiments were probatively irrelevant to the Freudian theory of slips of the tongue. For the mental sets that the investigator manipulated as his independent variable were *not repressed* ideation. And by being conscious (or preconscious) states instead, they failed to realize the initial conditions required by Freud's theory. In fact, the observed misreadings can all be explained by a rival psychological theory that allows *only* conscious motivational influences as generators of slips (Grünbaum 1983, chap. 4). Hence it remains to be seen what a properly designed test would show.

3. In view of my account of the epistemic defects inherent in the psychoanalytic method, it would seem that the validation of Freud's cardinal hypotheses has to come, if at all, mainly from well-designed *extra*-clinical studies, either epidemiologic or even experimental. But that appraisal is largely a task for the future.

NOTES

1. Sigmund Freud, "An Outline of Psycho-Analysis." In *Standard Edition of the Complete Psychological Works of Sigmund Freud,* translated by J. Strachey *et al.* (London: Hogarth Press, 1940, vol. 23, p. 158). Hereafter any references given to Freud's writings in English will be to this *Standard Edition* under its acronym "S.E." followed by the year of first appearance, the volume number, and the page(s). Thus, the 1940 paper just cited in full would be cited within the text in abbreviated fashion as follows: S.E. 1940, 23:158.

2. For further documentation of this conclusion, see my Introduction chapter, "Critique of the Hermeneutic Conception of Psychoanalytic Theory and Therapy" in (Grünbaum 1983).

   Since those who are expert in mathematics are called "mathematicians," I have assumed that the advocates of hermeneutics could be labeled quite *neutrally* by the term "hermeneutician," entirely without prejudice to the merits of their doctrine. Though I am told that some of them designate themselves as "hermeneuts," I employ the former term, which seems to be linguistically more appropriate.

3. See the Introduction chapter of (Grünbaum 1983) for a detailed scrutiny of Habermas' account of the validation of psychoanalytic propositions.

4. See the Introduction chapter of (Grünbaum 1983) for a number of additional reasons.

5. Elsewhere I have argued in detail that the treatment setting is, in fact, anything but a suitable arena for probatively cogent tests of general psychoanalytic hypotheses (cf. Grünbaum 1980 and 1983a).

6. For a very brief digest of the summary literature on treatment-outcome, see (Grünbaum 1977, pp. 235–250; 1980, pp. 344–345). Detailed argued accounts are given in (Smith, Glass & Miller 1980), in (Rachman & Wilson 1980), and in (Strupp, Hadley & Gomes-Schwartz 1977).

7. For my much fuller statement of these reasons, see (Grünbaum 1983a).

8. In the context of the therapeutic theories espoused by the post-Freudian neo-revisionists, I have advisedly depicted the undoing of repressions as just "one means" of effecting therapy. The need for this qualification has been stressed by Eagle (1983): As he points out, the Kohutian self-psychologists place less therapeutic emphasis on insight into prior repressions than on the therapist's "empathic mirroring," coupled with the patient's feelings of identification and idealization toward the doctor. But precisely insofar as there is such divergence from the orthodox psycho-therapeutic tenet, the warrant for labeling the revised doctrine "psycho-analytic" becomes seriously questionable.

   In any case, Eagle (1983) has argued tellingly that the etiologic and therapeutic claims of self-psychology and of object relations theory rest epistemically on bases even more dubious than those of Freud's corresponding hypotheses. Hence it would be unavailing to adduce the post-Freudian neo-revisionist credos in an attempt to blunt the force of the doubts I have raised against orthodox psychoanalysis.

9. I have argued in (Grünbaum 1983c, sec. 4) that neither Freud's own account of his *Irma* specimen dream (S.E. 1900, 4:chap. II), nor Erik Erikson's (1954) attempt to give an orthodox psychoanalytic interpretation of it, can serve to accredit free association as a reliable means for certifying dream motives.

REFERENCES

Brown, D. 1980. "Tchaikovsky," *The New Grove's Dictionary of Music and Musicians,* ed. Stanley Sadie. London: Macmillan, Vol. 18, pp. 626–628.

Considine, D. M. 1976. *Van Nostrand's Scientific Encyclopedia,* 5th ed. New York: Van Nostrand, p. 1335.

Dorian, F. 1981. "Tchaikovsky's Death a Suicide! A Biographical Correction," *Pittsburgh Symphony Orchestra Program Magazine* (Oct. 23), pp. 224–227.

Eagle, M. 1983. "Psychoanalysis and Modern Psychodynamic Theories," *Personality and the Behavior Disorders,* rev. ed., ed. N. S. Endler and J. McV. Hunt. New York: Wiley.

—. 1983a. "The Epistemological Status of Recent Developments in Psychoanalytic Theory," *Physics, Philosophy and Psychoanalysis,* ed. R. S. Cohen and L. Laudan. Boston: Reidel, pp. 31–55.

Efron, A. 1967. "Magnetic Hysteresis," *The Harper Encyclopedia of Science,* rev. ed., ed. J. R. Newman. New York: Harper & Row, p. 694.

Eissler, K. R. 1969. "Irreverent Remarks About the Present and the Future of Psychoanalysis," *International J. of Psycho-Analysis 50,* pp. 461–471.

Erikson, E. 1954. "The Dream Specimen of Psychoanalysis," *J. of the American Psychoanalytic Assn. 2,* pp. 5–56.

Freud, S. 1954. *The Origins of Psychoanalysis.* New York: Basic Books.

Gadamer, H. G. 1975. *Truth and Method.* New York: Seabury Press.

Glymour, C. 1980. *Theory and Evidence.* Princeton: Princeton University Press.

Grünbaum, A. 1977. "How Scientific Is Psychoanalysis?" *Science and Psychotherapy,* ed. R. Stern, L. S. Horowitz and J. Lynes. New York: Haven Publishing, pp. 219–254.

—. 1980. "Epistemological Liabilities of the Clinical Appraisal of Psychoanalytic Theory," *Noûs 14,* pp. 307–385.

—. 1981. "The Placebo Concept," *Behaviour Research and Therapy 19,* pp. 157–167. See also (Grünbaum, in press) below.

—. 1984. *The Foundations of Psychoanalysis: A Philosophical Critique.* Berkeley: University of California Press.

—. 1983a. "Retrospective Versus Prospective Testing of Aetiological Hypotheses in Psychoanalytic Theory," *Minnesota Studies in the Philosophy of Science,* vol. X, ed. J. Earman. Minneapolis, University of Minnesota Press, pp. 315–347.

—. 1983b. "Is Object Relations Theory Better Founded Than Orthodox Psychoanalysis?" *J. of Philosophy* 80, pp. 46–51.

—. 1983c. "Logical Foundations of Psychoanalytic Theory," *Festschrift for Wolfgang Stegmüller, Erkenntnis* 19, pp. 109–152.

—. 1984. "Explication and Implications of the Placebo Concept," *Rationality in Science and Politics,* ed. G. Andersson. Boston: Reidel.

Habermas, J. 1970. *Zur Logik der Sozialwissenschaften.* Frankfurt: Suhrkamp Verlag.

—. 1971. *Knowledge and Human Interests,* translated by J. J. Shapiro. Boston: Beacon Press.

Jones, E. 1959. *Editorial Preface to S. Freud, Collected Papers,* vol. 1. New York: Basic Books.

Klein, G. S. 1976. *Psychoanalytic Theory.* New York: International Universities Press.

Laplanche, J. & Pontalis, J. B. 1973. *The Language of Psychoanalysis.* New York: Norton.

Loftus, E. 1980. *Memory.* Reading, Mass.: Addison-Wesley.

Luborsky, L. & Spence, D. P. 1978. "Quantitative Research on Psychoanalytic Therapy," *Handbook of Psychotherapy and Behavior Change,* 2nd ed., ed. S. L. Garfield and A. E. Bergin. New York: Wiley.

MacKinnon, D. W. & Dukes, W. F. 1964. "Repression," *Psychology in the Making,* ed. L. Postman. New York: Knopf.

Malan, D. H. 1976. *Toward the Validation of Dynamic Psychotherapy.* New York: Plenum.

Marmor, J. 1968. "New Directions in Psychoanalytic Theory and Therapy," *Modern Psychoanalysis,* ed. J. Marmor. New York: Basic Books.

—. 1970. "Limitations of Free Association," *Archives of General Psychiatry* 22, pp. 160–165.

Menaker, E. 1982. *Otto Rank: A Rediscovered Legacy.* New York: Columbia University Press.

Möller, H. J. 1976. *Methodische Grundprobleme der Psychiatrie.* Stuttgart: Verlag W. Kohlhammer.

—. 1978. *Psychoanalyse-Erklärende Wissenschaft oder Deutungskunst?* Munich: W. Fink Verlag.

Moore, M. 1983. "The Nature of Psychoanalytic Explanation," *Mind and Medicine: Explanation and Evaluation in Psychiatry and the Biomedical Sciences,* ed. L. Laudan, *Pittsburgh Series in the Philosophy and History of Science,* vol. 8. Berkeley: University of California Press, pp. 5–78.

Motley, M. T. 1980. "Verification of 'Freudian Slips' and Semantic Prearticulatory Editing via Laboratory-Induced Spoonerisms," *Errors in Linguistic Performance: Slips of the Tongue, Ear, Pen, and Hand,* ed. V. A. Fromkin. New York: Academic Press, pp. 133–147.

Page, L. & Adams, N. I. 1940. *Electrodynamics.* New York: Van Nostrand.

Rachman, S. J. & Wilson, G. T. 1980. *The Effects of Psychological Therapy,* 2nd ed. New York: Pergamon Press.

Ricoeur, P. 1970. *Freud and Philosophy.* New Haven: Yale University Press.

—. 1981. *Hermeneutics and the Human Sciences,* translated by J. B. Thompson. New York: Cambridge University Press.

Smith, M. L., Glass, G. V. & Miller, T. I. 1980. *The Benefits of Psychotherapy.* Baltimore: Johns Hopkins University Press.

Steele, R. S. 1979. "Psychoanalysis and Hermeneutics," *International Review of Psycho-Analysis* 6, pp. 389–411.

Strupp, H. H., Hadley, S. W. & Gomes-Schwartz, B. 1977. *Psychotherapy for Better or Worse: The Problem of Negative Effects.* New York: Jason Aronson.

Waelder, R. 1962. Review of *Psychoanalysis, Scientific Method and Philosophy,* ed. S. Hook, *J. of the American Psychoanalytic Assn.* 10, pp. 617–637.

27

THE PROBLEMATICAL SELF IN KANT AND KOHUT

RICHARD D. CHESSICK

The purpose of this paper is to call attention to an important parallel between two major thinkers, both of whom were trying to break out of the scientific paradigms of their time because of their deep conviction that important moral and psychological issues were insufficiently explained by the prevailing scientific and philosophical approach of their era. Each thinker, Kant and Kohut, presented an evolving series of writings, difficult and at times obscure, which rested on a fundamentally new orientation. This new orientation also changed as it evolved, so that eventually not one but two significantly different philosophical systems appeared from the pen of each author. These earlier and later systems in both cases not only significantly differed but were not always consistent with each other, an inconsistency often not noted or at least glossed over by the authors.

In each case the crucial notion of self changed as the author evolved his thought from one major work to the next. Both authors first presented a crucial notion of the self as closely related to experience—although not identical with the moment to moment fluctuation of our empirically known self states—and then in later writings added more and more experience-distant attributes and functions to their notion of the self. The result of this was that their earlier concepts of the self were replaced by much more complicated later concepts in which the self became an independent or supraordinate concept outside of the previously accepted notions of the mind or mental apparatus of the time.

Thus, Kant's earlier notion of the noumenal self in the negative sense, presented in the *Critique of Pure Reason* (1781), shifted to his use of the noumenal self in the positive sense,

Reprinted from *Psychoanalytic Quarterly*, 49, 456–473. (1980).

employed in the *Critique of Practical Reason* (1788), in order to deal with moral, ethical, and cultural problems. This will be explained in detail below. Kohut's earlier notion of the self was an experience-near concept described as, if not within then at least alongside of the mental apparatus of Freud. Kohut initially used Freud's metapsychological terminology with modifications, presented as "the psychology of the self in the narrow sense." He then shifted into a more experience-distant and supraordinate concept requiring a terminology of its own, conceived of as an independent center of initiative and postulating its own forces and poles, and called it the "psychology of the self in the broad sense." This will be documented below.

Kant was grappling with the impasse in philosophy that resulted from the work of Hume, in which classical British empiricism was shown to lead to a dead end that could result only in complete scepticism. He tried to resolve this unacceptable end point by focusing philosophy and psychology away from concentration on empirically experienced "reality" to what could be known or could not be known to be behind this reality. In his "Copernican revolution" he hoped to demonstrate that our experience actually depended on the structure of the human mind and its functions and limitations rather than, as was previously done, conceiving of the mind simply as a *tabula rasa* for the registration of empirical sensations and impressions. His focus on the function of the mind itself represented a revolutionary step forward in the sophistication of our understanding of our experiences and began a tradition of trying to understand the contribution of the mind to our phenomenally experienced world. It is generally agreed among philosophers that, since Kant, one may argue for his views or against them, but one can never ignore them.

According to Kant (1781), we experience the mind through our "inner sense" or "empirical apperception," our consciousness of the flux of inner appearances of the state of the self. There is no permanent or abiding "self" in this, as both Hume and Kant agreed. Thus the *phenomenal* self, the self studied in psychology, is known to us empirically as a succession of mental states in time, for time is the *a priori* form of our inner sense, according to Kant.

This is distinguished from the *noumenal* or transcendental self, the self which knows, the self enduring and as it "really" is. Thus, for Kant, we can think about reality "out there" and about the knowing self, but we cannot ever directly know either of them or make direct statements describing them. For Kant, this unknown self or portion of the mind also modifies the mind in some inner way and leads to our empirical introspected inner sense of self which is always experienced in the flow of time. This unknown self is called the *noumenal* or intelligible self by Kant, and it is flatly postulated to be the "cause" of our empirical introspective experiences of self states, that constitute the *phenomenal* self. Thus, the key unproven postulate of Kant is that an antecedent, unknowable, permanent, on-going "I" lies behind our experienced activity of the mind.

Both Kant and Freud flatly assume that there is a reality "outside" of or "behind" the world of appearance and that there is a part of the mind behind the *phenomenal* self. For Freud, a concept analogous to Kant's *noumenal* self, which cannot be directly known but yet profoundly influences our experienced sense of self, was, in the topographic theory, the system unconscious; in the structural theory it becomes the id (and portions of the ego and superego). Freud (1938) writes, "The core of our being, then, is formed by the obscure *id,* which has no direct communication with the external world and is accessible even to our own knowledge only through the medium of another agency" (p. 197).

Furthermore, this aspect of the mind which is not directly knowable produces, through the faculty of understanding, what Kant calls the synthetic unity of thought. The unity of consciousness, "I," the conscious sense of self, or what Kant calls the "I am I" is an essential part of all thinking and is required for what Kant calls the synthetic unity of the manifold. Thus, our knowledge of objects comes not from a stream of unconnected sensory representations but is presented to us in a certain coherence or unity of connectedness. It is the task of the faculty of understanding to present this synthetic unity of the manifold, and, furthermore, *these experiences must appear as belonging to a single consciousness,* the "I" or the self. Kant labels this the synthetic unity of apperception.

The crucial argument of Kant's incredibly difficult but fundamental "transcendental deduction of the pure concepts of the understanding" rests on the premise of the transcendental unity of self-consciousness, the sense of "I am I," the cohesive sense of a single continuous self. This continuing core of self-consciousness is clearly required to distinguish one's self-boundaries and self-experiences from experiences coming from the external world. Kant points out that Hume's fundamental mistake was to overlook the inextricable interdependence of self-awareness and awareness of perceptual objects. Conversely, he argues that if the subjective unity of the consciousness begins to shatter for various reasons, the individual becomes confused as to the distinction between one's self and self-experiences, and experiences of the external world. Thus, even for Kant, fragmentation of the sense of self implies a diffusion of ego boundaries and a loss of reality testing.

For Kant, the *noumenal* self inwardly affects us, producing inner sense data, from which the understanding—using "the transcendental synthesis of the imagination"—produces a consciousness of the self, a sense of self as we appear to ourselves. One has two kinds of empirical experiences of the self: 1) "I am I," which is required for all thought—the synthetic unity of apperception, and 2) self states appearing in a unified manifold in time—this is akin to William James's (1890) famous flow of consciousness, or stream of thought.

An obvious contrasting alternative to Kant would be some kind of intellectual intuition faculty that could apprehend the noumenal self and noumenal objects directly, perhaps like Husserl's (1913) eidetic intuition. This would imply a *positive sense* of the use of noumena, to mean transcendent objects and a transcendent self that could be grasped directly. Thus noumena used in the positive sense means that the reality or things-in-themselves behind our experiential world consists of entities that can be described and given various structures and functions. At times Kant seems to flirt with this doctrine, suggesting that our experience of the synthetic unity of apperception could give us a direct grasp of the intelligible or noumenal self; but on the whole this contradicts the thrust of his philosophy, which leads us to noumena in the *negative sense,* that is, as an unknown something that somehow generates our experience, but about which *nothing further* can be said.

When he is most consistent, Kant uses the noumenal self as a regulative concept, an "idea of reason" which is "limiting," meaning that it is implied by the extension of reason beyond the limits of the world of experience. For this reason, "pure rational psychology" is considered by Kant to be a bogus discipline, because it proposes to discuss the noumenal self as some kind of "substance." This pseudo-science arises as a result of pure reason's natural drive toward unity, beyond the concepts of experience. For Kant, the natural scientist, there can *only* be an empirical psychology, an introspective study of one's inner states as they are presented in the phenomena of our introspection; there can be no purely rational psychology of the noumenal self underneath these experiences.

Thus, when Kant is most consistent in his doctrine of noumenal self and phenomenal self, he would define these as follows: the *phenomenal self* consists solely of the empirically experienced self states of classical psychology as revealed by introspective investigation of inner states or experiences; the *noumenal self* is a nonempirical "limiting concept" that reason leads us to from a study of our phenomenal self. The noumenal self, as a limiting concept, is experience-near, in the sense that it is directly suggested to reason by our experience; it is a regulative concept in Kant's terms, useful to reason in describing and classifying our phenomenal self experiences. Because it is only such a purely rational concept, nothing more can be said about it. When Kant uses the concept of noumenal self this way, he speaks of it as *the noumenal self in the negative sense.* This is the *only* nonempirical (Kant would call it transcendental) self that is justifiably arrived at by the action of reason on our empirical data in its efforts to develop unifying and explanatory concepts.

As is well known, in the rest of Kant's philosophy he ignores his own arguments and uses the concept of noumenal self in a quite difference sense. In his moral philosophy, noumenal self is employed as an independent agent, and a good deal is postulated about it. This shift is usually described as a movement on Kant's part—a quite incautious movement—from the *noumenal self in the negative sense* to the *noumenal self in the positive sense.* It is a shift from a notion of noumenal self suggested to reason from immediate empirical experience to a far more complex and experience-distant concept of noumenal self, a shift not justifiable by Kant's own philosophy in the *Critique of Pure Reason.*

This noumenal self used in a positive sense approaches what Kohut (1978) refers to as an axiomatic self, flatly postulated by a number of later philosophers and used by Kant to deal with matters of faith. When we use the notion of self in this manner, we have thus moved significantly away from the realm of science. This is the meaning of Kohut's (1977) statement that the self "in its essence" cannot be defined; such a definition would postulate an axiomatic self, which Kohut rightly considers to be unscientific.

The notion of the noumenal self as a limiting concept suggested to reason by experience, however, is well within the area of science, for it is not arbitrary but rather is inextricably bound up with the limitations of our empirical inner sense of self states. As an example of a limiting concept—which gives no "determinate or constitutive knowledge" (Kant's phrase for what we would call the empirical knowledge of the natural sciences)—let us take the following definition of infinity, or what Kant would call "the cosmological idea of totality." Infinity can be defined as a "limit" suggested to reason by any ever-increasing or ever-decreasing series of real numbers. This "limit" is never reached or experienced, it is only possible to approach it closer and closer by experience. The existence of such a limit is "suggested" to reason by our experience of such real number series—and of course it forms a fundamental notion of calculus. When employed, it allows for great scientific advances, but infinity "in its essence" can never be experienced, nor can any empirical statement be made about it.

I believe that Kant had this in mind from his studies of the recently discovered calculus of Leibniz and Newton when he talked about the noumenal self as a limiting concept in philosophy. There is no question, as Ewing (1967) points out, that any *further* definition of the noumenal self says something about the noumenal self and thus by definition cannot be admitted, since all the pure concepts of the understanding required for any description are applicable only to the world of phenomena.

Noumena was called by Kant a "problematical concept." We have no means of showing its objective reality or validity, but we are led to this concept by the exercise of reason, for such a concept has an important unifying function, leading to a more complete comprehensive and exhaustive explanation of the phenomena of experience.

Kohut's (1971) early concept of "self" is a similar-limiting notion in metapsychology, but the "sense of self" for Kohut is arrived at by an entirely different methodology—the methodology of empathy or vicarious introspection performed by the therapist when sitting with a patient. Thus the therapist empathically identifies with the patient's more or less cohesive sense of self at any given time; in this procedure the self itself is undefined and is a limiting concept about which nothing can directly be said. In this sense Kohut conceives of the self as a separate aspect of the mind, but clinically a more experience-near concept, as compared to Freud's "mental apparatus." I will discuss this in more detail later.

Inconsistently, Kant writes in the *Critique of Pure Reason* (1781, p. 472) that man "knows himself also through pure apperception," which allows the statement: "He is thus to himself, on the one hand, phenomenon, and on the other hand, in respect of certain faculties the action of which cannot be ascribed to the receptivity of sensibility, a purely intelligible object"; yet in a later statement (p. 558) he points out that the notion of self is "a mere idea which cannot be represented *in concreto.*" In this latter section of the *Critique of Pure Reason* he is more consistent by labeling the notion of self "*as if* it were a real being; indeed it is attainable in no other way." We must conclude that Kant's notion of the self is murky and inconsistent, although certain basic principles are generally adhered to in his *Critique of Pure Reason* (and abandoned in the later critiques).

For Kant, as Norman Kemp Smith (1962) points out, the self is the sole source of all unity. "As a pure and original unity it precedes experience; to its synthetic activities all conceptual unity is due; and by reflection upon the constancy of these activities it comes to consciousness of its own identity" (p. 208). Although Kant is committed by faith to a belief in the spiritual and abiding character of the self, and this belief frequently colors in illegitimate ways the expression of his views, he himself declares that there is no sufficient proof of the spirituality, or unitary and ultimate character of the self. Smith writes, "Like everything else the unity of apperception must be noumenally conditioned, but it cannot be shown that in itself, *as self consciousness or apperception,* it represents any noumenal reality" (p. 262). For Kant, in psychology we must proceed *as if* the self were a simple concrete entity endowed with personal identity; this gives us the greatest possible satisfaction of the natural rational need to connect phenomenal causes and effects.

To summarize, Kant distinguishes between the empirical and phenomenal self on the one hand, and the noumenal or real or intelligible self on the other. Through inner sense one can be aware of oneself and of one's states only as they appear under the subjectivity imposed form of time in the phenomenal world. The noumenal self, like Freud's unconscious, is timeless, and a person is not acquainted with his noumenal self or any of its characteristic activities. The noumenal self is given the task of pure apperception which leads to a synthetic unity of the consciousness, a cohesive sense of one's self experiencing one's experiences. The processes of synthesis are performed by a department of the noumenal self sometimes called the productive imagination, in accordance with certain concepts which are innate and belong to understanding. By this procedure all experiences, both of bodies outside ourselves and of our own inner states, are presented in an orderly synthetic unity of the manifold, with a clear distinction of an "I" who is experiencing the phenomena, as distinct from the reality around one.

Broad (1978) concludes that "Kant's account of the nature of the human self and of its knowledge of itself is extremely complicated, and it is doubtful whether a single consistent doctrine can be extracted from his various utterances" (p. 234). This is primarily because in the *Critique of Pure Reason* Kant leans toward the negative sense of the noumenal self, but in his ethical works such as the *Critique of Practical Reason* he employs a positive sense of the noumenal self which he then uses as a transcendant object in order to account for free will.

What is interesting to psychiatrists is that Kant, like Kohut, struggled with the inner sense of self and attempted to distinguish what we can and cannot know about the self. Kant, like Freud (1938), believed in an unknowable core of the individual being which could profoundly influence the conscious flow of inner and outer experiences, not only by stimulating these experiences but also by determining the nature of how and in what manner they are to be perceived. It is because of the unique noumenal self, or the unique unconscious, of each individual human being that we may vastly differ in our experiences of and reaction to ourselves and the world around us, even though in the biological or physical sense we are all reacting to the same natural stimuli.

Kohut (1978) explains that the fundamental advance of psychoanalytic fact-finding is to take the further step into a new methodology by which the therapist vicariously introspects with the patient and experiences the inner self and the world around the patient in a manner congruent to that of the patient. This yields important data about the state of the patient at any given time which cannot be obtained in any other manner of approach. Kohut's early notion of the sense of self is not "axiomatic" but comes from emphatic identification with the patient's sense of self at any given time. It is in truly understanding how the patient's sense of self waxes and wanes, or coheres and fragments, that we gain an explanation of why and how the patient perceives the inner and outer world around him and behaves accordingly.

This is more experience-near than Freud's metapsychology, because additional apparatuses or structures are not postulated as homunculi within the head of the individual determining the outcome of his behavior; the patient's perception and behavior are directly attributable to the patient's sense of self at any given time. This approach side-steps what Freud (1937, p. 225) called "the Witch Metapsychology" to a considerable extent, but of course understanding then depends fundamentally on the capacity of the therapist to empathize with the patient's inner state at any given time.

The parallel between Kant's noumenal self lying behind our synthetic unity of consciousness in our inner states as phenomenally perceived, and Kohut's self as an organizing principle behind empathically perceived psychological manifestations steadily increases as Kohut matures in his views. Thus Kohut (1977) writes in the *Restoration of the Self*:

> We can collect data concerning the way in which the set of introspectively or empathically perceived inner experiences to which we later refer as "I" is gradually established, and we can observe certain characteristic vicissitudes of this experience. We can describe various cohesive forms in which the self appears, can demonstrate the several constituents that make up the self—its two poles (ambitions and ideals) and the area of talents and skills that is interposed between the two poles—and explain their genesis and functions. And we can, finally, distinguish between various self types and can explain their distinguishing features on the basis of the predominance of one or the other of their constituents. We can do all that, but we will still not know the essence of the self as differentiated from its manifestations (p. 311).

For Kohut the self is "a generalization derived from empirical data," but, just like Kant's noumenal self, it also has clearly both a stimulating and synthesizing set of functions. The kind of empirical data from which it is derived, the data of vicarious introspection, is different from the empirical data—Kant's introspected inner states—which lead up to the limiting concept of the noumenal self, but the concept of the underlying and unknowable self is the same.

Remarkably, Kohut at times, like Kant, slips into the concept of self in the positive sense, as when he speaks of it as empty and depleted, or as yearning for mirroring or merger. In a fashion similar to Kant the self in these situations is used as an "as if" concept, and the anthropomorphic language has been criticized. For example, in a footnote to Kohut and Wolf (1978) the criticism of Nathaniel K. London is mentioned: "He thinks our language often suggests an anthropomorphization of the concept 'self,' in the same way that 'ego' used to be anthropomorphized" (p. 415, n.); in essence Kohut and Wolf plead guilty to the accusation but claim that it is "in the service of evocativeness and conciseness" (p. 416, n.).

In *The Analysis of the Self* Kohut (1971, p. 130) mentions that the cohesive experience of the self in time is the same as the experience of the self as a continuum, which seems to be the same as Kant's notion of inner states; in the same paragraph Kohut also mentions the "breadth and depth" of cohesiveness of the self, but without definition.

The concept of the fragmentation of the self is never made particularly clear. It seems to be equated with psychotic-like phenomena, at which time reality contact even with the therapist is in danger of being lost. It is characterized as a regressive phenomenon, predominantly autoerotic, a state of self nuclei—in contrast to the state of the cohesive self: "the growth of the self experience as a physical and mental unit which has cohesiveness in space and continuity in time" (p. 118). Here Kohut seems to disagree with Kant's contention that time is the sole form of our inner sense, for Kohut adds space.

Kohut's original notion of the cohesiveness of the self has to do with a "firm cathexis with narcissistic libido" (1971, p. 119), leading to a subjective feeling of well-being and an improvement of the functioning of the ego. In later writings this metapsychological explanation is dropped; signs of fragmentation of the self then have to do with a subjective feeling of self-state anxiety, and objective and subjective signs of deteriorating ego function. As Kohut (1971) explains, this is accompanied by frantic activities of various kinds in the work and sexual areas, especially in an effort to "counteract the subjectively painful feeling of self fragmentation by a variety of forced actions, ranging from physical stimulation and athletic activities to excessive work in . . . profession and business" (p. 119). Thus fragmentation of the self that Kohut in his early work calls "the dissolution of the narcissistic unity of the self" (pp. 120–121) is manifested by certain characteristic subjective sensations such as hypochondria and frantic activities "in order to stem the tide of regression." Kohut sees a regression from the cohesiveness of the self to its fragmentation as parallel to a regression "from narcissism to autoerotism" (p. 253). A clinical description of this is based on the self as "an organizing center of the ego's activities." When the self fragments, the personality which has not participated in the regression attempts to deal with the central fragmentation, but "the experience of the fragmented body-mind-self and self-object cannot be psychologically elaborated" (p. 30).

In *The Restoration of the Self* (1977) the self as a supraordinate concept becomes elaborated in its bipolar nature, showing itself primarily when self cohesion is not firm. Metapsychological energic concepts are dropped out, and the self is now seen as occupying "the central position" within the personality. Thus fragmentation of the self is defined by the experiences which it produces.

There is also a core self or nuclear self about which Kohut (1977) writes, "This structure is the basis for our sense of being an independent center of initiative and perception, integrated with our most central ambitions and ideals and with our experience that our body and mind form a unit in space and a continuum in time" (p. 177). In this later book the self is a "supraordinated configuration whose significance transcends that of the sum of its parts" (p. 97).

Remarkably, there is an almost exact parallel to Kant's use of the noumenal self in the negative and positive senses. Kohut first presents the self in the negative sense as an experience-near abstraction from psychoanalytic experience. As his work evolves, he focuses more and more on the self, finally placing the self "into the center of our being from which all initiative springs and where all experiences end" (1978, p. 95). This emphasis on the self would be the same as Kant's noumenal self used in the positive sense to explain free will—again a center of our being from which all initiative springs and where all experiences end. When Kohut moves to the bipolar self and its constituents he introduces a new concept. The self is no longer a depth-psychological concept that can be metapsychologically defined using classical terminology, and the self is no longer thought of as either within the mental apparatus or even as a fourth "agency" of the mind. "The area of the self and its vicissitudes," as Kohut (1978, p. 753) calls it, is essentially a separate science from Freud's psychoanalysis, just as the study of the phenomenal world in the *Critique of Pure Reason* is a separate discipline from the study of the noumenal world in the *Critique of Practical Reason.* Kohut (1978) himself labels this "the science of the self" (p. 752, n.), and the conclusion is inevitable that he has attempted to found a new science.

Perhaps the most remarkable parallel of all between Kant and Kohut is in Kohut's (1977) discussion of free will. Choice, decision, and free will are explained by Kohut by "the positing of a psychic configuration—the self—that, *whatever the history of its formation,* has become a center of initiative: a unit that tries to follow its own course" (p. 245). This notion and the analogy that follows in the same paragraph regarding "the universe *in toto*" are two of the three classical "ideas of reason" as described by Kant (1781) and used in his moral philosophy to explain the possibility of choice and free will.

Thus Kohut, like Kant, although he claims to maintain an experience-near definition of the self (just as Kant's philosophy points primarily to the noumenal self in the negative sense), relies more and more on the definition of the self as a supraordinate concept, which more resembles the noumenal self in the positive sense as an explanatory concept. We see the evolution of this in Kohut, beginning, for example, in his 1972 presentation (Chapter 31 in *The Search for the Self* [1978]), in which he definitely offers the earlier definition, and moving toward his focus on the self in *The Restoration of the Self* (1977) as a supraordinate concept that solves the philosophical dilemma regarding the phenomena of free will. The turning point in this shift is labeled by Kohut (1978, p. 935) himself as coming first in 1974 in his essay, "Remarks about the Formation of the Self" (Chapter 45 in *The Search for the Self*).

In the psychology of the self in the broad sense, Kohut has presented us with a complementary theory as he intends to do, at the cost of changing his definition of the self from an experience-near abstraction from psychoanalytic data to an independent postulated center of initiative; in this shift he has made a major philosophical change exactly parallel to that of Kant from the *Critique of Pure Reason* to the *Critique of Practical Reason.*

There is general agreement among philosophers that this shift in the case of Kant violates Kant's very own philosophy, which states that nothing at all can be known or said about the noumenal self. The original concept of the self of Kohut was a simpler experience-near abstraction, marked in its fragmentation by certain clinical phenomena, and is certainly consistent with traditional psychoanalytic theory. Kohut's later use of the self, however, is not consistent with this theory, because, although he continues to derive his concepts from psychoanalytic experience, postulating the self as a center of initiative implies that a mysterious something besides the instinctual drives—either instead of them or in addition to them—is a main energic spring of human behavior and thought. And, indeed, Kohut regards manifestations of the drives already as "disintegration products" rather than fundamental to human nature.

It seems to me virtually certain that Freud would not have accepted Kohut's theory of the psychology of the self in the broad sense as "complementary" but rather as a rival theory which uses a different treatment procedure from that of Freud's classical psychoanalysis. The new procedure is based by Kohut (1977) on the Zeigarnik phenomenon, which postulates some kind of inner motivation of undeveloped structures to resume their development when given the opportunity; the energy behind this motivation has nothing to do with Freud's instinctual drives, and the origin of it is not explained. The basis of therapy in the psychology of the self assumes that proper understanding and development of "selfobject transferences," or transference-like structures in the treatment, make it possible for this force to take over and thus for development of the self to resume via transmuting internalization; this is clearly fundamentally different from the resolution of conflicts via interpretation of a transference neurosis. Thus Slap and Levine (1978), in a rather extreme statement, write, "Although Kohut refers to it as psychoanalysis, his therapeutic method depends on suggestion and learning, but not insight, conflict resolution, or making the unconscious conscious" (p. 507).

In conclusion I wish to point out the important *differences* between Kant and Kohut. Kant began with certain preconceived dogmatic assumptions about religious faith, and actually the hidden purpose of his philosophy was to establish the validity of his pietistic beliefs in morality and religion. There is no reason to suppose that Kohut began with any kind of analogous hidden agenda; a careful study of the evolution of his writings reveals an unfolding and change in his notion of the self, primarily based on the elegant explanatory power of the self postulated as a center of initiative and psychic organization. Kohut is entranced by this explanatory power in a way not so dissimilar to Freud's extension of the explanatory power of the Oedipus complex into history, literature, biography, and so on.

The purpose of this paper has been to explore the basic concept of the self in the philosophies of Kant and Kohut and to show how each author developed two separate philosophies based on two fundamentally different definitions of the self that each employed. These philosophies, Kant's critical philosophy and Kant's ethical philosophy, as well as Kohut's psychology of the self in the narrow sense and psychology of the self in the broad sense, in each case represent a fundamental change of metaphysical viewpoint.

The early philosophies, Kant's critical philosophy and Kohut's psychology of the self in the narrow sense, postulate the self as a limiting concept, as an abstraction from empirical data and a limit toward which the data point; no provision is made for any discussion of the self in a positive sense as a motivational source. In their later philosophies, Kant's ethical philosophy and Kohut's psychology of the self in the broad sense, the self is made an explanatory concept and given energic and motivational powers that are at the center of the destiny of the individual. The values of the later philosophies lie in the elegant explanatory concepts provided as well as in an extension into the realm of faith, free will, and morality. The disadvantages lie in the more controversial nature of the use of and focus on the self and the inconsistency between the early and late philosophies.

The anthropomorphizing of the self with the notion of its unfolding of nuclear goals and ideals is parallel to Kant's concept of the noumenal self inevitably unfolding and fulfilling its destiny behind the empirical phenomena of everyday personality. This aspect of Kant's philosophy was brought to its completion by Schopenhauer (*cf.*, Chessick, 1977), who viewed man as determined in the grip of his "noumenal character," but it is already clearly described in the *Critique of Pure Reason* by Kant.

Compare this with Kohut and Wolf (1978): "Once the self has crystallized in the interplay of inherited and environmental factors, it aims towards the realization of its own specific programme of action . . ." (p. 414). This clearly represents a whole new scientific paradigm. It is better for the progress of human knowledge to directly face this situation; otherwise, students of the subject will become hopelessly confused in attempting to somehow reconcile the early and the late Kohut, or to reconcile Freud's psychoanalysis and the psychology of the self in the broad sense. Like Kant's noumenal self in the positive sense, Kohut's self in the broad sense becomes crucial to joy in life and the making of right choices; there is no room for such a postulated entity in the *Critique of Pure Reason* or in the psychology of the self in the narrow sense. As Kohut (1978) himself recognizes, this supraordinate self is beyond the laws of psychic determinism and outside the limits of traditional psychoanalysis. Just as Kant's ethical philosophy is developed for the moral use of placing faith on a firm foundation, so Kohut's psychology of the self in the broad sense addresses itself to the moral purpose of alleviating the tragedy of man suffocating in an increasingly inhuman environment that he himself continues to create.

REFERENCES

Broad, C. D. (1978): *Kant: An Introduction.* Cambridge and New York: Cambridge University Press.

Chessick, R. (1977): *Great Ideas in Psychotherapy.* New York: Jason Aronson.

Ewing, A. C. (1967): *A Short Commentary on Kant's Critique of Pure Reason.* Chicago: University of Chicago Press.

Freud (1937): *Analysis Terminable and Interminable.* Standard Edition, XXIII, pp. 216–253.

—— (1938): *An Outline of Psycho-Analysis.* Standard Edition, XXIII, pp. 144–207.

Husserl, E. (1913): *Ideas, General Introduction to Pure Phenomenology.* Translated by W. R. B. Gibson. New York: Macmillan, 1931, 1952.

James, W. (1890): *The Principles of Psychology.* In: *Great Books of the Western World, Vol. LIII.* Edited by R. Hutchins. Chicago: Encyclopedia Britannica, 1952.

Kant, I. (1781): *Critique of Pure Reason.* Translated by N. K. Smith. New York: St. Martin's Press, 1965.

—— (1788): *Critique of Practical Reason and Other Writings in Moral Philosophy.* Translated by L. W. Beck. Chicago: University of Chicago Press, 1949.

Kohut, H. (1971): *The Analysis of the Self. A Systematic Approach to the Psychoanalytic Treatment of Narcissistic Personality Disorders.* New York: International Universities Press, Inc.

—— (1977): *The Restoration of the Self.* New York: International Universities Press, Inc.

—— (1978): *The Search for the Self, Selected Writings of Heinz Kohut: 1950–1978.* Two volumes. Edited by P. Ornstein. New York: International Universities Press, Inc.

—— and Wolf, E. S. (1978): *The Disorders of the Self and Their Treatment: An Outline.* Int. J. Psa., LIX, pp. 413–425.

Slap, J. W. and Levine, F. J. (1978): *On Hybrid Concepts in Psychoanalysis.* This Quarterly, XLVII, pp. 499–523.

Smith, N. K. (1962): *A Commentary to Kant's Critique of Pure Reason.* New York: Humanities Press.

28

HUMANISM AND PSYCHOTHERAPY: A PERSONAL STATEMENT OF THE THERAPIST'S ESSENTIAL VALUES

HANS H. STRUPP

Most therapists and students of psychotherapy now seem to agree that the therapist's personality plays an important role in the formation of the patient-therapist relationship which in turn has a critical bearing on therapeutic outcomes. Within the matrix of variables subsumed under the heading of "therapist's personality," we must recognize a subset relating to the area of *values*. According to the dictionary, values represent "the ideals, customs, institutions, etc., of a society toward which the people of the group have an affective regard. These values may be positive, as cleanliness, freedom, education, etc., or negative, as cruelty, crime or blasphemy" (Random House Dictionary, 1967). It is obvious that psychotherapists, like other members of the culture, uphold a spectrum of values, many irrelevant or only tangentially relevant to the enterprise of psychotherapy. Other values, however, may have a critical impact on the patient-therapist relationship and thus the outcome of psychotherapy. What are such critical values? How do they affect the patient-therapist interaction and the outcome? Is there any evidence to document the impact of the therapist's values?

Traditionally, therapists have been trained to keep silent about many of their personal values, the rationale being that the therapist's personal values, preferences, and predilections tend to contaminate and complicate the patient-therapist interaction. Thus, rather than burdening the patient with the therapist's values, it is considered more important and therapeutic for the patient to discover his or her own.

Reprinted from *Psychotherapy: Theory, Research and Practice, 17,* 396–400. (1980).

While this position has merit, it is unrealistic and perhaps even harmful. For one thing, it is impossible for a therapist to interact with another human being for a period of time without the other person becoming aware of the therapist's values on a number of subjects, no matter how strenuously the therapist may try to present a "neutral" facade. For another, a totally neutral or opaque therapist may be deleterious because what the patient urgently needs is a relationship with a *real* human being rather than an impersonal analytic technician. In any case, some of the therapist's values seem to be essential for the therapeutic enterprise whereas others are not. While there may be a number of values to which all psychotherapists subscribe (*e.g.*, commitment to alleviate suffering and fostering personality growth), there is considerable disagreement on many others (*e.g.*, therapist's self-disclosures on a variety of topics, advocacy of particular ethical or religious positions, etc.).

It is apparent that an important part of the problem revolves around the therapist's conception of psychotherapy, its modus operandi and goals. In this paper I shall restrict my discussion to the "traditional" verbal psychotherapies, and more particularly to those on the psychodynamic model. Within this framework one may distinguish two extreme positions. The first, espoused by Freud (and now generally considered superseded), likens psychotherapy to a set of technical operations, analogous to surgery, in which the therapist, as a person, plays a negligible role. (Nonetheless, it is abundantly clear that analytic therapy is undergirded by a specific set of ethical principles.) At the other extreme, we can identify the view of psychotherapy as a unique human encounter, exemplified by client-centered, humanistic, existentialist writers, in which the therapist's personality is clearly of the utmost importance. Between these poles there are innumerable variations. In my view, the therapist's personality, including his or her values, *is* inextricably intertwined with the technical operations brought to bear on the dyadic interaction. Accordingly, it is meaningless to speak of techniques in the abstract, just as it is meaningless to speak of the therapist's personality in the abstract (see also Szasz, 1965, p. 39). For conceptual purposes it may be useful to make such differentiations but the patient always experiences the therapist as a whole person—to be sure a person who plays a particular role and whose behavior is circumscribed by certain constraints inherent in the therapist's professional role—but as a whole person nonetheless. Human experience does not come in pieces; it is a Gestalt.

This is perhaps a major reason why the research literature on the therapist's values (as well as therapist's personality) has been so unsatisfactory. Investigators have typically attempted to isolate single variables, hypothesizing that they may account for significant parts of the variance in measurable outcomes. Predictably, they do not. This does not mean that particular aspects of the therapist's personality and values are not important; it merely means that traditional research approaches are inadequate for studying the problem. Thus it should occasion no surprise that reviewers of this literature come to pessimistic conclusions (Parloff *et al.*, 1978).

With respect to the problem of values, only a few basic facts seem clear: (1) Psychotherapy is not a value-free enterprise; (2) therapists do communicate their values to patients; (3) in successful therapy the patient tends to assimilate (identify with) the therapist's values. Parloff *et al.* conclude: "This paucity of empirical research on value similarity and therapy outcome belies the importance of the hypothesis that relates to the two dimensions. Values seem to be an inherent part of the therapy process and therefore appear to be necessarily affected by the outcome of therapy. Understanding the particular relationships that link the values of therapist and patient seems to us a priority area of research" (p. 271). The trouble seems to be that we don't know how to research the problem.

In short, the empirical literature provides little guidance. I agree with the foregoing reviewers that, although there is as yet little progress to record, the area is of the utmost importance. With this thought, I turned to my clinical experience, both as a patient and as a therapist, for possible enlightenment. To this I add my extensive observations of patient-therapist interactions in a research context. I also profited greatly from studying the writings of the authors cited in this paper. My points obviously can be no more than suggestions but perhaps they are not without merit.

My thesis is that there is a set of important values underlying and guiding the therapeutic enterprise. While these values are shared by many well-trained therapists, they are typically not directly communicated to the patient. The patient nevertheless experiences them deeply and makes them his/her own. These values I propose to designate as *essential therapeutic values.* From these essential values one may differentiate a congeries of values which some therapists may wish to promote and which some patients may wish to acquire. In my view, they are not central to the psychotherapeutic enterprise. They may be called *optional values.* Finally, there is a host of *idiosyncratic values* which are more or less unique to the individual therapist. Both of the latter classes are of limited concern here, and most therapists would probably agree that patients should be spared the therapist's views on a variety of topics that are more or less irrelevant to the problems for which therapy is undertaken.

ESSENTIAL THERAPEUTIC VALUES

A major—perhaps *the* major—tenet of modern psychotherapy is the proposition put forth by Freud and amply elaborated in his writings that the purpose of therapy is to strengthen the patient's adaptive capacities, to provide whatever assistance may be necessary to enable the patient to lead a more satisfying life as a responsible citizen in our culture. Implicit in this formulation is a set of crucially important values, among them:

1. People have the right to personal freedom and independence.
2. As adult members of a particular society, they have rights and privileges but they also have responsibilities toward others.
3. To the greatest extent possible, people should be responsible for conducting their own lives, without undue dependence on others.
4. People are responsible for their actions but not their feelings, fantasies, etc.
5. People's individuality should be fully respected, and they should not be controlled, dominated, manipulated, coerced, or indoctrinated.
6. People are entitled to make their own mistakes and to learn from their life experiences.

The essence of the therapeutic enterprise as an education in autonomy and individual freedom has been incisively discussed by Thomas Szasz in *The Ethics of Psychoanalysis* (1965). I shall attempt to summarize his major propositions:

1. Psychotherapy (a term I prefer to "psychoanalysis") is a form of education, not medical treatment. Its aim is "to augment the client's capacity for self-determination and making choices" (p. 6). A common feature of psychiatric symptoms is that "[all]" entail an essential restriction of the patient's freedom to engage in conduct available to others similarly situated in society" (p. 14). The purpose of psychotherapy is "to liberate the patient from the automatic, unconscious influences exerted on him by his infantile introjects or, in plain English, from the ideas that had been drilled into him as a child" (p. 17).

2. The revolutionary conception of the therapist, created by Freud, is that of the *patient's agent,* not society's or the family's (p. 21). The therapist "must support the patient's aspirations toward freedom from coercive objects" [both internal and external] (p. 23). The therapeutic relationship "thus not only provide[s] the conditions for a certain kind of learning experience, but [it] will furnish a model of the autonomous, noncoercive relationship" (p. 24). "[A]utonomous psychotherapy (Szasz's preferred term) is an actual small-scale demonstration of the nature and feasibility of the ethic of autonomy in human relationships" (p. 24). The therapist "conducts himself autonomously and responsibly, subordinates himself to the terms of a contract regardless of the patient's subsequent conduct, and avoids coercing the patient in any way" (pp. 24–25).
3. The psychotherapist is an expert in decoding the patient's communications and the meaning of her/his "mental illness" (p. 38). "He treats the client as a *person*; he does not *do* anything *to* the patient nor does he use any methods *on* him" (p. 38). "In other words, psychotherapeutic technique issues from the personality of the therapist or becomes part of it" (p. 40). "Much of the analyst's work consists of attempts to comprehend and decode the patient's disguised communications and of encouraging the patient, by means of the analytic contract, to address the analyst clearly and explicitly in his everyday language and to decode his own concealed messages" (p. 56).
4. Szasz is a strong proponent of the view that *control* of another person's behavior and *understanding* are antithetical. The therapist's stance reflects a strong commitment to understanding the patient, a goal that is primarily achieved through *sharing information* (p. 149). By engaging in actions that augment the patient's autonomy and self-responsibility, the therapist teaches the patient to develop a more self-reliant attitude. Szasz concludes that psychotherapy is a supremely moral exercise or a moral therapy: "Because it deals with the nature and value of varying styles of personal conduct, it could not be anything else" (p. 202).

While Szasz captures important elements of the Freudian heritage, he slights the ideals of brotherly love and human relatedness which are coequal to knowledge (reason, truth, *logos*) and reduction of suffering (Fromm, 1950, p. 18). Fromm observes that these values constitute the essential ethical core of all great religions on which Eastern and Western culture are based. He further notes that the great religious teachers are in basic agreement about the aims of human development and the norms which ought to guide human conduct (p. 19). Like Szasz, Fromm stresses a *non-authoritarian, humanistic* system of ethics, which he regards as the essence and foundation of Freud's thinking. With respect to the goals of therapy, Fromm rejects "adjustment" to prevailing social and cultural norms in favor of a conception of mental health whose aims are independence, integrity, and the ability to love (p. 74). In this sense, psychoanalytic therapy has a definite religious function "provided that by religious we refer to the attitude common to the original teachings of humanistic religions" (p. 76). Fromm gives the clearest expression to this credo in the following passage:

> Whatever complaints the neurotic patient may have, whatever symptoms he may present are rooted in his inability to love, if we mean by love a capacity for the experience of concern, responsibility, respect, and understanding of another person and the intense desire for that other person's growth. *Analytic therapy is essentially an attempt to help the patient gain or regain his capacity for love.* If this aim is not fulfilled nothing but surface changes can be accomplished (p. 87; italics in original).

Allen Bergin (1980) in a searching article deplores the alienation of American psychology from religious values, in particular, he regards the prevailing mental health ideologies as rooted in "clinical pragmatism" and "humanistic idealism." These he contrasts with "theistic realism," a position founded on the supremacy of God and the acceptance of divine authority. In my view, his contrast of the two positions does considerable injustice to the former. For example, there is nothing in Fromm's humanistic framework that espouses self-satisfaction as central to personal growth, open marriage or no marriage, recreational sex without long-term responsibilities, etc. (Bergin's Table 1, p. 456). As Fromm puts it: ". . . the problem of religion is not the problem of God but the problem of man; religious formulations and religious symbols are attempts to give expression to certain kinds of human experiences. What matters is the nature of these experiences" (p. 113). In order to recognize that psychotherapy is supported by a system of religious values, it does not seem necessary to adopt the essentially authoritarian religious position advocated by Bergin. I share Fromm's view that "Man's aim in humanistic religion is to achieve the greatest strength, not the greatest powerlessness; virtue is self-realization, not obedience . . . The prevailing mood [of humanistic religion] is that of joy, while the prevailing mood in authoritarian religion is that of sorrow and of guilt" (p. 37).

MY INTERPRETATION

In the remainder of this paper I would like to set forth, as succinctly as possible, my views of the psychoanalytic therapist's position on the problem of essential therapeutic values. Obviously it is a personal view and an ideal. However, I firmly believe that it is in keeping with the best of the Freudian heritage.

1. The basic commitment of psychoanalytic therapy is to the dual goal of personal freedom and human relatedness. With regard to the former it extols individual autonomy, responsibility, fairness, decency, and honesty in interpersonal relations. With regard to the latter, it proceeds on the basic premise that harmony in human relations, epitomized by intimacy, is the major goal of therapy.

2. Psychoanalytic therapy adopts the working hypothesis that the patient's suffering is rooted in unfortunate life experiences, particularly in early childhood, which have created more or less pervasive impediments to the realization of the foregoing basic human values. Psychotherapy is possible to the extent that on some level the patient still struggles with these issues and seeks a better solution. The task of therapy is to help the patient overcome the inner obstacles (*e.g.*, those due to deprivations, traumas, an archaic superego). It seeks to achieve its objective not by indoctrination, exhortation, persuasion or other forms of coercive interventions but by helping the patient to discover for herself/himself the manner in which s/he unwittingly stands in his/her own path. The technical tools employed by psychoanalytic psychotherapy are forged from contemporary understanding of the mechanisms and forces relating to self-deceptions, cognitive distortions, symbolic meanings, symptom formation and the spectrum of maladaptive forms of behavior. To this end, psychotherapy uses participant observation—*i.e.*, the empirical approach. In that important sense, it is an empirical science with a firm commitment to observational data.

3. In keeping with the preceding formulation, the therapist helps the patient in two major ways. (a) He or she provides the model of a human relationship that faithfully

reflects to the greatest extent possible the essential therapeutic values mentioned above. The therapist becomes the patient's "ally" and his/her attitude is one of caring, commitment, reliability, trustworthiness, and honesty. S/he treats the patient as an equal, a partner in a unique human enterprise which provides safety, security, protection from interpersonal harm, one that is free from domination, exploitation, and other forms of coercion. The therapist steers clear of participation in neurotic involvements with the patient, resists seduction, provocations, and other maneuvers by which the patient frequently pursues neurotic goals, thereby seeking to defeat the therapeutic effort. In the best sense of the word, the therapist provides the patient with the model of what a good human relationship can be like. At the same time, the therapist does not view the therapeutic relationship as an end in itself but rather as a valuable preparation for independent living and intimacy with others. (b) Within this framework, the therapist brings to bear an abiding commitment to a deep *understanding* of the patient's inner world—his or her struggles, suffering, strivings for self-realization, autonomy, and relatedness. This effort at understanding is aided by the therapist's knowledge of the basic interpersonal constellations that underlie neurotic conflicts, such as childhood struggles with authority figures, dependency, and separation. This process is not only a cognitive function but is greatly aided by the therapist's ability to listen and empathically understand the patient's subjective world.

4. The "cure" resulting from psychoanalytic psychotherapy flows directly from the foregoing conceptualization—from the alliance with a trustworthy human being, the sense of being understood, and the assimilation of both the experiences during the therapeutic relationship and the hitherto obscure meanings which have guided the patient's life and led to conflicts, self-defeating maneuvers, anxieties, etc. This experience allows a profound reorganization of the patient's personal paradigms and leads to a revised view of himself in relation to others.

To the extent that the therapist's commitment to essential therapeutic values is realized a number of issues that are frequently discussed in the therapy literature become more or less irrelevant. Among these I would include: the therapist's gender, socioeconomic status, sexual preferences, religious beliefs, and many others. It may be argued that the therapist's values in these areas cannot be kept out of the therapeutic encounter and that the patient, willy-nilly, may be influenced by them. To be sure, the patient will inevitably learn something about the therapist's values in these areas. However, I believe that if psychotherapy is conceptualized in the manner I suggested and if the therapist conducts himself or herself to the greatest extent possible in accordance with this conceptualization, the issue of indoctrination or the alleged dangers of a laissez-faire stance are largely inconsequential.

In my view, what is unique about the enterprise of psychoanalytic psychotherapy is the basic belief that, given the opportunities sketched in this article (as well as by other authors), people will search for and find their own solutions to basic life problems. That too, I realize, is a position on values. It makes psychoanalytic psychotherapy an educational as well as a moral enterprise, but one enlightened by the insights we have learned from Freud and his followers about human conflicts and their vicissitudes. In a word, the essential commitment of psychotherapy is to human growth and relatedness. This is hardly original, but at a time when there is much talk about psychotherapy as "health care technology," psychotherapists as "service providers" or "change agents," and therapeutic outcomes as a marketable product, a restatement may not be amiss.

REFERENCES

Bergin, A. E. Psychotherapy and religious values. *Journal of Consulting and Clinical Psychology*, **48**, 95–105, 1980.

Fromm, E. *Psychoanalysis and Religion.* New Haven, Conn.: Yale University Press, 1950.

Parloff, M. B., Waskow, I. E. & Wolfe, B. E. Research on therapist variables in relation to process and outcome. *In* S. L. Garfield & A. E. Bergin (Eds.), *Handbook of psychotherapy and behavior change: An empirical analysis.* Second edition. New York: Wiley, 1978.

Szasz, T. S. *The Ethics of Psychoanalysis.* New York: Basic Books, 1965.

29

SOME LIMITS TO THE INTEGRATION OF PSYCHOANALYTIC AND BEHAVIOR THERAPY

STANLEY B. MESSER AND MEIR WINOKUR

Despite persistent attempts to link psychoanalytic and behavior therapy on conceptual and clinical levels, considerable difficulties remain in securing these bonds. Having first been trained as psychoanalytically oriented therapists and then finding ourselves working alongside behavior therapists, we were drawn to behavior therapy's promise of relatively rapid and seemingly painless ways of ameliorating human suffering. This contrasted sharply with the long and arduous route taken in the process of psychoanalytic therapy. Increased exposure to the theories and techniques of behavior therapy, however, did not readily lead us to the anticipated incorporation of behavioral techniques into our therapeutic repertoires. Our difficulties led us to wonder why this intuitively reasonable marriage should be so difficult to consummate.

We are familiar with the frequent criticisms leveled at each therapy by proponents of the other. Psychodynamic interpretations are seen by some behavior therapists as offering the client an illusory sense of understanding at the expense of the clarity, precision, and predictability offered by behavioral assessment and intervention (Lewis, 1970). Likewise, behavior therapy is derided by some analysts as sterile and dehumanizing, as bypassing feelings, thoughts, and interpersonal relations (Bieber, 1973). These overstated criticisms do not speak to our concerns: Behavior therapy, in our view, does not necessarily dehumanize, nor are psychodynamics necessarily imprecise. The difficulties in integrating the two seem to lie elsewhere.

In addressing ourselves to the gap that exists between psychoanalysis and behavior therapy, we recognize that we are not dealing with unitary entities. There are, in fact, a variety of

Reprinted from the *American Psychologist, 35,* 818–827. (1980).

The authors note that this article profited from the comments of George Atwood, Arnold Lazarus, Donna Messer, Margaret Mikesell, Donald Spence, and G. Terence Wilson. The point of view and ideas expressed are the joint responsibility of the authors, who shared equally in writing this article.

psychoanalytic and behavioral therapies, which can be arrayed along a spectrum ranging from orthodox psychoanalysis based on the "pure gold" of interpretation at one pole, to behavior therapy based exclusively on Skinnerian operant conditioning at the other. Between these poles the gap is indeed very wide. Toward the center of the spectrum, we would place the psychoanalytic therapies that contain varying degrees of the "copper of suggestion" (Freud, 1918/1955)—including such elements as abreaction, manipulation and clarification (Bibring, 1954), defense strengthening, and the building of object relations (Blanck & Blanck, 1974)—along with cognitive behavior therapy and multi-modal therapy, which include a good deal of attention to thoughts and feelings (Lazarus, 1976; Meichenbaum, 1977). Between these forms of psychoanalytic and behavior therapy the gap is narrower. Nevertheless, the nature, timing, and goals of the interventions of cognitive behavior therapists seem to us quite different from those of analytic therapists. Even where the gap is apparently at its narrowest, we find that it is yet quite wide.

This gap remains wide despite conceptual and practical shifts in each camp that have to some extent brought the two closer together. In placing more emphasis on the adaptive social context in which behavior occurs—that is, by assigning greater importance to the reality events to which a person is reacting and adapting (Hartmann, 1964; Langs, 1973)—psychoanalysis has moved one step closer to the behaviorist's predilection to look to environmental events as the central agent controlling behavior. Behavior therapy, by becoming more interested in thoughts, imagery, and other mediating processes (e.g., Kendall & Hollon, 1979), has come closer to the analyst's interest in internal, covert processes.

This conceptual shift allowed Wachtel (1977) to attempt a fuller integration between behavioral and psychoanalytic therapy, on both theoretical and clinical levels, than was previously possible. In brief, Wachtel and others (Feather & Rhoads, 1972; Rhoads & Feather, 1974) ask the behavior therapist to apply psychoanalytic understanding in assessing the client's problems and to pay more careful attention to what transpires between therapist and client during therapy sessions. In this marriage, the psychoanalytically oriented therapist is encouraged to focus more on the present than on the past, more on the interpersonal than on the intrapsychic, and to be more willing to actively employ techniques such as systematic desensitization, thereby encouraging the client to try out certain behaviors.

While Wachtel's approach to integration is quite convincing, we believe it underestimates the difficulties standing in the way of a successful match for these two reticent partners. It was the experience of observing cognitive behavior therapists at work and reading what they wrote that most helped us crystallize the nature of the problem and identify the content of the nagging breach lying between the two therapies. Although there is no guarantee that a particular behavior therapist would conduct therapy in quite the way we observed, we have the acknowledgment of several behavior therapists that the procedures we describe might indeed be employed in such a fashion. If there are major and compelling differences in assumptions about reality and human possibilities and limitations between *cognitive* behavior therapy and psychoanalytic therapy, these differences would appear still more marked were we to construct hypothetical interventions that a more traditional behavior therapist might make. In the following, we juxtapose behavioral and psychoanalytic diagnostic formulations and interventions. We do not address all of the differences between these two approaches (e.g., degree of manipulation, directiveness, activity) but instead focus on those aspects of the case that illustrate differences in the perspectives and visions of reality the approaches embody. The case then serves as a springboard for a discussion of these alternate vantage points.

AN ILLUSTRATIVE CASE DISCUSSION

> Mrs. J., a 37-year-old mother of two children, is currently separated from her husband and dating another man. For about two years she has had considerable fluctuation of moods and

> concerns about her adequacy. She alternates between feeling good about herself and feeling very low, depressed, self-blaming, and physically unattractive. During these low periods, she has a strong compulsion to eat and recently gained 20 pounds. The most significant events in her recent history are that her father, to whom she was close, died about ten months ago. She describes her mother as having frustrated her a great deal, as not being well attuned to her needs, and as having shifted a lot of the mothering chores to the client's older sister. Her father is described as basically loving, caring, and generous. "I loved him dearly, and he loved me."

As part of a behavioral assessment, the client might be asked to self-monitor the antecedents of her eating behavior by noting the conditions preceding her overeating (e.g., after an argument with her boyfriend, when bored, etc.) and her associated thoughts ("It's only a sandwich," "I deserve a reward," "I feel unhappy") and asked to keep track of the target behavior by counting caloric intake and weight gain or loss (Mahoney & Mahoney, 1976). With this information in hand, the therapist might then suggest a plan to decrease caloric intake and to increase amount of exercise. He or she would also point to the client's rationalization for overeating and encourage her to stop deluding herself as to the eventual consequences, namely, weight gain. The rationale for this intervention would be to improve the client's self-esteem and sense of control over one area of her life.

Nor would the therapy stop there. The cognitive behavior therapist would also want to know what feelings were associated with eating, which in this case could well be depression. More specifically, this depression would include negative self-statements ("dysfunctional thoughts") of the following sort: "I am fat, ugly, and immature," "I am worthless," "I can't control myself," "No one loves me," "I feel miserable and with good reason, and I'll always be this way." The behavior therapist might then examine these assumptions and beliefs, helping the client to see their overstated, irrational elements by exposing their illogic and by giving homework assignments designed to enhance her self-image. Response alternatives for her to employ in the situations that seemed to elicit these feelings would be suggested, thereby helping her to avoid rumination and overeating (Beck, Rush, Shaw, & Emery, 1979).

What kinds of considerations might a dynamically oriented therapist entertain about the compulsive eating and depression? The brief case outline is enough for him or her to postulate that the eating binges are related to loss of two important figures in one year. Could this be part of a pathological mourning process (Lindemann, 1944)? A therapeutic strategy suggests itself: One would want to find out about the symbolic meaning of food and eating. Overeating may represent a defense against experiencing and expressing painful feelings such as emptiness, or it may be a regressive move away from anger at the men who have left her, a feeling too anxiety provoking to be acknowledged. With this formulation in mind, the therapist might seek to help the client tolerate the painful feelings and to work through her sense of loss. The dynamic therapist would see his or her role as a source of support, as might a cognitive behavior therapist, in addition to being a temporary replacement for the lost figures and the nurturance they provided.

Note how this approach is based on a theoretical conception regarding mourning and "object" loss, implying that pain is inevitable and has to be accepted before it can be reduced; that is, whereas the behavior therapist views sorrow as a negative affect to be extinguished rapidly, the dynamically oriented therapist sees sorrow as a natural concomitant of the person's life history and current circumstances to be fully experienced, accepted, and worked through in connection with the real and perceived losses. Contrast this view with behavior therapists Wilson and Evans's (1977, p. 550) suggestion that there is rarely a good cause for arousing emotions during therapy; when they are aroused, it is not to help the client get in touch with feelings, but to extinguish them.

The behavior therapist does not ignore feelings, but responds to them differently from the psychoanalytic therapist. Detecting the client's excessive anger toward her boyfriend, who she feels treats her too casually, the behavior therapist might institute "anger management procedures" involving cognitive preparation for anger, cognitive skill acquisition, and practice in applying these skills (Novaco, 1977). The therapist, after identifying the person or situation that triggers the anger (slights by the boyfriend), would point out its excessive and unnecessary quality. The client would be taught to view the boyfriend differently and to modify the exaggerated importance she attributes to such slights. Coping self-statements and relaxation skills might be taught, and a sense of humor toward his behavior would be encouraged as a response that competes with anger.

The dynamic therapist, hearing the same material, picks up hints of hostility toward her mother for not nurturing her sufficiently, and toward father for "abandoning" her, and looks for parallels in her relationship with her boyfriend, husband, and therapist. Unlike the behavior therapist, he or she helps bring out the presumed sources of the anger (the drive) by interpreting her defenses against it (e.g., displacement) and looks for a way to thread together the past and the present. Instead of trying to dissipate these feelings or helping her to control them, the therapist tries to foster their integration into the personality, that is, their acceptance as part of the client's identity and self-image. And by having her perceive these feelings in relation to their several primary sources, the therapist facilitates the client's continuity of experience.

The differences between the two approaches do not necessarily reside in the presence or absence of such elements as empathy or interpretation; rather, they rest in the *form* of empathy and the *type* of interpretations they offer. Behavior therapists who use social learning theory as a conceptual base have recognized that the role of the therapist goes beyond that of technician and includes elements of persuasion, interpersonal attraction, and arousal of expectancy (Wilson & Evans, 1977). These therapists do attempt to be empathic in the sense of establishing a facilitative emotional climate by being warm, understanding, and friendly, thereby trying to ensure that things run along smoothly and that the client feels comfortable, listens to the therapist, and is willing to be influenced. The behavior therapist does not, however, use empathy to understand the nuances of clients' subjective sense of things, in that he or she is primarily interested in their reality situation. Psychoanalytic therapists, by contrast, tune in to unrecognized, unexpressed, or unconscious thoughts and feelings and are empathic in the sense of trying to convey an understanding of the individual's subjective experience and illuminating the person's particular dilemma.

Similarly, interpretations are offered within a behavioral format, but they seem to be of a rather general kind instead of constructed on the basis of listening to the idiosyncratic way in which clients perceive themselves and their environment. In this regard, when Kanfer and Phillips (1970), who represent more traditional behavior therapy, refer to the need for sensitivity and clinical acumen in the behavior therapist, it is not usually in the service of picking up the meaning of the client's communications, but is to enable the therapist to select desensitization hierarchies or to find effective reinforcers. It is our impression that even those engaged in cognitive restructuring (Ellis & Grieger, 1977; Goldfried, 1979) limit themselves to offering the client a somewhat restricted number of relatively standard constructions (e.g., fear of social disapproval, perfectionism). A good psychoanalytic interpretation, while relying on theoretical schemata (e.g., Oedipal complex, separation anxiety), attends to the specifics of an individual person's thoughts, memories, fantasies, and feelings and their idiosyncratic connection. Great attention is given both to the choice of words and to the timing of the therapist's comments.

To return to the client: She also complains of being insufficiently self-confident and assertive. She always feels that she has to put on a show for others and that she is a phony. The behavior therapist begins by assessing the source of the problem and then applies a relevant behavioral technique. Does the person not know what to say? The therapist can discuss what might be said or done in certain situations. Does she not know how to assert herself? Retraining via modeling, behavior rehearsal, and periodic feedback are instituted. Is the client's anxiety inhibiting her from being assertive? Desensitization or coping relaxation may be employed. Is she worried about negative consequences, such as the other person's thinking less of her? The therapist tries to convince her she is wrong or tries rational restructuring. If she feels that assertiveness is immoral or improper, referral to a minister may be made (Goldfried & Davison, 1976). The client's possibly valid perception of her own inauthenticity is viewed as secondary. By virtue of such interventions, the behavior therapist implicitly emphasizes social functioning over and above inner feeling. The client is not helped to do battle with or to explore these feelings. Since the aim is their amelioration, she is helped to feel better about herself as quickly and as painlessly as possible.

At this point it should be clear that therapists lean toward certain values and away from others, values that set different therapists on different courses. Cognitive behavior therapy *does* pay attention to the domains typically thought to be of particular interest to dynamic therapists—affect, cognition, imagery, and interpersonal relations. The difference resides not so much in *what* is covered but in the angle or perspective taken on these events, their relative importance in a hierarchy of values, and in implicit assumptions about the nature of human reality and human possibility.

PERSPECTIVES ON REALITY

Three related perspectives on reality that characterize the difference between these two approaches to therapy include realism versus idealism, objectivism versus subjectivism, and "extraspection" versus introspection (Rychlak, 1968). Regarding the first polarity, the realist thinks of the world as "out there," as having an existence of its own almost independent of the perceiver. In contrast, the idealist claims that there is no external world of reality independent of the perception and cognition (the "ideas") of the perceiver, that we look out on a world essentially of our own making. The baseball umpire as idealist would say, "I call 'em as I see 'em," but as realist would say, "I call 'em as they are."

With regard to the second polarity, viewing events "objectively" means sharing a frame of reference, having a common understanding of events or experience that is open to being checked and that can be generalized. In the words of physicist J. Robert Oppenheimer (1956), "The criterion of truth must come from . . . that very special kind of objectivity which characterizes science, namely, that we are quite sure we understand one another and that we can check up on one another" (p. 130). Subjectivity, conversely, implies that experience is unique and private and thus cannot be generalized beyond the individual. Knowing what goes on in one person's mind will not tell us what goes on in another's. Finally, in viewing other people from an extraspective frame of reference, one constructs a hypothesis about them from one's own vantage point as observer, regardless of the subject's viewpoint. By contrast, introspectively oriented theorists or therapists formulate their constructs by taking the subject's point of view seriously. People, from this viewpoint, inform us as to their nature.

Applying these closely related dimensions to the therapy described above, the behavior therapist takes an orientation that is relatively realistic, objective, and extraspective, in contrast with the more idealistic, subjective, and introspective outlook of the dynamic psychotherapist. In casting the formulation and treatment of obesity in measurable calories and pounds, in calling the negative self-statements irrational or illogical, and in emphasizing social behavior such as assertiveness, the therapist is perceiving the client in objective, realistic, and extraspective terms. The dynamic therapist, by emphasizing private, often unconscious events such as repressed hostility toward the father, by exploring the symbolic meaning of overeating, and by focusing on the client's feelings of phoniness and their idiosyncratic meaning in the context of her life history, leans toward subjectivity, idealism, and introspection.

Differing perspectives taken in the conduct of therapy quite naturally lead to different emphases in assessing outcome. The behavior therapist may want to know whether Mrs. J. lost weight, overcame her depression, began asserting herself appropriately, and showed better control over her outbursts of anger. The dynamic therapist, while interested in such outcomes, might focus on other aspects of change. Is Mrs. J. more in touch with and more tolerant of ambivalent feelings about her parents, including guilt, anger, and tenderness, and has she thereby worked through her grief? Does she have a different perspective on the excessive outbursts toward her boyfriend, seeing them as displaced from others? And as a consequence of experiencing her deeper feelings and acknowledging the distortion, does she feel more genuine and authentic? Finally, does she have a more integrated and balanced view of her life?

Although both therapists may measure outcomes objectively and thus adhere to the canons of science, the behavior therapist seems to assess such outcomes in more extraspective and realistic terms and the dynamic therapist within more introspective and idealistic modes. Similarly, Strupp and Hadley (1977) point out that therapists assess mental health outcomes consonant with the unique values embodied in their adopted theoretical vantage point. For the behavior therapist, ridding Mrs. J. of depression is, by itself, a positive outcome. The dynamic therapist, while likely judging this an improvement, wants to know about other intrapersonal changes related to the depressive affect, such as change in impulse-defense configurations and acceptance of and tolerance for feelings of loss. Could the conclusion of "no difference" in outcome of behavioral and analytic (and other) therapies (Luborsky, Singer, & Luborsky, 1975; Smith & Glass, 1977) be based on a failure to differentiate sufficiently the kinds of outcomes each therapy seeks to produce?

These three theoretical dimensions should be seen as applying in only a relative sense to the two therapies or to different therapists. In fact, the reconciliation that has come about in psychoanalytic and behavioral therapies can be described with reference to these terms. Insofar as the behavioral approach has become more cognitive—paying more attention to expectancies, irrational thoughts, imagery, and memories—it has moved toward the subjective, introspective, and idealistic modes (Goldfried & Davison, 1976; Mahoney, 1974; O'Leary & Wilson, 1975). Psychoanalysis, in being more willing to open its data to public scrutiny (Applebaum, 1977), in stressing the interpersonal versus the intrapsychic (Levenson, 1972) and taking into greater account the adaptive ego processes (Hartmann, 1964), has moved its position toward the objective, extraspective, and realistic poles. There have been changes in emphasis but not in these basic perspectives, which are likely to continue to place limits on the extent of possible integration.

VISIONS OF REALITY

While these perspectives refer to the angle from which reality can be viewed, they do not inform us as to the nature of that reality. Based on Frye's (1957) four mythic forms, Schafer (1976) presents four "visions of reality" that together constitute, he believes, the psychoanalytic world view: the romantic, ironic, comic, and tragic. Thus, in addition to differences between behavioral and psychoanalytic therapies in the *perspective* taken on events, there are differences with regard to the implied view of the *nature* of human reality and human possibility as such.

The romantic vision envisages life as a series of quests—"a perilous, heroic, individualistic journey," an essentially lonely, drawn-out, conflict-ridden, and difficult process "which ends after crucial struggles with exaltation" (Schafer, 1976, p. 31). Schafer illustrates cogently how the analytic process can be seen in these terms, how the analysand moves from the initial regressive wish for union with the analyst, through periods of heroic "dragon slaying," before hopefully arriving at a somewhat more temperate view of life's struggles and possibilities. The analytic therapist, operating in the romantic mode, holds an attitude of curiosity, adventure, and openness to new and unexpected developments in the client. We can find no counterpart to this drama in the behavioral domain, with its emphasis on the pragmatics of specified and realistic goals decided on at the beginning of therapy, brevity and economy of intervention, measurable outcomes, and strict adherence to scientific method.

The ironic vision, similarly, is incongruent with the behavioral world view. This vision is characterized chiefly as a readiness to seek out internal contradictions, ambiguities, and paradoxes. "It aims at detachment . . . spotting the antithesis to any thesis" (Schafer, 1976, p. 51). This emphasis on contradiction and ambiguity is in direct contrast to the behavioral emphasis on specific, relatively discrete problems, on straightforward strategy and clear-cut, unambiguous outcome criteria. One is reminded of the frequent criticism behavior therapists make of psychoanalysis as unnecessarily complex and contradictory. For the analyst, appreciation of ambiguity is a value; for the behavior therapist, it is an impediment to operationalization.

The tragic vision emphasizes the inescapable dangers, terrors, and absurdities of human existence. Pain and pleasure are inextricably mixed. Suffering is involved in learning and changing, and self-realization comes only through struggle and adversity. Conflict is endemic in life; it cannot be eliminated, but only confronted with the muted hope of partial mastery. Choices made are irreversible, outcomes are often ambiguous, lost objects are irreplaceable, and these facts can only partially be mitigated by psychotherapy. The dynamic therapist, by exposing conflicts such as the client's wish to return to her husband versus her desire for self-sufficiency and without encouraging one choice over the other, implicitly recognizes that in such a choice she gains one thing of value to her, but loses another. From the tragic and ironic viewpoints, the behavior therapist's telling her what to do and how to do it cannot help her work through and accept these grim realities. It is an essential part of dynamic therapy that the client recognize that the choice, with its attendant risks, is her own.

The psychoanalyst, therefore, is cautious about claims of singularly positive or happy outcomes. Even the successfully analyzed person remains vulnerable at times to neurotic responses; the permanence of gains is seen to depend on whether the analysand is spared "too searching a fate." Through analysis, Freud said, the patient can at best hope to exchange neurotic misery for everyday suffering. The incorporation of a developmental framework in psychoanalysis also contributes to its tragic view of life in that childhood fixations can never be entirely overcome or compensated for. The absence of a developmental framework in the behavioral approach leads to a more optimistic view of possible outcome; early deficits and traumas are not usually seen as placing a ceiling on possible change. Behavior therapists tend to assume that it is possible to achieve more total change through relearning. They de-emphasize the centrality of conflict and fixation and replace them with faulty learning or the absence of appropriate skills. Just about all skills can be taught!

The comic vision is in many ways antithetical to the tragic: It emphasizes the familiar, controllable, and predictable aspects of situations and people. Conflict is viewed as centered in situations, and it can be eliminated by effective manipulative action or via the power of positive thinking. Endings are happy ones free from guilt and anxiety. Security and sexual gratification, comfort and worldly success are, finally, achieved. This description of the comic mode is a remarkably close fit to the language and concepts of behavior therapy. Note that comic is not used here to connote "funny," "in a light vein," or "not serious"—as it does in common parlance.

Instead, it is used in the sense of "following the typical structure of dramatic comedy." No pejorative implication of "nonserious" is intended.

Nor do we mean to imply that the psychoanalytic undertaking does not have comic aspects; it does aim to clear the way toward "sustained hopefulness, the experience of progress, security and pleasure" (Schafer, 1976, p. 28). A successful analytic therapy should result in "a sense of being more alive in one's senses and sensuality, more worthy of one's benevolent attention, and freer to pursue and enjoy success and security however one defines them" (Schafer, 1976, p. 31). But if part of the goal of psychoanalytic therapy is essentially comic and ameliorative, another part is to help clients achieve a recognition of the inevitably tragic and ironic aspects of their own lives. One might say that the aim of analytic therapy is essentially comic but that this goal is tempered by a sense of the tragic and ironic. The analytic therapist aims not only to help clients feel better and function better but also to extend their perspective—their view of reality—and to recognize and accept that even with improvement, life is inevitably a mixture of comic, ironic, romantic, and tragic elements.

In trying to eliminate directly Mrs. J.'s obesity through exercise and control of caloric intake, the behavior therapist inherently embodies the comic vision. Similarly, in attempting to help her control her anger and hostility through coping techniques, or in exposing the illogic of the negative self-statements characterizing her depression, the therapist tries to invoke the power of positive thinking and engages in the direct action that follows from this viewpoint.

When the dynamic therapist allows Mrs. J. to experience grief, mourn her losses, see the death of her father and loss of her husband in their tragic grimness, the thrust is to help her change by facing the loss, reexperiencing it and working it through, with all the pain involved. Only rarely, the dynamic therapist would say, does growth in therapy, as in childhood, take place without some suffering. In all of this, the tragic element in life is recognized. "A healthy person must have the capacity to suffer and to be depressed," writes Hartmann (1964, p. 6). Compare this with the statement of a prominent eclectic behavior therapist: "The control or absence of unpleasant emotions coupled with an increase in positive feeling is a most worthy goal" (Lazarus, 1976, p. 5).

Where the behavioral approach, consonant with the comic view, leads to action, the psychoanalytic approach, following the tragic view, leads to reflection and inquiry. According to Schafer it is only through such reflection and inquiry and the therapist's willingness to persevere throughout the slow unfolding of the problem that empathy gradually emerges. The behavioral view in the comic mode denies the necessity for adversity in order for therapist empathy to develop. It is enough to have good will and an attitude of direct helpfulness and friendliness.

We do acknowledge, however, that there are many clients who are neither amenable to, nor suitable for, a kind of psychoanalytic therapy that emphasizes exploration of the person's inner life. For such clients techniques other than psychoanalytically oriented psychotherapy may often be indicated. It is for the large spectrum of clients for whom there are no clear indications of which approach is likely to be more effective that the visions and perspectives discussed above seem to be critical.

SOME PREVIOUS ATTEMPTS TO INTEGRATE PSYCHOANALYTIC AND BEHAVIOR THERAPY

Given the far-reaching difference between these two therapies in perspectives and visions, it is not surprising that efforts at integration have come to very little. One of the earliest and perhaps best known of such attempts was Dollard and Miller's (1950) conceptual tour de force in their application of behavioral stimulus–response language to psychoanalytic theory and therapy. Their effort has received a mixed reaction, and it has not had a substantial impact on the practice of either behavioral or psychoanalytic therapy (Lazarus, 1977; Wachtel, 1977).

Along with theoretical endeavors to bridge the gap between psychoanalytic and behavior therapy came practical efforts to relate one therapy to the other. Marks and Gelder (1966) concluded that the two therapies were each suitable to the treatment of different syndromes and thus were complementary and not conflicting modes of treatment. Enuresis and simple phobias, for example, were to be treated by behavior therapy, whereas depression and other difficulties involving unexpressed feelings and problems in interpersonal adjustment were to be treated by psychoanalytic methods. Some patients were seen as requiring both, a notion extended by Seagraves and Smith (1976), who have described several cases in which clients seen in psychodynamic therapy were referred to a behavior therapist for concurrent treatment of a psychoneurotic symptom such as phobia. This format has the advantage of permitting each therapist to work within his or her preferred mode of viewing reality, and it is thus less susceptible to the segregative effects of these outlooks.

The logical alternative to this "separate but equal" philosophy of Marks and Gelder and Seagraves and Smith is to weave both analytic and behavioral approaches into the fabric of the same treatment. Therapists who conduct psychodynamic treatment have, in fact, introduced behavioral techniques to eliminate symptoms, to enhance the therapeutic relationship, or to highlight resistances to therapy (Birk, 1970; Hersen, 1970; Leventhal, 1968; Woody, 1968). If our assessment is correct, the format in which the same therapist shifts from one approach to the other is likely to be much more difficult to effect, given the radical shift in perspective and vision involved.

Similar to the difficulties we predict for those who combine the two therapies are the problems expressed by clinical psychology students who are taught and who practice both therapies concurrently while working with different clients and supervisors. They frequently complain of confusion and anxiety in trying to shift from one form of therapy to another. This does not appear to be due merely to cognitive difficulty in mastering specific concepts or techniques. Rather, we detect a resistance to the outlook of one therapy or the other and the implicit recognition of some incompatibility between them. In fact, it does not take long before students sort themselves out as behaviorally or psychodynamically oriented, perhaps because they soon find one approach or the other more compatible with their own views of reality.

To alleviate the anxiety and confusion, we recommend that graduate students be exposed not just to the theory and practice of these two (and other) therapies but also to their philosophical underpinnings, their historical roots, their potentially differing outcomes, and their differing perspectives and visions of reality. In this way, given the chance to discuss, and come to terms with, alternate approaches, some may develop respect for more than one clinical orientation and thereby achieve some measure of integration in their future practice. For others, such exposure may confirm their strong inclination toward a particular viewpoint but, at the same time, increase their understanding of other points of view.

Just as therapists may sort themselves out on this basis, so too may clients. Bergin and Strupp (1972) have suggested that psychotherapy studies take into account personality dispositions of therapists and clients and the way they interact with types of therapy to determine therapeutic outcomes. Our analysis suggests that clients may do best with a therapist whose perspective and vision match their own.

CONCLUSIONS

In writing this article, we began to realize that we have in it the ingredients of a comic structure:

> What normally happens is that a young man wants a young woman, that his desire is resisted by some opposition . . . and that near the end of the play some twist in the plot will enable the hero to have his will. (Frye, 1957, p. 163)

In dramatic comedy, the obstacles to union typically involve the rigid standards of the older generation, who resist the couple's attempts to get together. The marriage of the couple can be seen to herald the dawning of a new social era. Following the comic mode, we should ideally be able to combine the two therapies into one new and better form and to replace the old psychoanalytic order controlled by "habit, ritual bondage, arbitrary law, and older characters" with a society controlled "by youth and pragmatic freedom" (Frye, 1957, p. 169).

Perhaps our efforts are motivated in part by romantic considerations. In trying to do something about that "gnawing gap," might we not be following a "persistent nostalgia, a search for some type of imaginative golden age" (Frye, 1957, p. 186)?

While there is, thus, a great deal of personal appeal in the idea of such a union, we are still left with the practical question of integration: Is it possible, is it desirable? What is very clear to us is that any form of integration is, at the very least, difficult. At particular choice points in a therapy, the therapist needs to decide whether to encourage action or to continue exploration, whether to listen and interpret or to challenge irrational assumptions and make specific suggestions. These are mutually exclusive options at any therapeutic moment. Different perspectives and visions propel the therapist in different directions.

Despite increased clarity about and tolerance for the behavioral point of view, we could neither undertake nor fully approve of any therapeutic activity that denied complexity, ambiguity, and the ubiquity of conflict in human affairs. Similarly, activity designed to remove negative feelings, or that artificially attempts to curtail mourning rather than to help the client accept and integrate such feelings, goes against our view of the psychologically sound and desirable. Nor could we picture ourselves actively convincing clients that their subjective view of things does not correspond to some ideal form of "rationality." Subjectivity and inner feeling have importance in their own right and are not to be minimized in the name of social desirability or appearance.

Although we are unable to reach either whole-hearted endorsement or full integration of the other therapy, there remains the possibility of limited integration through the opportune introduction of behavioral techniques into a basically psychoanalytic treatment. This seems to be the essence of Wachtel's (1977) approach: After the conflict has been partially worked through, techniques are introduced to help the client translate insight into action. If such an integrated approach were in fact shown to lead to better outcomes by agreed-on criteria, we would be happy to endorse the introduction of behavioral techniques into analytic practice.

Though Wachtel makes a convincing case in this regard, in the absence of outcome data, some reservations remain. We wonder whether such outcomes would reflect a trade-off between behavioral change and coping,and a deeper, more thorough resolution of problems. By encouraging clients to act, or by offering coping techniques such as relaxation or self-assertion, might not the therapist curtail the process of putting clients in touch with deeper feelings and resources that would help them become more whole, integrated, and genuine?

Furthermore, it seems to us that the consequences of such practical intervention can lead, in some clients, to a therapeutic misalliance. For instance, a client who has grown up with an intrusive or domineering parent might overtly agree to and enjoy a therapist's practical suggestions but harbor mixed feelings that he or she might be reluctant or unable to reveal. In this connection, we feel Wachtel underestimates the unconscious impact of behavioral interventions.

And, finally, in many instances the therapist does not know what clients should do any better than do the clients themselves. In such situations, continued exploration seems to us the most reasonable path. Thus, Wachtel minimizes the tragic vision both in embracing more ameliorative (comic) interventions and in overlooking the fact that these kinds of choices in themselves have tragic elements: By choosing one thing of value (rapid amelioration) we may lose another (deeper resolution).

These are several ways, however, in which we can incorporate aspects of the comic mode and the behaviorist's realistic, extraspective, and objective attitude. Despite our stated reservations, we are now willing to try out some of Wachtel's suggestions—to encourage clients to translate their insights into action, to have them take a risk and try out some behavior, as long as this encouragement has been preceded by clarification of both sides of the underlying conflict. This does not mean making a decision for the client, but rather supporting what he or she is now inclined and ready to do. We want to see whether such interventions may set into motion, as Wachtel suggests, a positive feedback loop leading to further insights and further adaptive action.

Also following the comic mode, we are more ready to support the prospect of psychoanalytic therapy being short-term, of some problems in some people being amenable to more rapid resolution than allowed for by the tragic and ironic visions (Malan, 1976; Mann, 1973; Winokur, Messer, & Schacht, in press). This can be achieved by focusing on some specific areas of conflict, much as the behavior therapist focuses on specific areas of behavior, choosing to ignore others. This approach, in addition, emphasizes the client's ego strength and capacity for growth and adaptation in spite of fixations and regressive tendencies. Furthermore, it insists on a statement of formulation and goals near the outset of therapy that can be assessed at its conclusion in relatively objective terms—a cornerstone of behavior therapy.

On the level of perspectives of reality, it seems to us feasible and even advisable to maintain a dual perspective on psychological events. We accept and recognize the usefulness of viewing events, at least some of the time, from extraspective, objective, and realistic viewpoints. This can serve as a counterweight to the overly introspective, subjective, and idealistic perspectives in which we and other analytically oriented therapists sometimes find ourselves enmeshed.

Within the realm of visions of reality, however, the exclusively comic view implicit in much of the behavioral approach remains inconsistent with our own therapeutic and general life experience, which dictates a mixed vision of reality.

REFERENCES

Applebaum, S. *The anatomy of change.* New York: Plenum Press, 1977.

Beck, A. T., Rush, A. J., Shaw, B. F., & Emery, G. *Cognitive therapy of depression.* New York: Guilford, 1979.

Bergin, A. E., & Strupp, H. H. *Changing frontiers in the science of psychotherapy.* Chicago: Aldine-Atherton, 1972.

Bibring, E. Psychoanalysis and the dynamic psychotherapies. *Journal of the American Psychoanalytic Association,* 1954, *2,* 745–770.

Bieber, I. On behavior therapy: A critique. *Journal of the American Academy of Psychoanalysis,* 1973, *1,* 39–52.

Birk, L. Behavior therapy—Integration with dynamic psychiatry. *Behavior Therapy,* 1970, *1,* 522–526.

Blanck, G., & Blanck, R. *Ego psychology: Theory and practice.* New York: Columbia University Press, 1974.

Dollard, J., & Miller, N. E. *Personality and psychotherapy: An analysis in terms of learning, thinking and culture.* New York: McGraw-Hill, 1950.

Ellis, A., & Grieger, R. (Eds.). *Handbook of rational-emotive therapy.* New York: Springer, 1977.

Feather, B. W., & Rhoads, J. M. Psychodynamic behavior therapy. *Archives of General Psychiatry,* 1972, *26,* 496–511.

Freud, S. Lines of advance in psychoanalytic therapy. In J. Strachey (Ed. and trans.), *Standard edition of complete psychological works* (Vol. 17). London: Hogarth, 1955. (Originally published, 1918.)

Frye, N. *Anatomy of criticism.* New York: Atheneum, 1957.

Goldfried, M. R. Anxiety reduction through cognitive-behavioral intervention. In P. C. Kendall & S. D. Hollon (Eds.), *Cognitive-behavioral intervention: Theory, research and procedures.* New York: Academic Press, 1979.

Goldfried, M. R., & Davison, G. C. *Clinical behavior therapy.* New York: Holt, Rinehart & Winston, 1976.

Hartmann, H. *Essays on ego psychology.* New York: International Universities Press, 1964.

Hersen, M. The use of behavior modification techniques within a traditional psychotherapeutic context. *American Journal of Psychotherapy,* 1970, *24,* 308–313.

Kanfer, F. H., & Phillips, J. S. *Learning foundations of behavior therapy.* New York: Wiley, 1970.

Kendall, P. C., & Hollon, S. D. (Eds.). *Cognitive-behavioral intervention: Theory, research and procedures.* New York: Academic Press, 1979.

Langs, R. *The technique of psychoanalytic psychotherapy.* New York: Aronson, 1973.

Lazarus, A. A. *Multimodal behavior therapy.* New York: Springer, 1976.

Lazarus, A. A. Has behavior therapy outlived its usefulness? *American Psychologist,* 1977, *32,* 550–554.

Levenson, E. A. *The fallacy of understanding.* New York: Basic Books, 1972.

Leventhal, A. M. Use of a behavioral approach within a traditional psychotherapeutic context: A case study. *Journal of Abnormal Psychology,* 1968, *73,* 178–182.

Levis, D. Integration of behavior therapy and dynamic psychiatry techniques: A marriage with a high probability of ending in divorce. *Behavior Therapy,* 1970, *1,* 531–537.

Lindemann, E. Symptomatology and management of acute grief. *American Journal of Psychiatry,* 1944, *101,* 141–148.

Luborsky, L., Singer, B., & Luborsky, L. Comparative studies of psychotherapies. *Archives of General Psychiatry,* 1975, *32,* 995–1008.

Mahoney, M. J. *Cognition and behavior modification.* Cambridge, Mass.: Ballinger, 1974.

Mahoney, M. J., & Mahoney, K. *Permanent weight control.* New York: Norton, 1976.

Malan, D. H. *The frontier of brief psychotherapy.* New York: Plenum Press, 1976.

Mann, J. *Time-limited psychotherapy.* Cambridge, Mass.: Harvard University Press, 1973.

Marks, I. M., & Gelder, M. G. Common ground between behavior therapy and psychodynamic methods. *British Journal of Medical Psychology,* 1966, *39,* 11–23.

Meichenbaum, D. *Cognitive behavior modification.* New York: Plenum Press, 1977.

Novaco, R. W. Stress inoculation: A cognitive therapy for anger and its application to a case of depression. *Journal of Consulting and Clinical Psychology,* 1977, *45,* 600–608.

O'Leary, K. D., & Wilson, G. T. *Behavior therapy: Application and outcome.* Englewood Cliffs, N.J.: Prentice-Hall, 1975.

Oppenheimer, J. R. Analogy in science. *American Psychologist,* 1956, *11,* 127–135.

Rhoads, J. M., & Feather, B. W. Application of psychodynamics to behavior therapy. *American Journal of Psychiatry,* 1974, *131,* 17–20.

Rychlak, J. F. *A philosophy of science for personality theory.* Boston: Houghton Mifflin, 1968.

Schafer, R. *A new language for psychoanalysis.* New Haven, Conn.: Yale University Press, 1976.

Seagraves, R. T., & Smith, R. C. Concurrent psychotherapy and behavior therapy: Treatment of psychoneurotic outpatients. *Archives of General Psychiatry,* 1976, *33,* 756–763.

Smith, M. L., & Glass, G. V. Meta-analysis of psychotherapy outcome studies. *American Psychologist,* 1977, *32,* 752–760.

Strupp, H. H., & Hadley, S. W. A tripartite model of mental health and therapeutic outcomes. *American Psychologist,* 1977, *32,* 187–196.

Wachtel, P. *Psychoanalysis and behavior therapy.* New York: Basic Books, 1977.

Wilson, G. T., & Evans, I. M. The therapist-client relationship in behavior therapy. In A. S. Gurman & A. M. Razin (Eds.), *The therapist's contribution to effective psychotherapy: An empirical approach.* New York: Pergamon Press, 1977.

Winokur, M., Messer, S. B., & Schacht, T. Contributions to the theory and practice of short term dynamic psychotherapy. *Bulletin of the Menninger Clinic,* in press.

Woody, R. H. Integrating behavior therapy and psychotherapy. *British Journal of Medical Psychology,* 1968, *41,* 261–266.

30

ON THEORY, PRACTICE, AND THE NATURE OF INTEGRATION

PAUL L. WACHTEL

It is really not very difficult to argue against an integration of psychodynamic and behavioral approaches. All one has to do is to define "psychodynamic" and "behavioral" in the right way, and they will indeed be incompatible. This the critics of integration have done, sometimes with flair and considerable sophistication. It will be the burden of this chapter to argue, however, that such criticisms do not really address the kind of integration I have proposed. They are, I suggest, articulate defenses of a less than satisfactory status quo, and they impede the creative fusion that I believe is necessary for a major advance in psychotherapeutic efficacy and in the theoretical understanding on which such enhanced efficacy must be based.

To some degree I myself have abetted the definitional confusion. For a variety of reasons, partly syntactic and aesthetic, partly having to do with the term "psychoanalysis" being more familiar and widely recognized, and partly, I confess, to arrest potential readers with a starker, more provocative challenge, I referred in the title of my book to psycho*analysis* and behavior therapy. It would have been less confusing to indicate (as I did do in the body of my book) that I was concerned with an integration of the psycho*dynamic* and behavioral approaches. The term "psychodynamic" is a broader—and less jealously guarded—one that includes not only Freudian theory and those variations of it that have been included in what might be called the official psychoanalytic movement, but also points of view that, although originally rooted in Freudian thought, have presented direct challenges to certain assumptions still widely held by Freudians.

It could reasonably be argued that "psychoanalysis" *is* the correct term for the points of view on which I rely. Horney and her followers did describe what they did as psychoanalysis, and

Reprinted from *Psychotherapy Therapy and Behavior Therapy: Is Integration Possible?* (pp. 111–130) by H. Arkowitz and S. Messer (Eds.), 1984, New York: Plenum Press.

many Sullivanians describe themselves as analysts. (Indeed, the journal of the William Alanson White Institute, the major Sullivanian training center, is called *Contemporary Psychoanalysis.*) Nonetheless, I do believe that it is more accurate—or at least less confusing—for someone like myself, who relies as much on Horney and Sullivan as on Freud, to describe my point of view as *psychodynamic* rather than specifically as psychoanalytic.

Freud himself varied on what he considered the essential defining features of psychoanalysis. In 1914 he said:

> Any line of investigation, *no matter what its direction,* which recognizes [the facts of transference and resistance] and takes them as the starting point of its work may call itself psycho-analysis, though it arrives at results other than my own. (Freud, 1914/1959, p. 298, italics mine)

A few years later a harder-line, more restrictive statement was offered—one that both upped the ante as to what a psychoanalyst must pay obeisance to and that was cast in a syntax of prohibition rather than of permission:

> The assumption that there are unconscious mental processes, the recognition of the theory of resistance and repression, the appreciation of the importance of sexuality and of the Oedipus complex—these constitute the principal subject-matter of psycho-analysis and the foundations of its theory. *No one who cannot accept them all* should count himself a psycho-analyst. (Freud, 1923/1959, p. 247, italics mine)

Freud's efforts to define the "sine qua nons" of the tradition he had launched were related to sectarian battles within the psychoanalytic movement. Fairly early, Freud was confronting the consequences of the extraordinarily stimulating effect his discoveries and theories produced; he spawned intellectual progeny he was eager to disown. He had, of course, every right to distinguish between his own theories and those of others whose ideas might be confused with his. I would largely agree with him that he is

> justified in maintaining that even to-day no one can know better than I what psycho-analysis is, how it differs from other ways of investigating the life of the mind, and precisely what should be called psycho-analysis and what would better be described by some other name. (Freud, 1914/1959, p. 287)

But if Freud could attempt with some justification to control what was to be called psychoanalysis, he had neither the right nor the power to control more generally how others were to reinterpret or selectively make use of his work. The more broadly psycho*dynamic* tradition consists of all those efforts to build a psychology starting from at least some of the central premises of Freudian thought, even if they diverged from Freud in substantial ways. After more than four decades of post-Freudian development, psychoanalysis itself—that is, modern Freudian orthodoxy—is hard to delineate precisely, and controversy (e.g., over whether Kohut's [1977] theorizing is properly Freudian psychoanalysis) abounds. The broader psycho*dynamic* umbrella is, of course, even harder to define. It is the essence of much of it that different proponents see different aspects of Freud's thought as the most crucial or most valuable. What is to one an unfortunate anachronism in Freud's otherwise brilliant work is to another the heart and soul of what makes psychoanalysis of continuing value.

Nonetheless, it is useful to delineate a broader psychodynamic point of view, many of whose proponents are steeped in Freud but are also critical of aspects of the Freudian mainstream. Despite the diversity of theoretical perspectives and of evaluations of Freud's own contribution, the notion of a psychodynamic tradition, encompassing Freudian psychoanalysis but including considerably more, is not really that vague. Agreement as to who would belong within such a category would be rather high. (And clearly, present-day behavior therapists would not fit within it.)

MISLEADING CHARACTERIZATIONS OF PSYCHODYNAMIC THOUGHT

There are certainly features of some versions of psychodynamic thought that would make an integration with behavior therapy rather difficult. Critics have seized upon these as if they were the essential defining features of a psychodynamic point of view. Some of these are almost totally red herrings. The contention, for example, that, unlike behavior therapy, psychoanalysis is a medical or disease model is thoroughly without merit. The close association of the official psychoanalytic organization in the United States with the medical profession was a matter of economics and guild protectionism and was counter both to the general policy of the International Psycho-Analytic Association and to Freud's (1926a/1959) own arguments. The psychoanalytic situation, in fact, was largely set up to *avoid* the kinds of interactions and expectations that are encountered in medicine. The psychoanalytic model is a psychological, not a medical model (Wachtel, 1977b).

More respectable, but still off the mark, is the contention that integration is impossible because psychoanalysis attributes causation to the past and because behavior therapy focuses on the present. It is certainly true that many analysts do contend that an exploration of the patient's past is essential for lasting and meaningful change. Such a view, however, though it was held by Freud, is not an essential characteristic of a psychodynamic point of view (Horney, 1939; Wachtel, 1977a).[1] Concern with unconscious motivation, with conflict—and even with the enormous shaping influence of early experience—can as readily be pursued via a model of cumulative skewing of development that gives great weight to present environmental input (Wachtel, 1973, 1977a, 1981a) as it can with a model that makes the influence of the past impervious to present realities. That is, one can trace how early experiences skew the kinds of later experiences one encounters, with the effect of maintaining the psychic structures previously existing. One can also trace how those psychic structures in turn lead to still further skewing of experience and to still further confirmation of existing structures in a continuing circle that at each point takes place in what is then the present. The mediational events in this continuing process can include unconscious conflicts and wishes, but they are always present wishes and conflicts, no matter however much they resemble those of the past.

A third objection is more interesting because it is based on a characterization that is indeed true for a very large majority of psychodynamic thinkers, whatever their specific persuasion. Franks (1978; Franks & Wilson, 1979) has described a methodological or epistemological difference between psychodynamic and behavioral thinkers. For the former, he suggests that "subjective data derived entirely from the clinical situation are typically regarded as valid" (Franks, 1978). The latter, he says, play by different rules.

The general picture this characterization presents of two groups of thinkers is largely accurate. Psychodynamic thinkers often do take as evidence for a particular formulation or general concept data that most behavior therapists do not find persuasive. As some analysts are beginning to articulate (e.g., Schafer, 1976), psychoanalysis is based on a methodology and epistemology that is more akin to that of history or literary studies than it is to that of the natural sciences. It seeks to explain by offering formulations that account for coherences in a diverse range of phenomena. It seeks also to show how the pictures offered by dreams, by slips of the tongue, by omissions and failures of memory, and by various otherwise puzzling behavioral patterns all converge—that is, to articulate unities behind the manifest diversity. The explanation is, to a large degree, one that *makes sense* out of the flux of events and that gives order and coherence.

[1]Indeed, one can argue that even where a strong concern with the past does characterize a particular psychodynamic thinker's approach, that does not preclude the use of behavioral measures. It is only where a strong stance of nonintervention is taken in order to permit the transference to emerge or unfold that a concern with the past is problematic for the purposes of integration (Wachtel, 1977b, 1982b).

It is a latticework of evidence in which each strand supports the others and in which each piece of evidence *becomes* evidence only in the context of the other pieces.

The dream, for example, that gives weight to an interpretation that an overly solicitous son in fact harbors warded-off hostile feelings toward his mother might *not* be evidence for such a view if the other data (slips, "inadvertent" behavior patterns, particular trends in the sequence of associations, etc.) did not also point that way. Indeed, in another context, the same dream might be usable as evidence for a *different* line of interpretation. And the same holds, by and large, for *each* piece of evidence. To a very great degree, pieces of evidence gain meaning and evidential gravity *from each other.*

This does not mean that evidence is used arbitrarily, that you can use anything to prove anything. Unfortunately, there are more dynamically oriented clinicians than one would wish who do make of their formulations a procrustean bed in which any potentially disturbing observations are put to rest; and it is probably also true that the mode of evaluating evidence in psychodynamic work makes it easier to "cheat" or to fool oneself that one has proven what one has not than is the case for behavior therapists.[2] But there is a discipline available that helps to minimize such occurrences if it is properly used. There *are* pieces that do not fit, that serve a cautionary or disconfirming function. When the paradigm is properly applied, such new observations can—in the fashion suggested before—lend a different cast to all the data previously seen as supportive of one's first formulation and force a new formulation that provides a coherent picture of this newer, larger body of data.

Thus the "good" psychoanalyst discards prior hypotheses just as the experimenter does when new results require it. And among the followers of both methodological paradigms, there are those whose ideas show a remarkable immunity to new observations, and there are those who actually learn from what they do. But if one can make a case that the methodologies and epistemologies are equally defensible, they are nonetheless different. Indeed, I have at times been astounded at how refractory some behavior therapists can be to what I regard as solidly convincing configurational evidence.

There is thus something useful in Franks and Wilson's distinction between the methodological or epistemological orientation of psychoanalysts and behavior therapists. If you define the essence of the psychodynamic and behavioral approaches as they do, the case for integration does look shaky.

Even here, it should be noted, their distinction refers to something statistical rather than essential. That is, although it is true that *most* psychoanalytic thinkers have a different orientation to evidence than do *most* behavior therapists, there is at least a small minority in each group whose canons of evidence overlap considerably. There are, for example, a number of psychoanalysts who have felt a need to establish psychoanalytic concepts by experimental evidence as well as by the more common configurational kind of evidence (see, for example, Shevrin & Dickman, 1980; Silverman, 1976; Wolitzky & Wachtel, 1973). And, I suggest, in clinical practice many behavior therapists show at least some inclination to think configurationally rather than requiring anything like experimental confirmation before they regard a hypothesis as confirmed. (They are much more likely to require such confirmation with regard to general *principles,* but as I have noted elsewhere [Wachtel, 1982c], the relation between those general principles and their actual clinical functioning is far looser than is usually suggested.)

Now, of course, one could say that to the degree that they deviate from experimental canons of evidence they are not really behavior therapists. But this is winning the anti-integration

[2]It really does not take all that much ingenuity—or wrongheadedness—to cheat within the behavioral paradigm either. Behavior therapy, too, has begun to develop divergent schools with mutual bitterness and accusations of highly selective renderings and interpretations of data.

argument by tautology. Or perhaps it would be fairer to say that Franks and Wilson argue against a different kind of integration than what I have advocated. Methodological or epistemological integration—that is, integration of ideas about evidence—may or may not be possible, but it is at the least very difficult. Certainly it is far more difficult than the kind of integration I have advocated.

Franks and Wilson suggest that at times it may be useful to attempt an integration at the level of clinical practice but not at a "conceptual" level. Even here they are rather skeptical and refer to this possibility as "technical opportunism," a term that could conceivably be defended as merely descriptive but whose connotation is hard to ignore. It is certainly true that there is yet scant evidence that an integration at the level of clinical practice will yield superior results. Though my own guess is obviously different, I regard as perfectly reasonable Franks and Wilson's hunch that in the long run advancement in clinical practice is more likely to follow from pursuing one of the presently established systems than from attempting an integration of techniques. But when they contrast their preferred scenario with "an indiscriminate deployment of what seems to work," I hope it is clear to the reader—and to them—that they are no longer referring to the kind of effort I have advocated.

My aim is not simply the practical application of a combination of clinical procedures, but rather to work toward a thorough conceptual integration. The particular way of proceeding clinically that I have developed out of my integrative efforts seems to me useful for now, but I am sure it will change. What seems more likely to be of enduring value is the construction of a frame of reference in which the ideas and the observations emanating from both[3] broad approaches can find a coherent place and in which the discoveries of each can push the other to expand. That frame of reference too is not a final or finished product; it continues and *must* continue to change and evolve in order to accommodate further observations and ideas. But, in my view, it is the development of a coherent way of thinking about clinical problems, a way open to input from a variety of sources, that will enable really effective clinical work at the practical level to proceed most expeditiously.

The development of a conceptual integration is, I think, usefully distinguished from a methodological or epistemological integration. Franks and Wilson conflate these two levels in arguing that a "conceptual" integration is impossible. They are quite right that "one's belief system" is hard to integrate with another that feels alien. Psychoanalysts and behavior therapists—to the degree that separate schools persist in coming years—will continue to hold different ideas about what constitutes "proof," as they will continue (at least as distinguishable statistical aggregates) to evidence different "visions" of life (see Messer & Winokur, 1980 . . .). But an integration at the conceptual—rather than the ideological or epistemological—level remains a useful and achievable goal. I will have more to say shortly about what such an integration is like, but first I would like return to its constituents. I have said something about what I think are *not* the essential defining features of a psychodynamic or behavioral view and about what I think are misleading or irrelevant differences for present purposes. Let me now indicate, at least briefly, what I do take to be the most significant characteristics of each approach.

THE PSYCHODYNAMIC POINT OF VIEW

I have argued that a number of characteristics commonly claimed to be essential to the psychodynamic point of view are not really essential after all. The "medical model," the emphasis on the past, and (to a lesser degree) a particular epistemological orientation are, I suggest,

[3]Although the integration of psychodynamic and behavioral approaches in particular is both the focus of this chapter and the starting point of my integrative efforts, other perspectives, such as that of family therapists, of Piaget, or of gestalt therapists have also begun to be included in the integrative effort under discussion here and will probably continue to be to an increasing degree. (See, for example, Wachtel, 1981a.)

misleading or unnecessarily constraining as defining properties of psychodynamic thought. To this negative list I would add such other candidates as the libido theory, Freud's mental geography, the requirement of neutrality or nonintervention by the therapist, and the insistence on insight as the primary source of psychological change (cf. Wachtel, 1977b, 1982c). Have I then succeeded in draining the term "psychodynamic" of all meaning and left just a hollow shell with no substance? I believe not. There remain a number of crucially important characteristics shared by all psychodynamic thinkers that clearly distinguish them from those in the behavioral tradition and represent, in my view, the most significant legacy of Freud's pioneering efforts.

Clearly, the single most essential defining property is a concern with unconscious processes. If anything is a sine qua non of the psychodynamic point of view, that is it. What Freud illuminated, more than anything else, was the degree to which we do not really know ourselves. Further, he points us to inquire into the *motives* for our self-deceptions and into their consequences: Our lack of awareness is not merely a failure to notice or to register. We *try* not to notice, and we *dare* not notice.[4] And, unfortunately, the immediate comfort this turning away brings us quite frequently has as its heir a disruption of our lives that is far out of proportion to the initial gain. The price of comfort is very high.

A second critical feature of the psychodynamic point of view is a focus upon *conflict.* What we want, it turns out, is not as simple as we would wish. In the prism of psychoanalysis our unitary actions or expressions of desire are resolved into components that, alone, would lead us in rather differing directions. Conceptions of conflict pervade the psychodynamic approach to motivation and, implicitly, suggest a quite different way of understanding what happens when a behavior therapist attempts to use reinforcements (Wachtel, 1977b, Chapter 11; 1982b). The psychodynamic conception of conflict is closely related to the concern with what is dynamically unconscious as well as to an increasing emphasis on the role of anxiety (Freud, 1926b/1959; Dollard & Miller, 1950). It need not, however, imply a strictly intrapsychic view of how conflict is generated or maintained (Wachtel, 1977b, 1982b).

A related feature of most psychodynamically oriented clinical work (though not as crucially defining a feature) is a concern with the *compromises* that conflict, anxiety, and self-deception lead to. From a psychodynamic perspective, even patterns of behavior or aspirations and guiding assumptions with which the person seems comfortable are likely to be called into question. This can at times be overdone, as behavior therapists have appropriately pointed out; the patient has a right to keep his goals and focus narrow, and some version of informed consent seems called for if the person's comfortable assumptions are to be systematically challenged. But if the analyst is attentive to the ethical complexities, this broader and deeper inquiry is one of the most valuable characteristics of the psychodynamic approach. Ignoring what the person is explicitly telling you is deplorable. But refusing to hear what cannot yet be put into words is unfortunate as well.

The psychodynamic perspective points not only to unconscious motives and to motivational conflict but to *unusual* and *non-normative* motives as well. Freud's researches have alerted us to the importance and the prevalence of wishes that differ substantially from what would conventionally be expected. Viewed psychodynamically, what people actually seek—as opposed to what they *say* they are seeking—can be rather surprising. Behavior therapists, in contrast, tend to assume that what people want is what they say they want and/or what is normatively expectable (Wachtel, 1977b).

Finally, a crucial feature of the psychodynamic approach is the rules of inference whereby such nonobvious, non-normative motives can be identified. It is these rules that make claims

[4]Sometimes, of course, simple failures to notice do occur. Freud distinguished between the dynamic and the descriptive unconscious. It is the former that plays such a key role in psychological difficulties and that Freud dedicated himself to illuminating.

regarding such motives not simply arbitrary assertions. Unfortunately, many of these rules have been passed along primarily by an oral tradition, and there is little good, explicit written material on the rules themselves. This has made it easy for opponents of psychoanalysis to view psychoanalytic claims about unconscious motives and thoughts as being essentially arbitrary. I have already indicated briefly some of the reasons why I think these inferences are *not* arbitrary. I hope before too long to complete a paper which examines this matter in more detail. For now, I simply wish to indicate that I regard such rules as essential contributions from the psychodynamic end to the synthesis under discussion in this chapter.

The reader will notice that such bellwether concepts as "transference" and "resistance"—the ideas Freud first designated as the essential defining characteristics of psychoanalysis—do not appear in the preceding list. Unlike "libido" or "neutrality," this is not because I think them faulty or inessential. In the case of resistance, it is merely that it is already subsumed under what has been outlined sketchily. Resistance is simply the manifestation in the therapy session of the conflict and motivated self-deception referred to previously (Wachtel, 1982b). The concept of transference—or at least the phenomena and concerns to which it refers—is certainly essential to address if one hopes to depict the psychodynamic point of view accurately. The term has, however, accumulated so much excess freight over the years and is so closely related to notions I do want to question, such as neutrality and nonintervention, that it cannot simply be listed without elaborate discussion. I have spelled out elsewhere alternative ways of understanding transference phenomena and how transference can be conceived so as to lend itself to the kind of integrative effort being discussed here (Wachtel, 1981a, 1982b).

THE BEHAVIORAL APPROACH

Indicating what I take to be the essential features of a behavioral approach is in some ways a more difficult task. As Franks and Wilson indicate, "there is much less of an abiding core to which all behavior therapists would subscribe." For present purposes, though, what is most important is to indicate those features of the behavioral approach that are central in the effort to achieve a psychodynamic and behavioral integration.

Perhaps most important in this regard is the emphasis on *active intervention.* Behavior therapists employ a wide variety of techniques to intervene in and alter maladaptive patterns of behavior. In their own way, so do analysts—both more and less than they think. They do more, in the sense that neutrality is a myth and influence is exerted in every choice to interpret, to remain silent, or to say, "Why do you ask?" They do less, in the sense that the clinical procedures of psychoanalysis are not nearly as powerful as one might hope and that they could be notably enhanced by the use of the intervention techniques developed by behavior therapists.

In psychoanalysis and in most psychodynamic therapy, the inquiry into the patient's difficulties and the intervention techniques are essentially the same. Understanding *is* the therapy. In behavior therapy, the understanding that is attained—by both patient and therapist—is *applied.* Explicit methods are utilized to assure that the patient garners the experiences that will enable him or her to change. These methods can also be used, I have argued, to make it more likely that the insights attained from a psychodynamic point of view in fact lead to the changes the patient is seeking (Wachtel, 1975, 1977b).[5]

[5]One can, of course, define psychodynamic therapy so as to include as an essential feature the presently common one of the therapist's striving for neutrality and/or an exclusively interpretive approach. To do so would, of course, make the use of active interventions incompatible with anything psychodynamic. Clearly, that is not the notion of psychodynamic therapy under discussion here. I regard the prevalent emphasis on neutrality as unfortunate and in no way required by the logic of the psychodynamic point of view per se (Wachtel, 1977b, 1982b).

A second feature of behavior therapy that is important in the present context is its concern with the environmental context of behavior, with relating the patient's behavior and experience to what is going on around him or her. Again, this is not something unique to behavior therapy. Even some versions of psychodynamic thought do this to a substantial degree (Wachtel, 1973), though usually not as thoroughly as behavior therapy. Family therapists, of course, are particularly concerned with relating behavior to context and have made valuable contributions in this regard that the present approach is still working to assimilate.

A third relevant feature is the emphasis by behavior therapists on an explicit contract between patient and therapist and a corresponding concern with specific target complaints. This leads, in conjunction with the emphasis on relating patients' difficulties to environmental events, to a kind of inquiry that has considerable merit both on ethical grounds and on practical ones. As discussed before, the articulation of a more explicit contract between patient and therapist need not exclude a concern with conflict or with examining the compromises and self-deceptions in the patient's life. But it does permit the patient to be a partner more fully in the therapeutic effort.

It is a common psychodynamic stereotype of behavior therapy that behavior therapists are authoritarian and manipulative and that they *work upon* the patient. Actually, in many respects the behavior therapist is *less* guilty of such an orientation. The emphasis by many dynamic therapists on therapeutic anonymity, the frequency with which questions are not explicitly answered, and other related features of most psychodynamic approaches contribute to an atmosphere in which the patient is in a childlike, one-down position. Behavior therapists, by and large, rather than dynamic therapists, are the ones who share explicitly with the patient what the rationale is for each thing that is being done and who concern themselves most explicitly with whether the work is moving in a direction that is consonant with the patient's own aims. Once anonymity and the idea that the transference should "emerge" or "unfold" without interference from the therapist are excluded as defining features of a psychodynamic approach (Wachtel, 1982b), it becomes possible to be similarly collaborative with the patient while maintaining a recognition of the important role of unconscious processes and motivational conflict.

As I noted earlier, I think it is misleading to identify a greater concern for evidence as an essential defining feature of behavior therapy, though I would agree that, as a group, behavior therapists are probably more alert to the need for, and pitfalls in gathering, such evidence. The characteristics of behavior therapy just noted, however—the effort to specify very clearly and precisely what changes the patient wants to achieve, and the effort to relate particular patterns of behavior to particular environmental contexts—do facilitate the evaluation of therapeutic efficacy. The effort to discuss patients' difficulties and the goals of the work in terms at least potentially amenable to evaluation—although sometimes leading to excessive narrowness or unwillingness to address what cannot be immediately measured—is a valuable feature of the behavioral approach that is capable of being incorporated into an integrated model. The goals of psychodynamic therapy are often discussed in such terms as "autonomy," "structural change," or "resolution" of conflicts or of the transference—notions that are notoriously hard to evaluate.

MESSER AND WINOKUR'S OBJECTIONS

The most interesting and sophisticated objection that has yet been made to the integration of psychodynamic and behavioral approaches has been offered by Messer and Winokur (1980). I believe that their objection can be effectively answered and that it really reflects a *comparative* orientation to psychodynamic and behavioral therapies, rather than one that fully takes into account the selective and emergent properties of a true integration. That is, they look at similarities and (especially) differences between psychodynamic and behavioral approaches, but do not as explicitly address how an integration—as a new, third orientation—might yield conceptions that reconcile those differences that presently exist. Nonetheless, their argument is an important one that must be addressed by any proponent of integration.

Messer and Winokur attempt to show that the values and the grounding vision that characterize psychoanalysts and behavior therapists are basically different. Even between the most ego- and reality-oriented analysts and the most cognitive or broad-spectrum behavior therapists, there is, they suggest, a "nagging breach" that is based on different conceptions of what is important in human life and what is possible. They pursue their comparative analysis by considering how an analytically and a behaviorally oriented therapist would pursue the same case as well as by a more general consideration of the basic orientation of each approach. Their descriptions seem to me, for the most part, to be fair-minded and accurate, and they do reveal some very significant differences. In some respects I have sensed similar differences myself in my own interactions with proponents of these two broad schools of thought. There are, however, a few points at which I would question their characterization, and I would like to address these before going on to consider my main objection to their line of argument—that differences *between* approaches do not necessarily preclude an integration *of* them.

In depicting the difference between the psychoanalytic and the behavioral vision, Messer and Winokur rely on a paper by Schafer (1976) that uses Northrup Frye's categories of mythic forms (Frye, 1957). Schafer argues that psychoanalysis can be seen as being characterized by four complementary visions of reality—the romantic, the ironic, the tragic, and the comic—and he elaborates the nature of each. This mode of characterization is useful in conveying various aspects of the psychoanalytic world view per se. But when it is employed by Messer and Winokur in an effort to compare the psychoanalytic vision with that of the behavior therapist, it is far less satisfactory. For *this* purpose, this set of categories has some insurmountable problems.

To begin with, the choices offered by this particular fourfold scheme lead to the vision of the behavior therapist being characterized as "comic." Messer and Winokur state explicitly that in this context the term is not meant to connote "funny," "in a light vein," or "not serious." But surely, as analysts they must recognize that connotations are not so easily dispelled. Whatever verbal disavowal may be offered, to characterize an entire approach to human problems simply as comic cannot fail to detract from any sense that that approach has something profound or serious to offer. Yes, Shakespeare's comedies can indeed be viewed as both profound *and* serious, but what Shakespearean scholar, writing commentaries on those plays, would be pleased at having his or her *own* work described simply as comic?

Moreover, even Messer and Winokur's explicit definition of "comic," meant to dispel the aforementioned connotation, is really a loaded one. In the comic vision, they say, conflict "can be eliminated by effective manipulative action or via the power of positive thinking." Why do they speak of effective *manipulative* action? Why do they not say effective action only? This is a small point perhaps but is not the word "manipulative" here both unnecessary and possessed of a possibly negative connotation? Similarly, "the power of positive thinking" is, after all, the title of a book that is not a scholarly work but a bit of pop preachiness for the *Reader's Digest* set—and, moreover, it is a book written by one of the favorite preachers of our most disgraced president, the man who presided over the wedding of Julie Nixon. In a paragraph devoted to dispelling the idea that comic implies a lack of seriousness or profundity, was there not a phrase with more scholarly associations that could have conveyed the same idea?

Further, Messer and Winokur go on to say about the comic vision that "endings are happy ones free from guilt and anxiety." This may be a more or less accurate picture of the structure of dramatic comedy. But does not the term "happy endings" nonetheless evoke the superficiality of

Hollywood at its worst, where even films not intended as comedies have foolish, hard-to-take-seriously happy endings? And does this really—as it seems to by the associative link they develop—characterize not just the comic vision but the world view of behavior therapists as well? By and large, behavior therapists do seem to be more optimistic in their outlook. They are less certain that tragedy and the involution of desire must haunt our days. But do they really expect simply happy endings, and do they really claim that after therapy patients are completely free from guilt and anxiety?

Finally, we come to a more subtle bias that is introduced as a consequence of the scheme Messer and Winokur use to analyze the competing visions. As an artifact of how they choose to slice the pie, it appears that psychoanalysis has *four* separate visions, whereas behavior therapy has but one. That alone, it seems, would make psychoanalysis far more comprehensive. Behavior therapy, with its single vision, seems superficial just by virtue of that. Of course, a vision of reality is not a "thing." It makes no sense to count visions or add them up. Yet, there is something initially compelling about seeing that the vision that guides behavior therapy is but one of the four visions guiding psychoanalysis.[6]

The problem, of course, lies in the terms in which the comparison is framed. The psychoanalytic world view is neatly dissected by this scheme, and the multiplicity of its perspectives is revealed. But the various facets of the behavioral vision are not similarly captured by this particular way of slicing things, so it is left with just "one" vision. In fact, the comic view of behavior therapists is a quite different one from the comic view of the analyst. Whereas for analysts this concept of Frye's intersects with but a small portion of their total world view, it is forced, within the constraints of this scheme, to cover the totality of the behavior therapist's vision. The behavior therapist's comic vision, however—being coterminous with the behavior therapist's vision per se—is (not surprisingly therefore) more complex. There is a sense, in fact, in which it can be said to be the container for the behavior therapist's sense of tragedy, of irony, and of romance. His or her vision is not totally devoid of these elements. Rather, they are organized differently; they are subsumed under a general orientation toward meliorating suffering rather than enduring it and under a basically optimistic (but not necessarily Pollyannaish) view of human possibilities.

Consider, for example, Messer and Winokur's discussion in their paper of the psychodynamic approach to a hypothetical patient, Mrs. J.

> When the dynamic therapist allows Mrs. J. to experience grief, mourn her losses, see the death of her father and loss of her husband in their tragic grimness, the thrust is to help her change by facing the loss, reexperiencing it and working it through, with all the pain involved. Only rarely, the dynamic therapist would say, does growth in therapy, as in childhood, take place without some suffering. In all this, the tragic element in life is recognized. (p. 824)

This certainly is a different picture than one would expect from a behavior therapist. Yet the gulf is not as thoroughly unbridgeable as it first might seem. After all, it is the essence of many behavioral measures to enable the patient to expose himself or herself to the experiences and situations he or she has previously avoided. Often, as in systematic desensitization, the attempt is made to minimize the pain, but some pain is almost inevitable and in certain techniques, such as flooding, things are arranged so that the pain is considerable. Behavior therapy is not predicated on avoidance of the painful but on confrontation and mastery.

[6]I do not mean to imply here that Messer and Winokur themselves count visions and argue on that basis. They do not. Rather, the point is that the scheme they use is likely to lead the *reader* to be struck by the seeming fact that the behavior therapist's vision is but one of the four visions of the analyst and to be led, perhaps without even recognizing it, to perceive behavior therapy in a way that introduces a negative bias.

WHAT IS AN INTEGRATION?

My point is not to deny the differences between the psychoanalytic and behavioral visions; the differences are real and in some ways substantial. My preceding objections notwithstanding, I regard Messer and Winokur's characterizations as largely accurate and in essence to be fair-minded. I do not think that the instances of bias I have pointed out were conscious efforts to mislead. They reflect, rather, an almost inevitable influence on our language of the passionate convictions that sustain any good work. I discussed them both to attempt a corrective and to indicate that the gap is not thoroughly beyond the reach of any conceivable effort at bridge building. At this point, however, I wish to approach the issue from a different angle. Let me alert the reader to the fact that it is in the following paragraphs that the most important part of my argument can be found.

Arguments showing that psychoanalysis and behavior therapy are *different* do not really bear on the question of whether they can be integrated. Indeed, were they not rather different, there would be little point in an integration. It is the very fact that each stresses certain things that the other does not that makes an integration more useful than either separately. And, of course, it is their differences that make an effort at integration interesting and challenging. It is no feat to put together what seems compatible and alike to everyone.

As I conceive it, an integration is not just a hodgepodge of eclecticism, a salad with a little of this and a little of that tossed in. The goal, rather, is the development of a new coherent structure, an internally consistent approach both to technical intervention and to the construction of theory. An integrative or synthetic effort is built on both an admiring and a critical attitude toward each separate approach. It is admiring in the sense that each has something useful and important to contribute, and it is critical in the sense that each is seen as *omitting* something useful and important (for the most part, something that is part of what is valuable about the other approach).

Messer and Winokur (1980), for example, capture well some of what I find valuable in psychoanalysis and somewhat missing in behavior therapy. They indicate, for example, that they could not approve of any approach that "denies complexity, ambiguity, and the ubiquity of conflict in human affairs" (p. 825). Neither could I.[7]

But I have come to feel that an approach that fails to appreciate the enormous significance of present contextual cues and contingencies, that fails to consider the therapist's responsibility to help the patient systematically to apply the lessons learned in the sessions to his or her daily life, that underestimates the factors that make it difficult for the patient to make that application spontaneously, or that has a deep-rooted bias against active intervention by the therapist is also unacceptable. As things stand now, we have the choice of embracing one set of follies (and of course strengths) or the other. The aim of an integration is to build upon the strengths of each without the limiting blinders. This can seem a grandiose aim (and in Messer and Winokur's terms it is comic—an effort to transcend the limitations, to take only the good). But one need not feel that the millennium is around the corner to strive for something better than we have or to expect some tangible gain from an integrative effort.

It is important to be clear that one can value the unique contributions of each approach without endorsing each and every feature of either. As a proponent of integration, I am frequently in the position of trying to persuade my behavioral colleagues of the virtues of a psychodynamic

[7]I wish to make it clear that I do not endorse the implicit message that behavior therapists deny all complexity and ambiguity. Messer and Winokur's specific way of stating their point here seems to me a bit unfair. But I do agree that there are complexities to which behavior therapists give *insufficient* attention, and my own inclinations are closer to those of Messer and Winokur. With regard to conflict in particular, a more categorical criticism of most behavior therapists does seem in order (cf. Wachtel, 1977b).

point of view, and vice versa. In this task I am at times embarrassed by things that are written by representatives of one or the other school. But that embarrassment stems from tactical rather than logical considerations. That is, it stems from a recognition that foolish excesses from either side make it harder to get people from the other side to see or hear what really is useful, and thus they play into an attitude of "See, I told you that stuff is worthless." But these embarrassing impediments to the *practical* task of persuading people on either side of the great divide are not necessarily impediments to the *theoretical* task of devising a new synthesis that incorporates the best of both. I agree with my psychoanalytic colleagues about many of the things they find objectionable in behavior therapy, and vice versa with regard to my behavioral colleagues. My charge as an integrationist is not to defend everything that analysts or behavior therapists say or do, but rather to show that each side contributes *something* useful that the other omits or plays down and to show how these *selected* features can be put together in a logically coherent fashion.

The total package that presently constitutes behavior therapy is indeed incompatible with the total package that is called psychoanalysis. One cannot be a psychoanalyst *and* a behavior therapist—at least not simultaneously. Messer and Winokur have helped to clarify further the nature of the differences. But one can take *elements* of each and combine them into a new synthesis that is still a *third* package, as it were.

The fallacy in most arguments against integration is a failure to appreciate that a synthesis is a different entity than either of its constituents. It is a clinical and theoretical approach with its own structure. It can be selective in what aspects of each approach it incorporates, drawing upon what seems potentially useful in constructing a new synergistic strategy, rather than upon what proponents of each as *separate* therapies regard as most important. The major constraint is that the elements must not be incompatible in the context of the new structure.[8]

Messer and Winokur state that behavior therapists are primarily interested in the external reality of their patients' lives and that psychoanalytic therapists are primarily interested in (conscious and unconscious) subjectivity. Representatives of each school might object to this, pointing to ways in which they do manifest the opposite perspective. But, as a broad characterization of emphasis, it is probably accurate. In the integrative approach discussed here, *both* perspectives are given substantial weight. This occurs not by striving for a balance by doing a little of this, a little of that—a kind of one-perspective-one-vote rule—but through the utilization of a conceptual structure that unites the two perspectives and reconciles their differences. That conceptual structure, for me, has centered on an effort to describe people's difficulties in terms of vicious circles, in which neither impulse nor defense and neither internal state nor external situation is primary; they are continually determining each other in a series of repeated transactions. I have described that conceptual structure as one of "cyclical psychodynamics" (Wachtel, 1982b, 1985) and have tried to show how it makes possible the reconciliation of what seem like opposing viewpoints (see also Wachtel, 1973b, 1977a, 1977b).

When the sharp dichotomy between "inner" and "outer" is challenged, one can see how even the deepest levels of subjectivity reflect, frequently in a symbolic way, the person's life situation. Thus, one patient began to dream of melting into his girlfriend and of being swallowed by her. Such fears and experiences of merger and boundary dissolution are frequently described by analysts as "deep" or "early" and are attributed to the intrapsychic residue of early experiences with mothering. The experiences the patient reported, however, could also be understood as symbolizing his present way of life: He was very inhibited and unassertive and felt unable to say

[8]What makes the approach described in this chapter an integration rather than a third approach is, first of all, the fact that its elements come primarily from the approaches being integrated rather than being original to it; what is unique is how they are put together. Secondly, this approach, rather than being a new "school," is founded on the conviction that schools have become more limiting than facilitating at this point. Finally, this approach is based upon respect for the earlier approaches rather than opposition to them.

no to his girlfriend or to spend any evenings alone or with friends if she wanted to see him. As he became more able to do so, he felt less swallowed up by her, and his sense of ego boundaries became firmer. Regardless of the origins of the experience he reported, it was not a purely intrapsychic event but a function as well of manifest events in his daily life.

At the same time, the situations one finds oneself in can often be understood not as thoroughly external events but as products of one's subjective particularities. That is, the events do not simply "happen" to us but are a predictable consequence of our internal state and the behavior it leads to. The stark impassiveness of a dominating husband, for example, both contributes to the wife's fear of assertiveness and stems from it. One woman I worked with was stunned to discover how much of a "pushover" her husband was once she started asserting herself. As she spontaneously put it, "I thought he was the situation I faced, but he was the situation I *made*."

Recently, the social learning formulations that have provided the theoretical background for much of the work in behavior therapy have stressed similar circular causal chains under the rubric of "reciprocal determinism" (Bandura, 1978). This seems to reflect an incorporation of earlier criticisms of social learning theory (Wachtel, 1973) and of earlier formulations of "social behaviorism," which Staats has argued—in a paper with extraordinary claims and an even more extraordinary history—have systematically preceded similar, more frequently cited formulations by Bandura (Staats, 1983).

Messer and Winokur note that "where the behavioral approach, consonant with the comic view, leads to action, the psychoanalytic approach, following the tragic view, leads to reflection and inquiry." For an integrative approach, *both* action and reflection are central. Messer and Winokur suggest this combination may be difficult to effect because of "the radical shift in perspective and vision involved" (1980). I would agree: It *is* difficult. My own efforts thus far, though encouraging, still remain far from the fully integrated ideal toward which I strive. But the difficulty is not so much the seemingly intractable one of irreconcilable visions as it is a practical one of finding just what is the best way to proceed (a difficult, painstaking task, but one that it is reasonable to expect might yield to continued effort). After all, by Messer and Winokur's own account, psychoanalysis has managed to contain and integrate four rather different visions of reality. As a synthesis of several visions, psychoanalysis is itself evidence that a powerful overarching vision can reconcile polarities among its constituent elements.

The challenge is to achieve a new sustaining vision of sufficient breadth and power. That task has only begun. I am optimistic about the possibilities of a synthesis rooted in the study of vicious circles, of how defensive efforts contribute to the very wishes and feelings they defend against, of how significant people in the present serve as "accomplices" in maintaining neurotic patterns, of how recognition of this can enable a conception of skewing of development to replace earlier notions of fixation and developmental arrest, of how such a perspective permits a transcendence of the dichotomy between an inner world and outer reality, of how conceptions of transference are altered by the application of Piagetian notions of "schema," "assimilation," and "accommodation," and finally, of how all of these conceptual modifications point to a greater variety of ways to intervene in the processes that produce neurotic misery.

The references cited in this chapter point to some of my own efforts in this direction. These efforts have been preceded and paralleled (and greatly aided) by important work on the part of a relative handful of innovative theorists and clinicians (see Goldfried & Padawer [1982] for a good review of this body of work). There are indications now of interest in the possibilities of integration on the part of a larger number of people. This greatly increases the likelihood of significant advances. The challenge will soon have to be faced of how to coordinate and bring together these various efforts. Working between rather than within established traditions is difficult, personally as well as intellectually. A support group that provided workers on the interface with a shared identity would be very useful. Both a journal and an organization could help to give this work a home, to attract young researchers and clinicians to this effort, and to enable a wider audience to become aware of the work and of new developments in it. But there are dangers as well. It would be unfortunate if integrative psychotherapy were to become a new "school," with gradually encrusting borders. Its strength lies precisely in its continued openness to the work of others. Devising the proper organizational framework to represent such a multifaceted and open-ended effort may be as important a challenge as is the development of the ideas and techniques themselves.[9]

REFERENCES

Bandura, A. (1978). On paradigms and recycled ideologies: Analogue research revisited. *Cognitive Therapy and Research, 2,* 79–104.

Franks, C.M. (1978). On the importance of conceptual integrity and its mutual advantages to two fundamentally incompatible systems. Paper read at the annual meeting of the Association for Advancement of Behavior Therapy. Chicago.

Franks, C.M. & Wilson, G.G. (1979). Behavior therapy: An overview. In C.M. Franks and G.T. Wilson (Eds.), *Annual review of behavior therapy.* New York: Brunner/Mazel.

Freud, S. (1957). *On the history of the psycho-analytic movement. In Standard Edition* (Vol. 14). London: Hogarth Press, p. 298. (Originally published, 1914.).

Freud, S. (1959). *Two encyclopedia articles.* In *Standard Edition* (Vol. 18). London: Hogarth Press, p. 247. (Originally published, 1923.).

Freud, S. (1959). (d) The question of lay analysis. In *Standard Edition* (Vol. 20). London: Hogarth Press. (Originally published 1926a.)

Frye, N. (1957). *Anatomy of criticism.* New York: Athaneum.

Goldfried, M.R., & Pawader, W. (1982). Current status and future directions in psychology. In M.R. Goldfried (Ed.), *Converging themes in psychotherapy.* New York: Springer.

Horney, K. (1939). *New ways in psychoanalysis.* New York: Norton.

Kohut, H. (1977). *The restoration of the self.* New York: International Universities Press.

Messer, S., & Winokur, M. (1980). Some limits to the integration of psychoanalytic and behavior therapy. *American Psychologist, 35,* 818–827.

Schafer, R. (1976). *A new language for psychoanalysis.* New Haven, CT: Yale University Press.

Shevrin, H., & Dickman, S. (1980). The psychological unconscious: A necessary assumption for all psychological therapy: *American Psychologist, 35,* 421–435.

Silverman, L.H. (1976). Psychoanalytic theory: "The reports of my death are greatly exaggerated." *American Psychologist, 31,* 621–637.

Staats, A.W. (1983). Science standards or separatism? Questions on the conduct of psychology. Unpublished manuscript, University of Hawaii.

Wachtel, P.L. (1973a). On fact, hunch, and stereotype: A reply to Mische. *Journal of Abnormal Psychology, 82,* 537–540.

Wachtel, P.L. (1973b). Psychodynamics, behavior therapy, and the implacable experimenter: An inquiry into the consistency of personality. *Journal of Abnormal Psychology, 82,* 324–334.ls

Wachtel, P.L. (1975). Behavior therapy and the facilitation of psychoanalytic exploration. *Psychotherapy: Theory, Research and Practice, 12,* 68–72.

[9]Shortly after the completion of this chapter, the Society for the Exploration of Psychotherapy Integration (SEPI) was founded.

Wachtel, P.L. (1977a). Interaction cycles, unconscious processes, and the person-situation issue. In D. Magnusson & N. Endler (Eds.), *Personality at the crossroads; Current issues in interactional psychology.* Hillsdale, NJ: Erlbaum.

Wachtel, P.L. (1977b). *Psychoanalysis and behavior therapy:* Toward an integration. New York: Basic Books.

Wachtel, P.L. (1981a). Transference, schema, and assimilation: The relevance of Piaget to the psychoanalytic theory of transference. *The Annual of Psychoanalysis, 8,* 59–76.

Wachtel, P.L. (1982a). Resistance and the process of therapeutic change. In P.L. Wachtel (Ed.), *Resistance: Psychodynamic and behavioral approaches.* New York: Plenum Press.

Wachtel, P.L. (1982b). Vicious circles: The self and the rhetoric of emerging and unfolding. *Contemporary Psychoanalysis, 18*(2), 259–293.

Wachtel, P.L. (1982c). What can dynamic therapies contribute to behavior therapy? *Behavior Therapy, 13,* 594–609.

Wachtel, P.L. (1985). Integrative psychodynamic therapy. In S. Lynn & J. Garske (Eds.), *Contemporary psychotherapies: Models and methods.* Columbus, OH: Charles E. Merrill.

Wolitzky, D.L. & Wachtel, P.L. (1973). Perception and personality. In B. Wolman (Ed.), *Handbook of general psychology.* Englewood Cliffs, NJ: Prentice-Hall.

RECOMMENDED READING

Arkowitz, H., & Messer, S. B. (1984. *Psychoanalytic therapy and behavior therapy: Is integration possible?* New York: Plenum Press.

Brenner, C. (1968). Psychoanalysis and science. *Journal of the American Psychoanalytic Association, 16,* 675–696.

Chessick, R. (1981). The relevance of Nietzsche to the study of Freud and Kohut. *Contemporary Psychoanalysis, 17,* 359–373.

Eagle, M. (1984). *Recent developments in psychoanalysis: A critical evaluation.* New York: McGraw-Hill.

Edelson, M. (1984). *Hypothesis and evidence in psychoanalysis.* Chicago: University of Chicago Press.

Erwin, E. (1981). The truth about psychoanalysis. *Journal of Philosophy, 78,* 549–560.

Farrell, B. A. (1981). *The standing of psychoanalysis.* London: Oxford University Press.

Grünbaum, A. (1984). *The foundations of psychoanalysis: A philosophical critique.* Berkeley: University of California Press.

Grünbaum, A. (1986). Is Freud's theory well founded? *Behavioral and Brain Sciences, 9,* 217–284. (Includes 39 reviews of Gruñbaum, 1984).

Grünbaum, A. (1992). *Validation in the clinical theory of psychoanalysis.* Madison, CT: International Universities Press.

Holt, R. (1985). The current status of psychoanalytic theory. *Psychoanalytic Psychology, 2,* 289–326.

Hook, S. (Ed.). (1959). *psychoanalysis, scientific method, and philosophy.* New York: New York University Press.

Holzman, P. S. (1985). Psychoanalysis: Is therapy destroying the science? *Journal of the American Psychoanalytic Association, 27,* 725–770.

Messer, S. B., Sass, L. A., & Woolfolk, R. L. (Eds.). (1988). *Hermeneutics and psychological theory: Interpretive perspectives on personality, psychotherapy, and psychopathology.* New Brunswick, NJ: Rutgers University Press.

Messer, S. B., & Winokur, M. (1981). What about the question of integration? A reply to Apfelbaum and to Ellis. *American Psychologist, 36,* 800–802.

Messer, S. B., & Winokur, M. (1986). Eclecticism and the shifting visions of reality in three systems of psychotherapy. *International Journal of Eclectic Psychotherapy, 5,* 115–124.

Protter, B. (1988). Ways of knowing in psychoanalysis: Some epistemic considerations for an autonomous theory of psychoanalytic praxis. *Contemporary Psychoanalysis, 24,* 498–526.

Ricoeur, P. (1970). *Freud and philosophy.* New Haven, CT: Yale University Press.

Schacht, T. (1984). The varieties of integrative experience. In H. Arkowitz & S. B. Messer (Eds.), *Psychoanalytic and behavior therapy: Is integration possible?* New York: Plenum Press.

Strupp, H. H. (1983). Are psychoanalytic therapists beginning to practice behavior therapy or is behavior therapy turning psychoanalytic? *British Journal of Cognitive Psychotherapy, 1,* 17–27.

Strupp, H. H., & Hadley, S. W. (1977). A tripartite model of mental health and therapeutic outcomes: With special reference to negative effects in psychotherapy. *American Psychologist, 32,* 187–196.

Wachtel, P. (1987). *Action and insight* (pp. 185–212). New York: Guilford Press.

Wallerstein, R. S. (1987). Psychoanalysis, psychoanalytic science, and psychoanalytic research—1986. *Journal of the American Psychoanalytic Association, 36,* 3–30.

Wollheim, R., & Hopkins, J. (1983). *Philosophical essays on Freud.* Cambridge, England: Cambridge University Press.

VI

PHILOSOPHICAL ISSUES OF THE FAMILY SYSTEMS APPROACH

INTRODUCTION: PHILOSOPHICAL PROBLEMS OF THE SYSTEMS APPROACH

RONALD B. MILLER

One finds adherents to a general systems theory approach to behavior in social psychology, social work, community psychology, social psychiatry, as well as among family therapists in clinical psychology. Its goals are not that different from the early Vienna Circle—to unify the sciences by showing their interactions and to find a common language or set of concepts to describe disparate phenomena. Using the concepts of system, information, feedback, homeostasis, and emphasizing observable measurable phenomena, systems theorists have tried to avoid what they see as both the imprecision of the humanistic and psychoanalytic approaches and the overly concrete and simplistic aspects of the biological and behavioral approaches. They reject the study of individual personality, psychopathology, and therapy, and argue for the understanding of interpersonal patterns of interaction that constitute a system that has its own properties and inertia (homeostasis). It is much more interested in what happens *between* people than it is in what happens *within* people. Family systems approaches assume that the system must be changed for the behavior of anyone in the system to change (Watzlawick, Bavelas, & Jackson, 1967). Of course, not all family therapy is based on the systems approach. Therapy sessions in which several members of the family are present may be conducted from any of the theoretical frameworks in clinical psychology, from the humanistic to the biological. The goals and techniques will, of course, vary greatly within the common condition of meeting with the (whole) family. The philosophical issues to be discussed in this section are restricted to those engendered by the systems approach to family therapy, or what has come to be called by some "strategic family therapy."

Gregory Bateson (1972) was the intellectual leader of this movement. An anthropologist by training, he saw anthropology as an extension of biology, and so the same with any phenomenon that he studied. He became interested in the culture of the mental hospital and with

Donald Jackson, Jay Haley, and Janet Weakland Bavelas developed the double-bind theory of schizophrenia (Bateson, Jackson, Haley, & Weakland, 1956). His work spawned a tremendous interest in the application of communications and cybernetic theory to clinical topics. Throughout his writings, he raises the question of epistemology and how this influences both the patient's and the clinician's views of clinical reality. Chapter 31 is typical of his work, weaving in and out of philosophy, systems theory, and clinical description. He rejects dualistic thinking on the mind–body question, insisting that the information theory supercedes this dichotomy. Although it is not dualistic, systems theory is clearly mechanistic. It assumes that very specific concrete explanatory principles will be found that render behavior completely predictable.

Information is what is real, and it is sometimes what psychologists have called mental and sometimes what they have called physical, but it is always information. In addition, Bateson questions the common distinction between ontology and epistemology because how people construe reality becomes their reality. What people believe to be true and what is true are identical for humans. Bateson believes that there are correct and incorrect ways of construing reality and that these incorrect methods lead to personal problems such as alcoholism or schizophrenia. Thus, epistemology is not only a basis for the discipline to define itself but also for each individual to define herself or himself.

The articles that follow are clearly reverent of Bateson's intellectual contribution as well as critical of key concepts within his work. In chapter 32, Held and Pols subject Bateson's use of the concept of epistemology to philosophical analysis and find it to be misleading. They observe that most readers respond to the ontological question of what is clinical reality (individuals or systems, linear or circular causality), which is generally regarded to be a metaphysical question. The truly epistemological question of what knowledge is, and how it is obtained, has received far less attention among the epistemologists of family systems theory. Bateson can collapse the two into one by putting forth a subjective view of knowledge and reality (what is real is what people construe to be real). However, he also claims that some constructions are right and others wrong. This appears to be a logical problem in that Bateson seems to be saying that reality is subjective, but his theory permits him to distinguish correct from incorrect views of that reality.

Gerald Erickson's critique is, on the other hand, from the hermeneutical perspective (see chapter 33). It addresses the moral implications of family systems theory and suggests that Bateson's view leads to an excessively conformist or authoritarian form of therapeutic intervention. The elimination of the self, and the blurring of the living and nonliving environment, is a source of great concern. Erikson believes that this approach does not sufficiently address the clinical problems of domestic violence, child abuse, and social inequality and that by avoiding assigning responsibility for these problems to individuals in the society, it is a conservative political ideology. He finds a social network approach to be more acceptable, as it acknowledges the importance of the social environment in the development of psychopathology while also emphasizing the historical and personal elements in America's current social problems. He believes that the moral consequences of the theory are more important than metaphysical speculation on the nature of ultimate reality.

Keeney and Sprenkle's article (see chapter 34) concerns another aspect of the objective versus subjective dimensions of systems theory. They note that the primary interpretation of Bateson has been along pragmatic, objectivist lines (Watzlawick et al., 1967) but that there is also an aesthetic interpretation of systems that is more phenomenological and existential in its holism. They contrast these two approaches to defining clinical problems and intervening in social systems and agree with both Rychlak's and Wachtel's suggestions that these opposing interpretations are complementary rather than competing. The aesthetic and the pragmatic are responses to different concerns and questions, not to the same question. It is a logical error that leads to theoretical conflict, not the incompatibility of the views themselves.

The systems approach allows for an environmentalist approach to clinical work without endorsing behavioral or cognitive–behavioral theory. Yet, its pragmatic wing shares with the cognitive–behavioral perspective an empirical approach to research and a mechanistic view of the goals of scientific theory. The philosophical agenda is quite similar to that of the cognitive–behavioral approach. By insisting that all members of a social group be defined as part of a problem, rather than just the weaker members, systems theory would at first seem to endorse a social justice agenda for psychology. Blaming the victim is less of an option. However, to the extent that it seeks a mechanistic explanation of human behavior, and a quantitative, empirical research methodology, it is likely to be identified with those who see their job as controlling other people. This tends to be a more conservative, repressive, moral, and political agenda. Again, there is a parallel with the moral position of the cognitive–behavioral approach. Natural science models developed in the context of a fact–value dichotomy are not likely to generate a moral agenda of their own and thus will remain parasitic on the independently developed moral values of the individual clinicians.

REFERENCES

Bateson, G. (1972). *Steps to an ecology of mind.* New York: Ballantine Books.

Bateson, G., Jackson, D., Haley, J., & Weakland, J. (1956). Toward a theory of schizophrenia. *Behavioral Science, 1,* 251–264.

Watzlawick, P., Bavelas, J., & Jackson, D. (1967). *Pragmatics of human communication.* New York: Norton.

31

THE CYBERNETICS OF "SELF": A THEORY OF ALCOHOLISM

GREGORY BATESON

The present essay is based upon ideas which are, perhaps all of them, familiar either to psychiatrists who have had dealings with alcoholics, or to philosophers who have thought about the implications of cybernetics and systems theory. The only novelty which can be claimed for the thesis here offered derives from treating these ideas seriously as premises of argument and from the bringing together of commonplace ideas from two too-separate fields of thought.

In its first conception, this essay was planned to be a systems-theoretic study of alcoholic addiction, in which I would use data from the publications of Alcoholics Anonymous, which has the only outstanding record of success in dealing with alcoholics. It soon became evident, however, that the religious views and the organizational structure of A.A. presented points of great interest to systems theory, and that the correct scope of my study should include not only the premises of alcoholism but also the premises of the A.A. system of treating it and the premises of A.A. organization.

My debt to A.A. will be evident throughout—also, I hope, my respect for that organization and especially for the extraordinary wisdom of its co-founders, Bill W. and Dr. Bob.

In addition, I have to acknowledge a debt to a small sample of alcoholic patients with whom I worked intensively for about two years in 1949–52, in the Veterans Administration Hospital, Palo Alto, California. These men, it should be mentioned, carried other diagnoses—mostly of "schizophrenia"—in addition to the pains of alcoholism. Several were members of A.A. I fear that I helped them not at all.

Reprinted from *Psychiatry, 34,* 1–18. (1971).

THE PROBLEM

It is rather generally believed that "causes" or "reasons" for alcoholism are to be looked for in the sober life of the alcoholic. Alcoholics, in their sober manifestations, are commonly dubbed "immature," "maternally fixated," "oral," "homosexual," "passive-aggressive," "fearful of success," "over-sensitive," "proud," "affable," or simply "weak." But the logical implications of this belief are usually not examined:

(1) If the sober life of the alcoholic somehow drives him to drink or proposes the first step toward intoxication, it is not to be expected that any procedure which reinforces his particular style of sobriety will reduce or control his alcoholism.

(2) If his style of sobriety drives him to drink, then that style must contain error or pathology; and intoxication must provide some—at least subjective—correction of this error. In other words, compared with his sobriety, which is in some way "wrong," his intoxication must be in some way "right." The old tag "*In vino veritas*" may contain a truth more profound than is usually attributed to it.

(3) An alternative hypothesis would suggest that when sober, the alcoholic is somehow more sane than the people around him, and that this situation is intolerable. I have heard alcoholics argue in favor of this possibility, but I shall ignore it in this essay. I think that Bernard Smith, the non-alcoholic legal representative of A.A., came close to the mark when he said, "the [A.A.] member was never enslaved by alcohol. Alcohol simply served as an escape from *personal* enslavement in the false ideals of a meterialistic society" (A.A., 1957, p. 279, italics added). It is not a matter of revolt against insane ideals around him but of escaping from his own insane premises, which are continually reinforced by the surrounding society. It is possible, however, that the alcoholic is in some way more vulnerable or sensitive than the normal to the fact that his insane (but conventional) premises lead to unsatisfying results.

(4) The present theory of alcoholism, therefore, will provide a *converse matching* between the sobriety and the intoxication, such that the latter may be seen as an appropriate subjective correction for the former.

(5) There are, of course, many instances in which people resort to alcohol and even to extreme intoxication as an anesthetic giving release from ordinary grief, resentment, or physical pain. It might be argued that the anesthetic action of alcohol provides a sufficient converse matching for our theoretical purposes. I shall, however, specifically exclude these cases from consideration as being not relevant to the problem of addictive or repetitive alcoholism; and this in spite of the undoubted fact that "grief," "resentment," and "frustration" are commonly used by addicted alcoholics as *excuses* for drinking.

I shall demand, therefore, a converse matching between sobriety and intoxication more specific than that provided by mere anesthesia.

SOBRIETY

The friends and relatives of the alcoholic commonly urge him to be "strong," and to "resist temptation." What they mean by this is not very clear, but it is significant that the alcoholic himself—while sober—commonly agrees with their view of his "problem." He believes that he could be, or, at least, ought to be "the captain of his soul."[1] But it is a cliché of alcoholism that

[1]This phrase is used by A.A. in derision of the alcoholic who tries to use will power against the bottle. The quotation, along with the line, "my head is bloody but unbowed," comes from the poem "Invictus" by William Ernest Henley, who was a cripple but not an alcoholic. The use of the will to conquer pain and physical disability is probably not comparable to the alcoholic's use of will.

after "that first drink," the motivation to stop drinking is zero. Typically the whole matter is phrased overtly as a battle between "self" and "John Barleycorn." Covertly the alcoholic may be planning or even secretly laying in supplies for the next binge, but it is almost impossible (in the hospital setting) to get the sober alcoholic to plan his next binge in an overt manner. He cannot, seemingly, be the "captain" of his soul and overtly will or command his own drunkenness. The "captain" can only command sobriety—and then not be obeyed.

Bill W., the co-founder of Alcoholics Anonymous, himself an alcoholic, cut through all this mythology of conflict in the very first of the famous "Twelve Steps" of A.A. The first step demands that the alcoholic agree that he is powerless over alcohol. This step is usually regarded as a "*surrender*" and many alcoholics are either unable to achieve it or achieve it only briefly during the period of remorse following a binge. A.A. does not regard these cases as promising: they have not yet "hit bottom"; their despair is inadequate and after a more or less brief spell of sobriety they will again attempt to use "self-control" to fight the "temptation." They will not or cannot accept the premise that, drunk or sober, the total personality of an alcoholic is an alcoholic personality which cannot conceivably fight alcoholism. As an A.A. leaflet puts it, "trying to use will power is like trying to lift yourself by your bootstraps."

The first two steps of A.A. are as follows:

1. We admitted we were powerless over alcohol—that our lives had become unmanageable.
2. Came to believe that a Power greater than ourselves could restore us to sanity. [A.A., 1939]

Implicit in the combination of these two steps is an extraordinary—and I believe correct—idea: the experience of defeat not only serves to convince the alcoholic that change is necessary; it *is* the first step in that change. To be defeated by the bottle and to know it is the first "spiritual experience." The myth of self-power is thereby broken by the demonstration of a greater power.

In sum, I shall argue that the "sobriety" of the alcoholic is characterized by an unusually disastrous variant of the Cartesian dualism, the division between Mind and Matter, or, in this case, between conscious will, or "self," and the remainder of the personality. Bill W.'s stroke of genius was to break up with the first "step" the structuring of this dualism.

Philosophically viewed, this first step is *not* a surrender; it is simply a change in epistemology, a change in how to know about the personality-in-the-world. And, notably, the change is from an incorrect to a more correct epistemology.

EPISTEMOLOGY AND ONTOLOGY

Philosophers have recognized and separated two sorts of problem. There are first the problems of how things are, what is a person, and what sort of a world this is. These are the problems of ontology. Second, there are the problems of how we know anything, or more specifically, how we know what sort of a world it is and what sort of creatures we are that can know something (or perhaps nothing) of this matter. These are the problems of epistemology. To these questions, both ontological and epistemological, philosophers try to find true answers.

But the naturalist, observing human behavior, will ask rather different questions. If he be a cultural relativist, he may agree with those philosophers who hold that a "true" ontology is conceivable, but he will not ask whether the ontology of the people he observes is "true." He will expect their epistemology to be culturally determined or even idiosyncratic, and he will expect the culture as a whole to make sense in terms of their particular epistemology and ontology.

If, on the other hand, it is clear that the local epistemology is *wrong*, then the naturalist should be alert to the possibility that the culture as a whole will never really make "sense," or will make sense only under restricted circumstances, which contact with other cultures and new technologies might disrupt.

In the natural history of the living human being, ontology and epistemology cannot be separated. His (commonly unconscious) beliefs about what sort of world it is will determine how he sees it and acts within it, and his ways of perceiving and acting will determine his beliefs about its nature. The living man is thus bound within a net of epistemological and ontological premises which—regardless of ultimate truth or falsity—become partially self-validating for him (Ruesch and Bateson, 1951, ch. 8).

It is awkward to refer constantly to both epistemology and ontology and incorrect to suggest that they are separable in human natural history. There seems to be no convenient word to cover the combination of these two concepts. The nearest approximations are "cognitive structure" or "character structure," but these terms fail to suggest that what is important is a body of habitual assumptions or premises implicit in the relationship between man and environment, and that these premises may be true or false. I shall therefore use the single term "epistemology" in this essay to cover both aspects of the net of premises which govern adaptation (or maladaptation) to the human and physical environment. In George Kelly's vocabulary, these are the rules by which an individual "construes" his experience.

I am concerned especially with that group of premises upon which Occidental concepts of the "self" are built, and, conversely, with premises which are corrective to some of the more gross Occidental errors associated with that concept.

THE EPISTEMOLOGY OF CYBERNETICS

What is new and surprising is that we now have partial answers to some of these questions. In the last twenty-five years extraordinary advances have been made in our knowledge of what sort of thing the environment is, what sort of thing an organism is, and, especially, what sort of thing a *mind* is. These advances have come out of cybernetics, systems theory, information theory, and related sciences.

We now know, with considerable certainty, that the ancient problem of whether the mind is immanent or transcendent can be answered in favor of immanence, and that this answer is more economical of explanatory entities than any transcendent answer: it has at least the negative support of "Occam's Razor."

On the positive side, we can assert that *any* on-going ensemble of events and objects which has the appropriate complexity of causal circuits and the appropriate energy relations will surely show mental characteristics. It will *compare,* that is, be responsive to *difference* (in addition to being affected by the ordinary physical "causes" such as impact or force). It will "process information" and will inevitably be self-corrective either toward homeostatic optima or toward the maximization of certain variables.

A "bit" of information is definable as a difference which makes a difference. Such a difference, as it travels and undergoes successive transformation in a circuit, is an elementary idea.

But, most relevant in the present context, we know that no part of such an internally interactive system can have unilateral control over the remainder or over any other part. The mental characteristics are inherent or immanent in the ensemble as a *whole.*

Even in very simple self-corrective systems, this holistic character is evident. In the steam engine with a "governor," the very word "governor" is a misnomer if it be taken to mean that this part of the system has unilateral control. The governor is, essentially, a sense organ or transducer which receives a transform of the *difference* between the actual running speed of the engine and some ideal or preferred speed. This sense organ transforms these differences into differences in some efferent message, for example, to fuel supply or to a brake. The behavior of the governor is determined, in other words, by the behavior of the other parts of the system, and indirectly by its own behavior at a previous time.

The holistic and mental character of the system is most clearly demonstrated by this last fact, that the behavior of the governor (and, indeed, of every part of the causal circuit) is partially determined by its own previous behavior. Message material (i.e., successive transforms of difference) must pass around the total circuit, and the *time* required for the message material to return to the place from which it started is a basic characteristic of the total system. The behavior of the governor (or any other part of the circuit) is thus in some degree determined not only by its immediate past, but by what it did at a time which precedes the present by the interval necessary for the message to complete the circuit. There is thus a sort of determinative *memory* in even the simplest cybernetic circuit.

The stability of the system (i.e., whether it will act self-correctively or oscillate or go into run-away) depends upon the relation between the operational product of all the transformations of difference around the circuit and upon this characteristic time. The "governor" has no control over these factors. Even a human governor in a social system is bound by the same limitations. He is controlled by information from the system and must adapt his own actions to its time characteristics and to the effects of his own past action.

Thus: in no system which shows mental characteristics can any part have unilateral control over the whole. In other words, *the mental characteristics of the system are immanent, not in some part, but in the system as a whole.*

The significance of this conclusion appears when we ask, "Can a computer think?" or, "Is the mind in the brain?" And the answer to both questions will be negative unless the question is focused upon one of the few mental characteristics which are contained within the computer or the brain. A computer is self-corrective in regard to some of its internal variables. It may, for example, include thermometers or other sense organs which are affected by differences in its working temperature and the response of the sense organ to these differences may affect the action of a fan which in turn corrects the temperature. We may therefore say that the system shows mental characteristics in regard to its internal temperature. But it would be incorrect to say that the main business of the computer—the transformation of input differences into output differences—is "a mental process." The computer is only an arc of a larger circuit which always includes a man and an environment from which information is received and upon which efferent messages from the computer have effect. This total system, or ensemble, may legitimately be said to show mental characteristics. It operates by trial and error and has creative character.

Similarly, we may say that "mind" is immanent in those circuits of the brain which are complete within the brain. Or that mind is immanent in circuits which are complete within the system, brain *plus* body. Or, finally, that mind is immanent in the larger system—man *plus* environment.

In principle, if we desire to explain or understand the mental aspect of any biological event, we must take into account the system—that is, the network of *closed* circuits, within which that biological event is determined. But when we seek to explain the behavior of a man or any other organism, this "system" will usually *not* have the same limits as the "self"—as this term is commonly (and variously) understood.

Consider a man felling a tree with an axe. Each stroke of the axe is modified or corrected, according to the shape of the cut face of the tree left by the previous stroke. This self-corrective (i.e., mental) process is brought about by a total system, tree-eyes-brain-muscles-axe-stroke-tree; and it is this total system that has the characteristics of immanent mind.

More correctly, we should spell the matter out as: (differences in tree)-(differences in retina)-(differences in brain)-(differences in muscles)-(differences in movement of axe)-(differences in tree), etc. What is transmitted around the circuit is transforms of differences. And, as noted above, a difference which makes a difference in an *idea* or unit of information.

But this is *not* how the average Occidental sees the event-sequence of tree-felling. He says, "*I* cut down the tree" and he even believes that there is a delimited agent, the "self," which performed a delimited "purposive" action upon a delimited object.

It is all very well to say that "billiard ball A hit billiard ball B and sent it into the pocket"; and it would perhaps be all right (if we could do it) to give a complete hard science account of the events all around the circuit containing the man and the tree. But popular parlance includes *mind* in its utterance by invoking the personal pronoun, and then achieves a mixture of mentalism and physicalism by restricting mind within the man and reifying the tree. Finally the mind itself becomes reified by the notion that, since the "self" acted upon the axe which acted upon the tree, the "self" must also be a "thing." The parallelism of syntax between "*I* hit the billiard ball" and "the ball hit another ball" is totally misleading.

If you ask anybody about the localization and boundaries of the self, these confusions are immediately displayed. Or consider a blindman with a stick. Where does the blindman's self begin? At the tip of the stick? At the handle of the stick? Or at some point halfway up the stick? These questions are nonsense, because the stick is a pathway along which differences are transmitted under transformation, so that to draw a delimiting line *across* this pathway is to cut off a part of the systemic circuit which determines the blindman's locomotion.

Similarly, his sense organs are transducers or pathways for information, as also are his axons, etc. From a systems-theoretic point of view, it is a misleading metaphor to say that what travels in an axon is an "impulse." It would be more correct to say that what travels is a difference, or a transform of a difference. The metaphor of "impulse" suggests a hard-science line of thought which will ramify only too easily into nonsense about "psychic energy," and those who talk this kind of nonsense will disregard the information content of *quiescence.* The quiescence of an axon *differs* as much from activity as its activity does from quiescence. Therefore quiescence and activity have equal informational relevance. The message of activity can only be accepted as valid if the message of quiescence can also be trusted.

It is even incorrect to speak of the "message of activity" and the "message of quiescence." Always the fact that information is a transform of difference should be remembered, and we might better call the one message "activity—not quiescence" and the other "quiescence—not activity."

Similar considerations apply to the repentant alcoholic. He cannot simply elect "sobriety." At best he could only elect "sobriety—not drunkenness," and his universe remains polarized, carrying always both alternatives.

The total self-corrective unit which processes information, or, as I say, "thinks" and "acts" and "decides," is a *system* whose boundaries do not at all coincide with the boundaries either of the body or of what is popularly called the "self" or "consciousness"; and it is important to notice that there are *multiple* differences between the thinking system and the "self" as popularly conceived:

(1) The system is not a transcendent entity as the "self" is commonly supposed to be.

(2) The ideas are immanent in a network of causal pathways along which transforms of difference are conducted. The "ideas" of the system are in all cases at least binary in structure. They are not "impulses" but "information."

(3) This network of pathways is not bounded with consciousness but extends to include the pathways of all unconscious mentation—both autonomic and repressed, neural and hormonal.

(4) The network is not bounded by the skin but includes all external pathways along which information can travel. It also includes those effective differences which are immanent in the "objects" of such information. It includes the pathways of sound and light along which travel transforms of differences originally immanent in things and other people—and especially *in our own actions.*

It is important to note that the basic—and I believe erroneous—tenets of popular epistemology are mutually reinforcing. If, for example, the popular premise of transcendence is discarded, the immediate substitute is a premise of immanence in the body. But this alternative will be unacceptable because large parts of the thinking network are located outside the body. The so-called "Body-Mind" problem is wrongly posed in terms which force the argument toward paradox: if mind be supposed immanent in the body, then it must be transcendent. If transcendent, it must be immanent. And so on (cf. Collingwood).

Similarly, if we exclude the unconscious processes from the "self" and call them "ego-alien," then these processes take on the subjective coloring of "urges" and "forces"; and this pseudo-dynamic quality is then extended to the conscious "self" which attempts to "resist" the "forces" of the unconscious. The "self" thereby becomes itself an organization of seeming "forces." The popular notion which would equate "self" with consciousness thus leads into the notion that ideas are "forces"; and this fallacy is in turn supported by saying that the axon carries "impulses." To find a way out of this mess is by no means easy.

We shall proceed by first examining the structure of the alcoholic's polarization. In the epistemologically unsound resolution, "I will fight the bottle," what is supposedly lined up against what?

ALCOHOLIC "PRIDE"

Alcoholics are philosophers in that universal sense in which all human beings (and all mammals) are guided by highly abstract principles of which they are either quite unconscious, or unaware that the principle governing their perception and action is philosophic. A common misnomer for such principles is "feelings" (Bateson, 1963).

This misnomer arises naturally from the Anglo-Saxon epistemological tendency to reify or attribute to the body all mental phenomena which are peripheral to consciousness. And the misnomer is, no doubt, supported by the fact that the exercise and/or frustration of these principles is often accompanied by visceral and other bodily sensations. I believe, however, that Pascal was correct when he said, "The heart has its *reasons* of which the reason knows nothing."

But the reader must not expect the alcoholic to present a consistent picture. When the underlying epistemology is full of error, derivations from it are inevitably either self-contradictory or extremely restricted in scope. A consistent corpus of theorems cannot be derived from an inconsistent body of axioms. In such cases, the attempt to be consistent leads either to the great proliferation of complexity characteristic of psychoanalytic theory and Christian theology or to the extremely narrow view characteristic of contemporary behaviorism.

I shall therefore proceed to examine the "pride" which is characteristic of alcoholics to show that this principle of their behavior is derived from the strange dualistic epistemology characteristic of Occidental civilization.

A convenient way of describing such principles as "pride," "dependency," "fatalism," and so forth, is to examine the principle as if it were a result of deutero-learning[2] (Bateson, 1942) and to ask what contexts of learning might understandably inculcate this principle.

(1) It is clear that the principle of alcoholic life which A.A. calls "pride" is not contextually structured around past achievement. They do not use the word to mean pride in something accomplished. The emphasis is not upon "I succeeded," but rather upon "I can . . ." It is an obsessive acceptance of a challenge, a repudiation of the proposition "I cannot."

(2) After the alcoholic has begun to suffer from—or be blamed for—alcoholism, this principle of "pride" is mobilized behind the proposition "I can stay sober." But, noticeably, success in this achievement destroys the "challenge." The alcoholic becomes "cocksure," as A.A. says. He relaxes his determination, risks a drink, and finds himself on a binge. We may say that the contextual structure of sobriety changes with its achievement. Sobriety, at this point, is no longer the appropriate contextual setting for "pride." It is the risk of the drink that now is challenging and calls out the fatal "I can. . . ."

(3) A.A. does its best to insist that this change in contextual structure shall never occur. They restructure the whole context by asserting over and over again that "*once an alcoholic, always an alcoholic.*" They try to have the alcoholic place alcoholism within the self, much as a Jungian analyst tries to have the patient discover his "psychological type" and to learn to live with the strengths and weaknesses of that type. In contrast, the contextual structure of alcoholic "pride" places the alcoholism *outside* the self: "*I* can resist drinking."

(4) The challenge component of alcoholic "pride" is linked with *risk-taking.* The principle might be put in words: "I can do something where success is improbable and failure would be disastrous." Clearly this principle will never serve to maintain continued sobriety. As success begins to appear probable, the alcoholic must challenge the risk of a drink. The element of "bad luck" or "probability" of failure places failure beyond the limits of the self. "If failure occurs, it is not *mine.*" Alcoholic "pride" progressively narrows the concept of "self," placing what happens outside its scope.

(5) The principle of pride-in-risk is ultimately almost suicidal. It is all very well to test once whether the universe is on your side, but to do so again and again, with increasing stringency of proof, is to set out on a project which can only prove that the universe hates you. But, still and all, the A.A. narratives show repeatedly that, at the very bottom of despair, *pride* sometimes prevents suicide. The final quietus must not be delivered by the "self" (cf. Bill's Story, A.A., 1939).

PRIDE AND SYMMETRY

The so-called pride of the alcoholic always presumes a real or fictitious "other" and its complete contextual definition therefore demands that we characterize the real or imagined relationship to this "other." A first step in this task is to classify the relationship as either

[2]This use of formal contextual structure as a descriptive device does not necessarily assume that the principle discussed is wholly or in part actually *learned* in contexts having the appropriate formal structure. The principle could have been genetically determined and it might still follow that the principle is best described by the formal delineation of the contexts in which it is exemplified. It is precisely this fitting of behavior to context that makes it difficult or impossible to determine whether a principle of behavior was genetically determined or learned in that context.

"symmetrical" or "complementary" (Bateson, 1936). To do this is not entirely simple when the "other" is a creation of the unconscious, but we shall see that the indications for such a classification are clear.

An explanatory digression is, however, necessary. The primary criterion is simple:

If, in a binary relationship, the behaviors of A and B are regarded (by A and B) as *similar* and are linked so that more of the given behavior by A stimulates more of it in B, and *vice versa,* then the relationship is "symmetrical" in regard to these behaviors.

If, conversely, the behaviors of A and B are *dissimilar* but mutually fit together (as, for example, spectatorship fits exhibitionism), and the behaviors are linked so that more of A's behavior stimulates more of B's fitting behavior, then the relationship is "complementary" in regard to these behaviors.

Common examples of simple symmetrical relationship are: armaments races, keeping up with the Joneses, athletic emulation, boxing matches, and the like. Common examples of complementary relationship are: dominance-submission, sadism-masochism, nurturance-dependency, spectatorship-exhibitionism, and the like.

More complex considerations arise when higher logical typing is present. For example: A and B may compete in gift-giving, thus superposing a larger symmetrical frame upon primarily complementary behaviors. Or, conversely, a therapist might engage in competition with a patient in some sort of play therapy, placing a complementary nurturant frame around the primarily symmetrical transactions of the game.

Various sorts of "double binds" are generated when A and B perceive the premises of their relationship in different terms—A may regard B's behavior as competitive when B thought he was helping A. And so on.

With these complexities we are not here concerned, because the imaginary "other" or counterpart in the "pride" of the alcoholic does not, I believe, play the complex games which are characteristic of the "voices" of schizophrenics.

Both complementary and symmetrical relationships are liable to progressive changes of the sort which I have called *schismogenesis* (Bateson, 1936). Symmetrical struggles and armaments races may, in the current phrase, "escalate"; and the normal pattern of succoring-dependency between parent and child may become monstrous. These potentially pathological developments are due to undamped or uncorrected positive feedback in the system, and may—as stated—occur in either complementary or symmetrical systems. However, in *mixed* systems schismogenesis is necessarily reduced. The armaments race between two nations will be slowed down by acceptance of complementary themes such as dominance, dependency, admiration, and so forth, between them. It will be speeded up by the repudiation of these themes.

This antithetical relationship between complementary and symmetrical themes is, no doubt, due to the fact that each is the logical opposite of the other. In a merely symmetrical armaments race, nation A is motivated to greater efforts by its estimate of *the greater strength* of B. When it estimates that B is weaker, nation A will relax its efforts. But the exact opposite will happen if A's structuring of the relationship is complementary. Observing that B is *weaker* than they, A will go ahead with hopes of conquest (cf. Bateson, 1946, and Richardson, 1935).

This antithesis between complementary and symmetrical patterns may be more than simply logical. Notably, in psychoanalytic theory (cf. Erikson, 1937), the patterns which are called "libidinal" and which are modalities of the erogenous zones are all *complementary.* Intrusion, inclusion, exclusion, reception, retention, and the like—all of these are classed as "libidinal." Whereas rivalry, competition, and the like fall under the rubric of "ego" and "defense."

It is also possible that the two antithetical codes—symmetrical and complementary—may be physiologically represented by contrasting states of the central nervous system. The progressive changes of schismogenesis may reach climactic discontinuities and sudden reversals. Symmetrical rage may suddenly turn to grief; the retreating animal with tail between his legs may suddenly "turn at bay" in a desperate battle of symmetry to the death. The bully may suddenly become the coward when he is challenged, and the wolf who is beaten in a symmetrical conflict may suddenly give "surrender" signals which prevent further attack.

The last example is of special interest. If the struggle between the wolves is symmetrical—that is, if wolf A is stimulated to more aggressive behavior by the aggressive behavior of B—then if B suddenly exhibits what we may call "negative aggression," A will not be able to continue to fight unless he can quickly switch over to that complementary state of mind in which B's weakness would be a stimulus for his aggression. Within the hypothesis of symmetrical and complementary modes, it becomes unnecessary to postulate a specifically "inhibitory" effect for the surrender signal.

Human beings who possess language can apply the label "aggression" to all attempts to damage the other, regardless of whether the attempt is prompted by the other's strength or weakness; but at the prelinguistic mammalian level these two sorts of "aggression" must appear totally different. We are told that from the lion's point of view, an "attack" on a zebra is totally different from an "attack" on another lion (Lorenz).

Enough has now been said so that the question can be posed: Is alcoholic pride contextually structured in symmetrical or complementary form?

First, there is a very strong tendency toward symmetry in the normal drinking habits of Occidental culture. Quite apart from addictive alcoholism, two men drinking together are impelled by convention to match each other, drink for drink. At this stage, the "other" is still real and the symmetry, or rivalry, between the pair is friendly.

As the alcoholic becomes addicted and tries to resist drinking, he begins to find it difficult to resist the social context in which he should match his friends in their drinking. The A.A. says, "Heaven knows, we have tried hard enough and long enough to drink like other people!"

As things get worse, the alcoholic is likely to become a solitary drinker and to exhibit the whole spectrum of response to challenge. His wife and friends begin to suggest that his drinking is a *weakness*, and he may respond, with symmetry, both by resenting them and by asserting his strength to resist the bottle. But, as is characteristic of symmetrical responses, a brief period of successful struggle weakens his motivation and he falls off the wagon. Symmetrical effort requires continual opposition from the opponent.

Gradually the focus of the battle changes, and the alcoholic finds himself committed to a new and more deadly type of symmetrical conflict. He must now prove that the bottle cannot kill him. His "head is bloody but unbowed." He is still the "captain of his soul"—for what it's worth.

Meanwhile, his relationships with wife and boss and friends have been deteriorating. He never did like the complementary status of his boss as an authority; and now as he deteriorates his wife is more and more forced to take a complementary role. She may try to exert authority, or she becomes protective, or she shows forbearance, but all those provoke either rage or shame. His symmetrical "pride" can tolerate no complementary role.

In sum, the relationship between the alcoholic and his real or fictitious "other" is clearly symmetrical and clearly schismogenic. It escalates. We shall see that the religious conversion of the alcoholic when saved by A.A. can be described as a dramatic shift from this symmetrical habit, or epistemology, to an almost purely complementary view of his relationship to others and to the universe or God.

PRIDE OR INVERTED PROOF?

Alcoholics may appear to be stiffnecked, but they are not stupid. The part of the mind in which their policy is decided certainly lies too deep for the word "stupidity" to be applicable.

These levels of the mind are prelinguistic and the computation which goes on there is coded in *primary process.*

Both in dream and in mammalian interaction, the only way to achieve a proposition which contains its own negation ("I will not bite you," or "I am not afraid of him") is by an elaborate imagining or acting out of the proposition to be negated, leading to a *reductio ad absurdum.* "I will not bite you" is achieved between two mammals by an experimental combat which is a "not combat," sometimes called "play." It is for this reason that "agnostic" behavior commonly evolves into friendly greeting (Bateson, 1969).

In this sense, the so-called pride of the alcoholic is in some degree ironic. It is a determined effort to test something like "self-control" with an ulterior but unstateable purpose of proving that "self-control" is ineffectual and absurd. "It simply won't work." This ultimate proposition, since it contains a simple negation, is not to be expressed in primary process. Its final expression is in an action—the taking of a drink. The heroic battle with the bottle, that fictitious "other," ends up in a "kiss and make friends."

In favor of this hypothesis, there is the undoubted fact that the testing of self-control leads back into drinking. And, as I have argued above, the whole epistemology of self-control which his friends urge upon the alcoholic is monstrous. If this be so, then the alcoholic is right in rejecting it. He has achieved a *reductio ad absurdum* of the conventional epistemology.

But this description of achieving a *reductio ad absurdum* verges upon teleology. If the proposition "It won't work" cannot be entertained within the coding of primary process, how then can the computations of primary process direct the organism to try out those courses of action which will demonstrate that "It won't work"?

Problems of this general type are frequent in psychiatry and can perhaps only be resolved by a model in which, under certain circumstances, the organism's discomfort activates a positive feedback loop to *increase* the behavior which preceded the discomfort. Such positive feedback would provide a verification that it was really that particular behavior which brought about the discomfort, and might increase the discomfort to some threshold level at which change would become possible.

In psychotherapy such a positive feedback loop is commonly provided by the therapist who pushes the patient in the direction of his symptoms—a technique which has been called the "therapeutic double bind." An example of this technique is quoted later in this essay, where the A.A. member challenges the alcoholic to go and do some "controlled drinking" in order that he may discover for himself that he has no control.

It is also usual that the symptoms and hallucinations of the schizophrenic—like dreams—constitute a corrective experience, so that the whole schizophrenic episode takes on the character of a self-initiation. Barbara O'Brien's account of her own psychosis is perhaps the most striking example of this phenomenon, which has been discussed elsewhere (Bateson, 1961, Introduction).

It will be noted that the possible existence of such a positive feedback loop, which will cause a runaway in the direction of increasing discomfort up to some threshold (which might be on the other side of death), is not included in conventional theories of learning. But a tendency to verify the unpleasant by seeking repeated experience of it is a common human trait. It is perhaps what Freud called the "death instinct."

THE DRUNKEN STATE

What has been said above about the treadmill of symmetrical pride is only one half of the picture. It is the picture of the state of mind of the alcoholic *battling* with the bottle. Clearly this state is very unpleasant and clearly it is also unrealistic. His "others" are either totally imaginary or are gross distortions of persons on whom he is dependent and whom he may love. He has an alternative to this uncomfortable state—he can get drunk. Or, *"at least,"* have a drink.

With this complementary surrender, which the alcoholic will often see as an act of spite—a Parthian dart in a symmetrical struggle—his entire epistemology changes. His anxieties and resentments and panic vanish as if by magic. His self-control is lessened, but his need to compare himself with others is reduced even further. He feels the physiological warmth of alcohol in his veins and, in many cases, a corresponding psychological warmth toward others. He may be either maudlin or angry, but he has at least become again a part of the human scene.

Direct data bearing upon the thesis that the step from sobriety into intoxication is also a step from symmetrical challenge into complementarity are scarce, and always confused both by the distortions of recall and by the complex toxicity of the alcohol. But there is strong evidence from song and story to indicate that the step is of this kind. In ritual, partaking of wine has always stood for the social aggregation of persons united in religious "communion" or secular *Gemütlichkeit.* In a very literal sense, alcohol supposedly makes the individual see himself as and act as *a part of* the group. That is, it enables complementarity in the relationships which surround him.

HITTING BOTTOM

A.A. attaches great importance to this phenomenon and regards the alcoholic who has not hit bottom as a poor prospect for their help. Conversely, they are inclined to explain their failures by saying that the individual who goes back to his alcoholism has not yet "hit bottom."

Certainly many sorts of disaster may cause an alcoholic to hit bottom. Various sorts of accidents, an attack of delirium tremens, a patch of drunken time of which he has no memory, rejection by wife, loss of job, hopeless diagnosis, and so on—any of these may have the required effect. A.A. says that "bottom" is different for different men and some may be dead before they reach it.[3]

It is possible, however, that "bottom" is reached many times by any given individual; that "bottom" is a spell of panic which provides a favorable moment for change, but not a moment at which change is inevitable. Friends and relatives and even therapists may pull the alcoholic out of his panic, either with drugs or reassurance, so that he "recovers" and goes back to his "pride" and alcoholism—only to hit a more disastrous "bottom" at some later time, when he will again be ripe for a change. The attempt to change the alcoholic in a period *between* such moments of panic is unlikely to succeed.

The nature of the panic is made clear by the following description of a "test."

> We do not like to pronounce any individual as alcoholic, but you can quickly diagnose yourself. Step over to the nearest barroom and try some controlled drinking. Try to drink and stop abruptly. Try it more than once. It will not take long for you to decide, if you are honest with yourself about it. It may be worth a bad case of jitters if you get a full knowledge of your condition. [A.A., 1939, p. 43]

We might compare the test quoted above to commanding a driver to brake suddenly when travelling on a slippery road: he will discover fast that his control is limited. (The metaphor "skid row" for the alcoholic section of town is not inappropriate.)

[3]Personal communication from a member.

The panic of the alcoholic who has hit bottom is the panic of the man who thought he had control over a vehicle but suddenly finds that the vehicle can run away with him. Suddenly, pressure on what he knows is the brake seems to make the vehicle go faster. It is the panic of discovering that *it* (the system, self *plus* vehicle) is bigger than he is.

In terms of the theory here presented, we may say that hitting bottom exemplifies systems theory at three levels:

(1) The alcoholic works on the discomforts of sobriety to a threshold point at which he has bankrupted the epistemology of "self-control." He then gets drunk—because the "system" is bigger than he is—and he may as well surrender to it.

(2) He works repeatedly at getting drunk until he proves that there is a still larger system. He then encounters the panic of "hitting bottom."

(3) If friends and therapists reassure him, he may achieve a further unstable adjustment—becoming addicted to their help—until he demonstrates that this system won't work, and "hits bottom" again but at a lower level. In this, as in all cybernetic systems, the sign (plus or minus) of the effect of any intrusion upon the system depends upon timing.

(4) Lastly, the phenomenon of hitting bottom is complexly related to the experience of double bind (Bateson et al., 1956). Bill W. narrates that he hit bottom when diagnosed as a hopeless alcoholic by Dr. William D. Silkworth in 1939, and this event is regarded as the beginning of A.A. history (A.A., 1957, p. vii). Dr. Silkworth also "supplied us with the tools with which to puncture the toughest alcoholic ego, those shattering phrases by which he described our illness: *the obsession of the mind* that compels us to drink and *the allergy of the body* that condemns us to go mad or die" (Bill W. in A.A., 1957, p. 13; italics in the original). This is a double bind correctly founded upon the alcoholic's dichotomous epistemology of mind *versus* body. He is forced by these words back and back to the point at which only an involuntary change in deep unconscious epistemology—a spiritual experience—will make the lethal description irrelevant.

THE THEOLOGY OF ALCOHOLICS ANONYMOUS

Some outstanding points of the theology of A.A. are:

(1) *There is a Power greater than the self.* Cybernetics would go somewhat further and recognize that the "self" as ordinarily understood is only a small part of a much larger trial-and-error system which does the thinking, acting, and deciding. This system includes all the informational pathways which are relevant at any given moment to any given decision. The "self" is a false reification of an improperly delimited part of this much larger field of interlocking processes. Cybernetics also recognizes that two or more persons—any group of persons—may together form such a thinking-and-acting system.

(2) This Power is felt to be personal and to be intimately linked with each person. It is "God as *you* understand him to be."

Cybernetically speaking, "my" relation to any larger system around me and including other things and persons will be different from "your" relation to some similar system around you. The relation "part of" must necessarily and logically always be complementary but the meaning of the phrase "part of" will be different for every person.[4] This difference will be especially important in systems containing more than one person. The system or "power" must necessarily appear different from where each person sits. Moreover, it is expectable that such systems, when they

[4]This diversity in styles of integration could account for the fact that some persons become alcoholic while others do not.

encounter each other, will recognize each other as systems in this sense. The "beauty" of the woods through which I walk is my recognition both of the individual trees and of the total ecology of the woods as *systems*. A similar esthetic recognition is still more striking when I talk with another person.

(3) A favorable relationship with this Power is discovered through "hitting bottom" and "surrender."

(4) By resisting this Power, men and especially alcoholics bring disaster upon themselves. The materialistic philosophy which sees "man" as pitted against his environment is rapidly breaking down as technological man becomes more and more able to oppose the largest systems. Every battle that he wins brings a threat of disaster. The unit of survival—either in ethics or in evolution—is not the organism or the species but the largest system or "power" within which the creature lives. If the creature destroys its environment, it destroys itself.

(5) But—and this is important—the Power does not reward and punish. It does not have "power" in that sense. In the biblical phrase, "All things work together for good to them that love God." And, conversely, to them that do not. The idea of power in the sense of unilateral control is foreign to A.A. Their organization is strictly "democratic" (their word), and even their deity is still bound by what we might call a systemic determinism. The same limitation applies both to the relationship between the A.A. sponsor and the drunk whom he hopes to help and to the relationship between A.A. central office and every local group.

(6) The first two "steps" of Alcoholics Anonymous taken together identify the addiction as a manifestation of this Power.

(7) The healthy relation between each person and this Power is complementary. It is in precise contrast to the "pride" of the alcoholic, which is predicated upon a symmetrical relationship to an imagined "other." The schismogenesis is always more powerful than the participants in it.

(8) The quality and content of each person's relation to the Power is indicated or reflected in the social structure of A.A. The secular aspect of this system—its governance—is delineated in "Twelve Traditions" (A.A., 1957), which supplement the "Twelve Steps," the latter developing man's relationship to the Power. The two documents overlap in the Twelfth Step, which enjoins aid to other alcoholics as a necessary spiritual exercise without which the member is likely to relapse. The total system is a Durkheimian religion in the sense that the relationship between man and his community parallels the relationship between man and God. "A.A. is a power greater than any of us" (A.A., 1957, p. 288).

In sum, the relationship of each individual to the "Power" is best defined in the words *"is part of."*

(9) Anonymity. It must be understood that anonymity means much more in A.A. thinking and theology than the mere protection of members from exposure and shame. With increasing fame and success of the organization as a whole, it has become a temptation for members to use the fact of their membership as a positive asset in public relations, politics, education, and many other fields. Bill W., the co-founder of the organization, was himself caught by this temptation in early days and has discussed the matter in a published article (A.A., 1957, pp. 286–294). He sees first that any grabbing of the spotlight must be a personal and spiritual danger to the member, who cannot afford such self-seeking; and beyond this that it would be fatal for the organization as a whole to become involved in politics, religious controversy, and social reform. He states clearly that the errors of the alcoholic are the same as the "forces which are today ripping the world apart at its seams," but that it is not the business of A.A. to save the world. Their single purpose is "to carry the A.A. message to the sick alcoholic who wants it" (loc. cit.). He concludes that anonymity is "the greatest symbol of self-sacrifice that we know."

Elsewhere the twelfth of the "Twelve Traditions" states that "anonymity is the spiritual foundation of our traditions, ever reminding us to place principles before personalities."

To this we may add that anonymity is also a profound statement of the systemic relation, part-to-whole. Some systems theorists would go even further, because a major temptation for systems theory lies in the reification of theoretical concepts. Anatol Holt says he wants a bumper sticker which would (paradoxically) say, "Stamp out nouns" (Wenner-Gren Foundation).

(10) Prayer. The A.A. use of prayer similarly affirms the complementarity of part-whole relationship by the very simple technique of asking for that relationship. They ask for those personal characteristics, such as humility, which are in fact exercised in the very act of prayer. If the act of prayer be sincere (which is not so easy), God cannot but grant the request. And this is peculiarly true of "God, *as you understand him.*" This self-affirming tautology, which contains its own beauty, is precisely the balm required after the anguish of the double binds which went with hitting bottom.

Somewhat more complex is the famous "Serenity Prayer": "God grant us the serenity to accept the things we cannot change, courage to change the things we can, and wisdom to know the difference."[5]

If double binds cause anguish and despair and destroy personal epistemological premises at some deep level, then it follows, conversely, that for the healing of these wounds and the growth of a new epistemology, some converse of the double bind will be appropriate. The double bind leads to the conclusion of despair, "There are no alternatives." The Serenity Prayer explicitly frees the worshipper from these maddening bonds.

In this connection it is worth mentioning that the great schizophrenic, John Perceval, observed a change in his "voices." In the beginning of his psychosis they bullied him with "contradictory commands" (or as I would say, double binds), but later he began to recover when they offered him choice of clearly defined alternatives (cf. Bateson, 1961).

(11) In one characteristic, A.A., differs profoundly from such natural mental systems as the family or the redwood forest. It has a *single* purpose—"to carry the A.A. message to the sick alcoholic who wants it"—and the organization is dedicated to the maximization of that purpose. In this respect, A.A. is no more sophisticated than General Motors or an Occidental nation. But biological systems, other than those premised upon Occidental ideas (and especially *money*), are multipurposed. There is no single variable in the redwood forest of which we can say that the whole system is oriented to maximizing that variable and all other variables are subsidiary to it; and, indeed, the redwood forest works toward optima, not maxima. Its needs are satiable, and too much of anything is toxic.

There is, however, this: that the single purpose of A.A. is directed outward and is aimed at a noncompetitive relationship to the larger world. The variable to be maximized is a complementarity and is of the nature of "service" rather than dominance.

THE EPISTEMOLOGICAL STATUS OF COMPLEMENTARY AND SYMMETRICAL PREMISES

It was noted above that in human interaction, symmetry and complementarity may be complexly combined. It is therefore reasonable to ask how it is possible to regard these themes as so fundamental that they shall be called "epistemological," even in a natural history study of cultural and interpersonal premises.

[5]This was not originally an A.A. document and its authorship is unknown. Small variations in the text occur. I have quoted the form which I personally prefer (A.A., 1957, p. 196).

The answer seems to hang upon what is meant by "fundamental" in such a study of man's natural history; and the word seems to carry two sorts of meaning.

First, I call *more fundamental* those premises which are the more deeply embedded in the mind, which are the more "hard programmed" and the less susceptible to change. In this sense, the symmetrical pride or hubris of the alcoholic is fundamental.

Second, I shall call more fundamental those premises of mind which refer to the larger rather than the smaller systems or gestalten of the universe. The proposition "grass is green" is less fundamental than the proposition "color differences make a difference."

But, if we ask about what happens when premises are changed, it becomes clear that these two definitions of the "fundamental" overlap to a very great extent. If a man achieves or suffers change in premises which are deeply embedded in his mind, he will surely find that the results of that change will ramify throughout his whole universe. Such changes we may well call "epistemological."

The question then remains regarding what is epistemologically "right" and what is epistemologically "wrong." Is the change from alcoholic symmetrical "pride" to the A.A. species of complementarity a correction of his epistemology? And is complementarity *always* somehow better than symmetry?

For the A.A. member, it may well be true that complementarity is always to be preferred to symmetry and that even the trivial rivalry of a game of tennis or chess may be dangerous. The superficial episode may touch off the deeply embedded symmetrical premise. But this does not mean that tennis and chess propose epistemological error for everybody.

The ethical and philosophic problem really concerns only the widest universe and the deepest psychological levels. If we deeply and even unconsciously believe that our relation to the largest system which concerns us—the "Power greater than self"—is symmetrical and emulative, then we are in error.

LIMITATIONS OF THE HYPOTHESIS

Finally, the above analysis is subject to the following limitations and implications:

(1) It is not asserted that all alcoholics operate according to the logic which is here outlined. It is very possible that other types of alcoholics exist and almost certain that alcoholic addiction in other cultures will follow other lines.

(2) It is not asserted that the way of Alcoholics Anonymous is the *only* way to live correctly or that their theology is the only correct derivation from the epistemology of cybernetics and systems theory.

(3) It is not asserted that all transactions between human beings ought to be complementary, though it is clear that the relation between the individual and the larger system of which he is a part must necessarily be so. Relations between persons will (I hope) always be complex.

(4) It is, however, asserted that the non-alcoholic world has many lessons which it might learn from the epistemology of systems theory and from the ways of A.A. If we continue to operate in terms of a Cartesian dualism of mind *versus* matter, we shall probably also continue to see the world in terms of God *versus* man; elite *versus* people; chosen race *versus* others; nation *versus* nation; and man *versus* environment. It is doubtful whether a species having *both* an advanced technology *and* this strange way of looking at its world can endure.

REFERENCES

[Alcoholics Anonymous.] *Alcoholics Anonymous*; New York, Works Publishing, 1939.

[Alcoholics Anonymous.] *Alcoholics Anonymous Comes of Age;* Harper, 1957.

Bateson, Gregory, *Naven;* Cambridge Univ. Press, 1936.

Bateson, Gregory. "Social Planning and the Concept of 'Deutero-learning,' " in *Conference on Science, Philosophy, and Religion, Second Symposium*; Harper, 1942.

Bateson, Gregory. "The Pattern of an Armaments Race—Part I: An Anthropological Approach," *Bull. Atomic Scientists* (1946) 2(5):10–11.

Bateson, Gregory, et al. "Toward a Theory of Schizophrenia," *Behavioral Science* (1956) 1:251–264.

Bateson, Gregory. (Ed.) *Perceval's Narrative*; Stanford Univ. Press, 1961.

Bateson, Gregory. "A Social Scientist Views the Emotions," in P. Knapp (Ed.), *Expression of the Emotions in Man*; Internat. Univ. Press, 1963.

Bateson, Gregory. "Metalogue: What Is an Instinct?," in T. Sebeok (Ed.), *Approaches to Animal Communication*; The Hague, Mouton, 1969.

Collingwood, Robin George. *The Idea of Nature*; Oxford Univ. Press, 1945.

Erikson, Erik H. "Configurations in Play—Clinical Notes," *Psychoanal. Quart.* (1937) 6:139–214.

Lorenz, Konrad. *On Aggression*; Harcourt, Brace & World, 1966.

O'Brien, Barbara. *Operators and Things: The Inner Life of a Schizophrenic*; Cambridge, Mass., Arlington Books, 1958.

Richardson, Lewis Fry. "Generalized Foreign Politics," *British J. Psychology,* Monogr. Supplements, 1939.

Ruesch, Jurgen, and Bateson, Gregory. *Communication: The Social Matrix of Psychiatry*; Norton, 1951.

Wenner-Gren Foundation. Conference on the effects of conscious purpose on human adaptation, 1968; Knopf, in press.

32

THE CONFUSION ABOUT EPISTEMOLOGY AND "EPISTEMOLOGY"—AND WHAT TO DO ABOUT IT

BARBARA S. HELD AND EDWARD POLS

Although less than two years ago the question of the correct epistemology for the family therapy movement dominated the major journals of the field, such debates are now less frequent. Perhaps most family therapists grew tired of words that had impressive sounds but few apparent practical implications (3). On the other hand, there may have been many family therapists who, although willing to admit that there might be something of value to their practice in that controversy, nevertheless felt that it was all too confusing and mystifying to be worth prolonging.

There is, in any event, a noticeable absence of public controversy these days. Whether this is a calm before another epistemological storm or merely a sign that the members of this field are ready to move on to other questions is not for us to say. Nor do we wish to argue whether epistemology should or should not be a major focus of discussion in family therapy. We intend to take a more modest position in this paper, namely, that there has been considerable confusion about the meaning of the term *epistemology*, and that this confusion has distorted many aspects of the discussion. We raise the question of epistemology in family therapy once again only to try to remove the confusion and so make it easier for family therapists to make informed decisions about the relevance of the whole question to their professional function.

Reprinted from *Family Process, 24,* 509–517. (1985).

The authors note that the question of first and second authorship has been determined on the basis of the field to which the article is addressed. Material relevant to the field of family therapy has been written mainly by the first author, philosophical material mainly by the second author. The authors, however, collaborated on every aspect of the paper.

In the title as well as throughout the article, the authors used quotation marks when a word was used in an unusual or dubious sense.

TWO MEANINGS OF THE TERM *EPISTEMOLOGY*

The debate about epistemology has been unnecessarily confused by an unconventional use of the term *epistemology.* There is another meaning of that term that has been the prevailing and standard one in philosophy and in other disciplines that make use of philosophical terms. The writers that have taken part in the debate seldom use the term in its prevailing meaning, although many of them seem to be aware that there is indeed a prevailing meaning different from the one now used in family therapy. They have sometimes made use, however, of doctrines that belong to epistemology, in the prevailing meaning of the term, without identifying them as such. Discussions have thus involved both *epistemology* (the prevailing meaning) and "epistemology" (the unconventional meaning), even though their focus has been generally on the latter. The confusion has therefore been compounded.

As a first step toward removing the confusion, we will call epistemology in the prevailing meaning *epistemology (meaning 1).* And, as an acknowledgment that the unconventional meaning is the usual one in family therapy circles, we will relieve it of its pejorative quotation marks and call it *epistemology (meaning 2).* Next we give capsule definitions, which will then be made more precise. Epistemology (meaning 1) is the discipline or study that concerns itself with the nature of knowledge—in the first place, with *what* knowledge is as distinct, say, from mere belief or prejudice; in the second place, with *how* we know. It is therefore concerned, among other things, with providing standards for *real* knowledge as opposed to the spurious. Epistemology (meaning 2) is more concerned with what we know (or think we know). If we are studying something that *really is* what is often called an ecosystem or a cybernetic system, it would be foolish to treat it as though it were a linear context or situation. These capsule definitions already suggest that the waters are deeper than they seem, for we have had to introduce the troublesome notion of reality into both definitions.

Epistemology (Meaning 2)

It will be convenient to go first into the details of epistemology (meaning 2), for that is the sense that has dominated recent discussion. What it has meant there can be seen in several versions of a doctrine generally identified with Bateson (6). According to that doctrine, a person may have epistemological (meaning 2) assumptions (or premises), and these assumptions determine "habits of punctuating the stream of experience so that it takes on one or another sort of coherence and sense" (1, p.163). Thus, the *way* one makes distinctions, the *way* one punctuates experience *is* one's epistemology (meaning 2). In the context of the quotation from Bateson, for example, the distinction between free will and determinism is an instance of such punctuation: to see persons as determined is to give the stream one sort of coherence and sense, to see them as free is to give it another sort. Those who insist that persons are determined might therefore be said to have a deterministic epistemology (meaning 2); those who insist that persons are free might be said to have a free-will epistemology (meaning 2).

Clearly, then, epistemology (meaning 2) is concerned, among many other things, with such matters as free will and determinism, and therefore with the problem of causality. This conclusion is reinforced by noting that the debate about linear vs. nonlinear (recursive, circular, cybernetic) causality is generally understood, in family therapy circles, to be a debate about epistemology. Many family therapists distinguish between a linear and a nonlinear epistemology[1] in a context that is clearly that of meaning 2 (5, 9, 11, 13). In general, on the basis of the

[1]It will be helpful to recall in more detail just how the two views have been defined in the family therapy domain. Linear causality has been defined as the Newtonian, mechanistic, deterministic, "anticontextual," "atomistic" (13, p.14) view, in which

doctrine of Bateson and his followers, persons have different epistemologies (meaning 2), and this means that they punctuate experience differently about such matters as causality.

The distinction between linear and nonlinear causality as made in the literature is obviously not clear. It does not, for instance, settle the question whether a supposedly nonlinear context is or is not simply an enormously complex system of linear components too numerous to yield to analysis. Nor does it establish any sense in which a nonlinear context may be said to be nondeterministic in contrast with a supposedly deterministic linear sequence. Although the second author believes that an adequate understanding of causality does indeed require a distinction between a more fundamental and a less fundamental kind of causality, the distinction he has provided elsewhere (18, 19) is different from the one between linear and nonlinear. But we will not take up a position here about what an adequate doctrine of causality might look like. We want, instead, to make the less debatable point that epistemology (meaning 2) is in fact what philosophers call *metaphysics* or—sometimes—*ontology*.

Persons differing radically about such matters as causality and determinism are usually said to differ in their metaphysics (or ontology), not in their epistemology. We have found only passing references to this usage (4, 7, 12), which, in any case, has not been adopted in the family therapy field. We will undertake no thoroughgoing definition of metaphysics here. In its origins the term signifies not that which is *beyond* the physical, but rather those fundamental issues that are taken up *after* the study of physics and the other sciences. Materialism is thus a metaphysical doctrine no less than idealism is, and scientific determinism is a metaphysical doctrine just as surely as a free-will doctrine is. In Greek philosophy, what is now called metaphysics was understood to be the study of what was then called *being* and is now more usually called (at least in the sciences) *the real*—the term *ontology* (a much later term) comes, of course, from the Greek word for being. We shall not be far wrong if we say that nowadays a metaphysical doctrine—that is, an epistemology (meaning 2)—is generally understood to be a doctrine about what is or is not real in some fundamental sense. There is that troublesome term *real* again.

But is it ever possible to know what is real? That question, however, belongs to epistemology (meaning 1), and that fact explains why historically metaphysics and epistemology (meaning 1) have been intertwined. In due course we shall see that this also explains why this recent confusion about epistemology (meaning 1) and epistemology (meaning 2) has arisen. We therefore now turn to epistemology (meaning 1).

Epistemology (Meaning 1)

A good example of an epistemology (meaning 1) is not some doctrine about causality but rather the doctrine that *the observer (or knower) punctuates experience, or gives structure to reality.* In other words, someone who makes the claim that knowing, by definition, involves a punctuating of experience, or a structuring of reality, by the knower is propounding an epistemology (meaning 1). One way of punctuating experience would be to take up a position about causality, but taking up a position about causality is not necessarily taking up a position about knowing. It becomes

simple, isolated cause and effect sequences are thought to prevail. For example, if A happens, then B happens, then C, and finally D; that is, "causal A led to result D in a continuous line" (26, as cited by 17, p.270). In contrast, nonlinear or circular causality has been defined as the introduction of feedback from output back into the input, so that a system becomes self-regulating (2, p.37). That is, "part of a system's output is reintroduced into the system as information about the output" (26, p.31), so that now, "D loops, and is fed back to A," thus making a "continuous line or event impossible. Events that exchange information in a system or context could no longer be viewed as sequential or lineal deterministic chains of events. . . . A now has a context (A, B, C, and D) and is part of a system in which it both acts and is acted upon by the components of its system" (17, p.270). In the context of therapy, circularity means "the capacity of the therapist to conduct his investigation on the basis of feedback from the family in response to the information he solicits about relationships and, therefore, about difference and change" (23, p.8).

clear, therefore, that the doctrine about knowledge put forward by Bateson and his followers is an epistemology (meaning 1)—an epistemology in the classical and prevailing sense.

Let us give that doctrine a number of alternative formulations, arranged in a spectrum from one that seems fairly close to common sense through others that grow increasingly more abstract and more extreme. It is important that we have found all of these formulations, except the last, in the epistemology debate of the last few years, although they are not always identified as epistemological formulations. Further investigation may turn up the last one as well, and it is in any case only a more precise version of two of the others.

1. "Our world of experience is socially constructed." (Keeney attributes this position to Milton Erickson, among others [13, p.5].)

2. There are "various habits of punctuating the stream of experience so that it takes on one or another sort of coherence and sense" (1,p.163).

3. "Language is a tool for imposing distinctions upon our world" (Keeney [13, p.25], interpreting what he calls general semanticists. The view, however, is a common one among contemporary linguistic philosophers. For a more extreme version see no. 8.)

4. Symbolic systems, which are also ways of punctuating, organize sensory data (which in turn contribute to the organization of the symbolic systems); through such systems we construct and maintain a reality (13, p.46). "Language does not so much *reflect* reality as *create* it" (25, p.16).

5. "Ordering sequences in one way or another creates what, without undue exaggeration, may be called different realities" (24, p.62). "We each create rather than reflect reality" (21, p.55). "One's theory or view creates one's reality. . . . 'truth' or 'reality' become more one's creation than one's discovery" (15, p.66). The authors attribute these latter two statements to Watzlawick and his collaborators.

6. What we call objectivity is always a function of an organizing subjectivity. This can be expressed somewhat differently by saying that an *independent* objectivity is not attainable by a knower. It can also be expressed by saying that what we normally call reality is nonobjective (21, pp.55–56).

7. Reality is always a function of an organizing subjectivity; alternatively, an independent reality either does not exist or else is not attainable by the knower (21, pp.55–56; 25, pp.42,119).

8. Reality is a function of our language, and in that sense reality is linguistic; an extra-linguistic reality is therefore not attainable. (This formulation is obviously related to no. 3 and no. 4, but it places a more decisive emphasis on the role of language. It is a common doctrine in contemporary linguistic philosophy (20, 22, 27). Linguistic philosophers, in effect, substitute the notion of language-user for the notion of subjectivity.)

Notice that it is a more radical claim to say, as no. 7 and no. 8 say, that *reality* does not exist independently of the knower than it is to say, as formulations no. 1 through no. 5 in effect say, that our *experience* of reality, being structured by ourselves, may be different from what reality in fact is. But, in any case, it should be clear that this is a spectrum of formulations of a general doctrine about knowledge and its limitations. The doctrine is therefore an epistemology (meaning 1), not an epistemology (meaning 2). It says nothing about what kind of distinction or punctuation is to be preferred—nothing, for instance, about whether a linear causality or a nonlinear causality is to be preferred or whether both are necessary to a complete causal account of what we are studying. In short, it is an epistemological doctrine in the classical and prevailing sense. It has a good deal of pragmatism in its ancestry, and it goes back ultimately to Kant, although he himself would probably accept only the first sentence of formulation no. 6, and then only with qualifications.[2]

[2]For Kant, incidentally, the terms objectivity and reality were not equivalent. He took scientific knowledge to be objective, but since he thought objectivity was a function of subjectivity, he also thought that reality, as it is "in itself," was not attainable by the knower.

The doctrine expressed by our spectrum is, however, only one among many such doctrines, and we must therefore give it a name so that we can distinguish it from other epistemological (meaning 1) doctrines. Let us name the doctrine by way of the most extreme formulation in our spectrum. Let us call it *epistemology (meaning 1)-NR* ("NR" for "no independent reality attainable by the knower"). Because it is a version of the epistemology (meaning 1) that lies behind almost all discussion of epistemological (meaning 2) questions in family therapy circles, it is important to observe that the NR doctrine is not obviously or self-evidently the truth about the nature of knowledge, about how we know. Although the doctrine has many adherents among contemporary philosophers, it also has some severe critics. It is clearly important, not only for family therapists, but also for all those engaged in any scientific discipline to notice that there are alternative epistemologies (meaning 1). To put it differently, we cannot be clear about epistemology (meaning 1) unless we notice that the truth in that field is not easy to establish.

In particular, we should single out for comparison another epistemological (meaning 1) doctrine that is opposed to the NR doctrine. Let us call it *epistemology (meaning 1)-R* ("R" for "independent reality sometimes attainable by the knower"). The R doctrine, like the NR doctrine, may be expressed in a spectrum of formulations. It is possible, for instance, to agree that, in quantum physics, reality may be in part a function of subjectivity (i.e., of the knower, of the observer) and yet to maintain that in most other circumstances it is not only possible to attain a reality independent of subjectivity, but it is furthermore essential to the scientific enterprise that we should do so. It is also possible, within the framework of an R doctrine, to work with hypotheses (or paradigms, models, explanations) that may not in the end turn out to be adequate to the reality we are investigating. The scientific method, as pursued over the ages, does not commit one to an epistemology (meaning 1)-NR.

Most confusions have a rational explanation. We are now in a position to see how the confusion about epistemology (meaning 1) and epistemology (meaning 2) arose in the first place. Evidently the source of it is epistemology (meaning 1)-NR, for if we say that the *known* is always a by-product of the *knower*, we can no longer speak with any conviction of what we know as being distinct from, or independent of, ourselves as knowers (13). A proponent of epistemology (meaning 1)-NR would therefore find it natural enough to allow a term, *epistemology*, devised for talk about knowing to usurp the function of a term, *metaphysics*, or *ontology*, that originally implied the distinctness, or independence, of what is known.

LOGICAL CONSEQUENCES OF ADOPTING A POSITION ON EPISTEMOLOGY (MEANING 1) OR EPISTEMOLOGY (MEANING 2)

It is of course not essential to the successful pursuit of family therapy to settle all the problems of epistemology (meaning 1) or all those of epistemology (meaning 2)—that is, metaphysics. It is, however, essential to be aware that if one does take up an epistemological (meaning 1) position or a position on a metaphysical issue (e.g., linear vs. nonlinear causality), one's choice will have consequences.

The most important consequence of embracing epistemology (meaning 1)-NR, is that this decision makes it impossible to claim that this or that epistemological (meaning 2) position is the "correct" one. Let us call the epistemological (meaning 2) view that causality is best understood as nonlinear *epistemology (meaning 2)-NL*. Let us call the view that causality is best understood as linear *epistemology (meaning 2)-L*.

Epistemology (meaning 1)-NR tells us that both the meaning 2 doctrine-NL and the meaning 2 doctrine-L are at best two ways of seeing reality (spectrum nos. 1–3), and at worst two ways of making reality (spectrum nos. 4, 5, 7, 8). It gives us no grounds for preferring either.

And it tells us that, if we put forward some ground for a preference, that too is of our own making. Perhaps Keeney (13) acknowledges that there are no clearly scientific grounds for such a preference by considering it to be an aesthetic matter. Certainly those who choose to make a "linear" intervention, or merely to think of themselves as making such an intervention, cannot be said, on the basis of epistemology (meaning 1)-NR, to be acting "incorrectly." No epistemology (meaning 2) can be flatly correct or incorrect on the basis of epistemology (meaning 1)-NR.

On the other hand, there will also be consequences if someone decides to try to find the "real" truth about epistemology (meaning 2). We take up no position here about whether or not that is a sensible goal. But it seems clear that some have talked occasionally as though they were looking for the "real" truth (e.g., in observing relationships in therapy or engaging in systematic research), even though they have previously adopted an epistemology (meaning 1) that precludes that search. In any event, if someone does cling to NL as the truth about human behavior, that person cannot logically embrace epistemology (meaning 1)-NR as the truth about the nature of human knowledge. We cannot logically say, on the one hand, *this is the true reality* and, on the other hand, either *there is no true reality* or *there is no true reality available to us.*

PRACTICAL IMPLICATIONS FOR THERAPY

As for the practical consequences of all this for family therapy, it should be noticed that to adopt the view, as does the first author, that in doing therapy one should strive to take account of as many recursive loops, relationships, or contexts as possible (including one's own perceptions and actions and the systemic/recursive bases for those perceptions and actions) that play a role in a situation is not necessarily to embrace an epistemology (meaning 2)-NL. One can adopt such a view in therapy rationally enough, even if one feels that both epistemology (meaning 1) and epistemology (meaning 2) lie outside the province of family therapy. To aim at the practical objective of taking account of all possible factors is compatible with this modesty of outlook and compatible also with a healthy skepticism about whether there is now any adequate causal theory—linear, nonlinear, or some other kind—about how all those factors are related to one another. The counter argument to the effect that, however one thinks one operates in family therapy, one is in fact functioning according to an implicit NL doctrine (since this doctrine reflects the true state of relationships) is not sound because, as we stated earlier, the NL doctrine has not been sufficiently distinguished from the L doctrine for it to be clear either that it is everybody's implicit doctrine or that it is the true doctrine.

But even if one does feel that epistemology (meaning 2)—that is, metaphysics—is of central concern to the family therapist, there is no reason to be dogmatic about the truth of this or that doctrine of causality. The question of causality and the related question of determinism vs. free will have not yet been settled in any discipline, including the disciplines of philosophy, physics, and psychology. In family therapy, for instance, most agree that to assume a linear causality is to take a simple deterministic position, but there is no clear consensus about how to handle the question of determinism when one rejects the linear position. Keeney (13), for example, argues that "it is important to realize that 'control' refers to the whole self-corrective system, not a unilateral influence from a therapist or any other member. However, the therapist's presence helps determine how a cybernetic system is organized" (p. 132). Dell, however, advocates abandoning entirely the linear/circular distinction, which he correctly perceives to be muddled (5, 8), for one of structure determinism, a concept based upon his idea of "coherence."[3]

[3]Within a structure-determined framework, entities behave in accordance with their own organization, or the way in which their aspects "fit together." Thus, "individuals always behave out of their coherence; they can behave in no other way. Control

Meanwhile, as a practical matter, one must make some assumptions about cause and effect to function as a therapist (10, 16). That will be true even if one prefers to avoid epistemological (meaning 2) issues. To the extent that such assumptions treat the context as though it were divisible into discrete causal elements, some may think them linear in a pejorative sense, even if one protests that one is not advancing a general theory about causality. But an assumption is linear in some undesirable sense only if there is some clear and comprehensive causal doctrine with which it can be contrasted. No such doctrine has been supplied.

To summarize our discussion in this section: (a) an epistemology (meaning 1)-NR position provides no clear rational basis for preferring either linear or nonlinear causality in epistemology (meaning 2), or metaphysics; (b) the distinction between linear and nonlinear remains very unclear; (c) despite valiant and laudable attempts to see their assumptions, distinctions, and behaviors as "approximations of more encompassing recursive patterns" (13, p.58), family therapists must make the assumption that they are capable of making effective interventions, even if that assumption is called linear by some; (d) no consensus about causality (and hence determinism) has been reached in philosophy, or in physics, or in psychology.

CONCLUSIONS

We may now ask what was the point of the epistemological phase of the family therapy movement? Although some might argue that the epistemology debates in part reflect a political struggle within the field (8), others might argue more optimistically that these debates have been an attempt to raise the philosophical consciousness of family therapists by making them examine their own philosophical positions (11, 14). But the confusion we have examined may have produced the opposite effect. Rather than engaging in more philosophical self-examination, many family therapists seem to have become either disillusioned with the value of these ideas or intimidated by them. They may therefore now be tempted to deny the importance of pondering such questions as, for example, one's assumptions about the causal role of the therapist in the change process.

We believe that family therapists need not feel obliged to solve epistemological and metaphysical problems in order to function effectively. We do, however, think it is important to think as clearly and effectively as possible about these matters if one does address them. They are important questions about nature and about our rational capacity to cope with nature.

REFERENCES

1. BATESON, G., *Steps to an Ecology of Mind,* New York, Ballantine Books, 1972.
2. BERTALANFFY, L. VON, "General Systems Theory and Psychiatry—An Overview," in W. Gray, F. J. Duhl, and N. D. Rizzo (eds.), *General Systems Theory and Psychiatry,* Boston, Little, Brown, 1969.
3. COYNE, J. C., "A Brief Introduction to Epistobabble," *Fam. Ther. Networker* 6: 27–28, 1982.
4. DELL, P. F., "Researching the Family Theories of Schizophrenia: An Exercise in Epistemological Confusion," *Fam. Proc.* 19: 321–335, 1980.

is impossible. Their coherence determines how they will behave" (5, p.37). In fact, Dell (5) goes so far as to obliterate altogether traditional causal notions of any sort.

> The individual's behavioral coherence is the lock—and the therapist's interventions are the keys. . . . It is always the lock that determines which keys will work. There is no Truth (i.e., One True Key). There is no Causality (i.e., the key that *makes* the lock open). There is only Fit (i.e., those keys that are complementary to the lock). [p.35]

5. ——, "Beyond Homeostasis: Toward a Concept of Coherence," *Fam. Proc.* 21: 21–41, 1982.

6. ——, "Family Theory and the Epistemology of Humberto Maturana," in F. W. Kaslow (ed.), *The International Book of Family Therapy,* New York, Brunner/Mazel, 1982.

7. ——, "The First International Conference on Epistemology, Psychotherapy and Psychopathology: Charge to the Conference," *J. Strat. Syst. Ther.* 3: 43–49, 1984.

8. ——, "Whither Family Theory?" Workshop Presented at the Seventh Annual Family Therapy Network Symposium, "Getting Unstuck," Washington, D. C. March, 17, 1984, Recorded by Creative Audio, Highland, Ind.

9. DE SHAZER, S., *Patterns of Brief Family Therapy: An Ecosystemic Approach,* New York, Guilford Press, 1982.

10. GURMAN, A. S., "Family Therapy Research and the 'New Epistemology'," *J. Mar. Fam. Ther.* 9: 227–234, 1983.

11. HOFFMAN, L., *Foundations of Family Therapy: A Conceptual Framework for Systems Change,* New York, Basic Books, 1981.

12. KEENEY, B. P., "Bateson's Epistemology," *J. Strat. Syst. Ther.* 1: 45–55, 1981.

13. ——, *Aesthetics of Change,* New York, Guilford Press, 1983.

14. LIDDLE, H. A., "On the Problems of Eclecticism: A Call for Epistemologic Clarification and Human-Scale Theories," *Fam. Proc.* 21:243–250, 1982.

15. LIDDLE, H. A. and SABA, G. W., "Teaching Family Therapy at the Introductory Level: A Conceptual Model Emphasizing Pattern Which Connects Training and Therapy," *J. Mar. Fam. Ther.* 8:63–73, 1982.

16. MINUCHIN, S.; ROSMAN, B. L.; and BAKER, L., *Psychosomatic Families: Anorexia Nervosa in Context,* Cambridge, Harvard University Press, 1978.

17. PENN, P., "Circular Questioning," *Fam. Proc.* 21: 267–280, 1982.

18. POLS, E., *Meditation on a Prisoner: Towards Understanding Action and Mind,* Carbondale and Edwardsville, Southern Illinois University Press, 1975.

19. ——, *The Acts of Our Being: A Reflection on Agency and Responsibility,* Amherst, University of Massachusetts Press, 1982.

20. QUINE, W. V. O., *From a Logical Point of View,* 2d ed. rev., New York and Evanston, Harper and Row, 1961 (1953).

21. REAMY-STEPHENSON, M., "The Assumption of Non-Objective Reality: A Missing Link in the Training of Strategic Family Therapists," *J. Strat. Syst. Ther.* 2: 51–67, 1983.

22. SELLARS, W., *Science, Perception and Reality,* London, Routledge and Kegan Paul; New York, Humanities Press, 1963.

23. SELVINI-PALAZZOLI, M.; BOSCOLO, L.; CECCHIN, G.; and PRATA, G., "Hypothesizing—Circularity—Neutrality: Three Guidelines for the Conductor of the Session," *Fam. Proc.* 19: 3–12, 1980.

24. WATZLAWICK, P., *How Real is Real?,* New York, Random House, 1976.

25. ——, *The Language of Change: Elements of Therapeutic Communication,* New York, Basic Books, 1978.

26. WATZLAWICK, P.; BEAVIN, J. H.; and JACKSON, D. D., *Pragmatics of Human Communication: A Study of Interactional Patterns, Pathologies and Paradoxes,* New York, Norton, 1967.

27. WITTGENSTEIN, L., *Philosophical Investigations,* trans. G. E. M. Anscombe, New York, MacMillan, 1953.

33

AGAINST THE GRAIN: DECENTERING FAMILY THERAPY

GERALD D. ERICKSON

IS THERE A FAMILY IN THIS THERAPY?

The traps laid by systemic family analysis are springing up everywhere and they permit no easy escape. The currently hegemonic circular-systemic paradigm, marked as it is by three powerful and negative ideals of our time—anti-humanism, anti-subjectivism, and anti-historicism (Sheridan, 1980)—has inevitably led to forms of analysis whereby families are taken as closed systems, where relations among members are given primacy, a division of these relations into manifest/latent functions taken as a given, and wherein only the therapist is privileged to interpret the latent function. None of the major human problems of our era can be adequately addressed by, or treated within, a systemic paradigm, whether child abuse, the situations of formerly hospitalized individuals, gender inequality, problems of spousal violence, or social inequality (Bograd, 1984; Dell, 1986b; McCannell, 1986). Such problems either cannot be perceived within a systemic view (how many sexually abusive fathers or step-fathers have been reframed as "cuddlers"?), or, if attention is called to them, must necessarily disappear into a set of interlocking and circular relations, the sum of which are said to serve a purpose of coherence and fit, of being homeostatic and helpful, of being required by the family, of being wanted and desired. The final chill of the systemic mode is provided by the totalizing view that:

> the family has to fit with its environment, just as the individual has to fit within the family, or the separate organs have to fit together in the system that is the biological self. And all have to fit together in the ecology of the whole. (Hoffman, 1981, p. 348)

Reprinted from the *Journal of Marital and Family Therapy, 14,* 225–236. (1988).

While systems-based approaches to families and family therapy have come under attack from those upholding a feminist perspective (e.g., James & McIntyre, 1983; O'Hare & Taylor, 1983), there is no reason to suppose that a theory that cannot accommodate the interests of women should at the same time be adequate for men and children of either gender. Responses to the feminist critique have tended to acknowledge the difficulty in applying the systemic perspective to women's issues and the social context in general, while at the same time claiming that this is a matter of bias that may be corrected by including the therapist in the analysis (MacKinnon & Miller, 1987; Taggart, 1985). Calling for the therapist to exert greater effort and insight to bring a bias under control seems, however, to be another version of blaming the victim. The feminist perspective provides the most striking example of the incongruity of a systemic view and therapy as a social context, but the soundness of making this incongruity a feminist problem must be questioned. In contrast, an argument will be made here that the neglect of social context and persons qua persons, is inherent in the theory and not correctable; further, that the real problem lies in determining when and under what circumstances a closed-systems analysis and therapy may be useful and helpful, i.e., when a systems perspective may be considered as a limited approach.

With respect to any systemic case description, the fundamental assumption in this paper is that the total set, the structure of family relations is *produced* by the analysis and *not discovered* by the therapist. Thus, family members and their subjective intentions, their individual and shared sense of a past, their creation of meaning, all vanish and are replaced by a particular understanding of a set of relations as called forth by a therapist. This may be seen as a creative act, as "systems analysis," but it may also be seen as an act of mystification and sophistry wearing a mask of science.

With these preliminary broad strokes as background and as sounding themes, I would like to turn now to an account of how it is, in the imagery adopted, that it is possible to have a family therapy that does not contain families, where, so to speak, the death of the family has been accompanied by the birth of the therapist.

Bateson's Perspective

Gregory Bateson is nearly uniformly appealed to as both the intellectual force and arbiter of correct thinking among those adopting a circular-systemic paradigm. Quite often, simply his name and a brief quotation are offered as justifying a particular position. His writing may be said to function as the thermostat which maintains systemic analysis within a prescribed range, a boundary setting which is, of late, proving difficult for adherents to stay within. The conundrum which is the "epistemological core" of Bateson's perspective is that: "all social systems and all ecological systems are circularly organized and circularly connected into larger and larger systems . . . (and that) . . . no part can have unilateral control over the remainder or any other part" (Dell, 1986a, p. 514). This core is, at the same time, both an invitation to "see" the world from a particular standpoint and an assertion of values. A "no unilateral control" principle, for example, automatically values "noncontrol," and thus, such concepts as interlocking fit, cooperation, holism, fields, and self-regulation. Buried in the "core" is a universe of value judgments and interpretive stances. It offers an image, but it is a nonempirical image which cannot be tested.

It may be helpful to observe that Bateson employed the idea of system in at least three ways (Lipset, 1980), and usually all at once, in presenting his perspective of the world: (a) in the 19th century biological sense of the world as an organic whole, as everything being connected to everything else (later extended by Bateson to a grand ecological conception); (b) as an interpretation of cybernetics in considering social systems as self-regulating machinery; (c) by means of the model provided by structural linguistics as extended to nonlinguistic fields, i.e., to social anthropology.[2] I will argue that this last usage is the key to understanding current systemic theory and practice, and will expand on this below. For now, it need only be said that the three usages of "system" appear hopelessly confused in the theoretical grounding of family therapy, with the first taken as a given, the second as a problematic (does it truly fit all social systems?), and the third is largely ignored (though, by far, the operationally most powerful of the three). They seemed to form a whole *only* for Bateson, for *his* life, for *his* perspective. No one is obliged to adopt or accept his perspective; it is like any perspectivist account in being an interpretation of the world arising, in this instance, from Bateson's life experience and learning, in roughly the temporal ordering of his learning. Indeed, no one else *can* adopt it fully because his emphasis on "circularity" is from the self-regulating machine model and the "systemic" from a nonmachine model, a linguistic model. It is futile to disagree with Bateson's perspective; it was a powerfully liberating set of ideas for many, but it cannot be falsified as it relates to the world of therapy and, thus, must remain in the realm of conjectures and metaphysics.

Saying that Bateson's perspective cannot be falsified is not to say that we do not owe him a tremendous debt. As Nehamas said of Nietzsche, he not only offered "a new way of looking at the world, but equivalently, a new aspect of the world to look at" (Nehamas, 1985, p. 59). His perspective offered a note of hopeful possibility to therapists that they might move beyond the rigidities and stultifications of mid-to-late 19th-century culture and categories of atomized individualism. The dilemma of many contemporary therapists (for example, those who conduct feminist analysis), however, is to consider that they are caught between the old world of the *Diagnostic and Statistical Manual III* (1980), and the systemic perspective, neither of which can convey any complete sense of a world anyone actually lives in.

The Structuralist Model[3]

It was suggested, above, that there is a particular key to understanding current systemic theory and practice; moreover, a key that has been largely overlooked—the model of "system" as originally developed within structural linguistics early in the 20th century and later extended to primarily nonlinguistic fields. It may be a large claim to say that for the most part, systemic family therapists are unaware of the basic features of the model that informs their therapy; nevertheless, this seems to be true. Given the anti-historicist bias of the systemic concept, however, this may not be surprising. Strictly speaking, the structuralist model is known to the extent that it was employed by Bateson as part of his perspective and because it has provided a source of intellectual energy within and across disciplinary boundaries for several decades. However, the full implications of the model for therapy have seldom been approached and some further exegesis seems needed.

While the history of family therapy has not been written, and is not being undertaken here, we can note that wherever one looks in the current historical narratives of family therapy, one of three versions is likely to be encountered. The first, and most truncated, is a colonizer account usually presented in heroic-mythic form whereby a small number of psychiatrists, awakening from their Freudian slumbers, come to recognize the importance of the family as a unit of practice and begin to work "underground," finally surfacing at conferences in the 1950's (Guerin, 1976). This type of narrative immediately displaces the natives (e.g., those with prior experience in family practice) and establishes a small elite group with claims to all the ground. A second type of account is more teleological and dialectical in nature, recognizing the multifaceted nature of family therapy by locating a number of sources and influences from the past (child guidance movement, marriage counselling, group therapy, social group work), and demonstrating how these sources have been precursors to higher stages of development, namely ourselves and our therapies (Goldenberg & Goldenberg, 1985). A third type adopts a more technical and scientific point of view, locating the origins in the era of World War II and the development of inertial guidance systems, followed by the cybernetic revolution and the adoption of a general systems theory (Hoffman, 1981). The analysis which follows is closest to the spirit of a point frequently made by Haley (1972): The idea undergirding family therapy was a new idea in the world and the task was to dislodge old ideas, not accommodate to them. The disagreement is about the nature of the "new idea."

I suggest that the horizon be moved backward in time, so that the frontier of understanding may perhaps be moved forward. The point of origin, insofar as there are points of origin that may be isolated, of the "new idea" is to be found in the period 1907–1911 and the revolutionary work in linguistics by Ferdinand de Saussure (1959). The chaos that was linguistics in the early part of the century was first dismantled and then re-ordered in a new way by de Saussure. The means by which he formulated a new understanding and program of action in linguistics was comprised of a powerful set of concepts which have been found to be equally fruitful in nonlinguistic fields. These concepts, especially those of synchrony, diachrony and system, have been found to open new areas of analysis with respect to any phenomenon that can be said to be structured like a language, e.g., the unconscious (Schneiderman, 1983), kinship (Levi-Strauss, 1945), political ideology (Dowling, 1984), fashions in clothing (Culler, 1982), films (Metz, 1974), literary texts (Hawkes, 1977).

While there are many accounts of Saussure's contributions to modern thought (Culler, 1976; Eagleton, 1983; Kurzwell, 1980; Macksey & Donato, 1970), and the original book based on his lecture series is readily available,[4] several aspects of his linguistics are salient here. He is widely acknowledged as introducing a new way of thinking, a new form or mode of analysis, a mode that was revolutionary because it could not be taken as an addition, or as complementary, to existing forms of analysis, but only as an alternative (Jefferson & Robey, 1986). The mode of thought that he introduced is, when combined with some self-regulating machinery metaphor, in fact the mode that governs systemic therapy.

Foremost in his framework was the idea of language as a "system." His view was that language was a system of differences. He went on to say that there are two ways of understanding a language system—the diachronic (how a system changes through time) and the synchronic (how a system functions at a given moment in time). The first emphasizes how a system develops, with a focus on the individual elements and how they may change individually; the second, the synchronic, is focused exclusively on the *simultaneous relations* among the constituent elements at the moment of analysis, without reference to the past or historical development. These two forms of analysis are entirely distinct, lead to different kinds of knowledge and cannot be combined.

All family therapy, to a greater or lesser extent, rests on a synchronic perspective,[5] on an analysis of current relations, a downplaying of historical causation and a complete rejection of the diachronic. It has been customary in much of family therapy to link the diachronic with psychoanalytic theory and individual therapy and both, together, with "linear thinking." "Linear thinking" is, thus, a code word for faulty thinking and faulty thinkers. That is, values and ideology have become entangled and confused, even when dressed up in cybernetic clothing, with modes of analysis. This is perhaps inevitable since, as we shall see, the synchronic perspective contains, when applied to families, a fairly complete load of conservative ideology.

An argument can be made that a synchronic perspective was necessary for the expansion and development of family therapy. Systems based family therapy begins with the discourse analysis of the communications of schizophrenics and their mothers by Bateson and his colleagues in the early 1950's. The claim that the discourse of schizophrenia, and the person called schizophrenic, are to be understood as elements in a closed system, a system that may be completely grasped in the present as sequences of communications/behavior, and that these elements cannot be understood other than as being connected with the matrix called "family," is the founding synchronic gesture of family therapy. It was the moment when structuralism (the general term for any extension of Saussurian concepts to nonlinguistic fields) entered the therapy field as a means of examining a system of signs, a system of differences. A family "grammar" was produced, complete with punctuation and a set of binary oppositions, e.g., report/command, complementary/symmetrical, anological/digital, homeostasis/morphostasis. Some years earlier, Levi-Strauss (1945) had produced a landmark paper on "Structural Analysis in Linguistics and Anthropology." The development by Bateson and his colleagues was clearly part of a much wider movement to adopt structural linguistic concepts in the social sciences (Gardner, 1985).

There are certain concomitants of the synchronic/systemic perspective, of structuralism, that may be set out, the better to understand current difficulties in family therapy. The structuralist method has been stated in succinct fashion by Sheridan:

> It approaches its object . . . a social system . . . with an initial act of isolation. Such questions as the intentions of a creative subject, the functional origins of a system, the effects of external factors on the object, or the object on its environment are set aside as irrelevant. The isolated object is then analysed in terms of a "combinatory," that is, a system of relations between elements in which it is the relations, rather than the elements, that are significant. (Sheridan, 1980, p. 203)

With respect to persons as elements, Whitaker only states directly what is a necessary feature of structuralism when he says: "I don't think there is any such thing as a person. I think a person is just a fragment of a family . . ." (Giacomo & Weissmark, 1986, p. 504). This is precisely what is meant by anti-humanism; the human subject is set aside or bracketed off (along with *all* matters of content) and relations are given primacy. The system then comes to have the attributes of a person (autonomy, self-regulation, change, resisting, cooperating, seeking solutions) and the family itself, as a set of persons, dissolves into a system of rules and sequences, "hanging in the air," per Eagleton's apt phrase (Eagleton, 1983, p. 112).

With the focus on synchronicity, a very large question of therapy remains: What rule or sequence of interaction should be changed for what purpose? By itself, the structuralist method can only arrive at one answer: *Whatever is (synchronically), is right.* Hence, the emphasis on positive connotation in systemic analysis. The question may be formulated as follows: If both the family as a set of persons, and external reality, are excluded as points of departure for analysis, then what ground is there for the interpretation of meaning within the system and for intervention? The answer can only be that the structure of relations, and therefore, the meaning of relations and decisions about change, are produced solely by the analyst, the therapist. All analysis of family systems is fundamentally an interpretation; there can be no purely objective knowledge of synchronic states, and, to rephrase an old axiom, one cannot *not* interpret. We may follow Steiner, then, in saying that: "To interpret is to judge. No matter what decipherment is made . . . no interpretation is value free" (Steiner, 1986, p. 1262). Accepting that, we may ask, then, whether therapists can have a sufficiently God-like perspective to perform the task.

The modern idea of the therapist, of course, was born with Freud. Psychoanalysis is also a purely interpretive activity and, while a fairly complete homology could be drawn demonstrating the similarity of forms in psychoanalysis and a systemic perspective in family therapy, the concern, here, is solely with the singular centrality of the therapist within the structuralist method. We may sketch an approximation of the general model, as it is employed in family therapy:

1. The family is asked to provide a narrative of themselves and their current situation. This narrative is carefully guided through quite narrow channels (Maranhao, 1986), varying with what particular interpretations the therapist customarily makes, e.g., one is looking for a

sequence with a peripheral member, another for too-close members, another for a mother who may be behaving as someone's aunt, yet another to micro differences of perceptions among members, and so forth. *Any* interpretation is possible and any interpretation is as correct as any other in not being falsifiable. But, since any interpretation is possible, therapy should quickly dissolve into an "anything goes" welter of purely subjective interpretations, with each therapist functioning as a personal school-of-thought. While the therapy field, at times, resembles a free-for-all, there clearly are some boundaries of permissible interpretations.

There are no means of discriminating among interpretations other than through an appeal to what Fish (1986) has termed an "interpretive community," or to one or more subcommunities. Interpretations create "facts," but they are only facts to the extent that others accept a particular mode of interpretation (Fish, 1986). The entire set of family therapists, to a minimal extent, may be thought of as a single interpretive community; all members will at least value a focus on the family, subscribe to the notion of the importance of including a social context in understanding symptoms, and perhaps a few other variables. But this wider community is made up of many subcommunities with distinctive flavors of acceptable facts. These smaller communities compete with one another for members and offer contrary interpretations of similar situations. One explanation of the power of Bateson's perspective is that it is taken as a guide to the ordering of facts for several subcommunities. Other central figures have, first, to at least nod to his perspective while proclaiming their own. New subcommunities of interpretation arise periodically, as others fall from sight; a small number endure over the years and function as "schools of thought." Just now, a feminist interpretive community is forming; a "radical" interpretive community may form. It may be predicted that these subcommunities will take their place with the structural, strategic, "Milano," social-learning, experiential, Bowen, psychodynamic, and others, perhaps minimally affecting them on some points, but largely functioning as independent "fact"-generating clusters.

2. Whatever narrative is provided by the family is taken as the *manifest* content of the set of family relations; this content conceals what the family does not know and cannot know. The correct and true understanding is *latent* in the simultaneous relations and can be grasped only by those adepts who have a special vision, a synchronic vision, in fact, a special ability to conduct systemic analysis.

3. The interventions of the therapist fix upon the set of relations that they, themselves, produce, i.e., through the interpretation of the latent meaning, the ordering of the sequence, the setting of the boundary. Family members cannot share in any responsibility for the understanding or the intervention; what is latent is not only outside the awareness of members, but resides in what is among them at the moment, in the space between the nodes, and members can have no vantage point, no place to stand, for perception of the whole. Thus, one never reads any account of any family members' systemic understanding. It might be supposed that therapists possessing a powerful means of ordering observations would be interested in educating families to grasp a sense of their own problematic situations. A systemic perspective, however, is not a means to empower family members, but rather, is a means of empowering the therapist.

It is no accident that one-way screens and video equipment are part of the furnishings of family therapy centers. The narrative content is enacted on one side and the meaning produced on the other. With observers in action, the therapist in the interviewing room may be dissolved into the set of family relations and, thus, becomes another element in a sequence that needs correcting.

Reading the Family Like a Book

The above may be rewritten more baldly as an analogue of structural textual analysis: The family text, the narration of members, is set aside and isolated from the world as so much content;

family members, as authors of the text are bracketed off as fragments of a family organization; the set of family relations, family structure, is determined by the reader and is defined as what is real and of paramount interest. Family discourse (their individual and joint stories) is important in revealing epistemological errors and the misconstruction of their world. The signifiers of the family are split off from their "signifieds" by the reader and a new set of "signifieds" inserted. Hence, the centrality of the therapist is at the cost of the marginalization of the family. The synchronic reading provides the grounding that the reader is properly located in an interpretive community; the cybernetic metaphor, the faith that the structures produced can be changed by interfering in the synchronous mesh.

The ideal therapist, the master reader, would indeed be "neutral," without gender, beyond social class, of no ethnicity, having no views of proper behavior and no norms of family life, focusing exclusively on a closed system of family relations in an objective, value-free manner. However, actually existing master therapists seem to be those who offer plausible interpretations of family systems and are able to persuade others of the power and practical utility of their interpretations (always with the implied message, "You, too, may be powerful."). Master therapists are master interpreters, thus, the emphasis on the names and persona of specific therapists. Hopes that some strategies of interpretation may be demonstrated to be of greater value than others through outcome or process research seems, if not entirely in vain, much more difficult than has been considered. Since meanings are plural, where can the therapist stand for an objective view? Perhaps, therapists of the future will be able to do several alternative "readings" concurrently.

The Wilder Culture of the Systemic

The centrality of the family therapist is, of course, supported by, and consistent with, aspects of the wider culture. Quite aside from being a feature of a much broader structuralist movement in the social sciences and the arts, it is especially congruent with that whole range of managerial and scientistic developments that have come to the fore since World War II: A systems scientist, moving into and out of families in the manner of a management consultant, possessing esoteric knowledge not available to the customers, having the power to bring about change that the subjects of concern may not even be aware of needing to change, forming elites within a wider elite movement—all that sums up to at least a promise of power, and especially for professionals on the edge, a move towards the center. Those who are already powerful do not need family therapy. It is, indeed, ironic that Bateson's name and thought should be invoked to provide a theoretical underpinning to systemic therapy; ironic that he, who so disliked the very idea of power, should be linked to a therapeutic movement marked by the unilateral power claims of its adherents.

While the structuralist method of structural linguistics is a foundation of family therapy, it apparently has come to be seen, in some quarters, as too limited, too sterile, as a paradigm in need of a fresh beginning, if not redemption. The current scene is marked by attempts to smuggle a diachronic perspective (history and time) through a side door by means of new "scientific" metaphor. Thus, we hear of "evolution," "mutations," and "structure determinism" from biology and "nonequilibrium dynamics" and "singularities" from physics. (Hoffman, 1981) One synchronic state, it is said, may be transformed into another through these mechanisms and history permitted back on stage. Such metasynchronic moves may be seen as typical efforts to save a paradigm that is failing, that can no longer account for the data at hand, that has become so complex with language and interpretations that even the disciples can no longer follow the arguments. In keeping with a therapist-centered perspective, personal names and new images (and no evidence) are advanced as a rationale to stretch the theory into diachronic territory, e.g., Prigogine (1978), Maturana (1975), Varela (1975). If a sufficiently powerful interpreter permits the move, (and with scientific terminology), that is all that is required. The added metaphors, obscure as they may be, are taken as self-justifying and inherently a theoretical advance. Thus, changes in the theory of clinical practice become a matter of fashion, as set out by the couturiers and designers of therapy.

I have attempted, to this point, to formulate a series of arguments intended to undermine the structuralist/synchronic perspective as the central organizing framework for family therapy. It may be already regarded as a museum piece (Eagleton, 1983) in other fields, but is largely still taken as a firm set of assumptions by many family therapists.

It is not to be supposed that the arguments presented here are sufficient by themselves to decenter family therapy, or that systemic therapists will tremble and mend their ways. The material presented is simply part of a growing critique and set of evaluations of family therapy from differing points of view (e.g., Bernal & Diamond, 1984; Bograd, 1984; Erickson, 1984a, Liddle, 1984; McIntyre, 1985; McCannell, 1986). Perhaps this critique will provide others with a space from which to launch their own personal evaluations. However, this, too, is only an interpretation and part of the background for another perspective. But everyone will agree that some interpretations are better than others, and on that the argument rests.

CONCLUSION: CENTERING THE NETWORK

The analysis presented here leads inescapably to the conclusion that the circular-systemic/structuralist paradigm will remain for some time as an important organizing framework for interpretation and practice. The interpretive community is too broad and extensive, the power conferred on the adherents too great, the aesthetics and rhetoric too attractive for it to be otherwise. It is to be wondered that so little has been done in moving beyond the structuralist method, even from within the method, itself. If we accept that family therapy is based on acts of interpretation, then a whole new range of theory and methodology is available form hermeneutics (Ricoeur, 1981), reader response theory (Tompkins, 1980), new variants in psychoanalytic theory (Schneiderman, 1983), post-structuralist theory (Derrida, 1981), feminist theory (Kristeva, 1981), and the like. There are many new potential models for understanding the relation of family discourse and therapist interpretation.

Saying that, however, everything that follows is mere opinion. There are too many contingencies to read the future. We are still left with the basic quandary and the major challenge: If events in childhood "matter"' for adult functioning (not to speak of mattering for children), if gender matters, if actual events in adulthood matter, if actual social/political/ideological situations matter, then any notion that a general synchronic basis for family therapy is possible is swept away and no amount of theoretical cosmetics will be able to save the systemic. On the other hand, it was the synchronic perspective that unleashed the energy and dynamic in family therapy, that undergirds a good deal of creative practice yet, today. There is no going back to that Galapagos-like terrain of the mental health field where the interpretive communities of the old turtles still lie in wait with "facts" of ego strengths and borderline personalities. Yet, there is no clear way forward, either. Is there an escape from being "spellbound" by structuralist thinking? (Merquior, 1986).

The concept of system is only *fully* useful when considered synchronically, yet leads, unvaryingly, to anti-humanism, cybernetic tinkering, and whatever interpretive bias governs the therapist in the family. These results are all, no doubt, attractive and even pleasurable matters; being imprisoned systemically seems preferable to many alternative conceptual jails. But the question arises: If not "system," then what? What, then, is to be done to avoid therapeutic nihilism? That is, to state a number of values, what would a family therapy look like that made no pretense of being value-free, that included a temporal dimension, that included both persons and relations, that was contextual, that induced the reduction of power differentials between therapist and family, that hoped for, and promoted, the empowerment of families, that valued equality over authoritarianism, and that valued an educational method as well as the therapeutic? The most cursory glance will demonstrate that such family therapy is everywhere about us (see, for example, Karpel, 1986). What is lacking, however, is a framework around which a nonsystemic interpretive community can coalesce. With respect to this, there seems little alternative to adopting a social network perspective. Such a perspective offers the advantages of generating three kinds of information: (a) about persons, (b) about relationships, and (c) about the structure of relationships and how structures, persons and relationships have changed over time in particular social contexts. Further, the therapist assumes a new guise of one helper among other helpers, analysis is conducted jointly with the family, and family therapy, itself, becomes one form of network-gathering among many potential gatherings (Erickson, 1984b); it is not inherently superior to any other form. Further, since a social network has both temporal and spatial dimensions, unbounded and always in flux, changing through time in measurable ways, it cannot readily be taken as an object and cannot be mistaken as having a "commanding entity" (Jefferson & Robey, 1986, p. 115) somewhere at the "core."

If a network perspective is to assume a more central role in interpretive activities and related practice, however, several problems need to be addressed. These problems are largely problems of vocabulary. It is most unfortunate that the concept "network," itself, entered the family practice world as a "therapy," as an extension of family therapy to "wider" systems. As such, it occupies a place in the general interpretive community as the most minor sort of adjunctive therapy (and, interesting though it is, apparently rarely practiced). The other side of the term—the social side—has been nearly preempted by the managerial culture and converted into "networking," seemingly, a way of using other people to one's advantage. These appear to be major handicaps, but perhaps may turn out to be rather trivial in the larger term. Rather trivial because the more interesting and fruitful areas of theory and practice development are occurring *outside* and apart from systemic family therapy currently and have been for several years. As one example, the already massive research findings and literature on social support (Gottlieb, 1983) are antithetical to a systemic perspective and cannot be integrated into systemic practice. Similarly, new developments in work with schizophrenia (Anderson, Hogarty, & Reiss, 1986), child and spousal abuse (Pressman, 1987), and high risk populations, in general, are taking place elsewhere. A network perspective can include social support interpretations as well as shelter and expand work with special populations.

The notion of a network of relationships of persons as a point of departure for analysis and practice can accommodate a conceptualization of family therapy as *one form* of therapeutic activity following from the analysis. The idea of network, however, is diachronic in nature, since an historical account of any current state is necessary. A network is also without boundaries and a contradiction to systemic closed systems analysis. There remains a question of whether a synchronic mode is possible in a decentered form. There is no theoretical objection to such a move, only the caveat that a knowledge different in kind and in meaning is produced, and with all the limitations presented above. What can be seen on the horizon, as the systemic paradigm slowly dissolves into incoherence, is a family therapy developing within a network space, as a major form of network intervention, but removed from the center, to a space where "system" will survive and may be employed for selected situations.

In any event, new facts are being created as family therapy is being decentered, opening the doors to more open spaces and out of the terrible poverty of the systemic trap.

REFERENCES

American Psychiatric Association. (1980). Diagnostic and statistical manual of mental disorders (3rd ed.). Washington, DC: Author.

Anderson, C., Hogarty, D. & Reiss, G. (1986). *Schizophrenia and the family.* New York: Guilford Press.

Bateson, G. (1972). *Steps to an ecology of mind.* New York: Ballantine Books.

Bernal, B. & Diamond, G. (1984). Notes on a socio-historical perspective of family therapy. *Journal of Structural and Systemic Therapy, 4,* 42–47.

Bograd, M. (1984). Family systems approaches to wife battering. *American Journal of Orthopsychiatry, 54,* 558–568.

Culler, J. (1976). *Saussure.* (Modern Masters Series). Glasgow, Scotland: Fontana Books.

Culler, J. (1982). *On deconstruction: Theory and criticism after structuralism.* Ithaca, NY: Cornell University Press.

Dell, P. (1986a). In defense of linear causality. *Family Process, 25,* 513–523.

Dell, P. (1986b). Toward a foundation for addressing violence. *Family Process, 25,* 527–531.

Derrida, J. (1981). *Positions.* Chicago: Chicago University Press.

Dowling, W. (1984). *Jameson, Althusser, Marx: An introduction to the political unconscious.* Ithaca, NY: Cornell University Press.

Eagleton, T. (1983). *Literary theory: An introduction.* Oxford, England: Basil Blackwell.

Erickson, G. D. (1984a). A menu note on the cybernetic network. *Family Process, 23,* 200–204.

Erickson, G. D. (1984b). A framework and themes for social network intervention. *Family Process, 23,* 187–197.

Fish, S. (1986). *Is there a text in this class?* Cambridge, MA: Harvard University Press.

Gardner, H. (1985). *The mind's new science: A history of the cognitive revolution.* New York: Basic Books.

Giacomo, D. & Weissmark, M. (1986). Systemic practice. *Family Process, 25,* 504–550.

Goldenberg, I. & Goldenberg, H. (1985). *Family therapy: An overview.* Monterey, CA: Brooks-Cole.

Gottlieb, B. (1983). *Social support strategies.* London, England: Sage Publications.

Guerin, P. (1976). *Family therapy.* New York: Gardner Press.

Haley, J. (1972, March). *Historical development of family therapy.* Seminar presentation, University of Manitoba, Winnipeg, Manitoba, Canada.

Hawkes, T. (1977). *Structuralism and semiotics.* Berkeley, CA: University of California Press.

Hoffman, L. (1981). *Foundations of family therapy.* New York: Basic Books.

James, K. & McIntyre, D. (1983). The reproduction of families: The social role of family therapy. *Journal of Marital and Family Therapy, 9,* 119–129.

Jefferson, A. & Robey, D. (Eds.), (1986). *Modern literary theory.* London, England: B. T. Batsford.

Karpel, M. (1986). *Family resources: The hidden partner in family therapy.* New York: Guilford Press.

Kristeva, J. (1981). Women's time. *Signs, 7,* 13–35.

Kurzwell, E. (1980). *The age of structuralism.* New York: Columbia University Press.

Levi-Strauss, C. (1945, April). *L'Analyse structurale en linguistique et en anthropologie.* [Structural analysis in linguistics and anthropology]. *Word, 1,* 33–53.

Liddle, H. (1984). Beyond family therapy: Challenging the boundaries, roles and mission of a field. *Journal of Structural and Systemic Therapy, 4,* 4–14.

Lipset, D. (1980). *Gregory Bateson: Legacy of a scientist.* Boston, MA: Beacon Press.

MacKinnon, L. K. & Miller, D. (1987). The new epistemology and the Milan approach: Feminist and sociopolitical considerations. *Journal of Marital and Family Therapy, 13,* 139–155.

Macksey, R. & Donato, E. (1970). *The structuralist controversy: The language of criticism and the sciences of man.* Baltimore, MD: Johns Hopkins Press.

Maranhao, T. (1986). *Therapeutic discourse and Socratic dialogue.* Madison, WI: University of Wisconsin Press.

Maturana, H. (1975). The organization of the living: A theory of the living organization. *International Journal of Man-Machine Studies, 7,* 313–332.

Maturana, H. R. & Varela, F. J. (1980). Autopoiesis: The organization of the living. In H. R. Maturana & F. J. Varela, (Eds.), *Autopoiesis and cognition: The realization of the living.* Boston, MA: Reidel Publishing.

McCannell, K. (1986). Family politics, family policy and family practice: A feminist perspective. *Canadian Journal of Community Mental Health, 5,* 61–73.

McIntyre, D. (1985). Domestic violence: A case of the disappearing victim? *Australian Journal of Family Therapy, 5,* 249–258.

Merquior, J. G. (1986). *From Prague to Paris: A critique of structuralist and post-structuralist thought.* London, England: Verso Press.

Metz, C. (1974). *Film language.* London, England: Oxford University Press.

Nehamas, A. (1985). *Nietzsche: Life as literature.* Cambridge, MA: Harvard University Press.

O'Hare, J. & Taylor, K. (1983). The reality of incest. *Women and Therapy, 2,* 215–229.

Pressman, B. (1987). *Family violence: Origins and treatment.* Guelph, Canada: University of Guelph.

Prigogine, I. (1978). Time, structure, and fluctuations. *Science, 201,* 778–785.

Ricoeur, P. (1981). *Hermeneutics and the human sciences.* (J. B. Thompson, Trans. & Ed.) Cambridge, England: Cambridge Press.

Saussure, F. de (1959). *Course in general linguistics.* Ed. by Charles Bally and Albert Sechehave, 1915. Trans. by Wade Baskin, New York: Philosophical Library.

Schneiderman, S. (1983). *Jacques Lacan: The death of an intellectual hero.* Cambridge, MA: Harvard University Press.

Sheridan, A. (1980). *Foucault: The will to truth.* London: England: Tavistock Publications.

Steiner, G. (1986). Viewpoint: A new meaning of meaning. *Times Literary Supplement, 4,* 1262.

Taggart, M. (1985). The feminist critique in epistemological perspective: Questions of context in family therapy. *Journal of Marital and Family Therapy, 11,* 113–126.

Tompkins, J. (1980). *Reader-response criticism from formalism to post-structuralism.* London, England & Baltimore, MD: Johns Hopkins University Press.

Varela, F. J. (1975). A calculus for self-reference. *International Journal of General Systems, 2,* 5–24.

NOTES

[1]Because there are many family therapies, the subject matter of this paper is not concerned with any particular model or school of thought, but rather, with the common thread of the idea of "system" which is present in all models. Since the idea is most clearly expressed in current usage by the terms "systemic" or "circular-systemic," I have used those terms as point of departure and base for analysis. The fit of the analysis with any specific family therapy model is, thus, inexact and intended to be so: Let the reader decide how exact.

[2]Was Bateson a structuralist? He certainly did not identify himself as such, but there is evidence that he was acquainted with structuralist thought and adapted it to his own work (see for example, the account of his "fundamentalist synchronic position" in Lipset [1980, p. 146], his correspondence with Levi-Strauss, the foremost structuralist anthropologist of the era [Lipset, 1980, p. 270], and the frequent use of the terminology of structural linguistics [e.g., "signs"] in *Steps to an Ecology of Mind* [Bateson, 1972]).

[3]The "structuralist model" does not, of course, refer to "structural family therapy."

[4]Saussure never lived to write the book, *Course on General Linguistics*; it was compiled by his students from lecture notes taken between 1907–1911.

[5]One of the enduring curiosities of family therapy is the rhetoric of "open" systems and the absolute necessity of conducting synchronic analysis with reference to closed systems, only. It represents a basic and unbridgeable gap between the "general systems" metaphor and the circular-systemic perspective. Of late, the "second cybernetics" has emphasized a "closed" approach to systemic analysis, "autopoiesis" being understood as a capacity for self-production through a closed system of relations (Maturana & Varela, 1980).

34

ECOSYSTEMIC EPISTEMOLOGY: CRITICAL IMPLICATIONS FOR THE AESTHETICS AND PRAGMATICS OF FAMILY THERAPY

BRADFORD P. KEENEY AND DOUGLAS H. SPRENKLE

The history of family therapy's individuation includes its characterizing and understanding individuals within the context of relationship ecologies. Despite the emergence of that broader view, controversies between reductionism and holism have remained. Specifically, there are family therapists who, like the early behaviorists, accentuate the importance of constraining one's focus to the level of observable and quantifiable sequences of behavior. Others claim that such punctuation is not adequate to account for the complexity of human experience and interaction, which in their opinion, requires more metaphorical forms of description.

In family therapy, reductionistic approaches do not argue with the "truthfulness" of metaphorical accounts of human behavior but claim that those forms of description are often not useful in creating and implementing strategies for therapeutic change. That form of reductionism typically arises from a pragmatic perspective that is primarily concerned with reducing or simplifying phenomena for practical purposes. In contrast to that position, holistic arguments have arisen from several perspectives including phenomenological, psychodynamic, existential, and systems. They do not question the "effectiveness" of pragmatically inspired therapies within the context demarcated by the practicing therapists but question whether the demarcated context is the appropriate context within which to evaluate the therapy.

Reprinted from *Family Process, 21*, 1–19. (1982).

The authors express their appreciation to the Menninger Foundation for sponsoring the conference "Size and Shape in Mental Health" held in Topeka, Kansas, September 7–9, 1979. Organized by Gregory Bateson and the first author, its participants included Mary Catherine Bateson, Wendell Berry, John Perry, Richard Rabkin, Gary Snyder, and Lyman Wynne. The conference helped to provoke some of the ideas presented in this paper.

For example, if a woman complains of severe anxiety attacks, a more pragmatic therapist may contract with the client to alleviate her symptom. Therapy would then be evaluated empirically by quantifiable comparisons of symptomatic occurrence. On the other hand, a less pragmatic therapist would be more concerned with evaluating the larger gestalt of which that symptom is a part, be the gestalt an individual's psyche, pattern of social interaction, or family ecology.

The pragmatic emphasis in family therapy is exemplified by practical approaches to human problem-solving that seek to be as economical and simple as possible. Proponents of that position are principally concerned with focusing on behavioral outcomes and typically describe the patterns of their work as analogous to playing a game of chess, in which victories and losses are observable outcomes that can be tallied. Accordingly, they evaluate ideas, tools, and techniques on the basis of their utility in achieving successful outcomes and attempt to package their learnings in explicit and economical forms of description.

That form of pragmatic reductionism is more apparent in our field when therapists argue that therapy must usually focus on the "presenting problem" with respect to designing interventions and evaluating the therapy. They acknowledge, however, that a larger gestalt may indeed be the unit that must change but that it will change most effectively through a therapist's limited focus on presented problems, usually cast in digital form. Their primary concern is with what therapeutic ideas and behaviors contribute to practical and effective problem-solving.

In contrast to the pragmatic position of family therapy, which seeks to reduce phenomena into manageable and practical bits and pieces, we suggest there is also a tendency to move in the opposite direction. Such a position, characterized by a sensitivity to holism and complexity, is motivated by aesthetics. Its emphasis is upon increasing and expanding the therapist's understanding and appreciation of the formal patterns characterizing therapeutic contexts. Therapists embodying the aesthetic perspective tend to speak of their work in terms of a journey or pilgrimage in which their principal concern includes their own growth as well as their clients or colleagues.

The aesthetic-based therapist does not argue with the pragmatist's technical considerations of therapy but does not consider them to be primary. This therapist is directed less by pragmatics and more by aesthetics. Are the patterns of therapy elegant? What is health? What are the errors of purposeful behavior on the part of therapist as well as client? These questions are motivated by a more aesthetic base and differ from the principal questions of the pragmatist, who may be asking: Are the patterns of therapy effective? What is the problem to be solved? What are the errors of a therapy without an adequately contracted goal? And so on.

An integrated ecosystemic approach to therapy asks pragmatic and aesthetic questions and is therefore guided by both orientations. One might even argue that in their finest moments "masters" of family therapy always work from both positions. The argument of this paper is that therapy based on ecosystemic epistemology arises from a position that is responsive to issues of both pragmatics and aesthetics. That view presupposes, however, that the pragmatic and aesthetic are different logical levels such that questions of the aesthetic cannot be answered from the pragmatic and vice versa.

Furthermore, if these two levels of concern are mixed, confusion may arise. For example, a pragmatist may criticize, discount, and even reject some ideas on the basis of their being too abstract, obscure, or irrelevant to the practice of therapy. On the other hand, an aesthetic-minded therapist or theorist may reject some ideas on the basis of their being too simplistic, purposeful, and ugly with regard to the creation and experience of pattern. For example, criticism of pragmatic family therapies has been largely voiced by Bateson. Predictably, the response of the pragmatists to his criticism has always been on the pragmatic level. It can be seen that the debate is irresolvable as long as each position argues from a mutually exclusive level—both criticisms are correct within the context of the respective perspective from which the criticism derives. At the same time, both criticisms are incomplete from the larger context subsuming two different levels of perspective.

At times the "isolated pragmatic position" (i.e., one that excludes aesthetic issues) in family therapy seems to echo the position of radical behaviorism that argues against the importance of nonempirical, nonquantifiable, and impractical questions. In the history of psychology, the reductionist arguments were responded to by holists such as Maslow. Maslow's position was not to say that the mechanistic, reductionistic, behaviorists were completely wrong but to suggest that they were correct within the boundaries of a particular context. He pointed out that on the analytical level, which is concerned with concrete particulars, reductionism is certainly appropriate. However, on the level of synthesis with its concern for wholes, he argued that reductionism must yield to holism. Maslow's (29) quest was for a way of thinking "both about particulars and about wholes without falling into either meaningless particularism or vague and useless generality" (p. 317).

This paper shares a similar goal, an epistemology that includes both reductionism and holism, pragmatism and aesthetics. To be more specific, our concern is with an epistemology that is sensitive to issues of pragmatics and aesthetics pertaining to ecosystems. Such an epistemology would necessarily have to embody two identifiable patterns: (a) the practitioner's moving in a reductionistic and specific direction when guided by ecosystem pragmatics and (b) the moving in a holistic (and more ambiguous) direction when concerned with ecosystem aesthetics. The way in which such therapy is integrated would depend upon the form of dialectic between these two juxtaposed patterns.

This form of epistemology, previously identified as "ecosystemic epistemology" (see 17) is rooted in the ideas of cybernetics, ecology, and systems theories. A large part of family therapy, particularly the more pragmatically inspired forms, has used some of these ideas to explain and advance its practice. The underlying assumption of this paper is that the pragmatically based forms of family therapy, which claim to be extensions of the ideas of cybernetics, ecology, and systems theory, have often overshadowed the level of ecosystem aesthetics. That may not be a new criticism, as is demonstrated by Pearson's (22, p. 145) earlier warning that family therapy risks becoming buried in a "new cybernetic scientism" that "strips away the contextualized meanings which surround family-system processes." In other words, family therapists have sometimes derived heuristic tools and strategies at the cost of ignoring ecosystem aesthetics. That stands in contrast to Bateson's (2, p. 505) reminder that "the ecological ideas implicit in our plans are more important than the plans themselves, and it would be foolish to sacrifice these ideas on the alter of pragmatism."

This discussion will therefore focus on identifying several critical implications that ecosystemic epistemology generates for family therapy, implications that are often largely ignored by an overemphasis on pragmatics. Namely, the following domains will be addressed: (a) the function of language in the relation between epistemology and clinical practice; (b) healthy and pathological family ecologies; (c) art and technique in therapy; and (d) the issue of manipulation.

The reader must be warned that this paper will repeatedly make the same type of error made by those overemphasizing the pragmatic level. That follows since some of the discussion will be singularly cast from the aesthetic level of ecosystemic epistemology, thus carrying with it the possible implication that the pragmatic level is either wrong or ugly. That is not the final conclusion the authors intend. Our concern is that the pragmatic be juxtaposed with the aesthetic. Our paper is purposefully biased in the direction of the aesthetic owing to the paucity given that level of ecosystemic epistemology, but the reader should remember that an ecosystemic epistemology includes both the pragmatic and aesthetic as components in an interactive system of ideas and actions.

The reader must also be reminded that the following ideas may elicit criticism on the basis of obscurantism, idealism, or utopianism or may trigger questions such as, "What are the immediate practical consequences of these ideas in clinical practice?" That will inevitably occur if the ideas are approached from the level or context of pragmatics. Such questions may be taken as an indication of how skillfully the reader operates as a pragmatist. This paper does not argue that the questions are wrong. Instead, it suggests an additional form of question arising from the level of aesthetics in ecosystemic epistemology.

The field of family therapy, as well as occidental culture, is deeply entrained to pragmatic questions, but not so habituated to questions of the aesthetic. It is to that deficiency this paper addresses itself. Initially, a brief analysis of the relation of theory and epistemology to clinical practice will be presented in order to demonstrate how pragmatics and aesthetics inevitably are connected parts in clinical contexts.

RELATION OF THEORY AND EPISTEMOLOGY TO CLINICAL PRACTICE

The relation between theory and clinical practice is an issue that repeatedly permeates serious discussion of family therapy. For example, Whitaker (35), Haley (14), and Bandler and Grinder (1) have all protested, in different ways, that theory can hinder clinical work. Unfortunately, their theories about the relation of other theories to clinical practice may lead the reader to overlook the necessary connections between ideas and action or, more broadly, between aesthetics and pragmatics. Any effort to disassociate this relation reinforces the false occidental dualism of mind and body. This epistemological error may consequently lead to maintaining various forms of pathology at individual, social, cultural, and planetary levels (see Bateson, 2).

When therapists argue that "theory" is not immediately useful to clinical practice, they are partly correct in the sense that a theory of therapy (or diagnosis or research) is of a different logical level from therapeutic action. However, to regard theory (whether organic, psychodynamic, behavioral, or systems) as completely irrelevant to the clinician ignores the ways in which theory and clinical practice interact. An earlier work on the relation of ecosystemic epistemology to family therapy (17) suggested that it is impossible to have no epistemology, for even the idea that one has no epistemology arises from a particular epistemology. Therefore, a therapist must always be operating from an epistemological base.

Theory, here defined as a description of the relation between one's epistemology and habits of action, may or may not be part of the therapist's repertoire of understanding. One relevant distinction to make is whether therapists consciously know the relation between their epistemological base and habitual patterns of clinical action. Any question regarding whether it is useful to have an explicit description of this relation (i.e., theory) presupposes a pragmatic orientation independent of aesthetic concerns. Questions presupposing the primacy of theory, on the other hand, will involve criteria of aesthetics with regard to the relation between epistemological premises and habits of action.

Independent of whether one is primarily concerned with the pragmatics or aesthetics of theory, it is again important to acknowledge that theory is always part and parcel of one's behavior. As Hanson (15) has proposed, "seeing is a 'theory-laden' undertaking" (p. 90), or as Popper (23) puts it, theory is a "net set to catch what we call the world" (p. 59). In that basic sense all strategies of perception and action presume underlying ideas, theories, and epistemologies that in part generate the strategies.

A pragmatically inspired therapist is somewhat analogous to a chef whose interests are more connected with cookbooks than theories of food science. Extending the analogy, although a chef may argue that formal theories of food science are irrelevant to his cooking, his choice of recipe and culinary action reflect particular premises regarding nutrition, as well as rules governing cookery. From the pragmatic side, although a cook and therapist always embody some form of theory and epistemology, it is correct that they are more explicitly focused on the level of engineering change. Nevertheless, the ways in which a cook or therapist induce changes, whether in culinary or family relationship contexts, are determined by formal premises regarding the nature of the change agent and his or her relation to the context being changed.

This paper argues that although there is a distinction between epistemology and action, as well as aesthetics and pragmatics, there is always a relation between the two levels such as their interaction modifies and tempers one another. An overemphasis on the differences between epistemology (or theory) and clinical practice, however, may blur their necessary connection. An important set of questions needs to be asked concerning the forms of interaction between these two different levels.

In regard to this interaction the pragmatist may consequently ask; "Is the interaction useful?"; "Is the interaction economical?"; "How does it direct me at this particular moment in this particular situation?" The answers to these questions could be predicted to arise pragmatically from a reductionistic strategy in which quantitatively shaped hypotheses are empirically researched. Contrarily, the aesthetic side may ask: "Is the interaction ecologically healthy or beautiful?" "Is there promotion of understanding?" "Will the interaction seriously disturb the ecology in the long run?" These questions would be answered from standards or fundamentals inherent in the realm of the aesthetic that cannot easily be given digital and pragmatic expression.

From the perspective of the aesthetic, which is a higher level of abstraction than the pragmatic, it is important that an understanding of theory precede the imposition of its pragmatic consequences. Unfortunately, as Bateson (6) has observed with reference to the clinical application of cybernetics, ecology, and systems theory, such understanding is sometimes ignored.

> Theory is becoming available to action-oriented people, whose first impulse is. . . . "Take it to the wards and try it. Don't waste years trying to understand the theory. Just use whatever hunches seem to follow from it." Such people are likely to be frustrated and their patients hurt. . . . Theory is not just another gadget which can be used without understanding. [6, p. 237]

These comments implicitly suggest one of the ways in which the interaction of theory and clinical action could temper clinical action. Namely, understanding theory facilitates more effective or less harmful therapy. On the other hand, the pragmatists have long demonstrated the utility of checking theoretical hunches in the context of stubborn data. That method of verification should not suggest that investigators or therapists randomly poke at phenomena in order to verify hunches. Similarly, one should not wait in the library until enough understanding is achieved before trying to rescue lost souls. The trick and the art lie in the simultaneous influence of epistemology on clinical practice and clinical practice on epistemology. A more metaphorical way of saying this is that the shape of the interaction should be seen as more a metalogue between the aesthetic and pragmatic, rather than a combination of lineal effects.

THE FUNCTION OF LANGUAGE IN EPISTEMOLOGY AND CLINICAL PRACTICE

Epistemology, or one's "way of knowing," interfaces with clinical practice in the language of a therapist. A therapist's description of his work, whether in the process of therapy or in post hoc explanation, requires appropriate linguistic forms that indicate the epistemological base directing his action. The importance of language as a focal point for discussing the relation of epistemology to clinical practice is emphasized by Selvini-Palazzoli (27). She argues that "linguistic conditioning" too often encapsulates one's ideas in a static, lineal epistemology that leads us to conceptualize families in a lineal rather than a "systemic-circular sense." Her assertion exemplifies the trend among family therapists to announce their subscription to a cybernetic form of causality when describing human interaction rather than a lineal one.

Selvini-Palazzoli's work presupposes that one's epistemology and premises for action are constrained by the deep structure or underlying forms of language. One basic implication is that owing to the structure of occidental language, there is no way of avoiding slicing the world into namable pieces. The naming of "parts" consequently leads one to engage in some form of dualism, even when one is attempting not to be dualistic. For example, the distinction between cybernetic and lineal causality suggests a dualism that may only change the appearance of the "lineal or dualistic trap" one is trying to escape. Given that dualistic constraint of language, however, Bateson (4, p. 244) suggests that there are "better and worse ways of doing this splitting of the universe into nameable parts." The contradictory objective seems to be to use dualistic language in order to escape other (more intolerable) dualisms.

Ecosystemic epistemology attempts a nondualistic conceptualization of cybernetics that recognizes complete circuits or whole ecosystems, rather than isolated parts that act, react, interact, or transact with each other. This perspective attempts to avoid any over-emphasis upon dualisms between individual and family, identified patient and therapist, symptom and context, behavior and interactional pattern, lineal and cybernetic, pragmatic and aesthetic, that may overshadow the connectivity of whole systems. For example, a therapist is always viewed as part and parcel of the unit of treatment—i.e., both are connected as parts of a complete cybernetic circuit.[1]

Cyberneticians note that a dualistic usage of language may lead to dismemberment of whole systems. That is illustrated when family therapists (and researchers) break up the natural history of family process into different discrete functions, resulting too often in losing sight of the totality or connectiveness of the interactive process. For example, scholars have distinguished parts of family process that are called communication, conflict, problem-solving, power, perception, homeostasis, and so on. If we draw boundaries between these parts of family process, we may lose awareness that they are just various representations of a unitary interactive system. Similarly, on the level of individual organization, the vocabulary that discriminates fear, rage, love, and hate too often implies that they operate separately, rather than being a system of feelings.

Ecosystemic epistemology, embodying nondualistic cybernetics, attempts to mend those static dualisms. In other words, to keep sight of complete cybernetic circuits we have to be careful how we pattern our observations and descriptions in order to avoid rigidly demarcating the circuitry (system) into isolated elements or mechanisms. It is also important to remember that nouns are always static nominalizations of relationship and process. An immediate implication is that an ecosystemic description of contexts of human relationship requires that we do

[1]Unfortunately, since Wiener's original formulation of cybernetics in 1948, an important distortion of its original meaning occurred as it traveled through such contexts as engineering, social science, and the media—analogous to the process of message distortion in rumor transmission. In the distorted form, cybernetics fell prey to the lineal trap of occidental linguistic conditioning. In particular, when the engineers got hold of the term, they used it as a referent to the study of black boxes that are delimited by parts called input and output. However, Bateson and Mead (7) claim that Wiener wasn't principally concerned with the mere input-output relations of black boxes, but with the events within the larger circuit of which the observer is part.

The dualistic distortion of cybernetics that posits the observer outside the phenomenon observed leads to the idea that the outsider is in a position possibly unilaterally to manipulate or control the system he's observing. Wiener's cybernetic ideas were not strictly dualistic in that sense. Rather, he viewed such an observer as part of the whole circuit, subject to the part-whole constraints of the system. Hence, criticism of cybernetics as the scientism of manipulation and control without any roots in the existential constraints of context and praxis carries with it the erroneous presupposition that cybernetics demarcates the observer from being observed (or the operator from that being operated on).

not nominalize interactions that comprise whole systems. To say that you are a leader, communicator, therapist, and so forth is to freeze (nominalize) a description of relationship into an isolated reification with assumed locus within the boundaries of one of the relata.

What we might term the "cybernetic use of language" involves preserving (and provoking) an awareness of whole interactive systems. Yet how can one use occidental language (which imposes dualisms) to depict systemic wholeness? One way is to engage in a dialectic in which dualistic linguistic formulations can be simply refuted. Watts (31, pp. 159–160) points out that the Madhyamika system of Nagarjuna is such a dialectical tool that refutes any dualism one might propose or encounter.

> . . . because language is dualistic or relational, any affirmation or denial whatsoever can have meaning only in relation to its own opposite. Every statement, every definition, sets up a boundary or limit; it classifies something, and thus it can always be shown that what is inside the boundary must coexist with what is outside. . . . The Madhyamika dialectic uses this as an infallible method for pointing out the relativity of any metaphysical premise. . . . [31, p. 160]

In other words, this approach is based on the catch that any statement proposed is necessarily dualistic by virtue of the linguistic form in which it is packaged. Thus, to get unstuck from one dualistic frame is inevitably to get stuck in another frame. The process of a dialectic encourages one to keep getting unstuck continuously. The implication is that a family therapist could embody a form of dialectic similar to the Madhyamika system to avoid getting stuck in any particular dualistic frame or lineal trap.

The therapeutic work of Selvini-Palazzoli provides a starting point in that direction. For example, she notes that one way of starting the process of getting unstuck from the lineal model of "treating a depressed patient" and moving to the cybernetic model of "treating an interactional pattern" is to transform one's description from "he is depressed" to "he seems depressed." She refers to this method as substituting the verb "to seem" for the verb "to be." However, to avoid getting stuck in potential dualisms proposed by the verb "to seem," she suggests replacing it with the verb "to show." We now move from "he seems depressed" to "he is showing us what illusively appears as depression." What Selvini-Palazzoli does, in process, is to unencapsulate linguistic framings by a form of dialectic. "To be" is challenged by "to seem," which is again challenged by "to show," and so on. Incidentally, it should be pointed out that a more elaborated form of dialectic is provided by what Bandler and Grinder (1) call their "meta-model"—a heuristic set of questions that enables one to challenge the incomplete, distorted, or absurd linguistic forms of client's statements.

The application of this form of dialectic to theory can be exemplified by how we think about "people communicating." From the perspective of whole cybernetic systems, it becomes nonsense to ask whether people communicate. In other words, we do not communicate per se, but rather we become a part of a communicating system. Paraphrasing Birdwhistell (10), one does not originate communication; one participates in it. This suggests that the first axiom of communication proposed by Watzlawick, Beavin, and Jackson (32), "one cannot not communicate," contains an epistemological error owing to its linguistic form. Viewed cybernetically, one can neither communicate nor not communicate. A revision of the axiom might be stated as, "One cannot not be a part of a communicating system." Of course, that statement potentially encapsulates a dualism between self and the "communicating system." The point is that one cannot escape dualistic framings when using occidental linguistic forms. At best, a dialectic can be proposed that continuously unravels each asserted linguistic frame. Any attempt to localize a delimited agent, such as the "self," performing purposive action (e.g., communicating, felling a tree, doing therapy) upon another delimited object is to chop up the whole cybernetic circuit. Ecosystemic epistemology therefore suggests that we do not statically demarcate those whole systems into isolated parts or functions.

The examples essentially demonstrate a way in which one battleground of ecosystemic epistemology is being cast in terms of the proper use of language. Going further, one could identify ecosystemic epistemology as including a set of ideals that attempts to disseminate ideas in terms of: (a) translating reified nouns (e.g., ego, anxiety, roles, enmeshment, paradox, symptom, therapist, family, theory, epistemology, clinical practice) into linguistic forms that signify relationship and process;[2] and (b) shifting the boundaries of individuals, families, and other ecosystems toward the context of completed circuits. However, because ecosystemic epistemology is itself cast in dualistic forms of language, a dialectic must be utilized to prevent it from falling into static lineal traps. In this sense, ecosystemic epistemology must *continuously* unravel and challenge its own propositions.

We will now shift to delineating how ecosystemic epistemology proposes other critical implications for family therapy. Again, the following discussion will be biased from the level of ecosystem aesthetics. The reader is further reminded that ecosystem pragmatics and aesthetics are always interacting components in ecosystemic epistemology.

HEALTHY AND PATHOLOGICAL FAMILY ECOLOGIES

One concern of the aesthetic level of ecosystemic epistemology is to characterize health and pathology from a general, holistic, systems perspective. In response to that concern it is immediately interesting to observe that the etymology of the word "health" demonstrates that it is connected to a family of words including whole, wholesome, hallow, and holy. Healthy family ecologies, therefore, in the more general sense, can be described in terms of the wholeness of relationship systems rather than exclusive consideration of the individual, interactive, or social components. Ecosystemic epistemology accordingly regards signs of healthy family ecologies as communication about the whole ecology, of which the family and its members are parts. Dualisms between health and pathology are mended when one views symptoms as well as signs of health as simply relationship metaphors—communication or indicators of the ecology of relationship systems (see 17).

On an aesthetic level, ecology is based upon the fundamental doctrine that all things in nature are complexly, but systematically, interrelated—morally, mentally, and physically. Roszak (26, p. 38) proposes that, if you extend this idea as far as it will go, you can imagine the earth at large, including ourselves and our culture, as a single, evolving system of life. The cybernetician Lovelock (19) terms this idea, "Gaia," a metaphor for thinking of the planet and its interlocking systems as a whole organism. The way in which systems are connected can be used as an aesthetic way to think about health and pathology.

The family is therefore a system within a system within a system, ad infinitum. The ways in which these cascades of Chinese box-like systems are connected to one another represent what cyberneticians call "coupling of systems." Long ago, Lewis Carroll (11) poked fun at the inappropriate coupling of biological systems when he described Alice's difficulty in trying to understand an unusual game of croquet. In Carroll's game, Alice is coupled with a "Flamingo mallet," which is coupled with a "hedgehog ball." As Bateson comments:

[2]The reader should again be reminded that ecosystemic epistemology does not merely suggest transposing one set of terms for another (e.g., family for individual), but is primarily concerned with the linguistic forms or context within which any set of terms are cast.

> Alice's difficulty arises from the fact that she does not "understand" the Flamingo, i.e., she does not have systemic information about the "system" which confronts her. Similarly, the flamingo does not understand Alice. They are at "cross purposes." [8, p. 15]

Bateson goes on to suggest that the problem of coupling man through consciousness with the environment of which he is necessarily a part is comparable to Alice's dilemma. When consciousness lacks or distorts information about these relationships, pathology may be generated. As Mary Catherine Bateson (8) has illustrated, an infant's body is a system coupled to the system of a family's life of which she is a part. For these systems the mother's and child's body processes can be coupled for breast feeding. In addition, the supermarket's milk supply (which is unlimited with respect to the child's demands) can be coupled to these systems. The latter form of coupling may perpetuate pathology by producing "a distortion in perception of the system that complements the belief that the sea is infinite" (p. 120). This example suggests that the ways in which systems are coupled reinforce or generate the epistemological premises upon which individuals shape their perception and action.

Similarly, all family ecologies can be characterized by the forms of coupling that link individuals and other subsystems to family systems as well as to larger social and cultural networks. Along these lines, Berry (9) states, "the parts are healthy insofar as they are joined harmoniously to the whole" (p. 110). This aesthetic level of description requires further elaboration of how the parts can be harmoniously connected. One example is provided by Minuchin's (21) discussion of social boundaries in terms of the connection of family subsystems to one another on a social organizational level. His boundary metaphors do not attend, however, to how individuals experience being connected to parts of ecosystems. In other words, an unattended subject concerns the forms of experience through which an individual becomes connected to a larger ecosystem.

One way of talking about how individuals and families become connected to the larger ecosystem of which they are a part is to use the aesthetic notion of sacramental experience. For Bateson (3, p. 25), sacrament is a technical matter referring to a combination of conscious thought and primary process that provides a way through which we enact our part in the ecosystem, or what Berry metaphorically calls our "oneness in the Creation." Sacramental experiences can therefore be described as characterizing a complementary relationship between "self" and the larger system subsuming it. In family life, the participation of all family members in growing a garden provides opportunities for sacramental experience in which members may experience being both parts of their family and the earth's territory. Perhaps the prescription of family rituals by therapists basically provides opportunities for family members to experience being connected to their whole context.

Bateson (2) states that the relation between an individual and the larger system of which he is a part must necessarily be complementary, or the ecology will suffer innumerable offenses. That idea is expanded by Berry (9) who claims that "there is, in practice, no such thing as autonomy. Practically, there is only a distinction between responsible and irresponsible dependence" (p. 111). The argument is that one can only be in a complementary relation with the system incorporating him and the choice of complementarity can be cast as healthy or pathological.[3]

Whitaker (36) aesthetically describes healthy families in terms of a context in which members experience "the creative tension between individuation and belongingness" (p. 113).

[3]Note that "complementary relationship" is another way of stating a part-whole relationship. Thus, any system subsumed by a larger system represents a part-whole or complementary relationship. The idea of autonomy assumes that a person can be independent of another person. However, the relationship of any set of persons is a whole of which no member can be separate. On this larger level of relationship systems, autonomy is a meaningless idea.

The dialectic between "self and we-ness" requires that the family provide flexible role structures in which "all the role functions in the family should be available to everybody in the family" (p. 111). In such families, children have opportunities for acting as if they were parents—whereupon they sacramentally experience being the parents. In other words, they have the experience of being parents (and parents being the children), while at the same time not really being the parents (and parents not really being the children). When one experiences being all the parts (or roles) that constitute a family, one can be described as, sacramentally speaking, having become one in that family. The "we-ness" and belongingness is being a family part (or role), and the individuation has to do with being able to change one's part.

On the other hand, from the aesthetic level, pathological family ecologies are descriptions of rigid systems in which the coupled subsystems are linked through what Minuchin terms enmeshed and disengaged boundaries. Such families apparently do not provide opportunities for the sacramental experience of being connected to other role functions, subsystems, and larger ecosystems. Pathological family ecologies can be characterized accordingly by inflexible role positions that lead to disconnections (morally, mentally, or physically) between husband and wife, marriage and family, family and community, community and earth, or any other possible permutation.

Although we previously stated that there is no such thing as autonomy, that statement was from the level of whole relationship systems. On the reductionist level of discrete parts, it may be argued that there is no such thing as "no autonomy." At this level, the individual systems, rather than their social relationship, are depicted. Whitaker's notion of health as a "creative tension between individuation and belongingness" implies a dialectic between the two levels. Thus, a more correct way of defining pathology would be to characterize it as the inability of an ecosystem to embody transformations between individual and social relationship levels.

From that view, ecological disconnections refer to a break in the pathways between levels of a system. In other words, in a pathological family ecology one gets stuck in one level. For example, no exit in a social relationship implies "enmeshment," whereas quicksand at the individual level suggests "disengagement." On a broader level, pathology at the family organizational level suggests the family's inability as a whole to be connected to the larger systems of neighborhood or community.

Poster (24, p. 121) connects with that line of reasoning by suggesting that only *after* the family was reduced to the conjugal unit, work was removed from the household, and the family severed from its ties with the community did the family begin manifesting the form of intense emotional dysfunction characterized by pathological family systems. Similarly Slater (29) says:

> In a simple community when a family crisis occurs people run into the street and the community gathers around to mediate, nourish and absorb. As a community becomes larger and less integrated the capacity of the family to generate drama does not change, but it can no longer be shared. The community becomes privatized, the family isolated, the streets empty. . . . Referral agencies, mental hospitals, prisons, and nursing homes are a few of the tardy, impersonal, inhumane, and generally rather dilapidated mechanisms we have evolved to replace this naive responsivity. [29, p. 36]

Berry (9) proposes that wherever there is a point of ecological disconnection, "the collaboration of corporation, government and experts sets up a profit-making enterprise that results in the further dismemberment and impoverishment of the Creation" (p. 137). In that way the solutions and cures may perpetuate the problems—an extension of the Mental Research Institute (see 33) view of problem formation. An important pragmatic question concerns the extent to which therapy as an institution creates, perpetuates, or maintains the very problems it purports to cure or solve. For example, Bateson's (2) analysis of alcoholic addiction demonstrates how family, friends, and therapists may intervene in ways that reinforce the dismemberment of "self" (mind) and "alcoholism" (body)—resulting in the problem being perpetuated and escalated. Thus, a concern with ecosystem aesthetics leads to examining the pragmatic effects of family therapy in terms of whether it facilitates or hinders ecological connections.

ART AND TECHNIQUE IN THERAPY

Any concern over what therapists actually do in their clinical practice eventually leads to an examination of their specified techniques. Going further, concern about coupling the implementation of their technique with the systems they treat, as well as all systems subsuming them, leads to an examination of their art. Accordingly, we will now discuss ecosystem aesthetics and pragmatics in terms of the therapist's art and technique.

One of Whitaker's (37) frustrations in teaching family therapy involves the tendency of his students to translate what he says, usually cast in aesthetic terms, into pragmatic versions of technique. For example, if he points out that the family will begin to change following the therapist's declaration of impotence, neonate therapists may take this to mean that when they want to induce change in a family they need to "simulate" impotence. An authentic experience becomes reduced (i.e., mistranslated) to a practical method or trick.

A brief perusal of the field indicates that numerous schools of therapy are based on attempts to reduce therapeutic artistry to packageable techniques that can be explicitly taught (and evaluated). From the aesthetic side, it must be asked whether these maps of artistic territory are simply distilled tricks that do not capture adequately the whole relevant context of the artist's work. The holistic response is in contrast to the reductionist position that various forms of artistry in therapy can be reduced to underlying basic forms, techniques, and method.

It might be argued that therapists can be differentiated on the basis of their commitment to aesthetics or pragmatics. Those who exclusively practice (and teach and evaluate) particular sets of skills and techniques as the royal road to therapeutic change would then be characterized as pragmatic "technicians." Such therapists occasionally imply that therapy is analogous to fixing a car or repairing a broken chair, and sometimes suggest that any focus on the "personal life of the therapist" is a distraction. They may even harshly criticize training contexts that spend time on the "personal growth" of the therapist. For technicians, their work is a craft involving useful skills—a representation of an "I-it" operation. "I will cure it."

On the other hand, art, rooted more in aesthetics than pragmatics, is an I-Thou operation in which training and practice of therapy focuses on one's own character building. The skill is incidental and secondary to growth of self, as opposed to the technician's focus on acquisition of tools and skills, with the self remaining the same. Paraphrasing Bateson (5), art can be ecologically defined as the problem of judging the ecological implications of a course of action as it becomes incorporated and assimilated into the total context. Thus, for an artist, the actions that arise from the practice of a skill have importance only in terms of its ecological function in the larger contexts of which the action is a part—its effects on one's character and social context, as well as planet. "We" are affirmed through *our* relation of "I-Thou."

It can be noted that training to become an artist actually invokes a dialectic between pragmatics and aesthetics, or what some might want to call left- and right-brain interaction. In the case of Zen Buddhism, the pupil chooses a technique to master (e.g., archery, calligraphy, tea-serving). Learning that technique is then governed by pragmatic constraints such as daily practice of particular skill components. Any explicit attention to the "personal growth" of the pupil that distracts from learning the techniques would be summarily dismissed. At the same time, however, the pupil is continuously bombarded by experiential dilemmas such as Koans.

The broader context tempers his mastery of technique from including an arrogant sense of pride or hubris. In western vernacular, his ego is kept in check by an interaction between pragmatic and aesthetic levels of concern. More specifically, dualisms between "self" and delimited objects are curbed. The overall effect is that technical mastery is juxtaposed with a form of experience that maintains the zen pupil's (and teacher's) complementary place as a humble part in a greater ecosystem.[4]

The process of learning to be an artist also demonstrates a point about the nature of change. The artist can only make a choice concerning the type of context within which his life will be governed. Commitment to the constraints of this context, however, results in slow change. For example, a student of physics must patiently wait years while studying mathematics and science until finally the bits of information begin to coalesce into meaningful patterns—he awakens to discover he is becoming a physicist. Similarly a music student must practice what may seem to be trivial and to require strenuous discipline until the joy of being "musical" finally evolves. The choice that makes a difference is the context in which we choose to set ourselves. The immediate moments are always consequences of the context of which we have chosen to be a part. As Bateson (5) puts it, there is "no free will at the immediate level," although "you will undergo change rather slowly according to the context you set yourself for learning in."

One implication for family therapy is that although pragmatically inspired techniques may provide immediate symptomatic relief to some piece of an ecosystem, the issue of the individual or family being committed to an alternative context of learning may easily be bypassed. The decision to change one's context of learning, however, is analogous to the Zen situation (or the aspiring musician). One chooses a new context of learning in which change requires time. All one can do in the immediate moment is practice and wait. Those forms of change focus on deep levels of mind, involving conversion of underlying epistemological premises.

One might now see that the pragmatic and aesthetic are coupled to different temporal frames. The pragmatic, typically connected to a shorter framework of time, is more concerned with brief forms of therapy and often requires that the therapist be impatient with outcomes that deviate from what was initially defined as the intended goal. On the other side, aesthetics is more connected to a broader time frame and requires patience on the part of therapist (and client) with regard to emergent changes.

What is important in the aesthetic context is a commitment to practice. Ironically, it can be argued that pragmatists use techniques to effect quick changes, whereas a primary concern with the aesthetic leads to using technique to postpone immediate change. On a broader time scale, however, artists practice technique as a means of effecting what they prefer to think is more profound change. In that broader frame, both orientations are pragmatic but are on different time scales, with different sensitivities to the aesthetic.

The differences in perspective are further exemplified by the story about someone complaining to Picasso that his portrait of Gertrude Stein did not look like her. Picasso is said to have replied, "Never mind, it will." One can choose to be different (or "see" differently) only by commitment to a different context in which one patiently practices and waits.

The difference between strictly pragmatic (sometimes called "band-aid methods") and strictly aesthetic (sometimes called "character rebuilding") approaches to therapy is also exemplified by how therapists view "symptoms." When a symptom is depicted as an ugly, bothersome nuisance to be quieted, alleviated, or exorcised, the therapeutic focus will inevitably be more surgical, technical, and brief-oriented. On the other hand, if the presenting discomfort is viewed

[4]A more ecological form of description would suggest that the technique or skill is harmoniously coupled to the whole ecology. The coupling can be seen, in part, as the complementary relationship of the skill to the larger context, which includes the therapist. Accordingly, both technique and therapist are complementary parts of a larger context.

as "the motor for growth," immediate symptom alleviation may be avoided and even seen as unethical. The views of Bateson, Laing, and Perry, among others, who depict psychosis as a self-healing journey, lead them to provide nonproblem-solving contexts (i.e., shelters) for people "suffering" such change. The general idea that what we label "symptom" may be the signal or metaphor of beginning growth is summarized by Esterson (13):

> He is like someone who has been living with a tourniquet on his arm. When the tourniquet is released and the blood begins to flow, the first experience is pain. The pain is a sign of returning life, not of the onset of disease. [13, p. 361]

At this time it is important to acknowledge that the reader may have mistakenly taken our discussion to imply that artists and technicians are two types of therapist. That is not the authors' intended outcome. Rather, the point this paper is moving toward is that an ecosystemic understanding of aesthetics and pragmatics requires that art be seen as a higher logical level than technique. One implication is that a concern for technique and pragmatics without any regard for the broader aesthetic context leads to the vulgarization of technique and pragmatic effort. Similarly, efforts to achieve aesthetic standards without serious regard for technical mastery inevitably lead to vulgar art. Each extreme represents the use of only half of one's brains. In contrast, ecosystemic epistemology involves the total interactive system with levels of pragmatics and aesthetics.

THE ISSUE OF MANIPULATION

The relation of pragmatics and aesthetics becomes most apparent in discussions regarding the idea and practice of interpersonal manipulation. In these discussions, however, it should always be made clear that if one defines manipulation as mere influence, then the truism, "one cannot not manipulate," is nondebatable since we are always influencing one another or communicating on a relationship level. The term, manipulation, as used by some therapists, however, suggests something more specific. They refer to *purposeful* intention to manipulate another. That definition is congruent with standard dictionary formulations that to manipulate is to induce change in order to serve one's purpose.

Cyberneticians have demonstrated that purposive consciousness may blind one to an awareness of ecological (inter)connections. In the case of brief problem-solving therapies, the homeostatic network surrounding the "problem" (social, psychological, economic, and so on) may not always be adequately comprehended. In 1968, a private conference in Vienna entitled "The Effects of Conscious Purpose on Human Adaptation" (8) addressed the pathology underlying purposive manipulation of various contexts. It found that conscious purpose, with its aim of achieving specific goals, cannot always take into account the whole ecological context and that this cognitive deficiency often leads to ecological disconnections or inappropriate coupling of systems.

The pragmatic problem, when tempered by the aesthetic side, is not one associated with conscious purpose or control. The problem is how to let an individual, family system, or social organization achieve its adjustments without mucking up the ecology.[5] For example, Whitaker (34) has made the interesting point that "it's important to know that we are also most valuable in those moments where we're not straining to be helpful" (p. 9). An implied counter point is that purposefulness in trying to help may itself become destructive. Unfortunately, knowing that purposefulness is not helpful may not be helpful.

[5]"Mucking up the ecology" refers to generating or maintaining inappropriately coupled system levels.

The trick seems to be partially related to not being in a hurry for change or problem-solving. In therapy, that is illustrated by the experiential family therapists who approach therapy primarily for their own growth. For example, if you approach a family with the idea, "You've got to change in the next ten sessions," more than likely the family will remain the same. But if you approach the family from the position, "I have infinite time and attention to give to you now," or "I am more concerned with my own growth," they may change quickly. The same principle applies to trying to get a small baby to go to sleep. The dilemma is that when you believe that you don't have much control, outcomes sometimes occur that may be interpreted as your having more control.

These considerations lead us to using the "green-thumb" metaphor for helping to account for successful gardeners, political leaders, and therapists. In the case of therapy, green-thumb therapists speak of respecting their client's intentions (often unconscious) and see their work as mobilizing the client's own resources. They do not impose packaged cures upon them. Furthermore, they see the client as activating the therapist's own growth and evolution.

One of the tragedies in family therapy is that some therapists use ecosystemic ideas to derive pragmatic strategies without any consideration for the aesthetic. The consequence is that they use ecosystemic ideas in a lineal and monadic fashion that is analogous to the inappropriate coupling of Alice's flamingo and hedgehog. One consequence of an inappropriate coupling of ecosystemic ideas to the therapist's action within the context being treated is suggested by an observation of Rappaport (25). He notes that "simple cybernetic models of adaptation may themselves be atomistic, and that concern with the homeostatic maintenance of some variables may distract us not only from other variables, but from consideration of the structure from which they have been abstracted" (p. 55). Therefore, family therapists who identify the "homeostatic cycle" in which a piece of behavior labeled problematic is maintained may indeed find a shortcut to immediate symptom alleviation but may be acting with ignorance of the larger ecology. That is another way of stating that the cybernetic nature of the therapist's self and the context of which he is part is distorted in the therapist's screen of consciousness. Such distortion inappropriately couples the therapist to the context of which he is a part.

Cyberneticians have lamented that their theory gets twisted into lineal forms of pragmatic plans that lead to more ecological disturbances. Rappaport (25) responds to this:

> It could be argued that increased knowledge of ecosystems results in decreased respect for them, and thus leads them to be guilty of, and subsequently to be punished for, what might be called ecological hubris. It is perhaps the case that knowledge will never be able to replace respect in man's dealing with ecological systems. [25, p. 59]

"Respect" for ecosystems assumes that the therapist and client are artifacts of an interactional pattern. The emphasis upon the pattern or dance rather than the dancers leads one to realize that both therapist and client are parts that constitute the whole of an ever-changing and evolving relationship context. That view enables us more correctly to identify the issue of manipulation in therapy. Ecosystemic epistemology suggests that it is a mistake to describe either therapist or client as unilaterally steering ("manipulating") the interactional dance in which they participate. For example, although it may sometimes appear that one dancer "leads" and another "follows," closer examination shows this to be questionable, since the follower may lead the leader to lead.

A similar metaphor comes from the cybernetician Holt (cited in 8, p. 249) who holds that "in my eyes the rock sculpts the sculptor, as much as the sculptor sculpts the rock." Such metaphors of relationship remind us of the interconnectedness of all parts of any ecosystem.

One might argue that "ecological humility" is an inevitable outcome of ecosystemic epistemology since there is no emphasis on any part of the whole relationship system. On an experiential level, this form of humility involves an awareness that any particular feeling, perception, or thought is always a response to a whole situation that is only partially represented in consciousness. In other words, conscious knowing is limited to an awareness of a fragment of the whole system or context within which we are an interactant. Ecological humility acknowledges the incompleteness of conscious knowing and sees it as only part of larger mental systems with diverse levels, including the aesthetic.

One outcome of pragmatically inspired schools of therapy is that they typically present solutions and cures in left-brain, discursive (digital) terms. That form of presentation assumes that problems and solutions can be known and approached through conscious, purposive thinking. As Bateson (3) has pointed out, however, the solution, cure, or answer is always partly unknowable. Any attempt to "know" the answer involves translating it into the left-brain, manipulative side. Bateson (3) remarks that "once they're switched over, no matter how right they were poetically and aesthetically, they go dead, and become manipulative techniques" (p. 26).

On the aesthetic side, the artist works to experience art, not to create a procrustean bed. For example, Gary Snyder (30) once mentioned that he seldom recorded his best poems because they were "too perfect" for the situation from which they emerged. From the level of aesthetics, the therapist's participation in therapy has more to do with being alive than creating specific outcomes. The immediate implication for therapy is that efforts to make therapeutic problem-solving explicitly conscious (e.g., creating packaged cookbook cures) may result in manipulative techniques that are not adequately coupled to the ecology of which they are part.

Our earlier discussion of the use of language suggested that ecosystemic epistemology attempts to avoid static, dualistic formulations. The proposal was to critique continuously and amend one's linguistic frames, whatever they may momentarily be. That means that any written record of such a dialectical process would be contradictory, always incomplete, and multi-leveled. This approach provides an alternative way of using language to talk about therapy.

An example of this style of discourse is storytelling that attempts to recreate contexts in vivid, analogic terms. As Simon (28) points out, this form of discourse presents us with "levels and layers of meaning"—a kind of "dance between fact and fiction; between the sciences and the arts" (p. 24). Simon goes on to use Bateson's metaphor suggesting that "if the 'melody' without is harmonious with a 'melody' within; then we are likely to achieve a kind of phenomenological understanding—what in German is called *Verstehende*" (28, p. 28). Thus, one can choose to tell a story that embodies a network of patterns that are isomorphic with the patterning within the therapeutic situation you wish to discuss.

It is perhaps appropriate now to present two stories. The first is an excerpt from Key's (18) tale about an imaginary space trip—it is concerned with pragmatics and manipulatory change. The second is a zen lesson about aesthetics and ecological connectiveness told by Herrigel (16).

I

> Adjust the focus of your space-reducing attachment, Ladies and Gentlemen. You will now observe that the earth herself is a living creature, and that what you have called men are the microbes on her skin. . . . Adjust your fine screws, Ladies and Gentlemen, and you will see amongst the microbes some that are smaller than others. These are viruses, and their cell-structure is incomplete so that they are only fully operative when they become part of other cells. In their own language, you may remember, they are called Experts.
>
> Observe, if you will, Ladies and Gentlemen, the operative cycle of an Expert. You will see one of them entering a normal, differentiated cell. Observe that it goes straight to the nucleus. It has the power to do this because it is incomplete, and when it gets to the nucleus it starts to rearrange the structure there. Remember, Ladies and Gentlemen, the well-known law that only what is partial can change what is complete. Your physicists split the atom, you may remember, by bombarding it with parts of atoms, because whole atoms leave it unchanged. [18, pp. 117–119]

II

> "You are under an illusion," said the Master after awhile, "if you imagine that even a rough understanding of these dark connections would help you. These are processes which are beyond the reach of understanding. Do not forget that even in Nature there are correspondences which cannot be understood, and yet are so real that we have grown accustomed to them, just as if they could not be any different. I will give you an example which I have often puzzled over. The spider dances her web without knowing that there are flies who will get caught in it. The fly, dancing nonchalantly on a sunbeam, gets caught in the net without knowing what lies in store. But through both of them 'It' dances, and inside and outside are united in this dance. So, too, the archer hits the target without having aimed—more I cannot say." [16, pp. 82–83]

The reader should be reminded that art always includes technique—i.e., the aesthetic must include the pragmatic level. One can never play any music with a sense of "mastery" unless some form of technique has been previously assimilated. Therefore, to see the choice as "pragmatics versus no pragmatics" is not equivalent to "pragmatics versus aesthetics." Any attempt to be in the context of art without sufficient technique can only lead to free-associative muddle. Any emphasis on pragmatics without regard for the aesthetic may become a loose buzz-saw. The path to art and aesthetics is through using both our brains, left and right, as one whole circuit. A sense of that circuitry is what Bateson calls "wisdom." For the therapist as artist, technique and art are not two. For ecosystemic epistemology, aesthetics and pragmatics are not two.

Before closing, it should be warned that some people use the term "ecosystemic epistemology" to represent a framework, backdrop, or stage for understanding the sequences of action that make up the drama of therapy. That again presupposes a separation of ideas from action and the aesthetic from the pragmatic, which is incorrect. Ecosystemic epistemology does not pertain exclusively to the sequences of action or to patterns of ideas. Its focus is always upon relation between ideas and action, the aesthetic and pragmatic. In the context of relationship, the relata are never two.

On the aesthetic level, ecosystemic epistemology leaves us without any finite distinctions. On that level we must even finally admit that there is no dualism (i.e., difference on the same logical level) between lineal and ecosystemic epistemologies or between the pragmatic and the aesthetic. There are inevitably occasions when we seek simplification. In these times we become reductionistic; create overspecified goals and means; speak of things, parts, lineal sequences, and atomistic cybernetics. In addition to having one foot in the domain of the pragmatic and secular, we also need to be part of the aesthetic and sacred with its holistic emphasis on processes, wholes, systems, underspecified goals and ends, and obscurity. Without the aesthetic, we forget to bring a certain amount of love (as well as hate) to what we look at and interact with. Simultaneously, we must remember that without the pragmatic, we get lost in our dreams and passion.

The sin of Job, as Bateson (2) has reminded us, was his hubris. Job, who boasted, "What a clever man am I," encountered Satan, who was actually a part of Job. Satan's remedy was to expose Job to natural history. God, the whole of Job, finally says, "What do you really know?" His sermon, Bateson points out, tells Job that he does not know any natural history.

> Who is this that darkeneth counsel by words without understanding. . . .
> Does thou know when the wild goats of the rock bring forth?
> Or canst thou tell when the hinds do calve?
>
> Job 34

Ecosystemic epistemology suggests that any attempt to embody pragmatics without aesthetics or aesthetics without pragmatics will lead to Job's false sense of righteousness. Ecological humility occurs when the two become legitimate within the context of a never-terminated metalogue. Such a context may facilitate the realization that, as the poet William Blake put it, "Without contraries is no progression."

And, finally, Isak Dinesen (12) has already stated, with aesthetic elegance, what this discussion has attempted to point toward.

> You speak like a person who would pronounce half of the notes of the scale—say, *do, re* and *mi*—to be sacred, but *fa, sol, la* and *ti* to be only profane, while Madam, no one of the notes is sacred in itself, and it is the music, which can be made out of them, which is alone divine. If your garter be sanctified by my old hand, so is my hand by your fine silk garter. The lion lies in wait for the antelope at the ford, and the antelope is sanctified by the lion, as is the lion by the antelope, for the play of the Lord is divine. Not the bishop, or the knight, or the powerful castle is sacred in itself, but the game of chess is a noble game, and herein the knight is sanctified by the bishop, as the bishop by the queen. Neither would it be an advantage if the bishop were ambitious to acquire the higher virtues of the queen, or the castle, those of the bishop. So are we sanctified when the hand of the Lord moves us to where he wants us to be. Here he may be about to play a fine game with us, and in that game I shall be sanctified by you, as you by any of us. [12, pp. 14–15]

REFERENCES

1. Bandler, R. and Grinder, J., *The Structure of Magic*, I, Palo Alto, Science and Behavior Books, 1975.
2. Bateson, G., *Steps to an Ecology of Mind*, New York, Ballantine Books, 1972.
3. ——, "Ecology of Mind: The Sacred," in R. Fields (ed.), *Loka*, New York, Anchor Books, 1975.
4. ——, "Afterword," in J. Brockman (ed.), *About Bateson*, New York, E. P. Dutton, 1977.
5. ——,"Direction and Determinism in Change," Lecture at Rackham Auditorium, University of Michigan, Ann Arbor, Michigan, April 4, 1977.
6. ——, "Theory versus Empiricism," in M. Berger, *Beyond the Double Bind*, New York, Brunner/Mazel, 1978.
7. Bateson, G. and Mead, M., "For God's Sake, Margaret," *CoEvolution Quart.* 10: 32–44, 1976.
8. Bateson, M. *Our Own Metaphor. A Personal Account of a Conference on the Effects of Conscious Purpose on Human Adaptation*, New York, Alfred A. Knopft, 1972.
9. Berry, W., *The Unsettling of America*, New York, Avon Books, 1977.
10. Birdwhistell, R., "Contribution of Linguistic-Kinesic Studies to the Understanding of Schizophrenia," in A. Auerback (ed.), *Schizophrenia*, New York, Ronald Press, 1959.
11. Carroll, L., *Alice in Wonderland*, ed. by D. Gray, New York, W.W. Norton, 1971.
12. Dinesen, I., *Seven Gothic Tales*, New York, Vintage Books, 1961.
13. Esterson, A, "On Breakdown in Psychiatry," in J. Fosshage and P. Olsen (eds), *Healing: Implications of Psychiatry*, New York, Human Sciences Press, 1978.
14. Haley, J., "Ideas Which Handicap Therapists," in M. Berger, *Beyond the Double Bind*, New York, Brunner/Mazel, 1978.
15. Hanson, N., *Patterns of Discovery*, Cambridge, Cambridge University Press, 1958.
16. Herrigel, E., *Zen in the Art of Archery*, New York, Vintage Books, 1971.
17. Keeney, B., "Ecosystemic Epistemology: An Alternative Paradigm for Diagnosis," *Fam. Proc.* 18: 117–129, 1979.
18. Keys, J., *Only Two Can Play This Game*, New York, Julian Press, 1972.
19. Lovelock, J. *Gaia: A New Look at Life on Earth*, Oxford, Oxford University Press, 1979.

20. Maslow, A., *Motivation and Personality*, New York, Harper and Row, 1970.

21. Minuchin S., *Families and Family Therapy*, Cambridge, Mass., Harvard University Press, 1974.

22. Pearson, G., "Prisons of Love: The Reification of the Family in Family Therapy," in N. Armistead (ed.), *Reconstructing Social Psychology*, Baltimore, Penguin, 1974.

23. Popper, K., *The Logic of Scientific Discovery*, London, Hutchinson, 1968.

24. Poster, K., *Critical Theory of the Family*, New York, Seabury Press, 1978.

25. Rappaport, R., "Sanctity and Adaptation," *CoEvolution Quart.* 2: 54–67, 1974.

26. Roszak, T., *Person/Planet*, New York, Anchor Press, 1977.

27. Selvini-Palazzoli, M.; Cecchin, G.; Prata, G.; and Boscolo, L., *Paradox and Counterparadox*, New York, Aronson, 1978.

28. Simon, H., "In Praise of Muddleheaded Anecdotalism," *Western J. Speech Communic.* 42: 21–28, 1978.

29. Slater, P., *Earthwalk*, New York, Bantam, 1974.

30. Snyder, G., Personal communication, September, 1979.

31. Watts, A., *Psychotherapy East and West*, New York, Ballantine, 1961.

32. Watzlawick, P.; Beavin, J.; and Jackson, D., *Pragmatics of Human Communication*, New York, W. W. Norton, 1967.

33. Watzlawick, P.; Weakland, J.; and Fisch, R., *Change: Principles of Problem Formation and Problem Resolution*, New York, W. W. Norton, 1974.

34. Whitaker, C., "Process Techniques of Family Therapy," Unpublished manuscript, 1974.

35. ____, "The Hindrance of Theory in Clinical Work," in P. Guerin, Jr. (ed.), *Family Therapy: Theory and Practice*, New York, Gardner Press, 1976.

36. ____, "On Family Therapy" (Interview with Bruce Howe), *Pilgrimage*, 7: 107–114, 1979.

37. ____, Personal communication, September, 1979.

RECOMMENDED READING

Aponte, H. J. (1985). The negotiation of values in therapy. *Family Process, 24,* 323–338.

Bateson, G. (1972). *Steps to an ecology of mind.* New York: Ballentine Books.

Dell, P. F. (1982). Beyond homeostasis: Toward a concept of coherence. *Family Process, 21,* 21–41.

Dell, P. F. (1985). Understanding Bateson and Maturana: Toward a biological foundation for the social sciences. *Journal of Marital and Family Therapy, 11,* 1–20.

Dell, P. F. (1987). Maturana's constitutive ontology of the observer. *Psychotherapy, 24,* 462–465.

Foester, H. Von. (1985). Apropos epistemologies. *Family Process, 24,* 517–521.

Held, B. S. (1990). What's in a name? Some confusions and concerns about constructivism. *Journal of Marital and Family Therapy, 16,* 179–186.

Held, B. S., & Pols, E. (1985) Rejoinder: On contradiction. *Family Process, 24,* 521–524.

Held, B. S., & Pols, E. (1987). Dell on Maturana: A real foundation for family therapy? *Psychotherapy, 24,* 455–461.

Held, B. S., & Pols, E. (1987). The philosophy of Dell and Maturana. *Psychotherapy, 24,* 466–468.

Hoffman, L. (1990) Constructing realities: An art of lenses. *Family Process, 29,* 1–12.

Keeney, B. P. (1982). Not pragmatics, not aesthetics. *Family Process, 21,* 429–434.

Keeney, B. P. (1982). What is an epistemology of family therapy? *Family Process, 21,* 153–168.

Pols, E. (in press). *Radical realism: Its consequences for science, common sense, and first philosophy.* Ithaca: Cornell University Press.

Pols, E. (1969). Philosophical knowledge of the person. In M. Greene (Ed.), *The anatomy of knowledge.* Amherst: University of Massachusetts Press.

Watzlawick, P., Bavelas, J., & Jackson, D. (1967). *Pragmatics of human communication* (pp. 19–47). New York: Norton.

Zygmond, M. J., & Boorhem, H. (1989). Ethical decision making in family therapy. *Family Process, 28,* 269–280.

VII

PHILOSOPHY OF SCIENCE AND THE RESEARCH ENDEAVOR IN CLINICAL PSYCHOLOGY

INTRODUCTION: PHILOSOPHICAL PROBLEMS OF CLINICAL RESEARCH

RONALD B. MILLER

One of the major themes of this book has been how the conceptualization of science influences the acceptance or rejection of a theoretical approach to clinical psychology. Of course, the philosophy of science is a critical element not only in how a clinical psychologist approaches clinical research but in the knowledge base of the discipline as a whole. There are three key areas of concern here: (a) the nature of scientific knowledge; (b) the nature of practical knowledge in a profession (hereafter referred to as clinical knowledge); and (c) the intersection of scientific knowledge with clinical knowledge.

In chapter 35, Manicas and Secord review and summarize for psychologists the contemporary thinking of analytical philosophers of science and how it relates to the various disciplines within psychology. Although it is a difficult article that requires several readings to absorb, it attempts to give a comprehensive picture of the epistemological, and to some extent the metaphysical and moral, status of psychology. Manicas and Secord discuss the realist perspective in the philosophy of science that views reality as a hierarchy of increasingly complex substance. Each new level of complexity contains emergent properties that cannot be entirely explained as a configuration of parts from the previous level of complexity.

Thus, psychology must be a separate independent science, even though it is in part based on the arrangement of physical matter explored in chemistry and biology. Because science must deal with general laws, and clinical psychologists must deal with individuals, then clinical, developmental, and social psychology are, at least in part, not sciences per se but biographical investigations. These are legitimate areas for scholarly investigation and knowledge building, but not scientific knowledge. A knowledgeable clinician must understand the culture of the client in day-to-day terms. This knowledge also cannot be considered scientific. These are intriguing suggestions too little followed-up by clinical psychologists.

Paul Meehl (1951, 1954, 1990) has been one of the most incisive minds contributing to the development of the fields of clinical psychology over the past 40 years. His work covers a tremendous breadth of topics, from psychoanalysis to psychometrics and parapsychology to philosophy and law. One feature of his contribution has been a consistent interest in the philosophy of science and its relationship to clinical psychology. In chapter 36, Meehl offers a philosophical account of why research in the "soft" areas of psychology (social, developmental, personality, abnormal, and clinical) has made so little progress over the last 40 years. His analysis is clearly in the neopositivist tradition of looking for ways for psychology to be more similar to the physical sciences. In addition to the many problems of doing research on humans, including the possibility that many aspects of human behavior may not be amenable to research at all, Meehl notes that psychology's basic problem is that its logic and methodology rarely result in rejecting the research hypothesis. This is partly attributable to an overreliance on tests of significance, which Meehl finds to be a weak measure of lawful relationships; it is also partly caused by the sheer number of variables that might influence a psychological, as opposed to a physical, research outcome. In the case of research on human behavior, there is always the possibility that an unanticipated variable will interfere with the action of a hypothesized cause–effect relationship and lead the researcher to conclude that the causal relationship exists despite disconfirming data. Meehl's solution is the development of *consistency tests* in which, for the variables in question, a theory is used to predict specific point values, rank orders, or function forms and is then evaluated in terms of the accuracy of the predictions or the goodness of fit of the data with the set of predicted values.

Gergen is the leading spokesman in American psychology for social constructionism. In chapter 37, rather than trying to correct old methodologies to make them more scientific, as Meehl has done, Gergen offers a hermeneutical (although he does not use the term) view of psychology that is influenced by both analytical hermeneutics and appears sympathetic to a psychosocial hermeneutics. He reviews a host of studies that support the view that psychological constructs or findings are simply reified social processes. There are a number of interesting clinical topics addressed by his review, including the socially determined meaning of suicide, schizophrenia, domestic violence, anger, self, and identity. He directs psychology's attention to anthropological forms of research, particularly ethnography, and to historical and literary forms of interpretation that he believes will better serve psychology.

In chapter 40, Levine reaches a similar conclusion but from a very different perspective. By analyzing the parallels between investigative reporting and research on human behavior, he argues that there is much psychologists could learn from journalism, law, anthropology, and biography about a method of research that is suited to the task of studying human beings, as opposed to imported from another discipline. Such realistic research revitalizes both the profession and the professional.

It does seem that the day of the case study may be returning as a central knowledge vehicle in clinical psychology. If Lewin (1935) was right that there is nothing as practical as a good theory, then perhaps there is no better test of theoretical knowledge than practical application. There seems no better way to communicate the success or failure of practical applications than through a series of intensive case studies. Perhaps what is needed is more attention to the ways of improving case studying methodology rather than superceding it with more "scientific" quantitative methods.

On the other hand, philosophical analysis can also lead to the development of new research programs and designs that, although sympathetic to the concerns of humanistic psychology, are nevertheless quantitative and controlled. In chapter 39, Lamiell uses a conceptual analysis of the logic of personality research to develop an empirical method for investigating personal identity and other idiographic concerns that have long been avoided by researchers. He advocates a distinction between personality research that investigates how people become the individuals that they are and individual-differences research that investigates how people differ on variables that are defined by their ability to be measured across individuals. He calls this sort of personality research *idiothetic* because he anticipates that there will be commonalities in the *processes* by which people become unique individuals.

Mahrer (chapter 38), a leading figure in humanistic psychotherapy, expresses his dissatisfaction with psychotherapy research that is aimed at proving or refuting the validity of theories of psychotherapy. He finds such research ineffective in improving or promoting such theories because supporters seem wedded to their theories regardless of the outcomes of the research. He recommends that researchers should simply try to discover more about what can happen in psychotherapy and to experience it more fully. He uses an existential–phenomenological framework to generate new research questions that may be explored using more controlled observational methods. This can be contrasted with Jennings (see chapter 20) and Packer (see chapter 19), who use the phenomenological–existential tradition to develop nontraditional, qualitative, interpretative forms of psychological investigation.

Finally in chapter 41, Howard discusses the role of values in psychologists' conceptions of science and their choice of theories and research topics. He argues that values permeate psychology more thoroughly than in the physical sciences because both the scientist and the subjects of the study are purposive agents whose values affect their behavior. Howard has extended this work to include empirical studies of the effects of value decisions on behavior. He shows how a philosophical critique leads to a radically different research question. He blends a neopositivist methodology with a humanistic conceptual system, much in the style of Rychlak's (1988) work on logical learning theory.

One of the major questions facing clinical psychology over the next decade will be whether to embrace a qualitative research methodology as suggested by those in the hermeneutic tradition (e.g., Polkinghorne, 1983) or to continue in the neopositivist tradition with conventional approaches to validity and reliability of measurement, controlled designs, sampling theory, and so on. This is the debate that raged in psychology in the 1930s and 1940s (see Allport, 1937) and was snuffed out by the clamor to logical positivist philosophy of science. Whether psychologists shall rise to the task of philosophical discourse about their methodological assumptions or continue splintering into rival camps of practitioners versus academic researchers or scientists versus humanists who have little communication with one another is the challenge before them.

REFERENCES

Allport, G. W. (1937). *Personality: A psychological interpretation.* New York: Holt.

Lewin, K. (1935). *A dynamic theory of personality.* New York: McGraw-Hill.

Meehl, P. E. (1951). *An atlas for the clinical use of the MMPI.* Minneapolis: University of Minnesota Press.

Meehl, P. E. (1954). *Clinical versus actuarial prediction: A theoretical analysis and a review of evidence.* Minneapolis: University of Minnesota Press.

Meehl, P. E. (1990). *Selected philosophical and methodological papers.* Minneapolis: University of Minnesota Press.

Polkinghorne, D. E. (1983). *Methodology for the human sciences: Systems of inquiry.* Albany: State University of New York Press.

Rychlak, J. F. (1988). *The psychology of rigorous humanism* (2nd ed.). New York: New York University Press.

35

IMPLICATIONS FOR PSYCHOLOGY OF THE NEW PHILOSOPHY OF SCIENCE

PETER T. MANICAS AND PAUL F. SECORD

This article provides psychologists with an overview of exciting developments in the philosophy of science that have occurred during the last two decades or so and briefly points up their implications for psychology as a science, a discipline, and a profession. These new philosophical developments provide a framework for psychology and the social sciences that will help to reconcile conflicting views and approaches within psychology and in its relation to the various biological and social science disciplines.

In the monumental *Psychology: A Study of a Science,* edited by Sigmund Koch (Volumes 1–6, 1959–1963), one eminent psychologist after another, after many years—or even a lifetime of research—admitted to strong doubts about where they had been and what had been achieved, and some suggested that our most basic assumptions about the nature of psychology as a science and a method had to be questioned. They were right, although at that time new directions were not at all clear.

Koch's diagnosis was incisive. He argued that psychology was unique insofar as

> its institutionalization preceded its content and its methods preceded its problems. . . .
>
> The "scientism" that many see and decry in recent psychology was thus with it from the start. . . . From the earliest days of the experimental pioneers, man's stipulation that psychology be adequate to science outweighed his commitment that it be adequate to man. (1959, Vol. 3, p. 783)

Even more crucially, Koch went on to point out that psychology bases "its understanding of vital questions of methods on an extrinsic philosophy of science which (in some areas) is twenty years or more out of date" (p. 788).

Reprinted from the *American Psychologist, 33,* 399–413. (1983).

Psychology has become far more sophisticated in its methodologies and procedures and has generated a large body of knowledge in the decades since then, but the philosophy of science that is implicit in contemporary psychology has not changed all that much. Moreover, in the last decade or so, we find Taylor in 1973 and Toulmin in 1978 observing (here in Taylor's words) that "psychology is a vast and ramified discipline [containing] many mansions, [yet] intellectually divided against itself." The past decade or so has seen the fragmentation of psychology into "dozens of highly specialized, and largely non-interacting sub-disciplines" (Toulmin, 1978). Toulmin attributed this, rightly, in our view, to the still dominating neopositivist theory of the behavioral sciences that succeeded the old positivism of the 1930s and 1940s.

But if, as these writers have argued, the root issue remains the very conception of science, of its methods, tasks, and limits, then the time may be ripe for a resolution. In recent decades a virtual Copernican Revolution has taken place in the philosophy of science, a radical change that has profound implications for the human sciences. We see these changes arriving at an extraordinary convergence on a new heuristic for the human sciences. This heuristic, which derives from a wide variety of disparate quarters—from continental hermeneutics, post-Wittgensteinian action theory and philosophy of mind, phenomenology, structuralism, and neo-Marxism—is not merely consistent with the new philosophy of science, but as we shall argue, is firmly grounded in the fundamental insights of that new philosophy (Bhaskar, 1975, 1979).

What follows is a sketch of the main features of the new theory of science and its implications for psychology. We believe that adopting this new perspective would resolve many of the tensions and conflicts which have plagued modern psychology from its beginnings. What we suggest is not some arbitrary and ecumenical redistribution of labor; our proposals for psychology are integrative and result from a radically new understanding of the nature of science and of the world as we know it.

THE NEW THEORY OF SCIENCE

To minimize misunderstanding, it may be helpful to begin with what, on our view, is the dominating philosophy of science. Called the "standard view" by Scheffler (1967), it remains widely held among psychologists and other social scientists.

The Standard View of Science

1. A *foundationist* epistemology, although made relative in practice, sees scientific propositions as founded on "data." The test of the truth of propositions is "correspondence" between theory and data in the sense proposed by Carnap (1956) and later modified. In other words, while perhaps no one any longer supposes that there is a preinterpreted "given" or even some transhistorical, theory-neutral data base, it is generally held that some propositions at least, are basic in that they constitute the test sentences for scientific theory. More roughly stated, hypotheses are to be tested against the "facts."
2. Theories are understood to be *interpreted calculi* or *hypothetico-deductive systems.* Theoretical terms, or *hypothetical constructs,* gain their meaning implicitly through their systemic relations to other terms in the theory, or explicitly by being connected to observations (through "operational definitions," "correspondence rules," or a "dictionary").

3. Research is more or less atheoretical, with many researchers avoiding theory as far as possible and seeking to test only hypotheses related to variables that can be closely tied to observations. Few investigators attempt to develop full-blown theories. Hypothetical constructs may or may not be understood realistically—as representing real mechanisms productive of predictive outcomes or not. In this regard the use of *model* is ambiguous. Sometimes a model is taken to be a representation of real mechanisms; sometimes models are understood heuristically or instrumentally, as purely mathematical, or as "convenient fictions" (Achinstein, 1969). Both views share in emphasizing predictability as the acid test of theory.

4. A Humean conception of causality and of lawfulness is taken for granted. On this view, causal relations are regular contingent relations between events. When strict universality is not possible, "reliable regularities between independent and dependent variables" or "probabilistic relationships among complex, interacting variables" may be all that can be achieved.

5. Attending the Humean conception of lawfulness, the standard view holds to a conception of explanation as subsumption under law. On this view explanation and prediction are exactly symmetrical. A full, complete (or ideal) explanation is *deductive-nomological.* In research practice, explanations are inductive-statistical, so that one achieves a better explanation when the probability statement "predicts the dependent variable more accurately by identifying additional independent variables, by better defining the relationship among these independent variables (and) by specifying more accurately the relationship of each of the dependent variables. . . ." (Hempel, 1963).

The foregoing ideas are strongly identified with recent logical empiricism (Scriven, 1969). But some of them have a much longer history, a fact of considerable relevance in explaining their place as the conventional wisdom about science. As more recent empiricism developed, from the late 1920s on, a number of problems and issues came to a head. Key doctrines came under attack; some were clarified, some amended, and some were dropped altogether (Brown, 1977; Suppe, 1974). One example may suffice here. In 1958, Hempel amended the "received view" of scientific theories in articulating the theoretician's dilemma: If theoretical terms are defined in terms of observations, they cannot function as explanatory; if, on the other hand, they are not, then how did they have empirical support? Attempts to resolve this dilemma culminated in the notion of theories sketched as Point 2 above (Hempel, 1963).

The Kuhnian or Paradigmatic Critique

By the late 1950s, alternatives to the standard view were available and included books by Stephen Toulmin (1953, 1961), David Bohm (1957), Mario Bunge (1959), and Norwood Hanson (1958), but these were largely ignored by psychologists. Not until Kuhn's *The Structure of Scientific Revolutions* (1962/1970) was read and absorbed did "paradigms" became the rage and key themes in logical empiricist philosophy of science come under scrutiny by the larger community, especially in psychology and the social sciences.

Kuhn attacked empiricist epistemology, the received view of theory, and logical empiricist ideas about scientific change and development (Brown, 1977). He argued, along with Toulmin, Hanson, and many others, that observation was "theory-laden" and that science must be understood as a social activity in which disciplines develop their own rules of practice. These philosophers made clear that observations were not "given" but were profoundly shaped by the observer's preconceptions and theoretical notions. They demonstrated convincingly that scientific meanings could not be found in observations alone, as the logical empiricists had maintained. And the idea that there could be unambiguous logical connections between theory and observation was overthrown. Finally, that scientists were human observers was demonstrated to make science a social activity, which subjected it to normative or paradigmatic influences operating apart from the internal criteria of science.

All this was salutary, as far as it went; but as its critics saw, the paradigm account of science precipitously courted irrationalism (Feyerabend, 1975; Lakatos & Musgrave, 1970). The problem was clear enough: If there is no theory-neutral data base (foundationism) and if disciplines constitute their own scientific practice, what are the criteria of truth? Does the paradigm view lead to a consensus theory of truth in which, in fact, there are no independent checks on the nature of the consensus? Indeed, as one social scientist put it, "working scientists . . . continue to be skeptical about this new interpretation of how science develops. . . . Even if Kuhn's view turns out to be correct, it is possible that it might be necessary for scientists to believe in the more traditional view in order to proceed with the work of science" (Cole, 1980). This suggestion—that in order to do science one must have a false view of it—is bizarre on its face, and it powerfully suggests a confused understanding of science. In our view, not only has logical empiricism not been exorcized, perhaps for the reasons which Cole indicated, but as well, the paradigm alternative is itself seriously deficient.

The Realist Critique

An alternative to the standard and paradigmatic views of science is now available. Whereas its origins lie in another philosophical line critical of the standard view, the *realist* theory constitutes a constructive alternative view of science. The earliest anticipations are to be found in the various writings of Michael Scriven (1956, 1962, 1964), Michael Polanyi (1964, 1967), and in Bunge, Bohm, and Toulmin, already mentioned. The decisive advance was taken, in our judgment, by Rom Harré (1970, 1972; Harré & Madden, 1975) and as influenced by Harré and others, by Roy Bhaskar (1975, 1978, 1979, 1982).

Our characterization of this view is necessarily brief and thus is put forth virtually without the supporting arguments available in the extensive literature. Nevertheless, since we believe that this new view has profound implications for psychology and the social sciences, it is important to try to convey its substance. This third view, variously called simply, *the realist theory of science* (Bhaskar, 1975), *transcendental realism* (Bhaskar, 1979), or as suggested by Donald Campbell (Note 1), *fallibilist realism,* has the following essential features.

1. It agrees with Kuhn and those epistemologies influenced by hermeneutics (Gadamer, 1975) that foundationism, even in its recent weakened forms, must be categorically rejected. Instead, it argues that knowledge is a social and historical product; hence the inevitability of a nonvicious hermeneutic circle (Bhaskar, 1979, pp. 195–203). This means that there is no preinterpreted "given" and that the test of truth cannot be "correspondence." Epistemologically, there can be nothing *known* to which our ideas (sentences, theories) can correspond. But versus the unknowable Kantian thing-in-itself, it is precisely the task of science to invent theories that aim to represent the world. Thus, in the spirit of Kuhn (but as more cogently argued by Toulmin, 1972), the practices of the sciences generate their own *rational* criteria in terms of which theory is accepted or rejected. The crucial point is that it is possible for these criteria to be rational precisely because on realist terms, there is a world that exists independently of cognizing experience. Since our theories are constitutive of the known world but *not* of the *world,* we may always be wrong, but *not* anything goes. As Bhaskar has noted, one must be a realist ontologically to be a fallibilist epistemologically.

2. The realist theory holds naturalism to be nonreductive or emergent; both the world and science are stratified. The basis for this view is the idea that the "things" of the world are complex composites. A simple if crude example may be helpful. Ordinary table salt is not, usually, *just* NaCl, since the purest of it contains other "things." But more important, at another *level,* the compound NaCl is a complex of elements, Na and Cl. Sodium and chlorine each have causal properties, and NaCl has causal properties that are not true of either sodium or of chlorine. But at still another level, sodium and chlorine are themselves complexes of electrons, neutrons, quarks, and so on. Later we will see, analogously, that the activities of persons in society may be seen as a set of interacting, interwoven structures at different levels. Establishing the existence and properties of these novel "things"—the theoretical things of science—is the product of theoretical and experimental work in precisely the sense that science demands the construction of confirmable explanatory theories about such structures and their properties (Harré, 1970).

Accepting a realist view of science allows us to see the problem of reduction in three different senses (Bhaskar, 1975, pp. 115ff.):

1. A lower-order domain provides the basis for the existence of some higher-order attribute; for example, our speech apparatus is the basis for the power of speech.
2. The principles of a higher-order science are explained in terms of a lower-order science; at least a partial translation is possible. For example, certain perceptual capacities may be explained in terms of the neurophysiological properties of the visual system.
3. From a knowledge of principles in a lower-order science, behavior in the higher-order domain is predicted. For example, behavioral experience involving mental processes may be predicted from the principles of brain chemistry alone.

Clearly the third sense makes the strongest claim; yet it has many supporters among behavioral scientists, at least as a promissory note. Senses 2 and 3 are often confused: Evidence supporting Sense 2 is often erroneously offered in support of Sense 3. Bhaskar notes that the principles and laws of chemistry can be explained in terms of those of physics, but the latter cannot be used to predict the next eruption of Mt. Vesuvius. It is the failure of reduction in this third sense that allows sciences to remain autonomous. Mitosis and growth cannot be predicted without biological laws, even if some principles of biology can be reduced to chemistry. A parallel issue in psychology is whether behavior can be predicted without invoking mental processes, a question we will return to shortly.

3. In contrast to logical empiricism and to Kuhnian views, in the new heuristic the Humean analysis of causation and of lawfulness is rejected. Instead of the usual characterization, $R_i = f(S_i)$ or $R_i = f(S_i \cdots S_n)$, where R is the dependent variable that is some function of an independent variable S of set of S's, we write, "If S_i, then ceteris paribus, i necessarily acts in virtue of its structure N." That is, given the "independent variable" S as a condition, i necessarily acts in a certain fashion because of its structure. In other words, scientific laws in this non-Humean framework are *not* about events or classes of events, regularly or stochastically conjoined, but are about the causal properties of structures that exist and operate in the world. This difference is crucial.

On the Humean conception, a dispositional property, for example, the solubility of salt, should manifest itself when "triggered," in this case, when put in water. If it does not, of course, the implicit ceteris paribus clause may be invoked. But within Humean strictures, this move is objectionable: Unless the ceteris paribus clause can be definitely specified, the "law" becomes a tautology—true no matter what obtains. This problem cannot arise under the realist view, because, to be specific about the conditions of the ceteris paribus clause, one *must* have a theory about the causal properties of the structure under conditions of closure, spelling out when the conditions of the ceteris paribus clause are satisfied (Sellars, 1961). That is, one must have a theoretical understanding of the nature of the structure such that one can specify the conditions under which the dispositional property will *not* be realized.

That is why we say a law has the form, "If S_i, then ceteris paribus, necessarily *i* phi's in virtue of its structure *N*." If *theoretical* salt, NaCl, is put in theoretical water, H_2O, then ceteris paribus, it must dissolve—it cannot do otherwise. Theory tells us quite precisely that this is a causal property of NaCl (and of H_2O), and it tells us why. To be sure, *actual* salt (any concrete instance of salt) only *tends* to dissolve in actual water. This is because, of course, the conditions of the ceteris paribus clause are not always met. Thus, not only is the world stratified but it is a complex of structures and structured processes. On the realist view, "things" of the world never operate under conditions of complete closure. This explains why we have the experience of *patterns,* of tendencies, and of probabilities. Events are the conjunctures of structured processes and are always the outcome of complex causal configurations at the same and at many different levels.

If this is the case, then we can also say that causal processes may have surprising effects. They need not, for example, yield the outcomes which they usually do. Thus, if *S* is followed by non-*R*, then, on the realist view, there may still be some structure whose causal properties may be having effects. There is no reason to suppose what is implied in the Humean doctrine; namely, that in the absence of predictable outcomes, the "law" does not apply, that once initiated by S_i, the causal property did not play a role in the outcome, or that the *theoretical* relation between S_i and *N* is for that reason false.

These considerations also allow us to see the significance and rationale of experiment in science. Since the structures of the world never operate under conditions of complete closure, we can test our theories about them by intervening to create (as far as possible) closures. To do this, of course, we need theories about the structures and their causal properties. The patterns of experience are where we begin. Led by a hypothesis that there is some causally efficacious mechanism at work, we construct theory about it. The theory tells us what we can expect if, with ingenuity, we can isolate the theorized mechanism. A good experiment confirms a theory precisely because if it establishes the right conditions and eliminates interfering causal mechanisms, the experiment yields what would *not* have been observed without the experiment. In contrast to the standard Humean view, we experiment not because we are interested in getting more reliable, more precise, and more probable empirical regularities but rather because we believe that the laws of nature apply and operate even in the absence of experimental closure.

More generally, then, the dominating views of science, logical empiricism, and the newer Kuhnian perspective cannot sustain the distinction, implicit in the practices of the well-established natural sciences, between the development of theories representing the structures of nature (including the experimental test of our theories about the structures of nature) and the application of these theories to explain, diagnose, and predict those particulars and events of interest to us. But the realist theory can sustain this distinction. These considerations suggest a fourth crucial contrasting feature of the new view of science versus the old.

4. The realist theory of science rejects in toto the covering law model of scientific explanation and the attending instrumentalist idea that explanation and prediction are symmetrical. On the realist view, events such as the collapse of a bridge or the cancerous growth of an organ are the conjunctions of causal processes operating in open systems. Such outcomes are the result of different mechanisms of very different kinds combining in many different ways. But if so, the covering law model is, at best, seriously misleading.

Scientific explanation is not subsumption. Rather, it is causal explanation, and it demands that we show how in each particular case a particular causal configuration occurred that had just the achieved result. In general, explanation requires the resolution of the event into its components and theoretical redescription of them: It requires causal analysis. As part of this process, it requires retrodiction to possible causes and the elimination of alternatives that might have figured into the particular configuration. Explanation thus requires knowledge of the causal properties of the configured structures *and* a historical grasp of the particular and changing configuration.

Accordingly, we may often be in a position to explain some event once it has occurred, when it would have been impossible—even in principle—to predict it. Although the relatively enduring structures of the world have definite (and knowable) causal properties, it is only under closure that explanation and prediction are symmetrical. In an open world, the configurations of structures and structured processes are not predictable. Indeed, for the standard view of science, the world is a determined concatenation of contingent events; for the realist, it is a contingent concatenation of real structures. And this difference is monumental. The past is, in a sense, "determined." That is, what happened can be causally *explained.* But the future is *not* determined precisely because the complexly related structures and systems of the world are constantly being reconfigured.

It would be easy to miss the force of the radical contrast we are drawing and to suppose that what we have put forth is, perhaps in other words, a reformulation of the standard view. Thus, it may be said that everyone recognizes uncertainty in prediction, that interaction hypotheses are widely employed, and that the typical effort of psychology (and the social sciences) is to aim at discovering reliable explanatory relationships between a wide variety of variables. These statements are doubtless true, but it is exactly these activities and the ideas that support them that we are here challenging and contrasting with the new heuristic.

One way to clarify further is to suggest why the alternative view is easily missed. One important reason is the uncritical collapse of the distinction, crucial for realist theory, between so-called empirical laws (generalizations) and causal laws. Roughly, empirical laws are statements of regularities, strict or probabilistic, between terms that are more or less readily available to direct empirical confirmation. A familiar example from learning theory of the 1930s is the various lawlike statements about the learning curve, plotted in terms of number of errors on successive trials. This was so often in such a great variety of situations found to take a negatively accelerated form that it was generally regarded as a "law of learning." Now, in hindsight, and with a better understanding of learning mechanisms, it is obvious that such a "law" has no explanatory power whatsoever. Another type of regularity is probabilistic, for example, "the probability of emitting the response will increase with the number of reinforcements." Or consider the probabilistic formulae in decision theory. Typically these probabilistic descriptions require analysis at a deeper, structural level to be fully understood.

Most methodology books in psychology and the social sciences recognize (rightly) that philosophers have repeatedly struggled to find an effective way to conceptualize causal laws in a manner distinct from contingent correlations (generalizations). Most methodological books also call attention to the fact that one cannot, without further justification, assume that a high correlation is a causal relation.

The standard view holds that, for explanation, certain conditions must be fulfilled; for example, that there must be a contiguity of time and place between the independent and dependent variables and that "the third variable problem" must be solved: Some unspecified variable must not have produced the relationship. Given that such constraints are satisfied (to the best of our ability), such regularities are, in the standard view, thought to be explanatory. Of course, in predicting particular instances, it is readily acknowledged that regularities are but "relational tendencies."

Consider the best candidate for this sort of account, $pv = k$. The correlation is perfect, but what does it explain? To explain (say) exploding gas chambers or the explosion of some particular chamber filled with gas, one would need more than—indeed, *other* than—$pv = k$, which is merely descriptive. One would need to show (at least) that, for example, the temperature of the gas in the chamber was increased *sufficiently* where "sufficiently" would be relative to the tensile strength (a causal property!) of the container. This sort of objection (important to the covering-law model of explanation) is not, however, the present problem. Rather, one should notice that $pv = k$ is *itself* a consequence of what is needed to explain the explosions of containers, that *because* gases are clouds of molecules that behave in certain theoretically defined ways, that is, because there are causal laws about gases (in addition to empirical laws about them), gases have the *tendencies* they have, and that indeed, the empirical laws about them hold to the extent that they do.

In other words, we can say that gases, in general, have a tendency to maintain a constant relation between pressure and volume *and* to explode their containers when they are heated. Both of these are tendencies because both assertions contain ceteris paribus clauses. We can say that they are tendencies because, as theory tells us, if the CP clauses *were* satisfied, it is necessary that $pv = k$, and quite impossible that containers of such and such a tensile strength *not* explode when the gas is sufficiently heated.

A similar analysis is available for every empirical law or generalization. Consider *sulphur is yellow.* The optical properties of sulphur, emitting photons of such and such a frequency, together with the (less-well-understood) mechanisms of human percipience, will generally result in our experiencing sulphur as yellow. On the present analysis, laws give us the optical properties of material substances *and* the perceptual properties of percipients, and these explain both generalizations familiar to experience and why these generalizations hold to the extent that they do. Thus, we see the cruciality of the distinction between the discovery of the causal properties of the generative mechanisms (structures) of the world and the application of this knowledge to analyze, explain, and predict.

We are mistakenly led into collapsing this distinction because the patterns or ordinary experience do obtain: They are patterns that allow for generalization. So we are quite content to explain the saltiness of water by noting that salt was put into it and it dissolved, sulphur is usually yellow in appearance, that guilty people often comply more readily, revolutionary upheavals seem reasonably related to differences in the rates of expectation and satisfaction, and so on. Nevertheless, these tendencies become intelligible only insofar as causal laws are natural necessities and are sharply distinguished from the empirical regularities they generate. Still, it may yet be thought that empirical regularities *explain* events. If so, it may be because it is still supposed that events may be explained by showing them to be the outcomes of a single law or set of laws of one science; that, for example, there is an economic explanation of a recession, a psychological explanation of a divorce, and so on.

But it seems that there is only one science in which such a view is even plausible. That science is celestial mechanics. And this is because the events of interest to us, the position and velocity of some planet, are governed by laws operating under relative *closure.* That is, there is a sense in which we explain these events by simply instantiating variables into a deterministic system under closure. Even so, we presuppose some very theoretical and *explanatory* properties of space/time structures in our "explanation." In any case, it is hard to imagine how much damage has been done by taking celestial mechanics as the paradigm of a scientific explanation. We take it that no one would be fooled into thinking that the explanation of a collapsed bridge, a cancerous growth in an organ, or a volcanic eruption would take the same form. But if so, it is puzzling that one should suppose that the laws of economics or history should explain recessions and revolutions (Manicas, 1981).

IMPLICATIONS FOR PSYCHOLOGY

The implications of the realist view for psychology are enormous. One implication may be emphasized at this point. Undoubtedly, persons are complex particulars and the events of interest to us, for example, instances of behavior or kinds of behavior, are the result of complex transactions of many different kinds of structures at many different levels, including (as we shall next argue) those particular structures of interest to psychology. But if so, it would surely be a vain hope to suppose that behaviors might be explained merely by appeal to anything that can usefully be described as a psychological law. But let us emphasize that this conclusion does not depend upon the special powers that distinguish persons as agents from other animals—or indeed from hurricanes. It is as true of complex physical events as of behavioral episodes.

It may be that every psychologist has always known this, however persistent has been the hope (fear, on the part of some) that psychology could, in principle, explain behavior by identifying (under some description) its lawfully conjoined antecedents. Consider here the exactly appropriate illustration by Campbell and Misanin:

> Few, if any psychologists now believe that those conditions once labelled basic drives, such as hunger, thirst, sex, and maternal behavior, are predominantly governed by some common underlying generalized drive state. Even if there is some activating or energizing state common to many basic drives, it is clear that the specific behaviors elicited by those drives are controlled by a complex of interactions among environmental stimuli, hormonal states, physiological imbalance, previous experience, etc., and that the basic drive concept is of little value in unravelling these complexities (Campbell & Misanin, 1969).

The point here is precisely that specific behaviors—like most events in the world—cannot be explained as the simple manifestation of some single law or principle. What we have is interacting levels of stratification. Indeed, the acts of persons are open-systemic events in which a wide variety of systems and structures are involved, systems that are physical, biological, psychological, and, as we shall argue, sociological as well. This posture leads to the conclusion that laboratory psychology should not be aimed at explaining behavior—action in the world; its purpose is far more circumscribed. The explanation of behavior, as we shall see, is properly a multidisciplinary effort and, though based on the behavioral sciences, necessarily transcends them to involve both biology and the social sciences.

Our stress on openness and the multiplicity of systems may easily be misunderstood. Psychologists might say, "What else is new? We've known all along that there are complex interactions among variables. That's why we've developed ANOVA, multiple regression analysis, and path analysis." But that complaint would miss the point. These techniques are unquestionably valuable tools, especially in a descriptive sense, but their routine application is unlikely to zero in on natural mechanisms that underlie behavior. Nor are such results by themselves properly considered explanations. Identification of structures and their dynamics can only be accomplished by the multilevel application of imaginative theory that simultaneously guides observation, analysis, and experiment.

Rejection of a misguided ideal for psychology does not make psychology as a science impossible. On the contrary, once we are clearer about the nature of the sciences, we can see that psychology is best construed as a family of related sciences with different tasks and different methodologies. But psychology in this sense is autonomous, in that there is an important difference between the subject matters of psychological and physical sciences.

Whether a science is autonomous in the present sense is a direct function of the nature of stratification in the world. That is, if from a knowledge of the causal properties and antecedent conditions of structures in one domain of science we cannot explain events at the next level, then that level defines another science with an irreducible subject matter. As Bhaskar (1979) writes, even if we could explain organic life in terms of physical and chemical elements out of which organic things are formed, and perhaps even reproduce this process in laboratories, biology would not be otiose. Living things do not cease to be real; knowledge of biological structures and processes would still be necessary to account for the world as we know it.

The Problem of Consciousness

It is hardly a novelty to assert that the problem of consciousness continues to bedevil inquiry in psychology and the human sciences (Taylor, 1982; Toulmin, 1982). In experimental psychology, one manifestation among many is the ongoing debate over whether imagery plays an essential part in certain cognitive skills, or whether it is a mere epiphenomenon (Cooper & Shepard, 1973; Pylyshyn, 1973). But, more tellingly, at the level of social behavior, it is surely difficult to deny that consciousness, along with agency, intention, and action (as against movement) constitute the crucially relevant difference in the subject matter of the human sciences (Boden, 1973).

Psychologists have adopted various strategies for coping with consciousness, but it may not be unfair to classify these under two main heads. One strategy is to minimize consciousness, either by a behaviorist end-run (Skinner, 1969, pp. 156ff.; Gibson, 1979) or by reductionist strategies—for example, arguing that conscious phenomena may be in principle reducible to brain chemistry (Churchland, 1981). The other strategy assigns to consciousness a central role, but in effect often rejects the causal model altogether. Humans are to some extent self-determining, according to this move, supported by some clinicians, humanists, and existentialists.

Our intention is not to assess the many arguments and conclusions in the recent literature. In our view, both sides are right and both sides are wrong, but more interestingly, this is because both sides of the argument have been infected by the mistaken assumption that it is the aim of a scientific psychology to explain our everyday actions by showing that they can be derived from a single set of laws or principles of behavior as discovered in the experimental laboratory. However, once, this assumption is dropped, we can see how both sides are right and both sides are wrong.

Humanistically oriented psychology is correct in insisting that because the phenomena of consciousness are real, psychology constitutes a different level of stratification from the physical sciences. Moreover, from this they rightly see that to explain action, one has to include those phenomena in any explanation. But they are mistaken in supposing that this is incompatible with the existence of psychological laws, construed here, let us emphasize, as statements about the causal properties of psychological structures.

On the other hand, the other side is correct in arguing that as a science, psychology should study the causal properties of psychological structures and processes but is mistaken in construing these as statements of invariance between antecedents and specific behaviors. Indeed, if we take our clue from the new heuristic and keep clearly in mind the distinction between discovering the causal properties and relations of structures in complex entities and applying this knowledge to explain, predict, and diagnose the particulars of the world, we can readily identify a resolution.

Experimental Psychology

In the history of psychology, "experimental psychology" has been used to refer to various and not necessarily compatible enterprises. And this is one of the problems in resolving the disputes among protagonists of widely varying approaches. We shall argue, as the foregoing account of science implies, that experimental psychology is necessarily a theoretical science. To be sure, there are experimentalists in psychology who are antitheoretical. But if we are correct, they radically misinterpret their experimental efforts. Such experimental work is, of course, closely associated with versions of positivism, especially versions of behaviorism; thus, it is not surprising that if we reject positivist understandings of science, this conception of experimental work as atheoretical should also fall. Positivistically oriented experimentation aims at establishing functional relationships between variables, and is not concerned with underlying causal mechanisms.

On the realist view, however, causal mechanisms are at the core of science. And the areas to which psychology has devoted its major effort during its century-long history are precisely the appropriate ones: memory, learning, perception, and the relation of such cognitive processes to their biological underpinnings. But whether these topics are approached from a positivist or from a realist perspective makes a crucial difference.

As Bhaskar (1975) writes, natural science aims at producing knowledge of "real structures which endure and operate independently of our knowledge, our experience, and the conditions which allow access to them" (p. 25). Science aims at discovering lawful processes, but such laws are not about events, but about the causal powers of those structures which exist and operate in the world. In cellular biology, the physico-chemical properties of cells are a case in point; cells have certain structures that are reflected in the power of cells to perform certain functions.

The description of relational, structural processes is a description of natural powers or mechanisms that are the core of scientific theory. Dynamite has the power to explode by virtue of its structures; only when we can describe these dynamically can we grasp its nature. Thus, this philosophical view turns logical empiricism upside down. Theoretical entities are not hypothetical, but real; observations are not the rock bottom of science, but are tenuous and always subject to reinterpretation.

To bring this closer to the concerns of psychologists, a familiar example from linguistics may be helpful. Chomsky's generative grammar is seen (rightly or wrongly) as a theoretical structure that enables persons to generate sentences, and that thus provides a core explanation of lingustic competence. But explaining linguistic performance requires a host of other variables, including many situational ones. Every linguistic performance is different from every other; no two are the same. We believe that psychology as an experimental science is best understood in analogous terms—as concerned with the structure of our competencies and not our realization of them in our everyday behavior.

Psychologists who misread us here are apt to be startled. We are not proposing to disenfranchise psychologists whose specialty is clinical, child, industrial, organizational, social, or whatever. If the new heuristic is taken seriously, then, as an experimental science, psychology can deal only with what we are calling competencies or powers. Explaining their actualization requires more than experimental science provides, and thus there is a place for the other psychological sciences that pertain to human action in life settings. And practitioners would ideally specialize in putting the findings of psychological science together with information about concrete individuals and their social settings in order to gain understanding of their behavior. But the same is true of physics, which provides the theoretical knowledge for an atomic bomb. It takes engineering technology to construct one and make it explode.

So experimental psychology is experimental for precisely the reasons that physics or chemistry is experimental. It aims at knowledge of those structures that in complex interaction give humans the special powers they have (acquire and develop) and that they exercise in acting in the world (Taylor, 1971; Harré & Secord, 1972, esp. chap. 12). So conceived—and let us stress this—experimental psychology does not explain everyday behavior, even though, of course, it is capable of shedding light on the complex mechanisms (neurophysiological, perceptual, cognitive, etc.) that taken together, underlie performances by individuals acting in the world.

The acts of persons in life settings are open-systemic events that involve an enormous range of codetermining structures and systems. One needs knowledge only of physics to account for the fall of a person from a precipice; one needs knowledge of biological structures and processes to comprehend birth or death; one needs psychology to have an understanding of the structures and processes that underlie performances—and of course, this is made more difficult by the fact that the relevant intrinsic structures of persons are complexly related and causally codetermining. But before proceeding further we need briefly to discuss statistical and probabilistic explanations.

Statistical and Probabilistic Explanations

The use of statistical probabilities in quantum mechanics is often cited as a justification for using probabilities in psychology. In fact, probabilities are used in psychology in a considerable variety of ways. But none of these are like their usage in quantum mechanics. There, the nature of electrons in principle requires that nothing can be said concerning the microparticles in a collection of electrons that goes beyond what is said of the macrobehavior of the collection itself. This principled constraint does not apply to psychology, however. Sets of actions by a single individual, or a set of actions by many individuals, *can* in principle be broken down into their contituent unities.

In effect, the statistically significant difference between the mean performance of two or more sets of individuals so common to experiments is a kind of probability usage. What it amounts to is making a crude generalization by attributing individual variances to "error" when, in fact, there are usually real differences between individuals. Another use of statistics is at the macrolevel, as in economics, demography, or educational sociology.

Do findings based on such methods constitute explanations? This question has been frequently debated, but the answer depends on what one takes as a scientific explanation. From the perspective of the new philosophy of science, however, they clearly do not constitute explanations. For from that viewpoint, explanations must be based on a dynamic structure/process that has causal force. Mere description is insufficient. Yet, this does not mean that statistical methodologies and probabilistic approaches are useless. Far from it. Often they are an earlier necessary stage in the process of description and discovery, and they may, for example, lead to the discovery of powers or competencies that are at first understood only at the macrolevel, but that later may be explained in terms of generative mechanisms.

Not all of psychology, however, is experimental psychology, and not all psychologists need to have the same tasks and methods. In the remainder of this article, three additional tasks and three commensurate methodologies are distinguished, each logically associated with specialties within the behavioral sciences. These specialties include psychologists whose concern is the understanding of concrete persons, of individual personalities and their life histories. Another group is the social psychologists, focusing on the actions of individuals in the social contexts and structures of the world. This takes us into the realm of the sociological, which is concerned with persons or aggregates of persons acting in life situations. But first we must discuss what Bhaskar (1982) has called the new heuristic in the social sciences.

The New Heuristic in the Social Sciences

Parallel and often complementary to the debate in the theory of the natural sciences has been a violent debate in the social sciences. This is probably less familiar to psychologists, but it is nevertheless crucial to the understanding of social behavior. Although phenomenology, ethnomethodology, dramaturgy, action theory, structuralism, critical theory and neo-Marxism, and the new heuristics constitute an enormously mixed bag, it is not untrue to say that each has contributed key elements to the new heuristic, preserving what was of central importance to mainstream conceptions and integrating them into a roomier and more critically defensible posture. Again, this story is much too large to tell here, but as before, it is possible to identify the central insights. (See especially, Bhaskar, 1975, 1979, 1982; Giddens, 1976, 1977, 1979; Bourdieu, 1977).

Perhaps the most important feature of the new heuristic is the new integration of central themes of the "subjectivist" versus "objectivist" approaches in social theory. The opposition between these terms is resolved by drawing a radical distinction between human action and social structure. Unless human action and social structure constitute radically different levels of description and conceptualization, with neither reducible to the other, their articulation and integration within a single system cannot be accomplished. But this, too, is of a piece with the new realist theory of science. As above, we held that psychology must be an autonomous science if we are to account for the world as we know it, so too must we reject reductionism in the social sciences. This means that methodological individualism is false; social phenomena cannot be explained solely in terms of knowledge about individuals (Bhaskar, 1979, chapter 2).

Action theory, phenomenology, ethnomethodology, and "interpretive sociologies" in general have emphasized the idea that action is meaningful and intentional and have insisted, rightly, that such behavior is social behavior, that "meanings" are always social meanings, and that intentionality necessarily involves "ongoing reflexive monitoring of conduct" in a socially managed milieu. Nevertheless, these orientations have tended, if subtly, to deny the "objective" character of society.

An opposite tendency has prevailed in the "objectivist" camp. Structural functionalism (Durkheim, Parsons) and recent continental structuralism (e.g., Levi-Strauss, 1976; Althusser, 1969; Godelier, 1972) have rightly emphasized the "reality" of society, but have tended to deny, again, if subtly, the efficacious causal role of agency.

The new heuristic weds these perspectives by arguing that social structure is simultaneously the relatively enduring product but also the medium of motivated human action. This conception allows both views to flourish without contradiction. Thus, social structures (e.g., language) are reproduced and transformed by action, but they preexist for individuals. They enable persons to become persons and to act (meaningfully and intentionally), yet at the same time, they are "coercive," limiting the ways we can act. It is thus that action is social, for, as acquiring the particular skills, competencies, habits, and forms of thought presuppose human capacities, they also presuppose society in the double sense that in acting we use and we express social structures. Social structures are, accordingly, constituted by the motivated human acts that either reproduce or transform the very structures that are its medium. Spoken language is reproduced through its use; it is also changed in use. But social structure is rarely intentionally reproduced; social change and history is the cumulative product of the largely unintended consequences of our intentional acts. People marry for psychological reasons, not to reproduce the structural form that the family takes, an unintended consequence of their acts.

This way of viewing the matter allows us to see clearly both the strengths and limitations of the subjectivist and objectivist views. As Bhaskar writes:

> Society is not the unconditioned creation of human agency (voluntarism), but it does not exist independently of it (reification). And individual action neither completely determines (individualism) nor is completely determined by (determinism) social forms. [On the transformational model of social activity] unintended consequences unacknowledged conditions, and tacit skills . . . limit the actor's understanding of the social world while unacknowledged (unconscious) motivation limits one's understanding of oneself (Bhaskar, 1982, p. 286).

This new heuristic leads to a very clear distinction between the social sciences and social psychological science (Bhaskar, 1982). The social sciences focus on the structures produced by human agency, studying how these relate to each other and to enduring practices. Thus, economists abstract the economic aspects of behavior to build functional models of how the economic system works; sociologists study the structures of social institutions and their interlocking with other aspects of society.

Social psychological science focuses on individuals in their interactions with one another and with social institutions and on how this activity relates to the larger social structures. Engagements in social activities (practices) may be described and analyzed either from the point of view of the agent—in hermeneutic terms involving her or his motivations, beliefs, competencies, understandings, and so on, or in terms of her or his place (function) in the social structures. Social psychology has, as it were, the onerous task of joining these two perspectives. In this sense social psychology is generally thought of as an interdisciplinary inquiry concerned at once with the insights and contributions of psychology and the social sciences. This theoretical and empirical task has been neglected by most social psychologists, including many with sociological backgrounds (e.g., symbolic interactionism, ethnomethodology, Goffman's microsociology; see Layder, 1981, 1982; Secord, 1982). But the power of analyses by those few who have seen this clearly, like Kurt Lewin, Solomon Asch, and Muzafer Sherif, lies in just this perspective.

Social psychology, then, is ideally a mediating discipline between general psychology, on the one hand, and the social sciences, on the other. There is nothing new in this; it is reflected in the fact that both psychology and sociology have long claimed it as their own discipline. But from the point of view of the new heuristic, social psychology has not served this mediating role very well. The most popular practice of social psychologists whose discipline is psychology has been to detach individuals from their social world and to study them in relative isolation. Consider many of the dominant research themes of both past and present: attitudes and attitude change, perceptual defense, person perception, cognitive consistency theory, dissonance theory, equity theory, and currently, attribution theory.

In all of these, the focus is usually on looking inward at cognitive processes rather than outward at situations and social structures. Of course such research is a perfectly legitimate scientific endeavor and, in principle, is even consistent with the new heuristic, in that it can be seen as focused on social competencies. Since all human powers are realized socially, their particular forms and contents will be culturally and historically variable. As Mead so well put it, "social psychology presupposes an approach to experience from the standpoint of the individual, but undertakes to determine in particular that which belongs to this experience because the individual himself belong to a social structure" (1934, p. 1).

Lest we paint too one-sided a picture, some research topics in social psychology roughly fit its mediating role: taken in a different way, equity theory falls here as well as under the previous heading. Other candidates, past and present, are small group behavior (once perhaps the dominant concern of the discipline), social exchange processes, interpersonal attraction, social roles, conformity to social norms, social power, altruistic behavior, ecological psychology, and environmental psychology.

But topics alone do not give the whole picture. Social psychologists have largely followed the standard line in their methodological approaches, and this adherence has often blocked any possibility of gaining knowledge of the links between social behavior and social structure. Thus, endless experiments on "bargaining" or on the "prisoner's dilemma" have only the most tenuous connection to negotiation in life settings: Structuring these investigations in the standard experimental paradigm has virtually eliminated the essential features of negotiation.

More central to the new heuristic is the concept of the person as we know and understand persons in our everyday lives (Harré & Secord, 1972, p. 87), and in this respect social psychology is not an experimental science in the way that experimental psychology is, since it must look to actual life situations. But beyond that, a truly mediating discipline would spell out the articulation between individual behavior, on the one hand, and social structure, on the other (Layder, 1981, 1982; Secord, 1982).

Our view of experimentation in social psychology may seem at odds with common consensus, so further comment is required. From midcentury onward social psychology has commonly been regarded as an experimental discipline (at least by those trained in psychology, if not in sociology). And, as already noted, if general psychologists experiment to discover and detail the competencies that are (one hopes) species-universal, social psychologists can legitimately experiment by introducing social variables into the laboratory or the field, especially those pertinent to the society native to the participants.

But it is important to recognize that social variables enormously complicate experimentation, making closure extraordinarily difficult to achieve, and further that even when their experiments are technically successful, in the realist view of science social psychologists have no more warrant than general experimenters for believing that their experiments explain everyday behavior. The fruits of such experimentation provide only partial knowledge and understanding of social behavior in life situations. Phenomena in open systems require knowledge of additional conditions and contexts, and frequently biographical/historical knowledge as well. This is why many astute observers from other areas of psychology (e.g., Neisser, 1980), from sociology (e.g., Giddens, 1979), and from philosophy and political theory (e.g., Bernstein, 1976) see experimental social psychologists as looking in the wrong place at the wrong phenomena. These observers, we assume, have at the very least an implicit grasp of what we have described as the central role of social psychology.

Psychology as Biographical and Diagnostic

The professional activities of a great many psychologists have only been briefly referred to so far, and much of our discussion has only been indirectly related to their concerns. Their fields of interest include clinical, humanist, developmental, personality, along with many related psychological specialties that are sometimes referred to as applied psychologies (e.g., industrial, personnel, medical psychology). Most of these perspectives can be seen as bringing to bear all of the foregoing discussion in the attempt to understand individual persons and their behavioral patterns as they occur in the concrete social world.

Consider the conflict within psychology over the problem of consciousness and the explanation of behavior. Humanistic psychological orientations rejected behaviorist and reductionist strategies pertaining to consciousness and put the concept of the person in the center of their frame. They thus urged, rightly, we think, that to understand persons we need to adopt a hermeneutical approach, that we must seek "to define correctly the interpretations of the agent" (Taylor, 1973). This insight, shared by phenomenology, action theory, and interpretive sociologies, argues that to understand a person we must grasp the person's meanings and understandings, the agent's vision of the world, his or her plans, purposes, motivations, and interests. This is not to say that once this is accomplished, behavior is fully understood; such knowledge provides only one piece of the puzzle, but a necessary one.

Except as a counter to the claims of those with a radical behaviorist orientation, this idea does not demand esoteric philosophical argument, although a great deal of recent philosophy, from Wittgenstein to existential phenomenology and critical theory, has provided pertinent philosophical arguments. We know a great deal about one another; otherwise, it would be hard to imagine how we could get along at all. What might be surprising to a Martian investigator—some real discovery about human motivation or desire—will not be a discovery to us. This knowledge is reflected in human languages, whose concepts and distinctions are the product of a long evolutionary and historical experience, an experience in which, as Scriven has noted, "the easy material" regarding human understanding has been "winnowed out" and where the "nonsense" has not survived the press of continued experience (Scriven, 1964).

Put in simple terms, the insight of the hermeneutical perspective is this: If our aim is to explain behavior as it occurs in ordinary life there is no escaping the ordinary description of behavior and experience. Certainly causal mechanisms and structures discovered by experimental psychology of other sciences apply to such behavior, but by themselves they do not provide sufficient explanation, and they certainly do not enable us to dispense with ordinary language and to substitute a pure scientific language of behavior. We hasten to add that the reverse cannot be done either. Ordinary language cannot substitute for the language of causal mechanisms and structures.

Of course, our ordinary concepts and distinctions remain revisable; some might be abandoned or modified, others added through insights made by remarkable individuals, poets, novelists, philosophers, and psychologists. Consider here the impact of Freud on our ordinary self-understandings. Moreover, to say that we know a great deal about one another is not to say that our understandings are perfect, or even as adequate as we might like. And no doubt, a too characteristic narrowness and provinciality is to some extent, at least, broken down by humanist education (Joynson, 1974).

Finally, our everyday understandings or interpretations can in any particular instance be wrong. There are two aspects to this fallibility. The first regards the entire shift of modern epistemology and its rejection of the idea of "brute data." It is by now commonplace that there is no such thing as a noninterpreted "given" that can serve as the foundation of knowledge. This applies not only as regards our knowledge of the other person as agent, but also to our understanding of the natural world as well. That is, all our perceptions, categories, and frames of meaning are mediated and are culturally and historically loaded. But this does not eliminate the possibility of objectivity, construed here as warranted assertibility. Nor are we accordingly driven to a morass of relativism.

The other aspect of our fallibility stems from the continuous possibility of self-deception, so that as there is no chance for incorrigible knowledge of others, neither is there the possibility of incorrigible self-knowledge (Solomon, 1974).

These points raise some very crucial questions for psychology as a science. But the question that defined the conflict between humanists and their opponents is not one of these. The question is not whether some hermeneutic psychological science might replace our ordinary understandings of ourselves and others, understandings we regularly if imperfectly have available to us. Rather the question is, what would be involved in achieving a better understanding, a better account of our acts and the acts of others? Put bluntly, it is a question of what is the character of hermeneutical science?

Much depends, of course, on what one means by science. Science functions honorifically, and thus important political (institutional) dimensions are involved. Scientific knowledge is too frequently thought of as the only kind of knowledge, or at least as the best—truest, surest. At the same time, having the credentials associated with the acquisition of such knowledge gives us access not otherwise available, to research monies, to authority, to status. These political dimensions are too complex to pursue here. But the scientific dimensions are clear. The entire drift of current reexaminations of science and its epistemology makes the claims of science much less secure than empiricists' demands would ever have allowed. In the new heuristic, whether palatable or not, scientific knowledge is much closer to knowledge that is more familiarly accessible, through common sense, literature, and other modes of experience (Bernstein, 1976, esp. Part IV).

To be sure, the idea of science as a mode of controlled inquiry remains and is important. The public, critical, and systematic character of scientific inquiry must be acknowledged, and in this sense, hermeneutical science differs from the sort of hermeneutical understanding we take for granted and with which it is continuous. But more can be said.

On the view of science sketched earlier, we distinguished between sciences that aim at discovering the structures and mechanisms at work in the world, and on the other hand, sciences that apply this knowledge to explain, predict, and diagnose the phenomena of the world.

Meteorology applies knowledge derived from physics, astronomy, geology, and other sciences to offer explanations and predictions of concrete meteorological phenomena, for example, the cause of some drought. Many systems are involved in this event, including often, the past activities of human actors, as, for example in the Sahel. And we recognize that meteorology is not an exact science. History, similarly, seeks to explain historical events as concrete episodes involving particular persons in society, in particular times and places. It uses knowledge derived from the special social sciences, a host of auxiliary sciences, for example, numismatics, paleography, and knowledge drawn from common experience as well.

A hermeneutic science of individual persons is then the psychological analogue to history or to meteorology. It is engaged in understanding the concrete person and his or her life history and particular patterns of behavior, including as reflexively applied, self-understanding. But evidently, although the task remains hermeneutics and close to our common task as social beings, as a scientific effort it requires also that the inquirer use whatever special knowledge is available regarding implicated psychological structures and mechanisms as these operated in the individual biography. And since the person is born and matures in a social world, this understanding inevitably also includes references to what is known about social structures pertinent to that biography. Finally, in contrast to our prescientific mode of understanding, hermeneutic inquiry as a science would be constrained by the systematic, public demands of establishing the evidential credibility of its accounts. Although this picture may seem somewhat idealized, it conforms closely, we believe, to the best actual practices of the various person oriented psychologies. Moreover, it helps to explain both the fallibility and uncertainty that characterize such practice, and the feeling, sometimes hostilely expressed by experimental psychologists, that such psychology is more like a critically informed and systematic application of common sense than a radically unique and special "science." But given the correctness of the view of science defended here, no other more rigorous person-oriented science is possible.

One must also distinguish between the explanatory, diagnostic, and therapeutic aspects of such science. As an explanatory science, the parallel to history is extremely close. Insofar as history seeks to explain some particular event, it offers an account that traces and connects the complicated conjunctions of motivated acts and their intended and unintended consequences within a structurally limited arena of space and time. The account generally takes the form of a narrative, and the explanation requires also the ability of the historian to enter that situation and to communicate to an audience not only what happened, but what it was like (Hexter, 1971, pp. 208–221). The appeal of a psychoanalytic account (whether valid or not) lies in just this feature.

The relation between common sense and hermeneutic science parallels the relation between Everyman the historian versus the professional historian. Hexter (1971) argues that in writing history, the historian appeals to two "records": first, to the record of the past in concrete evidence, "whatever is publicly accessible to examination and evaluation" (pp. 66ff.), and to the second record, namely, "everything that historians bring to their confrontation with the record of the past" (p. 79). This second record, of course, every inquirer brings when confronting the world, whether of nature, of society, of individual persons. For Hexter, however, a key difference between Everyman the historian and the professional concerns the treatment of the first record, "a difference in grounds on which they expect and receive credence" (p. 65). And so it is with laypersons and their professional analogue, clinicians, who must be far more critical than laypersons with respect to what is taken as descriptive fact or evidence.

Similar considerations apply to the diagnostic aspect except that emphasis has now shifted to what is wrong or amiss. This still demands an understanding of causes. Diagnoses, of course, are called when, from an ordinary point of view, others are enigmatic, their behaviors (beliefs, etc.) are anomalous, bizarre, and unintelligible, or when they seek or need help. It is thus also that therapy enters.

Of course it may be that we shall not be able to achieve a significantly better grasp of the psychological structures implicated in such cases, and that in a real sense, these remain, from a theoretical point of view, intractable. Nevertheless, even under these conditions, it may be desirable to have persons specifically qualified to help persons deal with such problems. Participation in self-knowledge, use of behavioral techniques proved efficacious in practice, and other strategies and technologies are surely legitimate to the extent that they are ameliorative.

More optimistically, as we learn more about basic human powers and competencies and the structures that underlie them, we may learn more about the causes of incompetencies, disabilities, and the like. Some of these (e.g., aphasia) are manifestly neurological in form, but some may not be. In any case, the diagnostic and therapeutic sciences, like medicine, require knowledge both of the concrete individual and of the relevant structures, even if, unlike medicine, the problems that call for psychological amelioration need not be physiologically manifest or even physiological at all.

CONCLUSION

Summarizing what we have said in a succinct and intelligible fashion is virtually impossible. But perhaps we can draw a few conclusions. Philosophy of science has most commonly been the work of philosophers, not scientists. Both epistemology and ontology are central concerns in such philosophy, and these topics have a long history spanning many centuries. A few philosophically oriented scientists may perhaps be partly influenced in their choice of criteria by philosophical writings, but more commonly, scientists contrast with philosophers in generating their own criteria for validity out of their daily practices in scientific research. With this framework in mind, we may ask about the relative compatibility between scientific practices and logical positivism/empiricism versus a realist view of science.

It seems clear that the appeal to scientists of positivism/empiricism has rested on its emphasis on the senses, on observation as a "factual" basis for science. The hard-nosed scientist, like the proverbial Missourian, wants to be shown the evidence. But other themes of the philosophy perhaps only appeared palatable, or their full implication might not have been grasped. The idea of a rigorous logical linkage between observations, hypotheses, and theory sounds fine in principle, but had scientists become aware of the paradoxes and dilemmas created by that idea (eventually pointed out by philosophers), they might have been less ready to accept it.

As for the ontology of logical positivism, which emphasizes hypothetical entities rather than real ones, philosophers have had centuries of argument and practice in convincing others that we cannot know the real world, and perhaps scientists found this idea especially convenient when they were criticizing the work of other scientists (while secretly believing that their own postulated entities were real enough). With respect to Humean causation, few scientists should really feel comfortable with the idea that cause is at bottom illusory, nothing more than the concomitance of events. The idea of necessary and sufficient cause—causal or generative mechanisms or structures—would seem to be something that hard-nosed scientists would dearly love to have at the basis of their science.

What this leads up to is the conclusion that the realist theory of science should be more palatable to the working scientist than positivism or neopositivism. It allows scientists to believe that they are grappling with entities that, although often not observable directly, are real enough. And scientists know that they do not follow rules in jumping from observations or empirical generalizations to theoretical propositions, and further, that even in the confirmatory stage, spelling out a theory (even if in mathematical language) is a slippery and hazardous process.

Finally, the realist theory as presented here, following Bhaskar, provides a means of sharply distinguishing between the task of the scientist and the task of the clinician or technician. The former practices science by creating at least partially closed systems; the latter uses the discoveries of science, but in order to bring about changes in the everyday world, also employs a great deal of knowledge that extends beyond science. This principle defines their respective roles more clearly, and certainly has no unfavorable connotations for either side. It would seem that once they understand it, scientists would happily adopt a realist theory of science.

REFERENCE NOTE

1. Campbell, D. Personal communication, April 4, 1981.

REFERENCES

Achinstein, P. Approaches to the philosophy of science. In P. Achinstein & S. Barker (Eds.). *The legacy of logical positivism.* Baltimore: Johns Hopkins Press, 1969.

Althusser, L. *For Marx.* London: Allen Lane, 1969.

Bernstein, R. *The restructuring of social and political theory.* New York: Harcourt Brace Jovanovich, 1976.

Bhaskar, R. *A realist theory of science.* Leeds, England: Leeds Books, 1975. (An edition published in 1978 by Harvester Press contains a postscript clarifying Bhaskar's use of the term "law.")

Bhaskar, R. On the possibility of social scientific knowledge and the limits of behaviorism. *Journal for the Theory of Social Behavior.* 1978, *8,* 1–28.

Bhaskar, R. *The possibility of naturalism.* Brighton, Great Britain: Harvest Press, 1979.

Bhaskar, R. Emergence, explanation and emancipation. In P. F. Secord (Ed.), *Explaining social behavior: Consciousness, behavior, and social structure.* Beverly Hills, Calif.: Sage, 1982.

Boden, M. The structure of intentions. *Journal for the Theory of Social Behavior,* 1973, *3,* 23–46.

Bohm, D. *Cause and chance in modern physics.* London: Routledge & Kegan Paul, 1957.

Bourieu, P. *An outline of a theory of practice.* New York: Cambridge University Press, 1977.

Brown, H. I. *Perception, theory and commitment.* Chicago: University of Chicago Press, 1977.

Bunge, M. *Causality.* Cambridge, Mass.: Harvard University Press, 1959.

Campbell, D. A., & Misanin, J. R. Basic drives. In P. H. Mussen & M. R. Rosenzweig (Eds.), *Annual Review of Psychology* (Vol. 20). Palo Alto, Calif.: Annual Reviews, 1969.

Carnap, R. The methodological character of theoretical concepts. In *Minnesota studies in the philosophy of science* (Vol. 1). Minneapolis: University of Minnesota Press, 1956.

Churchland, P. M. Eliminative materialism and propositional attitudes. *The Journal of Philosophy,* 1981, *78.* 67–89.

Cole, S. *The sociological method: An introduction to the science of sociology.* Chicago: Rand McNally, 1980.

Cooper, L. A., & Shepard, R. N. Chronometric studies of the rotation of mental images. In W. G. Chase (Ed.), *Visual information processing.* New York: Academic Press, 1973.

Feyerabend, P. K. *Against method.* London: NLB, 1975.

Gadamer, H. G. *Truth and method.* London: Sheed & Ward, 1975.

Gibson, J. J. *The ecological approach to visual perception.* Boston: Houghton Mifflin, 1979.

Giddens, A. *New rules of sociological method.* London: Hutchinson, 1976.

Giddens, A. *Studies in social and political theory.* London: Hutchinson, 1977.

Giddens, A. *Central problems in social theory.* London: Macmillan, 1979.

Godelier, M. System structure and contradiction in capital. In R. Blackburn (Ed.), *Ideology in social science.* London: Fontana, 1972.

Hanson, N. R. *Patterns of discovery.* Cambridge, England: Cambridge University Press, 1958.

Hanson, N. R. *Observation and explanation.* New York: Harper & Row, 1971.

Harré, R. *The principles of scientific thinking.* Chicago: University of Chicago Press, 1970.

Harré, R. *Philosophies of science.* Oxford, England: Oxford University Press, 1972.

Harré, R., & Madden, E. H. *Causal powers.* Totowa, N.J.: Littlefield Adams, 1975.

Harré, R. & Secord, P. F. *The explanation of social behavior.* Oxford, England: Basil Blackwell, 1972.

Hempel, C. G. The theoretician's dilemma: A study in the logic of theory construction. In *Minnesota studies in the philosophy of science* (Vol. 2). Minneapolis: University of Minnesota Press, 1958.

Hempel, C. G. *Aspects of scientific explanation.* New York: Free Press, 1963.

Hexter, J. H. *The history primer.* New York: Basic Books, 1971.

Joynson, R. B. *Psychology and common sense.* London: Routledge & Kegan Paul, 1974.

Koch, S. *Psychology: A study of a science* (6 vols.) New York: McGraw-Hill, 1959–63.

Kuhn, T. S. *The structure of scientific revolutions* (2nd ed.). Chicago: University of Chicago Press, 1970. (1st ed., 1962.)

Lakatos, I., & Musgrave, A. (Eds.). *Criticism and the growth of knowledge.* New York: Cambridge University Press, 1970.

Layder, D. *Structure, interaction and social theory.* London: Routledge & Kegan Paul, 1981.

Layder, D. Grounded theory: A constructive critique. *Journal for the Theory of Social Behavior,* 1982, *12,* 103–123.

Levi-Strauss, C. *The savage mind.* London: Weidenfield & Nicolson, 1976.

Manicas, P. T. Review of *States and social revolutions* by T. Skocpol. *History and Theory.* 1981, *20,* 204–218.

Mead, G. H. *Mind, self, and society.* Chicago: University of Chicago Press, 1934.

Neisser, U. On "social knowing." *Personality and Social Psychology Bulletin.* 1980, 6, 601–605.

Polanyi, M. *Personal knowledge.* New York: Harper & Row, 1964.

Polanyi, M. *The tacit dimension.* London: Routledge & Kegan Paul, 1967.

Pylyshyn, Z. W. What the mind's eye tells the mind's brain: A critique of mental imagery. *Psychological Bulletin.* 1973, *80,* 1–24.

Scheffler, I. *Science and subjectivity.* New York: Bobbs-Merrill, 1967.

Scriven, M. A possible distinction between traditional scientific disciplines and the study of human behavior. In H. Feigl & M. Scriven (Eds.), *Minnesota studies in the philosophy of science* (Vol. 1). Minneapolis: University of Minnesota Press, 1956.

Scriven, M. Explanations, predictions and laws. In H. Feigl and G. Maxwell (Eds.), *Minnesota studies in the philosophy of science,* (Vol. 3). Minneapolis: University of Minnesota Press, 1962.

Scriven, M. Views of human nature. In T. W. Wann (Ed.), *Behaviorism and phenomenology.* Chicago: University of Chicago Press, 1964.

Scriven, M. Logical positivism and the behavioral sciences. In P. Achinstein & S. Barker (Eds.), *The legacy of logical positivism.* Baltimore: Johns Hopkins Press, 1969.

Secord, P. F. Integrating the personal and the social. In P. F. Secord (Ed.), *Explaining social behavior: Consciousness, human action and social structure.* Beverly Hills, Calif.: Sage Publications, 1982.

Sellars, W. The language of theories. In H. Feigl & G. Maxwell (Eds.), *Current issues in the philosophy of science.* New York: Holt, Rinehart & Winston, 1961.

Skinner, B. F. *Contingencies of reinforcement.* New York: Appleton-Century-Crofts, 1969.

Solomon, R. C. Freud and unconscious motivation. *Journal for the Theory of Social Behavior,* 1974 4, 191–216.

Suppe, F. *The structure of scientific theories.* Urbana: University of Illinois, 1974.

Taylor, C. Interpretations and the sciences of man. *Review of Metaphysics,* 1971, *25,* (1).

Taylor, C. Peaceful coexistence in psychology. *Social Research,* 1973, *40,* (1).

Taylor, C. Consciousness. In P. F. Secord (Ed.), *Explaining social behavior: Consciousness, human action and social structure.* Beverly Hills, Calif.: Sage, 1982.

Toulmin, S. *The Philosophy of science.* New York: Harper & Row, 1953.

Toulmin, S. *Foresight and understanding.* New York: Harper & Row, 1961.

Toulmin, S. *Human understanding.* Princeton, N.J.: Princeton University Press, 1972.

Toulmin, S. Wittgenstein: The Mozart of psychology. *New York Review of Books,* 1978, *25*(14).

Toulmin, S. The genealogy of "consciousness." In P. F. Secord (Ed.), *Explaining social behavior: Consciousness, human action and social structure.* Beverly Hills, Calif.: Sage, 1982.

36

THEORETICAL RISKS AND TABULAR ASTERISKS: SIR KARL, SIR RONALD, AND THE SLOW PROGRESS OF SOFT PSYCHOLOGY

PAUL E. MEEHL

I had supposed that the title gave an easy tipoff of my topic, but some puzzled reactions by my Minnesota colleagues show otherwise, which heartens me because it suggests that what I am about to say is not trivial and universally known. The two knights are Sir Karl Raimund Popper (1959, 1962, 1972; Schilpp, 1974) and Sir Ronald Aylmer Fisher (1956, 1966, 1967), whose respective emphases on subjecting scientific theories to grave danger of refutation (that's Sir Karl) and major reliance on tests of statistical significance (that's Sir Ronald) are, at least in current practice, not well integrated—perhaps even incompatible. If you have not been accustomed to thinking about this incoherency, and my remarks lead you to do so (whether or not you end up agreeing with me), this article will have served its scholarly function.

I consider it unnecessary to persuade you that most so-called "theories" in the soft areas of psychology (clinical, counseling, social, personality, community, and school psychology) are scientifically unimpressive and technologically worthless. Documenting that statement would of course require a considerable amount of time, but you can quickly get the flavor by having a look at Braun (1966); Fiske (1974); Gergen (1973); Hogan, DeSoto, and Solano (1977); McGuire (1973); Meehl (1960/1973a, 1959/1973f); Mischel (1977); Schlenker (1974); Smith (1973); and Wiggins (1973). These are merely some high visible and forceful samples; I make no claim to bibliographic completeness on the large theme of "What's wrong with 'soft' psychology." A

Reprinted from the *Journal of Consulting and Clinical Psychology*, 46, 806–834. (1978).

The research reported here was assisted by Grant MH 24224 from the National Institute of Mental Health and the University of Minnesota Psychiatry Research Fund. Completion of the article was aided by a James McKeen Cattell Fund sabbatical award.

beautiful hatchet job, which in my opinion should be required reading for all PhD candidates, is by the sociologist Andreski (1972). Perhaps the easiest way to convince yourself is by scanning the literature of soft psychology over the last 30 years and noticing what happens to theories. Most of them suffer the fate that General MacArthur ascribed to old generals—They never die, they just slowly fade away. In the developed sciences, theories tend either to become widely accepted and built into the large edifice of well-tested human knowledge or else they suffer destruction in the face of recalcitrant facts and are abandoned, perhaps regretfully as a "nice try." But in fields like personology and social psychology, this seems not to happen. There is a period of enthusiasm about a new theory, a period of attempted application to several fact domains, a period of disillusionment as the negative data come in, a growing bafflement about inconsistent and unreplicable empirical results, multiple resort to ad hoc excuses, and then finally people just sort of lose interest in the thing and pursue other endeavors.

Since I do not want to step on toes lest my propaganda falls on deaf ears, I dare not mention what strike me as the most egregious contemporary examples, so let us go back to the late 1930s and early 1940s when I was a student. In those days we were talking about level of aspiration. You could not pick up a psychological journal—even the *Journal of Experimental Psychology*—without finding at least one and sometimes several articles on level of aspiration in schizophrenics, or in juvenile delinquents, or in Phi Beta Kappas, or whatever. It was supposed to be a great powerful theoretical construct that would explain all kinds of things about the human mind from psychopathology to politics. What happened to it? Well, I have looked into some of the recent textbooks of general psychology and have found that either they do not mention it at all—the very phrase is missing from the index—or if they do, it gets cursory treatment in a couple of sentences. There is no doubt something to the notion. We all agree (from common sense) that people differ in what they demand or expect of themselves, and that this probably has something to do, sometimes, with their performance. But it did not get integrated into the total nomological network, nor did it get clearly liquidated as a nothing concept. It did not get killed or resurrected or transformed or solidified; it just kind of dried up and blew away, and we no longer wanted to talk about it or do experimental research on it. A more recent example is the theory of "risky shift," about which Cartwright (1973) wrote, after reviewing 196 papers that appeared in the 1960s:

> As time went by . . . it gradually became clear that the cumulative impact of these findings was quite different from what had been expected by those who produced them. Instead of providing an explanation of why "groups are riskier than individuals," they in fact cast serious doubt on the validity of the proposition itself (p. 225).
>
> It is now evident that the persistent search for an explanation of "the risky shift" was misdirected and that any adequate theory will have to account for a much more complicated set of data than originally anticipated. But it is not clear how theorizing should proceed, since serious questions have been raised as to whether, or in what way, "risk" is involved in the effects to be explained (p. 226).
>
> After 10 years of research, [the] original problem remains unsolved. We still do not know how the risk-taking behavior of "real-life" groups compares with that of individuals (p. 231).

I do not think that there is any dispute about this matter among psychologists familiar with the history of the other sciences. It is simply a sad fact that in soft psychology theories rise and decline, come and go, more as a function of baffled boredom than anything else; and the enterprise shows a disturbing absence of that *cumulative* character that is so impressive in disciplines like astronomy, molecular biology, and genetics.

There are some solid substantive reasons for this that I will list here, lest you think that I am beating up on the profession, unaware of the terrible intrinsic difficulty of our subject matter. Since (in 10 minutes of superficial thought) I easily came up with 20 features that make human psychology hard to scientize, I invite you to pick your own favorites. Differences as to which difficulties are emphasized will not, I am sure, cause any disagreement about the general fact. This is not the place to develop in detail the thesis that the human mind is hard to scientize, let alone to prove it. Each of the 20 difficulties is, I am aware, debatable; and one could find competent psychologists who would either deny a difficulty's reality—at least in the form I state it—or who, although admitting it exists, would maintain that we have, or will be able to develop shortly, methods adequate to overcome or circumvent it. Each of these alleged difficulties in scienting the human mind is sufficiently controversial to deserve a methodological article by itself. This being so, to substitute a once-over lightly (and hence inevitably dogmatic) defense of each as a real difficulty is, for those who accept it, a work of supererogation, and for the others, it is doomed to failure. I therefore confine myself to listing and explaining the problems, repeating that my purpose in so doing is to prevent the rest of my article from being taken as a kind of malicious and unsympathetic attack on psychologists (of which, after all, I *am* one!) based on an inadequate appreciation of the terrible difficulties under which we work. In a few cases I have explained at some length and replied to objections, these being cases in which a difficulty is not widely recognized in our profession or in which it is generally held to have been exposed of by a familiar (but erroneous) refutation or solution. Regrettably, some psychologists use "philosophical" arguments that are a generation or more out of date.

Since I am listing and summarizing rather than developing or proving, it seems appropriate to present the set of difficulties as follows:

1. RESPONSE-CLASS PROBLEM

This involves the well-known difficulties of slicing up the raw behavioral flux into meaningful intervals identified by causally relevant attributes on the response side, a problem that exists already in the Skinner box (Skinner, 1938, p. 70), worsens in field study by an ethologist, and reaches almost unmanageable proportions in studying human social behavior of the kind to which clinical, social, and personology psychologists must address themselves (see, e.g., MacCorquodale & Meehl, 1954, pp. 218–231, after a quarter century still considered by some as best statement of the problem; Hinde, 1970, pp. 10–13; Meehl, 1954, pp. 40–44 and chap. 6 passim; Skinner, 1938, pp. 33–43).

2. SITUATION-TAXONOMY PROBLEM

As is well-known, the importance of an adequate classification and sampling of environments and situations has received less attention than Problem 1, above, despite emphasis by several major contributors such as Roger Barker (1968), Egon Brunswik (1955), and Saul B. Sells (1963). It seems likely that the problems of characterizing the stimulus side, even though often neglected by the profession or dealt with superficially, are about as intractable as the characterization of the response class. It is not even clear whether identificaion and measurement of the relevant stimulus dimensions (e.g., size) is the same task as concocting a taxonomy of "situations" and "environments," nor whether the answer to this question would quickly generate rules for an adequate statistical ecology applicable to research design. So I am perhaps lumping under this "situation-taxonomy" rubric three distinguishable but related problems. I am inclined to think that most (not all) of the current methodological controversy concerning traits versus situations is logically and mathematically reducible to this and the preceding category, since I think that traits are disposition clusters, and dispositions always involve at least implicit reference to the stimulus side; but this is not the place to push that view.

3. UNIT OF MEASUREMENT

One sometimes hears this conflated with one or both of the preceding, but, of course, it is not the same. There are questions in rating scales and in psychometrics (as well as in certain branches of nondifferential psychology) in which disagreements persist about such fundamental matters as the necessity of a genuine interval or ratio scale for the use of certain kinds of sampling statistical inference.

4. INDIVIDUAL DIFFERENCES

Perhaps the shortest way to discuss this one is to point out the oddity that what is one psychologist's subject matter is another psychologist's error term (Cronbach, 1957)! More generally, the fact is that organisms differ not only with respect to the strengths of various dispositions, but, more common and more distressing for the researcher, they differ as to *how* their dispositions are shaped and organized. As a result, the individual differences involed in "mental chemistry" are tougher to deal with than, say, the fact that different elements have different atomic numbers or that elements with the same atomic number vary in atomic weights (isotopes).

5. POLYGENIC HEREDITY

It is generally conceded that the measurement and causal inference problems that arise in biometrical genetics are, with some exceptions, more difficult than those found in the kind of single factor dominant or recessive gene situation on which the science of genetics was originally founded. Except for Mendelizing mental deficiencies and perhaps some psychiatric disorders that are transmitted in a Mendelizing fashion, most of the attributes studied by soft-field psychologists are influenced by polygenic systems. Usually we must assume that several totally different and unrelated polygenic systems influence a manifest trait like social introversion. Introversion may be based in part on a unitary (although polygenic) variable, as shown by Gottesman (1963) and others. However, as an acquired disposition of the adult-acculturated individual, it presumably results from a confluence of different polygenic contributes such as basic anxiety readiness, mesomorphic toughness, garden-variety social introversion, dominance, need for affiliation, and the like.

6. DIVERGENT CAUSALITY

As pointed out 35 years ago by the physical chemist Irving Langmuir (1943; London, 1946; Meehl, 1954, pp. 60–61; Meehl, 1967/1970b, especially Footnotes 1–8 on pp. 395–396), there are complex systems whose causal structure and boundary conditions are such that slight differences—including those that are, for practical predictive and explanatory purposes, effectively "random" (whatever their inner deterministic nature may be)—tend to "wash out," "cancel each other," or "balance" over the long run. On the other hand, there are other systems in which such slight perturbations or differences in the exact characer of the initial conditions are, so to speak, amplified over the long run. Langmuir christened the former kind of causality as "convergent," as when we say that the average errors in making repeated measurements of a table length tend to cancel out and leave us with a stable and highly trustworthy mean value of the result. On the other hand, an object in unstable equilibrium can lean slightly toward the right instead of the left, as a result of which a deadly avalanche occurs burying a whole village. Although both sorts of systems are found at all levels of Comte's Pyramid of the Sciences, it seems regrettably true that the incidence of important and pervasive types of divergent causality is greater in the sciences of behavior.

7. IDIOGRAPHIC PROBLEM

It is not necessary to "settle" the long-continued methodological controversies regarding idiographic versus nomothetic methods in psychology and history (e.g., whether they are philosophically, metaphysically fundamentally different) to agree with strong proponents of the idiographic method, such as Gordon Allport (Allport, 1937) or my long-time friendly adversary on the prediction issue, Robert R. Holt (1958), that the human personality—unless one approaches it with the postulate of impoverished reality—has in its content, structure, and, conceivably, even in individual differences as to some of its "laws," and very much in its origins, properties and relations that make the study of personality rather more similar to such disciplines as history, archeology (historical), geology, or the reconstruction of a criminal case from police evidence than the derivation of the molar gas laws from the kinetic theory of heat or the mechanisms of heredity from molecular biology. Some would argue that such explanatory derivations aside, even the mere inductive subsumption of particulars (episodes, molar traits, persons) under descriptive generalizations is a more difficult and problematic affair in these disciplines than in most branches of physical and biological science.

8. UNKNOWN CRITICAL EVENTS

Related to divergent causality and idiographic understanding but distinguishable from them is the fact that critical events in the history of personality development are frequently hard to ascertain. There is reason to believe that in some instances they are literally never ascertained by us or known to the individual under study, even somebody who has spent 500 hours on the analytic couch. They are sometimes observable events that, however, were not in fact observed and recorded, such as the precise tone of voice and facial expression that a patient's father had when he was reacting to an off-color joke that the patient innocently told at the dinner table at age 7. Every thoughtful clinician realizes that the standard life history that one finds in a medical chart is, from the standpoint of thorough causal comprehension, so thin and spotty and selective as to border on the ludicrous. But there is also what I would view as an important causal source of movement in one rather than another direction of divergent causality, namely, inner events, such as fantasies, resolutions, shifts in cognitive structure, that the patient may or may not report and that he or she may later be unable to recall.

9. NUISANCE VARIABLES

Other things equal, it is handy for research and theorizing if we can sort out the variables into three classes, namely, (a) variables that we manipulate (in the narrow sense of the word *experimental*), (b) variables that we do not manipulate but can hold constant or effectively exclude from influence by one or another means isolating the system under study, and (c) variables that are quasirandom with respect to the phenomena under study, so that they only contribute to measurement error or the standard deviation of a statistic. Unfortunately, there are systems, especially social and biological systems of the kind that clinical psychologists and personologists study, in which there is operative a nonnegligible class of variables that are not random but systematic, that exert a sizable influence, and are themselves also sizably influenced by other variables, either exogenous to the system (F. M. Fisher, 1966) or contained in it, such that we have to worry about the influence of these variables, but we cannot always ascertain the direction of the causal arrow. Sometimes we cannot even get sufficiently trustworthy measurements of these variables so as to "partial out" or "correct" their influence even if we are willing to make conjectures about the direction of causality. There are some circumstances in which we can extrapolate from experimental studies or from well-corroborated theory to make a high-confidence decision about the direction of causal influence, but there are many other circumstances—in soft psychology, the prepondering ones—in which this is not possible. Further, lacking special configurations such as highly atypical cells in a multivariate space or correlation coefficients that impose strong constraints on a causal interpretation, or provisional assumptions as relied on in path analysis (Li, 1975), the system is statistically and causally indeterminate. (Why these constraints are regularly treated as "assumptions" instead of refutable conjectures is itself a deep and fascinating question that I plan to examine some other time.) The well-known difficulties in assessing the influence of socioeconomic status (SES) on children's IQ when unscrambling the hereditary and environmental contributors to intelligence is perhaps the most dramatic one, but other less emotion-laden examples can be found on all sides in the behavioral sciences. (See Meehl, 1970a, 1971/1973b).

10. FEEDBACK LOOPS

A special case in engineering is the usual in psychology, that a person's behavior affects the behavior of other persons and hence alters the schedule imposed by the "social Skinner box." The complexities here are so refractory to quantitative decomposition that yoked box setups came to be used even for the (relatively simple) animal case as a factual substitute for piecewise causal–dispositional analysis. In the human social case, they may be devastating.

11. AUTOCATALYTIC PROCESSES

The chemist is familiar under the label *autocatalysis* with a rare but important kind of preparation in which one of the end products of the chemical processes is itself capable of catalyzing the process. Numerous common examples spring to mind in psychology, such as anxiety and depression as affects of economic failure as a social impact. Much of neurosis is autocatalytic in the cognitive-affective-volitional system, as are counterneurotic healing processes. When this kind of complicated setup is conjoined with the critical event, idiographic, and divergent causality factors, and also with the individual differences factor (that parameters relating the growth of one state of schedule to a dependent variable, which itself in turn acts autocatalytically, show individual differences), the task of unscrambling such a situation becomes terribly difficult.

12. RANDOM WALK

There is a widespread and understandable tendency to assume that the class of less-probable outcomes, given constancy of other classes of causally efficacious variables, should in principle be explicable by detecting a class of systematic input differences. Thus, for instance, we try to understand the genetic/environmental contributions to schizophrenia by studying discordant monozygotic twins. If I develop a florid clinical schizophrenia and my monozygotic twin remains sane and wins the Pulitzer Prize for poetry, it is a sensible strategy for the psychologist to consider my case *and similar cases* with an eye for "systematic differences" (such as who was born first, who was in what position in the uterus, or who had a severe case of scarlet fever with delirium) as responsible for dramatic difference in final outcomes. When one reflects on the rather meager yield of such assiduous ferreting out of systematic differences by, say Gottesman and Shields (1972) in their excellent book, one experiences bafflement. On the one hand, the concordance rate for monozygotic twins is only a little over 50%, indicating a very large nongenetic component in causality. Yet, on the other hand, we find feeble or null differences when we look at the list of "obvious, plausible" differentiators between the twins who fall ill and the twins who remain well. Of course, one can always say—and would no doubt be partly right in this—that we just have not been clever enough to hit on the right ones; or even if, qualitatively, they are the right ones, we do not have sufficiently construct-valid measures of them to show up in the statistics.

There is, however, an alternative explanation that when one reflects on it, is plausible (at least to a clinical practitioner like myself) and that has analogues in organic medicine and in other historical sciences like geology or the theory of evolution, to wit, that we are mistaken to look for a "big systematic variable" of the kind that is already in our standard list of influences, such as organic disease, parental preference, or SES of an adoptive home. Rather, we might emphasize that a human being's life history involves as one form of divergent causality, something akin to the stochastic process known as a "random walk" (Bartlett, 1955, pp. 15–20, 47–50, 89–96; Feller, 1957, pp. 73, 311; Kemeny, Snell, & Thompson, 1957, pp. 171–177; Read, 1972, pp. 779–782). At several points that are individually minor but collectively critical determinative, it is an almost "chance" affair whether the patient does A or not A, whether this girl friend says she will or will not go out with him on a certain evening, or whether he happens to hit it off with the opthamologist that he consults about some peculiar vision disturbances that are making him anxious about becoming blind, and the like. If one twin becomes psychotic at the end of such a random walk, it is possible that he was suffering from what was only, so to speak, "bad luck"—not a concept that appears in any standard list of biological and social nuisance variables!

Luck is one of the most important contributors to individual differences in human suffering, satisfaction, illness, achievement, and so forth, an embarrassingly "obvious" point that social scientists readily forget (Gunther, 1977; Jencks, 1972, pp. 8–9, 227–228; Popper, 1974, pp. 36–37; Stoddard, 1929; for further discussion of this see Meehl, 1972/1973g, pp. 402–407, Meehl, 1973d, pp. 220–221). Of course, the fact that a process resembles a random walk does not mean that it is not susceptible to quantitative treatment. Witness the extensive formal development of this sort of process in the field of finite mathematics by engineers and others. The point is that its analytical treatment will not look like the familiar kind of search for a systematic class of differentiating variables like SES as a nuisance variable in relationship to educational outcomes and intelligence.

13. SHEER NUMBER OF VARIABLES

I suppose that this is the most commonly mentioned of the difficulties of social science, and I assume that my readers would accept it without further elaboration. But it is worth mention that the number of variables is large from several different viewpoints. Thus we deal on one side with a *large number of phenotypic traits,* conceiving a phenotypic trait as a related family of response dispositions that (a) are correlated to some stipulated degree pairwise and that (b) have some kind of logical, semantic, social, or other "meaning" overlap or resemblance that entitles us to class them together. Or, again, we consider a large number of dimensions on the stimulus side and on the response side that are relevant in formulating a law of behavior acquisition, as well as in the subsequent control and activation dispositions thus acquired. From still another viewpoint, the list of historical causal influences is long and heterogeneous, ranging from such diverse factors as a mutated gene or a never-diagnosed subclinical tuberculosis to a mother who mysteriously absented herself the day after a patient first permitted himself the fantasy that a brutal father would go away, and the like. It should be noted that this matter of sheer number of variables would not be so important (except as a contributor to residual "random variation" in various kinds of outcomes) if they were each small contributors and independent, like the sources of error in the scattering of shots at a target in classical theory of errors. But in psychology this is not typically the situation. Rather, the variables, although large in number, are each nuisance variables that carry a significant amount of weight, interact with each other, and contribute to idiographic development via the divergent causality mode.

14. IMPORTANCE OF CULTURAL FACTORS

This source of individual differences, both in acquired response clusters (traits) and in the parameters of acquisition and activation functions, especially when taken together with the genetic factors contributing, for instance, to social competence, mental health, intellect, and so on, makes for unusual complications in understanding how somebody got to be the way he is. We are, for instance, so accustomed to referring to nuisance variables like SES in considering the design of experiments that involve SES-related individual differences that we readily forget something every reflective person knows—that the measures of things like SES are general and not tailor-made for what is idiographically more significant in the development of a particular person. So when we speak of "controlling for SES," that is a loose use of language in comparison with "controlling the temperature" in a Skinner box or controlling the efflux of calories in a physics lab by use of a bomb calorimeter. A treatise on the principles of internal medicine (such as Harrison et al., 1966) sometimes refers to cultural factors, including those that are not at all understood—in the way that, say, dietary deficiency might be mediated by extreme poverty in a backward country—and simply says that for some reason this disease is found more frequently among the rich than among the poor. But the *important* causal chains of prime interest to the physician, even in his role as an advisor of preventive medicine, do not typically involve worry about whether somebody is fifth-generation upper class or the third child of parents who became anxious after the birth of the second oldest sibling. However, this kind of consideration might be crucial in reconstructing the life history of such a person.

15. CONTEXT-DEPENDENT STOCHASTOLOGICALS

Cronbach and Meehl (1955/1973) and subsequent writers adopted (from the neopositivist philosophers of science) the phrase *nomological network* to designate the system of lawlike relationships conjectured to hold between theoretical entities (states, structures, events, dispositions) and between theoretical entities and their observable indicators. The "network" metaphor is chosen to emphasize the structure of such systems, in which the *nodes* of the network, representing the postulated theoretical entities, are connected by the *strands* of the network, representing the lawful relationships hypothesized to hold between the entities. What makes such a set of theoretical statements a system (rather than a mere conjunction of unrelated assertions, a "heap of hypotheses") is the semantic fact of their shared terms, an overlap in the propositions' inner components, without which, of course, no deductive fertility and no derivation chains to observational statements would be formally possible. The network is empirical (and "scientifically respectable"), because a proper subset of the theoretical terms is coordinated in fairly direct ways ("operationally") with terms designating perceptual or instrument reading predicates. These latter predicates normally possess the admirable properties of *quick decision, minimal theory dependence,* and *high interpersonal consensus.*

Despite the current distaste for these "objectivist" conceptions, I remain an old-fashioned unreconstructed positivist to the limited extent that I think science—both "normal science" and "revolutionary, paradigm-replacing science"—differs from less promising, noncumulative, and personalistic enterprises like politics, psychotherapy, folklore, ethics, metaphysics, aesthetics, and theology *in part* because of its skeptical insistence on reliable (intersubjective, replicable) protocols that describe observations. Skinner is in better shape than Freud partly because Norman Campbell (1920/1957, p. 29) was right in saying that the kinds of judgments for which universal assent can be obtained are (a) judgments of temporal simultaneity, consecutiveness, and "betweenness"; (b) judgments of coincidence and "betweenness" in space; and (c) judgments of number. I cannot view the increasingly fashionable dismissal of these objectivity-oriented views as other than obscurantist in tendency. (See Kordig, 1971, 1973.)

However, the nomological network, even though correlated directly, here and there, with observational data, is not "operational" throughout, since some of the nodes and strands are connected with the observational data base only via other subregions of the network. As Hempel said (1952):

> A scientific theory might therefore be likened to a complex spatial network: Its terms are represented by the knots, while the threads connecting the latter correspond, in part, to the definitions and, in part to the fundamental and derivative hypotheses included in the theory. The whole system floats, as it were, above the plane of observation and is anchored to it by rules of interpretation. These might be viewed as strings which are not part of the network but link certain points of the latter with specific places in the plane of observation. By virtue of those interpretive connections, the network can function as a scientific theory: From certain observational data, we may ascend, via an interpretive string, to some point in the theoretical network, thence proceed, via definitions and hypotheses, to other points, from which another interpretive string permits a descent to the plane of observation. (p. 36)

Even though the core of these ideas is sound and important, the word *nomological* is in soft psychology at best an extension of meaning and at worst a misleading corruption of the logician's terminology. Originally it designated strict laws as in W. E. Johnson's (1921/1964) earlier use of "nomic necessity" (p. 61). The lawlike relationships we have to work with in soft psychology are rarely (never?) of this strict kind, errors of measurement aside. Instead, they are correlations, tendencies, statistical clusterings, increments of probabilities, and altered stochastic dispositions. The ugly neologism *stochastological* (as analogue to *nomological*) is at least shorter than the usual "probabilistic relation" or "statistical dependence," so I shall adopt it. We are so accustomed to our immersion in a sea of stochastologicals that we may fail to notice what a terrible disadvantage this sort of probabilistic law network puts us under, both as to the clarity of our concepts and, more importantly, the testability of our theories. (One still hears the tiresome complaint that a theoretical system cannot be simultaneously concept definatory and factually assertive, despite repeated explanations of how this works. See, e.g., Braithwaite, 1960, pp. 76–87; Campbell, 1920/1957, pp. 119–158; Carnap, 1936–1937/1950, 1952/1956, 1966, pp. 225–226, 265–274;

Feigl, 1956, pp. 17–19; Hempel, 1952, 1958, pp. 81–87; Lewis, 1970; Maxwell, 1961, 1962; Meehl, 1977, pp. 35–37; Nagel, 1961, pp. 87, 91–93; Pap, 1958, pp. 318–321, 1962, pp. 46–52; Popper, 1974, pp. 14–73; Ramsey, 1931/1960; Sellars, 1948.)

When the observational corroborators of the theory consist wholly of percentages, crude curve fits, correlations, significance tests, and distribution overlaps, it is difficult or impossible to see clearly when a given batch of empirical data refutes a theory or even when two batches of data are (in any interesting sense) "inconsistent." All we can usually say with quasi-certainty is that context-dependent statistics should *not* be numerically identical in different studies of the same problem. (A dramatic recent example of this was the discovery that some of Sir Cyril Burt's correlation coefficients were *too consistent* to have been derived from the different tests and populations that he reported!)

In heading this section "Context-Dependent Stochastologicals," I mean to emphasize the aspect of this problem that seems to me most frustrating to our theoretical interests, namely, that the statistical dependencies we observe are always somewhat, and often strongly, dependent on the institution-cum-population setting in which the measurements were obtained. Lacking a "complete (causal) theory" of what influences what, *and how much,* we simply cannot compute expected numerical changes in stochastic dependencies when moving from one population or setting to another. Sometimes we cannot even rationally predict the direction of such changes. If the difference between two Pearson correlations were safely attributable to random sampling fluctuation alone, we could use the statistician's standard tools to decide whether Jones's study "fails to replicate" Smith's. But the usual situation is not one of simple cross-validation shrinkage (or "boostage")—rather, it involves the validity generalization problem. For this, there are no standard statistical procedures. We may be able, relying on strong theorems in general statistics plus a backlog of previous experience and a smattering of theory, to say some fairly safe things about restriction of range and the like. However, thoughtful theorists realize how little *quantitatively* we can say with sufficient confidence to warrant counting an unexpected shift in a stochastic quantity as a strong "discorroborator." This being so, we cannot fairly count an "in the ball park" predicted value as a strong corroborator. For example, Meehl's Mental Measure correlates .50 with SES in Duluth junior high school students, as predicted from Fisbee's theory of sociability. When Jones tries to replicate the finding on Chicano seniors in Tucson, he gets $r = .34$. Who can say anything theoretically cogent about this difference? Does any sane psychologist believe that one can do much more than shrug?

Although probability concepts (in the theory) and statistical distributions (in the data) sometimes appear in both classical and quantum physics, their usual role differs from that of context-dependent stochastologicals in social science. Without exceeding space limitations or my competence, let me briefly suggest some differences. When probabilities appear in physics and chemistry, they often drop out in the course of the derivation chain, yielding a quasi-nomological at its termination (e.g., derivation of gas laws or Graham's diffusion law from the kinetic theory of heat, in which the postulates are nomological, the "conditions" are probability distributions, and the resulting theorems are again nomological). Second, when the predicted observational result still contains statistical notions, their numerical values are either not context dependent or the context dependencies permit precise experimental manipulation. A statistical scatter function for photons or electrons can be finely tuned by altering a very limited number of experimental variables (e.g., wavelength, slit width, screen distance), and the law of large numbers assures that the expected "probabilistic" values of, say, photon incidence in a specified band will be indiscernibly different from the observed (finite but huge) numbers.

All of this is very unlike the stochastologicals of soft psychology, in which strong context dependence prevails, but we do not know (a) the complete list of contextual influences, (b) the function form of context dependency for those influences that we can list, (c) the numerical values of parameters in those function forms that we know or guess, or (d) the values of the context variable if we are so fortunate as to get past Ignorances a–c. Finally, unlike physics, our sample sizes are usually such that the Bernoulli theorem does not guarantee a close fit between theoretical and observed frequencies—perhaps one of the few good uses for significance tests?

16. OPEN CONCEPTS

As a consequence of the factors listed supra, especially those numbered 4, 7, 9, 15, it is usually not possible in the soft areas of social science to provide rigorous, explicit, or—the holy word when I was in graduate school—operational definitions for theoretical concepts. This difficulty occurs not because psychologists are intellectually lazy or sloppy, although most of us are at times (some routinely and on principle). Rather, it arises from the intrinsic nature of the subject matter, that is, from the organism's real compositional nature and structure and the causal texture of its environment. As has often been pointed out, one can concoct quick and easy "operational definitions" of psychological terms, but they will usually lack theoretical interest and, except for some important special cases (e.g., purely predictive task-tailored psychometrics and *some* kinds of operant behavior control), generalizable technological power (Lazarus, 1971; Loevinger, 1957). It is remarkable evidence of cultural lag in intellectual life that one can still find quite a few psychologists who are hooked on the dire necessity of strictly operational definitions, and who view open concepts as somehow methodologically sinful, although it is now a quarter of a century since the late Arthur Pap published his brilliant article on open concepts (Pap, 1953, see also chap. 11 of Pap, 1958). To do justice, and highlight the cultural lag, I should mention the related article of Waismann that antedated Pap's by 8 years (Waismann, 1945) and even Carnap's of 40 years ago (1936–1937/1950). I cannot name a single logician or a philosopher (or historian) of science who today defends strict operationism in the sense that some psychologists claim to believe in it. (They don't really—but you have to listen awhile to catch the deviations in *substance* when pseudooperationists are not discoursing dogmatically about *method.*)

The problem of open concepts and their relation to empirical falsifiability warrants a separate article, with which I am currently engaged, but suffice it to say here that the uavoidability of open concepts in social and biological science tempts us to sidestep it by fake operationism on the one side (if we are of the tough-minded, superscientific orientation) or to be contented with fuzzy verbalisms on the other side (if we are more artsy-craftsy or literary), thinking that it is the best we can get. The important point for methodology of psychology is that just as in statistics one can have a *reasonably precise theory of probable inference,* being "quasi-exact about the inherently inexact," so psychologists should learn to be sophisticated and rigorous in their metathinking about open concepts at the substantive level. I do not mean to suggest in saying this that the logicians' theory of open concepts is in a highly developed state, but it is far more developed than one would think from reading or listening to most psychologists.

I have elsewhere (Meehl, 1977) distinguished three kinds of openness that are involved in varying degrees in various psychological concepts and that may all be present in the same theoretical construct, namely, (a) openness arising from the indefinite extensibility of our provisional list of operational indicators of the construct; (b) openness associated with each indicator singly, because of the empirical fact that indicators are only probabilistically, rather than nomologically, linked to the inferred theoretical construct; and (c) openness due to the fact that most of our theoretical entities are introduced by an implicit or contextual definition, that is, by their role in the accepted nomological network, rather than by their inner nature. By their "inner nature" I mean nothing spooky or metaphysical but merely their ontological structure or composition as the latter will, with the progress of research, be formulatable in terms of the theoretical entities of more basic sciences in Comte's pyramid. In social and biological science, one should keep in mind that *explicit definition* of theoretical entities is seldom achieved in terms of the initial observational variables of those sciences, but it becomes possible instead by theoretical reduction or fusion. Explicit definition is achieved, if ever, in terms of some more basic underlying science (Meehl, 1977, see also Cronbach & Meehl (1955/1973); Meehl, 1959/1973f, 1973h, pp. 285–288).

A final remark, which also deserves fuller treatment in another place, is that when we deal with open concepts, as in personality psychometrics of traits or taxa, the statistical phenomenon of *psychometric drift* as a result of bootstrap oeprations, refinement of measures, and theoretical reflection on the big matrix of convergent and discriminative validities (Campbell & Fiske, 1959) also generates, via our reliance on implicit or contextual definitions of theoretical entities, an associated *conceptual drift,* a meaning shift. When we reassign weight to fallible indicators of an entity to the extent that the very meaning of the term designating that entity is specified by its role in the network, such reassignment of weights—especially under drastic revisions of the system as dropping a previously relied-upon indicator—constitutes a change in the theoretical concept. Difficult interpretative and research strategy problems arise here, because, on the one hand (especially in psychometrics) we encounter the danger that the resulting conceptual drift has pulled us away from what we started out to measure, but we also recognize that in psychology, as in the other sciences, part of the research aim is precisely that of bringing about revisions of concepts on the basis of revisions of the nomological network that implicitly defines them. We want, as Plato said, to carve nature at its joints; and the best test to this achievement is increased order in our material.

17. INTENTIONALITY, PURPOSE, AND MEANING

We do not need to settle the philosopher's question of what is the essential condition for the existence of intentionality, nor buy Brentano's famous criterion that intentionality is the distinctive mark of the mental, to recognize that human beings think and plan and intend, that if rats do so they do it at a much lower level, that sunflowers probably do not, and that stones certainly do not. The formulation of powerful functional relationships for systems that do not possess the capacity to think, worry, regret, plan, and intend is obviously on the average an easier task. (But see Vico, 1744/1948, for a view so different that an American social scientist of our time can hardly grasp it.)

18. RULE GOVERNANCE

Related to intentionality but sufficiently important to deserve a special listing is the fact that human behavior is rule governed. People do something not merely "in accordance with" a generalization but because they feel bound to obey the generalization stated in the form of a rule. Nobody has succeeded in coming up with a fully satisfactory definition of when a rule is a rule, but a sufficiently good approximation is to say that a rule differs from an empirical generalization in that a rule is not liquidated by being broken, whereas an empirical generalization is thereby liquidated (assuming that the conditions stated in its antecedent clause are granted, and the violation event is admitted into the corpus). Continued controversies in psycholinguistics reflect the importance of this kind of consideration in any discussion of human conduct.

19. UNIQUELY HUMAN EVENTS AND POWERS

In addition to being rule governed, there are several other human features that we do not share with chimpanzees, let alone sponges or boulders. I recall the late Richard M. Elliott saying that the main reason that psychology had done so poorly in its "theories" of humor is that man is the only animal that laughs. I think he had a good point here, since we have learned so much about aspects of human functioning, such as digestion and reproduction, by the experimental study of animals. There are a number of other things that human beings do that no infrahuman animal does, so far as we know. Only man speculates about nonpractical, theoretical matters; only man worships; only man systematically goes about seeking revenge, years later, for an injury done to him; only man carries on discussions about how to make decisions; and there are some features of cultural transmission that only man engages in, although the evidence now indicates that numerous other species transmit learned forms of behavior to subsequent generations.

20. ETHICAL CONSTRAINTS ON RESEARCH

This one is so obvious as to need no exposition. One can readily conceive quasi-definitive experiments on the IQ–heredity controversy, or whether there are family dynamics sufficient to make just anyone into a manic-depressive, that cannot be performed because to do so would be immoral.

Not to be overly pessimistic, let me mention (without proof) five noble traditions in clinical psychology that I believe have permanent merit and will still be with us 50 or 100 years from now, despite the usual changes. Some of these are currently unpopular among those addicted to one of the contemporary fly-by-night theories, but that does not bother me. These five noble traditions are (a) descriptive clinical psychiatry, (b) psychometric assessment, (c) behavior genetics, (d) behavior modification (I lump under this rubric positive contingency management, aversion therapy, and desensitization), and (e) psychodynamics. This list should convince you that I am not using methodological arguments to grind any substantive ax. I am probably one of the few psychologists alive today who would list all five of these as great, noble, and enduring intellectual traditions. I particularly emphasize the last, psychodynamics, since I am often perceived as a dust bowl empiricist who does not think that anything can be true or useful if it is not either based on laboratory experiments or statistical correlations. There is not a single experiment reported in my 23-volume set of the standard edition of Freud nor is there a *t* test. But I would take Freud's clinical observations over most people's *t* tests any time. I am confident that psychoanalytic concepts will be around after rubber band theory, transactional theory, attachment theory, labeling theory, dissonance theory, attribution theory, and so on, have subsided into a state of innocuous desuetude like risky shift and level of aspiration. At the very least, psychoanalysis is an interesting theory, which is more than I can say about some of the "theories" that are currently fashionable.

These five noble traditions differ greatly in the methods they use and their central concepts, and I am hard put to say what is common among them. Some of them, such as behavior modification, are not conceptually exciting to those of us who are interested in ideas like Freud's, but they more than make up for that by their remarkable technological power. I shall focus the remainder of my remarks on one feature that they have in common with the developed sciences (physical or biological); to wit, they were originally developed with negligible reliance on *statistical significance testing*. Even the psychometric assessment tradition in its early stages paid little attention to significance testing except (sometimes) for finding good items. Binet did not know anything about *t* tests, but he drew graphs of the developmental change of items. I suggest to you that Sir Ronald has befuddled us, mesmerized us, and led us down the primrose path. I believe that the almost universal reliance on merely refuting the null hyopthesis as the standard method for corroborating substantive theories in the soft areas is a terrible mistake, is basically unsound, poor scientific strategy, and one of the worst things that ever happened in the history of psychology.

It is easiest to see this from the methodological viewpoint of Sir Karl Popper, but fortunately we have here a rare instance in which Sir Karl's position yields the same result as the Bayesians', and both give the same result as "scientific common sense" practiced by those chemists and biologists who know nothing about philosophy of science or Bayesian statistics and could not care less about either. Briefly and simplistically, the position of Popper and the neo-Popperians is that we do not "induce" scientific theories by some kind of straightforward upward seepage from the clearly observed facts, nor do we "confirm" theories as the Vienna poisitivists supposed. All we can do is to subject theories—including the wildest and "unsupported" armchair conjectures (for a Popperian, completely kosher)—to grave danger of refutation, in accordance with the formally valid fourth figure of the implicative syllogism: $p \rightarrow q$, $\sim q$, $\therefore \sim p$, Popper's famous *modus tollens.*

A theory is corroborated to the extent that we have subjected it to such risky tests; the more dangerous tests it has survived, the better corroborated it is. If I tell you that Meehl's theory of climate predicts that it will rain sometime next April, and this turns out to be the case, you will not be much impressed with my "predictive success." Nor will you be impressed if I predict more rain in April than in May, even showing three asterisks (for $p < .001$) in my t-test table! If I predict from my theory that it will rain on 7 of the 30 days of Arpil, and it rains on exactly 7, you might perk up your ears a bit, but still you would be inclined to think of this as a "lucky coincidence." But suppose that I specifiy *which* 7 days in April it will rain and ring the bell; then you will start getting seriously interested in Meehl's meteorological conjectures. Finally, if I tell you that on April 4th it will rain 1.7 inches (.66 cm), and on April 9th, 2.3 inches (.90 cm) and so forth, and get seven of these correct within reasonable tolerance, you will begin to think that Meehl's theory must have a lot going for it. You may believe that Meehl's theory of the weather, like all theories, is, when taken literally, false, since probably all theories are false in the eyes of God, but you will at least say, to use Popper's language, that it is beginning to look as if Meehl's theory has considerable *verisimilitude,* that is, "truth-likeness." (An adequate reconstruction of the verisimilitude concept has yet to be provided by our logician friends, see, e.g., Popper, 1976, but few reflective psychologists will doubt that some such notion of "nearness to the truth" is unavoidable when we evaluate theories. It is crucial to recognize that verisimilitude is an ontological, not an epistemological, concept that must not be conflated with confirmation, probability, evidence, proof, corroboration, belief, support, or plausibility.)

Popperians would speak of low logical or prior probability, of the high content (forbidding much), because it specifies exactly which days it will rain how many inches. A Bayesian (who would reject Popper's philosophy on the grounds that we want our "theoretical prior" to be *high* to get a nice boost out of Bayes' theorem when the facts turn out right) would express Popper's point by saying that we want what Pap (1962, p. 160) calls the *expectedness,* the prior on the observations that is found in the denominator of Bayes' theorem to be low. An unphilosophical chemist or astronomer or molecular biologist would say that this was just good sensible scientific practice, that a theory that makes precise predictions and correctly picks out *narrow intervals on point values* out of the range of experimental possibilities is a pretty strong theory. There are revisions (as I think, necessary) of the classic Popperian position urged on us by his heretical exstudents P. K. Feyerabend and the late Imre Lakatos, but psychologists must reach at least the stage of Bayes and Popper before they can profitably go on to the refinements and criticisms of these gentlemen.

The most important caveat I would adjoin to Sir Karl's falsifiability requirement arises from the considerations pressed by Feyerabend (1962, 1965, 1970, 1971), Lakatos (1970, 1974a, 1974b), and others concerning the crucial role of auxiliary theories in subjecting the main substantive theory of interest to danger of *modus tollens.* As is well-known (and not disputed by Popper), when we spell out in detail the logical structure of what purports to be an observational test of a theoretical conjecture T, we normally find that we cannot get to an observational statement from T alone. We require further a set of often complex and problematic auxiliaries A, plus the empirical realization of certian conditions describing the experimental particulars, commonly labeled collectively as C. So that the derivation of an observation from a substantive theory T amounts always to the longer formula $(T.A.C) \rightarrow 0$, rather than the simplified schema $(T \rightarrow 0)$ that most of us learned in undergraduate logic courses. This presents a problem not perhaps for Popper's main thesis (although some critics do say this) but for its application as a criterion of the scientific status of theories (or the scientific approach of a particular theoretician or investigator?). The *modus tollens* now reads: Since $(T.A.C) \rightarrow 0$, and we have falsified 0 observationally, we have the consequence $\sim (T.A.C)$. Unfortunately, this result does not entail the falsity of T, the substantive theory of interest but only the falsity of the conjunction $(T.A.C.)$; that is, we have proved a disjunction of the falsities of the conjuncts. So the failure to get the expected observation 0 proves that $\sim T \vee \sim A \vee \sim C$, which is not quite what we would like to show.

One need not subscribe to the famous Duhemian thesis regarding falsification of science as a whole (Grünbaum, 1960, 1962, 1969, 1976) or to the Lakatosian exposition (Lakatos, 1970, 1974a, 1974b) about the protective belt of auxiliaries against which the *modus tollens* is directed versus the hard core of the theory against which the *modus tollens* is, prior to a Kuhnian revolution (Kuhn, 1970a, 1970b, 1970c), forbidden to be directed, to see that there is a difficult problem presented to even a neo-Popperian (like myself), because in social science the auxiliaries A and the initial and boundary conditions of the system C are frequently as problematic as the theory T itself. *Example:* Suppose that a personologist or social psychologist wants to investigate the effect of social fear on visual perception. He attempts to mobilize anxiety in a sample of adolescent males, chosen by their scores on the Social Introversion (*Si*) scale of the Minnesota Multiphasic Personality Inventory (MMPI), by employing a research assistant who is a raving beauty, instructing her to wear Chanel No. 5, and adopt a mixed seductive and castrative manner toward the subjects. An interpretation of a negative empirical result leaves us wondering whether the main substantive theory of interest concering social fear and visual perception has been falsified, or whether only the auxiliary theories that the *Si* scale is valid for social introversion and that attractive but hostile female experimenters elicit social fear in introverted young males have been falsified. Or perhaps even the particular conditions were not met; that is, she did not consistently act the way she was instructed to or the MMPI protocols were misscored.

There is nothing qualitatively unique about this problem for the inexact sciences, but it is quantitatively more severe for us than for the chemist or astronomer, for at least two reasons, which I shall set forth without either proving or developing them here. First, independent testing of the auxiliary theories (which often means validation of psychometric instruments or ascertaining efficacy of social stimulus inputs) is harder to carry out. Due to unavoidable looseness of the nomological network (Cronbach & Meehl, 1955/1973) plus the factors in the list of 20 difficulties supra, the range of research circumstances in which auxiliaries A are problematic is greater than in the exact sciences or in some but not all of the biological sciences. Second, a point to which philosophers of science have devoted little attention, in physics or chemistry there is usually a more intimate connection, sometimes one of contributing to derivability, between the substantive theory of interest T and components of the auxiliaries A. This is sometimes even true in advanced branches of biology. *Example:* There is a complicated, well-developed, and highly corroborated theory of how a cyclotron works, and the subject matter of that auxiliary "theory of the instrument" is for the most part identical to the subject matter of the physical theories concerning nuclear particles, and so on, being investigated by the physicist. Devices for bringing about a state of affairs, for isolating the system under study, and for observing what occurs as a result are all themselves legitimated by theory.

It seems there is a sense in which auxiliary theories used by physical and biological scientists are at least subtly informed by what may be loosely called *the spirit,* the leading ideas, the core, and pervasive concepts of the main substantive theory *T*, although not rigorously derivable from *T*. When this is not so, scientists are likely to consider the (*T.A.*) system as "unaesthetic," "incoherent," even ad hoc. These fascinating matters remain to be analyzed and reconstructed by logicians, but most scientists and historians of science are—however informally—well aware of their influence. (See, e.g., Holton, 1973.)

In the social sciences, no such intimate connection, and almost never a relation of theoretical derivability, exists; hence, the auxiliary theory (such as a theory that the Rorschach is valid for detecting subclinical schizoid cognitive slippage or that Chanel-doused beauteous research assistants are anxiety elicitors) must stand on its own feet. Almost nothing we know or conjecture about the substantive theory helps us to any appreciable degree in firming up our reliance on the auxiliary. The situation in which *A* is merely conjoined to *T* in setting up our test of *T* makes it hard for us social scientists to fulfill a Popperian falsifiability requirement—to state before the fact what would count as a strong falsifier.

I shall illustrate this problem further with a simple example whose adequate exposition will appear elsewhere (Golden & Meehl, in press). Suppose that I wish to test my dominant gene conjecture (Golden & Meehl, 1978; Meehl, 1972, 1972/1973g, 1977) concerning *schizotaxia* as the central nervous system condition for the development by social learning of *schizotypy* (Meehl, 1962/1973c), which in turn is the personality precondition for the development of a *clinical schizophrenia*—although the latter must then occur only in one fourth of the persons carrying the gene, given the roughly 12% concordance for first-degree relatives as regards diagnosable clinical schizophrenia. (See also Böök, 1960; Heston, 1966, 1970; Slater, 1958/1971). I might rely on some complex neurological or projective or structured test "sign" as having such-and-such estimated construct validity for the schizotypal personality makeup. Such a quantitative estimate might be made relying on a combination of empirical evidence concerning discordant monozygotic twins of known schizophrenics, protocols of persons tested as college freshmen who subsequently decompensate into a recognizable schizophrenia, and the like. Such numerical estimates will all suffer not only from the usual test unreliability and random sampling fluctuations, but they will also have some unknown degree of systematic bias. For instance, it clearly will not do to assume that the taxon *all compensated schizotypes* would average the same scores on a Rorschach or MMPI indicator variable as do the compensated (discordant) monozygotic twins, the latter being a biased selection, since they have the same potentiating genes that their decompensated twins have. However, there must be something else about them—of an environmental sort—that works strongly in their favor and helps keep them discordant, that is, clinically well. One simply has no way of ascertaining the net impact of these two opposed kinds of forces on the psychometric results.

Suppose that we take some combination of earlier findings on preschizophrenics, remitted schizophrenics, compensated discordant monozygotic twins of schizophrenics, and so forth, and we ascertain that while the valid positive rate p_s among these safely presumed schizotypes varies (even if the sample sizes are huge, it will always vary in an amount unexplainable by random sampling fluctuation), it nevertheless shows a "reasonably close" agreement. (Again, we think like physicists or physiologists instead of like social scientists fooling around with *t* tests.) So we strike some kind of rough average $\bar{p}_s$ of these several valid positive rates, knowing that it is the best we can do at this point with data on different groups of schizotypes, who, despite their differences, must all have somewhat been tagged as such. Given that estimated valid positive rate, and given a false positive rate p_u (also systematically biased because of the undiagnosed compensated schizotypes in any "control population"), we record our numerical predictions for the incidence of our psychometric sign among parent pairs of schizophrenic probands (where, on the dominant gene theory, we expect not only a 50% schizotype incidence but something stronger; to wit, at least one member of each parent pair must be a schizotype). We also compute it for siblings and dizygotic twins and—although here things get a bit feeble—with sufficiently large samples, maybe second-degree relatives. Thus, for instance, the expected sign-positive rate among parents (and sibs, if they all cooperate) is given by the simple expression $p^+ = \frac{1}{2}p_s + \frac{1}{2}p_n$.

Now the substantive dominant gene theory *T*, when conjoined with the auxiliary theroy *A* concerning psychometric validity, and assuming that we have identified the right relatives and the probands were all schizophrenics [= C], generates point predictions and therefore takes a high Popperian risk *when the conjunction* (T.A.C) *is considered as the "theory" under test.* Hence, the verification of those numerical point predictions as to the values of the psychometric incidence in relatives of different degrees of consanguinity provides a strong Popperian test for that conjunctive "theory." One would then normally say that successful negotiation of this hurdle, the failure to be clobbered *modus tollens* by the outcome of the empirical study, provides a moderate to strong corroboration of the conjunctive theory. Hence, (*T.A.C*) is doing well; that is, it has escaped falsification despite taking a high risk by making several numerical point predictions.

So far, so good, and Popper as well as his critics would have no complaint. However, the classical Popperian requirement on playing the scientific game fairly involves the theoretician's saying, before doing the research, what would count as a strong basis for rejecting the theory. If "the theory' is taken to be the substantive theory *T* (which it is, if one is not being philosophically disengenuous) rather than the psychometric auxiliary and diagnostic validity conjectures *A* and C, then one will be committing what amounts in spirit to a Popperian sin against falsificationism as a method. Of the empirical research does not pan out as predicted, one does not abandon *T*; instead he tells us that either *T* is incorrect, *A* is incorrect, or the diagnoses were untrustworthy!

I am not persuaded from his writings nor from conversations that I have had with him that Sir Karl adequately appreciates the degree to which this theory and auxiliary problem permeate research in the inexact sciences, especially the social sciences in their soft areas. Whether it presents a general problem for the Popperian formulation of scientific method is beyond the scope of this article and my competence. It is perhaps worth saying, however, for the benefit of philosophically oriented readers, that the above described situation—certainly no rarity in our field or in biology—may represent a social fact about the way science works that presents grave difficulties for the Popperian reconstruction. That is, the stipulation beforehand that one will be pleased about substantive theory *T* when the numerical results come out as forecast, but will not necessarily abandon it when they do not, seems on the face of it to be about as blatant a violation of the Popperian commandment as you could commit. For the investigator, in a way, is doing what Popper says we ought not to do, and what astrologers and Marxists and psychoanalysts allegedly do, playing "heads I win, tails you lose." But it seems in accordance with much scientific practice and, as far as I have sampled, with most persons' scientific common sense or intuitions, to say that if the combination (*T.A.C*) generates a high-risk numerical point prediction, such a result really does support all three of the components. The reason it does so seems pretty clear, despite its commonsense, nonnormalized character: Because of the lack of intimate inner connection in the inexact sciences between the components of these conjunctions, it would strike us as a *very strange coincidence* if the substantive therory T should have low verisimilitude (which would, were T true, also generate mispredictions of the numerical point values) and yet the two (largely unrelated) "wrongs" of T and A are somehow systematically balanced so as to generate the same numerical prediction generated from the conjecture that T and A both have relatively high verisimilitude.

Such a delicate quantitative counterbalancing of theoretical errors is not impossible, but it seems quite implausible, assuming that nature is (as Einstein says) "subtle but not malicious." So I think we are not being unreasonable to congratulate ourselves on arriving at a successful prediction of high-risk point values or other antecedently improbable observational patterns from the conjunction ($T.A.C.$), despite the fact that we seem to be hedging when we say before the fact that we will not consider our substantive theory T falsified by a bad result if it does not pan out. These are problems that need further exploration by statisticians and philosophers of science, especially in light of work on the history of science, and with special attention to the question of whether there are important differences between the inexact and the exact sciences, or even between the biological and social sciences, as to how a Popperian or neo-Popperian methodology should be explained and applied.

But, you may say, what has all this got to do with significance testing? Isn't the social scientist's use of the null hypothesis simply the application of Popperian (or Bayesian) thinking in contexts in which probability plays such a big role? No, it is not. One reason it is not is that the usual use of null hypothesis testing in soft psychology as a means of "corroborating" substantive theories does not subject the theory to grave risk of refutation *modus tollens*, but only to a rather feeble danger. The kinds of theories and the kinds of theoretical risks to which we put them in soft psychology when we use significance testing as our method are *not* like testing Meehl's theory of weather by seeing how well it forecasts the number of inches it will rain on certain days. Instead, they are depressingly close to testing the theory by seeing whether it rains in April at all, or rains several days in April, or rains in April more than in May. It happens mainly because, as I believe is generally recognized by statisticians today and by thoughtful social scientists, the null hypothesis, taken literally, is always false. I shall not attempt to document this here, because among sophisticated persons it is taken for granted. (See Morrison & Henkel, 1970, especially the chapters by Bakan, Hogben, Lykken, Meehl, and Rozeboom.) A little reflection shows us why it has to be the case, since an output variable such as adult IQ, or academic achievement, or effectiveness at communication, or whatever, will always, in the social sciences, be a function of a sizable but finite number of factors. (The smallest contributions may be considered as essentially a random variance term.) In order for two groups (males and females, or whites and blacks, or manic depressives and schizophrenics, or Republicans and Democrats) to be *exactly* equal on such an output variable, we have to imagine that they are exactly equal *or* delicately counterbalanced on all of the contributors in the causal equation, which will never be the case.

Following the general line of reasoning (presented by myself and several others over the last decade), from the fact that the null hypothesis is always false in soft psychology, it follows that the probability of refuting it depends wholly on the sensitivity of the experiment—its logical design, the net (attenuated) construct validity of the measures, and, most importantly, the sample size, which determines where we are on the statistical power function. Putting it crudely, if you have enough cases and your measures are not totally unreliable, the null hypothesis will always be falsified, *regardless of the truth of the substantive theory.* Of course, it could be falsified in the wrong direction, which means that as the power improves, the probability of a corroborative result approaches one-half. However, if the theory has no verisimilitude—such that we can imagine, so to speak, picking our empirical results randomly out of a directional hat apart from any theory—the probability of refuting by getting a significant difference in the wrong direction also approaches one-half. Obviously, this is quite unlike the situation desired from either a Bayesian, a Popperian, or a commonsense scientific standpoint. As I have pointed out elsewhere (Meehl, 1967/1970b; but see criticism by Oakes, 1975; Keuth, 1973; and rebuttal by Swoyer & Monson, 1975), an improvement in instrumentation or other sources of experimental accuracy tends, in physics or astronomy or chemistry or genetics, to subject the theory to a greater risk of refutation *modus tollens,* whereas improved precision in null hypothesis testing usually decreases this risk. A successful significance test of a substantive theory in soft psychology provides a feeble corroboration of the theory because the procedure has subjected the theory to a feeble risk.

But, you may say, we do not look at just one, we look at a batch of them. Yes, we do; and how do we usually do it? In the typical *Psychological Bulletin* article reviewing research on some theory, we see a table showing with asterisks (hence, my title) whether this or that experimenter found a difference in the expected direction at the .05 (one asterisk), .01 (two asterisks!), or .001 (three asterisks!!) levels of significance. Typically, of course, some of them come out favorable and some of them come out unfavorable. What does the reviewer usually do? He goes through what is from the standpoint of the logician an almost meaningless exercise; to wit, he *counts noses.* If, say, Fisbee's theory of the mind has a batting average of 7:3 on 10 significance tests in the table, he concludes that Fisbee's theory seems to be rather well supported, "although further research is needed to explain the discrepancies." This is scientifically a preposterous way to reason. It completely neglects the crucial asymmetry between confirmation, which involves an inference in the formally invalid third figure of the implicative syllogism (this is why inductive inferences are ampliative and dangerous and why we can be objectively wrong even though we proceed correctly), and refutation, which is in the valid fourth figure, and which gives the *modus tollens* its privileged position in inductive inference. Thus the adverse *t* tests, seen properly, do Fisbee's theory far more damage than the favorable ones do it good.

I am not making some nit-picking statistician's correction. I am saying that the whole business is so radically defective as to be scientifically almost pointless. This is not a technical hassle about whether Fisbee should have used the varimax rotation, or how he estimated the communalities, or that perhaps some of the higher order interactions that are marginally significant should have been lumped together as a part of the error term, or that the covariance matrices were not quite homogeneous. I am not a statistician, and I am not making a statistical complaint. I am making a philosophical complaint or, if you prefer, a complaint in the domain of scientific method. I suggest that when a reviewer tries to "make theoretical sense" out of such a table of favorable and adverse significance test results, what the reviewer is actually engaged in, willy-nilly or unwittingly, is meaningless substantive constructions on the properties of the statistical power function, and almost nothing else.

This feckless activity is made worse by the almost universal practice of what I call *stepwise low validation.* By this I mean that we rely on one investigation to "validate" a particular instrument and some other sudy to validate another instrument, and then we correlate the two instruments and claim to have validated the substantive theory. I do not argue that this is a scientific nothing, but it is about as close to a nothing as you can get without intending to. Consider that I first show that Meehl's Mental Measure has a validity coefficient (against the criterion I shall here for simplicity take to be quasi-infallible or definitive) of, say, .40—somewhat higher than we usually get in personology and social psychology! Then I show that Glotz's Global Gauge has a validity for its alleged variable of the same amount. Relying on these results, having stated the coefficient and gleefully recorded the asterisks showing that these coefficients are not zero (!), I now try to corroborate the Glotz-Meehl theory of personality by showing that the two instruments, each having been duly "validated," correlate .40, providing, happily, some more asterisks in the table. Now just what kind of a business is this? Let us suppose that each instrument has a reliability of .90 to make it easy. That means that the portion of construct-valid variance for each of the devices is around one fifth of the reliable variance and the same for their overlap when correlated with each other. I do not want to push the discredited (although recently revived) principle of indifference, but without other knowledge, it is easily possible, and one could perhaps say rather likely, that the correlation between the two occurs in a region of each one's components that has literally nothing to do with either of the two criterion variables used in the validity studies relied on. This is, of course, especially dangerous in light of the research that we have on the contribution of methods variance.

I seem to have trouble conveying to my students and colleagues just how dreadful a mess of flabby inferences this kind of thing involves. It is as if we were interested in the effect of sunlight on the mating behavior of birds, but not being able to get directly at either of these two things, we settle for correlating a proxy variable like field-mice density (because the birds tend to destroy the field mice) with, say, incidence of human skin cancer (since you can get that by spending too much time in the sun!) You may think this analogy dreadfully unfair; but I think it is a good one. Of course, the whole idea of simply counting noses is wrong, because a theory that has seven facts for it and three facts against it is *not* in good shape, and it would not be considered so in any developed science.

You may say, "But, Meehl, R. A. Fisher was a genius, and we all know how valuable his stuff has been in agronomy. Why shouldn't it work for soft psychology?" Well, I am not intimidated by Fisher's genius, because my complaint is not in the field of mathematical statistics; and as regards inductive logic and philosophy of science, it is well-known that Sir Ronald permitted himself a great deal of dogmatism. I remember my amazement when the late Rudolf Carnap said to me, the first time I met him, "But, of course, on this subject Fisher is just mistaken; surely you must know that." My statistician friends tell me that it is not clear just how useful the significance test has been in biological science either, but I set that aside as beyond my competence to discuss. The shortest answer to this rebuttal about agronomy, and one that has general importance in thinking about soft psychology, is that we must carefully distinguish *substantive theory* from *statistical hypothesis.* There is a tendency in the social sciences to conflate these in talking about our inferences. (A neglected article by Bolles, 1962, did not cure the psychologists' disease.) The substantive theory is the theory about the causal structure of the world, the entities and processes underlying the phenomena; the statistical hypothesis is a much more restricted and "operational" conjecture about the value of some parameter, such as the mean of a specified statistical population. The main point in agronomy is that the logical distance, the difference in meaning or content, so to say, between the alternative hypothesis and substantive theory T is so small that only a logician would be concerned to distinguish them. *Example:* I want to find out whether I should be putting potash on the ground to help me raise more corn. Now everybody knows from common sense as well as biology that the corn gets its nutrients from the soil, and furthermore that the yield of corn at harvest time is not causally efficacious in determining what I did in the spring, random numbers aside. If I refute the statistical null hypothesis that plots of corn with potash do not differ in yield from plots without potash, I have thereby proved the alternative hypothesis—that there *is* a difference between these two sorts of plots; and the only substantive conclusion to draw, given such a difference, is that the potash made the difference. Such a situation, in which the content of the substantive theory is logically quasi-identical with the alternative hypothesis, which was refuted by our significance test, is completely different from the situation in soft psychology. Fisbee's substantive theory of the mind is not equivalent, or anywhere near equivalent, to the alternative hypothesis. All sorts of competing theories are around, including my grandmother's common sense, to explain the nonnull statistical difference. So the psychologist can take little reassurance about the use of significance tests from knowing that Fisher's approach has been useful in studying the effect of fertilizer on crop yields.

Although this presents a pretty depressing picture, I daresay that the Skinner disciples among you will be inclined to think,

> well, that's just one more way of showing what we have known all along. The point is to prove that you have achieved experimental control over your subject matter, as Skinner says. If you have, I am not much interested in tabular asterisks; if you haven't, I'm not interested in them either.

But that is easy for Skinnerians because their theory (it is a theory in Sir Karl Popper's sense) is close to a pure dispositional theory and does not usually present us with the kind of evidentiary evaluation problem that we get with entity-postulating theories such as those of Freud, Hull, Albert Ellis, or, to come closer to home, my conjectures about schizophrenia or hedonic deficit (Meehl, 1972, 1974, 1975, 1962/1973c, 1972/1973g). Those of us whose cognitive passions are incompletely satisfied by dispositional theories, whether Skinnerian or psychometric, should ask ourselves what *kind* of inferred entity construction we want and how it could generate the sorts of intellectual "surprises" that Robert Nozick (1974, pp. 18–22) considers typical of invisible hand theories, which have proved so eminently successful in the physical and biological sciences and—somewhat less so—in economics. Some directions of solution (before I go on to the one that I am using in my own research) follow.

We could take the complex from of Bayes's theorem more seriously in concrete application to various substantive theories to take into account, even if crudely in the sense of setting upper and lower bounds to the probabilities involved, the logical asymmetry between confirmation and refutation (see, e.g., Maxwell, 1974). Second, it may be that the Fisherian tradition, with its soothing illusion of quantitative rigor, has inhibited our search for stronger tests, so we have thrown in the sponge and abandoned hope of concocting substantive theories that will generate stronger consequences than merely "the Xs differ from the Ys." Thus, for instance, even when we cannot generate numerical point predictions (the ideal case found in the exact sciences), it may be that we can at least predict the order of numerical values or the rank order of the first-order numerical differences, and the like.

Sometimes in the other sciences it has been possible to concoct a middling weak theory that, while incapable of generating numerical point values, entails a certain *function form,* such as a graph should be an ogive or that it should have three peaks and that these peaks should be increasingly high, and that the distance on the abscissa between the first two peaks should be less than the distance between the second two. In the early history of quantum theory, physicists relied on Wien's law, which related "some (unknown) function" of wavelength to energy multiplied by the fifth power of wavelength. In the cavity radiation experiment, the empirical points were simply plotted at varying temperatures, and it was evident by inspection that they fell on the same curve, even though a formal expression for that curve was beyond the theory's capabilities (Eisberg, 1961, pp. 50–51).

Talking of Wien's law is a good time for me to recommend to psychologists who disagree with my position to have a look at any textbook of theoretical chemistry or physics, where one searches in vain for a statistical significance test (and finds few confidence intervals). The power of the physicist does not come from exact assessment of probabilities that a difference exists (which physicists would view as a ludicrous thing to show), nor by the verbal precision of so-called "operational definitions" in the embedding text. The physicist's scientific power comes from two other sources, namely, the immense deductive fertility of the formalism and the accuracy of the measuring instruments. The scientific trick lies in conjoining rich mathematics and experimental precision, a sort of "invisible hand wielding fine calipers." The embedding text is sometimes surprisingly loose, free-wheeling, even metaphorical—as viewers of television's *Nova* are aware, seeing Nobel laureates discourse whimsically about the charm, strangeness, and gluons of nuclear particles (see, e.g., Nambu, 1976). One gets the impression that when you have a good science going, with potent mathematics and accurate instruments, you can be relaxed and easygoing about the words. Nothing is as stuffy and pretentious as the verbal "pseudorigor" of the soft branches of social science. In my modern physics text, I am unable to find one single test of statistical significance. What happens instead is that the physicist has a sufficiently powerful invisible hand theory that enables him to generate an expected curve for his experimental results. He plots the observed points, looks at the agreement, and comments that "the results are in reasonably good accord with theory." Moral: *It is always more valuable to show approximate agreement of observations with a theoretically predicted numerical point value, rank order, or function form, than it is to compute a "precise probability" that something merely differs from something else.* Of course, we do not have precise probabilities when we do significance testing because of the falsity of the assumptions generating the table's values and varying robustness of our tests under departures from these assumptions.

The only possible "solution" to the theory-refutation problem that I have time to discuss in any detail is what I call *consistency tests* (Meehl, Note 3). Unfortunately, this approach is not easily available for most theoretical problems in soft psychology, although I am not prepared to say that it is confined to the domain in which I have been developing it, namely, taxometrics, that is, the application of psychometric procedures to detection of a taxonic situation and classification of individuals into the taxon or outside of it. From our conjectures about the latent causal situation, we derive formulas for estimating the theoretical quantities of interest, such as the proportion of schizotypes in a given clinical population, the mean values of the schizotypal and nonschizotypal classes, the optimal cut ("hitmax") on each phenotypic indicator variable for classifying individuals, and the proportion of valid and false positives achieved by that cut, But we realize that our conjectures about the latent situation may be false or that the indicators relied on may have too low validity, or that they may be more correlated within the taxa than desired, and so forth. Second, even if the basic formal structure postulated is approximated by the state of nature (e.g., there is a schizoid taxon, the indicators have sizable validity, the intra-taxon distributions are quasi-normal or at least unimodal, the correlation of the indicators within the groups is small, and the departures from these various hypotheses are within the tolerance allowed by the method's robustness), it may still be that we have suffered some kind of systematic bias on one of the indicators due to a nuisance variable such as social class, or that we have had bad luck in the sample, so the method's numerical deliverances on this occasion are untrustworthy.

Whether the abstract causal structure postulated is unsound or the numerical values found in this sample are seriously in error, we need some method of checking the data internally to find out whether these unfortunate possibilities have materialized. We do this by deriving theorems within the formalism specifying how various numerical values (observed or calculated from the observed) should be related to each other, so that when they are not related as the consistency theorem demands, we are alerted to the danger that something is rotten in the state of Denmark (see Meehl, 1973d). Unfortunately, most of the work, both mathematical and empirical, is as yet only available in mimeographed reports from our laboratory (Golden, 1976; Golden & Meehl, Note 1, Note 2; Meehl, Note 3, Note 4). What survives scrutiny will be found in a book in preparation with my former student and research colleague Robert Golden (Golden & Meehl, in press).

One taxometric procedure, which I have christened *maxocov-hitmax* (Meehl, 1973d) relies on the following theorem: If three fallible indicator variables are negligibly correlated within a diagnostic taxon and within the extra taxon population, then the covariance of any pair of these maximized in that class interval on the third indicator that contains the hitmax (optimal, fewest misses) cut on the third indicator. That is, cov(yz) has its largest value for the subset of patients falling in the hitmax interval on x. Starting from this relation we go through a sequence of calculations yielding estimates of the base rate P of the taxon, the frequency distributions of all three of the fallible indicators, the location of all three hitmax cuts, and the inverse probability of taxon membership (via Bayes' theorem) for a patient who has any given combination of the three signs plus or minus.

Our Monte Carlo runs and our single application to a real case in which we know the true answer and pretend not to know it, namely, biological sex diagnosed by three MMPI femininity keys, have been most encouraging and suggest that the method is powerful and quite robust under departures from the simplifying hypotheses. But applying it to a situation in which we do not know the true answer (such as "What is the proportion of unrecognized schizotypes in a mixed psychiatric population?"), how much faith should we have in our numerical results? The best way I know to go about this, since mere replication of the inferred parameter estimates does not answer the question, is by the use of consistency tests. For example, one of the consistency tests in this kind of two-category taxonic situation is this: If we form the product of the differences between the inferred latent means on y and z (schizotypes minus non-schizotypes) and then multiply this product $\Delta\bar{y}\ \Delta\bar{z}$ by the product of the inferred schizotypal base-rate P and its complement Q, then it can be shown that this theoretically calculated quantity should equal the grand covariance of y and z computed directly from the observations. We call this the "total covariance consistency test."

Of course, such a relation is not required to be literally true, because it is known in advance that (a) the impoverished theory has imperfect verisimilitude and (b) all statistical estimates are subject to both systematic and random error. (We are *not* going to do a significance test!) What we have is a problem of robustness and detection of excessive departures from the postulated latent conditions. Golden and I arbitrarily said that we would consider a particular sample as delivering sufficiently accurate information if the estimates of base rate and hit rate were within .10 of the true values, and estimated latent means and standard deviations within one class interval of the truth. (Actually we did much better than that on the average. For example, with sample sizes greater than 400, equal variances, two sigma differences of latent means, and zero intrataxon correlations, the average error for P was only .01 and for latent means and sigmas, less than one fourth standard deviation which is one-half the smallest integral class interval.) But if these tolerances strike you as excessively large, I remind you how much more powerful such numerical claims are in soft psychology than the usual flabby "the boys are taller than the girls" or "the schizophrenics are shyer than the manic depressives." We then imposed tolerances on each of the four promising consistency tests derived within the formalism. For example, if the total covariance consistency test $T_1 = \text{cov}(yz) - PQ\,(\bar{y}_s - \bar{y}_n)\,(\bar{z}_s - \bar{z}_n)$ yields a discrepancy greater than $.64 + .74s^2$, a "robustness cut" chosen by a combination of analytical derivation with preliminary Monte Carlo trials, then this particular sample is considered "numerically inconsistent" with Consistency Test T^1. Now if any one of the four consistency tests is, so to speak, rejected by a given sample, this is a red flag warning us that we ought not to have much faith in the parametric estimates of interest.

The important question then is, how sensitive are the consistency tests to sample departures from the parametric truth in excess of the tolerance allowed? How often will we draw a sample in which the inferred parameters are in error by more than the tolerance limit imposed but all four consistency tests are satisfied within *their* tolerance limits, leading us mistakenly to trust our results? Second, how often is at least one of the four consistency tests numerically inconsistent (i.e., outside its tolerance limit) leading us to *mis*-trust the sample when in fact all of the sample estimates of the parameters are within their tolerances? The first of these we might call a "false negative" failure on the part of the consistency tests to function jointly; the second is then a false positive.

I restrict my data presentation to Monte Carlo runs in which the samples are generated from a multivariate normal model, although I want to emphasize that our methods are not generally confined to the normal case. Normality was imposed because of Monte Carlo generating problems. In Table 1, the numbers "Set 1.1, 1.2, . . ." in the first column merely name conditions of fixed population properties and sample sizes, and 25 Monte Carlo samples were drawn per set. The column heads indicate the various population properties, such as taxon base-rate P, the two latent taxon means and standard deviations, the mean difference in standard deviation units, the ratio of latent standard deviations, and the within-group correlations. The important result (F) indicates how many of the 25 samples under the given set conditions were failures of the consistency tests. Thus, the four consistency tests were applied to each sample, which was classified as probably trustworthy (or probably not) in accordance with the tolerance rules for consistency tests. Then the sample was classified as to whether it was *in fact* trustworthy, that is, whether the main latent parameters were all estimated within their allowed tolerance.

Despite the high average accuracy of our taxometric method when evaluated as mean percent errors in estimating each of the latent parameters (base rate, hit rates, means, standard deviations), if a naive trusting taxometrist relied blindly on the method, hoping to be accurate on all seven parameters on any sample drawn, he would be missed distressingly often were he to lack consistency tests. Among our 600 Monte Carlo samples, all seven latent parameters of the artificial population were estimated to an accuracy within the tolerance levels in 372 samples; that is, on 228 samples at least one parameter was inaccurate. This shows that a trustworthy device for detecting such bad samples is much to be desired. It will not do a taxonomic scientist much good to be "usually quite accurate" if the procedure relied on is nevertheless often (38% of the time) somewhat inaccurate *and the investigator is without a method that warns him when the untoward event has, on a given occasion, occurred.*

In Table 2 the 600 Monte Carlo samples are tallied with respect to each sample's parameter estimation accuracy and whether it passed all four consistency tests. It is encouraging that overall the consistency tests were 94% accurate. Furthermore, the 6% of the samples in which the consistency tests erred were all samples in which they erred conservatively; that is, one or more of the consistency tests was suspiciously outside its tolerance limits, yet none of the latent parameters estimated by the methods was outside *its* tolerance limits. We have not as yet drawn a single Monte Carlo sample (among 600) in which the four consistency tests were conjunctively reassuring but the sample was in fact misleading. This finding suggests that we were unduly stringent, so that if some small amount of leeway were permitted for errors of the other kind, the consistency tests could be somewhat relaxed and, perhaps concurrently, the tolerance limits on the parameter estimates could be somewhat tightened.

There is some interchangeability between original estimators and consistency tests, and the maxcov-hitmax method itself was originally derived by me as a consistency test before I

TABLE 1
Description of Sample Sets

Set	Variable	N	P	M_e	M_t	SD_e	SD_t	D'	SD_t/SD_e	r	F^a
1.1	N	1,000	.5	8	12	2	2	2	1	0^b	0
1.2		800	.5	8	12	2	2	2	1	0^b	0
1.3		600	.5	8	12	2	2	2	1	0^b	0
1.4		400	.5	8	12	2	2	2	1	0^b	0
2.1	P	1,000	.6	8	12	2	2	2	1	0^b	3
2.2		1,000	.7	8	12	2	2	2	1	0^b	2
2.3		1,000	.8	8	12	2	2	2	1	0^b	8
2.4		1,000	.9	8	12	2	2	2	1	0	0
3.1	D'	1,000	.5	9	12	2	2	1.5	1	0^b	0
3.2		1,000	.5	10	12	2	2	1	1	0^b	15
3.3		1,000	.5	11	12	2	2	.5	1	0	0
3.4		1,000	.5	12	12	2	2	0	1	0	0
4.1	SD_t/SD_e	1,000	.5	8	12	1.9	2.1	2	1.1	0^b	0
4.2		1,000	.5	8	12	1.7	2.3	2	1.3	0^b	0
4.3		1,000	.5	8	12	1.5	2.5	2	1.7	0^b	0
4.4		1,000	.5	8	12	1	3	2	3	0	0
5.1	r	1,000	.5	8	12	2	2	2	1	$.1^b$	0
5.2		1,000	.5	8	12	2	2	2	1	$.3^b$	0
5.3		1,000	.5	8	12	2	2	2	1	$.5^b$	8
5.4		1,000	.5	8	12	2	2	2	1	.8	0
										r_e/r_t	
6.1	$r_e/r_t = 4$	1,000	.8	8	12	2	2	2	1	.5/.125	0
6.2	N	800	.8	8	12	2	2	2	1	.5/.125	0
6.3		600	.8	8	12	2	2	2	1	.5/.125	0
6.4		400	.8	8	12	2	2	2	1	.5/.125	0

Note. N = sample size; P = base rate of the taxon; M_e = mean of the extra taxon class on each indicator; M_t = mean of the taxon on each indicator; SD_e = standard deviation of the extra taxon class on each indicator; SD_t = standard deviation of the taxon on each indicator; $D' = (M_t - M_e)/S$, where $S = SD_e + SD_t/2$; r = latent correlation between indicator pairs; F = number of failures of consistency tests in 25 samples.
[a]94% correct.
[b]Parameter estimates are always or nearly always accurate.

realized that it could better be used as an original search device (see Meehl, Note 3, pp. 28–29; Note 4, pp. 2–6).

Not in reliance on these results, which I present merely as exemplars of a general methodological thesis, I want now to state as strongly as I can a prescription that we should adopt in soft psychology to help get away from the feeble practice of significance testing: *Wherever possible, two or more nonredundant estimates of the same theoretical quantity should be made, because multiple approximations to a theoretical number are always more valuable, provided that methods of setting permissible tolerances exist, than a so-called exact setting of confidence intervals.* This is a special case of what my philosopher colleague Herbert Feigl refers to as "triangulation in logical space." It is, as you know, standard procedure in the developed sciences. We have, for instance, something like a dozen independent ways of estimating Avogadro's number, and since they all come out "reasonably close" (again, I have never seen a physicist do a *t* test on such a thing!), we are confident that we know how many molecules there are in a mole of chlorine.

TABLE 2
Consistency Test Result

Actual situation	Sample: Trustworthy	Suspicious	Total
Accurate	336	36	372
Inaccurate	0	228	228
Total	336	264	600

This last point may lead you to ask, "If consistency tests are as important as Meehl makes them out to be, why we don't hear about them in chemistry and physics?" I have a perfect answer to that query. It goes like this: *Consistency tests are so much a part of standard scientific method in the developed disciplines, taken so much for granted by everybody who researches in chemistry or physics or astronomy or molecular biology or genetics, that these scientists do not even bother having a special name for them!* It shows the sad state of soft psychology when a fellow like me has to cook up a special metatheory expression to call attention to something that in respectable science is taken as a matter of course.

Having presented what seems to me some encouraging data, I must nevertheless close with a melancholy reflection. The possibility of deriving consistency tests in the taxonic situation rests on the substantive problems presented by fields like medicine and behavior genetics, and it is not obvious how we would go about doing this in soft areas that are nontaxonic. It may be that the nature of the subject matter in most of personology and social psychology is inherently incapable of permitting theories with sufficient conceptual power (especially mathematical development) to yield the kinds of strong refuters expected by Popperians, Bayesians, and unphilosophical scientists in developed fields like chemisty. This might mean that we could most profitably confine ourselves to low-order inductions, a (to me, depressing) conjecture that is somewhat corroborated by the fact that the two most powerful forms of clinical psychology are atheoretical psychometrics or prediction on the one hand and behavior modification on the other. Neither of these approaches has the kind of conceptual richness that attracts the theory-oriented mind, but I think we ought to acknowledge the possibility that there is never going to be a really impressive theory in personality, or social psychology. I dislike to think that, but it might just be true.

ADDENDUM

My colleague, Thomas J. Bouchard, Jr., on reading a draft of this article faulted me for what he saw as a major inconsistency between my neo-Popperian emphasis on falsifiability and my positive assessment of Freud. There is no denying that for such a quantitatively oriented product of the "dust-bowl empiricist" tradition as myself, I do not have a soft spot in my heart (Minnesota colleagues would probably say in my head) for psychoanalysis. So, the most honest and straightforward way to deal with Bouchard's complaint might be simply to admit that the evidence on Freud is inadequate and that Bouchard and I are simply betting on different horses. But I cannot resist the impulse to say just a bit more on this vexatious question, because while I am acutely aware of a pronounced (and possibly irrational) difference in the "educated prior" I put on Freud as contrasted with rubber band theory or labeling theory or whatever, I am not persuaded that my position is as grossly incoherent as it admittedly appears. Passing the question whether attempts to study psychoanalytic theory by the methods of experimental or differential psychology have on the whole tended to support rather than refute it (see, e.g., Fisher & Greenberg, 1977; Rapaport, 1959; Sears, 1943; Silverman, 1976), my own view is that the best place to study psychoanalysis is the psychoanalytic session itself, as I have elsewhere argued in a far too condensed way (Meehl, 1970/1973e).

I believe that some aspects of psychoanalytic theory are not presently researchable because the intermediate technology required—which really means instruments-cum-theory—does not exist. I mean auxiliaries and methods such as a souped-up, highly developed science of psycholinguistics, and the kind of mathematics that is needed to conduct a rigorous but clinically sensitive and psychoanalytically realistic job of theme tracing in the analytic protocol. This may strike some as a kind of cop-out, but I remind you that Lakatos, Kuhn, Feyerabend, and others have convincingly made the point that there are theories in the physical and biological sciences that are untestable when first propounded because the theoretical and technological development necessary for making certain kinds of observations bearing on them had not taken place. It is vulgar positivism (still held by many psychologists) to insist that any respectable empirical theory must be testable, if testable means *definitively testable right now.*

But I do think that there is another class of consequences of psychoanalytic theory, close to the original "clinical connections" alleged by Freud, Ferenczi, Jones, Abraham, and others that does not involve much of what Freud called *the witch metapsychology,* where no complicated statistics are needed, let alone the invention of any *new* formal modes of protocol analysis. Here the problem is mainly that *none of us has bothered to carry out some relatively simple-minded kinds of analyses on a random sample of psychoanalytic protocols collected from essentially naive patients to whom no interpretations have as yet been offered.* This second category is, in my view, a category of research studies that we could have done, but have not done. *Example:* We can easily ascertain whether manifest dream content of a certain kind is statistically associated (in the simple straightforward sense of a patterned fourfold table) with such and such kinds of thematic material in the patient's subsequent associations to the dream. I would not even object to doing significance tests on a batch of such tables, but to explain why would unduly enlarge what is already an addendum.

I cheerfully admit, in this matter, to the presence of a large distance between my subjective personalistic probability (based on my experiences as analysand and practitioner of psychoanalytic therapy) and the present state of the "intersubjective public evidence." That is what I mean by saying that Bouchard and I are betting on different horses. But one must distinguish, as I know from subsequent conversations that he does, between criticism (a) that what *is* proper evidence *does* presently exist and is *adverse* to a conjecture and (b) an anti-Popperian claim that falsifiability in principle does not matter. If I thought (as does Popper) that Freudian theory was in principle not falsifiable, then I would have to confess to a major inconsistency. But I do think it is falsifiable, although I agree that *some parts* of it cannot *at present* be tested because of the primitive development of the auxiliary theories and the measurement technologies that would be jointly necessary.

A final point on this subject is one that I hesitate to include because it is very difficult to explain in the present state of philosophy of science, and I could be doing my main thesis damage by presenting a cursory and somewhat dogmatic statement of it. Nevertheless, having made the above statements about psychoanalytic theory and having contrasted it favorably with some of the (to me, trivial and flabby) theories in soft psychology, I fear I have an obligation to say it, however, ineptly. Once one sees that it is inappropriate to conflate the concepts *rational* and *statistical,* then it is a fuzzy open question, in the present state of the metatheoretician's art, just when a mass of nonquantitative converging evidence can be said to have made a stronger case for a conjecture than the weak kinds of nonconverging quantitative evidence usually represented by the significance testing tradition. I say "when" rather than "whether," because it is blindingly obvious that *sometimes* qualitative evidence of certain sorts is superior in its empirical weight to what a typical social, personality, or clinical psychologist gets in support of a substantitve theory by the mere refutation of the null hypothesis. Take, for instance, the evidence in a well-constructed criminal case, such as the evidence that Bruno Hauptmann was the kidnapper of the Lindbergh baby. I do not see how anybody who reads the trial transcript of the Hauptmann case could have a reasonable doubt that he was guilty as charged. Yet I cannot recall any of the mass of data that convicted him as being of a quantitative sort (one cannot fairly except the serial numbers on the gold notes, they being not "measures" but "football numbers").

All of us believe a lot of things that we would not have the vaguest idea how to express as a probability value (*pace* strong Bayesians!) or how to compute as an indirect test of statistical significance. I believe, for instance, that Adolf Hitler was a schizotype; I do not believe that Kaspar Hauser was the son of a prince; I believe that the domestic cat probably was evolved from *Felis lybica* by the ancient Egyptians; I hold that my sainted namesake wrote the letter to the Corinthians but did not write the letter to the Hebrews; I am confident that my wife is faithful to me; and so forth. The point is really a simple one—that there are many areas of both practical and theoretical inference in which nobody knows how to calculate a numerical probability value, and nobody knows how to state the manner or degree in which various lines of evidence converge on a certain conjecture as having high verisimilitude. There are propositions in history (such as, "Julius Caesar crossed the Rubicon") that we all agree are well corroborated by the available documents but without any *t* tests *or the possibility of calculating any,* whereas Fisbee's theory of social behavior is only weakly corroborated by the fact that he got a significant *t* test when he compared the boys and the girls or the older kids and the younger kids on the Hockheimer-Sedlitz Communication Scale. Now I consider my betting on the horse of psychoanalysis to be in the same kind of ball park as my beliefs about Julius Caesar or the evolution of the cat. But, I repeat, this may be a terribly irrational leap of faith on my part. For the purposes of the present article and Bouchard's criticism of it, I hope it is sufficient to say that one could arguably hold that significance testing in soft psychology is a pretentious endeavor that falls under a tolerant neo-Popperian criticism, and could nevertheless enter his personalistic prediction that *when adequate tests become available to us, a sizable portion of psychoanalytic theory will escape refutation.* So I do not think I am actually contradicting myself, but I am personalistically betting on the outcome of a future horse race.

REFERENCE NOTES

1. Golden, R., & Meehl, P. E. *Detecting latent clinical taxa, IV: Empirical study of the maximum covariance method and the normal minimum chi-square method, using three MMPI keys to identify the sexes* (Tech. Rep. PR-73-2). Minneapolis: University of Minnesota Psychiatry Research Labortory, 1973. (a)
2. Golden, R., & Meehl, P. E. *Detecting latent clinical taxa, V: A Monte Carlo study of the maximum covariance method and associated consistency tests* (Tech. Rep. PR-73-3). Minneapolis: University of Minnesota Psychiatry Research Laboratory, 1973. (b)
3. Meehl, P. E. *Detecting latent clinical taxa by fallible quantitative indicators lacking an accepted criterion* (Tech. Rep. PR-65-2). Minneapolis: University of Minnesota Psychiatry Research Laboratory, 1965.
4. Meehl, P. E. *Detecting latent clinical taxa, II: A simplified procedure, some additional hitmax cut locators, a single-indicator method, and miscellaneous theorems* (Tech. Rep. PR-68-4). Minneapolis: University of Minnesota Psychiatry Research Laboratory, 1968.

REFERENCES

Allport, G. W. *Personality: A psychological interpretation.* New York: Holt, 1937.

Andreski, S. *Social sciences as sorcery.* London: Deutsch, 1972.

Barker, R. G. *Ecological psychology.* Stanford, Calif.: Stanford University Press, 1968.

Bartlett, M. S. *An introduction to stochastic processes.* Cambridge, England: Cambridge University Press, 1955.

Bolles, R. C. The difference between statistical hypotheses. *Psychological Reports,* 1962, *11,* 639–645.

Böök, J. A. Genetical aspects of schizophrenic psychoses. In D. D. Jackson (Ed.), *The etiology of schizophrenia.* New York: Basic Books, 1960.

Braithwaite, R. B. *Scientific explanation.* New York: Harper, 1960.

Braun, J. R. (Ed.). *Clinical psychology in transition* (Rev. ed.). Cleveland, Ohio: World, 1966.

Brunswik, E. Representative design and probabilistic theory. *Psychological Review,* 1955, *62,* 236–242.

Campbell, D. T., & Fiske, D. W. Convergent and discriminant validation by the multitrait-multimethod matrix. *Psychological Bulletin,* 1959, *56,* 81–105.

Campbell, N. R. *Foundations of science.* New York: Dover Publications, 1957. (Originally published as *Physics, the elements,* 1920.)

Carnap, R. Testability and meaning. New Haven, Conn.: Yale University Graduate Philosophy Club, 1950. (Originally published, 1936–1937.)

Carnap, R. Meaning postulates. In R. Carnap, *Meaning and necessity.* Chicago: University of Chicago Press, 1956. (Originally published, 1952.)

Carnap, R. *Philosophical foundation of physics.* New York: Basic Books, 1966.

Cartwright, D. Determinants of scientific progress: The case of the risky shift. *American Psychologist,* 1973, *28,* 222–231.

Cronbach, L. J. The two disciplines of scientific psychology. *American Psychologist,* 1957, *12,* 671–684.

Cronbach, L. J., & Meehl, P. E. Construct validity in psychological tests. In P. E. Meehl, *Psychodiagnosis: Selected papers.* Minnesota Press, 1973. (Originally published, 1955.)

Eisberg, R. M. *Fundamentals of modern physics.* New York: Wiley, 1961.

Feigl, H. Some major issues and developments in the philosophy of science of logical empiricism. In H. Feigl & M. Scriven (Eds.), *The foundations of science and the concepts of psychology and psychoanalysis: Minnesota studies in the philosophy of science* (Vol. 1). Minneapolis: University of Minnesota Press, 1956.

Feller, W. *An introduction to probability theory and its applications* (2nd ed.). New York: Wiley, 1957.

Feyerabend, P. K. Explanation, reduction, and empiricism. In H. Feigl & G. Maxwell (Eds.), *Minnesota studies in the philosophy of science* (Vol. 3): *Scientific explanation, space and time.* Minneapolis: University of Minnesota Press, 1962.

Feyerabend, P. K. Problems of Empiricism, Part I. In R. G. Colodny (Ed.), *Beyond the edge of certainty.* Englewood Cliffs, N.J.: Prentice-Hall, 1965.

Feyerabend, P. K. Against method: Outline of an anarchistic theory of knowledge. In M. Radner & Winokur (Eds.), *Minnesota studies in the philosophy of science* (Vol. 4): *Analyses of theories and methods of physics and psychology.* Minneapolis: University of Minnesota Press, 1970.

Feyerabend, P. K. Problems of empiricism, Part II. In R. G. Colodny (Ed.), *The nature and function of scientific theories.* Pittsburgh, Pa.: Univeristy of Pittsburgh Press, 1971.

Fisher, F. M. *The identification problem in econometrics.* New York: McGraw-Hill, 1966.

Fisher, R. A. *Statistical methods and scientific inference.* Edinburgh, Scotland: Oliver & Boyd, 1956.

Fisher, R. A. *The design of experiments* (8th ed.). Edinburgh, Scotland: Oliver & Boyd, 1966.

Fisher, R. A. *Statistical methods for research workers* (13th ed.). Edinburgh, Scotland: Oliver & Boyd, 1967.

Fisher, S., & Greenberg, P. *The scientific credibility of Freud's theories and therapy.* New York: Basic Books, 1977.

Fiske, D. W. The limits of the conventional science of personality. *Journal of Personality,* 1974, *24*, 1–11.

Gergen, K. J. Social psychology is history. *Journal of Personality and Social Psychology,* 1973, *26*, 309–320.

Golden, R. *Psychometric verisimilitude.* Unpublished doctoral dissertation: University of Minnesota, 1976.

Golden, R. R., & Meehl, P. E. Testing a single dominant gene theory without an accepted criterion variable. *Annals of Human Genetics,* 1978, in press.

Golden, R. E., & Meehl, P. E. *Taxometric analysis of causal entities: Detection of the schizoid taxon.* New York: Academic Press, in press.

Gottesman, I. I. Heritability of personality: A demonstration. *Psychological monographs,* 1963, *77*(9, Whole No. 572).

Gottesman, I. I., & Shields, J. *Schizophrenia and genetics: A twin study vantage point.* New York: Academic Press, 1972.

Grünbaum, A. The Duhemian agrument. *Philosophy of Science,* 1960, *11*, 75–87.

Grünbaum, A. Falsifiability of theories: Total or partial? *Synthese,* 1962, *14*, 17–34.

Grünbaum, A. Can we ascertain the falsity of a scientific hypothesis? *Studium Generale,* 1969, *22*, 1061–1093.

Grünbaum, A. Ad hoc auxiliary hypotheses and falsificationism. *British Journal for the Philosophy of Science,* 1976, *27*, 329–362.

Gunther, M. *The luck factor.* New York: Macmillan, 1977.

Harrison, T. R., et al. (Eds.), *Principles of internal medicine.* New York: McGraw-Hill, 1966.

Hempel, C. G. *Fundamentals of concept formation in empirical science.* Chicago: University of Chicago Press, 1952.

Hempel, C. G. The theoretician's dilemma. In H. Feigl, M. Scriven, & G. Maxwell (Eds.), *Minnesota studies in the philosophy of science* (Vol. 2): *Concepts, theories, and the mind-body problem.* Minneapolis: Univeristy of Minnesota Press, 1958.

Heston, L. L. Pyschiatric disorders in foster home reared children of schizophrenic mothers. *British Journal of Psychiatry,* 1966, *112*, 819–825.

Heston, L. L. The genetics of schizophrenia and schizoid disease. *Science,* 1970, *167*, 249–256.

Hinde, R. A. *Animal behavior* (2nd ed.). New York: McGraw-Hill, 1970.

Hogan, R., DeSoto, C. B., & Solano, C. Traits, texts, and personality research. *American Psychologist,* 1977, *32*, 255–264.

Holt, R. R. Clinical and statistical prediction: A reformulation and some new data *Journal of Abnormal and Social Psychology,* 1958, *56*, 1–12.

Holton, G. *Thematic origins of scientific thought: Kepler to Einstein.* Cambridge, Mass.: Harvard University Press, 1973.

Jencks, C. *Inequality.* New York: Basic Books, 1972.

Johnson, W. E. *Logic, Part I.* New York: Dover Publications, 1964. (Originally published, 1921.)

Kemeny, J. G., Snell, J. L., & Thompson, G. L. *Introduction to finite mathematics.* Englewood Cliffs, N.J.: Prentice-Hall, 1957.

Keuth, H. On prior probabilities of rejecting statistical hypotheses. *Philosophy of Science,* 1973, *40*, 538–546.

Kordig, R. The comparability of scientific theories. *Philosophy of Science,* 1971, *38*, 467–485.

Kordig, C. R. Discussion: Observational invariance. *Philosophy of Science,* 1973, *40*, 558–569.

Kuhn, T. S. Logic of discovery of psychology of research? In I. Lakatos & A. Musgrave (Eds.), *Criticism and the growth of knowledge.* Cambridge, England: Cambridge University Press, 1970. (a)

Kuhn, T. S. Reflections on my critics. In I. Lakatos & A. Musgrave (Eds.), *Criticism and the growth of knowledge.* Cambridge, England: Cambridge University Press. 1970. (b)

Kuhn, T. S. *The structure of scientific revolutions* (2nd ed.). Chicago: University of Chicago Press, 1970. (c)

Lakatos, I. Falsification and the methodolgy of scientific research programs. In I. Lakatos & A. Musgrave (Eds.), *Criticism and the growth of knowledge.* Cambridge, England: Cambridge University Press, 1970.

Lakatos, I. Popper on demarcation and induction. In P. A. Schilpp (Ed.), *The philosophy of Karl Popper* (Vol. 1). LaSalle, Ill.: Open Court, 1974. (a)

Lakatos, I. The role of crucial experiments in science. *Studies in History and Philosophy of Science,* 1974, 4, 309–325. (b)

Langmuir, I. Science, common sense and decency. *Science,* 1943, 97, 1–7.

Lazarus, A. A. *Behavior therapy and beyond.* New York: McGraw-Hill, 1971.

Lewis, D. How to define theoretical terms. *Journal of Philosophy,* 1970, 67, 427–446.

Li, C. C. *Path analysis.* Pacific Grove, Calif.: Boxwood Press, 1975.

Loevinger, J. Objective tests as instruments of psychological theory. *Psychological Reports Monograph,* 1957, 9, 635–694.

London, I. D. Some consequences for history and psychology of Langmuir's concept of convergence and divergence of phenomena. *Psychological Review,* 1946, 53, 170–188.

MacCorquodale, K., & Meehl, P. E. Edward C. Tolman. In W. K. Estes et al., *Modern learning theory: A critical analysis of five examples.* New York: Appleton-Century-Crofts, 1954.

Maxwell, G. Meaning postulates in scientific theories. In H. Feigl & G. Maxwell (Eds.), *Current issues in the philosophy of science.* New York: Holt, Rinehart & Winston, 1961.

Maxwell, G. The necessary and the contingent. In H. Feigl & G. Maxwell (Eds.), *Scientific explanation, space and time: Minnesota studies in the philosophy of science.* (Vol. 3). Minneapolis: University of Minnesota Press, 1962.

Maxwell, G. Corroboration without demarcation. In P. A. Schilpp (Ed.), *The philosophy of Karl Popper.* LaSalle, Ill.: Open Court, 1974.

McGuire, W. I. The yin and the yang of progress in social psychology: Seven koans. *Journal of Personality and Social Psychology,* 1973, 26, 446–456.

Meehl, P. E. *Clinical versus statistical prediction: A theoretical analysis and a review of the evidence.* Minneapolis: University of Minnesota Press, 1954.

Meehl, P. E. Nuisance variables and the ex post facto design. In M. Radner & S. Winokur (Eds.), *Minnesota studies in the philosophy of science* (Vol. 4) *Analyses of theories and methods of physics and psychology.* Minneapolis: University of Minnesota Press, 1970. (a)

Meehl, P. E. Theory-testing in psychology and physics: A methodological paradox. In D. E. Morrison & R. E. Henkel (Eds.), *The significance test controversy.* Chicago: Aldine, 1970. (b) (Originally published, 1967.)

Meehl, P. E. A critical afterword. In I. I. Gottesman & J. Shields, *Schizophrenia and genetics.* New York: Academic Press, 1972.

Meehl, P. E. The cognitive activity of the clinician. In P. E. Meehl, *Psychodiagnosis: Selected papers.* Minneapolis: University of Minnesota Press, 1973. (a) (Originally published, 1960.)

Meehl, P. E. High school yearbooks: A reply to Schwarz. In P. E. Meehl, *Psychodiagnosis: Selected papers.* Minneapolis: University of Minnesota Press, 1973. (b) (Originally published, 1971.)

Meehl, P. E. Schizotaxia, schizotypy, schizophrenia. In P. E. Meehl, *Psychodiagnosis: Selected papers.* Minneapolis: University of Minnesota Press, 1973. (c) (Originally published, 1962.)

Meehl, P. E. MAXCOV-HITMAX: A taxonomic search method for loose genetic syndromes. In P. E. Meehl, *Psychodiagnosis: Selected papers.* Minneapolis: University of Minnesota Press, 1973. (d)

Meelh, P. E. Some methodological reflections on the difficulties of psychoanalytic research. *Psychological Issues,* 1973, *8,* 104–115. (e) (Originally published, 1970.)

Meehl, P. E. Some ruminations on the validation of clinical procedures. In P. E. Meehl, *Psychodiagnosis: Selected papers.* Minneapolis: University of Minnesota Press, 1973. (f) (Originally published 1959.)

Meehl, P. E. Specific genetic etiology, psychodynamics, and therapeutic nihilism. In P. E. Meehl, *Psychodiagnosis: Selected papers.* Minneapolis: University of Minnesota Press, 1973. (g) (Originally published, 1972.)

Meehl, P. E. Why I do not attend case conferences. In P. E. Meehl, *Psychodiagnosis: Selected papers.* Minneapolis: University of Minnesota Press, 1973. (h)

Meehl, P. E. Genes and the unchangeable core. *Voices: The Art and Science of Psychotherapy,* 1974, *38,* 25–35.

Meehl, P. E. Hedonic capacity: Some conjectures. *Bulletin of the Menninger Clinic,* 1975, *39,* 295–307.

Meehl, P. E. Specific etiology and other forms of strong influence: Some quantitative meanings. *Journal of Medicine and Philosophy,* 1977, *2,* 33–53.

Mischel, W. On the future of personality measurement. *American Psychologist,* 1977, *32,* 246–254.

Morrison, D. E. & Henkel, R. E. (Eds.). *The significance test controversy.* Chicago: Aldine, 1970.

Nagel, F. *The structure of science.* New York: Harcourt, Brace & World, 1961.

Nambu, Y. The confinement of quarks. *Scientific American,* 1976, *235,* 48–60.

Nozick, R. *Anarchy, state and utopia.* New York: Basic Books, 1974.

Oakes, W. F. On the alleged falsity of the null hypothesis. *Psychological Record,* 1975, *25,* 265–272.

Pap, A. Reduction-sentences and open concepts. *Methodos,* 1953, *5,* 3–30.

Pap, A. *Semantics and necessary truth.* New Haven, Conn.: Yale University Press, 1958.

Pap, A. *An introduction to the philosophy of science.* New York: Free Press, 1962.

Popper, K. R. *The logic of scientific discovery.* New York: Basic Books, 1959.

Popper, K. R. *Conjectures and refutations.* New York: Basic Books, 1962.

Popper, K. R. *Objective knowledge.* Oxford, England: Oxford Univeristy Press, 1972.

Popper, K. R. Autobiography. In P. A. Schilpp (Ed.), *The philosophy of Karl Popper.* LaSalle, Ill.: Open Court, 1974.

Popper, K. R. A note on verisimilitude. *British Journal for the Philosophy of Science,* 1976, *27,* 147–195.

Ramsey, F. P. Theories. In R. B. Braithwaite (Ed.), *F. P. Ramsey's The foundations of mathematics and other logical essays.* Paterson, N.J.: Littlefield, Adams, 1960. (Originally published, 1931.)

Rapaport, D. The structure of psychoanalytic theory: A systematizing attempt. In S. Koch (Ed.), *Psychology: A study of a science* (Vol. 3). *Formulations of the person and the social context.* New York: McGraw-Hill, 1959.

Read. R. C. *A mathematical background for economists and social scientists.* Englewood Cliffs, N.J.: Prentice-Hall, 1972.

Schilpp, P. A. (Ed.), *The philosophy of Karl Popper.* LaSalle, Ill.: Open Court, 1974.

Schlenker, B. R. Social psychology and science. *Journal of Personality and Social Psychology,* 1974, *29,* 1–15.

Sears, R. R. *Survey of objective studies of psychoanalytic concepts.* New York: *Social Science Research Council Bulletin* No. 51, 1943.

Sellars, W. Concepts as involving laws and inconceivable without them. *Philosophy of Science,* 1948, *15,* 287–315.

Sells, S. B. An interactionist looks at the environment. *American Psychologist,* 1963 *18*, 696–702.

Silverman, L. H. Psychoanalytic theory: "The reports of my death are greatly exaggerated." *American Psychologist,* 1976, *31*, 621–637.

Skinner, B. F. *The behavior of organisms.* New York: Appleton-Century, 1938.

Slater, E. The monogenic theory of schizophrenia. In J. Shields & I. I. Gottesman (Eds.), *Man, mind, and heredity: Selected papers of Eliot Slater on psychiatry and genetics.* Baltimore, Md.: Johns Hopkins University Press, 1971. (Originally published, 1958.)

Smith, M. B. Criticisms of a social science. *Science,* 1973, *180*, 610–612.

Stoddard, L. *Luck, your silent partner.* New York: Liveright, 1929.

Swoyer, C., & Monson, T. C. Theory confirmation in psychology. *Philosophy of Science,* 1975, *42*, 487–502.

Vico, G. *The new science of Giambattista Vico* (3rd rev. ed.) (T. C. Bergin and M. H. Fisch, trans.). Ithaca: Cornell University Press, 1948. (Originally published, 1744.)

Waismann, F. Verifiability. *Proceedings of the Aristotelian Society,* 1945, *19*, 119–150.

Wiggins, J. Despair and optimism in Minneapolis. *Contemporary Psychology,* 1973, *18*, 605–606.

37

THE SOCIAL CONSTRUCTIONIST MOVEMENT IN MODERN PSYCHOLOGY

KENNETH J. GERGEN

This article attempts to bring into focus the central contours of a contemporary movement of challenging implication. It would be misleading to say either that the movement is of recent origin or that its proponents are legion. The roots of the movement may properly be traced to earlier eras, and one might prefer to speak of a shared consciousness rather than a movement. However, in its current metamorphosis this emerging body of thought contains implications of substantial significance. Not only are broad vistas of inquiry opened for study, but the foundations of psychological knowledge also are thrown into critical relief. When the implications are fully elaborated, it becomes apparent that the study of social process could become generic for understanding the nature of knowledge itself. Social psychology would not stand, in this case, as a derivative of general psychology. Rather, the latter would be viewed as a form of social process, both the grounds and outcomes of which stand to be elucidated by social inquiry. In similar fashion, epistemological inquiry along with the philosophy of science could both give way, or become subsumed by, social inquiry. These are indeed bold conjectures, and as we shall see, to make good on them may require relinquishing much that is sacred. However, it is the plausibility of these conjectures that I hope to demonstrate in this article while simultaneously clarifying the contours and origins of the social constructionist movement.[1]

Reprinted from the *American Psychologist, 40,* 255–265. (1985).

[1]Although the term *constructivism* is also used in referring to the same movement (cf. Watzlawick, 1984), this term is also used in reference to Piagetian theory, to a form of perceptual theory, and to a significant movement in 20th century art. The term *constructionism* avoids these various confusions and enables a linkage to be retained to Berger and Luckmann's (1966) seminal volume, *The Social Construction of Reality.*

THE SOCIAL CONSTRUCTIONIST ORIENTATION

Social constructionist inquiry is principally concerned with explicating the processes by which people come to describe, explain, or otherwise account for the world (including themselves) in which they live. It attempts to articulate common forms of understanding as they now exist, as they have existed in prior historical periods, and as they might exist should creative attention be so directed. At the metatheoretical level most such work manifests one or more of the following assumptions.

1. What we take to be experience of the world does not in itself dictate the terms by which the world is understood. What we take to be knowledge of the world is not a product of induction, or of the building and testing of general hypotheses. The mounting criticism of the positivist–empiricist conception of knowledge has severely damaged the traditional view that scientific theory serves to reflect or map reality in any direct or decontextualized manner (cf. Feyerabend, 1976; Hanson, 1958; Kuhn, 1962/1970; Quine, 1960; Taylor, 1971). How can theoretical categories be induced or derived from observation, it is asked, if the process of identifying observational attributes itself relies on one's possessing categories? How can theoretical categories map or reflect the world if each definition used to link category and observation itself requires a definition? How can words map reality when the major constraints over word usage are furnished by linguistic context? How is it possible to determine whether competing theories refer to the same entities, without reference to some other theory not contained in those under comparison? If each theoretical proposition depends for its intelligibility on an array of related propositions, what aspect of the propositional network would be challenged by a disconfirmation of any single proposition? These and other telling questions have largely gone unanswered, and the lack of answers has left the empirical sciences without a viable logic of justification (Weimer, 1979).

Running counterpoint with this developing doubt has been a steadily intensifying concern with the constraints over understanding engendered by linguistic convention. Wittgenstein's (1963) *Philosophical Investigations* must be viewed as seminal in this regard. By asking such questions as where does an individual feel grief or happiness, could a person have a profound feeling in one second, and can the features of hope be described, Wittgenstein brought into poignant clarity the extent to which the use of mental predicates is convention bound. His work has served to inspire an impressive array of philosophic studies into the linguistic constraints governing the use of such concepts as mind (Ryle, 1949), intention (Anscombe, 1976), sense data (Austin, 1962b), and motivation (Peters, 1958). Such inquiry has also elucidated a variety of important problems created through the reification of the language. In effect, many classic problems both in psychology and philosophy appear to be products of linguistic entanglement; with clarity concerning the nature and functions of the language the problems may often be decomposed.

Social constructionism has been nurtured by the soil of such discontent. It begins with radical doubt in the taken-for-granted world—whether in the sciences or daily life—and in a specialized way acts as a form of social criticism. Constructionism asks one to suspend belief that commonly accepted categories or understandings receive their warrant through observation. Thus, it invites one to challenge the objective basis of conventional knowledge. For example, in Kessler and McKenna's (1978) investigation of the social construction of gender, the attempt is made to break down the seemingly incorrigible fact that there are two genders. By examining the variations in the way differing cultures and subcultural groups understand gender, the referents for the terms *man* and *woman* are obscured. Possibilities are opened for alternative means of understanding gender differences or of abandoning such distinctions altogether. In Averill's (1982) extensive work on emotion one is forced to question the assumption that anger is a biological state of the organism and is invited to consider it as a historically contingent social performance. Sarbin (1984) extended this line of thinking to the entire array of emotional terms. Emotions are not objects "out there" to be studied, ventured Sarbin; emotion terms acquire their meaning not from real world referents but from their context of usage.

Similar kinds of critiques have been launched against the taken-for-granted character of suicide (Atkinson, 1977), beliefs (Needham, 1972), schizophrenia (Sarbin & Mancuso, 1980), altruism (Gergen & Gergen, 1983), psychological disorder (Garfinkel, 1967), childhood (Kessen, 1979), domestic violence (Greenblat, 1983), menopause (McCrea, 1983), and situational causes (Gergen & Gergen, 1982). In each case, the objective criteria for identifying such "behaviors," "events," or "entities" are shown to be either highly circumscribed by culture, history, or social context or altogether nonexistent.

2. The terms in which the world is understood are social artifacts, products of historically situated interchanges among people. From the constructionist position the process of understanding is not automatically driven by the forces of nature, but is the result of an active, cooperative enterprise of persons in relationship. In this light, inquiry is invited into the historical and cultural bases of various forms of world construction. For example, historical investigation has revealed broad historical variations in the concept of the child (Aries, 1962), of romantic love (Averill, 1985), of mother's love (Badinter, 1980), and of self (Verhave & van Hoorne, 1984). In each case constructions of the person or relationships have undergone significant change across time. In certain periods childhood was not considered a specialized phase of development, romantic and maternal love were not components of human makeup, and the self was not viewed as isolated and autonomous. Such changes in conception do not appear to reflect alterations in the objects or entities of concern but seem lodged in historically contingent factors. Ethnographic study yields much the same conclusion. Conceptions of psychological process differ markedly from one culture to another (see Heelas & Lock's 1981 edited volume). Accounts of emotion among the Ifaluk (Lutz, 1982), of identity among the Trobrianders (Lee, 1959), of knowledge among the Illongot (Rosaldo, 1980), and of the self among the Maori (Smith, 1981) all serve as challenges to the ontology of mind in contemporary Western culture. They invite us to consider the social origins of taken-for-granted assumptions about the mind—such as the bifurcation between reason and emotion, the existence of motives and memories, and the symbol system believed to underlie language. They direct our attention to the social, moral, political, and economic institutions that sustain and are supported by current assumptions about human activity.

Constructionist inquiry has further been directed to the axioms or fundamental propositions underlying descriptions of persons in present-day society (Davis & Todd, 1982; Gergen, 1984a; Ossario, 1978; Semin & Chassein, in press; Shotter & Burton, 1983; Smedslund, 1978). It is first asked whether the folk models of mind within a culture necessarily determine or constrain the conclusions reached within the profession. How can the psychologist step outside cultural understandings and continue to "make sense"? Further, it is asked, are there generic rules governing accounts of human action from which common conventions are derived? Such work is of special interest as it begins to outline the possible constraints over what psychological research can say. If it is possible to isolate propositions or assumptions grounding discourse about persons, then we are furnished with a basis for understanding what psychological theory *must* say if it is to be reasonable or communicable.

3. The degree to which a given form of understanding prevails or is sustained across time is not fundamentally dependent on the empirical validity of the perspective in question, but on the vicissitudes of social processes (e.g., communication, negotiation, conflict, rhetoric). As proposed in this case, perspectives, views, or descriptions of persons can be retained regardless of variations in their actual conduct. Regardless of the stability or repetition of conduct, per-

spectives may be abandoned as their intelligibility is questioned within the community of interlocutors. Observation of persons, then, is questionable as a corrective or guide to descriptions of persons. Rather, the rules for "what counts as what" are inherently ambiguous, continuously evolving, and free to vary with the predilections of those who use them. On these grounds, one is even led to query the concept of truth. Is the major deployment of the term *truth* primarily a means for warranting one's own position and discrediting contenders for intelligibility (Gergen, 1984b)?

In this vein, Sabini and Silver (1982) have demonstrated how people manage the definition of morality in relationships. Whether an act is defined as envy, flirtation, or anger floats on a sea of social interchange. Interpretation may be suggested, fastened upon, and abandoned as social relationships unfold across time. In the same way, Mummendey and her colleagues (Mummendey, Bonewasser, Loschper, & Linneweber, 1982) have shown how decisions are reached as to whether an action constitutes aggression. Thus, aggression ceases to exist as a fact in the world and becomes a labeling device for social control. Other investigators (cf. Cantor & Brown, 1981; Harré, 1981; Lalljee, 1981) have discussed social negotiation processes underlying the attribution of causality to persons' actions. Earlier work on self-identity (Gergen, 1977) has focused on the manner in which self-definition is realigned over time as social circumstances are altered. Communications specialists Pearce and Cronen (1980) have outlined a general theory for the negotiation of reality. Others have concentrated on the family (Reiss, 1981) and the media (Adoni & Mane, 1984) as they contribute to prevailing forms of interpretation.

Much this same line of thinking has been increasingly employed by historians and sociologists of science to understand scientific conduct. For example, Mendelsohn (1977) has argued that the epistemological assumptions of modern science were developed largely as a means of gaining social control. Bohme (1977) has discussed the informal rules used within scientific communities to determine what they count as facts. Investigators such as Latour and Woolgar (1979) and Knorr-Cetina (1981) have carried out participant observation in natural science laboratories—much as anthropologists exploring tribal customs. As they contend, what passes for "hard fact" in the natural sciences typically depends on a subtle but potent array of social microprocesses. In effect, the move is from an experiential to a social epistemology (Campbell, 1969; Sullivan, 1984).

4. Forms of negotiated understanding are of critical significance in social life, as they are integrally connected with many other activities in which people engage. Descriptions and explanations of the world themselves constitute forms of social action. As such they are intertwined with the full range of other human activities. The opening, "Hello, how are you?" is typically accompanied by a range of facial expressions, bodily postures, and movements without which the expression could seem artificial, if not aberrant. In the same way, descriptions and explanations form integral parts of various social patterns. They thus serve to sustain and support certain patterns to the exclusion of others. To alter description and explanation is thus to threaten certain actions and invite others. To construct persons in such a way that they possess inherent sin is to invite certain lines of action and not others. Or to treat depression, anxiety, or fear as emotions from which people involuntarily suffer is to have far different implications than to treat them as chosen, selected, or played out as on a stage.

It is in this vein that many investigators have been concerned with the prevailing images or metaphors of human action employed within the field of psychology. Queries have been raised over the broad social implications of viewing persons as machines (Shotter, 1975), as self-contained individuals (Sampson, 1977, 1983), or as economic bargainers in social relations (Wexler, 1983). Attacks have also been levied against the damaging effects on children of the prevailing constructions of the child's mind (Walkerdine, 1984), the sexism implicit in investigation that assumes the superiority of universal principles in moral decision making (Gilligan, 1982), the effects of theories of cognitive mechanism in their implicit unconcern with material circumstances in society (Sampson, 1981), and the anomic effects of psychological assessment in organizations (Hollway, 1984).

SOCIAL CONSTRUCTIONISM IN HISTORICAL PERSPECTIVE

The significance of the constructionist movement is more fully appreciated against the backdrop of history. Although a full treatment of the relevant background is beyond the scope of this article, it does prove useful to understand constructionism in relation to two major and competing intellectual traditions. These traditions can largely be distinguished in terms of basic epistemological orientations or models of knowledge. On the one hand, thinkers such as Locke, Hume, the Mills, and various logical empiricists in the present century have traced the source of knowledge (as mental representation) to events in the real world. Knowledge copies (or should ideally copy) the contours of the world. This *exogenic perspective* (Gergen, 1982) thus tends to view knowledge as a pawn to nature. Proper knowledge maps or mirrors the actualities of the real world. In contrast, philosophers such as Spinoza, Kant, Nietzsche, and various phenomenologists have tended to adopt an *endogenic perspective* regarding the origins of knowledge. In this case, knowledge depends on processes (sometimes viewed as innate) endemic to the organism. Humans harbor inherent tendencies, it is said, to think, categorize, or process information, and it is these tendencies (rather than features of the world in itself) that are of paramount importance in fashioning knowledge.

The exogenic–endogenic antinomy has also played a major role in the history of psychological theory. As I have outlined elsewhere (Gergen, 1982), early German theorists often wrestled in vain with means of cementing the two perspectives. The attempt of classical psychophysical research to plot the precise relationship between external and internal worlds is but one case in point. As psychology developed in the United States, guided as it was by both pragmatist and positivist philosophy, it took on a strong exogenic character. Behaviorism (along with neobehaviorism) placed (and continues to place) the major determinants of human activity in the environment. If the organism is to adapt successfully, it is claimed, its knowledge must adequately represent or reflect that environment. Until recently the endogenic perspective failed to flourish on American soil. A handful of Gestalt psychologists, with their emphasis on autochthonous tendencies of perceptual organization, and a stalwart band of phenomenologists virtually prevented the orientation from otherwise perishing.

Yet, within the past two decades we have witnessed what appears to be a major reversal in emphasis. The endogenic perspective has returned in full force in the guise of cognitive psychology. The seeds for this evolution in social psychology were planted by Kurt Lewin, whose central concern with the psychological field was essentially a holdover from continental rationalism. In the hands of his students this emphasis reinstituted itself in such concepts as social (as opposed to physical) reality (Festinger, 1954), the social comparison process (Festinger, 1954), motivated perception (Pepitone, 1949), emotions as perceived (Schachter, 1964), and cognitive dissonance (Festinger, 1957). The centrality of this work in social psychology also served to hone the sensibilities of subsequent generations of researchers. Concerns with logical inference, cognitive schemata, information storage and retrieval, and cognitive heuristics have all extended the Lewinian premise: Human action is critically dependent on the cognitive processing of information, that is, on the world as cognized rather than the world as it is. Of course, much the same shift in explanatory emphasis has taken place within psychology more generally. The contours of the "cognitive revolution" are widely recognized.

Yet, it is my view that in spite of the richness of conceptualization and the profundity of its heritage, the endogenic perspective has not yet achieved full ascendency—nor can it in principle. There is much to be said on this account, but again a brief sketch is necessitated. First, cognitivism has not yet—neither in social psychology nor in psychology more generally—overturned the exogenic perspective because the exogenic perspective forms the metatheoretical basis of the science itself. That is, the contemporary conception of psychological science is a by-product of empiricist or exogenic philosophy—committed as it has been to rendering an account of objective knowledge of the world. The experimental psychologist thus sets out to employ methods for establishing objective knowledge about cognitive processes. To the extent that the investigator claims to achieve an accurate representation of the world (thus rendering support for exogenics), it threatens the view that it is the world as represented (cognized) rather than the world in itself which is of importance. In seeking objective truth (that which is true independent of subjective appraisal) the cognitive researcher thus denigrates the importance of the very processes he or she seeks to elucidate. The exogenic basis of the scientific activity undermines the validity of the endogenic theories under examination.

Nor, would it seem, can cognitivism ultimately achieve hegemony in psychological discourse. This may be anticipated in part by the example furnished by the history of the philosophy of knowledge. This history has been one of continuous and unresolved disputation between exogenic (or empiricist, in this context) and endogenic (rationist, idealist, phenomenological) thinkers. Essentially, the history of the philosophy of knowledge can largely be written in terms of a continuous series of pendulum swings. We have witnessed the conflict between Plato's pure forms of knowledge versus Aristotle's concern with the role of sensory experience; between the authority granted to experience by Bacon, Locke, and Hume versus the rational capacities granted to the mind by Descartes, Spinoza, and Kant; between the emphasis placed by Schopenhauer and Nietzche on will and passion in the generation of knowledge, and the attempts of logical positivists to ground all knowledge in observables. What is to prevent the same historical trajectory in psychology? We have most recently witnessed in the cognitive revolution a shift from an exogenic to an endogenic perspective. As the inherent flaws of cognitivism are once again revealed in future psychological work, are we again to anticipate a return to some form of (suitably enlightened) environmentalism? (Gibsonian affordance theory [Gibson, 1979] may already be foreshadowing the new swing.) And such problems are sure to emerge. For example, when cognitivism is extended to its natural conclusion it reverts into an unhappy and unacceptable solipsism. And, cognitivism remains perennially unable to resolve such thorny problems as the origin of ideas or concepts and the manner in which cognitions influence behavior (cf. Gergen, 1985). Compelling explanations for how cognitions could either be "built up" from experience or genetically programmed remain to be fashioned. Nor have theorists been able to solve the Cartesian dilemma of explaining how "mind stuff" can influence or dictate discrete bodily movements.

It is against this backdrop that one can appreciate the emergence of social constructionism. Rather than recapitulating yet again the movement of the pendulum, the challenge (for many) has been to transcend the traditional subject–object dualism and all its attendant problems (cf. Rorty, 1979) and to develop a new framework of analysis based on an alternative (nonempiricist) theory of the functioning and potentials of science. This movement begins in earnest when one challenges the concept of knowledge as mental representation. Given the myriad of insolubles to which such a concept gives rise, one is moved to consider what passes as knowledge in human affairs. At least one major candidate is that of linguistic rendering. We generally count as knowledge that which is represented in linguistic propositions—stored in books, journals, floppy disks, and the like. These renderings, to continue an earlier theme, are constituents of social practices. From this perspective, knowledge is not something people possess somewhere in their heads, but rather, something people do together. Languages are essentially shared activities. Indeed, until the sounds or markings come to be shared within a community, it is inappropriate to speak of language at all. In effect, we may cease inquiry into the psychological basis of language (which account would inevitably form but a subtext or miniature language) and focus on the performance use of language in human affairs.[2]

As we have seen, analyses of the social constructionist variety have been devoted to such broad topics as gender, aggression, mind, causality, person, self, child, motivation, emotion, morality, and so on. Typically the concern has been with the language forms that pervade the society, the means by which they are negotiated, and their implications for other ranges of social activity. In such endeavors social psychologists begin to join hands, as well, with a new range of disciplines. Rather than looking toward the natural sciences and experimental psychology for kinship, an affinity is rapidly sensed with a range of what may be termed *interpretive disciplines,* that is, disciplines chiefly concerned with rendering accounts of human meaning systems (cf. Rabinow & Sullivan, 1979). On the most immediate level, social constructionist inquiry is conjoined with ethnomethodological work (cf. Garfinkel, 1967; Psathas, 1979) with its emphasis on the methods employed by persons to render the world sensible, and with much dramaturgical analysis (cf. Goffman, 1959; Sarbin & Scheibe, 1983) and its focus on the strategic deployment of social conduct. Similarly, treatments of the social basis of scientific knowledge, including the history and sociology of knowledge, become relevant (Knorr, Krohn, & Whitley, 1981; Knorr-Cetina & Mulkay, 1983). Anthropological inquiry acquires a renewed interest for psychology. Of special interest is the work of symbolic anthropologists concerned with the construction of the world, including persons, developed in non-Western cultures (cf. Geertz, 1973; Shweder & Miller, 1985). Similarly, psychology gains a temporal dimension as its analyses become articulated with historical research in the constructionist mode (Nowell-Smith, 1977; White, 1978). And psychology stands to gain much by opening consideration on literary theory, including accounts of metaphor (Lakoff & Johnson, 1980), narratology (Genette, 1980), and the deconstruction of meaning (Culler, 1982). Such work informs as to the means by which various linguistic figures or tropes serve to organize or guide the attempt to "describe" reality.

CONSTRUCTIONISM AND THE PROBLEMATICS OF PSYCHOLOGICAL EXPLANATION

Thus far we have considered grounding assumptions of the constructionist orientation, along with its historical roots and contemporary emergence. It remains now to touch upon the implications of constructionism both for the character of psychological inquiry and for the nature of science more generally. With regard to psychology the implications are far reaching, and many years will be required before they are fully explored. To appreciate the arguments at issue consider the typical constructionist analysis of psychological processes or mechanisms. In Averill's (1982) hands the concept of anger is largely cut away from a deterministic physiology and becomes a form of social role; anger as a term thus does not refer to a mental state but constitutes part of the role itself. In a related analysis (Mills, 1940), doubt is cast on the concept of motivation as a primal power capable of moving people to action, and the focus shifts to people's talk about their motives and its social implications. The mind (Coulter, 1979) becomes a form of social myth; the self-concept (Gergen, 1985) is removed from the head and placed within the sphere

[2]If the emphasis is shifted, much cognitive research becomes relevant to constructionist pursuits. Research on social prototypes, implied personality theory, attributional schemata, the concept of intelligence, and the like do not from the present standpoint, inform us about another world—namely, an internal, cognitive one. Rather they might elucidate the nature of social discourse and thus raise interesting questions about the function of such terms in scientific and social life.

of social discourse. In each case, then, what have been taken by one segment of the profession or another as "facts about the nature of the psychological realm" are suspended; each concept (emotion, motive, etc.) is cut away from an ontological base within the head and is made a constituent of social process. In agreement with Wittgenstein's (1963) later analyses, one ceases to view mental predicates as possessing a syntactic relationship with a world of mental events; rather, as Austin (1962a) and other post-Wittgensteinians have proposed, such terms are cashed out in terms of the social practices in which they function.

From this perspective, then, all psychological theorizing and the full range of concepts that form the grounds for research become problematic as potential reflectors of an internal reality and become themselves matters of analytic interest. Professional agreements become suspect; normalized beliefs become targets of demystification; "the truth" about mental life is rendered curious. Or, in a slightly different light, the contemporary views of the profession on matters of cognition, motivation, perception, information processing, and the like become candidates for historical and cross-cultural comparison. From the constructionist perspective they often constitute a form of ethnopsychology, historically and culturally situated, institutionally useful, normatively sustained, and subject to deterioration and decay as social history unfolds.

As is clear, constructionism will inevitably confront strong resistance within psychology more generally. It forms a potential challenge to traditional knowledge claims; psychological research itself is placed in the uncomfortable position of a research object. Yet for social analysts the shift is one of heady proportion. No longer would social inquiry confront the threat of becoming a derivative enterprise—merely elaborating the social implications of more fundamental psychological processes. Rather, what is taken to be psychological process at the very outset becomes a derivative of social interchange. The explanatory locus of human action shifts from the interior region of the mind to the processes and structure of human interaction. The question "why" is answered not with a psychological state or process but with consideration of persons in relationship. Few are prepared for such a wrenching, conceptual dislocation. However, for the innovative, adventurous and resilient, the horizons are exciting indeed.

CONSTRUCTIONISM AND THE CHARACTER OF SCIENCE

Although many will find it difficult to relinquish the use of psychological mechanisms, structures, and processes as major explanatory vehicles, this loss may be coupled with a challenge of no small consequence. The challenge is essentially that of grappling with a new conception of knowledge. To appreciate the point it should be realized that problems inherent in both the endo- and exogenic orientations are also deeply engrained in the contemporary conception of scientific knowledge and its acquisition. In particular, the empiricist assumptions that form the undergirding rationale for research in psychology (and virtually all contemporary science) are drawn chiefly from the exogenic intellectual tradition. This orientation, with its emphasis on knowledge as an internal representation of the state of nature, is manifestly apparent in the traditional attempt to establish scientific knowledge through processes of empirical verification and falsification. However, if constructionism is to transcend the exogenic-endogenic antinomy, and the interminable conflict it has thus far spawned, then it must also eschew the empiricist account of scientific knowledge. As it abandons the subject–object dichotomy central to disciplinary debate, so must it challenge dualism as the basis for a theory of scientific knowledge.

What is confronted, then, is the traditional, Western conception of objective, individualistic, ahistoric knowledge—a conception that has insinuated itself into virtually all aspects of modern institutional life. As this view is increasingly challenged one must entertain the possibility of molding an alternative scientific metatheory based on constructionist assumptions. Such a metatheory would remove knowledge from the data-driven and/or the cognitively necessitated domains and place it in the hands of people in relationship. Scientific formulations would not on this account be the result of an impersonal application of decontextualized, methodological rules, but the responsibility of persons in active, communal interchange.

Elsewhere, the contours of this emerging metatheory have been referred to as *sociorationalist* (Gergen, 1982; Gergen & Morawski, 1980). In this view the locus of scientific rationality lies not within the minds of independent persons but within the social aggregate. That which is rational is the result of negotiated intelligibility. For social thinkers the further development of the metatheory should be of especially high priority. For, if the character of sociorationalist process is among the focal concerns of the social investigator, then the critical task of understanding the generation and evolution of knowledge falls centrally to scholars within the social sphere. Much philosophic inquiry—including the philosophy of science—thus falls subject to social constructionist analysis. To a certain degree philosophers of science are already aware of this prospect. In recent years philosophic inquiry into foundations of scientific knowledge has waned. Confidence in empiricist assumptions has largely been eroded, and there is no obvious contender on the horizon (Bernstein, 1978).[3] Such inquiry has become increasingly replaced by historical analysis. Kuhn's (1962/1970) seminal treatise on revolutions in scientific knowledge is essentially a historical account, and much subsequent discussion of rationality and progress in science has largely proceeded on historical as opposed to philosophic grounds. Such history is essentially social, and its elaboration requires close attention to processes of human interchange. It remains, however, for social analysts more generally to become aware of the pivotal position that they might legitimately occupy.

Thus far feminist thinkers have been among those most acutely aware of such possibilities. For feminists, the empiricist orientation to knowledge has not generally been a congenial perspective—advocating as it does manipulation, suppression, and alienation of those one wishes to understand (Jaeger, 1983). Further, from the feminist perspective, empiricist science seems to have been oft employed by males to construct views of women that contribute to their subjugation (Bleier, 1984; Weisstein, 1971). Both the process and the products of empiricist science have thus come under attack. As a result many feminists have searched for alternative forms of understanding—both of science and of other human beings. Constructionism, because of its emphasis on the communal basis of knowledge, processes of interpretation, and concern with the valuational underpinnings of scientific accounts, has been an attractive alternative. Thus, feminists have been frontrunners in employing interpretive research strategies (Acker, Barry, & Esseveld, 1983; Bowles, 1984), documenting the scientific construction of gender (Morawski, in press), demonstrating the pragmatic use of constructionist inquiry (Sassen, 1980), and exploring the foundations for constructionist metatheory (Unger, 1983).

Yet, the possibility of an alternative theory of knowledge can hardly demand broad appeal. The investments in and sense of security fostered by the enduring traditions are profound. Acute misgivings can be anticipated within these circles regarding criteria of knowledge and the companionate problem of appropriate methodology. Traditional empiricism holds experience to be the touchstone of objectivity; hypotheses are said to be confirmed or challenged by virtue of sense data. Yet, from the constructionist viewpoint, both the concepts of experience and sense data are placed in question. From what grounds do they derive their truth warrants? Are the so-called "reports of one's experience" not linguistic constructions guided and shaped by historically contingent conventions of discourse? Yet, although casting doubt on the process of objective

[3]Recent interest has been generated in a "realist" alternative to empiricist metatheory (Bhaskar, 1978; Manicas & Secord, 1983). However, although opposed to the Humean basis of scientific explanation, realist philosophy of science shares with empiricism a range of fundamental assumptions. It thus suffers from most of the criticisms lodged against empiricism.

warranting, constructionism offers no alternative truth criteria. Accounts of social construction cannot themselves be warranted empirically. If properly executed such accounts can enable one to escape the confines of the taken for granted. They may emancipate one from the demands of convention. However, the success of such accounts depends primarily on the analyst's capacity to invite, compel, stimulate, or delight the audience, and not on criteria of veracity. Required, then, are alternative criteria for evaluating knowledge claims—criteria that might reasonably take into account existing needs for systems of intelligibility, limitations inherent in existing constructions, along with a range of political, moral, aesthetic, and practical considerations.

By the same token, social constructionism offers no "truth through method." In large degree the sciences have been enchanted by the myth that the assiduous application of rigorous method will yield sound fact—as if empirical methodology were some form of meat grinder from which truth could be turned out like so many sausages. Yet, as analysts such as Quine, Taylor, Hanson, and Feyerabend have shown, such enchantment is of doubtful merit. Previous security is without firm foundation. For one seeking such security social constructionism will scarcely be palatable. Yet this is not to imply that constructionism eschews investigative methods. Whether rendering the conduct of organisms intelligible or demystifying existing forms of understanding, research methods can be used to produce "objectifications" or illustrations useful in advancing the pragmatic consequences of one's work. In this sense it would seem that virtually any methodology can be employed so long as it enables the analyst to develop a more compelling case. Although some methods may hold the allure of large samples, others can attract because of their purity, their sensitivity to nuance, or their ability to probe in depth. Such assets do not thereby increase the "objective validity" of the resulting constructions. However, like vivid photographs of startling vignettes drawn from daily life, when well wrought they may add vital power to the pen.

Others may eschew the constructionist orientation for what appears to be its rampant relativism. Yet, as we have seen, the attempts to justify objective foundations for knowledge have yet to furnish reason for optimism. One might well argue that the scientist's claims to privileged knowledge have served as mystifying devices within the society more generally. Constructionism offers no foundational rules of warrant and in this sense is relativistic. However, this does not mean that "anything goes." Because of the inherent dependency of knowledge systems of communities of shared intelligibility, scientific activity will always be governed in large measure by normative rules. However, constructionism does invite practitioners to view these rules as historically and culturally situated—thus subject to critique and transformation. There is stability of understanding without the stultification of foundationalism. Further, unlike the moral relativism of the empiricist tradition, constructionism reasserts the relevance of moral criteria for scientific practice. To the extent that psychological theory (and related practices) enter into the life of the culture, sustaining certain patterns of conduct and destroying others, such work must be evaluated in terms of good and ill. The practitioner can no longer justify any socially reprehensible conclusion on the grounds of being a "victim of the facts"; he or she must confront the pragmatic implications of such conclusions within society more generally.

Should the challenge of developing an alternative metatheory be accepted, a variety of interesting changes may be anticipated in the character of professional life. The problem of forging a compelling account of the social genesis of knowledge is not inconsequential. New theoretical tools are required—concepts that lie between the problematic explanatory domains of psychology and sociology. The functions of language, both as a system of reference and as a form of social participation must be elaborated. A general account must be furnished of the social dimensions of natural science, social science, and philosophy. The demarcation (if any) between science and nonscience must be carefully examined. The extent to which scientific accounts may be (if ever) corrected or modified through observation must be assessed. In effect, an array of challenging problems will be confronted, problems that are essentially conceptual rather than empirical. For such tasks dialogue is essential between psychologists and like-minded colleagues in sociology, anthropology, history, philosophy, and literary studies. Should such dialogue occur, we might reasonably anticipate the development of new theoretical departures, metatheory for a new conception of science, and a general refurbishment of intellectual resources.

REFERENCES

Acker, J., Barry, K., & Esseveld, J. (1983). Objectivity and truth. Problems in doing feminist research. *Women's Studies International Forum, 4,* 423–435.

Adoni, H., & Mane, S. (1984). Media and the social construction of reality. *Communication Research, 11,* 323–340.

Anscombe, G. E. M. (1976). *Intention.* Oxford, England: Blackwell (Original work published 1957)

Aries, P. (1962). *Centuries of childhood: A social history of family life.* New York: Vintage.

Atkinson, J. M. (1977). *Discovering suicide: Studies in the social organization of sudden death.* London: Macmillan Press.

Austin, J. L. (1962a). *How to do things with words.* Cambridge, MA: Harvard University Press.

Austin, J. L. (1962b). *Sense and sensibilia.* London: Oxford University Press.

Averill, J. (1982). *Anger and aggression.* New York: Springer-Verlag.

Averill, J. (1985). The social construction of emotion: With special reference to love. In K. J. Gergen & K. E. Davis (Eds.), *The social construction of the person.* New York: Springer-Verlag.

Badinter, E. (1980). *Mother love, myth and reality.* New York: Macmillan.

Berger, P., & Luckmann, T. (1966). *The social construction of reality.* Garden City, NY: Doubleday.

Bernstein, R. (1978). *The restructuring of social and political theory.* Philadelphia: University of Pennsylvania Press.

Bhaskar, R. (1978). *A realist theory of science* (2nd ed.). Atlantic Highlands, NJ: Humanities Press.

Bleier, R. (1984). *Science and gender, a critique of biology and its theories on women.* New York: Pergamon.

Bohme, G. (1977). Cognitive norms, knowledge interests and the constitution of the scientific object. In E. Mendelsohn & P. Weingart (Eds.), *The social production of scientific knowledge.* Dordrecht, The Netherlands: Reidel.

Bowles, G. (1984). The use of hermeneutics for feminist scholarship. *Women's Studies International Forum, 7,* 185–188.

Campbell, D. (1969). Ethnocentrism of disciplines and the Fishscale model of omniscience. In M. Sherif & C. W. Sherif (Eds.), *Inter-disciplinary relationships in the social sciences* (pp. 140–152). Chicago: Aldine.

Cantor, D., & Brown, J. (1981). Explanatory roles. In C. Antaki (Ed.), *The psychology of ordinary explanations* (pp. 221–242). London: Academic Press.

Coulter, J. (1979). *The social construction of the mind.* New York: Macmillan.

Culler, J. (1982). *On deconstruction.* Ithaca, NY: Cornell University Press.

Davis, K. E., & Todd, M. J. (1982). Friendship and love relationships, In K. Davis (Ed.), *Advances in descriptive psychology* (Vol. 2, pp. 79–122). Greenwich, CT: JAI Press.

Festinger, L. (1954). A theory of social comparison processes. *Human Relations, 7,* 117–140.

Festinger, L. (1957). *A theory of cognitive dissonance.* Evanston, IL: Row, Peterson.

Feyerabend, P. K. (1976). *Against method.* New York: Humanities Press.

Garfinkel, H. (1967). *Studies in ethnomethodology.* Englewood Cliffs, NJ: Prentice-Hall.

Geertz, C. (1973). *Interpretation of cultures.* New York: Basic Books.

Genette, R. (1980). *Narrative discourse.* Ithaca, New York: Cornell University Press.

Gergen, K. J. (1977). The social construction of self-knowledge. In T. Mischel (Ed.), *The self, psychological and philosophical issues.* Oxford, England: Blackwell.

Gergen, K. J. (1982). *Toward transformation in social knowledge.* New York: Springer-Verlag.

Gergen, K. J. (1984a). Aggression as discourse. In A. Mummendey (Ed.), *Social psychology of aggression* (pp. 51–68). New York: Springer-Verlag.

Gergen, K. J. (1984b) *Warranting voice and the elaboration of the self.* Paper presented at the Wales Conference on Self & Identity, Cardiff, Wales.

Gergen, K. J. (1985). Theory of the self: Impasse and evolution. In L. Berkowitz (Ed.), *Advances in experimental social psychology.* New York: Academic Press.

Gergen, K. J., & Gergen, M. M. (1982). Form and function in the explanation of human conduct. In P. Secord (Ed.), *Paradigms in the social sciences* (pp. 127–151). Beverly Hills, CA: Sage.

Gergen, K. J., & Gergen, M. M. (1983). The social construction of helping relationships. In J. D. Fisher, A. Nadler, & B. DePaulo (Eds.), *New directions in helping* (Vol. 1, pp. 144–163). New York: Academic Press.

Gergen, K. J., & Morawski, J. (1980). An alternative metatheory for social psychology. In L. Wheeler (Ed.), *Review of personality and social psychology* (pp. 326–352). Beverly Hills: Sage.

Gibson, J. J. (1979). *The ecological approach to visual perception.* Boston: Houghton Mifflin.

Gilligan, C. (1982). *In a different voice.* Cambridge, MA: Harvard University Press.

Goffman, E. (1959). *The presentation of self in everyday life.* New York: Doubleday.

Greenblat, C. S. (1983). A hit is a hit is a hit . . . Or is it? In R. J. Finkelhor, R. J. Gelles, G. T. Hotaling, & M. A. Straus (Eds.), *The dark side of families: Current family violence research* (pp. 132–158). Beverly Hills, CA: Sage.

Hanson, N. R. (1958). *Patterns of discovery.* London: Cambridge University Press.

Harré, R. (1981). Expressive aspects of descriptions of others. In C. Antaki (Ed.), *The psychology of ordinary explanations* (pp. 139–156). London: Academic Press.

Heelas, P., & Lock, A. (Eds.). (1981). *Indigenous psychologies.* London: Academic Press.

Hollway, W. (1984). Fitting work: Psychological assessment in organizations. In J. Henriques, W. Hollway, C. Urwin, V. Louze, & V. Walkerdine (Eds.), *Changing the subject* (pp. 26–59). London: Methuen.

Jaeger, A. (1983). *Feminist politics and human nature.* New York: Rowman & Allanheld.

Kessen, W. (1979). The American child and other cultural inventions. *American Psychologist, 34,* 815–820.

Kessler, S., & McKenna, W. (1978). *Gender: An ethnomethodological approach.* New York: Wiley.

Knorr, K. D., Krohn, R., & Whitley, R. (Eds.). (1981). *The social process of scientific investigation.* Dordrecht, The Netherlands: Reidel.

Knorr-Cetina, K. D. (1981). *The manufacture of knowledge.* Oxford, England: Pergamon.

Knorr-Cetina, K. D., & Mulkay, M. (1983). *Science observed.* Beverly Hills, CA: Sage.

Kuhn, T. S. (1970). *The structure of scientific revolutions* (2nd rev. ed.). Chicago: University of Chicago Press. (Original work published 1962)

Lakoff, G., & Johnson, M. (1980). *Metaphors we live by.* Chicago: University of Chicago Press.

Lalljee, M. (1981). Attribution theory and the analysis of explanations. In C. Antaki (Ed.), *The psychology of ordinary explanations* (pp. 119–138). London: Academic Press.

Latour, B., & Woolgaar, S. (1979). *Laboratory life, the social construction of scientific facts.* Beverly Hills, CA: Sage.

Lee, D. (1959). *Freedom and culture.* New York: Prentice-Hall.

Lutz, C. (1982). The domain of emotion words in Ifaluk. *American Ethnologist, 9,* 113–128.

Manicas, P. T., & Secord, P. E. (1983). Implications for psychology of the new philosophy of science. *American Psychologist, 38,* 399–413.

McCrea, F. B. (1983). The politics of menopause: The "discovery" of a deficiency disease. *Social Problems, 31,* 111–123.

Mendelsohn, E. (1977). The social construction of scientific knowledge. In E. Mendelsohn & P. Weingert (Eds.), *The social production of scientific knowledge.* Dordrecht, The Netherlands: Reidel.

Mills, C. W. (1940). Situated actions and vocabularies of motives. *American Sociological Review, 5,* 904–913.

Morawski, J. (in press). The measurement of masculinity and femininity: Engendering categorical realities. *Journal of Personality.*

Mummendey, A., Bonewasser, M., Loschper, G., & Linneweber, V. (1982). It is always somebody else who is aggressive. *Zeitschrift fur Sozialpsychologie, 13,* 341–352.

Needham, R. (1972). *Belief, language & experience.* Chicago: University of Chicago Press.

Nowell-Smith, P. H. (1977). The constructionist theory of history. *History and Theory, Studies in the Philosophy of History, 16,* 4.

Ossario, P. (1978). *What actually happens.* Columbia: University of South Carolina Press.

Pearce, W. B., & Cronen, V. E. (1980). *Communication, action and meaning.* New York: Praeger.

Pepitone, A. (1949). Motivation effects in social perception. *Human Relations, 3,* 57–76.

Peters, R. S. (1958). *The concept of motivation.* London: Routledge & Kegan Paul.

Psathas, G. (1979). *Everyday language.* New York: Irvington.

Quine, W. V. O. (1960). *Word and object.* Cambridge, MA: M.I.T. Press.

Rabinow, P., & Sullivan, W. (Eds.). (1979). *Interpretive social science: A reader.* Berkeley: University of California Press.

Reiss, D. (1981). *The family's construction of reality.* Cambridge, MA: Harvard University Press.

Rorty, R. (1979). *Philosophy and the mirror of nature.* Princeton, NJ: Princeton University Press.

Rosaldo, M. (1980). *Knowledge and passion, Ilongot notions of self and social life.* Cambridge, England: Cambridge University Press.

Ryle, G. (1949). *The concept of mind.* London: Hutchinson.

Sabini, J., & Silver, M. (1982). *The moralities of everyday life.* London and New York: Oxford University Press.

Sampson, E. E. (1977). Psychology and the American ideal. *Journal of Personality and Social Psychology, 35,* 767–782.

Sampson, E. E. (1981). Cognitive psychology as ideology. *American Psychologist, 36,* 730–743.

Sampson, E. E. (1983). Deconstructing psychology's subject. *Journal of Mind and Behavior, 4,* 135–164.

Sarbin, T. R. (1984, August). *Emotion: A contextualist view.* Invited address delivered at the meeting of the American Psychological Association, Toronto, Ontario, Canada.

Sarbin, T. R., & Mancuso, J. C. (1980). *Schizophrenia: Medical diagnosis or verdict?* Elmsford, NY: Pergamon.

Sarbin, T. R., & Scheibe, K. E. (Eds.). (1983). *Studies in social identity.* New York: Praeger.

Sassen, G. (1980). Success anxiety in women: A constructivist interpretation of its social significance. *Harvard Educational Review, 50,* 13–24.

Schachter, S. (1964). The interaction of cognitive and physiological determinants of emotional state. In L. Berkowitz (Ed.), *Advances in experimental social psychology* (Vol. 1, pp. 49–81). New York: Academic Press.

Semin, G. R., & Chassein, J. (in press). The relationship between higher order models and everyday conceptions of personality. *European Journal of Social Psychology.*

Shotter, J. (1975). *Images of man in psychological research.* London: Methuen.

Shotter, J., & Burton, M. (1983). Common sense accounts of human action: Descriptive formulations of Heider, Smedslund, & Ossario. In L. Wheeler (Ed.), *Review of personality and social psychology* (Vol. 4, pp. 272–296). Beverly Hills, CA: Sage.

Shweder, R. A., & Miller, J. (1985). The social construction of the person: How is it possible? In K. J. Gergen & K. E. Davis (Eds.), *The social construction of the person.* New York: Springer-Verlag.

Smedslund, J. (1978). Bandura's theory of self-efficacy: A set of common sense theorems. *Scandinavian Journal of Psychology, 19,* 1–14.

Smith, J. (1981). Self as experience in Maori culture. In P. Heelas & A. Lock (Eds.), *Indigenous psychologies* (pp. 145–160). London: Academic Press.

Sullivan, E. V. (1984). *A critical psychology.* New York: Plenum.

Taylor, C. (1971). Interpretation and the sciences of man. *Review of Metaphysics, 25*(1).

Unger, R. K. (1983). Through the looking glass: No wonderland yet! (The reciprocal relationship between methodology and models of reality). *Psychology of Women Quarterly, 8,* 9–32.

Verhave, R., & van Hoorne, W. (1984). The temporalization of the self. In K. J. Gergen & M. M. Gergen (Eds.), *Historical social psychology* (pp. 325–346). Hillsdale, NJ: Erlbaum.

Walkerdine, V. (1984). Developmental psychology and the child-centered pedogogy. In J. Henriques, W. Hollway, C. Urwin, V. Louze, & V. Walkerdine (Eds.), *Changing the subject* (pp. 153–202). London: Methuen.

Watslawick, P. (Ed.). (1984). *The invented reality.* New York: Norton.

Weimer, W. B. (1979). *Notes on the methodology of scientific research.* Hillsdale, NJ: Erlbaum.

Weisstein, N. (1971). Psychology constructs the female. In V. Gornick & B. K. Moran (Eds.), *Women in sexist society* (pp. 96–104). New York: Basic Books.

Wexler, P. (1983). *Critical social psychology.* Boston: Routledge & Kegan Paul.

White, H. (1978). *Tropics of discourse.* Baltimore, MD: Johns Hopkins University Press.

Wittgenstein, L. (1963). *Philosophical investigations* (G. E. M. Anscombe, Trans.). New York: Macmillan.

38

DISCOVERY-ORIENTED PSYCHOTHERAPY RESEARCH: RATIONALE, AIMS, AND METHODS

ALVIN R. MAHRER

In their companion introductions to the special issues on psychotherapy research for the *American Psychologist* and the *Journal of Consulting and Clinical Psychology*, both VandenBos (1986) and Kazdin (1986a) flagged the accelerating breadth of development in this research field over the past four decades. One of these developments, mentioned both inside and outside these special issues, is a small but vigorous interest in what is coming to be known as discovery-oriented psychotherapy research (Elliot, 1983a, 1983b, 1984; Gendlin, 1986; Glaser, 1978; Glaser & Strauss, 1967; Greenberg, 1986; Kazdin, 1986b; Mahrer, 1985, 1988; Rennie, Phillips, & Quartaro, 1988; Rice & Greenberg, 1984; Stiles, Shapiro, & Elliott, 1986; Strupp, 1986).

In this kind of research, the pivotal question is how to study psychotherapy to discover the discoverable, to learn the secrets of psychotherapy. If this question is kept centered, what begins to emerge is an increasing differentiation between research that is discovery-oriented and research that is oriented toward the testing of hypotheses. The differentiation is across the board, from the opening intent to do the research to the design and methodology of the study, and from the framing of the research question to the sense that is made of the findings. The purpose of this article is to introduce discovery-oriented psychotherapy research as an alternative to hypothesis-testing research; to present the rationale, aims, and goals of this approach; to outline the methods in sufficient detail for adoption by psychotherapy researchers; and thereby to stimulate research

Reprinted from the *American Psychologist, 43*, 694–702. (1988).

The author extends his appreciation to Howard M. Schachter, Anastassios Stalikas, and Wayne C. Nadler for assistance in the preparation of this article, and to Robert Elliott, Clara E. Hill, and Donald J. Kiesler for suggesting helpful readings.

that is genuinely enthusiastic, interesting, practical, and conceptually challenging and that allows us to discover what is there to be discovered.

HYPOTHESIS-TESTING RESEARCH

The preponderance of mainstream psychotherapy research is designed to test hypotheses. In the field of psychotherapy, there are at least two main aims of this kind of research, and my thesis is that hypothesis-testing is disappointingly ineffective for both.

The Confirmation or Disconfirmation of Theoretical Propositions

One of the major aims of hypothesis-testing research is to confirm or disconfirm theoretical propositions. The rationale is that a network of theoretical assumptions is logically bound to a set of propositions that provides the empirical basis for the testing of hypotheses (cf. Brodbeck & Feigl, 1968). If the proposition is confirmed, the theory is a little more secure. If the proposition is disconfirmed or refuted (Popper, 1968), the theory may be in trouble.

A serious problem lies in going from the findings to the theoretical proposition and from there to the network of theoretical assumptions, that is, the theory of psychotherapy. Although theoretical propositions may bear some degree of consistency or inconsistency with the findings, rarely if ever does logical necessity include significant modification or abandonment of the theoretical proposition. It is even rarer to find it necessary to significantly modify or abandon the network of theoretical assumptions (Armstrong, 1982; Brush, 1974; Danziger, 1985; Feyerabend, 1975; Gould, 1981; Kuhn, 1962; Lakatos, 1976; Orne, 1969; Popper, 1968; Rosenthal, 1966). "No theory can be proven true by empirical data. And, just as it is impossible to prove a theory, so also is it impossible to prove one false" (Greenwald, Pratkanis, Leippe, & Baumgardner, 1986, p. 226). I know of no established theory of psychotherapy that declared bankruptcy because of research that failed to confirm, disconfirmed, or falsified its theoretical propositions and network of theoretical assumptions; nor is there a logical necessity for that to occur.

Theories of psychotherapy wax and wane because of considerations that have virtually nothing to do with the testing of hypotheses bearing on their theoretical propositions. "It is simply a sad fact that in soft psychology theories rise and decline, come and go, more as a function of baffled boredom than anything else" (Meehl, 1978, p. 807; cf. Feyerbend, 1975; Kuhn, 1962; Mahrer, 1978; Polanyi, 1958). The careers of theories of psychotherapy are under no logical necessity of being seriously affected by the results of hypothesis-testing research.

Indeed, there are solid reasons why no theory of psychotherapy need be in any genuinely grave danger from hypothesis-testing research. "One reason is that the usual use of null hypothesis testing in soft psychology as a means of 'corroborating' substantive theories does not subject the theory to grave risk of refutation *modus tollens,* but only to a rather feeble danger" (Meehl, 1978, p. 821, cf. Greenwald, 1975; Weimer, 1979). Meehl argued convincingly that the use of null hypotheses and significance tests leave the theoretical propositions in a state of virtual imperviousness to the findings.

Second, the space between a theory of psychotherapy and a derived or deduced testable hypothesis is so extensive, loose, and filled with implicit and explicit clauses and conditions that the theory is in no grave danger from whatever findings are obtained. Especially in the field of psychotherapy,

> no theory on its own ever gives rise to predictions of a testable sort. A theory itself is a set of general postulates together with their deductive consequences, and to obtain a testable pre-

diction about a system we need to feed in both statements of the initial conditions of the system and auxiliary hypotheses. (Newton-Smith, 1981, p. 80)

When the findings are in, the theory of psychotherapy is in little danger.

Third, such research is rarely targeted on core theoretical propositions so that the theory of psychotherapy is in any real danger from the findings. Instead, the research is almost inevitably constrained to propositions that the theory of psychotherapy could easily live without.

Fourth, the propositions of theories of psychotherapy are generally so loose, floppy, and rarely, if ever, framed in explicit terms that they are safely immune from any attempts by researchers to disconfirm or refute what is not there to be disconfirmed or refuted (Grünbaum, 1979; Nagel, 1959). Furthermore, the case may be made that whereas there may be some qualified theories in the behavioral and social sciences, in the field of psychotherapy so-called theories are little more than loose connections of beliefs, ideologies, and second rate mythologies whose qualifications as scientific theories are amateur at best (Feyerabend, 1975; Mahrer, 1987, in press).

Fifth, it has probably never happened that the proponents of a theory of psychotherapy have spelled out the research grounds under which they would publicly foreswear their theory or renounce an important theoretical proposition (cf. Newton-Smith, 1981).

Sixth, rival theories are in no genuinely grave danger when pitted against one another by a researcher because it is rare that the rival theories agree that the contestant selected by the researcher are legitimate representatives of the theory. It is also rare that the proponents of rival theories accept the rules of the contest, that the theories agree on the consequences of losing, and especially that the theorists accept the referees and judges. The net result is that the contest is legitimate mainly in the eyes of the researcher while placing the losing theories at little risk.

Seventh, not only are firm believers easily able to refute and discount unfriendly findings of hypothesis-testing research, always managing to stay safely out of range, but their research lieutenants can inevitably be counted on to generate counterbalancing friendly studies.

Indeed, any theory that sponsors research can develop a methodology that ensures friendly results and pronounces alien research as dismissibly and discountably unscientific. The theory is "protected from the effects of contrary evidence because no evidence from outside the charmed methodological circle is accepted as valid . . . methods based on assumptions about the nature of the subject matter only produce observations which must confirm these assumptions" (Danziger, 1985, p. 10). Not only does the theory set the rules for what is to be accepted and rejected as scientific or unscientific, but the theory also can guarantee findings that are hypothesis-friendly by appropriate adjustments and readjustments of the research procedures, by continual reanalyses of the findings until they are friendly, and by persistent redoing of the study until it produces the right results (Armstrong, 1982; Brush, 1974; Gould, 1981; Greenwald et al., 1986; Lakatos, 1976; Orne, 1969; Rosenthal, 1966). "Putting it crudely, if you have enough cases and your measures are not totally unreliable, the null hypothesis will always be falsified, regardless of the truth of the substantive theory" (Meehl, 1978, p. 822). The net result is an increasingly successful partnership between theories of psychotherapy and the confirmatory empirical findings that their research produces. According to Feyerabend (1975), the theory

> is successful not because it agrees so well with the facts; it is successful because no facts have been specified that could constitute a test, and because some such facts have even been removed. Its "success" is *entirely man-made*. . . . This is how empirical "evidence" may be *created* by a procedure which quotes as its justification the very same evidence it has produced. (p. 44)

Behavioral theories of psychotherapy can justifiably claim to be supported by empirical research because they set their own rules for doing theory-friendly studies and for ensuring that they are in no danger from alien hypothesis-testing research.

To make matters even worse, reviewers engage in the confounding game of counting up the number of studies that are in favor and against, adding appropriate weights for carefulness and rigor, and then arriving at pronouncements about the research-supported status of the theoretical proposition.

> The writings of behavioral scientists often read as though they assumed—what is hard to believe anyone would explicitly assert if challenged—that successful and unsuccessful predictions are practically on all fours in arguing for and against a substantive theory . . . as if one could, so to speak, "Count noses," so that if a theory has somewhat more confirming than disconfirming instances, it is in pretty good shape evidentially. . . . We know that this is already grossly incorrect on purely formal grounds, it is a mistake a fortiori. (Meehl, 1967, p. 112; cf. Edelson, 1984; Smith & Glass, 1977)

All in all, theories of psychotherapy are safely impervious from the findings of hypothesis-testing research. Psychoanalysis is in no grave danger from the analysis of variance. I suggest that hypothesis testing is essentially unable to fulfill its self-assigned mission of confirming or disconfirming psychotherapeutic propositions or theories. Indeed, in the field of psychotherapy, the mission itself is fruitless. What is left for hypothesis-testing research in psychotherapy?

Contribution to the Cumulative Body of Knowledge in Psychotherapy

Hypothesis-testing research is justified as contributing to a supposed cumulative body of knowledge in psychotherapy. Picture a scientific body of knowledge containing at least two admissible classes of psychotherapeutic knowledge. One consists of scientifically stamped facts, hard and objective, empirical and tested, the tough data base of psychotherapeutic knowledge. The other class consists of psychotherapeutic laws and principles, canons and tenets. Hypothesis-testing research is apotheosized as the royal gatekeeper, guardian, and contributor to this cumulative body of psychotherapeutic knowledge. My thesis is that hypothesis-testing research is an inadequate means of contributing to an essentially nonexistent and mythical body of psychotherapeutic knowledge. The whole mission is both groundless and fruitless.

One of the problems is that precious little from outside the accepted body of knowledge is granted entry by hypothesis-testing research. Hypothesis testing contributes virtually nothing because most of the hypotheses are already in the body of knowledge, given their legitimacy by one lobby group or another. Nor is the hypothesis in any danger of exclusion by the findings of hypothesis-testing research provided that it is protected by a strong enough lobby.

Kiesler (1971) identified two major classes of hypotheses for psychotherapy researchers, both of which are already part and parcel of the cumulative body of knowledge because of powerful support groups. One class consists of the articulated clinical wisdom of the great thinkers in psychotherapy. "Here we find Freud, Sullivan, Rogers, Wolpe and the like—all originally practitioners of the art—attempting via explicit formulations to bring order out of chaos" (Kiesler, 1971, p. 39). Their followers already accept their formulations as entrenched landmarks in the body of knowledge. In contrast, the self-appointed role of psychotherapy researchers is to lend their weight of research confirmation or disconfirmation to the pieces of accepted knowledge and thereby to show that they either belong or do not belong. The problem is that proponents of these great clinical thinkers will continue to retain their formulated clinical wisdom in the body of psychotherapeutic knowledge, with the findings of hypothesis-testing research as lightweight irrelevancies.

The second class consists of the accepted knowledge base of such traditional academic fields as learning, perception, motivation, cognition, personality, biology, physiology, neurology, and social psychology (Kiesler, 1971). The problem here is that the factual knowledge and theories in these fields are already stamped as a legitimate part of the body of knowledge by powerful scientific lobbies. "The history of the social sciences reveals that whenever a theory showed itself to be promising, a conceptual leap was made from the empirical to the epistemological and the ontological" (Stigliano, 1986, p. 42) The aim of hypothesis-testing researchers is to convince psychotherapists to accept, cherish, respect, and apply to psychotherapy what is already firmly entrenched in the body of knowledge by the powerful lobbies of academic proponents of learning, perception, motivation, cognition, personality, biology, physiology, neurology, and social psychology. All in all, hypothesis-testing research does little more than confirm or fail to confirm the knowledge we already firmly believe we have, as supported by powerful lobby groups.

In fact, if hypothesis-testing research confirms the piece of knowledge, it is perhaps more firmly entrenched in the body of knowledge. If hypothesis-testing research fails to confirm the piece of knowledge, it should be on its way out of the body of knowledge, according to the research catechism, but it is typically unaffected as far as its proponents are concerned. The net result is that hypothesis-testing research either has no serious effect on the body of knowledge in psychotherapy, or far from contributing to a supposed cumulative body of knowledge, the research contributes to a shrinking body of knowledge that we hold with greater confidence. On the basis of hypothesis-testing research, we know less and less, but with higher and higher confidence.

The proof of the pudding is to take a look at the body of knowledge that all our hypothesis-testing has produced. If we look at the larger body of knowledge in the social and behavioral sciences, the pantry is embarrassingly bare (Deutsch, Platt, & Senghors, 1971; Hesse, 1980; Kristol & Bell, 1981; MacIntyre, 1981; Stigliano, 1986); "The National Science Foundation was considering terminating funding for the social and behavioral sciences because no data base has emerged from the decades of studies which have been carried out" (Stigliano, 1986, p. 37).

When one takes a look at the corner of the cumulative body of knowledge that relates to psychotherapy, one finds a loosely conglomerated mixed bag. There are pieces of knowledge authoritatively contributed by the fields of learning, perception, motivation, cognition, personality, biology, physiology, neurology, and social psychology. There is also an ever looser bag of psychotherapeutic truths, axioms, lore, tenets, laws, principles, canons, dictates, constructs, and firmly held beliefs. These vary all the way from the "law of effect" to the psychoanalytic "unconscious" and to such axiomatic truths as "in paranoia there are unconscious conflicts involving homosexual impulses." Even a moderately critical appraisal indicates that the body of scientific psychotherapeutic knowledge is bordering on nonexistent.

Instead of a single grand body of scientific psychotherapeutic knowledge, it is inviting to picture that each psychotherapeutic approach has its own package of cherished truths, dignified as a body of knowledge, with grossly varying weights attached to the findings of hypothesis-testing research, which stands relatively helpless in its assigned task of contributing to any cumulative body of knowledge in psychotherapy.

My conclusion is that hypothesis-testing research is poorly equipped for and disappointingly ineffective either in confirming or disconfirming theoretical propositions or in contributing to the supposed cumulative body of knowledge in psychotherapy. Yet hypothesis-testing is just about all we do. My recommendation is that hypothesis testing be left in the hands of those who can see no alternative and that the balance of researchers adopt the rationale, aims, and methods of discovery-oriented psychotherapy research.

AN ALTERNATIVE APPROACH TO PSYCHOTHERAPY RESEARCH

In the field of psychotherapy, the discovery-oriented approach is only a gleam in the eye of a few psychotherapy researchers (e.g., Elliott, 1983a, 1983b, 1984; Gendlin, 1986; Glaser, 1978;

Glaser & Strauss, 1967; Mahrer, 1985; Rennie et al., 1988; Rice & Greenberg, 1984). Indeed, if one looks at the field of psychotherapy through the eyes of devout hypothesis-testers there is no such thing as discovery-oriented research as a distinctly viable alternative, for all good research can only be hypothesis-testing in one form or another. When hypothesis-testing is done properly it includes discovery. It can include discovery in the form of correlational investigations that may even study multidimensional and factorial relations among variables (Cronbach, 1957; Kiesler, 1971). Hypothesis testing graciously grants a measure of respectability to coming up with (i.e., discovery of) useful hypotheses from naturalistic or single case studies.

> Intensive study of the single case (either controlled or uncontrolled, with or without measurements) is a valuable *source of hypotheses*. . . . Discovery of hypotheses is a legitimate and essential scientific activity. But idiographic study has little place in the confirmatory aspect of scientific activity, which looks for laws applying to individuals generally. (Kiesler, 1971, p. 66)

Hypothesis-testing researchers tend to regard discovery-oriented methods as a somewhat useful secondary tool for the serious work of scientific hypothesis testing. In contrast, my aim is to nominate the discovery-oriented approach as a distinctly viable alternative for psychotherapy researchers, with its own rationale, aims, and methods. I submit that there are at least two aims and purposes of discovery-oriented research that are different from those of hypothesis-testing research (cf. Polkinghorne, 1983). One of these is to provide a closer, discovery-oriented look at psychotherapeutic phenomena, and the other is to discover the relations among psychotherapeutic conditions, operations, and consequences. The aims and purposes of discovery-oriented research thereby are distinct from the confirmation or disconfirmation of theoretical propositions or from contribution to a cumulative body of psychotherapeutic knowledge. Indeed, this "approach does not strive to contribute to any version of a bank of human data containing the cumulative record of eternal verities" (Kremer, 1986, p. 66). The whole basis for designing hypothesis-testing studies revolves around some predetermined, formulated idea or expectation or prediction or hypothesis that one then proceeds to test. "To design an experiment, one must first have an idea which he wishes to test" (Lathrop, 1969, p. 28). In contrast, the whole basis for designing discovery-oriented studies is the intention to learn more; to be surprised; to find out what one does not already expect, predict, or hypothesize; to answer a question whose answer provides something one wants to know but might not have expected, predicted, or hypothesized. To design a discovery-oriented investigation, one must first have a motivating interest in discovering what may be discovered by taking a closer look into psychotherapy or by inquiring into the interconnections among psychotherapeutic conditions, operations, and consequences. Accordingly, the purpose of the balance of this article is to show why and how to carry out this alternative approach to psychotherapy research.

TAKING A CLOSER, DISCOVERY-ORIENTED LOOK

The aim is to take a closer, in-depth look at psychotherapy and to discover what is there to be discovered. There are five steps to be followed by the researcher.

Selecting the Target of the Investigation

The first step is to select some area in psychotherapy into which you want to take a closer look. What psychotherapeutic event or phenomenon excites you, piques your interest, or invites your taking a closer look? What is it that you would like to see in more detail, that you would like to investigate by getting down into it? Think of all the phenomena of psychotherapy, no matter how big and loose or small and tight. Think in terms of simple words rather than technical jargon constructs (such as locus of control, transference, self-efficacy, or ego alienness). Set aside general psychotherapeutic laws or principles or hypotheses. Just let yourself concentrate on whatever interests you enough so that you are drawn to taking a closer look into it.

Would you be interested in taking a closer look at what actually happened in Sigmund Freud's work with patients? If there were recordings of those sessions, I would be fascinated to discover what transpired. I am also interested in taking a closer look at what is going on when patients are in an extremely intense state of feeling and emotion or when patients are in the throes of genuinely impressive change or when patients are recounting incidents from very early childhood. Some of the targets may be big, such as an entire session by Freud. Some of the targets may be small, such as a patient's erupting into a spontaneous outburst of strong, hearty laughter. In any case, the aim is to take a closer look in order to discover what may be there to be discovered.

Obtaining Instances of the Target of the Investigation

The second step is to obtain instances of the target of your investigation, of that area into which you want to take a closer look. Usually this means audiotapes or videotapes of your target. Try to obtain a large number of these tapes, particularly high-grade, fine instances of the target. Sometimes you are limited to one or only a few instances of your target. It would be fortunate to have even a single precious recording of one of Freud's sessions. Some targets are themselves rare or very hard to produce, such as instances of patients undergoing profoundly significant personality change. It is not easy to obtain 50 instances of patients erupting into sudden spontaneous outbursts of strong, hearty laughter. It might be easier to obtain a large number of instances of patients being in an extremely intense state of feeling and emotion, or of patients recounting incidents from very early childhood. Whatever the selected target into which you want to take a closer look, it is helpful to obtain as many and as good instances as you can.

Obtaining an Instrument for Taking a Closer Look

The third step is to obtain (select or develop) an instrument that allows you to take a closer look at whatever target you selected. Some instruments may consist of a procedure. For example, you may get a closer look at moments in which patients have attained high levels of feeling and emotion by the procedure of interviewing the patients and therapists to find out more about those moments (e.g., Elliott, 1984). The instrument might be a tape recorder. Wouldn't it be wonderful to have audiotapes and videotapes of Freud's sessions? Audiotapes and videotapes are useful instruments for taking closer looks. You can use all sorts of technical instruments to get closer looks. For example, you need an instrument that records dreams so that you can get a closer look at the dreams by means of the video dream recorder. You need instruments to measure the exact body location and intensity of a feeling as it occurs in both therapist and patient in the ongoing session.

I rely on category systems that are custom designed to provide a closer look at the selected target of investigation. Suppose that you wanted to take a closer look at what patients are saying and doing during spontaneous outbursts of strong, hearty laughter. Start with a search of the research and clinical literatures to provide some provisional hypotheses. Then obtain a large and representative number of audiotaped excerpts of such instances. With a group of judges, go through each of the excerpts one by one, slowly and carefully describing what the patient is saying and doing in each instance. Use terms that are close to the data and are simple, rather than using high-level constructs wrapped in the jargon of any therapeutic approach. With each succeeding instance, frame provisional categories, refine the categories you have already obtained, reorganize the system on the basis of each new instance against the backdrop of the developing category system complemented by the provisional hypotheses from the literature. In this serially progressive procedure, by the time you and the judges have completed your analysis of a large number of instances, you will have developed a category system that is generated from actual data and is increasingly rigorous and comprehensive. It is a category system of what patients are judged to be saying and doing during moments of spontaneous outbursts of strong, hearty laughter. My colleagues and I have followed this same procedure in developing category systems for taking closer looks at other targets of investigation. For example, one of the more robustly useful is a category system of good moments in psychotherapy—moments of patient change, progress, improvement, movement, and process—that are valued and prized from the perspectives of a broad range of therapeutic approaches (Mahrer, 1985, 1988; Mahrer & Nadler, 1986).

The instrument (e.g., category system) is the means for taking the closer look. It is careful and rigorous enough to keep the researcher honest, and it provides a better quality of data than trying to look into the target without the instrument. Nor is the instrument to be opposed to simple clinical study and analysis because it was born out of clinical study and analysis in the very process of its development.

On the other hand, the kind of instrument you use opens up a particular kind of closer look and reveals a particular class of data. A category system of what patients are saying and doing in moments of strong, hearty laughter will likely reveal nothing about changes in galvanic skin responses or heart rates. A category system of the good moments in psychotherapy sessions provides that kind of data and little else. Whatever instrument you use to take a closer look is limited to its own class of data.

Gathering the Data

The fourth step is to gather the data. Apply the instrument to all the instances of your selected target. If you have plenty of instances, apply the category system to instances that were not used in developing the category system. If you have only a limited number of instances, use a different set of judges and apply the category system to the instances used in constructing the category system. In any case, the application of the category system in a careful and rigorous way will yield the data for taking the closer look. Now you must make discovery-oriented sense of the data.

Making Discovery-Oriented Sense of the Data

It takes a particular attitude or perspective to see what there is to be discovered in the data. All the instrument can do is to organize and display the data in as hard and objective a manner as the instrument is able. Making discovery-oriented sense of the data is the job of the researcher. It calls for some helpful guidelines.

Welcoming receptivity to the discoverable. The clinical researcher is to be exceedingly open to what is new in the data, to what is out of the ordinary, different, unexpected, exceptional, surprising, challenging, disconcerting. The researcher must be vigilant to what does not seem to fit, to what is hard to grasp, organize, explain. By taking this stance, the clinical researcher will be sensitive to the discoverable.

This way of seeing and listening to the data means that the investigator is to be a clinical researcher, with sufficient knowledge of what is ordinary, mainstream, or expected. Indeed, it helps to have a group of independent clinical researchers. The clinical researcher should also be passively naive in taking plenty of time to allow the data to show what is there to be discovered.

This process involves a blend of passive naiveté and knowledgeable understanding in being sensitive to what is new, different, unexpected, exceptional, surprising, and discoverable.

You must scan the data, be open to cues and leads, try out various patternings, attend to repeated instances, organize and reorganize the data, and go back to the data again and again until you receive the discoverable.

Declining traps that mask the discoverable. There are several traps that tend to obfuscate the discoverable. Researchers should decline to mask the discoverable with easy explanations and rushed understandings, especially from their favorite psychotherapeutic approach. Another trap is to lose the discoverable by rising to higher levels of generalization that fit, make sense of, and manage to assimilate the discoverable. A third trap is to bypass the discoverable under central tendencies and normative schemas; statistical means and common themes easily hide the discoverable. Fourth, the researcher should decline the rush toward general laws, truths, and principles. All of these traps are easy and appealing, but they obfuscate the discoverable and are to be declined in the task of making discovery-oriented sense of the data.

By following these five steps, the clinical researcher can take a closer look into psychotherapy, a look that offers a good chance to discover something new. Researchers can take a closer, discovery-oriented look at Freud's actual work with patients, at what may be going on when patients are in an extremely intense state of feeling and emotion or are undergoing profoundly significant personality change, at what patients are saying and doing during spontaneous outbursts of strong, hearty laughter, or at any other events that are of genuine interest to researchers who want to see what may be discovered by taking a closer look into psychotherapy. However, this is only one way of doing discovery-oriented psychotherapy research.

DISCOVERING INTERCONNECTIONS AMONG CONDITIONS, OPERATIONS, AND CONSEQUENCES

There are lots of ways of carving up or imposing a schema or perspective on psychotherapy. The way that is selected in this research approach is to organize psychotherapy into conditions, operations, and consequences (Mahrer, 1985, in press). Furthermore, each of these three terms is taken as referring to more or less specific and concrete events rather than abstractions that are loose and general, and to events that occur in psychotherapy sessions rather than to anything occurring outside of these sessions.

Accordingly, *conditions* refer to the patient in the session, to what the patient is doing and to how the patient is being. The condition is when the patient is on the verge of tears, says that his or her headache is starting to pound, begins to protest and complain in a loud voice, starts the session with a deep sigh, puts the therapist on the spot with a few well-aimed questions, or sinks into a conspicuous silence. Discovery-oriented researchers describe conditions in this way rather than identifying the patient as a borderline, phobic, or incest survivor or as being in the termination phase of treatment.

Operations refer to what the therapist does right here in these statements. The therapist gives an interpretation, tells the patient to say it with more feeling, or provides an empathic reflection. Operations do not refer to supportive therapy, assertion training, or desensitization.

Consequences refer to what the patient does and how the patient is subsequent to the therapist operation. Consequences refer to the patient's outburst of hearty laughter, expression of insightful understanding, or recounting of his or her first day at school. Consequences do not refer to Minnesota Multiphasic Personality Inventory (MMPI) profile or a post-therapy symptom checklist.

The aim of this research is to discover the interconnections among in-therapy conditions, operations, and consequences. In a way, this sounds somewhat like the bellwether question of psychotherapy research, which was nicely articulated by Paul (1967): "*What* treatment, by *whom*, is most effective for *this* individual with *that* specific problem, and under *which* set of circumstances" (p. 111; cf. Kiesler, 1971). This question is widely accepted as the solid foundation of what psychotherapy researchers should be investigating (Parloff, 1979). However, it is not the question asked by discovery-oriented researchers. The smaller difference is that discovery-oriented researchers are examining specifically concrete meanings of conditions, operations, and consequences whose referential meanings are in-session events. The larger difference is that they are engaged in a discovery-oriented search for the interconnections. If one begins with the more or less accepted psychotherapy research question, tightens it to include specifically concrete in-session referential meanings, and encases the modified traditional question in a discovery-oriented framework, one emerges with three general questions for discovering the interconnections among psychotherapeutic conditions, operations, and consequences.

1. Given this *operation*, carried out under this condition, what are the consequences? That is, if the therapist does this operation, when the patient is being this way, what will happen?

2. Given this *consequence*, what operations under what conditions can achieve this consequence? That is, what can the therapist do to effect this desired consequence?

3. Given this *condition*, what operation can achieve this consequence? That is, when the patient is this way, what does the therapist want to achieve, and what does the therapist do to achieve this consequence?

There are three steps in carrying out this research approach: (a) specifying the question, (b) obtaining data, and (c) examining the data.

Specifying the Discovery-Oriented Research Question

The first step is to start with one of the general research questions and to frame a specific discovery-oriented research question.

Given this operation, carried out under this condition, what are the consequences? This is B. F. Skinner's favorite discovery-oriented research question. Skinner "had little use for making hypotheses or predictions about what the effect of a manipulation *ought* to be. You can just make the manipulation and *see* what its effect is" (Mook, 1982, p. 410).

How does the psychotherapy researcher select a manipulation (operation), carried out under some condition, to see what its effect (consequence) is? One way is to begin with cherished therapeutic axioms and convert them into discovery-oriented research questions. Consider this axiom, "When the client focuses on meaningful material, and the therapist provides an empathic reflection, the consequence is enhanced self-exploration." This yields the following research question: When the client focuses on meaningful material, and the therapist provides an empathic reflection, what are the consequences—including enhanced self-exploration? The axiom that "when the patient talks about himself or herself, and the therapist self-discloses, the consequence is enhanced self-disclosure" becomes the following research question: "When the patient talks about himself or herself, and the therapist self-discloses, what are the consequences—including enhanced self-disclosure?" Another axiom is that when there is an appropriate therapeutic relationship, and the therapist offers interpretations, the cumulative consequence is increased insight and understanding. As a research question, this becomes "When there is an appropriate therapeutic relationship, and the therapist offers interpretations, what are the consequences—including increased insight and understanding?"

Another way of framing discovery-oriented research questions is by asking reasonably appealing "what ifs." When a therapist is exasperated with a patient, what if the therapist gives vent to his or her exasperation? When the patient is perched on the scary edge of falling apart, what would the consequences be if the therapist encouraged the patient to go ahead? When the therapist has private thoughts, what would the consequences be if the therapist disclosed them openly and freely?

Given this consequence, what operations under what conditions can achieve this consequence? Proceeding from this general research question to a particular and specific one calls for the researcher's selecting in-session consequences that are impressive, welcomed, desired, and significant, especially those that are taken as indicating therapeutic change, process, movement, progress, or improvement. Given that a patient's persistent headache has now cleared and is gone, what therapist operations under what conditions appear to have been instrumental in achieving this consequence? Given a patient's welcomed increase in self-assuredness, energy and enthusiasm, feeling level, or strength and toughness, what therapist operations under what conditions led to this desirable consequence? The researcher merely specifies a particular consequence, something the patient is or does that is welcomed and desired, and the discovery-oriented research question is in place.

Given this condition, what operation can achieve this consequence? The researcher turns this into a specific research question by identifying some concrete condition (or problem), figuring out the related consequence that is welcomed and desired, and looking for the right operations that can effect that consequence. For example, in the beginning of a session (condition), what therapist operations enable the patient to achieve a state of strong experiencing and feeling (consequence)? When the patient withdraws into an enveloping silence (condition), what therapist operations succeed in lifting the patient out of the silence and into providing useful therapeutic material (consequence)? Greenberg and his colleagues (Greenberg, 1984a) translated this general question into the following specific research question: When a client is in a condition regarded in gestalt therapy as a conflict split, what therapist–client operations are effective in achieving the desired consequence of a resolution of the conflict? Answering this question exemplifies the task analysis method (Greenberg, 1984b) wherein the discovery-oriented target is to identify therapist–client operations for moving from a designated in-therapy condition to a designated in-therapy consequence.

Obtaining the Data

Once the general research question is refined and put into a specific discovery-oriented question, the second step is to obtain the relevant data. Perhaps the best way of obtaining the data is from actual tapes and transcripts of therapists and patients. It is this step that punctuates the need for rich tape libraries in that each of the three general research questions yields specific discovery-oriented research questions whose answers are best provided by a rich tape library (cf. Gendlin, 1986; Mahrer, in press).

Consider three specific questions, each taken from one of the three general questions: (a) When the client focuses on meaningful material, and the therapist provides an empathic reflection, what are the consequences? (b) Given that the patient's persistent headache was extinguished at this point in the session, what therapist operations under what conditions were instrumental in achieving this consequence? (c) In the beginning of a session, what therapist operations enable the patient to achieve a state of strong experiencing and feeling? It seems clear that the most appropriate data for each of the three questions call for a rich library of tapes, yet it is the rare researcher who has access to tapes offering ample instances of the right conditions, operations, and consequences.

One of the three general questions, however, lends itself to manufacturing the data by experimental manipulation. This is the first general question; that is, given this operation, carried out under this condition, what are the consequences? It is feasible, for example, to instruct therapists that when the patient focuses on meaningful material, the therapist is to provide an empathic reflection, or when the therapist is exasperated with the patient, the therapist is to give vent to his or her exasperation. Although data for this first general question may be obtained either by experimental manipulation or through selection from a research tape library, data for the other two questions are beyond experimental manipulation and are best obtained through a research tape library.

In this research, much of the carefulness and rigor lie in specifying the meanings of the terms used in defining the conditions, operations, and consequences. The researcher must be reasonably precise in defining conditions such as "when there is an appropriate therapeutic relationship" or "when a client is in a gestalt conflict split," in defining therapist operations such as self-disclosure or empathic reflections, and in defining consequences such as the extinguishing of a persistent headache or the achievement of a state of strong experiencing and feeling.

Examining the Data to Obtain a Discovery-Oriented Answer

The method of examining the data varies with the general research question. Consider the general research question: Given this consequence, what operations under what conditions can achieve this consequence? For each instance of the target consequence, the method is to examine the antecedent therapist and patient statements, opening the window progressively larger and larger. It is helpful to use a number of independent clinical researchers to examine the antecedent operations and conditions.

A different method is called for in examining the data for the second general question: Given this operation, carried out under this condition, what are the consequences? With a large number of instances, it is helpful to use a category system tailor-made for those consequences according to the guidelines described earlier. The third general question is: Given this condition, what operation can achieve this consequence? Once again, it is useful to have a large number of instances and to use another category system tailor-made from, and for, the therapist (and patient) operations intervening between the conditions and the consequences.

Each of these three methods enables the clinical researcher to examine the data to answer the research question. However, as is required when the researcher takes a closer look into the psychotherapeutic phenomenon, it is important to examine the data so as to be exceedingly open to the discoverable, to what is new, out of the ordinary, different, unexpected, exceptional, or surprising. It is also important for the researcher to be sensitive to and avoid the common traps that bypass, hide, and lose the discoverable. By means of this third step, the clinical researcher examines the data to obtain a discovery-oriented answer to the research question and thereby to discover the interconnections among psychotherapeutic conditions, operations, and consequences.

CONCLUDING IMPLICATIONS

Hypothesis-testing research is essentially inadequate and unproductive for serious confirmation or disconfirmation of the propositions that make up theories of psychotherapy and also for contributing to a purportedly cumulative body of psychotherapeutic knowledge. Nor is hypothesis-testing research useful in discovering what is to be discovered in the field of psychotherapy. Hypothesis testing should be left in the hands of those who see no alternative way of doing psychotherapeutic research; otherwise, it should be abandoned.

Discovery-oriented research is a distinctive alternative whose rationale, aims, and methods contrast sharply with those of hypothesis-testing research. There are two approaches to this research. One consists of providing a closer, discovery-oriented look into psychotherapeutic events and phenomena, and the other consists of the discovery of the interconnections among psychotherapeutic conditions, operations, and consequences. Each of these two kinds of discovery-oriented research has its own characteristic methodology and procedural steps. The challenge is that the development of the field of psychotherapy will benefit more from discovery-oriented than from hypothesis-testing research, and that rigorous and productive discovery-oriented research will unseat hypothesis testing as the scientific means of inquiry in the field of psychotherapy research.

The findings of discovery-oriented research are of prime quality for (a) rigorously scientific theory building in the field of psychotherapeutic conceptualization, (b) generating advances throughout the field of psychotherapeutic practice, (c) opening up new avenues of psychotherapeutic research, and (d) integratively blending theory, practice, and research in the field of psychotherapy. Psychotherapy researchers are encouraged to develop the methodologies and procedures of discovery-oriented psychotherapy research and to adopt this way of discovering what is to be discovered in the field of psychotherapy.

These are the two kinds of research that comprise the discovery-oriented approach to psychotherapy research. Although they both differ from the rationale, aims, and methods of hypothesis-testing research, each has its own characteristic rationale, aims, and steps. Some psychotherapy researchers will remain steadfast in their allegiance to hypothesis testing. Others may assert that discovery-oriented aims and methods are already in place in the larger program of hypothesis testing. Still others may hold that they already do discovery-oriented psychotherapy research, although it may be described in different words. However, for those who are willing to consider discovery-oriented research as a distinctly viable alternative to hypothesis testing, I submit that we are headed toward a new period of discovering what is discoverable in the field of psychotherapy.

REFERENCES

Armstrong, J. S. (1982). Research on scientific journals: Implications for editors and authors. *Journal of Forecasting, 1,* 83–104.

Brodbeck, M., & Feigl, H. (1968). *Reading in the philosophy of the social sciences.* New York: MacMillan.

Brush, S. G. (1974). Should the history of science be rated X? *Science, 193,* 1164–1172.

Cronbach, L. J. (1957). The two disciplines of scientific psychology. *American Psychologist, 12,* 671–684.

Danziger, K. (1985). The methodological imperative in psychology. *Philosophy of the Social Sciences, 15,* 1–13.

Deutsch, K., Platt, J., & Senghors, D. (1971). Predictability in the social sciences. *Science, 107,* 1113–1116.

Edelson, M. (1984). *Hypothesis and evidence in psychoanalysis.* Chicago: University of Chicago Press.

Elliott, R. (1983a). Fitting process research to the practicing psychotherapist. *Psychotherapy: Theory, Research, and Practice, 20,* 47–55.

Elliott, R. (1983b). "That in your hands": A comprehensive process analysis of a significant event in psychotherapy. *Psychiatry, 46,* 113–129.

Elliott, R. (1984). A discovery-oriented approach to significant change events in psychotherapy: Interpersonal Process Recall and Comprehensive Process Analysis: In L. N. Rice & L. S. Greenberg (Eds.), *Patterns of change* (pp. 249–286). New York: Guilford.

Feyerabend, P. (1975). *Against method.* London: Verso.

Gendlin, E. T. (1986). What comes after traditional psychotherapy research? *American Psychologist, 41,* 131–136.

Glaser, B. G. (1978). *Theoretical sensitivity: Advances in the methodology of grounded theory.* Mill Valley, CA: The Sociology Press.

Glaser, B. G., & Strauss, A. (1967). *The discovery of grounded theory: Strategies for qualitative research.* Chicago: Aldine.

Gould, S. J. (1981). *The mismeasure of man.* New York: Norton.

Greenberg, L. S. (1984a). A task analysis of interpersonal conflict resolution. In L. N. Rice & L. S. Greenberg (Eds.), *Patterns of change* (pp. 67–123). New York: Guilford.

Greenberg, L. S. (1984b). Task analysis: The general approach. In L. N. Rice & L. S. Greenberg (Eds.), *Patterns of change* (pp. 124–148). New York: Guilford.

Greenberg, L. S. (1986). Change process research. *Journal of Consulting and Clinical Psychology, 54,* 4–9.

Greenwald, A. G. (1975). Consequences of prejudice against the null hypothesis. *Psychological Bulletin, 82,* 1–20.

Greenwald, A. G., Pratkanis, A. R., Leippe, M. R., & Baumgardner, M. H. (1986). Under what conditions does theory obstruct research progress? *Psychological Review, 93,* 216–229.

Grünbaum, A. (1979). Is Freudian psychoanalytic theory pseudo-scientific by Karl Popper's criterion of demarcation? *American Philosophical Quarterly, 16,* 131–141.

Hesse, M. (1980). Theory and value in the social sciences. In P. Petit & C. Hookway (Eds.)., *Action and interpretation* (pp. 1–16). New York: Cambridge University Press.

Kazdin, A. E., (1986a). Editor's introduction to the special issue. *Journal of Consulting and Clinical Psychology, 54,* 3.

Kazdin, A. E. (1986b). Comparative outcome studies of psychotherapy: Methodological issues and strategies. *Journal of Consulting and Clinical Psychology, 54,* 95–105.

Kiesler, D. J. (1971). Experimental designs in psychotherapy research. In A. E. Bergin & S. L. Garfield (Eds.), *Handbook of psychotherapy and behavior change: An empirical analysis* (pp. 36–74). New York: Wiley.

Kremer, J. W. (1986). The human science approach as discourse. *Saybrook Review, 6,* 65–105.

Kristol, I., & Bell, D. (1981). *The crisis in economic theory.* New York: Basic Books.

Kuhn, T. (1962). *The structure of scientific revolutions.* Chicago: University of Chicago Press.

Lakatos, I. (1976). *Proofs and refutations.* London, England: Cambridge University Press.

Lathrop, R. G. (1969). *Introduction to psychological research: Logic, design, analysis.* New York: Harper & Row.

MacIntyre, A. (1981). *After virtue.* Notre Dame, IN: University of Notre Dame Press.

Mahrer, A. R. (1978). *Experiencing: A humanistic theory of psychology and psychiatry.* New York: Brunner/Mazel.

Mahrer, A. R. (1985). *Psychotherapeutic change: An alternative approach to meaning and measurement.* New York: Norton.

Mahrer, A. R. (1987). These are the components of any theory of psychotherapy. *Journal of Integrative and Eclectic Psychotherapy, 6,* 28–31.

Mahrer, A. R. (1988). Research and clinical applications of "good moments" in psychotherapy. *Journal of Integrative and Eclectic Psychotherapy, 1,* 81–93.

Mahrer, A. R. (in press). *The integration of psychotherapies: A guide for practicing psychotherapists.* New York: Human Sciences Press.

Mahrer, A. R., & Nadler, W. P. (1986). Good moments in psychotherapy: A preliminary review, a list, and some promising research avenues. *Journal of Consulting and Clinical Psychology, 54,* 10–16.

Meehl, P. E. (1967). Theory-testing in psychology and physics: A methodological paradox. *Philosophy of Science, 34,* 103–115.

Meehl, P. E. (1978). Theoretical risks and tabular asterisks: Sir Karl, Sir Ronald, and the slow progress of soft psychology. *Journal of Consulting and Clinical Psychology, 46,* 806–834.

Mook, D. G. (1982). *Psychological research: Strategy and tactics.* New York: Harper & Row.

Nagel, E. (1959). Methodological issues in psychoanalytic theory. In S. Hook (Ed.), *Psychoanalysis, scientific method, and philosophy* (pp. 38–56). New York: Grove Press.

Newton-Smith, W. H. (1981). *The rationality of science.* London: Routledge & Kegan Paul.

Orne, M. T. (1969). Demand characteristics and the concept of quasi-controls. In R. Rosenthal & R. L. Rosnow (Eds.), *Artifact in behavioral research* (pp. 97–128). New York: Academic Press.

Parloff, M. B. (1979). Can psychotherapy research guide the policy-maker? *American Psychologist, 34,* 296–306.

Paul, G. L. (1967). Strategy of outcome research in psychotherapy. *Journal of Consulting Psychology, 31,* 109–118.

Polanyi, M. (1958). *Personal knowledge: Towards a post-critical philosophy:* Chicago: University of Chicago Press.

Polkinghorne, D. (1983). *Methodology for the human sciences.* Albany, NY: State University of New York Press.

Popper, K. (1968). *The logic of scientific discovery.* London: Hutchinson.

Rennie, D. L., Phillips, J. R., & Quartaro, G. K. (1988). Grounded theory: A promising approach to conceptualization in psychology? *Canadian Psychology, 29,* 139–150.

Rice, L. N., & Greenberg, L. S. (1984). *Patterns of change.* New York: Guilford.

Rosenthal, R. (1966). *Experimenter effects in behavioral research.* New York: Appleton.

Smith, M. L., & Glass, G. V. (1977). Meta-analysis of psychotherapy outcome studies. *American Psychologist, 32,* 752–760.

Stigliano, A. (1986). An ontology for the human sciences. *Saybrook Review, 6,* 33–63.

Stiles, W. A., Shaprio, D. A., & Elliott, R. (1986). "Are all psychotherapies equivalent?" *American Psychologist, 41,* 165–180.

Strupp, H. H. (1986). Psychotherapy: Research, practice, and public policy (How to avoid dead ends). *American Psychologist, 41,* 120–130.

VandenBos, G. R. (1986). Psychotherapy research: A special issue. *American Psychologist, 41,* 111–112.

Weimer, E. B. (1979). *Notes on the methodology of scientific research.* Hillsdale, NJ: Erlbaum.

39

TOWARD AN IDIOTHETIC PSYCHOLOGY OF PERSONALITY

JAMES T. LAMIELL

Within the introductory pages of most personality texts, one often finds some statement to the effect that consensus is lacking in the field on many issues. The mere existence of personality texts, however, and thus of an identifiable subdiscipline of psychology, suggests that at least some very basic concerns are shared by all or most personality theorists, concerns that therefore define the overriding (i.e., metatheoretical) objectives of the scientific study of personality. Based on his consideration of a wide variety of personality theories, Levy (1970) suggests that these basic concerns might reasonably be defined as follows:

> Colloquially, it might be said that in personality we are interested in learning the best way to describe what kind of a person a man is, how he got that way, what keeps him that way, what might make him change, and how we might use all this to explain why he behaves as he does and predict how he will behave in the future. (p. 29)

This article is predicated on the assumption that Levy's remarks do indeed identify a set of basic concerns that are (and have long been) widely shared among personality theorists. With this in mind, I argue below that the individual differences research paradigm, which has thoroughly dominated empirical personality research throughout the present century, is fundamentally inadequate for the purposes of a science of personality. The argument, in a nutshell, is that the assessment of differences between individuals on various common attributes, and the study

Reprinted from the *American Psychologist, 36,* 276–289. (1981).

For their reactions to countless earlier versions of this work, the author is especially grateful to the following individuals: Gerald Clore, Michael Coles, Donald Fiske, Mark Foss, Leslie Lamiell, Frank Landy, Thomas Lapic, Joseph McGrath, Leon Rappoport, Joseph Rychlak, Edward Seidman, Harry Triandis, Steve Trierweller, and Robert Wyer. The author is also grateful to the anonymous reviewers of earlier versions, many of whose criticisms were very helpful.

of the stabilities (and instabilities) of those differences over time and across situations, fails to confront what is clearly the most basic problem of all within the discipline: the development of a framework for empirically *describing* the personality of any given individual. Failing in this regard, it is difficult to see how individual differences research could possibly be adequate for addressing the remaining metatheoretical issues identified by Levy (1970), however useful it may be for other purposes.

After developing this argument below, I propose an alternative paradigm for the scientific study of personality. For lack of a better term, but for reasons that will become apparent, this proposed alternative has been labeled *idiothetic.* Without overly anticipating the later discussion, it suffices to note here that this term is intended to suggest an orientation in which (a) the problem of personality description would be approached in an explicitly idiographic manner (cf. Allport, 1962) and in which (b) nomothetic principles would be sought with respect to questions of personality development.

THE NEED FOR AN ALTERNATIVE TO THE INDIVIDUAL DIFFERENCES PARADIGM

As just mentioned, the most basic (though clearly not the only) problem for a science of personality is that of empirically describing the personalities of individuals, that is, identifying those qualities, attributes, or characteristics which are manifested by individuals at certain levels with some degree of regularity or consistency over time and across situations. To see why individual differences research does not and cannot resolve this basic problem, it will be helpful to review briefly the essential features of such research. This discussion will also facilitiate the later presentation of the proposed alternative framework for the study of personality.

Brief Overview of the Individual Differences Strategy

Individual differences research typically begins with the investigator's attempt to measure the status of each of a number of persons on some underlying attribute of a set of empirical observations. This process can be formally described in terms of the following general model:

$$S_{pa} = \underset{i=1}{\overset{m}{f}} (V_{pi})(R_{ia}), \tag{1}$$

where S_{pa} refers to the raw score assigned to person p to represent his or her status on some underlying attribute a, V_{pi} refers to a variable i in terms of which some empirical statements about person p can be expressed, and R_{ia} refers to the relevance of the information contained in variable i to attribute a. Equation 1 thus states that the score assigned to person p to represent his or her status on attribute a is some function (traditionally additive) of m empirical statements about person p, each of which is weighted by its presumed relevance to a.

The number and nature of the V_is depends, of course, on the particular assessment procedure in use. For example, they might consist of coded responses to projective test stimuli, check marks on the items of a self-report inventory, observer ratings on m different variables, or direct observations on those variables. Moreover, observations on the V_is might be recorded categorically (e.g., true/false, occurred/did not occur) or continuously (e.g., on scales ranging from "strongly agree" to "strongly disagree" or from "occurred very frequently" to "did not occur at all").

As Equation 1 indicates, there must also be some implicit or explicit definition of the relevance of the information contained in each V_i to the attribute being measured (cf. Bem &

Allen, 1974; Bem & Funder, 1978; Funder, 1980). These "relevance values" can be determined intuitively, deduced rationally from a theory, or defined according to strictly empirical criteria (cf. Hase & Goldberg, 1967). Examples of the latter would include the loadings defined for the V_is on the basis of a factor analysis of their intercorrelations or the scale values of the V_is defined on the basis of a multidimensional scaling analysis of pairwise (dis)similarity judgments (cf. Shweder, 1975). In essence, the R_{ia} values of Equation 1 reflect the process of abstraction that is normally an integral part of personality measurement (cf. Goldfried & Kent, 1972). That is, they indicate the degree to which a given V_i is presumed to "contain" or "reveal" the underlying attribute being measured.

It should be noted here that while several possibilities exist for interpreting the S_{pa} value assigned to any one individual (Cattell, 1944; Norman, 1967), the interpretation implicit in individual differences research is that "all meaning for a given score of a person derives from comparing his score with those of other persons" (Kleinmuntz, 1967, p. 45). Although slightly oversimplified, this means that single S_{pa} values are interpreted in terms of contrasts of the general sort ($S_{pa} - S_{p'a}$), where $S_{p'a}$ refers, collectively, to the measured status of persons other than person p on attribute a.[1] Contrasts of this kind are greatly facilitated by (if not strictly dependent on) the use of standardized "tests," that is, procedures whereby all of the persons in one's sample are scored on the same V_is and whereby the R_{ia} values applied to the V_is are held constant across persons.

Having generated data that reflect differences between individuals along some common attribute a, an investigator normally seeks to determine the stability of those differences over time and across situations. Empirical evidence that speaks to this question, which might be presented in the form of reliability and validity coefficients, omega-square ratios, and/or coefficients of generalizability (cf. Golding, 1975), has long been widely accepted as (a) grounds for generalizations about the degree of temporal/transsituational consistency with which the individuals assessed have manifested the attribute in question and, thus, as (b) grounds for an inference concerning the relevance or irrelevance of that attribute to a description of the personalities of those individuals.

There can be little doubt that this orientation toward the basic problem of personality description has been and continues to be widely endorsed by personality investigators.[2] The rationale just described was, after all, precisely the one on which Mischel (1968) based his highly influential discussion of the evidence relevant to the critical presumption inherent within the very concept of personality: the "consistency of particular predispositions *within any individual*" (Mischel, 1968, p. 9, italics added).

Similarly, and with explicit references to the validity coefficients that Mischel (1968) and many others have brought to bear on the issue, Bem and Allen (1974) comment on the "sharp discrepancy between our intuitions, which tell us that *individuals* do in fact display pervasive cross-situational consistences in their behavior, and the vast empirical literature, which tells us

[1]On infrequent occasions, some investigatorts have explored the possibilities offered by "ipsative" measurement, in which the score assigned to an individual on a given attribute is interpreted by contrasting it either with the scores assigned to that same individual on other attributes (cf. Block, 1957; Edwards, 1959; Heilbrun, 1963) or with the scores assigned to that individual on the same attribute at different points in time (cf. Baldwin, 1942, 1946). However, ipsative measurement has never been widely accepted as an adequate basis for scientific personality research (cf. Beck, 1953; Eysenck, 1954; Falk, 1956; Nunnally, 1967) and, as a result, has never played a very prominent role in the literature.

[2]It is worth noting here that even those studies which have used individualized assessment devices, such as role construct repertory (REP) tests and Q-sorts, have tended to end in the assessment and study of individual differences. For example, the information contained in REP test protocols has been used to define individual differences in such attributes as cognitive complexity (Crockett, 1965) and cognitive differentiation/integration (Landfield, 1976). Similarly, Q-sort protocols have been used in personality research as the basis for identifying typological or dimensional differences between persons (cf. Block, 1961; Stephenson, 1953). An excellent discussion of this literature can be found in Tyler (1978).

that they do not" (pp. 507–508, italics added). Bem and Allen go on to suggest that findings more consonant with our intuitions—that is, higher validity coefficients—can be obtained in individual differences research, provided that the investigator is willing to abandon the assumption that any single attribute will be relevant to a description of the personalities of all individuals. An extension of this line of thinking can be found in the recent work by Kenrick and Stringfield (1980).

The Bem and Allen proposal has not, of course, been the only major response to the issues raised by Mischel (1968). Some personologists have emphasized the need for improved theorizing and more sophisticated procedures for assessing individual differences (see, e.g., Alker, 1972; Block, 1968, 1971, 1977; Epstein, 1979; Hirschberg, 1978; Hogan, DeSoto, & Solano, 1977; McGowan & Gormly, 1976; Block, Note 1). Others have stressed the importance of studying the interactive variables on behavior (e.g., Argyle & Little, 1972; Bowers, 1973; Buss, 1977; Ekehammar, 1974; Endler & Magnusson, 1976; Magnusson & Endler, 1977; Mischel, 1973, 1977, 1979).

Whatever improvements of or departure from classical personology might be reflected in the relatively recent developments just discussed, there is no indication in the current literature of any real departure from the basic notion that gave rise to those developments in the first place, namely, that empirical evidence concerning the stability of differences between individuals on common attributes (a) will adequately support generalizations about the degree to which individuals are consistent in their manifestations of those attributes and (b) therefore is directly relevant to the problem of describing the personalities of individuals. Indeed, the arguments developed in the above-cited literature would seem, if anything, to have reinforced most personality investigators' beliefs in the essential correctness of this notion.

The Need for an Alternative to the Individual Differences Strategy

One important assumption on which traditional individual differences research has been based is that it will ultimately lead to the isolation of those (presumably few) attributes that are necessary and sufficient to describe the personality of any given individual (cf. Mehrabian & O'Reilly, 1980). As is well-known, the validity of this assumption has been called into question from time to time during the past several decades (Allport, 1937, 1962, 1966, 1967; Bem & Allen, 1974; Kenrick & Stringfield, 1980; Rosenzweig, 1950, 1951, 1952, 1958; Tyler, 1959, 1978).

I make no attempt in the present article, however, to recapitulate the arguments developed by those authors. The vast majority of personality investigators have been "unimpressed" (Sanford, 1963, p. 547) by the arguments in the past (cf. Beck, 1953; Eysenck, 1954; Falk, 1956; Holt, 1962; Kleinmuntz, 1967; Nunnally, 1967), and there is no compelling reason to suspect any imminent reversal of this trend. The discussion that follows focuses instead on a much more serious problem, namely, the previously discussed rationale for determining the relevance of particular attributes to a description of the personalities of individuals.

It was noted earlier that for most personologists the problem of describing an individual's personality is essentially one of identifying those qualities or attributes that he or she manifests with some degree of regularity over time and across situations. The reliability and validity coefficients (as well as omega-square ratios and generalizability coefficients) generated by individual differences research do not confront this problem, and it is this basic fact that undermines the adequacy of such research for the purposes of a science of personality.

All of the so-called personality coefficients just mentioned index, in one way or another, the degree of consistency with which selected attributes are manifested by *groups* of individuals.

In the last analysis, it is the simple fact that all of those coefficients are *aggregate* indices, computed on the basis of data summed *across* individuals, that virtually precludes their appropriateness as grounds on which to infer anything about the consistency or inconsistency of any *one* individual (cf. Epstein, 1980). Indeed, such an inference could be justified only under the rare (if not altogether nonexistent) circumstances when the personality coefficient is perfect (i.e., unity) because it is only then that the degree of consistency (in relative position on some attribute) manifested by the group of individuals happens to directly reflect the degree of consistency (in relative position) manifested by any given individual in the group.

Obviously, the personality coefficients generated in individual differences research are rarely, if ever, perfect, and there is little reason to believe that their deviations from unity can be entirely attributed to error in the measurement of the attribute(s) in question. However, personality investigators have long maintained the view that *whatever* its size, a conventional personality coefficient serves as grounds for a generalization about the consistency or inconsistency of the individuals in one's sample with respect to the attribute(s) studied.

This view is simply erroneous. In fact, a personality coefficient that deviates for any systematic reason from 1.00 is prima facie evidence that the individuals in one's sample were not *equally* consistent (or inconsistent) in their manifestations of the attribute(s) in question. Consequently, such a coefficient could not possibly support any inference about the consistency or inconsistency of those individuals *in general.* It merely reflects the (in)consistency of the individuals in the aggregate—as a group—which is an entirely different matter (for a concrete empirical illustration of this point, see Lamiell & Trierweiler, Note 2).

If one agrees that (a) the most basic problem in the science of personality is to develop an adequate means of describing the personality of any given individual and that (b) to describe an individual's personality is to identify those qualities or attributes that he or she manifests at certain levels with some degree of regularity over time and across situations, then it should be clear why individual differences research fails to confront the most basic problem in the science of personality. Given a reliability coefficient, validity coefficient, omega-square ratio, or generalizability coefficient that deviates from unity for any systematic reason, *it is simply not possible to tell* how consistent or inconsistent any one individual was in the levels at which he or she has manifested the underlying attribute in question. Consequently, it is not possible to determine, for any one individual, whether or not (or to what degree) the attribute in question is relevant to a description of his or her personality.

It is interesting to note that the ambiguities of conventional personality coefficients in this regard have been hinted at in the past in the writings of other authors (Baldwin, 1942, 1946; Block, 1971; Carlson, 1971; Epstein, 1979). Unfortunately, the problem has yet to be satisfactorily resolved. Contemporary personality researchers continue to interpret these coefficients as if they were based on or conveyed information about (in)consistency at the level of the individual (see, e.g., Epstein, 1979, pp. 1105–1106; Kenrick & Stringfield, 1980, p. 93; Zanna, Olson, & Fazio, 1980, pp. 437–438). Moreover, the few departures from the use of such coefficients that can be found in the literature actually change the original question in subtle but important ways.

For example, in his recent study of stability in behavior, Epstein (1979) reports (in addition to conventional reliability coefficients) correlations between attributes within individuals over time. Such intrasubject correlations can, as Epstein points out, reveal the pattern of covariation between pairs of attributes within an individual. They do not, however, reflect (in)consistencies in the degree to which that individual manifests any one of the attributes, which was the original question.

A high intrasubject correlation is, by definition, evidence of variability—not consistency—within an individual on two attributes over measurement occasions (on what grounds, therefore, can one claim that either of the two attributes is pertinent to a description of that individual's personality?). Moreover, a low intrasubject correlation could mean that an individual was highly variable on two attributes in ways that did not happen to coincide *or* that the individual was highly consistent on one or both attributes. In the limiting case, perfect consistency in the manifestation of one or both attributes would result in a zero intrasubject correlation for that pair of attributes.

In short, intrasubject correlations such as those reported by Epstein (1979) are no more adequate than conventional (i.e., intersubject) personality coefficients for the purpose of identifying those attributes that are manifested by individuals with some degree of consistency over time and across situations.[3]

Given the inadequacy of the individual differences paradigm with respect to the basic problem of personality description,[4] it is difficult to see how research conducted within this paradigm can adequately address the remaining metatheoretical issues identified by Levy (1970). How can empirical research that does not even describe the personalities of individuals possibly illuminate the process of personality development or, consequently, the way in which an understanding of that process could be used to explain and predict an individual's behavior? Based on what I have presented thus far, I believe that individual differences research is fundamentally ill suited for the pursuit of these objectives and that some alternative paradigm for the scientific study of personality is therefore needed.

Redistinguishing Differential Psychology From Personality Psychology

Does the above discussion imply that individual differences research has no utility whatsoever? Certainly not. The information contained in reliability, validity, and generalizability coefficients (as well as omega-square ratios) can be of great utility when one's objective is specifically to account for individual *differences* in various domains of human activity. This was precisely the objective in the early days of mental testing, at which time and for which purposes the technology of individual differences research was originally developed (cf. Mischel, 1976; Tyler, 1978).

The above discussion does suggest, however, that it would be very worthwhile to revive a distinction which has unfortunately become rather obscured over the years: that between *differential* psychology (cf. Anastasi, 1976) and *personality* psychology. The basic task of the former can be viewed as one of identifying and validating individual differences *constructs,* that is, concept-measurement method units (Campbell & Fiske, 1959). To the extent that the differential psychologist can show that an individual differences construct is both reliable and valid (or generalizable), he or she succeeds in demonstrating that within some specified domain of behavior, it is possible to predict or "postdict," with a degree of error that can be specified only in the aggregate (i.e., "the long run"), the relative performances of "some, most, or all of the people some, most, or 'an awful lot' of the time" (cf. Bem & Allen, 1974; Epstein, 1979; Kenrick & Stringfield, 1980). Note that to the differential psychologist, the concepts of reliability, validity,

[3]Nor can this problem be satisfactorily resolved in terms of Q-correlations based on attribute profiles obtained for single individuals on different measurement occasions (cf. Block, 1961, 1971; Harris, 1980). Such correlations can be used to address the question of (in)consistency at the level of the individual with respect to a *set* of attributes or characteristics. Again, however, this is rather different from the question of (in)consistency at the level of the individual with respect to any *one* attribute or characteristic.

[4]As a way of emphasizing my point, the reader is invited to reflect briefly on the results of three major studies recently reported in the personality literature (Epstein, 1979; Harris, 1980; Kenrick & Stringfield, 1980). As carefully as these studies were designed, executed, and reported, it is still not possible to tell on the basis of the results presented how (in)consistent any one of the subjects in any of the studies was with respect to any one of the attributes investigated.

and generalizability refer to properties of the individual differences constructs, and one establishes these properties with data aggregated *across* persons.

To address the basic problem of empirical personality description, however, an investigator must be able to detect temporal and transsituational consistencies *within* persons, that is, at the level of the individual. By mistaking empirical evidence that reflects the properties of individual differences constructs for evidence concerning consistencies and inconsistencies at the level of the individual, personality investigators have completely underminded their ability to detect the latter.

The central metatheoretical concerns of personality psychology cannot be addressed with empirical research aimed at determining the properties of individual differences constructs. The mere labeling of these constructs with personalitylike terms (e.g., friendliness, dominance, etc.) in no way alters this fact. It is for this reason that a clear distinction between differential psychology and personality psychology should be maintained.

The individual differences research paradigm is well suited to the concerns of differential psychology. The remainder of this article is devoted to the presentation of an alternative research paradigm that is at least formally suited to the concerns of scientific personality psychology.

TOWARD AN IDIOTHETIC PSYCHOLOGY OF PERSONALITY

The framework for personality research to be proposed here is grounded in the basic notion that an individual's personality is best described in terms of information about what that person tends to do—not in direct contrast with what others tend to do, but in direct contrast with what that person tends *not* to do but *could* do (cf. Lamiell, 1980; Lamiell, Foss, Cavenee, 1980; Shweder, 1980). In the discussion that follows, a formal measurement rationale consistent with this basic notion is presented. Subsequently, I consider that major implications of adopting this general orientation as the basis for scientific personality research.

A Formal Rationale for Idiographic Measurement

I noted earlier that any empirically based procedure for operationally defining an individual's status on some underlying attribute of a set of observations can be described in terms of the following general model:

$$S_{pa} = \underset{i=1}{\overset{m}{f}} (V_{pi})(R_{ia}). \tag{1}$$

This model is applicable in the present context as well. No less here than in individual differences measurement, one's measured status on some attribute a is empirically defined as some function of m empirical statements about person p, each of which is weighted by its presumed relevance of which is weighted by its presumed relevance to a.

It is at this point, however, that the present approach and the individual differences view part company. The crucial difference between the two lies in the nature of the contrasts by which single S_{pa} values are given meaning. As we saw earlier, the logic of individual differences measurement is such that the meaning of the score assigned to any one person depends in part on the scores assigned to other persons. Under the present rationale, however, the meaning of a single S_{pa} value is directly dependent on the extreme alternative values that could *possibly* be assigned to person p within the constraints imposed by the measurement operation itself. A concrete, if greatly over-simplified, example may help to clarify what is being argued here (an application of this approach to more complex data has been presented by Lamiell & Trierweiler, Note 2).

Suppose that the 11 items shown in Table 1 have been sampled by an investigator to represent a domain of activities that adolescents of high school age engage in. (Note that the term *sampled* is used here. It is extremely unlikely that an investigator would ever be able to deal, in practice, with a complete domain of alternative possible activities.) In the context of Equation 1, this set of 11 items would constitute the V_i component.

Suppose further that in the view of either the investigator or a given adolescent (depending on whose perspective is being taken in the research), the activities referred to in these 11 items were construed in terms of the attribute "compliant versus rebellious" and that the coordinates of the activities on this underlying attribute have been defined (e.g., on the basis of a multidimensional scaling of pairwise similarity judgments) as in the middle column of Table 1. These coordinates would operationally define the R_{ia} component of Equation 1.

Finally, suppose that some hypothetical adolescent I shall call "Mary" reports her activity over a given week as in the third column of Table 1.

By arbitrarily coding Mary's *yes* responses as 1 and her *no* responses as 0, the obtained information about Mary with respect to the 11 activities can be quantitatively represented. Applying Equation 1 to these data (and assuming the traditional additive integration function), one can see that Mary's protocol yields in this instance an S_{pa} value of .61. In effect, this value

TABLE 1
Illustrative Application of Proposed Measurement Rationale

Perceived behavioral alternatives	Conceptualization of perceived behavioral alternatives	Recorded behavior over a given week
1. Drinking beer/liquor	−.24	No (0)
2. Engaging in premarital sex	−.20	No (0)
3. Studying/reading	.18	Yes (1)
4. Participating in extracurricular activities	.32	Yes (1)
5. Engaging in acts of vandalism	−.26	No (0)
6. Doing nothing in particular	−.23	Yes (1)
7. Smoking marijuana	−.28	No (0)
8. Participating in church-related activities	.36	No (0)
9. Skipping school	−.28	No (0)
10. Shoplifting	−.29	No (0)
11. Participating in volunteer work in community	.34	Yes (1)

Note: Assuming an additive integration function, the application of Equation 1 to these data yields an S_{pa} value of .61 (see text for details). The data are based on a study by Lamiell, Foss, and Cavenee (1980).

summarizes the obtained information about Mary with respect to a set of empirical referents for the attribute "compliant versus rebellious."

Nothing in what has been said thus far runs contrary to the conventions of individual differences measurement. Under the rationale proposed here, however, the meaning of the .61 value obtained by Mary would not be defined with reference to the values obtained by other persons using the same measurement operations. Rather, the value's meaning would be defined with reference to the extreme *alternative* S_{pa} values (denoted $S'_{pa\ max}$ and $S'_{pa\ min}$) that could *possibly* have been assigned to Mary within the constraints imposed by the measurement operation itself.

Given (a) the sample of activities (b) the dichotomous scoring of available information regarding these activities, (c) the specification of particular relevance values for these activities, and (d) the use of an additive integration function, one can see that in the present example Mary might have been as "compliant" as 1.20 or as "rebellious" as -1.78. The former value would have been obtained had Mary reported *yes* for Activities 3, 4, 8, and 11 and *no* for Activities 1, 2, 5, 6, 7, 9, and 10. The latter value would have been obtained for the exact opposite response pattern.

Having defined the maximum and minimum values that can possibly be obtained on a measure of some underlying attribute of a set of empirical observations, an individual's status with respect to that attribute on any given measurement occasion can be formally expressed as follows:

$$I_{pa} = \frac{S_{pa} - S'_{pa\ min}}{S'_{pa\ max} - S'_{pa\ min}}, \tag{2}$$

where I_{pa} refers to the idiographically defined status of person p on attribute a, S_{pa} is defined according to Equation 1, and $S'_{pa\ max}$ and $S'_{pa\ min}$ are defined in the manner just discussed.

Under the terms of this measurement model, $S'_{pa\ min}$ serves as the functional zero point on the scale used to operationally define attribute a. The absolute difference between S_{pa} and $S'_{pa\ min}$ thus defines the deviation of an individual's protocol from the functional zero point, and the absolute difference between $S'_{pa\ max}$ and $S'_{pa\ min}$ defines the length of the scale. The ratio of these two differences thus provides a quantitative expression of the degree to which an individual's protocol reflects some attribute a, relative to how much that protocol *could* have reflected attribute a given the constraints imposed by the measurement operation itself. In short, Equation 2 expresses the status of an individual on a given measurement occasion with respect to attribute a—not in contrast with the status of others on attribute a, but instead with reference to what his or her measured status could possibly have been given the procedure for measuring attribute a.

In this example, the absolute difference between Mary's obtained S_{pa} value (.61) and $S'_{pa\ min}$ (-1.78) is equal to 2.39. This quantity expresses the deviation of Mary's reported activity pattern from the functional zero point of the scale. The absolute difference between $S'_{pa\ max}$ and $S'_{pa\ min}$ is 2.98, and this quantity defines the length of the scale. The ratio of these two quantities is .802, and it is this value that would be used in the present perspective to define Mary's status over the week in question with respect to the attribute "compliant versus rebellious."

In effect, what has just been presented is a formal rationale for idiographic personality measurement (cf. Allport, 1962; see also Cattell's [1944] discussion of "interactive measurement," which he distinguishes from both normative and ipsative measurement). It is a rationale by which the measured status of an individual on a single attribute at a given point in time hinges entirely on information available for *that* individual at *that* point in time with respect to a set of empirical referents for *that* attribute.

With the above discussion as "spadework," we are now in a position to consider the major implications of adopting idiographic measurement as the foundation for a science of personality.

Dispensing With the Comparison of Individuals Along Common Attributes

Perhaps the most obvious implication of the measurement rationale illustrated above is that it would enable an investigator to dispense completely with the comparison of individuals along common attributes. Technically, the reason for this is that the meaning of the S_{pa} value assigned to an individual at a given point in time is not derived by comparing it with $S_{p'a}$ values, that is, with the measured status of other persons on the same attribute. Consequently, there is no need to assume that attribute *a* is applicable to all—or even to any—other persons (cf. Bem & Allen, 1974; Kenrick & Springfield, 1980). It is interesting to note the compatibility of this view with Tyler's (1978) recent observation that "in a developed technology for assessing *individuals*, we will not give everybody the same test" (p. 113, italics added).

In principle, any subset of the 18,000 or so personality adjectives identified by Allport and Odbert (1936) could be used to characterize the actions of an individual in a given situation. Which subset is in fact applied will be directly dependent on the perception and construal of that individual's alternative possibilities for action in that situation. Thus, for example, an individual would be characterized as "friendly" if, in a given situation, he or she engaged in actions construed by the characterizer as "friendly" when actions construed by the characterizer as "unfriendly" were perceived as viable alternative possibilities.[5]

Now it is certainly true that the alternative possibilities for action which occur to an individual (or to an observer of that individual) in a given situation depend in a large part on his or her knowledge (and memory) of how other persons have acted under similar circumstances. As the above example makes clear, however, it does not follow that the degree to which an individual manifests some underlying attribute of a set of possible actions either must be or is most usefully defined in direct contrast to the degree to which identified others manifest that same attribute. Within the framework being proposed here, knowledge about individual differences in action can—indeed should—serve as the basis for defining the V_is of Equation 1, that is, the alternative possibilities for action. However, once those V_is (and their corresponding relevance values) have been specified, one has all the information one needs to characterize an individual's actions in a given situation, that is, to interpret meaningfully the S_{pa} value assigned to an individual on a given measurement occasion.

Before leaving this topic, I should emphasize that there is nothing in the logic of idiographic measurement that precludes the comparability of persons along common attributes. It seems perfectly reasonable to assume that under certain conditions, different persons will perceive essentially the same alternative possibilities for action and will, as a result of cultural norms and other factors, construe those alternative possibilities in essentially the same way. Under these conditions, a single set of "items" and "relevance values" might reasonably be applied to all of the individuals being studied. Moreover, under these specific conditions, differences between two individuals in their actions might well reflect differences in their personalities.

The point is that the comparability of persons along common attributes is not critical to the systematic, empirical characterization of any one person's actions at a given point in time. The essence of idiographic measurement is not that it rejects the assumption of universal applicability (cf. Bem & Allen, 1974; Kenrick & Stringfield, 1980) but that it renders this assumption immaterial.

[5]If no viable alternative possibilities are perceived for (or by) an individual in a given situation, then his or her actions in that situation are not likely to be regarded as informative about (or indicative of) his or her personality. This deduction is, of course, consistent with findings reported in the attribution literature (cf. Kruglanski, 1980).

In the long run, a matter of far greater significance than that just discussed is the fact that idiographic measurement provides an investigator with a means of empirically identifying those qualities or attributes that are manifested by an individual with some degree of regularity or consistency over time and across situations. This is, of course, the essence of personality description. In the light of the earlier discussion of personality coefficients, the importance of this topic is no doubt apparent.

To illustrate how an investigator would actually approach this task from an idiographic perspective, consider the data shown in Figure 1, obtained as part of a recent study by Lamiell and Trierweiler (Note 2). The specific purpose and procedural details of that study need not concern us here. It is sufficient to note that the data in Figure 1 are based on a straightforward application of the measurement rationale illustrated previously. In this case, however, four underlying dimensions (rather than just one) were identified for a set of 18 activities through multidimensional scaling procedures. Self-reports of activity frequencies during specified two-day intervals (recorded on continuous 10-point scales rather than dichotomously, as in the above example) were then obtained from each of 19 undergraduate respondents on three separate occasions. Figure 1 presents the data for three of those respondents.

Glancing at Figure 1, one can see that Respondent 1 (left panel) tended to be relatively consistent over time with respect to Attribute II and relatively inconsistent with respect to Attributes I, III, and IV; that is, shifts in the idiographically defined status of Respondent 1 on Attribute II across the three measurement occasions were small in comparison with shifts in the idiographically defined status of that same respondent on Attributes I, III, and IV. Applying this same rationale, one can see that Respondent 10 (center panel) was relatively consistent over time with respect to Attributes I and IV and relatively inconsistent with respect to Attributes II and III. Finally, Respondent 17 (right panel) was most consistent with respect to Attribute I and quite inconsistent with respect to Attributes II, III, and IV.

Obviously, one would not seriously attempt to draw firm conclusions about the personalities of any one of these three respondents on the basis of such a limited set of observations. The intent here is merely to illustrate how one would apply the formal measurement rationale outlined

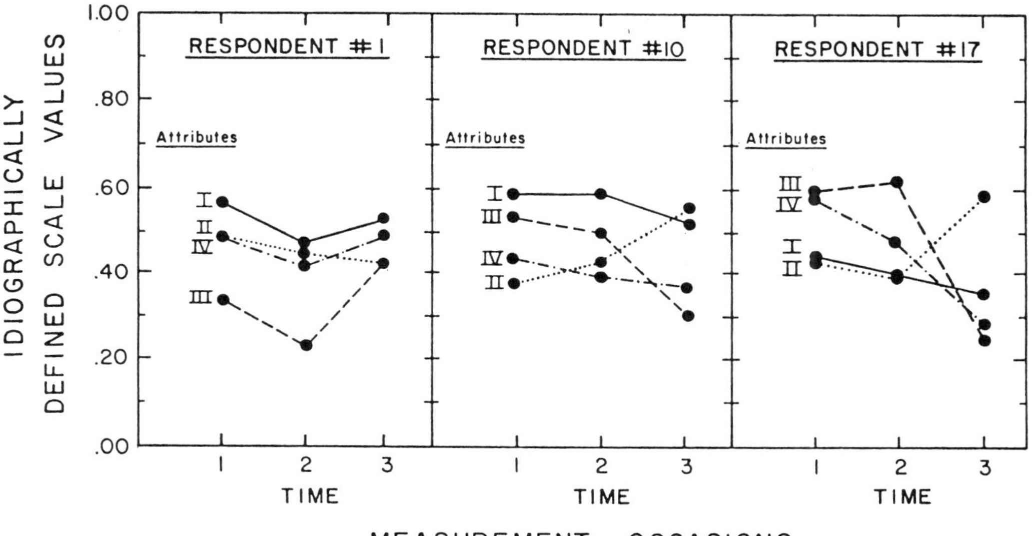

Figure 1: Idiographic measures for three respondents on four attributes at three points in time.

above to the problem of personality description. In connection with this illustration, two matters deserve special comment.

First, in data of the sort shown in Figure 1, the observed shifts in any one respondent's status on a given attribute do not depend in any way on the shifts of the other respondents with respect to that attribute. This could not be assumed had the data in Figure 1 been derived in accordance with the normative measurement rationale employed in individual differences research.

By the logic of a normative measurement rationale, an individual's measured status on a given attribute could change over time despite perfect consistency on the part of that individual with respect to the set of empirical referents for that attribute, that is, the $[(V_{pi})(R_{ia})]$ units of Equation 1. This could happen merely as a result of inconsistencies on the part of others with whom that individual happens to be compared. Similarly, an individual's status on a given attribute could, by the logic of individual differences measurement, remain constant over time despite marked changes in that individual with respect to the set of empirical referents for that attribute. This could happen if the others with whom the person is compared happen to change in the same way.

In idiographic measurement, ambiguities of this sort are eliminated; that is, the degree of consistency with which an individual manifests various attributes is completely independent of the (in)consistencies of other individuals with respect to those attributes and hinges entirely on the (in)consistencies of *that individual* with respect to the set(s) of empirical referents for those attributes.

A second point is that in the last analysis, the nature of the knowledge produced in the scientific study of personality will depend in part on the *quality* of the "raw" observations that are accumulated (cf. Fiske, 1978a, 1978b, 1979) as well as on the *perspective* from which they are accumulated (i.e., the investigator's or the subject's; cf. Golding, 1978; Harré & Secord, 1973; Kelly, 1955; Rychlak, 1968). However, the nature of that knowledge will also depend to a considerable degree on how those observations are organized once they are obtained, that is, on the way in which raw data are transformed into data (Coombs, 1964).

Unlike the personality coefficients generated within the individual differences paradigm, data of the sort shown in Figure 1 would permit an investigator to identify those qualities or attributes that are manifested by individuals with some degree of regularity or consistency; that is, they would provide the investigator with an empirical basis for personality description. If the present article has but one point to stress, it is that the creation of such data—by one means or another—is absolutely necessary for the purposes of a science of personality.

Idiographic Measurement and the Search for General Principles of Personality

Historically, the single most persistent response to previous proponents of idiography has been that whatever descriptive advantages idiography might have, it would ultimately undermine the overriding objective of establishing general principles of personality (cf. Beck, 1953; Eysenck, 1954; Falk, 1956; Holt, 1962; Kleinmuntz, 1967). Nunnally, (1967) has provided perhaps the most forceful expression of this view:

> The idiographists may be entirely correct, but if they are it is a sad day for psychology. Idiography is an antiscience point of view: it discourages the search for general laws and instead encourages the description of particular phenomena (people).
>
> Efforts to measure personality traits are based on the hypothesis that the idiographists are not entirely correct, that there are some general traits of human personality. The nomothetic point of view should be tested to the limit; otherwise, to accept an idiographic point of view

in advance is to postulate that only chaos prevails in the description of human personalities. (p. 472)

Because this view has so thoroughly dominated empirical personality psychology for so long, very little research of a truly idiographic nature has been reported in the literature—even by those who have advocated such research most earnestly (cf. Hall & Lindzey's [1978] discussion of Gordon Allport's career). Moreover, it has never been made clear how to reconcile what little idiographic research has been done (cf. Allport, 1965; Levinson, Darrow, Klein, Levinson, & McKee, 1978; White, 1972, 1975) with the nomothetic objectives of a science of personality.

The key to any such reconciliation lies in understanding that there is nothing in the search for general principles of personality which logically requires that the status of an individual on a given attribute be defined relative to the measured status of others on the same attribute. Indeed, one might argue, on the basis of what has been said thus far, that the nearly exclusive reliance by personality researchers on a normative measurement rationale is impeding rather than facilitating the search for general principles of personality.

In any event, there is nothing inherently "antiscientific" about an orientation which presumes that certain basic principles govern the emergence of, maintenance of, and changes in the personalities of individuals in general without presuming that the particular attributes which define the personalities of individuals must be common to all of those individuals (cf. Tyler, 1978). Stated otherwise, there is no logical a priori reason to reject a paradigm for the scientific study of personality in which generality is sought with reference to the *process* of personality development but in which comparability in the *substance* of individual's personalities is neither presumed nor precluded.

Suppose, for example, that data of the sort illustrated in Figure 1 had been carefully accumulated for numerous individuals over extended periods of time. Unlike the differential psychologist, the personality investigator might reasonably be quite uninterested in determining the degree of consistency with which certain common attributes were manifested by subjects in the aggregate. To the best of my knowledge, there is no personality theorist who is particularly concerned with that issue one way or the other. However, the personality investigator might well be very interested in whatever each individual's data might reveal about the basic process of personality development. This is an issue with which most personality theorists are directly concerned (cf. Hall & Lindzey, 1978; Levy, 1970). Moreover, as a means of formally testing hypotheses relevant to this issue with data of the kind envisioned here, time series analysis (Glass, Willson, & Gottman, 1975; Gottman, 1973) comes readily to mind.

To the extent that theoretically derived hypotheses pertinent to questions of personality development could repeatedly be confirmed in (theoretically relevant portions of) the data of single individuals, one could very well accumulate empirical support for general principles of personality, the (in)comparability of individuals on substantive attributes notwithstanding. By its very nature, such research would be logically compatible with the objectives of learning the best way to describe what kind of a person a given individual is, how he or she got that way, what keeps him or her that way, what might make him or her change, and how an understanding of all of this might contribute to the explanation and prediction of the behavior of individuals.

Programmatic research of the type just described would be idiographic in the sense that it would be predicted on an idiographic measurement rationale and would literally involve the study of single individuals over time. It would also be nomothetic, however, in that it would seek to confirm, *across* individuals, the applicability of certain basic principles to an understanding of theoretically relevant phenomena. In a word, the research would be *idiothetic.*

Obviously, no one can claim that such research would lead unfailingly to general principles of personality. No one knows for certain that general principles of personality can convincingly be established by *any* means. The reader can be certain, however, that such research would be neither logically incompatible with the search for such principles nor in any other way "antiscientific."

A Note on the Role of the Psychological Situation

During the past decade, considerable attention has been given to the problem of specifying the role of the psychological situation in the scientific study of personality (see, e.g., Bem & Funder, 1978; Buss, 1977; Ekehammar, 1974; Endler, 1975; Endler & Magnusson, 1976; Frederiksen, 1972; Howard, 1979; Magnusson & Ekehammar, 1975; Magnusson & Endler, 1977; Mischel, 1973, 1977, 1979; Pervin, 1977; Wachtel, 1977).

Space limitations preclude a thorough discussion of this topic here. It is worth nothing, however, that from an idiothetic perspective, a psychological situation would be defined in empirical research in terms of the attribute (or, possibly, the attributes) that is central to the construal of one's perceived alternative possibilities for action within a given interval of time.

Thus, for example, a "competitive" psychological situation would be defined as an interval of time during which the attribute "competitiveness versus noncompetitiveness" is central to the construal of the individual's perceived alternative possibilities for action. Similarly, a "love and affection" situation (cf. Rotter, 1955) would be defined as an interval of time during which the attribute "affectionate versus nonaffectionate" is central to the construal of one's perceived alternative possibilities for action. From this perspective, an individual would be said to remain in the same psychological situation to the extent that there is constancy in the attribute(s) that is central to the construal of his or her perceived alternative possibilities for action, whether or not there is constancy in the perceived alternative possibilities themselves.

This perspective on the role of the psychological situation in the scientific study of personality seems to be quite compatible with the approach recently taken by Bem and Funder (1978) and, more generally, with what some authors have termed an *organismic*—as contrasted with *mechanistic*—interactionism (cf. Bowers, 1973; Buss, 1977; Endler, 1975; Howard, 1979). Its utility, of course, remains to be firmly established.

CONCLUDING REMARKS

In his recent discussion of the past, present, and future (?) of personality theory, Rychlak (1976b) notes that a distinguishing feature of the personality theorist has always been his or her concern with the identity of the individual. He elaborates this point as follows:

> It is the ability to both have an idea or be doing something and yet at the same time grasp transcendentally that one *is* thinking and doing these things, to comment on them, and *to know that one could be doing and thinking otherwise,* that leads a personality theorist to postulate the identity factor. (p. 220, latter italics added)

Rychlak's conception of the individual identity seems quite similar to Tyler's (1978) recent discussion of *individuality:*

> Through encounters with a very large number of situations and persons exemplifying different possibilities for structuring reality, one puts together one's own repertoire of possibility-processing structures. (p. 232)

> What characterizes an individual is the pattern of responses, the likelihood that different tasks and situations *will be dealt with in one way rather than another.* (pp. 159–160, italics added)
>
> More than on anything else, one's individuality depends on the choices one makes. (p. 204)

Both Rychlak and Tyler emphasize the general failure of personality research to come to grips with the concepts of identity and individuality. As a result, Rychalk argues, the research has simply not served the personality theorist very well at all, a point seemingly corroborated by Sechrest's (1976) observation that despite the proliferation of empirical research, personality psychology has failed to achieve any major theoretical advances in decades. The present article has attempted to clarify the fundamental reason for this problem and to outline one possible approach to its resolution.

To recapitulate, it has been noted that most personality theorists are concerned with describing the personalities of individuals and, subsequently, with understanding how personalities develop, are maintained, and change. The presumption of personality *theorists* is that an understanding of these matters would (a) contribute importantly to the explanation of why any given individual acts the way he or she does and (b) provide a means of anticipating how any given individual will behave in the future.

Unfortunately, the vast majority of personality *researchers* have long been working within the constraints of a paradigm which, however useful it may be for other purposes, is inherently ill suited to the most fundamental of the above concerns: describing the personalities of individuals. Consequently, research conducted within this paradigm cannot possibly adequately address the remaining concerns of the personality theorist. The end result, of course, is that a large conceptual gap continues to exist between the theoretical and empirical branches of the discipline.

With the objective of eventually narrowing this gap, I have proposed and illustrated a formal rationale for idiographic personality measurement and have discussed the potential utility of adopting this rationale as the basis for scientific personality research. The compatibility of the proposed measurement rationale with Rychlak's (1976b) concept of identity and with Tyler's (1978) concept of individuality cannot be overlooked. It is a rationale based squarely on the notion that the "kind of person" one *is* is directly reflected in the kind of person one *is not* but *could be* and is only incidentally, if at all, reflected in the kind of person someone else is.

To be sure, what has been presented to this point is nothing more than a blueprint for future personality research (cf. Estein, 1980; Mischel, 1977, 1979). As the reader is doubtless well aware, the field of personality psychology is currently beset with numerous difficulties and controversies (Fiske, 1978b), and I certainly make no pretense here to have resolve them all.

This much seems clear, however: If the overriding metatheoretical concerns of a science of personality are at all well represented by the quotation of Levy (1970) cited at the outset of this article, then some viable alternative to the individual differences paradigm is going to have to be developed. Above all else, a viable alternative will be one within which the search for general principles of personality can proceed without simultaneously compromising the fidelity with which the investigator can address theoretically relevant questions *at the level of the individual.*

Although its empirical utility obviously awaits systematic documentation, the framework proposed here seems to provide at least a reasonable starting point. As this paradigm develops, the scientific study of personality will likely become less and less synonymous with the assessment and study of individual differences (which is the business of differential psychology) and increasingly synonymous with the search for the general principles that govern *the development of personal identities* (cf. Breger, 1974; Rychlak, 1976a). There are good reasons for believing that this is what most personality theorists have wanted to understand all along.

REFERENCE NOTES

1. Block, J. *Some enduring and consequential structures of personality.* Paper presented at "Explorations in Personality—78," Michigan State University, November 17, 1978.
2. Lamiel, J. T., & Trierweiler, S. J. *The study of consistencies and inconsistencies in personality: An alternative approach.* Unpublished manuscript, University of Illinois at Urbana-Champaign, Department of Psychology, 1980.

REFERENCES

Alker, H. A. Is personality situationally specific or intrapsychically consistent? *Journal of Personality,* 1972, *40,* 1–16.

Allport, G. W. *Personality: A psychological interpretation.* New York: Holt, Rinehart & Winston, 1937.

Allport, G. W. The general and the unique in psychological science. *Journal of Personality,* 1962, *30,* 405–422.

Allport, G. W. *Letters from Jenny.* New York: Harcourt, Brace & World, 1965.

Allport, G. W. Traits revisited. *American Psychologist,* 1966, *21,* 1–10.

Allport, G. W. *Pattern and grwoth in personality.* New York: Holt, Rinehart & Winston, 1967.

Allport, G. W., & Odbert, H. S. Trait-names: A psycho-lexical study. *Psychological Monographs,* 1936, *47*(1, Whole No. 211).

Anastasi, A. *Psychological testing.* New York: Macmillan, 1976.

Argyle, M., & Little, B. R. Do personality traits apply to social behaviour? *Journal for the Theory of Social Behaviour,* 1972, *2,* 1–35.

Baldwin, A. L. Personal structure analysis: A statistical method for investigating the single personality. *Journal of Abnormal and Social Psychology,* 1942, *37,* 163–183.

Baldwin, A. L. The study of individual personality by means of the intraindividual correlation. *Journal of Personality,* 1946, *14,* 151–168.

Beck, S. J. The science of personality: Nomothetic or idiographic? *Psychological Review,* 1953, *60,* 353–359.

Bem, D. J., & Allen, A. On predicting some of the people some of the time: The search for cross-situational consistencies in behavior. *Psychological Review,* 1974, *81,* 506–520.

Bem, D. J., & Funder, D. C. Predicting more of the people more of the time: Assessing the personality of situations. *Psychological Review,* 1978, *85,* 485–501.

Block, J. A comparison between ipsative and normative ratings of personality. *Journal of Abnormal and Social Psychology,* 1957, *54,* 50–54.

Block, J. *The Q-sort method in personality assessment and psychiatric research.* Springfield, Ill.: Charles C Thomas, 1961.

Block, J. Some reasons for the apparent inconsistency of personality. *Psychological Bulletin,* 1968, *70,* 210–212.

Block, J. *Lives through time.* Berkeley, Calif.: Bancroft, 1971.

Block, J. Advancing the psychology of personality: Paradigmatic shift or improving the quality of research? In D. Magnusson & N. S. Endler (Eds.), *Personality at the crossroads: Current issues in interactional psychology.* Hillsdale, N.J.: Erlbaum, 1977.

Bowers, K. S. Situationism in psychology: An analysis and a critique. *Psychological Review,* 1973, *80,* 307–336.

Breger, L. *From instinct to identity: The development of personality.* Englewood Cliffs, N.J.: Prentice-Hall, 1974.

Buss, A. R. The trait-situation controversy and the concept of interaction. *Personality and Social Psychology Bulletin,* 1977, *3,* 196–201.

Campbell, D. T., & Fiske, D. W. Convergent and discriminant validation by the multitrait-multimethod matrix. *Psychological Bulletin,* 1959, *56,* 81–105.

Carlson, R. Where is the person in personality research? *Psychological Bulletin,* 1971, *75,* 203–219.

Cattell, R. B. Psychological measurement: Normative, ipsative, interactive. *Psychological Review,* 1944, *51,* 292–303.

Coombs, C. H. *A theory of data.* New York: Wiley, 1964.

Crockett, W. H. Cognitive complexity and impression formation. In B. Maher (Ed.), *Progress in experimental personality research* (Vol. 2). New York: Academic Press, 1965.

Edwards, A. L. *Manual for the Edwards Personal Preference Schedule.* New York: Psychological Corporation, 1959.

Ekehammar, B. Interactionism in personality from a historical perspective. *Psychological Bulletin,* 1974, *81,* 1026–1048.

Endler, N. S. The case for person-situation interactions. *Canadian Psychological Review,* 1975, *16,* 12–21.

Endler, N. S., & Magnusson, D. Toward an interactional psychology of personality. *Psychological Bulletin,* 1976, *83,* 956–974.

Epstein, S. The stability of behavior: I. On predicting most of the people much of the time. *Journal of Personality and Social Psychology,* 1979, *37,* 1097–1126.

Epstein, S. The stability of behavior: II. Implications for psychological research. *American Psychologist,* 1980, *35,* 790–806.

Eysenck, H. J. The science of personality: Nomothetic! *Psychological Review,* 1954, *61,* 339–342.

Falk, J. Issues distinguishing idiographic from nomothetic approaches to personality theory. *Psychological Review,* 1956, *63,* 53–62.

Fiske, D. W. Cosmopolitan constructs and provincial observations: Some prescriptions for a chronically ill specialty. In H. London (Ed.), *Personality: A new look at metatheories.* New York: Wiley, 1978. (a)

Fiske, D. W. *Strategies for personality research.* San Francisco: Jossey-Bass, 1978. (b)

Fiske, D. W. Two worlds of psychological phenomena. *American Psychologist,* 1979, *34,* 733–739.

Frederiksen, N. Toward a taxonomy of situations. *American Psychologist,* 1972, *27,* 114–123.

Funder, D. C. The "trait" of ascribing traits: Individual differences in the tendency to trait ascription. *Journal of Research in Personality,* 1980, *14,* 376–385.

Glass, G. V., Willson, V. L., & Gottman, J. M. *Design and analysis of time series experiments.* Boulder: Colorado Associated University Press, 1975.

Goldfried, M. R., & Kent, R. N. Traditional versus behavioral personality assessment: A comparison of methodological and theoretical assumptions. *Psychological Bulletin,* 1972, *77,* 409–420.

Golding, S. L. Flies in the ointment: Methodological problems in the analysis of the percentage of variance due to persons and situations. *Psychological Bulletin,* 1975, *82,* 278–288.

Golding, S. L. Toward a more adequate theory of personality: Psychological organizing principles. In H. London (Ed.), *Personality: A new look at metatheories.* New York: Wiley, 1978.

Gottman, J. M. N-of-one and N-of-two research in psychotherapy. *Psychological Bulletin,* 1973, *80,* 93–105.

Hall, C. S., & Lindzey, G. *Theories of personality* (3rd ed.). New York: Wiley, 1978.

Harré, H., & Secord, P. F. *The explanation of social behavior.* Totowa, N.J.: Littlefield, Adams, 1973.

Harris, J. G., Jr. Nomovalidation and idiovalidation: A quest for the true personality profile. *American Psychologist,* 1980, *35,* 729–744.

Hase, H. D., & Goldberg, L. R. Comparative validity of different strategies of constructing personality inventory scales. *Psychological Bulletin,* 1967, *67,* 231–248.

Heilbrun, A. B., Jr. Evidence regarding the equivalence of ipsative and normative personality scales. *Journal of Consulting Psychology,* 1963, *27,* 152–156.

Hirschberg, N. A correct treatment of traits. In H. London (Ed.), *Personality: A new look at metatheories.* New York: Wiley, 1978.

Hogan, R. DeSoto, C. B., & Solano, C. Traits, tests, and personality research. *American Psychologist,* 1977, *32,* 255–264.

Holt, R. Individuality and generalization in the psychology of personality. *Journal of Personality,* 1962, *30,* 377–404.

Howard, J. A. Person-situation interaction models. *Personality and Social Psychology Bulletin,* 1979, *5,* 191–195.

Kelly, G. A. *The psychology of personal constructs.* New York: Norton, 1955.

Kenrick, D. T., & Stringfield, D. O. Personality traits and the eye of the beholder: Crossing some traditional philosophical boundaries in the search for consistency in all of the people. *Psychological Review,* 1980, *87,* 88–104.

Kleinmuntz, B. *Personality measurement: An introduction.* Homewood, Ill.: Dorsey Press, 1967.

Kruglanski, A. W. Lay epistemo-logic—Process and contents: Another look at attribution theory. *Psychological Review,* 1980, *87,* 70–87.

Lamiell, J. T. On the utility of looking in the "wrong" direction. *Journal of Personality,* 1980, *48,* 82–88.

Lamiell, J. T., Foss, M.A., & Cavenee, P. On the relationship between conceptual schemes and behavior reports: A closer look. *Journal of Personality,* 1980, *48,* 54–73.

Landfield, A. W. Interpretive man: The enlarged self-image. In J. K. Cole & A. W. Landfield (Eds.), *Nebraska Symposium on Motivation* (Vol. 24). Lincoln: University of Nebraska Press, 1976.

Levinson, D. J., Darrow, C. N., Klein, E. B., Levinson, M. H., & McKee, B. *The seasons of a man's life.* New York: Knopf, 1978.

Levy, L. *Conceptions of personality: Theories and research.* New York: Random House, 1970.

Magnusson, D., & Ekehammar, B. Perceptions and reactions to stressful situations. *Journal of Personality and Social Psychology,* 1975, *31,* 1147–1154.

Magnusson, D., & Endler, N. S. Interactional psychology: Present status and future prospects. In D. Magnusson & N. S. Endler (Eds.), *Personality at the crossroads: Current issues in interactional psychology.* Hillsdale, N.J.: Erlbaum, 1977.

McGowan, J., & Gormly, J. Validation of personality traits: A multicriteria approach. *Journal of Personality and Social Psychology,* 1976, *34,* 791–795.

Mehrabian, A., & O'Reilly, E. Analysis of personality measures in terms of basic dimensions of temperament. *Journal of Personality and Social Psychology,* 1980, *38,* 492–503.

Mischel, W. *Personality and assessment.* New York: Wiley, 1968.

Mischel, W. Toward a cognitive social learning reconceptualization of personality. *Psychological Review,* 1973, *80,* 252–283.

Mischel, W. *Introduction to personality* (2nd ed.). New York: Holt, Rinehart & Winston, 1976.

Mischel, W. On the future of personality measurement. *American Psychologist,* 1977, *32,* 246–254.

Mischel, W. On the interface of cognition and personality: Beyond the person-situation debate. *American Psychologist,* 1979, *34,* 740–754.

Norman, W. T. On estimating psychological relationships: Social desirability and self-report. *Psychological Bulletin,* 1967, *67,* 273–293.

Nunnally, J. C. *Psychometric theory.* New York: McGraw-Hill, 1967.

Pervin, L. A. The representative design of person-situation research. In D. Magnusson & N. S. Endler (Eds.), *Personality at the crossroads: Current issues in intractional psychology.* Hillsdale, N.J.: Erlbaum, 1977.

Rosenzweig, S. Norms and the individual in the psychologist's perspective. In M. L. Reymert (Ed.), *Feelings and emotions: The Mooseheart Symposium.* New York: McGraw-Hill, 1950.

Rosenzweig, S. Idiodynamics in personality theory with special reference to projective methods. *Psychological Review,* 1951, *58,* 293–311.

Rosenzweig, S. The investigation of repression as an instance of experimental idiodynamics. *Psychological Review,* 1952, *59,* 339–345.

Rosenzweig, S. The place of the individual and of idiodynamics in psychology: A dialogue. *Journal of Individual Psychology,* 1958, *14,* 3–20.

Rotter, J. B. The role of the psychological situation in determining the direction of human behavior. In M. R. Jones (Ed.), *Nebraska Symposium on Motivation* (Vol. 3). Lincoln: University of Nebraska Press, 1955.

Rychlak, J. F. *A philosophy of science for personality theory.* Boston: Houghton Mifflin, 1968.

Rychlak, J. F. (Ed.). *Dialectic: Humanistic rationale for behavior and development.* Basel, Switzerland: Karger, 1976. (a)

Rychlak, J. F. Personality theory: Its nature, past, present and—future? *Personality and Social Psychology Bulletin,* 1976, *2,* 209–224. (b)

Sanford, N. Personality: Its place in psychology. In S. Koch (Ed.), *Psychology: A study of a science* (Vol. 5). New York: McGraw-Hill, 1963.

Sechrest, L. Personality. *Annual Review of Psychology,* 1976, *27,* 1–27.

Shweder, R. A. How relevant is an individual differences theory of personality? *Journal of Personality,* 1975, *43,* 455–484.

Shweder, R. A. Factors and fictions in person perception: A reply to Lamiell, Foss, and Cavenee. *Journal of Personality,* 1980, *48,* 74–81.

Stephenson, W. *The study of behavior.* Chicago: University of Chicago Press, 1953.

Tyler, L. E. Toward a workable psychology of individuality. *American Psychologist,* 1959, *14,* 75–81.

Tyler, L. E. *Individuality: Human possibilities and personal choice in the psychological development of men and women.* San Francisco: Jossey-Bass, 1978.

Wachtel, P. L. Interaction cycles, unconscious processes, and the person-situation issue. In D. Magnusson & N. S. Endler (Eds.), *Personality at the crossroads: Current issues in interactional psychology.* Hillsdale, N.J.: Erlbaum, 1977.

White, R. W. *The enterprise of living: Growth and organization in personality.* New York: Holt, Rinehart & Winston, 1972.

White, R. W. *Lives in progress: A study of the natural growth of personality* (3rd ed.). New York: Holt, Rinehart & Winston, 1975.

Zanna, M. P., Olson, J. M., & Fazio, R. H. Attitude–behavior consistency: An individual difference perspective. *Journal of Personality and Social Psychology,* 1980, *38,* 432–440.

40

INVESTIGATIVE REPORTING AS A RESEARCH METHOD: AN ANALYSIS OF BERNSTEIN AND WOODWARD'S *ALL THE PRESIDENT'S MEN*

MURRAY LEVINE

Bernstein and Woodward's (1974) development of the Watergate story was more than muckraking. It gave us an unparalleled view of people in power and of governmental structures through which political power was exercised and restrained. Watergate raised the national consciousness about the potential misuse of power and introduced concepts (e.g., cover-up) that have served to guide our understanding of behavior in governmental and political organizations and, by extension, in other formal organizations as well.

The authors developed the story by using investigative reporting methods, very well described in *All the President's Men.* Investigative reporting deserves analysis as a research method. Existing textbooks (e.g., Anderson & Benjaminson, 1976) tend to be how-to-do-it treatises with little analysis of the methods themselves. While Bernstein and Woodward's (1974) book is superbly written, dramatic, and highly absorbing, it includes no reflection on the methods themselves.

Investigative reporting has much in common with qualitative and clinical research in the social and psychological sciences (see Balaban, 1973, 1978; Bogdan & Taylor, 1975; Diesing, 1971; Douglas, 1976; Erikson, 1964; Waelder, 1960; Whyte, 1955). The various treatises on the subject of qualitative research include defenses of that approach in relation to the predominant quantitative and experimental methodologies (e.g., Cronbach, 1975; Giorgi, 1970; Makkreel, 1975; Truzzi, 1974; Campbell, Note 1). These works contain many insights, much wisdom, and

Reprinted from the *American Psychologist, 35,* 626–638. (1980).

The author wishes to thank David I. Levine for his capable criticism and careful editing of an earlier draft of this article.

sophisticated analyses of the nature of social science and its methods. However, the qualitative approach still has an uncertain methodological status and is denigrated by some as little more than a useful art form. Bernstein and Woodward's work deserves the accolade of art, but there was, in addition, a distinct method to their approach. By making that method explicit, we may develop some further insight into qualitative research approaches.

Investigative reporting is a search for evidence to justify publication of a story; many forms of evidence are described in the book's pages. In addition to evidence obtained through interviews and documents, the authors used evidence similar to that used by clinicians—their own emotions, the emotions of others, and details of language (see Erikson, 1964; Waelder, 1960). Douglas (1976) has pointed out that the evidence in qualitative research and in the law (e.g., Cleary, 1972) is similar in nature to the evidence people commonly use in coming to understand their social worlds. What, then, distinguishes professional research?

The self-conscious emphasis on controlled and disciplined observation and inference distinguishes the professional researcher from the ordinary citizen. There are distinctive controls in the researcher's work, if control is defined as a probe of the limits of inferences that can reasonably be drawn from any set of observations (Group for the Advancement of Psychiatry, 1959). Control means more than an emphasis on reliability (e.g., confirmation by two or more sources). In telling the fascinating inside story, Bernstein and Woodward provide unusual insights into the many controls that the journalistic enterprise introduces into the investigative process.

Watergate required a theory to make sense of the mass of disconnected pieces of information and indeed to guide the subsequent investigation. From the beginning, Bernstein and Woodward operated with a more or less explicit theory, the scope of which enlarged as the investigation proceeded. The theory that Bernstein and Woodward used in their investigation can be considered similar in structure and function to the models used in modern science (Harré & Secord, 1972; Hesse, 1966). A model is a concrete image of how some set of structures and processes might act to produce a particular phenomenon. Bernstein and Woodward explained Watergate by showing how it happened, and in the process they provided a theoretically useful model of the corruption of power. We now have a concept and an image—Watergate—which allows us to raise the question of whether or not we are dealing with another Watergate when we encounter a new set of phenomena that requires explanation and understanding. Moreover, the model has implications for testable action in the real world, since it enables us to consider legislation and other controls over power.

Every human enterprise unfolds within a social context that shapes it. The social organization and culture of newspapers and that of the typical settings in which clinical and social researchers work are quite different. These differences are important in understanding to what extent investigative reporting methods can be transposed or adapted to the social science enterprise. Many factors limit the degree to which investigative reporting methods can be useful in the context of social science or clinical research. However, in the use of evidence, in the use of formal and informal controls, and in the need for theory and models to guide the inquiry, investigative reporting has, I contend, much in common with qualitative approaches in social and clinical research. In the following sections, I shall examine the Bernstein and Woodward (1974) book in an effort to illustrate this thesis and to systematize our understanding of qualitative methods.

EVIDENCE

Investigative journalism is a search for evidence to justify the publication of a story about an event or a set of events. Ethical and legal considerations. and the journalists' shared cultural need for statements grounded in fact, require that investigative reporters document the details of a story with reliable evidence. Some evidence, though useful in guiding the investigator, is not sufficiently objective or reliable to be useful in documenting the story. Published stories are usually warranted only by evidence (e.g., documents, statements of participants in the events) with greater probative value. However, both hard and soft evidence are interwoven in the investigative process.

Documents and Records

"Rosenfeld [an editor] always felt better when he knew that somewhere, no matter how inaccessible, there was a piece of paper that could support a story" (Bernstein & Woodward, 1974, p. 90). The pieces of paper were many and varied. They consisted of private documents (e.g., address books, p. 24) as well as public and quasi public records (e.g., library slips, pp. 32–33; records of long-distance telephone calls, p. 39; bank records, p. 39; credit-card records, p. 127; bills, p. 243; and cancelled checks, p. 43). The search for documents is based on the premise that all of us leave records of our presence, our movements, and our associations in this complex society. The usefulness of records is limited by their accessibility, by the investigator's knowledge about their location and the kinds of information different records contain, and by the imaginativeness with which records and documents may be used for a variety of investigative purposes.

Reconstruction of the organizational structure of the Committee to Re-elect the President (CRP) from its telephone roster (Bernstein & Woodward, 1974, p. 60; see also p. 286) was one of the most ingenious uses of a public document. The reconstruction provided leads to informants and, more important, enable the reporters to ascertain who had responsibility for decisions. A variety of other documents and records linked people and events, provided background for understanding specific events, and furnished leads to other evidence. Historians and lawyers are much more familiar with the use, and the pitfalls in the use, of documentary evidence than social scientists and clinical researchers are (Barzun, 1974; Winks, 1968), but documents can illuminate social science problems when used appropriately (A. Levine & M. Levine, 1977; M. Levine, 1979).

That documents may be of use to social scientists is one conclusion, but the cultural norms and ethics governing access to documents are quite different for social scientists and for journalists. The difference may be gleaned from Anderson and Benjaminson's (1976) classification of records:

> There are three kinds of records. There are those the law entitles the public to see, those the law prohibits the public from seeing, and those not mentioned by the law. Good investigators do not admit the existence of a category of records they will never see. As far as they are concerned, the only important distinctions among the three kinds of records involve the methods best suited to getting them and the relative difficulty in doing so. (p. 39)

Some journalist believe that their public mission allows them to obtain access to information by any means short of committing a crime; they may be willing to skirt even that line as well (see Bernstein & Woodward, 1974, pp. 232–236; 248–250). Differences between investigative journalists and social scientists in terms of professional culture, ethical principles, and legal constraints (e.g., New York State Public Health Law, Article 24A; 42 USC. 289; CFR Title 45, Part 46) may limit the adaptability of investigative methods for social scientists, although Douglas (1976) holds an opposite opinion.

Informants and Interview Data

The testimony of participants in events constitutes primary data for investigative reporters as well as for lawyers and social scientists. Interviewers may have been direct participants, or they may have indirect knowledge through conversations with participants or through personal observation of some of the activities. Bernstein and Woodward also used informants to provide general information on the culture, habits, values, styles, practices, and reputations of individuals and organizations. Such background information was crucial in helping the reporters understand other evidence, in providing them additional leads, and in assuring them that they were moving in the right direction.

The peculiar conditions of interviewing required that the reporters vary their methods of obtaining and recording the interview data. Standardized procedures and standardized interview protocols would have made no sense at all. The reporters had some idea of what each informant might provide, but information was often unexpected. Moreover, different interviewing techniques were required for cooperative or noncooperative interviewees. Of particular interest was the technique of confronting reluctant interviewees with adverse information requiring comment, confirmation, or denial. The response to this confrontational approach sometimes yielded still further data of importance.

In a situation as complex as Watergate, few knew the whole story. The reporters had to develop it by gathering information from numerous informants and then coordinating, correlating, and cross-checking what different individuals with access to the same material said, fitting together pieces much as one might fit the pieces of a jigsaw puzzle together. Contradictions from different sources were treated not as proof of unreliability, but as additional information.

Informants' Networks

In building the story, the two reporters assumed that everyone was part of a social network and that members of that network could provide information about other members and their relationships. For example, when Bernstein first learned of the burglary, he spoke to anyone at the Watergate complex he could reach—desk clerks, bellmen, maids, and waiters (Bernstein & Woodward, 1974, pp. 14–15). To learn more about McCord, the reporters checked a roster of 15 people who served with McCord in any army unit (see also pp. 54, 61, 286, 333). Sometimes such dragnet searches proved fruitless (p. 55). Sometimes the source for building a network was found in personal documents. Thus by checking every name and telephone number found in the burglars' address books, the reporters found a connection to Howard Hunt in the White House (pp. 23–24).

Much of the investigation assumed that in any social enterprise people were connected to each other for a purpose. By determining the nature of their transactions, one could begin to understand the complex of issues. The first clue was frequently an indication of some business or some acquaintance between the parties (e.g., Bernstein & Woodward, 1974, pp. 30, 44–45, 131, 157, 159). When Donald Segretti emerged as an important figure in the "dirty tricks" campaign, the reporters again began with a dragnet network of acquaintances and soon were able to trace links of friendship between Segretti and a number of White House and CRP figures (pp. 130–131). They also uncovered the "rat fucking" practiced by Segretti, Chapin, and Ziegler, who had known each other in college. Chapin and Ziegler later worked on Nixon's political campaign in California under Haldeman's direction and then joined an advertising agency where Haldeman was vice-president (p. 131).

Investigators' Networks

The reporters' own networks were of crucial importance in providing information. Woodward's "Deep Throat" was a long-time acquaintance with whom he had spent many evenings prior to Watergate discussing power and politics in government (Bernstein & Woodward, 1974,

p. 136). Many friends in and out of government and a number of other reporters offered information (e.g., pp. 23, 34, 131, 142). Once it became known that they were interested in the story, Bernstein and Woodward received information from a variety of volunteer informants. Some sources were considered suspect, or at least the information had to be treated carefully because the parties were known to have vested interests (p. 153). Unsolicited tips from the general public had to be checked out. These were less helpful than one might otherwise believe (p. 117), although sometimes such leads did produce useful data (pp. 290–293).

Credibility of Informants

An investigative reporter must assess the reliability of informants and interviewees. The nature of an informant's position, his or her reputation, and the reporters' previous experience with that person were important in assessing information. Moreover, the informants' demeanor and emotional state provided further clues to the validity or meaning of what they revealed. Witness demeanor and witness credibility are important issues in the law of evidence. Testimony in open court is required in part so that a jury can observe a witness's demeanor (Cleary, 1972, pp. 582, 602).

Woodward relied a great deal on his informant Deep Throat, who was in a position to have important information, and who never said anything that was incorrect (Bernstein & Woodward, 1974, p. 75). Deep Throat's manner of conducting himself was important. "He was dispassionate and seemed committed to the best version of the obtainable truth" (p. 137). Similarly, Woodward, who had not met Hugh Sloan before, was impressed by Sloan's care and his unwillingness to mention the names of persons he had no reason to think had done anything wrong. The detail an informant could provide added to the credibility of his or her story. Shipley, who named Segretti, had notes showing dates, times, places, and people involved in events (p. 119).

Beyond an informant's demeanor and position, it was sometimes necessary to assure an informant's credibility in other ways. Woodward, for example, made a dozen telephone calls to other attorneys and to the local bar association to assure himself and his editor of one informant's personal reputation (p. 161; see also p. 329). In other instances the reporters used other knowledge they had to judge the reliability of a source of information (pp. 306, 365). An informant's position and relationship to others were important. "Sloan was devoted to Stans. . . . Sloan hesitated. He was trying to plead Stans' case and instead was getting him in deeper" (p. 99). Sometimes the reporters had to be concerned about attacks on their own credibility from informants who might deliberately give them false information (p. 211; see also p. 358).

Nonverbal Communication

Nonverbal communication was almost as critical as verbal communication, not only helping the investigators assess the information they received from informants but also in providing clues to the state of the system they were studying. It was important, in understanding the story and the stakes involved, to appreciate the emotional states of their informants (Bernstein & Woodward, 1974, pp. 46, 48, 61, 79, 80, 91, 104, 181, 211, 295, 325).

> What information the reporters were getting at this time came in bits and pieces, almost always from people who did not want to discuss the matter. Their fright, more than anything else, was persuading Bernstein and Woodward that the stakes were higher than they originally perceived. Indeed, they too were unsettled by the reactions to their visits. (Bernstein & Woodward, 1974, p. 62)

An informant's affect, especially taken in relation to other information, provided revealing clues, sometimes pointing to other data and sometimes confirming previous information. When Woodward asked McGregor about Liddy, McGregor angrily told a story that another informant had said would be used as a cover story (pp. 48–49). The unexpected anger was a clue supporting the belief that the cover story was false.

Informants' emotions read in context helped to elaborate the meanings of statements and events. When Bernstein was discussing "dirty tricks" with a Justice Department attorney, the man became outraged. His affect impressed Bernstein because it was uncharacteristic, an additional clue that the White House staff was violating all accepted standards of political conduct (p. 134).

An informant's affect influenced the degree of conviction the reporters felt in the validity of a report. Sometimes the feeling tone aroused suspicion of lies or concealment. In other instances the tone was a clue to the importance of the issue, or it raised questions about causes. In their sensitivity to the emotional states of their interviewees, the reporters shared much with clinicians.

There are distinct lessons here suggesting the amount of information that is lost when subjects fill out questionnaires and are not seen in person as they tell their stories in their own words. The data may be soft or subjective, but the perceived emotional state of an informant provides critical information for clinicians as well as for investigative reporters.

Details of Language

Investigative reporters as well as clinicians are sensitive to the details of subjective reports and pay careful attention to the language and context of communications. In some instances unsolicited comments raised questions, as when White House press aide Clawson denied something no one had asked him about directly (Bernstein & Woodward, 1974, p. 25; see also p. 163). In some instances, apparent denials of published stories contained hidden confirmations. Nixon's early statement denied that anyone "presently employed" in the White House had anything to do with the burglary (p. 59; see also pp. 73, 108–109, 146, 150). A source who usually denied incorrect stories might confirm a story simply by remaining silent when asked (p. 179).

Public figures are apparently reluctant to tell outright lies, but they are not beyond making statements and using words that attempt to conceal the truth. Woodward at one point confronted Kissinger with the information that Kissinger had personally authorized wiretaps. Because Kissinger used the words "almost never" and "almost inconceivable" Woodward felt Kissinger's angry comments were not denials (pp. 345–346; see also pp. 175, 356).

The context of communications can also provide important information beyond the words involved. When a story broke about the President's appointments secretary, Ziegler, Dole, and McGregor used similar language in their rebuttals. The reporters and their editors took the concerted response as a sign that the counterattacks were probably ordered by the President, or at least made with his knowledge and consent (Bernstein & Woodward, 1974, pp. 172–173; see also pp. 62, 212).

Much of what the reporters used as evidence in directing their inquiries would be classified as hearsay, or not of sufficient probative value to be admissible in a trial court, although it would be admitted before a grand jury, which has a broader investigative role. While every such clue was useful in shaping the story, professional discipline demanded more evidence for confirmation before a piece was submitted for publication.

Some Limits of Clinical Evidence

Accuracy was critical in pursuing the Watergate story. If the reporters proved incorrect in one of their assertions, they and their newspaper would be vulnerable to libel suits. More important, their reputations within their own organization and profession would have been damaged, and potential sources would have been reluctant to provide them with information in the future. To a remarkable degree the reporters were accurate, as subsequent events demonstrated. However, at one critical point they appeared to have made an error, which temporarily damaged their credibility and certainly damaged their confidence. The error was caused in part by their reliance on the sort of indirect communications just described.

The reporters had strong reasons to believe that H. R. Haldeman, Nixon's top aide, not only was among the people who controlled the secret espionage fund but may well have been a key culprit. Although there was good reason to suspect Haldeman, the reporters knew enough about how he operated to understand that he would have preserved "deniability." They needed some very direct evidence to tie him to the Watergate events. In an interview with Hugh Sloan, Bernstein tried to get him to confirm Haldeman's role, because Sloan knew who authorized expenditures from the secret fund. Sloan refused to do so in straightforward fashion, but he conceded as much in a roundabout way. Later, in an attempt to confirm that Sloan had testified under oath to the grand jury that Haldeman was the person in control of the fund, Bernstein interviewed an FBI agent. The agent agreed with Bernstein's assertion that Sloan had testified to Haldeman's involvement under oath to the grand jury. The agent, however, agreed it was *John* Haldeman who had been implicated. Although Bernstein rechecked, the slip was to prove ominous for the particular story. Bernstein attempted to obtain confirmation from another source, a Justice Department lawyer, who refused to give any direct information but agreed to use a complex set of signals. After the story was printed, it developed that the lawyer had misunderstood the code and had signaled exactly the opposite of what Bernstein thought he had meant.

The investigators knew something was wrong when a White House press secretary issued an unequivocal denial that Sloan had named Haldeman before the grand jury, and Sloan's attorney confirmed the denial. In analyzing their error, Bernstein and Woodward (1974) found that they had relied too strongly on indirect evidence and inference:

> They had assumed too much. Persuaded by their sources, and by their own deductions that Haldeman loomed behind "Watergate," they had grasped a slim reed—the secret fund. . . . But they had taken short cuts once they themselves had come to be convinced that Haldeman controlled the fund. They had heard what they wanted hear. (pp. 217–218)

Tracing their errors, they realized that they had not questioned Sloan closely enough, that they had depended on an FBI agent whose reliability was not known to them, and that the indirect codes for confirmation with the attorney left too much room for misunderstanding. They were right in their assumption that Haldeman had controlled the fund, but wrong in their belief that the statement had been made to the grand jury. They had opened themselves to questions about their accuracy.

Inferences drawn from indirect evidence and from an informant's demeanor are not always correct, especially in the absence of other evidence (e.g., Bernstein & Woodward, 1974, pp. 167–168). Despite subjective certainty and clarity, hunches and inferences must not be confused with evidence and certainly ought not to be weighed heavily in the absence of other evidence.

Field Interviewing

The problems of interviewing in the highly charged atmosphere of Watergate required the reporters to use every bit of information, including what they could glean from details of language and emotions. Many of the persons who were approached were willing to be interviewed. Others set conditions. Some would only give partial information or hints or would only confirm information the reporters already had. The reporters used a confrontation technique with hostile interviewees in an effort to elicit spontaneous responses because these might be the only information the interview would produce. These special circumstances placed a premium on flexibility and on maintaining rapport. The reporters had to exercise self-control and make sensitive use of their own emotional states as part of the interview process.

The reporters frequently called people they didn't know. Many were reluctant to respond (see Bernstein & Woodward, 1974, p. 84), and some were rude. After working hard to see Martha Mitchell, Woodward had to be content to talk with her while a vacuum cleaner was going (pp. 96–98). Another interviewee seemed more interested in the Sunday afternoon football game on television than in talking (p. 166). An acquaintance of Woodward's hung up on him (p. 24).

Although they always identified themselves as reporters, Bernstein and Woodward often had to sell themselves as human beings, to look for some way of appealing to potential interviewees, of obtaining a person's sympathy, or of helping the person to find some rationalization for participating (p. 26). The rapport-building process often required extensive social conversation before getting on to important subject matter. Because the interviews were sensitive, the reporters often took no notes as they delicately worked around the edges of the subject (p. 62). However, Bernstein once played on a reluctant interviewee's curiosity by using a notebook to help make her more accepting of the interview (p. 67). Some respondents made the interview into a guessing game, forcing the reporters to act as if they knew more than they did.

The interview process required great sensitivity to the respondent's motivations and feelings. A nervous interviewee would insist that everything be off the record (p. 26). A fearful bookkeeper who didn't want to be accused of giving out anyone's name used initials, but only after arriving at a tacit agreement that she would confirm or deny information to try to help her bosses, Sloan and Stans, whom she respected (see also p. 87). When Segretti expressed annoyance at the media, Bernstein and his colleague Meyers "calculatedly dumped on the opposition" (Bernstein & Woodward, 1974, p. 227; see also p. 271).

The reporters were aware that shifts in an interviewee's mood might have been simulated for effect. When Woodward confronted Kissinger about his role in ordering wiretaps, Kissinger replied cagily. At other points he responded angrily to Woodward's interrogation and accused Woodward of trapping him into talking. Woodward felt "Kissinger had an effective way of moving back and forth from anger to tranquility" (Bernstein & Woodward, 1974, p. 345).

The reporters not only had to deal with others' aggression toward them, they themselves had to be aggressive in obtaining information (see pp;. 49, 91, 94, 114, 193, 214, 254, 288–289, 292, 358–360, 361). Sometimes their own expression of anger was spontaneous and intuitive, but at other times it was calculated (see pp. 42, 55–56, 72–73). At one point, Woodward felt it necessary to confront Deep Throat because he was not forthcoming.

> He told Deep Throat both of them were playing a chicken shit game—Deep Throat for pretending to himself that he never fed Woodward primary information, and Woodward for chewing up tidbits like a rat under a picnic table that didn't have the guts to go after the main dish. (Bernstein & Woodward, 1974, p. 141)

On another occasion, Bernstein decided to try to get information by deliberately angering his informant (p. 184). Woodward pressured a 20-year-old college student by questioning the student's ethics in agreeing to do political spying (pp. 290–292).

The pressures on the reporters, and their belief that they had a right to information from others, sometimes led them to overreact and to act out (pp. 213–216). Many of the interview situations touched the two reporters' emotions deeply and required great self-control on their part lest their judgment or their relationship with the interviewee be affected. When the reporters received information they were seeking or information they found startling, it was necessary for them to remain calm so that no obvious emotions would interfere with the ongoing interview (pp. 44–45, 54, 71, 100, 102, 138, 180, 182, 212, 251, 337).

Bernstein's telephone interview with John Mitchell is a prime example. He called for comment on the story that Mitchell had controlled the secret political espionage fund while he was Attorney General. For Bernstein, the only constant in the interview had been the "adrenal feeling" as he "perceived the excruciating depths of Mitchell's hurt" (Bernstein & Woodward, 1974, pp. 109–110). Later Bernstein found himself in an agitated state, unable to hit the proper keys as he was typing out the conversation based on his notes. After another interview, during which he had drunk large quantities of coffee and had been excited by the information he had received, Bernstein found it difficult to keep the information straight (p. 71; see also pp. 211–212).

Because they cajoled, pressured, entreated, and confronted (e.g., pp. 49, 80, 148), the two reporters sometimes felt inner conflict, as when Bernstein obtained confidential records from a source in a credit bureau, although he personally felt the records ought to remain private. Nowhere was the conflict between the requirements of their role and their personal feelings more clearly revealed than in their relationship with Hugh Sloan. They both liked Sloan, but they felt as if they were "using" him. The reporters described themselves as feeling like "vultures" because Sloan was having a difficult time in his personal life while they were becoming famous.

In one sense, it seemed as if the reporters felt less responsibility for the well-being of the persons involved than they did for the story. However, both of them were acutely aware of the impact their stories had on those who figured in them, especially if the information was adverse (e.g., pp. 89, 116, 148). Incidents revealing hurt to others were sobering and added to Bernstein and Woodward's sense of need for care, self-control, and self-awareness.

The circumstances of interviews ranged from meticulously planned to most informal. Some took place in homes and offices, but other interviews were held in underground parking garages, in airplanes, in taxicabs, on doorsteps, in restaurants, and on park benches. The interviews took place at all hours of the day and night, whether they were conducted in person or by telephone. Many interviews were with total strangers, but in others the reporters took advantage of friends and causal acquaintances. Sometimes they went back to sources over and over again, to obtain new information or to recheck information. They returned delicately, knowing that what they had printed might have changed the relationship. In other instances it was obvious to all that there was an adversary relationship if not outright animosity, and since they had to be in contact with each other, both parties had to deal with their anger.

The wide variety of people and circumstances, the profound emotions, the uncertainties of the situation, the difficulties of getting information, and the extremely high stakes—all these exacerbated the problems of remaining oriented toward the facts. In clinical settings, controls for the clinician's emotional involvement are provided by the attempt to achieve insight through personal therapy and by supervision. There are analogous patterns in investigative reporting. The reporters were both helped and hindered by the controls and supports that are involved in working for a newspaper and working as a team. It is to an examination of these controls and supports that I now turn.

CONTROLS, SUPPORTS, AND THE SOCIAL SYSTEM OF THE NEWSPAPER

Given the ambiguities of evidence, the difficulties in obtaining evidence, a newspaper's responsibility to the public, and the stakes involved for the targets of its stories and for the newspaper itself, a newspaper requires controls. The major control is through the editorial review process. The editorial review process played a highly significant role in the development of the Watergate story.

Editorial Review

The editors performed a number of functions in addition to assigning the reporters to stories and approving the final copy. The several editors served in roles similar to that of the cross-examiner recommended for use in social science field studies (M. Levine, 1974). When Bernstein and Woodward discovered that Hunt had been reading material on Chappaquiddick, the metropolitan editor, Rosenfeld, was enthusiastic about the story, but he took it to the executive editor, Bradlee, for clearance. Bradlee functioned much as an editorial reviewer would in a journal. He criticized the sufficiency of the available evidence to support the inference the reporters wanted to draw, and he interrogated them about the credibility of one of their sources. Concluding that the evidence was insufficient to support certain assertions, Bradlee revised the story before authorizing its publication and did not place it on the front page (Bernstein & Woodward, 1974, pp. 33–34).

When they first determined that an intelligence fund within CRP had been used to make payments to the burglars, the reporters realized that they had information from but one source. Conferring with two editors, they decided to soften the statement in print. Eventually they evolved an unwritten rule that a charge of criminal misconduct would not be used unless there were at least two confirming sources (p. 81). The editors helped form this rule, which was intended to guarantee the reliability of information, and acted to control the precision of the inferences they were willing to print.

Metropolitan editor Rosenfeld's forte as a cross-examiner was locating holes in proposed stories. Not only did he carefully examine what the reporters wrote, but he passed them questions to be used with sources and demanded to be kept closely informed on all developments. Rosenfeld did not approve a story for publication until he had interrogated his reporters (pp. 93–94).

Whenever Bernstein and Woodward reported details about the involvement of high officials in the Watergate financing, Bradlee reviewed the story and asked if they were absolutely certain of the facts. Once they were able to reassure him, Bradlee approved publication, even though the reporters did not yet have the full account. As managers of a daily newspaper, the editors could not wait for a definitive account but had to approve significant pieces of the larger story as the pieces could be confirmed, not unlike journal editors who publish disconnected studies and leave it to others to put the separate articles into a coherent theoretical structure (Bernstein & Woodward, 1974, pp. 105–106, 135).

The editors were cautious about the language they permitted in each story. They were very concerned that they not be accused of bias. The image of neutrality was important (pp. 174, 205). The editorial staff also exercised a certain amount of control and provided support to see that ethically proper procedures were followed (pp. 107, 111, 112, 215, 216, 229, 289, 306). To some extent they were concerned because of their potential liability in a libel suit. That liability would extend throughout the newspaper's hierarchy.

Editorial control through cross-examination could fail to serve its intended purpose, as was discovered in the error in the story about Haldeman and the grand jury. Before the story was printed, "Bradlee served as prosecutor, demanding to know exactly what each source had said" (Bernstein & Woodward, 1974, p. 203). It was only after he had satisfied himself and had obtained the recommendation of the other editors that Bradlee approved the story. Even after Bradlee approved, another editor, Simons, asked the reporters to try to find another source before printing it. Simons and Rosenfeld repeatedly asked the reporters for assurances that the story was accurate and well documented (p. 204).

Despite all the precautions and the fact that the reporters had four sources, the details of the story proved to be in error. Neither they nor their editors had caught the problem (p. 218). Their position was no different from that of a social scientist whose experiment is published after it has undergone editorial review and for which another investigator later discovers an artifact accounting for the results.

The Research Team as a Control

In addition to editorial review, the reporters' partnership provided another level of control. At first, Bernstein and Woodward were reluctant to work together because they were so different tempermentally and stylistically. However, they soon discovered that their differences, although requiring accommodation, provided distinct advantages. They acted as critics of each other, one providing the brake for the other's enthusiasm. To strengthen their working relationship, they evolved a rule that gave either one veto power over any story they were to run. If one of them felt the story was not solidly grounded, they did not use it, sometimes even after they had obtained editorial approval (Bernstein & Woodward, 1974, pp. 135–136, 165, 182, 202, 273–274). This rule allowed both men to attend seriously to their own intuitions and, at the same time, spurred them to make more certain of the factual bases for their stories.

The Organizational Structure of the Newspaper

The organizational structure of the newspaper provides a variety of supports to deal with fast-breaking stories. Reporters do not have fixed assignments but can be assigned as needed. They do not work regular shifts but, instead, work as professionals, keeping their own hours, governed primarily by publication deadlines. Thus, Bernstein and Woodward were available to cover stories at all hours of the day or night and on weekends. The resources of the newspaper were such that a reporter could fly to Miami or to California in pursuit of a lead, sometimes at a moment's notice, as when Bernstein followed the Watergate burglars and their attorney into a taxicab and then onto an airplane in order to be able to talk to them about their guilty pleas (Bernstein & Woodward, 1974, p. 258). The newspaper could hire temporary help anywhere in the country to pursue assignments, such as reporter Meyers who waited for days for Segretti to return to his apartment (p. 127ff).

The competitive nature of the newspaper business drove the reporters to continued effort, and in this the attitude of their editors was a clear factor. The editors continued to press them for more material (pp. 153, 224–225). For example, when the *Los Angeles Times* published an important story that they had been after, Bradlee said little about it, but his manner showed that he was unhappy about having been scooped. "I can't kick ass for getting scooped, but I do let it be known that I feel let down and that I hate it. Don't forget that I hate it" (Bernstein & Woodward, 1974, p. 115).

The pressure to get one particular story culminated in an effort of dubious ethics, skirting the borders of illegality. Woodward had a tip that a grand juror was sufficiently angry that she was willing to talk. The newspaper's legal counsel advised that the burden of keeping the oath of secrecy of grand jury proceedings is placed on the juror. Although it was not illegal to ask such a person questions, the reporter would be pressing the juror to violate the law. When the issue of interviewing the jurors came up at an editorial conference, private doubts about the ethics of the procedure went unstated, but the reporters agreed to ask their questions without mentioning the grand jury and/or the interviewee's participation in it.

The tactic backfired. One of the jurors told the prosecutor, who informed Judge Sirica (pp. 232–237). The episode caused the reporters much anguish and embarrassment, for they realized that they had allowed expediency to overcome principles, exposing others to arrest and punishment (pp. 247–251).

Competition With Other Newspapers

In any scientific endeavor, there is usually a community of scientists working on the same or similar problems who provide social controls beyond the experimental controls. As each group obtains its findings, they are published, providing new information and new leads to the other teams. Other laboratories will examine the data critically and may attempt to replicate or confirm the findings, then reporting their results in later publications. The analogue exists in journalism.

Even in the early phase of Watergate, other newspapers followed the story and added pieces to the developing picture. For example, when the *New York Times* published a story listing telephone calls made from Barker's Miami phone to CRP in Washington, Bernstein used a source within the telephone company to confirm the finding. The source led him to the Miami District Attorney's office, which, in turn, led him to evidence of an illegal campaign contribution (Bernstein & Woodward, 1974, p. 36ff). Other examples can be provided of one team confirming the findings of another and then building on those findings (see pp. 113–115, 151, 166, 174, 175, 283, 287–288, 324–325).[1]

Confirmation was important for other reasons. After the *Post*'s story on Haldeman had been shown to be incorrect in certain details, the reporters' credibility was severely challenged. A *New York Times* story confirming the existence of a secret CRP fund, and showing that $900,000 in cash disbursements had been made from the fund, restored their position considerably (p. 219). Confirmation provided protection because prestigious and powerful members of the press backed their efforts (p. 259).

An interesting insight into the attitudes and relationships among competitive investigators can be gleaned from the account of a dinner meeting with Seymour Hersh of the *New York Times*. The reporters discussed the case in general, discussed their own viewpoints, and exchanged impressions of the principals, but they did not exchange information that would reveal their current investigative approaches. Hersh even held back the details of the story that was to be published the next morning (Bernstein & Woodward, 1974, p. 312). Such secretiveness extends beyond normal experience in informal exchanges with colleagues, but it resembles the attitudes displayed by Watson and Crick in *The Double Helix* (Watson, 1968).

Success and Failure of Social Control

It is clear that the editorial process is a source of control. It is a conservative influence in that the burden of proof is placed on the reporter to convince the editor, and the editor tests the proof by cross-examining the reporter. The organizational structure of the newspaper facilitates the investigative process by providing resources, support, and protection against outside pressure. By the same token, the newspaper can act to limit the independence of the investigative reporter in protection of its own interests.

[1]The reporters' attempt to independently replicate the Watergate story—in the sense of finding their own evidence, then interviewing the same informants from a different perspective—provided important social controls for the formal investigations as well. While there is no direct evidence on this point, their efforts were probably critical in moving the Justice Department to do its job and in moving the Senate Select Committee to make a more thorough investigation as well. In effect, the presence of an independent and competing investigative team served a control function analogous to that of a community of scientists working on the same scientific problem.

Although care is exercised to ensure accuracy, the pressures of competition and of a daily production schedule may lead to error in publication. Newspaper reports are subject to error because of an editor's enthusiasm or biases, or for other organizational reasons. However, publication itself becomes part of the corrective process because other investigators covering the story will confirm or disconfirm it. Thus, in investigative reporting, as in science, the more powerful control is not the research design but the social control inherent in independent review, criticism, and attempts at replication of the reported observations.

THE ROLE OF THEORY

It is a truism that facts have no meaning outside of a context that gives them meaning. The process of theory building is a process of infinite approximation, or the inductive development of a modifiable hypothesis or schema (Diesing, 1971; Makkreel, 1975). The provisional assumptions underlying the investigation take form in the investigator's freely roaming imagination.

Theory, or schema, played a key role at every step in the Watergate investigation. The need for an explanation frequently arose not because of some fact per se, but because the fact represented something intriguing or puzzling, sometimes simply on an intuitive basis and sometimes because previous expectations about how the world was constructed were not met. The puzzlement and interest generated by an observation that did not make sense propelled the investigation until an explanation arose that did. The Watergate burglary itself made no sense as a piece of political espionage, and its ties to the White House and other events made no sense until the "Plumbers' " operation was uncovered. That, in turn, made sense only in the context of the particular conceptions of power that were shared in the culture of those surrounding Nixon.

The pages of *All the President's Men* are filled with events that piqued the reporters' curiosity or gave them a feeling of incomplete understanding and a need for further investigation. There are at least thirty references to circumstances that Bernstein and Woodward described as not making sense, either because there was some departure from a norm in the events that did occur, or because things that ought to have happened did not. In a great number of instances their emotional reactions were stronger than mere curiosity. Sometimes they described themselves as "baffled" or "perplexed." At other times they were "unsettled" by people's reactions to them and were "amazed," "shocked," "stunned," or "unnerved" by information, descriptions, or actions that departed from their expectations. It was these subjective reactions that powered their need for explanation.

Within the first few days after the burglary, Bernstein, acting on the basis of his surprise that an informant close to the administration spoke with "scorn and derision" of the people surrounding Nixon (Bernstein & Woodward, 1974, p. 29), wrote a five-page memo detailing the "Chotiner Theory." His editor, interest aroused by speculation, encouraged him to pursue it (p. 30). This particular theory proved incorrect, but it was the catalyst necessary to launch and to guide an investigation.

One of the editors, Sussman, was described by the reporters as a theoretician at heart. Deeply interested in the Watergate puzzle, Sussman kept careful track of every detail and made the intellectual effort to put the pieces together at every opportunity. He served not as a cross-examiner of data but as a source of questions. Moreover, Sussman used a historical model, the Teapot Dome scandal, as a guide for his own thinking and as a source of hypotheses.

The need for explanations led to a search for facts to provide them (pp. 56, 179, 278, 298–299). The idea of a massive cover-up had come to Bernstein well before he had the facts available to support publication of the story (p. 91). Proof of the theory that the White House had been heavily involved in political espionage was necessary to account for the seeming senselessness of the Watergate burglary taken by itself (p. 118).

Information was accumulated in bits and pieces. Some of it was not direct evidence but, rather, was information about the personality and character of given actors. Informants helped the reporters understand the culture and social organization of the Nixon administration. Combined with more specific pieces of evidence, this information supported an early story pointing to massive political espionage and sabotage, directed by the White House, as a partial explanation of the Watergate burglary, an event that otherwise made no sense.

Bernstein and Woodward (1974) admitted the initial story was "interpretive—risky" (p. 150). "The story was based on strains of evidence, statements from numerous sources, deduction, a partial understanding of what the White House was doing, the reporters' familiarity with the 'switchblade mentality' of the President's men, and disparate pieces of information the reporters had been accumulating for months" (pp. 150–151). In a great deal of what Bernstein and Woodward did, it appeared necessary to suspend faith in the constructs they held, and to work to overcome their feelings of awe of the Presidency and their disbelief that public officials could act as they did. It was the development of new concepts that allowed the investigation to proceed, even though the new concepts came slowly and required modification of existing concepts.

The reporters were constantly developing alternative hypotheses to account for information they received and interpreting its implications. When the story first broke, an editor suggested it might not be political espionage but just a case of some "crazy Cubans" (p. 16). Indeed, the idea that the burglary might be the work of Republicans seemed highly implausible at first. One alternative interpretation was that the reporters were being deliberately misled or set up in some way (p. 90). The suspicion of a setup caused them to hold publication of the story of the White House taping system, even though they had some advance information about it, because they feared the tapes might have been manufactured or recorded in such a way as to be self-serving (p. 363).

THEORY AND INVESTIGATION IN THE SOCIAL SCIENCES

Though it has long been an aim in the social sciences to develop encompassing theory, and though we honor such giants as Freud, Marx, Weber, Durkheim, and Hull for their theories, some critics contend that grand, abstract theories obscure rather than clarify. Indeed, as thoughtful a quantitatively oriented social scientist as Cronbach (1975) has come to believe that it is not possible to develop laws in the social sciences that will hold generally because of the problem of higher order interactions. And, in point of fact, John Stuart Mill (1843/1965) anticipated this view more than 100 years ago by despairing of ever developing a precise social science, except perhaps in economics, because the complexity of the social world did not permit precise formulation and testing of hypotheses. Cronbach argues that the role of the social scientist is not to develop grand theory but to pin down the contemporary facts and, in common with colleagues in the humanities, to attempt to develop explanations and interpretations that make sense of the contemporary world.

In comparing investigative reporting with social science, I am struck by the fact that investigative reporters make it their business to immerse themselves in their stories, personally getting as close as possible to the events and trying to find the human interest elements of the stories. Social scientists who endeavor to develop theory prefer to construct measures that have the merit of abstracting the essence from circumstances; however, such measures also remove the researcher from direct contact with the phenomena of interest. Questionnaires and attitude scales that force individuals to respond in abstract terms provide the social scientist with abstractions rather than with close representations of the experiences themselves.

Representations of feelings and meanings provide the basis for our understanding of each other and of the social world (Makkreel, 1975), but are often inappropriate and less than useful in our attempts to understand the physical world. Modern abstract theoretical statements reduce such meaning–feeling variables to a minimum. That ultimate abstraction, the mathematical formula, eliminates such considerations entirely. A beautiful example of how abstract concepts entirely eliminate meaning–feeling statements from scientific discourse is provided by Lévi-Strauss when he quotes the zoologist Hediger describing his first encounter with a dolphin:

> "Flippy was no fish, and when he looked at you with twinkling eyes from a distance of less than two feet, you had to stifle the question as to whether it was in fact an animal. So new, strange and extremely weird was this creature, that one was tempted to consider it as some kind of bewitched being. But the zoologist's brain kept on associating it with cold fact, painful in this connection, that it was known to science by the dull name, *Tursiops truncatus.*" (Lévi-Strauss, 1962/1966, p. 38)

It may be useful to eliminate meanings and feelings from equations reflecting relations among nonhuman subjects. Certainly much of our intellectual effort in the social sciences is modeled on forms useful in the physical sciences. However, the advantages of an abstract, quantitative approach may paradoxically result in considerable disadvantage when it comes to aiding our understanding of the human condition.

Investigative reporting, participant–observer research, and research deriving from clinical interaction—all of these approaches have the distinct advantage of bringing us close to the phenomena of interest. Such methods are faulty when subject to no discipline. What I have tried to point out here is that investigative reporting does have a discipline to it in that its results are grounded in evidence whose reliability is probed in a number of ways. The inference process is also limited by social controls. The method requires theory to guide investigation, and it can result in concepts or models that have significance beyond the unique events for which they were developed.

There are a number of strands in contemporary social science[2] that lead toward a renewed interest in, and acceptance of, clinical and qualitative methods. We can understand these methods better by observing how skilled investigators use them, and to that end, Bernstein and Woodward have provided us with an exceptionally useful document. I hope that other investigators will similarly provide us with a careful record of their own approaches so that a teachable, disciplined method of doing field research, case studies, and clinical research may emerge.

REFERENCE NOTE

1. Campbell, D. T. *Qualitative knowing in action research* (Kurt Lewin Award Address, Society for the Psychological Study of Social Issues). Paper presented at the meeting of the American Psychological Association, New Orleans, August 1974.

[2]London (1961, 1974, 1975, 1977) has tried to develop both a philosophy of method and a system of discipline for dealing with data derived from direct human experience, using observers who were participants in events. His use of a novelist to make dramatic sense of experience (London, 1974) has not received the attention it deserves. Kvale (1976) has pointed out that meanings are psychology's data and has described some of the difficulties and advantages of working with meanings as data. Campbell (Note 1) also believes that the quantitative and the qualitative necessarily complement each other in the research enterprise. Harré and Secord (1972) have called for an anthropomorphic social psychology. They too are interested in the direct human experience of events as the key to finding explanatory concepts.

REFERENCES

Anderson, D., & Benjaminson, P. *Investigative reporting.* Bloomington: Indiana University Press, 1976.

Balaban, R. M. The contribution of participant observation to the study of process in program evaluation. *International Journal of Mental Health,* 1973, *2,* 59–70.

Balaban, R. M. Participant observation—Rediscovering a research method. In L. Goldman (Ed.), *Research methods for counselors.* New York: Wiley, 1978.

Barzun, J. M. *Clio and the doctors: Psycho-history, quanto-history and history.* Chicago: University of Chicago Press, 1974.

Bernstein, C., & Woodward, B. *All the President's men.* New York: Warner Books, 1974. (Paperback)

Bogdan, R., & Taylor, S. J. *Introduction to qualitative research methods.* New York: Wiley, 1975.

Cleary, E. W. (Ed.). *McCormick on evidence.* St. Paul, Minn.: West, 1972.

Cronbach, L. J. Beyond the two disciplines of psychology. *American Psychologist,* 1975, *30,* 116–127.

Diesing, P. *Patterns of discovery in the social sciences.* Chicago: Aldine-Atherton, 1971.

Douglas, J. D. Investigative social research. Beverly Hills, Calif.: Sage, 1976.

Erikson, E. H. *Insight and responsibility.* New York: Norton, 1964.

Giorgi, A. *Psychology as a human science.* New York: Harper & Row, 1970.

Group for the Advancement of Psychiatry. *Some observations on controls in psychiatric research* (Report No. 42). New York: Author, 1959.

Harré, R., & Secord, P. F. *The explanation of social behaviour.* Oxford, England: Blackwell, 1972.

Hesse, M. B. *Models and analogies in science.* Notre Dame, Ind.: Notre Dame University Press, 1966.

Kvale, S. Meanings as data and human technology. *Scandinavian Journal of Psychology,* 1976, *17,* 171–180.

Levine, A., & Levine, M. The social context of evaluative research: A case study. *Evaluation Quarterly,* 1977 *1,* 515–542.

Levine, M. Scientific method and the adversary model: Some preliminary thoughts. *American Psychologist,* 1974, *29,* 661–677.

Levine, M. Congress (and evaluation) ought to pay more attention to history. *American Journal of Community Psychology,* 1979, *7,* 1–17.

Lévi-Strauss, C. *The savage mind.* London: Weidenfeld & Nicolson, 1966. (Originally published, 1962.)

London, I. D. Respondent-evaluation applied to quotational analysis: A case study. *Psychological Reports,* 1961, *9,* 615–621.

London, I. D. The revenge of heaven: A brief methodological account. *Psychological Reports,* 1974, *34,* 1023–1030.

London, I. D. Interviewing in Sinology: Observations on and its meaning for social sciences. *Psychological Reports,* 1975 *36,* 683–691.

London, I. D. Convergent and divergent amplification and its meaning for social sciences. *Psychological Reports,* 1977 *41,* 111–123.

Makkreel, R. A. *Dilthey: Philosopher of the human studies.* Princeton, N.J.: Princeton University Press, 1975.

Mill, J. S. *On the logic of the moral sciences.* Indianapolis, Ind.: Bobbs-Merrill, 1965. (Originally published, 1843)

Truzzi, M. (Ed.). *Versteken: Subjective understanding in the social sciences.* Reading, Mass.: Addison-Wesley 1974.

Waelder, R. *Basic Theory of psychoanalysis.* New York: International Universities Press, 1960.

Watson, J. D. *The double helix.* New York: Atheneun, 1968.

Whyte, W. F. *Street corner society.* Chicago: University of Chicago Press, 1955.

Winks, R. W. (Ed.). *The historian as detective: Essays on evidence.* New York: Harper & Row, 1968.

41

THE ROLE OF VALUES IN THE SCIENCE OF PSYCHOLOGY

GEORGE S. HOWARD

The role that values play in scientific research has been an important topic in the philosophy of science for the past three decades. McMullin (1983) noted in his presidential address to the Philosophy of Science Association that 30 years ago Rudner (1953) argued that the making of value judgments is an essential part of the work of science. Apparently Rudner (1953) realized that his claim would be quite shocking, because of the regnant positivist orthodoxy, and in fact claimed that its acceptance would bring about "a first-order crisis in science and methodology" (p. 6). But McMullin (1983) indicated that the landscape has changed dramatically in the ensuing years:

> Thirty years later, the claim that science is value-laden might no longer even seem controversial, among philosophers of science, at least, who have become accustomed to seeing the pillars of positivism fall, one by one. One might even characterize the recent deep shifts in theory of science as consequences (many of them, at least) of the growing realization of the part played by value-judgment in scientific work. (p. 3)

Although philosophers of science still debate the role of values in scientific research, the controversy is no longer about *whether* values influence scientific practice, but rather about *how* values are embedded in and shape scientific practice.

I have several ambitions in this article. The first task involves unpacking the various meanings of the overly broad and inclusive term *value.* Once the sense in which any science is value laden is established, I delineate the epistemic values that currently undergird our conception of proper science. Although not totally noncontroversial, these epistemic values are generally

Reprinted from the American Psychologist, 40, 255–265. (1985).

accepted as appropriate by both philosophers of science and practicing scientists. Next, I argue that certain characteristics of psychology's subject matter—namely, human beings—suggest yet another constellation of values as appropriate for our discipline. I argue that humans possess characteristics that are unlike those of subject matters studied by other sciences. Thus, an appropriate science of human action must be somewhat different from other existent sciences. Therefore, although we share science's epistemic values with the natural scientist, there may well be a set of values that, although proper for the psychologist, are irrelevant for the natural scientist in his or her pursuit of understanding. Finally, I delineate some of the implications of such a position for research praxis in psychology.

TYPES OF VALUES

The term *value* has served as a catchall category for an enormous array of very different judgments, decisions, preferences, and orientations. For the purposes of our discussion, it is helpful to divide values into epistemic and nonepistemic values. As a preliminary distinction between these two types of values one might consider how each type of value *should* be involved in the conduct of science. One might reasonably hold that all values can legitimately and fruitfully affect the choice or selection of questions for study. Then, once a particular theoretical issue has been raised for scientific consideration, the epistemic values should guide our judgments regarding the determination of the adequacy of competing theoretical explanations. Although nonepistemic values can play a role in determining what questions one might choose to entertain, it is felt that nonepistemic values should not intrude on the scientific process of determining the relative merits of competing theoretical explanations. Because the older meanings of the term *value* are of the nonepistemic variety, they will be considered first.

Nonepistemic Values

The first meaning of *value* relates to such features of human experience as attraction, feeling, and emotion. In this sense, value differences represent differences of attitude or emotional response in certain individuals. What, then, is the place of this sort of **emotive** value in determining the relative merits of competing theoretical explanations in science? McMullin (1983) wrote,

> It seems plausible to hold that emotive values are alien to the work of natural science. There is no reason to think that human emotionality is a trustworthy guide to the structures of the natural world. Indeed, there is every reason, historically speaking, to view emotive values, as Bacon did, as potentially distortive "Idols," projecting in anthropomorphic fashion the pattern of human wants, desires, and emotions on a world where they have no place (i.e., the domain of theory choice in science). When "ideology" is understood as a systematization of such values, it automatically becomes a threat to the integrity of science. (p. 5)

A second sense of *value* is referred to as a *characteristic* value. A property or set of properties may count as a characteristic value in an entity of a particular kind because it is advantageous for an entity of that kind. Sharpness is desirable in a knife because of its function in cutting; because of its survival value, speed is a valued trait in wild animals; or a sharp memory for names might be valuable for a politician. One can ask properly scientific evaluative questions about characteristic values. For example. "How fast is a particular animal?" or "Which utensil is sharper?" In the final section of this article I consider the possibility of pursuing nonevaluative, characteristic values as a proper component of the science of psychology. Questions of this sort might sound something like the following: "Why should one value honesty in a person?" or "How important is cognitive flexibility to a psychotherapist?"

Another construal of *value* concerns what we might refer to as *ethical* values. Obviously, ethical demands such as honesty, openness, and integrity are required for the communal work of science to proceed. Although recent history has amply demonstrated that this is not always the case (e.g., Norman, 1984), it is assumed that scientists will be ethical in the conduct of their research endeavors. Once again, however, the scientific merit of competing theories should not be judged by appeal to ethical values.

The final construal of *value* considered here is the *truth*-value of science, which McMullin (1983) explicated as follows:

> In the classic account, it was in fact the goal of the entire enterprise. Unlike other values, it was deemed to have nothing of the personal about it. On the contrary, it connoted an objective relation of the proposition and world and thus was constitutive of the very category of fact itself. But this was not thought to weaken the maxim that science should be value-free, because the values that were thus being enjoined from intrusion into the work of science were the particular ones that would tend to compromise the objectivity of the effort and not the transcendental one which defined the tradition of science itself. (pp. 6–7)

Of course, this construal of the truth-value of a scientific proposition or a theory historically implied a correspondence or matching between the scientific language and mind-independent reality. Such a construal has been roundly attacked by, among others, Wittgenstein (1953/1967), Putnam (1981), Lauden (1981), and Rorty (1979) and no longer appears to be a philosophically viable conception of scientific endeavors. Rather, when a scientist "accepts" a theory he or she is not claiming that it is true.

> The predicate in terms of which theory is valued is not truth, as the earlier account held it to be. We speak of a theory being "well-supported," "rationally acceptable," or the like. To speak of it as *true* would suggest that a later anomaly that would force a revision or even abandonment of the theory can in principle be excluded. (McMullin, 1983, p. 7)

This modified construal of the truth-value of a theory now enables us to state the relationship between epistemic values and the "truth" of a theory.

McMullin argued that truth is still a sort of ideal or "horizon-concept" of the scientific enterprise, even though we may never be able to assert truth in a definitive manner of any component of science along the way. Stated in this fashion, McMullin's position could be characterized as a *modest realist* position and can be distinguished from both a strict realist account (viz., science discovers the truth about the world) and the antirealist (or instrumentalist) account (viz., consideration of the truth-value of scientific propositions represents a fundamental misunderstanding of the scientific enterprise). (Readers can learn more of this currently debated philosophical issue from Bhaskar, 1975, and Lauden, 1981.)

It is generally felt that certain nonepistemic (i.e., emotive and characteristic) values should not influence the conduct of science and that often when they do intrude, it is to the detriment of the undertaking. That nonepistemic values influence many important aspects of research in psychology has been amply demonstrated (cf. Bevan, 1980, 1982). However, epistemic values are generally held to properly function in scientific enterprises, and it is to them we now turn.

Epistemic Values

Our consideration of truth-value, as a never-achieved ideal or horizon-concept, enables us to appreciate the way in which epistemic values are thought to move scientific pursuits closer to their proper goals. But first, the skeleton of a most important argument must be constructed.

This argument involves consideration of the proper aims and goals of science; the role of theory; and the relationship between theories and evidence. Consideration of these points will lead to the crucial proposition of this section of the article—namely, that the assessment of theories involves value judgment in an essential way.

The basic aim or goal of science is understanding, and this understanding is achieved through theoretical knowledge (e.g., Kuhn, 1977; McMullin, 1983; Toulmin, 1961). Because (a) empirical "facts" can support a multitude of incompatible theoretical positions, and (b) observations in science are, in fact, theory dependent (Hansen, 1958), the link between theory and observation must be tentative. That is, one can never choose between competing theories by simply looking toward the "brute facts" and "allowing the facts to speak for themselves," as the standard positivist view has held. The question, then, immediately arises: What are the criteria whereby choices among theories are made? McMullin (1983) held that "the appraisal of theory is in important respects closer in structure to value-judgment than it is to the rule-governed inference that the classic tradition in philosophy of science took for granted" (pp. 8–9).

Before elaborating further on epistemic values, it is necessary to draw a distinction between theoretical science and practical or applied science. Rudner (1953) argued that the acceptance of a scientific hypothesis

> is going to be a function of the importance, in the typically ethical sense, of making a mistake in accepting or rejecting the hypothesis. Thus, to take a crude but easily manageable example, if the hypothesis under consideration were to the effect that a toxic ingredient of a drug was not present in lethal quantity, we would require a relatively high degree of confirmation or confidence before accepting the hypothesis, for the consequences of making a mistake here are exceedingly grave by our moral standards. (p. 2)

Rudner took hypothesis acceptance to mean "approve as a basis for a specific kind of action" (p. 2). However, McMullin (1983) saw these criteria as appropriate for practical science but *not* for theoretical science:

> But acceptance in this sense is not part of theoretical science, strictly speaking. When a physicist "accepts" a particular theory, this can mean that he believes it to be the best-supported of the alternatives available or that he sees it as offering the most fruitful research-program for the immediate future. These are *epistemic* assessments; they attach no values to the theoretical alternatives other than those of likelihood or probable fertility. On the other hand, if theory is being applied to practical ends, and the theoretical alternatives carry with them outcomes of different value to the agents concerned, we have the typical decision-theoretic grid involving not only likelihood estimates but also "utilities" of one sort or another. Such utilities are irrelevant to theoretical science proper and the scientist is not called upon to make value-judgments in their regard as part of his scientific work. (p. 8)

Epistemic values, then, are those criteria employed by scientists to choose among competing theoretical explanations.[1] Scientists hope that by systematically employing epistemic values the

[1]The psychological literature on the criteria for theory choice is extensive (e.g., Allport, 1955; Baldwin, 1967; Estes et al., 1954; Goodson & Morgan, 1976; Marx & Hillix, 1973). Although the tendency in this literature is to see these characteristics of good theories as logical rules that can be straightforwardly exercised, the excellent piece by Goodson and Morgan (1976) highlights nicely why the criteria might best be viewed as general guideposts in each scientist's journey toward understanding. An appropriate justification for this more "subjective" stance may be found in Goodson and Morgan's (1976) final paragraph:

> It may seem paradoxical that the ultimate criterion for scientific research, with its insistence upon control of variables and clarity of concepts, should reside in something as subjective and as difficult to define as that which is implied by the term *understanding.* Yet because the process of science must culminate in some fashion, it seems not only reasonable but necessary that it terminate in the context that gave it motivation: man's subjective experience. (p. 298)

quality of their theoretical explanations will move closer to the ideal or horizon-concept of truth. The warrant for such belief lies in the history of science. Historically, theoretical explanations possessing these epistemic values have tended to represent superior scientific endeavors. Kuhn (1977) and McMullin (1983) considered five agreed-upon epistemic values and one additional contender.

The most salient epistemic value for the working scientist would likely be *predictive accuracy*. Although some degree of inaccuracy should be tolerated in the early stages of a theory, in the long run a theory must demonstrate predictive accuracy if it is to be acceptable. A second desideratum is *internal coherence*. That is, a theory should hang together properly, having no logical inconsistencies or unexplained coincidences. A third desired value is *external consistency*. The theory must be consistent with the theories and also the general background of scientific expectation. Theories that contradict other accepted theories from the same or related disciplines are subject to a certain amount of skepticism. *Unifying power* is a fourth valued characteristic of scientific theories. The ability to bring together hitherto disparate areas of knowledge is a valued trait for theories. Another crucial criterion is *fertility*. Theories are fertile not only because they make correct, novel predictions but also because they function like a metaphor might in literature and provide the scientist with imaginative resources to overcome anomalies and to make new and powerful extensions of our knowledge base (McMullin, 1976). A final epistemic value might be *simplicity*. Although less widely accepted than the others among contemporary philosophers, it still possesses some appeal as an almost aesthetic preference among certain scientists (most notably, perhaps, would be Einstein).[2]

Individual scientists emphasize different subsets of these epistemic values in their evaluations of competing theoretical positions. This realization sheds light on the reason for theoretical controversy in science:

> The fact that theory-appraisal is a sophisticated form of value-judgment explains one of the most obvious features of science, a feature that could only appear as a mystery in the positivist scheme of things. Controversy, far from being rare and wrong-headed, is a persistent and pervasive presence in science at all levels. Yet if the classical logicist view of science had been right, controversy would be easily resolvable. One would simply employ an algorithm, a "method," to decide which of the contending theories is best confirmed by the evidence available. At any given moment there would then be a "best" theory, to which scientists properly versed in their craft ought to adhere. (McMullin, 1983, p. 17)

Therefore, one can conceive of science as the cauldron in which competing theoretical perspectives struggle for acceptance. Epistemic values function something like environmental presses in weeding out unfit theories in this competition. However, rather than being rigidly adhered to, as the strict logicist would long for, various subsets of epistemic values are sometimes ruthlessly applied in instances of theory evaluation, whereas at other times they are held in abeyance.

Having now considered both epistemic and nonepistemic values, we can take a final look at the role of "truth" as a value in scientific theorizing. Thus, "truth-value" operates something like a superordinate value by which the usefulness (in moving theoretical explanations toward "truth") of the two general classes of values can be assessed. The astute reader will detect a certain circularity in the logic of the preceding sentence and may be troubled by it. However, the realist holds that some such form of circularity is inevitable for science to proceed, and it is the program of the realist philosopher and/or historian of science to demonstrate that such

[2]Other possible epistemic values sometimes assume crucial roles in particular perspectives on theory choice. For example, for Popper (1935/1959) the testability and potential falsifiability of a theory is crucial. Although I would not argue with someone who chose to include testability is the *sine qua non* of all scientific theories and more than anything else distinguishes science from nonscience. Further, one cannot speak of the predictive accuracy of a theory unless it is testable in some way.

circularity is nonvicious in nature. For more thorough treatments of the realists' defense, see McMullin (1983, 1984), Newton-Smith (1981), Putnam (1975), and Hacking (1983).

The astute observer will also note that considerable subjectivity has been included in this account of theory choice in science. Many would argue that this subjective element is essential for any complete and correct account of the practice of theoretical science. In fact, far from apologizing for this subjectivity as bias, I accept Kuhn's (1977) observation:

> Still, no very acute ear for language is required to generate discomfort with the ways in which the terms "objectivity" and, more especially, "subjectivity" have functioned in this paper. Let me briefly suggest the respects in which I believe language has gone astray. "Subjective" is a term with several established uses: in one of these it is opposed to "objective," in another to "judgmental." When my critics describe the idiosyncratic features to which I appeal as subjective, they resort, erroneously I think, to the second of these senses. When they complain that I deprive science of objectivity, they conflate that second sense of subjective with the first. (p. 337)

Theory choice involves the judgmental application of epistemic values. Kuhn (1977) pointed out that the leaders in scientific communities are constantly challenged to explain the judgmental bases for their theory choices: "Such judgments are eminently discussable, and the man who refuses to discuss his own cannot expect to be taken seriously" (p. 332).

Given the role values in theory choice, in what sense is science objective? The list of epistemic values above was not meant to be exhaustive. One might properly contend that there are other epistemic values, such as the reproducibility of an experiment or the accuracy of measurement, that permeate scientific practice. This is quite true and represents a way in which science is objective. However, recall that (a) data remain theory-dependent; (b) theories are underdetermined by data; and (c) theory choice involves the judgmental application of epistemic values. One quickly realizes that the objectivity of sciences must be understood as emanating from a nexus of judgmental presuppositions, and the efficacy of the entire enterprise is a function of the adequacy of those fundamental assumptive stances. (The importance of this caveat will become clear in the next section.)

Therefore, although nonepistemic values (e.g., pragmatic, political, social, religious) can and do exert influences on the directions sciences take (as sociologists of science have made us painfully aware), it is the application of epistemic values that underlies our assertion that scientific knowledge represents the most secure knowledge available to us of the world we seek to understand.

Of course the arguments outlined above are incomplete, and the interested reader is urged to study the original sources for the complete arguments. The position traced above represents a reasonably noncontroversial, middle-of-the-road position in contemporary philosophy of science. However, it is clear, either from the examples chosen by the philosophers cited above or from their explicit statements, that the model of science they are sketching is meant to apply to the natural sciences. It is widely acknowledged that the problems of objectivity-subjectivity and the value-laden nature of facts take on added complexity in the social sciences. This represents one reason why philosophers of science often choose to confine their observations to the natural sciences. It seems appropriate to speculate—as I will in the next section—about some ways in which values may operate in a somewhat different manner in the science of psychology than in the disciplines of the natural sciences.

The crucial point of the above analysis is that epistemic values function as values, not as strict rules, to guide the work of science. McMullin (1983), Kuhn (1977), and others demonstrated that theory development in the most mature natural sciences is influenced by the selective application of epistemic criteria. This is, of course, a different picture of the operation of science than a traditional logicist would have chosen to paint.

A PLACE FOR VALUES IN PSYCHOLOGICAL RESEARCH

Allow me to begin by asserting that psychology's claim to being a science must, like any other science, lie in its adherence to the epistemic values of science. We also share with other scientists a basic commitment to other related values such as nature being lawful, knowledge being worthwhile, and so forth. However, in this section of the article I will argue for a further influence of values in psychological research—an additional influence that is irrelevant for most other sciences. The need for this additional value element in psychological research is, I believe, a direct result of some of the unique characteristics of human beings. The present article aims to present what appears to be a major problem in studying humans scientifically, without claiming to offer a wholly satisfactory solution.

The significance of much of the research and theory in psychology has been seriously questioned over the last 20 years. Perhaps the first to see clearly the nature of the difficulties psychology confronted in becoming a coherent scientific discipline was Sigmund Koch (1959), who argued that psychology's difficulties occurred because

> its institutionalization preceded its content and its methods preceded its problems. . . .The "scientism" that many see and decry in recent psychology was thus with it from the start. . . . From the earliest days of the experimental pioneers, man's stipulation that psychology be adequate to science outweighed his commitment that it be adequate to man. (Vol. 3, p. 783)

Koch (1964, 1981) went on to claim that psychology based its understanding of vital questions of method on a philosophy of science that was already out of date at that time. For example, behaviorism, which dominated psychological research at that time, took a jaundiced view toward consciousness: "Psychology, as the behaviorist views it, is a purely objective, experimental branch of natural science which needs consciousness as little as do the sciences of chemistry and physics" (Watson, 1914). But, it turns out that consciousness is anything but irrelevant for modern physics; for example, Wigner (1970) claimed that "it is not possible to formulate the laws [of quantum theory] in a fully consistent way without reference to consciousness" (p. 172).[3] Rather than simply asserting that consciousness (or any other construct) should or should not be a part of research with humans, let us take Koch's critique seriously and consider first the characteristics and nature of human beings. The task then becomes one of constructing a model of research faithfully reflecting the noteworthy characteristics of humans. Implicit in this approach is the possibility that if humans possess characteristics that are unlike the characteristics of subject matters studied by other sciences, then an appropriate science of human behavior might need to be somewhat different from other extant sciences. Specifically, I contend that psychology should

[3]To fully explain the role of consciousness in quantum physics would take us far afield of the goals of this article. However, a marvelous quote by the physicist Capra (1982) catches the importance of the consciousness of the scientist in the behavior of the subject matter.

> Human consciousness plays a crucial role in the process of observation, and in atomic physics determines to a large extent the properties of the observed phenomena. This is another important insight of quantum theory that is likely to have far-reaching consequences. In atomic physics the observed phenomena can be understood only as correlations between various processes of observation and measurement, and the end of this chain of processes lies always in the consciousness of the human observer. The crucial feature of quantum theory is that the observer is not only necessary to observe the properties of the atomic phenomenon, but is necessary even to bring about these properties. My conscious decision about how to observe, say, an electron will determine the electron's properties to some extent. *If I ask a particle question, it will give me a particle answer: if I ask it a wave question, it will give me a wave answer!* (pp. 86–87, italics added)

Although this same relationship between the consciousness of the experimenter and the characteristics manifested by the subject matter undoubtedly also exists for psychological research, our problems cut deeper still. In psychology, the consciousness of the subject also represents an important determinant of what the subject "is," whereas in physics this is not the case because (as far as we can tell) light has no opinion as to whether it "is" a wave or a particle. This additional problem for psychological investigations is an important part of the arguments of the second half of this article.

retain the epistemic values insofar as possible and compromise them only to the degree necessary to accommodate our subject matter's unique characteristics.

Agency and Causal Powers

The active agent model advocated here borrows heavily from the work of Harré and his colleagues (Harré, 1974; 1980, 1984; Harré & Madden, 1975; Harré & Secord, 1972). Harré's brand of active agency holds that the most appropriate scientific understanding of everyday human action comes from an analysis of human beings by virtue of their unique causal powers. Humans are language users, and the most striking feature of a language user is the ability to monitor the control of his or her own actions. In this model, the person is a watcher, a commentator, and a critic, as well as an agent. In its most blatant form, the active agent approach holds that the things humans say to themselves are important causal elements in the genesis of behavior. Further, the maintenance and modification of ongoing activity are accomplished through the active monitoring of one's own social actions. A general teleological principle lies at the heart of all of Harré's work—namely, that social behavior is to be conceived as deliberate action directed toward certain ends. In this sense, Harré made contact with some accepted thought in psychology. For example, George Kelly (1962) felt that people anticipate events, and so all behavior can best be understood as future oriented and anticipatory. That is, "It is not the past and present but the *future* which determines behavior, and it is the hypotheses held by the individual that allow him or her to anticipate that future and behave accordingly" (Smith & Vetter, 1982, p. 239).

In the active agent model, social behavior is seen as the execution of performances. An agent may adopt many different "roles" (e.g., in my case, son, uncle, teacher, learner, host, guest, spouse) that serve to pattern actions in various contexts. Specific "rules" of behavior are associated with each role and serve as blueprints for action when the social self of that role is put to use. For example, "when one is serving as a host (the role), one should be pleasant and cordial" might constitute an individual's personally held rule.

Manicas and Secord (1983) emphasized that many of the tensions between theoretical approaches in psychology are attributable to the mistaken notions in the older philosophy of science that has long undergirded research in psychology. Newer notions in the philosophy of science allow for a revised conception of the role of psychological theory in the understanding of individuals. Manicas and Secord (1983) recognized the importance of agency in humans and allowed for the study of relevant constructs, such as shared social scripts, in their view of a proper social psychology. Because language use is so important to an understanding of human action and because social and cultural influences shape how we think and use language, a complete understanding of humans demands that attention be given to this human capacity.

But in what way do human agency and language use make psychology any different from other forms of scientific inquiry, such as the natural sciences?

Reflexivity and Human Values in Human Action

Howard (1984) has discussed two characteristics of humans that mark them as unique among the various subject matters studied by sciences: reflexivity[4] and human values. Stephen

[4]Reflexive is defined as "directed or turned back upon itself" (*Webster's Seventh New Collegiate Dictionary*, 1965). Psychologists are well aware of the phenomenon of reactivity in research and have made tremendous strides toward ameliorating its debilitating effects in psychological studies (Argyris, 1968: Orne, 1962; Rosenthal & Rosnow, 1969; Webb, Campbell, Schwarts, & Sechrest, 1966). Reactivity problems in psychological research are owing to the reflexive nature of human beings. But reflexivity, as the superordinate category, has important implications, which extend beyond reactivity concerns, that are delineated in the remainder of this article.

Toulmin (1981) captured a sense in which psychology as science needs to confront the problem of reflexivity when he pointed out that in the era of classical science, as exemplified by Newtonian physics, an object of study never knew it was being studied. Therefore, the object would continue to behave without any perverseness leading it to react to the knowledge that it was being observed. The scientist was traditionally thought as one who studies a system without intervening in the operations of the system. The notion of rational objectivity in science required a lack of reciprocal interaction between observer and object. The scientist was to observe nature, but nature was not to reflect upon itself being observed. But is the subject matter of psychology (namely, human beings) suited to these demands of rational objectivity? Bannister (1966) did not think so and colorfully made the point:

> I am reminded of a recurrent theme in certain types of science fiction story. The master-chemist has finally produced a bubbling green slime in his test tubes, the potential of which is great but the properties of which are mysterious. He sits alone in his laboratory, test tube in hand, brooding about what to do with the bubbling green slime. Then it slowly dawns on him that the bubbling green slime is sitting alone in the test tube brooding about what to do with him. This special nightmare of the chemist is the permanent work-a-day world of the psychologist—the bubbling green slime is always wondering what to do about you. (p. 22)

Many psychologists brusquely categorize the problem as one requiring greater experimental control. Putative solutions involve keeping subjects naive (or even deceived) regarding the purposes of the study or even to the fact that they are being studied. But this view mistakes the tip of the iceberg for the iceberg. The problem of reflexivity cuts deeper still and is concerned not only with how our behavior is altered because we are being studied but also with how the results of studies can alter our behavior in *nonexperimental* contexts. Human beings care about the findings of psychological investigations. Because we care, research results might precipitate changes in humans' behavior. Possible examples include individuals who actively resist agreeing with others' opinions when making uncertain judgments because of their knowledge of the results of the Asch conformity studies. Or perhaps simply informing depressed clients that depressed people tend to be more self-critical would make them more aware of their self-derogating tendencies and aid them in actually reversing these tendencies.

In contrast to the circumscribed examples of human reflexivity suggested above, there is an extensive literature on the social construction of the child (or the child as a cultural invention). Stimulated by Kessen's (1979) influential paper "The American Child and Other Cultural Inventions," Kessel and Siegel (1983) brought together a diverse group of thinkers to probe the implications of such a conception of childhood development. Consistent with the reflexive powers of active agents described above, Wartofsky (1983) argued against the view of childhood as an Aristotelian "natural kind," as some essential or fixed nature that characterizes all individuals of a given kind and makes them the kind of individuals they are. Rather, Wartofsky (1983) made a case for the cultural or social construction of the child as a historical variable:

> Contrary to the Aristotelian theory of "natural kinds," I would argue that, for human beings at any rate, the self-conception, or the social conception, of childhood is itself constituted—in part, but not entirely (for reasons I will give later)—of what children are. That is to say, the kind of individual or the kind of entity of which childhood can be predicated—what it is to be a child—is in large part a function of what childhood is taken to be. Children are, or become, what they are taken to be by others, and what they come to take themselves to be, in the course of their social communication and interaction with others. In this sense, I take "child" to be a social and historical kind, rather than a natural kind, and therefore also a constructed kind rather than one given, so to speak, by nature in some fixed or essential form. What is involved in such sociohistorical or cultural construction of the child and in the self-construction or self-constitution of the child I will discuss later. But I want to note here

> that such cultural constitution, or construction and self-construction, is not simply a matter of reflection in thought, but also of the whole range of practices, interactions, and institutions that comprise the social and historical life-world. (p. 190)

To varying degrees, the other essays in the Kessel and Siegel (1983) work play on variations of the same theme (e.g., Kessel, 1983; Kessen, 1983; White, 1983).

Howard (1984) noted that reflexivity problems did not generally pose difficulties for natural scientists by considering the hypothetical situation in which a chemist investigates the temperature at which sodium and chlorine combine to form salt:

> Nor would it be reasonable to think that the sodium would become aware that this is an experiment, and bond with chlorine at a higher (or lower) temperature deliberately (or inadvertently) because it is being studied. Finally, if one were to "tell" the chemicals the findings of previous studies on their binding temperatures, it is unlikely their reactions would be altered one iota. (p. 105)

Any discussion of human reflexivity begins with a consideration of language as the mechanism underlying the operation of the phenomenon and ends with the role of values in steering reflexive human action (cf. Sperry, 1977, 1983). These steering values are often embedded in one's culture and influence not only individuals' everyday actions, but science as well. For example, Stephanie Shields (1977) reviewed much of the research on sex differences between men and women over the past century and made some telling observations about how the findings reflect the beliefs, biases, and values of the period. Rather than correcting, refining, or remedying the biases within the profession at a given point in time, research more often was used to document and support those biases. Current beliefs and assumptions appear to be important determinants of what issues we will choose to study, what findings we expect to obtain, what results we actually obtain, and how we interpret the meaning of those findings. A researcher with an entirely different perspective on the problem might conduct another set of studies that would provide an entirely different set of results and, consequently, a totally different answer to the research question. Therefore, one might view the findings of research investigations as demonstrating not what necessarily occurs in the world, but what is *possible* if human beings were considered from a particular perspective. Consequently, our results might not signal what will or must occur, but rather serve to demonstrate how people might think, feel, and act if considered from a particular perspective.

Koch (1981) indicated that several of the models of humans that are implicit in much of the research in psychology are impoverished and distort the best qualities of human beings. He pointed out that it is dehumanizing to think of people as if they were only reinforcement maximizers, information processors, and so forth. The crux of Koch's critique is that if researchers entertain these stultified models of humans as basic to their understandings of the meaning of their research findings, then they will gradually accumulate scientific evidence that appears to support their belief that these models do adequately capture the essence of humans. And when we convey these results to the scientific and nonscientific communities, human beings might become persuaded to believe that they actually *are* (or worse, that they *must be*) the way the research suggests.

We have come full circle when we consider that in viewing themselves in this particular manner, humans might actually become more like the model because they have reason to expect that they will act in accord with the scientific evidence. By viewing people solely as reinforcement maximizers, for example, we might actually be unwitting contributors to a self-fulfilling prophecy wherein humans actually become more like the model. This circle, which has possibilities for either human benefit or detriment, represents our third type of reflexivity. Koch was concerned that the models we have selected for our understanding of humans have been overly simplistic and therefore incapable of accurately representing human complexity and subtlety. Thus, these views of human beings are typically impoverished and thereby dehumanizing. But are there no options available to ameliorate this problem?

Consider what might occur if we viewed research in psychology as giving us knowledge regarding human *possibilities* rather than human realities or human necessities. For a moment, view research findings as what might be true for people, rather than what is true or what must be true for humans. Research evidence provides us with a sense for human possibilities, given the limiting constraints of the scientist's model. And what might those constraints be?

The first major limitation we have already considered: the assumptions, biases, and theoretical perspective of the scientist. We have considered this phenomenon above; the assumptions we hold in approaching a topic of inquiry are important determinants of what answers we obtain to our questions. Second, the current set of accepted research tools (both research designs and statistical analyses) becomes the means by which we can answer those questions. Because our supply of research tools is constantly expanding, we are always limited by what tools are currently developed, documented, and accepted for general practice. As new tools are developed and refined, previously unanswerable questions become testable. Further, employing new tools often leads to different answers to questions that were considered with an older set of research tools. The third constraint relates to the human element of science. None of us wishes to make a bad mistake in public; and science is in the public domain. It is safe to conduct research within the constraints of currently accepted assumptions using the tried-and-true set of research tools. Unfortunately, few researchers interpret their findings with the humility due evidence constrained by so many factors. Fewer researchers strive to develop new assumptive stances or to create innovative tools to probe research questions from new perspectives. Koch made us aware that human beings are complex, multifaceted beings. The challenge to psychologists is, I believe, to develop an array of theoretical perspectives and research tools capable of appreciating and understanding humans in all their complexity.

THE ROLE OF SUBJECTIVITY IN THE SCIENCE OF PSYCHOLOGY

Progress is made in science through the succession of increasingly more appropriate theories that explain particular phenomena. It is becoming increasingly apparent to some philosophers of science that a more accurate description of this progression would be that increasingly better theories are being created rather than discovered. The form and characteristics of any creation are, in part, a reflection of the creator. This is true even in the natural sciences, where the theory bears the mark of the theorist. But I am arguing that subjectivity cuts yet a second way in psychological theory and research: Human action, the explanandum of the theory, can also change in reaction to the theory. Therefore, although the psychologist shares with the natural scientist the task of explaining the present action of his or her object of study, the psychologist has a further injunction: to consider what human beings might become in response to our research.

Viewed from this perspective, psychologists are seen as agents in the formation of human beings. Applied psychologists have long been aware of the need for social responsibility in their actions. But the traditional view of the scientist in any discipline was that of a neutral truth seeker who followed a value-free pursuit of knowledge. For the reasons presented herein, I believe researchers should modify their ambition to become disinterested parties or value-free agents. It seems that a more adequate solution would involve acknowledging and accepting the place of values in their endeavors.

Perhaps a brief hypothetical example of research of this more value-inspired sort might be helpful. Stanley Milgram's (1974) work on obedience has probably engendered as much controversy as any other program of research in psychology. The controversy stems from at least two sources: (a) whether or not Milgram was ethically justified in deceiving his subjects and subjecting them to psychological risk, and (b) what his findings might imply about humans' tendencies toward acquiescing to authority. Considering only the controversy generated by the latter point for a moment, we might conclude that most people agree that it would have been preferable for individuals not to conform to authority in such circumstances. Given this value preference, several lines of value-inspired research are possible: (a) What are the circumstances that enhance individuals' rejecting inappropriate demands by authority figures? (b) What lines of thinking typically lead an individual to defy authority? (c) Assuming trends emerge in the studies of (b), can training programs of various types increase thinking of that sort and thereby increase disobedience to inappropriate uses of authority? and (d) Are there any trends in the developmental histories of those subjects who obey (versus those who disobey) the authority figure that translate into recommendations for child rearing? There are, of course, an enormous number of problems (not the least of which are ethical difficulties) associated with conducting each of these lines of inquiry. However, the crucial point is that each line of inquiry would be undertaken in the hope that the findings might lead to knowledge that could translate into desired results for humans.

The value-directed course for psychological research being recommended is similar to work in progress in related disciplines that deal with humans. For example, the pharmacologist does not blindly experiment with drugs and dispassionately observe the pharmacological effects of new drug combinations. Rather, human difficulties (such as hypertension, depression, and so forth) are considered, and drugs are developed that might produce specific pharmacological effects to influence the symptomatology of the disease. Because of prior, value-impregnated decisions, the researcher knows what types of drug effects will represent an appropriate solution to his or her investigation. The challenge is to find a drug (or develop some new compound) that produces the desired outcomes. By pursuing a similar path, psychological research might profit by being guided in its efforts by *characteristic values*. From this perspective, the earlier distinction between theoretical and practical science seems to dissolve. Perhaps where human beings are concerned, that which is most practical is of most theoretical interest.

The shift in roles for research psychologists, from neutral truth seekers to chroniclers and molders of human action, implies a greater acknowledgment of subjectivity and value judgment in science. McMullin (1983), Feyerabend (1975), Kuhn (1977), and Lauden (1984) made us abundantly aware that values have always been present in the world of scientific facts. McMullin (1983) colorfully depicted our common gut reaction to allowing values and subjectivity into the realm of science:

> What is left of the vaunted objectivity of science, the element of the factual, in all this welter of value-judgment? Once the camel's nose is inside, the tent rapidly becomes uncomfortable. Is there any reasoned way to stop short of a relativism that would see in science no more than the product of a contingent social consensus, bearing testimony to the historical particularity of culture and personality much more than to an objective truth about the world? (p. 20).

McMullin answered his own question in the affirmative by asserting faith in the continued use of the epistemic values in selecting among various competing theories. To the extent that nonepistemic values and other nonepistemic factors have been instrumental in the original theory-decision, they are gradually sifted out. The nonepistemic will not survive this selective process in the long run. The process of science serves to limit the effects of sources of distortive intrusion into the slow process of shaping our thought to the world. Thus, McMullin (1983) salvaged the picture of theoretical natural sciences evolving toward truth as an ideal or horizon-concept. But can psychology, in view of our treatment of reflexivity and values, ride on the coattails of such an argument?

To the extent that one believes that there are immutable, law-like relationships in human behavior. McMullin's argument furnishes support for the belief that the influence of nonepistemic values should continually be minimized in psychological research. When one views humans as evolving in response to individual biographical and social influences, the wisdom of extending McMullin's argument to the human sciences becomes suspect. If human nature is influenced by how science views it, not only should we consider whether nonepistemic values *can* be removed from psychological research, but we must also consider if nonepistemic values *should* be removed.

So now we have reached the crux of the issue. Are there any models of humans and models of science that adopt a value-impregnated stance? To my mind, Harré's (1984) position represents a strong challenge to the received view in psychology because he saw the choice to be made between a consideration of causal mechanisms and moral orders:

> Two images of human psychology compete for our attention. Academic psychologists, particularly those who work in the "experimental" tradition, make the implicit assumption that men, women and children are high-grade automata, the patterns of whose behavior are thought to obey something very like natural laws. . . . It is assumed that there are programs which control action and the task of psychology is to discover the "mechanisms" by which they are implemented. Lay folk, clinical psychologists, lawyers, historians and all of those who have to deal in a practical way with human beings tend to think of people as agents struggling to maintain some sort of reasoned order in their lives against a background flux of emotions, inadequate information and the ever-present tides of social pressures.
>
> I shall try to show that the great differences that mark off these ways of thinking about human psychology are not ultimately grounded in a reasoned weighing of the evidence available to any student of human affairs. They turn in the end on unexamined political and moral assumptions. . . . Although these profoundly different ways of interpreting and explaining human thought and action have their origin in preferred linguistic forms rather than any compelling facts of the matter, they do have profoundly different practical consequences. They carry with them very distinctive stances as to the moral, political and clinical problems with which modern people are beset. (p. 4)

Harré's stance moves concepts such as personal power, agency, moral responsibility, will, and self determination to the forefront. Harré (1984) believed that "the self as agent is not a mysterious thing but *a belief which endows the believer* with certain powers of action" (p. 180, emphasis added), and that "what personal development is possible will depend on the theories actors hold. Certain person-theories will promote self-knowledge and self-mastery, others will inhibit them" (p. 256). One can gain the sense from these brief snatches of Harré's thought that he took the reflexive nature of humans, and the value-impregnated view of a science of humans, quite seriously indeed. Whereas positions such as Harré's hold promise as models for psychological research, only time will determine the eventual fruitfulness of such approaches. (See also Argyris, 1977; Tyler, 1983.)

POSTSCRIPT

Mahatma Ghandi once wrote that there were seven sins in the world: wealth without work, pleasure without conscience, knowledge without character, commerce without morality, science without humanity, worship without sacrifice, and politics without principle. What did Ghandi mean by science without humanity? It appears that the meaning might be very different for every science. For example, the possibility of the nuclear destruction of the human race represents a legacy that many physicists sorely regret. But psychology's ill-conceived bequest might be of a quite different sort. Our legacy could be an impoverished vision of humanity. By viewing humans from an unduly narrow perspective, we may perpetuate a paralyzing myopia that serves to diminish rather than expand humans' potential as individuals and as a species. Our challenge, then, is to construct a science of humans built upon an image of humanity that reflects and reveres human nature in all its diversity, complexity, and subtlety. An understanding of human values is crucial if we are to achieve a proper grasp of the nature of humans and to adequately comprehend that uniquely human activity—science.

REFERENCES

Allport, F. (1955). *Theories of perception and the concept of structure.* New York: Wiley.

Argyris, C. (1968). Some unintended consequences of rigorous research. *Psychological Bulletin, 70,* 185–197.

Argyris, C. (1977). *Inner contradictions of rigorous research.* New York: Academic Press.

Baldwin, A. (1967). *Theories in child development.* New York: Wiley.

Bannister, D. (1966). Psychology as an exercise in paradox. *Bulletin of the British Psychological Society, 19,* 21–26.

Bevan, W. (1980). On getting in bed with a lion. *American Psychologist, 35,* 779–789.

Bevan, W. (1982). A sermon of sorts in three plus parts. *American Psychologist, 37,* 1303–1322.

Bhaskar, R. (1975). *A realist view of science.* Leeds, England: Leeds Books.

Capra, F. (1982). *The turning point.* New York: Simon & Schuster.

Estes, W. K., Koch, S., MacCorquodale, D., Meehl, P. E., Muller, C. G., Schoenfeld, W. N., & Verplanck, W. S. (1954). *Modern learning theory.* New York: Appleton-Century-Crofts.

Feyerabend, P. K. (1975). *Against method.* London: Redwood Barn.

Goodson, F. E., & Morgan, G. A. (1976). Evaluation of a theory. In M. H. Marx & F. E. Goodson (Eds.), *Theories in contemporary psychology* (pp. 286–299). New York: Macmillan.

Hacking, I. (1983). *Representing and intervening.* Toronto, Canada: University of Toronto Press.

Hansen, N. R. (1958). *Patterns of discovery.* Cambridge, England: Cambridge University Press.

Harré, R. (1974). Blueprint for a new science. In A. Nigel (Ed.), *Reconstructing social psychology* (pp. 3–25). Baltimore: Penguin Books.

Harré, R. (1980). *Social being: A theory for social psychology.* Totowa, NJ: Littlefield, Adams.

Harré, R. (1984). *Personal being.* Cambridge, MA: Harvard University Press.

Harré, R., & Madden, E. H. (1975). *Causal powers: A theory of natural necessity.* Oxford, England: Basil Blackwell.

Harré, R., & Secord, P. F. (1972). *The explanation of social behavior.* Oxford, England: Basil Blackwell.

Howard, G. S. (1984). On studying humans. *The Counseling Psychologist, 12,* 101–109.

Kelly, G. (1962). *The psychology of personal constructs.* New York: Norton.

Kessel, F. S. (1983). On cultural construction and reconstruction in psychology: Voices in conversation. In F. S. Kessel & A. W. Siegel (Eds.), *The child and other cultural inventions* (pp. 224–259). New York: Praeger.

Kessel, F. S., & Siegel, A. W. (Eds.). (1983). *The child and other cultural inventions.* New York: Praeger.

Kessen, W. (1979). The American child and other cultural inventions. *American Psychologist, 34,* 815–820.

Kessen, W. (1983). The child and other cultural inventions. In F. S. Kessel & A. W. Siegel (Eds.), *The child and other cultural inventions* (pp. 26–39). New York: Praeger.

Koch, S. (1959). *Psychology: A study of a science* (Vol. 3). New York: McGraw-Hill.

Koch, S. (1964). Psychology and emerging concepts of knowledge as unitary. In T. W. Wann (Ed.), *Behaviorism and phenomenology* (pp. 1–41). Chicago: University of Chicago Press.

Koch, S. (1981). Psychology and its human clientele: Beneficiaries or victims? In R. A. Kasschau & F. S. Kessel (Eds.), *Psychology and society: In search of symbiosis* (pp. 24–47). New York: Holt, Rinehart & Winston.

Kuhn, T. (1977). *The essential tension.* Chicago: University of Chicago Press.

Lauden, L. (1981). A confutation of convergent realism. *Philosophy of Science, 48,* 19–49.

Lauden, L. (1984). *Science and values: An essay on the aims of science and their role in scientific debate.* Berkeley, CA: University of California Press.

Manicas, P. T., & Secord, P. F. (1983). Implications for psychology of the new philosophy of science. *American Psychologist, 38,* 399–413.

Marx, M. H., & Hillix, W. A. (1973). *Systems and theories in psychology.* New York: McGraw-Hill.

McMullin, E. (1976). The fertility of theory and the unit for appraisal in science. In P. Feyerabend, R. W. Cohen, & M. W. Wartofsky (Eds.), *Essay in honor of Imre Lakatos, Boston Studies, 39* (pp. 395–432). Dordrecht, The Netherlands: Reidel.

McMullin, E. (1983). Values in science. In P. D. Asquith & T. Nickles (Eds.), *Proceedings of the 1982 Philosophy of Science Association* (Vol. 2, pp. 3–23). East Lansing, MI: Philosophy of Science Association.

McMullin, E. (1984). A case for scientific realism. In J. J. Leplin (Ed.), *Essays on scientific realism* (pp. 53–71). Berkeley: University of California Press.

Milgram, S. (1974). *Obedience to authority.* New York: Harper & Row.

Newton-Smith, W. (1981). *The rationality of science.* London: Rutledge.

Norman, C. (1984). Reduce fraud in seven easy steps. *Science, 224,* 581. (See also *Science,* May 27, 1983, p. 936)

Orne, M. T. (1962). On the social psychology of the psychological experiment: With particular reference to demand characteristics and their implications. *American Psychologist, 17,* 776–783.

Popper, K. (1959). *The logic of scientific discovery.* London: Hutchinson. (Original work published 1935)

Putnam, H. (1975). *Mind, language and reality.* Cambridge, England: Cambridge University Press.

Putnam, H. (1981). The corroboration of theories. In I. Hacking (Ed.), *Scientific revolutions* (pp. 60–79). Oxford, England: Oxford University Press.

Rorty, R. (1979). *Philosophy and the mirror of nature.* Princeton, NJ: Princeton University Press.

Rosenthal, R., & Rosnow, R. L. (Eds.). (1969). *Artifact in behavioral research.* New York: Academic Press.

Rudner, R. (1953). The scientist *qua* scientist makes value-judgments. *Philosophy of Science, 20,* 1–6.

Shields, S. (1975). Functionalism, Darwinism and the psychology of women: A study in social myth. *American Psychologist, 30,* 739–754.

Smith, B. D., & Vetter, H. J. (1982). *Theoretical approaches to personality.* Englewood Cliffs, NJ: Prentice-Hall.

Sperry, R. (1983). *Science and moral priority.* New York: Columbia University Press.

Sperry, R. W. (1977). Bridging science and values: A unifying view of mind and brain. *American Psychologist, 32,* 237–245.

Toulmin, S. (1961). *Foresight and understanding.* New York: McGraw-Hill.

Toulmin, S. (1981). Evolution, adaptation, and human understanding. In M. B. Brewer & B. E. Collins (Eds.), *Scientific inquiry and the social sciences* (pp. 18–36). San Francisco: Jossey-Bass.

Tyler, L. E. (1983). *Thinking creatively.* San Francisco: Jossey-Bass.

Wartofsky, M. (1983). The child's construction of the world and the world's construction of the child: From historical epistemology to historical psychology. In F. S. Kessel & A. W. Siegel (Eds.), *The child and other cultural inventions* (pp. 188–215). New York: Praeger.

Watson, J. B. (1914). *Behavior.* New York: Holt.

Webb, E. J., Campbell, D. T., Schwartz, R. D., & Sechrest, L. (1966). *Unobtrusive measures.* Skokie, IL: Rand McNally.

Webster's seventh new collegiate dictionary. (1965). Springfield, MA: Merriam.

White, S. (1983). Psychology as a moral science. In F. S. Kessel & A. W. Siegel (Eds.), *The child and other cultural inventions* (pp. 1–25). New York: Praeger.

Wigner, E. P. (1970). *Symmetries and reflections. Scientific essays.* Cambridge, MA: M.I.T. Press.

Wittgenstein, L. (1967). *Philosophical investigation.* Oxford, England: Blackwell. (Original work published 1953)

RECOMMENDED READING

Bechtel, W. B. (1988). *Philosophy of science: An overview for cognitive science.* Hillsdale, NJ: Erlbaum.

Faulconer, J. E., & Williams, R. N. (1985). Temporality in human action: An alternative to positivism and historicism. *American Psychologist, 40,* 1179–1188.

Gergen, K. J. (1986). Correspondence vs. autonomy in the language of understanding human action. In D. Fiske & R. Shweder (Eds.), *Metatheory in social science: Pluralism and subjectivities* (pp. 137–162). Chicago: University of Chicago Press.

Haan, N. (1982). Can research on morality be "scientific"? *American Psychologist, 37,* 1096–1104.

Hoshmand, L. L. T. (1989). Alternate research paradigms: A review and teaching proposal. *Counseling Psychologist, 17,* 3–79.

Howard, G. S. (1986). *Dare we develop a human science?* Notre Dame, IN: Academic Publications.

Howard, G. S. (1989). *A tale of two stories: Excursions into a narrative approach to psychology.* Notre Dame, In: Academic Publications.

Howard, G. S. (1986) Can there be an empirial science of volitional action? *American Psychologist, 41,* 1241–1251.

Lamiell, J. T. (1986). *The psychology of personality: An epistemological inquiry.* New York: Columbia University Press.

Levine, M. (1974). Scientific method and the adversary model: Some preliminary thoughts. *American Psychologist, 29,* 661–677.

Levine, M. (1982). Method or madness: On the alienation of the professional. *Journal of Community Psychology, 10,* 3–14.

Mahrer, A. R. (1989). *Experiencing: A humanistic theory of psychology and psychiatry* (pp. 97–144). Ottawa, Ontario, Canada: University of Ottawa Press. (Original work published 1978)

Mahrer, A. R. (1985). *Psychotherapeutic change: An alternative approach to meaning and measurement.* New York: Norton.

Manicas, P. (1987). *A history and philosophy of the social sciences.* Oxford, England: Basil Blackwell.

Manicas, P. (1989). Explanation and quantification. In B. Glassner & J. Moreno (Eds.), *The qualitative–quantitative distinction in the social sciences* (pp. 179–205). Dordrecht, the Netherlands: Reidel.

Manicas, P. (1984). Reply to comments. *American Psychologist, 39,* 922–926.

Meehl, P. E. (1990). Selected philosophical and methodological papers. Minneapolis: University of Minnesota Press.

Meehl, P. E. (1986). What social scientists don't understand. In D. W. Fiske & R. A. Shweder (Eds.), *Metatheory in social science: Pluralisms and subjectivities* (pp. 315–338). Chicago: University of Chicago Press.

Meehl, P. E. (1983). Subjectivity in psychoanalytic inference: The nagging persistence of Wilhelm Fliess's Achensee question. In J. Earman (Ed.), *Minnesota studies in the philosophy of science: Vol. 10. Testing scientific theories* (pp. 349–411). Minneapolis: University of Minnesota Press.

McNamee, S., & Gergen, K. J. (in press). *Social construction and the therapeutic process.* London: Sage.

Polkinghorne, D. E. (1983). *Methodology for the human sciences: Systems of inquiry.* Albany: State University of New York Press.

Schiebe, K. E. (1978). The psychologist's advantage and its nullification: Limits of human predictability. *American Psychologist, 33,* 869–881.

Semin, G., & Gergen, K. J. (Eds.). (1990). *Everyday understanding: social and scientific implications.* London: Sage.

POSTSCRIPT: THE ROLE OF PHILOSOPHY IN THE EDUCATION OF CLINICAL PSYCHOLOGISTS

RONALD B. MILLER

It is perhaps with some degree of exhaustion that readers arrive at this concluding chapter, weary from the difficulty and complexity of the issues, the unfamiliarity of the subject matter and language, and the sheer breadth of the topics covered. I hope that this fatigue is outweighed, as it has been for me and many of my students, by an excitement and enthusiasm that comes from having discovered that one was not alone in that vague but nagging sense that something very important has been missing from one's training and education as a psychologist. Relief, too, in discovering that there is a place within the discipline of psychology for discussion of the questions one has about the assumptions and premises of other courses or texts, and about which one has been told, in effect, "These are the premises of our work, and if you want to be a psychologist, you won't question them."

Most psychology students have discovered by the completion of their first course in psychology that the field is very fragmented. Clinical psychology graduate students quickly discover that their newly adopted profession is riddled with schisms. Research-oriented academicians rarely talk to the students' clinical supervisors, and they even more rarely have anything good to say about each other's work. Then, of course, there are the divisions among clinical practitioners of different theoretical persuasions (i.e., theoretical preciousness), to say nothing of the divisions along professional lines among clinical psychologists, counseling psychologists, school psychologists, mental health counselors, clinical social workers, psychiatric nurses, rehabilitation counselors, and psychiatrists. These schisms have tended to produce very isolated communities of discourse; although there have been efforts in recent years to bridge these chasms with "integrated" or "eclectic" approaches to treatment, psychologists and other mental health professionals seem to lack understanding of how such fundamental differences can be examined or resolved.

It was suggested in chapter 1 that because these differences are, in fact, philosophical, it would stand to reason that an improved understanding of philosophy would further one's ability to make sense out of the divisions within the discipline. I hope that readers have also experienced some of the relief that comes from discovering that theoretical differences can be examined and discussed right through to their most fundamental philosophical assumptions, without a rupture in communications. This is not to say that in discussing one's own most cherished and fundamental beliefs and values, the discussion may not on occasion deteriorate into an angry exchange or rhetoric. Philosophy is not a guarantee against human beings being emotional about their beliefs. Rather, it is a way to proceed—to resume the dialogue—once people calm down. Without it, the only recourse is to separate oneself from the other, for there is nothing more to say.

Professions, by their very nature, tend to be self-protective, isolated, and not particularly self-critical. As psychology becomes increasingly professionalized, there will be more, rather than less, pressure to think in terms of theoretical preciousness; there will also be less of a tendency to question fundamental assumptions and a narrower focus to graduate education. Including the philosophical foundations of clinical psychology in the curriculum is one way to counter these forces and broaden the profession's understanding of itself.

I am convinced that philosophical analysis is just as important, if not more, to the training of a professional psychologist as is statistical analysis. Statistical analysis provides a means of testing some hypotheses, but philosophical analysis is necessary in order to properly formulate a hypothesis in the first place, select the appropriate research strategy, and interpret the results. Although philosophizing is not something that the clinician is well advised to do with clients, it is something the clinician cannot do without in the attempt to make theoretical sense out of that clinical experience.

A GRADUATE COURSE IN THE PHILOSOPHY OF CLINICAL PSYCHOLOGY

Almost a decade ago (Miller, 1983), I proposed that a graduate course in the philosophy of clinical psychology would be a valuable addition to the curriculum of graduate programs in clinical psychology and the other mental health professions. The purpose of such a course would be to teach the student how to identify philosophical assumptions implicit in psychological theories and how to analyze and construct philosophical arguments (i.e., how to participate in philosophical discourse). As with any course, there are a number of ways in which this could be done effectively, but two factors probably should be constant in any such course.

First, there must be much opportunity for discussion and for the classroom experience itself to be a model of philosophical discourse. Therefore, it needs to be taught in a true seminar format. Written assignments should also be consistent with this goal. I encourage students to "do" philosophy in their papers rather than write summaries of what other philosophers have done. They are encouraged to examine the philosophical assumptions of the theoretical approach to personality and psychotherapy that they find most interesting and to evaluate the logic of the philosophical arguments for and against such a position.

Second, it is recommended that psychologists collaborate, if possible, with a professional philosopher in preparing and teaching the course. Philosophy and psychology have been independent disciplines for 100 years now; for a psychologist to do justice to the philosophy of clinical psychology without such assistance is asking too much of any one intellect. Such interdisciplinary efforts, particularly between faculty in the humanities and an applied field such as clinical psychology are extremely enriching for faculty in terms of questioning the most fundamental assumptions of one's discipline or graduate training.

Obviously, in such a course, one may choose to emphasize classic works in philosophy more than contemporary sources or to narrow the focus to two or three approaches to clinical psychology rather than the five represented in this book. On the other hand, some may wish a broader course including Eastern philosophy or more theological issues. It is also possible to limit the focus of the course to just one branch of contemporary philosophy (e.g., Anglo-American analytical philosophy, continental phenomenological–existential philosophy). Although I think this is less preferable than a coverage of both, it is possible to teach psychology students to do philosophy this way, and that is what is important.

Given the centrality of philosophical issues to the discipline, it is unrealistic to expect everything that is important to be covered in a one-semester graduate course. Just as an undergraduate course in statistics has become a prerequisite for admission into graduate school in clinical psychology, I would urge that clinical psychology graduate programs consider requiring some upper-level undergraduate preparation in the humanities as well. I have found that students who have had at least one upper-level undergraduate course in philosophy, intellectual history, or literary criticism, and so forth, have a much better appreciation of the sorts of issues to be raised by a course such as is being suggested here.

Of course, one does not have to restrict the discussion of philosophical issues in clinical psychology to a separate course. Indeed, in some ways it would be more preferable if such a discussion were integrated into one of the following courses: theories of psychotherapy, theories of personality, theories of psychopathology, clinical psychology, or history and systems of psychology. Perhaps as the reconciliation between philosophy and psychology that Feigl (see chapter 2) called for approaches, this will be possible. In the meantime, at the very least, one can hope that the philosophy of clinical psychology will no longer be trivialized or undermined by *terminal philosophical ambivalence, theoretical preciousness,* or *philosophy by fiat* in the student's other courses.

A graduate course in the philosophy of clinical psychology prepares the student for the task that most graduate curricula demand of the student but do little to prepare the student for integrating extremely diverse, conflicting, and seemingly incommensurable theories and data. Despite the fact that such a course does not provide any tangible clinical information or skill, it is nevertheless of great practical value in the development of both the individual professional psychologist and the profession as a whole. It instills a confidence in one's work that comes from having one's intellectual roots clearly defined and firmly planted and provides a perspective on the place of one's work in the intellectual traditions of civilization.

REFERENCE

Miller, R. (1983). A call to armchairs. *Psychotherapy: Theory, Research and Practice, 20,* 208–219.

INDEX

ABOUT THE EDITOR

Ronald B. Miller received his bachelor of arts degree from Oberlin College and his doctorate in clinical psychology from the University of Vermont in 1976. He was a Woodrow Wilson Fellow in the department of moral philosophy in 1970–1971 at Saint Andrews University in Scotland. Dr. Miller has been on the faculty of Saint Michael's College in Colchester, Vermont, since 1983 and is an associate professor of psychology there. Dr. Miller is also director of the master's program in clinical psychology at St. Michael's College, a program that he helped found in 1983. In addition, Dr. Miller has a private practice, specializing in psychotherapy, couples and family therapy, and school consultation.